COPYRIGHTED

COPYRIGHTED.

T. A. Hendricks

CAMPAIGN OF '84.

BIOGRAPHIES

OF

S. GROVER CLEVELAND,

THE DEMOCRATIC CANDIDATE FOR PRESIDENT,

AND

THOMAS A. HENDRICKS,

THE DEMOCRATIC CANDIDATE FOR VICE-PRESIDENT,

WITH A

DESCRIPTION OF THE LEADING ISSUES

AND THE

PROCEEDINGS OF THE NATIONAL CONVENTION,

TOGETHER WITH A

HISTORY OF THE POLITICAL PARTIES OF THE UNITED STATES

COMPARISONS OF PLATFORMS ON ALL IMPORTANT QUESTIONS,

AND

POLITICAL TABLES FOR READY REFERENCE.

BY GEN'L BENJAMIN LA FEVRE,

Member of the House of Representatives from Ohio.

CHICAGO AND NEW YORK:

BAIRD & DILLON.

1884.

Entered according to Act of Congress, in the year 1884, in the Office of the Librarian of Congress, at Washington, D. C.

Bound by
HENRY ALTEMUS,
4th and Cherry Streets,
Philadelphia.

CONTENTS.

Biographies, etc.

HISTORY OF THE POLITICAL PARTIES.

POLITICAL PLATFORMS.

PART I.

BIOGRAPHIES OF

S. GROVER CLEVELAND

AND

THOMAS A. HENDRICKS.

STEPHEN GROVER CLEVELAND

New York presents a grand array of noble names, which have alike shed a lustre on the Democratic party and the nation. Its great men have been conspicuous in the camps of the soldier in the pulpit, at the bar, and in the legislative halls of the state and nation. The political history of our country is filled with the names of men from this state who have left their imprints upon this age and generation, and become known and famous throughout the civilized world.

Martin Van Buren who succeeded Andrew Jackson as President, Horatio Seymour, Horace Greeley, General McClellan, and Samuel J. Tilden, nominees for that elevated position all hailed from that state, while General Hancock, another nominee, although not belonging to it, was and is an actual resident of New York. The country believes, and it will go through all time as a matter of history, that Mr. Tilden failed to become President, not because he was defeated at the ballot box, but because he was sacrificed by the Electoral Commission at Washington, and that four years of Republican misrule was forced upon the country by that unjust and illegal decision.

The Democratic National Convention, which convened at Chicago, July 8, to make nominations, after carefully surveying the field and digesting the merits of the respective candidates, again selected a candidate from the Empire state in the person of Stephen G. Cleveland, the present Governor. When we consider the galaxy of grand names before the Convention for its consideration, and the influences by which they were presented and supported, it cannot fail to impress us with the force and reputation of the man who could win amongst such compeers. Probably never before had a National Convention the opportunity of making a selection from such a number of distinguished personages.

Delaware presented its Bayard, a time-honored name in that state, and an acknowledged leader among men. Conservative in his views, deliberate in his action, profound in thought, and brilliant in intellect, he is a statesman who ornaments his high position of United States Senator.

Thurman, of Ohio, whose giant intellect and broad-gauge views won him the position of a leading senator—a man whose acute knowledge of jurisprudence elevated him to the head of the Bar, and whose will-power is coequal with his judgment, was one of the contestants. Indiana presented McDonald, stalwart in faith, careful and plodding in details, whose record in the Senate was without blot or blemish. Pennsylvania, through ex-Senator Wallace, named Mr Randall, who in the councils of his native city, in the State Senate, and for nearly a quarter of a century in Congress, has been favorably known by the people. As an organizer, a parliamentarian and legislator he is the acknowledged leader of the House of Representatives. The present accomplished Speaker of the House, Mr. Carlisle, of Kentucky, one of the intellectual giants of Congress, a Chesterfield in manners, and a Napoleon in strategy—Morrison, of Illinois, with true western push, and advanced ideas of political economy, formed a brilliant pair on the nominating roster. Any one of these men would have been a worthy leader of the Democracy to victory, and, therefore, the selection of Stephen G. Cleveland from the number was an enviable honor, apart from that which attains to the Presidential office.

It is not the purpose of this biographical notice to trace with minute exactness an ancestry, about which the American people care but little, as under a government like ours the faded pages of ancestral records weigh but little against the living realities of the present. A Government of the people takes the people as they are, and for what they are worth, as component parts thereof, and not from any heritage from buried generations. It recognizes no royalty of birth, no caste because of ancestry, but, actuated by the spirit of our laws, it rates him for his intrinsic worth, and no matter how humble his origin—

"The man's a man for a' that."

Before entering upon a biographical sketch of Mr Cleveland, we will introduce him to our readers as he was presented to the Chicago Convention by Mr. Lockwood.

Cleveland's Name Presented.

MR. CHAIRMAN AND GENTLEMEN OF THE CONVENTION: It is with no ordinary feeling of responsibility, that I appear before this Convention as representative of the Democracy of the State of New York [applause] for the purpose of placing in nomination a gentleman from the State of New York as a candidate for the Presidency of the United States. This responsibility is made greater when I remember that the richest pages of American history have been made up from the records of Democratic administration. [Applause.] This responsibility is made still greater when I remember that the only blot in the political history done at Washington, an outrage upon the rights of the American people, was in 1876, and that that outrage and that injury to justice is still unavenged [applause], and this responsibility is not lessened when I recall the fact that the gentleman whose name I shall present to you has been my political associate from my youth. Side by side have we marched to the tune of Democratic music, side by side have we studied the principles of Jefferson and Jackson, and we love the faith in which we believe: and during all this time he has occupied a position comparatively as a private citizen, yet always true and always faithful to Democratic principles. No man has greater respect or admiration for the honored names which have been presented to this convention than myself; but, gentlemen, the world is moving, and moving rapidly. From the North to the South, new men, men who have acted but little in politics, are coming to the front [applause], and to-day there are hundreds and thousands of young men in this country, men who are to cast their first vote, who are independent in politics, and they are looking to this convention, praying silently that there shall be no mistake made here. They want to drive the Republican party from power. They want to cast their vote for a Democrat in whom they believe. [Applause.] These people know from the record of the gentleman whose name I shall present that Democracy with him means honest government, pure government, and protection to the rights of the people of every class and every condition.

A little more than three years ago I had the honor, at the city of Buffalo, to present the name of this same gentleman for the office of Mayor of that city. It was presented then for the same reason, for the same causes that we present now, it was because the Government of that city had become corrupt, and had become debased, and political integrity sat not in high places. The people looked for a man who would represent the contrary, and without any hesitation they named Grover Cleveland as the man [at this point there was a wild burst of applause. Some of the New York delegation, practically the entire Wisconsin delegation and some few scattering delegates, stood up and made all the demonstrations possible in Cleveland's favor. As soon as the uproar subsided and comparative order was regained, Mr. Lockwood continued.]. The result of that election and his holding that office was that in less than nine months the State of New York found herself in a position to want just such a candidate and for such a purpose, and when at the Convention in 1882 his name was placed in nomination for the office of Governor of the State of New York, the same people, the same class of people, knew that that meant honest government, it meant pure government, it meant Democratic government, and it was ratified by the people. [Cheers.]

And, gentlemen, now, after eighteen months' service there, the Democracy of the State of New York come to you and ask you to give to the country, to give the Independent and Democratic voters of the country, to give the young men of the country the new blood of the country, and present the name of Grover Cleveland as the standard-bearer for the next four years. I shall indulge in no eulogy of Mr Cleveland. I shall not attempt any further description of his political career. It is known. His Democracy is known. His statesmanship is known throughout the length and breadth of the land. And all I ask of this convention is to let no passion, no prejudice influence its duty which it owes to the people of this country. Be not deceived. Grover Cleveland can give the Democratic party the thirty-six electoral votes of the State of New York on election day. He can by his purity of character, by his purity of administration, by his fearless and undaunted courage to do right, bring to you more votes than can anybody else. Gentlemen of the Convention, but one word more. Mr. Cleveland's candidacy before this Convention is offered upon the ground of his honor, his integrity, his wisdom, and his Democracy [cheers], upon that ground we ask it, believing that, if ratified by this Convention, he can be elected, and take his seat at Washington as a Democratic President of the United States.

General BRAGG spoke as follows:

GENTLEMEN OF THE CONVENTION: It is with feelings of no ordinary pride that I fill the post that has been assigned to me to-day. Grown gray personally fighting the battles of the Democratic party, I stand to-day to voice the sentiment of young men of my State when I speak for Grover Cleveland, of New York. [Cheers.] His name is upon their lips. His name is in their hearts. He is the choice not only of that band of young men, but he is the choice of all those who desire for the first time as young men to cast their vote in November for the candidate nominated by this Convention. They love him, gentlemen, and respect him, not only for himself, for his character, for his integrity, and judgment and iron will, but they love him most for the enemies he has made.

This broad nation witnessed the disgraceful spectacle of a Senator of the United States trading his proud possession for gain. Mahone and Riddleberger would scarcely be allowed to stand upon this platform to teach you whom you ought to nominate. Go to the Senate of the State of New York since Governor Cleveland has been Governor, and there you find two worthy conferees playing in a small theatre Mahone and Riddleberger over again. And why? Because the Governor of the State of New York had more nerve than the machine. They may speak of him, aye, the worst of the species may defile a splendid statue, but they only disgrace themselves. Wherever the thin disguise can be reached, you will find it covering nothing but personal grievance, disappointed ambition, as a cutting off of access to the flesh-pots to those who desire to fatten upon them. I do not assume here to speak for labor. The child of a man who always earned his daily bread by his daily labor, brought up for more than a quarter of a century, from boyhood to manhood among laborers that have made the great Northwest what it is. I do not assume to speak for labor. Labor is not represented in political conventions by the soft hand of the political trickster, no matter where you find him. The men who follow conventions and talk about the rights of labor, are the Swiss contingent who place their tent wherever the prospect of profit is greatest—while honest, intelligent, horny-handed labor will be found following the old Democratic flag, thanking God that its self-styled leaders have gone where they belong. They come here to talk of labor! Yes, their labor has been upon the crank of the machine (immense applause and laughter), and their study has been political chicanery in the midnight conclave.

Governor Cleveland's Ancestry.

Governor Cleveland's great grand-father was Aaron Cleveland. He was born on the ninth of February, 1744, one hundred and forty years ago, in the town of East Haddam, the principal of the numerous

Haddams that lie along the Connecticut river a short distance from Middletown. During the greater portion of his life he carried on business in the town of Norwich, where he followed his calling as a hatter. The records of the place make frequent mention of him, not as a hat maker, but as an active participant in the public affairs of the town, as a versatile speaker, an able writer, and an active politician. He was one of the early opponents of slavery, and he became notorious by introducing a bill in the Connecticut Legislature, in which he represented the town of Norwich, for its abolition. The bill provoked a prolonged and exciting discussion, in which Aaron Cleveland bore a conspicuous part, and was finally defeated, as he expected; for he presented it without the most remote idea of success, but merely to put himself and the other members on the record. Apart from his business, and his political ventures, he found time to prosecute the study of divinity, and abandoning the hat business, and leaving the politics of state and town in other hands, he removed to Vermont, and became a somewhat noted Congregational minister From thence he returned to his native State, locating at New Haven, where he died in 1815. Throughout his life he had openly opposed the institution of slavery, and was well known as the Anti-Slavery Agitator. His son, Charles Cleveland, was born in Norwich in 1772, and at an early age removed to Massachusetts and settled in Boston. There he became a noted city missionary, and was known throughout the State as "Father Cleveland." A daughter, the youngest of thirteen children, was married to the celebrated Doctor Samuel H. Cox, and his son, the Rev Arthur Cleveland Coxe, is now Bishop of the Protestant Episcopal Church of Western New York. The reader will notice that the third generation has remodelled the name by the addition of a final e.

William, the second son of Aaron Cleveland, and the grandfather of the presidential nominee was a silversmith, and plied his vocation at Beacon Hill, adjoining Norwich. Like his father, he belonged to the Congregational Church, in which he was a deacon for a quarter of a century. In the latter part of his life he retired from business and removed to Buffalo, New York. He died at Black Rock in 1857

Richard Falling Cleveland, the second son of William Cleveland, and the father of Stephen Grover Cleveland, the nominee, was born in Norwich, June 19, 1804. He is described as a pale, intellectual youth, who had a passion for reading and study, and he was entered at Yale College in 1820, and graduated with honors in 1824. The graduating class consisted of sixty-seven members, but few of whom are now living. Within a few months after graduating, he located in Baltimore and pursued the calling of a teacher. He appears to have inherited the desire to enter the ministry, and whilst teaching he pursued his studies in that direction. In 1828, four years after he removed to Wilmington, he was ordained a Presbyterian minister and at once took charge of a Church near the homestead in Windham, near Norwich. He left his affections behind him in Baltimore, and in the following year he returned to that city and married the daughter of Abner Neal of that place. He did not return to Windham but preached in sundry places in the South, and afterwards settled at Caldwell, New Jersey From thence he removed to Fayetteville in 1841, and in 1847 he was appointed Secretary of the Home Missionary Society. Six years afterwards he was installed at Holland Patent, where he died, October 1, 1853, in his fiftieth year.

Mrs. Cleveland, mother of the Governor, died at the same place, July 19, 1882. They had nine children, four boys and five girls, as follows: Anna, (Mrs. Dr. Hastings) missionary to Ceylon; William N., an Alumnus of Hamilton, teacher in the New York City Blind Asylum, now a Presbyterian Minister at Forestport, N. Y., 1832; Mary, (Mrs. W E. Hoyt), 1833, Richard Cecil, 1835, Stephen Grover, (Governor of New York and Presidential nominee), 1837; Margaret, (Mrs. N. B. Bacon), 1838, Lewis Frederick, 1841; Susan, (Mrs. S. Yeomans), 1843; Rose, (unmarried), 1846.

His Birth-Place.

It was during the stay of the family in New Jersey that Governor Cleveland was born, and the old, dingy, obscure town of Caldwell is the place of his birth. The little, unpretentious two-and-a-half story house, with a dirty white coating and clumsy shutters, still stands to mark the place where, in 1837, he first became an actor on the busy stage of life, and from whence and when he has matured and advanced until now he is the honored Governor of the Empire State. Less than a thousand souls live in this quiet hamlet, which but for the accidents of politics would probably never have been heard of outside of the records of Oneida county It was made famous in a day by the nomination of Governor Cleveland for the Presidency True it is that neither the place nor its humble people ever knew much of him, either as boy or man, for his life there can be spanned by the circle of a few months. It has held the family hearthstone for many years and that now makes it a place of note. The father died here, when he had said his long prayers and given good old doctrinal sermons to his slender flock only three weeks. His mother made it her home until her death, soon after her son was elected Governor of New York. The only maiden sister he has, still keeps up the humble cottage, which will now figure in song, story and picture as the early and only real home of the Democratic Presidential nominee.

Recollections.

It is not easy to find out much about Mr Cleveland's early life, although he spent most of his boyhood days within a dozen miles of this neat little city Over at Clinton, a secluded village some ten miles across the flat country from here, he went to school some time before his parents moved up to "the Patent." But he is remembered there only as the son of a poor Presbyterian preacher, who wore shabby clothes and was always ready to fight, not only for himself, but for his younger companions, when he or they were nagged by the older or more fortunate boys. There are not many reminiscences of his father to be had there or here. He is remembered as a rigid disciple of the Blue Stocking faith, one of those strong, severe characters, which "would have perished at the stake for tenets he would not forsake." The mother is also readily recalled as a positive force in this pious household. The blood of a good, Southern Maryland family runs in her veins, and it was a good strain with which to warm the frigid qualities of the cold New England stock which was top in the head of the household. Hence the ten strong children who were born of the union, were offspring equipped with the qualities of body and mind for a stiff battle with the world. Not brilliant, but able, substantial people, were all of them. Whether or not it was the Southern blood that changed the temper of the children I cannot say, but I believe that out of the five boys none of them turned to the ministry as their ancestors in the male line had done for generations before. One or two of the girls married preachers, but most of them chose to look for a better material chance in life than can be found in the product of mite societies and of donation gatherings. His recollections of his native town must be very meagre and the associations very vague and shadowy, for he was but three years of age when he left there. His father was a Presbyterian preacher whose salary was small and whose family was large, and keenly feeling "the wants that pinch the poor," and desiring a larger field of labor, with an increased income, he removed, by way of the Hudson river and the Erie canal, to Fayetteville, which was then a thriving straggling country town about six miles from Pompey Hill, the birth-place of ex-Governor Seymour. In those days the means of transportation were slow and limited, and the appearance of this humble family as it slowly floated to a new home, would not have indicated to an observer the probability that one of the urchins composing the party would become the Mayor of an important city, and the Governor of the greatest State. The struggle for life is filled with mutations, but by means of its friction the sparks of latent genius fly upward and onward.

> "Greatness and fame from no positions rise,
> Act well thy part, there all the honor lies."

His Early Education.

At Fayetteville, Grover Cleveland, as he was called, commenced his education in an old-fashioned country school, where he very probably fell into the ways of the village boys, and exhibited the usual compound of good and evil that distinguish the average school-boy. That he availed himself of the poor opportunities then offered in a common school is evidenced by the fact that before he had reached fourteen years of age he had mastered all the studies that the schoolmaster taught, and feeling that a longer continuance there was useless, he urgently entreated his father to send him to an academy not far from there. But the elder Cleveland thought that inasmuch as his son had mastered the curriculum of the school, he did not need an academic finishing which would consume time and money that might be more profitably invested. So the son's aspirations were nipped in the bud, and the academy project was abandoned.

Clerk in a Country Store.

The father s income was small, and he intended that the son should support himself without delay So he was placed in a country store to deal out the thousand and one articles contained in such an institution, for which he was to receive one dollar per week for the first year, and if he proved active and honest his wages to be doubled for the following year Here in this village center he dealt out molasses and mackerel, soap and sugar, and expatiated on the cotton prints to the village girls, proving himself a valuable assistant until the expiration of the second year.

Origin.

Governor Cleveland is of Yankee origin and hails originally from "the land of steady habits." His father graduated at Yale in 1824, taught in Baltimore after the custom of Jared Sparks and other college graduates of an early day, married a daughter of Abner Neal, of that city, after he had become a Presbyterian minister and was pastor of the church at Caldwell, N. J. March 18, 1837, the day when the child was born, which was named Stephen Grover Cleveland, and who as Grover Cleveland, the Democratic candidate for president , was to become far more widely known than any of his preaching and rhyme-writing ancestors. Stephen Grover, for whom the boy was named was a Presbyterian minister, who preceded preacher Cleveland as the occupant of the Presbyterian pulpit at Caldwell. Perhaps the best known Cleveland, after Grover, is his cousin, Arthur Cleveland Coxe, Episcopal bishop of Western New York. A grand uncle, Charles, city missionary of Boston, who was better known as "Father" Cleveland, lived to be one hundred years old, lacking seventeen days.

Grover, as he was always called for sake of euphony, was the fifth of nine brothers and sisters. His brothers Frederic and Cecil were lost at sea in the burning steamship Missouri, October 22, 1872, off Abaco, the chief of the Bahamas. Frederic was the lessee of the Royal Victoria Hotel, at Nassau, New Providence.

The Rev C. T Barry, the pastor of the Presbyterian Church, lives in the old parsonage, in good old fashioned style, and in unostentatious simplicity. The house sets back from the road about a hundred feet and two noble ash trees stand like sentinels before it. The grounds which contain about two acres are well kept, and the whole place has an air of neatness and respectability The house itself is a two-story and a-half, with a front porch and low windows. The front door opens into a spacious hall and the rooms on each side of it are cosy and comfortable. The ceilings are low The doors are very wide and the whole place savors of antiquity.

The Church Record.

In the old church baptismal record we find the record of the birth and baptizing of the Democratic nominee," and Mr. Barry pointed to an entry which read as follows: "Stephen Grover Cleveland, baptized July 1, 1837 , born March 18, 1837 "

"During his six years' pastorate," said Mr Barry, "Mr. Cleveland's father had a child baptized every year. When Grover Cleveland was elected Governor of New York I wrote and told him that I had these interesting facts, and he sent me a very graceful reply Here is the room in which Governor Cleveland was born, and Mr Barry pushed open the door and led the visitor into a room now used as a library The room was about fifteen feet square, with two windows and a low ceiling. An excellent steel engraving of James G. Blaine stood upon a table looking in the direction of the spot where his opponent was born.

Cleveland's Boyhood.

The removal of the elder Cleveland to Clinton gave Grover the long-wished-for opportunity to attend a high school and he pursued his studies industriously and laid the foundation of his future success so far as school knowledge and discipline supply the material, until the family moved up on the Black River to what was then known as the Holland Patent—a village of five or six hundred people—fifteen miles north of Utica. The elder Cleveland preached but three Sundays in this place, when he suddenly died. Grover first heard of his father's death while walking with his sister in the streets of Utica. But he went no farther than the academy, his father's death forcing him out into the world to do something for his family and himself. This event produced the usual break-up of the family, and we next hear of Grover Cleveland setting out for New York City to accept at a small salary the position of under teacher in an asylum for the blind, where at the time the since well-known Gus. Schell was executive officer.

A Teacher of the Blind.

In the city of New York stands an imposing structure of Sing Sing granite, fronting about two hundred feet, with buttresses and turrets approaching the Elizabethan style, in which has been expended more than two millions of dollars for the education of the blind.

New York took the first steps on this continent to educate the blind, and this society was organized more than fifty years ago. The building has been standing probably forty years, though the Mansard roof upon it has been added recently. When it was built it stood far outside of New York proper. The Ninth Avenue Elevated Railroad runs right before it and has a station at the corner on Thirty-fourth street.

Reminiscences of Him.

A person well acquainted with the Institution gives the following information as to Grover Cleveland's tutorship there. When asked at what time he taught in the Institution, he said: "About thirty years, but there is not a single personal recollection of him in the institution. It seems that he and a brother were both teachers here about one year each and at the same time." "Have you looked the archives up?" "Yes and there I find the names of both the Clevelands. But there have been so many teachers in the institution that no record is left of these, but I suspect from a Mr. Allen having been the secretary of this institution and that being the name of Grover Cleveland's uncle, that they got their places through the influence of this uncle. It was from the blind asylum that Grover went to Buffalo and settled there."

Its History.

The institution at which Cleveland taught in New York was begun by Dr John Russ, who came from Massachusetts and began to practice medicine in New York. Dr. Howe, of Boston, sent him in a ship to take supplies to the Greeks, who were fighting the Turks, as at that day the American people were not afraid to extend their help not only to South America but to Europe in the arms of tyranny After spending three years in Greece, where he established a hospital, Dr Russ returned to New York and began to educate blind boys. He refused to leave this great field for a blind institution which was afterward organized in Boston, and he introduced the trades here of making baskets, mats and carpets.

Dr. Russ had scarcely left the New York Blind Institution when young Cleveland came in to teach. It seems that Boston and New York started their blind institutions the same year, 1832, while Pennsylvania began the following year

Noted School Teachers.

Our Presidents present very peculiar contrasts in education and a very large percentage of our statesmen began at school teaching. Teaching school was in the first half of this century what writing for the newspapers is now—a method of tiding over the early years of one's life until a more substantial opportunity can be presented. William H. Seward and Lyman Trumbull went South to be tutors. John Adams studied law under cover of teaching school at Worcester, Mass. Jefferson had all the instincts of a school teacher though he was led into public life. I found the last of the kin of James Madison, his nephew's daughters, teaching school in Virginia a few years ago. Aaron Burr was the son of the first schoolmaster of Princeton. John Quincy Adams taught at Harvard College. I think Andrew Jackson made a feeble effort at school teaching for a little while in Western North Carolina, though there is some doubt about this. Millard Fillmore, I believe, had a little spell of school teaching in Western New York. Fillmore's only son, by the way, is alive in Buffalo, without any posterity, and Mr Bissel, law partner of Governor Cleveland, told me during the convention that the name of Fillmore would expire with him. When Grover Cleveland went to Buffalo Fillmore had just ceased to be President and had returned to the city, where he established the practice of law.

Breaks Away from Tutorship.

He stayed there two years, and it has been found possible to discover the same indelible record of hard work, faithfully performed and well remembered by those who were cognizant of it, and who are still alive. From tending country store to teaching the blind is a long way on the road of self-discipline. But to teach he did not believe was his mission, and consequently at the expiration of two years he abandoned it and literally started out to seek his fortune in the Far West—only reversing the usual order, and instead of coming to the great city, he left it. His first idea was to go to Cleveland. On his way, he stopped at Buffalo, N. Y., where young Cleveland paid his respects to his uncle Lewis F Allen, a noted stock-breeder, who was favorably impressed with the young man, whom he saw for the first time, and he asked him for his advice and guidance. As he has since said, the name seemed a good omen.

Wants to be a Lawyer.

The uncle did not speak enthusiastically. "What is it you want to do my boy?" he asked,

"Well sir, I want to study law."

"Good gracious," remarked the old gentleman. "Do you indeed? What ever put that in your head? How much money have you got?"

To tell the truth he hadn't got any.

"See here," said the uncle, after a long consultation. "I want somebody to get up my herd-book this year. You come and stay with me and help me and I'll give you $50 for the year's work and you can look around."

The offer was a tempting one, for employment was what he was in search of, but he replied:—"I have agreed to go to Cleveland with my companion and I cannot desert him now in the midst of the journey" It was finally agreed that Grover should interview his friend upon this subject, and if possible gain his consent. Mr. Cleveland, much to his gratification, found that his comrade was willing to release him from his agreement to go to Ohio, and Grover Cleveland became a resident of Buffalo.

A Mixed Calling.

Here it is that we find the American boy now annotating short horns out at Black Rock, quite two miles from Buffalo. But he kept his eye out for a chance to enter a law office while he was editing the stock book, and one day he walked boldly into the room of Messrs, Rogers, Bowen & Rogers, and told them what he wanted. There were a number of young men in the place already. But young Cleveland's persistency won, and he was finally permitted to come as an office boy and have the use of the law library

For this he received the nominal sum of $3 or $4 a week, out of which he had to pay his board and washing. The walk to and from his uncle's was a long and at that time a rugged one. The first winter was a memorably severe one, and his shoes were broken, and he had no overcoat. But he never intermitted a day. It began to be noticed that he was the most punctual and regular of the lads in the office. Often at night he was compelled to stand by the warm chimney in the loft where he slept and dry his feet after tramping the two miles through the snow His senior employer had taken a copy of Blackstone on the first day of the boy's office experience and, planting it before him with a bang that made the dust fly, said: "That's where they all begin." There was a titter ran round the little circle of clerks, for it was a foreboding thing to begin with to the average lad. It appears, however, that he stuck to the Blackstone so well that he mastered it and so absorbed was he in it one night that they locked him in and all went off. He spent that night with the book and never forgot it.

His political preference at this time led him to join the Democratic party, to which he has ever since persistently adhered.

The Discipline of Hardship.

This uneventful period of Grover Cleveland's life, so devoid of adventure and barren of romance, was the period at which all the forces of his later life were gestating. The privations and miseries of a penniless novitiate gave way slowly before his determined assiduity and pluck. He tells in his own way with a beaming, reminiscent humor of the first honor that came to him when his uncle, in getting out the second volume of his "Breed Book," announced to him that he intended to acknowledge in it his valuable assistance. But these privations and miseries, it may readily be seen by the temperament of the man, were only so many stimuli. His was not the hypersensitive nature that winced and wore under physical discomforts.

"See here," said his uncle to him one bitter December night when the lad had walked out to Black Rock through the sleet and snow: "this is pretty cold weather for you to be traveling without an overcoat."

"Oh," says the young man, "I'm going to buy one when I earn the money"

"Why, look at your feet, they must be sopping, eh!"

"Oh, that's nothing. I'm getting some copying to do now and I'll have a pair of boots by and by"

In those days boys had to demonstrate what was in them before they received many favors.

"You just go right over there to the tailor's and get the stoutest overcoat he's got. D'ye hear."

Very likely Grover had begun to demonstrate what was in him, but whether to the mind of the uncle it was a capacity for compiling herd books or the capacity to contain Blackstone cannot now be learned.

His Old Uncle.

The old uncle, L. F Allen, who gave him good advice, but very little else, when he reached here some thirty years ago on his way to Cleveland, Ohio, still lives there and is now past four-score years. He persuaded his nephew to stop at this point and helped him to get a chance to study law by working mighty hard for it. He is an eccentric man, of strict business habits, and doesn't seem to take much interest in politics. He really knows less of the life of his relative than almost any man of repute you meet.

A Financial Move.

It must have been about this time, or just as he was to set out from home on his journey West, that he borrowed from the Hon. Ingham Townsend, of Floyd, Oneida County, a certain sum of money, to which the following letter, written many years afterward, (it was on Jan. 21, 1867,) refers:

I am now in condition to pay my note which you hold, given for money borrowed some years ago. I suppose I might have paid it long before, but I have never thought you were in need of it, and I had other purposes for my money I have forgotten the date of the note. If you will send me it I will mail you the principal and interest. The loan you made me was my start in life, and I shall always preserve the note as an interesting reminder of your kindness. Let me hear from you soon. With many kind wishes to Mrs. Townsend and your family, I am yours, very respectfully.

GROVER CLEVELAND.

His Banker.

Mr. Townsend died in the town of Floyd in March, 1883, so that he had lived long enough to see the recipient of his bounty elected Governor of the State of New York. His age was then eighty-one, and he had in his time assisted many young men with money to make their first start in the world. When he gave the money to young Cleveland he told him he need never return it, but that, should he ever meet a young man in need as he himself has been, he might turn the money over to him should he have it to spare. Grover Cleveland had not been long in this law office at Buffalo when the firm engaged him at a fixed, liberal salary and found that he was entirely capable of earning it. It was about the year 1858 that the young student secured admission to the Bar. He had been four years with the Rogers firm, and after his admission he remained with them four years longer, thus securing a thorough training and equipment for his profession.

What they say at Syracuse.

This quiet little village of twelve hundred inhabitants was once the home of Grover Cleveland, the nominee of the Democratic party for the Presidency. Dr D. P Hutchins, an old resident, who had an office in Deacon McViccar s store when Grover was a clerk there, when asked for some reminiscences of the Governor's boyhood, said that " Grove," as they used to call him, was always considered a good boy, courteous and dignified in his manners and was exceedingly popular. He held his position in the store about one year. He made an efficient clerk and was highly recommended by Mr McViccar when he left the latter's employ

H. Howard Edwards, also a long resident, and a playmate of the Governor's, when questioned concerning his recollections of Cleveland's boyhood, said there was nothing during the time he lived here to indicate his future distinction. " Why," said Mr Edwards, " we used to be together constantly, go a-fishing together, sleep together, and I cannot recall anything that impressed me with his future greatness. He was very slim when he was a boy, short and had small features. He was full of fun, and, I tell you, we had lots of fun together "

Captain H. S. Pratt, another old resident was found in bed, but said, " Grove was one of the finest boys I ever knew. Everybody respected him, even the ' old folks' and you never heard of a practical joke on him, he was chuck full of fun and I recollect he had a weakness for ringing the school bell when he got a chance. He and his brother ' Will ' used to have a long rope attached to the hammer of the bell and the way they used to make that bell ring after dark was a caution."

There is a warm feeling towards the Cleveland family on the part of all who remember them.

As a Lawyer.

Four years in the office of Rogers, Bowen & Rogers as a student equipped him with sufficient elementary knowledge and experience to become managing clerk at the end of that time. And so four years more pass. It is interesting to know exactly what kind of character he had now made for himself and how he was regarded by his associates. It is not difficult to ascertain this with reasonable accuracy, seeing that most of those associates are alive and accessible and speak with noticeable candor and unanimity

Said one of them to the writer : " Grover won our admiration by his three traits of indomitable industry, unpretentious courage and unswerving honesty. I never saw a more thorough man at anything he undertook. Whatever the subject was, he was reticent until he had mastered all its bearings and made up his own mind—and then nothing could swerve him from his conviction. It was this quality of intellectual integrity more than anything else perhaps that made him afterwards listened to and respected when more brilliant men who were opposed to him were applauded and forgotten.

Admission to the Bar.

In 1859, when he was in his twenty-second year, he had completed his legal studies, passed the necessary examination, and was admitted to the bar

After being admitted to the bar he engaged in practice, and despite the many obstacles that confront a young lawyer, and the almost certain vexatious delay in waiting for clients, he soon obtained considerable practice. He had no influential family name to entice clients to the office, no powerful relatives to give him substantial support, and every lawyer who reads this will appreciate the position of the young man of humble name, without means, and unknown to the general public, first entering upon his professional career. Old and established names and firms, whose reputations are well known to the public, are generally sought by those desiring legal advice and assistance to the exclusion of those just entering the profession. And so Grover Cleveland found it, as day after day he tendered his services to a people almost without recognition. But he did not become discouraged, and succumb to what some would consider adverse fate, but stuck persistently to his calling, serving the few who came with devotion and ability until his reputation as a lawyer widened, bringing with it an increase of patronage. Fortunately for him he was entrusted with some important cases, which he conducted so successfully that his fellow members of the bar recognized him as one destined to rise in the legal profession. At the end of three years he had acquired a fair practice and a good standing at the bar and he was looked upon with marked favor by his fellow citizens.

The First Step into Public Life.

In 1863 the question of who should be appointed Assistant District-Attorney for the county of Erie was warmly discussed by the young lawyers in Messrs. Rogers & Bowen's office. There were several that were both eligible and anxious, but it does not appear that young Cleveland advanced his own claims. Indeed, it is a fact that after the matter had been pretty well canvassed, they all agreed that he was the person who ought to have it, and they urged him to accept it. This simple incident speaks volumes for the already developed character of the young man. He was appointed, and from that moment his public record began. During the three years that he was in the District-Attorney's office, the great bulk of its duties fell upon his shoulders, and then it was that his enormous vital strength and tireless industry made themselves felt. One may say now that it is well perhaps that the District-Attorney himself was rather disposed to let youth and vigor shoulder the great part of the responsibility It was just the training that young Cleveland needed, and he went into it with all the zeal of youthful aspirations.

Cleveland Drafted.

It was during the performance of the duties of this office, and at a time when a large number of important cases with which he alone was thoroughly familiar were demanding his attention, that he was drafted. There was no question at all of what his duty was. He promptly supplied a substitute. So well and faithfully had he conducted the affairs of the county that at the end of three years he was nominated by the Democrats for the District-Attorneyship. Here, again, it is an undisputable fact that he did not solicit the nomination, hesitated to accept it, and did not turn his hand over to secure his election. It is said in Buffalo that on the day of election he was trying a case in court, while his friends were electioneering for him on the street, and the Judge on the Bench, who was presumably an admirer of his, peremptorily adjourned the case and told Cleveland to go and attend to his interests.

Defeated.

In the canvass that followed he was beaten by the Republican candidate, Lyman K. Bass, one of his very near personal friends with whom he afterwards formed a law partnership. This was in 1865. In 1866, the year following his defeat, Mr Cleveland formed a partnership in the law with the late Mayor I. K. Vanderpoel, which lasted till 1869, but on the election of Mr Vanderpoel as Police Justice soon afterward he became a member of the firm of Laning, Cleveland & Folsom, of which the head was the late Senator A. P Laning.

The latter association, however, ended at the expiration of two years, owing to Mr. Cleveland having been nominated and elected in 1869 to be Sheriff of Erie County

As Sheriff.

The friends of Governor Cleveland brought out his name in connection with the office of Sheriff of Erie county, and without any effort on his part he was nominated by the Democratic Convention, and elected for three years. In that important position he fully sustained his character for integrity and ability, and whilst performing the duties of the office, he earned an additional meed of public respect for his courageous disregard of partisan interests and his conscientious regard for the public welfare. A correspondent of the New York *World* gives the following interesting items relating to his official actions as Sheriff:

Two Executions.

It was as Sheriff of Erie county that the Governor became known in a political or official way and many interesting anecdotes are told by those who remember those days. During his term of office as Sheriff, the Governor swung two men into eternity The first one was the notorious Jack Gaffney a reckless young Irishman, who kept a saloon at the corner of Washington and Carroll streets, almost opposite the *Courier* office. Gaffney was seated in a low dive on Canal street—"Ted" Sweeney's—playing cards with a kindred spirit named Patrick Fahey The two quarrelled over the stakes, and Gaffney shot and killed Fahey in cool blood. He was sentenced by the General Term in December to hang February 7 following. During these two months there was the greatest effort made on the part of the reporters to find out how the condemned man spent his time, but the Sheriff turned a deaf ear to them, and not a few times gave them to understand that they wanted to know too much. He kept them out of the jail entirely after a while, and they were in sore straits. The interest in the case was intensified at the last from the fact that Governor Hoffman respited the condemned man for a week, and that the most strenuous efforts were made to get a commutation of sentence for the doomed man. Meanwhile the vigilant Sheriff was more rigid in his discipline than ever, and he even went so far as to station an old Dutchman outside with strict orders to keep reporters off the premises. This outside guard was used to relieve the guard inside Gaffney's cell, so that he was well posted on what was going on inside. One of the reporters, who now, by the way, is a city editor of that city, conceived the idea of "working" the grim German sentinel outside.

How it Worked.

He did not try to do it all at once, but by a skilful working of his points he became acquainted with him as the young man who attended the spiritual adviser. By degrees he became aware that the grim sentinel had a weakness for beer. It was easy work after that, for he contrived to meet him every night after he was relieved and together the two talked over the events of the day in the jail over their beverage. The German was full of information in just the proportion that he was full of beer, and the facts that filled many a breezy column of his paper were costing the enterprising news gatherer dear. Sheriff Cleveland was wild. He questioned every one about the jail, but could get no satisfaction. At last his eye fell upon the sentinel and he was spotted. It was the night before the execution the two were seen together That settled it, for in the morning the sentinel was gone and in his place was another. Gaffney swung on the morning of the 14th of February, 1872. Many citizens of the city remember the execution and the quickness with which the Governor disappeared after he had cut the cord.

The Second Execution.

The second execution performed by the Governor while Sheriff was five months later. The murderer was one of the most despicable wretches that ever deserved a shameful death—Patrick Morrissey. He lived with his poor old mother in the vicinity of the old "Packet" dock, in the rear of what was known as the Alhambra Theatre. He was a thoroughly heartless man and was given to frequent and continued debauches, during which he submitted his dependent mother to the most shameful cruelty While on one of these sprees he sought out his mother's hovel and demanded from her the few pence she had earned by her own exertions to buy bread. She refused him, when he struck her to the floor. At the time she was cutting a loaf of bread for his supper As she struggled to her feet she said to him, "You had better kill your mother and be done with it." As she uttered the words he grasped the knife from her hands and with the words, "I will kill you then," buried it in her breast. The horror of the matricide made people of the city shudder, and the jury by which he was tried lost no time in bringing in a verdict of murder in the first degree. Morrissey was sentenced to hang on the 6th day of September Prominent among the witnesses on that famous trial was Albert Haight, now a Supreme Court Judge. The execution took place on the day named in the warrant, and the present Governor was the executioner"

His Habits as Sheriff.

Whilst holding this important office, Grover Cleveland's habits of life seem to have been as simple as the general conduct of the man has been—unassuming. He dwelt in a quiet boarding house, and when its mistress got a well-to-do son-in-law and quit business he used to take his Sunday morning breakfast at the Terrapin Lunch, a plain restaurant, where probably a terrapin was never seen. Old Major Randall, of the Lake Shore Rail road, was his intimate friend and companion. He died soon after Cleveland was made Governor. It was his oft-expressed ambition to live to see "Grove," as he called him, President. He was made Sheriff of this county by an accident. In fact, he never had an office that he was not forced into. In 1869 David Williams, superintendent of the Lake Shore Railroad, wanted to run for Congress. This district was close and he wouldn't make the effort with any of the aspirants for the Sheriffalty It was the most important office to be filled and there was a bitter contest for it. The leaders got together and decided that Cleveland must run to help Williams. There wasn't much chance of an election, and to all appearances his defeat seemed a foregone conclusion, but they insisted that he must make the sacrifice for the party He was then regarded as a good lawyer, with a good practice, but he became the candidate and not only helped Williams, but by a hundred votes he defeated his opponent, to the surprise of both parties.

His Financial Start.

The fees of the Sheriff's office were large and the income from it gave him his first financial start. He then made money at the law and saved something. His reputation is not that of a money-getter and money-saver Had he been ambitious in this direction he could and would have been a rich man.

His Return to the Bar.

At the expiration of his official term as Sheriff in 1873, he became a member of the firm of Messrs. Bass, Cleveland & Bissell, with Lyman K. Bass and Wilson S. Bissell as associates. This was a strong and popular firm, and commanded a large and lucrative practice. At the close of Mr. Bass's Congressional career his failing health induced him to seek a residence in Colorado, resulting in a dissolution of the copartnership and the formation of another under the name of Cleveland & Bissell. In December, 1881, Mr. George J. Sicard was admitted as a partner in the firm, which was then styled Cleveland, Bissell & Sicard, and thus continues to the present time.

Legal Distinction.

It was while thus associated that Grover Cleveland achieved his distinction as a lawyer second to few in the western part of the State for legal acumen and intellectual honesty His jury and bench trials were distinguished by clear views, direct, simple logic and a thorough mastery of all the intricacies of the cases, and his invariable avoidance of extrinsic issues and purely technical devices secured for him the respect of his own profession and the admiration of the public. These qualities, combined with the fidelity and independence of his official action while in office, brought him prominently before the public of Buffalo when that city, unable to extricate itself from a municipal octopus, was casting about for a stanch reform leader.

Mr Cleveland has had four or five law partnerships with the strong men of this city and all say he was a valuable business companion. His career as a lawyer is well defined in this region and his reputation well established. It seems queer that the general agreement has not reflected itself outside of Western New York. Mr Milburn a bright young man, now a partner in the law firm where the present Governor studied, writes as follows:

"It amuses me to hear this talk about Mr Cleveland's lack of ability. He is the strongest character I ever knew without a national reputation. He is a fine lawyer. He is incapable of wilful wrong and nothing on earth could sweep him from his conviction of duty That he is thoroughly honest cannot be questioned and without being what might be called a brilliant man he has always been regarded as an able and safe one in every relation of life."

His Standing at Home.

This terse summing up of the nominee's position at home is simply duplicated by the Judges and lawyers with whom he has mingled. Among the laymen he seems to stand equally high. Republicans and Democrats alike speak of him as a man of the strongest character and highest attainments. Mr James N Matthews who edits the *Express*, the leading Republican paper of the City by the Lake, speaks forth this sentiment as follows:

"I know of no Democrat better equipped for the position for which he has been named than Grover Cleveland. He is an able, honest and incorruptible man. He is self-reliant and has excellent judgment. I shall do all I can honestly and honorably to defeat his election, for I am earnestly for Mr Blaine. But when people speak of him as an obscure man it is but fair to say that he has long stood in the front rank with the very leaders of thought and action in this part of New York."

As Mayor.

While in private life he gave his whole attention to the practice of his profession, and kept out of the political arena until 1881 At that period circumstances were shaping themselves so as to draw Mr. Cleveland into a wider sphere of life than he had yet been an actor There was a popular revolt against the administration of the municipal affairs of the city of Buffalo, and in the disquieted condition of affairs the old party lines were somewhat broken. It had been badly ruled by a combination or ring of Republican managers, and many of its voters rebelled against an extension of this fraud and mismanagement. Buffalo was not a great city, but in the matter of municipal corruption and combinations it could have given points to others with many times its number of people. It was ring-ridden. Its revenues were stolen or wasted and no Mayor had been found for many years who had at once the ability and the boldness necessary to attack these abuses.

They Found their Man.

To find such an individual was no easy task. There were many who were profuse in their promises, but such pledges had been so often broken, that the people intended that no one should be promoted to the place, who could not give good security by means of an unsullied reputation, and a good record. They selected Grover Cleveland, and seeing their opportunity, called him out from his retirement from politics to be their candidate for Mayor of the city Buffalo is usually Republican by from 2,000 to 5,000 majority, and Mr. Cleveland's election on the Democratic ticket by a majority of 5,000 was simply a tribute to his personal integrity

As in the Sheriff's Office, here again the office sought the man, and the man they selected proved worthy of the confidence they reposed in him.

Grover Cleveland's election on a Democratic and reform ticket in November, 1881, suddenly lifted him from local into national prominence. The incidents of that election and subsequent administration are familiar throughout the country. The election itself was an almost unparalleled triumph, seeing that it was secured by the largest majority ever known, thus demonstrating the unbounded confidence which the people had in the special fitness of their candidate to carry out the reform and in his unassailable integrity

His Mother's Advice.

After Grover was elected Mayor of Buffalo the mother wrote him rather disapproving his entering public life. After saying what her ambitions were for him and expressing a natural tinge of gratification at his election, she concluded her epistle by saying : "But now that you have taken upon yourself the burthens of public office do right, act honestly, impartially and fearlessly" The injunction was obeyed and his courage has won him a phenomenal success.

It would appear from a close study of this man's conduct and general traits of character from boyhood up, right here, where his early days were spent, and in Buffalo, where his latter life has been an open book to its people, that his hard struggle for a place in the world has ever given him supreme self-reliance. He was about seventeen when he left Holland Patent and went to New York to help teach the blind. He had early established the reputation of being a nervy, manly sort of a young fellow, somewhat diffident, but not afraid to face any emergency which might confront him. He seems to have assumed more than any other member of the family the care of his mother and sisters.

The Candidate of Reform.

It is strictly true that Mayor Cleveland was swept into office on one of those tidal waves of popular protest against ring rule that are as restless as they are sudden. But it was after all a local contest, and one has yet to account for the national importance which the Buffalo election assumed and the widespread interest that was felt in the new champion. There is only one way in which to explain this. Mr. Cleveland had not yet attracted attention outside of his metropolitan field. But there was one issue that in a sense was the issue of the hour everywhere, and that was whether it was any longer possible to secure by a popular election that kind of integrity and sagacity that would administer the people's affairs with the honesty and discretion that was necessary to good government. The Buffalo canvass for the Mayoralty defined that issue in the sharpest manner. The nomination of Grover Cleveland was avowedly and defiantly the gage of battle thrown down by reform. There were only two points to be determined—did the people want reform ? that is did they wish their business conducted honestly, and would the man they had selected for the experiment so conduct it ? So vitally important were these two questions that vaster and intenser themes were for the moment forgotten by the country, and it turned aside momentarily to watch this contest in Buffalo. The people answered one question and Grover Cleveland answered the other. The reply in one case was with votes, in the other with acts.

An Honest Mayor.

Whatever else may have been searched for, it is pretty well settled that they had found an honest man, and, what is of more consequence, the honest man was brave enough to carry his private convictions into his public duties with no regard to partisanship on the one hand or the influence and threats of political scoundrels on the other. There was no uncertain sound in his inaugural message. It rang clear and simple.

"We hold," said he, "the money of the people in our hands, to be used for their purposes and to further their interests as members of the municipality, and it is quite apparent that, when any part of the funds which the taxpayers have thus intrusted us are diverted to other purposes, or when, by design or neglect, we allow a greater sum to be applied to any municipal purpose that is necessary, we have, to that extent, violated our duty There surely is no difference in his duties and obligations, whether a person is intrusted with the money of one man or many. And yet it sometimes appears as though the office-holder assumes that a different rule of fidelity prevails between him and the taxpayers than that which should regulate his conduct when, as an individual, he holds the money of his neighbor."

The First Move.

He passed the first few weeks of his term of office in attentively studying the details of every department of the city administration. His previous experiences as Assistant District Attorney and as Sheriff taught him what to look for and where to look for it. He found the ordinary municipal abuses, sanctioned by long habit and immunity, flourishing as usual. One morning he surprised the city by issuing an order that all the officials should keep strict business hours, like the employés of private firms. Before the office-holders had recovered from this shock, he began a series of vetoes which equally astonished the Common Council. This Board had a Republican majority, and attempted to override the vetoes, but Mayor Cleveland's terse, logical, business-like messages were published, and public opinion was too strong for the opposition Councilmen. They attempted to entrap him by passing a resolution apportioning for the celebration of Decoration Day a sum of money reserved by the charter for other purposes, believing that Mayor Cleveland would not dare to interfere with Decoration Day, or that he would become unpopular if he did. Down came the veto as promptly as ever, and in his message the Mayor so thoroughly exposed the trick, that his popularity, instead of diminishing, rapidly increased.

His Popularity.

His administration of the office fully justified the partiality of the friends who insisted upon nominating him, and vindicated the good judgment of the people who so powerfully insisted upon electing him. It is not too much to say that in the first half of the first year he almost revolutionized Buffalo's municipal government. With no more power than his predecessors had, he inaugurated reforms before only hoped for, and corrected abuses which had become almost venerable. Accounts against the city were thoroughly audited, since he pointed out what is required of an officer whose duty is to audit. The wholesome rule of competition was adopted for important work that used to be given out in the form of a political patronage. So far as one man can see, he saw to it that the city got the full value for its money He knew his power and was not afraid to use it. He conquered the most corrupt combinations ever formed in the council and rebuked the conspirators in terms that brought the blush of shame to the most brazen of Aldermen. His veto messages have become municipal classics.

Opposed to All Jobs.

His veto of the street-cleaning job is regarded as the real beginning of his public career.

An Example of His Work.

When Mr. Cleveland entered upon the office of Mayor the Common Council had determined to build an intercepting sewer and had advertised for proposals. The lowest bid for the work was $1,568,000. Mr Cleveland thought the sewer could be built cheaper if a committee of citizens had charge of its construction. Through his efforts, though opposed in the Council, a law was passed allowing a commission to be appointed. This commission, composed of representative citizens, conferred with the most eminent sewer engineers of the country, and on their advice have adopted a plan that will meet all requirements at an estimated cost of $764,370. The plan has been accepted by the Council and the sewer will be constructed accordingly The saving to the city on this item alone is $803,630.

On June 19 the Council voted to award the street-cleaning contract for five years, to George Talbot at his bid of $422,500. There were several lower bids, by thoroughly responsible men. Mayor Cleveland vetoed the award, severely condemning the attempted waste of the people's money The contract was subsequently awarded to the lowest bidder—Capt. Thomas Maytham—at $313,500. The saving to the city by this veto was $109,000. The amount saved on these two items during the first six months of Mayor Cleveland's administration was nearly $1,000,000. In many other cases Mayor Cleveland had interposed the veto power to prevent misuse of public funds. He has refused to permit expenditure for livery for the Street Commissioner and other city officials, and has brought about order and economy in all departments of the city government. Many thousands of dollars have been saved in this way

"This," said the veto, "is a time for plain speech, and my objection to your action shall be plainly stated. I regard it as the culmination of a most barefaced, impudent and shameless scheme to betray the interests of the people and to worse than squander the public money. We are fast gaining positions in the grades of public stewardship. There is no middle ground. Those who are not for the people, either in or out of your honorable body, are against them and should be treated accordingly"

It would take a good many columns to reproduce here all those simple and straightforward messages of his which, coming from Buffalo and dealing only with local matters, have nevertheless been reproduced all over the country by the press and made the political text and the new hope of the party of reform.

His Name Grew with the People.

These acts brought him into prominence and started him towards his present place. It was on account of his fearless fight in spite of large odds against public plunderers that he was pushed and elected Governor by these people. It is because they know him to be perfectly honest and incorruptible that to-day all men, regardless of differing political affiliations, are rejoicing over his successes. Though his law office and his bachelor quarters over there are silent, both are saluted as the abode of a man who has done well on a small beginning. If the record of his life is soon told, his own people point to it with pride and give bond to the country that he will do even better in the future. This is the tenor of all the speeches and the talk of the people.

Grover Cleveland, elevated to this position by a majority of 5,000, entered cheerfully and earnestly upon his work. He had not sought the position. He had not been an active political worker in the accepted sense of that word. He knew nothing about the manipulation of caucuses and conventions. He was connected with no halls or other organizations for extorting public plunder from the officers chosen by the popular voice, and his political experience had been confined to a single term in the comparatively important office of Sheriff of the county eleven years before.

The Secret of His Success.

But he succeeded where other men had faltered or failed. And what was the secret of this success? It was simply due to the fact that the day he became Mayor of Buffalo in name he became also Mayor in fact. He did not enter upon its duties to register the edicts of a party caucus or to obey the orders of party bosses. He looked upon the office of Mayor as the business agency of the people of his city He attacked corrupt combinations in a manner which soon convinced the trading members of a City Council that he understood each item of a bill and that he had determined to reject all corrupt or unnecessary expenditure and administer the city business as faithfully as if it were his own. He used the veto power with intelligent persistence. Schemes conferring special privileges or making unwise, extravagant or sentimental appropriations or for unnecessarily increasing offices were relentlessly slaughtered. The people of Buffalo, accustomed to the waste and profligacy incident to municipal government, discovered that they had at last found a man who looked upon office as something more than a mere play-spell or an opportunity to reward his friends, and they noised his fame abroad.

His Retirement from the Office.

He went out of the office with more friends and stronger friends than he had when he went in, and he had also made some enemies, but they were of that kind which are more to a man's honor than to his discredit. In the fifteen years that he had been practicing law he had come to have a mind thoroughly disciplined and thoroughly well-adapted to the exigencies that might arise in the administration of the affairs of a large city He was his own city counsellor What he said he had a reason for in his own mind, thus giving it an individuality, concreteness and strength, whether in the shape of veto, message, or simple opinion, that may not always be found in those who hold like positions. Here, Gov Cleveland first showed the real metal there was in him.

Here he met the first trials of an administrative office, and first came in contact with the temptations that arise from party leanings and party appeals. He never flinched, never faltered once—never said an ambiguous word or performed an ambiguous act, but kept straight along in the path of strict and conscientious duty. When his administration had closed, the people of Buffalo said, "Well done, thou good and faithful servant." Next came the people of the whole State of New York and said, "Come up higher" There had been no display about his holding the office of Mayor of Buffalo. There had been no electioneering juggling about his candidacy for it, and after he received it, no one could point to a single act of self-glorification or self-advancement. He was the plain, honest, faithful, industrious man that he had been for fifteen years before in Buffalo—a good and true man put in a place of trust and found genuine.

Through all his term of office he watched the interests of the people with ceaseless vigilance, promptly approving what he thought was right, and disapproving what he believed to be wrong; and it is a fact worthy of record, that while Mayor of Buffalo, not an enactment was passed over his veto.

A Voice from the Press.

The New York *Sun*, speaking of him editorially, said:

"Grover Cleveland, now Mayor of Buffalo and the Democratic candidate for Governor of New York, is a man worthy of the highest public confidence. No one can study the record of his career since he has held office in Buffalo without being convinced that he posesses those highest qualities of a public man, sound principles of administrative duty, luminous intelligence and courage to do what is right no matter who may be pleased or displeased thereby"

(Here follow extracts from Mayor Cleveland's inaugural.)

"We wish," said the *Sun*, "that the utterance we have now quoted might be read and pondered by every citizen of the State. No matter what political faith a man may have been educated in, no matter by what party name he may now prefer to be called, no one can consider such principles and sentiments as these declared by Mr. Cleveland without feeling that such a public officer is worthy of the confidence and support of the whole people, and that the interests of the Empire State will be entirely safe in his hands."

As Governor.

The year 1882, brought with it the Gubernatorial Campaign in New York. The Republican Party in order to give prestige to its ticket placed Mr. Folger, President Arthur's Secretary of the Treasury, in nomination. Mr Folger was personally a good and strong man,but as he had been selected by the machine ring of his party, and in case of his election would have to obey its behests and carry out its mandates, his nomination did not give universal satisfaction within the party The cry of reform that had cleared the Augean stables at Buffalo, rang out through the State, and very naturally the Democratic party thought that he who had worked such healthful changes in a city, was a proper and safe man to put at the head of the great Commonwealth. His supporters made such a showing and so successfully convinced the Democrats of the State of their earnestness and the worth of their man that Mr. Cleveland was nominated for Governor over well-known and active competitors. His reputation, merely local as it had been, was still found quite large enough to spread out over a State.

A Remarkable Campaign.

The campaign was remarkable even for New York, with its astonishing and kaleidoscopic changes in politics. Many of the leading Republicans of the State ranged themselves on the side of Cleveland's candidacy. The independent element of all parties came to his support, factions in his own party disappeared, and the resulting majority of one hundred and ninety-two thousand, the largest ever given a candidate for Governor in any State in the Union carried Mr. Cleveland into the Governorship. Thus the plain, plodding citizen of Buffalo, whose capacity was neither generally known nor suspected outside the limits of his community, became one of the leading men of the country in less than a year after he had emerged from his hiding place.

How the Nomination was Received.

On the morning after the nomination of Grover Cleveland the Buffalo *Express*, the leading Republican newspaper in the interior of the State, announced that it would support him instead of the Republican candidate. Within a week many other leading Republican organs and politicians took the same bold ground. Republicans–so divided upon almost every other subject, as District Attorney Woodford and George William Curtis—agreed in repudiating the Folger and forgery ticket. Thousands of Republicans, led by the Young Men's Club of Brooklyn, voted for Grover Cleveland, and thousands more refrained from voting for any Governor. He swept the State like a tidal wave, carrying all before him.

It was not his party alone that had placed him in the Executive Chair, but the people of the Commonwealth had joined hands with the Democracy to purify the government. So the reform Mayor of Buffalo became the reform Governor of New York. He was taken because of his record. He had been judged by his works. He promised nothing except to do his whole duty in the work of reform.

He is Inaugurated Governor.

Mr. Cleveland went to Albany just before the beginning of 1883 to assume the office of Governor in the most quiet and unostentatious manner. On the day of his inauguration he walked to the Capitol and avoided all appearance of parade. His address evinced a deep sense of the responsibility which had come upon him, and a distrust of his ability to meet it fully, coupled with an evident determination to do his best. He was obliged at once to address the Legislature and to face the requirements of its action. One of his first acts was to appoint the Railroad Commissioners provided for by the law passed the year before. The admirable character of his selections showed his judgment of men and their fitness for special duties. The same characteristic was displayed as well as a conscientious disregard of mere partisans considerations in the important appointments which came later in the session. In naming Mr Shanahan as Superintendent of Public Works, Mr Perry as Commissioner to the new Capitol, and Mr. Andrews as Superintendent to the Capitol Buildings he disregarded political influence and looked to fitness alone. In advancing Assistant Superintendent McCall to the head of the Insurance Department he exemplified the principle of civil service reform to which he was fully committed. In his letter of acceptance he had said :

An Exposition of Facts.

"Subordinates in public place should be selected and retained for their efficiency and not because they may be used to accomplish partisan ends. The people have a right to demand here, as in cases of private employment, that their money be paid to those who will render the best service in return, and that the appointment to and tenure of such places should depend upon ability and merit. If the clerks and assistants in public departments were paid the same compensation and required to do the same amount of work as those employed in prudently conducted private establishments, the anxiety to hold these public places would be much diminished and the cause of civil service reform materially aided. The expenditure of money to influence the action of the people at the polls or to secure legislation is calculated to excite the gravest concern. When this pernicious agency is successfully employed a representative form of government becomes a sham, and laws passed under its baleful influence cease to protect, but are made the means by which the rights of the people are sacrificed and the public Treasury despoiled. It is useless and foolish to shut our eyes to the fact that this evil exists among us, and the party which leads in an honest effort to return to better and purer methods will receive the confidence of our citizens and secure their support. It is willful blindness not to see that the people care but little for party obligations when they are invoked to countenance and sustain fraudulent and corrupt practices. And it is well for our country and for the purification of politics that the people, at times fully roused to danger, remind their leaders that party methods should be something more than a means used to answer the purposes of those who profit by political occupation."

A Synopsis of His Policy.

He not only acted in conformity with these sentiments in making appointments but promptly approved the civil service reform bills which public sentiment and the persistency of an earnest minority compelled the Legislature to pass, following it at once with a most admirable appointment of Commissioners. He has aided and sustained the commission at all points in a most unreserved and honest manner. In dealing with the acts of the Legislature generally Governor Cleveland early developed his peculiarity of studying carefully every measure laid before him, not only with a view to judging of its effect and bearing upon public interests, but to ascertain that it was consistent with the existing laws and free in its form from such defects as would produce trouble in its operation. He adopted a practice quite unusual of sending back measures whose purpose he approved but which were defective in form, to have them corrected. In his vetoes, which were quite numerous, he displayed the utmost candor and a complete disregard of the question whether certain persons or interests would not be aggrieved by the failure of measures which he believed were not demanded by the wider interests of the public. It was during this session of 1883 that Mr Cleveland made his conscientious and courageous veto of the Five Cent Fare bill in the face of a very strong public sentiment, but in accordance with what he was convinced was his duty as an interpreter of the obligations of the State. At the close of the session he came for the first time in direct collision with the power of Tammany He had made a number of appointments chiefly affecting New York City, among them Commissioners of Emigration, Quarantine Commissioners, and Harbor Masters. These were not pleasing to Tammany, and were attacked especially by Senator Grady. The Governor sent a communication to the Senate urging the importance of disposing of these appointments before the session closed, and reflecting indirectly on the motives of the opposition. This drew from Grady a bitter tirade against the Governor, and the Legislature adjourned without a confirmation of the appointments. As the political canvass of last year came on Gov Cleveland wrote a personal letter to John Kelly conveying to the Tammany "boss" his wish that Grady should not be sent again to the Senate, recognizing the unquestionable fact that Kelly was the dispenser of nominations in Tammany Hall, and placing his objection not only on the ground of his own comfort but of the public interest. These incidents sufficiently indicate the occasion of Tammany's hostility to the Governor and of Grady's special opposition to him.

The following is a copy of his letter to Mr Kelly:

EXECUTIVE CHAMBER,
ALBANY, Oct. 20, 1883.

HON. JOHN KELLY.—

MY DEAR SIR—It is not without hesitation that I write this. I have determined to do so, however, because I see no reason why I should not be entirely frank with you. I am anxious that Mr. Grady should not be returned to the Senate. I do not wish to conceal the fact that my personal comfort and satisfaction are involved in this matter. But I know that good legislation, based upon a pure desire to promote the interests of the people, and the improvement of legislative methods are also deeply involved. I forbear to write in detail of the other considerations having relation to the welfare of the party and the approval to be secured by a change for the better in the character of its representatives. These things will occur to you without suggestion from me.

Yours very truly,

GROVER CLEVELAND.

This letter will explain Mr. Grady's antagonism to Governor Cleveland since that period.

His Unswerving Policy.

All through his career as Governor of the principal State of the Union there is observable at every turn the same simple, cardinal principles that preserved and honored his youth and that gave him a firm foothold among his fellow citizens while yet but a humble attorney Bill after bill sent him by the Legislature was vetoed, but each veto had with it a reason, and every reason was so convincing that not one rejected bill passed over his protest. He made a conscientious examination of every bill—an examination accompanied by a sharp legal insight—and as he had been his own city counsellor while Mayor of Buffalo, so he is his own Attorney-General while Governor of the State. In all his work he has gone straight ahead regardless of the bearing his conduct might have on his own political fortunes, apparently bound only to the discharge of a duty he owes to the whole people. He vetoed the Five-Cent-Fare Bill, about which there has been such an outcry, when he must have known that his act would be used against him in any future political undertaking. He did it for constitutional reasons. He stated them plainly, and thus saved the State the expense of going to the courts with the prospect of being defeated in the end. Nobody has ever attacked him on the ground that the position he took was unsound, nor that he failed to do a sworn duty. He vetoed a general street railroad bill because it was not drawn with sufficient care, but when it had been corrected he signed it. He vetoed a bill removing some of the restrictions against investing in certain lines of dangerous securities on the part of savings banks because he believed the deposits of innocent people might be endangered. He disapproved of three of the New York City Reform bills and gave satisfactory reasons therefor. The remainder of these bills he signed, but did not sign some of them till they had been returned and properly drawn. In these reform bills which he signed there are provisions that will save to New York City not less than $150,000 per annum. Thus his friends point to actual results when they call him the reform Governor. Whether in signing bills or in rejecting them, he has shown a diligence, a patience and competent inquiry which have elicited the warmest esteem of the fair-minded people of the State. They look upon him as a strong, determined man in whom there is full security.

The Five-Cent Car Fare Bill.

His veto of the Five-Cent bill has been widely complained of, but no one has intimated that he was not governed by a strict sense of justice to all the interests involved.

The following letter from President White, of Cornell University, is one of several that speak of that veto with commendation:

ITHACA, N Y., April 20, 1883.

Returning to Ithaca after an absence of ten days I find your kind letter and inclosure. I will say to you frankly that I am coming to have a very great respect and admiration for our new Governor His course on the Elevated Railroad bill first commended him to me. Personally, I should have been glad to have seen that company receive a slap. But the method of administering it seemed to me very insidious and even dangerous, and glad was I to see that the Governor rose above all the noise and clap-trap which was raised about the question, went to the fundamental point of the matter and vetoed the bill. I think his course at that time gained the respect of every thinking man in the State. As to his veto of the Buffalo Fire Department bill, that, I think, begins to lift him into national prominence, and when you add such a significant sign as his reported dealing with the Palmyra statesmen, he really begins to "loom up." It is refreshing to find that a spark of the old Jeffersonian statesmanship is really alive among us. Party allegiance in this State and elsewhere among thinking men is, I think, growing decidedly loose. Great numbers of men are quietly on the lookout for men who can grapple, not with the old abolition question or the civil war question, but with the question of a real reform in our civil service—the question of the present and future. No man and no party can be built up or kept up on clap-trap, but on real determination and power to move in this new line parties and men can alone be brought to supremacy

Thus far every party which has arrived at power and kept it for any length of time has represented some real principle, something which commended itself if not to a majority at least to an aggressive body of voters, even though that body be small. The present time is no exception to this rule.

Congratulating you on the record of the Governor thus far, and, in common with vast numbers of our fellow-citizens, longing that he may be the man whom we are all looking for, I remain, very truly yours,

AND. D. WHITE.

Henry A. Richmond, Esq., Buffalo, N Y

P. S.—I ought to have included in the Governor's titles to respect his recent appointment to the Capitol Commission, which, from all accounts is exceedingly honorable to him, not only as regards the man he did appoint, but the man he did not appoint, and, also, since writing the above, his appointment to the Insurance Department. A. D. W

As Governor he has carried out the simple business policy he had inaugurated and adhered to as Mayor His first message was rather halting. It was evident that he scarcely felt sure of his ground. The interests of the State of New York were large and extensive, and as he had never been called upon to make a special study of them the easy and nonchalant dogmatism so common to Gubernatorial messages was lacking.

His Executive Ability.

But when it came to action he made no serious misstep. He watched the course of the Legislature closely and pruned its work mercilessly He exercised the veto power with wise discretion and was especially intelligent and watchful in all legislation relating to municipal affairs. Before the session was half over he had secured the ill-will of the New York city managers in his own party but had won in return the support of the independent and reform element, regardless of political opinion. Every detail of government has been closely studied and watched. His nominations have been quite uniformly creditable, because he has rejected the services of insignificant politicians. He has dealt openly and above board.

In the matter of pardons his policy of publishing a detailed statement of his reasons made the impression that he was exercising this power in an unusual degree. But on comparison with the records of previous Governors for the same periods it was found that he had released fewer convicts than any of his recent predecessors.

Muncipal Reform.

In his prompt approval of the bills for reforming and reorganizing the city service in New York he has shown his comprehension of the needs of municipal government and made himself effectively the leader of the movement. The moral effect of his prompt action on the one bill taking from the despotic and trading Board of Aldermen the confirming power and throwing the responsibility entirely upon the Mayor enabled the reform element in the Legislature to continue their work with the assurance that every necessary and reasonable aid would be given them by the Executive.

During the late session of the Legislature the Governor's attitude throughout was one of sympathy and support for the effort to reform the methods of municipal administration in this city, and to extend the operation of the State civil service laws. It was known from the start that he was in sympathy with the work in which Senators Gibbs and Robb and Assemblymen Roosevelt and others took a leading part, though the opposition to it was chiefly in his own party. He made valuable suggestions, met every one with frankness, and gave his approval without hesitation to all the reform bills that were placed before him in reasonably perfect shape or in time to have defects remedied. He continued the practice of studying every measure carefully and disapproving, without thinking of personal or political effect, those which in his judgment ought not to become laws. He scrutinized appropriations with special care, and his excision of items from the supply bill showed his discriminating economy and his relentless keeness in scenting out jobs.

His Industry.

Mr. Cleveland's character as Governor has been one of unremitting hard work and faithful devotion to public duty He has shirked nothing, proved unequal to no requirement, and never lost sight of the rule of action which he laid down as

Mayor of Buffalo in a communication to the Common Council "It seems to me," he said, "that a successful and faithful ministration of the Government of a city may be accomplished by constantly bearing in mind that we are the trustees and agents of our fellow-citizens, holding their funds in sacred trust to be expended for their benefit, that we should at all times be prepared to render an honest account to them touching the manner of its expenditure, and that the affairs of the city should be conducted as far as possible upon the same principles as a good business man manages his private concerns."

What His Administration Shows.

The administration of Grover Cleveland as Governor has been highly satisfactory and fully in accordance with his views expressed in his letter accepting the nomination. All the appointments to office which he has made bear the stamp of that high, conscientious spirit which has always actuated him. His industry is beyond all question. Never has there been a man less approachable by politicians in quest of fat offices. His moral courage is great, as witness his veto of the Five Cent Fare bill, which he treated regardless of the shower of abuse which he knew to be coming. Many of his other vetoes have been singularly objectionable to New York ward politicians. Many of the bills he has signed. have had a like effect. For instance, those curtailing the emoluments of the County Clerk, of the Register and of the Sheriff. If he is elected President he may be expected to follow in the path of political rectitude which has always distinguished him, and he will be opposed by none but the schemers and tricksters of his party

Why it was he didn't "Go for a Soldier."

There is nothing discreditable about Gov. Cleveland's war record. At the opening of the war it was a question whether he should go to the army or not. He was entirely ready and willing to do so, but his father had died some time before and left a widowed mother, poor and with a large family, several of whom were daughters. Provision had to be made for their support, and yet the family felt obliged to contribute in some way to the cause of the Union. A sort of family council was held. Grover had just been admitted to the bar at Buffalo and was beginning to have some practice. Two younger brothers volunteered to go to the army and leave Grover at home to support their mother and sisters. This was agreed to all around, and the two brothers went to the front and served with honor till the war closed. When peace was declared they returned home, but were soon afterward lost at sea. Grover Cleveland was the first man drafted in Buffalo. He promptly supplied a substitute, who made a faithful soldier. Gov Cleveland has always been a friend of the soldiers, and was what was called a War Democrat. While Mayor of Buffalo there was an attempt to make capital out of the fact that he had vetoed a bill appropriating public money for a soldiers' monument in the city. When the facts came out it proved to be true that he did it on the ground that the City Council had no right to appropriate public funds for a purpose of that kind, but he suggested that the result might be reached by a public subscription. The hint was adopted, a subscription paper was taken around and the first and largest subscriber was Mayor Cleveland. Since he has been Governor of New York he has approved a bill providing that the heads of the various State departments shall, when making appointments, give preference to honorably discharged soldiers and sailors of the United States. Some irritation was created last winter because of his vetoing a bill in reference to Grand Army badges. In the bill was a provision making the wearing of such a badge by any person not entitled to do so by reason of membership of some post a crime, punishable by imprisonment. The Governor thought the penalty unnecessarily severe. It was also logically observed that the child of a veteran might be imprisoned for wearing his father's badge.

The Governor's Veto of the Five Cent Fare Bill.

One of the charges against the administration of Governor Cleveland is his veto of the above bill, and the facts in the case have been so perverted in order to excite the prejudices of the poor working men against him, as a friend and protector of grasping monopolies as against labor, that a plain statement of the case is here presented. When those outside of the corporations interested, shall have read this, and become possessed of the true merits of the case, there can be little doubt that he will be sustained by every unprejudiced and honorable voter

The act is commonly known as the "Five Cent Fare bill," and forbade the collection or charge of more than five cents on any railroad in New York City for conveying a person any distance between the Battery and Harlem. At the time of its presentation the Governor was so impressed with its importance and the public interest which it excited that he exercised the greatest care and most diligent inquiry into the measure before rendering his decision.

His Reason.

"I am convinced," he said, "that in all cases the share which falls upon the Executive regarding the legislation of the State should be in no manner evaded, but fairly met by the expression of his carefully guarded and unbiassed judgment. In his conclusion he may err, but if he has fairly and honestly acted, he has performed his duty and given to the people of the State his best endeavor"

The Governor goes on to explain in justification of his veto that the Elevated Roads of the city are now under the sole operation of the Manhattan Elevated Railroad as lessee of the New York Elevated Railroad and the Metropolitan. He cites the provisions laid down in the act of April 20, 1866, authorizing the construction of the West Side road, which specified that no more than five cents per mile might be charged for fare of one person. That road has since gone into the hands of the New York Elevated Railroad Com pany, and a law was passed on June 17 1875, transferring the rights of the road to the new company, and further providing that it be "hereby confirmed in the possession and enjoyments of said rights, powers, privileges and franchises as fully and at large as they were so granted in and by the acts to the West Side and Yonkers Patent Railway Company The Court of Appeals, referring to the law, said:

"The effect of this act was to secure to the Elevated Railroad Company all the rights, privileges and franchises of the West Side and Yonkers Patent Railway Company under the purchase by and transfer to it."

By another section of this act the New York Elevated Railroad was empowered to receive from each passenger a sum not exceeding 10 cents a mile for five miles or less.

The Rapid Transit Act.

In 1875 another act was passed, commonly known as the Rapid Transit Act, providing for the appointment of a Board of Commissioners, whose office embraced authority to fix and determine the time within which the new elevated roads should be completed, and to formulate a scale of maximum rates to be charged as fare on such roads, and regulate the hours during which special trains should be run at reduced rates of fare. In accordance with the act the Mayor of this city appointed a Board of Commissioners, who expended a great deal of time and labor in the consideration of the proposed roads. They even fixed and determined specifically the route of the new New York Elevated Railroad, and prescribed with the utmost particularity the manner and form of its construction and operation. A deliberate and specific agreement was made with the company that it should charge as fares upon its cars, at such hours as were not embraced within the time specified for the running of "commission" trains, at a rate "for all distances under five miles not to exceed 10 cents, and not to exceed two cents for each mile or fraction of a mile over five miles, until the fare should amount to not exceeding 15 cents for a through passenger from and between the Battery and intersection of Third avenue and One Hundred and Twenty-ninth street, and from and between the Battery and High Bridge not to exceed 17 cents for a through passenger, and that for the entire distance from and between the Battery and Fifty-ninth street the fare shall not exceed 10 cents per passenger."

A further agreement was made that

commission trains should be run during certain hours of the morning and evening, upon which—for the benefit of workingmen and the laboring classes—the fare should not exceed five cents for conveyance between the Battery and Fifty-ninth street, nor should exceed seven cents for a through passenger from the Battery to Harlem during those hours. The railroad company further agreed that when the net income of the proposed road, after all expenditures, taxes and charges are paid, should amount to a sum sufficient to pay exceeding 10 per cent. per annum on the capital stock of the company that in such case and within six months thereafter, and so long as said net earnings amount to a sum sufficient to pay more than 10 per cent., the said company would run commission trains on its road at all hours during which it should be operated, at the rates of fare mentioned.

These agreements were at the time of their formulation highly satisfactory to the Commissioners, who accordingly transmitted them to the Mayor, accompanied by a highly congratulatory report, upon the receipt of which the Mayor submitted the papers to the Board of Aldermen, who approved the act. This was in the fall of 1875. The New York Elevated Railroad Company thereupon constructed its road from the Battery to Harlem, a distance of ten miles.

The New Bill Ignored the Old Contract.

The new bill, however, which was presented to the Governor for signature last year, provided that, notwithstanding all the laws which had been passed and rigidly complied with on the part of the railroad company, a new scale of rates should be forced upon it, insisting that passengers should be carried the whole length of the road for five cents, a sum about half that which was specified in the agreement. In his consideration of the bill Governor Cleveland was compelled, out of a single spirit of honesty, to say:

"I am of the opinion that in the legislation and proceedings which I have detailed, and in the fact that pursuant thereto the road of the company was constructed and finished, there exists a contract in favor of this company which is protected by that clause of the Constitution of the United States which prohibits the passage of a law by any State impairing the obligation of contracts."

He went on to say that section 33 of the General Railroads act provided that the Legislature may, when any railroad shall be opened for use, from time to time alter or reduce the rates of freight, fare or other profits upon said road, but the sum shall not without the consent of the company be so reduced as to bring down the profits on the invested capital to less than 10 per cent. per annum. In his communication to the Legislature vetoing the proposed bill modifying the rates of fare the Governor said that even if the State had the power to reduce the rates of fare on the elevated roads, it promised in its agreement not to do so except under certain circumstances and after a certain specified examination.

Constitutional Objections.

"I am not satisfied," he said, "that these circumstances exist. It is conceded that no such examination has been made. The constitutional objections which I have suggested to the bill under consideration are not, I think, removed by the claim that the proposed legislation is in the nature of an alteration of the charters of these companies, and that this is permitted by the State Constitution and by the provisions of some of the laws to which I have referred. I suppose that while the charters of corporations may be altered or repealed, it must be done in subordination to the Constitution of the United States, the supreme law of the land. This leads to the conclusion that the alteration of a charter cannot be made the pretext for the passage of a law which impairs the obligation of a contract. If I am mistaken in supposing that there are legal objections to this bill, there is another consideration which furnishes to my mind a sufficient reason why I should not give it my approval.

A Breach of Faith.

"It seems to me that to arbitrarily reduce these fares at this time under existing circumstances involves a breach of faith on the part of the State and a betrayal of confidence which the State has invited. The fact was notorious that for many years rapid transit was the great need of the inhabitants of the city of New York, and was of direct importance to the citizens of the State. Projects which promised to answer the people s wants in this direction failed and were abandoned. The Legislature, appreciating the situation, willingly passed statute after statute calculated to aid and encourage a solution of the problem. Capital was timid and hesitated to enter a new field full of risks and dangers. By the promise of liberal fares, as will be seen in all the acts passed on the subject, and through other concessions gladly made, capitalists were induced to invest their money in the enterprise, and rapid transit but lately became an accomplished fact. But much of the risk, expense and burden attending the maintenance of these roads is yet unknown and threatening.

"In the meantime the people of the city of New York are receiving the full benefit of their construction, a great enhancement of the value of the taxable property of the city has resulted, and in addition to taxes, more than $120,000, being 5 per cent. in increase, pursuant to the law of 1868, has been paid by the companies into the city treasury on the faith that the rate of fare agreed upon was secured to them. I am not aware that the corporations have, by any default, forfeited any of their rights, and if they have, the remedy is at hand under existing laws."

"It is manifestly important that invested capital should be protected, and that its necessity and usefulness in the development of enterprises valuable to the people should be recognized by conservative conduct on the part of the State government. We have especially in our keeping," continued Mr Cleveland, "the honor and good faith of a great State, and we should see to it that no suspicion attaches, through any act of ours, to the fair fame of the commonwealth."

How the New York World puts it.

The New York World in speaking of this veto gives the following illustration of how the bill, had it become a law, would have affected car drivers.

"The pay of a driver on a Harlem Railroad line is, say, $2 per day. The round trip from the bridge to the City Hall and back takes 3 hours and 20 minutes. Five round a trips day occupy 16 hours and 40 minutes, or, say, 17 hours.

These five round trips average 40 cents per trip. If the Governor had signed that unsatisfactory and unjust bill—unjust to the employeé and not to the employer—the company would have divided up the pay into trips, and have paid 40 cents per round trip. Three and a half round trips would consume the 12 hours to which a driver's work would have been limited, and for this service he would have received only $1.40.

To make his full $2 he would have had to work over-hours and must still have made his five trips per day occupying 16 hours and 40 minutes.

More than that. In the winter, during the delay consequent to a severe snowstorm, when the round trip instead of taking 3 hours and 20 minutes, frequently occupies 5 hours, the drivers would have received no more than the 40 cents, and would have earned in 12 hours, for two and a half trips, only $1 Or if in ordinary times, through a large fire or any other cause, a driver who worked the old 17 hours in order to get as much as he now gets, should miss a trip, the amount for that trip would have been deducted from his pay

The drivers and conductors ought to hold a mass-meeting to thank Gov CLEVELAND for vetoing a bill so absurd and so adverse to their interests. Demagogues may bluster and promise, but no legislative enactment has ever yet been invented that will secure a man fifteen hours' pay for eight hours' labor."

Personal Appearance.

He is a tall, stoutly built gentleman, weighing over two hundred and fifty pounds, aged forty-seven years and a bachelor. He is vigorous, robust, of a nervous temperament, light complexion, thin brown hair, rapidly tending to baldness, and is a prepossessing-looking bachelor. He has good executive ability. He shuns society, and chiefly delights in association with his own sex. He has dark, penetrating eyes and heavy eyebrows. His movements are deliberate and dignified, but devoid of the heaviness which sometimes accompanies men of his type. His manner is so curt and brusque, his 'yea' 'yea,' and his 'nay' 'nay,' that he often offends those who speak with him for the first time, but the longer he is known the more warmly he is esteemed, respected and admired. He does not wear his heart upon his sleeve for daws to peck at, but under his stern demeanor he conceals a kindly, generous and charitable nature. One of his oldest and most intimate friends characteristically defined him as "an up and up man." Everybody who has ever had any dealings with him is aware that he means precisely what he says and says exactly what he means. In appearance, no less than in character, he is one of the old Continental school of politicians, and seems to have come down to us from a former generation to teach us what strong, brave, honest, resolute men our forefathers were who founded this Republic. Mr Cleveland is a member of the large social clubs of Buffalo. In September, 1882, he was elected vice president of the State Bar Association from the Eighth Judicial district.

His face, no less than his figure and actions, indicates strenuous vital force and that admirable co-ordination of faculties which is best expressed in the phrase, "a cool head." Those traits which are in part the result of early and constant self-training have given him the air of conscious and quiet power which belongs only to the triumphant antagonist in the world's fight. His figure betokens herculean strength— massiveness is the best word for it—and there is in the smoothly shaven face, the same token of equal solidity of character, with the suggestion of physical vigor in the soft brown mustache that strongly contrasts with the scantiness of hair on his head. There is a decided tendency to corpulency—as is usually the case in vital temperaments—and a double chin is beginning to hang down over the simple white necktie. There is nothing phlegmatic in the man's manner. His face lights up with a sympathetic smile and without becoming animated or brilliant he is at once interesting, unaffected and intensely real.

A Visitor's Description.

A visitor at the Executive Mansion thus describes an interview with the Governor

"The moment he found that I did not want to ask him about the future and was quite content to listen to the past, he talked freely and familiarly There was nothing in his humble origin and struggling career that he was ashamed of. I fancied he was rather proud of his early struggles. And it was not impossible in an hour's conversation to make some kind of measurement of the man's mind and character I said to myself, this is the executive not the reflective man. I don't suppose he is ever perplexed with questions of ethics. Such men have a steady poise of judgment that saves a world of words. The right pathway is never obscured or hidden. With them the doctrinaire has a hard time of it, for instead of chasing a principle through all the mazes of possibilities for the sake of the hunt, they hold the dogs of dialectics in leash and, with unerringly clear sight and constant good nature, whip them all back to the true scent. I was always struck with a single sentence in the second volume of Carlyle's 'French Revolution," which, after those two volumes of bloody chaos, announce the arrival of Napoleon. The purport of that sentence, as I now recall it, is that 'a man having now come upon the scene events began to straighten themselves out.' And I suppose that whatever events become chaotic and life gets into confusion that it is absolutely necessary to have a man at the helm. And history shows that it is the executive man, equipped with convictions and endowed with courage who assumes the chieftainship in moments of public doubt. Distracted on everything else, the people are willing to rest their issues on indubitable strength of character, capable of both representing and leading. He may not bring any new truth with him, or a more brilliant method, but the trust is that he will with clear eye, pure heart and strong hand keep the columns in close order along the approved path of safety and advance."

A True American Citizen.

Grover Cleveland, both in his record and in his person, impresses one as peculiarly the outcome and result of what is best and most enduring in American life. As we have already seen, he started like the typical American boy to hew his own way The almost insuperable difficulties of his youth, the hardships of poverty, pangs of hunger, the frosts of winter never deterred him. They were in fact, as they always are to the true metal, only the blows that compacted and shaped the man. We hear a great deal nowadays about men being all American. Obviously there are some American things which a man had better be without. It is not pleasant to contemplate a man whose character reflects the heterogeneous and discordant elements of our complex life. Nor is it safe to trust with heavy responsibilities that man whose chief element of Americanism is impatience of restraint, disrespect for the past and an unswerving desire to be smart rather than right. The best elements of our American life have always come up from the hardy, vigorous stratum that was nearest to the soil and in some way dependent on it. The abiding glory of the country has been in its defiant boys with God-fearing ancestors, boys who had organized in them by a race of humble but devout pioneers the patience and industry to achieve and the reverence to respect. It is to men of this fibre that the republic has always gone in its emergencies—turning in extremity from its politicians, its doctrinaries and its workers of statecraft, back to the elemental, vital, honest forces that underlie all its achievements and that are oftenest found in the sturdy, modest, indomitable workers who have not sought the political race.

At his Home.

A writer who visited Buffalo for the purpose of learning facts concerning the Governor, says:

I had an opportunity to converse with several persons who had known their Mayor long and well. I found a sterling regard for the man everywhere, and it was a regard uninfluenced by political bias. Among those best able to form independent opinions, this regard was obviously founded on character. Among the people themselves there was a well-defined conviction that he was a man to depend upon. As one rough fellow said to me in the hotel saloon: "Well, I don't know about his learnin' or how he stands on a lot of questions that we don't understand, and don't want to, but he's a safe man, and he's pretty sure to understand them better than we do, and he'll do the right thing."

Solidity of Character.

I suppose that this kind of faith in character is one of the most inestimable discoveries that a man can make, and I was interested to find that the element of popularity did not grow out of the subject good-fellowship, or mere manners. I failed to hear any one say that Grover Cleveland had any magnetism, or that he fascinated a crowd, or that he drew people after him with a personal glamour. On the contrary, I formed a very distinct notion that there was a class of men that he repelled, and that disliked him as easily, as naturally and as sincerely as a thief hates a magistrate or a smuggler hates a dead calm Indeed it was impossible to discover either in the man's record or in the reputation that had grown up about him anything dramatic. The resultant heroism of his life is that common heroism of the "common" work-a-day world which does its duty, not for effect, but for a principle and a purpose, and which, if it does not so easily catch the eye and the ear, is after all the enduring force that the people come to look for and rely upon when there is great work to be done. I looked into his law offices on Main street—this later laboratory where were evolved the legal functions that came into the public service of his own community They were curiously solid and unpretentious, and upstairs were the bachelor rooms where for years Grover Cleveland had slept and worked. I examined them minutely, for one often obtains a glimpse of character by such *entourage*. And they were instantly indicative of the simple tastes, methodical habits and studious life of the occupant. Two or three pictures, evidently selected not for decoration, but because the owner prized the subject and admired the treatment, hung on the walls. But there was elsewhere not a superfluous article in the room. Elegance had been forgotten in the successful attempt to secure comfort and convenience and seclusion.

Cleveland on Citizenship.

Views expressed when Mayor of Buffalo on the Release of the Irish Suspects.

When it became known in this country that Mr. Lowell had abandoned the Americans imprisoned in Ireland without formal accusation, trial or conviction, the public indignation found expression in mass meetings to protest against his course, and about the time that the controversy culminated such a meeting was called in Buffalo. It was held April 9th, 1882, in St. James' Hall, and the Governor, who had been then three months Mayor of Buffalo, presided. On taking the chair he delivered the following address, which is certainly as frank and outspoken an utterance in regard to the duties of the American Government to its citizens abroad as anyone need ask for:

His Foreign Policy.

"Fellow citizens: This is the formal mode of address on occasions of this kind, but I think we seldom realize fully its meaning or how valuable a thing it is to be a citizen. From the earliest civilization to be a citizen has been to be a free man, endowed with certain privileges and advantages and entitled to the full protection of the State. The defence and protection of the personal rights of its citizens has always been the paramount and most important duty of a free, enlightened government. And perhaps no government has this sacred trust more in its keeping than this—the best and freest of them all—for here the people who are to be protected are the source of those powers which they delegate upon the express compact that the citizen shall be protected. For this purpose we choose those who for the time being shall manage the machinery which we have set up for our defence and safety.

The True Doctrine of Protection.

"And this protection adheres to us in all lands and places as an incident of citizenship. Let but the weight of a sacrilegious hand be put upon this sacred thing and a great, strong government springs to its feet to avenge the wrong. Thus it is that the native-born American citizen enjoys his birthrights. But when, in the westward march of empire, this nation was founded and took root, we beckoned to the Old World and invited hither its immigration and provided a mode by which those who sought a home among us might become our fellow-citizens. They came by thousands and hundreds of thousands, they came and

'Hewed the dark old woods away,
And gave the virgin fields to-day;'

they came with strong sinews and brawny arms to aid in the growth and progress of a new country, they came and upon our altars laid their fealty and submission, they came to our temples of justice and under the solemnity of an oath renounced all allegiance to every other State, potentate and sovereignty and surrendered to us all the duty pertaining to such allegiance. We have accepted their fealty and invited them to surrender the protection of their native land.

"And what should be given them in return? Manifestly, good faith and every dictate of honor demands that we give them the same liberty and protection here and elsewhere which we vouchsafe to our native-born citizens. And that this has been accorded to them is the crowning glory of American institutions. It needed not the statute which is now the law of the land, declaring that 'all naturalized citizens while in foreign lands are entitled to and shall receive from this government the same protection of person and property which is accorded to native-born citizens,' to voice the policy of our nation.

The Rights of Our Citizens.

"In all lands where the semblance of liberty is preserved, the right of a person arrested to a speedy accusation and trial is, or ought to be, a fundamental law as it is a rule of civilization. At any rate, we hold it to be so, and this is one of the rights which we undertake to guarantee to any native-born or naturalized citizen of ours, whether he be imprisoned by order of the Czar of Russia or under the pretext of a law administered for the benefit of the landed aristocracy of England. We do not claim to make laws for other countries, but we do insist that whatsoever those laws may be, they shall, in the interests of human freedom and the rights of mankind so far as they involve the liberty of our citizens, be speedily administered. We have a right to say and do say, that mere suspicion without examination on trial is not sufficient to justify the long imprisonment of a citizen of America. Other nations may permit their citizens to be thus imprisoned. Ours will not. And this in effect has been solemnly declared by statute.

"We have met here to-night to consider this subject and inquire into the cause and the reasons and the justice of the imprisonment of certain of our fellow citizens now held in British prisons without the semblance of a trial or legal examination. Our law declares that the government shall act in such cases. But the people are the creators of the government. The undaunted apostle of the Christian religion, imprisoned and persecuted, appealing centuries ago to the Roman law and the rights of Roman citizenship, boldly demanded 'Is it lawful for you to scourge a man that is a Roman and uncondemned?' So, too, might we ask, appealing to the law of our land and the laws of civilization: 'Is it lawful that these, our fellows, be imprisoned, who are American citizens and uncondemned?' I deem it an honor to be called upon to preside at such a meeting and I thank you for it. What is your further pleasure?"

Grover Cleveland's Romance.

Grover Cleveland came of a somewhat singular and peculiar family. All his ancestors were strong people, but turning to the church for a living they were always poor. The city is full of reminiscences of his fight for a place in the city of his adoption, but the story of his boyhood days have to be gathered from another locality But very few persons know why he never married, perhaps none do. The mishap that left him to tread the wine-press of life alone was a painful one, but it left the sting before he came to Buffalo. Ever since his residence in Buffalo he has lived with his law books and his profession. Although he is reputed to be a good, genial companion, fond of life and the world, he has shunned society and lived for his mother and sisters, who needed his help. Probably more preachers were reared out of his family than any other in the country They all taught the doctrines of the Presbyterian Church for a small price and died poor. Mr. Cleveland's father left some ten children, which were about his only available assets when he died. Hence it went out that he was too poor to marry until so well grounded in his bachelor ways that he could not be tempted from them by the comeliest girl in the land. There are no traditions that he ever courted a lass. Yet it is true that he did and that the picture of that one still remains by his side. It is true that he was and, as the world goes, still he is poor. As is already stated in this narrative it was not until a few years ago that he felt able to pay back the money be borrowed to bring him West in 1855. He only got his legal education by a pretty tough fight with adversity and it took him four years of drudgery in the office of Rogers & Bowen before he was admitted to practice.

Governor Cleveland's Fortune.

It has been generally supposed by a majority of people in Buffalo that Grover Cleveland was a wealthy man. He has always lived in style, boarding at the Tifft House when here, and the centre of a group of bachelor friends, all of whom are possessed of independent fortunes. Since his election as Governor, but especially since he has been mentioned as a candidate of the Democratic party for President, this rumor has assumed more than its former proportions. It has for a few days been harped upon by prominent anti-monopolists and labor leaders that the Governor was possessed of a fortune of more than $100,000, upon a greater part of which he paid no taxes.

To gain some information upon this vexed subject an inquirer after the truth visited the Assessor's office and made a thorough investigation. It was found that the books there make the Governor's fortune far smaller than do his enemies. The sum total against him is a tax upon $5,000 worth of personal property. No mention of any real or landed estate is made and it is safe to say he owns none inside the corporate limits of the city. It cannot be truthfully said that Governor

Cleveland is possessed of a hurtful amount of property

A Love Story.

When Governor Cleveland was just able to support himself he became enamored of a young woman who was a relative of the late Judge Verplanck. The girl was not disposed to look favorably on his suit and this made him love her the more. She delighted in tantalizing him by permitting other young men to escort her home from the old Eagle Street Theatre, which was then the only place of amusement of any account in the city The girl was comparatively wealthy and looked down on Grover, who was a poor lawyer. After awhile she got to thinking fondly of him, and it is said that they were engaged to be married when she was taken ill with a fever and died. Cleveland did not recover from the shock for several months, and though he has a bachelor s liking for pretty ladies his friends say that he will never marry One lady became so infatuated with him that she proposed to him. He rejected her advances and it is said that she became crazy and is now confined in an asylum.

A friend of the Governor told a reporter a romantic story of how a lady living near Poughkeepsie engaged in correspondence with the Governor since he was elected Mayor, and that a tender feeling had sprung up between them. They have met but four times, once when Cleveland was Sheriff, a few years later at Saratoga, after Cleveland was elected Mayor and once since he has been Governor. This friend said that it was quite likely that the lady would be married by Cleveland if elected President, and that she would grace the White House parlors at his reception. The lady is described as being a charming brunette, about thirty-five years old, with pleasing manners and considerable property. This incident is given for what it is worth as one of the rumors of the day

Personal Peculiarities.

All the traits of assiduous industry, unostentatious dignity, thoroughness and simplicity, noted in Grover Cleveland's early career are observable in his present life at Albany On the day before his inauguration as Governor he came down from Buffalo quietly with his law partner, Mr. Bissell, went to the Executive Mansion and spent the night. On the morrow the city was excited with the approaching ceremonies. The streets were crowded, but there was to be no military parade, no procession. The Governor-elect walked from the Executive Mansion in company with his friend to the Capitol, which is a mile distant, joining the throngs that were going that way He entered the building unrecognized, but quite at his ease, sauntered up the Executive Chamber and was there met by Gov Cornell. The moment the inaugural ceremony was over he passed into the spacious Executive Chamber which is set apart for his use, ordered that the doors should be opened to admit anybody, and went immediately to work.

Pristine Democracy.

Never was any important public event so completely stripped of its fuss and feathers. Never was a more radical change effected in the official routine of the Executive Department. Hitherto there were all sorts of delays and impediments in the path to the Governor Cards had to be sent in, ushers conducted citizens into anterooms and left them to cool their heels on the State's tessellated floor But the moment Grover Cleveland took possession he issued on order to admit anybody at once who wished to see him. And up to the present time he has been quite able himself to prevent this return to republican simplicity from being abused. His habits are indicative of his dislike of ostentation and official parade and of his methodical and industrious training. He walks from the Executive Mansion every morning at 9 o'clock to the Capitol and goes straight to work. At 1 30 he walks back to his lunch, which takes an hour. He then returns on foot to work again and remains until 6, when he goes to dinner. He is back at 8 and generally stays until 11 or 12. He keeps no horses or extra servants and has not been known to ride since he has been in Albany except for an occasional pleasure jaunt. The amount of work thus accomplished—as his private secretary, Mr. Daniel S. Lamont, testifies—is something enormous.

He is not a rich man, in spite of his frugal bachelor habits. He does much free legal work for poor clients and has a way of assisting them which, though most creditable to his conscience, does not put money in his purse. He is also a liberal benefactor of all the charities of Buffalo, a city peculiarly active in this work.

His Strength as a Candidate.

Mr. Cleveland's strength as a candidate is due to his strong conservatism, his unsullied character, his sympathy with straightforward, business methods in politics, his exceptional standing with the independent reform element the country over and his ability to inspire people with the belief that he may be trusted to do nothing for purely partisan purposes. Few men unite in themselves so many considerations of fitness and expediency If elected he may be trusted to expose jobs turn out and keep out thieves and give the country a manly, conservative administration of his own.

As a Lawyer and a Man.

Mr. Cleveland's rank at the bar is a high one. He is careful and methodical as a business man, which, united to his faculty of going to the bottom of all questions, gives him the principal elements essential to success in his profession. He presents his case well and closely, whether the argument is made before a court or a jury, but does not indulge in any exhibition of pyrotechnics. His vocabulary is ample but not overwhelming or exhaustive, as is so often the case with professional legal talkers. He is a hard worker, and a large, reliable and commanding practice is his reward.

In the presentation of Grover Cleveland's record to the readers of this biography, it has been the object to reflect him as he is apart from any bias or one-sided statements, and hence the following extract is published.

It will be remembered that George William Curtis is a leader in the Republican Party, and was a delegate from New York in the Chicago Convention that nominated James G. Blaine. The following appears as his leading editorial in *Harpers' Weekly:*

What Mr. Curtis Says.

"The nomination of Governor Cleveland defines sharply the actual issue of the presidential election of this year He is a man whose absolute official integrity has never been questioned, who has no laborious and doubtful explanations to undertake, and who is universally known as the Governor of New York elected by an unprecedented majority which was not partisan, and represented both the votes and the consent of an enormous body of Republicans, and who as the Chief Executive of the State has steadily withstood the blandishments and the threats of the worst elements of his party, and has justly earned the reputation of a courageous, independent and efficient friend and promoter of administrative reform. His name has become that of the especial representative among our public men of the integrity, purity and economy of administration which are the objects of the most intelligent and patriotic citizens. The bitter and furious hostility of Tammany Hall and of General Butler to Governor Cleveland is his passport to the confidence of good men, and the general conviction that Tammany will do all that it can to defeat him, will be an additional incentive to the voters who cannot support Mr. Blaine, and who are unwilling not to vote at all, to secure the election of a candidate whom the political rings and the party traders instinctively hate and unitedly oppose."

Public Interests Before Party.

So firm and "clean" and independent in his high office has Gov Cleveland shown himself to be, that he is denounced as not being a Democrat by his Democratic opponents. This denunciation springs from the fact that he has not hesitated to prefer the public welfare to the mere interest of his party. Last autumn, when the Democratic District-Attorney of Queen County was charged with misconduct, the Governor heard the accusation and the defense, and decided that it was his duty to remove the officer. He was asked by his party friends to defer the removal until after the election, as otherwise the party would lose the district by the opposition of the Attorney's friends. The Governor understood his duty and removed the officer some days before the election, and the party did lose the district. This kind of courage and devotion to public duty in the teeth of the most virulent opposition of traders of his own party is unusal in any public man, and it shows precisely the executive quality which is demanded at a time when every form of speculation and fraud presses upon the public treasury under the specious plea of party advantage.

The argument that in an election it is not a man but a party that is supported, and that the Democratic party is less to be trusted than the Republican, is futile at a time when the Republican party has nominated a candidate whom a great body of the most conscientious Republicans cannot support, and the Democratic party has nominated a candidate whom a great body of the most venal Democrats practical bolt. Distrust of the Democratic party springs from the conduct of the very Democrats who madly oppose Governor Cleveland because they know that they cannot use him. The mere party argument is vain also, because no honorable man will be whipped in to vote for a candidate whom he believes to be personally disqualified for the Presidency on the ground that a party ought to be sustained. The nomination of Gov Cleveland is due not so much to the preference of his party as to the general demand of the country for a candidacy which stands for precisely the qualities and services which are associated with his name."

What the Evening Telegraph Says.

We also give a portion of an editorial which appeared in the *Evening Telegraph* of Philadelphia, a staunch Republican paper, and a supporter of the Republican nominees:

The Democrats have nominated a very strong ticket—probably the strongest ticket that it was possible for them to nominate; and if it is to be beaten, it will be necessary for the Republicans to give some positive assurances that the party as a party, and despite the efforts of time-servers and tricksters to use it for improper personal and grossly unpatriotic ends, intends that the very best of its past shall indicate with unmistakable clearness its future. It is sheer folly to underrate the merit of the deliverances of the Democratic Convention yesterday, or to attempt to misinterpret their plain meaning or the plain peril which they represent. For the first time since the Democratic Party went out of power in 1861, it comes before the country with its baser elements forced into the background, if not into subjection, with men of clean, strong and patriotic records as their candidates, and with a challenge to thinking and patriotic men to regard what is good in it instead of obtruding upon them the unsavory features of its history and the most evil of its desires. It may be said, and with entire truth, that Cleveland is an expediency nomination, but there are expediencies and expediencies. It was expediency that dictated the nomination of General Hancock four years ago. It was hoped that Hancock s splendid record as a soldier would win votes that might not be winable by a demonstration in the line of true statesmanship. It is no disparagement to General Hancock to say that his nomination was a trick, and that those who were most actively instrumental in procuring it hoped to turn it to an evil account should it be ratified at the polls. The nomination of Grover Cleveland was made on quite other grounds. This man was selected because it is believed he has a public and private record that is unimpeachable, and particularly because, since he has been Governor of the great State of New York, he has shown himself to be a careful and zealous guardian of the true interests of the public, even at the cost of the friendship of men in his own party who have the power to wield a multitude of votes.

Incidents--Leading the Blind.

The following incident of recent occurrence is related of the Governor:

The crier in one of the courts of Albany is a blind man, who lives in the same part of the city as the Governor. He is somewhat aged and has become so familiar with the road from his home over to the court-house that he generally goes alone. But one morning, some months ago, he missed his way, and the Governor coming along took him by the arm and brought him along with him as far as the Capitol building. As they were about to separate, the old gentleman asked the name of his considerate guide.

"My name is Cleveland," said the Governor

"Are you in business in the city?"

"Yes, I have an office up here in the Capitol."

"Oh, you are not the Governor?'

"Yes. I am the Governor"

The poor old fellow was almost beside himself and went on his way with a story to tell as long as he lived.

"Which might be the Governor?"

The Governor is full of the milk of human kindness and his heart is big enough to take in all mankind. Though a bachelor he has a most benignant face and can talk to you like a father. The pictures of him do not give his face as it is generally seen. He sometimes looks serious, but never cross or even austere. As soon as you see him you feel that you need not have any trepidation in speaking to him. When he sits down there is not much room left between the arms of a pretty wide chair, and he looks wonderfully comfortable and homelike. The other day when there were three or four gentlemen callers sitting or walking about in the Executive office, a bunch of country women dropped in on their sight-seeing tour. After gazing about in some perplexity, as if they were looking for something they could not find to their entire satisfaction, the eldest and the supposable head of the party, ventured up to the Governor as the most approachable man she saw, and ventured to ask —"Which might be the Governor?' "Right here," said he, as he thumped himself on the bosom and went on with the business in hand. "Oh!" the lady ejaculated, and retired amid her blushes to the expectant group in the corner, and then they all looked over and said "oh'" in chorus.

Never Disturbed.

When the Governor gets well settled in his chair, takes a good long breath, and adjusts his glasses on the lower part of his nose, he looks as wise, as mellow, and as sunshiny as Benjamin Franklin. He looks as though it would take a very considerable shock to knock him off his balance. When asked the other day if he read the papers that abused him.

"Sometimes," said he, with a smile that broke out all over his face.

"Do you ever get disturbed over any thing they say?"

"Not much. Every man has a right to enjoy his own mind. I remember an old fellow who was a neighbor of my father, and we would sometimes try to get him to come over to our church. He was a strong Baptist, and he would always say: 'No, you folks are Presbyterians, and if I go over to your church I couldn't enjoy my mind.' Of course that was the end of the argument."

Regarding Newspaper Slanders.

In reply as to the slanders published about him, the Governor recently said:—"Well, I have been more surprised at the way I have been misrepresented as to the laboring men than anything else. I don't see how the idea ever got out in the first place that I have been opposed to the interests of laboring men. I cannot remember one single act in my life that could be reasonably construed into any thing inimical to their best interests. It has been just the other way with me. I have always taken particular pains, whenever it was in my power, to see their interests well guarded. But I have no fear as to the outcome. I have observed that laboring men have minds of their own as well as political principles, and when there has been a full investigation of my official life the facts will be made known, and I am not uneasy as to the result. They talk about the workingmen as if they were a lot of sheep to be corralled or scattered by this man or that. Most workingmen are natural Democrats. Democracy means the rule of the people, and the Democratic party has always been the natural friend of the workingmen. I do not think any great number of those who are in my party will fail to vote for me, first, because they are naturally disposed to go with their party, and second, because they will learn long before election day that my attitude towards them has been misrepresented."

Opinions on Public Questions.

Because Governor Cleveland took no active part in politics until recently, it must not be inferred that he became invested with important offices without any knowledge or experience of public men and measures. Ever since he attained his majority he had been an ardent supporter of the Democratic party, and kept himself fully posted on all state and national matters. He was little accustomed to making speeches and writing letters on public questions, but when he began it was with some purpose. Appreciation of the business side of office and politics has been a marked feature of his utterances. In his inaugural address as Mayor of Buffalo, he said—

The People's Money.

We hold the money of the people in our hands to be used for their purposes and to further their interests as members of the municipality, and it is quite apparent that when any part of the funds which the tax-payers have entrusted to us are diverted to other purposes or when by design or neglect we allow a greater sum to be applied to any municipal purpose than is necessary, we have, to that extent, violated our duty There surely is no difference in his duties and obligations whether a person is entrusted with the money of one man or of many, and yet it sometimes appears as though the office-holder assumes that a different rule of fidelity prevails between him and the tax-payer than that which should regulate his conduct when, as an individual, he holds the money of his neighbors. It seems to me that a successful and faithful ministration of the government of our city may be accomplished by constantly bearing in mind that we are the trustees and agents of our fellow-citizens, holding their funds in sacred trust to be expended for their benefit, that we should at all times be prepared to render an honest account to them touching the manner of its expenditure, and that the affairs of the city should be conducted, as far as possible, upon the same principles as a good business man manages his private concerns.

His Civil Service Views.

In his letter, accepting the nomination for Governor of New York, he gave his views on Civil Service, and on an efficient and honest administration of public officers, showing most conclusively that he had given the subject careful thought, and had formed a decided opinion in its favor:

Subordinates in public places should be selected and retained for their efficiency, and not because they may be used to accomplish partisan ends. The people have a right to demand here, as in cases of private employment, that their money be paid to those who will render the best service in return, and that the appointment to and tenure of such places should depend upon ability and merit. If the clerks and assistants in public departments were paid the same compensation, and required to do the same amount of work as those employed in prudently conducted private establishments the anxiety to hold these public places would be much diminished, and the cause of civil service reform materially aided.

His Opposition to Corruption at the Polls.

The expenditure of money to influence the action of the people at the polls, or to secure legislation is calculated to excite the gravest concern. When this pernicious agency is successfully employed a representative form of government becomes a sham, and laws passed under its baleful influence cease to protect, but are made the means by which the rights of the people are sacrificed and the public treasury despoiled. It is useless and foolish to shut our eyes to the fact that this evil exists among us, and the party which leads in an honest effort to return to better and purer methods will receive the confidence of our citizens and secure their support. It is wilful blindness not to see that the people care but little for party obligations, when they are invoked to countenance and sustain fraudulent and corrupt practices. And it is well for our country and for the purification of politics that the people, at times fully roused to danger, remind their leaders that party methods should be something more than a means used to answer the purposes of those who profit by political occupation.

Col. Frank H. Burr, one of the best descriptive writers of the day, gives the following relating to Governor Cleveland:

Shunning Society.

This style of living was not kept up after he became well-to-do to be saving, for he has the reputation of being a rather open-handed man and not given to hoarding money. It is apparent, from the talk of all his friends, that he loves congenial companionship and is a most pleasant conversationalist, thoroughly capable of entertaining a company of any character. I found it current talk in Buffalo that he had always been much courted in society, but that he could rarely be induced to enter the charmed circle. There is a good deal of interesting chat about the plans that have been set to capture this bachelor and their universal failure. One story runs that only recently some friends had two charming ladies visiting them from the Eastern States, and that the lady of the house gave an evening party especially for the purpose of bringing the Governor within the influence of these attractive girls. He shunned the temptation, as he has done many of the kind, and did not attend. He said to a lady who chaffed him about his bachelor life, that if she could find a girl whom she would certify was just right he would enter into bonds to marry her if she would have him. This good-natured raillery has given rise to the rumor that he is thinking of making a change in his domestic relations.

It is singular to find a man who has led a bachelor life so well thought of by all classes as Mr Cleveland is in Buffalo. He has the confidence and respect of everybody except a few ward politicians whom he has disappointed. His political methods, as you find them developed at his home, are not calculated to commend him to the average politician. His self-reliance, candid faith in his own judgment and unflinching honesty have earned him the reputation among this class of being ungrateful to those who have helped to make him a power.

A Pen Portrait.

After gathering the home impressions of the man and the features of his early life in this locality, I spent a half day at Albany with the man who has so recently filled the public eye plumb full. He is a good deal such a man as you would expect to find from his experiences, training, birth and general habits of life. He is a large and powerfully built, well proportioned and rather good-looking man. The picture printed as a frontispiece gives a very fair idea of his general appearance, although his expression of countenance is entirely free from the stern, bull-dog look that the wood-cuts give him. He has a pleasant cast of countenance and is rather a winning talker. He has not the quality of magnetism about him, but impresses you with his candor and openness. He is an attractive man, without being too familiar, and is the most democratic official I ever saw.

No Ceremony.

The humblest man or woman is admitted to his presence as readily as the highest. He impressed me as a person having the judicial quality of mind developed to a very high degree—one of those strong-headed men with a good opinion of his own understanding of anything he considered. There is not the least characteristic of a politician about him. This is of course the natural result of a life that has been busy and entirely devoted of late years to the enjoyment of the fruits of professional labor and to dealing with men upon the basis of perfect fairness. He is a singular man and has led a peculiar life. If the majority of his years have been tending up hill, his latter days certainly have not, and he seems to be shaping himself to take solid comfort among the rewards of his toil.

His Inauguration as Governor.

Governor Cleveland was inaugurated at the Capitol in Albany Jan. 1, 1883, in the presence of a vast concourse of his fellow citizens. After being escorted to the platform by Governor Cornell, the incoming executive was presented by his predecessor to the people in the following neat address:

FELLOW CITIZENS:—The people of the State are its sovereign Rulers. Those whom they elect to perform official trusts, to make laws or execute them, are but the exponents of their views, the custodians of their interests, and the instruments of their supreme will. He is wise, therefore, who in any representative capacity, recognizes and obeys the influence or expression of that will in these ceremonial forms to do as presented the fitting illustration of the maxim, that the just powers of government are derived from the consent of the governed. All successful places emanate from enlightened public sentiment, and whatever motive attends the choice of official servants, that will only succeed, which has for its real and ultimate object the maintenance and promotion of good and honest government.

By the operation of the Constitution, the limit of an executive term has again been reached, and we stand to-day in the presence of rightful authority, expressed in lawful manner to witness the transfer of the high office of Chief Magistrate of the State to one who has been chosen to execute the responsible and trying duties that belong to it. Three years ago, the place now passed to my constitutional successor, was accepted with a due sense of the responsibility involved.

My pledge was then given to faithfully and impartially discharge the obligations assumed. There was no reservation of purpose, to redeem that pledge with vigilance and fidelity, and it has been my constant aim, to meet every requirement of just and economical administration to the service of the state.

Neither private interest nor personal favor has been permitted to stand in the way of public duty. In taking leave now, of the scenes and labors that have occupied the last three years, it affords me profound satisfaction, to congratulate the people of this majestic commonwealth on the high degree of prosperity and peace that prevail within these borders.

Our public debt is nearly extinguished, the rate of taxation has been materially reduced, and new sources of public revenue have been developed. The public works have been conducted with the utmost economy, consistent with safety and efficiency,encroachments on private rights have been stayed, and important steps have been taken to secure just accountabilities in the management of corporations.

In other essential respects, also, the public welfare has been fostered and frugality in public expenditures secured. These and like results have been accomplished and sustained by the aid of advanced public sentiment. And they will be derelict who, in the direction of affairs, fail to respect the demands of enlightened public opinion. To you, Governor Cleveland, God-speed in every endeavor to secure to this people the richest blessings of beneficent government. It is your good fortune to come to these important duties by an expression of the public will almost unprecedented in the history of the State. The emphasis thus given to your election is clearly indicative of public expectation in the discharge of your official functions. May the Infinite Ruler endow you with wisdom and strength equal to the great responsibilities which now devolve upon you. The faithful discharge of conscious duty will be ample satisfaction and reward, and whatever circumstances or events occur, the public, whose servant you are, will not be unmindful or turn away

Governor Cleveland's Inaugural Address.

Placing his right hand in the breast of his close-fitting black coat, and directly facing Mr Cornell, Governor Cleveland spoke as follows:

Governor Cornell: I am profoundly grateful for your pleasant words and kind wishes for my success. You speak in full view of the labors that are past and duty well performed, and no doubt you generously suppose that what you have safely encountered and overcome, another may not fear to meet. But I cannot be unmindful of the difficulties that beset the path upon which I enter, and I shall be quite content, if when the end is reached, I may like you, look back upon an official career, honorable to myself, and useful to the people of the States.

I cannot forbear at this time to also express my appreciation of the hearty kindness and consideration with which you have at other times sought to make easier my performance of official duties.

Then turning to the deeply interested audience, Mr. Cleveland continued.

Fellow Citizens: You have assembled to-day to witness the retirement of an officer tried and trusted, from the highest place in the state, and the assumption of these duties by one yet to be tried. This ceremony, simple and unostentatious as becomes the spirit of your institution, is yet of vast importance to you and to the people of this great commonwealth.

The interests now transferred to new hands are yours, and the duties newly assumed should be performed for your benefit and for your good, hence, you have the right to demand and enforce, by the means placed in your hands, which you well know how to use. And if the public servant should always know that he is jealously watched by the people, he surely would be none the less faithful to his trusts.

This vigilance on the part of the citizen, and an active interest and participation in practical concerns, are the safeguards of its rights. But sluggish interference with practical privileges, invite the machinations of those who wait to betray the people s interests. Thus when the conduct of public affairs receives your attention, do not omit to perform your duties as citizens, but protect your own best interests. While this is true, and while those whom you put in place should be held to strict account, their opportunities for usefulness should not be impaired, nor their efforts for good thwarted by unfounded and querulous complaint and cavil.

Let us together, but in our different places, take part in the regulation and demonstration of the Government of our state, and thus become, not only the keepers of our own interests, but contributors to the progress and prosperity which will await us.

I enter upon the discharge of the duties of the office to which my fellow citizens have called me, with a profound sense of gratitude to the kind Providence which I believe will aid an honest design, and the forbearance of the just people, which I trust will recognize a patriotic endeavor.

EXTRACTS FROM GOVERNOR CLEVELAND'S MESSAGE JAN. 7, 1883.

Apportionments.

The last Legislature neglected its plain duty in failing to re-apportion the State into Congressional districts according to the United States census of 1880 and pursuant of the allottment of Congress to our quota of members of the House of Representatives. It is to be hoped that this work will be speedily undertaken. To make an apportionment of the population of a state into 34 districts, having due regard to geographical situation, and contiguity of territory, requires but little time, and no great amount of ingenuity, if attempted with fair and honest intention.

It is submitted, that the appointment of subordinates in the several state Departments, and their tenure of office or employment should be based upon fitness and efficiency, and that this principle should be embedded in Legislative enactment to the end that the State may conform to the reasonable public demand on that subject.

Municipal Government.

The formation and administration of the Government of cities are subjects of public interest and of great importance to many of the inhabitants of the state. The formation of such Governments is proper matter for most careful legislation. They should be so organized as to be simple in their details and to cast upon the people affected thereby, the full responsibility of their administration. The different Departments should be in such accord as in their operations to lead toward the same results.

Divided councils, and divided responsibilities of the people, on the part of municipal officers, it is believed, gives rise to much that is objectionable in the government of cities. If to remedy this evil, the chief executive should be made answerable to the people for the proper conduct of the city's affairs, it is quite clear, that his power in selecting those who manage the different departments should be greatly enlarged. The protection of the people in their primaries will, it is hoped, be secured by the early passage of the law for that purpose, which will rid the present system from the evils which surround it, tending to defraud the people of rights closely connected with their privileges as citizens.

Special Legislation.

It is confidently expected that those who represent the people in the present Legislature address themselves to the enactment of such laws as are for the benefit of all the citizens of the State, to the exclusion of special legislation and interference with affairs which should be managed by the localities to which they pertain. It is not only the right of the people to administer their local government, but it should be made their duty to do so. Any departure from this doctrine is an abandonment of the principles upon which our institutions are founded, and a concession to the infirmity and partial failure of the theory of a representative form of government. If the aid of the Legislature is invoked to further projects which should be subject to local control and management, suspicion should at once be aroused, and interference should be promptly and sternly refused.

If local rule is in any instance bad, weak or inefficient, those who suffer from mal-administration have the remedy within their own control. If through their neglect or inattention it falls into unworthy hands, or if bad methods and practices gain a place in its administration, it is neither harsh nor unjust to remit those who are responsible for those conditions to their self-invited fate, until their interest, if no better motive, prompts them to an earnest and active discharge of the duties of good citizenship.

His Appeal to Legislators.

Let us enter upon the discharge of our duties, fully appreciating our relations to the people, and determined to serve them faithfully and well. This involves a jealous watch of the public funds, and a refusal to sanction their appropriation, except for public needs. To this end, all unnecessary offices should be abolished, and all employment of doubtful benefit discontinued. If to this we add the enactment of such wise and well-considered laws as will meet the varied wants of our fellow-citizens and increase their prosperity, we shall merit and receive the approval of those whese representatives they are, and with the conscientiousness of duty well performed, shall leave our impression for good on the Legislation of the State.

His Wide Popularity.

The admiration and support of Governor Cleveland reaches far beyond the limits of his party, and the indciations are that his success in the present campaign will be as triumphant as when he was chosen Governor of New York.

The Independent Republican Convention which met at New York on July 22d, in its address to the people of the country recognizes the importance of the issue, and the value ot the Democratic nominee.

The following is an extract from said address :

Their Exposition of the Case.

As there is no destructive issue upon public policy presented for the consideration of the country, the character of the candidates becomes of the highest importance with all citizens who do not hold that party victory should be secured at any cost. While the Republican nomination presents a candidate whom we cannot support, the Democratic party presents one whose name is the synonym of political courage and honesty and of administrative reform. He has discharged every official trust with sole regard to the public welfare and with just disregard of mere partisan and personal advantage, which with the appearance and confidence of both parties have raised him from the chief executive administration of a great city to that of a great State. His unreserved, intelligent and sincere support of reform in the civil service has firmly established that reform in the State and cities of New York, and his personal convictions, proved by his official acts more decisive than any possible platform declaration, are the guarantee that in its spirit and in its letter the reform would be enforced in the national administration His high sense of duty, his absolute and unchallenged official integrity, his inflexible courage in resisting party pressure and public outcry, his great experience in the details of administration and his commanding executive ability and independence are precisely the qualities which the political situation demands in the chief executive officer of the Government to resist corporate monopoly on the one hand and demagogue commission on the other, and at home and abroad, without menace or fear, to protect every right of American citizens and to respect every right of friendly states by making political morality and private honesty the basis of constitutional administration.

He is a Democrat who is, happily free from all association with the fierce party differences of the slavery contest, and whose financial views are in harmony with those of the best men in both parties; and coming into public prominence at a time when official purity, courage and character are of chief importance, he presents the qualities and the promise which independent voters desire and when a great body of Republicans, believing those qualities to be absolutely indispensable in the administration of the Government at this time, do not find in the candidate of their own party

Such independent voters do not propose to ally themselves inextricably with any party Such Republicans do not propose to abandon the Republican party, nor to merge themselves in any other party, but they do propose to aid in defeating a Republican nomination which, not for reasons of expediency only, but for high moral and patriotic considerations with a due regard for the Republican name and for the American character, was unfit to be made. They desire not to evade the proper responsibility of American citizens by declining to vote, and they desire also to make their votes as effective as possible for honest and pure and wise administration.

How can such voters who at this election cannot conscientiously support the Republican candidate, promote the objects which they desire to accomplish more surely than by supporting the candidate who represents the qualities, the spirit and the purpose which they all agree in believing to be of controlling importance in the election? No citizen can rightfully avoid the issue or refuse to cast his vote. The ballot is a trust. Every voter is a trustee for good government, bound to answer to his private conscience for his public acts. This Conference, therefore, assuming that Republicans and Independent voters who for any reason cannot sustain the Republican nomination desire to take the course which, under the necessary conditions and constitutional methods of a Presidential election, will most readily and surely secure the result at which they aim, respectfully recommends to all such citizens to support the electors who will vote for Grover Cleveland in order most effectually to enforce their conviction that nothing could more deeply stain the American name and prove more disastrous to the public welfare than the deliberate indifference of the people of the United States to increasing public corruption and to the want of official integrity in the highest trusts of the Government.

What They Say Abroad.

To those who may imagine that because Governor Cleveland's public life has been entirely confined to his native State, he is unknown to the people generally outside of that Commonwealth, we publish the following extracts showing that his good name and reputation not only are as broad as his native land, but extend to other nations, where he is regarded as one possessing wonderful executive abilities, and is, in the true sense of the word, a Reformer.

[*From the Pall Mall Gazette.*]

Unless all observers are mistaken and all the signs misleading, Governor Cleveland, who was nominated as the Democratic candidate by the party convention at Chicago, will be elected President of the American Republic in November. The Republicans have split their party by selecting Mr Blaine, and the attempt to curry favor with the Irish by printing as Republican campaign documents every expression of English opinion adverse to the great American Jingo, has been so barefaced as to provoke a reaction. The Americans do not want to have a President sent to Washington by the men who send dynamite to London. It may be noted, however, for the confusion of those who are constantly assuring us that an industrial democracy is free from all craving for territorial extension, that the policy of contraction is energetically repudiated by both the great American parties. Mr. Blaine is the Beaconsfield of the States, and as for Governor Cleveland, this is what the platform of his party has to say about the foreign policy of the Democrats:

"As the result of this policy we recall the acquisition of Louisiana, Florida, California, and of the adjacent Mexican territory by purchase alone. Contrast these grand acquisitions of Democratic statesmanship with the purchase of Alaska, the sole fruit of a Republican administration of nearly a quarter of a century"

And yet, in face of this eager competition of American parties on the eye of a Presidential election as to which has annexed the most territory, there are those who imagine that the English democracy when once it is fully enfranchised will be enthusiastic for the contraction of England!

Another Tribute.

The London *Globe*, one of the leading British papers, whose criticisms of American matters are always read with interest on this side of the ocean, in commenting on the nomination of Governor Cleveland says:

"The Democrats may be congratulated on having made a wise choice, and there seems every probability at present of their carrying the Presidency From an outside point of view, Governor Cleveland is somewhat to be preferred to Mr Blaine. The latter has Irish and filibustering leanings, and is a much stronger Protectionist than his rival. It is also possible that Governor Cleveland will, if elected, really set his hand in earnest to civil service reform—a crusade not to be expected of Mr. Blaine. The latter, indeed, now stands as the champion of vested interests in corruption, while Governor Cleveland has been forced by circumstances to place dependence on the purity ticket."

The reader will note that his reputation as a reformer has reached beyond his own country, and those who have carefully watched his public career in distant lands are convinced that in whatever position he may be placed, he will be an avowed enemy to public plunder and corruption both within and outside of his party.

Still Another Tribute.

[*From the London Standard*].

The Chicago Democratic Convention have ended their task by nominating Governor Cleveland as their candidate for the Presidency A more satisfactory result could hardly have been desired. Mr. Cleveland is little known out of his own State, but he bears the character of being a man of ability, and his "record" is unstained. The fight will, in reality, be one between "clean" and "unclean"—that is to say, old-fashioned politics. The last eight years of Republican rule have not been popular Indian frauds, sutler frauds, mail frauds, whiskey frauds, have been prominent, the whole being crowned with a Presidential election fraud, which was the worst of all. The struggle, however, as it was in 1828, lies between men, rather than between parties, and if the country prefers Mr Blaine, with his unpleasant record and evil possibilities, to Mr. Cleveland, with his unblemished reputation, it will be because they fear that a party which for twenty-four years has been out of office will be too greedy for "the spoils" to practice within the White House the virtues they profess.

The above paragraph shows very clearly that England has little or no interest in the platforms or principles of the different political parties, and that she does not expect to be benefited as a nation by the success of a particular party So far as industries are at stake, our British cousins simply attend to their own interests and do not expect other nations to assist them. Hence the idea that either free trade or protection in this country is of momentous importance to them is simply "a wind of words." The *Standard* compares the men as men fitted for the position.

THOMAS ANDREWS HENDRICKS.

By constitutional provision, upon the death or disqualification of the President, the Vice-President assumes the office, vested with all the powers as though he had been directly chosen for that position. Four times in the history of the nation has this officer become the Chief Executive, and four times have the people been taught the necessity of nominating a man for the second place competent to fill the first. Could the future have been known with its results, it is doubtful if either of the men selected as candidates for the Vice-Presidency would have received the nomination.

The Democratic Party, by its action in the National Convention at Chicago, appears to have been impressed with the importance of the second place on the ticket, and governed its actions accordingly in the selection of one eminently fitted by devotion to party and country, by broad statesmanship, ripe experience as a legislator, and thoroughly conversant with the affairs of state. A life-long experience with governmental affairs, a thorough knowledge of our government, its needs and its aspirations, a legislative career reaching over thirty years, a portion of which is the most eventful in our history and an extended acquaintance with public men, make him eminently fitted for the highest honors that can be bestowed by our countrymen.

He is Well Known.

Thomas A. Hendricks is well known to all men and to all parties, as his participation in public affairs and his opinions on all important questions of public policy form a part of our historic records. In private as well as in public life he has been a man of strong convictions, never entertaining an idea that he could not defend, and never accepting a proposition that could not be demonstrated. Always true to his party allegiance, at the same time his broad and progressive ideas made him a national statesman. In the halls of legislation he served his constituents with unwavering devotion, and watched their interests with unceasing vigilance. Yet at the same time on all questions of national import he was for his country as a whole. Representing a government of the people, he stood closely by the people in defence of their legal rights and for such measures as enlarged their freedom, elevated their manhood, and promoted their general welfare. As a Senator, he made for himself a national reputation which will endure for all time.

He was ever active and aggressive. and his career was characterized by frankness and boldness. He was active in opposition to the measures overturning the old State Governments, the imposition of test oaths, the Civil Rights bill, the Freedman's Bureau bill and kindred legislation. He shaped his political conduct upon the theory that the prosperity of the white people of the South, even though they had been rebels, was a matter of more importance than the prosperity of the negroes. If either race was to go to the wall he thought it should be the black race, but he held that the natural supremacy of the white race was a guarantee for all. His arguments on the great questions of the day have been adopted as the authoritative statement of Democratic opinion in the summaries of Congressional debate. For many years he has been the leader of his party in his state, and his fellow citizens have shown their appreciation of his valuable services by giving him repeated positions of trust and honor. There is probably no man in Indiana who has a stronger personal following than Mr. Hendricks, or whose opinions exert a greater influence. Eight years ago his fellow citizens placed him on the ticket with Samuel J. Tilden, and those who best know the inward workings of that campaign, and its termination before the Electoral Commission, feel assured that the ticket elected by the people was sacrificed by that arbitration. It is not our purpose to discuss that matter in this brief notice, but the law of retributive justice would seem to have demanded his presentation again for the position to which he, and millions of his people, believe he was rightfully elected.

Thomas A. Hendricks is more than an ordinary statesman. His ability to grasp the issues of the hour and to predict their effects upon the future, is attested by the Congressional records giving his services in the House and in the Senate. Never in the history of our country did political excitement run more high than when he took his place in the upper House of Congress. With a disrupted nation and a bloody war, which had existed for two years, with the North and South arrayed against each other, with millions of men in the field—with a demoniac howl against the Democracy throughout the free states because they strove to be national instead of sectional,—with the bayonets of the Federal army as a support of the Republican party, and with the soldiers as a detective police, to throw into prisons without warrant or indictment any who might refuse to sanction the policy of the dominant party—in such a time, and under such circumstances, the Democracy of Indiana chose Mr. Hendricks to represent their State in the Senate. But then as now, there, as in his own state, he stood true to his convictions, and acted as the Senator of a nation, instead of the champion of a faction.

His Nomination as Vice-President.

After Mr. Cleveland had been chosen for the first place on the National ticket, the question as to who was the best man for the second place became the topic of the moment. That the delegations had deliberated as to a Vice-President, prior to the selection of Mr. Cleveland, there can be no doubt from the fact that no delay was had in completing the ticket. There were many in that convention who were for "the old ticket" of 1876, and had Mr Tilden consented to be a candidate, there is little doubt that it would have been nominated. But when that could not be had, there seemed to be a general feeling that the honored name of Hendricks which graced the old ticket, should again be placed upon the Democratic banner The recess that was taken only tended to solidify this sentiment and when the convention again met, it was a foregone conclusion that Thomas A. Hendricks would be the nominee.

Ex-Senator Wallace of Pennsylvania said that he nominated as a candidate for Vice-President a man conversant with public affairs throughout his whole life, an honored statesman, a pure and upright citizen, a victim of the grossest fraud ever perpetrated on the American people—Thomas A. Hendricks.

Governor Waller seconded the nomination of Hendricks, and said that the Democratic party would, in defiance of fraud and in accordance with law, place him in the chair of Vice-President.

The presentation of Mr. Hendricks' name was greeted with enthusiastic cheers, the Convention repeating, in a lesser degree, the scene which took place at the morning session in honor of the same gentleman.

The announcement that Mr. Hendricks might not accept the second place, only increased the enthusiasm, and one by one, all the names of the other candidates were withdrawn, leaving him the sole nominee. Mr. Waller continued his eulogy, and said that neither Connecticut's Governor nor Connecticut had a desire to force on Indiana a candidate against her will, but this was not an Indiana convention [laughter and applause], but one of the Democracy of the country, and the Democrats had the right to take any man that they saw fit for their ticket. If there was any Democrat who said he wonld not, under the circumstances here presented, take the nomination, he would of course withdraw his name, but Mr. Hendricks deserved it for the wrong that had been done in 1876. [Applause.] The party would have selected the same statesman from the East that it had eight years ago but for his lack of health. Mr Hendricks was, thank God, in good health, and his selection was demanded by the party now

Somebody asked that the rule be enforced requiring the call of States to proceed, and ex-Senator Wallace, declaring that Mr Hendricks had once been elected Vice-President, and it was the party's demand now that he occupy his rightful seat again, moved that the rule be suspended and that the nomination be made by acclamation.

He was an Alabamian who now mildly suggested that a roll-call be taken on the honorable names that had been presented. The convention, however was set on having Hendricks, and no attention was paid to him. Judge John T Harris, of Virginia, seconded Mr Wallace s motion. The withdrawal of all names save that of Hendricks now began, amid the applause of the audience. Searles withdrew the name of Rosecrans, and Colorado that of McDonald. Ex-Governor Hubbard of Texas, seconded Hendricks's nomination in a vigorous speech from the platform, in which he declared that the old ticket had been the desire of the Texas delegation when elected, and it still had a longing for it "Gov. Hendricks will surely carry Indiana," said he, and again there was a shout. "He deserves it give it to him, for God's sake," Black's name was withdrawn, and Smith M. Weed begged the convention not to give the nomination to Mr Hendricks with a hurrah, but let the roll be called. Wallace withdrew his motion and substituted one that the nominations be closed, which was adopted with a hurrah. and State after State recorded in his favor, giving him the entire vote of the convention.

Before proceeding to his biography in detail we propose to give the reader an intelligent idea of the man as the representative of the party which has just nominated him, by quoting from his public record.

His Record.

Mr. Hendricks's broad and sound financial views, the correctness of which has been fully demonstrated by the facts, show that he was in advance of all others in his belief that our bonds could be placed at a lower rate of interest than was then paid. That the reader may fully understand his position on the financial question, and his faith in government securities more than one year before the war had closed, we make the following extract from the Congressional records:

March 3, 1864, when a bill "To provide ways and means to support the government" was before the Senate, Mr. Hendricks said: "It has been expected in the country that a five per cent. loan would be provided for, and I was surprised when the report came from the Committee on Finance providing for a six per cent. loan. The six per cent. bonds are worth in the market above par, which indicates very clearly that the Government could negotiate a loan at less than that rate of interest. It seems to me that the Government should negotiate its loans at the very lowest rate of interest possible. As compared with the debts of other Governments our debt is being contracted at a very high rate of interest, and it thus imposes a very great burden on the people. If we can secure a loan at five per cent. instead of six we ought to do it. It seems to me, if the public credit is maintained as it has been for the last few months, that a loan can be secured at five per cent. With the present depreciation of the currency five per cent. payable in coin, as this bill provides, would be equal to nearly eight per cent. in currency.

My proposition is to issue these bonds at a rate of interest not to exceed five per cent. If the chairman of the Committee on Finance will say that he is satisfied such a loan cannot be negotiated, of course that would influence my judgment very much on this proposition but until he says so, I am satisfied that such a loan can be negotiated, and if so it ought to be done. We ought not to continue to increase our debt at the enormons rate of interest we now pay unless it be absolutely necessary. If we can secure a five per cent. loan instead of six per cent. or a higher rate, we should do it. I should like to know from the chairman of the Committee on Finance whether, in his judgment, on an examination of almost all the cities money can be readily had on an interest of six per cent per annum payable in paper As I said before, at the time the answer was made to the Senator by Mr. Hunter, that was not the case; but loans were negotiated at from seven to nine or ten per cent.

Now, sir, the difference between paper and gold is quite thirty-three per cent.; one dollar in gold being worth $1.59 in the paper currency of the country, and the ordinary commercial rate of interest being six per cent. payable in paper. Under these circumstances, I want to know why it is that the Secretary of the Treasury cannot negotiate this loan payable in gold at less than six per cent. If the banks of the country can use their capital at six per cent. and no greater rate of interest payable in paper, which is worth so much less than gold, why is it that the Secretary of the Treasury must pay in gold what is equal to more than nine per cent. in paper?

If the Secretary of the Treasury were to say to the Senate that he could not negotiate a loan for less than nine per cent., when the ordinary interest of the country is but six per cent., payable in depreciated currency, I would say the opinion of the Secretary of the Treasury was not entitled to the respect of the Senate. That would be my response to that proposition. But I want to ask the chairman of the Committee on Finance if the Secretary of the Treasury were to say to us that in view of the present state of the rate of interest in the country he could not probably negotiate for less than nine per cent., whether he would insert in this bill "nine" instead of "six per cent.," contrary to his own convictions.

Mr President, I have not designed to discuss this question as a party man, nor do I intend to be led off into a party discussion. We are now considering a question that goes to the pockets of the taxpayers of the country. If we can negotiate a loan at five per cent., instead of six per cent., it is our duty to do it. Our debt is being contracted at a higher rate of interest than perhaps the debt of any country in the world. I do not intend that it shall be considered a sufficient answer to me that any former Administration was compelled to negotiate a loan at a very high rate of interest. In reply to the Senator from Michigan, I do not recollect the circumstance to which he refers. I will not dispute it, but my reply is, that I have no knowledge of the circumstance to which he refers.

The chairman of the Committee on Finance has called attention again to the fact that this is but a limitation, it fixes the maximum of interest, and the Secretary of the Treasury may possibly negotiate it at a less rate. I will ask the Senator if he knows of any case in which a loan has been negotiated at a less rate of interest than the maximum fixed in the bill allowing the loan?

Mr. FESSENDEN. No, I do not.

Mr. HENDRICKS. The senator says he does not. Of course he does not. I knew that would be his reply As soon as it is fixed in the bill, it becomes the opinion of the country, and the rule in the Department, too, that that shall be the rate, and when we say that it shall not exceed six per cent. it is the same as saying that the loan shall be negotiated at six per cent. That becomes both the maximum and the minimum.

There has been a desire to obtain the Government securities within the last few months. We have an illustration of it here in this bill. A six per cent. loan was sought after with such avidity that $11,000,000 were subscribed for beyond the amount allowed by law, and this bill provides for that excess. There was an earnest desire to secure the loan, and that Government security is now worth in the market three or four per cent. above par.

With this prominent, striking fact before us, it seems to me remarkable that the chairman of the Committee on Finance should say to us we cannot negotiate a loan at less than six per cent. This loan is now worth at six per cent., payable in coin, nine per cent. in currency. Money is loaned in the banks and in all commercial transactions at six per cent., but the Government pays what is equivalent to nine per cent. I say we ought not to do it. If we make a loan at five per cent., payable in coin, it is equal to seven or eight per cent. in the ordinary currency of the country

I have made this proposition in good faith, not as a party man. I disclaim party considerations and influence upon a question like this. Our debt is going up to an enormous amount, and we should consider well at every step where we add one hundred or two hundred or three hundred million dollars to our already enormous debt, whether we can secure the loan at a less rate than that heretofore provided for

I believe if we put a six per cent. loan in this bill, the Secretary of the Treasury cannot negotiate it at less than six per cent., because that then becomes the rate in the public opinion, and the men who have money to loan will say to the Secretary, "We will let you have it at the amount of interest which the bill allows, but we will not let you have it at less." If the bill were to say five per cent., I believe the Secretary could secure it at that rate.

I should not have indulged in another word in this debate, for I have expressed my views on the amendment which I have offered in good faith, were it not for the last suggestion of the Senator from Maine. He has said to the Senate that the last loan was taken and public confidence grew up in respect to it notwithstanding the efforts of the men in the country with whom I act politically to beat down public confidence in regard to that loan. Sir, I have not said anything in this debate to call for any such suggestion from the Senator and with great respect to him personally, I think that part of his argument is not worthy the position he holds in the Senate. I know of no effort on my own part and of no effort on the part of the public men with whom I act as a party man to destroy the confidence of the people in the Government securities. Public confidence in those securities depends very much on our military operations, and the confidence in that loan was insipred more by the successes of our army upon the Mississippi and the Cumberland than by any political speeches, and the Senator ought to know it. After the victories of July last, the confidence of the public in the Government securities went up, very naturally. And now as the Senator claims that the rebellion is upon its last legs, why is it that he says the confidence in the public securities is not greater to-day than it was even at that hour? As the hour approaches, in the opinion of the Senator, at which the rebellion will cease to have power to resist the authority of the Government, the confidence in the Government securities is to go down, at least not to increase. Sir, the success of our armies has given this confidence, and no efforts of political parties in the country.

I am very sorry that upon a question that affects only the tax-payers of the country, the Senator should have deemed it necessary to go into any political discussion. I do not intend to be led into it even by the chairman of the Committee on Finance.

His Early History.

Thomas Andrews Hendricks, was born on a little farm in the vicinity of Zanesville, Muskingum County, Ohio, on the 9th of September, 1819, so that he is now approaching his sixty-sixth year, His father, the late Major John Hendricks, was a native of Pennsylvania, and was amongst the first settlers of Ligonier Valley, in the county of Westmoreland. He was an enterprising, thrifty man, and a fine specimen of those early squatters who filled the primeval forests and tilled the virgin soil. His father was noted for his social graces and hospitality, and was conspicuous in the Presbyterian Church; and these circumstances left an impress on the young man's character. He took an active part in public affairs, held several positions in the county, and was elected to the State Legislature. His wife, the mother of the nominee, was Jane Thomson, of Scotch descent, her grandfather, John Thomson, having emigrated to this country before the Revolutionary war, in which he bore an honorable and conspicuous part. In 1820, six months after the birth of his son Thomas, he sold his property in Westmoreland county, and removed to Madison on the Ohio river, in the State of Indiana, where his brother, William Hendricks, also resided, the second Governor of Indiana, the first Representative to Congress from that State, and afterwards the predecessor of his nephew Thomas, in the Senate of the United States. Shortly after the father, John, removed to Indiana he was appointed by the government at Washington, Surveyor of Public Lands, a positon which he filled to the satisfaction of the administration. In the year 1822, when Thomas was only three years of age, his father concluded to go further west, and accordingly removed into the interior of the State and purchased a home in Shelby County, near Shelbyville, the present site of the County seat, which was then, and still is, one of the most delightful and productive spots in the State of Indiana. Here John Hendricks built him a substantial brick house, which is still standing, in which his family was reared, amid the best influences that could be enjoyed in those pioneer days. Indianapolis had just been laid out and established as the future capital of the State, and Mr. Hendricks' house was one of the principal centres of education and Christian refinement in the central part of Indiana. He was the father and founder of the Presbyterian Church in Indianapolis, of the good Scotch type, and in that faith the boy Thomas was reared and nurtured.

His Early Days.

Young Hendricks attended the village school where he exhausted the local educational opportunities, and as soon as he reached the required age he entered the college at South Hanover, near Madison, one of the pioneer educational institutions of the West, from which he graduated in 1841, at the age of twenty-two years. During his collegiate term he was noted amongst his preceptors and students for the ease with which he prepared himself in his several studies, which was due to his analytical mind and retentive memory He always had time to join in games for recreation, as well as to read many books in no way appertaining to his college studies. He excelled in mathematics and logic, and gave promise of high literary talent.

The Student and Lawyer.

Prior to leaving college he decided to make the law his profession and he at once commenced the study of law with Judge Major, one of the most prominent members of the Bar of Central Indiana, then and still residing at Shelbyville. Here for about a year he diligently pursued his legal studies, giving promise that he had selected a profession for which he was peculiarly fitted, and in 1842, he went to Chambersburg, Pennsylvania, at the request of his uncle, Judge Thomson, of that place, where he completed his studies under his direction and was admitted to practice. Shortly after graduating in the law he left the home of his uncle, returned to Indiana, and hung out his shingle as a lawyer in Shelbyville. But clients came slowly and at long intervals, and the bright and pleasant dreams of the visionary student faded away before the stern realties of actual business. His success was not rapid, and at one time the young lawyer depairing of success, almost resolved to strike out in another field of labor. His friends dissuaded him from so doing, so he continued at his calling, and his close attention to the interests of those who patronized him, his correct habits and his pleasant and engaging address, all conspired to give him popularity, so that gradually his practice increased and his reputation spread, until in the end he had a lucrative practice and a high position in his profession.

By hard work at his profession and habits of strict economy, he accumulated a moderate fortune. About the same time he commenced to practice law, he entered the political field and being a good debater and an oratorical speaker, he soon became a prominent factor in the politics of his state. It is quite probable that his political speeches and his commingling with the public men of the day, added very largely to the number of his clients and augmented the receipts from his profession.

In Mr. Hendricks' profession—the law—all acknowledge him to be great. This is the vocation to which nature particularly adapted him, and it is his favorite one. He has, since first entering public life, returned to the practice of his profession with facility and zeal immediately upon the termination or intermission of official engagements. He thoroughly mastered its elementary principles and the minutiæ of its practice. With this foundation and with a natural legal mind he is never at a loss, and is always strong in any cause without special book preparation. Before court or jury he is equally at home. In a trial he is never off his guard nor disconcerted by any unlooked for turn in the fortune of a case. He encounters any such crisis with as much promptness, fortitude and address as if it had been anticipated and prepared for

He enters Public Life.

Mr Hendricks continued in the practice of the law until 1848, during which period he obtained a high reputation as a lawyer, and his practice not only was large in his own district, but it had extended throughout the state. Probably no one in the profession in Indiana of his age held a more promising place at the bar than young Hendricks, and his forensic efforts were models of eloquence and legal knowledge. He has always been reckoned one of the most powerful men before a jury in his state, and he has carried away many a case from the cold and logical instructions of the court to a spell-bound jury

An Incident.

On one occasion an excited individual called at his office to procure his legal services. Mr Hendricks was sitting in a lazy chair reading a volume of State Reports when he entered, and inviting the visitor to a chair, asked him the nature of his business.

I want you to assist me in resisting the payment of a note, and I have been recommended to you as the best lawyer of the place."

"Well," said Mr. Hendricks, "state the circumstances and facts just as they are."

The visitor then explained to him, that he purchased some stock six months since, and gave his note for the amount, which would fall due in a few weeks. As he lost money by the transaction he did not propose to pay the note if he could avoid it, and he wished the attorney to legally transfer his property to another party, so that it could not be seized for the debt.

"You received the goods according to agreement," said Mr. Hendricks.

"Yes, sir."

"And gave your note in good faith?"

"Yes, sir."

"And you wish me to aid you in defrauding an honest creditor?"

"I wish to save my money, as many others do," replied the would-be client, "and I will divide the amount of the note with you for your services."

"And what will be my share?" asked the lawyer

"Why the note is for $600, and your share will be one half that sum."

"See here, young man," said Mr Hendricks rising from his chair and advancing towards his visitor, "I will give you my opinion and advice without any fee. My opinion is that you are a rogue and a scoundrel, who richly deserves to be placed behind the bars of a prison, and my advice is that unless you pay that note when it becomes due, and thus meet your honest obligations like a man, the court will place you where you properly belong. There may be persons who would aid you in your rascally scheme, and enable you to cheat your fellow-man, but you have called at the wrong office. Good night, sir—take my advice and you will never regret it."

During the presidential campaign in 1844, when Mr. Hendricks was but 24 years of age, he took a conspicuous part, and worked efficiently for the success of the ticket. He took the stump for Polk and Dallas, and made a number of speeches throughout the State. Being an effective speaker, and a ready writer, his services were in great demand, and the announcement of his presence at a political meeting was sure to draw a large concourse of people. His speeches in those days were models of their kind, and gave him a notoriety that hastened his advent into public life. He had a decided liking for politics, and even at that early day he was one of the best posted men in the State in local and national issues. His activity in this field brought him in contact, and gave him an acquaintance with the leading men of the State. He then formed friendships which have proven most valuable, and which have lasted to the present time, and many of his most enthusiastic admirers and ardent supporters are those who met him nearly forty years ago.

In the State Legislature.

From 1843 to 1860, Mr Hendricks resided at the City of Shelbyville, where as lawyer and politician he was one of the leading citizens. His Democratic convictions were of the most decided character. Its anti-centralization policy, its conservatism so like that which characterized the tried governments of the old world, and its close affiliation with the direct interests of the populace made it his ideal of the party for a government of the people. Indeed his great personal popularity in his district was in a great measure due to the fact that he always stood close by the masses and their rights, and was quick to resent any effort to curtail their powers. He had read all the party lore, he had been a close student in our political history, and had followed the party of his choice throughout all its doings. His admiration of Jefferson led him to study his writings and his character, and hence he has always been a genuine Jeffersonian Democrat. He is no advocate of "isms," no follower of visionary theories, but sticks closely to the old party landmarks. Hence his safe conservatism and strict adherence to the vital issues of his party

A Natural Leader.

His fellow-citizens, beholding these traits even in his early years, naturally turned towards him as a natural leader, and counsellor, and in 1848 they with great unanimity nominated him for the State legislature before he was 28 years of age. Three years prior to this, September 25, 1845, he was married, near Cincinnati, to Miss Eliza C. Morgan, by whom he had a son, born in 1848, but who lived only three years. This was his only child, and his death left a lasting impression on the bereaved father. The position in the legislature was not sought by him, and he accepted it with reluctance, for he had a lucrative legal practice, which must necessarily suffer in his absence at the State Capital. But withal there was a fascination in politics that captivated him, and sacrificing his financial prospects for political promotion, he, for two years represented his people in the lower house, with the same zeal that he attended to his legal business. But the position proved unsatisfactory to him. He felt himself beyond the position, and resolved to return to his office and books at the close of his term. Whilst in the House he was always at his post, and was watchful of every class of legislation, and he became noted as opposed to all sorts of extravagance and useless expenditure of the public money True to his party, to his State, and to himself, he was one of the leading members whose opinion had much weight in moulding legislation. From his first entry as a public officer he has favored an honest and economical administration of public affairs, and thus is a fitting personage to place on the national ticket with Governor Cleveland.

A Member of the Constitutional Convention.

But the people did not intend that he should retire to private life, when he declined a re-election to the State legislature in 1850. In the meantime an act had been passed to organize a Constitutional Convention, and his name was at once brought out in connection with that body. The Indianapolis Senatorial district elected him a member of the convention, a position to which his legal knowledge and safe judgment made him a valuable member. Mr. Hendricks was then but thirty years old, and was perhaps the youngest member of that august body. Here with Schuyler Colfax, William S. Holman, and the leading lawyers and statesmen of Indiana, he took a prominent and leading part in the proceedings, and much of the instrument that emanated from that convention bears the impress of his handiwork. It was this convention that framed the present constitution of the State.

An examination of the records of that body attests the valuable aid Mr. Hendricks gave his fellow-members, and the close attention he bestowed on every detail of its labors. One conspicuous feature exhibited there, as elsewhere, is his opposition as a general rule to special legislation.

There were influences bearing on this body, as upon all similar convocations favoring special classes and interests, all tending to the centralization of power into the hands of the few and creating monopolies to give capital an undue influence over labor. They found no friend for such in Mr Hendricks, who opposed every effort in that direction, and the entire absence of such special legislation in the new consti tution is as much due to him as to any other member Some of his arguments on that occasion are models in eloquence, in purity of style, in close and cogent reasoning, and in devotion to his State. Mr Colfax said that no man in that body gave more valuable service than he, and Mr. Holman, who is not verbose in laudation spoke of him as an invaluable member

Elected to Congress.

The prominence of Mr Hendricks in the Constitutional Convention gave him additional notoriety and popularity It was his first opportunity to demonstrate his worth and ability and the people saw in him one of the rising men of the commonwealth. The State legislature gave no scope for his broad ideas—it was too narrow and confined for one with such broad statesmanship and legal acumen. But this convention brought him into his proper sphere and enabled his constituents to note the power of him whom they had selected. His friends presented him as a candidate for Congress from that district, which then extended over a vast scope of country, owing to the sparse population. It was the Central Congressional District of that State, reaching from Tipton on the north, to Brown County on the south, and from Marion on the east, to Hendricks on the West. The nominating convention selected him, and in August 1851, he was elected over his competitor, Colonel Rush, of Hancock County, by a majority of nearly 4000 votes.

In Congress.

On the first Monday in December, 1852, he took his seat in that great national body, and commenced a career in statesmanship which has given him a reputation as extended as the bounds of the nation. A new member of the House of Representatives, no matter what his genius or ability, or standing in state and local politics finds himself in the vocative when he takes his seat in the lower House at Washington. It was a new school in which there is much to study and to learn, ere he can become an active and useful participant, and he who flops up to seek notoriety in his incipiency is as a rule, so completely ignored and squelched, that as a result he regrets his impetuosity, and in the future "makes haste slowly" So Mr. Hendricks quietly performed his several duties during that winter, without rushing into debate, studying his new position and gradually preparing himself for future efforts. In the Committee room he was a steady and careful worker, and on the floor an active member. He never rose to address the house without a specific object, and when he did, he reached his point by the most direct route. His powers of condensation, so noticeable at the present, were shown in his early efforts in the House.

Re-elected to Congress.

Under the provisions of the new State Constitution the time for electing members of Congress was changed, and a member had to be selected in the following year. The Democratic Convention of his District unanimously nominated him, and in 1852, he was re-elected. A new apportionment had changed the district from its former geographical boundaries, giving him to some extent a new constituency. His opponent in the congressional campaign of 1852 was Mr. Bradley, an able and brilliant Whig. By an agreement between them Messrs. Hendricks and Bradley held joint discussions throughout the district, which was the first of that kind of campaigning in Indiana. The campaign was an exciting one, and this novel manner of conducting it drew large audiences composed of both political parties at the places selected for this joint discussion. It was predicted by many of the friends of both gentlemen that the experiment would not succeed—that disorder and perhaps bloodshed might ensue from bringing men under the pressure of political excitement into contact. The result showed that their fears were unfounded. The speakers were courteous to each other and did not permit party feeling to sunder personal friendship, and the crowds partook of the general good humor. As was expected, Mr. Hendricks was re-elected by a handsome majority

The Missouri Compromise.

It was during his second term in Congress that the Missouri Compromise came before Congress, and that body as well as the country at large felt the most profound interest in the proceedings. The friends of the Compromise regarded it as the anchor which had prevented the nation from drifting on the rocks of discord and dissolution, whilst others considered it the cause of such constant dissension in the halls of legislation that its repeal was necessary for the security of our government. It is not our purpose to enter into a discussion of the question, as it forms such an important part of the history of that period, and has so often been given in its fullest details that every general reader is conversant with it. Suffice it to say that Henry Clay had almost secured the devotion of the people as the father of that measure, and with that regard which well established principles will obtain, the people were taught to look with suspicion and fear upon any interference with this compact. Opinions on this question did not drift in strict party channels, but men divided on it as a great question outside of party lines. In its defence, as well as in the opposition, Whig and Democrat worked shoulder to shoulder. It was a new departure, which created a new dividing line between individuals wholly upon this single issue.

Its Repeal.

The discussions in both Houses of Congress on the question were of an exciting character, and well calculated to inflame the public mind. Mr. Hendricks, as a Representative, took part in the House proceedings and favored its repeal. He advocated his position from a constitutional and legal standpoint, and divesting himself of all personality, and ignoring all local influences, he chose rather to be the advocate of a nation than the attorney of a district, Mr. Hendricks was not misinformed as to public opinion at home, but he well knew that his convictions were in opposition to the views of many of his constituents. The time-serving politician would have had no difficulty in shaping his course under such circumstances. He would have stifled conscience, abandoned what he considered right, and yielded to the clamor of his constituents. Not so with Mr Hendricks. He acted as he thought the present demanded, leaving the future to provide for itself, and however much we may differ as to the propriety and wisdom of his course, all agree that he was honest in his convictions.

He sought to explain his vote in favor of its repeal to his constituents, and to convince them that his action was right in the premises, but that vote lost him a large following in his district. He received the nomination for a third term in Congress but was defeated at the election by Lucien Barbour who has died since, and who was the first Republican Congressman from the Central district of Indiana. However much his people may have, differed as to his vote on the repeal of the Missouri Compromise, he was satisfied He (as a majority now do) believed that the original bill was unconstitutional, and apart from any merit it might possess, should be repealed. He considered the Constitution of the United States long enough, broad enough, and strong enough to govern our people, and that any unconstitutional legislation, however valuable it might prove for the time, was not only a wilful wrong against government, but a direct attack upon the fundamental principles of the Government.

On the 4th of March, 1855, his term expired, and he left the nation's capital to return to his homestead, and again feel the sweet and refreshing repose of private life.

At Home.

Again we find him in Shelbyville, surrounded by his law books and his briefs, the same pleasant, social every-day man as before. It is not every one who can stand political honors. The adulation of sycophants, the importance of duties, the eminence of the position, and the *eclat* that appertains to the office, have a tendency to turn men's heads, and give them false ideas of their greatness. They are too apt to forget that it is the position or office and not the man that brings attention and patronage, and they do not discover their mistake until they are relegated to private life, and find that they are disrobed of all that flattered their vanity. Not so with Mr. Hendricks. In all stations and on all occasions you find him the same, plain, unassuming, companionable gentleman, neither proud nor pedantic—the very beau ideal of an American citizen.

At His Profession.

A very few months found him with an extensive practice. His former clients returned, and his reputation brought a large influx of new ones. Lawyer Hendricks was as popular as Congressman Hendricks, and to him it was no doubt more pleasant, for it is more easy to serve clients than constituents, more congenial to tender legal advice than to attempt to ride on the deceitful billows of public opinion. And so the spring, with its pale green tints and early flowers, ripened into redolent summer, when at the close of a hot August day he was sitting on the porch of his cozy home, a messenger called and placed in his hand an unpretentious package. That was thirty-five years ago, when many things, both in private and official life, were done differently from what they now are. At the present time appointments are, by means of the telegraph, heralded all over the country, even before they are made, and the fortunate individual is amongst the last to receive the notice. What the President will do is more thoroughly discussed through the newspapers than what he does, and a man is put on trial before his countrymen before the indictment is made out. In those days it was the very opposite, and such matters were "State secrets," which even the omnipresent correspondents could not find out. He opened the packet which bore the seal of the president of the United States, and within it found an autograph letter from President Pierce tendering him the office of

Commissioner of the Land Office.

The offer of the position was a complete surprise to Mr. Hendricks who had not made application for it or for any other position at the disposal of the Executive. The President knew him personally, and Mr. Hendricks' friends had, unknown to him, endorsed him for the place. Life in Washington had no particular charms for him, he preferred his own quiet home in Indiana, and as this position would not only necessitate his return to that city, but would occupy all of his time there, he was at first disposed to decline the proffered position. He wrote to the President, asking for a few days to decide, and in the meantime consulted his father and a few of his most intimate friends. The father who no doubt felt flattered that his son had been selected for such an honorable and important position, urged him to accept, and his friends argued that inasmuch as he had entered public life, and in all probability would continue in politics, he should take the place as a stepping stone to other and higher positions. Accordingly he wrote his acceptance to the President, was duly appointed and commissioned for the office, and in September he left his office and his home, and took charge of the General Land Office. Robert McClelland, of Michigan, was then Secretary of the Interior, and was his immediate superior officer, and as he knew Mr. Hendricks well, it is more than probable that he used his influence with the President to have him appointed. During the remainder of that administration the most friendly relations existed between them resulting in a friendship that extended through after years.

His Administration of the Office.

His administration of the affairs of the office showed that he possessed fine executive ability, and never before was the business so promptly executed. He made himself familiar with every department of the business, knew the details of all its branches, and very soon was well posted on the efficiency of all his subordinates. Whilst holding this position he rendered several important decisions relating to our public lands, and gave the office a standing and importance it had never before attained. He placed the office on a strict business basis, by which means he was able to accomplish the work at less expense and with greater despatch. The imprint of his worth may still be seen in that office, although it has been a quarter of a century since he retired from its duties.

He continued during the remainder of Mr. Pierce's administration, and when Mr. Buchanan was inaugurated, he asked the Commissioner to remain. He did so for over two years of his administration, when he became weary of the increasing duties which for four years had required his undivided attention, and felt that he needed that relaxation and comfort which can only be found at home. He tendered his resignation to President Buchanan, through Jacob Thompson, then Secretary of the Interior, and in 1859 he again sought the city of Shelbyville, to rest from his labors and eventually to follow his profession.

Nominated for Governor.

But he was not permitted to continue at his profession. The campaign of 1860, an eventful one in the history of both party and country, agitated the country to its remotest extremity.

The Democratic Convention held at Charleston failed to make a harmonious nomination. Stephen A. Douglas, a prominent leader of the Democracy had taken issue with the policy of President Buchanan, and a segment of the party sustained him in his opinions of public policy. His followers were known as Anti-Lecompton Democrats, and the delegates favorable to the nomination of Mr. Douglas left the convention and afterwards met and placed him in nomination at Baltimore. Thus the party was hopelessly divided—one branch sustaining Mr. Breckenridge and the other Mr. Douglas. Abraham Lincoln had been suddenly lifted into notoriety by his joint discussions with Mr. Douglas, and the Republicans placed him in nomination. Thus a divided Democracy had to contend with the solid Republican party. On one side a party entirely sectional in its character, endeavored to solidify the north in its favor, whilst the Democracy put forth its greatest efforts to harmonize its discordant elements, and stem the tide of popular clamor. At the same time the State of Indiana had a governor to elect in October, and the importance of a victory at the first election was felt by the contending parties. The party looked over the field and unanimously nominated Mr. Hendricks for Governor.

Oliver P Morton was the nominee of the Republicans, and the campaign was one of the most exciting ever held in the State. Sectional prejudices ran so high, that men with broad national conservative views were accused of fealty to the government, and enemies of their own section. The result was that Mr Hendricks was defeated by a large majority, and the government of the State passed into the hands of the Republicans. Even his personal popularity could not stem the rushing tide, and his State yielded to the popular clamor. He had led the forlorn tribe for his State and his country and lost.

He Removes to Indianapolis.

Shortly after the election, he left Shelbyville and removed to Indianapolis, and opened a law office, where he at once took a leading position at the bar of the State Capital. The reader will note how he alternated between politics and law, and really during all his public life never actually abandoning either Here he immediately secured an extensive practice which increased beyond his ability to transact, and he formed a partnership with Oscar B. Hard, a prominent attorney who subsequently became Attorney-General of the Commonwealth. This firm became widely known, and much of its time was occupied with important cases before the higher courts. At this time, 1862, the legislature of the State was Democratic, and Jesse D. Bright, United States Senator from Indiana, having been expelled from that body, an election was held to choose one to fill his unexpired term of about three weeks, and David H. Turpin was elected to fill the vacancy

Chosen United States Senator.

It devolved on the same legislature to elect a Senator for the ensuing term of six years, from March 4th following, and Mr. Hendricks received the unanimous vote of his party, and was elected. And thus again as the reader will note, his relegation to private life was of short duration. From the lower house of the State legislature he had arisen till he now was selected to fill one of the highest and most honorable positions within the gift of his countrymen. It was at a momentous period of our national history, and the conservative class hailed with delight his advent to the chief council of the nation.

He took his seat in the National Senate on the 4th of March, 1863, and served until 1869—four years as the collegue of Senator Lane and for two years with Senator Morton. With Mr Hendricks' Senatorial services and record the country is familiar He became in great measure the leader of the small Democratic minority in that body

His Course as Senator.

It is not our purpose to follow the career of Mr Hendricks as United States Senator It is a matter of history with which the reader is no doubt familiar. Suffice it to say that his course throughout was marked by the same general characteristics which he had shown in his prior public and private life. Although a strict party man, he was not a party menial, and often on great national questions he rose above party, and saw only his country and its institutions as a grand whole. He met every question presented for consideration frankly and fairly, giving his views without prevarication, and his votes as his judgment dictated. He never consumed the time of the Senate in useless debate—never discussed a question that he did not fully comprehend, and never courted or succumbed to an excited public opinion.

There was nothing dramatic in his manner, and he never did anything for effect. He had nothing of the spread eagle style, but on the contrary always appeared before that body in the character of a broad Statesman and a Constitutional lawyer. That the reader may be his own judge in these matters, we will now reproduced him from his official record giving a few of his opinions as expressed on the floor of the Senate.

Senator Hendricks' Views.

Senator Hendricks is a sound Constitutional lawyer, and his legal views always obtained the attention and respect of his fellow Senators. The following speech is given that the reader may judge of his power and ability from this standpoint. The question at issue was whether interest on claims against the United States should be allowed.

Mr HENDRICKS said :—

Mr President, I am not going to discuss the question whether the Government, which is presumed always to be ready when a claim is properly presented, ought to pay interest or not. But our policy with a few exceptional cases, has been not to pay interest. When the Government has owed a private citizen for many years and has delayed him in the application, and oftentimes allowed him to meet with financial ruin before it complied with its just obligations to him, still it has refused to pay him interest; and why? Upon the theory that the Government is always ready to pay its debts when properly presented. But it seems in this case that there was no claim for interest presented, it was not demanded. The Senator says that the slave power was in the way. Why, sir the slave power paid Massachusetts all she asked. Did the Senator from Massachusetts expect that the slave power would go beyond the asking and voluntarily pay more than Massachusetts wanted?

Mr. President, I think this claim ought to be put upon the ground that Massachusetts was so earnest in her support of the war of 1812. It does appear that she did not advance anything, according to the argument of the Senator, until the booming of the cannon was heard just beyond the hills that line her coast and until her own soil was invaded, and then it seems she raised a militia for the purpose of protecting her own borders, not to aid in the general cause except so far as the defense of her own borders was connected with the general cause; and I suppose she paid this militia that was called out for the special purpose of protecting her own borders, not like Indiana in the recent war, not like Ohio in the recent war, advancing funds so as to fill the Army immediately to fight the battles of the country upon other than her own soil, but Massachusetts, showing her devotion to the cause and the flag of the country in the war of 1812, did not want her own soil invaded, and she took active means, prompt steps to prevent that, and she paid that particular force for that particular service and then she asked Congress to pay it back. It was paid. It was paid a long time before a good many other claims arising in that war were paid, very long before. Why, sir, as young a man as I am myself I recollect when I was a member of the House of Representatives to have presented a claim for an old gentleman whose vessel had been taken under such circumstances that Congress had to pay for it, and yet nobody thought to pay him interest.

He was a young man in command of his vessel upon the Delaware when it was taken from him, and he was left without the means of support almost, except his hands, and when it was paid he was old and gray and blind, and Congress never thought of paying him interest, and when it was asked the slave power, as the Senator says controlling Congress at that time, would not listen to him. He lived in Indiana, and it never occurred to him that it was the slave power that was opposed to the blind, gray-headed old man who did not get interest. Why? Upon the theory that the Government of the United States is always ready to pay when a claim is established to the satisfaction of its conscience. When did Massachusetts present her claim in such form as that it could not be questioned any longer? Was it before 1820? It seems that in 1820 she presented it in such a shape that there was a partial allowance made. Did Massachusetts in 1820 present the claim so as that the conscience of the Government was in default in not paying the whole? Then in 1836 some additional evidence was presented and additional payment was made; and then in 1859 a final allowance, when the State having presented all the evidence she could produce received the money from the Government upon a declaration that it is the last payment that is to be made. But this is a mistake. It is not the last. The Senator says he will not stop at all. Why did he allow that to go into the law and into the reports that this is upon the balance, the final payment? He did not intend it I suppose. Now, the truth of the business is that in 1820 the State of Massachusetts presented her evidence as well as she could, I suppose, and she was paid according to the claim then established, in 1836 she added to her evidence, I suppose, and she was paid according to the claim as then presented.

Mr. President, until four years since there was no claim urged by the State of Massachusetts for interest but she received the money as it was appropriated by Congress, upon a statement made by the Secretary of War and referred to by the law, that that was the balance of the claim. The one side, that is, the Government, in her legislation and by her Department ascertains that this is the balance; and the State accepting it upon that statement, in my judgment, is not now in a condition to demand interest.

But, Mr. President, this law of 1859 shows the fact to have been as I supposed it to be, that in 1820 the State of Massachusetts was not in a condition to demand all that was due to her from the Government, in other words, she had not presented her claim to Congress in such form as satisfied the conscience of Congress that this payment ought to be made; so that in 1836 there was a resolution passed authorizing the State of Massachusetts to present evidence in support of her claim. Up to that time she had not presented evidence. I ask the Senator from Massachusetts if the Government of the United States is under any moral obligation to pay interest to a State or any other body or person until that person or State is in a condition to demand the money? If the accounts of the State when presented are not supported by such evidence as makes it the duty of the public officers to pay the money is the Government in default? This was service rendered peculiarly under the eye of Massachusetts. This military service was not under the control and management of the officers of the United States, but it was her own militia upon her own pay-rolls, as I suppose, and it was for her, if she had a claim against the Government for this irregular service, to present it with such evidence as would justify the representatives of the States and of the people in making the payment from the public Treasury I submit to Senators can interest be demanded upon any principle of conscience and equity from the United States until the claim is supported by such evidence as makes it a duty on the part of the Government to pay?

Then, in 1836, Congress—I suppose at the request of Massachusetts—provided that Massachusetts might furnish evidence of her claim, Then she prepares her evidence, and in 1859, through the Secretary of War that evidence is brought before Congress and the appropriation is made of the sum of money then found due. I want to know from the Senator from Massachusetts when was this claim presented in such shape as that it became the duty of Congress to make the appropriation for the $800,000? The Senator says that no written report has been made on this subject, none was necessary

Why Mr. President, when a claim is made against the Government for interest what must be established? Not that the principal was found to be due some time, but it must be shown that the Government was in default in making payment, that it unreasonably delayed the party after the claim was in proper shape, presented against it. Can a citizen, can a State, in conscience demand interest of the Government until the State or person has made the claim so clear by evidence as that the Government in conscience cannot refuse it? The claim for interest is in the nature of damages; and in the nature of damages for what? For delay of payment, for unreasonable and wrongful delay, for default in payment. When does the default occur on the part of the Government? Not when the debt first has its origin, but when the debt is presented against the Government in such shape so established by evidence as that the public officers are in the wrong if they refuse to pay it. In this case the officers appealed to were the members of the legislative body When then, I ask, was this evidence of the claim presented to Congress in such shape as that Congress was in default in this matter? I think that the Senator from Massachusetts cannot say to the Senate that no written report has ever been made upon this subject, because it was not necessary. I want to know of him now when did the State of Massachusetts present her case to Congress supported by such evidence as made it the duty of Congress to appropriate eight hundred and odd thousand dollars? It clearly had not been done up to 1836, because in 1836 a resolution was passed authorizing Massachusetts to present her evidence. Then she prepared her testimony, I suppose in support of her claim, and it came finally to be acted upon in 1859, and payment was then received by Massachusetts as the balance of the claim, urging no interest, thinking of no interest, not regarding that as a part of her claim until a railroad company becomes interested in it and that corporation urges it as a claim against the Government. The conscience of the Government was not charged with wrong by the State of Massachusetts until her assignment is made to a corporation, and I want to know before the Senator from Massachusetts undertakes to say that we are in fault in this matter when the evidence was completed in support of this claim.

But, Mr. President, it is not the policy of the Government to pay interest on claims when allowed. I will not discuss the right or the wrong of that. A State has no better right to interest than the humblest citizen of this country He who furnishes corn to feed the cavalry horses or provisions to feed the soldiers during war is as much entitled to interest upon his advances as a State that makes an advance of money to support the cause, and especially if it be made to defend her own borders.

Now, we had better decide the question whether we choose to reverse the whole policy of the Government on this question. I am free to say that I cannot answer very satisfactorily the demand that may be made for interest by any party after a claim has been presented with sufficient evidence to support it. I do not know why the Government should not pay interest after that time; but we have said during our whole history that we will not pay interest. Shall we reverse it? The citizen comes to Congress and he can scarcely have a hearing. Session after session he attends, he beseeches, he prays, he begs that he may be paid what the Government owes him; it may be for a horse taken, it may be for provisions supplied, whatever it is he importunes, and he stays about the Capitol hoping from day to day that he may receive that which the Government owes him. At the end of years he gets his money upon a claim which was established in the first place by sufficient evidence, but nobody talks of giving him the interest, and by the time he gets the money perhaps he is broken up in the prosecution of the claim. I have thought sometimes that the Government was the worst debtor that the citizen could possibly find, so difficult, so tedious, and so expensive is the prosecution of a claim against the Government, but after all we say to him, "We owe you no interest." Why? Upon the theory that the Government is always ready to pay, but in the case I have referred to it does not pay, has not paid except upon very uureasonable delay Now, if that citizen thus presenting a claim well supported in every respect and commanding the conscience of the Government cannot receive interest why shall a State?

The State that I represent is somewhat interested in this question, for during the war she made advances for Army purposes, she sold her bonds, and paid interest upon those bonds, and when a settlement was made in the Departments she was only allowed the amount advanced. Of course if Massachusetts is paid interest this must be returned to Indiana. We cannot see a discrimination of that sort because there is nothing peculiar in the case of Massachusetts. There is much that was peculiar in the case of Maryland where she sold her trust funds, which were yielding interest, in order to raise money; but in this case of Massachusetts there is nothing peculiar to justify the payment of interest; and if it be paid to her, then Indiana must have her interest, of course. I should not be doing my duty to my State if I did not most earnestly insist upon it, and do that now. I want it to be understood that if this claim be carried then Indiana must be provided for, and I should say all the States ought to be provided for that have made advances, and if you go upon the theory of this proposition that interest is to be allowed before a State has perfected her evidence in support of her claim, then of course Indiana must be paid from the date that she made the advances, not from the day that she demanded the money back again.

A Case in Point.

Mr President, the circumstances of a case very much change the zeal of gentlemen. A few days ago there was a claim of a girl here whose house was taken that upon the site of the house there might be built a fortification, and the entire property taken for military purposes. No Senator in this body was more earnest in opposition to that claim than the Senator from Massachusetts, and his hostility rested upon the most heartless technicality that it is possible to conceive. If I oppose this claim to-night urged for interest upon the theory that the Government is always to be presumed ready to pay every demand when properly presented, that technicality is not so harsh, so cold, so heartless as the technicality that a loyal person—using the language of the Senator from Massachusetts—in a southern State whose property was taken for public use cannot make demand against the Government for the simple reason that that person was a public enemy Devoted to the country, standing by the flag all the while, never deserting the old Government, but always true—the Senator from Massachusetts says to such a person, "Unfortunately your home was in a southern State, and you are by law branded with the character of a public enemy It is not true in fact; you were as loyal as I," says the gentleman from Massachusetts, "as loyal as any son of Massachusetts, yet you had the misfortune to live in a southern State, and therefore the law marks you as a public enemy To stand by the flag you had to stand against public sentiment, you had to make a stand where it was difficult to stand, and in that respect you have greater merit than a man living in the North, and yet unfortunately you lived in a southern State, your property was taken for public uses, your property aided the cause of the country, and you cannot be paid because you are a public enemy" That was the argument made by the honorable Senator the other day to save the Treasury from the payment of a claim presented here upon the most satisfactory evidence. Now he says that no technicality is to be urged against a claim for interest. I urge against the State of Massachusetts—a sovereign State, one of the Confederacy—the very technicality which is arrayed against the humblest citizen that comes to the Halls of Congress for relief the Government is always ready to pay its debts when they are presented in such form and supported by such evidence as makes it an obligation of conscience to pay them.

President Johnson in his message of July 15th, 1867, closed with the following paragraph:

"It is worthy the consideration of Congress and the country whether, if the Federal Government by its action were to assume such obligations, so large an addition to our public expenditures would not seriously impair the credit of the nation or on the other hand, whether the refusal of Congress to guaranty the payment of the debts of these States, after having displaced or abolished their State governments, would not be viewed as a violation of good faith and a repudiation by the national Legislature of liabilities which these States had justly and legally incurred."

When the message was before the Senate, and the legal status of the States that had been in open rebellion against the government was under discussion, Senator Hendricks closed his opinion with the following remarks, which as the reader will observe were concurred in by Senator Howard (Republican) of Michigan.

His Exposition of the Law.

Before this subject passes from the consideration of the Senate, I desire simply to add that in my view of this subject the Government of the United States can rightfully come under no obligation to pay the debts of the southen States existing prior to the war. I think the war was prosecuted, as it was declared by Congress, for the purpose of maintaining the rightful authority of the Government of the United States; for the purpose of maintaining the Constitution and perpetuating the Union, that that being accomplished by the war, the States restored to their rightful position in the Union, or rather their rightful position being maintained no obligation whatever rests upon the Government of the United States in regard to their debts. But, sir, I think it is worthy of consideration and reflection what obligations may fall upon the United States in the event that we maintain the doctrine that the States of the South do not rightfully exist, and that in some way or other they have ceased to be legal States, and that they exist, if at all, by the sufferance and permission of the United States, and upon that position we establish down there a government of our own.

In other words, if we strike out of existence the State government, its machinery of officers and of courts, and establish instead a government of our own, placing there our own officers, taking control through our own officers, appointed by the United States, of the revenue of these States, and in every way control the States, it is worthy of reflection whether that is not an absorption practically and by force, and in that event what may become of the obligations of the Government. Rightfully there can no obligation rest upon the United States, in my judgment, and the States being held in their relation to the Union as defined by the Constitution, we can incur no obligation. However much their relations may have been interupted by a rebellion which they bring on, we can not be responsible to any parties for any loss resulting to them from that. I agree thus far fully with the Senator from Maine, but if we, in fact, strike their State governments out of existence upon the proposition that they are illegal and *de jure*, do not exist at all, and exist only *de facto*—that is our position as declared last spring and now—

and if upon that proposition we assume over them all the powers that may be exercised by any Government, we, by our officers, controlling the revenues which might go to the payment of their debts, we by our officers, declaring how much of those revenues of necessity must go to the purposes which we declare and enforce, them it is a practical question of great moment for us whether that is not an absorption upon which obligations may rest upon us. I hope, sir, we shall not go so far; but I am not prepared to say that it is unwise for the President, when he sees that Congress has now declared that these State governments do not exist *de jure* at all, and that they exist *de facto* only by our permission and only so far as we do permit, when we are legislating in the direction of taking posession and absorbing these State governments, and making them a part of Federal machinery, it is not unwise in my judgment, for the President, when he sees this course of legislation initiated, to admonish us of the possible obligations that may be incurred.

MR. HOWARD. Mr President, the Senator from Indiana and myself, I think, do not differ at all upon some of the points raised in this discussion. We do not differ as to the original and continued liability of the rebel States, for instance, for all debts contracted *ante bellum*. Such obligations arose under legitimate governments, recognized by the United States, and are, of course, still binding upon the governments and the people of those States and will always remain as long as there is a people constituting a State. That is natural justice, and that, I understand, is the public law It is matter of plain common sense and common justice. We agree in this. Then as to all obligations contracted by these several States during the war against the United States and in and of that treasonable war, I take it that we both agree that there is no principle of constitutional law or of public law which in any possible event could make it obligatory upon the Government of the United States to pay those debts.

MR. HENDRICKS. I agree with the Senator in that.

His Tariff Views.

Mr. Hendrick's views upon the tariff question are in strict harmony with those enunceated at Chicago. During his senatorial career he fully expressed himself on that question, and we append some of his own utterances in that body.

January 29, 1867, when a bill affecting import duties was before the Senate, he addressed it on the merits of the bill. Some extracts from his speech are given below.

"I am not in favor of the bill. I think the western country is taxed enough now I saw a statement the other day which I believe in substance, though it may not be literally true. The statement was that the products of the western country, if carried to a market wherever in the world the best prices could be found, could be sold, and from their proceeds twice as much brought back to the people of the western States if there were no tariff as under this proposed bill. In other words, the earnings of Western labor under this bill will not bring to the people of that section half as much of the comforts and necessaries of life as if there were no taxation like this. As a representative of Western labor I could not vote for such a bill. I would cheerfully vote for a revenue bill, and am willing reasonably to discriminate in favor of the industries that have a right to claim discrimination, but we have undertaken in this bill to protect every thing. Some minerals that a good many Senators have never heard of before have been provided for in this bill. Why, sir, it is as if we undertook almost to create minerals.

"It is suggested that we shall wait to see what the House is going to do with the internal revenue system. From that intimation I understand we have got to change the internal taxes of the country. This is the fourth session that I have been in this body, and I believe at every session the revenue system of the Government has been changed, the internal revenue and the tariff. Nothing is understood to be fixed, nothing is stable any longer in this country. We give an intoxicating support to a particular industry for a while, and then we change the tax upon that, and so prices go up and come down according to the action of Congress, and Congress changes its action at every session. My opinion is that the manufacing interests as well as the agricultural interests of this country now ask for stability more than anything else, and I cannot conceive of anything more vicious than the changing at every session of Congress of the revenue system of the Government."

How it Works.

It has been a remarkable spectacle that we have witnessed here for a week past. If you propose to tax a particular article the friends of that article say, "You must give us a compensation in some other direction." If you tax wool the manufacturer of woolen goods says to us, "You must tax the manufactured article from abroad so that we can pay the increased price upon the raw material and still make a profit." If you put an internal revenue tax upon any article of manufacture the producer of that article will say to us, "You must put a prohibitory tariff, at least a tariff so prohibitory as to allow us to raise our prices so that we shall lose nothing by this internal tax," and the argument being carried into practical legislation an entire interest of the country is exempt from the burdens of Government. Take the manufacturer of woolen goods. For the protection of the farmer a duty is imposed upon wool. He says at once, "Then put an additional duty upon manufactured woolen goods," and he raises his price so as to make a profit, notwithstanding the increased price of the wool. Lay an internal tax upon the manufacturer of woolen goods, and he says at once, "Increase the tariff so as that my profits may be the same still," and in the end, according to this argument, he is to bear none of the burdens of Government.

But, Mr President, I did not intend to go into the argument of this bill. I do not intend to discuss it now, I do not know but that it will be better that it should pass. I would like the western people to fairly feel for once this policy. They have not understood it yet; but let this bill go into operation and I think they will understand it. I can say to gentlemen that in my opinion, from the day a system is firmly adopted here which taxes western labor for the benefit of another section of the country agitation will commence that will not stop until this system is swept out of existence. I think the true interest of the manufacturer is to take such protection as is reasonable, such as will be agreeable to the people of the western country, and such as will throw upon all interests of the country their fair portion of the public burdens. Why, sir, there is nothing that is not now agitated in Congress. When the negro ceases to be agitated here then comes the tariff, then comes the banks, and that question is to be agitated—an abandonment of the present system of banking—until at this very hour in the country no man knows what is going to stand. The banks do not know whether they dare loan out any money to-day. They do not know but that next month they will be required to call in their credits. It seems to me it is the duty of the Finance Committee to give the country to understand that there's something settled, some one thing settled and fixed.

I think the Senator refers to the gentlemen on his own side of the Chamber. It has not been a controversy between the Senator from Maine and Senators on this side. It has been a controversy among the various interests, and it has been a strife as to what interest can get the better share of this Bill. Everybody can see that. An amendment comes from one interest, and then a corresponding or compensating amendment must come from some other interest. It has been a system of exchanges, bargain, equalization; and what there is in the bill now I doubt very much whether the Senator from Maine has a very clear understanding of himself, he had, no doubt, when the bill was reported to the Senate. I think he will find something to do in correcting all the inequalities in this bill if it should be referred to his committee, even if the bill should ever come back again.

For the interests that I represent here all that I ask is equal legislation; that when a man raises some corn or some wheat or cattle or pork in the western States he shall have some fair show in the markets of the world. I do not think this Government was established to take the profits from profitable labor to build up unprofitable labor. It is an absurdity in political economy. If agriculture in this country is naturally, and because of our condition and position, profitable, and some other pursuit is not profitable, I cannot understand the wisdom of taking the profits from agriculture and handing them over to build up a labor that is not profitable. But, sir, we need a revenue, we need to maintain the credit of the Government; and I think all the eastern interests are sufficiently protected when we have a revenue system adjusted with a view to the maintenance of the public credit.

It seems to me that the condition of the Treasury to-day ought to attract the attention of Senators. There is locked up in the Treasury to-day about ninety-three millions of gold. The tariff already established has brought into the Treasury $93,000,000 of gold that no demands upon the Treasury will send out again into the channels of trade, while a currency of eight or nine hundred millions dollars, nearly one hundred millions, under your present legislation, is locked up.

Now, Senators say we must increase the tariff, because we are going to fail to meet the public obligations. Upon what statement of fact do Senators assume that? The present tariff has been in existence two years. The first year it brought into the Treasury between eighty and ninety million dollars, and during the fiscal year ending on the 30th of June it brought in $179,000,000, $90,000,000 more than during that year could be used, and $40,000,000 more than can be required the next year. And yet Senators say they are justified in the opinion that the present tariff will not meet the demands of the Government.

The Senator from Ohio asked the question, what will be the responsibility upon Congress should we not increase the tariff and should there be a failure to meet the demands upon the Treasury? Mr. President, I would rather meet that result than to have a revenue system that locks up $93,000,000 of gold in the public Treasury. I would rather see the Government strained to meet her obligations than to see her holding in her coffers one ninth of the currency of the country We need this gold now, we need the currency now, as I think, to keep up our trade, to keep it well alive, and I cannot vote for any tariff that proposes upon the short and unsatisfactory experiment we have had of the last bill to increase it.

Mr. President, I am in favor of leaving things for a while as they are. I was not in favor of the present banking system, but it is established, it is fixed upon the country, business is being carried on under its influence, and using the currency that it furnishes; and I think it is madness at the present to disturb it, to agitate it. I cannot agree altogether with many persons in the popular idea that we must rapidly return to a specie currency or a specie basis. I think that has to be done very gradually indeed. As a Democrat, of course I have been accustomed to the doctrine of a specie currency, and that if we have any paper currency it should be a currency that could be redeemed at any time in specie, but we all know that that is not now possible without bringing on a financial crisis; and my judgment is, that we had better for the present leave the laws as they are. I would rather vote to reduce the taxes. When I see such an excess of money above the present demands of the Government brought into the Treasury and locked up and nobody able to tell what to do with it, I would rather reduce than increase. No Senator can to-day tell us what to do with the gold that is in the Treasury. Some talk about authorizing the Secretary to sell it in New York. As soon as he does that he disturbs prices all over the country, and that is not right.

There are a great many inconveniences brought about by hasty legislation. The present condition of the Treasury, I think, is an illustration of it. Take the tax upon whisky. Everybody knows now that it is not only unjust to the interest, but it is a failure with a view to revenue. All over the country everybody believes it was an unjust tax, and therefore men will cheat the Government. We all know that if the tax was one dollar a gallon we should receive twice as much revenue as we do now; but see the difficulty! If we reduce it to one dollar, or to sixty or seventy cents, as perhaps it ought to be, then all the men in the country who are holding liquors are broken up and an entire interest destroyed, so far as the holders are concerned. I refer to this as an illustration of the difficulty of coming down after we have once raised the taxes to a high standard. We ought to be very careful about doing it. For these reasons I shall vote for the proposition of the Senator from Kentucky

Hendricks' Speech.

When the Republican party persecuted Andrew Johnson, who had succeeded to the Presidential chair because he would not violate his obligation and become the pliant tool and do the bidding of the Republican leaders, Mr Hendricks, arising above party prejudices and petty jealousies, made a most manly defence for him, as the following extracts from his speech in the Senate will attest. On the 17th of January 1867, Mr Hendricks said:

Mr President, from my youth up I have looked to the Senate of the United States as a body so elevated, so far removed from the prejudices and passions of the times, that no injustice whatever would be done in its action. I have been surprised during the course of this debate to hear what I have regarded as most unjust accusations against the President of the United States, and none perhaps so marked as that of the Senator from Massachusetts, [Mr Sumner.] When discussing this bill the other day that Senator felt himself authorized to say after quoting the line—

"New actions teach new duties:"

"We have a new occasion now teaching a new duty That new occasion is the misconduct of the Executive of the United States, and the new duty which this occasion teaches is that Congress should exercise all its powers in throwing a shield over our fellow-citizens. We see that the Executive is determined to continue this warfare upon the incumbents of office; shall we not if possible protect them? I say that it is our duty growing out of this hour"

The misconduct of the Executive throws upon Congress new duties, is the burden of the argument of the Senator from Massachusetts; and what is that "misconduct?" Not the disregard of any obligation that the Constitution throws upon him, not the violation of any law, except in two particular instances to which he did not refer, but the violation of duty on the part of the President to which he refers is the exercise on his part of a constitutional power which has been recognized from the very first session of the Congress of the United States—the exercise of his power of removal from office and appointment of other men.

Mr. President, I have never sympathized with the general removal from office. I have never seen a faithful officer removed that I have not sympathized with him, except in cases where according to our doctrine of rotation in office, that party had held the office, as we understand, long enough. But what is this doctrine of the Senator from Massachusetts? Is it the English doctrine, a doctrine, however, which has been repudiated in the English courts, that a man shall have a right in his office as against everybody else, to hold it as against the party or power in the Government that confers it? Is it the doctrine that because a man is once in office he shall continue in office? I recognize the full force of the argument in favor of the incumbent where he has done his duty But if he has done his duty, after he has held the office a reasonable length of time, I think he does not have a claim above everybody else in the country.

But what is this charge that the Senator brings against the President? It has been brought down to an exact statement by the Senator from Pennsylvania: out of all the civil officers of the country under his control he has removed one man out of six; he has called into office of the men that sympathized with him in what he regards to be the proper policy one man out of six, leaving five office-holders out of six against him. And this is charged against him as an outrage and a wrong by a

Senator who uniformly supported the policy of Mr Lincoln.

Is it not known to every Senator that in 1861 there was a proscription because of opinion more sweeping and terrible than had ever been known in the country? Until 1861, when was it ever held that every man must be turned out of office who did not agree with the party in power? Scarcely a man was left in office in 1861 to represent the sentiments of the large minority in the country. I bring this up as no accusation against Mr Lincoln's administration. I did not claim that the men who voted against him ought to be kept in office, and I conceded his right to call into the executive offices men who sympathized sincerely with him in his political views, that he should have confidence not only in his Secretaries but in every executive officer who was to aid him in the execution of the laws; and I never charged him with a wrong because he left no Democrats in office. When the Democrats were beaten in 1860, and the Republican party was successful, I thought it right enough for Mr. Lincoln to call men to him and to his support in all the offices of the country—men who truly sympathized with him in his political views—that he should have confidence in all from the highest to the lowest: and I never thought of charging it as an outrage by him, and as a reason why by legislation the whole policy of the Government should be changed in that regard.

The proscription since 1861 has been surpassing anything ever observed before. It has not only extended to the high offices of the country, but to the smaller offices, until it has gone to the courts, and for the past five years in the Federal courts, where the marshal and the clerk control the subject, you would scarcely see a juror called into the box or placed upon the grand jury who did not agree in political opinion with the party in power. The proscription has gone into the courts, and juries have been organized upon political principles. The men called into the grand jury-room to inquire of the violation of law, and who ought to be free from partisan feelings, have been selected with a view to their party politics. I have thought that a wrong. I have felt, as a practitioner of the law, that party politics ought never to find its way into the court. Stopping short of that and leaving it to be left only in the executive offices, I have no charge to make against the late Administration. But the gentlemen who supported that Administration in this proscriptive policy certainly are not justified in saying that Mr. Johnson, the present Chief Magistrate, is chargeable with wrong if he calls his friends into one sixth of the public offices.

But, sir, is the Senate of the United States the place in which to make the charge of proscription? Of all the employés of this body I know of but one man who sympathizes with the conservative sentiment of the country; and on the first or second day of the session, because of political party views, three of the distinguished chiefs or heads of committees were stricken from their places and assigned to the foot of the committees. I should have no criticism to make upon that if those committees were in charge of matters relating to the political questions of the day, but they had no reference to such questions. The three committees to which I refer have no charge of any question that now agitates the country or divides Congress and the President, but simply because brother Senators differ upon a political question the majority of the Senate proscribe them, and in the middle of a Congress assign them from the head of a committee to the foot of it. And yet Senators say that it is an outrage to proscribe men because of political opinions.

Why, sir, in this very city, under the eye of the President, nearly all the offices are filled by men that oppose him. The postmaster in this city is understood to be one of the leaders of the opposition to the President and of the adherents of Congress. The collecting officer in this District is another instance; and of all the clerks in the Departments my information is that there is not perhaps one out of ten that supports the President of the United States. And yet he is charged with proscription, he is charged with doing a wrong, because some of the officers of the country have been removed and men sympathizing with his policy have been placed in their stead.

I know very well the argument which is used: that Mr Johnson has proscribed men who belong to the party that put him in power. Well, sir, who have been appointed in their places as a general thing? Not Democrats, not men who opposed the Lincoln and Johnson ticket in 1864, but, as a general thing, the men who have been appointed by this Administration are men who voted for Mr Lincoln and Mr. Johnson in 1864, and in removing one man and putting in another the President has simply selected among the men who supported him in the contest of 1864. And is it wholly unreasonable that he should make such a selection? Have questions not come up since 1864 that did not enter into the contest of that year? Did the question that now divides the Congress and the President enter into the contest of 1864, and was Mr. Johnson elected upon that question? I submit to the candid judgment of every Senator whether the question that divides you from the President formed an issue in the contest of 1864? It did not. Since Mr. Johnson's election and since he has come to be President of the United States, a question has arisen because of the close of the war, and that question is in what mode shall the States be restored to all their proper relations to the Federal Government.

Upon that great question the President of the United States has assumed his ground Congress has assumed an opposite ground, and here is a difference, a difference upon a question that has arisen since the President came into power, an unexpected difference of opinion. Undoubtedly his views are honestly entertained by him, and so on the other hand are the views of the majority of Congress honestly entertained by them. That question having arisen, and the President of the United States being charged with the duty to see that the laws are executed, are you willing to deny to him that which you have claimed for every Administration that went before him—the right to put into the public offices of the country men who sympathise with him and in whom he can have entire confidence?

It is charged now as a wrong that he removes one Republican from office and puts another one in. I do not say that this is the case in all instances, for there are instances of appointment to office of men who opposed his election in 1864; but they are very few compared with the appointments that have been made. The great body of appointments that have been made are of men who supported the Lincoln and Johnson ticket in 1864.

Then, sir, this bill proposes to deny to Mr Johnson as President of the United States that which has been conceded to every President that went before him, to place in the offices of the country, to aid him in the execution of the laws, men who sympathize with him in his views.

A very significant question was asked by the Senator from Pennsylvania [Mr. Cowan] yesterday: To whom do the offices belong? He answered it well in saying they belong to the law. The man that is appointed is appointed simply to execute the law, to discharge his duty under the law The office does not belong to him except for the time during which he holds it, he has no patent by which he can hold it beyond the will of the power that conferred it. But suppose the propositions of Senators be correct, that the offices belong to the people, is there nothing, then, due to the large minority in this country? At the recent elections, in October and November last, eighteen hundred thousand voters of this country endorsed the policy of the President; about twenty-two hundred thousand endorsed the policy of Congress. Out of the four million voters casting their votes, eighteen hundred thousand men at the polls said they believed the President was right. Do Senators say that those eighteen hundred thousand men, representing nine millions of the people of this country outside of the seceding States—do Senators say, that that large portion of our population have no rights in the offices of the country; that it is a wrong, for which the President shall be arraigned before the judgment of the country if he does not leave all the offices in the hands of men who oppose his views? The President has thus far not asked to aid him in the execution of the laws a proportion of the officers of the country equal to the popular vote in his favor He has asked for but one-sixth; while of the voters of the country there is nearly one-half who sustain him. In the great States of New York, Pennsylvania, and Indiana, giving a popular vote of about one million, forty-four thousand votes cover the majority A change of forty-four thousand in the enormous vote of these three great States would have thrown them in favor of the President—three States that give about seventy-two electoral votes. And yet Senators say, that if the President of the United States respects, in the little matter of appointments to office, this enormous sentiment of the country, he is to be charged with a wrong.

MR. WILLIAMS. I should like to ask the honorable Senator from Indiana what proportion of the one million eight hundred thousand men to whom he refers voted and determined in 1864 that the war for the Union was a failure?

MR. HENDRICKS. I have not made any calculation upon that subject; and, sir I know of no portion of the voters of the country who voted that sentiment. I know of no expression of that opinion. I know of a resolution, to which I suppose the Senator means to refer, declaring that thus far, up to a certain time, the war had proved a failure to restore the Union. Eight months after that, in my judgment, that resolution ought to have been proved untrue, and the result of the war ought to have proved that the Union was restored. But, sir, the Union is not yet restored; and until the Senator from Oregon is ready to bring all of the States into their proper relations in the Federal Union upon the basis of the Constitution, until he is ready to admit into the Senate and House of Representatives loyal men who are able to take the oath prescribed by law, he cannot say that the restoration of the Union is completed.

But, sir, I have spoken of the one million eight hundred thousand men who at the late elections voted in favor of the policy of the President of the United States, to say the least of it a very great minority, and when Senators claim that the offices belong to the people, what are the rights of this large minority?

I think that in the late elections the difference between the Congress of the United States and the President of the United States did make a very marked issue in the contest, and upon that issue the majority which I have mentioned went in favor of Congress. I am now speaking of the large minority that sustained the President. It is known that upon that question ten of the States were not allowed to express any opinion. In the States that did at the ballot-box express their opinion Congress received the majority which I have mentioned. When you speak of the offices belonging to the people, let me ask what are the rights of this minority of one million eight hundred thousand men? It is not asked, and has not been asked as a general proposition, that the offices should be given to the men who opposed the election of the present Chief Magistrate. It is simply asked that of the men who voted for him in 1864 he should be allowed to bring into office a reasonable number of those who now support him and are in sympathy with him. Is that unjust? Is it an unfair thing to demand, so that the Senator from Massachusetts is authorized to denounce it as misconduct on the part of the President? Is a thing that was so generally sustained by the majority party in 1861 wrong in 1866? I do not understand it so.

Why is it that the President of the United States by public opinion has been sustained in removing men and putting those in office who sympathize with him? It is because in the due execution of the laws he should have his friends to aid him. That is the sentiment of the country upon that question; and now, if it has devolved upon the present Chief Magistrate to see that the laws are executed, why may he not claim that for himself; why may not his friends claim that for him which has been conceded to every Administration that went before him?

But now, when we come to understand the facts, we find that only four hundred and fifty out of two thousand four hundred and fifty or about that number of office-holders have been removed, leaving nearly two thousand men in office opposed to the President or supposed to be opposed to him, and he having called into office only about four hundred and fifty of his friends to support him. This the honorable Senator from Massachusetts calls the "misconduct" of the President. If the Senator had confined his remark to the two cases which have been referred to, where the President after the adjournment of the Senate appointed men who had been rejected by this body, I should have no criticism to make upon his argument. I think that when the judgment of the Senate is expressed upon any nomination that judgment ought not to be reversed by the Executive, but as a question of law I understand the President took the opinion of the Attorney General, a very accomplished gentleman, high in the profession to which he belongs, an ornament to the western bar, an ornament of which we are all proud and the present Attorney General, I understand, gave it as his opinion that the action of the Senate did not disqualify the party for an appointment after the adjournment. I think it would have been proper for the Attorney General to have gone beyond the question of law and to have said to the President that he owed it to the judgment of the Senate not to appoint a man who had been rejected for that particular office. The legal right and the power of the President under the Constitution to make those two appointments I believe has not been questioned by any Senator.

On the question of propriety I agree with the Senators who have expressed the opinion that such appointment ought not to be made, and if Senators wish to prevent them in the future and will present a resolution expressing the sentiment of the Senate upon that question I shall have no objection to vote for it and let it be known as the opinion of the Senate that a man once rejected by the Senate shall not after the adjournment be appointed to that office. I think he ought not to be; but certainly the facts stated by the Senator from Pennsylvania on that particular question in reference to the appointment of the postmaster of St. Louis and the revenue officer at Philadelphia ought to be considered by the Senator from Massachusetts before he passes a harsh judgment upon the President even upon those cases.

But this bill has very little relation to that particular subject. It goes into the whole matter and undertakes to regulate the exercise of this constitutional power on the part of the President from first to last. And now, without referring to the justice and right of the thing, I ask Senators if it is well, because there is a difference of opinion between the President and the Senate, that the Senate shall undertake to take from the President any power which the Constitution confers upon him? It is too late now to question the power of the President on the subject of removals from office. A uniform practice of so many years does not leave it an open question. It is a settled question, settled, I believe, by every department of the Government. It was settled, I think, by the legislative department at the first session of Congress. It has been settled by the uniform action of the executive department. I think it has been settled also by the judiciary, by the judgment of the Supreme Court upon a claim made by the judges in one of the Territories after they had been removed from office by the President. I have not had occasion to look to that case for some time, and I cannot give the particular facts; but my impression of the decision is that the Supreme Court decided that after removal by the President the parties were not in office and could not claim their salaries.

His Senatorial term expired March 4, 1869, and he again cast aside his official robes and returned to his law office in Indianapolis.

Again in Politics.

In the autumn prior to the expiration of his Senatorial term, he received the nomination for Governor of his State, and the Republican convention selected Conrad Baker as his opponent. After an exciting campaign Baker was elected by about 800 majority, and Senator Hendricks again went to his law office, the firm being Hendricks, Hard & Hendricks, the latter a cousin, Abram W., a Republican without guile and a man of the finest ability The firm was one of two or three leading ones in the city, enjoyed a very lucrative practice, and Mr. Hendricks added to a comfortable competence he had acquired by his shrewdness and providence. During this period he continued at the law, and for two years he was permitted to enjoy the comforts of home, unalloyed by the labors and vexations of office. He never failed, however, to give his party his able support and advice, and whether as a Lawyer or Public Servant, he was alive to the success of the Democratic party

Governor of Indiana.

In 1872 the State was again rent with a political contest. The Liberal movement of that year on the part of dissatisfied Republicans gave the Democracy an apparent opportunity for success, and again the State Convention nominated Mr Hendricks for Governor. His Republican opponent was Gen. Thomas M. Browne. There was a good deal of temperance sentiment in the State, to which Mr. Hendricks made himself acceptable. The purpose of the temperance folks was to secure a local option law, and this Mr. Hendricks allowed himself to be understood he would approve, which he afterwards did in the shape of what is known as "the Baxter law." As the result of another remarkably close election, Mr. Hendricks was chosen Governor by a plurality of 1,200 votes, while all the other officers of the State, except the Superintendent of Public Instruction, were Republicans. That Mr Hendricks' election was caused by the influence here spoken of was made evident from the fact that in the next month Grant carried Indiana by 6,000 majority. It has been said by no less a distinguished authority than Gov Hendricks himself that any man competent to be a notary public could be Governor of Indiana, and so there was not much to test the executive abilities of Gov Hendricks during his term of office. He made an urbane, careful, satisfactory Governor, and retired from the position with the respect of all parties in the State.

Tilden and Hendricks.

In the Convention that nominated this ticket Senator Hendricks was a candidate far the first place. The circumstances of the nomination of Gov Hendricks on the ticket with Gov Tilden by the St. Louis Convention are fresh in the public mind. He was a candidate for the Presidency, as he also was in 1868 at the New York Tammany Hall Convention, but there he was antagonized by a part of his own State delegation, headed by Richard J. Bright. This opposition from his own delegation defeated him. In 1876 a strong and vigorous opposition to Mr Hendricks was organized in his own state and made its appearance in St. Louis. The nomination of Mr Tilden and his own nomination for the second place was a great humiliation to Mr Hendricks and a sore disappointment. After the election, in November, Mr Hendricks made no secret of his disagreement with Mr. Tilden's course. He wrote a letter the purport of which was that he was opposed to the Electoral Commission, and that if he were Gov Tilden he should take the oath of office and demand it of President Grant, leaving the Supreme Court to adjudicate the dispute. Of course, the inauguration of Hayes and Wheeler settled the future for Mr. Hendricks, and he proceeded quietly with his law business. Mr Hendricks was again a candidate for the Presidential nomination in Cincinnati, in 1880, and this time had the ardent and enthusiastic support of his entire State delegation. But his nomination was impossible, He probably could have secured the nomination of Joseph E. McDonald. But Mr. Hendricks again remembered 1868, and he would not give the word of assent. The result was the nomination of Hancock and, with the idea of placating Indiana, William H. English. This action sent Mr. Hendricks into his tent, where he remained until nearly the end of the campaign, when he emerged because of a bitter attack upon him personally made by the Republican press. But there was no harmony between the Democratic leaders, as the campaign of that year in Indiana went against the Democratic Party. After the election of

Garfield Mr. Hendricks was interviewed, and in answer to the question whether he was out of politics answered that he should never be out of politics until he was in his grave. The Democratic Party had been too kind to him to permit him to deafen his ears to its voice whenever it demanded his service.

The Past Eight Years.

After Mr. Hayes' inauguration he went to California, where he was warmly received and his health completely restored from the wear and tear of electoral suspense. Upon his return he went to Europe and in the fall came home and went into the practice of the law with his former partners, O. B. Hood and A. W. Hendricks, with the additional partner, Hon. Conrad Baker, who had preceded him in the Gubernatorial office. The four years of his executive term was the only period when Mr Hendricks did not practice law, and yet he resumed the profession with such diffidence, lest he had lost ground therein, that the gaining of his first case was very much of a surprise to him. It was a famous canal case, which had run the gauntlet of the courts for a dozen years and had its root and finding in matters dating back twenty-seven years. Perhaps the most important case which has engaged his attention was that of the Pennsylvania Railway, in which he held his own with such distinguished talent as that of Judge Hoadly, Stanley Matthews and Mr McDonald. His argument at Newport covered one hundred pages of printed matter, and is a marvel of legal acumen and intellectual scope. Another great case was that of the Toledo and Western.

Literary Labors.

The work Mr. Hendricks accomplished was not confined to the law. In addition, he attended to considerable private business. He also made some valuable contributions to current literature and traveled extensively, making a tour of Europe. So versatile and arduous were his labors, in fact, that three times in the last eight years his health broke down. He would not be fatigue and exposure in the campaign o 1882. It was the attack of phlegmonous erysipelas, which came so near costing him his life. His perfect recovery, thanks to a splendid constitution and well-regulated life, was a disappointment to the physicians who said he would die, and the forced rest and subsequent sojourn abroad give him promise of many years of usefulness to come.

"Cleveland and Hendricks."

When the Democratic Convention met at Chicago in July last, to form a Presidential ticket, the State of Indiana again presented his name as a candidate, and his availability was again discussed. But the political importance of the Empire State gave it, as heretofore the preference of a candidate, and Governor Cleveland was selected from the array of brilliant names before it. Mr. Hendricks was not (and indeed never was) a candidate for the Vice Presidency, and the impression prevailed that he might not accept the place, but notwithstanding this, he was unanimously nominated, and is now before the people for their suffrages. His countrymen have asked him to fill the place, and in this instance, as in others, he has waived his own preferences, and obeyed their orders.

Prophetic Utterances.

In the light of the action of the Chicago Convention it is interesting to repea Mr. Hendricks' utterances in 1877, eve if he did not expect this tardy endorsement. At his reception by the Manhattan Club, New York, he said .

"A great and sincere people will pas their final verdict upon the outrageou act. Democratic principles will be car ried out by the Democrats and by suc fair-minded Republicans as will not mak themselves a party to the wrong done la winter This will be accomplished by th majority of the voters in the several State * * and Indiana will again do he duty."

It remains for the Democracy now make good the words which, for the lac of a renomination of the "old ticket tial fraud will gradually be lost sight of in the absorbing question of reform. In the opinion of Mr. Hendricks it is the question and it grows out of the stupendous abuses of Republican administration. There must be reform in all matters of government and to this view the Democratic party is in existence and must be placed in power for that express purpose.

Revenue Reform.

"The question of revenue reform suggests itself to every mind when the fact is considered that the change in the internal revenue and tax laws made by the Republican Congress before this, a little more than one year ago, left the revenues of the government in excess of the demands of an economical administration at least fifty millions a year. No party in the world can stand up before an intelligent people and defend the collection from the people of more money than the government has a right to use when economically administered. Of course this important point will attract attention. Administrative reform is not less a question of vital interest. Every now and then something wrong is looming up in some department—carelessness and inefficiency characterize many of the departments of public service. It is an honor to any young man to get an appointment from the government, of course, but position is not given him in a department for him to make it a lounging place. He must work with care and diligence and earnestness in order that all the interests of the government shall be amply and fully protected, just as the active and honest young man in the store, or on the farm, or in the railroad office gives the best capabilities of his mind and industry to the promotion of the interests which he is paid to take care of.''

In his Home.

A visitor thus describes his home, and other interesting details.

"Since Mr. Hendricks' marriage he has lived in many houses, but never in one built after a plan of his making or selection. Now he resides in a substantial two-story brick dwelling, built by the late General Low and the double of one erected by the General's father-in-law, the late Hon. O. H. Smith. It is not a house of many rooms, but they are large and handsome and have an air of comfort foreign to most more pretentious dwellings. The hall is especially spacious, and with the open door and inviting chairs and sofa makes a pleasant reception room in the summer Mr Hendricks' private or political library is up stairs, and there he has a table and telephone and receives the politicians who crave a special hearing. When the campaign opens he will probably have headquarters in a more accessible quarter, although his house is not out of the way. It faces the State House grounds on Tennessee street and is but a stone's throw (around the corner) from the *Sentinel* office.

The best likeness of Mr. Hendricks is one which was photographed by Van Loo. The portrait of the ex-Senator in the State library, painted by Freeman, conveys the idea of a high liver, which is not just, Mr Hendricks being rather abstemious than otherwise in his habits. The Van Loo does justice to the pose of the finely-formed head, the brow is clear the eyes are penetrating and the expression is pleasing and intellectual. The picture even conveys an idea of the delicacy of complexion and soft, brown tint of hair which marks his Scotch descent. His head and face have changed a good deal in the last eight years. They seem larger. The forehead is broad and smooth and the cheeks slope gently to the chin, which is innocent of beard. The mouth is not large and the lips are thin. It is altogether a classic mouth and chin, and the nose is well formed and delicate in expression. The eyes are blue, mixed with gray, and express more penetration than reserve. They are schooled to express interest in whatever subject is presented and tell no tales. The head is poised on a manly figure, with unusual depth of chest, and its perfect proportions are revealed in the firm, elastic step. The face in repose is free from wrinkles. In conversation it lights up amazingly, and joined to a pleasing deference of manner has given him the reputation of a Talleyrand. That he does not deserve, for on occasions he is extremely outspoken. In all, the autotype of Trajan, familiar in the shops, is a better portrait of Mr Hendricks than the generality of those he has had taken. My picture of him would not be complete without referring to his taste in dress. Those who saw him in Chicago will join me in saying it is perfect.

He was nurtured in the Presbyterian faith, and was a member of that communion until the organization of St. Paul's Episcopal Church in Indianapolis in the year 1862. He became a member of that parish and was elected Senior Warden. He has never belonged to but one secret society the Odd Fellows, being a charter member of the Wellsville Lodge, but for a long time has ceased to actively participate in its work. After the election in 1876 Mr. Hendricks made an extensive tour of Europe, meeting with cordial receptions everywhere and making the acquaintance of many of the most distinguished European politicians. He was particularly impressed with Gambetta, of whom he has frequently spoken in terms of high admiration.

How He opens the Campaign.

As the Chandler letter may be taken for the key-note of the campaign, long ahead of the opening of the canvass, so in Mr Hendricks' speech at the ratification meeting at his home, he said one thing which has already become a watchword. It was this:

"I will tell you what we need—Democrat and Republicans will alike agree upon that—we need to have the books in the government-offices opened for examination." * * "What is the remedy? To have a President who will appoint a head of a bureau that will investigate the condition of the books and bring the guilty to trial."

"The books must be opened" is a natural sequence to "Cleveland, Hendricks and Reform" and "Revenue and Administrative Reform." It may be, some lengthier axioms from Mr. Hendricks' utterances may be in order, such as, "Government shall exist for man, and not man for government;" "We will not enslave man, even that he shall admit and practice the truth;" "Where there is no freedom of action there can be no freedom of judgment;" "Heaven's law leaves man able to obey, but free to disobey;" "Habits of tyranny become usages;" "We cannot exclude all from a privilege or right because it is abused by a few;" "When once in the box the ballot has no color"

Mr Hendricks' views in regard to the service young men should render as employes of the government, are a practical compendium of civil-service reform, and they are backed by life-long devotion to the welfare of young men, which has been paid in kind. In 1872, when he was the first Democratic Governor elected in the North after the war, he suddenly took heart at the close of a dispiriting canvass when one hundred young men—first voters—marched in a Democratic procession along Washington Street. Due attention to the training of young men in Democratic faith and good works is one of the strong points in Mr. Hendricks' party management.

PROCEEDINGS OF CHICAGO CONVENTION, 1884.

Democratic National Committee.

The Democratic National Committee met at Chicago, July 7, at 12 o clock, Chairman Barnum presiding. The States represented were as follows:

Alabama....................H. O. Semple.
Arkansas................John J. Sumpter.
California................James T Farley.
Colorado........ ....T M. Patterson.
Connecticut.......William H. Barnum.
Delaware.............Ignatius C. Grubb.
Florida......................Samuel Puliston.
Georgia................George T Barnes.
Illinois........................W C. Goudy.
Indiana..................Austin H. Brown.
Iowa............................M. M. Ham.
Kansas..................Charles W Blair
Kentucky..........Henry D. McHenry.
Louisiana.......................B. F Jonas.
Maine.................Edmund F Wilson.
Maryland...........Outerbridge Horsey
Massachusetts.....Frederick O. Prince.
Michigan.................Edward Kanter.
Minnesota......................P H. Kelly
Mississippi.....................W T Morton.
Missouri..................John G. Prather.
Nebraska..................Sterling Marten.
Nevada.......................R. P Keating.
New Hampshire.......Alvah Sulloway
New Jersey...........Orestes Cleveland.
New York...........Abraham S. Hewitt.
North Carolina.........N. W Ransom.
Ohio.............William W Armstrong.
Oregon...........................A. Noltner.
Pennsylvania.....Ex-Senator Wallace.
Rhode Island...............J B. Barnaby.
South Carolina..........F W Dawson.
Tennessee............Robert F Looney.
Texas......................F T Stockdale.
Vermont............Bradley B. Smalley.
Virginia.................John S. Barbour.
West Virginia...Alexander Campbell.
Wisconsin..............William F Vilas.

Mr. Barnes, of Georgia, nominated Augustus O. Bacon, of Georgia, for temporary chairman of the Convention. Mr. Stockdale, of Texas, nominated Governor Robert B. Hubbard, of Texas, Mr Martin, of Mississippi, nominated Charles E. Hooker, of Mississippi.

Governor Hubbard Selected.

The committee proceeded to ballot, with the following result: Whole number of votes cast, 37, Hubbard received 22, Bacon 9, Hooker 6. On motion of Mr. Prince the nomination of Governor Hubbard was made unanimous. On motion of Mr. Hewitt, Mr. Prince was elected temporary secretary of the Convention. The following were elected assistant secretaries: E. L. Merritt, of Illinois, George W Guthrie, of Pennsylvania, G. S. Johnson, of Iowa, Robert M. Bashford, of Wisconsin; Charles M. Vallandigham, of Missouri, Henry J. Lynn, of Tennessee, Michael J Barrett, of New Jersey

The committee then adjourned to 10 o'clock on the following day

THE CONVENTION.

The First Day's Session.

The Convention was called to order at 12:37 by Hon. William H. Barnum, of Connecticut, chairman of the Democratic National Committee. He presented Rev. Dr. Marquis, of Chicago, who opened the deliberations of the Convention with prayer.

Mr. Barnum said:—Gentlemen of the Convention: Harmony seems to be the sense of this Convention; the very air itself seems saturated with the desire and the determination to nominate a ticket for president and vice-president satisfactory to the North as well as to the South, to the East as well as to the West—nay, more, a ticket that will harmonize the Democracy of this nation and insure victory in November. No effort has been made to nominate a temporary chairman of this

Convention in the interest of any candidate, but, on the contrary, one who will proceed with absolute impartiality. With this spirit and to that end I have been directed by the unanimous vote of the National Committee to nominate the Hon. Richard B. Hubbard, of Texas, for temporary chairman, and Hon. Richard B Hubbard was elected. The Chair appointed Senator B. F Jonas, of Louisiana, Hon. George B. Barnes, of Georgia, and Abram S. Hewitt, of New York, a committee to wait upon Mr Hubbard and conduct him to the chair. Mr Hubbard was received with vociferous applause and Mr Barnum advancing to the front, said :

" I have the distinguished honor to present Hon. Richard B. Hubbard, of Texas, as the absolutely impartial temporary chairman of this Convention."

Chairman Hubbard's Speech.

Mr Hubbard came forward amid loud applause and said: "Mr Chairman and gentlemen of the Democratic Convention of the Union—I am profoundly grateful for the confidence which you have reposed in me in ratifying the nomination of the National Executive Committee, who have done your bidding for the last four years by your authority I accept it, my fellow-Democrats, not as a tribute to the humble citizen and your fellow-Democrat who speaks to you to day, but rather as a compliment to the great State from whence I come. We accept it as a tribute to the fact that Texas, with her two million of people, gladly at each recurring election, places in the ballot-box over one hundred thousand Democratic majority

" Fellow-Democrats, we have met upon an occasion of great and absorbing interest to our party as well as to our common country The occasion would not justify me nor demand that I should attempt to speak to you of its great history and its distinctive principles through two-thirds of the most glorious history of our country I could not stop to discuss, if I would, its munificent policy of progress, the part which it has taken in building up our country,.its progress, its territory and its wealth. I can only say to you to-day, in brief, that the Democratic Party, in all the essential elements, is the same as it was when it was founded by the framers of the Constitution nearly three-quarters of a century ago.

" Men die as the leaves of autumn, but principles are underlying liberty and self-government, the right of representation and taxation going hand in hand, economy in the administration of the Government, so that the Government shall make the burdens as small as they may be upon the millions who constitute our countrymen. These and other principles underlie the Democratic Party and cannot be effaced from the earth, though their authors may be numbered with the dead.

"The Democratic party is loyal to the Union. The 'bloody shirt,' in the vulgar parlance of the times, has at each recurring election been flaunted in the face of Southern Democrats and in your own faces. With Logan on the ticket I presume it will be again. Blaine could hardly afford it, as he did not indulge much in that 'unpleasantness.' They will endeavor to stir up the bad blood of the past. My countrymen, the war is over for a quarter of a century, and they know it, Why our boys have married the young maidens of the North and children have been born since those days. They will continue to go to the altar, and, side by side at dying beds, they will talk of that bourne whence no traveler returns, will lie down and be buried together. Why, the boys in the blue and the gray have slept together for a quarter of a century upon a thousand fields of common glory. Let their bones alone. They are representing the best blood of the land, and, though differing in the days that should be forgotten, the good men of all parties in our country to-day, I thank God, have united in the great common progress of our race to forget the war memories of the war times."

At the conclusion of Gov Hubbard's speech, Mr Prince, of Massachusetts, Secretary of the National Convention, then made the following report on temporary organization:

For temporary Chairman, Richard B. Hubbard, of Texas; for temporary Secretary, Frederick O. Prince, of Massachusetts; Assistant Secretaries, E. L. Merrit, of Illinois; George O, Guthrie, of Pennsylvania, G. L. Johnston, of Iowa, Robert M. Bashford, of Wisconsin; Charles M. Vallandingham. of Missouri; H. J Lynn, of Tennessee; Michael D. Barret, of New Jersey The Report was unanimously adopted.

Mr. Smalley, of Vermont, then said he was instructed by the National Committee to offer the following resolution:

Resolved, That the rules of the last Democratic Convention govern this body until otherwise ordered, subject to the following modification That in voting for candidates for President and Vice-President no State shall be allowed to change its vote until the roll of the States has been called and every State has cast its vote.

Mr. Grady, of New York, offered the following amendment to the resolution:

When the vote of a State as announced by the chairman of the delegation from such State is challenged by any member of the delegation, then the Secretary shall call the names of the individual delegates from the State, and their individual preferences as expressed shall be recorded as the vote of such State.

After discussion the question was then put, the chairman of each State delegation announcing its vote as follows:

States.	*Yeas*	*Nays*	*States.*	*Yeas*	*Nays*
Alabama,	15	5	Mississippi,	18	—
Arkansas,	—	14	Missouri,	8	24
California,	16	—	Nebraska,	5	5
Colorado,	4	2	Nevada,	6	—
Connecticut,	2	10	New Hampshire	—	8
Delaware,	6	—	New Jersey,	14	4
Florida,	2	6	New York,	—	72
Georgia,	12	12	North Carolina,	10	12
Illinois,	22	22	Ohio,	25	21
Indiana,	30	—	Oregon,	—	6
Iowa,	6	20	Pennsylvania,	21	39
Kansas,	3	15	Rhode Island,	—	8
Kentucky,	20	6	South Carolina,	3	14
Louisiana,	—	16	Tennessee,	17	7
Maine,	2	10	Texas,	12	10
Maryland,	—	16	Vermont,	—	8
Massachusetts	21	7	Virginia,	6	18
Michigan,	12	12	West Virginia,	9	3
Minnesota,	—	14	Wisconsin,	5	17

The Secretary announced the result of the vote as follows: Total number of votes cast, 795; yeas, 332; nays, 463.

The call of the roll on the original resolution was then dispensed with and it was unanimously adopted.

This question having been disposed of the roll of the States was called and the chairmen of the several delegations named the delegates chosen as members of the Committees on Credentials and Resolutions. On the completion of the call of the roll the Convention adjourned until 11 A. M. to-morrow

The Platform Committee.

The following is the Committee on Platform: Alabama, L. P Walker; Arkansas, Benjamin F Duval, California, T J. Currie; Connecticut, A. E. Burr, Florida, P P Bishop; Georgia, E. P Howell, Illinois, William R. Morrison, Indiana, G. V Menzies, Iowa E. H. Thayer; Kansas, Thomas P Finlan, Kentucky, Henry Watterson, Louisiana, E. H. Burke, Maine, David R. Hastings; Maryland, C. J Gwynn, Massachusetts, B. F Butler, Michigan, S. E. Farsney, Minnesota, J. C. Wise; Missouri, W H. Phelps; Nebraska, J S. Sterling Morton; Nevada, D. E. McCarthy New Hampshire, Henry Bingham; New Jersey, James A. McPherson, New York, Abram S. Hewitt; North Carolina, J. S. Carr, Ohio, George L. Converse, Pennsylvania, Malcom Hay, South Carolina, Leroy F Youmans; Tennessee, Albert T McNeil, Texas, D. C. Giddings; Vermont, James A. Brown; Virginia, P W McKenny, West Virginia, Henry G. Davis, Wisconsin, J. G. Jenkins.

The committee on Permanent Organization met in the evening and decided to recommend to the Convention the name of Colonel W F Vilas, of Wisconsin, as permanent Chairman, and that the remaining officers of the temporary organization be made permanent.

SECOND DAY'S SESSION.

The Convention was opened with prayer by the Right Reverend Bishop McLaren, of the Diocese of Chicago.

Mr. Cummings, of Massachusetts, offered a resolution instructing the Committee on Resolutions to give a hearing to the committee of the Irish National League in favor of excluding aliens from acquiring real estate in America.

Mr. Taylor, of Arkansas, submitted the report of the Committee on Credentials, in which he stated that in Massachusetts, a contest appearing in the Twelfth Congressional District, your committee, after a full investigation of the facts, unanimously recommended that the parties, Joseph

Callan, E. McLearned, A. L. Perry and George H. Bloch, be admitted to this Convention, and each shall be entitled to a half vote.

Mr Heenan, of Michigan, offered a resolution for the reduction of taxation to a revenue basis. Referred.

Mr Taylor, of Arkansas, chairman of the Committee on Credentials, reported the list of delegates with an amendment giving territorial delegates the right to vote in the Convention.

Mr. Randolph, of New Jersey moved an amendment that the territorial delegates be not allowed to vote. The amendment was rejected and the report adopted.

Mr. Gallup, of New York, offered a resolution demanding such a revision of the tariff as shall lessen the duty upon those articles which supply daily the wants of the farmer, mechanic, artisan and laborer A number of other resolutions were offered and it was finally decided to refer them all to the Committee on Platform.

Permanent Organization.

The report of the Committee on Permanent Organization was then made, the name of W H. Vilas. of Wisconsin, being presented as President, with a list of vice-presidents (one from each state) and several secretaries and assistants, and that the secretaries and clerks of the temporary organization be continued under the permanent organization.

The Chair then appointed as a committee to escort Mr Vilas to the chair the Hon. Thomas A. Hendricks, of Indiana Hon. W W Armstrong, of Ohio , Hon. W H. Parsons, of Georgia; Hon. John N. Henderson, of Texas Hon. John A. Day, of Missouri , Hon. Mr Sparks, of Illinois, and the Hon. Smith M. Weed, of New York.

Mr. Vilas, in taking the chair, returned thanks for the honor done him, not as a recognition of himself, but of the young Democracy of the Northwest. It was their fair due. It was a tribute to their lofty zeal and patriotism. They hailed it as a presage and prototype of the coming triumph.

This Convention was assembled to consider a great cause; to pronounce a momentous judgment. Its import and value lay not in the hope of mere party victory, in clutching the spoils of office. The opportunity was pregnant with mighty possibilities of good to men. The air was already filled with vapors of visionary schemes addressed to various interests and factions. It is the party of Jefferson and Jackson to-day as formerly, and the principles they promulgated are its principles now. It is the party of the people; of economy and honesty in the administration of Government. It has shaken off the venial and time-serving, and has recruited from the ranks of its opponents the best and wisest. The Democracy are ready to continue such exchange. In conclusion, he counseled moderation in their action and bespoke a generous forbearance for himself in the discharge of his duties.

"I thank God, fellow-citizens, that though we have been out of power for a quarter of a century, we are to-day, in all that makes adherence, and confidence and zeal, as much a party organized for aggressive war as when the banners of victory were perched above our heads.

"The Democratic party, fellow-citizens, since the war time, commencing with reconstruction, with our hands manacled, with our ballot-boxes surrounded by the gleaming bayonet, with carpet-bag rulers, with the voice of free men who pay their taxes to the Government, stifled—the Democratic party has lived to see through all this misrule the day come when in a great majority of our states the Democratic party has resumed its control, its power. It has your House of Representatives, and but for treason stalking in the Senate Chamber, we would have that, too.

"We want men there whose very lives and whose very names would be a platform to this people; we want men there who shall, in all the departments of the Government, in its Department of Justice, in its postal affairs, its Interior Department, everywhere, follow its servants with the eye of the ministers of justice, and see that every cent that belongs to the Government shall remain with the Government; that no tribute shall be demanded, except the tribute that is due the Government; that no assessment shall be levied upon 100,000 office-holders, who are paid one hundred millions annually, five millions to go into a corrupt political fund. These, we thank God, will be corrected when the Democratic party shall get into power once more.

We read of the enunciation of principles by the Republican party. They tell us they have civil service reform, and yet they demand, in the next breath, from every federal office-holder of the 100,000, his tribute to the corrupt fund that shall be paid out to the voter at the polls. They tell us that they have a pure government, and yet not a solitary felon has been condemned in the flock of those who have stolen their millions from the treasury

Mr Snowden, of Pennsylvania, offered a resolution for the call of the roll of the States and for the placing in nomination of candidates for President and Vice President. Mr. Clunie, of California, moved its reference to the committee on platform. The nominations should not be made until after the adoption of the platform. The motion was rejected.

A motion was made to lay on the table Mr. Snowden's motion to make nominations now. The question was taken by a vote by States and resulted in the negative. The vote on call of States was finally announced as yeas 282, nays 521; so the Convention refused to lay the motion on the table.

The vote in detail was as follows:

State.	Yeas.	Nays	State.	Yeas.	Nays
Alabama	1	19	New Hampshire	—	8
Arkansas	—	14	New Jersey	14	4
California	16	—	New York .	—	72
Colorado	6	—	North Carolina	—	22
Connecticut	—	12	Ohio	19	24
Delaware	6	—	Oregon .	5	1
Florida	—	8	Pennsylvania	24	35
Georgia	8	16	Rhode Island	1	7
Illinois	17	26	South Carolina	11	7
Indiana	30	—	Tennessee	23	1
Iowa	—	26	Texas	14	12
Kansas	13	5	Vermont	—	8
Kentucky	3	23	Virginia . .	—	24
Louisiana	—	16	West Virginia	2	10
Maine	3	8	Wisconsin	—	22
Maryland	—	16	Arizona .	—	2
Massachusetts	6	13	Dist. Columbia	—	2
Michigan	—	26	Dakota	2	—
Minnesota	—	14	Idaho	—	2
Mississippi	11	7	Montana .	—	2
Missouri	7	25	New Mexico	—	2
Nebraska	1	8	Washington	2	—
Nevada	6	—	Wyoming	2	—

Delaware.—Attorney General Geeorg Gray nominated Bayard of Delaware, which was seconded by Col. C. E. Hooker, of Mississippi.

Indiana.—Thomas A. Hendricks nominated McDonald, of Illinois, which was seconded by General Black.

Kentucky.—James A. McKenzie nominated Carlisle.

New York.—Mr Lockwood nominated Grover Cleveland, Carter Harrison seconding the nomination.

Ohio.—John W Breckenridge, of California, nominated A. G. Thurman, which was seconded by Durbin Ward, of Ohio.

A motion to suspend the order of business was made and carried and then at 6.20 the convention took a recess until 10.30 A. M. to-morrow.

EVENING SESSION.

At 8.05 the convention was called to order and a resolution was offered by Mr. Henry, of Mississippi, expressing the regret and intense admiration of the convention at reading the statesmanlike, patriotic letter of Samuel J Tilden, in which he made known the overpowering and providential necessity which constrained him to decline the nomination to the Presidency, condemning the fraud and violence by which Tilden and Hendricks were cheated out of their offices in 1876; expressing regret that the nation has been deprived of the lofty patriotism and splendid executive and administrative ability of Mr. Tilden, and appointing a committee to convey these sentiments to that gentleman. Adopted.

At 9 P M. Morrison, of Illinois, chairman of the committee on resolutions, stepped to the platform to present the report of that committee.

The reading of the platform was concluded at ten o'clock.

THIRD DAY'S SESSION.

The convention was called to order at 11:10 and the proceedings were opened with prayer by the Rev. George C. Lorimer, of the Immanuel Baptist Church, of Chicago.

The unfinished business of yesterday, being the call of States for nominations, was resumed.

Mr Hoadly of Ohio was placed in nomination by Thomas E. Powell of Ohio.

Senator Wallace of Pennsylvania, nominated Samuel J. Randall of Pennsylvania.

The nomination was seconded by Governor Abbett of New Jersey.

John W Cumming of Massachusetts seconded the nomination of Mr Bayard.

The names of the candidates were then announced as follows—each name being greeted with cheers, but by far the greatest demonstration being for Cleveland:

Thomas Francis Bayard......of Delaware,
Joseph E. McDonald............of Indiana,
John G Carlisle..................of Kentucky
Grover Cleveland...... ......of New York.
Allen G Thurman....................of Ohio.
Samuel J Randall.........of Pennsylvania.
George Hoadly.................... .of Ohio.

The candidates having been all presented the convention at 2.25 took a recess until evening.

General Butler presented the minority report which was debated, and defeated by a vote of 714½ to 97½ The Platform was then adopted.

After a motion to adjourn was lost, the call of States for the nomination of President was ordered, and resulted as follows:

First Ballot.

Cleveland	392
Bayard	170
Randall	78
McDonald	56
Thurman	88
Hoadly	3
Carlisle	27

Another motion to adjourn was made at 1 10 A. M. The motion, having been seconded by New York, was agreed to, and the Convention adjourned until 10 A. M. tomorrow

FOURTH DAY'S SESSION.

The Convention was called to order at 11 o clock, and prayer was offered by Rev Dr Clinton Locke, of Grace Church, Chicago.

Details of the Second Ballot.

The second ballot commenced at 11.20, with the following result

Cleveland Nominated on the Second Ballot.

The votes of the States in detail were then (1 o'clock) announced by the Clerk for verification.

The general result was announced as follows at 1.10 P. M.

Whole number of votes cast	820
Necessary to choice	547
Cleveland	683
Bayard	81½
Randall	4
Hendricks	45½
McDonald	2
Thurman	4

The Nomination made Unanimous.

The question was then put on Mr. Menzies' motion to make the nomination unanimous which was triumphantly carried.

The Convention then at 1:25 took a recess until 5 o clock P M.

EVENING SESSION.

At half-past 5 o'clock the evening session was called to order, and the first business done was the adoption of a resolution electing Mr Vilas (Chairman of the Convention) as Chairman of the committee to notify the nominees of their selection as candidates

Naming Candidates for Vice-President.

The Convention then proceeded to the call of the roll for the nomination of a candidate for Vice-President.

Mr Searles of California, nominated General William S. Rosecrans.

Mr Branch (Col.) nominated Joseph E. McDonald, of Indiana.

Mr Bacon (Ga.) said he was commissioned by his delegation to present the name of General John C. Black, of Illinois.

Judge Black expressed his appreciation of the high and unmerited compliment paid him. It was almost absolutely a surprise to him, but he had come here as the spokesman and representative of another citizen of the Republic. He had put his hand in the hand of Joseph E. McDonald, and while that gentlemen's name was before the Convention, he (Black) could not appear as in any sense his rival for any position. He, therefore, respectfully declined the nomination.

Mr. Pinlow (Kan.) presented the name of Governor George W Glick.

Ex-Senator Wallace (Pa.) said that he nominated as a candidate for Vice President a man conversant with public affairs throughout his whole life, an honored statesman, a pure and upright citizen, a victim of the grossest fraud ever perpetrated on the American people—Thomas A. Hendricks. [Cheers.]

Mr. Searles (Cal.) withdrew the nomination of Rosecrans.

The other nominees were all withdrawn.

one, by one, so that Mr. Hendricks' name alone remained before the Convention.

Hendricks Unanimously Nominated.

The motion was agreed to, and the Clerk proceeded to call the roll of States. The result was the unanimous nomination of Thomas A. Hendricks as the candidate for Vice-President.

The Chairman announced that there had been 816 votes cast, all of them being for Thomas A. Hendricks, and that Mr Hendricks was therefore the candidate of the National Democratic Convention for Vice-President of the United States.

The Convention then, at 7.25, adjourned *sine die.*

The Vote Tabulated.

The following table gives the vote of each State for Presidential candidates on each of the two ballots :

States and Territories.	1ST BALLOT.						2D BALLOT.		
	Cleveland.	Bayard.	McDonald.	Thurman.	Randall.	Carlisle.	Cleveland.	Bayard.	Hendricks.
Alabama.	4	14	1	1			5	14	
Arkansas.	14						14		
California				16			16		
Colorado			5	1			6		
Connecticut	12						12		
Delaware		6						6	
Florida.	8						8		
Georgia.	10	12			2		22	2	
Illinois.	28	2	11	1	1		43		
Indiana.			30				30		
Iowa.	23	1	1	1			26		
Kansas.	11	5		2			17	1	
Kentucky.						26	4	21	
Louisiana.	13	1		1			15		
Maine	12						12		
Maryland	6	10					16		
Massachusetts	5	21		2			8	7½	12½
Michigan.	14	1		11			23		3
Minnesota	14						14		
Mississippi	1	15		1	1		2	14	2
Missouri	15	10	1	3	3		32		
Nebraska.	8	1		1			7	1	
Nevada				6					5
New Hampshire	8						8		
New Jersey	4	3			11		5	2	11
New York.	72						72		
North Carolina		22					22		
Ohio.	21			23			46		
Oregon.	2	4					6		
Pennsylvania.	5				55		42	2	11
Rhode Island.	6	2					7	1	
South Carolina	8	10					10	8	
Tennessee	2	8	3	9	1		24		
Texas	11	10	1	4			26		
Vermont	8						8		
Virginia	13	9	1	1			23		1
West Virginia.	7	2		2	1		10	2	
Wisconsin	12	1	2	2		1	22		
Arizona	2						2		
Dakota.	2						2		
Idaho	2						2		
Montana	2						2		
New Mexico	2						2		
Utah.	2						2		
Washington.	1				1		2		
Wyoming.	2						2		
Dist. of Columbia					2		2		
Total . .	392	170	56	88	78	27	683	81½	45½

Democratic Platform.

Adopted at Chicago, July 10, 1884.

The Democratic party of the Union, through its representatives in National Convention assembled, recognizes that, as the nation grows older new issues are born of time and progress and old issues perish. But the fundamental principles of the Democracy, approved by the united voice of the people, remain, and will ever remain, as the best and only security for the continuance of free government. The preservation of personal rights, the equality of all citizens before the law, the reserved rights of the states and the supremacy of the Federal Government within the limits of the Constitution will ever form the true basis of our liberties, and can never be surrendered without destroying that balance of rights and powers which enables a continent to be developed in peace, and social order to be maintained by means of local self-government, but it is indispensable for the practical operation and enforcement of these fundamental principles that the Government should not always be controlled by one political power. Frequent change of administration is as necessary as constant recurrence to the popular will. Otherwise abuses grow and the Government, instead of being carried on for the general welfare, becomes an instrumentality for imposing heavy burdens on the many who are governed for the benefit of the few who govern. Public servants thus become arbitrary rulers.

This is now the condition of the country, hence a change is demanded.

The Republican Party.

The Republican party, so far as principle is concerned, is a reminiscence. In practice, it is an organization for enriching those who control its machinery. The frauds and jobbery which have been brought to light in every department of the Government are sufficient to have called for reform within the Republican party, yet those in authority, made reckless by the long possession of power, have succumbed to its corrupting influence, and have placed in nomination a ticket against which the independent portion of the party are in open revolt.

Therefore a change is demanded. Such a change was alike necessary in 1876, but the will of the people was then defeated by a fraud which can never be forgotten nor condoned. Again in 1880 the change demanded by the people was defeated by the lavish use of money contributed by unscrupulous contractors and shameless jobbers who had bargained for unlawful profits or for high office. The Republican party during its legal, its stolen and its bought tenures of power has steadily decayed in moral character and political capacity. Its platform promises are now a list of its past failures. It demands the restoration of our navy it has squandered hundreds of millions to create a navy that does not exist. It calls upon Congress to remove the burdens under which American shipping has been depressed, it imposed and has continued those burdens. It professes the policy of reserving the public lands for small holdings by actual settlers, it has given away the people's heritage, till now a few railroads and non-resident aliens, individual and corporate, possess a larger area than that of all our farms between the two seas. It professes a preference for free institutions, it organized and tried to legalize a control of state elections by Federal troops. It professes a desire to elevate labor; it has subjected American working-men to the competition of convict and imported contract labor It professes gratitude to all who were disabled or died in the war, leaving widows and orphans, it left to a Democratic House of Representatives the first effort to equalize both bounties and pensions. It proffers a pledge to correct the irregularities of our tariff, it created and has continued them. Its own Tariff Commission confessed the need of more than 20 per cent. reduction, its Congress gave a reduction of less than 4 per cent. It professes the Protection of American manufactures, it has subjected them to an increasing flood of manufactured goods and a hopeless competition with manufacturing nations, not one of which taxes raw materials. It professes to protect all American industries, it has impoverished many to subsidize a few It professes the Protection of American labor, it has depleted the returns of American agriculture—an industry followed by half our people. It professes the equality of men before the law, attempting to fix the status of colored citizens.

The acts of its congress were overset by the decisions of its courts. It "accepts anew the duty of leading in the work of progress and reform," its caught criminals are permitted to escape through continued delays or actual connivance in the prosecution. Honeycombed with corruption, outbreaking exposures no longer shock its moral sense. Its honest members, its independent journals, no longer maintain a successful contest for authority in its coun sels, or a veto upon bad nominations. That change is necessary is proved by an existing surplus of more than $100,000,000, which has yearly been collected from a suffering people. Unnecessary taxation is unjust taxation. We denounce the Republican party for having failed to relieve the people from crushing war taxes, which have paralyzed business, crippled industry, and deprived labor of employment and of just reward. The Democracy pledges it self to purify the administration from corruption, to restore economy, to revive respect for law and to reduce taxation to the lowest limit consistent with due regard to the preservation of the faith of the nation to its creditors and pensioners, knowing full well, however, that legislation affecting the occupations of the people should be cautious and conservative in method, not in advance of public opinion, but responsive to its demands. The Democratic party is pledged to revise the tariff in a spirit of fairness to all interests.

Tariff Reduction.

But in making a reduction in taxes it is not proposed to injure any domestic industries, but rather to promote their healthy growth. From the foundation of this Government, taxes collected at the custom-house have been the chief source of federal revenue, such they must continue to be. Moreover, many industries have come to rely upon legislation for successful continuance, so that any change of law must be at every step regardful of the labor and capital thus involved. The process of reform must be subject in the execution to this plain dictate of justice.

All taxation shall be limited to the requirements of economical government. The necessary reduction in taxation can and must be effected without depressing American labor or the ability to compete successfully with foreign labor, and without imposing lower rates of duty than will be ample to cover any increased cost of production which may exist in consequence of the higher rate of wages prevailing in this country. Sufficient revenue to pay all the expenses of the Federal Government economically administered, including pensions, interest and principal of the public debt, can be got, under our present system of taxation, from custom-house taxes on fewer imported articles, bearing heaviest on articles of luxury, and bearing lightest on articles of necessity We therefore denounce the abuses of the existing tariff and, subject to the preceding limitations, we demand that federal taxation shall be exclusively for public purposes, and shall not exceed the needs of the Government economically administered. The system of direct taxation known as the "internal revenue" is a war tax, and, so long as the law continues, the money derived therefrom should be sacredly devoted to the relief of the people from the remaining burdens of the war, and be made a fund to defray the expense of the care and comfort of worthy soldiers disabled in the line of duty in the wars of the Republic, and for the payment of such pensions as Congress may from time to time grant to such soldiers, a like fund for the sailors having been already provided, and any surplus should be paid into the treasury.

Commerce with South America.

We favor an American continental policy based upon more intimate commercial and political relations with the fifteen sister republics of North, Central and South America, but entangling alliances with none. We believe in honest money, the gold and silver coinage of the Constitution, and a circulating medium convertible into such money without loss. Asserting the equality of all men before the law, we hold that it is the duty of the Government in its dealings with the people to mete out equal and exact justice to all citizens, of whatever nativity, race, color or persuasion, religious or political. We believe in a free ballot and a fair count and we recall to the memory of the people the noble struggle of the Democrats in the Forty-fifth and Forty-sixth Congresses, by which a reluctant Republican opposition was compelled to assent to legislation making everywhere illegal the presence of troops at the polls, as the conclusive proof that a Democratic administration will preserve liberty with order The selection of federal officers for the territories should be restricted to citizens previously resident therein. We oppose sumptuary laws which vex the citizen and interfere with individual liberty. We favor honest civil service reforms and the compensation of all United States officers by fixed salaries, the separation of church and state, and the diffusion of free education by common schools, so that every child in the land may be taught the rights and duties of citizenship. While we favor all legislation which will tend to the equitable distribution of property, to the prevention of monopoly and to the strict enforcement of individual rights against corporate abuses, we hold that the welfare of society depends upon a scrupulous regard for the rights of property as defined by law We believe that labor is best rewarded where it is freest and most enlightened. It should therefore be fostered and cherished. We favor the repeal of all laws restricting the free action of labor, and the enactment of laws by which labor organizations may be incorporated, and of all such legislation as will tend to enlighten the people as to the true relation of capital and labor. We believe that the public lands ought, as far as possible, to be kept as homesteads for actual settlers, that all unearned lands, heretofore improvidently granted to railroad corporations by the action of the Republican party, should be restored to the public domain, and that no more grants of land shall be made to corporations, or to be allowed to fall into the ownership of alien absentees. We are opposed to all propositions which, upon any pretext, would convert the general Government into a machine for collecting taxes to be distributed among the states,or the citizens thereof.

Jeffersonian Principles.

In reaffirming the declarations of the Democratic platform of 1856, that "the liberal principles embodied by Jefferson in the Declaration of Independence and sanctioned in the Constitution, which make ours the land of liberty and the asylum of the oppressed of every nation, have ever been cardinal principles in the Democratic faith," we, nevertheless, do not sanction the importation of foreign labor or the admission of servile races unfitted by habits, training, religion or kindred for absorption into the great body of our people or for the citizenship which our laws confer

American civilization demands that against the immigration or importation of Mongolians to these shores our gates be closed. The Democratic party insists that it is the duty of the Government to protect with equal fidelity and vigilance the rights of its citizens, native and naturalized, at home and abroad, and, to the end that this protection may be assured, United States papers of naturalization issued by courts of competent jurisdiction must be respected by the executive and legislative departments of our own Government and by all foreign powers. It is an imperative duty of this Government to efficiently protect all the rights of persons and property of every American citizen in foreign lands, and demand and enforce full reparation for any invasion thereof.

An American citizen is only responsible to his own Government for any action done in his own country or under her flag, and can only be tried, therefore, on her own soil and according to her laws, and no power exists in this Government to expatriate an American citizen to be tried in any foreign land for any such act.

This country has never had a well defined and executed foreign policy save under Democratic administration. The policy has ever been, in regard to foreign nations, so long as they do no act detrimental to the interests of the country or hurtful to our citizens, to let them alone. That, as the result of this policy, we recall the acquisition of Louisiana, Florida, California, and of the adjacent Mexican territory by purchase alone and contrast these grand acquisitions of Democratic statesmanship with the purchase of Alaska, the sole fruit of a Republican administration of nearly a quarter of a century.

Federal Responsibilities.

The Federal Government should care for and improve the Mississippi River and other great water ways of the Republic, so as to secure for the interior states easy and cheap transportation to tidewater. Under a long period of Democratic rule and policy our merchant marine was fast overtaking and on the point of outstripping that of Great Britain. Under twenty years of Republican rule and policy our commerce has been left to British bottoms, and almost has the American flag been swept off the high seas. Instead of the Republican party's British policy, we demand for the people of the United States an American policy Under the Democratic rule and policy, our merchants and sailors, flying the stars and stripes in every port, successfully searched out a market for the varied products of American industry Under a quarter of a century of Republican rule and policy, despite our manifest advantages over all other nations in high paid labor favorable climate and teeming soils, despite freedom of trade among all these United States, despite their population by the foremost races of men and an annual immigration of the young, thrifty and adventurous of all nations, despite our freedom here from the inherited burdens of life and industry in old world monarchies, their costly war navies, their vast tax-consuming, non-producing standing armies; despite twenty years of peace, that Republican rule and policy have managed to surrender to Great Britain, along with our commerce, the control of the markets of the world.

Instead of the Republican party's British policy, we demand in behalf of the American Democracy, an American policy; instead of the Republican party's discredited scheme and false pretenses of friendship for American labor expressed by imposing taxes, we demand in behalf of the Democracy, freedom for American labor, by reducing taxes to the end that these United States may compete with unhindered powers for the primacy among nations in all the arts of peace and fruits of liberty

With profound regret we have been apprised by the venerable statesman, through whose person was struck that blow at the vital principle of republics (acquiescence in the will of the majority), that he cannot permit us again to place in his hands the leadership of the Democratic hosts, for the reason that the achievement of reform in the administration of the Federal Government is an undertaking now too heavy for his age and failing strength. Rejoicing that his life has been prolonged until the general judgment of our fellow-countrymen is united in the wish that wrong were righted in his person for the Democracy of the United States, we offer to him, in his withdrawal from public cares, not only our respectful sympathy and esteem, but also that best homage of freemen, the pledge of our devotion to the principles and the cause now inseparable in the history of the Republic from the labors and the name of Samuel J. Tilden. With this statement of the hopes, principles and purposes of the Democratic party the great issue of reform and change in administration is submitted to the people in calm confidence that the popular voice will pronounce in favor of new men and new and more favorable conditions for the growth of industry, the extension of trade, the employment and due reward of labor and of capital, and the general welfare of the whole country.

THE ISSUES OF 1884.

The Democratic party with its long historic record, reaching back to the primitive days of the Republic, has so often asserted its fundamental principles, and in the administration of the government has so fully defined its policy that a passing notice is all that is necessary to present them to the reader. Its maxim of "the greatest good to the greatest number" has been the prominent idea of the party since the days of Jefferson, and hence its great following by the masses of the laboring classes. The Democratic party as the representative of free institutions, or of a government of the people, became from the beginning the natural antagonist of aristocracy, and the champion of legitimate industry. It not only welcomed to our shores the oppressed of other nations, but after clothing them with the garb of citizenship it has stood between labor and capital, demanding an equitable division of their joint earnings. To hold in check the syndicates of capital, and to compel corporations to deal justly with employees, has ever been its aim and end. The great national doctrines enunciated by Jefferson, whose broad and practical views gave our nation a home prosperity and a foreign prestige, still form the keystone of the Democratic arch through which the present millions march onward to a bright future. To preserve national honor, to perpetuate our institutions as handed down to us by the noble framers of our government, to give stability to industry and trade, to legislate for the whole nation and not for a chosen few—these are a few of the prominent ideas of the Democratic party. Individual interests will differ, the different callings of life beget a friction, and cause collisions between rival elements. Governments when just, instead of favoring one interest to the prejudice of others, bring about such a compromise as aids all by protecting all.

The two great political parties substantially agree as to the true intent and purpose of government. They both declare their purpose to be to secure the perpetuity of our institutions, the prosperity of our people, and the rapid and safe development of our resources. Each recognizes the constitutional rights of our people, and the supremacy of legal enactments in accordance therewith. Executive officers and legislators without regard to party must protect and defend our institutions, and carry on the government as they shall deem best for its present and future good. It is at this point that party lines diverge on the question of *policy*. The division is not as to what we need as a nation, but as to the best way to secure it. Thus, we need money to carry on the government, but the question as to the best way to procure it is probably the real dividing line between the great parties. At the present time our receipts are from duties on imports, from internal revenue taxes, and from the sale of public lands. As regards the money raised by the taxation of articles produced in our own country, there is a large following in both the Democratic and Republican parties that the necessity for said tax no longer exists, and its collection should be discontinued.

Protection laws are unstable.

An essential of a just law is that it affects all alike, and measured from this stand point our tariff legislation is undoubtedly very unjust. Protection instead of being designed for the common good, is special and discriminating, and is therefore partial. It favors the one at the expense of the other, and all tariff legislation having a view to protect must necessarily do so. When it discards favoritism and ceases to discriminate, it cannot protect, because a law which affords equal protection to all the home industries would leave them in precisely the same condition as if they had no legal protection. As has been truly said, "the attempt to protect everything protects nothing. The history of our country shows further, that these partial laws cannot be permanent, and the knowledge that they are liable to change at any session of Congress tends to disorganize business and thus destroy the general prosperity Capitalists are slow to invest in any business, which is subject to the mutations of popular legislation, thus placing them and those whom they employ at the mercy of each congressional delegation. A tariff which favors one class today may be changed to favor another tomorrow, and thus capitalists become bankrupt and labor is paralyzed under the hypocritical name of protection. The Democratic party is pledged against such favoritism, and sham protection, and favors such tariff legislation as will give stability to all our industries, and through that, prosperity to the whole country What the country needs is a rest from such legislation as vainly strives to regulate that which is only governed by the stern laws of supply and demand, when business will take its natural channel, labor receive its proper compensation, and prosperity will bless and restore what protective laws have blasted.

The Duties are Principally Paid by the Consumer.

Those who advocate a Protective Tariff assert that the importer pays the duty, and thus foreign Governments pay the principal portion of our taxes. The absurdity of this proposition is evident from the fact that if it were true, all nations would immediately resort to such a tariff in order that they might be relieved from taxation. But even for a moment admitting it to be true, no possible benefit could be derived from such a system, as the reciprocal feature would require us to pay the taxes of other nations in the same amount that they might pay ours.

It may be laid down as a verity, that the consumer of an article pays its full value, including all costs and charges incident to its production and delivery to the last purchaser, and hence whatever we consume of foreign product or manufacture we pay for to the uttermost farthing. We are even obliged to pay more than the value in a foreign market with the duties and freight added, because these commodities of necessity pass through more hands than domestic produce, and each demands his percentage on the actual cost. The wealthy who can afford to purchase in large quantities of first hands, purchase at less rates than the poor who are compelled to buy in small quantities, at much higher rates, and hence the laboring poor of the country, who are least able to pay, have to bear the major part of this taxation. Duties on imports are therefore a direct tax on the labor of the country much more onerous and unjust to the poor than a direct taxation would be. To put the case plainly, the consumer of an imported article pays, in addition to its market price at home, the expense of transportation and insurance, the amount of duty levied under the tariff law, the cost of maintaining our custom houses and their accessories, the commissions of agents, the percentage of wholesale dealers, the profits of jobbers, and the augmented prices of the retail dealers, so that the original price is often quadrupled ere it is purchased by the sweat of labor. It compounds its rates as it passes from hand to hand, and the consumer must pay both principal and interest.

But the Protectionist replies, that notwithstanding this, the consumer purchases at a cheaper rate than he can buy the same goods manufactured at home—that foreign manufacturers must undersell our market before they can find purchasers. If this were true, it would successfully refute the position taken by the Democratic Party on the tariff question, and completely disarm the opponents of Protection so far as this principle applies. But it is not the fact, as may be shown in a single sentence. The idea that goods manufactured in the old countries are superior to ours, is entertained by a great majority of our people, and hence they are willing to pay a higher price for them than for similar articles made at home. There was a time when the proposition was true, but the rapid development of the country, and its advance in all the skilled industries, enables it now to make almost every article of utility or luxury as good as it is made abroad. But the prejudice still exists, and it is kept alive by the agents of foreign establishments, so that in many cases foreign trash is purchased in preference to home staples, because it is "imported," and thus foreign goods in many cases do not compete with our own, but are purchased at higher prices under the delusive impression that they are superior because of foreign manufacture. A Protective Tariff with its school of trained theorists, and its army of officers fed and fattened out of fees is the breeder of this fallacy, through which our manufacturers suffer more than if they were exposed to an open competitive market. A lady will pay $3.00 per yard for an imported silk no better in quality than that produced at home and sold for $2.00 per yard, because it is "imported." A gentleman pays $50 for a suit of imported fabric, inferior in quality to what he can obtain for $35 of American make. The Cincinnati hog merchant sells bacon at 8 cents per pound, but knowing this sophistry by which foreign goods are sold, he ships it to Belfast, and then re-ships it to New York, and obtains 20 cents a pound for his *genuine* Irish Bacon.

Protection does not Protect.

So long as we are schooled to the belief that goods manufactured in foreign countries are superior to our own, and we are willing to pay enhanced prices for them, protection cannot protect our industries. Apart from this it may be conceded that some of our industries are temporarily stimulated by protective duties, and that producers thereby realize large profits on their products, but it is done at the expense of the domestic consumers who pay the increased price. Protection proposes to promote industry at the expense of the products of industry, and justifies the increased expenditure on the grounds that the additional amount paid would have been expended for something else. It is impossible for such a tariff to equally protect capital and labor, which, although in one sense are so closely allied, yet at the same time have antagonistic interests. Capital without labor is non-producing—labor without the aid of capital is inoperative. But the unity of interest ceases here, and the contest between the two elements begins. Capital desires cheap labor in order to produce cheap goods. Labor desires such remuneration as will secure the necessities of life at fair prices, and asks for an equitable division of profits. If our import system makes the capitalist wealthy and the operative poor, or vice versa, it is not equitable, and cannot add to the general prosperity. Whenever it protects the one at the expense of the other it is working a personal and a public evil. The Democratic Party resists this protective policy on the grounds that it is neither practical, equitable nor honest. It is directly in the interest of corporations, of capitalists and syndicates of speculators. It protects that which can protect itself, and leaves the laboring poor at the mercy of soulless money making corporations. It protects the one by laying tribute on every article that enters into competition with his business, it secures for him the entire home market for his goods, and enables him to fix his prices on what he sells, under the plea of Protection to American Industry, while at the same time it allows him to supplant American labor which demands fair wages with cheap labor from abroad. There is no protective tariff on labor—the foreign workman comes in free of duty, and at low wages drives home labor from its callings. If a tariff is intended to protect American labor, it must not only tax the products of foreign labor, but also the labor itself when employed in this country, otherwise it cannot protect our own industry. It is in behalf of American labor that the Democratic Party opposes a tariff for the protection of capital at the expense of the working man. A manufactory in this country filled with foreign operatives employed at lower prices than are paid to native labor, is the class of industry that is protected by our tariff, and on account of which hundreds of millions of dollars are annually paid by our consumers. The products of such an establishment are as truly foreign as though they had been manufactured in Sheffield or Lyons. The natural effect of such a tariff is, first, to force native labor out of employment, and second, to tax the people of the country for thus depressing our industries.

A Protective Tariff is on the Principle of Slavery.

The great value of property is the right to exchange it for the property of another, as by this exchange both parties are benefited—each disposing of what he does not need, and receiving that which he does need, and any system of law that denies to an individual or a people the rights of exchange, violates the great principle of liberty As well might government determine what you should make, as how you should dispose of the products of your labor It might as well dictate who should be merchants, mechanics, or artisans, as to direct as to the sale or exchange of their goods. "No man can be free," says an able writer, "who, by arbitrary enactment is not allowed, in trying to exchange his products for another, to obtain all that the laws of value acting freely would give him, or who has some part of the product of his labor arbitrarily taken from him for the use and enjoyment of some other man who has not earned it.

The argument that is generally put forth by the advocates of the policy of protection, in justification of legislation restricting freedom of exchange, or in defence of the pithily expressed proposition that "it is better to compel an individual to buy a hat for five dollars, rather than to allow him to purchase it for three, is that any *present* loss or injury resulting from such restriction to the individual will be more than compensated to him, or to society, through some future and indirect accruing benefit. But it should be borne in mind that this is the same argument that has always been made use of in past times as a warrant for every crime against liberty It ought not therefore to be a matter of surprise, that the intellectuality of this latter third of the nineteenth century, recognizing the antagonism of any other position to the great cause of human progress, should have ranged itself by an overwhelming majority on the side of industrial and commercial freedom, equally and for like reasons and motives as it has on the side of intellectual, religious and political freedom ; that no man intellectually great by general acknowledgment, who has given any special attention to this subject, and who is not avowedly working in the interests of despotism, or private gain, can be pointed out in either hemisphere, that is not unqualifiedly in favor of removing speedily and to the greatest extent compatible with the requirements of governments for revenue, all restrictions on the commercial intercourse of both nations and individuals , and that there is not to-day a first-class college or institution of learning in the whole world which would admit or invite to its chair of political economy, a person who theoretically believed in the theory or expediency of restricting exchanges as a means of increasing popular welfare and abundance."

The Party opposed to Centralization of Power.

The Democratic party opposes a protective tariff because it tends to a centralization of power not warranted by the Constitution. In countries where the government is a despotism, without any limitation or restraint, such a policy would be in strict accordance with its powers, but under a free government, where the powers of the ruler are the vested rights of the people, it is a question whether its legislators have the right to levy discriminating taxes other than to defray public expenditures. As ours is a government of the people, for the people as a whole, and not for any particular portion or class, it becomes a question whether any legislation discriminating between them, and thus affecting their rights as citizens is not a direct violation of our Constitution. At all events it is committing a wrong upon one class to benefit another, and is not equitable, if legal. It takes from those who can least afford to pay, and gives to those who do not need it.

What the Supreme Court says.

The Democratic policy as regards this great question cannot be more accurately stated, than in the words of Justice Miller, of the Supreme Court of the United States, in an opinion of that Court, given in Wallace Reports, volume xx. "The theory of our governments, State and National, is opposed to the deposit of unlimited power anywhere. The executive, the legislative and the judicial branches of these governments are all of limited and defined powers. They are limitations of such powers which grow out of the essential nature of all free governments, implied reservation of individual rights, without which the social compact could not exist, which is respected by all governments entitled to the name. Of all the powers conferred upon governments that of taxation is most liable to abuse. Given a purpose or object for which taxation may be lawfully used, and the extent of its exercise is in its very nature unlimited. This power can as readily be employed against one class of individuals and in favor of another, so as to ruin the one class and give unlimited wealth and prosperity to the other if there are no implied limitations of the uses for which the power may be exercised. To lay with one hand the power of the government on the property of the citizen, and with the other to bestow it upon favored individuals to aid private enterprise and build up private fortunes, is none the less robbery because it is done under the forms of the law and is called taxation. This is not legislation; it is a decree under legislative forms. Nor is it taxation. Beyond a cavil there can be no lawful tax which is not laid for a public purpose. It may not be easy to draw the line in all cases so as to decide what is a public purpose in this sense and what is not. If it be said that a benefit results to the local public of a town, by establishing manufactures, the same may be said of any other business or pursuit which employs capital or labor. The merchant, the mechanic, the inn-keeper, the banker, the builder, the steamboat owner, are equally promoters of the public good and equally deserving the aid of the citizens by forced contributions. No line can be drawn in favor of the manufacturer which would not open the public treasury to the importunities of two-thirds of the business men of the city or town." Here is an exposition of Democratic doctrine given by the Supreme Court within ten years, to which there was but one dissenting opinion. It confirms the great party principle that protection to aid private interests in manufacturing or in any other line of business is beyond the province of State and National governments, and when such legislation is had, to use the words of Justice Miller, "it is none the less robbery because it is done under the forms of law and is called taxation."

A distinguished judge of the Supreme Court of Michigan in his work on the "Principles of Constitutional Law," says: "Constitutionally a tax can have no other basis than the raising of a revenue for public purposes, and whatever governmental action has not this basis is tyrannical and unlawful. A tax on imports, therefore, the purpose of which is not to raise a revenue, but to discourage and indirectly prohibit some particular import for the benefit of some home manufacture, may well be questioned as being merely colorable, and, therefore, not warranted by Constitutional principles."

Another learned jurist says "If there is any proposition about which there is an entire and uniform weight of judicial authority, it is that taxes are to be imposed for the use of the people of the State in the varied and manifold purposes of government, and not for private objects or the special benefit of individuals. The State cannot discriminate among occupations, for a discrimination in favor of one is a discrimination adverse to all others. While the State is bound to protect all, it ceases to give that just protection when it affords undue advantages, or gives special and exclusive preferences to particular individuals and particular and special industries at the cost and charge of the rest of the community."

Does Protection Increase Wages?

The argument advanced that we need a Protective tariff in order that our laborers may receive fair wages, is another of the fallacies adduced by the Republican party in order to control the votes of the operatives in our manufactories. It is asserted that in the absence of this protective policy the influx of foreign goods at low prices will first reduce the rates of labor, and finally compel the manufacturers to close their business. When we reflect that only a very small percentage of our people are engaged in occupations which admit of being protected against foreign competition, it is also important to observe how very few of the many products of home manufacture can possibly be directly benefited by a protective tariff. That which can be exported promptly and regularly, and sold in competition abroad with similar foreign products, cannot be directly benefited by any tariff legislation—on the contrary it must prove a decided detriment. The influx of foreign goods does not affect the general result, for supposing that in consequence of the abandonment of protection, large quantities of foreign goods should come to our market, they must be sold and paid for, before they can compete with our own. They are not given away to the people for nothing. Product for product is the imperative law of exchange, and we can only purchase from abroad, with what we produce at home, and hence the absurdity of the proposition that without a protective tariff we should be deluged with foreign goods. The whole question is met with the self-evident fact that if more goods are imported under a low tariff than under a high one, we must produce more at home to enable us to purchase them, in which case our domestic industries would be stimulated and increased, or else we must obtain a higher price for what we manufacture and produce, either of which would add to our national prosperity We cannot purchase foreign goods unless we have the money, and that money must be obtained through our own industry The whole thing is compensation because people as a rule purchase only what they need, and what they have the money to buy Labor is not for labor, but for its recompense, and human wants multiply just as the means to gratify them are obtained. The luxuries of one generation become the necessities of the succeeding one, so that if the price of labor was quadrupled, the demand for additional comforts and luxuries would increase in the same ratio.

The cheaper goods are, the more will be consumed, and nothing is more irrational than the supposition that the cheapness of goods, or the increased ability to purchase, diminishes or restricts the opportunity to labor. To quote a standard authority: "Wages are the laborers' share of product." No employer of labor can continue for any great length of time to pay wages, unless his product is large. If it is not, and he attempts it, it is only a question of time when his affairs will be wound up by the sheriff. Or, on the other hand, if a high rate of wages continues permanently to be paid in any industry and in any country, it is in itself proof positive that the product of labor is large, that the laborer is entitled to a generous share of it, and that the employer can afford to give it to him. And if to-morrow the tariff of the United States was swept out of existence, this natural advantage which, supposing the same skill and intelligence, is the sole advantage which the American laborer has over his foreign competitor, would not be diminished to the extent of the fraction of an iota. Consider for example, the American agriculturist. He pays higher wages than his foreign competitor. In fact the difference between the wages paid in agriculture in the United States and Europe are greater than in any other form of industry The tariff cannot help him, but by increasing the cost of all his instrumentalities of production, greatly injures him. With a surplus product in excess of any home demand to be disposed of, no amount of other domestic industry can determine his prices. How then can he undersell all the other nations and at the same time greatly prosper individually? Simply because of his natural advantages of sun, soil and climate, aided by cheap transportation and the use of ingenious machinery, which combined give him a greater product in return for his labor than can be obtained by the laborers in similar competitive industries in any other country. What has he to ask of government other than that it will interfere with him to the least possible extent?"

HON. E. CROSSLAND, of Kentucky, in his speech in the House of Representatives, March 16, 1872, thus defines the protective policy:

We have heard all our lives politicians argue that American industry, American manufactures, and American labor must be protected. What does this mean, the people inquire? Why, simply this, "and nothing more" or less: that there are a few men in the United States who have money enough to buy machinery They erect large factories and engage in the business of making iron and steel, manufacturing salt, spinning and weaving cotton, and making cotton cloth, weaving and making woolen cloth, making leather, and manufacturing for wholesale shoes and boots, manufacturing books, paper, medicine, &c. Across the ocean, in England and other countries, there are men who are also engaged in manufacturing. They are willing to sell what they make at a small profit, and having more than there is a demand for at home, they desire to bring it over to this country and sell it to our people for small profits, or exchange it with them for bread and meat, tobacco, and other products of this country, each getting a fair price for their products, but the American manufacturer wishes to sell his goods for more than their worth, and notwithstanding the fact that they are already protected by the wide waste of waters that lie between us and Scotland, England and Germany, by long, perilous and expensive transportation that foreign goods must pay, incited by greed and avarice, comes to Washington and makes his appeal to Congress for statutory protection. And they, acting under the double influence of prejudice to foreigners and partiality for the home manufacturer, losing sight of the interest of the great majority engaged in other pursuits, enact laws, and say that before the foreign-made goods shall be sold to the people there must be paid an average of forty-eight per cent. on their value, so as to enable the American manufacturer to sell his goods for forty-eight per cent. more than they are worth, and in this no man under the sun is protected or benefitted except the owners of the money invested in the various branches of manufactures.

It Shuts us out from the Commerce of the World.

Besides, as I have said, this high taxation on foreign products or manufactures drives them to seek markets where they are less taxed and restricted, and to exchange them for such articles as they do not produce in such abundance as to supply the home demand, and in this way we drive off purchasers of our large surplus of products, and the farmer is obliged to sell his produce at home, where the supply largely exceeds the demand, and the consequence is he receives a low price for it. And under this most iniquitous system of exclusion the foreign goods are taxed so high that they do not come in quantities sufficient to make healthy competition. The manufacturer, having no competition, sells his goods for the highest prices, because the people cannot buy them elsewhere, and then, having no competition, no one to bid against him for the farmer s produce, he takes it at his own price, and thus everything the people buy is high, and all they sell is low, and they are kept in poverty and the manufacturer made rich. Protectionists urge what they call the general prosperity of the people as an evidence that the tariff does not oppress them. We do see the people, by the hardest labor and the strictest economy, able to live, but what we do not see is the general prosperity that would pervade all classes when they could sell the results of their labor for good prices, and not then be obliged to pay away half or two thirds of it to the monopolists called manufacturers. Our farmers raised last year eighteen hundred million bushels of grain, and we exported less than seventy million bushels.

The home market in the United States can never absorb this immense annual production; a large surplus is inevitable, and must find a market somewhere, or the prosperity of this great class must end; and the cost of transportation from the farms to the markets is greatly increased by this unjust taxation. Railroad iron, cars and engines are all made of taxed articles; steamboats and all other means of transportation, from the farm-wagon to the grand steamers that plow the ocean main, all are taxed. The railroad companies and steamboat owners must make profits on their investments, and to do this high freights must be charged, and all paid by the farmer. Here is an interest greater than all others in this land, an industry to which all classes must look for food, for bread and meat, identical with all others, (except that of the monopolists;) the class that feeds us all, ought it not above all others to be fostered and protected? Yet you hear no application from the farmers or mechanics to oppress another class in their interests. No lobbyists are here asking the Committee of Ways and Means to tax other industries to protect them, no, that sturdy class love justice, and all they ask for is justice and fairness in life s great struggle. They are willing to labor and thus earn a livelihood, all they ask is equality Unlike the monopolists, they ask for no exclusive privileges.

HON MR. JOHNSON presents the party views of Protection as follows

The True Definition of Protection.

I do not know how else to define protection except to say that it is a cunningly devised scheme by which a portion and but a small portion of the community, under the pretense of raising a revenue for the support of the Government, get rich at the expense of the large majority of the people.

That being the idea that I have of what constitutes protection, I will inquire for a moment, whom does it protect? Unless it protects some considerable portion of the community, it ought not to be retained upon our statute-books; and if it protects only a small part of the community at the expense of the great body of the people, still less ought it to be the policy of the country.

I am unable to see whom it protects except the manufacturer himself. If a man converts raw cotton into cotton cloth, or if he converts iron ore into pig iron, he is the person to be protected. He gets the benefit of the duty which is assessed upon these articles when they are brought in from abroad, but he is the only man who gets it, nobody else does. It is simply the man whose capital is employed in converting the raw material into the manufactured article that gets the benefit of the duty His employés, and every other man, woman, and child in the community suffers the loss for the benefit of this one man. While it protects him, it injures the farmer, the planter, the teacher, the mechanic, the lawyer, the doctor, the merchant, the laborer, and every other class of the community

The Home Market Fallacy.

One favorite theory of the protectionists is that they create a home market. Their idea is that the agricultural community must have a market here composed of manufacturers to sell their products to, and that the manufacturing community must in return sell their products to the farmers, and thus home markets will be created for both. But it must be apparent to everybody that this home market is entirely too small for either industry You can never get a condition of things in this country in which all of its vast agricultural products can find a market here. We can never have enough manufacturers and attendant laborers to consume all that our rich lands in this great and extensive country can raise. There must be some market abroad, therefore, as well as a home market for our agricultural products. And if we did have manufacturers and attendant laborers enough to consume the surplus our farmers make, it is certain that they could manufacture infinitely more than the agricultural community could want or purchase. We could not sell enough to our whole people to make manufacturers entirely prosperous. We must have, therefore, to be prosperous, in addition to the home market, a foreign market for our manufacturer as well as for our agricultural products.

The scheme, then, of a home market as being sufficient and as affording all that we ought to ask, is of course not to be entertained. We must so arrange our system as to have not only a good home market, but at the same time a good foreign market, both for agricultural products and manufactured articles.

Our True Policy.

It is manifest, therefore, that the policy of our country should be to cheapen production so that whatever we have got to sell we can sell in the markets of the world in competition with other manufacturers. We should be able to go anywhere that England goes and sell our products at the same rate she sells hers. If we cannot do that we cannot compete with her. When we make the cost of productions high, we to that extent limit our market and exclude ourselves from the rest of the world.

The protective system, of necessity, has the effect of withdrawing wealth from one portion of the community and concentrating it in a particular class. The wealth of the country outside of the real estate is nearly a fixed quantity It increases slowly with business. If, therefore, we legislate in such a way as to give one portion of the community a large share of this fixed quantity, as a matter of course it can only be done by abstracting it from the rest.

But it is said that this not only benefits the manufacturer but benefits the laborer, the employé of the manufacturer because it enables the manufacturer to give him higher wages. Well, sir, wages, like everything else, are great or small by comparison. A dime is just as good as a dollar when it will buy as much. It is no answer to say that in this country wages are a dollar, or a dollar and a half, or two dollars a day, and that in Europe they are less, unless the purchasing power of the dollar, or dollar and a half, or two dollars in this country is greater than the purchasing power of a smaller sum in Europe. While the nominal amount of wages may be greater, yet if their actual value is not greater the laborer is not benefited. But while the nominal value of wages is greater, yet all the expenses attending living are increased by this protective system. Why? The laborer must have woolens, cottons, leather, and the products of these things to clothe himself and family, he has to pay rent; he has to pay taxes, and when he buys articles of prime necessity for his support, he buys them with the tariff duty added to their cost, he buys them with the protective burden upon them; he buys them at the increased price which is necessitated by the high rate of duties that is imposed upon them. If you give him a dollar a day and sell him cottons at twice as much as he can buy them for abroad you see at once that his wages, while nominally better, are not really so.

The People want Low Prices.

But, sir, against what does protection protect? It only protects against low prices. The people want low prices, they want everything they use at reasonable cost. When protection is asked for, it is a protection not against the English manufacturer, but a protection against low prices. It is a protection against the right of the people to purchase what they want and must have on the best terms for them. It is a protection against the people living as easily as they can and at as little cost as possible.

What else does protection secure? Do high tariffs produce low prices? That claim is astonishing. Unless it enables the manufacturer to sell his commodity at a higher price, how, I ask, is it possible to benefit even him? He says, "I am not getting enough for my goods, I make cottons, and I can only get ten cents a yard, I cannot afford to do that, I want protection, fix your duty upon cottons so that I can get fifteen cents a yard, and then I will be protected." So a man who makes iron says, "I can only sell my iron at twenty dollars a ton, which does not pay, but I can afford to make it if I can get twenty-five dollars a ton; protect me, therefore, and let me get twenty-five dollars a ton." Unless protection has that effect, how does it benefit the manufacturer? How can any one conceive it possible that a man should be benefited unless he is enabled to sell his commodities at a greater price than he did before?

It is said by the advocates of protection that it increases the wages of the laborers. How is that? If the wages of labor are raised, of course the cost of the article made must be enhanced. If the manufacturer give his hands one dollar a day this month and two dollars a day next month, can he sell for less when the labor costs him two dollars than when it only costs him one? They say, "Protect us and we can give higher wages." Higher wages, of course, indicate increased cost of production, and having given higher wages, and made your articles cost more than they would otherwise, we will still sell them for less than we did before." This proposition is one that hardly needs refutation.

HON. MR. GARRETT, of Tennessee, states the question as follows:

In a Government like ours, instituted by the people for the people, and under a written compact or Constitution, sealed as ours has been by an expenditure of blood and treasure unequalled in the history of the civilized world, whose territory extends over so vast an area, possessing so many diversified interests to be fostered and encouraged, the task of providing laws equally just to all, it will be readily seen, is one difficult in the extreme, if not altogether impossible. The law-maker, then, should seek to evolve from all measures brought to his consideration "the greatest good to the greatest number," and to do this his mind should be free from prejudices for or against any section or industry The wants and wishes of the wealthy manufacturer the merchant prince, or the lordly banker, should weigh no more with him, nay, not so much, as the wants and wishes of the humblest citizen, who, obeying the fiat of the great Ruler of the universe, "in the sweat of thy face shalt thou eat bread" gathers a harvest from the bosom of mother earth, delves beneath her surface to bring forth hidden riches, or in the workshop fashions the productions of the one or the other into articles of use or luxury, and unless the legislator remembers and acts upon this principle he is unfaithful to his trust and unfit to represent a free people, he has violated the theory of republican institutions as well as his official oath.

Now, what benefits have the people to show for this increased taxation? Where are the great internal improvements, the increased facilities for commerce or for education that should result from this expenditure? Nowhere but upon paper projects, which these *proteges* of the Government have inaugurated, and the funds for carrying which into execution they have wrung from an impoverished people and stolen.

What Mr. Kerr Says:

The gentleman from Pennsylvania protests that he wishes to legislate in the interests of the whole country, and he boasts of the comfortable homes of his bounty-fed neighbors, their well-furnished parlors, their pianos, and other musical instruments, and their comfortable houses lighted with gas, supplied with hot and cold water, well carpeted, and filled with convenient and handsome furniture. If this boast is well founded, whose bounty enables them thus to enjoy life? If in these professions he is sincere, why does he not offer to reduce the taxes and bounty paid by the people on all these things which are indispensable to the general prosperity, happiness and improvement of the people? Why does he cling with such hungry tenacity to grossly protective taxes on copper, iron, steel, lumber, leather, all kinds of clothing, carpeting, earthenware, glassware, and nearly everything that protectionists manufacture? Why does he constantly defend laws which discriminate against agriculture? Is he willing that the common people of the South and West, the millions of common laborers mechanics, and farmers all over the country, may live in log huts, poor-houses, with no parlors, no carpets, no pianos, no comforts beyond the hard necessities of mere life and toil? Does he want to keep them in such conditions by compelling them to pay bountiful tribute to the petted and pampered favorites of this State and city? That is his way of legislating for "the whole country." I repel it, and denounce it as unjust, sectional, selfish, and lawless. I plead for the poor, for the sons of toil, for the "hewers of wood and drawers of water," and demand equal laws, equal burdens, taxation for revenue only, and justice for all.

ROBERT J. WALKER, then Secretary of the Treasury, in his great report of December 3, 1845, uttered a pregnant truth when he said:

"A protective tariff is a question regarding the enhancement of the profits of capital, and not the augmentation of the wages of labor, It is a question of percentage, and is to decide whether money vested in our manufactures shall, by special legislation, yield a profit of ten, twenty or thirty per cent., or whether it shall remain satisfied with dividends equal to those accruing from the same capital invested in agriculture, commerce, or navigation."

The Effect on Agriculture.

The products of agriculture in the country at large cannot be otherwise than injuriously affected by tariffs. This has been the uniform experience of our country It was the experience of Great Britain, now admitted by all her statesmen and economic writers. Give agriculture absolute freedom from Government interference, with moderate taxation for revenue alone, and its prosperity will be certain, speedy, and permanent. But protective tariffs discriminate against it and in favor of manufactures. It is compelled to pay them tribute to swell their generous profits and diminish its own moderate earnings. The commodities they consume are constantly aggravated in price by the tariff, and their own products of the soil are made to cost them very much more than they should, and they are thus left at the mercy of the favored manufacturers, who, by the gross and criminal partiality of the Government, are enabled to dictate prices, to monopolize the markets, to keep out competition, and by enhancement of the cost of production to make successful foreign commerce impossible. By the increased cost of production in our country, caused chiefly by the tariff, but in part also by our depreciated currency, we are always at a disadvantage in all the great markets of other countries. Thus the protected few in this country are able to regulate directly the prices the people shall pay them for their manufactured products, and indirectly to exclude the farmers and other producers of values from the markets of the world.

Protection in our country has produced more poverty than it ever relieved. Pennsylvania and Massachusetts, that have for ten years confessed themselves dependent for material well-being and prosperity upon the bounty of the whole country, and have levied tribute to the extent of many hundred millions of dollars upon all the people, have more poverty, more pauperism, more embarrassed poor to-day than ever before in their history except in periods of financial crises or from causes having no immediate connection with tariffs. To-day we have an average of over two hundred thousand constant paupers in our country, notwithstanding our boundless territory and youthful vigor and inexhaustible resources, and we spend in their subsistence and protection out of public revenues over $11,000,000 annually, and in private and voluntary charities many millions more. Protective and restrictive laws, under one name and pretense or another, continued for centuries, are the potential causes of so much pauperism in the countries of the Old World. Out of those laws arose systems and institutions oppressive to the poor and the multitude. By their aid, the few increased in revenues, powers, titles, and dignity, at the expense of the people.

MR. ATKINSON, a very intelligent manufacturer and revenue reformer, whose statements are always worthy of the utmost respect, says:

"I think it cannot be denied that although wages are nominally higher, yet very many workingmen and women find themselves compelled to work as many hours for no better shelter and subsistence than before these great improvements (in machinery) had been made. I think it cannot be denied that it is more imprudent for young people to be married than it used to be, even if they are free from luxurious nonsense, that men of moderate means and small salaries find it more and more difficult to live in comfort and independence. I think it cannot be denied that society is becoming sorted into classes, more clearly divided, and each knowing and caring less about the other than ever before. I think it cannot be denied that the chief benefit of our progress in the useful arts in the last ten years has inured to the few and not to the many, and that this inequitable distribution is due to bad laws."

The Rights of Labor.

Tariffs for protection are direct assaults upon the personal liberty of labor. There is an element of tyranny and brigandage in every one. The right to live and to labor is no more inherent, original, and sacred than the right to control and dispose of the fruits of labor The right to buy or sell where you please is no more undeniable than the right of immunity from assault and battery at the hands of every strong man you meet. Free exchange of the products of different lands and sections among men is no less necessary for the well-being of individuals and society than is free action of the atmosphere to the health of human beings. Then why shall Government deny these sacred rights? Is Government wiser in the practical affairs of life than all the members who compose society? Has it any right to take the earnings of one and give them to another? That would be to take property without compensation. All men are equal in elementary rights. It is infamous, it is tyranny for Government to have favorites among its citizens. Nothing but the brutal sophism that "might makes right" can justify such a thing. Labor, and the true friends of labor, must learn these great principles. They are eternal and beneficent as truth itself.

Natural justice demands that the Government shall be supported by the citizens in proportion to their ability to pay Taxation should bear a just relation to the property of the tax-payer. If this honest policy were adopted, the poor would pay a very moderate portion of the revenues. The dividends of the rich and the monopolists would be diminished by larger contributions to the Government. But under our present cruel tariff, the poor, the great body of consumers, the agriculturists and artisans, are compelled to pay both taxes and tribute, to contribute the bulk of the public revenue and also to fill the plethoric coffers of the monopolists with bounty This is outrageous robbery and will not always be endured by freemen. Favored classes may as well now take warning that persistence in such policy will sooner or later lead to fundamental changes in our system of taxation, whereby property, and not poverty and necessity, shall be made to support the Government. The sons of toil cannot be forever deceived or enslaved, either in mind or body. With their intelligent awakening may come a conflict, bitter but just, whose result will vindicate their rights. The time approaches in our country when the bounty fed few "who pay tribute to the Lord out of the pockets of the poor," must do justice, or themselves suffer wrongs.

What Mr. Bright says.

Hon. John M. Bright declares that whatever trifle the manufacturer may agree to pay he gets a thousand-fold remuneration in the royal protection of his Government. He is on the inside of the gates of commerce, and escapes the duty tribute to the support of his Government. The farmer, mechanic, and day laborer are the consumers of dutiable goods, and thus they pay the taxes for the support of the Government. The manufacturer's neck has never been indurated by the yoke of taxation. He chafed and fretted under the income tax until the Government gently lifted it off. This is bad enough, but it is not all. The farmer, mechanic, and laborer have not only to support the Government and pay its debts, but, on the top of these, they, in the consumption of protected goods, pay bounty and support the manufacturers in pompous munificence, who, under shelter of the Government, can raise the price of their goods to the high water mark of protection.

This protection is in the nature of a pension bounty, which goes to the manufacturer and not to the Government. The Government does not have the money to pay, and it can afford to be liberal at the people's expense. Of course the manufacturers do not complain of a burden which they do not feel.

The result is that the manufacturer is not only exempted from paying a fair proportion to the expenses of the Government, but through the artificial contrivance of the tariff he is sluicing and making enormous profits out of the other industries of the country Any system which works out such a result is manifestly wrong and calls for a remedy The pretext which called the protective policy into existence in our Government has long since ceased to exist. The doctrine was founded in the idea that it was a national duty to encourage the home manufacture of war materials to make us independent of foreign nations. When we grew to be great and powerful, and we were ashamed to own a ridiculous timidity, the protectionists changed the cry into protection for American labor!

The manufacturer, with the bleating eloquence of a starveling calf, was let to the Government udder, and he has been tugging away since, until he has grown to huge proportions, and now moves about with a lumbering, pig-metal tread, roaring like a very bull of Bashan, full-horned, and goring every other industry from the Government manger.

But it is not our purpose to make war on our manufacturing interests, but on the vicious policy of our Government, which victimizes other interests for their protection. Free trade, restricted by a purely revenue tariff, is, in fact, not the antagonist of manufacturing industry By its liberal policy it opens up new fields of trade, gives expansion to consumption, stimulates demand, elicits additional capital, demands larger quantities of raw materials, employs more operatives, invigorates commerce, swells the volume of importations, and multiplies the comforts of all the people.

Our manufacturers, with their exemption from revenue duties, with the incidental protection of a purely revenue tariff, and the natural protection of the three thousand miles of waves which roll between us and Europe and the four thousand miles between us and China, will still occupy the highest vantage ground of any other American industry.

But it seems that some of our manufacturers have been so long protected with Government bounty that they claim it by prescriptive right, and would extract their tribute from the other industries, with the insane and uncalculating cupidity of one "who would burn his neighbor's house to roast his own eggs."

Then let the Government retrench its extravagance, lay its tariff for revenue alone, and with a benign policy, like the cope of heaven, span every department of industry alike; and while the land may tremble with rumbling machinery, let the tariff blockades be struck down to give vent to our redundant commerce, let our argosies be turned loose to climb the waves of every sea, and go touching at every island, landing at every coast, sweeping every continent, gathering up the wealth of the Old World, and returning to empty their treasures into the lap of our own country

HON. MR. READ'S views:

I now desire to call the attention of the House for a short time to the subject of the present

Onerous Tariff,

which is oppressing the people of the country so sorely I would like, if I had the time, to investigate and analyze that subject thoroughly, or so far as my feeble ability would permit. I have the figures and facts before me, and if arranged in proper form, they would startle the taxpayers and consumers of the whole country; but I am admonished to confine my remarks to results, and put the facts in an aggregated form.

The tariff is a source of raising revenue for the purpose of defraying the expenses of Governments. It has been a question that has given the statesmen of both this country and Europe for many years great thought and attention. The object of all patriots and statesmen should be to procure for themselves and posterity the best form of government, and devise ways and means by which their Government can be best supported and give contentment to its subjects. More discord and discontent has grown out of the manner in which taxes ought to be raised than that of all others. Internal discords and strife have arisen, and frequently produced in many instances by an honest misconception of the true policy to be pursued, but more frequently for the imposition, practiced on the people by scheming politicians, and with a desire to foster and make wealth at the expense of the many

The present tariff was procured by the capitalists and submitted to by a patriotic, patient, and law-abiding people. Civil war was pending; patriotism suggested that the integrity of the Union must at all hazards be maintained, and that it could not be without money A high tariff was suggested, which looked to the patriot that if put in practical operation it would yield more money than would be necessary to meet the exigencies of the war. A high protective tariff bill was passed by Congress, and to the astonishment of the uninitiated, the result of its operation fell far short of expectation, a tax or tariff was placed on about four thousand articles of consumption, but the articles that yield revenue to the Government of any consequence are but few in number, say ten or fifteen, there may be a few more. The tariff had the effect to prohibit the importation of articles of goods that the consumer needed and wanted, and built up and protected a monopoly the effect of which is burdensome. The people have submitted to a prohibition of the various needed articles of consumption, and the consumer was thus driven to make his purchases of supplies of the monopolists of the country, and thereby subjected to a tax on any article of supplies necessary to the comfort of themselves and families, ranging from fifty to three hundred and fifty per cent.

But the Radicals say that this is not true, that a protective tariff is necessary to enable us to compete with foreign countries, and also to protect the laboring man and woman at home, that if the tariff is reduced it will depress labor, that we cannot compete with the pauper labor of foreign countries. God pity the poor laborer and mechanic of other countries if they are in a worse condition than the operatives of the manufactories of this country The poor have to live in other countries by their labor as well as ours, and they are fed as well as ours if the reports be true. Then how is it that the operatives can live cheaper in England and France than in this? It is because nearly all the articles consumed by the laboring classes of those countries are governed by the laws of free trade, and the articles of consumption are therefore cheaper than what they are in this. Subjected to a tariff of protection let us for a moment examine and see the effect of the present tariff upon the articles consumed by the operatives, or a portion of them, thus consumed.

Wages of Labor not Helped by Taxation.

Hon. William R. Morrison, of Illinois, the present Chairman of the Committee of Ways and Means in the House, in his speech of April 15, 1884, says:

"During more than half of the last ten years wages have been as low or lower than before the adoption of the taxing policy as a pretended means of making wages higher. They are lower still when compared with the use which those who earn wages are compelled to make of them, for they must use them to obtain the means of comfortable living. Counted by what our laborers are able to accomplish and produce in quantities, and especially in values, wages here are but little more in many industries than the wages paid by our chief commercial rivals. There is but one horizontal reduction for which our opponents are willing to legislate—the reduction of wages—and this their favorites, with or without regard to legislation, are now executing day by day with cruel regularity

"Of all the false pretenses with which protection mocks its victims the assumption that labor is helped or protected by taxing its earnings is the flimsiest. Protectionists, in common with our people, invite the surplus labor of all the world to come, untaxed, unrestricted, free, and join us on equal terms and share in the profits of the wonderful heritage this newer world affords. The captains and masters of industry, if not masters of Congress as well, take to themselves protection of a very different kind—they tax the people at home that they may have no competition from abroad."

Low Tariff Develops the Country Most.

When this is done manufacturing industries may add something to the wealth of the nation by reason of the tribute which other nations must pay to its endless resources and the unrivalled skill and intelligence of its people.

The grand aggregate of national wealth, counted in the census at $43,300,000,000 in 1880, was but $26,460,000,000 in 1870. "Behold," exclaims the protectionist, "the results of our system which so multiplies and nearly doubles the wealth and national savings in a single decade." Further investigation will show that in the ten years from 1850 to 1860 with very low tariff taxes wealth was more than doubled, and that was the only decade in our history which doubled wealth. Protection has prevented this industry from bringing anything to the wealth of the country from abroad. Had manufacturing industry produced more that could be sold profitably abroad it might have better claim to the credit of the country's growth and development, when for its own prosperity it has been dependent upon other domestic industries.

Hon. W T. Hamilton declares against an undue restriction upon trade.

When we consider that revenue is the primary object of this species of taxation, all these schemes to pervert it to the subservience of special interests are practical wrongs upon the people, and in principle altogether wrong.

There can be no question but that under the Constitution the object of this species of taxation is revenue , it must mean taxation, nothing more, nothing less. It cannot, in the philosophy and nature of things, mean that you lay this tax to protect, or, if you please, encourage certain named branches of industry, and not to raise revenue. If no revenue were required, and you possessed the power under the Constitution, I apprehend a far different system would prevail. Then the system of protection would be a question pure and simple, not embarrassed by duties for revenues, but the legislation of the country would go directly to the main question itself, whether any or what commodities should be imported at all, and under what restraints, if any, they should be allowed to be imported. This would open up a broad field for legislation, where the theories of protection could be carried out to their greatest extent, and where the industries, productions, and energies of the citizen would be unhappily placed under the control of Congress. Fortunately for the country, fortunately for her great industrial interests, no such power has ever been exercised or claimed as a distinct substantive power under the Constitution.

Is such a principle right in a Government claiming to be free, and where the primary object is claimed to be the benefit of man, and where he is supposed to be secure in the full enjoyment of the fruits of his toil and in deriving from it all the benefit and happiness he can ? Is this protection the golden thought that has been rioting upon the common mind for centuries and for so many years in this country? It is a finely formed, rotund, impressive, seductive word, gaudily, nay richly attired, veiled even as the Prophet of Khorassan, but when stripped it presents features narrow and contracted, repulsive with low cunning, morbid selfishness, and base instincts. There is nothing in it broad, nor good, nor benevolent, nor liberal.

State Elections of 1882 and 1883, compared with the Presidential Election of 1880.

STATES.	1880.†				1882.‡				1883.*			
	Garfield, Rep.	Hancock Dem.	Weaver Gbk.	Dow, Pro.	Rep.	Dem.	Gbk.	Pro.	Rep.	Dem.	Gbk.	Pro.
Alabama	56,221	91,185	4,642		46,386	100,591						
Arkansas	42,436	60,775	4,079		49,352	87,675	10,142					
California	80,348	80,426	3,392		67,175	90,694	1,020	5,772				
Colorado	27,450	24,647	1,435		27,552	29,897						
*Connecticut	67,071	64,415	868	40	64,853	59,014	607	1,034	51,749	46,146		
Delaware	14,133	15,275	120		10,088	12,053						
Florida	23,654	27,964			20,139	24,067	3,553			23,680		
Georgia	54,086	102,470	969		24,930	81,443	68					
Illinois	318,037	277,321	26,358	443	254,551	249,067	11,306	11,202				
Indiana	232,164	225,522	12,986		210,234	220,918	13,520					
Iowa	183,927	105,845	32,701	592	149,051	112,180	30,817		164,182	139,093	23,089	
Kansas	121,549	59,801	19,851	25	§98,166	§61,547	§23,2[illegible]0					
Kentucky	106,306	149,068	11,499	258	79,036	110,813	736		89,181	133,615		
Louisiana	38,637	65,067	439		33,953	49,892						
Maine	74,039	65,171	4,408	93	72,724	63,552	1,302	395				
Maryland	78,515	93,706	818		74,515	80,725	1,833		80,707	92,694		1,881
Massachusetts	165,205	111,960	4,548	682	§134,358	§116,678	§4,033	§2,141	160,092	150,228		13,950
Michigan	185,341	131,597	34,895	942	§157,925	§140,443	§1,572	§1,440	122,330	127,376		
Minnesota	93,903	53,315	3,267	286	92,802	46,653	3,781	1,545	72,404	57,859		
Mississippi	34,854	75,750	5,797		30,282	48,159						
Missouri	153,567	200,699	35,135		128,239	198,620	33,407					
Nebraska	54,979	28,523	3,950		43,495	28,562	16,991		52,305	47,795		
Nevada	8,732	9,613			‡7,362	‡6,906						
New Hampshire	44,852	40,794	528	180	38,299	36,879	449	338				
New Jersey	120,555	122,565	2,617	191	97,860	99,962	6,093	2,004	97,047	103,856	2,960	4,153
New York	555,544	534,511	12,373	1,517	§400,422	‖482,822	‖10,527	‖16,234	429,252	445,817	7,187	19,368
North Carolina	115,874	124,208	1,126		111,320	111,763						
Ohio	375,048	340,821	6,456	2,616	297,759	316,874	5,345	12,202	347,164	359,793	2,937	8,362
Oregon	20,619	19,948	249		21,481	20,069						
Pennsylvania	444,704	407,428	20,668	1,939	¶359,232	¶355,791	¶23,996	¶5,196	319,106	302,031	4,452	6,602
Rhode Island	18,195	10,779	236	20	10,056	5,311	120		13,068	10,907		
South Carolina	58,071	112,312	556			67,458	17,719					
Tennessee	107,677	128,191	5,917	43	**91,693	**123,929	**9,538					
Texas	57,893	156,428	27,405		41,761	142,087	41,825					
Vermont	45,567	18,316	1,215		35,839	14,466	1,535					
Virginia	84,020	128,586			100,690	94,184						
West Virginia	46,243	57,391	9,079		43,440	46,661						
Wisconsin	144,400	114,649	7,986	69	94,606	103,630	2,496	13,800				
Total	4,454,416	4,444,952	308,578	10,305	3,620,844	4,051,035	277,691	76,303	1,998,587	2,040,890	40,629	54,316
Plurality	9,464					130,195				42,303		
Total vote		9,219,947				8,025,975				4,134,458		

* In Connecticut, the vote for Sheriff is taken. In New York, the average vote on four of the five State officers chosen, excluding Secretary of State. In Nebraska, Democratic and Anti-Monopoly vote combined on Judge. † American, 707; scattering, 989. ‡ Scattering, 106. § In these States the vote on Lieutenant-Governor was taken, as being, from special causes, a fairer test of party strength. In the others the principal State officer was taken. Where State officers were not elected, the Congressional vote was taken. In Georgia, Congressmen-at-Large was taken. ‖ The vote for Chief Judge. ¶ The Regular and Independent Republican vote is combined. ** Vote of the two Democratic candidates is combined.

PART II.

HISTORY

OF

POLITICAL PARTIES.

HISTORY

OF THE

POLITICAL PARTIES OF THE UNITED STATES.

Colonial Parties—Whig and Tory.

The parties peculiar to our Colonial times hardly have a place in American politics. They divided people in sentiment simply, as they did in the mother country, but here there was little or no power to act, and were to gather results from party victories. Men were then Whigs or Tories because they had been prior to their emigration here, or because their parents had been, or because it has ever been natural to show division in individual sentiment. Political contests, however, were unknown, for none enjoyed the pleasures and profits of power, the crown made and unmade rulers. The local self-government which our forefathers enjoyed, were secured to them by their charters, and these were held to be contracts not to be changed without the consent of both parties. All of the inhabitants of the colonies claimed and were justly entitled to the rights guaranteed by the Magna Charta, and in addition to these they insisted upon the supervision of all internal interests and the power to levy and collect taxes. These claims were conceded until their growing prosperity and England's need of additional revenues suggested schemes of indirect taxation. Against these the colony of Plymouth protested as early as 1636, and spasmodic protests from all the colonies followed. These increased in frequency and force with the growing demands of King George III. In 1651 the navigation laws imposed upon the colonies required both exports and imports to be carried in British ships, and all who traded were compelled to do it with England. In 1672 inter-colonial duties were imposed, and when manufacturing sought to flank this policy, their establishment was forbidden by law.

The passage of the Stamp Act in 1765 caused high excitement, and for the first time parties began to take definite shape and manifest open antagonisms, and the words Whig and Tory then had a plainer meaning in America than in England. The Stamp Act was denounced by the Whigs as direct taxation, since it provided, that stamps previously paid for should be affixed to all legal papers. The colonies resented, and so general were the protests that for a time it seemed that only those who owed their livings to the Crown, or expected aid and comfort from it, remained with the Tories. The Whigs were the patriots. The war for the rights of the colonies began in 1775, and it was supported by majorities in all of the Colonial Assemblies. These majorities were as carefully organized then as now to promote a popular cause, and this in the face of adverse action on the part of the several Colonial Governors. Thus in Virginia, Lord Dunmore had from time to time, until 1773, prorogued the Virginia Assembly, when it seized the opportunity to pass resolves instituting a committee of correspondence, and recommending joint action by the legislatures of the other colonies. In the next year, the same body, under the lead of Henry, Randolph, Lee, Washington, Wythe and other patriots, officially deprecated the closing of the port of Boston, and set apart a day to implore Divine interposition in behalf of the colonies. The Governor dissolved the House for this act, and the delegates, 89 in number, repaired to a tavern, organized themselves into a committee, signed articles of association, and advised with other colonial committees the expediency of "appointing deputies to meet in a general correspondence"—really a suggestion for a Congress. The idea of a Congress, however, originated with Doctor Franklin the year before, and it had then been approved by town meetings in Providence, Boston and New York. The action of Virginia lifted the proposal above individual advice and the action of town meetings, and called to it the attention of all the colonial legislatures. It was indeed fortunate in the incipiency of these political movements, that the people were practically unanimous. Only the far-seeing realized the drift and danger, while nearly all could join their voices against oppressive taxes and imposts.

The war went on for colonial rights, the Whigs wisely insisting that they were willing to remain as colonists if their rights should be guaranteed by the mother country; the Tories, chiefly fed by the Crown, were willing to remain without guarantee —a negative position, and one which in the high excitement of the times excited little attention, save where the holders of such views made themselves odious by the enjoyment of high official position, or by harsh criticism upon, or treatment of the patriots.

The first Continental Congress assembled in Philadelphia in September, 1774, and there laid the foundations of the Republic. While its assemblage was first recommended by home meetings, the cause, as already shown, was taken up by the assemblies of Massachusetts and Virginia. Georgia alone was not represented. The members were called delegates, who declared in their official papers that they were "appointed by the good people of these colonies." It was called the "revolutionary government," because it derived its power from the people, and not from the functionaries of any existing government. In it each colony was allowed but a single vote, regardless of the number of delegates, and here began not only the unit rule, but the practice which obtains in the election of a President when the contest reaches, under the constitution and law, the National House of Representatives. The original object was to give equality to the colonies as colonies.

In 1775, the second Continental Congress assembled at Philadelphia, all the colonies being again represented save Georgia. The delegates were chosen principally by conventions of the people, though some were sent by the popular branches of the colonial legislatures. In July, and soon after the commencement of hostilities, Georgia entered the Confederacy.

The Declaration of Independence, passed in 1776, drew yet plainer lines between the Whigs and Tories. A gulf of hatred separated the opposing parties, and the Tory was far more despised than the open foe, when he was not such, and was the first sought when he was. Men who contend for liberty ever regard those who are not for them as against them—a feeling which led to the expression of a political maxim of apparent undying force, for it has since found frequent repetition in every earnest campaign. After the adoption of the Declaration by the Continental Congress, the Whigs favored the most direct and absolute separation, while the Tories supported the Crown. On the 7th of June, 1776, Richard Henry Lee, of Virginia, moved the Declaration in these words:

"*Resolved*, That these united colonies are, and of right ought to be, free and independent states; that they are absolved from all allegiance to the British Crown, and that all political connection between them and the State of Great Britain is, and ought to be, totally dissolved."

Then followed preparations for the formal declaration, which was adopted on the 4th of July, 1776, in the precise language submitted by Thomas Jefferson. All of the state papers of the Continental Congress evince the highest talent, and the evils which led to its exhibition must have been long but very impatiently endured to impel the study of the questions involved. Possibly only the best lives in our memory invite our perusal, but certain it is that higher capacity was never called to the performance of graver political duties in the history of the world.

It has been said that the Declaration is in imitation of that published by the United Netherlands, but whether this be true or false, the liberty-loving world has for more than a century accepted it as the best protest against oppression known to political history. A great occasion conspired with a great author to make it grandly great.

Dr. Franklin, as early as July, 1775, first prepared a sketch of articles of confederation between the colonies, to continue until their reconciliation with Great Britain, and in failure thereof to be perpetual. John Quincy Adams says this plan was never discussed in Congress. June 11, 1776, a committee was appointed to prepare the force of a colonial confederation, and the day following one member from each colony was appointed to perform the duty. The report was submitted, laid aside August 20, 1776, taken up April 7,

1777, and debated from time to time until November 15th, of the same year, when the report was agreed to. It was then submitted to the legislatures of the several states, these being advised to authorize their delegates in Congress to ratify the same. On the 26th of June, 1778, the ratification was ordered to be engrossed and signed by the delegates. Those of New Hampshire, Massachusetts Bay, Rhode Island, Connecticut, New York, Pennsylvania, Virginia and South Carolina signed July 9th, 1778; those of North Carolina July 21st; Georgia July 24th; Jersey November 26th, same year; Delaware February 22d and May 5th, 1779. Maryland refused to ratify until the question of the conflicting claims of the Union and of the separate States to the property of the crown-lands should be adjusted. This was accomplished by the cession of the lands in dispute to the United States, and Maryland signed March 1st, 1781. On the 2d of March, Congress assembled under the new powers, and continued to act for the Confederacy until the 4th of March, 1789, the date of the organization of the government under the Federal constitution. Our political life has therefore three periods, "the revolutionary government," "the confederation," and that of the "federal constitution," which still obtains.

The federal constitution is the result of the labors of a convention called at Philadelphia in May, 1787, at a time when it was feared by many that the Union was in the greatest danger, from inability to pay soldiers who had, in 1783, been disbanded on a declaration of peace and an acknowledgment of independence; from prostration of the public credit and faith of the nation; from the neglect to provide for the payment of even the interest on the public debt; and from the disappointed hopes of many who thought freedom did not need to face responsibilities. A large portion of the convention of 1787 still clung to the confederacy of the states, and advocated as a substitute for the constitution a revival of the old articles of confederation with additional powers to Congress. A long discussion followed, and a most able one, but a constitution for the people, embodying a division of legislative, judicial and executive powers prevailed, and the result is now daily witnessed in the federal constitution. While the revolutionary war lasted but seven years, the political revolution incident to, identified with and directing it, lasted thirteen years. This was completed on the 30th of April, 1789, the day on which Washington was inaugurated as the first President under the federal constitution.

The Particularists.

As questions of government were evolved by the struggles for independence, the Whigs, who of course greatly outnumbered all others during the Revolution, naturally divided in sentiment, though their divisions were not sufficiently serious to excite the establishment of rival parties—something which the great majority of our forefathers were too wise to think of in time of war. When the war closed, however, and the question of establishing the Union was brought clear to the view of all, one class of the Whigs believed that state government should be supreme, and that no central power should have sufficient authority to coerce a state, or keep it to the compact against its will. All accepted the idea of a central government; all realized the necessity of union, but the fear that the states would lose their power, or surrender their independence was very great, and this fear was more naturally shown by both the larger and the smaller states. This class of thinkers were then called Particularists. Their views were opposed by the

Strong Government Whigs

who argued that local self-government was inadequate to the establishment and perpetuation of political freedom, and that it afforded little or no power to successfully resist foreign invasion. Some of these went so far as to favor a government patterned after that of England, save that it should be republican in name and spirit. The essential differences, if they can be reduced to two sentences, were these: The Particularist Whigs desired a government republican in form and democratic in spirit, with rights of local self-government and state rights ever uppermost. The Strong Government Whigs desired a government republican in form, with checks upon the impulses or passions of the people; liberty, sternly regulated by law, and that law strengthened and confirmed by central authority—the authority of the national government to be final in appeals.

As we have stated, the weakness of the confederation was acknowledged by many men, and the majority, as it proved to be after much agitation and discussion thought it too imperfect to amend. The power of the confederacy was not acknowledged by the states, its congress not respected by the people. Its requisitions were disregarded, foreign trade could not be successfully regulated; foreign nations refused to bind themselves by commercial treaties, and there was a rapid growth of very dangerous business rivalries and jealousies between the several states. Those which were fortunate enough, independent of congress, to possess or secure ports for domestic or foreign commerce, taxed the imports of their sister states. There was confusion which must soon have approached violence, for no authority beyond the limits of the state was respected, and Congress was notably powerless in its attempts to command aid from the states to meet the payment of the war debt, or the interest thereon. Instead of general respect for there was almost general disregard of law on the part of legislative bodies, and the people were not slow in imitating their representatives. Civil strife became imminent, and Shay's Rebellion in Massachusetts was the first warlike manifestation of the spirit which was abroad in the land.

Alive to the new dangers, the Assembly of Virginia in 1786, appointed commissioners to invite all the states to take part in a convention for the consideration of questions of commerce, and the propriety of altering the Articles of Confederation. This convention met at Annapolis, Sept. 11th, 1786. But five states sent representatives, the others regarding the movement with jealousy. This convention, however, adopted a report which urged the appointment of commissioners by all the states, "to devise such other provisions as shall, to them seem necessary to render the condition of the Federal government adequate to the exigencies of the Union; and to report such an act for that purpose to the United States in Congress assembled, as, when agreed to by them and afterwards confirmed by the legislatures of every state, will effectually provide for the same." Congress approved this action, and passed resolutions favoring a meeting in convention for the "sole and express purpose of revising the Articles of Confederation, and report to Congress and the State legislatures." The convention met in Philadelphia in May, 1787, and continued its sessions until September 17th, of the same year. The Strong Government Whigs had previously made every possible effort for a full and able representation, and the result did not disappoint them, for instead of simply revising the Articles of Confederation, the convention framed a constitution, and sent it to Congress to be submitted to that body and through it to the several legislatures. The act submitting it provided that, if it should be ratified by nine of the thirteen states, it should be binding upon those ratifying the same. Just here was started the custom which has since passed into law, that amendments to the national constitution shall be submitted after approval by Congress, to the legislatures of the several states, and after approval by three-fourths thereof, it shall be binding *upon all*—a very proper exercise of constitutional authority, as it seems now, but which would not have won popular approval when Virginia proposed the Annapolis convention in 1786. Indeed, the reader of our political history must ever be impressed with the fact that changes and reforms ever moved slowly, and that those of slowest growth seem to abide the longest.

The Federal and Anti-Federal Parties.

The Strong Government Whigs, on the submission of the constitution of 1787 to Congress and the legislatures, and indirectly through the latter to the people, who elect the members on this issue, became the Federal party, and all of its power was used to promote the ratification of the instrument. Its ablest men, headed by Alexander Hamilton and James Madison, advocated adoption before the people, and their pens supplied much of the current political literature of that day. Eighty-five essays, still noted and quoted for their ability, under the *nom de plume* of "Publius," were published in "The Federalist." They were written by Hamilton, Madison and Jay, and with irresistible force advocated the Federal constitution, which was ratified by the nine needed states, and Congress was officially informed of the fact July 2d, 1788, and the first Wednesday in March, 1789, was fixed as the time "for commencing proceedings under the constitution."

This struggle for the first time gave the Federalists an admitted majority. The complexion of the State legislature prior to it showed them in fact to be in a minority, and the Particularist Whigs, or Anti-Federals opposed every preliminary step looking to the abandonment of the Articles of Confederation and the adoption of a Federal constitution. They were called Anti-Federals because they opposed a federal government and constitution and adhered to the rights of the States and those of local self-government. Doubtless party rancor, then as now, led men to oppose a system of government which it seems they must have approved after fighting for it, but the earlier jealousies of the States and the prevailing ideas of liberty certainly gave the Anti-Federals a popularity which only a test so sensible as that proposed could have shaken. They were not without popular orators and leaders. Patrick Henry, the earliest of the patriots, and "the-old-man-eloquent," Samuel Adams, took special pride in espousing their cause. The war questions between Whig and Tory must have passed quickly away, as living issues, though the newspapers and contemporaneous history show that the old taunts and battle cries were applied to the new situation with a plainness and virulence that must still be envied by the sensational and more bitterly partisan journals of our own day. To read these now, and some of our facts are gath ered from such sources, is to account for the frequent use of the saying touching "the ingratitude of republics," for when partisan hatred could deride the still recent utterances of Henry before the startled assembly of Virginians, and of Adams in advocating the adoption of the Declaration, there must at least to every surface view have been rank ingratitude. Their good names, however, survived the struggle, as good names in our republic have ever survived the passions of the law. In politics the Americans then as now, hated with promptness and forgave with generosity.

The Anti-Federals denied nearly all that the Federals asserted. The latter had for the first time assumed the aggressive, and had the advantage of position. They showed the deplorable condition of the country, and their opponents had to bear the burdens of denial at a time when nearly all public and private obligations were dishonored; when labor was poorly paid, workmen getting but twenty-five cents a day, with little to do at that; when even the rich in lands were poor in purse, and when commerce on the seas was checked by the coldness of foreign nations and restricted by the action of the States themselves; when manufactures were without protection of any kind, and when the people thought their struggle for freedom was about to end in national poverty Still Henry, and Adams and Hancock, with hosts of others, claimed that the aspirations of the Anti-Federals were the freest, that they pointed to personal liberty and local sovereignty Yet many Anti-Federals must have accepted the views of the Federals, who under the circumstances must have presented the better reason, and the result was as stated, the ratification of the Federal constitution of 1787 by three-fourths of the States of the Union. After this the Anti-Federalists were given a new name, that of "Close Constructionists," because they naturally desired to interpret the new instrument in such a way as to bend it to their views. The Federalists became "Broad Constructionists," because they interpreted the constitution in a way calculated to broaden the power of the national government.

The Confederacy once dissolved, the Federal party entered upon the enjoyment of full political power, but it was not without its responsibilities. The government had to be organized upon the basis of the new constitution, as upon the success of that organization would depend not alone the stability of the government and the happiness of its people, but the reputation of the party and the fame of its leaders as statesmen.

Fortunately for all, party hostilities were not manifested in the Presidential election. All bowed to the popularity of Washington, and he was unanimously nominated by the congressional caucus and appointed by the electoral college He selected his cabinet from the leading minds of both parties, and while himself a recognized Federalist, all felt that he was acting for the good of all, and in the earlier years of his administration, none disputed this fact.

As the new measures of the government advanced, however, the anti-federalists organized an opposition to the party in power. Immediate danger had passed. The constitution worked well. The laws of Congress were respected; its calls for revenue honored, and Washington devoted much of his first and second messages to showing the growing prosperity of the country, and the respect which it was beginning to excite abroad. But where there is political power, there is opposition in a free land, and the great leaders of that day neither forfeited their reputations as patriots, or their characters as statesmen by the assertion of honest differences of opinion. Washington, Adams, and Hamilton were the recognized leaders of the Federalists, the firm friends of the constitution. The success of this instrument modified the views of the anti-Federalists, and Madison of Virginia, its recognized friend when it was in preparation, joined with others who had been its friends—notably,* Doctor Williamson, of North Carolina, and Mr. Langdon, of Georgia, in opposing the administration, and soon became recognized leaders of the anti-Federalists. Langdon was the President *pro tem.* of the Senate. Jefferson was then on a mission to France, and not until some years thereafter did he array himself with those opposed to centralized power in the nation. He returned in November, 1789, and was called to Washington's cabinet as Secretary of State in March, 1790. It was a great cabinet, with Jefferson as its premier (if this term is suited to a time when English political nomenclature was anything but popular in the land;) Hamilton, Secretary of the Treasury; Knox, Secretary of War, and Edmund Randolph, Attorney-General. There was no Secretary of the Navy until the administration of the elder Adams, and no Secretary of the Interior.

The first session of Congress under the Federal constitution, held in New York, sat for nearly six months, the adjournment taking place September 29th, 1789. Nearly all the laws framed pointed to the organization of the government, and the discussions were able and protracted. Indeed, these discussions developed opposing views, which could easily find separation on much the same old lines as those which separated the founders of constitutional government

* Edwin Williams in Statesman's Manual.

from those who favored the old confederate methods. The Federalists, on pivotal questions, at this session, carried their measures only by small majorities.

Much of the second session was devoted to the discussion of the able reports of Hamilton, and their final adoption did much to build up the credit of the nation and to promote its industries. He was the author of the protective system, and at the first session gave definite shape to his theories. He recommended the funding of the war debt the assumption of the state war debts by the national government, the providing of a system of revenue from the collection of duties on imports, and an internal excise. His advocacy of a protective tariff was plain, for he declared it to be necessary for the support of the government and *the encouragement of manufactures* that duties be laid on goods, wares, and merchandise imported.

The third session of the same Congress was held at Philadelphia, though the seat of the national government had, at the previous one, been fixed on the Potomac instead of the Susquehanna—this after a compromise with Southern members, who refused to vote for the Assumption Bill until the location of the capital in the District of Columbia had been agreed upon; by the way this was the first exhibition of log-rolling in Congress. To complete Hamilton's financial system, a national bank was incorporated. On this project both the members of Congress and of the cabinet were divided, but it passed, and was promptly approved by Washington. By this time it was well known that Jefferson and Hamilton held opposing views on many questions of government, and these found their way into and influenced the action of Congress, and passed naturally from thence to the people, who were thus early believed to be almost equally divided on the more essential political issues. Before the close of the session, Vermont and Kentucky were admitted to the Union. Vermont was the first state admitted in addition to the original thirteen. True, North Carolina and Rhode Island had rejected the constitution, but they reconsidered their action and came in—the former in November, 1789, and the latter in May, 1790.

The election for members of the Second Congress resulted in a majority in both branches favorable to the administration. It met at Philadelphia in October, 1791. The exciting measure of the session was the excise act, somewhat similar to that of the previous year, but the opposition wanted an issue on which to rally, they accepted this, and this agitation led to violent and in one instance warlike opposition on the part of a portion of the people. Those of western Pennsylvania, largely interested in distilleries, prepared for armed resistance to the excise, but at the same session a national militia law had been passed, and Washington took advantage of this to suppress the "Whisky Rebellion" in its incipiency. It was a hasty, rash undertaking, yet was dealt with so firmly that the action of the authorities strengthened the law, and the respect for order. The four counties which rebelled did no further damage than to tar and feather a government tax collector and rob him of his horse, though many threats were made and the agitation continued until 1794, when Washington's threatened appearance at the head of fifteen thousand militia settled the whole question.

The first session of the Second Congress also passed the first methodic apportionment bill, which based the congressional representation on the census taken in 1790, the basis being 33,000 inhabitants for each representative. The second session which sat from November, 1792, to March, 1793, was mainly occupied in a discussion of the foreign and domestic relations of the country. No important measures were adopted.

The Republican and Federal Parties.

The most serious objection to the constitution before its ratification was the absence of a distinct bill of rights, which should recognize "the equality of all men, and their rights to life, liberty and the pursuit of happiness," and at the first session of Congress a bill was framed containing twelve articles, ten of which were afterwards ratified as amendments to the constitution. Yet state sovereignty, then imperfectly defined, was the prevailing idea in the minds of the Anti-Federalists, and they took every opportunity to oppose any extended delegation of authority from the states of the Union. They contended that the power of the state should be supreme, and charged the Federalists with monarchical tendencies. They opposed Hamilton's national bank scheme, and Jefferson and Randolph plainly expressed the opinion that it was unconstitutional—that a bank was not authorized by the constitution, and that it would prevent the states from maintaining banks. But when the Bill of Rights had been incorporated in and attached to the constitution as amendments, Jefferson with rare political sagacity withdrew all opposition to the instrument itself, and the Anti-Federalists gladly followed his lead, for they felt that they had labored under many partisan disadvantages. The constitution was from the first too strong for successful resistance, and when opposition was confessedly abandoned the party name was changed, also at the suggestion of Jefferson, to that of Republican. The Anti-Federalists were at first disposed to call their party the Democratic-Republicans, but finally called it simply Republican, to avoid the opposite of the extreme which they charged against the Federalists. Each party had its taunts in use, the Federalists being denounced as monarchists, the Anti-Federalists as Democrats; the one presumed to be looking forward to monarchy, the other to the rule of the mob.

By 1793 partisan lines under the names of Federalists and Republicans, were plainly drawn, and the schism in the cabinet was more marked than ever. Personal ambition may have had much to do with it, for Washington had previously shown his desire to retire to private life. While he remained at the head of affairs he was unwilling to part with Jefferson and Hamilton, and did all in his power to bring about a reconciliation, but without success. Before the close of the first constitutional Presidency, however, Washington had become convinced that the people desired him to accept a re-election, and he was accordingly a candidate and unanimously chosen. John Adams was re-elected Vice-President, receiving 77 votes to 50 for Geo. Clinton, (5 scattering) the Republican candidate. Soon after the inauguration Citizen Genet, an envoy from the French republic, arrived and sought to excite the sympathy of the United States and involve it in a war with Great Britain. Jefferson and his Republican party warmly sympathized with France, and insisted that gratitude for revolutionary favors commanded aid to France in her struggles. The Federalists, under Washington and Hamilton. favored non-intervention, and insisted that we should maintain friendly relations with Great Britain. Washington showed his usual firmness, and before the expiration of the month in which Genet arrived, had issued his celebrated proclamation of neutrality. This has ever since been the accepted foreign policy of the nation.

Genet, chagrined at the issuance of this proclamation, threatened to appeal to the people, and made himself so obnoxious to Washington that the latter demanded his recall. The French government sent M. Fauchet as his successor, but Genet continued to reside in the United States, and under his inspiration a number of Democratic Societies, in imitation of the French Jacobin clubs, were founded, but like all such organizations in this country, they were short-lived. Secret political societies thrive only under despotisms. In Republics like ours they can only live when the great parties are in confusion and greatly divided. They disappear with the union of sentiment into two great parties. If there were many parties and factions, as in Mexico and some of the South American republics, there would be even a wider field for them here than there.

The French agitation showed its impress upon the nation as late as 1794, when a resolution to cut off intercourse with Great Britain passed the House, and was defeated in the Senate only by the casting vote of the Vice-President. Many people favored France, and to such silly heights did the excitement run that these insisted on wearing a national cockade. Jefferson had left the cabinet the December previous, and had retired to his plantation in Virginia, where he spent his leisure in writing political essays and organizing the Republican party, of which he was the acknowledged founder. Here he escaped the errors of his party in Congress, but it was a potent fact that his friends in official station not only did not endorse the non-intervention policy of Washington, but that they actively antagonized it in many ways. The Congressional leader in these movements was Mr. Madison. The policy of Britain fed this opposition. The forts on Lake Erie were still occupied by the British soldiery in defiance of the treaty of 1783; American vessels were seized on their way to French ports, and American citizens were impressed. To avoid a war, Washington sent John Jay as special envoy to England. He arrived in June, 1794, and by November succeeded in making a treaty It was ratified in June, 1795, by the Senate by the constitutional majority of two-thirds, though there was much declamatory opposition, and the feeling between the Federal and Republican parties ran higher than ever before. The Republicans denounced while the Federals congratulated Washington. Under this treaty the British surrendered possession of all American ports, and as Gen'l Wayne during the previous summer had conquered the war-tribes and completed a treaty with them, the country was again on the road to prosperity

In Washington's message of 1794, he plainly censured all "self-created political societies," meaning the democratic societies formed by Genet, but this part of the message the House refused to endorse, the speaker giving the casting vote in the negative. The Senate was in harmony with the political views of the President. Party spirit had by this time measurably affected all classes of the people, and as subjects for agitation here multiplied, the opposition no longer regarded Washington with that respect and decorum which it had been the rule to manifest. His wisdom as President, his patriotism, and indeed his character as a man, were all hotly questioned by political enemies. He was even charged with corruption in expending more of the public moneys than had been appropriated—charges which were soon shown to be groundless.

At the first session of Congress in December, 1795, the Senate's administration majority had increased, but in the House the opposing Republicans had also increased their numbers. The Senate by 14 to 8 endorsed the message; the House at first refused but finally qualified its answers.

In March, 1796, a new political issue was sprung in the House by Mr. Livingstone of New York, who offered a resolution requesting of the President a copy of the instructions to Mr. Jay, the envoy who made the treaty with Great Britain. After a debate of several days, more bitter than any which had preceded it, the House passed the resolution by 57 to 35, the Republicans voting aye, the Federals no. Washington in answer, took the position that the House of Representatives was not part of the treaty-making power of the government, and could not therefore be entitled to any papers relating to such treaties. The constitution had placed this treaty making and ratifying power in the hands of the Senate, the Cabinet and the President.

This answer, now universally accepted as the proper one, yet excited the House and increased political animosities. The Republicans charged the Federals with being the "British party," and in some instances hinted that they had been purchased with British gold. Indignation meetings were called, but after much sound and fury, it was ascertained that the people really favored abiding by the treaty in good faith, and finally the House, after more calm and able debates, passed the needed legislation to carry out the treaty by a vote of 51 to 48.

In August, 1796, prior to the meeting of the Congressional caucus which then placed candidates for the Presidency in nomination, Washington issued his celebrated Farewell Address, in which he gave notice that he would retire from public life at the expiration of his term. He had been solicited to be a candidate for reelection (a third term) and told that all the people could unite upon him—a statement which, without abating one jot, our admiration for the man, would doubtless have been called in question by the Republicans, who had become implacably hostile to his political views, and who were encouraged to believe they could win control of the Presidency, by their rapidly increasing power in the House. Yet the address was everywhere received with marks of admiration. Legislatures commended it by resolution and ordered it to be engrossed upon their records; journals praised it, and upon the strength of its plain doctrines the Federalists took new courage, and prepared to win in the Presidential battle which followed. Both parties were plainly arrayed and confident, and so close was the result that the leaders of both were elected—John Adams, the nominee of the Federalists, to the Presidency, and Thomas Jefferson, the nominee of the Republicans, to the Vice-Presidency. The law which then obtained was that the candidate who received the highest number of electoral votes, took the first place, the next highest, the second. Thomas Pinckney of South Carolina was the Federal nominee for Vice-President, and Aaron Burr of the Republicans. Adams received 71 electoral votes, Jefferson 68, Pinckney 59, Burr 30, scattering 48. Pinckney had lost 12 votes, while Burr lost 38—a loss of popularity which the latter regained four years later. The first impressions which our forefathers had of this man were the best.

John Adams was inaugurated as President in Philadelphia, at Congress Hall, March 4th, 1797, and in his inaugural was careful to deny the charge that the Federal party had any sympathy for England, but reaffirmed his endorsement of the policy of Washington as to strict neutrality. To this extent he sought to soften the asperities of the parties, and measurably succeeded, though the times were still stormy The French revolution had reached its highest point, and our people still took sides. Adams found he would have to arm to preserve neutrality and at the same time punish the aggression of either of the combatants. This was our first exhibition of "armed neutrality." An American navy was quickly raised, and every preparation made for defending the rights of Americans. An alliance with France was refused, after which the American Minister was dismissed and the French navy began to cripple our trade. In May, 1797, President Adams felt it his duty to call an extra session of Congress, which closed in July. The Senate approved of negotiations for reconciliation with France. They were attempted but proved fruitless in May, 1798, a full naval armament was authorized, and soon several French vessels were captured before there was any declaration of war. Indeed, neither power declared war, and as soon as France discovered how earnest the Americans were she made overtures for an adjustment of difficulties, and these resulted in the treaty of 1800.

The Republicans, though warmly favoring a contest, did not heartily support that inaugurated by Adams, and contended after this that the militia and a small naval force were sufficient for internal defense. They denounced the position of the Federals, who favored the enlargement of the army and navy, as measures calculated to overawe public sentiment in time of peace. The Federals, however, through their prompt resentment of the aggressions of France, had many adherents to their party. They organized their power and sought to perpetuate it by the passage of the alien and sedition, and a naturalization law.

The alien and sedition law gave the President authority "to order all such aliens as he shall judge dangerous to the peace and safety of the United States, or shall have reasonable grounds to suspect are concerned in any treasonable or secret machinations against the government thereof, to depart out of the territory of the United States, within such time as shall be expressed in such order." The provisions which followed were in keeping with that quoted, the 3d section commanding every master of a ship entering a port of the United States, immediately on his arrival, to make report in writing to the collector of customs, the names of all aliens on board, etc. The act was to continue in force for two years from the date of its passage, and it was approved June 25th, 1798.

A resolution was introduced in the Senate on the 25th of April, 1798, by Mr. Hillhouse of Connecticut, to inquire what provision of law ought to be made, &c., as to the removal of such aliens as may be dangerous to the peace of the country, &c. This resolution was adopted the next day, and Messrs. Hillhouse, Livermore and Read were appointed the committee, and subsequently reported the bill. It passed the Senate by 16 to 7, and the House by 46 to 40, the Republicans in the latter body resisting it warmly. The leading opposing idea was that it lodged with the Executive too much power, and was liable to great abuse. It has frequently since, in arguments against centralized power, been used for illustration by political speakers.

The Naturalization law, favored by the Federalists, because they knew they could acquire few friends either from newly arrived English or French aliens, among other requirements provided that an alien must reside in the United States *fourteen years* before he could vote. The Republicans denounced this law as calculated to check immigration, and dangerous to our country in the fact that it caused too many inhabitants to owe no allegiance. They also asserted, as did those who opposed Americanism later on in our history, that America was properly an asylum for all nations, and that those coming to America should freely share all the privileges and liberties of the government.

These laws and the political resentments which they created gave a new and what eventually proved a dangerous current to political thought and action. They were the immediate cause of the Kentucky and Virginia resolutions of 1798, Jefferson being the author of the former and Madison of the latter.

These resolutions were full of political significance, and gave tone to sectional discussion up to the close of the war for the Union. They first promulgated the doctrine of nullification or secession, and political writers mistake who point to Calhoun as the father of that doctrine. It began with the old Republicans under the leadership of Jefferson and Madison, and though directly intended as protests against the alien and sedition, and the naturalization laws of Congress, they kept one eye upon the question of slavery—rather that interest was kept in view in their declarations, and yet the authors of both were anything but warm advocates of slavery. They were then striving, however, to reinforce the opposition to the Federal party, which the administration of Adams had thus far apparently weakened, and they had in view the brief agitation which had sprung up in 1793, five years before, on the petition to Congress of a Pennsylvania society "to use its powers to stop the traffic in slaves." On the question of referring this petition to a committee there arose a sectional debate. Men took sides not because of the party to which they belonged, but the section, and for the first time the North and South were arrayed against each other on a question not then treated either as partisan or political, but which most minds then saw must soon become both partisan and sectional. Some of the Southern debaters, in their protests against interference, thus early threatened civil war. With a view to better protect their rights to slave property, they then advocated and succeeded in passing the first fugitive slave law. This was approved February 12, 1793.

The resolutions of 1798 will be found in the book devoted to political platforms. So highly were these esteemed by the Republicans of that day, and by the interests whose support they so shrewdly invited, that they more than counterbalanced the popularity acquired by the Federals in their resistance to France, and by 1800 they caused a rupture in the Cabinet of Adams.

In the Presidential election of 1800 John Adams was the nominee for President and C. C. Pinckney for Vice-President. A "Congressional Convention" of Republicans, held in Philadelphia, nominated Thomas Jefferson and Aaron Burr as candidates for these offices. On the election which followed the Republicans chose 73 electors and the Federalists 65. Each elector voted for two persons, and the Republicans so voted that they unwisely gave Jefferson and Burr each 73 votes. Neither being highest, it was not legally determined which should be President or Vice-President, and the election had to go to the House. The Federalists threw 65 votes to Adams and 64 to Pinckney. The Republicans could have done the same, but Burr's intrigue and ambition prevented this, and the result was a protracted contest in the House, and one which put the country in great peril, but which plainly pointed out some of the imperfections of the electoral features of the Constitution. The Federalists proposed to confess the inability of the House to agree through the vote by States, but to this proposition the Republicans threatened armed resistance. The Federalists next attempted a combination with the friends of Aaron Burr, but this specimen of bargaining to deprive a nominee of the place to which it was the plain intention of his party to elect him, really contributed to Jefferson's popularity, if not in that Congress, certainly before the people. He was elected on the 36th ballot.

The bitterness of this strife, and the dangers which similar ones threatened, led to an abandonment of the system of each Elector voting for two, the highest to be President, the next highest Vice-President, and an amendment was offered to the Constitution, and fully ratified by September 25, 1804, requiring the electors to ballot separately for President and Vice-President.

Jefferson was the first candidate nominated by a Congressional caucus. It convened in 1800 at Philadelphia, and nominated Jefferson for President and Burr for Vice-President. Adams and Pinckney were not nominated, but ran and were accepted as natural leaders of their party, just as Washington and Adams were before them.

Downfall of the Federal Party.

This contest broke the power of the Federal party It had before relied upon the rare sagacity and ability of its leaders, but the contest in the House developed such attempts at intrigue as disgusted many and caused all to quarrel, Hamilton having early showed his dislike to Adams. As a party the Federal had been peculiarly brave at times when high bravery was needed. It had framed the Federal Government and stood by the powers given it until they were too firmly planted for even newer and triumphant partisans to recklessly trifle with. It stood for non-interference with foreign nations against the eloquence of adventurers, the mad impulses of mobs, the generosity of new-born freemen, the harangues of demagogues, and best of all against those who sought to fan these popular breezes to their own comfort. It provided for the payment of the debt, had the courage to raise revenues both from internal and external sources, and to increase expenditures, as the growth of the country demanded. Though it passed out of power in a cloud of intrigue and in a vain grasp at the "flesh-pots," it yet had a glorious history, and one which none untinctured with the better prejudices of that day, can avoid admiring.

The defeat of Adams was not unexpected by him, yet it was greatly regretted by his friends, for he was justly regarded as second to no other civilian in the establishment of the liberties of the colonies. He was eloquent to a rare degree, possessed natural eloquence, and made the most famous speech in advocacy of the Declaration. Though the proceedings of the Revolutionary Congress were secret, and what was said never printed, yet Webster gives his version of the noted speech of Adams, and we reproduce it in Book III. of this volume as one of the great speeches of noted American orators.

Mr. Jefferson was inaugurated the third President, in the new capitol at Washington, on the 4th of March, 1801, and Vice-President Burr took his seat in the Senate the same day Though Burr distinctly disavowed any participancy in the House contest, he was distrusted by Jefferson's warm friends, and jealousies rapidly cropped out. Jefferson endeavored through his inaugural to smooth factious and party asperities, and so well were his words chosen that the Federalists indulged, the hope that they would not be removed from office because of their political views.

Early in June, however, the first question of civil service was raised. Mr. Jefferson then removed Elizur Goodrich, a Federalist, from the Collectorship of New Haven, and appointed Samuel Bishop, a Republican, to the place. The citizens remonstrated, saying that Goodrich was prompt, reliable and able, and showed that his successor was 78 years old, and too infirm for the duties of the office. To these remonstrances Mr. Jefferson, under date of July 12th, replied in language which did not then, as he did later on, plainly assert the right of every administration to have its friends in office. We quote the following:

"Declarations by myself, in favor of political tolerance, exhortations to harmony and affection in social intercourse, and respect for the equal rights of the minority, have, on certain occasions, been quoted and misconstrued into assurances that the tenure of office was not to be disturbed. But could candor apply such a construction? When it is considered that, during the late administration, those who were not of a particular sect of politics were excluded from all office; when, by a steady pursuit of this measure, nearly the whole offices of the United States were monopolized by that sect; when the public sentiment at length declared itself, and burst open the doors of honor and confidence to those whose opinions they approved; was it to be imagined that this monopoly of office was to be continued in the hands of the minority? Does it violate their equal rights to assert some rights in the majority also? Is it political intolerance to claim a proportionate share in the direction of the public affairs? If a due participation of office is a matter of right, how are vacancies to be obtained? Those by death are few, by resignation none. Can any other mode than that of removal be proposed? This is a painful office; but it is made my duty, and I meet it as such. I proceed in the operation with deliberation and inquiry, that it may injure the best men least, and effect the purposes of justice and public utility with the least private distress, that it may be thrown as much as possible on delinquency, on oppression, on intolerance, on ante-revolutionary adherence to our enemies.

"I lament sincerely that unessential differences of opinion should ever have been deemed sufficient to interdict half the society from the rights and the blessings of self-government, to proscribe them as unworthy of every trust. It would have been to me a circumstance of great relief, had I found a moderate participation of office in the hands of the majority. I would gladly have left to time and accident to raise them to their just share. But their total exclusion calls for prompter corrections. I shall correct the procedure; but that done, return with joy to that state of things when the only questions concerning a candidate shall be: Is he honest? Is he capable? Is he faithful to the constitution?"

Mr. Adams had made few removals, and none because of the political views held by the incumbents, nearly all of whom had been appointed by Washington and continued through good behavior. At the date of the appointment of most of them, Jefferson's Republican party had no existence; so that the reasons given in the quotation do not comport with the facts. Washington's rule was integrity and capacity, for he could have no regard for politics where political lines had been obliterated in his own selection. Doubtless these office-holders were human, and adhered with warmth to the administration which they served, and this fact, and this alone, must have angered the Republicans and furnished them with arguments for a change.

Mr. Jefferson's position, however, made his later conduct natural. He was the acknowledged leader of his party, its founder indeed, and that party had carried him into power. He desired to keep it intact, to strengthen its lines with whatever patronage he had at his disposal, and he evidently regarded the cause of Adams in not rewarding his friends as a mistake. It was, therefore, Jefferson, and not Jackson, who was the author of the theory that "to the victors belong the spoils." Jackson gave it a sharp and perfectly defined shape by the use of these words, but the spirit and principle were conceived by Jefferson, who throughout his life showed far greater originality in politics than any of the early patriots. It was his acute sense of just what was right for a growing political party to do, which led him to turn the thoughts of his followers into new and popular directions. Seeing that they were at grave disadvantage when opposing the attitude of the government in its policy with foreign nations; realizing that the work of the Federalists in strengthening the power of the new government, in providing revenues and ways and means for the payment of the debt, were good, he changed the character of the opposition by selecting only notoriously arbitrary measures for assault—and changed it even more radically than this. He early saw that simple opposition was not progress, and that it was both wise and popular to be progressive, and in all his later political papers he sought to make his party the party favoring personal freedom, the one of liberal ideas, the one which, instead of shirking, should anticipate every change calculated to enlarge the liberties and the opportunities of citizens. These things were not inconsistent with his strong views in favor of local self-government; indeed, in many particulars they seemed to support that theory, and by the union of the two ideas he shrewdly arrayed political enthusiasm by the side of political interest. Political sagacity more profound than this it is difficult to imagine. It has not since been equalled in the history of our land, nor do we believe in the history of any other.

After the New Haven episode, so jealous was Jefferson of his good name, that while he confided all new appointments to the hands of his political friends, he made few removals, and these for apparent cause. The mere statement of his position had proved an invitation to the Federalists in office to join his earlier friends in the support of his administration. Many of them did it, so many that the clamorings of truer friends could not be hushed. With a view to create a new excuse, Jefferson declared that all appointments made by Adams after February 14th, when the House began its ballotings for President, were void, these appointments belonging of right to him, and from this act of Adams we date the political legacies which some of our Presidents have since handed down to their successors. One of the magistrates whose commission had been made out under Adams, sought to compel Jefferson to sign it by a writ of mandamus before the Supreme Court, but a "profound investigation of constitutional law" induced the court not to grant the motion. All commissions signed by Adams after the date named were suppressed.

Jefferson's apparent bitterness against the Federalists is mainly traceable to the contest in the House, and his belief that at one time they sought a coalition with Burr. This coalition he regarded as a violation of the understanding when he was nominated, and a supposed effort to appoint a provisional office he regarded as an usurpation in fact. In a letter to James Monroe, dated February 15th, speaking of this contest, he says:

"Four days of balloting have produced not a single change of a vote. Yet it is confidently believed that to-morrow there is to be a coalition. I know of no foundation for this belief. If they could have been permitted to pass a law for putting the government in the hands of an officer, they would certainly have prevented an election. But we thought it best to declare openly and firmly, one and all, that the day such an act passed, the Middle States would arm, and that no such usurpation, even for a single day, should be submitted to."

It is but fair to say that the Federalists denied all such intentions, and that James A. Bayard, of Delaware, April 3, 1806, made formal oath to this denial. In this he says that three States, representing Federalist votes, offered to withdraw their opposition if John Nicholas, of Virginia, and the personal friend of Jefferson, would secure pledges that the public credit should be supported, the navy maintained, and that subordinate public officers, employed only in the execution of details, established by law, should not be removed from office on the ground of their public character, nor without complaint against their conduct. The Federalists then went so far as to admit that officers of "high discretion and confidence," such as members of the cabinet and foreign ministers, should be known friends of the administration. This proposition goes to show that there is nothing very new in what are called our modern politics; that the elder Bayard, as early as 1800, made a formal proposal to bargain. Mr. Nicholas offered *his* assurance that these things would prove acceptable to and govern the conduct of Jefferson's administration, but he declined to consult with Jefferson on the points. General Smith subsequently engaged to do it, and Jefferson replied that the points given corresponded with his views and intentions, and that Mr. Bayard and his friends might confide in him accordingly. The opposition of Vermont, Maryland and Delaware was then immediately withdrawn, and Mr Jefferson was made President. Gen'l Smith, twelve days later, made an affidavit which substantially confirmed that of Bayard. Latimer, the collector of the port of Philadelphia, and M'Lane, collector of Wilmington, (Bayard's special friend) were retained in office. He had cited these two as examples of his opposition to any change, and Jefferson seemed to regard the pledges as not sacred beyond the parties actually named in Bayard's negotiations with Gen'l Smith.

This misunderstanding or misconstruction of what in these days would be plainly called a bargain, led to considerable political criticism, and Jefferson felt it necessary to defend his cause. This he did in letters to friends which both then and since found their way into the public prints. One of these letters, written to Col. Monroe, March 7th, shows in every word and line the natural politician. In this he says:

"Some (removals) I know must be made. They must be as few as possible, done gradually, and bottomed on some malversation or inherent disqualification. Where we shall draw the line between all and none, is not yet settled, and will not be till we get our administration together; and perhaps even then we shall proceed *ā talons*, balancing our measures according to the impression we perceive them to make. This may give you a general view of our plan."

A little later on, March 28, he wrote to Elbridge Gerry:

"Officers who have been guilty of gross abuses of office, such as marshals packing juries, etc., I shall now remove, as my predecessor ought in justice to have done. The instances will be few, and governed by strict rule, not party passion. The right of opinion shall suffer no invasion from me."

Jefferson evidently tired of this subject, and gradually modified his views, as shown in his letter to Levi Lincoln, July 11, wherein he says:

"I am satisfied that the heaping of abuse on me personally, has been with the design and the hope of provoking me to make a general sweep of all Federalists out of office. But as I have carried no passion into the execution of this disagreeable duty, I shall suffer none to be excited. The clamor which has been raised will not provoke me to remove one more, nor deter me from removing one less, than if not a word had been said on the subject. In the course of the summer, all which is necessary will be done; and we may hope that, this cause of offence being at an end, the measures we shall pursue and propose for the amelioration of the public affairs, will be so confessedly salutary as to unite all men not monarchists in principle." In the same letter he warmly berates the monarchical federalists, saying, "they are incurables, to be taken care of in a madhouse if necessary, and on motives of charity."

The seventh Congress assembled. Political parties were at first nearly equally divided in the Senate, but eventually there was a majority for the administration. Jefferson then discontinued the custom established by Washington of delivering in person his message to Congress. The change was greatly for the better, as it afforded relief from the requirement of immediate answers on the subjects contained in the message. It has ever since been followed.

The seventh session of Congress, pursuant to the recommendation of President Jefferson, established a uniform system of naturalization, and so modified the law as to make the required residence of aliens five years, instead of fourteen, as in the act of 1798, and to permit a declaration of intention to become a citizen at the expiration of three years. By his recommendation also was established the first sinking fund for the redemption of the public debt. It required the setting apart annually for this purpose the sum of seven millions and three hundred thousand dollars. Other measures, more partisan in their character, were proposed, but Congress showed an aversion to undoing what had been wisely done. A favorite law of the Federalists establishing circuit courts alone was repealed, and this only after a sharp debate, and a close vote. The provisional army had been disbanded by a law of the previous Congress. A proposition to abolish the naval department was defeated, as was that to discontinue the mint establishment.

At this session the first law in relation to the slave trade was passed. It was to prevent the importation of negroes, mulattoes and other persons of color into any port of the United States within a state which had prohibited by law the admission of any such person. The penalty was one thousand dollars and the forfeiture of the vessel. The slave trade was not then prohibited by the constitution, nor was the subject then generally agitated, though it had been as early as 1793, when, as previously stated, an exciting sectional debate followed the presentation of a petition from Pennsylvania to abolish the slave trade.

Probably the most important occurrence under the first administration of Jefferson was that relating to the purchase and admission of Louisiana. There had been apprehensions of a war with Spain, and with a view to be ready Congress had passed an act authorizing the President to call upon the executives of such of the states as he might deem expedient, for detachments of militia not exceeding eighty thousand, or to accept the services of volunteers for a term of twelve months. The disagreement arose over the south-western boundary line and the right of navigating the Mississippi. Our government learned in the spring of 1802, that Spain had by a secret treaty made in October, 1800, actually ceded Louisiana to France. Our government had in 1795 made a treaty with Spain which gave us the right of deposite at New Orleans for three years, but in October, 1802, the Spanish authorities gave notice by proclamation that this right was withdrawn. Excitement followed all along the valley of the Mississippi, and it was increased by the belief that the withdrawal of the privilege was made at the suggestion of France, though Spain still retained the territory, as the formalities of ceding it had not been gone through with. Jefferson promptly took the ground that if France took possession of New Orleans, the United States would immediately become allies of England, but suggested to Minister Livingston at Paris that France might be induced to cede the island of New Orleans and the Floridas to the United States. It was his belief, though a mistaken one, that France had also acquired the Floridas. Louisiana then comprised much of the territory west of the Mississippi and south of the Missouri.

The Federalists in Congress seized upon this question as one upon which they could make an aggressive war against Jefferson's administration, and resolutions were introduced asking information on the subject. Jefferson, however, wisely avoided all entangling suggestions, and sent Monroe to aid Livingston in effecting a purchase. The treaty was formed in April, 1803, and submitted by Jefferson to the Senate in October following. The Republicans rallied in favor of this scheme of annexation, and claimed that it was a constitutional right in the government to acquire territory —a doctrine widely at variance with their previous position, but occasions are rare where parties quarrel with their administrations on pivotal measures. There was also some latitude here for endorsement, as the direct question of territorial acquisition had not before been presented, but only hypothetically stated in the constitutional disputations then in great fashion. Jefferson would not go so far as to say that the constitution warranted the acquisition to foreign territory, but the scheme was nevertheless his, and he stood in with his friends in the political battle which followed.

The Federalists claimed that we had no power to acquire territory, and that the acquirement of Louisiana would give the South a preponderance which would "continue for all time (poor prophets they!), since southern would be more rapid than northern development;" that states created west of the Mississippi would injure the commerce of New England, and they even went so far as to say that the "admission of the Western World into the Union would compel the Eastern States to establish an eastern empire," Doubts were also raised as to the right of Louisianians, when admitted to citizenship under our laws, as their lineage, language and religion were different from our own. Its inhabitants were French and descendants of French, with some Spanish creoles, Americans, English and Germans—in all about 90,000, including 40,000 slaves. There were many Indians of course, in a territory then exceeding a million of square miles—a territory which, in the language of First Consul Napoleon, "strengthens forever the power of the United States," and which will give to England a maritime rival that will sooner or later humble her pride"—a military view of the change fully justified by subsequent history. Napoleon sold because of needed preparations for war with England, and while he had previously expressed a willingness to take fifty million francs for it, he got sixty through the shrewd diplomacy of his ministers, who hid for the time their fear of the capture of the port of New Orleans by the English navy

Little chance was afforded the Federalists for adverse criticism in Congress, for the purchase proved so popular that the people greatly increased the majority in both branches of the eighth Congress, and Jefferson called it together earlier for the purpose of ratification. The Senate ratified the treaty on the 20th of October, 1803, by a vote of 24 to 7, while the House adopted a resolution for carrying the treaty into effect by a vote of 90 to 25. Eleven million dollars of the purchase money was appropriated, the remaining four millions being reserved for the indemnity of American citizens who had sustained losses by French assaults upon our commerce—from which fact subsequently came what is known as the French Spoliation Bill.

Impeachment trials were first attempted before the eighth Congress in 1803. Judge Pickering, of the district court of the United States for New Hampshire, was impeached for occasional drunkenness, and dismissed from office. Judge Chase of the U. S. Supreme Court, and Judge Peters of the district court of Pennsylvania, both Federalists, were charged by articles proposed in the House with illegal and arbitrary conduct in the trial of parties charged with political offenses. The Federalists took alarm at these proceedings, and so vehement were their charges against the Republicans of a desire to destroy the judiciary that their impeachments were finally abandoned.

The Republicans closed their first national administration with high prestige. They had met several congressional reverses on questions where defeat proved good fortune, for the Federalists kept a watchful defence, and were not always wrong. The latter suffered numerically, and many of their best leaders had fallen in the congressional contest of 1800 and 1802, while the Republicans maintained their own additions in talent and number.

In 1804, the candidates of both parties were nominated by congressional caucuses. Jefferson and Clinton were the Republican nominees; Charles C. Pinckney and Rufus King, the nominees of the Federalists, but they only received 14 out of 176 electoral votes.

The struggle of Napoleon in Europe with the allied powers now gave Jefferson an opportunity to inaugurate a foreign policy. England had forbidden all trade with the French and their allies, and France had in return forbidden all commerce with England and her colonies. Both of these decrees violated our neutral rights, and were calculated to destroy our commerce, which by this time had become quite imposing.

Congress acted promptly, and on the 21st of December passed what is known as the Embargo Act, under the inspiration of the Republican party, which claimed that the only choice of the people lay between the embargo and war, and that there was no other way to obtain redress from England and France. But the promised effects of the measure were not realized, and so soon as any dissatisfaction was manifested by the people, the Federalists made the question a political issue. They declared it unconstitutional because it was not limited as to time; that it helped England as against France (a cunning assertion in view of the early love of the Republicans for the cause of the French), and that it laid violent hands on our home commerce and industries. Political agitation increased the discontent, and public opinion at one time turned so strongly against the law that it was openly resisted on the eastern coast, and treated with almost as open contempt on the Canadian border. The bill had passed the House by 87 to 35, the Senate by 19 to 9. In January, 1809, the then closing administration of Jefferson had to change front on the question, and the law was repealed on the 18th of March. The Republicans when they changed, went all the way over, and advocated full protection by the use of a navy, of all our rights on the high seas. If the Federals could have recalled their old leaders, or retained even a considerable portion of their power, the opportunity presented by the embargo issue could have brought them back to full political power, but lacking these leaders, the opportunity passed

---

Democrats and Federals.

During the ninth Congress, which assembled on the second of December, 1805, the Republicans dropped their name and accepted that of "Democrats." In all their earlier strifes they had been charged by their opponents with desiring to run to the extremes of the democratic or "mob rule," and fear of too general a belief in the truth of the charge led them to denials and rejection of a name which the father of their party had ever shown a fondness for. The earlier dangers which had threatened their organization, and the recollection of defeats suffered in their attempts to establish a government anti-federal and confederate in their composition, had been greatly modified by later successes, and with a characteristic cuteness peculiar to Americans they accepted an epithet and sought to turn it to the best account. In this they imitated the patriots who accepted the epithets in the British satirical song of "Yankee Doodle," and called themselves Yankees. From the ninth Congress the Jeffersonian Republicans called themselves Democrats, and the word Republican passed into disuse until later on in the history of our political parties, the opponents of the Democracy accepted it as a name which well filled the meaning of their attitude in the politics of the country.

Mr. Randolph of Roanoke, made the first schism in the Republican party under Jefferson, when he and three of his friends voted against the embargo act. He resisted its passage with his usual earnestness, and all attempts at reconciling him to the measure were unavailing. Self-willed, strong in argument and sarcasm, it is believed that his cause made it even more desirable for the Republicans to change name in the hope of recalling some of the more wayward "Democrats" who had advocated Jacobin democracy in the years gone by. The politicians of that day were never short of expedients, and no man so abounded in them as Jefferson himself.

Randolph improved his opportunities by getting most of the Virginia members to act with him against the foreign policy of the administration, but he was careful not to join the Federalists, and quickly denied any leaning that way. The first fruit of his faction was to bring forth Monroe as a candidate for President against Madison—a movement which proved to be quite popular in Virginia, but which Jefferson flanked by bringing about a reconciliation between Monroe and Madison. The now usual Congressional caucus followed at Washington, and although the Virginia Legislature in its caucus proviously held had been unable to decide between Madison and Monroe, the Congressional body chose Madison by 83 to 11, the minority being divided between Clinton and Monroe, though the latter could by that time hardly be considered as a candidate. This action broke up Randolph's faction in Virginia, but left so much bitterness behind it that a large portion attached themselves to the Federalists. In the election which followed Madison received 122 electoral votes against 47 for C. C. Pinckney, of South Carolina, and 6 for Geo. Clinton of New York.

Before Jefferson's administration closed he recommended the passage of an act to prohibit the African slave trade after January 1st, 1808, and it was passed accordingly. He had also rejected the form of a treaty received from the British minister Erskine, and did this without the formality of submitting it to the Senate—first, because it contained no provision on the objectionable practice of impressing our seamen; second, *because it was accompanied by a note from the British ministers, by which the British government reserved to itself the right of releasing itself from the stipulations in favor of neutral rights, if the United States submitted to the British decree, or other invasion of those rights by France." This rejection of the treaty by Jefferson caused public excitement, and the Federalists sought to arouse the commercial community against his action, and cited the fact that his own trusted friends, Monroe and Pinckney had negotiated it. The President's party stood by him, and they agreed that submission to the Senate was immaterial, as its advice could not bind him. This refusal to consider the treaty was the first step leading to the war of 1812, for embargoes followed, and Britain openly claimed the right to search American vessels for her deserting seamen. In 1807 this question was brought to issue by the desertion of five British seamen from the *Halifax*, and their enlistment on the U. S. frigate *Chesapeake*. Four separate demands were made for these men, but all of the commanders, knowing the firm attitude of Jefferson's administration against the practice, refused, as did the Secretary of State refuse a fifth demand on the part of the British minister. On the 23d of June following, while the *Chesapeake* was near the capes of Virginia, Capt. Humphreys of the British ship *Leopard* attempted to search her for deserters. Capt. Barron denied the right of search, but on being fired into, lowered his flag,

*From the Statesman's Manual, Vol. 1., by Edwin Williams.

Humphreys then took four men from the *Chesapeake*, three of whom had previously entered the British service, but were Americans by birth, and had been formally demanded by Washington. The act was a direct violation of the international law, for a nation's ship at sea like its territory is inviolable. The British government disavowed the act of its officer and offered apology and reparation, which were accepted. This event, however, strengthened Jefferson's rejection of the Monroe-Pinckney treaty, and quickly stopped adverse political criticism at home. Foreign affairs remained, however, in a complicated state, owing to the wars between England and the then successful Napoleon, but they in no wise shook the firm hold which Jefferson had upon the people, nor the prestige of his party. He stands in history as one of the best politicians our land has ever seen, and then as now no one could successfully draw the line between the really able politician and the statesman. He was accepted as both. His administration closed on the 3d of March, 1809, when he expressed great gratification at being able to retire to private life.

Mr. Madison succeeded at a time when the country, through fears of foreign aggression and violence, was exceedingly gloomy and despondent—a feeling not encouraged in the least by the statements of the Federalists, some of whom then thought political criticism in hours of danger not unpatriotic. They described our agriculture as discouraged, our fisheries abandoned, our commerce restrained, our navy dismantled, our revenues destroyed at a time when war was at any moment probable with either France, England or Spain.

Madison, representing as he did the same party, from the first resolved to follow the policy of Jefferson, a fact about which there was no misunderstanding. He desired to avert war as long as possible with England, and sought by skilful diplomacy to avert the dangers presented by both France and England in their attitude with neutrals. England had declared that a man who was once a subject always remained a subject, and on this plea based her determination to impress again into her service all deserters from her navy. France, because of refusal to accede to claims equally at war with our rights, had authorized the seizure of all American vessels entering the ports of France. In May, 1810, when the non-intercourse act had expired, Madison caused proposals to be made to both belligerents, that if either would revoke its hostile edict, the non-intercourse act should be revived and enforced against the other nation. This act had been passed by the tenth Congress as a substitute for the embargo. France quickly accepted Madison's proposal, and received the benefits of the act, and the direct result was to increase the growing hostility of England. From this time forward the negotiations had more the character of a diplomatic contest than an attempt to maintain peace. Both countries were upon their mettle, and early in 1811, Mr. Pinckney, the American minister to Great Britain, was recalled, and a year later a formal declaration of war was made by the United States.

Just prior to this the old issue, made by the Republicans against Hamilton's scheme for a National Bank, was revived by the fact that the charter of the bank ceased on the 4th of March, 1811, and an attempt was made to recharter it. A bill for this purpose was introduced into Congress, but on the 11th of January, 1811, it was indefinitely postponed in the House, by a vote of 65 to 64, while in the Senate it was rejected by the casting vote of the Vice-President, Geo. Clinton, on the 5th of February, 1811—this notwithstanding its provisions had been framed or approved by Gallatin, the Secretary of the Treasury. The Federalists were all strong advocates of the measure, and it was so strong that it divided some of the Democrats who enjoyed a loose rein in the contest so far as the administration was concerned, the President not specially caring for political quarrels at a time when war was threatened with a powerful foreign nation. The views of the Federalists on this question descended to the Whigs some years later, and this fact led to the charges that the Whigs were but Federalists in disguise.

The eleventh Congress continued the large Democratic majority, as did the twelfth, which met on the 4th of November, 1811, Henry Clay, then an ardent supporter of the policy of Madison, succeeding to the House speakership. He had previously served two short sessions in the U. S. Senate, and had already acquired a high reputation as an able and fluent debater. He preferred the House, at that period of life, believing his powers better calculated to win fame in the more popular representative hall. Calhoun was also in the House at this time, and already noted for the boldness of his views and their assertion.

In this Congress jealousies arose against the political power of Virginia, which had already named three of the four Presidents, each for two terms, and De Witt Clinton, the well-known Governor of New York, sought through these jealousies to create a division which would carry him into the Presidency. His efforts were for a time warmly seconded by several northern and southern states. A few months later the Legislature of New York formally opened the ball by nominating DeWitt Clinton for the Presidency. An address was issued by his friends, August 17th, 1812, which has since become known as the Clintonian platform, and his followers were known as Clintonian Democrats. The address contained the first public protest against the nomination of Presidential candidates by Congressional caucuses. There was likewise declared opposition to that "official regency which prescribed tenets of political faith." The efforts of particular states to monopolize the principal offices was denounced, as was the continuance of public men for long periods in office.

Madison was nominated for a second term by a Congressional caucus held at Washington, in May, 1812. John Langdon was nominated for Vice-President, but as he declined on account of age, Elbridge Gerry of Massachusetts, took his place. In September of the same year a *convention* of the opposition, representing eleven states, was held in the city of New York, which nominated De Witt Clinton, with Jared Ingersoll for Vice-President. This was the first national convention, partisan in character, and the Federalists have the credit of originating and carrying out the idea. The election resulted in the success of Madison, who received 128 electoral votes to 89 for Clinton.

Though factious strife had been somewhat rife, less attention was paid to politics than to the approaching war. There were new Democratic leaders in the lower House, and none were more prominent than Clay of Kentucky, Calhoun, Cheves and Lowndes, all of South Carolina. The policy of Jefferson in reducing the army and navy was now greatly deplored, and the defenceless condition in which it left the country was the partial cause, at least a stated cause of the factious feuds which followed. Madison sought to change this policy, and he did it at the earnest solicitation of Clay, Calhoun and Lowndes, who were the recognized leaders of the war party. They had early determined that Madison should be directly identified with them, and before his second nomination had won him over to their more decided views in favor of war with England. He had held back, hoping that diplomacy might avert a contest, but when once convinced that war was inevitable and even desirable under the circumstances, his official utterances were bold and free. In the June following the caucus which renominated him, he declared in a message that our flag was continually insulted on the high seas; that the right of searching American vessels for British seamen was still in practice, and that thousands of American citizens had in this way been impressed in service on foreign ships, that peaceful efforts at adjustment of the difficulties had proved abortive, and that the British ministry and British emissaries had actually been intriguing for the dismemberment of the Union.

The act declaring war was approved by the President on the 18th of June, 1812, and is remarkably short and comprehensive. It was drawn by the attorney-general of the United States, William Pinckney, and is in the words following:—

"*An act declaring war between the United Kingdom of Great Britain and Ireland, and the dependencies thereof, and the United States of America and their territories.*

"*Be it enacted, &c.* That war be, and the same is hereby declared to exist between the United Kingdom of Great Britain and Ireland, and the dependencies thereof, and the United States of America, and their territories; and that the President of the United States is hereby authorized to use the whole land and naval force of the United States to carry the same into effect, and to issue to private armed vessels of the United States commissions, or letters of marque and general reprisal, in such form as he shall think proper, and under the seal of the United States, against the vessels, goods, and effects, of the government of the United Kingdom of Great Britain and Ireland and the subjects thereof."

This was a soul-stirring message, but it did not rally all the people as it should have done. Political jealousies were very great, and the frequent defeats of the Federalists, while they tended to greatly reduce their numbers and weaken their power, seemed to strengthen their animosity, and they could see nothing good in any act of the administration. They held, especially in the New England states, that the war had been declared by a political party simply, and not by the nation, though nearly all of the Middle, and all of the Southern and Western States, warmly supported it. Clay estimated that nine-tenths of the people were in favor of the war, and under the inspiration of his eloquence and the strong state papers of Madison, they doubtless were at first. Throughout they felt their political strength, and they just as heartily returned the bitterness manifested by those of the Federalists who opposed the war, branding them as enemies of the republic, and monarchists who preferred the reign of Britain.

Four Federalist representatives in Congress went so far as to issue an address, opposing the war, the way in which it had been declared, and denouncing it as unjust. Some of the New England states refused the order of the President to support it with their militia, and Massachusetts sent peace memorials to Congress.

A peace party was formed with a view to array the religious sentiment of the country against the war, and societies with similar objects were organized by the more radical of the Federalists. To such an extreme was this opposition carried, that some of the citizens of New London, Conn., made a practice of giving information to the enemy, by means of blue lights, of the departure of American vessels.

The Hartford Convention.

This opposition finally culminated in the assembling of a convention at Hartford, at which delegates were present from all of the New England states. They sat for three weeks with closed doors, and issued an address which will be found in this volume in the book devoted to political platforms. It was charged by the Democrats that the real object of the convention was to negotiate a separate treaty of peace, on behalf of New England, with Great Britain, but this charge was as warmly denied. The exact truth has not since been discovered, the fears of the participants of threatened trials for treason, closing their mouths, if their professions were false. The treaty of Ghent, which was concluded on December 14th, 1814, prevented other action by the Hartford convention than that stated. It had assembled nine days before the treaty, which is as follows:

Treaty of Ghent.

This treaty was negotiated by the Right Honorable James Lord Gambier, Henry Goulburn, Esq., and William Adams, Esq., on the part of Great Britain, and John Quincy Adams, James A. Bayard, Henry Clay, Jonathan Russell, and Albert Gallatin, on behalf of the United States.

The treaty can be found on p. 218, vol. 8, of Little & Brown's Statutes at Large. The first article provided for the restoration of all archives, records, or property taken by either party from the other during the war. This article expressly provides for the restoration of "slaves or other private property" The second article provided for the cessation of hostilities and limitation of time of capture. The third article provided for the restoration of prisoners of war.

The fourth article defined the boundary established by the treaty of 1783, and provided for commissioners to mark the same.

The fifth, sixth, seventh, and eighth articles established rules to govern the proceedings of the commissioners.

The ninth article bound the United States and His Britannic Majesty to end all hostilities with Indian tribes, with whom they were then respectively at war.

The tenth article reads as follows:—

"Whereas the traffic in slaves is irreconcilable with the principles of humanity and justice; and, whereas, both His Majesty and the United States are desirous of continuing their efforts to promote its entire abolition, it is hereby agreed that both the contracting parties shall use their best endeavors to accomplish so desirable an object."

The eleventh and last article provides for binding effect of the treaty, upon the exchange of ratifications.

The position of New England in the war is explained somewhat by her exposed position. Such of the militia as served endured great hardships, and they were almost constantly called from their homes to meet new dangers. Distrusting their loyalty, the general government had withheld all supplies from the militia of Massachusetts and Connecticut for the year 1814, and these States were forced to bear the burden of supporting them, at the same time contributing their quota of taxes to the general government—hardships, by the way, not greater than those borne by Pennsylvania and Ohio in the late war for the Union, nor half as hard as those borne by the border States at the same time. True, the coast towns of Massachusetts were subjected to constant assault from the British navy, and the people of these felt that they were defenceless. It was on their petition that the legislature of Massachusetts finally, by a vote of 226 to 67, adopted the report favoring the calling of the Hartford Convention. A circular was then addressed to the Governors of the other States, with a request that it be laid before their legislatures, inviting them to appoint delegates, and stating that the object was to deliberate upon the dangers to which the eastern section was exposed, "and to devise, if practicable, means of security and defence which might be consistent with the preservation of their resources from total ruin, *and not repugnant to their obligations as members of the Union.*" The italicized portion shows that there was at least then no design of forming a separate treaty, or of promoting disunion. The legislatures of Connecticut and Rhode Island endorsed the call and sent delegates. Those of New Hampshire and Vermont did not, but delegates were sent by local conventions. These delegates, it is hardly necessary to remark, were all members of the Federal party, and their suspected designs and action made the "Hartford Convention" a bye-word and reproach in the mouths of Democratic orators for years thereafter. It gave to the Democrats, as did the entire history of the war, the prestige of superior patriotism, and they profited by it as long as the memory of the war of 1812 was fresh. Indeed, directly after the war, all men seemed to keep in constant view the reluctance of the Federalists to support the war, and their almost open hostility to it in New England. Peace brought prosperity and plenty, but not oblivion of the old political issues, and this was the beginning of the end of the Federal party. Its decay thereafter was rapid and constant.

The eleventh, twelfth and thirteenth Congresses had continued Democratic. The fourteenth began Dec. 4, 1815, with the Democratic majority in the House increased to 30. Clay had taken part in negotiating the treaty, and on his return was again elected to the House, and was for the third time elected speaker. Though 65 Federalists had been elected, but 10 were given to Federal candidates for speaker, this party now showing a strong, and under the circumstances, a very natural desire to rub out party lines. The internal taxes and the postage rates were reduced.

The Protective Tariff.

President Madison, in his message, had urged upon Congress a revision of the tariff, and pursuant to his recommendation what was at the time called a protective tariff was passed. Even Calhoun then supported it, while Clay proclaimed that protection must no longer be secondary to revenue, but of primary importance. The rates fixed, however, were insufficient, and many American manufactures were soon frustrated by excessive importations of foreign manufactures. The position of Calhoun and Lowndes, well known leaders from South Carolina, is explained by the fact that just then the proposal of a protective tariff was popular in the south, in view of the heavy duties upon raw cotton which England then imposed. The Federalists in weakness changed their old position when they found the Democrats advocating a tariff, and the latter quoted and published quite extensively Alexander Hamilton's early report in favor of it. Webster, in the House at the time and a leading Federalist, was against the bill. The parties had exchanged positions on the question.

Peace brought with it another exchange of positions. President Madison, although he had vetoed a bill to establish a National Bank in 1815, was now (in 1816) anxious for the establishment of such an institution. Clay had also changed his views, and claimed that the experiences of the war showed the necessity for a national currency. The bill met with strong opposition from a few Democrats and nearly all of the Federalists (the latter having changed position on the question since 1811), but it passed and was signed by the President.

A bill to promote internal improvements, advocated by Clay, was at first favored by Madison, but his mind changed and he vetoed the measure—the first of its kind passed by Congress.

The Democratic members of Congress, before the adjournment of the first session, held a caucus for the nomination of candidates to succeed Madison and Gerry It was understood that the retiring officers and their confidential friends favored James Monroe of Virginia. Their wishes were carried out, but not without a struggle, Wm. H. Crawford of Georgia receiving 54 votes against 65 for Monroe The Democrats opposed to Virginia's domination in the politics of the country, made a second effort, and directed it against Monroe in the caucus. Aaron Burr denounced him as an improper and incompetent candidate, and joined in the protest then made against any nomination by a Congressional caucus; he succeeding in getting nineteen Democrats to stay out of the caucus. Later he advised renewed attempts to break down the Congressional caucus system, and before the nomination favored Andrew Jackson as a means to that end. Daniel B. Tompkins was nominated by the Democrats for Vice-President. The Federalists named Rufus King of New York, but in the election which followed he received but 24 out of 217 electoral votes. The Federalists divided their votes for Vice-President.

Monroe was inaugurated on the 14th of March, 1817, the oath being administered by Chief Justice Marshall. The inaugural address was so liberal in its tone that it seemed to give satisfaction to men of all shades of political opinion. The questions which had arisen during the war no longer had any practical significance, while the people were anxious to give the disturbing ones which ante-dated at least a season of rest. Two great and opposing policies had previously obtained, and singularly enough each seemed exactly adapted to the times when they were triumphant. The Federal power had been asserted in a government which had gathered renewed strength during what was under the circumstances a great and perilous war, and the exigencies of that war in many instances compelled the Republicans or Democrats, or the Democratic-Republicans as some still called them, to concede points which had theretofore been in sharp dispute, and they did it with that facility which only Americans can command in emergencies: yet as a party they kept firm hold of the desire to enlarge the scope of liberty in its application to the citizens, and just here kept their original landmark.

It is not singular then that the administration of Monroe opened what has ever since been known in politics as the "Era of Good Feeling." Party differences rapidly subsided, and political serenity was the order of the day. Monroe made a tour of the States, with the direct object of inspecting fortifications and means of defence, and in this way spread the good feeling, without seeming to have any such object. He was everywhere favorably greeted by the people, and received by delegations which in many instances were specially made up of all shades of opinion.

The Cabinet was composed of men of rare political distinction, even in that day of great men. It was probably easier to be great then than now, just as it is easier to be a big political hero in the little State of Delaware than it is in the big States of New York or Pennsylvania. Yet these men were universally accepted as great without regard to their localities. All were Republicans or Democrats, with John Quincy Adams as Secretary of State, Wm. H. Crawford (Monroe's competitor for the nomination) as Secretary of the Treasury, John C. Calhoun as Secretary of War, William Wirt as Attorney General. All of these united with the President in the general desire to call a halt upon the political asperities which were then recognized as a public evil. On one occasion, during his tour, the citizens of Kennebunk and its vicinity, in Maine, having in their address alluded to the prospects of a political union among the people in support of the administration, the President said in reply:

"You are pleased to express a confident hope that a spirit of mutual conciliation may be one of the blessings which may result from my administration. This indeed would be an eminent blessing, and I pray it may be realized. Nothing but union is waiting to make us a great people. The present time affords the happiest presage that this union is fast consummating. It cannot be otherwise; I daily see greater proofs of it. The further I advance in my progress in the country, the more I perceive that we are all Americans —that we compose but one family—that our republican institutions will be supported and perpetuated by the united zeal and patriotism of all. Nothing could give me greater satisfaction than to behold a perfect union among ourselves—a union which is necessary to restore to social intercourse its former charms, and to render our happiness, as a nation, unmixed and complete. To promote this desirable result requires no compromise of principle, and I promise to give it my continued attention, and my best endeavors."

Even General Jackson, since held up to public view by historians as the most austere and "stalwart" of all politicians, caught the sweet infection of peace, and thus advised President Monroe:—

"Now is the time to exterminate that monster, called party spirit. By selecting [for cabinet officers] characters most conspicuous for their probity, virtue, capacity, and firmness, without regard to party, you will go far to, if not entirely, eradicate those feelings, which, on former occasions, threw so many obstacles in the way of government. The chief magistrate of a great and powerful nation should never indulge in party feelings. His conduct should be liberal and disinterested; always bearing in mind, that he acts for the whole and not a part of the community."

This advice had been given with a view to influence the appointment of a mixed political Cabinet, but while Monroe professed to believe that a free government could exist without political parties, he nevertheless sought to bring all of the people into one political fold, and that the Democratic. Yet he certainly and plainly sought to allay factions in his own party, and with this view selected Crawford for the Treasury—the gentleman who had been so warmly supported in the nominating struggle by the Clintonians and by all who objected to the predominating influence of Virginia in national politics.

Monroe, like his immediate predecessor, accepted and acted upon the doctrines of the new school of Republicans as represented by Clay and Calhoun, both of whom still favored a tariff, while Clay had become a warm advocate of a national system of internal improvements. These two statesmen thus early differed on some questions, but they were justly regarded as the leading friends and advisers of the administration, for to both still clung the patriotic recollections of the war which they had so warmly advocated and supported, and the issue of which attested their wisdom. Clay preferred to be called a Republican; Calhoun preferred to be called a Democrat, and just then the terms were so often exchanged and mingled that history is at fault in the exact designation, while tradition is colored by the bias of subsequent events and lives.

Monroe's first inaugural leaned toward Clay's scheme of internal improvements, but questioned its constitutionality. Clay was next to Jefferson the most original of all our statesmen and politicians. He was prolific in measures, and almost resistless in their advocacy, From a political standpoint he was the most direct author of the war of 1812, for his advocacy mainly brought it to the issue of arms, which through him and Calhoun were substituted for diplomacy. And Calhoun then stood in broader view before the country than since. His sectional pride and bias had been rarely aroused, and like Clay he seemed to act for the country as an entirety. Subsequent sectional issues changed the views held of him by the people of both the North and South.

We have said that Monroe leaned toward internal improvements, but he thought Congress was not clothed by the

Constitution with the power to authorize measures supporting it, and when the opportunity was presented (May 4, 1822) he vetoed the bill "for the preservation and repair of the Cumberland road," and accompanied the veto with a most elaborate message in which he discussed the constitutional aspects of the question. A plain majority of the friends of the administration, under the leadership of Clay, supported the theory of internal improvements from the time the administration began, but were reluctant to permit a division of the party on the question.

Mississippi and Illinois were admitted to the Union during the "Era of Good Feeling," without serious political disturbance, while Alabama was authorized to form a state constitution and government, and Arkansas was authorized as a separate territorial government from part of Missouri. In 1819 President Monroe made a tour through the Southern States to examine their defenses and see and get acquainted with the people. From the first inauguration of Monroe up to 1819 party lines can hardly be said to have existed, but in the sixteenth session of Congress, which continued until May, 1820, new questions of national interest arose, prominent among which were additional protective duties for our manufactures; internal improvements by the government; acknowledgments of the independence of the South American States.

The Monroe Doctrine.

Upon the question of recognizing the independence of the South American States, the President made a record which has ever since been quoted and denominated "The Monroe Doctrine." It is embodied in the following abstract of his seventh annual message, under date of Dec. 2d, 1823:

"It was stated, at the commencement of the last session, that a great effort was then making in Spain and Portugal to improve the condition of the people of those countries, and that it appeared to be conducted with extraordinary moderation. It need scarcely be remarked that the result has been, so far, very different from what was then anticipated. Of events in that quarter of the globe, with which we have so much intercourse, and from which we derive our origin, we have always been anxious and interested spectators. The citizens of the United States cherish sentiments the most friendly in favor of the liberty and happiness of their fellow men on that side of the Atlantic. In the wars of the European powers, in matters relating to themselves, we have never taken any part, nor does it comport with our policy to do so. It is only when rights are invaded or seriously menaced, that we resent injuries, or make preparation for our defense. With the movements in this hemisphere we are of necessity more immediately connected, and by causes which must be obvious to all enlightened and impartial observers. The political system of the allied powers is essentially different in this respect from that of America. This difference proceeds from that which exists in their respective governments. And to the defense of our own, which has been achieved by the loss of so much blood and treasure, and matured by the wisdom of their most enlightened citizens, and under which we have enjoyed unexampled felicity, this whole nation is devoted. We owe it, therefore, to candor, and to the amicable relations existing between the United States and those powers, to declare, that we should consider any attempt on their part to extend their system to any portion of this hemisphere as dangerous to our peace and safety. With the existing colonies or dependencies of any European power we have not interfered, and shall not interfere. But with the governments who have declared their independence, and maintained it, and whose independence we have, on great consideration, and on just principles, acknowledged, we could not view any interposition for the purpose of oppressing them, or controlling in any other manner their destiny, by any European power, in any other light than as the manifestation of an unfriendly disposition toward the United States. In the war between those new governments and Spain, we declared our neutrality at the time of their recognition, and to this we have adhered, and shall continue to adhere, provided no change shall occur which, in the judgment of the competent authorities of this government, shall make a corresponding change on the part of the United States indispensable to their security.

The late events in Spain and Portugal show that Europe is still unsettled. Of this important fact no stronger proof can be adduced, than that the allied powers should have thought it proper, on a principle satisfactory to themselves, to have interposed by force in the internal concerns of Spain. To what extent such interposition may be carried, on the same principle, is a question to which all independent powers, whose governments differ from theirs, are interested; even those most remote, and surely none more so than the United States. Our policy in regard to Europe, which was adopted at an early stage of the wars which have so long agitated that quarter of the globe, nevertheless remains the same, which is, not to interfere in the internal concerns of any of its powers; to consider the government, *de facto*, as the legitimate government for us: to cultivate friendly relations with it, and to preserve those relations by a frank, firm, and manly policy; meeting, in all instances, the just claims of every power, submitting to injuries from none But in regard to these continents, circumstances are eminently and conspicuously different. It is impossible that the allied powers should extend their political system to any portion of either continent without endangering our peace and happiness; nor can any one believe, that our southern brethren, if left to themselves, would adopt it of their own accord. It is equally impossible, therefore that we should behold such interposition, in any form, with indifference. If we look to the comparative strength and resources of Spain and those new governments, and their distance from each other, it must be obvious that she can never subdue them. It is still the true policy of the United States to leave the parties to themselves, in the hope that other powers will pursue the same course."

The second election of Monroe, in 1820, was accomplished without a contest. Out of 231 electoral votes, but one was cast against him, and that for John Quincy Adams. Mr. Tompkins, the candidate for Vice-President, was only a little less fortunate, there being 14 scattering votes against him. Neither party, if indeed there was a Federalist party left made any nominations.

The Missouri Compromise.

The second session of the 17th Congress opened on the 4th day of March, 1820, with James Monroe at the head of the Executive Department of the Government, and the Democratic party in the majority in both branches of the Federal Legislature. The Cabinet at that time was composed of the most brilliant minds of the country, indeed as most justly remarked by Senator Thomas H. Benton in his published review of the events of that period, it would be difficult to find in any government, in any country, at any time, more talent and experience, more dignity and decorum, more purity of private life, a larger mass of information, and more addiction to business, than was comprised in the list of celebrated names then constituting the executive department of the government. The legislative department was equally impressive. The exciting and agitating question then pending before Congress was on the admission of the State of Missouri into the Federal Union, the subject of the issue being the attempted tacking on of conditions restricting slavery within her limits. She was admitted without conditions under the so called compromise, which abolished it in certain portions of the then province of Louisiana. In this controversy, the compromise was sustained and carried entirely by the Democratic Senators and members from the Southern and slave-holding States aided and sanctioned by the Executive, and it was opposed by fifteen Senators from non-slave-holding States, who represented the opposite side on the political questions of the day. It passed the House by a close vote of 86 to 82. It has been seriously questioned since whether this act was constitutional. The real struggle was political, and for the balance of power. For a while it threatened the total overthrow of all political parties upon principle, and the substitution of geographical parties discriminated by the slave line, and thus destroying the proper action of the Federal government, and leading to a separation of the States. It was a federal movement, accruing to the benefit of that party, and at first carried all the Northern democracy in its current, giving the supremacy to their adversaries. When this effect was perceived, democrats from the northern non slave-holding States took early opportunity to prevent their own overthrow, by voting for the admission of the States on any terms, and thus prevent the eventual separation of the States in the establishment of geographical parties divided by a slavery and anti-slavery line.

The year 1820 marked a period of financial distress in the country, which soon became that of the government. The army was reduced, and the general expenses of the departments cut down, despite which measures of economy the Congress deemed it necessary to authorize the President to contract for a loan of five million dollars. Distress was the cry of the day; relief the general demand, the chief demand coming from debtors to the Government for public lands purchased under the then credit system, this debt at that time aggregating twenty-three millions of dollars. The banks failed, money vanished, instalments were coming due which could not be met; and the opening of Congress in November, 1820, was saluted by the arrival of memorials from all the new States praying for the relief to the purchaser of the public lands. The President referred to it in his annual message of that year, and Congress passed a measure of relief by changing the system to cash sales instead of credit, reducing the price of the lands, and allowing present debtors to apply payments already made to portions of the land purchased, relinquishing the remainder. Applications were made at that time for the establishment of the preemptive system, but without effect; the new States continued to press the question and finally prevailed, so that now the preemptive principle has become a fixed part of our land system, permanently incorporated with it, and to the equal advantage of the settler and the government.

The session of 1820–21, is remarkable as being the first at which any proposition was made in Congress for the occupation and settlement of our territory on the Columbia river—the only part then owned by the United States on the Pacific coast. It was made by Dr. Floyd, a representative from Virginia, who argued that the establishment of a civilized power on the American coast of the Pacific could not fail to produce great and wonderful benefits not only to our own country, but to the people of Eastern Asia, China and Japan on the opposite side of the Pacific Ocean, and that the valley of the Columbia might become the granary of China and Japan. This movement suggested to Senator Benton, to move, for the first time publicly in the United States, a resolution to send ministers to the Oriental States.

At this time treaties with Mexico and Spain were ratified, by which the United States acquired Florida and ceded Texas; these treaties, together with the Missouri compromise—a measure contemporaneous with them—extinguished slave soil in all the United States territory west of the Mississippi, except in that portion which was to constitute the State of Arkansas; and, including the extinction in Texas consequent upon its cession to a non-slaveholding power, constituted the largest territorial abolition of slavery that was ever up to that period effected by any political power of any nation.

The outside view of the slave question in the United States, at this time, is that the extension of slavery was then arrested, circumscribed, and confined within narrow territorial limits, while free States were permitted an almost unlimited expansion.

In 1822 a law passed Congress abolishing the Indian factory system, which had been established during Washington's administration, in 1796, under which the Government acted as a factor or agent for the sale of supplies to the Indians and the purchase of furs from them; this branch of the service then belonged to the department of the Secretary of War. The abuses discovered in it led to the discontinuance of that system.

The Presidential election of 1824 was approaching, the candidates were in the field, their respective friends active and busy, and popular topics for the canvass in earnest requisition. Congress was full of projects for different objects of internal improvement, mainly in roads and canals, and the friends of each candidate exerted themselves in rivalry of each other, under the supposition that their opinions would stand for those of their principals. An act for the preservation of the Cumberland Road, which passed both houses of Congress, met with a veto from President Monroe, accompanied by a state paper in exposition of his opinions upon the whole subject of Federal interference in matters of inter state commerce and roads and canals. He discussed the measure in all its bearings, and plainly showed it to be unconstitutional. After stating the question, he examined it under every head of constitutional derivation under which its advocates claimed the power, and found it to be granted by no one of them and virtually prohibited by some of them. This was then and has since been considered to be the most elaborate and thoroughly considered opinion upon the general question which has ever been delivered by any American statesman. This great state paper, delivered at a time when internal improvement by the federal government had become an issue in the canvass for the Presidency and was ardently advocated by three of the candidates and qualified by two others, had an immense current in its power, carrying with it many of the old strict constructionists.

The revision of the tariff, with a view to the protection of home industry, and to the establishment of what was then called "The American System," was one of the large subjects before Congress at the session of 1823–24, and was the regular commencement of the heated debates on that question which afterwards ripened into a serious difficulty between the federal government and some of the Southern States. The presidential election being then depending, the subject became tinctured with party politics, in which so far as that ingredient was concerned, and was not controlled by other considerations, members divided pretty much on the line which always divided them on a question of constructive powers. The protection of domestic industry not being among the powers granted, was looked for in the incidental; and denied by the strict constructionists to be a substantive term, to be exercised for the direct purpose of protection; but admitted by all at that time and ever since the first tariff act of 1789, to be an incident to the revenue raising power, and an incident to be regarded in the exercise of that power. Revenue the object, protection the incident, had been the rule in the earlier tariffs; now that rule was sought to be reversed, and to make protection the object of the law, and revenue the incident. Mr. Henry Clay was the leader in the proposed revision and the champion of the American system; he was ably supported in the House by many able and effective speakers; who based their argument on the general distress then alleged to be prevalent in the country Mr. Daniel Webster was the leading speaker on the other side, and disputed the universality of the distress which had been described; and contested the propriety of high or prohibitory duties, in the present active and intelligent state of the world, to stimulate industry and manufacturing enterprise.

The bill was carried by a close vote in both Houses. Though brought forward avowedly for the protection of domestic manufactures, it was not entirely supported on that ground; an increase of revenue being the motive with some, the public debt then being nearly ninety millions. An increased protection to the products of several States, as lead in Missouri and Illinois, hemp in Kentucky, iron in Pennsylvania, wool in Ohio and New York, commanded many votes for the bill; and the impending presidential election had its influence in its favor.

Two of the candidates, Messrs. Adams and Clay, voted for and avowedly supported General Jackson, who voted for the bill, was for it, as tending to give a home supply of the articles necessary in time of war, and as raising revenue to pay the public debt; Mr. Crawford was opposed to it, and Mr. Calhoun had withdrawn as a Presidential candidate. The Southern planting States were dissatisfied, believing that the new burdens upon imports which it imposed, fell upon the producers of the exports, and tended to enrich one section of the Union at the expense of another. The attack and support of the bill took much of a sectional aspect; Virginia, the two Carolinas, Georgia, and some others, being unanimous against it. Pennsylvania, New York, Ohio, and Kentucky being unanimous for it. Massachusetts, which up to this time had no small influence in commerce, voted, with all, except one member, against it. With this sectional aspect, a tariff for protection, also began to assume a political aspect, being taken under the care of the party, afterwards denominated as Whig. The bill was approved by President Monroe; a proof that that careful and strict constructionist of the constitution did not consider it as deprived of its revenue character by the degree of protection which it extended.

A subject which at the present time is exciting much criticism, viz: proposed amendments to the constitution relative to the election of President and Vice-President, had its origin in movements in that direction taken by leading Democrats during the campaign of 1824. The electoral college has never been since the early elections, an independent body free to select a President and Vice-President; though in theory they have been vested with such powers, in practice they have no such practical power over the elections, and have had none since their institution. In every case the elector has been an instrument, bound to obey a particular impulsion, and disobedience to which would be attended with infamy, and with every penalty which public indignation could inflict. From the beginning they have stood pledged to vote for the candidate indicated by the public will; and have proved not only to be useless, but an inconvenient intervention between the people and the object of their choice. Mr. McDuffie in the House of Representatives and Mr. Benton in the Senate, proposed amendments; the mode of taking the direct vote to be in districts, and the persons receiving the greatest number of votes for President or Vice-President in any district, to count one vote for such office respectively which is nothing but substituting the candidates themselves for their electoral representatives.

In the election of 1824 four candidates were before the people for the office of President, General Jackson, John Quincy Adams, William H. Crawford and Henry Clay. None of them received a majority of the 261 electoral votes, and the election devolved upon the House of Representatives. John C. Calhoun had a majority of the electoral votes for the office of Vice-President, and was elected. Mr. Adams was elected President by the House of Representatives, although General Jackson was the choice of the people, having received the greatest number of votes at the general election. The election of Mr. Adams was perfectly constitutional, and as such fully submitted to by the people; but it was a violation of the *demos krateo* principle; and that violation was equally rebuked. All the representatives who voted against the will of their constituents, lost their favor, and disappeared from public life. The representation in the House of Representatives was largely changed at the first general election, and presented a full opposition to the new President. Mr. Adams himself was injured by it, and at the ensuing presidential election was beaten by General Jackson more than two to one.

Mr. Clay, who took the lead in the House for Mr. Adams, and afterwards took upon himself the mission of reconciling the people to his election in a series of public speeches, was himself crippled in the effort, lost his place in the democratic party, and joined the Whigs (then called the national republicans). The democratic principle was victor over the theory of the Constitution, and beneficial results ensued. It vindicated the people in their right and their power. It re-established parties upon the basis of principle, and drew anew party lines, then almost obliterated under the fusion of parties during the "era of good feeling," and the efforts of leading men to make personal parties for themselves. It showed the conservative power of our goverment to lie in the people, more than in its constituted authorities. It showed that they were capable of exercising the function of self-government, and lastly, it assumed the supremacy of the democracy for a long time, and until lost by causes to be referred to hereafter. The Presidential election of 1824 is remarkable under another aspect—its results cautioned all public men against future attempts to govern presidential elections in the House of Representatives; and it put an end to the practice of caucus nominations for the Presidency by members of Congress. This mode of concentrating public opinion began to be practiced as the eminent men of the Revolution, to whom public opinion awarded a preference, were passing away, and when new men, of more equal pretensions, were coming upon the stage. It was tried several times with success and general approbation, because public sentiment was followed—not led—by the caucus. It was attempted in 1824 and failed; all the opponents of Mr. Crawford, by their joint efforts, succeeded, and justly in the fact though not in the motive, in rendering these Congress caucus nominations odious to the people, and broke them down. They were dropped, and a different mode adopted —that of party nominations by conventions of delegates from the States.

The administration of Mr. Adams commenced with his inaugural address, in which the chief topic was that of internal national improvement by the federal government. This declared policy of the administration furnished a ground of opposition against Mr. Adams, and went to the reconstruction of parties on the old line of strict, or latitudinous, construction of the Constitution. It was clear from the beginning that the new administration was to have a settled and strong opposition, and that founded in principles of government—the same principles, under different forms, which had discriminated parties at the commencement of the federal government. Men of the old school—survivors of the contest of the Adams and Jefferson times, with some exceptions, divided accordingly—the federalists going for Mr. Adams, the republicans against him, with the mass of the younger generation. The Senate by a decided majority, and the House by a strong minority, were opposed to the policy of the new President.

In 1826 occurred the famous debates in the Senate and the House, on the proposed Congress of American States, to contract alliances to guard against and prevent the establishment of any future European colony within its borders. The mission though sanctioned was never acted upon or carried out. It was authorized by very nearly a party vote, the democracy as a party being against it. The President, Mr. Adams, stated the objects of the Congress to be as follows: "An agreement between all the parties represented at the meeting, that each will guard, by its own means, against the establishment of any future European colony within its own borders, may be advisable. This was, more than two years since, announced by my predecessor to the world, as a principle resulting from the emancipation of both the American continents. It may be so developed to the new southern nations, that they may feel it as an essential appendage to their independence."

Mr. Adams had been a member of Mr. Monroe's cabinet, filling the department from which the doctrine would emanate. The enunciation by him as above of this "Monroe Doctrine," as it is called, is very different from what it has of late been supposed to be, as binding the United States to guard all the territory of the New World from European colonization. The message above quoted was written at a time when the doctrine as enunciated by the former President through the then Secretary was fresh in the mind of the latter, and when he himself in a communication to the American Senate was laying it down for the adoption of all the American nations in a general congress of their deputies. According to President Adams, this "Monroe Doctrine" (according to which it has been of late believed that the United States were to stand guard over the two Americas, and repulse all intrusive colonists from their shores), was entirely confined to our own borders; that it was only proposed to get the other States of the New World to agree that, each for itself, and by its own means, should guard its own territories; and, consequently, that the United States, so far from extending gratuitous protection to the territories of other States, would neither give, nor receive, aid in any such enterprise, but that each should use its own means, within its own borders, for its own exemption from European colonial intrusion.

No question in its day excited more intemperate discussion, excitement, and feeling between the Executive and the Senate, and none died out so quickly, than this, relative to the proposed congress of American nations. The chief advantage to be derived from its retrospect—and it is a real one—is a view of the firmness with which the minority maintained the old policy of the United States, to avoid entangling alliances and interference with the affairs of other nations; and the exposition, by one so competent as Mr. Adams, of the true scope and meaning of the Monroe doctrine.

At the session of 1825–26 attempt was again made to procure an amendment to the Constitution, in relation to the mode of election of President and Vice-President, so as to do away with all intermediate agencies, and give the election to the direct vote of the people. In the Senate the matter was referred to a committee who reported amendments dispensing with electors, providing for districts equal in number to the whole number of Senators and Representatives to which the State was entitled in Congress, and obviating all excuses for caucuses and conventions to concentrate public opinion by providing that in the event of no one receiving a majority of the whole number of district votes cast, that a second election should be held limited to the two persons receiving the highest number of votes; and in case of an equal division of votes on the second election then the House of Representatives shall choose one of them for President, as is prescribed by the Constitution. The idea being that the first election, if not resulting in any candidate receiving a majority, should stand for a popular nomination—a nomination by the people themselves, out of which the election is almost sure to be made on the second trial. The same plan was suggested for choosing a Vice-President, except that the Senate was to finally elect, in case of failure to choose at first and second elections. The amendments did not receive the requisite support of two-thirds of either the Senate or the House. This movement was not of a partisan character; it was equally supported and opposed respectively by Senators and Representatives of both parties. Substantially the same plan was recommended by President, Jackson in his first annual message to Congress, December 8, 1829.

It is interesting to note that at this Session of 1825 and '26, attempt was made by the Democrats to pass a tenure of office bill, as applicable to government employees and office-holders; it provided "that in all nominations made by the President to the Senate, to fill vacancies occasioned by an exercise of the President's power to remove from office, the fact of the removal shall be stated to the Senate at the same time that the nomination is made, with a statement of the reasons for which such officer may have been removed." It was also sought at the same time to amend the Constitution to prohibit the appointment of any member of Congress to any federal office of trust or profit, during the period for which he was elected; the design being to make the members wholly independent of the Executive, and not subservient to the latter, and incapable of receiving favors in the form of bestowals of official patronage.

The tariff of 1828 is an era in our political legislation; from it the doctrine of "nullification" originated, and from that date began a serious division between the North and the South. This tariff law was projected in the interest of the woolen manufacturers, but ended by including all manufacturing interests. The passage of this measure was brought about not because it was favored by a majority, but because of political exigencies. In the then approaching presidential election, Mr. Adams, who was in favor of the "American System," supported by Mr. Clay (his Secretary of State) was opposed by General Jackson. This tariff was made an administration measure, and became an issue in the canvass. The New England States, which had formerly favored free trade, on account of their commercial interests, changed their policy, and, led by Mr. Webster, became advocates of the protective system. The question of protective tariff had now not only become political, but sectional. The Southern States as a section, were arrayed against the system, though prior to 1816 had favored it, not merely as an incident to revenue, but as a substantive object. In fact these tariff bills, each exceeding the other in its degree of protection, had become a regular appendage of our presidential elections—carrying round in every cycle of four years, with that returning event; starting in 1816 and followed up in 1820–24, and now in 1828, with successive, augmentations of duties; the last being often pushed as a party measure, and with the visible purpose of influencing the presidential election. General Jackson was elected, having received 178 electoral votes to 83 received by John Quincy Adams. Mr. Richard Rush, of Pennsylvania, who was on the ticket with Mr. Adams, was defeated for the office of Vice-President, and John C. Calhoun, of South Carolina, was elected to that office.

The election of General Jackson was a triumph of democratic principle, and an assertion of the people's right to govern themselves. That principle had been violated in the presidential election in the House of Representatives in the session of 1824–25; and the sanction, or rebuke, of that violation was a leading question in the whole canvass. It was also a triumph over the high protective policy, and the federal internal improvement policy, and the latitudinous construction of the Constitution; and of the democracy over the federalists, then called national republicans; and was the re-establishment of parties on principle, according to the landmarks of the early years of the government. For although Mr. Adams had received confidence and office from Mr. Madison and Mr. Monroe, and had classed with the democratic party during the "era of good feeling," yet he had previously been federal; and on the re-establishment of old party lines which began to take place after the election of Mr. Adams in the House of Representatives, his affinities and policy became those of his former party; and as a party, with many individual exceptions, they became his supporters and his strength. General Jackson, on the contrary, had always been democratic, so classing when he was a Senator in Congress under the administration of the first Mr. Adams; and when party lines were most straightly drawn, and upon principle, and as such now receiving the support of men and States which took this political position at that time, and maintained it for years afterwards; among the latter, notably the States of Virginia and Pennsylvania.

The short session of 1829–30 was rendered famous by the long and earnest debates in the Senate on the doctrine of nullification, as it was then called. It started by a resolution of inquiry introduced by Mr. Foot of Connecticut; it was united with a proposition to limit the sales of the public lands to those then in the market—to suspend the surveys of the public lands—and to abolish the office of Surveyor-General. The effect of such a resolution, if sanctioned upon inquiry and carried into legislative effect, would have been to check emigration to the new States in the West, and to check the growth and settlement of these States and Territories. It was warmly opposed by Western members. The debate spread and took an acrimonious turn, and sectional, imputing to the quarter of the Union from which it came an old and early policy to check the growth of the West at the outset by proposing to limit the sale of the Western lands, by selling no tract in advance until all in the rear was sold out; and during the debate Mr. Webster referred to the famous ordinance of 1787 for the government of the north-western territory, and especially the anti-slavery clause which it contained.

Closely connected with this subject to which Mr. Webster's remarks, during the debate, related, was another which excited some warm discussion—the topic of slavery—and the effect of its existence or non-existence in different States. Kentucky and Ohio were taken for examples, and the superior improvement and population of Ohio were attributed to its exemption from the evils of slavery. This was an excitable subject, and the more so because the wounds of the Missouri controversy in which the North was the undisputed aggressor, were still tender. Mr. Hayne from South Carolina answered with warmth and resented as a reflection upon the Slave States this disadvantageous comparison. Mr. Benton of Missouri followed on the same side, and in the course of his remarks said, "I regard with admiration, that is to say, with wonder, the sublime morality of those who cannot bear the abstract contemplation of slavery, at the distance of five hundred or a thousand miles off." This allusion to the Missouri controversy, and invective against the free States for their part in it, by Messrs. Hayne and Benton, brought a reply from Mr Webster, showing what their conduct had been at the first introduction of the slavery topic in the Congress of the United States, and that they totally refused to interfere between master and slave in any way whatever. But the topic which became the leading feature of the whole debate, and gave it an interest which cannot die, was that of nullification—the assumed right of a State to annul an act of Congress—then first broached in the Senate—and in the discussion of which Mr. Webster and Mr. Hayne were the champion speakers on opposite sides—the latter voicing the sentiments of the Vice-President, Mr. Calhoun. This turn in the debate was brought about, by Mr. Hayne having made allusion to the course of New England during the war of 1812, and especially to the assemblage known as the Hartford Convention, and to which designs unfriendly to the Union had been attributed. This gave Mr. Webster an opportunity to retaliate, and he referred to the public meetings which had just then taken place in South Carolina on the subject of the tariff, and at which resolves were passed, and propositions adopted significant of resisistance to the act; and consequently of disloyalty to the Union. He drew Mr Hayne into their defence and into an avowal of what has since obtained the current name of "*Nullification.*" He said, "I understand the honourable gentleman from South Carolina to maintain, that it is a right of the State Legislature to interfere, whenever, in their judgment, this government transcends its constitutional limits, and to arrest the operation of its laws, * * * * that the States may lawfully decide for themselves, and each State for itself, whether, in a given case, the act of the general government transcends its powers, * * * * that if the exigency of the case, in the opinion of any State government require it, such State government may, by its own sovereign authority, annul an act of the general government, which it deems plainly and palpably unconstitutional." Mr. Hayne was evidently unprepared to admit, or fully deny, the propositions as so laid down, but contented himself with stating the words of the Virginia Resolution of 1798, as follows: "That this assembly doth explicitly and peremptorily declare, that it views the powers of the federal government as resulting from the compact, to which the States are parties, as limited by the plain sense and intention of the instrument constituting that compact, as no farther valid than they are authorized by the grants enumerated in that compact, and that, in case of a deliberate, palpable and dangerous exercise of other powers, not granted by the said compact, the States who are parties thereto have the right, and are in duty bound, to interpose for arresting the progress of the evil, and for maintaining, within their respective limits, the authorities, rights, and liberties appertaining to them."

This resolution came to be understood by Mr. Hayne and others on that side of the debate, in the same sense that Mr Webster stated, as above, he understood the gentleman from the South to interpret it. On the other side of the question, he argued that the doctrine had no foundation either in the Constitution, or on the Virginia resolutions—that the Constitution makes the federal government act upon citizens within the States, and not upon the States themselves, as in the old confederation: that within their Constitutional limits the laws of Congress were supreme —and that it was treasonable to resist them with force and that the question of their constitutionality was to be decided by the Supreme Court: with respect to the Virginia resolutions, on which Mr. Hayne relied, Mr. Webster disputed the interpretation put upon them—claimed for them an innocent and justifiable meaning—and exempted Mr. Madison from the suspicion of having framed a resolution asserting the right of a State legislature to annul an Act of Congress, and thereby putting it in the power of one State to destroy a form of government which he had just labored so hard to establish.

Mr. Hayne on his part gave (as the practical part of his doctrine) the pledge of forcible resistance to any attempt to enforce unconstitutional laws. He said, "The gentleman has called upon us to carry out our scheme practically Now, sir, if I am correct in my view of this matter, then it follows, of course, that the right of a State being established, the federal government is bound to acquiesce in a solemn decision of a State, acting in its sovereign capacity, at least so far as to make an appeal to the people for an amendment to the Constitution. This solemn decision of a State binds the federal government, under the highest constitutional obligation, not to resort to any means of coercion against the citizens of the dissenting State. * * * Suppose Congress should pass an agrarian law, or a law emancipating our slaves, or should commit any other gross violation of our constitutional rights, will any gentlemen contend that the decision of every branch of the federal government, in favor of such laws, could prevent the States from declaring them null and void, and protecting their citizens from their operation? * * Let me assure the gentlemen that, whenever any attempt shall be made from any quarter, to enforce unconstitutional laws, clearly violating our essential rights, our leaders (whoever they may be) will not be found reading black letter from the musty pages of old law books. They will look to the Constitution, and when called upon by the sovereign authority of the State, to preserve and protect the rights secured to them by the charter of their liberties, they will succeed in defending them, or 'perish in the last ditch.'"

These words of Mr. Hayne seem almost prophetic in view of the events of thirty years later. No one then believed in anything serious in the new interpretation given to the Virginia resolutions—nor in anything practical from nullification—nor in forcible resistance to the tariff laws from South Carolina—nor in any scheme of disunion.

Mr. Webster's closing reply was a fine piece of rhetoric, delivered in an elaborate and artistic style, and in an apparent spirit of deep seriousness. He concluded thus—"When my eyes shall be turned to behold, for the last time, the sun in heaven, may I not see him shining on the broken and disfigured fragments of a once glorious Union; on States dissevered, discordant, belligerent; on a land rent with civil feuds, or drenched, it may be, in fraternal blood. Let their last feeble and lingering glance, rather, behold the gorgeous ensign of the Republic, now known and honored throughout the earth, still full high advanced, its arms and trophies streaming in their original lustre, not a stripe erased or polluted, nor a single star obscured, bearing for its motto no such miserable interrogatory as, What is all this worth? nor those other words of delusion and folly, Liberty first and Union afterwards; but everywhere, spread all over in characters of living light, blazing in all its ample folds, as they float over the sea and over the land, and in every wind under the whole heavens, that other sentiment, dear to every true American heart—Liberty *and* Union, now and forever, one and inseparable!"

President Jackson in his first annual message to Congress called attention to the fact of expiration in 1836 of the charter of incorporation granted by the Federal government to a moneyed institution called The Bank of the United States, which was originally designed to assist the government in establishing and maintaining a uniform and sound currency. He seriously doubted the constitutionality and expediency of the law creating the bank, and was opposed to a renewal of the charter. His view of the matter was that if such an institution was deemed a necessity it should be made a national one, in the sense of being founded on the credit of the government and its revenues, and not a corporation independent from and not a part of the government. The House of Representatives was strongly in favor of the renewal of the charter, and several of its committees made elaborate, ample and argumentative reports upon the subject. These reports were the subject of newspaper and pamphlet publication; and lauded for their power and excellence, and triumphant refutation of all the President's opinions. Thus was the "war of the Bank" commenced at once in Congress, and in the public press; and openly at the instance of the Bank itself, which, forgetting its position as an institution of the government, for the convenience of the government, set itself up as a power, and struggled for continued existence, by demand for renewal of its charter. It allied itself at the same time to the political power opposed to the President, joined in all their schemes of protective tariff, and national internal improvement, and became the head of the American system. Its moneyed and political power, numerous interested affiliations, and control over other banks and fiscal institutions, was truly great and extensive, and a power which was exercised and made to be felt during the struggle to such a degree that it threatened a danger to the country and the government almost amounting to a national calamity.

The subject of renewal of the charter was agitated at every succeeding session of Congress down to 1836, and many able speeches made for and against it.

In the month of December, 1831, the National Republicans, as the party was then called which afterward took the name of "whig," held its convention in Baltimore, and nominated candidates for President and Vice-President, to be voted for at the election in the autumn of the ensuing year. Henry Clay was the candidate for the office of President, and John Sergeant for that of Vice-President. The platform or address to the people presented the party issues which were to be settled at the ensuing election, the chief subjects being the tariff, internal improvement, removal of the Cherokee Indians, and the renewal of the United States Bank charter. Thus the bank question was fully presented as an issue in the election by that part of its friends who classed politically against President Jackson. But it had also Democratic friends without whose aid the recharter could not be got through Congress, and they labored assiduously for it. The first Bank of the United States, chartered in 1791, was a federal measure, favored by General Hamilton, opposed by Mr. Jefferson, Mr. Madison, and the Republican party; and became a great landmark of party, not merely for the bank itself, but for the latitudinarian construction of the constitution in which it was founded, and the precedent it established that Congress might in its discretion do what it pleased, under the plea of being "*necessary*" to carry into effect some granted power. The non-renewal of the charter in 1811, was the act of the Republican party, then in possession of the government, and taking the opportunity to terminate, upon its own limitation, the existence of an institution whose creation they had not been able to prevent. The charter of the second bank, in 1816, was the act of the Republican party, and to aid them in the administration of the government, and, as such, was opposed by the Federal party—not seeming then to understand that, by its instincts, a great moneyed corporation was in sympathy with their own party, and would soon be with it in action—which the bank soon was—and now struggled for a continuation of its existence under the lead of those who had opposed its creation and against the party which effected it. Mr. Webster was a Federal leader on both occasions—against the charter in 1816; for the re-charter in 1832. The bill passed the Senate after a long and arduous contest; and afterwards passed the House, quickly and with little or no contest at all.

It was sent to the President, and vetoed by him July 10, 1832; the message stating his objections being an elaborate review of the subject; the veto being based mainly on the unconstitutionality of the measure. The veto was sustained. Following this the President after the adjournment removed from the bank the government deposits, and referred to that fact in his next annual message on the second day of December, 1833, at the opening of the first session of the twenty-third Congress. Accompanying it was the report of the Secretary of the Treasury, Hon. Roger B. Taney, afterwards Chief Justice of the Supreme Court of the United States, giving the reasons of the government for the withdrawal of the public funds. Long and bitter was the contest between the President on the one side and the Bank and its supporters in the Senate on the other side. The conduct of the Bank produced distress throughout the country, and was so intended to coerce the President. Distress petitions flooded Congress, and the Senate even passed resolutions of censure of the President. The latter, however, held firm in his position. A committee of investigation was appointed by the House of Representatives to inquire into the causes of the commercial embarrassment and the public distress complained of in the numerous distress memorials presented to the two Houses during the session; and whether the Bank had been instrumental, through its management of money, in producing the distress and embarrassment of which so much complaint was made; to inquire whether the charter of the Bank had been violated, and what corruptions and abuses, if any, existed in its management; and to inquire whether the Bank had used its corporate power or money to control the press, to interpose in politics, or to influence elections. The committee were granted ample powers for the execution of these inquiries. It was treated with disdain and contempt by the Bank management, refused access to the books and papers, and the directors and president refused to be sworn and testify The committee at the next session made report of their proceedings, and asked for warrants to be issued against the managers to bring them before the Bar of the House to answer for contempt; but the friends of the Bank in the House were able to check the proceedings and prevent action being taken. In the Senate, the President was sought to be punished by a declination by that body to confirm the President's nomination of the four government directors of the Bank, who had served the previous year; and their re-nomination after that rejection again met with a similar fate. In like manner his re-nomination of Roger B. Taney to be Secretary of the Treasury was rejected, for the action of the latter in his support of the President and the removal of the public deposits. The Bank had lost much ground in the public estimation by resisting the investigation ordered and attempted by the House of Representatives, and in consequence the Finance Committee of the Senate made an investigation, with so weak an attempt to varnish over the affairs and acts of the corporation that the odious appellation of "white-washing committee" was fastened upon it. The downfall of the Bank speedily followed; it soon afterwards became a total financial wreck, and its assets and property were seized on executions. With its financial failure it vanished from public view, and public interest in it and concern with it died out.

About the beginning of March, 1831, a pamphlet was issued in Washington, by Mr. John C. Calhoun, the Vice-President, and addressed to the people of the United States, explaining the cause of a difference which had taken place between himself and the President, General Jackson, instigated as the pamphlet alleged, by Mr. Van Buren, and intended to make trouble between the first and second officers of the government, and to effect the political destruction of himself (Mr. Calhoun) for the benefit of the contriver of the quarrel, the then Secretary of State, and indicated as a candidate for the presidential succession upon the termination of Jackson's term. The differences grew out of certain charges against General Jackson respecting his conduct during the Seminole war which occurred in the administration of President Monroe. The President justified himself in published correspondence, but the inevitable result followed—a rupture between the President and Vice-President—which was quickly followed by a breaking up and reconstructing the Cabinet. Some of its members classed as the political friends of Mr. Calhoun, and could hardly be expected to remain as ministers to the President. Mr. Van Buren resigned; a new Cabinet was appointed and confirmed. This change in the Cabinet made a great figure in the party politics of the day, and filled all the opposition newspapers, and had many sinister reasons assigned to it—all to the prejudice of General Jackson and Mr. Van Buren.

It is interesting to note here that during the administration of President Jackson,—in the year 1833,—the Congress of the United States, as the consequence of the earnest efforts in that behalf, of Col. R. M. Johnson, of Kentucky, aided by the recommendation and support of the President, passed the first laws, abolishing imprisonment for debt, under process from the Courts of the United States: the only extent to which an act of Congress could go, by force of its enactments; but by force of example and influence, has led to the cessation of the practice of imprisoning debtors, in all, or nearly all, of the States and Territories of the Union; and without the evil consequences which had been dreaded from the loss of this remedy over the person. The act was a total abolition of the practice, leaving in full force all the remedies against fraudulent evasions of debt.

The American system, and especially its prominent feature of a high protective tariff was put in issue, in the Presidential canvass of 1832; and the friends of that system labored diligently in Congress in presenting its best points to the greatest advantage; and staking its fate upon the issue of the election. It was lost; not only by the result of the main contest, but by that of the congressional election which took place simultaneously with it. All the States dissatisfied with that system, were satisfied with the view of its speedy and regular extinction, under the legislation of the approaching session of Congress, excepting only South Carolina. She has held aloof from the Presidential contest, and cast her electoral votes for persons who were not candidates—doing nothing to aid the election of General Jackson, with whom her interests were apparently identified. On the 24th November, 1832, two weeks after the election which decided the fate of the tariff, that State issued an "Ordinance to nullify certain acts of the Congress of the United States, purporting to be laws laying duties and imposts on the importation of foreign commodities." It declared that the Congress had exceeded its constitutional powers in imposing high and excessive duties on the theory of "protection," had unjustly discriminated in favor of one class or employment, at the expense and to the injury and oppression of other classes and individuals; that said laws were in consequence not binding on the State and its citizens; and declaring its right and purpose to enact laws to prevent the enforcement and arrest the operation of said acts and parts of the acts of the Congress of the United States within the limits of that State after the first day of February following. This ordinance placed the State in the attitude of forcible resistance to the laws of the United States, to take effect on the first day of February next ensuing—a date prior to the meeting of the next Congress, which the country naturally expected would take some action in reference to the tariff laws complained of. The ordinance further provided that if, in the meantime, any attempt was made by the federal government to enforce the obnoxious laws, except through the tribunals, all the officers of which were sworn against them, the fact of such attempt was to terminate the continuance of South Carolina in the Union—to absolve her from all connection with the federal government—and to establish her as a separate government, wholly unconnected with the United States or any State. The ordinance of nullification was certified by the Governor of South Carolina to the President of the United States, and reached him in December of the same year; in consequence of which he immediately issued a proclamation, exhorting the people of South Carolina to obey the laws of Congress; pointing out and explaining the illegality of the procedure; stating clearly and distinctly his firm determination to enforce the laws as became him as Executive, even by resort to force if necessary. As a state paper, it is important as it contains the views of General Jackson regarding the nature and character of our federal government, expressed in the following language: "The people of the United States formed the constitution, acting through the State Legislatures in making the compact, to meet and discuss its provisions, and acting in separate conventions when they ratified those provisions; but, the terms used in the constitution show it to be a government in which the people of all the States collectively are represented. We are one people in the choice of President and Vice-President. Here the States have no other agency than to direct the mode in which the votes shall be given. * * The people, then, and not the States, are represented in the executive branch. * * * In the House of Representatives the members are all representatives of the United States, not representatives of the particular States from which they come. They are paid by the United States, not by the State, nor are they accountable to it for any act done in the performance of their legislative functions. * * * * *

The constitution of the United States, then, forms a government, not a league; and whether it be formed by a compact between the States, or in any other manner, its character is the same. It is a government in which all the people are represented, which operates directly on the people individually, not upon the States—they retained all the power they did not grant. But each State, having expressly parted with so many powers as to constitute, jointly with the other States, a single nation, cannot, from that period, possess any right to secede, because such secession does not break a league, but destroys the unity of the nation, and any injury to that unity, is not only a breach which could result from the contravention of a compact, but it is an offence against the whole Union. To say that any State may at pleasure secede from the Union, is to say that the United States are not a nation; because it would be a solecism to contend that any part of a nation might dissolve its connection with the other parts, to their injury or ruin, without committing any offence."

Without calling on Congress for extraordinary powers, the President in his annual message, merely adverted to the attitude of the State, and proceeded to meet the exigency by the exercise of the powers he already possessed. The proceedings in South Carolina not ceasing, and taking daily a more aggravated form in the organization of troops, the collection of arms and of munitions of war, and in declarations hostile to the Union, he found it necessary early in January to report the facts to Congress in a special message, and ask for extraordinary powers. Bills for the reduction of the tariff were early in the Session introduced into both houses, while at the same time the President, though not relaxing his efforts towards a peaceful settlement of the difficulty, made steady preparations for enforcing the law. The result of the bills offered in the two Houses of Congress, was the passage of Mr. Clay's "compromise" bill on the 12th of February 1833, which radically changed the whole tariff system.

The President in his message on the South Carolina proceedings had recommended to Congress the revival of some acts, heretofore in force, to enable him to execute the laws in that State; and the Senate's committee on the judiciary had reported a bill accordingly early in the session. It was immediately assailed by several members as violent and unconstitutional, tending to civil war, and denounced as "the bloody bill"—the "force bill," &c. The bill was vindicated in the Senate, by its author, who showed that it contained no novel principle; was substantially a revival of laws previously in force; with the authority superadded to remove the office of customs from one building or place to another in case of need. The bill was vehemently opposed, and every effort made to render it odious to the people, and even extend the odium to the President, and to every person urging or aiding in its passage. Mr Webster justly rebuked all this vituperation, and justified the bill, both for the equity of its provisions, and the necessity for enacting them. He said, that an unlawful combination threatened the integrity of the Union; that the crisis called for a mild, temperate, forbearing but unflexibly firm execution of the laws; and finally, that public opinion sets with an irresistible force in favor of the Union, in favor of the measures recommended by the President, and against the new doctrines which threatened the dissolution of the Union. The support which Mr. Webster gave to these measures was the regular result of the principles which he laid down in his first speeches against nullification in the debate with Mr. Hayne, and he could not have done less without being derelict to his own principles then avowed. He supported with transcendent ability, the cause of the constitution and of the country, in the person of a President to whom he was politically opposed, whose gratitude and admiration he earned for his patriotic endeavors. The country, without distinction of party, felt the same; and the universality of the feeling was one of the grateful instances of popular applause and justice when great talents are seen exerting themselves for the good of the country. He was the colossal figure on the political stage during that eventful time; and his labors, splendid in their day, survive for the benefit of distant posterity.

During the discussion over the re-charter of the Bank of the United States, which as before mentioned, occupied the attention of Congress for several years, the country suffered from a money panic, and a general financial depression and distress was generally prevalent. In 1834 a measure was introduced into the House, for equalizing the value of gold and silver, and legalizing the tender of foreign coin, of both metals. The good effects of the bill were immediately seen. Gold began to flow into the country through all the channels of commerce, foreign and domestic; the mint was busy; and specie payment, which had been suspended in the country for thirty years, was resumed, and gold and silver became the currency of the land; inspiring confidence in all the pursuits of industry.

As indicative of the position of the democratic party at that date, on the subject of the kind of money authorized by the Constitution, Mr. Benton's speech in the Senate is of interest. He said: "In the first place, he was one of those who believed that the government of the United States was intended to be a hard money government; that it was the intention and the declaration of the Constitution of the United States, that the federal currency should consist of gold and silver, and that there is no power in Congress to issue, or to authorize any company of individuals to issue, any species of federal paper currency whatsoever. Every clause in the Constitution (said Mr. B.) which bears upon the subject of money—every early statute of Congress which interprets the meaning of these clauses—and every historic recollection which refers to them, go hand in hand in giving to that instrument the meaning which this proposition ascribes to it. The power granted to Congress to coin money is an authority to stamp metallic money, and is not an authority for emitting slips of paper containing promises to pay money The authority granted to Congress to regulate the value of coin, is an authority to regulate the value of the metallic money, not of paper. The prohibition upon the States against making anything but gold and silver a legal tender, is a moral prohibition, founded in virtue and honesty, and is just as binding upon the Federal Government as upon the State Governments; and that without a written prohibition; for the difference in the nature of the two governments is such, that the States may do all things which they are not forbid to do; and the Federal Government can do nothing which it is not authorized by the Constitution to do. The framers of the Constitution (said Mr. B.) created a hard money government. They intended the new government to recognize nothing for money but gold and silver; and every word admitted into the Constitution, upon the subject of money, defines and establishes that sacred intention.

Legislative enactment came quickly to the aid of constitutional intention and historic recollection. The fifth statute passed at the first session of the first Congress that ever sat under the present Constitution was full and explicit on this head. It declared, "that the fees and duties payable to the federal government shall be received in gold and silver coin only." It was under General Hamilton, as Secretary of the Treasury, in 1791, that the policy of the government underwent a change. In the act constituting the Bank of the United States, he brought forward his celebrated plan for the support of the public credit—that plan which unfolded the entire scheme of the paper system and immediately developed the great political line between the federalists and the republicans. The establishment of a national bank was the leading and predominant feature of that plan; and the original report of the secretary, in favor of establishing the bank, contained this fatal and deplorable recommendation: "The bills and notes of the bank, originally made payable, or which shall have become payable, on demand, in gold and silver coin, shall be receivable in all payments to the United States." From the moment of the adoption of this policy, the moneyed character of the government stood changed and reversed. Federal bank notes took the place of hard money; and the whole edifice of the government slid, at once, from the solid rock of gold and silver money, on which its framers had placed it, into the troubled and tempestuous ocean of paper currency

The first session of the 35th Congress opened December 1835. Mr. James K. Polk was elected Speaker of the House by a large majority over Mr. John Bell, the previous Speaker; the former being supported by the administration party, and the latter having become identified with those who, on siding with Mr. Hugh L. White as a candidate for the presidency, were considered as having divided from the democratic party. The chief subject of the President's message was the relations of our country with France relative to the continued non-payment of the stipulated indemnity provided for in the treaty of 1831 for French spoliations of American shipping. The obligation to pay was admitted, and the money even voted for that purpose; but offense was taken at the President's message, and payment refused until an apology should be made. The President commented on this in his message, and the Senate had under consideration measures authorizing reprisals on French shipping. At this point Great Britain offered her services as mediator between the nations, and as a result the indemnity was shortly afterwards paid.

Agitation of the slavery question in the United States really began about this time. Evil-disposed persons had largely circulated through the Southern states, pamphlets and circulars tending to stir up strife and insurrection; and this had become so intolerable that it was referred to by the President in his message. Congress at the session of 1836 was flooded with petitions and memorials urging federal interference to abolish slavery in the States; beginning with the petition of the Society of Friends of Philadelphia, urging the abolition of slavery in the District of Columbia. These petitions were referred to Committees after an acrimonious debate as to whether they should be received or not. The position of the government at that time is embodied in the following resolution which was adopted in the House of Representatives as early as 1790, and substantially re-affirmed in 1836, as follows: "That Congress have no authority to interfere in the emancipation of slaves, or in the treatment of them within any of the States; it remaining with the several States to provide any regulations therein which humanity and true policy may require."

In the Summer preceding the Presidential election of 1836, a measure was introduced into Congress, which became very nearly a party measure, and which in its results proved disastrous to the Democratic party in after years. It was a plan for distributing the public land money among the States either in the shape of credit distribution, or in the disguise of a deposit of surplus revenue; and this for the purpose of enhancing the value of the State stocks held by the United States Bank, which institution, aided by the party which it favored, led by Mr. Clay, was the prime mover in the plan. That gentleman was the author of the scheme, and great calculations were made by the party which favored the distribution upon its effect in adding to their popularity. The Bill passed the Senate in its original form, but met with less favor in the House where it was found necessary. To effectuate substantially the same end, a Senate Bill was introduced to regulate the keeping of the public money in the deposit banks, and this was turned into distribution of the surplus public moneys with the States, in proportion to their representation in Congress, to be returned when Congress should call for it; and this was called a deposit with the States, and the faith of the States pledged for a return of the money. It was stigmatized by its opponents in Congress, as a distribution in disguise—as a deposit never to be reclaimed; as a miserable evasion of the Constitution; as an attempt to debauch the people with their own money; as plundering instead of defending the country. The Bill passed both houses, mainly by the efforts of a half dozen aspirants to the Presidency, who sought to thus increase their popularity. They were doomed to disappointment in this respect. Politically, it was no advantage to its numerous and emulous supporters, and of no disservice to its few determined opponents. It was a most unfortunate act, a plain evasion of the Constitution for a bad purpose; and it soon gave a sad overthrow to the democracy and disappointed every calculation made upon it. To the States it was no advantage, raising expectations which were not fulfilled, and upon which many of them acted as realities. The Bill was signed by the President, but it is simple justice to him to say that he did it with a repugnance of feeling, and a recoil of judgment, which it required great efforts of his friends to overcome, and with a regret for it afterwards which he often and publicly expressed. In a party point of view, the passage of this measure was the commencement of calamities, being an efficient cause in that general suspension of specie payments, which quickly occurred, and brought so much embarrassment on the Van Buren administration, ending in the great democratic defeat of 1840.

The presidential election of 1836 resulted in the choice of the democratic candidate, Mr. Van Buren, who was elected by 170 electoral votes; his opponent, General Harrison, receiving seventy-three electoral votes. Scattering votes were given for Mr. Webster, Mr. Mangum, and Mr. Hugh L. White, the last named representing a fragment of the democracy who, in a spirit of disaffection, attempted to divide the democratic party and defeat Mr. Van Buren. At the opening of the second session of the twenty-fourth Congress, December, 1836, President Jackson delivered his last annual message, under circumstances exceedingly gratifying to him. The powerful opposition in Congress had been broken down, and he had the satisfaction of seeing full majorities of ardent and tried friends in each House. The country was in peace and friendship with all the world; all exciting questions quieted at home; industry in all its branches prosperous, and the revenue abundant. And as a happy sequence of this state of affairs, the Senate on the 16th of March, 1837, expunged from the Journal the resolution, adopted three years previously, censuring the President for ordering the removal of the deposits of public money in the United States Bank. He retired from the presidency with high honors, and died eight years afterwards at his home, the celebrated "Hermitage," in Tennessee, in full possession of all his faculties, and strong to the last in the ruling passion of his soul—love of country.

The 4th of March, 1837, ushered in another Democratic administration—the beginning of the term of Martin Van Buren as President of the United States. In his inaugural address he commented on the prosperous condition of the country, and declared it to be his policy to strictly abide by the Constitution as written—no latitudinarian constructions permitted, or doubtful powers assumed; that his political chart should be the doctrines of the democratic school, as understood at the original formation of parties.

The President, however, was scarcely settled in his new office when a financial panic struck the country with irresistible force. A general suspension of the banks, a depreciated currency, and insolvency of the federal treasury were at hand. The public money had been placed in the custody of the local banks, and the notes of all these banks, and of all others in the country, were received in payment of public dues. On the 10th of May, 1837, the banks throughout the country suspended specie payments. The stoppage of the deposit banks was the stoppage of the Treasury. Non-payment by the government was an excuse for non-payment by others. The suspension was now complete; and it was evident, and as good as admitted by those who had made it, that it was the effect of contrivance on the part of politicians and the so-called Bank of the United States (which, after the expiration of its national charter, had become a State corporation chartered by the Legislature of Pennsylvania in January, 1836) for the purpose of restoring themselves to power. The whole proceeding became clear to those who could see nothing while it was in progress. Even those of the democratic party whose votes had helped to do the mischief, could now see that the attempt to deposit forty millions with the States was destruction to the deposit banks; that the repeal of President Jackson's order, known as the "specie circular"—requiring payment for public lands to be in coin—was to fill the treasury with paper money, to be found useless when wanted; that distress was purposely created to throw blame of it upon the party in power; that the promptitude with which the Bank of the United States had been brought forward as a remedy for the distress, showed that it had been held in reserve for that purpose; and the delight with which the whig party saluted the general calamity, showed that they considered it their own passport to power. Financial embarrassment and general stagnation of business diminished the current receipts from lands and customs, and actually caused an absolute deficit in the public treasury. In consequence, the President found it an inexorable necessity to issue his proclamation convening Congress in extra session.

The first session of the twenty-fifth Congress met in extra session, at the call of the President, on the first Monday of September, 1837. The message was a review of the events and causes which had brought about the panic; a defense of the policy of the "specie circular," and a recommendation to break off all connection with any bank of issue in any form; looking to the establishment of an Independent Treasury, and that the Government provide for the deficit in the treasury by the issue of treasury notes and by withholding the deposit due to the States under the act then in force. The message and its recommendations were violently assailed both in the Senate and House by able and effective speakers, notably by Messrs. Clay and Webster, and also by Mr. Caleb Cushing, of Massachusetts, who made a formal and elaborate reply to the whole document under thirty-two distinct heads, and reciting therein all the points of accusation against the democratic policy from the beginning of the government down to that day. The result was that the measures proposed by the Executive were in substance enacted; and their passage marks an era in our financial history—making a total and complete separation of Bank and State, and firmly establishing the principle that the government revenues should be receivable in coin only.

The measures of consequence discussed and adopted at this session, were the graduation of price of public lands under the pre-emption system, which was adopted; the bill to create an independent Treasury, which passed the Senate, but failed in the House; and the question of the re-charter of the district banks, the proportion for reserve, and the establishment of such institutions on a specie basis. The slavery question was again agitated in consequence of petitions from citizens and societies in the Northern States, and a memorial from the General Assembly of Vermont, praying for the abolition of slavery in the District of Columbia and territories, and for the exclusion of future slave states from the Union. These petitions and memorials were disposed of adversely; and Mr. Calhoun, representing the ultra-Southern interest, in several able speeches, approved of the Missouri compromise, he urged and obtained of the Senate several resolutions declaring that the federal government had no power to interfere with slavery in the States; and that it would be inexpedient and impolitic to interfere, abolish or control it in the District of Columbia and the territories. These movements for and against slavery in the session of 1837–38 deserve to be noticed, as of disturbing effect at the time, and as having acquired new importance from subsequent events.

The first session of the twenty-sixth Congress opened December, 1839. The organization of the House was delayed by a closely and earnestly contested election from the State of New Jersey. Five Democrats claiming seats as against an equal number of Whigs. Neither set was admitted until after the election of Speaker, which resulted in the choice of Robert M. T. Hunter, of Virginia, the Whig candidate, who was elected by the full Whig vote with the aid of a few democrats—friends of Mr. Calhoun, who had for several previous sessions been acting with the Whigs on several occasions. The House excluding the five contested seats from New Jersey, was really Democratic; having 122 members, and the Whigs 113 members. The contest for the Speakership was long and arduous, neither party adhering to its original caucus candidate. Twenty scattering votes, eleven of whom were classed as Whigs, and nine as Democrats, prevented a choice on the earlier ballots, and it was really Mr. Calhoun's Democratic friends uniting with a solid Whig vote on the final ballot that gained that party the election. The issue involved was a vital party question as involving the organization of the House. The chief measure, of public importance, adopted at this session of Congress was an act to provide for the collection, safe-keeping, and disbursing of the public money. It practically revolutionized the system previously in force, and was a complete and effectual separation of the federal treasury and the Government, from the banks and moneyed corporations of the States. It was violently opposed by the Whig members, led by Mr. Clay, and supported by Mr. Cushing, but was finally passed in both Houses by a close vote.

At this time, and in the House of Representatives, was exhibited for the first time in the history of Congress, the present practice of members "*pairing off*," as it is called; that is to say, two members of opposite political parties, or of opposite views on any particular subject, agreeing to absent themselves from the duties of the House, for the time being. The practice was condemned on the floor of the House by Mr. John Quincy Adams, who introduced a resolution: "That the practice, first openly avowed at the present session of Congress, of pairing off, involves, on the part of the members resorting to it, the violation of the Constitution of the United States, of an express rule of this House, and of the duties of both parties in the transaction, to their immediate constituents, to this House, and to their country." This resolution was placed in the calendar to take its turn, but not being reached during the session, was not voted on. That was the first instance of this justly condemned practice, fifty years after the establishment of the Government; but since then it has become common, even inveterate, and is now carried to great lengths.

The last session of the twenty-sixth Congress was barren of measures, and necessarily so, as being the last of our administration superseded by the popular voice, and soon to expire; and therefore restricted by a sense of propriety, during the brief remainder of its existence, to the details of business and the routine of service. The cause of this was the result of the presidential election of 1840. The same candidates who fought the battle of 1836 were again in the field. Mr. Van Buren was the Democratic candidate. His administration had been satisfactory to his party, and his nomination for a second term was commended by the party in the different States in appointing their delegates; so that the proceedings of the convention which nominated him were entirely harmonious and formal in their nature. Mr. Richard M. Johnson, the actual Vice-President, was also nominated for Vice-President.

On the Whig ticket, General William Henry Harrison, of Ohio, was the candidate for President, and Mr. John Tyler, of Virginia, for Vice-President. The leading statesmen of the Whig party were again put aside, to make way for a military man, prompted by the example in the nomination of General Jackson, the men who managed presidential elections believing then as now that military renown was a passport to popularity and rendered a candidate more sure of election. Availability—for the purpose—was the only ability asked for. Mr. Clay, the most prominent Whig in the country, and the acknowledged head of the party, was not deemed available; and though Mr. Clay was a candidate before the convention, the proceedings were so regulated that his nomination was referred to a committee, ingeniously devised and directed for the afterwards avowed purpose of preventing his nomination and securing that of General Harrison; and of producing the intended result without showing the design, and without leaving a trace behind to show what was done. The scheme (a modification of which has since been applied to subsequent national conventions, and out of which many bitter dissensions have again and again arisen) is embodied and was executed in and by means of the following resolution adopted by the convention: "*Ordered*, That the delegates from each State be requested to assemble as a delegation, and appoint a committee, not exceeding three in number, to receive the views and opinions of such delegation, and communicate the same to the assembled committes of all the delegations, to be by them respectively reported to their principals; and that thereupon the delegates from each State be requested to assemble as a delegation, and ballot for candidates for the offices of President and Vice-President, and having done so, to commit the ballot designating the votes of each candidate, and by whom given, to its committee, and thereupon all the committees shall assemble and compare the several ballots, and report the result of the same to their several delegations, together with such facts as may bear upon the nomination; and said delegation shall forthwith re-assemble and ballot again for candidates for the above offices, and again commit the result to the above committees, and if it shall appear that a majority of the ballots are for any one man for candidate for President, said committee shall report the result to the convention for its consideration; but if there shall be no such majority, then the delegation shall repeat the balloting until such a majority shall be obtained, and then report the same to the convention for its consideration. That the vote of a majority of each delegation shall be reported as the vote of that State; and each State represented here shall vote its full electoral vote by such delegation in the committee." This was a sum in political algebra, whose quotient was known, but the quantity unknown except to those who planned it; and the result was—for General Scott, 16 votes; for Mr. Clay, 90 votes; for General Harrison, 148 votes. And as the law of the convention impliedly requires the absorption of all minorities, the 106 votes were swallowed up by the 148 votes and made to count for General Harrison, presenting him as the unanimity candidate of the convention, and the defeated candidates and all their friends bound to join in his support. And in this way the election of 1840 was effected—a process certainly not within the purview of those framers of the constitution who supposed they were giving to the nation the choice of its own chief magistrate.

The contest before the people was a long and bitter one, the severest ever known in the country, up to that time, and scarcely equalled since. The whole Whig party and the large league of suspended banks, headed by the Bank of the United States making its last struggle for a new national charter in the effort to elect a President friendly to it, were arrayed against the Democrats, whose hard-money policy and independent treasury schemes, met with little favor in the then depressed condition of the country. Meetings were held in every State, county and town; the people thoroughly aroused; and every argument made in favor of the respective candidates and parties, which could possibly have any effect upon the voters. The canvass was a thorough one, and the election was carried for the Whig candidates, who received 234 electoral votes coming from 19 States. The remaining 60 electoral votes of the other 9 States, were given to the Democratic candidate; though the popular vote was not so unevenly divided; the actual figures being 1,275,611 for the Whig ticket, against 1,135,761 for the Democratic ticket. It was a complete rout of the Democratic party, but without the moral effect of victory.

On March 4, 1841, was inaugurated as President, Gen'l Wm. H. Harrison, the first Chief Magistrate elected by the Whig party, and the first President who was not a Democrat, since the installation of Gen'l Jackson, March 4, 1829. His term was a short one. He issued a call for a special session of Congress to convene the 31st of May following, to consider the condition of the revenue and finances of the country, but did not live to meet it. Taken ill with a fatal malady during the last days of March, he died on the 4th of April following, having been in office just one month. He was succeeded by the Vice-President, John Tyler. Then, for the first time in our history as a government, the person elected to the Vice-Presidency of the United States, by the happening of a contingency provided for in the constitution, had devolved upon him the Presidential office.

The twenty-seventh Congress opened in extra session at the call of the late President, May 31, 1841. A Whig member—Mr. White of Kentucky—was elected Speaker of the House of Representatives. The Whigs had a majority of forty-seven in the House and of seven in the Senate, and with the President and Cabinet of the same political party presented a harmony of aspect frequently wanting during the three previous administrations. The first measure of the new dominant party was the repeal of the independent treasury act passed at the previous session; and the next in order were bills to establish a system of bankruptcy, and for distribution of public land revenue. The former was more than a bankrupt law; it was practically an insolvent law for the abolition of debts at the will of the debtor. It applied to all persons in debt, allowed them to institute the proceedings in the district where the petitioner resided, allowed constructive notices to creditors in newspapers —declared the abolition of the debt where effects were surrendered and fraud not proved; and gave exclusive jurisdiction to the federal courts, at the will of the debtor. It was framed upon the model of the English insolvent debtors' act of George the Fourth, and embodied most of the provisions of that act, but substituting a release from the debt instead of a release from imprisonment. The bill passed by a close vote in both Houses.

The land revenue distribution bill of this session had its origin in the fact that the States and corporations owed about two hundred millions to creditors in Europe. These debts were in stocks, much depreciated by the failure in many instances to pay the accruing interest—in some instances failure to provide for the principal. These creditors, becoming uneasy, wished the federal government to assume their debts. The suggestion was made as early as 1838, renewed in 1839, and in 1840 became a regular question mixed up with the Presidential election of that year, and openly engaging the active exertions of foreigners. Direct assumption was not urged; indirect by giving the public land revenue to the States was the mode pursued, and the one recommended in the message of President Tyler. Mr. Calhoun spoke against the measure with more than usual force and clearness, claiming that it was unconstitutional and without warrant. Mr. Benton on the same side called it a squandering of the public patrimony, and pointed out its inexpediency in the depleted state of the treasury, apart from its other objectionable features. It passed by a party vote.

This session is remarkable for the institution of the hour rule in the House of Representatives—a very great limitation upon the freedom of debate. It was a Whig measure, adopted to prevent delay in the enactment of pending bills. It was a rigorous limitation, frequently acting as a bar to profitable debate and checking members in speeches which really impart information valuable to the House and the country No doubt the license of debate has been frequently abused in Congress, as in all other deliberative assemblies, but the incessant use of the previous question, which cuts off all debate, added to the hour rule which limits a speech to sixty minutes (constantly reduced by interruptions) frequently results in the transaction of business in ignorance of what they are about by those who are doing it.

The rule worked so well in the House, for the purpose for which it was devised—made the majority absolute master of the body—that Mr. Clay undertook to have the same rule adopted in the Senate; but the determined opposition to it, both by his political opponents and friends, led to the abandonment of the attempt in that chamber.

Much discussion took place at this session, over the bill offered in the House of Representatives, for the relief of the widow of the late President—General Harrison—appropriating one year's salary. It was strenuously opposed by the Democratic members, as unconstitutional, on account of its principle, as creating a private pension list, and as a dangerous precedent. Many able speeches were made against the bill, both in the Senate and House; among others, the following extract from the speech of an able Senator contains some interesting facts. He said: "Look at the case of Mr. Jefferson, a man than whom no one that ever existed on God's earth were the human family more indebted to.

His furniture and his estate were sold to satisfy his creditors. His posterity was driven from house and home, and his bones now lay in soil owned by a stranger. His family are scattered: some of his descendants are married in foreign lands. Look at Monroe—the able, the patriotic Monroe, whose services were revolutionary, whose blood was spilt in the war of Independence, whose life was worn out in civil service, and whose estate has been sold for debt, his family scattered, and his daughter buried in a foreign land. Look at Madison, the model of every virtue, public or private, and he would only mention in connection with this subject, his love of order, his economy, and his systematic regularity in all his habits of business. He, when his term of eight years had expired, sent a letter to a gentleman (a son of whom is now on this floor) [Mr. Preston], enclosing a note of five thousand dollars, which he requested him to endorse, and raise the money in Virginia, so as to enable him to leave this city, and return to his modest retreat—his patrimonial inheritance—in that State. General Jackson drew upon the consignee of his cotton crop in New Orleans for six thousand dollars to enable him to leave the seat of government without leaving creditors behind him. These were honored leaders of the republican party They had all been Presidents. They had made great sacrifices, and left the presidency deeply embarrassed; and yet the republican party who had the power and the strongest disposition to relieve their necessities, felt they had no right to do so by appropriating money from the public Treasury Democracy would not do this. It was left for the era of federal rule and federal supremacy—who are now rushing the country with steam power into all the abuses and corruptions of a monarchy, with its pensioned aristocracy—and to entail upon the country a civil pension list."

There was an impatient majority in the House in favor of the passage of the bill. The circumstances were averse to deliberation—a victorious party, come into power after a heated election, seeing their elected candidate dying on the threshold of his administration, poor and beloved: it was a case for feeling more than of judgment, especially with the political friends of the deceased—but few of whom could follow the counsels of the head against the impulsions of the heart.

The bill passed, and was approved; and as predicted, it established a precedent which has since been followed in every similar case.

The subject of naval pensions received more than usual consideration at this session. The question arose on the discussion of the appropriation bill for that purpose. A difference about a navy—on the point of how much and what kind—had always been a point of difference between the two great political parties of the Union, which, under whatsoever names, are always the same, each preserving its identity in principles and policy, but here the two parties divided upon an abuse which no one could deny or defend. A navy pension fund had been established under the act of 1832, which was a just and proper law, but on the 3d of March, 1837, an act was passed entitled "An act for the more equitable distribution of the Navy Pension Fund." That act provided: I. That Invalid naval pensions should commence and date back to the time of receiving the inability, instead of completing the proof. II. It extended the pensions for death to all cases of death, whether incurred in the line of duty or not. III. It extended the widow's pensions for life, when five years had been the law both in the army and navy. IV It adopted the English system of pensioning children of deceased marines, until they attained their majority.

The effect of this law was to absorb and bankrupt the navy pension fund, a meritorious fund created out of the government share of prize money, relinquished for that purpose, and to throw the pensions, arrears as well as current and future, upon the public treasury, where it was never intended they were to be. It was to repeal this act, that an amendment was introduced at this session on the bringing forward of the annual appropriation bill for navy pensions, and long and earnest were the debates upon it. The amendment was lost, the Senate dividing on party lines, the Whigs against and the Democrats for the amendment. The subject is instructive, as then was practically ratified and reenacted the pernicious practice authorized by the act of 1837, of granting pensions to date from the time of injury and not from the time of proof; and has grown up to such proportions in recent years that the last act of Congress appropriating money for arrears of pensions, provided for the payment of such an enormous sum of money that it would have appalled the original projectors of the act of 1837 could they have seen to what their system has led.

Again, at this session, the object of the tariff occupied the attention of Congress. The compromise act, as it was called, of 1833, which was composed of two parts—one to last nine years, for the benefit of manufactures; the other to last for ever, for the benefit of the planting and consuming interest—was passed, as hereinbefore stated, in pursuance of an agreement between Mr. Clay and Mr. Calhoun and their respective friends, at the time the former was urging the necessity for a continuance of high tariff for protection and revenue, and the latter was presenting and justifying before Congress the nullification ordinance adopted by the Legislature of South Carolina. To Mr. Clay and Mr. Calhoun it was a political necessity, one to get rid of a stumbling-block (which protective tariff had become); the other to escape a personal peril which his nullifying ordinance had brought upon him, and with both, it was a piece of policy, to enable them to combine against Mr. Van Buren, by postponing their own contention; and a device on the part of its author (Mr. Clayton, of Delaware) and Mr. Clay to preserve the protective system. It provided for a reduction of a certain per centage each year, on the duties for the ensuing nine years, until the revenue was reduced to 20 per cent. ad valorem on all articles imported into the country. In consequence the revenue was so reduced that in the last year, there was little more than half what the exigencies of the government required, and different modes, by loans and otherwise, were suggested to meet the deficiency. The Secretary of the Treasury had declared the necessity of loans and taxes to carry on the government; a loan bill for twelve millions had been passed; a tariff bill to raise fourteen millions was depending; and the chairman of the Committee of Ways and Means, Mr. Millard Fillmore, defended its necessity in an able speech. His bill proposed twenty per cent. additional to the existing duty on certain specified articles, sufficient to make up the amount wanted. This encroachment on a measure so much vaunted when passed, and which had been kept inviolate while operating in favor of one of the parties to it, naturally excited complaint and opposition from the other, and Mr. Gilmer, of Virginia, in a speech against the new bill, said: "In referring to the compromise act, the true characteristics of that act which recommended it strongly to him, were that it contemplated that duties were to be levied for revenue only, and in the next place to the amount only necessary to the supply of the economical wants of the government. He begged leave to call the attention of the committee to the principle recognized as the language of the compromise, a principle which ought to be recognized in all time to come by every department of the government. It is, that duties to be raised for revenue are to be raised to such an amount only as is necessary for an economical administration of the government. Some incidental protection must necessarily be given, and he, for one, coming from an anti-tariff portion of the country, would not object to it."

The bill went to the Senate where it found Mr Clay and Mr. Calhoun in positions very different from what they occupied when the compromise act was passed—then united, now divided—then concurrent, now antagonistic, and the antagonism general, upon all measures, was to be special upon this one. Their connection with the subject made it their function to lead off in its consideration; and their antagonist positions promised sharp encounters, which did not fail to come. Mr. Clay said that he "observed that the Senator from South Carolina based his abstractions on the theories of books on English authorities, and on the arguments urged in favor of free trade by a certain party in the British Parliament. Now he, (Mr. Clay,) and his friends would not admit of these authorities being entitled to as much weight as the universal practice of nations, which in all parts of the world was found to be in favor of protecting home manufactures to an extent sufficient to keep them in a flourishing condition. This was the whole difference. The Senator was in favor of book theory and abstractions: he (Mr. Clay) and his friends, were in favor of the universal practice of nations, and the wholesome and necessary protection of domestic manufactures."

Mr. Calhoun in reply, referring to his allusion to the success in the late election of the tory party in England, said: "The interests, objects, and aims of the tory party there and the whig party here, are identical. The identity of the two parties is remarkable. The tory party are the patrons of corporate monopolies; *and are not you?* They are advocates of a high tariff; *and are not you?* They are supporters of a national bank; *and are not you?* They are for corn-laws—laws oppressive to the masses of the people, and favorable to their own power; *and are not you?* Witness this bill. * * * The success of that party in England, and of the whig party here, is the success of the great money power, which concentrates the interests of the two parties, and identifies their principles."

The bill was passed by a large majority, upon the general ground that the government must have revenue.

The chief measure of the session, and the great object of the whig party—the one for which it had labored for ten years—was for the re-charter of a national bank. Without this all other measures would be deemed to be incomplete, and the victorious election itself but little better than a defeat. The President, while a member of the Democratic party, had been opposed to the United States Bank; and to overcome any objections he might have the bill was carefully prepared, and studiously contrived to avoid the President's objections, and save his consistency—a point upon which he was exceedingly sensitive.

The democratic members resisted strenuously, in order to make the measure odious, but successful resistance was impossible. It passed both houses by a close vote, and contrary to all expectation the President disapproved the act, but with such expressions of readiness to approve another bill which should be free from the objections which he named, as still to keep his party together, and to prevent the resignation of his cabinet. In his veto message the President fell back upon his early opinions against the constitutionality of a national bank, so often and so publicly expressed.

The veto caused consternation among the whig members; and Mr. Clay openly gave expression to his dissatisfaction, in the debate on the veto message in terms to assert that President Tyler had violated his faith to the whig party, and had been led off from them by new associations. He said: "And why should not President Tyler have suffered the bill to become a law without his signature? Without meaning the slightest possible disrespect to him (nothing is further from my heart than the exhibition of any such feeling towards that distinguished citizen, long my personal friend), it cannot be forgotten that he came into his present office under peculiar circumstances. The people did not foresee the contingency which has happened. They voted for him as Vice President. They did not, therefore, scrutinize his opinions with the care which they probably ought to have done, and would have done, if they could have looked into futurity. If the present state of the fact could have been anticipated—if at Harrisburg, or at the polls, it had been foreseen that General Harrison would die in one short month after the commencement of his administration; so that Vice President Tyler would be elevated to the presidential chair, that a bill passed by decisive majorities of the first whig Congress, chartering a national bank, would be presented for his sanction; and that he would veto the bill, do I hazard anything when I express the conviction that he would not have received a solitary vote in the nominating convention, nor one solitary electoral vote in any State in the Union?"

The vote was taken on the bill over again, as required by the constitution, and so far from receiving a two-thirds vote, it received only a bare majority, and was returned to the House with a message stating his objections to it, where it gave rise to some violent speaking, more directed to the personal conduct of the President than to the objections to the bill stated in his message. The veto was sustained; and so ended the second attempt to resuscitate the old United States Bank under a new name. This second movement to establish the bank has a secret history. It almost caused the establishment of a new party, with Mr. Tyler as its head; earnest efforts having been made in that behalf by many prominent Whigs and Democrats. The entire cabinet, with the exception of Mr. Webster, resigned within a few days after the second veto. It was a natural thing for them to do, and was not unexpected. Indeed Mr. Webster had resolved to tender his resignation also, but on reconsideration determined to remain and publish his reasons therefor in a letter to the National Intelligencer, in the following words:

"Lest any misapprehension should exist, as to the reasons which led me to differ from the course pursued by my late colleagues, I wish to say that I remain in my place, first, because I have seen no sufficient reasons for the dissolution of the late Cabinet, by the voluntary act of its own members. I am perfectly persuaded of the absolute necessity of an institution, under the authority of Congress, to aid revenue and financial operations, and to give the country the blessings of a good currency and cheap exchanges. Notwithstanding what has passed, I have confidence that the President will co-operate with the legislature in overcoming all difficulties in the attainment of these objects; and it is to the union of the Whig party—by which I mean the whole party, the Whig President, the Whig Congress, and the Whig people—that I look for a realization of our wishes. I can look nowhere else. In the second place if I had seen reasons to resign my office, I should not have done so, without giving the President reasonable notice, and affording him time to select the hands to which he should confide the delicate and important affairs now pending in this department."

The conduct of the President in the matter of the vetoes of the two bank bills produced revolt against him in the party; and the Whigs of the two Houses of Congress held several formal meetings to consider what they should do in the new condition of affairs. An address to the people of the United States was resolved upon. The rejection of the bank bill gave great vexation to one side, and equal exultation to the other. The subject was not permitted to rest, however; a national bank was the life—the vital principle—of the Whig party, without which it could not live as a party; it was the power which was to give them power and the political and financial control of the Union. A second attempt was made, four days after the veto, to accomplish the end by amendments to a bill relating to the currency, which had been introduced early in the session. Mr. Sargeant of Pennsylvania, moved to strike out all after the enacting clause, and insert his amendments, which were substantially the same as the vetoed bill, except changing the amount of capital and prohibiting discounts on notes other than bills of exchange. The bill was pushed to a vote with astonishing rapidity, and passed by a decided majority In the Senate the bill went to a select committee which reported it back without alteration, as had been foreseen, the committee consisting entirely of friends of the measure; and there was a majority for it on final passage. Concurred in by the Senate without alteration, it was returned to the House, and thence referred to the President for his approval or disapproval. It was disapproved and it was promulgated in language intended to mean a repudiation of the President, a permanent separation of the Whig party from him, and to wash their hands of all accountability for his acts. An opening paragraph of the address set forth that, for twelve years the Whigs had carried on a contest for the regulation of the currency, the equalization of exchanges, the economical administration of the finances, and the advancement of industry—all to be accomplished by means of a national bank—declaring these objects to be misunderstood by no one and the bank itself held to be secured in the Presidential election, and its establishment the main object of the extra session. The address then proceeds to state how these plans were frustrated:

"It is with profound and poignant regret that we find ourselves called upon to invoke your attention to this point. Upon the great and leading measure touching this question, our anxious endeavors to respond to the earnest prayers of the nation have been frustrated by an act as unlooked for as it is to be lamented. We grieve to say to you that by the exercise of that power in the constitution which has ever been regarded with suspicion, and often with odium, by the people—a power which we had hoped was never to be exhibited on this subject, by a Whig President—we have been defeated in two attempts to create a fiscal agent, which the wants of the country had demonstrated to us, in the most absolute form of proof to be eminently necessary and proper in the present emergency. Twice have we with the utmost diligence and deliberation matured a plan for the collection, safekeeping and disbursing of the public moneys through the agency of a corporation adapted to that end, and twice has it been our fate to encounter the opposition of the President, through the application of the veto power. * * * We are constrained to say that we find no ground to justify us in the conviction that the veto of the President has been interposed on this question solely upon conscientious and well-considered opinions of constitutional scruple as to his duty in the case presented. On the contrary, too many proofs have been forced upon our observation to leave us free from the apprehension that the President has permitted himself to be beguiled into an opinion that by this exhibition of his prerogative he might be able to divert the policy of his administration into a channel which should lead to new political combinations, and accomplish results which must overthrow the present divisions of party in the country; and finally produce a state of things which those who elected him, at least, have never contemplated.

* * * * * *

In this state of things, the Whigs will naturally look with anxiety to the future, and inquire what are the actual relations between the President and those who brought him into power; and what, in the opinion of their friends in Congress, should be their course hereafter. * * * The President by his withdrawal of confidence from his real friends in Congress and from the members of his cabinet; by his bestowal of it upon others notwithstanding their notorious opposition to leading measures of his administrations has voluntarily separated himself from those by whose exertions and suffrage he was elevated to that office through which he has reached his present exalted station. * * * * The consequence is, that those who brought the President into power can be no longer, in any manner or degree, justly held responsible or blamed for the administration of the executive branch of the government; and the President and his advisers should be exclusively hereafter deemed accountable. * * * The conduct of the President has occasioned bitter mortification and deep regret. Shall the party, therefore, yielding to sentiments of despair, abandon its duty, and submit to defeat and disgrace? Far from suffering such dishonorable consequences, the very disappointment which it has unfortunately experienced should serve only to redouble its exertions, and to inspire it with fresh courage to persevere with a spirit unsubdued and a resolution unshaken, until the prosperity of the country is fully re-established, and its liberties firmly secured against all danger from the abuses, encroachments or usurpations of the executive department of the government."

This was the manifesto, so far as it concerns the repudiation of President Tyler, which Whig members of Congress put forth: it was answered (under the name of an address to his constituents) by Mr. Cushing, in a counter special plea—counter to it on all points—especially on the main question of which party the President was to belong to; the manifesto of the Whigs assigning him to the democracy—the address of Mr. Cushing, claiming him for the Whigs. It was especially severe on Mr. Clay, as setting up a caucus dictatorship to coerce the President; and charged that the address emanated from this caucus, and did not embody or represent the sentiments of all Whig leaders, and referred to Mr. Webster's letter, and his remaining in the cabinet as proof of this. But it was without avail against the concurrent statements of the retiring senators, and the confirmatory statements of many members of Congress. The Whig party recoiled from the President, and instead of the unity predicted by Mr Webster, there was diversity and widespread dissension. The Whig party remained with Mr. Clay; Mr. Webster retired, Mr Cushing was sent on a foreign mission, and the President, seeking to enter the democratic ranks, was refused by them, and left to seek consolation in privacy for his political errors and omissions.

The extra session, called by President Harrison, held under Mr. Tyler, dominated by Mr Clay commenced May 31, and ended Sept. 13, 1841—and was replete with disappointed calculations, and nearly barren of permanent results. The purposes for which it was called into being, failed. The first annual message of President Tyler, at the opening of the regular session in December, 1841, coming in so soon after the termination of the extra session, was brief and meagre of topics, with few points of interest.

In the month of March, 1842, Mr. Henry Clay resigned his place in the Senate, and delivered a valedictory address to that body He had intended this step upon the close of the previous presidential campaign, but had postponed it to take personal charge of the several measures which would be brought before Congress at the special session—the calling of which he foresaw would be necessary He resigned not on account of age, or infirmity, or disinclination for public life, but out of disgust—profound and inextinguishable. He had been basely defeated for the Presidential nomination, against the wishes of the Whig party of which he was the acknowledged head—he had seen his leading measures vetoed by the President whom his party had elected—the downfall of the Bank for which he had so often pledged himself—and the insolent attacks of the petty adherents of the administration in the two Houses: all these causes acting on his proud and lofty spirit, induced this withdrawal from public life for which he was so well fitted.

The address opened with a retrospect of his early entrance into the Senate, and a grand encomium upon its powers and dignity as he had found it, and left it. Memory went back to that early year, 1806, when just past thirty years of age, he entered the United States Senate, and commenced his high career—a wide and luminous horizon before him, and will and talent to fill it. He said: "From the year 1806, the period of my entering upon this noble theatre of my public service, with but short intervals, down to the present time, I have been engaged in the service of my country. Of the nature and value of those services which I may have rendered during my long career of public life, it does not become me to speak. History, if she deigns to notice me, and posterity—if a recollection of any humble service which I may have rendered, shall be transmitted to posterity—will be the best, truest, and most impartial judges; and to them I defer for a decision upon their value. But, upon one subject, I may be allowed to speak. As to my public acts and public conduct, they are for the judgment of my fellow citizens; but my private motives of action—that which prompted me to take the part which I may have done, upon great measures during their progress in the national councils, can be known only to the Great Searcher of the human heart and myself; and I trust I shall be pardoned for repeating again a declaration which I made thirty years ago: that whatever error I may have committed—and doubtless I have committed many during my public service—I may appeal to the Divine Searcher of hearts for the truth of the declaration which I now make, with pride and confidence, that I have been actuated by no personal motives—that I have sought no personal aggrandizement—no promotion from the advocacy of those various measures on which I have been called to act—that I have had an eye, a single eye, a heart, a single heart, ever devoted to what appeared to be the best interests of the country."

Mr. Clay led a great party, and for a long time, whether he dictated to it or not, and kept it well bound together, without the usual means of forming and leading parties. It was surprising that, without power and patronage, he was able so long and so undividedly to keep so great a party together, and lead it so unresistingly. He had great talents, but not equal to some whom he led. He had eloquence—superior in popular effect, but not equal in high oratory to that of some others. But his temperament was fervid, his will was strong, and his courage daring; and these qualities, added to his talents, gave him the lead and supremacy in his party, where he was always dominant. The farewell address made a deep impression upon the Senators present; and after its close, Mr. Preston brought the ceremony to a conclusion, by moving an adjournment, which was agreed to.

Again at this session was the subject of the tariff considered, but this time, as a matter of absolute necessity, to provide a revenue. Never before were the coffers and the credit of the treasury at so low an ebb. A deficit of fourteen millions in the treasury—a total inability to borrow, either at home or abroad, the amount of the loan of twelve millions authorized the year before—the treasury notes below par, and the revenues from imports inadequate and decreasing.

The compromise act of 1833 in reducing the duties gradually through nine years, to a fixed low rate; the act of 1837 in distributing the surplus revenue; and the continual and continued distribution of the land revenue, had brought about this condition of things. The remedy was sought in a bill increasing the tariff, and suspending the land revenue distribution. Two such bills were passed in a single month, and both vetoed by the President. It was now near the end of August. Congress had been in session for an unprecedentedly long time. Adjournment could not be deferred, and could not take place without providing for the Treasury The compromise act and the land distribution were the stumbling-blocks: it was resolved to sacrifice them together; and a bill was introduced raising the duties above the fixed rate of twenty per cent., and that breach of the mutual assurance in relation to the compromise, immediately in terms of the assurance, suspended the land revenue distribution—to continue it suspended while duties above the compromise limit continued to be levied. And as that has been the case ever since, the distribution of the land revenue has been suspended ever since. The bill was passed, and approved by the President, and Congress thereupon adjourned.

The subject of the navy was also under consideration at this session. The naval policy of the United States was a question of party division from the origin of parties in the early years of the government—the Federal party favoring a strong and splendid navy, the Republican a moderate establishment, adapted to the purposes of defense more than of offense. And this line of division has continued. Under the Whig regime the policy for a great navy developed itself. The Secretary of the Navy recommended a large increase of ships, seamen and officers, involving a heavy expense, though the government was not in a condition to warrant any such expenditure, and no emergency required an increase in that branch of the public service. The vote was taken upon the increase proposed by the Secretary of the Navy, and recommended by the President; and it was carried, the yeas and nays being well defined by the party line.

The first session of the twenty-eighth Congress, which convened December 1843, exhibited in its political complexion, serious losses in the Whig following. The Democratic candidate for Speaker of the House of Representatives, was elected over the Whig candidate—the vote standing 128 to 59. Thus an adverse majority of more than two to one was the result to the Whig party at the first election after the extra session of 1841. The President's message referred to the treaty which had lately been concluded with Great Britain relative to the northwestern territory extending to the Columbia river, including Oregon and settling the boundary lines; and also to a pending treaty with Texas for her annexation to the United States; and concluded with a recommendation for the establishment of a paper currency to be issued and controlled by the Federal government.

For more than a year before the meeting of the Democratic Presidential Convention in Baltimore, in May 1844, it was evident to leading Democrats that Martin Van Buren was the choice of the party To overcome this popular current and turn the tide in favor of Mr. Calhoun, who desired the nomination, resort was had to the pending question of the annexation of Texas. Mr. Van Buren was known to be against it, and Mr. Calhoun for it. To gain time, the meeting of the convention was postponed from December previous, which had been the usual time for holding such elections, until the following May. The convention met, and consisted of two hundred and sixty-six delegates, a decided majority of whom were for Mr. Van Buren, and cast their votes accordingly on the first ballot. But a chairman had been selected, who was adverse to his nomination; and aided by a rule adopted by the convention, which required a concurrence of two-thirds to effect a nomination, the opponents of Mr. Van Buren were able to accomplish his defeat. Mr. Calhoun had, before the meeting of the convention, made known his determination, in a public address, not to suffer his name to go before that assemblage as a candidate for the presidency, and stated his reasons for so doing, which were founded mainly on the manner in which the convention was constituted; his objections being to the mode of choosing delegates, and the manner of their giving in their votes—he contending for district elections, and the delegates to vote individually. South Carolina was not represented in the convention. After the first ballot Mr. Van Buren's vote sensibly decreased, until finally, Mr. James K. Polk, who was a candidate for the Vice Presidency, was brought forward and nominated unanimously for the chief office. Mr. Geo. M. Dallas was chosen as his colleague for the Vice Presidency. The nomination of these gentlemen, neither of whom had been mentioned until late in the proceedings of the convention, for the offices for which they were finally nominated, was a genuine surprise to the country. No voice in favor of it had been heard; and no visible sign in the political horizon had announced it.

The Whig convention nominated Henry Clay, for President; and Theodore Frelinghuysen for Vice-President.

The main issues in the election which ensued, were mainly the party ones of Whig and Democrat, modified by the tariff and Texas questions. It resulted in the choice of the Democratic candidates, who received 170 electoral votes as against 105 for their opponents; the popular majority for the Democrats being 238,284, in a total vote of 2,834,108. Mr. Clay received a larger popular vote than had been given at the previous election for the Whig candidate, showing that he would have been elected had he then been the nominee of his party; though the popular vote at this election was largely increased over that of 1840. It is conceded that the 36 electoral votes of New York State gave the election to Mr. Polk. It was carried by a bare majority; due entirely to the Gubernatorial candidacy of Mr. Silas Wright, who had been mentioned for the vice-presidential nomination in connection with Mr. Van Buren, but who declined it after the sacrifice of his friend and colleague; and resigning his seat in the Senate, became a candidate for Governor of New York. The election being held at the same time as that for president, his name and popularity brought to the presidential ticket more than enough votes to make the majority that gave the electoral vote of the State to the Democrats.

President Tyler's annual and last message to Congress, in December 1844, contained, (as did that of the previous year) an elaborate paragraph on the subject of Texas and Mexico; the idea being the annexation of the former to the Union, and the assumption of her causes of grievance against the latter; and a treaty was pending to accomplish these objects. The scheme for the annexation of Texas was framed with a double aspect—one looking to the then pending presidential election, the other to the separation of the Southern States; and as soon as the rejection of the treaty was foreseen, and the nominating convention had acted, the disunion aspect manifested itself over many of the Southern States—beginning with South Carolina. Before the end of May, a great meeting took place at Ashley, in that State, to combine the slave States in a convention to unite the Southern States to Texas, if Texas should not be received into the Union; and to invite the President to convene Congress to arrange the terms of the dissolution of the Union if the rejection of the annexation should be persevered in. Responsive resolutions were adopted in several States, and meetings held. The opposition manifested, brought the movement to a stand, and suppressed the disunion scheme for the time being—only to lie in wait for future occasions. But it was not before the people only that this scheme for a Southern convention with a view to the secession of the slave States was a matter of discussion; it was the subject of debate in the Senate; and there it was further disclosed that the design of the secessionists was to extend the new Southern republic to the Californias.

The treaty of annexation was supported by all the power of the administration, but failed; and it was rejected by the Senate by a two-thirds vote against it. Following this, a joint resolution was early brought into the House of Representatives for the admission of Texas as a State of the Union, by legislative action; it passed the House by a fair majority, but met with opposition in the Senate unless coupled with a proviso for negotiation and treaty, as a condition precedent. A bill authorizing the President and a commissioner to be appointed to agree upon the terms and conditions of said admission, the question of slavery within its limits, its debts, the fixing of boundaries, and the cession of territory, was coupled or united with the resolution; and in this shape it was finally agreed to, and became a law, with the concurrence of the President, March 3, 1845. Texas was then in a state of war with Mexico, though at that precise point of time an armistice had been agreed upon, looking to a treaty of peace. The House resolution was for an unqualified admission of the State; the Senate amendment or bill was for negotiation; and the bill actually passed would not have been concurred in except on the understanding that the incoming President (whose term began March 4, 1845, and who was favorable to negotiation) would act under the bill, and appoint commissioners accordingly.

Contrary to all expectation, the outgoing President, on the last day of his term, at the instigation of his Secretary of State, Mr. Calhoun, assumed the execution of the act providing for the admission of Texas—adopted the legislative clause—and sent out a special messenger with instructions. The danger of this had been foreseen, and suggested in the Senate; but close friends of Mr. Calhoun, speaking for the administration, and replying to the suggestion, indignantly denied it for them, and declared that they would not have the "audacity" to so violate the spirit and intent of the act, or so encroach upon the rights of the new President. These statements from the friends of the Secretary and President that the plan by negotiation would be adopted, quieted the apprehension of those Senators opposed to legislative annexation or admission, and thus secured their votes, without which the bill would have failed of a majority. Thus was Texas incorporated into the Union. The legislative proposition sent by Mr. Tyler was accepted: Texas became incorporated with the United States, and in consequence the state of war was established between the United States and Mexico; it only being a question of time and chance when the armistice should end and hostilities begin. Although Mr. Calhoun was not in favor of war with Mexico—he believing that a money payment would settle the differences with that country—the admission of Texas into the Union under the legislative annexation clause of the statute, was really his act and not that of the President's; and he was, in consequence, afterwards openly charged in the Senate with being the real author of the war which followed.

The administration of President Polk opened March 4, 1845; and on the same day, the Senate being convened for the purpose, the cabinet ministers were nominated and confirmed. In December following the 29th Congress was organized. The House of Representatives, being largely Democratic, elected the Speaker, by a vote of 120, against 70 for the Whig candidate. At this session the "American" party—a new political organization—first made its appearance in the National councils, having elected six members of the House of Representatives, four from New York and two from Pennsylvania. The President's first annual message had for its chief topic, the admission of Texas, then accomplished, and the consequent dissatisfaction of Mexico; and referring to the preparations on the part of the latter with the apparent intention of declaring war on the United States, either by an open declaration, or by invading Texas. The message also stated causes which would justify this government in taking the initiative in declaring war—mainly the non-compliance by Mexico with the terms of the treaty of indemnity of April 11, 1839, entered into between that State and this government relative to injuries to American citizens during the previous eight years. He also referred to the fact of a minister having been sent to Mexico to endeavor to bring about a settlement of the differences between the nations, without a resort to hostilities. The message concluded with a reference to the negotiations with Great Britain relative to the Oregon boundary; a statement of the finances and the public debt, showing the latter to be slightly in excess of seventeen millions; and a recommendation for a revision of the tariff, with a view to revenue as the object, with protection to home industry as the incident.

At this session of Congress, the States of Florida and Iowa were admitted into the Union; the former permitting slavery within its borders, the latter denying it. Long before this, the free and the slave States were equal in number, and the practice had grown up—from a feeling of jealousy and policy to keep them evenly balanced—of admitting one State of each character at the same time. Numerically the free and the slave States were thus kept even: in political power a vast inequality was going on—the increase of population being so much greater in the northern than in the southern region.

The Ashburton treaty of 1842 omitted to define the boundary line, and permitted, or rather did not prohibit, the joint occupation of Oregon by British and American settlers. This had been a subject of dispute for many years. The country on the Columbia River had been claimed by both. Under previous treaties the American northern boundary extended "to the latitude of 49 degrees north of the equator, and along that parallel indefinitely to the west." Attempts were made in 1842 and continuing since to 1846, to settle this boundary line, by treaty with Great Britain. It had been assumed that we had a dividing line, made by previous treaty, along the parallel of 54 degrees 40 minutes from the sea to the Rocky mountains. The subject so much absorbed public attention, that the Democratic National convention of 1844 in its platform of principles declared for that boundary line, or war as the consequence. It became known as the 54–40 plank, and was a canon of political faith. The negotiations between the governments were resumed in August, 1844. The Secretary of State, Mr. Calhoun, proposed a line along the parallel of 49 degrees of north latitude to the summit of the Rocky mountains and continuing that line thence to the Pacific Ocean; and he made this proposition notwithstanding the fact that the Democratic party—to which he belonged—were then in a high state of exultation for the boundary of 54 degrees 40 minutes, and the presidential canvass, on the Democratic side, was raging upon that cry.

The British Minister declined this proposition in the part that carried the line to the ocean, but offered to continue it from the summit of the mountains to the Columbia River, a distance of some three hundred miles, and then follow the river to the ocean. This was declined by Mr. Calhoun. The President had declared in his inaugural address in favor of the 54–40 line. He was in a dilemma; to maintain that position meant war with Great Britain; to recede from it seemed impossible. The proposition for the line of 49 degrees having been withdrawn by the American government on its non-acceptance by the British, had appeased the Democratic storm which had been raised against the President. Congress had come together under the loud cry of war, in which Mr. Cass was the leader, but followed by the body of the democracy, and backed and cheered by the whole democratic newspaper press. Under the authority and order of Congress notice had been served on Great Britain which was to abrogate the joint occupation of the country by the citizens of the two powers. It was finally resolved by the British Government to propose the line of 49 degrees, continuing to the ocean, as originally offered by Mr. Calhoun; and though the President was favorable to its acceptance, he could not, consistently with his previous acts, accept and make a treaty on that basis. The Senate, with whom lies the power, under the constitution, of confirming or restricting all treaties, being favorable to it, without respect to party lines, resort was had, as in the early practice of the Government, to the President, asking the advice of the Senate upon the articles of a treaty before negotiation. A message was accordingly sent to the Senate, by the President, stating the proposition, and asking its advice, thus shifting the responsibility upon that body, and making the issue of peace or war depend upon its answer. The Senate advised the acceptance of the proposition, and the treaty was concluded.

The conduct of the Whig Senators, without whose votes the advice would not have been given nor the treaty made, was patriotic in preferring their country to their party—in preventing a war with Great Britain—and saving the administration from itself and its party friends.

The second session of the 29th Congress was opened in December, 1847 The President's message was chiefly in relation to the war with Mexico, which had been declared by almost a unanimous vote in Congress. Mr. Calhoun spoke against the declaration in the Senate, but did not vote upon it. He was sincerely opposed to the war, although his conduct had produced it. Had he remained in the cabinet, to do which he had not concealed his wish, he would, no doubt, have labored earnestly to have prevented it. Many members of Congress, of the same party with the administration, were extremely averse to the war, and had interviews with the President, to see if it was inevitable, before it was declared. Members were under the impression that the war could not last above three months.

The reason for these impressions was that an intrigue was laid, with the knowledge of the Executive, for a peace, even before the war was declared, and a special agent dispatched to bring about a return to Mexico of its exiled President, General Santa Anna, and conclude a treaty of peace with him, on terms favorable to the United States. And for this purpose Congress granted an appropriation of three millions of dollars to be placed at the disposal of the President, for negotiating for a boundary which should give the United States additional territory.

While this matter was pending in Congress, Mr. Wilmot of Pennsylvania introduced and moved a proviso, "*that no part of the territory to be acquired should be open to the introduction of slavery.*" It was a proposition not necessary for the purpose of excluding slavery, as the only territory to be acquired was that of New Mexico and California, where slavery was already prohibited by the Mexican laws and constitution. The proviso was therefore nugatory, and only served to bring on a slavery agitation in the United States. For this purpose it was seized upon by Mr. Calhoun and declared to be an outrage upon and menace to the slave-holding States. It occupied the attention of Congress for two sessions, and became the subject of debate in the State Legislatures, several of which passed disunion resolutions. It became the watchword of party—the synonym of civil war, and the dissolution of the Union. Neither party really had anything to fear or to hope from the adoption of the proviso—the soil was free, and the Democrats were not in a position to make slave territory of it, because it had just enunciated as one of its cardinal principles, that there was "*no power in Congress to legislate upon slavery in Territories.*" Never did two political parties contend more furiously about nothing. Close observers, who had been watching the progress of the slavery agitation since its inauguration in Congress in 1835, knew it to be the means of keeping up an agitation for the benefit of the political parties—the abolitionists on one side and the disunionists or nullifiers on the other—to accomplish their own purposes. This was the celebrated Wilmot Proviso, which for so long a time convulsed the Union; assisted in forcing the issue between the North and South on the slavery question, and almost caused a dissolution of the Union. The proviso was defeated; that chance of the nullifiers to force the issue was lost; another had to be made, which was speedily done, by the introduction into the Senate on the 19th February, 1847, by Mr. Calhoun of his new slavery resolutions, declaring the Territories to be the common property of the several States; denying the right of Congress to prohibit slavery in a Territory, or to pass any law which would have the effect to deprive the citizens of any slave State from emigrating with his property (slaves) into such Territory. The introduction of the resolutions was prefaced by an elaborate speech by Mr. Calhoun, who demanded an immediate vote upon them. They never came to a vote; they were evidently introduced for the mere purpose of carrying a question to the slave States on which they could be formed into a unit against the free States; and so began the agitation which finally led to the abrogation of the Missouri Compromise line, and arrayed the States of one section against those of the other.

The Thirtieth Congress, which assembled for its first session in December, 1847, was found, so far as respects the House of Representatives, to be politically adverse to the administration. The Whigs were in the majority, and elected the Speaker; Robert C. Winthrop, of Massachusetts, being chosen. The President's message contained a full report of the progress of the war with Mexico; the success of the American arms in that conflict; the victory of Cerro Gordo, and the capture of the City of Mexico; and that negotiations were then pending for a treaty of peace. The message concluded with a reference to the excellent results from the independent treasury system.

The war with Mexico was ended by the signing of a treaty of peace, in February, 1848, by the terms of which New Mexico and Upper California were ceded to the United States, and the lower Rio Grande, from its mouth to El Paso, taken for the boundary of Texas. For the territory thus acquired, the United States agreed to pay to Mexico the sum of fifteen million dollars, in five annual installments; and besides that, assumed the claims of American citizens against Mexico, limited to three and a quarter million dollars, out of and on account of which claims the war ostensibly originated. The victories achieved by the American commanders, Generals Zachary Taylor and Winfield Scott, during that war, won for them national reputations, by means of which they were brought prominently forward for the Presidential succession.

The question of the power of Congress to legislate on the subject of slavery in the Territories, was again raised, at this session, on the bill for the establishment of the Oregon territorial government. An amendment was offered to insert a provision for the extension of the Missouri compromise line to the Pacific Ocean; which line thus extended was intended by the amendment to be permanent, and to apply to all future territories established in the West. This amendment was lost, but the bill was finally passed with an amendment incorporating into it the anti-slavery clause of the ordinance of 1787 Mr. Calhoun, in the Senate, declared that the exclusion of slavery from any territory was a subversion of the Union; openly proclaimed the strife between the North and South to be ended, and the separation of the States accomplished. His speech was an open invocation to disunion, and from that time forth, the efforts were regular to obtain a meeting of the members from the slave States, to unite in a call for a convention of the slave States to redress themselves. He said: "The great strife between the North and the South is ended. The North is determined to exclude the property of the slaveholder, and, of course, the slaveholder himself, from its territory On this point there seems to be no division in the North. In the South, he regretted to say, there was some division of sentiment. The effect of this determination of the North was to convert all the Southern population into slaves; and he would never consent to entail that disgrace on his posterity He denounced any Southern man who would not take the same course. Gentlemen were greatly mistaken if they supposed the Presidential question in the South would override this more important one. The separation of the North and the South is completed. The South has now a most solemn obligation to perform—to herself—to the constitution—to the Union. She is bound to come to a decision not to permit this to go on any further, but to show that, dearly as she prizes the Union, there are questions which she regards as of greater importance than the Union. This is not a question of territorial government, but a question involving the continuance of the Union." The President, in approving the Oregon bill, took occasion to send in a special message, pointing out the danger to the Union from the progress of the slavery agitation, and urged an adherence to the principles of the ordinance of 1787—the terms of the Missouri compromise of 1820—as also that involved and declared in the Texas case in 1845, as the means of averting that danger.

The Presidential election of 1848 was coming on. The Democratic convention met in Baltimore in May of that year; each State being represented in the convention by the number of delegates equal to the number of electoral votes it was entitled to; saving only New York, which sent two sets of delegates, and both were excluded. The delegates were, for the most part, members of Congress and office-holders. The two-thirds rule, adopted by the previous convention, was again made a law of the convention. The main question which arose upon the formation of the platform for the campaign, was the doctrine advanced by the Southern members of non-interference with slavery in the States or in the Territories. The candidates of the party were, Lewis Cass, of Michigan, for President, and General Wm. O. Butler, of Kentucky, for Vice-President.

The Whig convention, taking advantage of the popularity of Genl. Zachary Taylor, for his military achievements in the Mexican war, then just ended; and his consequent availability as a candidate, nominated him for the Presidency, over Mr. Clay, Mr. Webster and General Scott, who were his competitors before the convention. Millard Fillmore was selected as the Vice-presidential candidate.

A third convention was held, consisting of the disaffected Democrats from New York who had been excluded from the Baltimore convention. They met at Utica, New York, and nominated Martin Van Buren for President, and Charles Francis Adams for Vice President. The principles of its platform, were, that Congress should abolish slavery wherever it constitutionally had the power to do so—[which was intended to apply to the District of Columbia]—that it should not interfere with it in the slave States—and that it should prohibit it in the Territories. This party became known as "Free-soilers," from their doctrines thus enumerated, and their party cry of "free-soil, free-speech, free-labor, free-men." The result of the election, as might have been foreseen, was to lose New York State to the Baltimore candidate, and give it to the whigs, who were triumphant in the reception of 163 electoral votes for their candidates, against 127 for the democrats; and none for the free-soilers.

The last message of President Polk, in December following, gave him the opportunity to again urge upon Congress the necessity for some measure to quiet the slavery agitation, and he recommended the extension of the Missouri compromise line to the Pacific Ocean, passing through the new Territories of California and New Mexico, as a fair adjustment, to meet as far as possible the views of all parties. The President referred also to the state of the finances; the excellent condition of the public treasury; government loans, commanding a high premium; gold and silver the established currency; and the business interests of the country in a prosperous condition. And this was the state of affairs, only one year after emergency from a foreign war. It would be unfair not to give credit to the President and to Senator Benton and others equally prominent and courageous, who at that time had to battle against the bank theory and national paper money currency, as strongly urged and advocated, and to prove eventually that the money of the Constitution —gold and silver—was the only currency to ensure a successful financial working of the government, and prosperity to the people.

The new President, General Zachary Taylor, was inaugurated March 4, 1849. The Senate being convened, as usual, in extra session, for the purpose, the Vice President elect, Millard Fillmore, was duly installed; and the Whig cabinet officers nominated by the President, promptly confirmed. An additional member of the Cabinet was appointed by this administration to preside over the new "Home Department" since called the "Interior," created at the previous session of Congress.

The following December Congress met in regular session—the 31st since the organization of the federal government. The Senate consisted of sixty members, among whom were Mr. Webster, Mr. Calhoun, and Mr. Clay, who had returned to public life. The House had 230 members; and although the whigs had a small majority, the House was so divided on the slavery question in its various phases, that the election for Speaker resulted in the choice of the Democratic candidate, Mr. Cobb, of Georgia, by a majority of three votes. The annual message of the President plainly showed that he comprehended the dangers to the Union from a continuance of sectional feeling on the slavery question, and he averred his determination to stand by the Union to the full extent of his obligations and powers. At the previous session Congress had spent six months in endeavoring to frame a satisfactory bill providing territorial governments for California and New Mexico, and had adjourned finally without accomplishing it, in consequence of inability to agree upon whether the Missouri compromise line should be carried to the ocean, or the territories be permitted to remain as they were—slavery prohibited under the laws of Mexico. Mr. Calhoun brought forward, in the debate, a new doctrine—extending the Constitution to the territory, and arguing that as that instrument recognized the existence of slavery, the settlers in such territory should be permitted to hold their slave property taken there, and be protected. Mr. Webster's answer to this was that the Constitution was made for States, not territories; that it cannot operate anywhere, not even in the States for which it was made, without acts of Congress to enforce it. The proposed extension of the constitution to territories, with a view to its transportation of slavery along with it, was futile and nugatory, without the act of Congress to vitalize slavery under it. The early part of the year had witnessed ominous movements—

nightly meetings of large numbers of members from the slave States, led by Mr. Calhoun, to consider the state of things between the North and the South. They appointed committees who prepared an address to the people. It was in this condition of things, that President Taylor expressed his opinion, in his message, of the remedies required. California, New Mexico and Utah, had been left without governments. For California, he recommended that having a sufficient population and having framed a constitution, she be admitted as a State into the Union; and for New Mexico and Utah, without mixing the slavery question with their territorial governments, they be left to ripen into States, and settle the slavery question for themselves in their State constitutions.

With a view to meet the wishes of all parties, and arrive at some definite and permanent adjustment of the slavery question, Mr. Clay early in the session introduced compromise resolutions which were practically a tacking together of the several bills then on the calendar, providing for the admission of California—the territorial government for Utah and New Mexico—the settlement of the Texas boundary—slavery in the District of Columbia—and for a fugitive slave law. It was seriously and earnestly opposed by many, as being a concession to the spirit of disunion—a capitulation under threat of secession; and as likely to become the source of more contentions than it proposed to quiet.

The resolutions were referred to a special committee, who promptly reported a bill embracing the comprehensive plan of compromise which Mr. Clay proposed. Among the resolutions offered, was the following: "Resolved, that as slavery does not exist by law and is not likely to be introduced into any of the territory acquired by the United States from the Republic of Mexico, it is inexpedient for Congress to provide by law either for its introduction into or exclusion from any part of the said territory; and that appropriate territorial governments ought to be established by Congress in all of the said territory, and assigned as the boundaries of the proposed State of California, without the adoption of any restriction or condition on the subject of slavery" Mr. Jefferson Davis of Mississippi, objected that the measure gave nothing to the South in the settlement of the question; and he required the extension of the Missouri compromise line to the Pacific Ocean as the least that he would be willing to take, with the specific recognition of the right to hold slaves in the territory below that line; and that, before such territories are admitted into the Union as States, slaves may be taken there from any of the United States at the option of their owner.

Mr. Clay in reply, said: "Coming from a slave State, as I do, I owe it to myself, I owe it to truth, I owe it to the subject, to say that no earthly power could induce me to vote for a specific measure for the introduction of slavery where it had not before existed, either south or north of that line. * * * If the citizens of those territories choose to establish slavery, and if they come here with constitutions establishing slavery, I am for admitting them with such provisions in their constitutions; but then it will be their own work, and not ours, and their posterity will have to reproach them, and not us, for forming constitutions allowing the institution of slavery to exist among them."

Mr. Seward of New York, proposed a renewal of the Wilmot Proviso, in the following resolution: "Neither slavery nor involuntary servitude, otherwise than by conviction for crime, shall ever be allowed in either of said territories of Utah and New Mexico;" but his resolution was rejected in the Senate by a vote of 23 yeas to 33 nays. Following this, Mr. Calhoun had read for him in the Senate, by his friend James M. Mason of Virginia, his last speech. It embodied the points covered by the address to the people, prepared by him the previous year; the probability of a dissolution of the Union, and presenting a case to justify it. The tenor of the speech is shown by the following extracts from it: "I have, Senators, believed from the first, that the agitation of the subject of slavery would, if not prevented by some timely and effective measure, end in disunion. Entertaining this opinion, I have, on all proper occasions, endeavored to call the attention of each of the two great parties which divide the country to adopt some measure to prevent so great a disaster, but without success. The agitation has been permitted to proceed, with almost no attempt to resist it, until it has reached a period when it can no longer be disguised or denied that the Union is in danger. You have had forced upon you the greatest and gravest question that can ever come under your consideration: How can the Union be preserved? * * * * * Instead of being weaker, all the elements in favor of agitation are stronger now than they were in 1835, when it first commenced, while all the elements of influence on the part of the South are weaker. Unless something decisive is done, I again ask what is to stop this agitation, before the great and final object at which it aims—the abolition of slavery in the States—is consummated? Is it, then, not certain that if something decisive is not now done to arrest it, the South will be forced to choose between abolition and secession? Indeed as events are now moving, it will not require the South to secede to dissolve the Union. * * * * If the agitation goes on, nothing will be left to hold the States together except force." He answered the question, *How can the Union be saved?* with which his speech opened, by suggesting. "To provide for the insertion of a provision in the constitution, by an amendment, which will restore to the South in substance the power she possessed of protecting herself, before the equilibrium between the sections was destroyed by the action of the government." He did not state of what the amendment should consist, but later on, it was ascertained from reliable sources that his idea was a dual executive—one President from the free, and one from the slave States, the consent of both of whom should be required to all acts of Congress before they become laws. This speech of Mr. Calhoun's, is important as explaining many of his previous actions; and as furnishing a guide to those who ten years afterwards attempted to carry out practically the suggestions thrown out by him.

Mr. Clay's compromise bill was rejected. It was evident that no compromise of any kind whatever on the subject of slavery, under any one of its aspects separately, much less under all put together, could possibly be made. There was no spirit of concession manifested. The numerous measures put together in Mr. Clay's bill were disconnected and separated. Each measure received a separate and independent consideration, and with a result which showed the injustice of the attempted conjunction; for no two of them were passed by the same vote, even of the members of the committee which had even unanimously reported favorably upon them as a whole.

Mr. Calhoun died in the spring of 1850; before the separate bill for the admission of California was taken up. His death took place at Washington, he having reached the age of 68 years. A eulogy upon him was delivered in the Senate by his colleague, Mr. Butler, of South Carolina. Mr. Calhoun was the first great advocate of the doctrine of secession. He was the author of the nullification doctrine, and an advocate of the extreme doctrine of States Rights. He was an eloquent speaker—a man of strong intellect. His speeches were plain, strong, concise, sometimes impassioned, and always severe. Daniel Webster said of him, that "he had the basis, the indispensable basis of all high characters, and that was unspotted integrity, unimpeached honor and character!"

In July of this year an event took place which threw a gloom over the country The President, General Taylor, contracted a fever from exposure to the hot sun at a celebration of Independence Day, from which he died four days afterwards. He was a man of irreproachable private character, undoubted patriotism, and established reputation for judgment and firmness. His brief career showed no deficiency of political wisdom nor want of political training. His administration was beset with difficulties, with momentous questions pending, and he met the crisis with firmness and determination, resolved to maintain the Federal Union at all hazards. His first and only annual message, the leading points of which have been stated, evinces a spirit to do what was right among all the States. His death was a public calamity. No man could have been more devoted to the Union nor more opposed to the slavery agitation; and his position as a Southern man and a slaveholder—his military reputation, and his election by a majority of the people as well as of the States, would have given him a power in the settlement of the pending questions of the day which no President without these qualifications could have possessed.

In accordance with the Constitution, the office of President thus devolved upon the Vice-President, Mr. Millard Fillmore, who was duly inaugurated July 10, 1850. The new cabinet, with Daniel Webster as Secretary of State, was duly appointed and confirmed by the Senate.

The bill for the admission of California as a State in the Union, was called up in the Senate and sought to be amended by extending the Missouri Compromise line through it, to the Pacific Ocean, so as to authorize slavery in the State below that line. The amendment was introduced and pressed by Southern friends of the late Mr. Calhoun, and made a test question. It was lost, and the bill passed by a two-third vote; whereupon ten Southern Senators offered a written protest, the concluding clause of which was: "We dissent from this bill, and solemnly protest against its passage, because in sanctioning measures so contrary to former precedents, to obvious policy, to the spirit and intent of the constitution of the United States, for the purpose of excluding the slaveholding States from the territory thus to be erected into a State, this government in effect declares that the exclusion of slavery from the territory of the United States is an object so high and important as to justify a disregard not only of all the principles of sound policy, but also of the constitution itself. Against this conclusion we must now and for ever protest, as it is destructive of the safety and liberties of those whose rights have been committed to our care, fatal to the peace and equality of the States which we represent, and must lead, if persisted in, to the dissolution of that confederacy, in which the slaveholding States have never sought more than equality, and in which they will not be content to remain with less." On objection being made, followed by debate, the Senate refused to receive the protest, or permit it to be entered on the Journal. The bill went to the House of Representatives, was readily passed, and promptly approved by the President. Thus was virtually accomplished the abrogation of the Missouri compromise line; and the extension or non-extension of slavery was then made to form a foundation for future political parties.

The year 1850 was prolific with disunion movements in the Southern States. The Senators who had joined with Mr. Calhoun in the address to the people, in 1849, united with their adherents in establishing at Washington a newspaper entitled "The Southern Press," devoted to the agitation of the slavery question; to presenting the advantages of disunion, and the organization of a confederacy, of Southern States to be called the "United States South." Its constant aim was to influence the South against the North, and advocated concert of action by the States of the former section. It was aided in its efforts by newspapers published in the South, more especially in South Carolina and Mississippi. A disunion convention was actually held, in Nashville, Tennessee, and invited the assembly of a Southern Congress. Two States, South Carolina and Mississippi responded to the appeal; passed laws to carry it into effect, and the former went so far as to elect its quota of Representatives to the proposed new Southern Congress. These occurrences are referred to as showing the spirit that prevailed, and the extraordinary and unjustifiable means used by the leaders to mislead and exasperate the people. The assembling of a Southern "Congress" was a turning point in the progress of disunion. Georgia refused to join; and her weight as a great Southern State was sufficient to cause the failure of the scheme. But the seeds of discord were sown, and had taken root, only to spring up at a future time when circumstances should be more favorable to the accomplishment of the object.

Although the Congress of the United States had in 1790 and again in 1836 formally declared the policy of the government to be non-interference with the States in respect to the matter of slavery within the limits of the respective States, the subject continued to be agitated in consequence of petitions to Congress to abolish slavery in the District of Columbia, which was under the exclusive control of the federal government; and of movements throughout the United States to limit, and finally abolish it. The subject first made its appearance in national politics in 1840, when a presidential ticket was nominated by a party then formed favoring the abolition of slavery; it had a very slight following which was increased ten-fold at the election of 1844 when the same party again put a ticket in the field with James G. Birney of Michigan, as its candidate for the Presidency; who received 62,140 votes. The efforts of the leaders of that faction were continued, and persisted in to such an extent, that when in 1848 it nominated a ticket with Gerritt Smith for President, against the Democratic candidate, Martin Van Buren, the former received 296,232 votes. In the presidential contest of 1852 the abolition party again nominated a ticket, with John P Hale as its candidate for President, and polled 157,926 votes. This large following was increased from time to time, until uniting with a new party then formed, called the Republican party, which latter adopted a platform endorsing the views and sentiments of the abolitionists, the great and decisive battle for the principles involved, was fought in the ensuing presidential contest of 1856; when the candidate of the Republican party, John C. Fremont, supported by the entire abolition party, polled 1,341,812 votes. The first national platform of the Abolition party, upon which it went into the contest of 1840, favored the abolition of slavery in the District of Columbia and Territories; the inter-state slave trade, and a general opposition to slavery to the full extent of constitutional power.

Following the discussion of the subject of slavery, in the Senate and House of Representatives, brought about by the presentation of petitions and memorials, and the passage of the resolutions in 1836 rejecting such petitions, the question was again raised by the presentation in the House, by Mr. Slade of Vermont, on the 20th December 1837, of two memorials praying the abolition of slavery in the District of Columbia, and moving that they be referred to a select committee. Great excitement prevailed in the chamber, and of the many attempts by the Southern members an adjournment was had. The next day a resolution was offered that thereafter all such petitions and memorials touching the abolition of slavery should, when presented, be laid on the table; which resolution was adopted by a large vote. During the 24th Congress, the Senate pursued the course of laying on the table the motion to receive all abolition petitions; and both Houses during the 25th Congress continued the same course of conduct; when finally on the 25th of January 1840, the House adopted by a vote of 114 to 108, an amendment to the rules, called the 21st Rule, which provided:—"that no petition, memorial or resolution, or other paper, praying the abolition of slavery in the District of Columbia, or any state or territory, or the slave-trade between the States or territories of the United States, in which it now exists, shall be received by this House, or entertained in any way whatever." This rule was afterwards, on the 3d of December, 1844, rescinded by the House, on motion of Mr J. Quincy Adams, by a vote of 108 to 80; and a motion to re-instate it, on the 1st of December 1845, was rejected by a vote of 84 to 121. Within five years afterwards—on the 17th September 1850,—the Congress of the United States enacted a law, which was approved by the President, abolishing slavery in the District of Columbia.

On the 25th of February, 1850, there was presented in the House of Representatives, two petitions from citizens of Pennsylvania and Delaware, setting forth that slavery, and the constitution which permits it, violates the Divine law; is inconsistent with republican principles; that its existence has brought evil upon the country, and that no union can exist with States which tolerate that institution; and asking that some plan be devised for the immediate, peaceful dissolution of the Union. The House refused to receive and consider the petitions; as did also the Senate when the same petitions were presented the same month.

The presidential election of 1852 was the last campaign in which the Whig party appeared in National politics. It nominated a ticket with General Winfield Scott as its candidate for President. His opponent on the Democratic ticket was General Franklin Pierce. A third ticket was placed in the field by the Abolition party, with John P Hale as its candidate for President. The platform and declaration of principles of the Whig party was in substance a ratification and endorsement of the several measures embraced in Mr. Clay's compromise resolutions of the previous session of Congress, before referred to; and the policy of a revenue for the economical administration of the government, to be derived mainly from duties on imports, and by these means to afford protection to American industry. The main plank of the platform of the Abolition party (or Independent Democrats, as they were called) was for the non-extension and gradual extinction of slavery. The Democratic party equally adhered to the compromise measure. The election resulted in the choice of Franklin Pierce, by a popular vote of 1,601,474, and 254 electoral votes, against a popular aggregate vote of 1,542,403 (of which the abolitionists polled 157,926) and 42 electoral votes, for the Whig and Abolition candidates. Mr. Pierce was duly inaugurated as President, March [illegible] 1853.

The first political parties in the United States, from the establishment of the federal government and for many years afterwards, were denominated Federalists and Democrats, or Democratic Republicans. The former was an anti-alien party. The latter was made up to a large extent of naturalized foreigners; refugees from England, Ireland and Scotland, driven from home for hostility to the government or for attachment to France. Naturally, aliens sought alliance with the Democratic party, which favored the war against Great Britain. The early party contests were based on the naturalization laws; the first of which, approved March 26, 1790, required only two years' residence in this country; a few years afterwards the time was extended to five years; and in 1798 the Federalists taking advantage of the war fever against France, and then being in power, extended the time to fourteen years. (See Alien and Sedition Laws of 1798). Jefferson's election and Democratic victory of 1800, brought the period back to five years in 1802, and re-inforced the Democratic party. The city of New York, especially, from time to time became filled with foreigners; thus naturalized; brought into the Democratic ranks; and crowded out native Federalists from control of the city government, and to meet this condition of affairs, the first attempt at a Native American organization was made. Beginning in 1835; ending in failure in election of Mayor in 1837, it was revived in April, 1844, when the Native American organization carried New York city for its Mayoralty candidate by a good majority. The success of the movement there, caused it to spread to New Jersey and Pennsylvania. In Philadelphia, it was desperately opposed by the Democratic, Irish and Roman Catholic element, and so furiously, that it resulted in riots, in which two Romish Churches were burned and destroyed. The adherents of the American organization were not confined to Federalists or Whigs, but largely of native Democrats; and the Whigs openly voted with Democratic Natives in order to secure their vote for Henry Clay for the Presidency; but when in November, 1844, New York and Philadelphia both gave Native majorities, and so sapped the Whig vote, that both places gave majorities for the Democratic Presidential electors, the Whigs drew off. In 1845, at the April election in New York, the natives were defeated, and the new party disappeared there. As a result of the autumn election of 1844, the 29th Congress, which organized in December, 1845, had six Native Representatives; four from New York and two from Pennsylvania. In the 30th Congress, Pennsylvania had one. Thereafter for some years, with the exception of a small vote in Pennsylvania and New York, Nativism disappeared. An able writer of that day—Hon. A. H. H. Stuart, of Virginia—published under the nom-de-plume of "Madison" several letters in vindication of the American party (revived in 1852,) in which he said: "The vital principle of the American party is *Americanism*—developing itself in a deep-rooted attachment to our own country—its constitution, its union, and its laws—to American men, and American measures, and American interests—or, in other words, a fervent patriotism—which, rejecting the transcendental philanthropy of abolitionists, and that kindred batch of wild enthusiasts, who would seek to embroil us with foreign countries, in righting the wrongs of Ireland, or Hungary, or Cuba—would guard with vestal vigilance American institutions and American interests against the baneful effects of foreign influence."

About 1852, when the question of slavery in the territories, and its extension or its abolition in the States, was agitated and causing sectional differences in the country, many Whigs and Democrats forsook their parties, and took sides on the questions of the day This was aggravated by the large number of alien naturalized citizens constantly added to the ranks of voters, who took sides with the Democrats and against the Whigs. Nativism then re-appeared, but in a new form—that of a secret fraternity. Its real name and objects were not revealed—even to its members, until they reached a high degree in the order; and the answer of members on being questioned on these subjects was, "I don't know"—which gave it the popular name, by which it is yet known, of "Know-nothing." Its moving causes were the growing power and designs of the Roman Catholic Church in America; the sudden influx of aliens; and the greed and incapacity of naturalized citizens for office. Its cardinal principle was: "Americans must rule America"; and its countersign was the order of General Washington on a critical occasion during the war: "Put none but Americans on guard to-night." Its early nominations were not made public, but were made by select committees and conventions of delegates. At first these nominations were confined to selections of the best Whig or best Democrat on the respective tickets; and the choice not being made known, but quietly voted for by all the members of the order, the effect was only visible after election, and threw all calculation into chaos. For a while it was really the arbiter of elections.

On February 8, 1853, a bill passed the House of Representatives providing a territorial government for Nebraska, embracing all of what is now Kansas and Nebraska. It was silent on the subject of the repeal of the Missouri Compromise. The bill was tabled in the Senate; to be revived at the following session. In the Senate it was amended, on motion of Mr. Douglas, to read: "That so much of the 8th section of an act approved March 6, 1820, (the Missouri compromise) * * * which, being inconsistent with the principles of non-intervention by Congress with slavery in the States and Territories, as recognized by the legislature of 1850, commonly called the Compromise measures, is hereby declared inoperative and void; it being the true intent and meaning of this act not to legislate slavery into any Territory or State, nor to exclude it therefrom, but to leave the people thereof perfectly free to form and regulate their domestic institutions in their own way, subject only to the Constitution of the United States." It was further amended, on motion of Senator Clayton, to prohibit "alien suffrage." In the House this amendment was not agreed to; and the bill finally passed without it, on the 25th May, 1854.

So far as Nebraska was concerned, no excitement of any kind marked the initiation of her territorial existence. The persons who emigrated there seemed to regard the pursuits of business as of more interest than the discussion of slavery. Kansas was less fortunate. Her territory became at once the battle-field of a fierce political conflict between the advocates of slavery, and the free soil men from the North who went there to resist the establishment of that institution in the territory Differences arose between the Legislature and the Governor, brought about by antagonisms between the Pro-slavery party and the Free State party; and the condition of affairs in Kansas assumed so frightful a mien in January, 1856, that the President sent a special message to Congress on the subject, January 24, 1856; followed by a Proclamation, February 11, 1856, "warning all unlawful combinations (in the territory) to retire peaceably to their respective abodes, or he would use the power of the local militia, and the available forces of the United States to disperse them."

Several applications were made to Congress for several successive years, for the admission of Kansas as a state in the Union; upon the basis of three separate and distinct constitutions, all differing as to the main questions at issue between the contending factions. The name of Kansas was for some years synonymous with all that is lawless and anarchical. Elections became mere farces, and the officers thus fraudulently placed in power, used their authority only for their own or their party's interest. The party opposed to slavery at length triumphed; a constitution excluding slavery was adopted in 1859, and Kansas was admitted into the Union January 29, 1861

Under the fugitive slave law, which was passed by Congress at the session of 1850, as one of the Compromise measures, introduced by Mr. Clay, a long and exciting litigation occurred to test the validity and constitutionality of the act, and the several laws on which it depended. The suit was instituted by Dred Scott, a negro slave, in the Circuit Court of the United States for the District of Missouri, in April Term, 1854, against John F A. Sanford, his alleged owner, for trespass *vi et armis*, in holding the plaintiff and his wife and daughters in slavery in said District of Missouri, where by law slavery was prohibited; they having been previously lawfully held in slavery by a former owner—Dr Emerson—in the State of Illinois, from whence they were taken by him to Missouri, and sold to the defendent, Sanford. The case went up on appeal to the Supreme Court of the United States, and was clearly and elaborately argued. The majority opinion, delivered by Chief Justice Taney as also the dissenting opinions, are reported in full in Howard's U. S. Supreme Court Reports, Volume 19, page 393. In respect to the territories the Constitution grants to Congress the power "to make all needful rules and regulations concerning the territory and *other property* belonging to the United States." The Court was of opinion that the clause of the Constitution applies only to the territory within the original States at the time the Constitution was adopted, and that it did not apply to future territory acquired by treaty or conquest from foreign nations. They were also of opinion that the power of Congress over such future territorial acquisitions was not unlimited, that the citizens of the States migrating to a territory were not to be regarded as colonists, subject to absolute power in Congress, but as citizens of the United States, with all the rights of citizenship guarantied by the Constitution, and that no legislation was constitutional which attempted to deprive a citizen of his property on his becoming a resident of a territory. This question in the case arose under the act of Congress prohibiting slavery in the territory of upper Louisiana, (acquired from France, afterwards the State), and of which the territory of Missouri was formed. Any obscurity as to what constitutes citizenship, will be removed by attending to the distinction between local rights of citizenship of the United States according to the Constitution. Citizenship at large in the sense of the Constitution can be conferred on a foreigner only by the naturalization laws of Congress. But each State, in the exercise of its local and reserved sovereignty, may place foreigners or other persons on a footing with its own citizens, as to political rights and privileges to be enjoyed within its own dominion. But State regulations of this character do not make the persons on whom such rights are conferred citizens of the United States or entitle them to the privileges and immunities of citizens in another State. See 5 Wheaton, (U S. Supreme Court Reports), page 49.

The Court said in The Dred Scott case, above referred to, that:—"The right of property in a slave is distinctly and expressly affirmed in the Constitution. The right to traffic in it like the ordinary article of merchandise and property was guarantied to the citizens of the United States, in every State that might desire it for twenty years, and the government in express terms is pledged to protect it in all future time if the slave escapes from his owner. This is done in plain words—too plain to be misunderstood, and no word can be found in the Constitution which gives Congress a greater power over slave property, or which entitles property of that kind to less protection than the property of any other description. The only power conferred is the power coupled with the duty of guarding and protecting the owner in his rights. Upon these considerations, it is the opinion of the Court that the Act of Congress which prohibited a citizen from holding and owning property of this kind in the territory of the United States north of the line therein mentioned, is not warranted by the Constitution and is therefore void; and that neither Dred Scott himself, nor any of his family were made free by being carried into this territory; even if they had been carried there by the owner with the intention of becoming a permanent resident." The abolition of slavery by the 13th amendment to the Constitution of the United States ratified and adopted December 18, 1865, has put an end to these discussions formerly so numerous.

As early as 1854, the Kansas-Nebraska controversy on the territorial government bill, resulted in a division of the Whig party in the North. Those not sufficiently opposed to slavery to enter the new Republican party, then in its incipiency, allied themselves with the Know-Nothing order, which now accepting the name of American party established a separate and independent political existence. The party had no hold in the West; it was entirely Middle State at this time, and polled a large vote in Massachusetts, Delaware and New York. In the State elections of 1855 the American party made a stride Southward. In 1855, the absence of naturalized citizens was universal in the South, and even so late as 1881 the proportion of foreign-born population in the Southern States, with the exception of Florida, Louisiana, and Texas was under two per cent. At the early date—1855—the nativist feeling among the Whigs of that section, made it easy to transfer them to the American party, which thus secured in both the Eastern and Southern States, the election of Governor and Legislature in the States of New Hampshire, Massachusetts, Rhode Island, Connecticut, New York, California and Kentucky; and also elected part of its State ticket in Maryland, and Texas; and only lost the States of Virginia, Alabama, Mississippi, Louisiana, and Texas, by small majorities against it.

The order began preparations for a campaign as a National party, in 1856. It aimed to introduce opposition to aliens and Roman Catholicism as a national question. On the 21st of February, 1856, the National Council held a session at Philadelphia, and proceeded to formulate a declaration of principles, and make a platform, which were as follows:

"An humble acknowledgement to the Supreme Being, for his protecting care vouchsafed to our fathers in their successful Revolutionary struggle, and hitherto manifested to us, their descendants, in the preservation of the liberties, the independence, and the union of these States.

2d. The perpetuation of the Federal Union, as the palladium of our civil and religious liberties, and the only sure Bulwark of American independence.

3d. Americans must rule America, and to this end, native-born citizens should be selected for all state, federal, and municipal offices or government employment, in preference to all others; nevertheless,

4th. Persons born of American parents residing temporarily abroad, should be entitled to all the rights of native-born citizens; but,

5th. No person shall be selected for political station (whether of native or foreign birth), who recognizes any allegiance or obligation, of any description, to any foreign prince, potentate, or power, or who refuses to recognize the Federal and State constitutions (each within its sphere) as paramount to all other laws, as rules of political action.

6th. The unqualified recognition and maintenance of the reserved rights of the several States, and the cultivation of harmony and fraternal good will, between the citizens of the several States, and to this end, non-interference by congress with questions appertaining solely to the individual States, and non-intervention by each State with the affairs of any other State.

7th. The recognition of the right of the native-born and naturalized citizens of the United States, permanently residing in any territory thereof, to frame their constitution and laws, and to regulate their domestic and social affairs in their own mode, subject only to the provisions of the Federal Constitution, with the privilege of admission into the Union, whenever they have the requisite population for one representative in Congress.—Provided always, that none but those who are citizens of the United States, under the Constitution and laws thereof, and who have a fixed residence in any such territory, ought to participate in the formation of the Constitution, or in the enactment of laws for said Territory or State.

8th. An enforcement of the principle that no State or Territory ought to admit others than citizens of the United States to the right of suffrage, or of holding political office.

9th. A change in the laws of naturalization, making a continued residence of twenty-one years, of all not hereinbefore provided for, an indispensable requisite for citizenship hereafter, and excluding all paupers, and persons convicted of crime, from landing upon our shores; but no interference with the vested rights of foreigners.

10th. Opposition to any union between Church and State; no interference with religious faith, or worship, and no test oaths for office.

11th. Free and thorough investigation into any and all alleged abuses of public functionaries, and a strict economy in public expenditures.

12th. The maintenance and enforcement of all laws constitutionally enacted, until said laws shall be repealed, or shall be declared null and void by competent judicial authority

The American Ritual, or Constitution, rules, regulations, and ordinances of the Order were as follows:—

AMERICAN RITUAL.

Constitution of the National Council of the United States of North America.

ART. 1st. This organization shall be known by the name and title of THE NATIONAL COUNCIL OF THE UNITED STATES OF NORTH AMERICA, and its jurisdiction and power shall extend to all the states, districts, and territories of the United States of North America.

ART. 2d. The object of this organization shall be to protect every American citizen in the legal and proper exercise of all his civil and religious rights and privileges; to resist the insidious policy of the Church of Rome, and all other foreign influence against our republican institutions in all lawful ways; to place in all offices of honor trust, or profit, in the gift of the people, or by appointment, none but native-born Protestant citizens, and to protect, preserve, and uphold the union of these states and the constitution of the same.

ART. 3d. Sec. 1.—A person to become a member of any subordinate council must be twenty-one years of age; he must believe in the existence of a Supreme Being as the Creator and preserver of the universe. He must be a native-born citizen; a Protestant, either born of Protestant parents or reared under Protestant influence and not united in marriage with a Roman Catholic; provided, nevertheless, that in this last respect, the state, district, or territorial councils shall be authorized to so construct their respective constitutions as shall best promote the interests of the American cause in their several jurisdictions; and provided, moreover, that no member who may have a Roman Catholic wife shall be eligible to office in this order; and provided, further, should any state, district, or territorial council prefer the words "Roman Catholic" as a disqualification to membership, in place of "Protestant" as a qualification, they may so consider this constitution and govern their action accordingly

Sec. 2.—There shall be an interval of three weeks between the conferring of the first and second degrees; and of three months between the conferring of the second and third degrees—provided, that this restriction shall not apply to those who may have received the second degree previous to the first day of December next; and provided, further, that the presidents of state, district, and territorial councils may grant dispensations for initiating in all the degrees, officers of new councils.

Sec. 3.—The national council shall hold its annual meetings on the first Tuesday in the month of June, at such place as may be designated by the national council at the previous annual meeting, and it may adjourn from time to time. Special meetings may be called by the President, on the written request of five delegations representing five state councils; provided, that sixty days' notice shall be given to the state councils previous to said meeting.

Sec. 4.—The national council shall be composed of seven delegates from each state, to be chosen by the state councils; and each district or territory where a district or territorial council shall exist, shall be entitled to send two delegates, to be chosen from said council—provided that in the nomination of candidates for President and Vice President of the United States, and each state shall be entitled to cast the same number of votes as they shall have members in both houses of Congress. In all sessions of the national council, thirty-two delegates, representing thirteen states, territories, or districts, shall constitute a quorum for the transaction of business.

Sec. 5.—The national council shall be vested with the following powers and privileges:

It shall be the head of the organization for the United States of North America, and shall fix and establish all signs, grips, passwords, and such other secret work, as may seem to it necessary.

It shall have the power to decide all matters appertaining to national politics.

It shall have the power to exact from the state councils, quarterly or annual statements as to the number of members under their jurisdictions, and in relation to all other matters necessary for its information.

It shall have the power to form state, territorial, or district councils, and to grant dispensations for the formation of such bodies, when five subordinate councils shall have been put in operation in any state, territory, or district, and application made.

It shall have the power to determine upon a mode of punishment in case of any dereliction of duty on the part of its members or officers.

It shall have the power to adopt cabalistic characters for the purpose of writing or telegraphing. Said characters to be communicated to the presidents of the state councils, and by them to the presidents of the subordinate councils.

It shall have the power to adopt any and every measure it may deem necessary to secure the success of the organization; provided that nothing shall be done by the said national council in violation of the constitution; and provided further, that in all political matters, its members may be instructed by the state councils, and if so instructed, shall carry out such instructions of the state councils which they represent until overruled by a majority of the national council.

Art. 4. The President shall always preside over the national council when present, and in his absence the Vice President shall preside, and in the absence of both the national council shall appoint a president *pro tempore;* and the presiding officers may at all times call a member to the chair, but such appointment shall not extend beyond one sitting of the national council.

Art. 5. Sec. 1.—The officers of the National Council shall be a President, Vice-President, Chaplain, Corresponding Secretary, Recording Secretary, Treasurer, and two Sentinels, with such other officers as the national council may see fit to appoint from time to time; and the secretaries and sentinels may receive such compensation as the national council shall determine.

Sec. 2.—The duties of the several officers created by this constitution shall be such as the work of this organization prescribes.

Art. 6. Sec. 1.—All officers provided for by this constitution, except the sentinels, shall be elected annually by ballot. The president may appoint sentinels from time to time.

Sec. 2.—A majority of all the votes cast shall be requisite to an election for an office.

Sec. 3.—All officers and delegates of this council, and of all state, district, territorial, and subordinate councils, must be invested with all the degrees of this order.

Sec. 4.—All vacancies in the elective offices shall be filled by a vote of the national council, and only for the unexpired term of the said vacancy.

Art. 7 Sec. 1.—The national council shall entertain and decide all cases of appeal, and it shall establish a form of appeal.

Sec. 2.—The national council shall levy a tax upon the state, district, or territorial councils, for the support of the national council, to be paid in such manner and at such times as the national council shall determine.

Art. 8.—This national council may alter and amend this constitution at its regular annual meeting in June next, by a vote of the majority of the whole number of the members present. (Cincinnati, Nov. 24, 1854.)

RULES AND REGULATIONS.

Rule 1.—Each State, District, or Territory, in which there may exist five or more subordinate councils working under dispensations from the National Council of the United States of North America, or under regular dispensations from some State, District, or Territory, are duly empowered to establish themselves into a State, District, or Territorial council, and when so established, to form for themselves constitutions and by-laws for their government, in pursuance of, and in consonance with the Constitution of the National Council of the United States; provided, however, that all State, District, or Territorial constitutions shall be subject to the approval of the National Council of the United States. (June, 1854.)

Rule 2.—All State, District, or Territorial councils, when established, shall have full power and authority to establish all subordinate councils within their respective limits; and the constitutions and by-laws of all such subordinate councils must be approved by their respective State, District, or Territorial councils. (June, 1854.)

Rule 3.—All State, District, or Territorial councils, when established and until the formation of constitutions, shall work under the constitution of the National Council of the United States. (June, 1854.)

Rule 4.—In all cases where, for the convenience of the organization, two State or Territorial councils may be established, the two councils together shall be entitled to but thirteen delegates* in the National Council of the United States—the proportioned number of delegates to depend on the number of members in the organizations; provided, that no State shall be allowed to have more than one State council, without the consent of the National Council of the United States. (June, 1854.)

Rule 5.—In any State, District, or Territory, where there may be more than one organization working on the same basis, (to wit, the lodges and "councils,") the same shall be required to combine; the officers of each organization shall resign and new officers be elected; and thereafter these bodies shall be known as State councils, and subordinate councils, and new charters shall be granted to them by the national council. (June, 1854.)

Rule 6.—It shall be considered a penal offence for any brother not an officer of a subordinate council, to make use of the sign or summons adopted for public notification, except by direction of the President; or for officers of a council to post the same at any other time than from midnight to one hour before daybreak, and this rule shall be incorporated into the by-laws of the State, District, and Territorial councils. (June, 1854.)

Rule 7.—The determination of the necessity and mode of issuing the posters for public notification shall be intrusted to the State, District, or Territorial councils. (June, 1854.)

Rule 8.—The respective State, District, or Territorial councils shall be required to make statements of the number of members within their respective limits, at the next meeting of this national council, and annually thereafter, at the regular annual meeting. (June, 1854.)

Rule 9.—The delegates to the National Council of the United States of North America shall be entitled to three dollars per day for their attendance upon the national council, and for each day that may be necessary in going and returning from the same; and five cents per mile for every mile they may necessarily travel in going to, and returning from the place of meeting of the national council; to be computed by the nearest mail route: which shall be paid out of the treasury of the national council. (November, 1854.)

Rule 10.—Each State, District, or Territorial council shall be taxed four cents per annum for every member in good standing belonging to each subordinate council under its jurisdiction on the first day of April, which shall be reported to the national council, and paid into the national treasury, on or before the first day of the annual session, to be held in June; and on the same day in each succeeding year. And the first fiscal year shall be considered as commencing on the first day of Decem-

*Note.—See Constitution, Art. 3, Sec. 4, p. 5.

ber, 1854, and ending on the fifteenth day of May, 1855. (November, 1854.)

Rule 11.—The following shall be the key to determine and ascertain the purport of any communication that may be addressed to the President of a State, District, or Territorial council by the President of the national council, who is hereby instructed to communicate a knowledge of the same to said officers:

A	B	C	D	E	F	G	H	I	J	K	L	M
1	7	13	19	25	2	8	14	20	26	3	9	15
N	O	P	Q	R	S	T	U	V	W	X	Y	Z
21	4	10	16	22	5	11	17	23	6	12	18	24

Rule 12.—The clause of the article of the constitution relative to belief in the Supreme Being is obligatory upon every State and subordinate council, as well as upon each individual member. (June, 1854.)

Rule 13.—The following shall be the compensation of the officers of this council:

1st. The Corresponding Secretary shall be paid two thousand dollars per annum, from the 17th day of June, 1854.

2d. The Treasurer shall be paid five hundred dollars per annum, from the 17th day of June, 1854.

3d. The Sentinels shall be paid five dollars for every day they may be in attendance on the sittings of the national council.

4th. The Chaplain shall be paid one hundred dollars per annum, from the 17th day of June, 1854.

5th. The Recording Secretary shall be paid five hundred dollars per annum, from the 17th day of June, 1854.

6th. The Assistant Secretary shall be paid five dollars per day, for every day he may be in attendance on the sitting of the national council. All of which is to be paid out of the national treasury, on the draft of the President. (November, 1854.)

SPECIAL VOTING.

Vote 1st.—This national council hereby grants to the State of Virginia two State councils, the one to be located in Eastern and the other in Western Virginia, the Blue Ridge Mountains being the geographical line between the two jurisdictions. (June, 1854.)

Vote 2d.—The President shall have power, till the next session of the national council, to grant dispensations for the formation of State, District, or Territorial councils, in form most agreeable to his own discretion, upon proper application being made. (June, 1854.)

Vote 3d.—The seats of all delegates to and members of the present national council shall be vacated on the first Tuesday in June, 1855, at the hour of six o'clock in the forenoon; and the national council convening in annual session upon that day, shall be composed exclusively of delegates elected under and in accordance with the provisions of the constitution, as amended at the present session of this national council; provided, that this resolution shall not apply to the officers of the national council. (November, 1854.)

Vote 4th.—The Corresponding Secretary of this council is authorized to have printed the names of the delegates to this national council; also, those of the Presidents of the several State, District, and Territorial councils, together with their address, and to forward a copy of the same to each person named; and further, the Corresponding Secretaries of each State, District, and Territory are requested to forward a copy of their several constitutions to each other. (November, 1854.)

Vote 5th.—In the publication of the constitution and the ritual, under the direction of the committee—brothers Deshler, Damrell, and Stephens—the name, signs, grips, and passwords of the order shall be indicated by [* * *], and a copy of the same shall be furnished to each State, District, and Territorial council, and to each member of that body. (November, 1854.)

Vote 6th.—A copy of the constitution of each State, District, and Territorial council, shall be submitted to this council for examination. (November, 1854.)

Vote 7th.—It shall be the duty of the Treasurer, at each annual meeting of this body, to make a report of all moneys received or expended in the interval. (November, 1854.)

Vote 8th.—Messrs. Gifford of Pa., Barker of N. Y., Deshler of N. J., Williamson of Va., and Stephens of Md., are appointed a committee to confer with similar committees that have been appointed for the purpose of consolidating the various American orders, with power to make the necessary arrangement for such consolidation—subject to the approval of this national council, at its next session. (November, 1854.)

Vote 9th.—On receipt of the new ritual by the members of this national council who have received the third degree, they or any of them may, and they are hereby empowered to, confer the third degree upon members of this body in their respective states, districts, and territories, and upon the presidents and other officers of their state, district, and territorial councils. And further, the presidents of the state, district, and territorial councils shall in the first instance confer the third degree upon as many of the presidents and officers of their subordinate councils as can be assembled together in their respective localities; and afterwards the same may be conferred upon officers of other subordinate councils, by any presiding officer of a council who shall have previously received it under the provisions of the constitution. (November, 1854.)

Vote 10th.—To entitle any delegate to a seat in this national council, at its annual session in June next, he must present a properly authenticated certificate that he was duly elected as a delegate to the same, or appointed a substitute in accordance with the requirements of the constitutions of state, territorial, or district councils. And no delegate shall be received from any state, district, or territorial council which has not adopted the constitution and ritual of this national council. (November, 1854.)

Vote 11th.—The committee on printing the constitution and ritual is authorized to have a sufficient number of the same printed for the use of the order. And no state, district, or territorial council shall be allowed to reprint the same. (November, 1854.)

Vote 12th.—The right to establish all subordinate councils in any of the states, districts, and territories represented in this national council, shall be confined to the state, district, and territorial councils which they represent. (November, 1854.)

CONSTITUTION FOR THE GOVERNMENT OF SUBORDINATE COUNCILS.

Art. I. Sec. 1.—Each subordinate council shall be composed of not less than thirteen members, all of whom shall have received all the degrees of the order, and shall be known and recognised as ——— Council, No. ——, of the ——— of the county of ———, and State of North Carolina.

Sec. 2.—No person shall be a member of any subordinate council in this state, unless he possesses all the qualifications, and comes up to all the requirements laid down in the constitution of the national council, and whose wife (if he has one), is not a Roman Catholic.

Sec. 3. No application for membership shall be received and acted on from a person residing out of the state, or resides in a county where there is a council in existence, unless upon special cause to be stated to the council, to be judged of by the same; and such person, if the reasons be considered sufficient, may be initiated the same night he is proposed, provided he resides five miles or more from the place where the council is located. But no person can vote in any council, except the one of which he is a member.

Sec. 4. Every person applying for membership, shall be voted for by ballot, in open council, if a ballot is requested by a single member. If one-third of the votes cast be against the applicant, he shall be rejected. If any applicant be rejected, he shall not be again proposed within six months thereafter. Nothing herein contained shall be construed to prevent the initiation of applicants privately, by those empowered to do so, in localities where there are no councils within a convenient distance.

Sec. 5. Any member of one subordinate council wishing to change his membership to another council, shall apply to the council to which he belongs, either in writing or orally through another member, and the question shall be decided by the council. If a majority are in favor of granting him an honorable dismission, he shall receive the same in writing, to be signed by the president and countersigned by the secretary. But until a member thus receiving an honorable dismission has actually been admitted to membership in another council, he shall be held subject to the discipline of the council from which he has received the dismission, to be dealt with by the same, for any violation of the requirements of the order. Before being received in the council to which he wishes to transfer his membership, he shall present said certificate of honorable dismission, and shall be received as new members are.

Sec. 6. Applications for the second degree shall not be received except in second degree councils, and voted on by second and third degree members only, and applications for the third degree shall be received in third degree councils, and voted on by third degree members only.

Art. II.—Each subordinate council shall fix on its own time and place for meeting: and shall meet at least once a month, but where not very inconvenient, it is recommended that they meet once a week. Thirteen members shall form a quorum for the transaction of business. Special meetings may be called by the president at any time, at the request of four members of the order.

Art. III.—Sec. 1. The members of each subordinate council shall consist of a president, vice-president, instructor, secretary, treasurer, marshal, inside and outside sentinel, and shall hold their offices for the term of six months, or until their successors are elected and installed.

Sec. 2. The officers of each subordinate council (except the sentinels, who shall be appointed by the president), shall be elected at the first regular meetings in January and July, separately, and by ballot; and each shall receive a majority of all the votes cast to entitle him to an election. No member shall be elected to any office, unless he be present and signify his assent thereto at the time of his election. Any vacancy which may occur by death, resignation, or otherwise, shall be filled at the next meeting thereafter, in the manner and form above described.

Sec. 3. The President.—It shall be the duty of the president of each subordinate council, to preside in the council, and enforce a due observance of the constitution and rules of the order, and a proper respect for the state council and the national council; to have sole and exclusive charge of the charter and the constitution and ritual of the order, which he must always have with him when his council is in session, to see that all officers perform their respective duties; to announce all ballotings to the council; to decide all questions of order; to give the casting vote in all cases of a tie; to convene special meetings when deemed expedient; to draw warrants on the treasurer for all sums, the payment of which is ordered by the council; and to perform such other duties as are demanded of him by the constitutions and ritual of the order.

Sec. 4. The vice-president of each subordinate council shall assist the president in the discharge of his duties, whilst his council is in session; and, in his absence, shall perform all the duties of the president.

Sec. 5. The instructor shall perform the duties of the president in the absence of the president and vice-president, and shall, under the direction of the president, perform such duties as may be assigned to him by the ritual.

Sec. 6. The secretary shall keep an accurate record of the proceedings of the council. He shall write all communications, fill all notices, attest all warrants drawn by the president for the payment of money; he shall keep a correct roll of all the members of the council, together with their age, residence, and occupation, in the order in which they have been admitted; he shall, at the expiration of every three months, make out a report of all work done during that time, which report he shall forward to the secretary of the state council; and when superseded in his office shall deliver all books, papers, &c., in his hands to his successor.

Sec. 7 The treasurer shall hold all moneys raised exclusively for the use of the state council, which he shall pay over to the secretary of the state council at its regular sessions, or whenever called upon by the president of the state council. He shall receive all moneys for the use of the subordinate council, and pay all amounts drawn for on him, by the president of the subordinate council, if attested by the secretary.

Sec. 8. The marshal shall perform such duties, under the direction of the president, as may be required of him by the ritual.

Sec. 9. The inside sentinel shall have charge of the inner door, and act under the directions of the president. He shall admit no person, unless he can prove himself a member of this order, and of the same degree in which the council is opened, or by order of the president, or is satisfactorily vouched for.

Sec. 10. The outside sentinel shall have charge of the outer door, and act in accordance with the orders of the president. He shall permit no person to enter the outer door unless he give the password of the degree in which the council is at work, or is properly vouched for.

Sec. 11. The secretary, treasurer, and sentinels, shall receive such compensation as the subordinate councils may each conclude to allow.

Sec. 12. Each subordinate council may levy its own fees for initiation, to raise a fund to pay its dues to the state council, and to defray its own expenses. Each council may, also, at its discretion, initiate without charging the usual fee, those it considers unable to pay the same.

Sec. 13. The president shall keep in his possession the constitution and ritual of the order. He shall not suffer the same to go out of his possession under any pretence whatever, unless in case of absence, when he may put them in the hands of the vice-president or instructor, or whilst the council is in session, for the information of a member wishing to see it, for the purpose of initiation, or conferring of degrees.

Art. IV Each subordinate council shall have power to adopt such by-laws, rules, and regulations, for its own government, as it may think proper, not inconsistent with the constitutions of the national and state councils.

Form of Application for a Charter to Organize a new Council.

Post Office —— county,
Date ——.

To ——

President of the State Council of North Carolina:—

We, the undersigned, members of the Third Degree, being desirous of extending the influence and usefulness of our organization, do hereby ask for a warrant of dispensation, instituting and organizing us as a subordinate branch of the order, under the jurisdiction of the State Council of the State of North Carolina, to be known and hailed as Council No. ——, and to be located at ——, in the county of ——, State of North Carolina.

And we do hereby pledge ourselves to be governed by the Constitution of the State Council of the State of North Carolina, and of the Grand Council of the U. S. N. A., and that we will in all things conform to the rules and usages of the order.

Names. **Residences.**

FORM OF DISMISSION FROM ONE COUNCIL TO ANOTHER.

This is to certify that Brother ——, a member of —— Council, No. ——, having made an application to change his membership from this council to that of —— Council, No. ——, at ——, in the county of ——, I do hereby declare, that said brother has received an honorable dismission from this council, and is hereby recommended for membership in —— Council, No. ——, in the county of ——, N C.; provided, however, that until Brother —— has been admitted to membership in said council, he is to be considered subject to the discipline of this council, to be dealt with by the same for any violation of the requirements of the order. This the —— day of ——, 185—, and the —— year of American Independence.

—— President, —— Council,
No. ——.

—— Secretary

FORM OF CERTIFICATE FOR DELEGATES TO THE STATE COUNCIL.

—— Council, No. ——,
—— county of ——, N C.

This is to certify that —— and —— were at the regular meeting of this council, held on the ——, 185—, duly elected delegates to represent this council in the next annual meeting of the state council, to be held in ——, on the 3d Monday in November next. And by virtue of the authority in me reposed, I do hereby declare the said —— and —— to be invested with all the rights, powers, and privileges of the delegates as aforesaid. This being the —— day of ——, 185—, and the —— year of our national independence.

—— —— President of
—— Council, No.——

—— —— Secretary

FORM OF NOTICE

From the Subordinate Council to the State Council, whenever any Member of a Subordinate Council is expelled.

—— Council, No. ——,
—— county of ——, N. C.

To the President of the State Council of North Carolina:

Sir:—This is to inform you that at a meeting of this council, held on the —— day of ——, 185—, —— —— was duly expelled from membership in said council, and thus deprived of all the privileges, rights, and benefits of this organization.

In accordance with the provisions of the constitution of the state council, you are hereby duly notified of the same, that you may officially notify all the subordinate councils of the state to be upon their guard against the said ——, as one unworthy to associate with patriotic and good men, and (*if expelled for violating his obligation*) as a perjurer to God and his country. The said —— is about —— years of age, and is by livelihood a ——

Duly certified, this the —— day of —— 185—, and in the —— year of our national independence.

—— —— President o.
—— Council, No. ——.

—— Secretary.

FIRST DEGREE COUNCIL.

To be admitted to membership in this order, the applicant shall be—

1st. Proposed and found acceptable.

2nd. Introduced and examined under the guarantee of secrecy

3rd. Placed under the obligation which the order imposes.

4th. Required to enrol his name and place of residence.

5th. Instructed in the forms and usages and ceremonies of the order.

6th. Solemnly charged as to the objects to be obtained, and his duties.

[A recommendation of a candidate to this order shall be received only from a brother of approved integrity It shall be accompanied by minute particulars as to name, age, calling, and residence, and by an explicit voucher for his qualifications, and a personal pledge for his fidelity These particulars shall be recorded by the secretary in a book kept for that purpose. The recommendation may be referred, and the ballot taken at such time and in such a manner as the state council may prescribe; but no communication shall be made to the candidate until the ballot has been declared in his favor. Candidates shall be received in the ante-room by the marshal and secretary]

OUTSIDE.

Marshal.—Do you believe in a Supreme Being, the Creator and Preserver of the universe?

Ans.—I do.

Marshal.—Before proceeding further, we require a solemn obligation of secrecy and truth. If you will take such an obligation, you will lay your right hand upon the Holy Bible and cross.

(When it is known that the applicant is a Protestant, the cross may be omitted, or affirmation may be allowed.)

OBLIGATION.

You do solemnly swear (or affirm) that you will never reveal anything said or done in this room, the names of any persons present, nor the existence of this society, whether found worthy to proceed or not, and that all your declarations shall be true, so help you God?

Ans.—"I do."

Marshal.—Where were you born?

Marshal.—Where is your permanent residence?

(If born out of the jurisdiction of the United States, the answer shall be written, the candidate dismissed with an admonition of secrecy, and the brother vouching for him suspended from all the privileges of the order, unless upon satisfactory proof that he has been misinformed.)

Marshal.—Are you twenty-one years of age?

Ans.—"I am."

Marshal.—Were you born of Protestant parents, or were you reared under Protestant influence?

Ans.—"Yes."

Marshal.—If married, is your wife a Roman Catholic?

("No" or "Yes"—the answer to be valued as the Constitution of the State Council shall provide.)

Marshal.—Are you willing to use your influence and vote only for native-born American citizens for all offices of honor, trust, or profit in the gift of the people, to the exclusion of all foreigners and aliens, and Roman Catholics in particular, and without regard to party predilections?

Ans.—"I am."

INSIDE.

(The marshal shall then repair to the council in session, and present the written list of names, vouchers, and answers to the president, who shall cause them to be read aloud, and a vote of the council to be taken on each name, in such manner as prescribed by its by-laws. If doubts arise in the ante-room, they shall be referred to the council. If a candidate be dismissed, he shall be admonished to secrecy. The candidates declared elected shall be conducted to seats within the council, apart from the brethren. When all are present the president by one blow of the gavel, shall call to order and say:)

President.—Brother marshal, introduce the candidates to the vice-president.

Marshal.—Worthy Vice-President, I present to you these candidates, who have duly answered all questions.

Vice-President, rising in his place.—Gentlemen, it is my office to welcome you as friends. When you shall have assumed the patriotic vow by which we are all bound, we will embrace you as brothers. I am authorized to declare that our obligations enjoin nothing which is inconsistent with the duty which every good man owes to his Creator, his country, his family, or himself. We do not compel you, against your convictions, to act with us in our good work; but should you at any time wish to withdraw, it will be our duty to grant you a dismissal in good faith. If satisfied with this assurance, you will rise upon your feet (*pausing till they do so*), place the left hand upon the breast, and raise the right hand towards heaven.

(The brethren to remain seated till called up.)

OBLIGATION.

In the presence of Almighty God and these witnesses, you do solemnly promise and swear, that you will never betray any of the secrets of this society, nor communicate them even to proper candidates, except within a lawful council of the order; that you never will permit any of the secrets of this society to be written, or in any other manner made legible, except for the purpose of official instruction; that you will not vote, nor give your influence for any man for any office in the gift of the people, unless he be an American born citizen, in favor of Americans ruling America, nor if he be a Roman Catholic; that you will in all political matters, so far as this order is concerned, comply with the will of the majority, though it may conflict with your personal preference, so long as it does not conflict with the Constitution of the United States of America, or that of the state in which you reside; that you will not, under any circumstances whatever, knowingly recommend an unworthy person for initiation, nor suffer it to be done, if in your power to prevent it; that you will not, under any circumstances, expose the name of any member of this order, nor reveal the existence of such an association; that you will answer an *imperative notice* issued by the proper authority; obey the command of the state council, president, or his deputy, while assembled by such notice, and respond to the claim of a *sign* or *cry* of the order, unless it be physically impossible; and that you will acknowledge the State Council of ——— as the legislative head, the ruling authority, and the supreme tribunal of the order in the state of ———, acting under the jurisdiction of the National Council of the United States of North America.

Binding yourself in the penalty of excommunication from the order, the forfeiture of all intercourse with its members, and being denounced in all the societies of the same, as a wilful traitor to your God and your country.

(The president shall call up every person present, by three blows of the gavel, when the candidates shall all repeat after the vice-president in concert:)

All this I voluntarily and sincerely promise, with a full understanding of the solemn sanctions and penalties.

Vice-President.—You have now taken solemn oaths, and made as sacred promises as man can make, that you will keep all our secrets inviolate; and we wish you distinctly to understand that he that takes these oaths and makes these promises, and then violates them, leaves the foul, the deep and blighting stain of perjury resting on his soul.

President.—(Having seated all by one blow of the gavel.)—Brother Instructor, these new brothers having complied with the demand of the order, are entitled to the secrets and privileges of the same. You will, therefore, invest them with everything appertaining to the first degree.

Instructor.—Brothers: the practices and proceedings in our order are as follows:

We have pass-words necessary to be used to obtain admission to our councils; forms for our conduct while there; means of recognizing each other when abroad; means of mutual protection; and methods for giving notices to members.

At the outer door you will* (*make any ordinary alarm* to attract the attention of the outside sentinel).

When the wicket is opened you will pronounce the (*words—what's the pass*), in a whisper. The outside sentinel will reply (*Give it*), when you will give the term pass-word and be admitted to the anteroom. You will then proceed to the inner door and give (one rap). When the wicket is opened, give your name, the number of, and location of your council, the explanation of the term pass, and the degree pass-word.

If these be found correct, you will be admitted; if not, your name will be reported to the vice president, and must be properly vouched for before you can gain admission to the council. You will then proceed to the centre of the room and address the (*President*) with the countersign, which is performed thus (*placing the right hand diagonally across the mouth*). When this salutation is recognized, you will quietly take your seat.

This sign is peculiar to this degree, and is never to be used outside the council room, nor during the conferring of this degree. When retiring, you will address the (*Vice President*) in the same manner, and also give the degree pass-word to the inside sentinel.

The "term pass-word" is (*We are*).

(The pass-word and explanation is to be established by each State Council for its respective subordinates.)

The "explanation" of the "term-pass," to be used at the inner door, is (*our country's hope.*)

The "degree pass-word" is (*Native*).

The "traveling pass-word" is (*The memory of our pilgrim fathers*).

(This word is changed annually by the President of the National Council of the United States, and is to be made and used only when the brother is traveling beyond the jurisdiction of his own state, district, or territory. It and all other pass-words must be communicated in a whisper, and no brother is entitled to communicate them to another, without authority from the presiding officer.)

"The sign of recognition" is (*grasping the right lappel of the coat with the right hand, the fore finger being extended inwards.*)

The "answer" is given by (*a similar action with the left hand.*)

The "grip" is given by (*an ordinary shake of the hand*).

The person challenging shall (*then draw the fore finger along the palm of the hand*). The answer will be given by (*a similar action forming a link by hooking together the ends of the fore finger*); when the following conversation ensues—the challenging party first saying (*is that yours?*) The answer, (*it is.*) Then the response (*how did you get it?*), followed by the rejoinder (*it is my birth-right*).

Public notice for a meeting is given by means of a (*piece of white paper the shape of a heart*).

(In cities * the *** of the *** where the meeting is to be held, will be written legibly upon the notice; and upon the election day said *** will denote the *** where your presence is needed. This notice will never be passed, but will be *** or thrown upon the sidewalk with a *** in the centre.)

If information is wanting of the object of the gathering, or of the place, &c., the inquirer will ask of an undoubted brother (*where's when?*) The brother will give the information if possessed of it; if not it will be yours and his duty to continue the inquiry, and thus disseminate the call throughout the brotherhood.

If the color of *the paper* (be *red*), it will denote actual trouble, which requires that you come prepared to meet it.

The "cry of distress"—to be used only in time of danger, or where the American interest requires an immediate assemblage of the brethren—is (*oh, oh, oh.*) The response is (*hio, hio, h-i-o.*)

The "sign of caution"—to be given when a brother is speaking unguardedly before a stranger—is (*drawing the fore finger and thumb together across the eyes, the rest of the hand being closed*), which signifies "keep dark."

Brothers, you are now initiated into and made acquainted with the work and organization of a council of this degree of the order; and the marshal will present

* In the Ritual the words in parentheses are omitted. In the key to the Ritual, they are written in figures—the alphabet used being the same as printed below. So throughout.

Key to Unlock Communications.

A	B	C	D	E	F	G	H	I	J	K	L	M
1	7	13	19	25	2	8	14	20	26	3	9	15
N	O	P	Q	R	S	T	U	V	W	X	Y	Z
21	4	10	16	22	5	11	17	23	6	12	18	24

* Concerning what is said of cities, the key to the Ritual says: "Considered unnecessary to decipher what is said in regard to cities."

you to the worthy president for admonition.

President.—It has no doubt, been long apparent to you, brothers, that foreign influence and Roman Catholicism have been making steady and alarming progress in our country. You cannot have failed to observe the significant transition of the foreigner and Romanist from a character quiet, retiring, and even abject, to one bold, threatening, turbulent, and despotic in its appearance and assumptions. You must have become alarmed at the systematic and rapidly augmenting power of these dangerous and unnatural elements of our national condition. So it is, brothers, with others beside yourselves in every state of the Union. A sense of danger has struck the great heart of the nation. In every city, town, and hamlet, the danger has been seen and the alarm sounded. And hence true men have devised this order as a means of disseminating patriotic principles, of keeping alive the fire of national virtue, of fostering the national intelligence, and of advancing America and the American interest on the one side, and on the other of checking the strides of the foreigner or alien, or thwarting the machinations and subverting the deadly plans of the papist and Jesuit.

Note.—The President shall impress upon the initiates the importance of secrecy, the manner of proceeding in recommending candidates for initiation, and the responsibility of the duties which they have assumed.

Second Degree Council.

Marshal.—Worthy President: These brothers have been duly elected to the second degree of this order. I present them to you for obligation.

President.—Brothers: You will place your left hand upon your right breast, and extend your right hand towards the flag of our country, preparatory to obligation. (Each council room should have a neat American flag festooned over the platform of the President.)

OBLIGATION.

You, and each of you, of your own free will and accord, in the presence of Almighty God and these witnesses, your left hand resting upon your right breast, and your right hand extended to the flag of your country, do solemnly and sincerely swear, that you will not under any circumstances disclose in any manner, nor suffer it to be done by others, if in your power to prevent it, the name, signs, pass-words, or other secrets of this degree, except in open council for the purpose of instruction; that you will in all things conform to all the rules and regulations of this order, and to the constitution and by-laws of this or any other council to which you may be attached, so long as they do not conflict with the Constitution of the United States, nor that of the State in which you reside; that you will under all circumstances, if in your power so to do, attend to all regular signs or summons that may be thrown or sent to you by a brother of this or any other degree of this order; that you will support in all political matters, for all political offices, members of this order in preference to other persons; that if it may be done legally, you will, when elected or appointed to any official station conferring on you the power to do so remove all foreigners, aliens, or Roman Catholics from office or place, and that you will in no case appoint such to any office or place in your gift. You do also promise and swear that this and all other obligations which you have previously taken in this order shall ever be kept through life sacred and inviolate. All this you promise and declare, as Americans, to sustain and abide by, without any hesitation or mental reservation whatever. So help you God and keep you steadfast.

(Each will answer "I do."

President.—Brother Marshal, you will now present the brothers to the instructor for instructions in the second degree of the order.

Marshal.—Brother Instructor, by direction of our worthy president, I present these brothers before you that you may instruct them in the secrets and mysteries of the second degree of the order.

Instructor.—Brothers, in this degree we have an entering sign and a countersign. At the outer door proceed (*as in the first degree*). At the inner door you will make (*two raps*), and proceed as in the first degree, giving the second degree pass-word, which is *American,* instead of that of the first degree. If found to be correct, you will then be admitted, and proceed (*to the centre of the room*), giving the countersign, which is made thus (*extending the right arm to the national flag over the president, the palm of the hand being upwards*).

The sign of recognition in this degree is the same as in the first degree, with the addition of (*the middle finger*), and the response to be made in a (*similar manner.*)

Marshal, you will now present the brothers to the worthy president for admonition.

Marshal.—Worthy President, I now present these candidates to you for admonition.

President.—Brothers, you are now duly initiated into the second degree of this order. Renewing the congratulations which we extended to you upon your admission to the first degree, we admonish you by every tie that may nerve patriots, to aid us in our efforts to restore the political institutions of our country to their original purity. Begin with the youth of our land. Instil into their minds the lessons of our country's history—the glorious battles and the brilliant deeds of patriotism of our fathers, through which we received the inestimable blessings of civil and religious liberty. Point them to the example of the sages and the statesmen who founded our government. Implant in their bosoms an ardent love for the Union. Above all else, keep alive in their bosoms the memory, the maxims, and the deathless example of our illustrious WASHINGTON.

Brothers, recalling to your minds the solemn obligations which you have severally taken in this and the first degree, I now pronounce you entitled to all the privileges of membership in this the second degree of our order.

THIRD DEGREE COUNCIL.

Marshal.—Worthy President, these brothers having been duly elected to the third degree of this order, I present them before you for obligation.

President.—Brothers, you will place yourselves in a circle around me, each one crossing your arms upon your breasts, and grasping firmly each other's hands, holding the right hand of the brother on the right and the left hand of the brother on the left, so as to form a circle, symbolical of the links of an unbroken chain, and of a ring which has no end.

Note.—This degree is to be conferred with the national flag elevated in the centre of the circle, by the side of the president or instructor, and not on less than five at any one time, in order to give it solemnity, and also for the formation of the circle—except in the first instance of conferring it on the officers of the state and subordinate councils, that they may be empowered to progress with the work.

The obligation and charge in this degree may be given by the president or instructor, as the president may prefer.

OBLIGATION.

You, and each of you, of your own free will and accord, in the presence of Almighty God and these witnesses, with your hands joined in token of that fraternal affection which should ever bind together the States of this Union—forming a ring, in token of your determination that, so far as your efforts can avail, this Union shall have no end—do solemnly and sincerely swear [or affirm] that you will not under any circumstances disclose in any manner, nor suffer it to be done by others if in your power to prevent it, the name, signs, passwords, or other secrets of this degree, except to those to whom you may prove on trial to be brothers of the same degree, or in open council, for the purpose of instruction; that you do hereby solemnly declare your devotion to the Union of these States; that in the discharge of your duties as American citizens, you will uphold, maintain, and defend it; that you will discourage and discountenance any and every attempt, coming from any and every quarter, which you believe to be designed or calculated to destroy or subvert it, or to weaken its bonds; and that you will use your influence, so far as in your power, in endeavoring to procure an amicable and equitable adjustment of all political discontents or differences which may threaten its injury or overthrow. You further promise and swear [or affirm] that you will not vote for any one to fill any office of honor, profit or trust of a political character, whom you know or believe to be in favor of a dissolution of the Union of these States, or who is endeavoring to produce that result; that you will vote for and support for all political offices, third or union degree members of this order in preference to all others; that if it may be done consistently with the constitution and laws of the land, you will, when elected or appointed to any official station which may confer on you the power to do so, remove from office or place all persons whom you know or believe to be in favor of a dissolution of the Union, or who are endeavoring to produce that result; and that you will in no case appoint such person to any political office or place whatever. All this you promise and swear [or affirm] upon your honor as American citizens and friends of the American Union, to sustain and abide by without any hesitation or mental reservation whatever. You also promise and swear [or affirm] that this and all other obligations which you have previously taken in this order, shall ever be kept sacred and inviolate. To all this you pledge your lives, your fortunes, and your sacred honors. So help you God and keep you steadfast.

(Each one shall answer, "I do.")

President.—Brother Marshal, you will now present the brothers to the instructor for final instruction in this third degree of the order.

Marshal.—Instructor, by direction of our worthy president, I present these brothers before you that you may instruct them in the secrets and mysteries of this the third degree of our order.

Instructor.—Brothers, in this degree as in the second, we have an entering password, a degree password, and a token of salutation. At the outer door (*make any ordinary alarm.* The outside sentinel will *say U; you say ni;* the sentinel will rejoin *on*). This will admit you to the inner door. At the inner door you will make (*three*) distinct (*raps*). Then announce your name, with the number (or name) and location of the council to which you belong, giving the explanation to the password, which is (*safe*). If found correct, you will then be admitted, when you will proceed to the centre of the room, and placing the (*hands on the breast with the fingers interlocked*), give the token of salutation, which is (*by bowing to the president*). You will then quietly take your seat.

The sign of recognition is made by the same action as in the second degree, with the addition of (*the third finger*), and the response is made by (a similar action with *the left hand*.)

(The grip is given by taking hold of the *hand in the usual way*, and then by *slipping the finger around on the top of the thumb*, then extending the *little finger and pressing the inside of* the *wrist*. The person challenging shall say, *do you know what that is?* The answer is *yes*. The challenging party shall say, further *what is it?* The answer is, *Union*.

[The instructor will here give the grip of this degree, with explanations, and also the true password of this degree, which is (*Union*.)]

CHARGE.

To be given by the president.

Brothers, it is with great pleasure that I congratulate you upon your advancement to the third degree of our order. The responsibilities you have now assumed, are more serious and weighty than those which preceded, and are committed to such only as have been tried and found worthy. Our obligations are intended as solemn avowals of our duty to the land that gave us birth; to the memories of our fathers; and to the happiness and welfare of our children. Consecrating to your country a spirit unselfish and a fidelity like that which distinguished the patriots of the Revolution, you have pledged your aid in cementing the bonds of a Union which we trust will endure for ever. Your deportment since your initiation has attested your devotion to the principles we desire to establish, and has inspired a confidence in your patriotism, of which we can give no higher proof than your reception here.

The dangers which threaten American liberty arise from foes without and from enemies within. The first degree pointed out the source and nature of our most imminent peril, and indicated the first measure of safety. The second degree defined the next means by which, in coming time, such assaults may be rendered harmless. The third degree, which you have just received, not only reiterates the lessons of the other two, but it is intended to avoid and provide for a more remote, but no less terrible danger, from domestic enemies to our free institutions.

Our object is briefly this:—to perfect an organization modeled after that of the Constitution of the United States, and coextensive with the confederacy. Its object and principles, in all matters of national concern, to be uniform and identical whilst in all local matters the component parts shall remain independent and sovereign within their respective limits.

The great result to be attained—the only one which can secure a perfect guarantee as to our future—is UNION; permanent, enduring, fraternal UNION! Allow me, then, to impress upon your minds and memories the touching sentiments of the Father of his Country, in his Farewell Address:—

"The unity of government which constitutes you one people," says Washington, "is justly dear to you, for it is the main pillar in the edifice of your real independence, the support of your tranquillity at home, of your peace abroad, of your safety, your prosperity—even that liberty you so justly prize.

" * * It is of infinite moment that you should properly estimate the immense value of your *National Union*, to your collective and individual happiness. You should cherish a cordial, habitual, and immovable attachment to it; accustoming yourselves to think and speak of it, as the palladium of your political safety and prosperity; watching for its preservation with jealous anxiety; discountenancing whatever may suggest even a suspicion that it can in any event be abandoned; and indignantly frowning upon the dawning of every attempt to alienate any portion of our country from the rest, or to enfeeble the sacred ties which now bind together the various parts."

Let these words of paternal advice and warning, from the greatest man that ever lived, sink deep into your hearts. Cherish them, and teach your children to reverence them, as you cherish and reverence the memory of Washington himself. The Union of these states is the great conservator of that liberty so dear to the American heart. Without it, our greatness as a nation would disappear, and our boasted self-government prove a signal failure. The very name of liberty, and the hopes of struggling freedom throughout the world, must perish in the wreck of this Union. Devote yourselves, then, to its maintenance, as our fathers did to the cause of independence; consecrating to its support, as you have sworn to do, your lives, your fortunes, and your sacred honors.

Brothers: Recalling to your minds the solemn obligations which you have severally taken in this and the preceding degrees, I now pronounce you entitled to all the privileges of membership in this organization, and take pleasure in informing you that you are now members of the order of (*the American Union*.)

American, Whig, Republican and Democratic Nominations of 1856.

The American convention met the next day after the session of the National Council of the Order, on the 22d February, 1856. It was composed of 227 delegates; all the States being represented except Maine, Vermont, Georgia and South Carolina. Hon. Millard Fillmore was nominated for President, and Andrew J. Donelson for Vice-President.

The Whig Convention met at Baltimore, September, 17, 1856, and endorsed the nominations made by the American party, and in its platform declared that "without adopting or referring to the peculiar doctrines of the party which has already selected Mr. Fillmore as a candidate" * * * Resolved, that in the present exigency of political affairs, we are not called upon to discuss the subordinate questions of the administration in the exercising of the constitutional powers of the government. It is enough to know that civil war is raging, and that the Union is in peril; and proclaim the conviction that the restoration of Mr. Fillmore to the Presidency will furnish the best if not the only means of restoring peace."

The first National Convention of the new Republican party met at Philadelphia, June 18, 1856, and nominated John C. Fremont for President, and William L. Dayton for Vice-President. Since the previous Presidential election, a new party consisting of the disaffected former adherents of the other parties—Native and Independent Democrats, Abolitionists, and Whigs opposed to slavery—had sprung into existence, and was called by its adherents and friends, the Republican party.

This convention of delegates assembled in pursuance of a call addressed to the people of the United States, without regard to past political differences or divisions, who were opposed to the repeal of the Missouri Compromise. To the policy of President Pierce's administration: To the extension of slavery into free territory: In favor of the admission of Kansas as a free State: Of restoring the action of the federal government to the principles of Washington and Jefferson.

It adopted a platform, consisting of a set of resolutions, the principal one of which was: "That we deny the authority of Congress, of a territorial legislature, of any individual, or association of individuals, to give legal existence to slavery in any territory of the United States, while the present Constitution shall be maintained." And closed with a resolution: "That we invite the approbation and co-operation of the men of all parties, however different from us in other respects, in support of the principles herein declared; and believing that the spirit of our institutions, as well as the Constitution of our country, guaranties liberty of conscience and equality of rights among citizens, we oppose all legislation impairing their security."

The Democratic Convention, met at Cincinnati, in May 1856, and nominated James Buchanan for President, and John C. Breckenridge for Vice-President. It adopted a platform which contained the material portions of all its previous platforms, and also defined its position on the new issues of the day, and declared (1) that the revenue to be raised should not exceed the actual necessary expenses of the government, and for the gradual extinction of the public debt; (2) that the Constitution does not confer upon the general government the power to commence and carry on a general system of internal improvements; (3) for a strict construction of the powers granted by the Constitution to the federal government; (4) that Congress has no power to charter a national bank; (5) that Congress has no power to interfere with slavery in the States and Territories; the people of which have the exclusive right and power to settle that question for themselves. (6) Opposition to native Americanism.

At the election which followed, in November, 1856, the Democratic candidates were elected, though by a popular minority vote, having received 1,838,160 popular votes, and 174 electoral votes, against 2,215,768 popular votes, and 122 electoral votes for John C. Fremont, the Republican candidate, and Mr. Fillmore, the Whig and American candidate.

The aggregate vote cast for Mr. Fillmore, who was the nominee on both the Whig and American tickets, was 874,534, and his electoral vote was eight; that of the State of Maryland. This was the last national election at which the Whigs appeared as a party, under that name; they having joined with the American and with the Republican parties, and finally united with the latter after the downfall and extinction of the former. In the State elections of that year, (1856) the American party carried Rhode Island and Maryland; and in the 35th Congress, which met in December, 1857, the party had 15 to 20 Representatives and five Senators. When the 36th Congress met, in 1859, it had become almost a border State or Southern party, having two Senators; one from Kentucky and one from Maryland; and 23 Representatives, five from Kentucky, seven from Tennessee, three from Maryland, one from Virginia, four from North Carolina, two from Georgia, and one from Louisiana. The American party had none of the elements of persistence. It made another desperate effort, however, in the next Presidential campaign, but having failed to carry the South, disappeared finally from politics.

The new Republican party polled a very large vote—1,341,234 out of a total vote of 4,053,928—and its candidates received 114 votes out of 296, in the electoral college; having secured majorities in all the free States, except Illinois, Indiana, Pennsylvania, New Jersey and California.

The successful candidate, Mr. James Buchanan, was duly inaugurated as President of the United States, and entered upon the discharge of his duties as such, March 4, 1857

After the election of November, 1856, the Republican Association of Washington issued an address to the people, in which the results of the election were examined, and the future policy of the party stated. It is an interesting paper, as laying the foundation of the campaign of 1860, which followed, and is here given in full:

"Republican Association of Washington.

Address to the Republicans of the United States.

"WASHINGTON, *Nov.* 27, 1856.

"The Presidential contest is over, and at last we have some materials to enable us to form a judgment of the results.

"Seldom have two parties emerged from a conflict with less of joy in the victors, more of hope in the vanquished. The pro-slavery party has elected its Presidential candidate, only, however, by the votes of a minority, and that of such a character as to stamp the victory as the offspring of sectionalism and temporary causes. The Republicans, wherever able to present clearly to the public the real issue of the canvass—slavery restriction or slavery extension—have carried the people with them by unprecedented majorities; almost breaking up in some States the organization of their adversaries. A sudden gathering together of the people, alarmed at the inroads of the slave power, rather than a well organized party, with but a few months to attend to the complicated details of party warfare; obstructed by a secret Order, which had pre-occupied the field, and obtained a strong hold of the national and religious prejudices of the masses; opposed to an old party, commencing the canvass with the united support of a powerful section, hardened by long party drill, accustomed to victory, wielding the whole power of the federal administration—a party which only four years ago carried all but four of the States, and a majority of the popular vote—still, under all these adverse circumstances, they have triumphed in eleven, if not twelve of the free States, pre-eminent for enterprise and general intelligence, and containing one half of the whole population of the country; given to their Presidential candidate nearly three times as many electoral votes as were cast by the Whig party in 1852; and this day control the governments of fourteen of the most powerful States of the Union.

"Well may our adversaries tremble in the hour of their victory 'The Democratic and Black Republican parties,' they say, 'are nearly balanced in regard to power. The former was victorious in the recent struggle, but success was hardly won, with the aid of important accidental advantages. The latter has abated nothing of its zeal, and has suffered no pause in its preparations for another battle.'

"With such numerical force, such zeal, intelligence, and harmony in counsel; with so many great States, and more than a million voters rallied to their standard by the efforts of a few months, why may not the Republicans confidently expect a victory in the next contest?

The necessity for their organization still exists in all its force. Mr. Buchanan has always proved true to the demands of his party. He fully accepted the Cincinnati platform, and pledged himself to its policy —a policy of filibustering abroad, propagandism at home. Prominent and controlling among his supporters are men committed, by word and deed, to that policy; and what is there in his character, his antecedents, the nature of his northern support, to authorize the expectation that he will disregard their will? Nothing will be so likely to restrain him and counteract their extreme measures, as a vigorous and growing Republican organization, as nothing would be more necessary to save the cause of freedom and the Union, should he, as we have every reason to believe, continue the pro-slavery policy of the present incumbent. Let us beware of folding our arms, and waiting to see what he will do. We know the ambition, the necessities, the schemes of the slave power. Its policy of extension and aggrandizement and universal empire, is the law of its being, not an accident—is settled, not fluctuating. Covert or open, moderate or extreme, according to circumstances, it never changes in spirit or aim. With Mr. Buchanan, the elect of a party controlled by this policy, administering the government, the safety of the country and of free institutions must rest in the organization of the Republican party

What, then, is the duty before us? Organization, vigilance, action; action on the rostrum, through the press, at the ballot-box; in state, county, city, and town elections; everywhere, at all times; in every election, making Republicanism, or loyalty to the policy and principles it advocates, the sole political test. No primary or municipal election should be suffered to go by default. The party that would succeed nationally must triumph in states—triumph in the state elections, must be prepared by municipal success.

Next to the remaining power in the states already under their control, let the Republicans devote themselves to the work of disseminating their principles, and initiating the true course of political action in the states which have decided the election against them. This time we have failed, for reasons nearly all of which may be removed by proper effort. Many thousand honest, but not well-informed voters, who supported Mr. Buchanan under the delusive impression that he would favor the cause of free Kansas will soon learn their mistake, and be anxious to correct it. The timid policy of the Republicans in New Jersey, Pennsylvania, and Indiana, in postponing their independent action, and temporizing with a party got up for purposes not harmonizing with their own, and the conduct of Mr. Fillmore's friends in either voting for Mr. Buchanan, or dividing the opposition by a separate ticket, can hardly be repeated again. The true course of the Republicans is to organize promptly, boldly, and honestly upon their own principles, so clearly set forth in the Philadelphia platform, and, avoiding coalitions with other parties, appeal directly to the masses of all parties to ignore all organizations and issues which would divert the public mind from the one danger that now threatens the honor and interests of the country, and the subtlety of the Union—slavery propagandism allied with disunionism.

Let us not forget that it is not the want of generous sentiment, but of sufficient information, that prevents the American people from being united in action against the aggressive policy of the slave power. Were these simple questions submitted to-day to the people of the United States:—Are you in favor of the extension of slavery? Are you in favor of such extension by the aid or connivance of the federal government? And could they be permitted to record their votes in response, without embarrassment, without constraint of any kind, nineteen-twentieths of the people of the free States, and perhaps more than half of the people of the slave States, would return a decided negative to both.

Let us have faith in the people. Let us believe, that at heart they are hostile to the extension of slavery, desirous that the territories of the Union be consecrated to free labor and free institutions; and that they require only enlightenment as to the most effectual means of securing this end, to convert their cherished sentiment into a fixed principle of action.

The times are pregnant with warning. That a disunion party exists in the South, no longer admits of a doubt. It accepts the election of Mr. Buchanan as affording time and means to consolidate its strength and mature its plans, which comprehend not only the enslavement of Kansas, and the recognition of slavery in all territory of the United States, but the conversion of the lower half of California into a slave State, the organization of a new slavery territory in the Gadsden purchase, the future annexation of Nicaragua and subjugation of Central America, and the acquisition of Cuba; and, as the free States are not expected to submit to all this, ultimate dismemberment of the Union, and the formation of a great slaveholding confederacy, with foreign alliances with Brazil and Russia. It may assume at first a moderate tone, to prevent the sudden alienation of its Northern allies; it may delay the development of its plot, as it did under the Pierce administration, but the repeal of the Missouri compromise came at last, and so will come upon the country inevitably the final acts of the dark conspiracy When that hour shall come, then will the honest Democrats of the free States be driven into our ranks, and the men of the slave States who prefer the republic of Washington, Adams and Jefferson—a republic of law, order and liberty—to an oligarchy of slaveholders and slavery propagandists, governed by Wise, Atchison, Soulé, and Walker, founded in fraud and violence and seeking aggrandizement by the spoliation of nations, will bid God speed to the labors of the Republican party to preserve liberty and the Union, one and inseparable, perpetual and all powerful.

Washington, D. C., Nov 27, 1856.

The Kansas Struggle.

It was the removal of the interdiction against slavery, in all the territory north of 36° 30,' by the repeal of the Missouri Compromise which gave legality to the struggle for Kansas, and it was the doctrine of popular sovereignty which gave an impartial invitation to both sides to enter the struggle. The aggressive men of both parties hurried emigrants to the Territory Each accused the other of organized efforts, and soon in the height of the excitement these charges were rather confessed than denied.

A new question was soon evolved by the struggle, for some who entered from the South took their slaves with them. The Free State men now contended that slavery was a local institution and confined to the States where it existed, and that if an emigrant passed into the territory with his slaves these became free. The Southern view was, that slaves were recognized as property by the National Constitution; that therefore their masters had a right to take them there and hold them under constitutional guarantees, the same as any other property; that to assert anything else would be to deny the equality of the States within their common territory, and degrade them from the rank of equals to that of inferiors. This last proposition had such force that it would doubtless have received more general recognition if the North had not felt that the early compact dedicating the territories north of 36° 30 to freedom, had been violated. In answer to this proposition they therefore proclaimed in their platforms and speeches, and there was no other logical answer, "that freedom was National, and slavery Sectional."

We cannot enter upon a full description of the scenes in Kansas, but bloodshed and rapine soon followed the attempts of the opposing parties to get control of its government. What were called the "Border Ruffians" by the Free State men, because of active and warlike organization in Missouri and upon its borders, in the earlier parts of the struggle, seemed to have the advantage. They were supported by friends near at hand at all times, and warlike raids were frequent. The Free State men had to depend mainly upon New England for supplies in arms and means, but organizations were in turn rapidly completed to meet their calls, and the struggle soon became in the highest degree critical.

The pro-slavery party sustained the Territorial government appointed by the administration; the anti-slavery party repudiated it, because of its presumed committal to slavery The election for members of the Territorial legislature had been attended with much violence and fraud, and it was claimed that these things properly annulled any action taken by that body. A distinct and separate convention was called at Topeka to frame a State constitution, and the Free State men likewise elected their own Governor and Legislature to take the place of those appointed by Buchanan, and when the necessary preliminaries were completed, they applied for admission into the Union. After a long and bitter struggle Congress decided the question by refusing to admit Kansas under the Topeka Constitution, and by recognizing the authority of the territorial government. These proceedings took place during the session of 1856-7, which terminated immediately before the inauguraation of President Buchanan.

At the beginning of Buchanan's administration in 1857, the Republicans almost solidly faced the Democrats. There still remained part of the division caused by the American or Know-Nothing party, but its membership in Congress had already been compelled to show at least the tendency of their sentiments on the great question which was now rapidly dividing the two great sections of the Union. The result of the long Congressional struggle over the admission of Kansas and Nebraska was simply this: "That Congress was neither to legislate slavery into any Territory or State, nor to exclude it therefrom; but to leave the people thereof perfectly free to form and regulate their domestic institutions in their own way, subject only to the Constitution of the United States,"* and it was specially prescribed that when the Territory of Kansas shall be admitted as a State, it shall be admitted into the Union with or without slavery as the constitution adopted should prescribe at the time of admission.

This was, as it proved, but a temporary settlement on the principle of popular sovereignty, and was regarded at the time as a triumph of the views of Stephen A. Douglas by the friends of that great politician. The more radical leaders of the South looked upon it with distrust, but the blood of the more excitable in both sections was rapidly rising toward fever heat, and the border men from the Free and Slave States alike were preparing to act upon a compromise which in effect invited a conflict.

The Presidential election in 1856 had singularly enough encouraged the more aggressive of both sections. Buchanan's election was a triumph for the South; Fremont's large vote showed the power of a growing party as yet but partially organized, and crippled by schisms which grew out of the attempt to unite all elements of opposition to the Democrats. The general plan of the latter was now changed into an attempt to unite all of the free-soil elements into a party organization against slavery, and from that time forward until its total abolition slavery was the paramount issue in the minds of the more aggressive men of the north. Lincoln voiced the feelings of the Republicans when he declared in one of his Illinois speeches.—

"We will, hereafter, speak for freedom, and against slavery, as long as the Constitution guaranties free speech; until everywhere, on this wide land, the sun shall shine, and the rain shall fall, and the wind shall blow upon no man who goes forth to unrequited toil."

In the Congressional battle over the admission of Kansas and Nebraska, Douglas was the most conspicuous figure, and the language which we have quoted from Buchanan's inaugural was the literal meaning which Douglas had given to his idea of "popular" or "squatter sovereignty."

Prior to the Kansas struggle the Free

* President Buchanan's Inaugural Address.

Soilers of the North had regarded Douglas as an ally of the South, and his admitted ambition for the Presidency gave color to this suspicion. He it was who reported and carried through Congress the bill for the repeal of the Missouri Compromise, a measure which at that time was thought to obstruct Southern designs in the territories of the great West, but this repeal proved in fact the first plain steps toward the freedom of the territories. Having repealed that compromise, something must take its place, and what better than "popular sovereignty," thought Douglas. Territories contiguous to the Slave States, or in the same latitude, would thus naturally revert to slavery; while those farther north, and at that time least likely of early settlement, would be dedicated to freedom. There was a grave miscalculation just here. Slave-owners were not apt to change their homesteads, and could not with either profit or convenience carry their property to new lands which might or might not be fruitful in the crops best adapted to slave labor. Slave-owners were few in number compared with the free citizens of the North and the thousands of immigrants annually landing on our shores. People who had once moved from the New England or Middle States westward, were rather fond of it, and many of these swelled the tide which constantly sought homes in the territories; and where these did not go in person their sons and daughters were quite willing to imitate the early adventures of their parents. All these counted for the North under the doctrine of "popular sovereignty," and it was the failure of that doctrine to aid the South which from this time forward caused that section to mistrust the friendship of Douglas.

No political writer has since questioned his motives, and we doubt if it can be done successfully. His views may have undergone some change since 1850, and it would be singular if they had not; for a mind as discerning as his could hardly fail to note the changes going on all about him, and no where more rapidly than in his own State. He thought his doctrine at least adapted to the time, and he stood by it with rare bravery and ability If it had been accepted by the Republicans, it would have been fatal to their organization as a party. We doubt the ability of any party to stand long upon any mere compromise, made to suit the exigencies and avoid the dangers of the moment. It may be said that our government, first based on a confederacy and then a constitution, with a system of checks and balances, with a division of power between the people and the States, is but a compromise; but the assertion will not hold good. These things were adopted because of a belief at the time that they were in themselves right, or as nearly right as those who participated in their adoption were given to see the right. There was certainly no attempt at a *division of right and wrong*, and the closest investigation will show nothing beyond a surrender of power for the good of all, which is in itself the very essence and beginning of government.

We have said that Douglas fought bravely for his idea, and every movement in his most remarkable campaign with Lincoln for the U. S. Senate demonstrated the fact. The times were full of agitation and excitement, and these were increased when it became apparent that Buchanan's administration would aid the effort to make Kansas a slave State. Douglas was the first to see that the application of administration machinery to his principle, would degrade and rob it of its fairness. He therefore resented Buchanan's interference, and in turn Buchanan's friends sought to degrade him by removing him from the chairmanship of the Senate Committee on Territories, the position which had given him marked control over all questions pertaining to the organization of territories and the admission of new States.

The Lincoln and Douglas Debate.

The Senatorial term of Douglas was drawing near to its close, when in July, 1858, he left Washington to enter upon the canvass for re-election. The Republican State Convention of Illinois had in the month previous met at Springfield, and nominated Abraham Lincoln as a candidate for United States Senator, this with a view to pledge all Republican members of the Legislature to vote for him—a practice since gone into disuse in most of the States, because of the rivalries which it engenders and the aggravation of the dangers of defeat sure to follow in the selection of a candidate in advance. "First get your goose, then cook it," inelegantly describes the basic principles of improved political tactics. But the Republicans, particularly of the western part of Illinois, had a double purpose in the selection of Lincoln. He was not as radical as they, but he well represented the growing Republican sentiment, and he best of all men could cope with Douglas on the stump in a canvass which they desired should attract the attention of the Nation, and give shape to the sentiment of the North on all questions pertaining to slavery The doctrine of "popular sovereignty" was not acceptable to the Republicans, the recent repeal of the Missouri compromise having led them, or the more radical portion of them, to despise all compromise measures.

The plan of the Illinois Republicans, if

indeed it was a well-settled plan, accomplished even more than was anticipated, though it did not result in immediate success. It gave to the debate which followed between Lincoln and Douglas a world-wide celebrity, and did more to educate and train the anti-slavery sentiment, taken in connection with the ever-growing excitement in Kansas, than anything that could have happened.

Lincoln's speech before the convention which nominated him, gave the first clear expression to the idea that there was an "irrepressible conflict" between freedom and slavery Wm. H. Seward on October 25th following, at Rochester, N Y., expressed the same idea in these words:

"It is an *irrepressible conflict* between opposing and enduring forces, and it means that the United States will sooner or later become either an entire slaveholding Nation, or an entirely free labor Nation."

Lincoln's words at Springfield, in July, 1858, were

"If we could first know where we are, and whither we are tending, we could better judge what to do, and how to do it. We are now far into the fifth year, since a policy was initiated with the avowed object, and confident promise of putting an end to the slavery agitation. Under the operation of that policy, that agitation has not only not ceased, but has constantly augmented. In my opinion it will not cease, until a crisis shall have been reached and passed. 'A house divided against itself cannot stand.' I believe this government cannot endure permanently half slave and half free I do not expect the Union to be dissolved—I do not expect the house to fall—but I do expect it will cease to be divided. It will become all one thing, or all the other. Either the opponents of slavery will arrest the further spread of it, and place it where the public mind shall rest in the belief that it is in the course of ultimate extinction; or its advocates will push it forward, till it shall become alike lawful in all the States, old as well as new—North as well as South."

Douglas arrived in Chicago on the 9th of July, and was warmly received by enthusiastic friends. His doctrine of "popular sovereignty" had all the attractions of novelty and apparent fairness. For months it divided many Republicans, and at one time the New York *Tribune* showed indications of endorsing the position of Douglas—a fact probably traceable to the attitude of jealousy and hostility manifested toward him by the Buchanan administration. Neither of the great debaters were to be wholly free in the coming contest. Douglas was undermined by Buchanan, who feared him as a rival, and by the more bitter friends of slavery, who could not see that the new doctrine was safely in their interest; but these things were dwarfed in the State conflict, and those who shared such feelings had to make at least a show of friendship until they saw the result. Lincoln was at first handicapped by the doubts of that class of Republicans who thought "popular sovereignty" not bad Republican doctrine.

On the arrival of Douglas he replied to Lincoln's Springfield speech; on the 16th he spoke at Bloomington, and on the 17th, in the afternoon, at Springfield. Lincoln had heard all three speeches, and replied to the last on the night of the day of its delivery He next addressed to Douglas the following challenge to debate:

CHICAGO, July 24th, 1858.

HON. S. A. DOUGLAS:—*My Dear Sir:*—Will it be agreeable to you to make an arrangement to divide time, and address the same audience, during the present canvass? etc. Mr. Judd is authorized to receive your answer, and if agreeable to you, to enter into terms of such agreement, etc.

Your obedient servant,
A. LINCOLN.

Douglas promptly accepted the challenge, and it was arranged that there should be seven joint debates, each alternately opening and closing, the opening speech to occupy one hour, the reply one hour and a half, and the closing half an hour. They spoke at Ottawa, August 21st; Freeport, August 27th; Jonesboro', September 15th; Charleston, September 18th; Galesburg, October 7th, Quincy, October 13th; and Alton, October 15th. We give in Book III of this volume their closing speeches in full.

Great crowds attended, and some of the more enterprising daily journals gave phonographic reports of the speeches. The enthusiasm of the North soon ran in Lincoln's favor, though Douglas had hosts of friends, but then the growing and the aggressive party was the Republican, and even the novelty of a new and attractive doctrine like that of "popular sovereignty" could not long divert their attention. The prize suspended in view of the combatants was the United States Senatorship, and to close political observers this was plainly within the grasp of Douglas by reason of an apportionment which would give his party a majority in the Legislature, even though the popular majority should be twenty thousand against him—a system of apportionment, by the way, not confined to Illinois alone, or not peculiar to it in the work of any of the great parties at any period when party lines were drawn.

Buchanan closely watched the fight, and it was charged and is still believed by the friends of the "Little Giant," that the administration secretly employed its patronage and power to defeat him. Certain it is that a few prominent Democrats deserted the standard of Douglas, and that some of them were rewarded. In the heat of the battle, however, Douglas' friends were careless of the views of the administration. He was a greater leader than Buchanan, and in Illinois at least he overshadowed the administration. He lacked neither money nor friends. Special trains of cars, banners, cannon, bands, processions, were all supplied with lavish hands. The democracy of Illinois, nor yet of any other State, ever did so well before or since, and if the administration had been with him this enthusiasm might have spread to all other States and given his doctrine a larger and more glorious life. Only the border States of the South, however, saw opportunity and glory in it, while the office-holders in other sections stood off and awaited results.

Lincoln's position was different. He, doubtless, early realized that his chances for election were remote indeed, with the apportionment as it was, and he sought to impress the nation with the truth of his convictions, and this without other display than the force of their statement and publication. Always a modest man, he was never more so than in this great battle. He declared that he did not care for the local result, and in the light of what transpired, the position was wisely taken. Douglas was apparently just as earnest, though more ambitious; for he declared in the vehemence of the advocacy of his doctrine, that "he did not care whether slavery was voted up or voted down." Douglas had more to lose than Lincoln—a place which his high abilities had honored in the United States Senate, and which intriguing enemies in his own party made him doubly anxious to hold. Beaten, and he was out of the field for the Presidency, with his enthroned rival a candidate for re-election. Successful, and that rival must leave the field, with himself in direct command of a great majority of the party. This view must have then been presented, but the rapid rise in public feeling made it in part incorrect. The calculation of Douglas that he could at one and the same time retain the good will of all his political friends in Illinois and those of the South failed him, though he did at the time, and until his death, better represent the majority of his party in the whole country than any other leader.

At the election which followed the debate, the popular choice in the State as a whole was for Lincoln by 126,084 to 121,940 for Douglas; but the apportionment of 1850 gave to Douglas a plain majority of the Senators and Representatives.

At the Freeport meeting, August 27th, there were sharp questions and answers between the debaters. They were brought on by Lincoln, who, after alluding to some questions propounded to him at Ottawa, said:

"I now propose that I will answer any of the interrogatories, upon condition that he will answer questions from me not exceeding the same number, to which I give him an opportunity to respond. The judge remains silent; I now say that I will answer his interrogatories, whether he answer mine or not, and that after I have done so I shall propound mine to him.

"I have supposed myself, since the organization of the Republican party at Bloomington in May, 1856, bound as a party man by the platforms of the party, there, and since. If, in any interrogatories which I shall answer, I go beyond the scope of what is within these platforms, it will be perceived that no one is responsible but myself.

"Having said thus much, I will take up the judge's interrogatories as I find them printed in the *Chicago Times*, and answer them *seriatim*. In order that there may be no mistake about it, I have copied the interrogatories in writing, and also my answers to them. The first one of these interrogatories is in these words:

Question 1.—I desire to know whether Lincoln to-day stands, as he did in 1854, in favor of the unconditional repeal of the Fugitive Slave Law?

Answer.—I do not now, nor ever did, stand in favor of the unconditional repeal of the Fugitive Slave Law.

Q. 2.—I desire him to answer whether he stands pledged to-day, as he did in 1854, against the admission of any more slave States into the Union, even if the people want them?

A.—I do not now, nor ever did, stand pledged against the admission of any more slave States into the Union.

Q. 3—I want to know, whether he stands pledged against the admission of a new State into the Union, with such a Constitution as the people of the State may see fit to make?

A.—I do not stand pledged against the admission of a new State into the Union, with such a Constitution as the people of the State may see fit to make.

Q. 4.—I want to know whether he stands to-day pledged to the abolition of slavery in the District of Columbia?

A.—I do not stand to-day pledged to the abolition of slavery in the District of Columbia.

Q. 5.—I desire him to answer whether he stands pledged to the prohibition of the slave trade between the different States?

A.—I do not stand pledged to prohibition of the slave trade between the different States.

Q. 6.—I desire to know whether he stands pledged to prohibit slavery in all the Territories of the United States, North as well as South of the Missouri Compromise line?

A.—I am impliedly, if not expressly, pledged to a belief in the RIGHT and DUTY of Congress to prohibit slavery in all of the United States' Territories.

Q. 7.—I desire him to answer, whether he is opposed to the acquisition of any new territory, unless slavery is first prohibited therein?

A.—I am not generally opposed to honest acquisition of territory; and in any given case, I would or would not oppose such acquisition, according as I might think such acquisition would or would not aggravate the slavery question among ourselves.

"Now, my friends, it will be perceived upon an examination of these questions and answers, that so far, I have only answered that I was not *pledged* to this, that, or the other.

The judge has not framed his interrogatories to ask me anything more than this and I have answered in strict accordance with the interrogatories, and have answered truly, that I am not *pledged* at all upon any of the points to which I have answered. But I am not disposed to hang upon the exact form of his interrogatories. I am rather disposed to take up, at least some of these questions, and state what I really think upon them.

"The fourth one is in regard to the abolition of slavery in the District of Columbia. In relation to that, I have my mind very distinctly made up. I should be very glad to see slavery abolished in the District of Columbia. I believe that Congress possesses the constitutional power to abolish it. Yet, as a member of Congress, I should not, with my present views, be in favor of *endeavoring* to abolish slavery in the District of Columbia, unless it should be upon these conditions: FIRST, That the abolition should be gradual; SECOND, That it should be on a vote of a majority of qualified voters in the District; and THIRD, That compensation should be made to unwilling owners. With these three conditions, I confess I would be exceedingly glad to see Congress abolish slavery in the District of Columbia, and in the language of Henry Clay, 'sweep from our Capital that foul blot upon our nation.'"

I now proceed to propound to the judge the interrogatories, so far as I have framed them. I will bring forward a new instalment when I get them ready I will bring now only four. The first one is:—

1. If the people of Kansas shall, by means entirely unobjectionable in all other respects, adopt a State Constitution and ask admission into the Union under it *before* they have the requisite number of inhabitants, according to the English bill—some ninety-three thousand—will he vote to admit them?

2. Can the people of the United States Territory, in any lawful way, against the wish of any citizen of the United States, exclude slavery from its limits prior to the formation of a State Constitution?

3. If the Supreme Court of the United States shall decide that States cannot exclude slavery from their limits, are you in favor of acquiescing in, adopting and following such decision as a rule of political action?

4. Are you in favor of acquiring additional territory in disregard of how much acquisition may affect the nation on the slavery question?

To these questions Mr. Douglas said: "In reference to Kansas, it is my opinion that, as she has population enough to constitute a slave State, she has people enough for a free State. I hold it to be a sacred rule of universal application, to require a Territory to contain the requisite population for a member of Congress, before it is admitted as a State into the Union.

2. "It matters not what way the Supreme Court may hereafter decide, as to the abstract question whether slavery may or may not go into a Territory under the Constitution, the people have the lawful means to introduce it, or exclude it as they please, for the reason that slavery cannot exist a day, or an hour, anywhere, unless it is supported by local police regulations. These police regulations can only be established by the local legislature, and if the people are opposed to slavery, they will elect representatives to that body, who will, by unfriendly legislation, effectually prevent the introduction of it into their midst. If, on the contrary, they are for it, their legislation will favor its extension. Hence, no matter what the decision of the Supreme Court may be on that abstract question, still the right of the people to make a slave Territory or a free Territory is perfect and complete under the Nebraska bill.

"3. The third question which Mr. Lincoln presented is, if the Supreme Court of the United States shall decide that a State of this Union cannot exclude slavery from its own limits, will I submit to it? I am amazed that Mr. Lincoln should ask such a question.

He casts an imputation upon the Supreme Court of the United States by supposing that they would violate the constitution of the United States. I tell him that such a thing is not possible. It would be an act of moral treason that no man on the bench could ever descend to. Mr. Lincoln, himself, would never, in his partisan feelings, so far forget what was right as to be guilty of such an act.

4. With our natural increase, growing with a rapidity unknown in any other part of the globe, with the tide of emigration that is fleeing from despotism in the old world, to seek refuge in our own, there is a constant torrent pouring into this country that requires more land, more territory upon which to settle, and just as fast as our interests and our destiny require an additional territory in the North, in the South, or on the Island of the Ocean, I am for it, and when we require it, will leave the people, according to the Nebraska bill, free to do as they please on the subject of slavery, and every other question."

The bitterness of the feelings aroused by the canvass and boldness of Douglas, can both be well shown by a brief abstract from his speech at Freeport. He had persisted in calling the Republicans "*Black* Republicans," although the crowd, the great majority of which was there against him, insisted that he should say "*White* Republican." In response to these oft repeated demands, he said:—

"Now, there are a great many Black Republicans of you who do not know this thing was done. ("White, white, and great clamor)." I wish to remind you that while Mr. Lincoln was speaking, there was not a Democrat vulgar and blackguard enough to interrupt him. But I know that the shoe is pinching you. I am clinching Lincoln now, and you are scared to death for the result. I have seen this thing before. I have seen men make appointments for discussions and the moment their man has been heard, try to interrupt and prevent a fair hearing of the other side. I have seen your mobs before and defy your wrath. (Tremendous applause.)

"My friends, do not cheer, for I need my whole time.

"I have been put to severe tests. I have stood by my principles in fair weather and in foul, in the sunshine and in the rain. I have defended the great principle of self-government here among you when Northern sentiment ran in a torrent against me, and I have defended that same great principle when Southern sentiment came down like an avalanche upon me. I was not afraid of any test they put to me. I knew I was right—I knew my principles were sound—I knew that the people would see in the end that I had done right, and I knew that the God of Heaven would smile upon me if I was faithful in the performance of my duty."

As an illustration of the earnestness of Lincoln's position we need only quote two paragraphs from his speech at Alton:—

"Is slavery wrong? That is the real issue. That is the issue that will continue in this country when these poor tongues of Judge Douglas and myself shall be silent. It is the eternal struggle between these two principles—right and wrong—throughout the world. They are two principles that have stood face to face from the beginning of time; and will ever continue to struggle. The one is the common right of humanity, and the other the divine right of Kings. It is the same principle in whatever shape it develops itself. It is the same spirit that says, 'you work and toil, and earn bread, and I'll eat it.' No matter in what shape it comes, whether from the mouth of a King who seeks to bestride the people of his own nation and life by the fruit of their labor, or from one race of men as an apology for enslaving another race, it is the same tyrannical principle."

And again:—

"On this subject of treating it as a wrong, and limiting its spread, let me say a word. Has anything ever threatened the existence of this Union save and except this very institution of slavery? What is it that we hold most dear among us? Our own liberty and prosperity What has ever threatened our liberty and prosperity save and except this institution of slavery? If this is true, how do you propose to improve the condition of things? by enlarging slavery?—by spreading it out and making it bigger? You may have a wen or cancer upon your person and not be able to cut it out, lest you bleed to death, but surely it is no way to cure it, to engraft it and spread it over your whole body. That is no proper way of treating what you regard a wrong. You see this peaceful way of dealing with it as a wrong—restricting the spread of it, and not allowing it to go into new countries where it has not already existed. That is the peaceful way, the old-fashioned way, the way in which the fathers themselves set us the example."

The administration of Pierce had left that of Buchanan a dangerous legacy He found the pro-slavery party in Congress temporarily triumphant, it is true, and supported by the action of Congress in rejecting the Topeka constitution and recognizing the territorial government, but he found that that decision was not acceptable either to the majority of the people in the country or to a rapidly rising anti-slavery sentiment in the North. Yet he saw but one course to pursue, and that was to sustain the territorial government, which had issued the call for the Lecompton convention. He was supported in this view by the action of the Supreme Court, which had decided that slavery existed in Kansas under the constitution of the United States, and that the people therein could only relieve themselves of it by the election of delegates who would prohibit it in the constitution to be framed by the Lecompton convention. The Free State men refused to recognize the call, made little, if any, preparation for the election, yet on the last day a number of them voted for State officials and a member of Congress under the Lecompton constitution. This had the effect of suspending hostilities between the parties, yet peace was actually maintained only by the intervention of U. S. troops, under the command of Col. Sumner, who afterwards won distinction in the war of the rebellion. The Free State people stood firmly by their Topeka constitution, and refused to vote on questions affecting delegates to the Lecompton convention. They had no confidence in Governor Walker the appointee of President Buchanan, and his proclamations passed unheeded. They recognized their own Governor Robinson, who in a message dated December 7th, 1857, explained and defended their position in these words:

"The convention which framed the constitution at Topeka originated with the people of Kansas territory They have adopted and ratified the same twice by a direct vote, and also indirectly through two elections of State officers and members of the State Legislature. Yet it has pleased the administration to regard the whole proceeding as revolutionary "

The Lecompton convention, proclaimed by Governor Walker to be lawfully constituted, met for the second time, Sept. 4th, 1857, and proceeded to frame a constitution, and adjourned finally Nov 7th. A large majority of the delegates, as in the first, were of course pro-slavery, because of the refusal of the anti-slavery men to participate in the election. It refused to submit the whole constitution to the people, it is said, in opposition to the desire of President Buchanan, and part of his Cabinet. It submitted only the question of whether or not slavery should exist in the new State, and this they were required to do under the Kansas-Nebraska act, if indeed they were not required to submit it all. Yet such was the hostility of the pro-slavery men to submission, that it was only by three majority the proposition to submit the main question was adopted—a confession in advance that the result was not likely to favor their side of the controversy But six weeks' time was also allowed for preparation, the election being ordered for Dec. 21st, 1857 Still another advantage was taken in the printing of the ballots, as ordered by the convention. The method prescribed was to endorse the ballots, "Constitution with Slavery," and "Constitution with no Slavery, thus compelling the voter, however adverse his views, as to other parts of the Constitution, to vote for it as a whole. As a consequence, (at least this was given as one of the reasons,) the Free State men as a rule refused to participate in the election, and the result as returned was 6,143 votes in favor of slavery, and 589 against it. The constitution was announced as adopted, an election was ordered on the first Monday of January, 1858, for State officers, members of the Legislature, and a member of Congress. The opponents of the Lecompton constitution did not now refrain from voting, partly because of their desire to secure the representative in Congress, but mainly to secure an opportunity, as advised by their State officers, to vote down the Lecompton constitution. Both parties warmly contested the result, but the Free State men won, and with their general victory secured a large majority in the Legislature.

The ballots of the Free State men were now headed with the words "Against the Lecompton Constitution," and they returned 10,226 votes against it, to 134 for it with slavery, and 24 for it against slavery. This return was certified by J. W Denver, "Secretary and Acting Governor," and its validity was endorsed by Douglas in his report from the Senate Territorial Committee. It was in better accord with his idea of popular sovereignty, as it showed almost twice as large a vote as that cast under the Lecompton plan, the fairness of the return not being disputed, while that of the month previous was disputed.

But their previous refusal to vote on the Lecompton constitution gave their opponents an advantage in position strangely at variance with the wishes of a majority of the people. The President of that convention, J. Calhoun, forwarded the document to the President with an official request that it be submitted to Congress. This was done in a message dated 2d February, 1858, and the President recommended the admission of Kansas under it.

This message occasioned a violent debate in Congress, which continued for three months. It was replete with sectional abuse and bitterness, and nearly all the members of both Houses participated. It finally closed with the passage of the "Act for the admission of the State of Kansas into the Union," passed May 4th, 1858. This Act had been reported by a committee of conference of both Houses, and was passed in the Senate by 31 to 22, and in the House by 112 to 103. There was a strict party vote in the Senate with the exception of Mr. Douglas, C. E. Stuart of Michigan, and D. C. Broderick of California, who voted with the Republican minority In the House several anti-Lecompton democrats voted with the Republican minority These were Messrs. Adrian of New Jersey; Chapman of Pennsylvania; Clark of New York; Cockerill of Ohio; Davis of Indiana; Harris of Illinois; Haskin of New York; Hickman of Pennsylvania; McKibben of California;

Marshall of Illinois; Morgan of New York; Morris, Shaw, and Smith of Illinois. The Americans who voted with the Republicans were Crittenden of Kentucky; Davis of Maryland; Marshall of Kentucky; Ricaud of Maryland; Underwood of Kentucky. A number of those previously classed as Anti-Lecompton Democrats voted against their colleagues of the same faction, and consequently against the bill. These were Messrs. Cockerill, Gwesheck, Hall, Lawrence, Pendleton and Cox of Ohio; English and Foley of Indiana; and Jones of Pennsylvania. The Americans who voted against the bill were Kennedy of Maryland; Anderson of Missouri; Eustis of Louisiana; Gilmer of North Carolina, Hill of Georgia; Maynard, Ready and Zollicoffer of Tennessee; and Trippe of Georgia.

Lecompton Constitution.

The following are the political features of the Lecompton constitution:

ARTICLE VII.—*Slavery.*

SEC. 1. The right of property is before and higher than any constitutional sanction, and the right of the owner of a slave to such slave and its increase is the same, and as inviolable as the right of the owner of any property whatever.

SEC. 2. The legislature shall have no power to pass laws for the emancipation of slaves without the consent of the owners, or without paying the owners previous to their emancipation a full equivalent in money for the slaves so emancipated. They shall have no power to prevent emigrants to the state from bringing with them such persons as are deemed slaves by the laws of any one of the United States or territories, so long as any person of the same age or description shall be continued in slavery by the laws of this state: *Provided,* That such person or slave be the bona fide property of such emigrants: *And provided, also,* That laws may be passed to prohibit the introduction into this state of slaves who have committed high crimes in other states or territories. They shall have power to pass laws to permit the owners of slaves to emancipate them, saving the rights of creditors, and preventing them from becoming a public charge. They shall have power to oblige the owners of slaves to treat them with humanity, to provide for them necessary food and clothing, to abstain from all injuries to them extending to life or limb, and, in case of their neglect or refusal to comply with the direction of such laws, to have such slave or slaves sold for the benefit of the owner or owners.

SEC. 3. In the prosecution of slaves for crimes of higher grade than petit larceny, the legislature shall have no power to deprive them of an impartial trial by a petit jury.

SEC. 4. Any person who shall maliciously dismember, or deprive a slave of life, shall suffer such punishment as would be inflicted in case the like offence had been committed on a free white person, and on the like proof, except in case of insurrection of such slave.

Free Negroes.

Bill of Rights, SEC. 23. Free negroes shall not be allowed to live in this state under any circumstances.

ARTICLE VIII.—*Elections and Rights of Suffrage.*

SEC. 1. Every male citizen of the United States, above the age of twenty-one years, having resided in this state one year, and in the county, city, or town in which he may offer to vote, three months next preceding any election, shall have the qualifications of an elector, and be entitled to vote at all elections. And every male citizen of the United States, above the age aforesaid, who may be a resident of the state at the time this constitution shall be adopted, shall have the right of voting as aforesaid; but no such citizen or inhabitant shall be entitled to vote except in the county in which he shall actually reside at the time of the election.

The Topeka Constitution.

The following are the political features of the Topeka constitution:

Slavery.

Bill of Rights, SEC. 6. There shall be no slavery in this state, nor involuntary servitude, unless for the punishment of crime.

Amendments to the Constitution.

SEC. 1. All propositions for amendments to the constitution shall be made by the General Assembly.

SEC. 2. A concurrence of two-thirds of the members elected to each house shall be necessary, after which such proposed amendments shall be again referred to the legislature elected next succeeding said publication. If passed by the second legislature by a majority of two-thirds of the members elected to each house, such amendments shall be republished as aforesaid, for at least six months prior to the next general election, at which election such proposed amendments shall be submitted to the people for their approval or rejection; and if a majority of the electors voting at such election shall adopt such amendments, the same shall become a part of the constitution.

SEC. 3. When more than one amendment is submitted at the same time, they shall be so submitted as to enable the electors to vote upon each amendment separately. No convention for the formation of a new constitution shall be called, and no amendment to the constitution shall be, by the general assembly, made before the year 1865, nor more than once in five years thereafter.

Submission of Constitution to the People.

Schedule, SEC. 2. That this constitution shall be submitted to the people of Kansas for ratification on the 15th day of December next. That each qualified elector shall express his assent or dissent to the constitution by voting a written or printed ticket, labelled "Constitution," or "No Constitution," which election shall be held by the same judges, and conducted under the same regulations and restrictions as is hereinafter provided for the election of members of the general assembly.

The Douglas Amendment.

The following is the Douglas amendment, which really formed the basis of the bill for admission:

"It being the true intent and meaning of this act not to legislate slavery into any state or territory, nor to exclude it therefrom, but to leave the people thereof perfectly free to form and regulate their domestic institutions in their own way, subject only to the Constitution of the United States."

The bill which passed on the 4th of May was known as the English bill, and it met the approval of Buchanan. To the measure was attached "a fundamental condition precedent," which arose from the fact that the ordinance of the convention accompanying the constitution claimed for the new State a cession of the public lands six times greater than had been granted to other States, amounting in all to 23,500,000 acres. In lieu of this Congress proposed to submit to a vote of the people a proposition specifying the number of acres and the purposes for which the money arising from their sale were to be used, and the acceptance of this was to be followed by a proclamation that "thereafter, and without further proceedings from Congress the admission of the State of Kansas, into the Union, upon an equal footing with the original States in all respects whatever, shall be complete and absolute." The condition was never fulfilled, for the people at the election on the 2d of August, 1858, rejected it by a majority of 9,513, and Kansas was not admitted under the Lecompton constitution.

Finally, and after continued agitation, more peaceful, however, than that which characterized the earlier stages of the struggle, the territorial legislature of Kansas called an election for delegates to meet and form a constitution. They assembled in convention at Wyandot, in July, 1859, and reported a constitution prohibiting slavery. This was adopted by a majority exceeding 4000, and under it Kansas was admitted to the Union on the 29th of January, 1861.

The comparative quiet between the rejection of the English proposition and the adoption of the Wyandot constitution, was at one time violently disturbed by a raid made by John Brown at Harper's Ferry, with a view to excite the slaves to insurrection. This failed, but not before Gov. Wise, of Virginia, had mustered his militia, and called for the aid of United States troops. The more radical anti-slavery men of the North were at first shocked by the audacity of an offense which many looked upon as an act of treason, but the anxiety of Virginia to hang Brown and all his followers who had been captured alive, changed a feeling of conservatism in the North to one of sympathy for Brown and deeper hatred of slavery. It is but fair to say that it engendered hostility to the Union in the South. The right and wrong of slavery was thereafter more generally discussed than ever. The talent of the South favored it; while, with at least a large measure of truth it can be said that the talent of the North opposed it. So bitter grew the feeling that soon the churches of the sections began to divide, no other political question having ever before disturbed the Union.

We have not pretended to give a complete history of the Kansas trouble either in that State or in Congress, nor yet a full history of the many issues raised on questions which were but subsidiary to the main one of slavery. Our object is to show the relation of the political parties throughout that struggle, for we are dealing with the history of parties from a national view, and not with battles and the minor questions or details of parliamentary struggles. The contest had cemented the Democrats of the South as it had the Republicans of the North; it divided both the Democrats of the North and the Americans in all sections. John Bell, of Tennessee, and Sam Houston of Texas, recognized leaders of the Americans, had shown their sympathy with the new stand taken by Douglas, as early as 1854. Bell, however, was less decided than Houston, and took his position with many qualifications. Houston opposed even the repeal of the Missouri Compromise, and made the last speech against it in the Senate. He closed with these words:

"In the discharge of my duty I have acted fearlessly. The events of the future are left in the hands of a wise Providence, and, in my opinion, on the decision which we make upon this question must depend union or disunion."

These sentiments were shared by many Americans, and the great majority of them drifted into the Republican party. The Abolitionists from the beginning of the struggle, allied themselves with the Republicans, a few of their leaders proclaiming, however, that this party was not sufficiently advanced in its views.

The Charleston Convention.

Such was the condition of the parties when the Democratic national convention met at Charleston, S. C., on the 23d of April, 1860, it being then the custom of the Democratic party, as it is of all majority parties, to call its convention first. It was composed of delegates from all the thirty-three States of the Union, the whole number of votes being 303. After the example of former Democratic conventions it adopted the two-third rule, and 202 votes were required to make nominations for President and Vice-President. Caleb Cushing, of Mass., presided. From the first a radical difference of opinion was exhibited among the members on the question of slavery in the Territories. Almost the entire Southern and a minority of the Northern portion believed in the Dred Scott decision, and held that slave property was as valid under the constitution as any other class of property. The Douglas delegates stood firmly by the theory of popular sovereignty, and avowed their indifference to the fact whether it would lead to the protection of slave property in the territories or not. On the second day a committee on resolutions consisting of one member from each State, selected by the State delegates, was named, and then a resolution was resolved unanimously "that this convention will not proceed to ballot for a candidate for the Presidency until the platform shall have been adopted." On the fifth day the committee on resolutions presented majority and minority reports.

After a long discussion on the respective merits of the two reports, they were both, on motion of Mr. Bigler, of Pennsylvania, re-committed to the Committee on Resolutions, with a view, if possible, to promote harmony; but this proved to be impracticable. On the sixth day of the Convention (Saturday, April 28th,) at an evening session, Mr. Avery, of North Carolina, and Mr. Samuels, of Iowa, from the majority and minority of the committee, again made opposite and conflicting reports on the question of slavery in the Territories. On this question the committee had divided from the beginning, the one portion embracing the fifteen members from the slaveholding States, with those from California and Oregon, and the other consisting of the members from all the free States east of the Rocky Mountains. On all other questions both reports substantially agreed.

The following is the report of the majority made on this subject by Mr. Avery, of North Carolina, the chairman of the committee: "*Resolved*, That the platform adopted by the Democratic party at Cincinnati be affirmed with the following explanatory resolutions: 1st. That the Government of a Territory, organized by an act of Congress, is provisional and temporary, and during its existence all citizens of the United States have an equal right to settle with their property in the Territory, without their rights, either of person or property, being destroyed or impaired by Congressional or Territorial legislation. 2d. That it is the duty of the Federal Government, in all its departments, to protect, when necessary, the rights of persons and property in the Territories, and wherever else its constitutional authority extends. 3d. That when the settlers in a Territory having an adequate population form a State Constitution, the right of sovereignty commences, and being consummated by admission into the Union, they stand on an equal footing with the people of other States, and the State thus organized ought to be admitted into the Federal Union whether its constitution prohibits or recognizes the institution of slavery."

The following is the report of the minority, made by Mr. Samuels, of Iowa. After re-affirming the Cincinnati platform by the first resolution, it proceeds: "Inasmuch as differences of opinion exist in the Democratic party, as to the nature and extent of the powers of a Territorial Legislature, and as to the powers and duties of Congress, under the Constitution of the United States, over the institution of slavery within the Territories, *Resolved*, That the Democratic party will abide by the decisions of the Supreme Court of the United States upon questions of constitutional law."

After some preliminary remarks, Mr. Samuels moved the adoption of the minority report as a substitute for that of the majority. This gave rise to an earnest and excited debate. The difference between the parties was radical and irreconcilable. The South insisted that the Cincinnati platform, whose true construction in regard to slavery in the Territories had always been denied by a portion of the Democratic party, should be explained and settled by an express recognition of the principles decided by the Supreme Court. The North, on the other hand, refused to recognize this decision, and still maintained the power to be inherent in the people of a Territory to deal with the question of slavery according to their own discretion. The vote was then taken, and the minority report was substituted for that of the majority by a vote of one hundred and sixty-five to one hundred and thirty-eight. The delegates from the six New England States, as well as from New York, Ohio, Indiana, Illinois, Michigan, Wisconsin, Iowa, and Minnesota, fourteen free States, cast their entire vote in favor of the minority report. New Jersey and Pennsylvania alone among the free States east of the Rocky Mountains, refused to vote as States, but their delegates voted as individuals.

The means employed to attain this end were skillfully devised by the minority of the Pennsylvania delegation in favor of nominating Mr. Douglas. The entire delegation had, strangely enough, placed this power in their hands, by selecting two of their number, Messrs. Cessna and Wright, to represent the whole on the two most important committees of the Convention—that of organization and that of resolutions. These gentlemen, by adroitness and parliamentary tact, succeeded in abrogating the former practice of casting the vote of the State as a unit. In this manner, whilst New York indorsed with her entire thirty-five votes the peculiar views of Mr. Douglas, notwithstanding there was in her delegation a majority of only five votes in their favor on the question of Territorial sovereignty, the effective strength of Pennsylvania recognizing the judgment of the Supreme Court, was reduced to three votes, this being the majority of fifteen on the one side over twelve on the other.

The question next in order before the Convention was upon the adoption of the second resolution of the minority of the committee, which had been substituted for the report of the majority. On this question Georgia, Louisiana, Alabama, Arkansas, Texas, Florida, and Mississippi refused to vote. Indeed, it soon appeared that on the question of the final adoption of this second resolution, which in fact amounted to nothing, it had scarcely any friends of either party in the Convention. The Douglas party, without explanation or addition, voted against it. On the other hand, the old Democracy could not vote for it without admitting that the Supreme Court had not already placed the right over slave property in the Territories on the same footing with all other property, and therefore they also voted against it. In consequence the resolution was negatived by a vote of only twenty-one in its favor to two hundred and thirty-eight. Had the seven Southern States just mentioned voted, the negatives would have amounted to two hundred and eighty-two, or more than thirteen to one. Thus both the majority and the minority resolutions on the Territorial question were rejected, and nothing remained before the Convention except the Cincinnati platform.

At this stage of the proceedings (April 30th), the States of Louisiana, Alabama, South Carolina, Mississippi, Florida, Texas, and Arkansas, having assigned their reasons for the act, withdrew in succession from the Convention. After these seven States had retired, the delegation from Virginia made an effort to restore harmony. Mr. Russell, their chairman, addressed the Convention and portrayed the alarming nature of the crisis. He expressed his fears that we were on the eve of a revolution, and if this Convention should prove a failure it would be the last National Convention of any party which would ever assemble in the United States. "Virginia," said he, "stands in the midst of her sister States, in garments red with the blood of her children slain in the first outbreak of the 'irrepressible conflict.' But, sir, not when her children fell at midnight beneath the weapon of the assassin, was her heart penetrated with so profound a grief as that which will wring it when she is obliged to choose between a separate destiny with the South, and her common destiny with the entire Republic."

Mr. Russell was not then prepared to answer, in behalf of his delegation, whether the events of the day (the defeat of the majority report, and the withdrawal of the seven States) were sufficient to justify her in taking the irrevocable step in question. In order, therefore, that they might have time to deliberate, and if they thought proper make an effort to restore harmony in the Convention, he expressed a desire that it might adjourn and afford them an opportunity for consultation. The Convention accordingly adjourned until the next day, Tuesday, May 1st; and immediately after its reassembling the delegation from Georgia, making the eighth State, also withdrew.

In the mean time the Virginia delegation had consulted among themselves, and had conferred with the delegation of the other Southern States which still remained in the Convention, as to the best mode of restoring harmony. In consequence Mr. Howard, of Tennessee, stated to the Convention that "he had a proposition to present in behalf of the delegation from Tennessee, whenever, under parliamentary rules, it would be proper to present it." In this Tennessee was joined by Kentucky and Virginia. He should propose the following resolution whenever it would be in order: '*Resolved*, That the citizens of the United States have an equal right to settle with their property in the Territories of the United States; and that, under the decision of the Supreme Court of the United States, which we recognize as the correct exposition of the Constitution of the United States, neither the rights of person nor property can be destroyed or inpaired by Congressional or Territorial legislation.'"

On a subsequent day (May 3d), Mr. Russell informed the Convention that this resolution had, "he believed, received the approbation of all the delegations from the Southern States which remained in the Convention, and also received the approbation of the delegation from New York. He was informed there was strength enough to pass it when in order."

Mr. Howard, however, in vain attempted to obtain a vote on his resolution. When he moved to take it up on the evening of the day it had been offered, he was met by cries of "Not in order," "Not in order." The manifest purpose was to postpone its consideration until the hour should arrive which had been fixed by a previous order of the Convention, in opposition to its first order on the same subject, for the balloting to commence for a Presidential candidate, when it would be too late. This the friends of Mr. Douglas accomplished, and no vote was ever taken upon it either at Charleston or Baltimore.

Before the balloting commenced Mr. Howard succeeded, in the face of strong opposition, with the aid of the thirty-five votes from New York, in obtaining a vote of the Convention in re-affirmance of the two-thirds rule. On his motion they resolved, by 141, to 112 votes, "that the President of the Convention be and he is hereby directed not to declare any person nominated for the office of President or Vice-President, unless he shall have received a number of votes equal to two-thirds of the votes of all the electoral colleges." It was well known at the time that this resolution rendered the regular nomination of Mr. Douglas impossible.

The balloting then commenced (Tuesday evening, May 1st), on the eighth day of the session. Necessary to a nomination, under the two-thirds rule, 202 votes. On the first ballot Mr. Douglas received 145½ votes; Mr. Hunter, of Virginia, 42; Mr. Guthrie, of Kentucky, 35½; Mr. Johnson, of Tennessee, 12; Mr. Dickinson, of New York, 7; Mr. Lane, of Oregon, 6; Mr. Toucey, of Connecticut, 2½; Mr. Davis, of Mississippi, 1½, and Mr. Pearce, of Maryland, 1 vote.

The voting continued until May 3d, during which there were fifty-four additional ballotings. Mr. Douglas never rose to more than 152½, and ended in 151½ votes, 202 votes being necessary to a nomination.

Until 1824 nominations had been made by Congressional caucus. In these none participated except Senators and Democratic States, and Representatives from Democratic Congressional districts. The simple majority rule governed in these caucuses, because it was morally certain that, composed as they were, no candidate could be selected against the will of the Democratic States on whom his election depended. But when a change was made to National Conventions, it was at once perceived that if a mere majority could nominate, then the delegates from Anti-Democratic States might be mainly instrumental in nominating a candidate for whom they could not give a single electoral vote. Whilst it would have been harsh and inexpedient to exclude these States from the Convention altogether, it would have been unjust to confer on them a controlling power over the nomination. To compromise this difficulty, the two-thirds rule was adopted. Under its operation it would be almost impossible that a candidate could be selected, without the votes of a simple majority of delegates from the Democratic States. This was the argument of its friends.

It had now become manifest that it was impossible to make a nomination at Charleston. The friends of Mr. Douglas adhered to him and would vote for him and him alone, whilst his opponents, apprehending the effect of his principles should he be elected President, were equally determined to vote against his nomination.

In the hope that some compromise might yet be effected, the Convention, on the motion of Mr. Russell, of Virginia, resolved to adjourn to meet at Baltimore on Monday, the 18th June; and it was "respectfully recommended to the Democratic party of the several States, to make provision for supplying all vacancies in their respective delegations to this Convention when it shall re-assemble."

The Convention re-assembled at Baltimore on the 18th June, 1860, according to its adjournment, and Mr. Cushing, the President, took the chair.

Immediately after the reorganization of the Convention, Mr. Howard, of Tennessee, offered a resolution, "that the President of this Convention direct the sergeant-at-arms to issue tickets of admission to the delegates of the Convention, as originally constituted and organized at Charleston." Thus the vitally important question was distinctly presented. It soon, however, became manifest that no such resolution could prevail. In the absence of the delegates who had withdrawn at Charleston, the friends of Mr. Douglas constituted a controlling majority. At the threshold they resisted the admission of the original delegates, and contended that by withdrawing they had irrevocably resigned their seats. In support of this position, they relied upon the language of the resolution adjourning the Convention to Baltimore, which, as we have seen, "recommended to the Democratic party of the several States to make provision for supplying all vacancies in their respective delegations to this Convention, when it shall reassemble." On the other hand, the advocates of their readmission contended that a simple withdrawal of the delegates was not a final renunciation of their seats, but they were still entitled to reoccupy them, whenever, in their judgment, this course would be best calculated to restore the harmony and promote the success of the Democratic party; that the Convention had no right to interpose between them and the Democracy of their respective States; that being directly responsible to this Democracy, it alone could accept their resignation; that no such resignation had ever been made, and their authority therefore continued in full force, and this, too, with the approbation of their constituents.

In the mean time, after the adjournment from Charleston to Baltimore, the friends of Mr. Douglas, in several of these States, had proceeded to elect delegates to take the place of those who had withdrawn from the Convention. Indeed, it was manifest at the time, and has since been clearly proved by the event, that these delegates represented but a small minority of the party in their respective States. These new delegates, nevertheless, appeared and demanded seats. *

After a long and ardent debate, the Convention adopted a resolution, offered by Mr. Church, of New York, and modified on motion of Mr. Gilmore, of Pennsylvania, as a substitute for that of Mr. Howard, to refer "the credentials of all persons claiming seats in this Convention, made vacant by the secession of delegates at Charleston, to the Committee on Credentials." They thus prejudged the question, by deciding that the seats of these delegates had been made and were still vacant. The Committee on Credentials had been originally composed of one delegate from each of the thirty-three States, but the number was now reduced to twenty-five, in consequence of the exclusion of eight of its members from the States of Georgia, Alabama, Mississippi, South Carolina, Texas, Louisiana, Arkansas, and Florida. The committee, therefore, now stood 16 to 9 in favor of the nomination of Mr. Douglas, instead of 17 to 16 against it, according to its original organization.

The committee, through their chairman, Mr. Krum, of Missouri, made their report on the 21st June, and Governor Stevens, of Oregon, at the same time presented a minority report, signed by himself and eight other members.

It is unnecessary to give in detail these conflicting reports. It is sufficient to state that whilst the report of the majority maintained that the delegates, by withdrawing at Charleston, had resigned their seats, and these were still vacant; that of the minority, on the contrary, asserted the right of these delegates to resume their seats in the Convention, by virtue of their original appointment.

On the next day (June 22), the important decision was made between the conflicting reports. Mr. Stevens moved to substitute the minority report for that of the majority, and his motion was rejected by a vote of 100½ to 150. Of course no vote was given from any of the excluded States, except one half vote from each of the parties in Arkansas.

The resolutions of the majority were then adopted in succession. Among other motions of similar character, a motion had been made by a delegate in the majority to reconsider the vote by which the Convention had adopted the minority report, as a substitute for that of the majority, and to lay his own motion on the table. This is a common mode resorted to, according to parliamentary tactics, of defeating every hope of a reconsideration of the pending question, and rendering the first decision final.

Mr. Cessna with this view called for a vote on laying the motion to reconsider on the table. Should this be negatived, then the question of reconsideration would be open. The President stated the question to be first "on laying on the table the motion to reconsider the vote by which the Convention refused to amend the majority report of the Committee on Credentials by substituting the report of the minority." On this question New York, for the first time since the meeting at Baltimore, voted with the minority and changed it into a majority. "When New York was called," says the report of the proceedings, "and responded thirty-five votes" (in the negative) "the response was greeted with loud cheers and applause." The result of the vote was 113½ to 138½—"so the Convention refused to lay on the table the motion to reconsider the minority report." The Convention then adjourned until evening, on motion of Mr. Cochrane, of New York, amidst great excitement and confusion.

This vote of New York, appearing to indicate a purpose to harmonize the party by admitting the original delegates from the eight absent States, was not altogether unexpected. Although voting as a unit, it

* From Mr. Buchanan's Administration on the eve of [illegible] & Co., 1866.

was known that her delegation were greatly divided among themselves. The exact strength of the minority was afterwards stated by Mr. Bartlett, one of its members, in the Breckinridge Convention. He said: "Upon all questions and especially upon the adoption of the majority report on credentials, in which we had a long contest, the line was strictly drawn, and there were thirty on one side and forty on the other."

The position of New York casting an undivided vote of thirty-five, with Dean Richmond at their head, had been a controlling power from the commencement.

Strong expectations were, therefore, now entertained that after the New York delegation had recorded their vote against a motion which would have killed the minority report beyond hope of revival, they would now follow this up by taking the next step in advance and voting for its reconsideration and adoption. On the evening of the very same day, however, they reversed their course and voted against its reconsideration. They were then cheered by the opposite party from that which had cheered them in the morning. Thus the action of the Convention in favor of the majority report became final and conclusive.

Mr. Cessna, of Pennsylvania, at once moved "that the Convention do now proceed to nominate candidates for President and Vice-President of the United States."

Mr. Russell rose and stated, "It has become my duty now, by direction of a large majority of the delegation from Virginia, respectfully to inform you and this body, that it is not consistent with their convictions of duty to participate longer in its deliberations."

Mr. Lander next stated "that it became his duty, as one of the delegates from North Carolina, to say that a very large majority of the delegation from that State were compelled to retire permanently from this Convention, on account, as he conceived, of the unjust course that had been pursued toward some of their fellow-citizens of the South. The South had heretofore relied upon the Northern Democracy to give them the rights which were justly due them; but the vote to-day had satisfied the majority of the North Carolina delegation that these rights were now refused them, and, this being the case, they could no longer remain in the Convention."

Then followed in succession the withdrawal of the delegations from Tennessee, Kentucky, Maryland, California, Oregon, and Arkansas. The Convention now adjourned at half-past-ten o'clock until the next morning at ten.

Soon after the assembling of the Convention, the President, Mr. Cushing, whilst tendering his thanks to its members for their candid and honorable support in the performance of his duties, stated that notwithstanding the retirement of the delegations of several of the States at Charleston, in his solicitude to maintain the harmony and union of the Democratic party, he had continued in his post of labor. "To that end and in that sense," said he, "I had the honor to meet you, gentlemen, here at Baltimore. But circumstances have since transpired which compel me to pause. The delegations of a majority of the States have, either in whole or in part, in one form or another, ceased to participate in the deliberations of the Convention. * * * In the present circumstances, I deem it a duty of self-respect, and I deem it still more a duty to this Convention, as at present organized, * * * to resign my seat as President of this Convention, in order to take my place on the floor as a member of the delegation from Massachusetts. * * * I deem this above all a duty which I owe to the members of this Convention, as to whom no longer would my action represent the will of a majority of the Convention."

Governor Tod, of Ohio, one of the Vice-Presidents, then took the vacant chair, and was greeted with hearty and long-continued cheers and applause from members of the Convention.

Mr. Butler, of Massachusetts, now announced that a portion of the Massachusetts delegation desired to retire, but was interrupted by cries of "No," "No," "Call the roll." Mr. Cessna called for the original question, to wit, that the Convention now proceed to a nomination for President and Vice-President.

The President here ordered the Secretary to call the States. Maine, New Hampshire, and Vermont were called, and they gave an unbroken vote for Stephen A. Douglas. When Massachusetts was called, Mr. Butler rose and said he had a respectful paper in his hand which he would desire the President to have read. A scene of great confusion thereupon ensued, cries of "I object" being heard upon all sides. Mr. Butler, not to be baffled, contended for his right at this stage to make remarks pertinent to the matter, and cited in his support the practice of the Conventions at Baltimore in 1848 and 1852, and at Cincinnati in 1856. He finally prevailed, and was permitted to proceed. He then said he "would now withdraw from the Convention, upon the ground that there had been a withdrawal, in whole or in part, of a majority of the States; and further, which was a matter more personal to himself, he could not sit in a convention where the African slave trade, which was piracy according to the laws of his country, was openly advocated."

Mr. Butler then retired, followed by General Cushing and four others of the

Massachusetts delegation. All of these had voted with the South and against Douglas.

The balloting now proceeded. Mr. Douglas received 173½ votes; Mr. Guthrie 9; Mr. Breckinridge 6½; Mr. Bocock and Mr. Seymour each 1; and Mr. Dickerson and Mr. Wise each half a vote. On the next and last ballot Mr. Douglas received 181½ votes, eight of those in the minority having changed their votes in his favor.

To account for this number, it is proper to state that a few delegates from five of the eight States which had withdrawn still remained in the Convention. On the last ballot Mr. Douglas received all of their votes, to wit: 3 of the 15 votes of Virginia, 1 of the 10 votes of North Carolina, 1½ of the 3 votes of Arkansas, 3 of the 12 votes of Tennessee, 3 of the 12 votes of Kentucky, and 2½ of the 8 votes of Maryland, making in the aggregate 14 votes. To this number may be added the 9 votes of the new delegates from Alabama and the 6 from Louisiana, which had been admitted to the exclusion of the original delegates.

Mr. Douglas was accordingly declared to be the regular nominee of the Democratic party of the Union, upon the motion of Mr. Church, of New York, when, according to the report of the proceedings, "The whole body rose to its feet, hats were waved in the air, and many tossed aloft; shouts, screams, and yells, and every boisterous mode of expressing approbation and unanimity, were resorted to."

Senator Fitzpatrick, of Alabama, was then unanimously nominated as the candidate for Vice-President; and the Convention adjourned *sine die* on the 23d June, the sixth and last day of its session. On the same day, but after the adjournment, Mr. Fitzpatrick declined the nomination, and it was immediately conferred on Mr. Herschel V. Johnson, of Georgia, by the Executive Committee. Thus ended the Douglas Convention.

But another Convention assembled at Baltimore on the same 23d June, styling itself the "National Democratic Convention." It was composed chiefly of the delegates who had just withdrawn from the Douglas Convention, and the original delegates from Alabama and Louisiana. One of their first acts was to abrogate the two-third rule, as had been done by the Douglas Convention. Both acted under the same necessity, because the preservation of this rule would have prevented a nomination by either.

Mr. Cushing was elected and took the chair as President. In his opening address he said: "Gentlemen of the Convention, we assemble here, delegates to the National Democratic Convention, duly accredited thereto from more than twenty States of the Union, for the purpose of nominating candidates of the Democratic party for the offices of President and Vice-President of the United States, for the purpose of announcing the principles of the party, and for the purpose of continuing and re-establishing that party upon the firm foundations of the Constitution, the Union, and the coequal rights of the several States."

Mr. Avery, of North Carolina, who had reported the majority resolutions at Charleston, now reported the same from the committee of this body, and they "were adopted unanimously, amid great applause."

The Convention then proceeded to select their candidates. Mr. Loring, on behalf of the delegates from Massachusetts, who with Mr. Butler had retired from the Douglas Convention, nominated John C. Breckinridge, of Kentucky, which Mr. Dent, representing the Pennsylvania delegation present, "most heartily seconded." Mr. Ward, from the Alabama delegation, nominated R. M. T. Hunter, of Virginia; Mr. Ewing, from that of Tennessee, nominated Mr. Dickinson, of New York; and Mr. Stevens, from Oregon, nominated General Joseph Lane. Eventually all these names were withdrawn except that of Mr. Breckinridge, and he received the nomination by a unanimous vote. The whole number of votes cast in his favor from twenty States was 103½.

General Lane was unanimously nominated as the candidate for Vice-President. Thus terminated the Breckinridge Convention.

The Chicago Republican Convention.

The Republicans had named May 16th, 1860, as the date and Chicago as the place for holding their second National Convention. They had been greatly encouraged by the vote for Fremont and Dayton, and, what had now become apparent as an irreconcilable division of the Democracy, encouraged them in the belief that they could elect their candidates. Those of the great West were especially enthusiastic, and had contributed freely to the erection of an immense "Wigwam," capable of holding ten thousand people, at Chicago. All the Northern States were fully represented, and there were besides partial delegations from Delaware, Maryland, Kentucky, Missouri and Virginia, with occasional delegates from other Slave States, there being none, however, from the Gulf States. David Wilmot, of Penna., author of the Wilmot proviso, was made temporary chairman, and George Ashman, of Mass., permanent President. No differences were excited by the report of the committee on platform, and the proceedings throughout were characterized by great harmony, though there was a somewhat sharp contest for the Presidential nomination. The prominent candidates were Wm. H. Seward, of New York; Abraham Lincoln, of Illinois, Salmon P Chase, of Ohio; Simon Cameron, of Pennsylvania, and Edward Bates, of Missouri. There were three ballots, Mr. Lincoln receiving in the last 354 out of 446 votes. Mr. Seward led the vote at the beginning, but he was strongly opposed by gentlemen in his own State as prominent as Horace Greeley and Thurlow Weed, and his nomination was thought to be inexpedient. Lincoln's successful debate with Douglas was still fresh in the minds of the delegates, and every addition to his vote so heightened the enthusiasm that the convention was finally carried "off its feet," the delegations rapidly changing on the last ballot. Lincoln had been a known candidate but a month or two before, while Seward's name had been everywhere canvassed, and where opposed in the Eastern and Middle States, it was mainly because of the belief that his views on slavery were too radical. He was more strongly favored by the Abolition branch of the party than any other candidate. When the news of his success was first conveyed to Mr. Lincoln he was sitting in the office of the *State Journal*, at Springfield, which was connected by a telegraph wire with the Wigwam. On the close of the third ballot a despatch was handed Mr. Lincoln. He read it in silence, and then announcing the result said: "There is a little woman down at our house would like to hear this—I'll go down and tell her," and he started amid the shouts of personal admirers. Hannibal Hamlin, of Maine, was nominated for Vice-President with much unanimity, and the Chicago Convention closed its work in a single day.

The American Convention.

A "Constitutional Union," really an American Convention, had met at Baltimore on the 9th of May. Twenty States were represented, and John Bell, of Tennessee, and Edward Everett, of Massachusetts, were named for the Presidency and Vice-Presidency. Their friends, though known to be less in number than either those of Douglas, Lincoln or Breckinridge, yet made a vigorous canvass in the hope that the election would be thrown into the House, and that there a compromise in the vote by States would naturally turn toward their candidates. The result of the great contest is elsewhere given in our Tabulated History of Politics.

THE PRINCIPLES INVOLVED.

Lincoln received large majorities in nearly all of the free States, his popular vote being 1,866,452; electoral vote, 180. Douglas was next in the popular estimate, receiving 1,375,157 votes, with but 12 electors. Breckinridge had 847,953 votes, with 76 electors; Bell, with 570,631 votes, had 39 electors.

The principles involved in the controversy are given at length in the Book of Platforms, and were briefly these: The Republican party asserted that slavery should not be extended to the territories; that it could exist only by virtue of local and positive law; that freedom was national; that slavery was morally wrong, and the nation should at least anticipate its gradual extinction. The Douglas wing of the Democratic party adhered to the doctrine of popular sovereignty, and claimed that in its exercise in the territories they were indifferent whether slavery was voted up or down. The Breckinridge wing of the Democratic party asserted both the moral and legal right to hold slaves, and to carry them to the territories, and that no power save the national constitution could prohibit or interfere with it outside of State lines. The Americans supporting Bell, adhered to their peculiar doctrines touching emigration and naturalization, but had abandoned, in most of the States, the secrecy and oaths of the Know-Nothing order. They were evasive and non committal on the slavery question.

Preparing for Secession.

Secession, up to this time, had not been regarded as treasonable in all sections and at all times. As shown in many previous pages, it had been threatened by the Hartford Convention; certainly by some of the people of New England who opposed the war of 1812. Some of the more extreme Abolitionists had favored a division of the sections. The South, particularly the Gulf States, had encouraged a secret organization, known as the "Order of the Lone Star," previous to and at the time of the annexation of Texas. One of its objects was to acquire Cuba, so as to extend slave territory The Gulf States needed more slaves, and though the law made participancy in the slave trade piracy, many cargoes had been landed in parts of the Gulf without protest or prosecution, just prior to the election of 1860. Calhoun had threatened, thirty years before, nullification, and before that again, secession in the event of the passage of the Public Land Bill. Jefferson and Madison had indicated that doctrine of State Rights on which secession was based in the Kentucky and Virginia resolutions of 1798, facts which were daily discussed by the people of the South during this most exciting of all Presidential campaigns.

The leaders in the South had anticipated defeat at the election, and many of them made early preparations for the withdrawal of their States from the Union. Some of the more extreme anti-slavery men of the North, noting these preparations, for a time favored a plan of letting the South go in peace. South Carolina was the first to adopt a secession ordinance, and before it did so, Horace Greeley said in the New York *Tribune:*

"If the Declaration of Independence justified the secession from the British Empire of three millions of colonists in 1776, we can not see why it would not justify the secession of five millions of Southrons from the Federal Union in 1861."

These views, however, soon fell into disfavor throughout the North, and the period of indecision on either side ceased when Fort Sumter was fired upon. The Gulf States openly made their preparations as soon as the result of the Presidential election was known, as a rule pursuant to a previous understanding. The following, condensed from Hon. Edward McPherson's "*Political History of the United States of America during the Great Rebellion,*" is a correct statement of the movements which followed, in the several Southern States:

SOUTH CAROLINA.

November 5th, 1860. Legislature met to choose Presidential electors, who voted for Breckinridge and Lane for President and Vice President. Gov. William H. Gist recommended in his message that in the event of Abraham Lincoln's election to the Presidency, a convention of the people of the State be immediately called to consider and determine for themselves the mode and measure of redress. He expressed the opinion that the only alternative left is the "secession of South Carolina from the Federal Union."

7th. United States officials resigned at Charleston.

10th. U. S. Senators James H. Hammond and James Chestnut, Jr., resigned their seats in the Senate. Convention called to meet Dec. 17th. Delegates to be elected Dec. 6th.

13th. Collection of debts due to citizens of non-slaveholding States stayed. Francis W Pickens elected Governor.

17th. Ordinance of Secession adopted unanimously.

21st. Commissioners appointed (Barnwell, Adams, and Orr) to proceed to Washington to treat for the possession of U. S. Government property within the limits of South Carolina. Commissioners appointed to the other slaveholding States. Southern Congress proposed.

24th. Representatives in Congress withdrew.

Gov. Pickens issued a proclamation "announcing the repeal, Dec. 20th, 1860, by the good people of South Carolina," of the Ordinance of May 23d, 1788, and "the dissolution of the union between the State of South Carolina and other States under the name of the United States of America," and proclaiming to the world "that the State of South Carolina is, as she has a right to be, a separate, sovereign, free and independent State, and, as such, has a right to levy war, conclude peace, negotiate treaties, leagues, or covenants, and to do all acts whatsoever that rightfully appertain to a free and independent State.

"Done in the eighty-fifth year of the sovereignty and independence of South Carolina."

Jan. 3d, 1861. South Carolina Commissioners left Washington.

4th. Convention appointed T. J. Withers, L. M. Keitt, W W. Boyce, Jas. Chestnut, Jr., R. B. Rhett, Jr., R. W Barnwell, and C. G. Memminger, delegates to Southern Congress.

5th. Convention adjourned, subject to the call of the Governor.

14th. Legislature declared that any attempt to reinforce Fort Sumter would be considered an open act of hostility and a declaration of war. Approved the Governor's action in firing on the *Star of the West.* Accepted the services of the Catawba Indians.

27th. Received Judge Robertson, Commissioner from Virginia, but rejected the proposition for a conference and co-operative action.

March 26th. Convention met in Charleston.

April 3d. Ratified "Confederate" Constitution—yeas 114, nays 16.

8th. Transferred forts, etc., to "Confederate" government.

GEORGIA.

November 8th, 1860. Legislature met pursuant to previous arrangement.

18th. Convention called. Legislature appropriated $1,000,000 to arm the State.

Dec. 3d. Resolutions adopted in the Legislature proposing a conference of the Southern States at Atlanta, Feb. 20th.

January 17th, 1861. Convention met. Received Commissioners from South Carolina and Alabama

18th. Resolutions declaring it the right and duty of Georgia to secede, adopted—yeas 165, nays 130.

19th. Ordinance of Secession passed—yeas 208, nays 89.

21st. Senators and Representatives in Congress withdrew.

24th. Elected Delegates to Southern Congress at Montgomery, Alabama.

28th. Elected Commissioners to other Slaveholding States.

29th. Adopted an address "to the South and the world."

March 7th. Convention reassembled.

16th. Ratified the "Confederate" Constitution—yeas 96, nays 5.

20th. Ordinance passed authorizing the "Confederate" government to occupy, use and possess the forts, navy yards, arsenals, and custom houses within the limits of said State.

April 26th. Governor Brown issued a proclamation ordering the repudiation by the citizens of Georgia of all debts due Northern men.

MISSISSIPPI.

November 26th, 1860. Legislature met Nov. 26th, and adjourned Nov. 30th. Election for Convention fixed for Dec. 20th. Convention to meet Jan 7th. Convention bills and secession resolutions passed unanimously. Commissioners appointed to other Slaveholding States to secure "their co-operation in effecting measures for their common defence and safety."

Jan. 7th, 1861. Convention assembled.

9th. Ordinance of Secession passed—yeas 84, nays 15.

In the ordinance the people of the State of Mississippi express their consent to form a federal union with such of the States as have seceded or may secede from the Union of the United States of America, upon the basis of the present Constitution of the United States, except such parts thereof as embrace other portions than such seceding States.

10th. Commissioners from other States received. Resolutions adopted, recognizing South Carolina as sovereign and independent.

Jan. 12th. Representatives in Congress withdrew.

19th. The committee on the Confederacy in the Legislature reported resolutions to provide for a Southern Confederacy, and to establish a provisional government for seceding States and States hereafter seceding.

21st. Senators in Congress withdrew.

March 30th. Ratified "Confederate" Constitution—yeas 78, nays 7.

FLORIDA.

November 26th, 1860. Legislature met. Governor M. S. Perry recommended immediate secession.

Dec. 1st. Convention bill passed.

Jan. 3d, 1861. Convention met.

7th. Commissioners from South Carolina and Alabama received and heard.

10th. Ordinance of Secession passed—yeas 62, nays 7

18th. Delegates appointed to Southern Congress at Montgomery.

21st. Senators and Representatives in Congress withdrew.

Feb. 14th. Act passed by the Legislature declaring that after any actual collision between Federal troops and those in the employ of Florida, the act of holding office under the Federal government shall be declared treason, and the person convicted shall suffer death. Transferred control of government property captured, to the "Confederate" government.

LOUISIANA.

December 10th, 1860. Legislature met.

11th. Convention called for Jan. 23d. Military bill passed.

12th. Commissioners from Mississippi received and heard. Governor instructed to communicate with Governors of other southern States.

Jan 23d, 1861. Convention met and organized. Received and heard Commissioners from South Carolina and Alabama.

25th. Ordinance of Secession passed—yeas 113, nays 17 Convention refused to submit the ordinance to the people by a vote of 84 to 45. This was subsequently reconsidered, and the ordinance was submitted. The vote upon it as declared was 20,448 in favor, and 17,296 against.

Feb. 5th. Senators withdrew from Congress, also the Representatives, except John E. Bouligny. State flag adopted. Pilots at the Balize prohibited from bringing over the bar any United States vessels of war.

March 7th. Ordinance adopted in secret session transferring to "Confederate" States government $536,000, being the amount of bullion in the U. S. mint and customs seized by the State.

16th. An ordinance voted down, submitting the "Confederate" Constitution to the people—yeas 26, nays 74.

21st. Ratified the "Confederate" Constitution—yeas 101, nays 7 Governor authorized to transfer the arms and property captured from the United States to the "Confederate" Government.

27th. Convention adjourned *sine die.*

ALABAMA.

January 7th, 1861. Convention met.

8th. Received and heard the Commissioner from South Carolina.

11th. Ordinance of Secession passed in secret session—yeas 61, nays 39. Proposition to submit ordinance to the people lost—yeas 47, nays 53.

14th. Legislature met pursuant to previous action.

19th. Delegates elected to the Southern Congress.

21st. Representatives and Senators in Congress withdrew.

26th. Commissioners appointed to treat with the United States Government relative to the United States forts, arsenals, etc., within the State.

The Convention requested the people of the States of Delaware, Maryland, Virginia, North Carolina, South Carolina, Florida,

Georgia, Mississippi, Louisiana, Texas, Arkansas, Tennessee, Kentucky and Missouri to meet the people of Alabama by their delegates in Convention, February 4th, 1861, at Montgomery, for the purpose of consulting as to the most effectual mode of securing concerted or harmonious action in whatever measures may be deemed most desirable for their common peace and security. Military bill passed. Commissioners appointed to other Slaveholding States.

March 4th. Convention re-assembled.

13th. Ratified "Confederate" Constitution, yeas 87, nays 6. Transferred control forts, of arsenals, etc., to "Confederate" Government.

ARKANSAS.

January 16th, 1861. Legislature passed Convention bill. Vote of the people on the Convention was 27,412 for it, and 15,826 against it.

February 18th. Delegates elected.

March 4th. Convention met.

18th. The Ordinance of Secession defeated—yeas 35, nays 39. The convention effected a compromise by agreeing to submit the question of co-operation or secession to the people on the 1st Monday in August.

May 6th. Passed Secession Ordinance—yeas 69, nays 1. Authorized her delegates to the Provisional Congress, to transfer the arsenal at Little Rock and hospital at Napoleon to the "Confederate" Government.

TEXAS.

January 21st, 1861. Legislature met.

28th. People's State Convention met.

29th. Legislature passed a resolution declaring that the Federal Government has no power to coerce a Sovereign State after she has pronounced her separation from the Federal Union.

February 1st. Ordinance of Secession passed in Convention—yeas 166, nays 7. Military bill passed.

7th. Ordinance passed, forming the foundation of a Southern Confederacy. Delegates to the Southern Congress elected. Also an act passed submitting the Ordinance of Secession to a vote of the people.

23d. Secession Ordinance voted on by the people; adopted by a vote of 34,794 in favor, and 11,235 against it.

March 4th. Convention declared the State out of the Union. Gov. Houston issued a proclamation to that effect.

16th. Convention by a vote of 127 to 4 deposed Gov. Houston, declaring his seat vacant. Gov. Houston issued a proclamation to the people protesting against this action of the Convention.

20th. Legislature confirmed the action of the Convention in deposing Gov. Houston by a vote of 53 to 11. Transferred forts, etc., to "Confederate" Government.

23d. Ratified the "Confederate" Constitution—yeas 68, nays 2.

NORTH CAROLINA.

November 20th, 1860. Legislature met. Gov. Ellis recommended that the Legislature invite a conference of the Southern States, or failing in that, send one or more delegates to the neighboring States so as to secure concert of action. He recommended a thorough reorganization of the militia, and the enrollment of all persons between 18 and 45 years, and the organization of a corps of ten thousand men; also, a Convention, to assemble immediately after the proposed consultation with other Southern States shall have terminated.

December 9th, Joint Committee on Federal Relations agreed to report a Convention Bill.

17th. Bill appropriating $300,000 to arm the State, debated.

18th. Senate passed above bill—yeas, 41, nays, 3.

20th. Commissioners from Alabama and Mississippi received and heard—the latter, J. Thompson, by letter.

22d. Senate bill to arm the State failed to pass the House.

22d. Adjourned till January 7th.

January 8th, 1861. Senate Bill arming the State passed the House, yeas, 73, nays, 26.

30th. Passed Convention Bill—election to take place February 28th. No Secession Ordinance to be valid without being ratified by a majority of the qualified voters of the State.

31st. Elected Thos. L. Clingman United States Senator,

February 13th. Commissioners from Georgia publicly received.

20th. Mr. Hoke elected Adjutant General of the State. Military Bill passed.

28th. Election of Delegates to Convention took place.

28th. The vote for a Convention was 46,671; against 47,333—majority against a Convention 661.

May 1st. Extra session of the Legislature met at the call of Gov. Ellis. The same day they passed a Convention Bill, ordering the election of delegates on the 15th.

2d. Legislature adjourned.

13th. Election of delegates to the Convention took place.

20th. Convention met at Raleigh.

21st. Ordinance of Secession passed; also the "Confederate" Constitution ratified.

June 5th. Ordinance passed, ceded the arsenal at Fayetteville, and transferred magazines, etc., to the "Confederate" Government.

TENNESSEE.

January 6th, 1861. Legislature met.

12th. Passed Convention Bill.

30th. Commissioners to Washington appointed.

February 8th. People voted no Convention: 67,360 to 54,156.

May 1st. Legislature passed a joint resolution authorizing the Governor to appoint Commissioners to enter into a military league with the authorities of the "Confederate" States.

7th. Legislature in secret session ratified the league entered into by A. O. W. Totten, Gustavus A. Henry, Washington Barrow, Commissioners for Tennessee, and Henry W. Hilliard, Commissioner for "Confederate" States, stipulating that Tennessee until she became a member of the Confederacy placed the whole military force of the State under the control of the President of the "Confederate" States, and turned over to the "Confederate" States all the public property, naval stores and munitions of war. Passed the Senate, yeas 14, nays 6, absent and not voting 5; the House, yeas 42, nays 15, absent and not voting, 18. Also a Declaration of Independence and Ordinance dissolving the Federal relations between Tennessee and the United States, and an ordinance adopting and ratifying the Confederate Constitution, these two latter to be voted on by the people on June 8th were passed.

June 24th. Gov. Isham G. Harris declared Tennessee out of the Union, the vote for Separation being 104,019 against 47,238.

VIRGINIA.

January 7th, 1861. Legislature convened.

8th. Anti-coercion resolution passed.

9th. Resolution passed, asking that the *status quo* be maintained.

10th. The Governor transmitted a despatch from the Mississippi Convention, announcing its unconditional secession from the Union, and desiring on the basis of the old Constitution to form a new union with the seceding States. The House adopted—yeas 77, nays 61,—an amendment submitting to a vote of the people the question of referring for their decision any action of the Convention dissolving Virginia's connection with the Union, or changing its organic law. The Richmond *Enquirer* denounced "the emasculation of the Convention Bill as imperilling all that Virginians held most sacred and dear."

16th. Commissioners Hopkins and Gilmer of Alabama received in the Legislature.

17th. Resolutions passed proposing the Crittenden resolutions as a basis for adjustment, and requesting General Government to avoid collision with Southern States. Gov. Letcher communicated the Resolutions of the Legislature of New York, expressing the utmost disdain, and saying that "the threat conveyed can inspire no terror in freemen." The resolutions were directed to be returned to the Governor of New York.

18th. $1,000,000 appropriated for the defence of the State.

19th. Passed resolve that if all efforts to reconcile the differences of the country fail, every consideration of honor and interest demands that Virginia shall unite her destinies with her sister slaveholding States. Also that no reconstruction of the Union can be permanent or satisfactory, which will not secure to each section self-protecting power against any invasion of the Federal Union upon the reserved rights of either. (See Hunter's proposition for adjustment.)

21st. Replied to Commissioners Hopkins and Gilmer, expressing inability to make a definite response until after the meeting of the State Convention.

22d. The Governor transmitted the resolutions of the Legislature of Ohio, with unfavorable comment. His message was tabled by a small majority.

30th. The House of Delegates to-day tabled the resolutions of the Pennsylvania Legislature, but referred those of Tennessee to the Committee on Federal Relations.

February 20th. The resolutions of the Legislature of Michigan were returned without comment.

28th. Ex-President Tyler and James A. Seddon, Commissioners to the Peace Congress, presented their report, and denounced the recommendation of that body as a delusion and a sham, and as an insult and an offense to the South.

Proceedings of Virginia Convention.

February 4th. Election of delegates to the Convention.

13th. Convention met.

14th. Credentials of John S. Preston, Commissioner from South Carolina, Fulton Anderson from Mississippi, and Henry L. Benning from Georgia, were received.

18th. Commissioners from Mississippi and Georgia heard; both pictured the danger of Virginia remaining with the North; neither contemplated such an event as reunion.

19th. The Commissioner from South Carolina was heard. He said his people believed the Union unnatural and monstrous, and declared that there was no human force —no sanctity of human touch, —that could re-unite the people of the North with the people of the South—that it could never be done unless the economy of God were changed.

20th. A committee reported that in all but sixteen counties, the majority for submitting the action of the Convention to a vote of the people was 52,857. Numerous resolutions on Federal Relations introduced, generally expressing attachment to the Union, but denouncing coercion.

26th. Mr. Goggin of Bedford, in his speech, denied the right of secession, but admitted a revolutionary remedy for wrongs committed upon a State or section, and said wherever Virginia went he was with her.

March 2d. Mr. Goode of Bedford offered a resolution that, as the powers delegated to the General Government by Virginia had been perverted to her injury, and as the Crittenden propositions as a basis of adjustment had been rejected by their Northern confederates, therefore every consideration of duty, interest, honor and patriotism requires that Virginia should declare her connection with the Government to be dissolved.

5th. The thanks of the State were voted to Hon. John J. Crittenden, by yeas 107, nays 16, for his efforts to bring about an honorable adjustment of the national difficulties. Mr. Harvie of Amelia offered a resolution, requesting Legislature to make needful appropriations to resist any attempt of the Federal authorities to hold, occupy or possess the property and places claimed by the United States in any of the seceded States, or those that may withdraw or collect duties or imposts in the same.

9th. Three reports were made from the Committee on Federal Relations. The majority proposed to submit to the other States certain amendments to the Constitution, awaiting the response of non-slaveholding States before determining whether "she will resume the powers granted by her under the Constitution of the United States, and throw herself upon her reserved rights; meanwhile insisting that no coercion be attempted, the Federal forts in seceded States be not reinforced, duties be not collected, etc.," and proposing a Convention at Frankfort, Kentucky, the last Monday in May, of the States of Delaware, Maryland, North Carolina, Tennessee, Kentucky, Missouri and Arkansas. Henry A. Wise differed in details, and went further in the same direction. Messrs. Lewis E. Harvie, Robert L. Montague and Samuel C. Williams recommended the immediate passage of an Ordinance of Secession. Mr. Barbour of Culpeper insisted upon the immediate adoption by the non-slaveholding States of needed guarantees of safety, and provided for the appointment of three Commissioners to confer with the Confederate authorities at Montgomery.

19th. Committee on Federal Relations reported proposed amendments to the Constitution, which were the substitute of Mr. Franklin of Pa., in "Peace Conference," changed by using the expression "involuntary servitude" in place of "persons held to service." The right of owners of slaves is not to be impaired by congressional or territorial law, or any pre-existing law in territory hereafter acquired. Involuntary servitude, except for crime, to be prohibited north of 36°30′, but shall not be prohibited by Congress or any Territorial legislature south of that line. The third section has some verbal alterations, providing somewhat better security for property in transit. The fifth section prohibits the importation of slaves from places beyond the limits of the United States. The sixth makes some verbal changes in relation to remuneration for fugitives by Congress, and erases the clause relative to the securing of privileges and immunities. The seventh forbids the granting of the elective franchise and right to hold office to persons of the African race. The eighth provides that none of these amendments, nor the third paragraph of the second section of the first article of the Constitution, nor the third paragraph of the second section of the fourth article thereof, shall be amended or abolished without the consent of all the States.

25th. The Committee of the Whole refused (yeas 4, nays 116) to strike out the majority report and insert Mr. Carlile's "Peace Conference" substitute.

26th. The Constitution of the "Confederate" States, proposed by Mr. Hall as a substitute for the report of the committee, rejected—yeas 9, nays 78.

28th. The first and second resolutions reported by the committee adopted.

April 6th. The ninth resolution of the majority report came up. Mr. Bouldin offered an amendment striking out the whole, and inserting a substitute declaring that the independence of the seceded States should be acknowledged without delay, which was lost—yeas 68, nays 71.

9th. Mr. Wise's substitute for the tenth resolution, to the effect that Virginia recognizes the independence of the seceding States was adopted—yeas 128, nays 20.

April 17. Ordinance of Secession passed in secret session—yeas 88, nays 55, one excused, and eight not voting.

Same day the Commissioners adopted and ratified the Constitution of the Provisional Government of the "Confederate" States of America, this ordinance to cease to have legal effect if the people of Virginia voting upon the Ordinance of Secession should reject it.

25th. A Convention was made between Commissioners of Virginia, chosen by the Convention, and A. H. Stephens, Commissioner for "Confederates," stipulating that Virginia until she became a member of the Confederacy should place her military force under the direction of the President of the "Confederate" States; also turn over to "Confederate" States all her public property, naval stores, and munitions of war. Signed by J Tyler, W B. Preston, S. McD. Moore, James P Holcombe, Jas. C. Bruce, Lewis E. Harvie—for Virginia; and A. H. Stephens for "Confederate" States.

June 25th. Secession vote announced as 128,884 for, and 32,134 against.

July. The Convention passed an ordinance to the effect that any citizen of Virginia holding office under the Government of the United States after the 31st of July 1861, should be forever banished from the State, and be declared an alien enemy Also that any citizen of Virginia, hereafter undertaking to represent the State of Virginia in the Congress of the United States, should, in addition to the above penalties, be considered guilty of treason, and his property be liable to confiscation. A provision was inserted exempting from the penalties of the act all officers of the United States outside of the United States, or of the Confederate States, until after July 1st, 1862.

KENTUCKY.

December 12th, 1860. Indiana militia offer their services to quell servile insurrection. Gov. Magoffin declines accepting them.

January 17th, 1861. Legislature convened.

22d. The House by a vote of 87 to 6 resolved to resist the invasion of the South at all hazards.

27th. Legislature adopted the Virginia resolutions requiring the Federal Government to protect Slavery in the Territories and to guarantee the right of transit of slaves through the Free States.

February 2d. The Senate passed by a vote of 25 to 11, resolutions appealing to the Southern States to stop the revolution, protesting against Federal coercion and providing that the Legislature reassemble on the 24th of April to hear the responses from sister States, also in favor of making an application to call a National Convention for proposing amendments to the Constitution of the United States, also by a vote of 25 to 14 declared it inexpedient at this time to call a State Convention.

5th. The House by a vote of 54 to 40 passed the above resolutions.

March 22d. State Rights Convention assembled. Adopted resolutions denouncing any attempt on the part of the Government to collect revenue as coercion; and affirming that, in case of any such attempt, the border States should make common cause with the Southern Confederacy. They also recommended a border State Convention.

April 24th. Gov. Magoffin called an extra session of the Legislature.

May 20th. Gov Magoffin issued a neutrality proclamation.

September 11th. The House of Representatives by a vote of 71 to 26, adopted a resolution directing the Governor to issue a proclamation ordering the Confederate troops to evacuate Kentucky soil. The Governor vetoed the resolution, which was afterwards passed over his veto, and accordingly he issued the required proclamation.

October 29th. Southern Conference met at Russellville. H. C. Burnett elected Chairman, R. McKee Secretary, T. S. Bryan Assistant Secretary. Remained in secret session two days and then adjourned *sine die*. A series of resolutions reported by G. W Johnson were adopted. They recite the unconstitutional and oppressive acts of the Legislature, proclaim revolution, provide for a Sovereignty Convention at Russellville, on the 18th of November, recommend the organization of county guards, to be placed in the service of and paid by the Confederate States Government; pledge resistance to all Federal and State taxes, for the prosecution of the war on the part of the United States; and appoint Robert McKee, John C. Breckinridge, Humphrey Marshall, Geo. W. Ewing, H. W Bruce, Geo. B. Hodge, William Preston, Geo. W Johnson, Blanton Duncan, and P B. Thompson to carry out the resolutions.

November 18th. Convention met and remained in session three days.

20th. It passed a Declaration of Independence and an Ordinance of Secession. A Provisional Government consisting of a Governor, Legislative Council of ten, a Treasurer, and an Auditor were agreed upon. Geo. W Johnson was chosen Governor. Legislative Council were: Willis B. Machen, John W Crockett, James P. Bates, Jas. S. Chrisman, Phil. B. Thompson, J P Burnside, H. W Bruce, J. W. Moore, E. M. Bruce, Geo. B. Hodge.

MARYLAND.

Nov. 27th, 1860. Gov. Hicks declined to call a special session of the Legislature, in response to a request for such convening from Thomas G. Pratt, Sprigg Harwood, J. S. Franklin, N H. Green, Llewellyn Boyle, and J. Pinkney.

December 19th. Gov. Hicks replied to A. H. Handy, Commissioner from Mississippi, declining to accept the programme of Secession.

20th. Wm. H. Collins, Esq., of Baltimore, issued an address to the people, in favor of the Union, and in March a second address.

31st. The "Clipper" denied the existence of an organization in Maryland to prevent the inauguration of President Lincoln.

A. H. Handy of Mississippi addressed citizens of Baltimore in favor of disunion.

January 3d, 1861. Henry Winter Davis issued an address in favor of the Union.

3d. Numerous Union meetings in various part of the State. Gov. Hicks issued an address to the people against secession.

11th John C. Legrand in a letter to Hon. Reverdy Johnson replied to the Union speech of the latter.

14th. James Carroll, former Democratic candidate for Governor, announced his desire to go with the seceding States.

16th. Wm. A. Spencer, in a letter to Walter S. Cox, Esq., declared against the right of Secession but for a Convention.

16. Marshal Kane, in a letter to Mayor Berrett, denied that any organization exists to prevent the inauguration of President Lincoln, and said that the President elect would need no armed escort in passing through or sojourning within the limits of Baltimore and Maryland.

24th. Coleman Yellott declared for a Convention.

30th. Messrs. John B. Brooke, President of the Senate, and E. G. Kilbourn, Speaker of the House of Delegates, asked the Governor to convene the Legislature in response to public meetings. Senator Kennedy published his opinion that Maryland must go with Virginia.

February 18th. State Conference Convention held, and insisted upon a meeting of the Legislature. At a meeting in Howard Co., which Speaker E. G. Kilbourn addressed, a resolution was adopted that "immediate steps ought to be taken for the establishment of a Southern Confederacy, by consultation and co-operation with such other Southern and Slave States as may be ready therefor."

April 21st. Gov. Hicks wrote to Gen. Butler, advising that he do not land his troops at Annapolis. Butler replied that he intended to land there and march thence to Washington. Gov. Hicks protested against this and also against his having taken forcible possession of the Annapolis and Elkridge railroad.

24th. A special election of ten delegates to the Legislature took place at Baltimore. The total vote cast in all the wards was 9,249. The total vote cast at the Presidential election in November, 1860, was 30,148.

26th. Legislature reassembled at Frederick, Annapolis being occupied by Union troops.

29th. Gov. Hicks sent a message to the Legislature communicating to them the correspondence between himself and Gen. Butler and the Secretary of War relative to the landing of troops at Annapolis.

The House of Delegates voted against Secession, 53 to 13. Senate unanimously.

May 2d. The Committee on Federal Relations, "in view of the seizure of the railroads by the General Government and the erection of fortifications," presented resolutions appointing Commissioners to the President to ascertain whether any becoming arrangements with the General Government are practicable, for the maintenance of the peace and honor of the State and the security of its inhabitants. The report was adopted, and Otho Scott, Robt. M. McLane, and Wm. J. Ross were appointed such Commissioners.

Mr. Yellott in the Senate introduced a bill to appoint a Board of Public Safety. The powers given to the Board included the expenditure of the two millions of dollars proposed by Mr. Brune for the defence of the State, and the entire control of the military, including the removal and appointment of commissioned officers. It was ordered to a second reading by a vote of 14 to 8. The Board was to consist of Ezekiel F. Chambers, Enoch Louis Lowe, John V. L. MacMahon, Thomas G. Pratt, Walter Mitchell, and Thomas Winans. Gov. Hicks was made *ex-officio* a member of the Board. This measure was strongly pressed by the Disunionists for a long time, but they were finally compelled to give way and the bill never passed.

6th. The Commissioners reported the result of their interview with the President, and expressed the opinion that some modification of the course of the General Government towards Maryland *ought to be expected*.

10th. The House of Delegates passed a series of resolutions reported by the Committee on Federal Relations by a vote of 43 to 12. The resolutions declare that Maryland protests against the war, and does earnestly beseech and implore the President of the United States to make peace with the "Confederate" States; also, that "the State of Maryland desires the peaceful and immediate recognition of the independence of the Confederate States." Those who voted in the negative are Messrs. Medders, Lawson, Keene, Routzahn, Naill, Wilson of Harford, Bayless, McCoy, Fiery, Stake, McCleary, and Gorsuch.

13th. Both Houses adopted a resolution providing for a committee of eight members, (four from each House) to visit the President of the United States and the President of the Southern Confederacy. The committee to visit President Davis were instructed to convey the assurance that Maryland sympathizes with the Confederate States, and that the people of Maryland are enlisted with their whole hearts on the side of reconciliation and peace.

June 11th. Messrs. McKaig, Yellott and Harding, Commissioners to visit President Davis, presented their report; accompanying which is a letter from Jefferson Davis, expressing his gratification to hear that the State of Maryland was in sympathy with themselves, was enlisted on the side of peace and reconciliation, and avowing his perfect willingness for a cessation of hostilities, and a readiness to receive any proposition for peace from the United States Government.

20th. The House of Delegates, and June 22d, the Senate adopted resolutions unqualifiedly protesting against the arrest of Ross Winans and sundry other citizens of Maryland, as an "oppressive and tyrannical assertion and exercise of military jurisdiction within the limits of Maryland, over the persons and property of her citizens, by the Government of the United States."

MISSOURI.

January 15th, 1861. Senate passed Convention Bill—yeas 31, nays 2. Passed House also.

February 28th. Convention met; motion to go into secret session, defeated. A resolution requiring members to take an oath to support the Constitution of the United States and the State of Missouri, was lost —65 against 30.

March 4. Resolution passed, 64 yeas, 35 nays, appointing committee to notify Mr. Glenn, Commissioner of Georgia, that the Convention was ready to hear any communication from his State. Mr. Glenn was introduced, read Georgia's articles of secession, and made a speech urging Missouri to join her.

5th. Resolutions were read, ordering that the protest of St. Louis against coercion be reduced to writing, and a copy sent to the President of the United States; also, resolutions were adopted informing the Commissioner from Georgia that Missouri dissented from the position taken by that State, and refused to share the honors of secession with her.

6th. Resolutions were offered by several members and referred, calling a Convention of the Southern States which have not seceded, to meet at Nashville, April 15th, providing for such amendments to the Constitution of the United States as shall secure to all the States equal rights in the Union, and declaring strongly against secession.

9th. The Committee on Federal Relations reported a series of resolutions, setting forth that at present there is no adequate cause to impel Missouri to leave the Union, but that on the contrary she will labor for such an adjustment of existing troubles as will secure peace and the rights and equality of all the States; that the people of Missouri regard the amendments to the Constitution proposed by Mr. Crittenden, with their extension to territory hereafter to be required, a basis of adjustment which would forever remove all difficulties; and that it is expedient for the Legislature to call a Convention for proposing amendments to the Constitution.

The Senate passed resolutions that their Senators be instructed, and their Representatives requested, to oppose the passage of all acts granting supplies of men and money to coerce the seceding States into submission or subjugation; and that, should such acts be passed by Congress, their Senators be instructed, and their Representatives requested, to retire from the halls of Congress.

16th. An amendment of the fifth resolution of the majority report of the Committee on Federal Relations, asserting that Missouri would never countenance nor aid a seceding State in making war upon the General Government, nor provide men and money for the purpose of aiding the General Government to coerce a seceding State, was voted down.

27th. The following resolution was passed by a vote in the House of 62 against 42:—

Resolved, That it is inexpedient for the General Assembly to take any steps for calling a National Convention to propose amendments to the Constitution, as recommended by the State Convention.

July 22d. The Convention reassembled.

23d. Resolution passed, by a vote of 65 to 21, declaring the office of President, held by General Sterling Price at the last session of the Convention, vacant. A committee of seven were appointed to report what action they deem it advisable to take in the dislocated condition of the State.

25th. The committee presented their report. It alludes at length to the present unparalleled condition of things, the reckless course of the recent Government, and flight of the Governor and other State officers from the capitol. It declares the offices of Governor, Lieutenant-Governor, and Secretary of State vacant, and provides that their vacancies shall be filled by the Convention, the officers so appointed to hold their positions till August, 1862, at which time it provides for a special election by the people. It repeals the ninth section of the sixth article of the Constitution, and provides that the Supreme Court of the State shall consist of seven members; and that four members, in addition to the three now comprising the Court, shall be appointed by the Governor chosen by this Convention to hold office till 1862, when the people shall decide whether the change shall be permanent. It abolishes the State Legislature, and ordains that in case, before the 1st of August, 1862, the Governor chosen by this Convention shall consider the public exigencies demand, he shall order a special election for the members of the State Legislature. It recommends the passage of an ordinance repealing the following bills, passed by the Legislature in secret session, in May last: The military fund bill, the bill to suspend the distribution of the school fund, and the bill for cultivating friendly relations with the Indian tribes. It repeals the bill authorizing the appointment of one major-general of the Missouri militia, and revives the militia law of 1859.

A resolution was passed that a committee of seven be appointed by the President to prepare an address to the people of the State of Missouri.

November 26th. Jefferson Davis transmitted to the "Confederate" Congress a message concerning the secession of Missouri. It was accompanied by a letter from Governor Jackson, and also by an act dissolving the union with the United States, and an act ratifying the Constitution of the Provisional Government of the Confederate States; also, the Convention between the Commissioners of Missouri and the Commissioners of the Confederate States. Congress unanimously ratified the Convention entered into between the Hon. R. M. T. Hunter for the rebel Government and the Commissioners for Missouri.

Inter-State Commissioners.

The seceding States, as part of their plan of operation, appointed Commissioners to visit other slaveholding States. They were as follows, as announced in the newspapers:

South Carolina.

To Alabama, A. P. Calhoun.
To Georgia, James L. Orr, Ex-M. C.
To Florida, L. W. Spratt.
To Mississippi, M. L. Bonham, Ex-M. C.
To Louisiana, J. L. Manning.
To Arkansas, A. C. Spain.
To Texas, J. B. Kershaw.
To Virginia, John S. Preston.

Alabama.

To North Carolina, Isham W. Garrett.
To Mississippi, E. W. Pettus.
To South Carolina, J. A. Elmore.
To Maryland, A. F. Hopkins.
To Virginia, Frank Gilmer.
To Tennessee, L. Pope Walker.
To Kentucky, Stephen F. Hale.
To Arkansas, John Anthony Winston.

Georgia.

To Missouri, Luther J. Glenn.
To Virginia, Henry L. Benning.

Mississippi.

To South Carolina, C. E. Hooker.
To Alabama, Jos. W. Matthews, Ex-Gov.
To Georgia, William L. Harris.
To Louisiana, Wirt Adams.
To Texas, H. H. Miller.
To Arkansas, George R. Fall.
To Florida, E. M. Yerger.
To Tennessee, T. J. Wharton, Att'y-Gen.
To Kentucky, W. S. Featherstone, Ex-M. C.
To North Carolina, Jacob Thompson, Ex-M. C.
To Virginia, Fulton Anderson.
To Maryland, A. H. Handy, Judge.
To Delaware, Henry Dickinson.
To Missouri, —— Russell.

Southern Congress.

This body, composed of Deputies elected by the Conventions of the Seceding States, met at Montgomery, Alabama, February 4th, 1861, to organize a Southern Confederacy. Each State had a representation equal to the number of members of the Thirty-sixth Congress. The members were:

South Carolina.

Robert W. Barnwell, Ex-U. S. Senator.
R. Barnwell Rhett, " " "
James Chestnut, jr., " " "
Lawrence M. Keitt, Ex-M. C.
William W. Boyce, " "
Wm. Porcher Miles, " "
C. G. Memminger.
Thomas J Withers.

Alabama.

W. P. Chilton.
Stephen F. Hale.
David P. Lewis.
Thomas Fearn,
Richard W. Walker.
Robert H. Smith.
Colin J. McRae.
John Gill Shorter.
J. L. M. Curry, Ex-M. C.

Florida.

J. Patten Anderson, Ex-Delegate from Washington Territory.
Jackson Morton, Ex-U. S. Senator.
James Powers,

Mississippi.

W. S. Wilson.
Wiley P. Harris, Ex-M. C.
James T. Harrison.
Walter Brooke, Ex-U. S. Senator.
William S. Barry, Ex-M. C.
A. M. Clayton.

Georgia.

Robert Toombs, Ex-U. S. Senator.
Howell Cobb, Ex-M. C.
Martin J. Crawford, " "
Augustus R Wright, " "

Augustus H. Keenan.
Benjamin H. Hill.
Francis S. Bartow.
E. A. Nisbet.
Thomas R. R. Cobb.
Alexander H. Stephens, Ex-M. C.

Louisiana.

Duncan F. Kenner.
Charles M. Conrad, Ex-U. S. Senator.
Henry Marshall.
John Perkins, jr.
G. E. Sparrow.
E. De Clouet.

Texas.
(Admitted March 2d, 1861.)

Louis T. Wigfall, Ex-U. S. Senator.
John Hemphill, " " "
John H. Reagan, Ex-M. C.
T. N. Waul.
John Gregg.
W. S. Oldham.
W. B. Ochiltree.

Proceedings of the Southern Congress.

February 4th, 1861. Howell Cobb of Georgia elected President, Johnson J. Hooper of Alabama, Secretary. Mr. Cobb announced that secession "is now a fixed and irrevocable fact, and the separation is perfect, complete and perpetual."

6th. David L. Swain, M. W. Ransom, and John L. Bridgers, were admitted as Commissioners from North Carolina, under resolutions of the General Assembly of that State, passed January 29th, 1861, "to effect an honorable and amicable adjustment of all the difficulties that disturb the country, upon the basis of the Crittenden resolutions, as modified by the Legislature of Virginia," and to consult with the delegates to the Southern Congress for their "common peace, honor and safety."

7th. Congress notified that the State of Alabama had placed $500,000 at its disposal, as a loan to the provisional government of the Confederacy of Seceding States.

8th. The Constitution of the Provisional Government adopted. *

9th. Jefferson Davis, of Mississippi, elected Provisional President of the Confederate States of America, and Alexander H. Stephens, of Georgia, Vice-President. The question of attacking Fort Sumter has been referred to the Congress.

11th. Mr. Stephens announced his acceptance. Committee appointed to prepare a permanent Constitution.

12th. The Congress assumed "charge of all questions and difficulties now existing between the sovereign States of this Confederacy and the Government of the United States, relating to the occupation of forts, arsenals, navy yards, custom-houses, and all other public establishments." The resolution was directed to be communicated to the Governors of the respective States of the Confederacy.

15th. Official copy of the Texas Ordinance of Secession presented.

16th. President Davis arrived and received with salute, etc.

18th. President Davis inaugurated.

19th. Tariff law passed.

21st. Robert Toombs appointed Secretary of the State; C. G. Memminger, Secretary of the Treasury; L. Pope Walker, of

*The Provisional Constitution adopted by the Seceded States differs from the Constitution of the United States in several important particulars. The alterations and additions are as follows:

ALTERATIONS.

1st. The Provisional Constitution differs from the other in this: That the legislative powers of the Provisional Government are vested in the Congress now assembled. and this body exercises all the functions that are exercised by either or both branches of the United States Government.

2d. The Provisional President holds his office for one year, unless sooner superseded by the establishment of a permanent Government.

3d. Each State is erected into a distinct judicial district, the judge having all the powers heretofore vested in the district and circuit courts; and the several district judges together compose the supreme bench—a majority of them constituting a quorum.

4th. Whenever the word "Union" occurs in the United States Constitution the word "Confederacy" is substituted.

THE FOLLOWING ARE THE ADDITIONS.

1st. The President may veto any separate appropriation without vetoing the whole bill in which it is contained.

2d. The African slave-trade is prohibited.

3d. Congress is empowered to prohibit the introduction of slaves from any State not a member of this Confederacy.

4th. All appropriations must be upon the demand of the President or heads of departments.

OMISSIONS.

1st, There is no prohibition on members of Congress holding other offices of honor and emolument under the Provisional Government.

2d. There is no provision for a neutral spot for the location of a seat of government, or for sites for forts, arsenals, and dock-yards; consequently there is no reference made to the territorial powers of the Provisional Government.

3d. The section in the old Constitution in reference to capitation and other direct tax is omitted; also, the section providing that no tax or duty shall be laid on any exports.

4th. The prohibition on States keeping troops or ships of war in time of peace is omitted

5th. The Constitution being provisional merely, no provision is made for its ratification.

AMENDMENTS.

1st. The fugitive slave clause of the old Constitution is so amended as to contain the word "slave," and to provide for full compensation in cases of abduction of forcible rescue on the part of the State in which such abduction or rescue may take place.

2d. Congress, by a vote of two-thirds, may at any time alter or amend the Constitution.

TEMPORARY PROVISIONS.

1st. The Provisional Government is required to take immediate steps for the settlement of all matters between the States forming it and their other late confederates of the United States in relation to the public property and the public debt.

2d. Montgomery is made the temporary seat of government.

3d. This Constitution is to continue one year, unless altered by a two thirds vote or superseded by a permanent Government.

Alabama, Secretary of War; Stephen R. Mallory, Secretary of the Navy; Judah P. Benjamin, Attorney-General, and John H. Reagan, Postmaster-General; Philip Clayton, of Georgia appointed Assistant Secretary of the Treasury, and Wm. M. Browne, late of the Washington *Constitution*, Assistant Secretary of State.

March 2d. The Texas Deputies received.

The Confederate States.

The Confederate States was the name of the government formed in 1861 by the seven States which first seceded. Belligerent rights were accorded to it by the leading naval powers, but it was never recognized as a government, notwithstanding the persevering efforts of its agents near the principal courts. This result was mainly due to the diplomacy of the federal Secretary of State, Wm H. Seward, to the proclamations of emancipation in 1862-3, which secured the sympathy of the best elements of Great Britain and France for the federal government, and the obstinate persistence of the federal government in avoiding, as far as possible, any recognition of the existence, even *de facto*, of a confederate government. The federal generals in the field, in their communications with confederate officers, did not hesitate, upon occasion, even to give "president" Davis his official title, but no such embarrassing precedent was ever admitted by the civil government of the United States. It at first endeavored, until checked by active preparations for retaliation, to treat the crews of confederate privateers as pirates; it avoided any official communication with the confederate government, even when compelled to exchange prisoners, confining its negotiations to the confederate commissioners of exchange; and, by its persistent policy in this direction, it succeeded, without any formal declaration, in impressing upon foreign governments the belief that any recognition of the confederate States as a separate people would be actively resented by the government of the United States as an act of excessive unfriendliness. The federal courts have steadily held the same ground, that "the confederate states was an unlawful assemblage, without corporate power;" and that, though the separate States were still in existence and were indestructible, their state governments, while they chose to act as part of the confederate States, did not exist, even *de facto*. Early in January, 1861, while only South Carolina had actually seceded, though other Southern States had called conventions to consider the question, the Senators of the seven States farthest South practically assumed control of the whole movement, and their energy and unswerving singleness of purpose, aided by the telegraph, secured a rapidity of execution to which no other very extensive conspiracy of history can afford a parallel. The ordinance of secession was a negative instrument, purporting to withdraw the state from the Union and to deny the authority of the federal government over the people of the State; the cardinal object of the senatorial group was to hurry the formation of a new national government, as an organized political reality which would rally the outright secessionists, claim the allegiance of the doubtful mass, and coerce those who still remained recalcitrant. At the head of the senatorial group, and of its executive committee, was Jefferson Davis, Senator from Mississippi, and naturally the first official step toward the formation of a new government came from the Mississippi Legislature, where a committee reported, January 19th, 1861, resolutions in favor of a congress of delegates from the seceding States to provide for a southern confederacy, and to establish a provisional government, therefore. The other seceding States at once accepted the proposal, through their State conventions, which also appointed the delegates on the ground that the people had intrusted the State conventions with unlimited powers. The new government therefore began its existence without any popular ratio of representation, and with only such popular ratification as popular acquiescence gave. The provisional congress met Feb. 4th, at Montgomery, Ala., with delegates from South Carolina, Georgia, Alabama, Louisiana, Florida and Mississippi. The Texas delegates were not appointed until Feb. 14th. Feb, 8th, a provisional constitution was adopted, being the constitution of the United States, with some changes. Feb. 9th, Jefferson Davis, of Mississippi, was unanimously chosen provisional president, and Alexander H. Stephens, of Georgia, provisional vice-president, each State having one vote, as in all other proceedings of the body. By acts of Feb. 9th and 12th, the laws and revenue officers of the United States were continued in the confederate States until changed. Feb. 18th, the president and vice-president were inaugurated. Feb. 20th-26th, executive departments and a confederate regular army were organized, and provision was made for borrowing money. March 11th, the permanent constitution was adopted by Congress.

The Internal legislation of the provisional congress was, at first, mainly the adaptation of the civil service in the Southern States to the uses of the new government. Wherever possible, judges, postmasters, and civil as well as military and naval officers, who had resigned from the service of the United States, were given an equal or higher rank in the confederate service. Postmasters were directed to make their final accounting to the United States, May 31st, thereafter accounting to the Confederate States. April 29th, the provisional congress, which had adjourned March 16th, re-assembled at Montgomery, having been convoked by President Davis in consequence of President Lincoln's preparations to enforce federal authority in the South. Davis' message announced that all the seceding States had ratified the permanent constitution; that Virginia, which had not yet seceded and entered into alliance with the confederacy, and that other States, were expected to follow the same plan. He concluded by declaring that "all we ask is to be let alone." May 6th, an act was passed recognizing the existence of war with the United States. Congress adjourned May 22d, re-convened at Richmond, Va., July 20th, and adjourned August 22d, until November 18th. Its legislation had been mainly military and financial. Virginia, North Carolina, Tennessee and Arkansas, had passed ordinances of secession, and been admitted to the confederacy. (See the States named, and secession.) Although Missouri and Kentucky had not seceded, delegates from these States were admitted in December 1861. Nov. 6, 1861, at an election under the permanent constitution, Davis and Stephens were again chosen to their respective offices by a unanimous electoral vote. Feb. 18th, 1862, the provisional congress (of one house) gave way to the permanent congress, and Davis and Stephens were inaugurated February 22nd. The cabinet, with the successive Secretaries of each department, was as follows, including both the provisional and permanent cabinets:

State Department.—Robert Toombs, Georgia, February 21st, 1861; R. M. T. Hunter, Virginia, July 30th, 1861; Judah P. Benjamin, Louisiana, February 7th, 1862.

Treasury Department.—Charles G. Memminger, South Carolina, February 21st, 1861, and March 22d, 1862; James L. Trenholm, South Carolina, June 13th, 1864.

War Department.—L. Pope Walker, Mississippi, February 21st, 1861; Judah P. Benjamin, Louisiana, November 10th, 1861; James A. Seddon, Virginia, March 22d, 1862; John C. Breckinridge, Kentucky, February 15th, 1865.

Navy Department.—Stephen R. Mallory, Florida, March 4th, 1861, and March 22d.

Attorney General.—Judah P. Benjamin, Louisiana, February 21st, 1861; Thomas H. Watts, Alabama, September 10th, 1861, and March 22nd, 1862; George Davis, North Carolina, November 10th, 1863.

Postmaster-General.—Henry J. Elliot, Mississippi, February 21st, 1865; John H. Reagan, Texas, March 6th, 1861, and March 22d, 1862.

The provisional Congress held four sessions, as follows: 1. February 4-March 16th, 1861; 2. April 29-May 22d, 1861; 3. July 20-August 22d, 1861; and 4. November 18th, 1861-February 17th, 1862.

Under the permanent Constitution there were two Congresses. The first Congress held four sessions, as follows: 1. February 18-April 21st, 1862; 2. August 12-October 13th, 1862; 3. January 12-May 8th 1863; and 4. December 7, 1863-February 18th, 1864. The second Congress held two sessions, as follows: 1. May 2-June 15th, 1864; and 2. From November 7th, 1864, until the hasty and final adjournment, March 18th, 1865.

In the first Congress members chosen by rump State conventions, or by regiments in the confederate service, sat for districts in Missouri and Kentucky, though these States had never seceded. There were thus thirteen States in all represented at the close of the first Congress; but, as the area of the Confederacy narrowed before the advance of the Federal armies, the vacancies in the second Congress became significantly more numerous. At its best estate the Confederate Senate numbered 26, and the house 106, as follows: Alabama, 9; Arkansas, 4; Florida, 2; Georgia, 10; Kentucky, 12; Louisiana, 6; Mississippi, 1; Missouri, 7; North Carolina, 10; South Carolina, 6; Tennessee, 11; Texas, 6; Virginia, 16. In both Congresses Thomas S. Bocock, of Virginia, was Speaker of the House.*

For four months between the Presidential election and the inauguration of Mr. Lincoln those favoring secession in the South had practical control of their section, for while President Buchanan hesitated as to his constitutional powers, the more active partisans in his Cabinet were aiding their Southern friends in every practical way. In answer to the visiting Commissioners from South Carolina, Messrs. R. W. Barnwell, J. H. Adams and Jas. L. Orr, who formally submitted that State's ordinance of secession, and demanded possession of the forts in Charleston harbor, Buchanan said:—

"In answer to this communication, I have to say that my position as President of the United States was clearly defined in the message to Congress on the 3d inst. In that I stated that 'apart from the execution of the laws, so far as this may be practicable, the Executive has no authority to decide what shall be the relations between the Federal Government and South Carolina. He has been invested with no such discretion. He possesses no power to

* From Lalor's *Encyclopædia of Political Science*, published by Rand & McNally, Chicago, Ill.

change the relations heretofore existing between them, much less to acknowledge the independence of that State. This would be to invest a mere executive officer with the power of recognizing the dissolution of the Confederacy among our thirty-three sovereign States. It bears no resemblance to the recognition of a foreign *de facto* Government, involving no such responsibility. Any attempt to do this would, on his part, be a naked act of usurpation. It is, therefore, my duty to submit to Congress the whole question in all its bearings.

"Such is my opinion still. I could, therefore, meet you only as private gentlemen of the highest character, and was entirely willing to communicate to Congress any proposition you might have to make to that body upon the subject. Of this you were well aware. It was my earnest desire that such a disposition might be made of the whole subject by Congress, who alone possess the power, as to prevent the inauguration of a civil war between the parties in regard to the possession of the Federal forts in the harbor of Charleston."

Further correspondence followed between the President and other seceding State Commissioners, and the attitude of the former led to the following changes in his Cabinet: December 12th, 1860, LEWIS CASS resigned as Secretary of State, because the President declined to reinforce the forts in Charleston harbor. December 17th, JEREMIAH S. BLACK was appointed his successor.

December 10th, HOWELL COBB, resigned as Secretary of the Treasury—"his duty to Georgia requiring it." December 12th, PHILIP F. THOMAS was appointed his successor, and resigned, January 11th, 1861, because differing from the President and a majority of the Cabinet, "in the measures which have been adopted in reference to the recent condition of things in South Carolina," especially "touching the authority, under existing laws, to enforce the collection of the customs at the port of Charleston." January 11th, 1861, JOHN A. DIX appointed his successor.

29th, JOHN B. FLOYD resigned as Secretary of War, because, after the transfer of Major Anderson's command from Fort Moultrie to Fort Sumter, the President declined "to withdraw the garrison from the harbor of Charleston altogether."

December 31st, JOSEPH HOLT, Postmaster-General, was entrusted with the temporary charge of the War Department, and January 18th, 1861, was appointed Secretary of War.

January 8th, 1861, JACOB THOMPSON resigned as Secretary of the Interior, because "additional troops, he had heard, have been ordered to Charleston" in the Star of the West.

December 17th, 1860, JEREMIAH S. BLACK resigned as Attorney-General, and EDWIN M. STANTON, December 20th, was appointed his successor.

January 18th, 1861, JOSEPH HOLT resigned as Postmaster-General, and HORATIO KING, February 12th, 1861, was appointed his successor.

President Buchanan, in his annual message of December 3d, 1860, appealed to Congress to institute an amendment to the constitution recognizing the rights of the Southern States in regard to slavery in the territories, and as this document embraced the views which subsequently led to such a general discussion of the right of secession and the right to coerce a State, we make a liberal quotation from it:—

"I have purposely confined my remarks to revolutionary resistance, because it has been claimed within the last few years that any State, whenever this shall be its sovereign will and pleasure, may secede from the Union in accordance with the Constitution, and without any violation of the constitutional rights of the other members of the Confederacy. That as each became parties to the Union by the vote of its own people assembled in convention, so any one of them may retire from the Union in a similar manner by the vote of such a convention.

"In order to justify secession as a constitutional remedy, it must be on the principle that the Federal Government is a mere voluntary association of States, to be dissolved at pleasure by any one of the contracting parties. If this be so, the Confederacy is a rope of sand, to be penetrated and dissolved by the first adverse wave of public opinion in any of the States. In this manner our thirty-three States may resolve themselves into as many petty, jarring, and hostile republics, each one retiring from the Union without responsibility whenever any sudden excitement might impel them to such a course. By this process a Union might be entirely broken into fragments in a few weeks, which cost our forefathers many years of toil, privation, and blood to establish.

"Such a principle is wholly inconsistent with the history as well as the character of the Federal Constitution. After it was framed with the greatest deliberation and care, it was submitted to conventions of the people of the several States for ratification. Its provisions were discussed at length in these bodies, composed of the first men of the country. Its opponents contended that it conferred powers upon the Federal Government dangerous to the rights of the States, whilst its advocates maintained that, under a fair construction of the instrument, there was no foundation for such apprehensions. In that mighty struggle between the first intellects of this or any other country, it never occurred to any individual, either among its opponents or advocates, to assert or even to intimate that their efforts were all vain labor, because the moment that any State felt herself aggrieved she might secede from the Union. What a crushing argument would this have proved against those who dreaded that the rights of the States would be endangered by the Constitution. The truth is, that it was not until some years after the origin of the Federal Government that such a proposition was first advanced. It was afterwards met and refuted by the conclusive arguments of General Jackson, who, in his message of the 16th of January, 1833, transmitting the nullifying ordinance of South Carolina to Congress, employs the following language: 'The right of the people of a single State to absolve themselves at will and without the consent of the other States from their most solemn obligations, and hazard the liberty and happiness of the millions composing this Union, cannot be acknowledged. Such authority is believed to be utterly repugnant both to the principles upon which the General Government is constituted, and to the objects which it was expressly formed to attain.'

'It is not pretended that any clause in the Constitution gives countenance to such a theory. It is altogether founded upon inference, not from any language contained in the instrument itself, but from the sovereign character of the several States by which it was ratified. But it is beyond the power of a State like an individual, to yield a portion of its sovereign rights to secure the remainder? In the language of Mr. Madison, who has been called the father of the Constitution, 'It was formed by the States—that is, by the people in each of the States acting in their highest sovereign capacity, and formed consequently by the same authority which formed the State constitutions.' 'Nor is the Government of the United States, created by the Constitution, less a Government, in the strict sense of the term within the sphere of its powers, than the governments created by the constitutions of the States are within their several spheres. It is like them organized into legislative, executive, and judiciary departments. It operates, like them, directly on persons and things; and, like them, it has at command a physical force for executing the powers committed to it.'

"It was intended to be perpetual, and not to be annulled at the pleasure of any one of the contracting parties. The old Articles of Confederation were entitled 'Articles of Confederation and Perpetual Union between the States;' and by the thirteenth article it is expressly declared that 'the articles of this confederation shall be inviolably observed by every State, and the Union shall be perpetual.' The preamble to the constitution of the United States, having express reference to the Articles of Confederation, recites that it was established 'in order to form a more perfect union.' And yet it is contended that this 'more perfect union' does not include the essential attribute of perpetuity.

"But that the Union was designed to be perpetual, appears conclusively from the nature and extent of the powers conferred by the Constitution of the Federal Government. These powers embrace the very highest attributes of national sovereignty. They place both the sword and purse under its control. Congress has power to make war and to make peace; to raise and support armies and navies, and to conclude treaties with foreign governments. It is invested with the power to coin money, and to regulate the value thereof, and to regulate commerce with foreign nations and among the several States. It is not necessary to enumerate the other high powers which have been conferred upon the Federal Government. In order to carry the enumerated powers into effect, Congress possesses the exclusive right to lay and collect duties on imports, and, in common with the States, to lay and collect all other taxes.

"But the Constitution has not only conferred these high powers upon Congress, but it has adopted effectual means to restrain the States from interfering with their exercise. For that purpose it has in strong prohibitory language expressly declared that 'no State shall enter into any treaty, alliance, or confederation; grant letters of marque and reprisal; coin money; emit bills of credit; make anything but gold and silver coin a tender in payment of debts; pass any bill of attainder, *ex post facto* law, or law impairing the obligation of contracts.' Moreover, 'without the consent of Congress no State shall lay any imposts or duties on any imports or exports, except what may be absolutely necessary for executing its inspection laws,' and if they exceed this amount, the excess shall belong to the United States. And 'no State shall, without the consent of Congress, lay any duty of tonnage, keep troops or ships of war in time of peace, enter into any agreement or compact with another State, or with a foreign power, or engage in war, unless actually invaded or in such imminent danger as will not admit of delay.'

"In order still further to secure the uninterrupted exercise of these high powers against State interposition, it is provided 'that this Constitution and the laws of the United States which shall be made in pursuance thereof, and all treaties made or which shall be made under the authority of the United States, shall be the supreme law of the land; and the judges in every State shall be bound thereby, any thing in the Constitution or laws of any State to the contrary notwithstanding.'

"The solemn sanction of religion has been superadded to the obligations of official duty, and all Senators and Representatives of the United States, all members of State Legislatures, and all executive and judicial officers, 'both of the United States and of the several States, shall be bound by oath or affirmation to support this Constitution.'

"In order to carry into effect these powers, the Constitution has established a perfect Government in all its forms, legislative, executive, and judicial; and this Government to the extent of its powers acts directly upon the individual citizens of every State, and executes its own decrees by the agency of its own officers. In this respect it differs entirely from the Government under the old confederation, which was confined to making requisitions on the States in their sovereign character. This left it in the discretion of each whether to obey or refuse, and they often declined to comply with such requisitions. It thus became necessary, for the purpose of removing this barrier, and 'in order to form a more perfect union,' to establish a Government which could act directly upon the people and execute its own laws without the intermediate agency of the States. This has been accomplished by the Constitution of the United States. In short, the Government created by the Constitution, and deriving its authority from the sovereign people of each of the several States, has precisely the same right to exercise its power over the people of all these States in the enumerated cases, that each one of them possesses over subjects not delegated to the United States, but 'reserved to the States respectively or to the people.'

"To the extent of the delegated powers the Constitution of the United States is as much a part of the constitution of each State, and is as binding upon its people, as though it had been textually inserted therein.

"This Government, therefore, is a great and powerful Government, invested with all the attributes of sovereignty over the special subjects to which its authority extends. Its framers never intended to implant in its bosom the seeds of its own destruction nor were they at its creation guilty of the absurdity of providing for its own dissolution. It was not intended by its framers to be the baseless fabric of a vision, which, at the touch of the enchanter, would vanish into thin air, but a substantial and mighty fabric, capable of resisting the slow decay of time, and of defying the storms of ages. Indeed, well may the jealous patriots of that day have indulged fears that a Government of such high power might violate the reserved rights of the States, and wisely did they adopt the rule of a strict construction of these powers to prevent the danger. But they did not fear, nor had they any reason to imagine that the Constitution would ever be so interpreted as to enable any State by her own act, and without the consent of her sister States, to discharge her people from all or any of their federal obligations.

"It may be asked, then, are the people of the States without redress against the tyranny and oppression of the Federal Government? By no means. The right of resistance on the part of the governed against the oppression of their governments cannot be denied. It exists independently of all constitutions, and has been exercised at all periods of the world's history. Under it, old governments have been destroyed and new ones have taken their place. It is embodied in strong and express language in our own Declaration of Independence. But the distinction must ever be observed that this is revolution against an established Government, and not a voluntary secession from it by virtue of an inherent constitutional right. In short, let us look the danger fairly in the face; secession is neither more nor less than revolution. It may or it may not be a justifiable revolution; but still it is revolution."

The President having thus attempted to demonstrate that the Constitution affords no warrant for secession, but that this was inconsistent both with its letter and spirit, then defines his own position. He says:

"What, in the mean time, is the responsibility and true position of the Executive? He is bound by solemn oath, before God and the country, 'to take care that the laws be faithfully executed,' and from this obligation he cannot be absolved by any human power. But what if the performance of this duty, in whole or in part, has been rendered impracticable by events over which he could have exercised no control? Such, at the present moment, is the case throughout the State of South Carolina, so far as the laws of the United States to secure the administration of justice by means of the Federal judiciary are concerned. All the Federal officers within its limits, through whose agency alone these laws can be carried into execution, have already resigned. We no longer have a district judge, a district attorney, or a marshal in South Carolina. In fact, the whole machinery of the Federal government necessary for the distribution of remedial justice among the people has been demolished, and it would be difficult, if not impossible, to replace it.

"The only acts of Congress on the statute book bearing upon this subject are those of the 28th Februrry, 1795, and 3rd March, 1807. These authorize the President, after he shall have ascertained that the marshal, with his *posse comitatus*, is unable to execute civil or criminal process in any particular case, to call forth the militia and employ the army and navy to aid him in performing this service, having first by proclamation commanded the insurgents 'to disperse and retire peaceably to their respective abodes within a limited time.' This duty cannot by possibility be performed in a State where no judicial authority exists to issue process, and where there is no marshal to execute it, and where, even if there were such an officer, the entire population would constitute one solid combination to resist him.

"The bare enumeration of these provisions proves how inadequate they are without further legislation to overcome a united opposition in a single State, not to speak of other States who may place themselves in a similar attitude. Congress alone has power to decide whether the present laws can or cannot be amended so as to carry out more effectually the objects of the Constitution.

"The same insuperable obstacles do not lie in the way of executing the laws for the collection of customs. The revenue still continues to be collected, as heretofore, at the custom-house in Charleston, and should the collector unfortunately resign, a successor may be appointed to perform this duty.

"Then, in regard to the property of the United States in South Carolina. This has been purchased for a fair equivalent, 'by the consent of the Legislature of the State,' 'for the erection of forts, magazines, arsenals,' &c., and over these the authority 'to exercise exclusive legislation' has been expressly granted by the Constitution to Congress. It is not believed that any attempt will be made to expel the United States from this property by force; but if in this I should prove to be mistaken, the officer in command of the forts has received orders to act strictly on the defensive. In such a contingency the responsibility for consequences would rightfully rest upon the heads of the assailants.

"Apart from the execution of the laws, so far as this may be practicable, the Executive has no authority to decide what shall be the relations between the Federal Government and South Carolina. He has been invested with no such discretion. He possesses no power to change the relations heretofore existing between them, much less to acknowledge the independence of that State. This would be to invest a mere executive officer with the power of recognizing the dissolution of the Confederacy among our thirty-three sovereign States. It bears no relation to the recognition of a foreign *de facto* Government, involving no such responsibility. Any attempt to do this would, on his part, be a naked act of usurpation. It is, therefore, my duty to submit to Congress the whole question in all its bearings."

Then follows the opinion expressed in the message, that the Constitution has conferred no power on the Federal Government to coerce a *State* to remain in the Union. The following is the language: "The question fairly stated is, 'Has the Constitution delegated to Congress the power to coerce a State into submission which is attempting to withdraw, or has actually withdrawn from the Confederacy?' If answered in the affirmative, it must be on the principle that the power has been conferred upon Congress to make war against a State.

"After much serious reflection, I have arrived at the conclusion that no such power has been delegated to Congress or to any other department of the Federal Government. It is manifest, upon an inspection of the Constitution, that this is not among the specific and enumerated powers granted to Congress; and it is equally apparent that its exercise is not 'necessary and proper for carrying into execution' any one of these powers. So far from this power having been delegated to Congress, it was expressly refused by the Convention which framed the Constitution.

"It appears from the proceedings of that body that on the 31st May, 1787, the clause '*authorizing an exertion of the force of the whole against a delinquent State*' came up for consideration. Mr. Madison opposed it in a brief but powerful speech, from which I shall extract but a single sentence. He observed: 'The use of force against a State would look more like a declaration of war than an infliction of punishment, and would probably be considered by the party attacked as a dissolution of all previous compacts by which it might be bound.' Upon his motion the clause was unanimously postponed, and was never, I believe, again presented. Soon afterwards, on the 8th June, 1787, when incidentally adverting to the subject, he said: 'Any government for the United States, formed on the supposed practicability of using force against the unconstitutional proceedings of the States, would prove as visionary and fallacious as the government of Congress,' evidently meaning the then existing Congress of the old confederation."

At the time of the delivery of this message the excitement was very high. The extreme Southerners differed from it, in so far as it disputed both the right of revolution and secession under the circumstances, but quickly made a party battle-cry of the denial of the right of the National Government to coerce a State—a view which for a time won the President additional friends, but which in the end solidified all friends of the Union against his administration. To show the doubt which this ingenious theory caused, we quote from the speech of Senator Andrew Johnson, of Tennessee (subsequently Vice-President and acting President), delivered Dec. 18th, 1860, (Congressional Globe, page 119):—

"I do not believe the Federal Government has the power to coerce a State, for by the eleventh amendment of the Constitution of the United States it is expressly provided that you cannot even put one of the States of this confederacy before one of the courts of the country as a party. As a State, the Federal Government has no power to coerce it; but it is a member of the compact to which it agreed in common with the other States, and this Government has the right to pass laws, and to enforce those laws upon individuals within the limits of each State. While the one proposition is clear, the other is equally so. This Government can, by the Constitution of the country, and by the laws enacted in conformity with the Constitution, operate upon individuals, and has the right and power, not to coerce a State, but to enforce and execute the law upon individuals within the limits of a State."

Senator Jefferson Davis of Mississippi publicly objected to the message because of its earnest argument against secession, and the determination expressed to collect the revenue in the ports of South Carolina, by means of a naval force, and to defend the public property. From this moment they alienated themselves from the President. Soon thereafter, when he refused to withdraw Major Anderson from Fort Sumter, on the demand of the self-styled South Carolina Commissioners, the separation became complete. For more than two months before the close of the session all friendly intercourse between them and the President, whether of a political or social character, had ceased.

The Crittenden Compromise.

Congress referred the request in the message, to adopt amendments to the constitution recognizing the rights of the Slave States to take slavery into the territories to a committee of thirteen, consisting of five Republicans: Messrs. Seward, Collamer, Wade, Doolittle, and Grimes; five from slave-holding States: Messrs. Powell, Hunter, Crittenden, Toombs, and Davis; and three Northern Democrats; Messrs. Douglas, Bigler, and Bright. The latter three were intended to act as mediators between the extreme parties on the committee.

The committee first met on the 21st December, 1860, and preliminary to any other proceeding, they "resolved that no proposition shall be reported as adopted, unless sustained by a majority of each of the classes of the committee; Senators of the Republican party to constitute one class, and Senators of the other parties to constitute the other class." This resolution was passed, because any report they might make to the Senate would be in vain unless sanctioned by at least a majority of the five Republican Senators. On the next day (the 22d), Mr. Crittenden submitted to the committee "A Joint Resolution" (the same which he had two days before presented to the Senate), "proposing certain amendments to the Constitution of the United States," now known as the Crittenden Compromise. This was truly a compromise of conflicting claims, because it proposed that the South should surrender their adjudged right to take slaves into all our Territories, provided the North would recognize this right in the Territories south of the old Missouri Compromise line. The committee rejected this compromise, every one of its five Republican members, together with Messrs. Davis and Toombs, from the cotton States, having voted against it. Indeed, not one of all the Republicans in the Senate, at any period or in any form, voted in its favor.

The committee, having failed to arrive at a satisfactory conclusion, reported their disagreement to the Senate on the 31st December, 1860, in a resolution declaring that they had "not been able to agree upon any general plan of adjustment."

Mr. Crittenden did not despair of ultimate success, notwithstanding his defeat before the Committee of Thirteen. After this, indeed, he could no longer expect to carry his compromise as an amendment to the Constitution by the necessary two-thirds vote of Congress. It was, therefore, postponed by the Senate on his own motion. As a substitute for it he submitted to the Senate, on the 3d January, 1861, a joint resolution, which might be passed by a majority of both Houses. This was to refer his rejected amendment, by an ordinary act of Congress, to a direct vote of the people of the several States.

He offered his resolution in the following language: "Whereas the Union is in danger, and, owing to the unhappy division existing in Congress, it would be difficult, if not impossible, for that body to concur in both its branches by the requisite majority, so as to enable it either to adopt such measures of legislation, or to recommend to the States such amendments to the Constitution, as are deemed necessary and proper to avert that danger; and whereas in so great an emergency the opinion and judgment of the people ought to be heard, and would be the best and surest guide to their Representatives; Therefore, *Resolved*, That provision ought to be made by law without delay for taking the sense of the people and submitting to their vote the following resolution [the same as in his former amendment], as the basis for the final and permanent settlement of those disputes that now disturb the peace of the country and threaten the existence of the Union."

Memorials in its favor poured into Congress from portions of the North, even from New England. One of these presented to the Senate was from "the Mayor and members of the Board of Aldermen and the Common Council of the city of Boston, and over 22,000 citizens of the State of Massachusetts, praying the adoption of the compromise measures proposed by Mr. Crittenden." It may be proper here to observe that the resolution of Mr. Crittenden did not provide in detail for holding elections by which "the sense of the people" could be ascertained. To supply this omission, Senator Bigler, of Pennsylvania, on the 14th January, 1861, brought in "A bill to provide for taking the sense of the people of the United States on certain proposed amendments to the Constitution of the United States;" but never was he able to induce the Senate even to consider this bill.

President Buchanan exerted all his influence in favor of these measures. In his special message to Congress of the 8th of January, 1861, after depicting the consequences which had already resulted to the country from the bare apprehension of civil war and the dissolution of the Union, he says:

"Let the question be transferred from political assemblies to the ballot-box, and the people themselves would speedily redress the serious grievances which the South have suffered. But, in Heaven's name, let the trial be made before we plunge into armed conflict upon the mere assumption that there is no other alternative. Time is a great conservative power. Let us pause at this momentous point, and afford the people, both North and South, an opportunity for reflection. Would that South Carolina had been convinced of this truth before her precipitate action! I, therefore, appeal through you to the people of the country, to declare in their might that the Union must and shall be preserved by all constitutional means. I most earnestly recommend that you devote yourselves exclusively to the question how this can be accomplished in peace. All other questions, when compared with this, sink into insignificance. The present is no time for palliatives; action, prompt action is required. A delay in Congress to prescribe or to recommend a distinct and practical proposition for conciliation, may drive us to a point from which it will be almost impossible to recede.

"A common ground on which conciliation and harmony can be produced is surely not unattainable. The proposition to compromise by letting the North have exclusive control of the territory above a certain line, and to give Southern institutions protection below that line, ought to receive universal approbation. In itself, indeed, it may not be entirely satisfactory, but when the alternative is between a reasonable concession on both sides and a dissolution of the Union, it is an imputation on the patriotism of Congress to assert that its members will hesitate for a moment."

This recommendation was totally disregarded. On the 14th January, 1861, Mr. Crittenden made an unsuccessful attempt to have it considered, but it was postponed until the day following. On this day it was again postponed by the vote of every Republican Senator present, in order to make way for the Pacific Railroad bill. On the third attempt (January 16,) he succeeded, but by a majority of a single vote, in bringing his resolution before the body. Every Republican Senator present voted against its consideration. Mr. Clark, a Republican Senator from New Hampshire, moved to strike out the entire preamble and resolution of Mr. Crittenden, and in lieu thereof insert as a substitute a preamble and resolution in accordance with the Chicago platform. This motion prevailed by a vote of 25 to 23, every Republican Senator present having voted in its favor. Thus Mr. Crittenden's proposition to refer the question to the people was buried under the Clark amendment. This continued to be its position for more than six weeks, until the day before the final adjournment of Congress, 2d March, when the proposition itself was defeated by a vote of 19 in the affirmative against 20 in the negative.

The Clark Amendment prevailed only in consequence of the refusal of six Secession Senators to vote against it. These were Messrs. Benjamin and Slidell, of Louisiana; Mr. Iverson, of Georgia; Messrs. Hemphill and Wigfall, of Texas; and Mr. Johnson, of Arkansas. Had these gentlemen voted with the border slaveholding States and the other Democratic Senators, the Clark Amendment would have been defeated, and the Senate would then have been brought to a direct vote on the Crittenden resolution.

It is proper for reference that the names of those Senators who constituted the majority on this question, should be placed upon record. Every vote given from the six New England States was in opposition to Mr. Crittenden's resolution. These consisted of Mr. Clark, of New Hampshire; Messrs. Sumner and Wilson, of Massachusetts; Mr. Anthony, of Rhode Island; Messrs. Dixon and Foster, of Connecticut; Mr. Foot, of Vermont; and Mr. Fessenden, of Maine. The remaining twelve votes, in order to make up the 20, were given by Messrs. Bingham and Wade, of Ohio; Mr. Trumbull, of Illinois; Messrs. Bingham and Chandler, of Michigan; Messrs. Grimes and Harlan, of Iowa; Messrs. Doolittle and Durkee, of Wisconsin; Mr. Wilkinson, of Minnesota; Mr. King, of New York; and Mr. Ten Eyck, of New Jersey. The Republicans not voting were Hale of New Hampshire; Simmons of Rhode Island; Collamer of Vermont; Seward of New York, and Cameron of Pennsylvania. They refrained from various motives, but in the majority of instances because they disbelieved in any effort to compromise, for nearly all were recognized leaders of the more radical sentiment, and in favor of coercion of the South by energetic use of the war powers of the government. This was specially true of Hale, Seward, and General Cameron, shortly after Secretary of War, and the first Cabinet officer who favored the raising of an immense army and the early liberation and arming of the slaves.

On December 4th, 1860, on motion of Mr. Boteler of Virginia, so much of President Buchanan's message as related to the perilous condition of the country, was referred to a special committee of one from each State, as follows:

Corwin of Ohio; Millson of Virginia; Adams of Massachusetts; Winslow of North Carolina; Humphrey of New York; Boyce of South Carolina; Campbell of Pennsylvania; Love of Georgia; Ferry of Connecticut; Davis of Maryland; Robinson of Rhode Island; Whiteley of Delaware; Tappan of New Hampshire; Stratton of New Jersey; Bristow of Kentucky; Morrill of Vermont; Nelson of Tennessee; Dunn of Indiana; Taylor of Louisiana; Davis of Mississippi; Kellogg of Illinois; Houston of Alabama; Morse of Maine; Phelps of Missouri; Rust of Arkansas; Howard of Michigan; Hawkins of Florida; Hamilton of Texas; Washburn of Wisconsin; Curtis of Iowa; Burch of California; Windom of Minnesota; Stout of Oregon.

Messrs. Hawkins and Boyce asked to be excused from service on the Committee, but the House refused.

From this Committee Mr. Corwin reported, January 14th, 1861, a series of propositions with a written statement in advocacy thereof. Several minorrity reports were presented, but the following Joint Resolution is the only one which secured the assent of both Houses.

CONSTITUTIONAL AMENDMENT.

Be it resolved by the Senate and House of Representatives of the United States of America in Congress assembled, two-thirds of both Houses concurring, That the following article be proposed to the Legislatures of the several States as an amendment to the Constitution of the United States, which, when ratified by three-fourths of said Legislatures, shall be valid, to all intents and purposes, as a part of the said Constitution, namely:

ART. XII. No amendment shall be made to the Constitution which will authorize or give to Congress the power to abolish or interfere within any State, with the domestic institutions thereof, including that of persons held to labor or service by the laws of said State.

The Legislatures of Ohio and Maryland agreed to the amendment promptly, but events followed so rapidly, that the attention of other States was drawn from it, and nothing came of this, the only Congressional movement endorsed which looked to reconciliation. Other propositions came from the Border and individual states, but all alike failed.

The Peace Convention.

The General Assembly of Virginia, on the 19th of January, adopted resolutions inviting Representatives of the several States to assemble in a Peace Convention at Washington, which met on the 4th of February. It was composed of 133 Commissioners, many from the border States, and the object of these was to prevail upon their associates from the North to unite with them in such recommendations to Congress as would prevent their own States from seceding and enable them to bring back six of the cotton States which had already seceded.

One month only of the session of Congress remained. Within this brief period it was necessary that the Convention should recommend amendments to the Constitution in sufficient time to enable both Houses to act upon them before their final adjournment. It was also essential to success that these amendments should be sustained by a decided majority of the commissioners both from the Northern and the border States.

On Wednesday, the 6th February, a resolution was adopted,* on motion of Mr. Guthrie, of Kentucky, to refer the resolutions of the General Assembly of Virginia, and all other kindred subjects, to a committee to consist of one commissioner

* Official Journal of the Convention, pp. 9 and 10.

from each State, to be selected by the respective State delegations; and to prevent delay they were instructed to report on or before the Friday following (the 8th), "what they may deem right, necessary, and proper to restore harmony and preserve the Union."

This committee, instead of reporting on the day appointed, did not report until Friday, the 15th February.

The amendments reported by a majority of the committee, through Mr. Guthrie, their chairman, were substantially the same with the Crittenden Compromise; but on motion of Mr. Johnson, of Maryland, the general terms of the first and by far the most important section were restricted to the *present* Territories of the United States. On motion of Mr. Franklin, of Pennsylvania, this section was further amended, but not materially changed, by the adoption of the substitute offered by him. Nearly in this form it was afterwards adopted by the Convention. The following is a copy: "In all the present territory of the United States north of the parallel of thirty-six degrees and thirty minutes of north latitude, involuntary servitude, except in punishment of crime, is prohibited. In all the present territory south of that line, the status of persons held to involuntary service or labor, as it now exists, shall not be changed; nor shall any law be passed by Congress or the Territorial Legislature to hinder or prevent the taking of such persons from any of the States of this Union to said territory, nor to impair the rights arising from said relation; but the same shall be subject to judicial cognizance in the Federal courts, according to the course of the common law. When any Territory north or south of said line, within such boundary as Congress may prescribe, shall contain a population equal to that required for a member of Congress, it shall, if its form of government be republican, be admitted into the Union on an equal footing with the original States, with or without involuntary servitude, as the Constitution of such State may provide."

Mr. Baldwin, of Connecticut, and Mr. Seddon, of Virginia, made minority reports, which they proposed to substitute for that of the majority. Mr. Baldwin's report was a recommendation "to the several States to unite with Kentucky in her application to Congress to call a Convention for proposing amendments to the Constitution of the United States, to be submitted to the Legislatures of the several States, or to Conventions therein, for ratification, as the one or the other mode of ratification may be proposed by Congress, in accordance with the provisions in the fifth article of the Constitution."

The proposition of Mr. Baldwin, received the votes of eight of the twenty-one States. These consisted of the whole of the New England States, except Rhode Island, and of Illinois, Iowa, and New York, all being free States.

The first amendment reported by Mr. Seddon differed from that of the majority inasmuch as it embraced not only the present but all future Territories. This was rejected. His second amendment, which, however, was never voted upon by the Convention, went so far as distinctly to recognize the right of secession.

More than ten days were consumed in discussion and in voting upon various propositions offered by individual commissioners. The final vote was not reached until Tuesday, the 26th February, when it was taken on the first vitally important section, as amended.

This section, on which all the rest depended, was negatived by a vote of eight States to eleven. Those which voted in its favor were Delaware, Kentucky, Maryland, New Jersey, Ohio, Pennsylvania, Rhode Island, and Tennessee. And those in the negative were Connecticut, Illinois, Iowa, Maine, Massachusetts, Missouri, New York, North Carolina, New Hampshire, Vermont, and Virginia. It is but justice to say that Messrs. Ruffin and Morehead, of North Carolina, and Messrs. Rives and Summers, of Virginia, two of the five commissioners from each of these States, declared their dissent from the vote of their respective States. So, also, did Messrs. Bronson, Corning, Dodge, Wool, and Granger, five of the eleven New York commissioners, dissent from the vote of their State. On the other hand, Messrs. Meredith and Wilmot, two of the seven commissioners from Pennsylvania, dissented from the majority in voting in favor of the section. Thus would the Convention have terminated but for the interposition of Illinois. Immediately after the section had been negatived, the commissioners from that State made a motion to reconsider the vote, and this prevailed. The Convention afterwards adjourned until the next morning. When they reassembled (February 27,) the first section was adopted, but only by a majority of nine to eight States, nine being less than a majority of the States represented. This change was effected by a change of the vote of Illinois from the negative to the affirmative, by Missouri withholding her vote, and by a tie in the New York commissioners, on account of the absence of one of their number, rendering it impossible for the State to vote. Still Virginia and North Carolina, and Connecticut, Maine, Massachusetts, New Hampshire, and Vermont, persisted in voting in the negative. From the nature of this vote, it was manifestly impossible that two-thirds of both Houses of Congress should act favorably on the amendment, even if the delay had not already rendered such action impracticable before the close of the session.

The remaining sections of the amendment were carried by small majorities. The Convention, on the same day, through Mr. Tyler, their President, communicated to the Senate and House of Representatives the amendment they had adopted, embracing all the sections, with a request that it might be submitted by Congress, under the Constitution, to the several State Legislatures. In the Senate this was immediately referred to a select committee, on motion of Mr. Crittenden. The committee, on the next day (28th Feb.), reported a joint resolution proposing it as an amendment to the Constitution, but he was never able to bring the Senate to a direct vote upon it. Failing in this, he made a motion to substitute the amendment of the Peace Convention for his own.

Mr. Crittenden's reasons failed to convince the Senate, and his motion was rejected by a large majority (28 to 7). Then next in succession came the memorable vote on Mr. Crittenden's own resolution, and it was in its turn defeated, as we have already stated, by a majority of 20 against 19.

In the House of Representatives, the amendment proposed by the Convention was treated with still less consideration than it had been by the Senate. The Speaker was refused leave even to present it. Every effort made for this purpose was successfully resisted by leading Republican members. The consequence is that a copy of it does not even appear in the Journal.

The refusal to pass the Crittenden or any other Compromise heightened the excitement in the South, where many showed great reluctance to dividing the Union. Georgia, though one of the cotton States, under the influence of conservative men like Alex. H. Stephens, showed greater concern for the Union than any other, and it took all the influence of spirits like that of Robert Toombs to bring her to favor secession. She was the most powerful of the cotton States and the richest, as she is to-day. On the 22d of December, 1860, Robert Toombs sent the following exciting telegraphic manifesto from Washington:

Fellow-Citizens of Georgia: I came here to secure your constitutional rights, or to demonstrate to you that you can get no guarantees for these rights from your Northern Confederates.

The whole subject was referred to a committee of thirteen in the Senate yesterday. I was appointed on the committee and accepted the trust. I submitted propositions, which, so far from receiving decided support from a single member of the Republican party on the committee, were all treated with either derision or contempt. The vote was then taken in committee on the amendments to the Constitution, proposed by Hon. J. J. Crittenden of Kentucky, and each and all of them were voted against, unanimously, by the Black Republican members of the committee.

In addition to these facts, a majority of the Black Republican members of the committee declared distinctly that they had no guarantees to offer, which was silently acquiesced in by the other members.

The Black Republican members of this Committee of Thirteen are representative men of their party and section, and to the extent of my information, truly represent the Committee of Thirty-three in the House, which on Tuesday adjourned for a week without coming to any vote, after solemnly pledging themselves to vote on all propositions then before them on that date.

That committee is controlled by Black Republicans, your enemies, who only seek to amuse you with delusive hope until your election, in order that you may defeat the friends of secession. If you are deceived by them, it shall not be my fault. I have put the test fairly and frankly. It is decisive against you; and now I tell you upon the faith of a true man that all further looking to the North for security for your constitutional rights in the Union ought to be instantly abandoned. It is fraught with nothing but ruin to yourselves and your posterity.

Secession by the fourth of March next should be thundered from the ballot-box by the unanimous voice of Georgia on the second day of January next. Such a voice will be your best guarantee for LIBERTY, SECURITY, TRANQUILLITY and GLORY.

ROBERT TOOMBS.

IMPORTANT TELEGRAPHIC CORRESPONDENCE.

Atlanta, Georgia, December 26th, 1860.
Hon. S. A. Douglas or Hon. J. J. Crittenden:

Mr. Toombs's despatch of the 22d inst. unsettled conservatives here. Is there any hope for Southern rights in the Union? We are for the Union of our fathers, if Southern rights can be preserved in it. If not, we are for secession. Can we yet hope the Union will be preserved on this principle? You are looked to in this emergency. Give us your views by despatch and oblige

WILLIAM EZZARD.
ROBERT W. SIMS.
JAMES P. HAMBLETON.
THOMAS S. POWELL.
S. G. HOWELL.
J. A. HAYDEN.
G. W. ADAIR.
R. C. HONLESTER.

Washington, December 29th, 1860.

In reply to your inquiry, we have hopes that the rights of the South, and of every State and section, may be protected within the Union. Don't give up the ship. Don't despair of the Republic.

J. J. CRITTENDEN.
S. A. DOUGLAS.

Congress, amid excitement which the above dispatches indicate, and which was general, remained for several weeks comparatively inactive. Buchanan sent messages, but his suggestions were distrusted by the Republicans, who stood firm in the conviction that when Lincoln took his seat, and the new Congress came in, they could pass measures calculated to restore the property of and protect the integrity of the Union. None of them believed in the right of secession; all had lost faith in compromises, and all of this party repudiated the theory that Congress had no right to coerce a State. The revival of these questions, revived also the logical thoughts of Webster in his great reply to Hayne, and the way in which he then expanded the constitution was now accepted as the proper doctrine of Republicanism on that question. No partisan sophistry could shake the convictions made by Webster, and so apt were his arguments in their application to every new development that they supplied every logical want in the Northern mind. Republican orators and newspapers quoted and endorsed, until nearly every reading mind was imbued with the same sentiments, until in fact the Northern Democrats, and at all times the Douglas Democrats, were ready to stand by the flag of the Union. George W. Curtis, in *Harper's Weekly* (a journal which at the time graphically illustrated the best Union thoughts and sentiments), in an issue as late as January 12th, 1872, well described the power of Webster's grand ability * over a crisis which he did not live to see, Mr. Curtis says :—

"The war for the Union was a vindication of that theory of its nature which Webster had maintained in a memorably impregnable and conclusive manner. His second speech on Foot's resolution — the reply to Hayne—was the most famous and effective speech ever delivered in this country. It stated clearly and fixed firmly in the American mind the theory of the government, which was not, indeed, original with Webster, but which is nowhere else presented with such complete and inexorable reason as in this speech. If the poet be the man who is so consummate a master of expression that he only says perfectly what everybody thinks, upon this great occasion the orator was the poet. He spoke the profound but often obscured and dimly conceived conviction of a nation. He made the whole argument of the civil war a generation before the war occurred, and it has remained unanswered and unanswerable. Mr. Everett, in his discourse at the dedication of the statute of Webster, in the State-House grounds in Boston in 1859, described the orator at the delivery of this great speech. The evening before he seemed to be so careless that Mr. Everett feared that he might not be fully aware of the gravity of the occasion. But when the hour came, the man was there. 'As I saw him in the evening, if I may borrow an illustration from his favorite amusement,' said Mr. Everett, 'he was as unconcerned and as free of spirit as some here have often seen him while floating in his fishing-boat along a hazy shore, gently rocking on the tranquil tide, dropping his line here and there with the varying fortune of the sport. The next morning he was like some mighty admiral, dark and terrible, casting the long shadow of his frowning tiers far over the sea, that seemed to sink beneath him; his broad pennant streaming at the main, the Stars and Stripes at the fore, the mizzen, and the peak, and bearing down like a tempest upon his antagonist, with all his canvas strained to the wind, and all his thunders roaring from his broadsides.' This passage well suggests that indescribable impression of great oratory which Rufus Choate, in his eulogy of Webster at Dartmouth College, conveys by a felicitous citation of what Quintilian says of Hortensius, that there was some spell in the spoken word which the reader misses."

As we have remarked, the Republicans were awaiting the coming of a near and greater power to themselves, and at the same time jealously watching the movements of the friends of the South in Congress and in the President's Cabinet. It needed all their watchfulness to prevent advantages which the secessionists thought they had a right to take. Thus Jefferson Davis, on January 9th, 1860, introduced to the senate a bill "to authorize the sale of public arms to the several States and Territories," and as secession became more probable he sought to press its passage, but failed. Floyd, the Secretary of War, was far more successful, and his conduct was made the subject of the following historic and most remarkable report:—

Transfer of U. S. Arms South in 1859-60.

Report (Abstract of) made by Mr. B. Stanton, from the Committee on Military

* The text of Webster's speech in reply to Hayne, now accepted as the greatest constitutional exposition ever made by any American orator, will be found in our book devoted to Great Speeches on Great Issues.

Affairs, in House of Representatives, Feb. 18th, 1861.

The Committee on Military Affairs, to whom was referred the resolution of the House of Representatives of 31st of December last, instructing said committee to inquire and report to the House, how, to whom, and at what price, the public arms distributed since the first day of January, A. D. 1860, have been disposed of; and also into the condition of the forts, arsenals, dock-yards, etc., etc., submit the following report:

That it appears from the papers herewith submitted, that Mr. Floyd, the late Secretary of War, by the authority or under color of the law of March 3d, 1825, authorizing the Secretary of War to sell any arms, ammunition, or other military stores which should be found unsuitable for the public service, sold to sundry persons and States 31,610 flint-lock muskets, altered to percussion, at $2.50 each, between the 1st day of January, A. D. 1860, and the 1st day of January, A.D., 1861. It will be seen from the testimony of Colonel Craig and Captain Maynadier, that they differ as to whether the arms so sold had been found, "upon proper inspection, to be unsuitable for the public service."

Whilst the Committtee do not deem it important to decide this question, they say, that in their judgment it would require a very liberal construction of the law to bring these sales within its provisions.

It also appears that on the 21st day of November last, Mr. Belknap made application to the Secretary of War for the purchase of from one to two hundred and fifty thousand United States muskets, flint-locks and altered to percussion, at $2.15 each; but the Secretary alleges that the acceptance was made under a misapprehension of the price bid, he supposing it was $2.50 each, instead of $2.15.

Mr. Belknap denies all knowledge of any mistake or misapprehension, and insists upon the performance of his contract.

The present Secretary refuses to recognize the contract, and the muskets have not been delivered to Mr. Belknap.

Mr. Belknap testifies that the muskets were intended for the Sardinian government.

It will appear by the papers herewith submitted, that on the 29th of December, 1859, the Secretary of War ordered the transfer of 65,000 percussion muskets, 40-000 muskets altered to percussion, and 10-000 percussion rifles, from the Springfield Armory and the Watertown and Watervliet Arsenals, to the Arsenals at Fayetteville, N. C., Charleston, S. C., Augusta, Ga., Mount Vernon, Ala., and Baton Rouge, La., and that these arms were distributed during the spring of 1860 as follows:

	Percussion muskets.	Altered muskets.	Rifles.
To Charleston Arsenal,	9,280	5,720	2,000
To North Carolina Arsenal,	15 480	9,520	2,000
To Augusta Arsenal,	12,380	7,620	2,000
To Mount Vernon Arsenal,	9,280	5,720	2,000
To Baton Rouge Arsenal,	18,580	11,420	2,000
	65,000	40,000	10,000

All of these arms, except those sent to the North Carolina Arsenal,* have been seized by the authorities of the several States of South Carolina, Alabama, Louisiana and Georgia, and are no longer in possession of the United States.

It will appear by the testimony herewith presented, that on the 20th of October last the Secretary of War ordered forty columbiads and four thirty-two pounders to be sent from the Arsenal at Pittsburg to the fort on Ship Island, on the coast of Mississippi, then in an unfinished condition, and seventy columbiads and seven thirty-two pounders to be sent from the same Arsenal to the fort at Galveston, in Texas, the building of which had scarcely been commenced.

This order was given to the Secretary of War, without any report from the Engineer department showing that said works were ready for their armament, or that the guns were needed at either of said points.

It will be seen by the testimony of Captain Wright, of the Engineer department, that the fort at Galveston cannot be ready for its entire armament in less than about five years, nor for any part of it in less than two; and that the fort at Ship Island will require an appropriation of $85,000 and one year's time before it can be ready for any part of its armament. This last named fort has been taken possession of by the State authorities of Mississippi.

The order of the late Secretary of War (Floyd) was countermanded by the present Secretary (Holt) before it had been fully executed by the shipment of said guns from Pittsburg.†

It will be seen by a communication from the Ordnance office of the 21st of January last, that by the last returns there were remaining in the United States arsenals and armories the following small arms, viz:

Percussion muskets and muskets altered to percussion of calibre 69	499,554
Percussion rifles, calibre 54	42,011
Total	541,565

* These were afterwards seized.

† The attempted removal of these heavy guns from Allegheny Arsenal, late in December, 1860, created intense excitement. A *monster mass* meeting assembled at the call of the Mayor of the city, and citizens of all parties aided in the effort to prevent the shipment. Through the interposition of Hon. J. K. Moorhead, Hon. R. McKnight, Judge Shaler, Judge Wilkins, Judge Shannon, and others inquiry was instituted, and a revocation of the order obtained. The Secessionists in Congress bitterly complained of the "mob law" which thus interfered with the routine of governmental affairs.—McPherson's History.

Of these 60,878 were deposited in the arsenals of South Carolina, Alabama, and Louisiana, and are in the possession of the authorities of those States, reducing the number in possession of the United States to 480,687.

Since the date of said communication, the following additional forts and military posts have been taken possession of by parties acting under the authority of the States in which they are respectively situated, viz:

Fort Moultrie, South Carolina.
Fort Morgan, Alabama.
Baton Rouge Barracks, Louisiana.
Fort Jackson, Louisiana.
Fort St. Philip, "
Fort Pike, Louisiana.
Oglethorpe Barracks, Georgia.

And the department has been unofficially advised that the arsenal at Chattahoochee, Forts McRea and Barrancas, and Barracks, have been seized by the authorities of Florida.

To what further extent the small arms in possession of the United States may have been reduced by these figures, your committee have not been advised.

The whole number of the sea-board forts in the United States is fifty-seven; their appropriate garrison in war would require 26,420 men; their actual garrison at this time is 1,334 men, 1,308 of whom are in the forts at Governor's Island, New York; Fort McHenry, Maryland; Fort Monroe, Virginia, and at Alcatraz Island, California, in the harbor of San Francisco.

From the facts elicited, it is certain that the regular military force of the United States, is wholly inadequate to the protection of the forts, arsenals, dockyards, and other property of the United States in the present disturbed condition of the country. The regular army numbers only 18,000 men when recruited to its maximum strength, and the whole of this force is required for the protection of the border settlements against Indian depredations. Unless it is the intention of Congress that the forts, arsenals, dock-yards and other public property, shall be exposed to capture and spoliation, the President must be armed with additional force for their protection.

In the opinion of the Committee the law of February 28th, 1795, confers upon the President ample power to call out the militia, to execute the laws and protect the public property. But as the late Attorney-General has given a different opinion, the Committee to remove all doubt upon the subject, report the accompanying bill, etc.

OTHER ITEMS.

Statement of Arms distributed by Sale since the first of January, 1860, to whom sold and the place whence sold.

To whom sold.	*No.*	1860. *Date of Sale.*	*Arsenals. Where sold.*
J. W. Zacharie & Co.	4,000	Feb 3	St. Louis.
James T. Ames	1,000	Mar. 14	New York.
Captain G. Barry	80	June 11	St. Louis.
W. C. N. Swift	400	Aug. 31	Springfield.
do	80	Nov. 13	do.
State of Alabama	1 000	Sep. 27	Baton Rouge.
do	2,500	Nov. 14	do.
State of Virginia	5,000	Nov. 6	Washington.
Phillips county, Ark	50	Nov. 16	St. Louis.
G. B. Lamar	10,000	Nov. 24	Watervliet.

The arms were all flint-lock muskets altered to percussion, and were all sold at $2.50 each, except those purchased by Captain G. Barry and by the Phillips county volunteers, for which $2 each were paid.

The Mobile *Advertiser* says: "During the past year 135,430 muskets have been quietly transferred from the Northern Arsenal at Springfield alone, to those in the Southern States. We are much obliged to Secretary Floyd for the foresight he has thus displayed in disarming the North and *equipping the South for this emergency.* There is no telling the quantity of arms and munitions which were sent South from other Northern arsenals. There is no doubt but that every man in the South who can carry a gun can now be supplied from private or public sources. The Springfield contribution alone would arm all the militiamen of Alabama and Mississippi."

General Scott, in his letter of December 2d, 1862, on the early history of the Rebellion, states that "Rhode Island, Delaware and Texas had not drawn, at the end of 1860, their annual quotas of arms for that year, and Massachusetts, Tennessee, and Kentucky only in part; Virginia, South Carolina, Georgia, Florida, Alabama, Louisiana, Mississippi and Kansas were, by order of the Secretary of War, supplied with their quotas for 1861 in advance, and Pennsylvania and Maryland in part."

This advance of arms to eight Southern States is in addition to the transfer, about the same time, of 115,000 muskets to Southern arsenals, as per Mr. Stanton's report.

Governor Letcher of Virginia, in his Message of December, 1861, says, that for some time prior to secession, he had been engaged in purchasing arms, ammunition, etc.; among which were 13 Parrott rifled cannon, and 5,000 muskets. He desired to buy from the United States Government 10,000 more, when buying the 5,000, but he says "the authorities declined to sell them to us, although five times the number were then in the arsenal at Washington."

Had Jefferson Davis' bill relative to the purchase of arms become a law, the result might have been different.

This and similar action on the part of the South, especially the attempted seizure and occupation of forts, convinced many of the Republicans that no compromise could endure, however earnest its advocates from the Border States, and this earnestness was unquestioned. Besides their attachment to the Union, they knew that in the threatened war they would be the greatest sufferers, with their people divided neighbor against neighbor, their lands laid waste, and their houses destroyed. They had every motive for earnestness in the effort to conciliate the disagreeing sections.

The oddest partisan feature in the entire preliminary and political struggle was the attempt, in the parlance of the day, of "New York to secede from New York"—an oddity verified by Mayor Wood's recommendation in favor of the secession of New York city, made January 6th, 1861. The document deserves a place in this history, as it shows the views of a portion of the citizens then, and an exposition of their interests as presented by a citizen before and since named by repeated elections to Congress.

Mayor Wood's Secession Message.

To the Honorable the Common Council:

GENTLEMEN:—We are entering upon the public duties of the year under circumstances as unprecedented as they are gloomy and painful to contemplate. The great trading and producing interests of not only the city of New York, but of the entire country, are prostrated by a monetary crisis; and although similar calamities have before befallen us, it is the first time that they have emanated from causes having no other origin than that which may be traced to political disturbances. Truly, may it now be said, "We are in the midst of a revolution *bloodless* AS YET." Whether the dreadful alternative implied as probable in the conclusion of this prophetic quotation may be averted, "no human ken can divine." It is quite certain that the severity of the storm is unexampled in our history, and if the disintegration of the Federal Government, with the consequent destruction of all the material interests of the people shall not follow, it will be owing more to the interposition of Divine Providence, than to the inherent preventive power of our institutions, or the intervention of any other human agency.

It would seem that a dissolution of the Federal Union is inevitable. Having been formed originally on a basis of general and mutual protection, but separate local independence—each State reserving the entire and absolute control of its own domestic affairs, it is evidently impossible to keep them together longer than they deem themselves fairly treated by each other, or longer than the interests, honor and fraternity of the people of the several States are satisfied. Being a Government created by *opinion*, its continuance is dependent upon the continuance of the sentiment which formed it. It cannot be preserved by coercion or held together by force. A resort to this last dreadful alternative would of itself destroy not only the Government, but the lives and property of the people.

If these forebodings shall be realized, and a separation of the States shall occur, momentous considerations will be presented to the corporate authorities of this city. We must provide for the new relations which will necessarily grow out of the new condition of public affairs.

It will not only be necessary for us to settle the relations which we shall hold to other cities and States, but to establish, if we can, new ones with a portion of our own State. Being the child of the Union, having drawn our sustenance from its bosom, and arisen to our present power and strength through the vigor of our mother—when deprived of her maternal advantages, we must rely upon our own resources and assume a position predicated upon the new phase which public affairs will present, and upon the inherent strength which our geographical, commercial, political, and financial pre-eminence imparts to us.

With our aggrieved brethren of the Slave States, we have friendly relations and a common sympathy. We have not participated in the warfare upon their constitutional rights or their domestic institutions. While other portions of our State have unfortunately been imbued with the fanatical spirit which actuates a portion of the people of New England, the city of New York has unfalteringly preserved the integrity of its principles in adherence to the compromises of the Constitution and the equal rights of the people of all the States. We have respected the local interests of every section, at no time oppressing, but all the while aiding in the development of the resources of the whole country. Our ships have penetrated to every clime, and so have New York capital, energy and enterprise found their way to every State, and, indeed, to almost every county and town of the American Union. If we have derived sustenance from the Union, so have we in return disseminated blessings for the common benefit of all. Therefore, New York has a right to expect, and should endeavor to preserve a continuance of uninterrupted intercourse with every section.

It is, however, folly to disguise the fact that, judging from the past, New York may have more cause of apprehension from the aggressive legislation of our own State than from external dangers. We have already largely suffered from this cause. For the past five years, our interests and corporate rights have been repeatedly trampled upon. Being an integral portion of the State, it has been assumed, and in effect tacitly admitted on our part by non-resistance, that all political and governmental power over us rested in the State Legislature. Even the common right of taxing ourselves for our own government, has been yielded, and we are not permitted to do so without this authority. * * *

Thus it will be seen that the political connection between the people of the city and the State has been used by the latter to our injury. The Legislature, in which the present partizan majority has the power, has become the instrument by which we are plundered to enrich their speculators, lobby agents, and Abolition politicians. Laws are passed through their malign influence by which, under forms of legal enactment, our burdens have been increased, our substance eaten out, and our municipal liberties destroyed. Self-government, though guaranteed by the State Constitution, and left to every other county and city, has been taken from us by this foreign power, whose dependents have been sent among us to destroy our liberties by subverting our political system.

How we shall rid ourselves of this odious and oppressive connection, it is not for me to determine. It is certain that a dissolution cannot be peacefully accomplished, except by the consent of the Legislature itself. Whether this can be obtained or not, is, in my judgment, doubtful. Deriving so much advantage from its power over the city, it is not probable that a partizan majority will consent to a separation—and the resort to force by violence and revolution must not be thought of for an instant. We have been distinguished as an orderly and law-abiding people. Let us do nothing to forfeit this character, or to add to the present distracted condition of public affairs.

Much, no doubt, can be said in favor of the justice and policy of a separation. It may be said that secession or revolution in any of the United States would be subversive of all Federal authority, and, so far as the Central Government is concerned, the resolving of the community into its original elements—that, if part of the States form new combinations and Governments, other States may do the same. California and her sisters of the Pacific will no doubt set up an independent Republic and husband their own rich mineral resources. The Western States, equally rich in cereals and other agricultural products, will probably do the same. Then it may be said, why should not New York city, instead of supporting by her contributions in revenue two-thirds of the expenses of the United States, become also equally independent? As a free city, with but nominal duty on imports, her local Government could be supported without taxation upon her people. Thus we could live free from taxes, and have cheap goods nearly duty free. In this she would have the whole and united support of the Southern States, as well as all the other States to whose interests and rights under the Constitution she has always been true.

It is well for individuals or communities to look every danger square in the face, and to meet it calmly and bravely. As dreadful as the severing of the bonds that have hitherto united the States has been in contemplation, it is now apparently a stern and inevitable fact. We have now to meet it with all the consequences, whatever they may be. If the Confederacy is broken up the Government is dissolved, and it behooves every distinct community, as well as every individual, to take care of themselves.

When Disunion has become a fixed and certain fact, why may not New York disrupt the bands which bind her to a venal and corrupt master—to a people and a party that have plundered her revenues, attempted to ruin her commerce, taken away the power of self-government, and destroyed the Confederacy of which she was the proud Empire City? Amid the gloom which the present and prospective condition of things must cast over the country, New York, as a *Free City*, may shed the only light and hope of a future reconstruction of our once blessed Confederacy.

But I am not prepared to recommend the violence implied in these views. In stating this argument in favor of freedom, "peaceably if we can, forcibly if we must," let me not be misunderstood. The redress can be found only in appeals to the magnanimity of the people of the whole State. The events of the past two months have no doubt effected a change in the popular sentiment of the State and National politics. This change may bring us the desired relief, and we may be able to obtain a repeal of the law to which I have referred, and a consequent restoration of our corporate rights.

FERNANDO WOOD, Mayor.

January 6th, 1861.

Congress on the Eve of the Rebellion.

It should be borne in mind that all of the propositions, whether for compromise, authority to suppress insurrection, or new laws to collect duties, had to be considered by the Second Session of the 36th Congress, which was then, with the exception of the Republicans, a few Americans, and the anti-Lecompton men, supporting the administration of Buchanan. No Congress ever had so many and such grave propositions presented to it, and none ever showed more exciting political divisions. It was composed of the following persons, some of whom survive, and most of whom are historic characters:

SENATE.

JOHN C. BRECKINRIDGE, of Kentucky, *Vice-President*;

Maine—H. Hamlin,* W. P. Fessenden.
New Hampshire—John P. Hale, Daniel Clark.
Vermont—Solomon Foot, J. Collamer.
Massachusetts—Henry Wilson, Charles Sumner.
Rhode Island—James F. Simmons, H. B. Anthony.
Connecticut—L. S. Foster, Jas. Dixon.
New York—William H. Seward, Preston King.
New Jersey—J. C. Ten Eyck, J. R. Thomson.
Pennsylvania—S. Cameron, Wm. Bigler.
Delaware—J. A. Bayard, W. Saulsbury.
Maryland—J. A. Pearce, A. Kennedy.
Virginia—R. M. T. Hunter, James M. Mason.
South Carolina—Jas. Chesnut,† James H. Hammond.†
North Carolina—Thomas Bragg, T. L. Clingman.
Alabama—B. Fitzpatrick, C. C. Clay, Jr.
Mississippi—A. G. Brown, Jeff. Davis.
Louisiana—J. P. Benjamin, John Slidell.
Tennessee—A. O. P. Nicholson, A. Johnson.
Arkansas—R. W. Johnson, W. K. Sebastian.
Kentucky—L. W. Powell, J. J. Crittenden.
Missouri—Jas. S. Green, Trusten Polk.
Ohio—B. F. Wade, Geo. E. Pugh.
Indiana—J. D. Bright, G. N. Fitch.
Illinois—S. A. Douglas, L. Trumbull.
Michigan—Z. Chandler, K. S. Bingham.
Florida—D. L. Yulee, S. R. Mallory.
Georgia—Alfred Iverson, Robt. Toombs.
Texas—John Hemphill, L. T. Wigfall.
Wisconsin—Charles Durkee, J. R. Doolittle.
Iowa—J. M. Grimes, Jas. Harlan.
California—M. S. Latham, William M. Gwin.
Minnesota—H. M. Rice, M. S. Wilkinson.
Oregon—Joseph Lane, Edward D. Baker.

*Resigned January 17th, 1861, and succeeded by Hon. Lot M. Morrill.

† Did not attend.

HOUSE OF REPRESENTATIVES.

WILLIAM PENNINGTON, of New Jersey, *Speaker*.

Maine—D. E. Somes, John J. Perry, E. B. French, F. H. Morse, Israel Washburn, Jr.,* S. C. Foster.
New Hampshire—Gilman Marston, M. W. Tappan, T. M. Edwards.
Vermont—E. P. Walton, J. S. Morrill, H. E. Royce.
Massachusetts—Thomas D. Eliot, James Buffinton, Charles Francis Adams, Alexander H. Rice, Anson Burlingame, John B. Alley, Daniel W. Gooch, Charles R. Train, Eli Thayer, Charles Delano, Henry L. Dawes.
Rhode Island—C. Robinson, W. D. Brayton.
Connecticut—Dwight Loomis, John Woodruff, Alfred A. Burnham, Orris S. Ferry.
Delaware—W. G. Whiteley.
New York—Luther C. Carter, James Humphreys, Daniel E. Sickles, W. B. Maclay, Thomas J. Barr, John Cochrane, George Briggs, Horace F. Clark, John B. Haskin, Chas. H. Van Wyck, William S. Kenyon, Charles L. Beale, Abm. B. Olin, John H. Reynolds, Jas. B. McKean, G. W. Palmer, Francis E. Spinner, Clark B. Cochrane, James H. Graham, Richard Franchot, Roscoe Conkling, R. H. Duell, M. Lindley Lee, Charles B. Hoard, Chas. B. Sedgwick, M. Butterfield, Emory B. Pottle, Alfred Wells, William Irvine, Alfred Ely, Augustus Frank, Edwin R. Reynolds, Elbridge G. Spaulding, Reuben E. Fenton.
New Jersey—John T. Nixon, John L. N. Stratton, Garnett B. Adrain, Jetur R. Riggs, Wm. Pennington (Speaker).
Pennsylvania—Thomas B. Florence, E. Joy Morris, John P. Verree, William Millward, John Wood, John Hickman, Henry C. Longnecker, Jacob K. McKenty, Thaddeus Stevens, John W. Killinger, James H. Campbell, George W. Scranton, William H. Dimmick, Galusha A. Grow, James T. Hale, Benjamin F. Junkin, Edward McPherson, Samuel S. Blair, John Covode, William Montgomery, James K. Moorhead, Robert McKnight, William Stewart, Chapin Hall, Elijah Babbitt.
Maryland—Jas. A. Stewart, J. M. Harris, H. W. Davis, J. M. Kunkel, G. W. Hughes.
Virginia—John S. Millson, Muscoe R. H. Garnett, Daniel C. De Jarnette, Roger A. Pryor, Thomas S. Bocock, William Smith, Alex. R. Boteler, John T. Harris, Albert G. Jenkins, Shelton F. Leake, Henry A. Edmundson, Elbert S. Martin, Sherrard Clemens.

*Resigned and succeeded January [illegible], by Hon. Stephen Coburn.

South Carolina—John McQueen, Wm. Porcher Miles, Lawrence M. Keitt, Milledge L. Bonham, John D. Ashmore, Wm. W. Boyce.

North Carolina—W. N. H. Smith, Thos. Ruffin, W. Winslow, L. O'B. Branch, John A. Gilmer, Jas. M. Leach, Burton Craige, Z. B. Vance.

Georgia—Peter E. Love, M. J. Crawford, Thos. Hardeman, Jr., L. J. Gartrell, J. W. H. Underwood, James Jackson, Joshua Hill, John J. Jones.

Alabama—Jas. L. Pugh, David Clopton, Sydenh. Moore, Geo. S. Houston, W. R. W. Cobb, J. A. Stallworth, J. L. M. Curry.

Mississippi—L. Q. C. Lamar, Reuben Davis, William Barksdale, O. R. Singleton, John J. McRae.

Louisiana—John E. Bouligny, Miles Taylor, T. G. Davidson, John M. Landrum.

Ohio—G. H. Pendleton, John A. Gurley, C. L. Vallandigham, William Allen, James M. Ashley, Wm. Howard, Thomas Corwin, Benj. Stanton, John Carey, C. A. Trimble, Chas. D. Martin, Saml. S. Cox, John Sherman, H. G. Blake, William Helmick, C. B. Tompkins, T. C. Theaker, S. Edgerton, Edward Wade, John Hutchins, John A. Bingham.

Kentucky—Henry C. Burnett, Green Adams, S. O. Peyton, F. M. Bristow, W. C. Anderson, Robert Mallory, Wm. E. Simms, L. T. Moore, John Y. Brown, J. W. Stevenson.

Tennessee—T. A. R. Nelson, Horace Maynard, R. B. Brabson, William B. Stokes, Robert Hatton, James H. Thomas, John V. Wright, James M. Quarles, Emerson Etheridge, Wm. T. Avery.

Indiana—Wm. E. Niblack, Wm. H. English, Wm. M'Kee Dunn, Wm. S. Holman, David Kilgore, Albert G. Porter, John G. Davis, James Wilson, Schuyler Colfax, Chas. Case, John U. Pettit.

Illinois—E. B. Washburne, J. F. Farnsworth, Owen Lovejoy, Wm. Kellogg, I. N. Morris, John A. McClernand, James C. Robinson, P. B. Fouke, John A. Logan.

Arkansas—Thomas C. Hindman, Albert Rust,

Missouri—J. R. Barrett, T. L. Anderson, John B. Clark, James Craig, L. H. Woodson, John S. Phelps, John W. Noell.

Michigan—William A. Howard, Henry Waldron, F. W. Kellogg, De W. C. Leach.

Florida—George S. Hawkins.

Texas—John H. Regan, A. J. Hamilton.

Iowa—S. R. Curtis, Wm. Vandever.

California—Charles L. Scott, John C. Burch.

Wisconsin—John F. Porter, C. C. Washburne, C. H. Larrabee.

Minnesota—Cyrus Aldrich, Wm. Windom.

Oregon—Lansing Stout.

Kansas—Martin F. Conway, (sworn Jan. 30th, 1861).

MR. LINCOLN'S VIEWS.

While the various propositions above given were under consideration, Mr. Lincoln was of course an interested observer from his home in Illinois, where he awaited the legal time for taking his seat as President. His views on the efforts at compromise were sought by the editor of the New York *Tribune*, and expressed as follows:

"'I will suffer death before I will consent or advise my friends to consent to any concession or compromise which looks like buying the privilege of taking possession of the Government to which we have a constitutional right; because, whatever I might think of the merits of the various propositions before Congress, I should regard any concession in the face of menace as the destruction of the government itself, and a consent on all hands that our system shall be brought down to a level with the existing disorganized state of affairs in Mexico. But this thing will hereafter be, as it is now, in the hands of the people; and if they desire to call a convention to remove any grievances complained of, or to give new guarantees for the permanence of vested rights, it is not mine to oppose.'"

JUDGE BLACK'S VIEWS.

Jeremiah S. Black, of Pennsylvania, was then Buchanan's Attorney General, and as his position has since been made the subject of lengthy controversy, it is pertinent to give the following copious extract from his "Opinion upon the Powers of the President," in response to an official inquiry from the Executive:—

The existing laws put and keep the Federal Government strictly on the defensive. You can use force only to repel an assault on the public property, and aid the courts in the performance of their duty. If the means given you to collect the revenue and execute the other laws be insufficient for that purpose, Congress may extend and make them more effectual to that end.

If one of the States should declare her independence, your action cannot depend upon the rightfulness of the cause upon which such declaration is based. Whether the retirement of a State from the Union be the exercise of a right reserved in the Constitution or a revolutionary movement, it is certain that you have not in either case the authority to recognize her independence or to absolve her from her Federal obligations. Congress or the other States in convention assembled must take such measures as may be necessary and proper. In such an event I see no course for you but to go straight onward in the path you have hitherto trodden, that is, execute the laws t[illegible] extent of the defensive means placed in your hands, and act generally upon the assumption that the present constitutional relations between the States and the Federal Government continue to exist until a new order of things shall be established, either by law or force.

Whether Congress has the constitutional right to make war against one or more States, and require the Executive of the Federal Government to carry it on by means of force to be drawn from the other States, is a question for Congress itself to consider. It must be admitted that no such power is expressly given; nor are there any words in the Constitution which imply it. Among the powers enumerated in article I. section 8, is that "to declare war, grant letters of marque and reprisal, and to make rules concerning captures on land and water." This certainly means nothing more than the power to commence, and carry on hostilities against the foreign enemies of the nation. Another clause in the same section gives Congress the power "to provide for calling forth the militia," and to use them within the limits of the State. But this power is so restricted by the words which immediately follow, that it can be exercised only for one of the following purposes: 1. To execute the laws of the Union; that is, to aid the Federal officers in the performance of their regular duties. 2. To suppress insurrections against the States; but this is confined by article IV. section 4, to cases in which the State herself shall apply for assistance against her own people. 3. To repel the invasion of a State by enemies who come from abroad to assail her in her own territory. All these provisions are made to protect the States, not to authorize an attack by one part of the country upon another; to preserve their peace, and not to plunge them into civil war. Our forefathers do not seem to have thought that war was calculated "to form a more perfect union, establish justice, insure domestic tranquillity, provide for the common defence, promote the general welfare, and secure the blessings of liberty to ourselves and our posterity." There was undoubtedly a strong and universal conviction among the men who framed and ratified the Constitution, that military force would not only be useless, but pernicious as a means of holding the States together.

If it be true that war cannot be declared, nor a system of general hostilities carried on by the central government against a State, then it seems to follow that an attempt to do so would be *ipso facto* an expulsion of such State from the Union. Being treated as an alien and an enemy, she would be compelled to act accordingly. And if Congress shall break up the present Union by unconstitutionally putting strife and enmity, and armed hostility, between different sections of the country, instead of the "domestic tranquillity" which the Constitution was meant to insure, will not all the States be absolved from their Federal obligations? Is any portion of the people bound to contribute their money or their blood to carry on a contest like that?

The right of the General Government to preserve itself in its whole constitutional vigor by repelling a direct and positive aggression upon its property or its officers, cannot be denied. But this is a totally different thing from an offensive war to punish the people for the political misdeeds of their State governments, or to prevent a threatened violation of the Constitution, or to enforce an acknowledgment that the Government of the United States is supreme. The States are colleagues of one another, and if some of them shall conquer the rest and hold them as subjugated provinces, it would totally destroy the whole theory upon which they are now connected.

If this view of the subject be as correct as I think it is, then the Union must totally perish at the moment when Congress shall arm one part of the people against another for any purpose beyond that of merely protecting the General Government in the exercise of its proper constitutional functions. I am, very respectfully, yours, etc.,

J. S. BLACK.

To the President of the United States.

The above expressions from Lincoln and Black well state the position of the Republican and the administration Democrats on the eve of the rebellion, and they are given for that purpose. The views of the original secessionists are given in South Carolina's declaration. Those of the conservatives of the South who hesitated and leaned toward the Union, were best expressed before the Convention of Georgia in the

SPEECH OF ALEX. H. STEPHENS.

This step (of secession) once taken can never be recalled; and all the baleful and withering consequences that must follow, will rest on the convention for all coming time. When we and our posterity shall see our lovely South desolated by the demon of war, *which this act of yours will inevitably invite and call forth*; when our green fields of waving harvest shall be trodden down by the murderous soldiery and fiery car of war sweeping over our land; our temples of justice laid in ashes; all the horrors and desolations of war upon us; *who but this Convention will be held responsible for it?* and who but him who shall have given his vote for this unwise and ill-timed measure, as I honestly think and believe, *shall be held to strict account for this suicidal act by the present generation, and probably cursed and execrated by posterity for all coming time*, for the wide and desolating ruin that will inevitably follow this act you now propose to perpetrate? Pause, I entreat you, and consider for a moment what reasons you can give that will even satisfy yourselves in calmer moments—what reason you can give to your fellow sufferers in the calamity that it will bring upon us. *What reasons can you give to the nations of the earth to justify it?* They will be the calm and deliberate judges in the case; and what cause or one overt act can you name or point, on which to rest the plea of justification? *What right has the North assailed?* What interest of the South has been invaded? What justice has been denied? and what claim founded in justice and right has been withheld? Can either of you to-day name one governmental act of wrong, deliberately and purposely done by the government of Washington, of which the South has a right to complain? I challenge the answer. While on the other hand, let me show the facts (and believe me, gentlemen, I am not here the advocate of the North; but I am here the friend, the firm friend, and lover of the South and her institutions, and for this reason I speak thus plainly and faithfully for yours, mine, and every other man's interest, the words of truth and soberness), of which I wish you to judge, and I will only state facts which are clear and undeniable, and which now stand as records authentic in the history of our country. When we of the South demanded the slave-trade, or the importation of Africans for the cultivation of our lands, did they not yield the right for twenty years? When we asked a three-fifths representation in Congress for our slaves, was it not granted? When we asked and demanded the return of any fugitive from justice, or the recovery of those persons owing labor or allegiance, was it not incorporated in the Constitution, and again ratified and strengthened by the Fugitive Slave Law of 1850? But do you reply that in many instances they have violated this compact, and have not been faithful to their engagements? As individual and local communities, they may have done so; but not by the sanction of Government; for that has always been true to Southern interests. Again, gentlemen, look at another act: when we have asked that more territory should be added, that we might spread the institution of slavery, have they not yielded to our demands in giving us Louisiana, Florida and Texas, out of which four States have been carved, and ample territory for four more to be added in due time, if you by this unwise and impolitic act do not destroy this hope, and perhaps, by it lose all, and have your last slave wrenched from you by stern military rule, as South America and Mexico were; *or by the vindictive decree of a universal emancipation, which may reasonably be expected to follow?*

But, again, gentlemen, what have we to gain by this proposed change of our relation to the General Government? We have always had the control of it, and can yet, if we remain in it, and are as united as we have been. We have had a majority of the Presidents chosen from the South; as well as the control and management of most of those chosen from the North. We have had sixty years of Southern Presidents to their twenty-four, thus controlling the Executive department. So of the Judges of the Supreme Court, we have had eighteen from the South, and but eleven from the North; although nearly four-fifths of the judicial business has arisen in the Free States, yet a majority of the Court has always been from the South. This we have required so as to guard against any interpretation of the Constitution unfavorable to us. In like manner we have been equally watchful to guard our interests in the Legislative branch of Government. In choosing the presiding Presidents (*pro tem.*) of the Senate, we have had twenty-four to their eleven. Speakers of the House we have had twenty-three, and they twelve. While the majority of the Representatives, from their greater population, have always been from the North, yet we have so generally secured the Speaker, because he, to a great extent, shapes and controls the legislation of the country. Nor have we had less control in every other department of the General Government. Attorney-Generals we have had fourteen, while the North have had but five. Foreign ministers we have had eighty-six, and they but fifty-four. While three-fourths of the business which demands diplomatic agents abroad is clearly from the Free States, from their greater commercial interest, yet we have had the principal embassies so as to secure the world-markets for our cotton, tobacco, and sugar on the best possible terms. We have had a vast majority of the higher offices of both army and navy, while a larger proportion of the soldiers and sailors were drawn from the North. Equally so of Clerks, Auditors, and Comptrollers filling the executive department, the records show for the last fifty years that of the three thousand thus employed, we have had more than two-thirds of the same, while we have but one-third of the white population of the Republic.

Again, look at another item, and one, be assured, in which we have a great and vital interest; it is that of revenue, or means of supporting Government. From official documents, we learn that a fraction over three-fourths of the revenue collected for the support of the Government has uniformly been raised from the North.

Pause now while you can, gentlemen, and contemplate carefully and candidly these important items. Look at another necessary branch of Government, and learn from stern statistical facts how matters stand in that department. I mean the mail and Post-Office privileges that we now enjoy under the General Government as it has been for years past. The expense for the transportation of the mail in the Free States was, by the report of the Postmaster-General for the year 1860 a little over $13,000,000, while the income was $19,000,000. But in the Slave States the transportation of the mail was $14,716,000, while the revenue from the same was $8,001,026, leaving a deficit of $6,704,974, to be supplied by the North for our accommodation, and without it we must have been entirely cut off from this most essential branch of Government.

Leaving out of view, for the present, the countless millions of dollars you must expend in a war with the North; with tens of thousands of your sons and brothers slain in battle, and offered up as sacrifices upon the altar of your ambition—and for what, we ask again? Is it for the overthrow of the American Government, established by our common ancestry, cemented and built up by their sweat and blood, and founded on the broad principles of *Right, Justice* and *Humanity?* And as, such, I must declare here, as I have often done before, and which has been repeated by the greatest and wisest of statesmen and patriots in this and other lands, that it is the best and freest Government—the most equal in its rights, the most just in its decisions, the most lenient in its measures, and the most aspiring in its principles to elevate the race of men, that the sun of heaven ever shone upon. Now, for you to attempt to overthrow such a government as this, under which we have lived for more than three-quarters of a century—in which we have gained our wealth, our standing as a nation, our domestic safety while the elements of peril are around us, with peace and tranquillity accompanied with unbounded prosperity and rights unassailed—is the height of *madness, folly,* and *wickedness,* to which I can neither lend my sanction nor my vote."

The seven seceding States (South Carolina, Mississippi, Georgia, Florida, Alabama, Louisiana and Texas,) as shown by data previously given, organized their Provisional Government, with Jefferson Davis, the most radical secession leader, as President; and Alex. H. Stephens, the most conservative leader, as Vice President. The reasons for these selections were obvious; the first met the views of the cotton States, the other example was needed in securing the secession of other States. The Convention adopted a constitution, the substance of which is given elsewhere in this work. Stephens delivered a speech at Savannah, March 21st, 1861, in explanation and vindication of this instrument, which says all that need be said about it:

"The new Constitution has put at rest forever all the agitating questions relating to our peculiar institutions—African slavery as it exists among us—the proper status of the negro in our form of civilization. *This was the immediate cause of the late rupture and present revolution. Jefferson, in his forecast, had anticipated this as the 'rock upon which the old Union would split.'* He was right. What was conjecture with him, is now a realized fact. But whether he fully comprehended the great truth upon which that rock stood and stands, may be doubted. The prevailing ideas entertained by him and most of the leading statesmen at the time of the formation of the old Constitution, were that the enslavement of the African was in violation of the laws of nature: that it was wrong in principle, socially, morally, and politically. It was an evil they knew not well how to deal with, but the general opinion of the men of that day was, that somehow or other, in the order of Providence, the institution would be evanescent and pass away. This idea, though not incorporated in the Constitution, was the prevailing idea at the time. The Constitution, it is true, secured every essential guarantee to the institution while it should last, and hence no argument can be justly used against the constitutional guarantees thus secured, because of the common sentiment of the day. Those ideas, however, were fundamentally wrong. They rested upon the assumption of the equality of races. This was an error. It was a sandy foundation, and the idea of a government built upon it; when the 'storm came and the wind blew, it fell.'

"Our new Government is founded upon exactly the opposite idea; its foundations are laid, its corner-stone rests upon the great truth that the negro is not equal to the white man. That slavery—subordination to the superior race, is his natural and normal condition. This, our new Government, is the first, in the history of the world, based upon this great physical and moral truth. This truth has been slow in the process of its development, like all other truths in the various departments of science. It has been so even amongst us. Many who hear me, perhaps, can recollect well, that this truth was not generally admitted, even within their day. The errors of the past generation still clung to many as late as twenty years ago. Those at the North who still cling to these errors, with a zeal above knowledged, we justly denominate fanatics. * * *

"In the conflict thus far, success has been, on our side, complete throughout the length and breadth of the Confederate States. It is upon this, as I have stated, our actual fabric is firmly planted; and I cannot permit myself to doubt the ultimate success of a full recognition of this principle throughout the civilized and enlightened world.

"As I have stated, the truth of this principle may be slow in development, as all truths are, and ever have been, in the various branches of science. It was so with the principles announced by Galileo—it was so with Adam Smith and his principles of political economy—it was so with Harvey and his theory of the circulation of the blood. It is stated that not a single one of the medical profession, living at the time of the announcement of the truths made by him, admitted them. Now they are universally acknowledged. May we not, therefore, look with confidence to the ultimate universal acknowledgment of the truths upon which our system rests. It is the first government ever instituted upon principles of strict conformity to nature, and the ordination of Providence, in furnishing the materials of human society. Many governments have been founded upon the principle of certain classes; but the classes thus enslaved, were of the same race, and in violation of the laws of nature. Our system commits no such violation of nature's laws. The negro, by nature, or by the curse against Canaan, is fitted for that condition which he occupies in our system. The architect, in the construction of buildings, lays the foundation with the proper materials, the granite; then comes the brick or the marble. The substratum of our society is made of the material fitted by nature for it, and by experience we know that it is best, not only for the superior, but for the inferior race that it should be so. It is, indeed, in conformity with the ordinance of the Creator. It is not for us to inquire into the wisdom of His ordinances, or to question them. For His own purposes He has made one race to differ from another, as He has made 'one star to differ from another star in glory.'

"The great objects of humanity are best attained when conformed to His laws and decrees, in the formation of governments, as well as in all things else. Our Confederacy is founded upon principles in strict conformity with these laws. This stone which was first rejected by the first builders 'is become the chief stone of the corner' in our new edifice.

"The progress of disintegration in the old Union may be expected to go on with almost absolute certainty. We are now the nucleus of a growing power, which, if we are true to ourselves, our destiny, and high mission, will become the controlling power on this continent. To what extent accessions will go on in the process of time, or where it will end, the future will determine."

It was determined by the secession of eleven States in all, the Border States except Missouri, remaining in the Union, and West Virginia dividing from old Virginia for the purpose of keeping her place in the Union.

The leaders of the Confederacy relied to a great extent upon the fact that President Buchanan, in his several messages and replies to commissioners, and in the explanation of the law by his Attorney-General, had tied his own hands against any attempt to reinforce the garrisons in the Southern forts, and they acted upon this faith and made preparations for their capture. The refusal of the administration to reinforce Fort Moultrie caused the resignation of General Cass, and by this time the Cabinet was far from harmonious. As early as the 10th of December, Howell Cobb resigned as Secretary of the Treasury, because of his "duty to Georgia;" January 26th, John B. Floyd resigned because Buchanan would not withdraw the troops from Southern forts; and before that, Attorney General Black, without publicly expressing his views, also resigned. Mr. Buchanan saw the wreck around him, and his administration closed in profound regret on the part of many of his northern friends, and, doubtless, on his own part. His early policy, and indeed up to the close of 1860, must have been unsatisfactory even to himself, for he supplied the vacancies in his cabinet by devoted Unionists—by Philip F. Thomas of Maryland, Gen'l Dix of New York, Joseph Holt of Kentucky, and Edwin M. Stanton of Pennsylvania—men who held in their hands the key to nearly every situation, and who did much to protect and restore the Union of the States. In the eyes of the North, the very last acts of Buchanan were the best.

With the close of Buchanan's administration all eyes turned to Lincoln, and fears were entertained that the date fixed by law for the counting of the electoral vote—February 15th, 1861—would inaugurate violence and bloodshed at the seat of government. It passed, however, peaceably. Both Houses met at 12 high noon in the hall of the House, Vice-President Breckinridge and Speaker Pennington, both democrats, sitting side by side, and the count was made without serious challenge or question.

On the 11th of February Mr. Lincoln

left his home for Washington, intending to perform the journey in easy stages. On parting with his friends at Springfield, he said:

"*My Friends:* No one, in my position, can realize the sadness I feel at this parting. To this people I owe all that I am. Here I have lived more than a quarter of a century. Here my children were born, and here one of them lies buried. I know not how soon I shall see you again. I go to assume a task more difficult than that which has devolved upon any other man since the days of Washington. He never would have succeeded except for the aid of Divine Providence, upon which he at all times relied. I feel that I cannot succeed without the same Divine blessing which sustained him; and on the same Almighty Being I place my reliance for support. And I hope you, my friends, will all pray that I might receive that Divine assistance, without which I cannot succeed, but with which success is certain. Again, I bid you all an affectionate farewell."

Lincoln passed through Indiana, Ohio, New York, New Jersey and Pennsylvania on his way to the Capitol. Because of threats made that he should not reach the Capitol alive, some friends in Illinois employed a detective to visit Washington and Baltimore in advance of his arrival, and he it was who discovered a conspiracy in Baltimore to mob and assassinate him. He therefore passed through Baltimore in the night, two days earlier than was anticipated, and reached Washington in safety. On the 22d of February he spoke at Independence Hall and said:

"All the political sentiments I entertain have been drawn, so far as I have been able to draw them, from the sentiments which originated in, and were given to the world from, this hall. I never had a feeling, politically, that did not spring from the sentiments embodied in the Declaration of Independence.

* * * * * * * *

"It was not the mere matter of the separation of the Colonies from the motherland, but that *sentiment* in the Declaration of Independence, which gave liberty, not alone to the people of this country, but, I hope, to the world for all future time. It was that which gave promise that, in due time, the weight would be lifted from the shoulders of men. This is the sentiment embodied in the Declaration of Independence. Now, my friends, can this country be saved upon that basis? If it can, I will consider myself one of the happiest men in the world, if I can help to save it. If it cannot be saved upon that principle, it will be truly awful! But if this country cannot be saved without giving up the principle, I was about to say, 'I would rather be assassinated on the spot than surrender it.' * * * * * I have said nothing but what I am willing to live by, and if it be the pleasure of Almighty God, to die by!"

Lincoln's First Administration.

Such was the feeling of insecurity that the President-elect was followed to Washington by many watchful friends, while Gen'l Scott, Col. Sumner, Major Hunter and the members of Buchanan's Cabinet quickly made such arrangements as secured his safety. Prior to his inauguration he took every opportunity to quell the still rising political excitement by assuring the Southern people of his kindly feelings, and on the 27th of February,* "when waited upon by the Mayor and Common Council of Washington, he assured them, and through them the South, that he had no disposition to treat them in any other way than as neighbors, and that he had no disposition to withhold from them any constitutional right. He assured the people that they would have all of their rights under the Constitution—'not grudgingly, but freely and fairly.'"

He was peacefully inaugurated on the 4th of March, and yet Washington was crowded as never before by excited multitudes. The writer himself witnessed the military arrangements of Gen'l Scott for preserving the peace, and with armed cavalry lining every curb stone on the line of march, it would have been difficult indeed to start or continue a riot, though it was apparent that many in the throng were ready to do it if occasion offered.

The inaugural ceremonies were more than usually impressive. On the eastern front of the capitol, surrounded by such of the members of the Senate and House who had not resigned their seats and entered the Confederacy, the Diplomatic Corps, the Judges of the Supreme Court, headed by Chief Justice Taney, the author of the Dred Scott decision; the higher officers of Army and Navy, while close by the side of the new President stood the retiring one—James Buchanan—tall, dignified, reserved, and to the eye of the close observer apparently deeply grieved at the part his party and position had compelled him to play in a National drama which was now reaching still another crisis. Near by, too, stood Douglas (holding Lincoln's hat) more gloomy than was his wont, but determined as he had ever been. Next to the two Presidents he was most observed.

If the country could then have been pacified, Lincoln's inaugural was well calculated to do it. That it exercised a wholesome influence in behalf of the Union,

* From the "History of Abraham Lincoln and the Overthrow of Slavery," by Hon. Isaac N. Arnold.

and especially in the border States, soon became apparent. Indeed, its sentiments seemed for weeks to check the wild spirit of secession in the cotton States, and it took all the efforts of their most fiery orators to rekindle the flame which seemed to have been at its highest when Major Anderson was compelled to evacuate Fort Moultrie.

It is but proper in this connection, to make a few quotations from the inaugural address, for Lincoln then, as he did during the remainder of his life, better reflected the more popular Republican sentiment than any other leader. The very first thought was upon the theme uppermost in the minds of all. We quote:

"Apprehension seems to exist among the people of the Southern States that by the accession of a Republican Administration their property and their peace and personal security are to be endangered. There has never been any reasonable cause for such apprehension. Indeed, the most ample evidence to the contrary has all the while existed and been open to their inspection. It is found in nearly all the published speeches of him who now addresses you. I do but quote from one of those speeches when I declare that 'I have no purpose directly or indirectly, to interfere with the institution of slavery in the States where it exists. I believe I have no lawful right to do so, and I have no inclination to do so.' Those who nominated and elected me did so with full knowledge that I had made this and many similar declarations, and had never recanted them. And more than this, they placed in the platform for my acceptance, and as a law to themselves and to me, the clear and emphatic resolution which I now read:

'*Resolved*, That the maintenance inviolate of the rights of the States, and especially the right of each State to order and control its own domestic institutions according to its own judgment exclusively, is essential to the balance of power on which the perfection and endurance of our political fabric depend, and we denounce the lawless invasion by armed force of the soil of any State or Territory, no matter under what pretext, as among the gravest of crimes.'

I now reiterate these sentiments; and in doing so, I only press upon the public attention the most conclusive evidence of which the case is susceptible, that the property, peace, and security of no section are to be in anywise endangered by the now incoming Administration. I add, too, that all the protection which, consistently with the Constitution and the laws, can be given, will be cheerfully given to all the States when lawfully demanded, for whatever cause—as cheerfully to one section as to another."

After conveying this peaceful assurance, he argued the question in his own way, and in a way matchless for its homely force:

"Physically speaking, we cannot separate. We cannot remove our respective sections from each other, nor build an impassable wall between them. A husband and wife may be divorced, and go out of the presence and beyond the reach of each other; but the different parts of our country cannot do this. They cannot but remain face to face; and intercourse, either amicable or hostile, must continue between them. Is it possible, then, to make that intercourse more advantageous or more satisfactory *after* separation than *before*? Can aliens make treaties easier than friends can make laws? Can treaties be more faithfully enforced between aliens than laws can among friends? Suppose you go to war, you cannot fight always; and when after much loss on both sides, and no gain on either, you cease fighting, the identical old questions, as to terms of intercourse, are again upon you.

"This country, with its institutions, belongs to the people who inhabit it. Whenever they shall grow weary of the existing Government they can exercise their *constitutional* right of amending it, or their *revolutionary* right to dismember or overthrow it. I cannot be ignorant of the fact that many worthy and patriotic citizens are desirous of having the National Constitution amended. While I make no recommendation of amendments, I fully recognize the rightful authority of the people over the whole subject, to be exercised in either of the modes prescribed in the instrument itself; and I should under existing circumstances, favor rather than oppose a fair opportunity being afforded the people to act upon it. I will venture to add that to me the convention mode seems preferable, in that it allows amendments to originate with the people themselves, instead of only permitting them to take or reject propositions originated by others, not especially chosen for the purpose, and which might not be precisely such as they would wish to either accept or refuse. I understand a proposed amendment to the Constitution—which amendment, however, I have not seen—has passed Congress, to the effect that the Federal Government shall never interfere with the domestic institutions of the States, including that of persons held to service. To avoid misconstruction of what I have said, I depart from my purpose not to speak of particular amendments so far as to say that, holding such a provision now to be implied constitutional law, I have no objection to its being made express and irrevocable.

"The Chief Magistrate derives all his authority from the people, and they have conferred none upon him to fix terms for the separation of the States. The people themselves can do this also if they choose; but the Executive, as such, has nothing to do with it. His duty is to administer the present Government, as it came to his hands, and to transmit it, unimpaired by him, to his successor. * * *

"In *your* hands, my dissatisfied fellow-countrymen, and not in *mine*, is the momentous issue of civil war. The Government will not assail *you*. You can have no conflict without being yourselves the aggressors. *You* have no oath registered in heaven to destroy the Government, while I shall have the most solemn one to 'preserve, protect and defend it.'

"I am loth to close. We are not enemies but friends. We must not be enemies. Though passion may have strained, it must not break our bonds of affection. The mystic chords of memory, stretching from every battle-field and patriot grave to every living heart and hearth-stone, all over this broad land, will yet swell the chorus of the union, when again touched, as surely they will be, by the better angels of our nature."

Lincoln appointed a Cabinet in thorough accord with his own views, and well suited to whatever shades of difference there were in the Republican party. Wm. H. Seward, Secretary of State, and Salmon P. Chase represented the more advanced anti-slavery element; General Simon Cameron, Secretary of War, from the first saw only a prolonged war in which superior Northern resources and appliances would surely win, while Seward expressed the view that "all troubles would be over in three months;" Gideon Welles, Secretary of the Navy; Caleb B. Smith of the Interior; Edward Bates, Attorney General, and Montgomery Blair, Postmaster General, represented the more conservative Republican view—the two last named being well adapted to retaining the National hold on the Border States.

Political events now rapidly succeeded each other. As early as March 11, John Forsyth of Alabama and Martin J. Crawford of Georgia, submitted to the Secretary of State a proposition for an unofficial interview. Mr. Seward the next day, from "purely public considerations," declined. On the 13th the same gentlemen sent a sealed communication, saying they had been duly accredited by the Confederate government as Commissioners, to negotiate for a speedy adjustment of all questions growing out of the political separation of seven States, which had formed a government of their own, etc. They closed this remarkable document by requesting the Secretary of State to appoint as early a day as possible in order that they may present to the President of the United States the credentials which they bear, and the objects of the mission with which they are charged.

Mr. Seward's reply in substance, said that his "official duties were confined, subject to the direction of the President, to the conducting of the foreign relations of the country, and do not at all embrace domestic questions or questions arising between the several States and the Federal Government, is unable to comply with the request of Messrs. Forsyth and Crawford, to appoint a day on which they may present the evidences of their authority and the object of their visit to the President of the United States. On the contrary, he is obliged to state to Messrs. Forsyth and Crawford that he has no authority, nor is he at liberty to recognize them as diplomatic agents, or hold correspondence or other communication with them."

An extended correspondence followed, but the administration in all similar cases, refused to recognize the Confederacy as a government in any way. On the 13th of April the President granted an interview to Wm. Ballard Preston, Alex. H. Stuart, and George W. Randolph, who had been sent by the Convention of Virginia, then in session, under a resolution recited in the President's reply, the text of which is herewith given:—

GENTLEMEN: As a committee of the Virginia Convention, now in session, you present me a preamble and resolution in these words:

"Whereas, in the opinion of this Convention, the uncertainty which prevails in the public mind as to the policy which the Federal Executive intends to pursue toward the seceded States is extremely injurious to the industrial and commercial interests of the country, tends to keep up an excitement which is unfavorable to the adjustment of pending difficulties, and threatens a disturbance of the public peace: Therefore,

"*Resolved*, That a committee of three delegates be appointed to wait on the President of the United States, present to him this preamble and resolution, and respectfully ask him to communicate to this Convention the policy which the Federal Executive intends to pursue in regard to the Confederate States."

"In answer I have to say, that, having at the beginning of my official term expressed my intended policy as plainly as I was able, it is with deep regret and some mortification I now learn that there is great and injurious uncertainty in the public mind as to what that policy is, and what course I intend to pursue.

"Not having as yet seen occasion to change, it is now my purpose to pursue the course marked out in the inaugural address. I commend a careful consideration of the whole document as the best expression I can give of my purposes. As I then and therein said, I now repeat:

"The power confided to me will be used to hold, occupy, and possess the property and places belonging to the Government, and to collect the duties and imposts; but beyond what is necessary for these objects there will be no invasion, no using of force against or among the people anywhere."

"By the words 'property and places belonging to the Government' I chiefly allude to the military posts and property which were in the possession of the Government when it came into my hands.

"But if, as now appears to be true, in pursuit of a purpose to drive the United States authority from these places, an unprovoked assault has been made upon Fort Sumter, I shall hold myself at liberty to repossess, if I can, like places which had been seized before the Government was devolved upon me. And, in any event, I shall, to the best of my ability, repel force by force.

"In case it proves true that Fort Sumter has been assaulted, as is reported, I shall perhaps cause the United States mails to be withdrawn from all the States which claim to have seceded, believing that the commencement of actual war against the Government justifies and possibly demands it."

"I scarcely need to say that I consider the military posts and property situated within the States which claim to have seceded as yet belonging to the Government of the United States as much as they did before the supposed secession.

"Whatever else I may do for the purpose, I shall not attempt to collect the duties and imposts by any armed invasion of any part of the country—not meaning by this, however, that I may not land a force deemed necessary to relieve a fort upon the border of the country.

"From the fact that I have quoted a part of the inaugural address, it must not inferred that I repudiate any other part, the whole of which I reaffirm, except so far as what I now say of the mails may be regarded as a modification."

We have given the above as not only fair but interesting samples of the semi-official and official transactions and correspondence of the time. To give more could not add to the interest of what is but a description of the political situation.

The Border states and some others were "halting between two opinions." North Carolina at first voted down a proposition to secede by 46,671 for, to 47,333 against, but the secessionists called another convention in May, the work of which the people ratified, the minority, however, being very large.

Before Lincoln had entered office most of the Southern forts, arsenals, docks, custom houses, etc., had been seized, and now that preparations were being made for active warfare by the Confederacy, many officers of the army and navy resigned or deserted, and joined it. The most notable were General Robert E. Lee, who for a time hesitated as to his "duty," and General David E. Twiggs, the second officer in rank in the United States Army, but who had purposely been placed by Secretary Floyd in command of the Department of Texas to facilitate his joining the Confederacy, which he intended to do from the beginning. All officers were permitted to go, the administration not seeking to restrain any, under the belief that until some open act of war was committed it ought to remain on the defensive. This was wise political policy, for it did more than all else to hold the Border States, the position of which Douglas understood fully as well as any statesman of that hour. It is remarked of Douglas (in Arnold's "*History of Abraham Lincoln*") that as early as January 1, 1861, he said to General Charles Stewart, of New York, who had made a New Year's call at his residence in Washington, and inquired, "What will be the result of the efforts of Jefferson Davis, and his associates, to divide the Union?" "Rising, and looking," says my informant, "like one inspired, Douglas replied, 'The cotton States are making an effort to draw in the border States to their schemes of secession, and I am but too fearful they will succeed. If they do succeed, there will be the most terrible civil war the world has ever seen, lasting for years.' Pausing a moment, he exclaimed, 'Virginia will become a charnel house, but the end will be the triumph of the Union cause. One of their first efforts will be to take possession of this Capitol to give them prestige abroad, but they will never succeed in taking it—the North will rise *en masse* to defend it;—but Washington will become a city of hospitals—the churches will be used for the sick and wounded—even this house (Minnesota block, afterwards, and during the war, the Douglas Hospital) may be devoted to that purpose before the end of the war.' The friend to whom this was said inquired, 'What justification for all this?' Douglas replied, 'There is NO justification, nor any pretense of any—if they remain in the Union, I will go as far as the Constitution will permit, to maintain their just rights, and I do not doubt a majority of Congress would do the same. But,' said he, again rising on his feet, and extending his arm, 'if the Southern States attempt to secede from this Union, without further cause, I am in favor of their having just so many slaves, and just so much slave territory, as they can hold at the point of the bayonet, and NO MORE.'"

In the border states of Maryland, Virginia, North Carolina, Tennessee and Missouri there were sharp political contests between the friends of secession and of the Union. Ultimately the Unionists triumphed in Maryland, Kentucky and Missouri—in the latter state by the active aid of U. S. troops—in Maryland and Kentucky by military orders to arrest any members of the Legislature conspiring to take their states out. In Tennessee, the Union men, under the lead of Andrew Johnson, Governor ("Parson") Brownlow, Horace Maynard and others, who made a most gallant fight to keep the state in, and they had the sympathy of the majority of the people of East Tennessee. The Secessionists took Virginia out April 17th, and North Carolina May 20th. The leading Southerners encouraged the timid and hesitating by saying the North would not make war; that the political divisions would be too great there, and they were supported in this view by the speeches and letters of leaders like Clement L. Vallandigham. On the other hand they roused the excitable by warlike preparations, and, as we have stated, to prevent reconsideration on the part of those who had seceded, resolved to fire upon Sumter. Beauregard acted under direct instructions from the government at Montgomery when he notified Major Anderson on the 11th of April to surrender Fort Sumter. Anderson replied that he would evacuate on the 15th, but the original summons called for surrender by the 12th, and they opened their fire in advance of the time fixed for evacuation—a fact which clearly established the purpose to bring about a collision. It was this aggressive spirit which aroused and united the North, and made extensive political division therein impossible.

The Southern leaders, ever anxious for the active aid of the Border States, soon saw that they could only acquire it through higher sectional excitement than any yet cultivated, and they acted accordingly. Roger A. Pryor, in a speech at Richmond April 10th, gave expression to this thought, when he said in response to a serenade:—

"Gentlemen, I thank you, especially that you have at last annihilated this accursed Union, [applause,] reeking with corruption, and insolent with excess of tyranny. Thank God, it is at last blasted and riven by the lightning wrath of an outraged and indignant people. [Loud applause.] Not only is it gone, but gone forever. [Cries of 'You're right,' and applause.] In the expressive language of Scripture, it is water spilt upon the ground, which cannot be gathered up [Applause.] Like Lucifer, son of the morning, it has fallen, never to rise again. [Continued applause.] *For my part, gentlemen, if Abraham Lincoln and Hannibal Hamlin tomorrow were to abdicate their offices and were to give me a blank sheet of paper to write the conditions of reannexation to the defunct Union, I would scornfully spurn the overture.* * * * * I invoke you, and I make it in some sort a personal appeal—personal so far as it tends to our assistance in Virginia—I do invoke you, in your demonstrations of popular opinion, in your exhibitions of official intent, to give no countenance to this idea of reconstruction. [Many voices, emphatically, 'Never,' and applause.] In Virginia they all say, if reduced to the dread dilemma of this memorable alternative, they will espouse the cause of the South as against the interest of the Northern Confederacy, but they whisper of reconstruction, and they say Virginia must abide in the Union, with the idea of reconstructing the Union which you have annihilated. *I pray you, gentlemen, rob them of that idea.* Proclaim to the world that upon no condition, and under no circumstance, will South Carolina ever again enter into political association with the Abolitionists of New England. [Cries of 'Never," and applause.]

"Do not distrust Virginia. As sure as to-morrow's sun will rise upon us, just so sure will Virginia be a member of this Southern Confederation. [Applause.] *And I will tell you, gentlemen, what will put her in the Southern Confederation in less than an hour by Shrewsbury clock*—STRIKE A BLOW! [Tremendous applause.] *The very moment that blood is shed, old Virginia will make common cause with her sisters of the South.* [Applause.] It is impossible she should do otherwise."

Warlike efforts were likewise used to keep some of the states firmly to their purpose. Hon. Jeremiah Clemens, formerly United States Senator from Alabama, and a member of the Alabama Seceding Convention who resisted the movement until adopted by the body, at an adjourned Reconstruction meeting held at Huntsville, Ala., March 13, 1864, made this significant statement:—

Mr. Clemens, in adjourning the meeting, said he would tell the Alabamians how their state was got out of the Union. "In 1861," said Mr. C., "shortly after the Confederate Government was put in operation, I was in the city of Montgomery. One day I stepped into the office of the Secretary of War, General Walker, and found there, engaged in a very excited discussion, Mr. Jefferson Davis, Mr. Memminger, Mr. Benjamin, Mr. Gilchrist, a member of our Legislature from Loundes county, and a number of other prominent gentlemen. They were discussing the propriety of immediately opening fire on Fort Sumter, to which General Walker, the Secretary of War, appeared to be opposed. Mr. Gilchrist said to him, 'Sir, unless you sprinkle blood in the face of the people of Alabama they will be back in the old Union in less than ten days!' The next day General Beauregard opened his batteries on Sumter, and Alabama was saved to the Confederacy."

When the news flashed along the wires that Sumter had been fired upon, Lincoln immediately used his war powers and issued a call for 75,000 troops. All of the northern governors responded with promptness and enthusiasm; but this was not true of the governors of the southern states which at that time had not seceded, and the Border States.

We take from McPherson's admirable condensation, the evasive or hostile replies of the Governors referred to, and follow it with his statement of the military calls and legislation of both governments, but for the purposes of this work omit details which are too extended.

REPLIES OF SOUTHERN STATE GOVERNORS TO LINCOLN'S CALL FOR 75,000 TROOPS.

Governor BURTON, of Delaware, issued a proclamation, April 26, recommending the formation of volunteer companies for the protection of the lives and property of the people of Delaware against violence of any sort to which they may be exposed, the companies not being subject to be ordered by the Executive into the United States service, the law not vesting him with such authority, but having the option of offering their services to the General Government for the defence of its capital and the support of the Constitution and laws of the country.

Governor HICKS, of Maryland, May 14, issued a proclamation for the troops, stating that the four regiments would be detailed to serve within the limits of Maryland or for the defence of the capital of the United States.

Governor LETCHER, of Virginia, replied that "The militia of Virginia will not be furnished to the powers of Washington for any such use or purpose as they have in view. Your object is to subjugate the southern States, and a requisition made upon me for such an object—an object, in my judgment, not within the purview of the Constitution or the act of 1795—will not be complied with. You have chosen to inaugurate civil war, and having done so we will meet it in a spirit as determined as the Administration has exhibited toward the South."

Governor ELLIS, of North Carolina, replied April 15:

"Your dispatch is received, and if genuine—which its extraordinary character leads me to doubt—I have to say in reply that I regard the levy of troops made by the Administration, for the purpose of subjugating the States of the South, as in violation of the Constitution and a usurpation of power. I can be no party to this wicked violation of the laws of the country, and to this war upon the liberties of a free people. You can get no troops from North Carolina. I will reply more in detail when your call is received by mail."

Governor MAGOFFIN, of Kentucky, replied, April 15:

"Your dispatch is received. In answer I say emphatically, Kentucky will furnish no troops for the wicked purpose of subduing her sister Southern States."

Governor HARRIS, of Tennessee, replied, April 18:

"Tennessee will not furnish a single man for coercion, but fifty thousand, if necessary, for the defence of our rights or those of our southern brethren."

Governor JACKSON, of Missouri, replied:

"Your requisition is illegal, unconstitutional, revolutionary, inhuman, diabolical, and cannot be complied with."

Governor RECTOR, of Arkansas, replied, April 22:

"None will be furnished. The demand is only adding insult to injury."

ALL OTHER CALLS FOR TROOPS.

May 3, 1861—The President called for thirty-nine volunteer regiments of infantry and one regiment of cavalry, with a minimum aggregate of 34,506 officers and enlisted men, and a maximum of 42,034; and for the enlistment of 18,000 seamen.

May 3, 1861—The President directed an increase of the regular army by eight regiments of infantry, one of cavalry, and one of artillery—minimum aggregate, 18,054; maximum, 22,714.

August 6—Congress legalized this increase, and all the acts, orders, and proclamations respecting the Army and Navy.

July 22 and 25, 1861—Congress authorized the enlistment of 500,000 volunteers.

September 17, 1861—Commanding officer at Hatteras Inlet, N. C., authorized to enlist a regiment of loyal North Carolinians.

November 7, 1861—The Governor of Missouri was authorized to raise a force of State militia for State defence.

December 3, 1861—The Secretary of War directed that no more regiments, batteries, or independent companies be raised by the Governors of States, except upon the special requisition of the War Department.

July 2, 1862—The President called for three hundred thousand volunteers.

Under the act of July 17, 1862.

August 4, 1862—The President ordered a draft of three hundred thousand militia, for nine months unless sooner discharged; and directed that if any State shall not, by the 15th of August, furnish its quota of the additional 300,000 authorized by law, the deficiency of volunteers in that State will also be made up by special draft from the militia. Wednesday, September 3, was subsequently fixed for the draft.

May 8, 1863—Proclamation issued, defining the relations of aliens to the conscription act, holding all aliens who have declared on oath their intention to become citizens and may be in the country within sixty-five days from date, and all who have declared their intention to become citizens and have voted.

June 15, 1863 One hundred thousand men, for six months, called to repel the invasion of Maryland, West Virginia, Ohio, and Pennsylvania.

October 17, 1863—A proclamation was issued for 300,000 volunteers, to serve for three years or the war, not, however, exceeding three years, to fill the places of those whose terms expire "during the coming year," these being in addition to the men raised by the present draft. In States in default under this call, January 5, 1864, a draft shall be made on that day.

February 1, 1864—Draft for 500,000 men for three years or during the war, ordered for March 10, 1864.

March 14, 1864—Draft for 200,000 additional for the army, navy and marine corps, ordered for April 15, 1864, to supply the force required for the navy and to provide an adequate reserve force for all contingencies.

April 23, 1864—85,000 one hundred day men accepted, tendered by the Governors of Ohio, Indiana, Illinois, Iowa, and Wisconsin; 30,000, 20,000, 20,000, 10,000 and 5,000 being tendered respectively.

UNION MILITARY LEGISLATION.

1861, July 22—The President was authorized to accept the services of volunteers, not exceeding five hundred thousand, for a period not exceeding three years. July 27, this authority was duplicated.

1861, July 27—Nine regiments of infantry, one of cavalry, and one of artillery, added to the regular army.

August 5—Passed bill approving and legalizing the orders of the President respecting the army and navy, issued from 4th of March to that date.

1862, July 17—Authorized the President, when calling forth the militia of the States, to specify the period of such service, not exceeding nine months; and if by reason of defects in existing laws or in the execution of them, it shall be found necessary to provide for enrolling the militia, the President was authorized to make all necessary regulations, the enrollment to include all able bodied male citizens between eighteen and forty-five, and to be apportioned according to representative population. He was authorized, in addition to the volunteers now authorized, to accept 100,000 infantry, for nine months; also, for twelve months, to fill up old regiments, as many as may be presented for the purpose.

1863, February 7—Authorized the Governor of Kentucky, by the consent and under the direction of the President, to raise twenty thousand volunteers, for twelve months, for service within the limits of the State, for repelling invasion, suppressing insurrection, and guarding and protecting the public property—two regiments to be mounted riflemen. With the consent of the President, these troops may be attached to, and become a part of, the body of three years' volunteers.

1863, March 3—The conscription act passed. It included as a part of the national forces, all able bodied male citizens of the United States, and persons of foreign birth who shall have declared on oath their intention to become citizens under and in pursuance of the laws thereof, between the ages of twenty-one and forty-five years, except such as are rejected as physically or mentally unfit for the service; also, the Vice President, the judges of the various courts of the United States, the heads of the various executive departments of the Government, and the Governors of the several States; also, the only son liable to military service, of a widow dependent upon his labor for support; also, the only son of aged or infirm parent or parents, dependent upon his labor for support; also, where there are two or more sons of aged or infirm parents, subject to draft, the father, or if he be dead, the mother, may elect which son shall be exempt; also, the only brother of children not twelve years old, having neither father nor mother, dependent upon his labor for support; also, the father of motherless children under twelve years of age, dependent upon his labor for support; also, where there are a father and sons in the same family and household, and two of them are in military service of the United States as non-commissioned officers, musicians, or privates, the residue of such family; provided that no person who has been convicted of any felony shall be enrolled or permitted to serve in said forces. It divided the forces into two classes: 1st, those between twenty and thirty-five and all unmarried persons above thirty-five and under forty-five; 2d, all others liable to military duty. It divided the country into districts, in each of which an enrollment board was established. The persons enrolled were made subject to be called into the military service for two years from July 1, 1863, and continue in service for three years. A drafted person was allowed to furnish an acceptable substitute, or pay $300, and be discharged from further liability under that draft. Persons failing to report, to be considered deserters. All persons drafted shall be assigned by the Presid nt to military duty in such corps, regiments, or branches of the service as the exigencies of the service may require.

1864, Feb. 24—Provided for equalizing the draft by calculating the quota of each district or precinct and counting the number previously furnished by it. Any person enrolled may furnish an acceptable substitute who is not liable to draft, nor, at any time, in the military or naval service of the United States; and such person so furnishing a substitute shall be exempt from draft during the time for which such substitute shall not be liable to draft, not exceeding the time for which such substitute shall have been accepted. If such substitute is liable to draft, the name of the person furnishing him shall again be placed on the roll and shall be liable to draft in future calls, but not until the present enrollment shall be exhausted. The exemptions are limited to such as are rejected as physically or mentally unfit for the service; to persons actually in the military or naval service of the Government, and all persons who have served in the military or naval service two years during the present war and been honorably discharged therefrom.

The separate enrollment of classes is repealed and the two classes consolidated.

Members of religious denominations, who shall by oath or affirmation declare that they are conscientiously opposed to the bearing of arms, and who are prohibited from doing so by the rules and articles of faith and practice of said religious denomination, shall when drafted, be considered non-combatants, and be assigned to duty in the hospitals, or the care of freedmen, or shall pay $300 to the benefit of sick and wounded soldiers, if they give proof that their deportment has been uniformly consistent with their declaration.

No alien who has voted in county, State or Territory shall, because of alienage, be exempt from draft.

"All able-bodied male colored persons between the ages of twenty and forty-five years, resident in the United States, shall be enrolled according to the provisions of this act, and of the act to which this is an amendment, and form part of the national forces; and when a slave of a loyal master shall be drafted and mustered into the service of the United States, his master shall have a certificate thereof; and thereupon such slave shall be free, and the bounty of one hundred dollars, now payable by law for each drafted man, shall be paid to the person to whom such drafted person was owing service or labor at the time of his muster into the service of the United States. The Secretary of War shall appoint a commission in each of the slave States represented in Congress, charged to award to each loyal person to whom a colored volunteer may owe service a just compensation, not exceeding three hundred dollars, for each such colored volunteer, payable out of the fund derived from commutations, and every such colored volunteer on being mustered into the service shall be free. And in all cases where men of color have been enlisted, or have volunteered in the military service of the United States, all the provisions of this act so far as the payment of bounty and compensation are provided, shall be equally applicable, as to those who may be hereafter recruited. But men of color, drafted or enlisted, or who may volunteer into the military service, while they shall be credited on the quotas of the several States, or sub-divisions of States, wherein they are respectively drafted, enlisted, or shall volunteer, shall not be assigned as State troops, but shall be mustered into regiments or companies as United States colored troops."

1864, Feb. 29—Bill passed reviving the grade of Lieutenant General in the army, and Major General Ulysses S. Grant was appointed March 2d.

1864, June 15—All persons of color shall receive the same pay and emoluments, except bounty, as other soldiers of the regular or volunteer army from and after Jan. 1, 1864, the President to fix the bounty for those hereafter mustered, not exceeding $100.

1864, June 20—The monthly pay of privates and non-commissioned officers was fixed as follows, on and after May 1:

Sergeant majors, twenty-six dollars; quartermaster and commissary sergeants of cavalry, artillery, and infantry, twenty-two dollars; first sergeants of cavalry, artillery, and infantry, twenty-four dollars; sergeants of cavalry, artillery, and infantry, twenty dollars; sergeants of ordnance, sappers and miners, and pontoniers, thirty-four dollars; corporals of ordnance, sappers and miners, and pontoniers, twenty dollars; privates of engineers and ordnance of the first class, eighteen dollars, and of the second class, sixteen dollars; corporals of cavalry, artillery, and infantry, eighteen dollars; chief buglers of cavalry, twenty-three dollars; buglers, sixteen dollars; farriers and blacksmiths, of cavalry, and artificers of artillery, eighteen dollars; privates of cavalry, artillery and infantry, sixteen dollars; principal musicians of artillery and infantry, twenty-two dollars; leaders of brigade and regimental bands, seventy-five dollars; musicians, sixteen dollars; hospital stewards of the first class, thirty-three dollars; hospital stewards of the second class, twenty-five dollars; hospital stewards of the third class, twenty-three dollars."

July 4—This bill became a law:

Be it enacted, &c. That the President of

the United States may, at his discretion, at any time hereafter call for any number of men as volunteers for the respective terms of one, two, and three years for military service; and any such volunteer, or, in case of draft, as hereinafter provided, any substitute, shall be credited to the town, township, ward of a city, precinct, or election district, or of a county not so subdivided towards the quota of which he may have volunteered or engaged as a substitute; and every volunteer who is accepted and mustered into the service for a term of one year, unless sooner discharged, shall receive, and be paid by the United States, a bounty of one hundred dollars; and if for a term of two years, unless sooner discharged, a bounty of two hundred dollars; and if for a term of three years, unless sooner discharged, a bounty of three hundred dollars; one third of which bounty shall be paid to the soldier at the time of his being mustered into the service, one-third at the expiration of one-half of his term of service, and one-third at the expiration of his term of service. And in case of his death while in service, the residue of his bounty unpaid shall be paid to his widow, if he shall have left a widow; if not, to his children; or if there be none, to his mother, if she be a widow.

* * * * * * * *

SEC. 8. That all persons in the naval service of the United States, who have entered said service during the present rebellion, who have not been credited to the quota of any town, district, ward, or State, by reason of their being in said service and not enrolled prior to February twenty-four, eighteen hundred and sixty-four, shall be enrolled and credited to the quotas of the town, ward, district, or State, in which they respectively reside, upon satisfactory proof of their residence made to the Secretary of War.

"CONFEDERATE" MILITARY LEGISLATION.

February 28, 1861, (four days before the inauguration of Mr. Lincoln)—The "Confederate" Congress passed a bill providing—

1st. To enable the Government of the Confederate States to maintain its jurisdiction over all questions of peace and war, and to provide for the public defence, the President be, and he is hereby authorized and directed to assume control of all military operations in every State, having reference to a connection with questions between the said States, or any of them, and Powers foreign to themselves.

2d. The President was authorized to receive from the several States the arms and munitions of war which have been acquired from the United States.

3d. He was authorized to receive into Government service such forces in the service of the States, as may be tendered, in such number as he may require, for any time not less than twelve months, unless sooner discharged.

March 6, 1861—The President was authorized to employ the militia, military and naval forces of the Confederate States to repel invasion, maintain rightful possession of the territory, and secure public tranquillity and independence against threatened assault, to the extent of 100,000 men, to serve for twelve months.

May 4, 1861—One regiment of Zouaves authorized.

May 6, 1861—Letters of marque and reprisal authorized.

1861, August 8—The Congress authorized the President to accept the services of 400,000 volunteers, to serve for not less than twelve months nor more than three years after they shall be mustered into service, unless sooner discharged.

The Richmond *Enquirer* of that date announced that it was ascertained from official data, before the passage of the bill, that there were not less than 210,000 men then in the field.

August 21—Volunteers authorized for local defence and special service.

1862, January—Publishers of newspapers, or other printed matter are prohibited from giving the number, disposition, movement, or destination of the land or naval forces, or description of vessel, or battery, fortification, engine of war, or signal, unless first authorized by the President or Congress, or the Secretary of War or Navy, or commanding officer of post, district, or expedition. The penalty is a fine of $1,000 and imprisonment not over twelve months.

1862, February—The Committee on Naval Affairs were instructed to inquire into the expediency of placing at the disposal of the President five millions of dollars to build gunboats.

1862—Bill passed to "regulate the destruction of property under military necessity," referring particularly to cotton and tobacco. The authorities are authorized to destroy it to keep it from the enemy; and owners, destroying it for the same purpose, are to be indemnified upon proof of the value and the circumstances of the destruction.

1862, April 16—The first "conscription" bill became a law.

1864, February. The second conscription bill became a law.

The Richmond Sentinel of February 17, 1864, contains a synopsis of what is called the military bill, heretofore forbidden to be printed:

The first section provides that all white men residents of the Confederate States, between the ages of seventeen and fifty, shall be in the military service for the war.

The second section provides that all between eighteen and forty-five, now in service, shall be continued during the war in the same regiments, battalions, and companies to which they belong at the passage of this act, with the organization, officers, &c., provided that companies from one State organized against their consent, expressed at the time, with regrets, &c., from another State, shall have the privilege of being transferred to the same arm in a regiment from their own State, and men can be transferred to a company from their own State.

Section three gives a bounty eight months hence of $100 in rebel bonds.

Section four provides that no person shall be relieved from the operations of this act heretofore discharged for disability, *nor shall those who furnished substitutes be exempted, where no disability now exists*; but exempts religious persons who have paid an exemption tax. * * *

The tenth section provides that no person shall be exempt except the following: ministers, superintendents of deaf, dumb, and blind, or insane asylums; one editor to each newspaper, and such employees as he may swear to be indispensable; the Confederate and State public printers, and the journeymen printers necessary to perform the public printing; one apothecary to each drug store, who was and has been continuously doing business as such since October 10, 1862; physicians over 30 years of age of seven years' practice, not including dentists; presidents and teachers of colleges, academies and schools, who have not less than thirty pupils; superintendents of public hospitals established by law, and such physicians and nurses as may be indispensable for their efficient management.

One agriculturist on such farm where there is no white male adult not liable to duty employing fifteen able-bodied slaves, between sixteen and fifty years of age, upon the following conditions:

The party exempted shall give bonds to deliver to the Government in the next twelve months, 100 pounds of bacon, or its equivalent in salt pork, at Government selection, and 100 pounds of beef for each such able-bodied slave employed on said farm at commissioner's rates.

In certain cases this may be commuted in grain or other provisions.

The person shall further bind himself to sell all surplus provisions now on hand, or which he may raise, to the Government, or the families of soldiers, at commissioner's rates, the person to be allowed a credit of 25 per cent. on any amount he may deliver in three months from the passage of this act; Provided that no enrollment since Feb. 1, 1864, shall deprive the person enrolled from the benefit of this exemption.

In addition to the above, the Secretary of War is authorized to make such details as the public security requires.

The vote in the House of Representatives was—yeas, 41; nays, 31.

GUERRILLAS.

1862, April 21—The President was authorized to commission such officers as he may deem proper, with authority to form bands of partisan rangers, in companies, battalions or regiments, either as infantry or cavalry, to receive the same pay, rations, and quarters, and be subject to the same regulations as other soldiers. For any arms and munitions of war captured from the enemy by any body of partisan rangers, and delivered to any quartermaster at designated place, the rangers shall pay their full value.*

The following resolution, in relation to partisan service, was adopted by the Virginia Legislature, May 17, 1862:

Whereas, this General Assembly places a high estimate upon the value of the ranger or partisan service in prosecuting the present war to a successful issue, and regards it as perfectly legitimate; and it being understood that a Federal commander on the northern border of Virginia has intimated his purpose, if such service is not discontinued, to lay waste by fire the portion of our territory at present under his power.

Resolved by the General Assembly, That in its opinion, the policy of employing such rangers and partisans ought to be carried out energetically, both by the authorities of this State and of the Confederate States, without the slightest regard to such threats.

By another act, the President was authorized, in addition to the volunteer force authorized under existing laws, to accept the services of volunteers who may offer them, without regard to the place of enlistment, to serve for and during the existing war.

1862, May 27—Major General John B. Floyd was authorized by the Legislature of Virginia, to raise ten thousand men, not now in service or liable to draft, for twelve months.

1862, September 27—The President was authorized to call out and place in the military service for three years, all white men who are residents, between the ages of thirty-five and forty-five, at the time the call may be made, not legally exempt. And such authority shall exist in the President, during the present war, as to all persons who now are, or hereafter may become eighteen years of age, and all persons between eighteen and forty-five, once enrolled, shall serve their full time.

* 1864, February 15—Repealed the above act, but provided for continuing organizations of partisan rangers acting as regular cavalry and so to continue; and authorising the Secretary of War to provide for uniting all bands of partisan rangers with other organizations and bringing them under the general discipline of the provisional army.

THE TWENTY-NEGRO EXEMPTION LAW.

1862, October 11—Exempted certain classes, described in the repealing law of the next session, as follows:

The dissatisfaction of the people with an act passed by the Confederate Congress, at its last session, by which persons owning a certain number of slaves were exempted from the operation of the conscription law, has led the members at the present session to reconsider their work, and already one branch has passed a bill for the repeal of the obnoxious law. This bill provides as follows:

"*The Congress of the Confederate States do enact*, That so much of the act approved October 11, 1862, as exempts from military service 'one person, either as agent, owner, or overseer, on each plantation on which one white person is required to be kept by the laws or ordinances of any State, and on which there is no white male adult not liable to military service, and in States having no such law, one person, as agent, owner, or overseer on such plantation of twenty negroes, and on which there is no white male adult not liable to military service;' and also the following clause in said act, to wit: 'and furthermore, for additional police of every twenty negroes, on two or more plantations, within five miles of each other, and each having less than twenty negroes, and on which there is no white male adult not liable to military duty, one person, being the oldest of the owners or overseers on such plantations,' be and the same are hereby repealed; and the persons so hitherto exempted by said clauses of said act are hereby made subject to military duty in the same manner that they would be had said clauses never been embraced in said act."

THE POSITION OF DOUGLAS.

After the President had issued his first call, Douglas saw the danger to which the Capitol was exposed, and he promptly called upon Lincoln to express his full approval of the call. Knowing his political value and that of his following Lincoln asked him to dictate a despatch to the Associated Press, which he did in these words, the original being left in the possession of Hon. George Ashmun of Massachusetts:

"April 18, 1861, Senator Douglas, called on the President, and had an interesting conversation, on the present condition of the country. The substance of it was, on the part of Mr. Douglas, that while he was unalterably opposed to the administration in all its political issues, he was prepared to fully sustain the President, in the exercise of all his Constitutional functions, to preserve the Union, maintain the Government, and defend the Federal Capitol. A firm policy and prompt action was necessary. The Capitol was in danger, and must be defended at all hazards, and at any expense of men and money. He spoke of the present and future, without any reference to the past."

Douglas followed this with a great speech at Chicago, in which he uttered a sentence that was soon quoted on nearly every Northern tongue. It was simply this, "that there now could be but two parties, patriots and traitors." It needed nothing more to rally the Douglas Democrats by the side of the Administration, and in the general feeling of patriotism awakened not only this class of Democrats, but many Northern supporters of Breckinridge also enlisted in the Union armies. The leaders who stood aloof and gave their sympathies to the South, were stigmatized as "Copperheads," and these where they were so impudent as to give expression to their hostility, were as odious to the mass of Northerners as the Unionists of Tennessee and North Carolina were to the Secessionists—with this difference—that the latter were compelled to seek refuge in their mountains, while the Northern leader who sought to give "aid and comfort to the enemy" was either placed under arrest by the government or proscribed politically by his neighbors. Civil war is ever thus. Let us now pass to

THE POLITICAL LEGISLATION INCIDENT TO THE WAR.

The first session of the 37th Congress began July 4, 1861, and closed Aug. 6. The second began December 2, 1861, and closed July 17, 1862. The third began December 1, 1862 and closed March 4, 1863.

All of these sessions of Congress were really embarrassed by the number of volunteers offering from the North, and sufficiently rapid provision could not be made for them. And as illustrative of how political lines had been broken, it need only be remarked that Benjamin F. Butler, the leader of the Northern wing of Breckinridge's supporters, was commissioned as the first commander of the forces which Massachusetts sent to the field. New York, Pennsylvania, Ohio—the great West—all the States, more than met all early requirements. So rapid were enlistments that no song was as popular as that beginning with the lines:

"We are coming, Father Abraham,
Six hundred thousand strong."

The first session of the 37th Congress was a special one, called by the President. McPherson, in his classification of the membership, shows the changes in a body made historic, if such a thing can be, not only by its membership present, but that which had gone or made itself subject to expulsion by siding with the Confederacy. We quote the list so concisely and correctly presented:

MEMBERS OF THE 37TH CONGRESS.

March 4, 1861, to March 4, 1863.

HANNIBAL HAMLIN, of Maine, President of the Senate.

SENATORS.

Maine—Lot M. Morrill, Wm. Pitt Fessenden.

New Hampshire—John P. Hale, Daniel Clark.

Vermont—Solomon Foot, Jacob Collamer.

Massachusetts—Charles Sumner, Henry Wilson.

Rhode Island—James F. Simmons,* Henry B. Anthony.

Connecticut—James Dixon, Lafayette S. Foster.

New York—Preston King, Ira Harris.

New Jersey—John B. Thomson,* John C. Ten Eyck.

Pennsylvania—David Wilmot, Edgar Cowan.

Delaware—James A. Bayard, Willard Saulsbury.

Maryland—Anthony Kennedy, James A. Pearce.*

*Virginia.**

Ohio—Benjamin F. Wade, John Sherman.

Kentucky—Lazarus W. Powell, John C. Breckinridge.*

Tennessee—Andrew Johnson.

Indiana—Jesse D. Bright,* Henry S. Lane.

Illinois—O. H. Browning,* Lyman Trumbull.

Missouri—Trusten Polk,* Waldo P. Johnson.*

Michigan—Z. Chandler, K. S. Bingham.*

Iowa—James W. Grimes, James Harlan.

Wisconsin—James R. Doolittle, Timothy O. Howe.

California—Milton S. Latham, James A. McDougall.

Minnesota—Henry M. Rice, Morton S. Wilkinson.

Oregon—Edward D. Baker,* James W. Nesmith.

Kansas—James H. Lane, S. C. Pomeroy.

REPRESENTATIVES.

GALUSHA A. GROW, of Pennsylvania, Speaker of the House.

Maine—John N. Goodwin, Charles W. Walton,* Samuel C. Fessenden, Anson P. Morrill, John H. Rice, Frederick A. Pike.

New Hampshire—Gilman Marston, Edward H. Rollins, Thomas M. Edwards.

Vermont—E. P. Walton, Jr., Justin S. Morrill, Portus Baxter.

* See memorandum at the end of list.

Massachusetts—Thomas D. Eliot, James Buffinton, Benjamin F. Thomas, Alexander H. Rice, William Appleton,* John B. Alley, Daniel W. Gooch, Charles R. Train, Goldsmith F. Bailey,* Charles Delano, Henry L. Dawes.

Rhode Island—William P. Sheffield, George H. Browne.

Connecticut—Dwight Loomis, James E. English, Alfred A. Burnham,* George C. Woodruff.

New York—Edward H. Smith, Moses F. Odell, Benjamin Wood, James E. Kerrigan, William Wall, Frederick A. Conkling, Elijah Ward, Isaac C. Delaplaine, Edward Haight, Charles H. Van Wyck, John B. Steele, Stephen Baker, Abraham B. Olin, Erastus Corning, James B. McKean, William A. Wheeler, Socrates N. Sherman, Chauncey Vibbard, Richard Franchot, Roscoe Conkling, R. Holland Duell, William E. Lansing, Ambrose W. Clark, Charles B. Sedgwick, Theodore M. Pomeroy, Jacob P. Chamberlain, Alexander S. Diven, Robert B. Van Valkenburgh, Alfred Ely, Augustus Frank, Burt Van Horn, Elbridge G. Spalding, Reuben E. Fenton.

New Jersey—John T. Nixon, John L. N. Stratton, William G. Steele, George T. Cobb, Nehemiah Perry.

Pennsylvania—William E. Lehman, Charles J. Biddle,* John P. Verree, William D. Kelley, William Morris Davis, John Hickman, Thomas B. Cooper,* Sydenham E. Ancona, Thaddeus Stevens, John W. Killinger, James H. Campbell, Hendrick B. Wright, Philip Johnson, Galusha A. Grow, James T. Hale, Joseph Baily, Edward McPherson, Samuel S. Blair, John Covode, Jesse Lazear, James K. Moorhead, Robert McKnight, John W. Wallace, John Patton, Elijah Babbitt.

Delaware—George P. Fisher.

Maryland—John W. Crisfield, Edwin H. Webster, Cornelius L. L. Leary, Henry May, Francis Thomas, Charles B. Calvert.

Virginia—Charles H. Upton,* William G. Brown, John S. Carlile,* Kellian V. Whaley.

Ohio—George H. Pendleton, John A. Gurley, Clement L. Vallandigham, William Allen, James M. Ashley, Chilton A. White, Richard A. Harrison, Samuel Shellabarger, Warren P. Noble, Carey A. Trimble, Valentine B. Horton, Samuel S. Cox, Samuel T. Worcester, Harrison G. Blake, Robert H. Nugen, William P. Cutler, James R. Morris, Sidney Edgerton, Albert G. Riddle, John Hutchins, John A. Bingham.

Kentucky—Henry C. Burnett,* James S. Jackson,* Henry Grider, Aaron Harding, Charles A. Wickliffe, George W. Dunlap, Robert Mallory, John J. Crittenden, William H. Wadsworth, John W. Menzies.

See memorandum at end of list.

Tennessee—Horace Maynard,* Andrew J. Clements,* George W. Bridges.*

Indiana—John Law, James A. Cravens, W. McKee Dunn, William S. Holman, George W. Julian, Albert G. Porter, Daniel W. Voorhees, Albert S. White, Schuyler Colfax, William Mitchell, John P. C. Shanks.

Illinois—Elihu B. Washburne, Isaac N. Arnold, Owen Lovejoy, William Kellogg, William A. Richardson,* John A. McClernand,* James C. Robinson, Philip B. Fouke, John A. Logan.*

Missouri—Francis P. Blair, Jr., James S. Rollins, John B. Clark,* Elijah H. Norton, John W. Reid,* John S. Phelps,* John W. Noell.

Michigan—Bradley F. Granger, Fernando C. Beaman, Francis W. Kellogg, Rowland E. Trowbridge.

Iowa—Samuel R. Curtis,* William Vandever.

Wisconsin—John F. Potter, Luther Hanchett,* A. Scott Sloan.

Minnesota—Cyrus Aldrich, William Windom.

Oregon—Andrew J. Thayer.*

Kansas—Martin F. Conway.

MEMORANDUM OF CHANGES.

The following changes took place during the Congress:

IN SENATE.

Rhode Island—1862, Dec. 1, Samuel G. Arnold succeeded James F. Simmons, resigned.

New Jersey—1862, Dec. 1, Richard S. Field succeeded, by appointment, John R. Thompson, deceased Sept. 12, 1862. 1863, Jan. 21, James, W. Wall, succeeded, by election, Richard S. Field.

Maryland—1863, Jan. 14, Thomas H. Hicks, first by appointment and then by election succeeded James A. Pearce, deceased Dec. 20, 1862.

Virginia—1861, July 13, John S. Carlile and Waitman T. Willey, sworn in place of Robert M. T. Hunter and James M. Mason, withdrawn and abdicated.

Kentucky—1861, Dec. 23, Garrett Davis succeeded John C. Breckinridge, expelled December 4.

Indiana—1862, March 3, Joseph A. Wright succeeded Jesse D. Bright, expelled Feb. 5, 1863, Jan. 22, David Turpie, superseded, by election, Joseph A. Wright.

Illinois—1863, Jan. 30, William A. Richardson superseded, by election, O. H. Browning.

Missouri—1861, Jan. 24, R. Wilson succeeded Waldo P. Johnson, expelled Jan. 10. 1862, Jan. 29, John B. Henderson succeeded Trusten Polk, expelled Jan. 10.

Michigan—1862, Jan. 17, Jacob M. Howard succeeded K. S. Bingham, deceased October 5, 1861.

Oregon—1862, Dec. 1, Benjamin F. Harding succeeded Edward D. Baker, deceased Oct. 21, 1862.

IN HOUSE OF REPRESENTATIVES

Maine—1862, December 1, Thomas A. D. Fessenden succeeded Charles W. Walton, resigned May 26, 1862.

Massachusetts—1861, December 1, Amasa Walker succeeded Goldsmith F. Bailey, deceased May 8, 1862; 1861, December 2, Samuel Hooper succeeded William Appleton, resigned.

Connecticut—1861, December 2, Alfred A. Burnham qualified.

Pennsylvania—1861, December 2, Charles J. Biddle qualified; 1862, June 3, John D. Stiles succeeded Thomas B. Cooper, deceased April 4, 1862.

Virginia,—1861, July 13, John S. Carlile resigned to take a seat in the Senate; 1861, December 2, Jacob B. Blair, succeeded John S. Carlile, resigned; 1862, February 28, Charles H. Upton unseated by a vote of the House; 1862, May 6, Joseph Segar qualified.

Kentucky—1862, December, 1, George H. Yeaman succeeded James S. Jackson, deceased; 1862, March 10, Samuel L. Casey succeeded Henry C. Burnett, expelled December 3, 1861.

Tennessee—1861, December 2, Horace Maynard qualified; 1862, January 13, Andrew J. Clements qualified; 1863, February 25, George W. Bridges qualified.

Illinois—1861, December 12, A. L. Knapp qualified, in place of J. A. McClernand, resigned; 1862, June 2, William J. Allen qualified, in place of John A. Logan, resigned; 1863, January 30, William A. Richardson withdrew to take a seat in the Senate.

Missouri—1862, January 21, Thomas L. Price succeeded John W. Reid, expelled December 2, 1861; 1862, January 20, William A. Hall succeeded John B. Clark, expelled July 13, 1861; 1862, May 9, John S. Phelps qualified.

Iowa—1861, December 2, James F. Wilson succeeded Samuel R. Curtis, resigned August 4, 1861.

Wisconsin—1863, January 26, Walter D. McIndoe succeeded Luther Hanchett, deceased November 24, 1862.

Oregon—1861, July 30, George K. Shiel succeeded Andrew J. Thayer, unseated.

Louisiana—1863, February 17, Michael Hahn qualified; 1863, February 23, Benjamin F. Flanders qualified.

Lincoln, in his message, recited the events which had transpired since his inauguration, and asked Congress to confer upon him the power to make the conflict short and decisive. He wanted 400,000 men, and four hundred millions of money, remarking that "the people will save their government if the government itself will do its part only indifferently well." Congress responded by adding an hundred thousand to each request.

There were exciting debates and scenes during this session, for many of the Southern leaders remained, either through hesitancy or with a view to check legislation and aid their section by adverse criticism on the measures proposed. Most prominent in the latter list was John C. Breckinridge, late Vice President and now Senator from Kentucky. With singular boldness and eloquence he opposed every war measure, and spoke with the undisguised purpose of aiding the South. He continued this course until the close of the extra session, when he accepted a General's commission in the Confederate army. But before its close, Senator Baker of Oregon, angered at his general course, said in reply to one of Breckinridge's speeches, Aug. 1st:

"What would the Senator from Kentucky, have? These speeches of his, sown broadcast over the land, what clear distinct meaning have they? Are they not intended for disorganization in our very midst? Are they not intended to destroy our zeal? Are they not intended to animate our enemies? Sir, are they not words of brilliant polished TREASON, even in the very Capitol of the Republic?" [Here there were such manifestations of applause in the galleries, as were with difficulty suppressed.]

Mr. Baker resumed, and turning directly to Mr. Breckinridge, inquired:

"What would have been thought, if, in another Capitol, in another republic, in a yet more martial age, a Senator as grave, not more eloquent or dignified than the Senator from Kentucky, yet with the Roman purple flowing over his shoulders, had risen in his place, surrounded by all the illustrations of Roman glory, and declared that the cause of the advancing Hannibal was just, and that Carthage ought to be dealt with in terms of peace? What would have been thought if, after the battle of Cannæ, a Senator there had risen in his place, and denounced every levy of the Roman people, every expenditure of its treasure, and every appeal to the old recollections and the old glories?"

There was a silence so profound throughout the Senate and galleries, that a pinfall could have been heard, while every eye was fixed upon Breckinridge. Fessenden exclaimed in deep low tones, "he would have been hurled from the Tarpeian Rock!"

Baker resumed:

"Sir, a Senator himself learned far more than myself, in such lore, (Mr. Fessenden) tells me, in a low voice, "he would have been hurled from the Tarpeian Rock." It is a grand commentary upon the American Constitution, that we permit these words of the Senator from Kentucky, to be uttered. I ask the Senator to recollect, to what, save to send aid and comfort to the enemy, do these predictions amount to? Every word thus uttered, falls as a note of inspiration upon every Confederate ear. Every sound thus uttered, is a word, (and falling from his lips, a mighty word) of kindling and triumph to the foe that determines to advance."

The Republicans of the North were the distinctive "war party," *i. e.*, they gave unqualified support to every demand made by the Lincoln administration. Most of the Democrats, acting as citizens, did likewise, but many of those in official position, assuming the prerogative of a minority, took the liberty in Congress and State Legislature to criticise the more important war measures, and the extremists went so far, in many instances, as to organize opposition, and to encourage it among their constituents. Thus in the States bordering the Ohio and Mississippi rivers, organized and individual efforts were made to encourage desertions, and the "Knights of the Golden Circle," and the "Sons of Liberty," secret societies composed of Northern sympathizers with the South, formed many troublesome conspiracies. Through their action troops were even enlisted in Southern Indiana, Illinois and Missouri for the Confederate armies, while the border States in the Union sent whole regiments to battle for the South. The "Knights of the Golden Circle" conspired to release Confederate prisoners of war, and invited Morgan to raid their States. One of the worst forms of opposition took shape in a conspiracy to resist the draft in New York city. The fury of the mob was several days beyond control, and troops had to be recalled from the front to suppress it. The riot was really political, the prejudices of the mob under cover of resistance to the draft, being vented on the negroes, many of whom were killed before adequate numbers could be sent to their succor. The civil authorities of the city were charged with winking at the occurrence, and it was afterwards ascertained that Confederate agents really organized the riot as a movement to "take the enemy in the rear."

The Republican was as distinctively the war party during the Great Rebellion, as the Whigs were during the Revolution, the Democratic-Republicans during the War of 1812, and the Democrats during the War with Mexico, and, as in all of these war decades, kept the majority sentiment of the country with them. This is such a plain statement of facts that it is neither partisan to assert, nor a mark of party-fealty to deny. The history is indelibly written. It is stamped upon nearly every war measure, and certainly upon every political measure incident to growing out of the rebellion.

These were exciting and memorable scenes in the several sessions of the 37th Congress. During the first many Southern Senators and Representatives withdrew after angry statements of their reasons, generally in obedience to calls from their States or immediate homes. In this way the majority was changed. Others remained until the close of the first session, and then more quietly entered the rebellion. We have shown that of this class was Breckinridge, who thought he could do more good for his cause in the Federal Congress than elsewhere, and it is well for the Union that most of his colleagues disagreed with him as to the propriety and wisdom of his policy. If all had followed his lead or imitated his example, the war would in all probability have closed in another compromise, or possibly in the accomplishment of southern separations. These men could have so obstructed legislation as to make all its early periods far more discouraging than they were. As it was the Confederates had all the advantages of a free and fair start, and the effect was traceable in all of the early battles and negotiations with foreign powers. There was one way in which these advantages could have been supported and continued. Breckenridge, shrewd and able politician as he was, saw that the way was to keep Southern Representatives in Congress, at least as long as Northern sentiment would abide it, and in this way win victories at the very fountain-head of power. But at the close of the extra session this view had become unpopular at both ends of the line, and even Breckenridge abandoned it and sought to hide his original purpose by immediate service in the Confederate armies.

It will be noted that those who vacated their seats to enter the Confederacy were afterwards expelled. In this connection a curious incident can be related, occuring as late as the Senate session of 1882:

The widow of the late Senator Nicholson, of Tennessee, who was in the Senate when Tennessee seceded, a short time ago sent a petition to Congress asking that the salary of her late husband, after he returned to Tennessee, might be paid to her. Mr. Nicholson's term would have expired in 1865 had he remained in his seat. He did not appear at the special session of Congress convened in July, 1861, and with other Senators from the South was expelled from the Senate on July 11th of that year. The Senate Committee on Claims, after examining the case thoroughly, submitted to the Senate an adverse report. After giving a concise history of the case the committee say: "We do not deem it proper, after the expiration of twenty years, to pass special acts of Congress to compensate the Senators and Representatives who seceded in 1861 for their services in the early part of that year. We recommend that the claim of the petitioner be disallowed."

The Sessions of the 37th Congress changed the political course of many public men. It made the Southern believers in secession still more vehement; it separated the Southern Unionists from their former friends, and created a wall of fire between them; it changed the temper of Northern Abolitionists, in so far as to drive from them all spirit of faction, all pride of methods, and compelled them to unite with a republican sentiment which was making sure advances from the original declaration that slavery should not be extended to the Territories, to emancipation, and, finally, to the arming of the slaves. It changed many Northern Democrats, and from the ranks of these, even in representative positions, the lines of the Republicans were constantly strengthened on pivotal questions. On the 27th of July Breckinridge had said in a speech: "When traitors become numerous enough treason becomes respectable." Senator Andrew Johnson, of Tennessee, replied to this, and said: "God being willing, whether traitors be many or few, as I have hitherto waged war against traitors and treason, I intend to continue it to the end." And yet Johnson had the year before warmly supported Breckinridge in his presidential campaign.

Among the more conspicuous Republicans and anti-Lecompton Democrats in this session were Charles Sumner, a man who then exceeded all others in scholarly attainments and as an orator, though he was not strong in current debate. Great care and preparation marked every important effort, but no man's speeches were more admired throughout the North, and hated throughout the South, than those of Charles Sumner. An air of romance surrounded the man, because he was the first victim of a senatorial outrage, when beaten by Brooks of South Carolina; but, sneered his political enemies, "no man more carefully preserved his wounds for exhibition to a sympathetic world." He had some minor weaknesses, which were constantly displayed, and these centred in egotism and high personal pride—not very popular traits—but no enemy was so malicious as to deny his greatness.

Fessenden of Maine was one of the great lights of that day. He was apt, almost beyond example, in debate, and was a recognized leader of the Republicans until, in the attempt to impeach President Johnson, he disagreed with the majority of his party and stepped "down and out." Yet no one questioned his integrity, and all believed that his vote was cast on this question in a line with his convictions. The leading character in the House was Thaddeus Stevens, an original Abolitionist in sentiment, but a man eminently practical and shrewd in all his methods.

The chances of politics often carry men into the Presidential Chair, into Cabinets, and with later and demoralizing frequency into Senate seats; but chance never makes a Commoner, and Thaddeus Stevens was throughout the war, and up to the hour of his death, recognized as the great Commoner of the Northern people. He led in every House battle, and a more unflinching party leader was never known to parliamentary bodies. Limp and infirm, he was not liable to personal assault, even in days when such assaults were common; but when on one occasion his fiery tongue had so exasperated the Southerners in Congress as to make them show their knives and pistols, he stepped out into the aisle, and facing, bid them defiance. He was a Radical of the Radicals, and constantly contended that the government—the better to preserve itself—could travel outside of the Constitution. What cannot be said of any other man in history, can be said of Thaddeus Stevens. When he lay dead, carried thus from Washington to his home in Lancaster, with all of his people knowing that he was dead, he was, on the day following the arrival of his corpse, and within a few squares of his residence, unanimously renominated by the Republicans for Congress. If more poetic and less practical sections or lands than the North had such a hero, hallowed by such an incident, both the name and the incident would travel down the ages in song and story.*

The "rising" man in the 37th Congress was Schuyler Colfax, of Indiana, elected Speaker of the 38th, and subsequently Vice President. A great parliamentarian, he was gifted with rare eloquence, and with a kind which won friends without offending enemies—something too rare to last. In the House were also Justin S. Morrill, the author of the Tariff Bill which supplied the "sinews of war," Henry L. Dawes of Massachusetts, then "the man of Statistics" and the "watch-dog of the treasury." Roscoe Conkling was then the admitted leader of the New York delegation, as he was the admitted mental superior of any other in subsequent terms in the Senate, up to the time of his resignation in 1881. Reuben E. Fenton, his factional opponent, was also there. Ohio was strongly represented in both parties—Pendleton, Cox and Vallandigham on the side of the Democrats; Bingham and Ashley on the part of the Republicans. Illinois showed four prominent anti-Lecompton supporters of the administration—Douglas in the Senate; Logan, McClernand and Richardson in the House; while prominent among the Republicans were Lovejoy (an original Abolitionist), Washburne, a candidate for the Presidential nomination in 1880—Kellogg and Arnold. John F. Potter was one of the prominent Wisconsin men, who had won additional fame by accepting the challenge to duel of Roger A. Pryor of Virginia, and naming the American rifle as the weapon. Fortunately the duel did not come off. Pennsylvania had then, as she still has, Judge Kelley of Philadelphia, chairman of Ways and Means in the 46th Congress; also Edward McPherson, frequently since Clerk of the House, temporary President of the Cincinnati Convention, whose decision overthrew the unit rule, and author of several valuable political works, some of which we freely quote in this history. John Hickman, subsequently a Republican, but one of the earliest of the anti-Lecompton Democrats, was an admitted leader, a man of rare force and eloquence. So radical did he become that he refused to support the re-election of Lincoln. He was succeeded by John M. Broomall, who made several fine speeches in favor of the constitutional amendments touching slavery and civil rights. Here also were James Campbell, Hendricks B. Wright, John Covode, James K. Morehead, and Speaker Grow—the father of the Homestead Bill, which will be found in Book V., giving the Existing Political Laws.

At this session Senator Trumbull of Illinois, renewed the agitation of the slavery question, by reporting from the Judiciary Committee of which he was Chairman, a bill to confiscate all property and free all slaves used for insurrectionary purposes.* Breckinridge fought the bill, as indeed he did all bills coming from the Republicans, and said if passed it would eventuate in "the loosening of all bonds." Among the facts stated in support of the measure was this, that the Confederates had at Bull Run used the negroes and slaves against the Union army—a statement never well established. The bill passed the Senate by 33 to 6, and on the 3d of August passed the House, though several Republicans there voted against it, fearing a too rapid advance would prejudice the Union cause. Indeed this fear was entertained by Lincoln when he recommended

COMPENSATED EMANCIPATION

in the second session of the 37th Congress, which recommendation excited official discussion almost up to the time the emancipation proclamation was issued as a war necessity. The idea of compensated eman-

*This incident was related to the writer by Col. A. K. McClure of Philadelphia, who was in Lancaster at the time.

*Arnold's "History of Abraham Lincoln."

cipation originated with or was first formulated by James B. McKean of New York, who on Feb. 11th, 1861, at the 2d session of the 36th Congress, introduced the following resolution:

WHEREAS, The "Gulf States" have assumed to secede from the Union, and it is deemed important to prevent the "border slave States" from following their example; and whereas it is believed that those who are inflexibly opposed to any measure of compromise or concession that involves, or may involve, a sacrifice of principle or the extension of slavery, would nevertheless cheerfully concur in any lawful measure for the emancipation of the slaves: Therefore,

Resolved, That the select committee of five be instructed to inquire whether, by the consent of the people, or of the State governments, or by compensating the slaveholders, it be practicable for the General Government to procure the emancipation of the slaves in some, or all, of the "border States;" and if so, to report a bill for that purpose.

Lincoln was so strongly impressed with the fact, in the earlier struggles of the war, that great good would follow compensated emancipation, that on March 2d, 1862, he sent a special message to the 2d session of the 37th Congress, in which he said:

"I recommend the adoption of a joint resolution by your honorable bodies, which shall be substantially as follows:

Resolved, That the United States ought to co-operate with any State which may adopt gradual abolishment of slavery, giving to such State pecuniary aid, to be used by such State in its discretion, to compensate for the inconveniences, public and private, produced by such change of system.

"If the proposition contained in the resolution does not meet the approval of Congress and the country, there is the end; but if it does command such approval, I deem it of importance that the States and people immediately interested should be at once distinctly notified of the fact, so that they may begin to consider whether to accept or reject it. The Federal Government would find its highest interest in such a measure, as one of the most efficient means of self-preservation. The leaders of the existing insurrection entertain the hope that this Government will ultimately be forced to acknowledge the independence of some part of the disaffected region, and that all the slave States north of such part will then say, 'the Union for which we have struggled being already gone, we now choose to go with the southern section.' To deprive them of this hope, substantially ends the rebellion; and the initiation of emancipation completely deprives them of it as to all the States initiating it. The point is not that *all* the States tolerating slavery would very soon, if at all, initiate emancipation; but that, while the offer is equally made to all, the more northern shall, by such initiation, make it certain to the more southern that in no event will the former ever join the latter in their proposed confederacy. I say 'initiation,' because, in my judgment, gradual, and not sudden emancipation, is better for all. In the mere financial or pecuniary view, any member of Congress, with the census tables and Treasury reports before him, can readily see for himself how very soon the current expenditures of this war would purchase, at fair valuation, all the slaves in any named State. Such a proposition on the part of the General Government sets up no claim of a right by Federal authority to interfere with slavery within State limits, referring, as it does the absolute control of the subject in each case to the State and its people immediately interested. It is proposed as a matter of perfectly free choice with them.

"In the annual message last December, I thought fit to say, 'the Union must be preserved; and hence all indispensable means must be employed.' I said this not hastily, but deliberately. War has been made, and continues to be an indispensable means to this end. A practical reacknowledgment of the national authority would render the war unnecessary, and it would at once cease. If, however, resistance continues, the war must also continue; and it is impossible to foresee all the incidents which may attend, and all the ruin which may follow it. Such as may seem indispensable, or may obviously promise great efficiency toward ending the struggle, must and will come.

"The proposition now made, though an offer only, I hope it may be esteemed no offence to ask whether the pecuniary consideration tendered would not be of more value to the States and private persons concerned, than are the institution, and property in it, in the present aspect of affairs?

"While it is true that the adoption of the proposed resolution would be merely initiatory, and not within itself a practical measure, it is recommended in the hope that it would soon lead to important practical results. In full view of my great responsibility to my God and to my country, I earnestly beg the attention of Congress and the people to the subject."

Mr. Conkling called the question up in the House March 10th, and under a suspension of the rules, it was passed by 97 to 36. It passed the Senate April 2, by 32 to 10, the Republicans, as a rule, voting for it, the Democrats, as a rule, voting against it; and this was true even of those in the Border States.

The fact last stated excited the notice of President Lincoln, and in July, 1862, he sought an interview with the Border State Congressmen, the result of which is contained in *McPherson's Political History of the Great Rebellion*, as follows:

The President's Appeal to the Border States.

The Representatives and Senators of the border slaveholding States, having, by special invitation of the President, been convened at the Executive Mansion, on Saturday morning last, (July 12,) Mr. Lincoln addressed them as follows from a written paper held in his hand:

"GENTLEMEN: After the adjournment of Congress, now near, I shall have no opportunity of seeing you for several months. Believing that you of the border States hold more power for good than any other equal number of members, I feel it a duty which I cannot justifiably waive, to make this appeal to you.

"I intend no reproach or complaint when I assure you that, in my opinion, if you all had voted for the resolution in the gradual emancipation message of last March, the war would now be substantially ended. And the plan therein proposed is yet one of the most potent and swift means of ending it. Let the States which are in rebellion see definitely and certainly that in no event will the States you represent ever join their proposed Confederacy, and they cannot much longer maintain the contest. But you cannot divest them of their hope to ultimately have you with them so long as you show a determination to perpetuate the institution within your own States. Beat them at elections, as you have overwhelmingly done, and, nothing daunted, they still claim you as their own. You and I know what the lever of their power is. Break that lever before their faces, and they can shake you no more forever.

"Most of you have treated me with kindness and consideration, and I trust you will not now think I improperly touch what is exclusively your own, when, for the sake of the whole country, I ask, 'Can you, for your States, do better than to take the course I urge?' Discarding *punctilio* and maxims adapted to more manageable times, and looking only to the unprecedentedly stern facts of our case, can you do better in any possible event? You prefer that the constitutional relations of the States to the nation shall be practically restored without disturbance of the institution; and, if this were done, my whole duty, in this respect, under the Constitution and my oath of office, would be performed. But it is not done, and we are trying to accomplish it by war. The incidents of the war cannot be avoided. If the war continues long, as it must, if the object be not sooner attained, the institution in your States will be extinguished by mere friction and abrasion —by the mere incidents of the war. It will be gone, and you will have nothing valuable in lieu of it. Much of its value is gone already. How much better for you and for your people to take the step which at once shortens the war and secures substantial compensation for that which is sure to be wholly lost in any other event! How much better to thus save the money which else we sink forever in the war! How much better to do it while we can, lest the war ere long render us pecuniarily unable to do it! How much better for you, as seller, and the nation, as buyer, to sell out and buy out that without which the war could never have been, than to sink both the thing to be sold and the price of it in cutting one another's throats!

"I do not speak of emancipation *at once*, but of a *decision* at once to emancipate *gradually*. Room in South America for colonization can be obtained cheaply and in abundance, and when numbers shall be large enough to be company and encouragement for one another, the freed people will not be so reluctant to go.

"I am pressed with a difficulty not yet mentioned, one which threatens division among those who, united, are none too strong. An instance of it is known to you. General Hunter is an honest man. He was, and I hope still is, my friend. I valued him none the less for his agreeing with me in the general wish that all men everywhere could be freed. He proclaimed all men free within certain States, and I repudiated the proclamation. He expected more good and less harm from the measure than I could believe would follow. Yet, in repudiating it, I gave dissatisfaction, if not offence, to many whose support the country cannot afford to lose. And this is not the end of it. The pressure in this direction is still upon me, and is increasing. By conceding what I now ask you can relieve me, and, much more, can relieve the country in this important point.

"Upon these considerations I have again begged your attention to the message of March last. Before leaving the Capitol, consider and discuss it among yourselves. You are patriots and statesmen, and as such I pray you consider this proposition; and at the least commend it to the consideration of your States and people. As you would perpetuate popular government for the best people in the world, I beseech you that you do in nowise omit this. Our common country is in great peril, demanding the loftiest views and boldest action to bring a speedy relief. Once relieved, its form of government is saved to the world, its beloved history and cherished memories are vindicated, and its happy future fully assured and rendered inconceivably grand. To you, more than to any others, the privilege is given to assure that happiness and swell that grandeur, and to link your own names therewith forever."

At the conclusion of these remarks some conversation was had between the President and several members of the delegations from the border States, in which it was represented that these States could not be expected to move in so great a matter as that brought to their notice in the foregoing address while as yet the Congress had taken no step beyond the passage of a resolution, expressive rather of a sentiment than presenting a substantial and reliable basis of action.

The President acknowledged the force of this view, and admitted that the border States were entitled to expect a substantial pledge of pecuniary aid as the condition of taking into consideration a proposition so important in its relations to their social system.

It was further represented, in the conference, that the people of the border States were interested in knowing the great importance which the President attached to the policy in question, while it was equally due to the country, to the President, and to themselves, that the representatives of the border slave-holding States should publicly announce the motives under which they were called to act, and the considerations of public policy urged upon them and their constituents by the President.

With a view to such a statement of their position, the members thus addressed met in council to deliberate on the reply they should make to the President, and, as the result of a comparison of opinions among themselves, they determined upon the adoption of a majority and minority answer.

REPLY OF THE MAJORITY.

The following paper was yesterday sent to the President, signed by the majority of the Representatives from the border slave-holding States:—

WASHINGTON, *July* 14, 1862.

To the PRESIDENT:

The undersigned, Representatives of Kentucky, Virginia, Missouri, and Maryland, in the two Houses of Congress, have listened to your address with the profound sensibility naturally inspired by the high source from which it emanates, the earnestness which marked its delivery, and the overwhelming importance of the subject of which it treats. We have given it a most respectful consideration, and now lay before you our response. We regret that want of time has not permitted us to make it more perfect.

We have not been wanting, Mr. President, in respect to you, and in devotion to the Constitution and the Union. We have not been indifferent to the great difficulties surrounding you, compared with which all former national troubles have been but as the summer cloud; and we have freely given you our sympathy and support. Repudiating the dangerous heresies of the secessionists, we believed, with you, that the war on their part is aggressive and wicked, and the objects for which it was to be prosecuted on ours, defined by your message at the opening of the present Congress, to be such as all good men should approve. We have not hesitated to vote all supplies necessary to carry it on vigorously. We have voted all the men and money you have asked for, and even more; we have imposed onerous taxes on our people, and they are paying them with cheerfulness and alacrity; we have encouraged enlistments and sent to the field many of our best men; and some of our number have offered their persons to the enemy as pledges of their sincerity and devotion to the country.

We have done all this under the most discouraging circumstances, and in the face of measures most distasteful to us and injurious to the interests we represent, and in the hearing of doctrines avowed by those who claim to be your friends, must be abhorrent to us and our constituents. But, for all this, we have never faltered, nor shall we as long as we have a Constitution to defend and a Government which protects us. And we are ready for renewed efforts, and even greater sacrifices, yea, any sacrifice, when we are satisfied it is required to preserve our admirable form of government and the priceless blessings of constitutional liberty.

A few of our number voted for the resolution recommended by your message of the 6th of March last, the greater portion of us did not, and we will briefly state the prominent reasons which influenced our action.

In the first place, it proposed a radical change of our social system, and was hurried through both Houses with undue haste, without reasonable time for consideration and debate, and with no time at all for consultation with our constituents, whose interests it deeply involved. It seemed like an interference by this Government with a question which peculiarly and exclusively belonged to our respective States, on which they had not sought advice or solicited aid. Many of us doubted the constitutional power of this Government to make appropriations of money for the object designated, and all of us thought our finances were in no condition to bear the immense outlay which its adoption and faithful execution would impose upon the national Treasury. If we pause but a moment to think of the debt its acceptance would have entailed, we are appalled by its magnitude. The proposition was addressed to all the States, and embraced the whole number of slaves.

According to the census of 1860 there were then nearly four million slaves in the country; from natural increase they exceed that number now. At even the low average of $300, the price fixed by the emancipation act for the slaves of this District, and greatly below their real worth, their value runs up to the enormous sum of $1,200,000,000; and if to that we add the cost of deportation and colonization, at $100 each, which is but a fraction more than is actually paid by the Maryland Colonization Society, we have $400,000,000 more. We were not willing to impose a tax on our people sufficient to pay the interest on that sum, in addition to the vast and daily increasing debt already fixed upon them by the exigencies of the war, and if we had been willing, the country could not bear it. Stated in this form the proposition is nothing less than the deportation from the country of $1,600,000,000 worth of producing labor, and the substitution in its place of an interest-bearing debt of the same amount.

But, if we are told that it was expected that only the States we represent would accept the proposition, we respectfully submit that even then it involves a sum too great for the financial ability of this Government at this time. According to the census of 1860—

	Slaves.
Kentucky had	225,490
Maryland	87,188
Virginia	490,887
Delaware	1,798
Missouri	114,965
Tennessee	275,784
Making in the whole	1,196,112
At the same rate of valuation these would amount to	$358,933,500
Add for deportation and colonization $100 each	118,244,533
And we have the enormous sum of	$478,038,133

We did not feel that we should be justified in voting for a measure which, if carried out, would add this vast amount to our public debt at a moment when the Treasury was reeling under the enormous expenditure of the war.

Again, it seemed to us that this resolution was but the annunciation of a sentiment which could not or was not likely to be reduced to an actual tangible proposition. No movement was then made to provide and appropriate the funds required to carry it into effect; and we were not encouraged to believe that funds would be provided. And our belief has been fully justified by subsequent events. Not to mention other circumstances, it is quite sufficient for our purpose to bring to your notice the fact that, while this resolution was under consideration in the Senate, our colleague, the Senator from Kentucky, moved an amendment appropriating $500,000 to the object therein designated, and it was voted down with great unanimity. What confidence, then, could we reasonably feel that if we committed ourselves to the policy it proposed, our constituents would reap the fruits of the promise held out; and on what ground could we, as fair men, approach them and challenge their support?

The right to hold slaves is a right appertaining to all the States of this Union. They have the right to cherish or abolish the institution, as their tastes or their interests may prompt, and no one is authorized to question the right or limit the enjoyment. And no one has more clearly affirmed that right than you have. Your inaugural address does you great honor in this respect, and inspired the country with confidence in your fairness and respect for the law. Our States are in the enjoyment of that right. We do not feel called on to defend the institution or to affirm it is one which ought to be cherished; perhaps, if we were to make the attempt, we might find that we differ even among ourselves. It is enough for our purpose to know that it is a right; and, so knowing, we did not see why we should now be expected to yield it. We had contributed our full share to relieve the country at this terrible crisis; we had done as much as had been required of others in like circumstances; and we did not see why sacrifices should be expected of us from which others, no more loyal, were exempt. Nor could we see what good the nation would derive from it.

Such a sacrifice submitted to by us would not have strengthened the arm of this Government or weakened that of the enemy. It was not necessary as a pledge of our loyalty, for that had been manifested beyond a reasonable doubt, in every form, and at every place possible. There was not the remotest probability that the States we represent would join in the rebellion, nor is there now, or of their electing to go with the southern section in the event of a recognition of the independence of any part of the disaffected region. Our

States are fixed unalterably in their resolution to adhere to and support the Union. They see no safety for themselves, and no hope for constitutional liberty but by its preservation. They will, under no circumstances, consent to its dissolution; and we do them no more than justice when we assure you that, while the war is conducted to prevent that deplorable catastrophe, they will sustain it as long as they can muster a man or command a dollar. Nor will they ever consent, in any event, to unite with the Southern Confederacy. The bitter fruits of the peculiar doctrines of that region will forever prevent them from placing their security and happiness in the custody of an association which has incorporated in its organic law the seeds of its own destruction.

* * * * * * * *

Mr. President, we have stated with frankness and candor the reasons on which we forbore to vote for the resolution you have mentioned; but you have again presented this proposition, and appealed to us with an earnestness and eloquence which have not failed to impress us, to "consider it, and at the least to commend it to the consideration of our States and people." Thus appealed to by the Chief Magistrate of our beloved country, in the hour of its greatest peril, we cannot wholly decline. We are willing to trust every question relating to their interest and happiness to the consideration and ultimate judgment of our own people. While differing from you as to the necessity of emancipating the slaves of our States as a means of putting down the rebellion, and while protesting against the propriety of any extra-territorial interference to induce the people of our States to adopt any particular line of policy on a subject which peculiarly and exclusively belongs to them, yet, when you and our brethren of the loyal States sincerely believe that the retention of slavery by us is an obstacle to peace and national harmony, and are willing to contribute pecuniary aid to compensate our States and people for the inconveniences produced by such a change of system, we are not unwilling that our people shall consider the propriety of putting it aside.

But we have already said that we regarded this resolution as the utterance of a sentiment, and we had no confidence that it would assume the shape of a tangible, practical proposition, which would yield the fruits of the sacrifice it required. Our people are influenced by the same want of confidence, and will not consider the proposition in its present impalpable form. The interest they are asked to give up is to them of much importance, and they ought not to be expected even to entertain the proposal until they are assured that when they accept it their just expectations will not be frustrated. We regard your plan as a proposition from the Nation to the States to exercise an admitted constitutional right in a particular manner and yield up a valuable interest. Before they ought to consider the proposition, it should be presented in such a tangible, practical, efficient shape as to command their confidence that its fruits are contingent only upon their acceptance. We cannot trust anything to the contingencies of future legislation.

If Congress, by proper and necessary legislation, shall provide sufficient funds and place them at your disposal, to be applied by you to the payment of any of our States or the citizens thereof who shall adopt the abolishment of slavery, either gradual or immediate, as they may determine, and the expense of deportation and colonization of the liberated slaves, then will our State and people take this proposition into careful consideration, for such decision as in their judgment is demanded by their interest, their honor, and their duty to the whole country. We have the honor to be, with great respect,

C. A. Wickliffe, *Ch'n*,
Garrett Davis,
R. Wilson,
J. J. Crittenden,
John S. Carlile,
J. W. Crisfield,
J. S. Jackson,
H. Grider,
John S. Phelps,
Francis Thomas,
Chas. B. Calvert,
C. L. Leary,
Edwin H. Webster,
R. Mallory,
Aaron Harding,
James S. Rollins,
J. W. Menzies,
Thomas L. Price,
G. W. Dunlap,
Wm. A. Hall.

Others of the minority, among them Senator Henderson and Horace Maynard, forwarded separate replies, but all rejecting the idea of compensated emancipation. Still Lincoln adhered to and advocated it in his recent annual message sent to Congress, Dec. 1, 1862, from which we take the following paragraphs, which are in themselves at once curious and interesting:

"We have two million nine hundred and sixty-three thousand square miles. Europe has three million and eight hundred thousand, with a population averaging seventy-three and one-third persons to the square mile. Why may not our country, at some time, average as many? Is it less fertile? Has it more waste surface, by mountains, rivers, lakes, deserts, or other causes? Is it inferior to Europe in any natural advantage? If, then, we are at some time to be as populous as Europe, how soon? As to when this *may* be, we can judge by the past and the present; as to when it *will* be, if ever, depends much on whether we maintain the Union. Several of our States are already above the average of Europe —seventy-three and a third to the square mile. Massachusetts has 157; Rhode Island, 133; Connecticut, 99; New York and New Jersey, each, 80. Also two other great states, Pennsylvania and Ohio, are not far below, the former having 63 and the latter 59. The states already above the European average, except New York, have increased in as rapid a ratio, since passing that point, as ever before; while no one of them is equal to some other parts of our country in natural capacity for sustaining a dense population.

"Taking the nation in the aggregate, and we find its population and ratio of increase, for the several decennial periods, to be as follows:

		Ratio of increase.
1790........	3,929,827	
1800........	5,305,937	35.02 per cent.
1810........	7,239,814	36.45 "
1820........	9,638,131	33.13 "
1830........	12,866,020	33.49 "
1840........	17,069,453	32.67 "
1850........	23,191,876	35.87 "
1860........	31,443,790	35.58 "

This shows an annual decennial increase of 34.69 per cent. in population through the seventy years from our first to our last census yet taken. It is seen that the ratio of increase, at no one of these seven periods is either two per cent. below or two per cent. above the average; thus showing how inflexible, and, consequently, how reliable, the law of increase in our case is. Assuming that it will continue, gives the following results:

1870..................................	42,323,341
1880..................................	56,967,216
1890..................................	76,677,872
1900..................................	103,208,415
1910..................................	138,918,526
1920..................................	186,984,335
1930..................................	251,680,914

"These figures show that our country *may* be as populous as Europe now is at some point between 1920 and 1930—say about 1925—our territory, at seventy-three and a third persons to the square mile, being of capacity to contain 217,186,000.

"And we *will* reach this, too, if we do not ourselves relinquish the chance by the folly and evils of disunion, or by long and exhausting war springing from the only great element of national discord among us. While it cannot be foreseen exactly how much one huge example of secession, breeding lesser ones indefinitely, would retard population, civilization, and prosperity no one can doubt that the extent of it would be very great and injurious.

The proposed emancipation would shorten the war, perpetuate peace, insure this increase of population, and proportionately the wealth of the country. With these, we should pay all the emancipation would cost, together with our other debt, easier than we should pay our other debt without it. If we had allowed our old national debt to run at six per cent. per annum, simple interest, from the end of our revolutionary struggle until to-day, without paying anything on either principal or interest, each man of us would owe less upon that debt now than each man owed upon it then; and this because our increase of men through the whole period has been greater than six per cent.; has run faster than the interest upon the debt. Thus, time alone relieves a debtor nation, so long as its population increases faster than unpaid interest accumulates on its debt.

"This fact would be no excuse for delaying payment of what is justly due; but it shows the great importance of time in this connection—the great advantage of a policy by which we shall not have to pay until we number a hundred millions, what, by a different policy, we would have to pay now, when we number but thirty-one millions. In a word, it shows that a dollar will be much harder to pay for the war than will be a dollar for emancipation on the proposed plan. And then the latter will cost no blood, no precious life. It will be a saving of both."

Various propositions and measures relating to compensated emancipation, were afterwards considered in both Houses, but it was in March, 1863, dropped after a refusal of the House to suspend the rules for the consideration of the subject.

Emancipation as a War Necessity.

Before the idea of compensated emancipation had been dropped, and it was constantly discouraged by the Democrats and Border Statesmen, President Lincoln had determined upon a more radical policy, and on the 22d of September, 1862, issued his celebrated proclamation declaring that he would emancipate "all persons held as slaves within any State or designated part of a State, the people whereof shall be in rebellion against the United States"—by the first of January, 1863, if such sections were not "in good faith represented in Congress." He followed this by actual emancipation at the time stated.

Proclamation of Sept. 22, 1862.

I, ABRAHAM LINCOLN, President of the United States of America, and Commander-in-Chief of the army and navy thereof, do hereby proclaim and declare that hereafter, as heretofore, the war will be prosecuted for the object of practically restoring the constitutional relation between the United States and each of the States and the people thereof, in which States that relation is or may be suspended or disturbed.

That it is my purpose, upon the next meeting of Congress, to again recommend the adoption of a practical measure tendering pecuniary aid to the free acceptance or rejection of all slave States, so called, the people thereof may not then be in rebellion against the United States, and which States may then have voluntarily adopted, or thereafter may voluntarily adopt, immediate or gradual abolishment of slavery within their respected limits; and that the effort to colonize persons of African descent with their consent upon this continent or elsewhere, with the previously obtained consent of the Governments existing there, will be continued.

That on the first day of January, in the year of our Lord one thousand eight hundred and sixty-three, all persons held as slaves within any State or designated part of a State, the people whereof shall then be in rebellion against the United States, shall be then, thenceforward, and forever free; and the Executive Government of the United States, including the military and naval authority thereof, will recognize and maintain the freedom of such persons, and will do no act or acts to repress such persons, or any of them, in any efforts they may make for their actual freedom.

That the Executive will, on the first day of January aforesaid, by proclamation, designate the States and parts of States, if any, in which the people thereof respectively, shall then be in rebellion against the United States; and the fact that any State, or the people thereof, shall on that day be, in good faith, represented in the Congress of the United States by members chosen thereto at elections wherein a majority of the qualified voters of such State shall have participated, shall, in the absence of strong countervailing testimony, be deemed conclusive evidence that such State, and the people thereof, are not in rebellion against the United States.

That attention is hereby called to an act of Congress entitled "An act to make an additional article of war," approved March 13, 1862, and which act is in the words and figures following:

"*Be it enacted by the Senate and House of Representatives of the United States of America in Congress assembled*, That hereafter the following shall be promulgated as an additional article of war, for the government of the army of the United States, and shall be obeyed and observed as such.

"ARTICLE —. All officers or persons in the military or naval service of the United States are prohibited from employing any of the forces under their respective commands for the purpose of returning fugitives from service or labor who may have escaped from any persons to whom such service or labor is claimed to be due, and any officer who shall be found guilty by a court-martial of violating this article shall be dismissed from the service.

"SEC. 2. *And be it further enacted*, That this act "shall take effect from and after its passage."

Also to the ninth and tenth sections of an act entitled "An act to suppress insurrection, to punish treason and rebellion, to seize and confiscate property of rebels, and for other purposes," approved July 17, 1862, and which sections are in the words and figures following:

"SEC. 9. *And be it further enacted*, That all slaves of persons who shall hereafter be engaged in rebellion against the Government of the United States or who shall in any way give aid or comfort thereto, escaping from such persons and taking refuge within the lines of the army; and all slaves captured from such persons or deserted by them, and coming under the control of the Government of the United States; and all slaves of such persons found *on* [or] being within any place occupied by rebel forces and afterwards occupied by the forces of the United States, shall be deemed captives of war, and shall be forever free of their servitude, and not again held as slaves.

"SEC. 10. *And be it further enacted*, That no slave escaping into any State, Territory, or the District of Columbia, from any other State, shall be delivered up, or in any way impeded or hindered of his liberty, except for crime, or some offence against the laws, unless the person claiming said fugitive shall first make oath that the person to whom the labor or service of such fugitive is alleged to be due is his lawful owner, and has not borne arms against the United States in the present rebellion, nor in any way given aid and comfort thereto; and no person engaged in the military or naval service of the United States shall, under any pretence whatever, assume to decide on the validity of the claim of any person to the service or labor of any other person, or surrender up any such person to the claimant, on pain of being dismissed from the service."

And I do hereby enjoin upon and order all persons engaged in the military and naval service of the United States to observe, obey, and enforce, within their respective spheres of service, the act and sections above recited.

And the Executive will in due time recommend that all citizens of the United States who shall have remained loyal thereto throughout the rebellion shall (upon the restoration of the constitutional relation between the United States and their respective States and people, if that relation shall have been suspended or disturbed) be compensated for all losses by acts of the United States, including the loss of slaves.

In witness whereof, I have hereunto set my hand, and caused the seal of the United States to be affixed.

Done at the city of Washington this twenty-second day of September, in the year of our Lord one thousand eight hundred and sixty-two, and of the Independence of the United States the eighty-seventh.

ABRAHAM LINCOLN.

By the President:

WILLIAM H. SEWARD, *Secretary of State.*

Proclamation of January 1, 1863.

WHEREAS, on the twenty-second day of September, in the year of our Lord one thousand eight hundred and sixty-two, a proclamation was issued by the President of the United States, containing among other things, the following, to wit:

"That on the first day of January, in the year of our Lord one thousand eight hundred and sixty-three, all persons held as slaves within any State or designated part of a State, the people whereof shall then be in rebellion against the United States, shall be then, thenceforward, and forever, free; and the Executive Government of the United States, including the military and naval authority thereof, will recognize and maintain the freedom of such persons, and will do no act or acts to repress such persons, or any of them, in any efforts they may make for their actual freedom.

"That the Executive will, on the first day of January aforesaid, by proclamation, designate the States and parts of States, if any, in which the people thereof, respectively, shall then be in rebellion against the United States; and the fact that any State, or the people thereof, shall on that day be in good faith represented in the Congress of the United States, by members chosen thereto at elections wherein a majority of the qualified voters of such States shall have participated, shall, in the absence of strong countervailing testimony, be deemed conclusive evidence that such State, and the people thereof, are then in rebellion against the United States."

Now, therefore, I, ABRAHAM LINCOLN, President of the United States, by virtue of the power in me vested as Commander-in-Chief of the Army and Navy of the United States, in time of actual armed rebellion against the authority and Government of the United States, and as a fit and necessary war measure for suppressing said rebellion, do, on this first day of January, in the year of our Lord one thousand eight hundred and sixty-three, and in accordance with my purpose so to do, publicly proclaimed for the full period of one hundred days from the day first above mentioned, order and designate as the States and parts of States wherein the people thereof, respectively, are this day in rebellion against the United States, the following, to wit:

Arkansas, Texas, Louisiana, (except the parishes of St. Bernard, Plaquemines, Jefferson, St. John, St. Charles, St. James, Ascension, Assumption, Terre Bonne, Lafourche, St. Mary, St. Martin, and Orleans, including the city of New Orleans,) Mississippi, Alabama, Florida, Georgia, South Carolina, North Carolina, and Virginia, (except the forty-eight counties designated as West Virginia, and also the counties of Berkeley, Accomac, Northampton, Elizabeth City, York, Princess Ann, and Norfolk, including the cities of Norfolk and Portsmouth,) and which excepted parts are for the present left precisely as if this proclamation were not issued.

And by virtue of the power and for the purpose aforesaid, I do order and declare that all persons held as slaves within said designated States and parts of States are, and henceforward shall be, free; and that the Executive Government of the United States, including the military and naval authorities thereof, will recognize and maintain the freedom of said persons.

And I hereby enjoin upon the people so declared to be free to abstain from all violence, unless in necessary self-defence; and I recommend to them that, in all cases when allowed, they labor faithfully for reasonable wages.

And I further declare and make known that such persons, of suitable condition, will be received into the armed service of the United States to garrison forts, positions, stations, and other places, and to man vessels of all sorts in said service.

And upon this act, sincerely believed to be an act of justice, warranted by the Constitution upon military necessity, I invoke the considerate judgment of mankind and the gracious favor of Almighty God.

In witness whereof, I have hereunto set my hand and caused the seal of the United States to be affixed.

Done at the city of Washington this first day of January, in the year of our Lord one thousand eight hundred and sixty-three, and of the independence of the United States of America the eighty-seventh. ABRAHAM LINCOLN.

By the President:

WILLIAM H. SEWARD,

Secretary of State.

These proclamations were followed by many attempts on the part of the Democrats to declare them null and void, but all such were tabled. The House on the 15th of December, 1862, endorsed the first by a vote of 78 to 51, almost a strict party vote. Two classed as Democrats, voted for emancipation—Haight and Noell; seven classed as Republicans, voted against it—Granger. Harrison, Leary, Maynard, Benj. F. Thomas, Francis Thomas, and Whaley.

Just previous to the issuance of the first proclamation a meeting of the Governors of the Northern States had been called to consider how best their States could aid the general conduct of the war. Some of them had conferred with the President, and while that meeting and the date of the emancipation proclamation are the same, it was publicly denied on the floor of Congress by Mr. Boutwell (June 25, 1864,) that the proclamation was the result of that meeting of the Governors. That they fully endorsed and knew of it, however, is shown by the following

---

Address of loyal Governors to the President.

Adopted at a meeting of Governors of loyal States, held to take measures for the more active support of the Government, at Altoona, Pennsylvania, on the 22d day of September, 1862.

After nearly one year and a half spent in contest with an armed and gigantic rebellion against the national Government of the United States, the duty and purpose of the loyal States and people continue, and must always remain as they were at its origin—namely, to restore and perpetuate the authority of this Government and the life of the nation. No matter what consequences are involved in our fidelity, this work of restoring the Republic, preserving the institutions of democratic liberty, and justifying the hopes and toils of our fathers shall not fail to be performed.

And we pledge without hesitation, to the President of the United States, the most loyal and cordial support, hereafter as heretofore, in the exercise of the functions of his great office. We recognize in him the Chief Executive Magistrate of the nation, the Commander-in-chief of the Army and Navy of the United States, their responsible and constitutional head, whose rightful authority and power, as well as the constitutional powers of Congress, must be rigorously and religiously guarded and preserved, as the condition on which alone our form of Government and the constitutional rights and liberties of the people themselves can be saved from the wreck of anarchy or from the gulf of despotism.

In submission to the laws which may have been or which may be duly enacted, and to the lawful orders of the President, co-operating always in our own spheres with the national Government, we mean to continue in the most vigorous exercise of all our lawful and proper powers, contending against treason, rebellion, and the public enemies, and, whether in public life or in private station, supporting the arms of the Union, until its cause shall conquer, until final victory shall perch upon its standard, or the rebel foe shall yield a dutiful, rightful, and unconditional submission.

And, impressed with the conviction that an army of reserve ought, until the war shall end, to be constantly kept on foot, to be raised, armed, equipped, and trained at home, and ready for emergencies, we respectfully ask the President to call for such a force of volunteers for one year's service, of not less than one hundred thousand in the aggregate, the quota of each State to be raised after it shall have filled its quota of the requisitions already made, both for volunteers and militia. We believe that this would be a measure of military prudence, while it would greatly promote the military education of the people.

We hail with heartfelt gratitude and encouraged hope the proclamation of the President, issued on the 22d instant, declaring emancipated from their bondage all persons held to service or labor as slaves in the rebel States, whose rebellion shall last until the first day of January now next ensuing. The right of any person to retain authority to compel any portion of the subjects of the national Government to rebel against it, or to maintain its enemies, implies in those who are allowed possession of such authority the right to rebel themselves; and therefore the right to establish martial law or military government in a State or territory in rebellion implies the right and the duty of the Government to liberate the minds of all men living therein by appropriate proclamations and assurances of protection, in order that all who are capable, intellectually and morally, of loyalty and obedience, may not be forced into treason as the unwilling tools of rebellious traitors. To have continued indefinitely the most efficient cause, support, and stay of the rebellion, would have been, in our judgment, unjust to the loyal people whose treasure and lives are made a willing sacrifice on the altar of patrotism—would have discriminated against the wife who is compelled to surrender her husband, against the parent who is to surrender his child to the hardships of the camp and the perils of battle, in favor of rebel masters permitted to retain their slaves. It would have been a final decision alike against humanity, justice, the rights and dignity of the Government, and against sound and wise national policy. The decision of the President to strike at the root of the rebellion will lend new vigor to the efforts and new life and hope to the hearts of the people. Cordially tendering to the President our respectful assurance of personal and official confidence, we trust and believe that the policy now inaugurated will be crowned with success, will give speedy. and triumphant victories over our enemies, and secure to this nation and this people the blessing and favor of Almighty God. We believe that the blood of the heroes who have already fallen, and those who may yet give their lives to their country, will not have been shed in vain.

The splendid valor of our soldiers, their patient endurance, their manly patriotism, and their devotion to duty, demand from us and from all their countrymen the homage of the sincerest gratitude and the pledge of our constant reinforcement and support. A just regard for these brave men, whom we have contributed to place in the field, and for the importance of the duties which may lawfully pertain to us hereafter, has called us into friendly conference. And now, presenting to our national Chief Magistrate this conclusion of our deliberations, we devote ourselves to our country's service, and we will surround the President with our constant support, trusting that the fidelity and zeal of the loyal States and people will always assure him that he will be constantly maintained in pursuing with the utmost vigor this war for the preservation of the national life and the hope of humanity.

A. G. CURTIN,
JOHN A. ANDREW,
RICHARD YATES,
ISRAEL WASHBURNE, JR.,
EDWARD SOLOMON,
SAMUEL J. KIRKWOOD,
O. P. MORTON,
By D. G. ROSE, his representative,
WM. SPRAGUE,
F. H. PEIRPOINT,
DAVID TOD,
N. S. BERRY,
AUSTIN BLAIR.

Repeal of the Fugitive Slave Law.

The first fugitive slave law passed was that of February 12th, 1793, the second and last that of September 18th, 1850. Various efforts had been made to repeal the latter before the war of the rebellion, without a prospect of success. The situation was now different. The war spirit was high, and both Houses of Congress were in the hands of the Republicans as early as December, 1861, but all of them were not then ready to vote for repeal, while the Democrats were at first solidly against it. The bill had passed the Senate in 1850 by 27 yeas to 12 nays; the House by 109 yeas to 76 nays, and yet as late as 1861 such was still the desire of many not to offend the political prejudices of the Border States and of Democrats whose aid was counted upon in the war, that sufficient votes could not be had until June, 1864, to pass the repealing bill. Republican sentiment advanced very slowly in the early years of the war, when the struggle looked doubtful and when there was a strong desire to hold for the Union every man and county not irrevocably against it; when success could be foreseen the advances were more rapid, but never as rapid as the more radical leaders desired. The record of Congress in the repeal of the Fugitive Slave Law will illustrate this political fact, in itself worthy of grave study by the politician and statesman, and therefore we give it as compiled by McPherson :—

Second Session, Thirty-Seventh Congress.*

In Senate, 1861, December 26—Mr. Howe, of Wisconsin, introduced a bill to repeal the fugitive slave law; which was referred to the Committee on the Judiciary.

1862, May 24—Mr. Wilson, of Massachusetts, introduced a bill to amend the fugitive slave law; which was ordered to be printed and lie on the table.

June 10—Mr. Wilson moved to take up the bill; which was agreed to—Yeas 25, nays 10, as follows:

YEAS—Messrs. Anthony, Browning, Chandler, Clark, Cowan, Dixon, Doolittle, Fessenden, Foot, Grimes, Hale, Harlan, Harris, Howard, Howe, King, Lane of Kansas, Morrill, Pomeroy, Simmons, Sumner, Ten Eyck, Trumbull, Wade, Wilson, of Massachusetts.—25.

NAYS—Messrs. *Carlile, Davis, Latham,*

* On the 23d of July, 1861, the Attorney General, in answer to a letter from the United States Marshal of Kansas, inquiring whether he should assist in the execution of the fugitive slave law, wrote:

ATTORNEY GENERAL'S OFFICE, *July* 23, 1861.

J. L. MCDOWELL, *U. S. Marshal, Kansas:*

Your letter, of the 11th of July, received 19th, (under frank of Senator Lane, of Kansas,) asks advice whether you should give your official services in the execution of the fugitive slave law.

It is the President's constitutional duty to "take care that the laws be faithfully executed." That means all the laws. He has no right to discriminate, no right to execute the laws he likes, and leave unexecuted those he dislikes. And of course you and I, his subordinates, can have no wider latitude of discretion than he has. Missouri is a State in the Union. The insurrectionary disorders in Missouri are but individual crimes, and do not change the legal status of the State, nor change its rights and obligations as a member of the Union.

A refusal by a ministerial officer to execute any law which properly belongs to his office, is an official misdemeanor, of which I have no doubt the President would take notice. Very respectfully

EDWARD BATES.

McDougall, Nesmith, Powell, Saulsbury, Stark, Willey, *Wright*—10.*

The bill was to secure to claimed fugitives a right to a jury trial in the district court for the United States for the district in which they may be, and to require the claimant to prove his loyalty. The bill repeals sections 6, 7, 8, 9, and 10 of the act of 1850, and that part of section 5, which authorizes the summoning of the *posse comitatus*. When a warrant of return is made either on jury trial or confession of the party in the presence of counsel, having been warned of his rights, the fugitive is to be surrendered to the claimant, or the marshal where necessary, who shall remove him to the boundary line of the district, and there deliver him to the claimant. The bill was not further considered.

In House, 1861, December 20—Mr. Julian offered this resolution:

Resolved, That the Judiciary Committee be instructed to report a bill, so amending the fugitive slave law enacted in 1850 as to forbid the recapture or return of any fugitive from labor without satisfactory proof first made that the claimant of such fugitive is loyal to the Government.

Mr. Holman moved to table the resolution, which was disagreed to—yeas 39, nays 78, as follows:

YEAS—Messrs. *Ancona, Joseph Baily, Biddle, George H. Browne, Cobb, Cooper, Cox, Cravens, Crittenden, Dunlap, English. Fouke, Grider, Harding, Holman, Johnson, Law. Lazear, Leary, Lehman, Mallory, Morris, Noble, Noell, Norton, Nugen, Odell, Pendleton, Robinson, Shiel, John B. Steele, William G. Steele, Vallandigham, Wadsworth*, Webster, *Chilton A. White, Wickliffe, Woodruff, Wright*—39.

NAYS—Messrs. Aldrich, Alley, Arnold, Babbitt, Baker, Baxter, Beaman, Bingham, Francis P. Blair, Samuel S. Blair, Blake, Buffinton, Burnham, Chamberlain, Clark, Colfax, Frederick A. Conkling, Roscoe Conkling, Cutler, Davis, Dawes, Delano, Duell, Edwards, Eliot, Fessenden, Franchot, Frank, Gooch, Goodwin, Gurley, Hale, Hanchett, Harrison, Hooper, Hutchins, Julian, William Kellogg, Lansing, Loomis, Lovejoy, McKnight, McPherson, Marston, Mitchell, Moorhead, Anson P. Morrill, Justin S. Morrill, Olin, Patton, Pike, Pomeroy, Porter, John H. Rice, Riddle, Edward H. Rollins, Sargent, Sedgwick, Shanks, Shellabarger, Sherman, Sloan, Spaulding, Stevens, Benjamin F. Thomas, Train, Vandever, Wall, Wallace, Walton, Washburne, Wheeler, Whaley, Albert S. White, Wilson, Windom, Worcester—78.

The resolution was then adopted—yeas 78, nays 39.

1862, June 9—Mr. Julian, of Indiana, introduced into the House a resolution instructing the Judiciary Committee to report a bill for the purpose of repealing the fugitive slave law; which was tabled—yeas 66, nays 51, as follows:

YEAS—Messrs. *William J. Allen, Ancona, Baily, Biddle*, Francis P. Blair, Jacob B. Blair, *George H. Browne*, William G. Brown, Burnham, *Calvert*, Casey, Clements, *Cobb, Corning, Crittenden*, Delano, Diven, Granger, *Grider*, Haight, Hale, *Harding, Holman, Johnson*, William Kellogg, *Kerrigan, Knapp, Lazear*, Low, Maynard, *Menzies*, Moorhead, *Morris, Noble, Noell, Norton, Odell, Pendleton, John S. Phelps*, Timothy G. Phelps, Porter, *Richardson, Robinson, James S. Rollins*, Sargent, Segar, *Sheffield, Shiel, Smith, John B. Steele, William G. Steele*, Benjamin F. Thomas, Francis Thomas, Trimble, *Vallandigham*, Verree, *Vibbard, Voorhees, Wadsworth*, Webster, *Chilton A. White, Wickliffe, Wood*, Woodruff, Worcester, *Wright*—66.

NAYS—Messrs. Aldrich, Alley, Baker, Baxter, Beaman, Bingham, Blake, Buffinton, Chamberlain, Colfax, Frederick A. Conkling, Davis, Dawes, Edgerton, Edwards, Eliot, Ely, Franchot, Gooch, Goodwin, Hanchett, Hutchins, Julian, Kelley, Francis W. Kellogg, Lansing, Lovejoy, McKnight, McPherson, Mitchell, Anson P. Morrill, Pike, Pomeroy, Potter, Alexander H. Rice, John H. Rice, Riddle, Edward H. Rollins, Shellabarger, Sloan, Spaulding, Stevens, Train, Trowbridge, Van Horn, Van Valkenburgh, Wall, Wallace, Washburne, Albert S. White, Windom—51.

Same day—Mr. Colfax, of Indiana, offered this resolution:

Resolved, That the Committee on the Judiciary be instructed to report a bill modifying the fugitive slave law so as to require a jury trial in all cases where the person claimed denies under oath that he is a slave, and also requiring any claimant under such act to prove that he has been loyal to the Government during the present rebellion.

Which was agreed to—yeas 77, nays 43, as follows:

YEAS—Messrs. Aldrich, Alley, Arnold, Ashley, Babbitt, Baker, Baxter, Beaman, Bingham, Francis P. Blair, Blake, Buffinton, Burnham, Chamberlain, Colfax, Frederick A. Conkling, Davis, Dawes, Delano, Diven, Edgerton, Edwards, Eliot, Ely, Franchot, Gooch, Goodwin, Granger, Gurley, Haight, Hale, Hanchett, Hutchins, Julian, Kelley, Francis W. Kellogg, William Kellogg, Lansing, Loomis, Lovejoy, Lowe, McKnight, McPherson, Mitchell, Anson P. Morrill, Justin S. Morrill, Nixon, Timothy G. Phelps, Pike, Pomeroy, Porter, Potter, Alexander H. Rice, John H. Rice, Riddle, Edward H. Rollins, Sargent, Shanks, *Sheffield*, Shellabarger, Sloan, Spaulding, Stevens, Stratton, Benjamin F.

* Republicans in Roman; Democrats in italics.

Thomas, Train, Trimble, Trowbridge, Van Valkenburgh, Verree, Wall, Wallace, Washburne, Albert, S. White, Wilson, Windom, Worcester—77.

NAYS—Messrs. *William J. Allen*, *Ancona*, *Baily*, *Biddle*, Jacob B. Blair, William G. Brown, *Calvert*, Casey, Clements, *Cobb*, *Corning*, *Crittenden*, *Fouke*, *Grider*, *Harding*, *Holman*, *Johnson*, *Knapp*, Maynard, *Menzies*, *Noble*, Noell, *Norton*, *Pendleton*, *John S. Phelps*, *Richardson*, *Robinson*, *James S Rollins*, Segar, *Shiel*, *Smith*, *John B. Steele*, *William G. Steele*, Francis Thomas, *Vallandigham*, *Vibbard*, *Voorhees*, *Wadsworth*, Webster, *Chilton A. White*, *Wickliffe*, *Wood*, *Wright*.—43.

Third Session, Thirty-Seventh Congress.

In Senate, 1863, February 11—Mr. Ten Eyck, from the Committee on the Judiciary, to whom was referred a bill, introduced by Senator Howe, in second session, December 26, 1861, to repeal the fugitive slave act of 1850, reported it back without amendment, and with a recommendation that it do not pass.

First Session, Thirty-Eighth Congress.

In House, 1863, Dec. 14.—Mr. Julian, of Indiana, offered this resolution:

Resolved, That the Committee on the Judiciary be instructed to report a bill for a repeal of the third and fourth sections of the "act respecting fugitives from justice and persons escaping from the service of their masters," approved February 12, 1793, and the act to amend and supplementary to the aforesaid act, approved September 18, 1850.

Mr. Holman moved that the resolution lie upon the table, which was agreed to—yeas 81, nays 73, as follows:

YEAS—Messrs. *James C. Allen*, *William J. Allen*, *Ancona*, Anderson, *Baily*, *Augustus C. Baldwin*, Jacob B. Blair, *Bliss*, *Brooks*, *James S. Brown*, William G. Browne, *Clay*, Cobb, *Coffroth*, *Cox*, *Cravens*, Creswell, *Dawson*, Demming, *Denison*, *Eden*, *Edgerton*, *Eldridge*, *English*, *Finck*, *Ganson*, *Grider*, *Griswold*, *Hall*, *Harding*, *Harrington*, *Benjamin G. Harris*, *Charles M. Harris*, Higby, *Holman*, *Hutchins*, *William Johnson*, *Kernan*, *King*, *Knapp*, *Law*, *Lazear*, *Le Blond*, *Long*, *Mallory*, *Marcy*, Marvin, McBride, *McDowell*, *McKinney*, *William H. Miller*, *James R. Morris*, *Morrison*, *Nelson*, *Noble*, *Odell*, *John O'Neil*, *Pendleton*, William H. Randall, *Robinson*, *Rogers*, *James S. Rollins*, *Ross*, *Scott*, Smith, Smithers, *Stebbins*, *John B. Steele*, *Stuart*, *Sweat*, Thomas, *Voorhees*, *Wadsworth*, *Ward*, *Wheeler*, *Chilton A. White*, *Joseph W. White*, Williams, *Winfield*, *Fernando Wood*, *Yeaman*—81.

NAYS—Messrs. Alley, Allison, Ames, Arnold, Ashley, John D. Baldwin, Baxter, Beaman, Blaine, Blow, Boutwell, Boyd, Brandegee, Broomall, Ambrose W. Clark, Freeman Clark, Cole, Henry Winter Davis, Dawes, Dixon, Donnelly, Driggs, Dumont, Eckley, Eliot, Farnsworth, Fenton, Frank, Garfield, Gooch, Grinnell, Hooper, Hotchkiss, Asahel W. Hubbard, John H. Hubbard, Hulburd, Jenckes, Julian, Francis W. Kellogg, Orlando Kellogg, Loan, Longyear, Lovejoy, McClurg, McIndoe, Samuel F. Miller, Moorhead, Morrill, Amos Myers, Leonard Myers, Norton, Charles O'Neill, Orth, Patterson, Pike, Pomeroy, Price, Alexander H. Rice, John H. Rice, Edward H. Rollins, Schenck, Scofield, Shannon, Spalding, Thayer, Van Valkenburgh, Elihu B. Washburne, William B. Washburn, Whaley, Wilder, Wilson, Windom, Woodbidge—73.

1864, June 6, Mr. Hubbard, of Connecticut, offered this resolution:

Resolved, That the Committee on the Judiciary be instructed to report to this House a bill for the repeal of all acts and parts of acts which provide for the rendition of fugitive slaves, and that they have leave to make such report at any time.

Which went over under the rule. May 30, he had made an ineffectual effort to offer it, Mr. Holman objecting.

REPEALING BILLS.

1864, April 19, the Senate considered the bill to repeal all acts for the rendition of fugitives from service or labor. The bill was taken up—yeas 26, nays 10.

Mr. Sherman moved to amend by inserting these words at the end of the bill:

Except the act approved February 12, 1793, entitled "An act respecting fugitives from justice, and persons escaping from the service of their masters."

Which was agreed to—yeas 24, nays 17, as follows:

YEAS—Messrs. *Buckalew*, *Carlile*, Collamer, Cowan, *Davis*, Dixon, Doolittle, Foster, Harris, Henderson, *Hendricks*, Howe, Johnson, Lane of Indiana, *McDougall*, *Nesmith*, *Powell*, *Riddle*, *Saulsbury*, Sherman, Ten Eyck, Trumbull, Van Winkle, Willey---24.

NAYS—Messrs. Anthony, Brown, Clark, Conness, Fessenden, Grimes, Hale, Howard, Lane of Kansas, Morgan, Morrill, Pomeroy, Ramsey, Sprague, Sumner, Wilkinson, Wilson—17.

Mr. Saulsbury moved to add these sections:

And be it further enacted, That no white inhabitant of the United States shall be arrested, or imprisoned, or held to answer for a capital or otherwise infamous crime, except in cases arising in the land or naval forces, or in the militia when in actual service in time of war or public danger, without due process of law.

And be it further enacted, That no person engaged in the executive, legislative, or judicial departments of the Government of the United States, or holding any office or trust recognized in the Constitution of the United States, and no person in military or naval service of the United States, shall, without due process of law, arrest or imprison any white inhabitant of the United States who is not, or has not been, or shall not at the time of such arrest or imprisonment be, engaged in levying war against the United States, or in adhering to the enemies of the United States, giving them aid and comfort, nor aid, abet, procure or advise the same, except in cases arising in the land or naval forces, or in the militia when in actual service in time of war or public danger. And any person as aforesaid so arresting, or imprisoning, or holding, as aforesaid, as in this and the second section of this act mentioned, or aiding, abetting, or procuring, or advising the same, shall be deemed guilty of felony, and, upon conviction thereof in any court of competent jurisdiction, shall be imprisoned for a term of not less than one nor more than five years, shall pay a fine of not less than $1,000 nor more than $5000, and shall be forever incapable of holding any office or public trust under the Government of the United States.

Mr. HALE moved to strike out the word "white" wherever it occurs; which was agreed to.

The amendment of Mr. SAULSBURY, as amended, was then disagreed to—yeas 9, nays 27, as follows:

YEAS—Messrs. *Buckalew, Carlile,* Cowan, *Davis, Hendricks, McDougall, Powell, Riddle, Saulsbury*—9.

NAYS—Messrs. Anthony, Clark, Collamer, Conness, Doolittle, Fessenden, Foster, Grimes, Hale, Harris, Howard, Howe, Lane of Indiana, Lane, of Kansas, Morgan, Morrill, Pomeroy, Ramsey, Sherman, Sprague, Sumner, Ten Eyck, Trumbull, Van Winkle, Wilkinson, Willey, Wilson—27.

Mr. CONNESS moved to table the bill; which was disagreed to—yeas 9, (Messrs. *Buckalew, Carlile,* Conness, *Davis, Hendricks, Nesmith, Powell, Riddle, Saulsbury,*) nays 31.

It was not again acted upon.

1864, June 13—The House passed this bill, introduced by Mr. SPALDING, of Ohio, and reported from the Committee on the Judiciary by Mr. MORRIS, of New York, as follows:

Be it enacted, etc., that sections three and four of an act entitled "An act respecting fugitives from justice and persons escaping from the service of their masters," passed February 12, 1793, and an Act entitled "An act to amend, and supplementary to, the act entitled 'An act respecting fugitives from justice, and persons escaping from their masters,' passed February 12, 1793," passed September 18, 1850, be, and the same are hereby, repealed.

Yeas 86, nays 60, as follows:

YEAS—Messrs. Alley, Allison, Ames, Arnold, Ashley, John D. Baldwin, Baxter, Beaman, Blaine, Blair, Blow, Boutwell, Boyd, Brandegee, Broomall, Ambrose W. Clarke, Freeman Clark, Cobb, Cole, Creswell, Henry Winter Davis, Thomas T. Davis, Dawes, Dixon, Donnelly, Driggs, Eckley, Eliot, Farnsworth, Fenton, Frank, Garfield, Gooch, *Griswold*, Higby, Hooper, Hotchkiss, Asahel W. Hubbard, John K. Hubbard, Hulburd, Ingersoll, Jenckes, Julian, Kelley, Francis W. Kellogg, O. Kellogg, Littlejohn, Loan, Longyear, Marvin, McClurg, McIndoe, Samuel F. Miller, Moorhead, Morrill, Daniel Morris, Amos Myers, Leonard Myers, Norton, Charles O'Neill, Orth, Patterson, Perham, Pike, Price, Alexander H. Rice, John H. Rice, Schenck, Scofield, Shannon, Sloan, Spalding, Starr, Stevens, Thayer, Thomas, Tracy, Upson, Van Valkenburgh, Webster, Whaley, Williams, Wilder, Wilson, Windom, Woodbridge—86.

NAYS—Messrs. *James C. Allen, William J. Allen, Ancona, Augustus C. Baldwin, Bliss, Brooks, James S. Brown, Chanler, Coffroth, Cox, Cravens, Dawson, Denison, Eden, Edgerton, Eldridge, English, Finck, Ganson, Grider, Harding, Harrington, Charles M. Harris, Herrick, Holman, Hutchins, Kalbfleisch, Kernan, King, Knapp, Law, Lazear, Le Blond, Mallory, Marcy, McDowell, McKinney, Wm. H. Miller, James R. Morris, Morrison, Odell, Pendleton, Pruyn, Radford, Robinson, Jas. S. Rollins, Ross,* Smithers, *John B. Steele, Wm. G. Steele, Stiles, Strouse, Stuart, Sweat, Wadsworth, Ward, Wheeler, Chilton A. White, Joseph W. White, Fernando Wood*—60.

June 22—This bill was taken up in the Senate, when Mr. SAULSBURY moved this substitute:

That no person held to service or labor in one State, under the laws thereof, escaping into another, shall, in consequence of any law or regulation therein, be discharged from such service or labor, but shall be delivered up on claim of the party to whom such service or labor may be due; and Congress shall pass all necessary and proper laws for the rendition of all such persons who shall so, as aforesaid, escape.

Which was rejected—yeas 9, nays 29, as follows:

YEAS—Messrs. *Buckalew, Carlile,* Cowan, *Davis, McDougall, Powell, Richardson, Riddle, Saulsbury*—9.

NAYS—Messrs. Anthony, Brown, Chandler, Clark, Conness, Dixon, Foot, Grimes, Hale, Harlan, Harris, Hicks, Howard, Howe, Johnson, Lane of Indiana, Lane of Kansas, Morgan, Morrill, Pomeroy, Ramsey, Sprague, Sumner, Ten Eyck, Trumbull, Van Winkle, Wade, Willey—29.

Mr. JOHNSON, of Maryland, moved an amendment to substitute a clause repealing the act of 1850; which was rejected—yeas 17, nays 22, as follows:

YEAS—Messrs. *Buckalew*, *Carlile*, Cowan, *Davis*, Harris, Hicks, Johnson, Lane of Indiana, *McDougall*, *Powell*, *Richardson*, *Riddle*, *Saulsbury*, Ten Eyck, Trumbull, Van Winkle, Willey—17.

NAYS—Messrs. Anthony, Brown, Chandler, Clark, Conness, Dixon, Fessenden, Foot, Grimes, Hale, Harlan, Howard, Howe, Lane of Kansas, Morgan, Morrill, Pomeroy, Ramsey, Sprague, Sumner, Wade, Wilson—22.

The bill then passed—yeas 27, nays 12, as follows:

YEAS—Messrs. Anthony, Brown, Chandler, Clark, Conness, Dixon, Fessenden, Foot, Grimes, Hale, Harlan, Harris, Hicks, Howard, Howe, Lane of Indiana, Lane of Kansas, Morgan, Morrill, Pomeroy, Ramsey, Sprague, Sumner, Ten Eyck, Trumbull, Wade, Wilson—27.

NAYS—Messrs. *Buckalew*, *Carlile*, Cowan, *Davis*, Johnson, *McDougall*, *Powell*, *Richardson*, *Riddle*, *Saulsbury*, Van Winkle, Willey—12.

ABRAHAM LINCOLN, *President*, approved it, June 28, 1864.

Seward as Secretary of State.

Wm. H. Seward was a master in diplomacy and Statecraft, and to his skill the Unionists were indebted for all avoidance of serious foreign complications while the war was going on. The most notable case coming under his supervision was that of the capture of Mason and Slidell, by Commodore Wilkes, who, on the 8th of November, 1861, had intercepted the *Trent* with *San Jacinto*. The prisoners were Confederate agents on their way to St. James and St. Cloud. Both had been prominent Senators, early secessionists, and the popular impulse of the North was to hold and punish them. Both Lincoln and Seward wisely resisted the passions of the hour, and when Great Britain demanded their release under the treaty of Ghent, wherein the right of future search of vessels was disavowed, Seward yielded, and referring to the terms of the treaty, said:

"If I decide this case in favor of my own Government, I must disavow its most cherished principles, and reverse and forever abandon its essential policy. The country cannot afford the sacrifice. If I maintain those principles and adhere to that policy, I must surrender the case itself."

The North, with high confidence in their President and Cabinet, readily conceded the wisdom of the argument, especially as it was clinched in the newspapers of the day by one of Lincoln's homely remarks: "*One war at a time.*" A war with Great Britain was thus happily avoided.

With the incidents of the war, however, save as they affected politics and politicians, this work has little to do, and we therefore pass the suspension of the *writ of habeas corpus*, which suspension was employed in breaking up the Maryland Legislature and other bodies when they contemplated secession, and it facilitated the arrest and punishment of men throughout the North who were suspected of giving "aid and comfort to the enemy." The alleged arbitrary character of these arrests caused much complaint from Democratic Senators and Representatives, but the right was fully enforced in the face of every form of protest until the war closed. The most prominent arrest was that of Clement L. Vallandigham, member of Congress from Ohio, who was sent into the Southern lines. From thence he went to Canada, and when a candidate for Governor in Ohio, was defeated by over 100,000 majority.

Financial Legislation—Internal Taxes.

The Financial legislation during the war was as follows:

1860, *December* 17—Authorized an issue of $10,000,000 in TREASURY NOTES, to be redeemed after the expiration of one year from the date of issue, and bearing such a rate of interest as may be offered by the lowest bidders. Authority was given to issue these notes in payment of warrants in favor of public creditors at their par value, bearing six per cent. interest per annum.

1861, *February* 8—Authorized a LOAN of $25,000,000, bearing interest at a rate not exceeding six per cent. per annum, and reimbursable within a period not beyond twenty years nor less than ten years. This loan was made for the payment of the current expenses, and was to be awarded to the most favorable bidders.

March 2—Authorized a LOAN of $10,000,000, bearing interest at a rate not exceeding six per cent. per annum, and reimbursable after the expiration of ten years from July 1, 1861. In case proposals for the loan were not acceptable, authority was given to issue the whole amount in TREASURY NOTES, bearing interest at a rate not exceeding six per cent. per annum. Authority was also given to substitute TREASURE NOTES for the whole or any part of the loans for which the Secretary was by law authorized to contract and issue bonds, at the time of the passage of this act, and such treasury notes were to be made receivable in payment of all public dues, and redeemable at any time within two years from March 2, 1861.

March 2—Authorized an issue, should the Secretary of the Treasury deem it expedient, of $2,800,000 in coupon BONDS, bearing interest at the rate of six per cent.

per annum, and redeemable in twenty years, for the payment of expenses incurred by the Territories of Washington and Oregon in the suppression of Indian hostilities during the year 1855–'56.

July 17—Authorized a loan of $250,000,000, for which could be issued BONDS bearing interest at a rate not exceeding 7 per cent. per annum, irredeemable for twenty years, and after that redeemable at the pleasure of the United States.

TREASURY NOTES bearing interest at the rate of 7.30 per cent. per annum, payable three years after date; and

United States NOTES without interest, payable on demand, to the extent of $50,000,000. (Increased by act of February 12, 1862, to $60,000,000.)

The bonds and treasury NOTES to be issued in such proportions of each as the Secretary may deem advisable.

August 5—Authorized an issue of BONDS bearing 6 per cent. interest per annum, and payable at the pleasure of the United States after twenty years from date, which may be issued in exchange for 7.30 treasury notes; but no such bonds to be issued for a less sum than $500, and the whole amount of such bonds not to exceed the whole amount of 7.30 treasury notes issued.

February 6, 1862—Making $50,000,000 of notes, of denominations less than $5, a legal tender, as recommended by Secretary Chase, was passed January 17, 1862. In the House it received the votes of the Republicans generally, and 38 Democrats. In the Senate it had 30 votes for to 1 against, that of Senator Powell.

1862, *February* 25—Authorized the issue of $15,000,000 in *legal tender United States* NOTES, $50,000,000 of which to be in lieu of demand notes issued under act of July 17, 1861, $500,000,000 in 6 per cent. bonds, redeemable after five years, and payable twenty years from date, which may be exchanged for United States notes, and a temporary loan of $25,000,000 in United States notes for not less than thirty days, payable after ten days' notice at 5 per cent. interest per annum.

March 17—Authorized an increase of TEMPORARY LOANS of $25,000,000, bearing interest at a rate not exceeding 5 per cent. per annum.

July 11—Authorized a further increase of TEMPORARY LOANS of $50,000,000, making the whole amount authorized $100,000,000.

March 1—Authorized an issue of CERTIFICATES OF INDEBTEDNESS, payable one year from date, in settlement of audited claims against the Government. Interest 6 per cent. per annum, payable in gold on those issued prior to March 4, 1863, and in lawful currency on those issued on and after that date. Amount of issue not specified.

1862, *July* 11—Authorized an additional issue of $150,000,000 *legal tender* NOTES, $35,000,000 of which might be in denominations less than five dollars. Fifty million dollars of this issue to be reserved to pay temporary loans promptly in case of emergency.

July 17—Authorized an issue of NOTES of the fractional part of one dollar, receivable in payment of all dues, except customs, less than five dollars. Amount of issue not specified.

1863, *January* 17—Authorized the issue of $100,000,000 in United States NOTES for the immediate payment of the army and navy; such notes to be a part of the amount provided for in any bill that may hereafter be passed by this Congress. The amount in this resolution is included in act of March 3, 1863.

March 3—Authorized a LOAN of $300,000,000 for this and $600,000,000 for next fiscal year, for which could be issued bonds running not less than ten nor more than forty years, principal and interest payable in coin, bearing interest at a rate not exceeding 6 per cent. per annum, payable on bonds not exceeding $100, annually, and on all others semi-annually. And TREASURY NOTES (to the amount of $400,000,000) not exceeding three years to run, with interest not over 6 per cent. per annum, principal and interest payable in lawful money, which may be made a legal tender for their face value, excluding interest, or convertible into United States notes. And a further issue of $150,000,000 in United States NOTES for the purpose of converting the Treasury notes which may be issued under this act, and for no other purpose. And a further issue, if necessary, for the payment of the army and navy, and other creditors of the Government, of $150,000,000 in United States NOTES, which amount includes the $100,000,000 authorized by the joint resolution of Congress, January 17, 1863. The whole amount of bonds, treasury notes, and United States notes issued under this act not to exceed the sum of $900,000,000.

March 3—Authorized to issue not exceeding $50,000,000 in FRACTIONAL CURRENCY, (in lieu of postage or other stamps,) exchangeable for United States notes in sums not less than three dollars, and receivable for any dues to the United States less than five dollars, except duties on imports. The whole amount issued, including postage and other stamps issued as currency, not to exceed $50,000,000. Authority was given to prepare it in the Treasury Department, under the supervision of the Secretary.

1864, *March* 3—Authorized, in lieu of so much of the loan of March 3, 1863, a LOAN of $200,000,000 for the current fiscal year, for which may be issued bonds redeemable after five and within forty years, principal and interest payable in coin, bearing interest at a rate not exceeding 6 per cent. per annum, payable annually on bonds not over $100, and on all others semi-annually. These bonds to be exempt from taxation by or under State or municipal authority.

1864, *June* 30—Authorized a LOAN of $400,000,000, for which may be issued bonds, redeemable after five nor more than thirty years, or if deemed expedient, made payable at any period not more than forty years from date—interest not exceeding six per cent. semi-annually, in coin.

Pending the loan bill of June 22, 1862, before the House in Committee of the Whole, and the question being on the first section, authorizing a loan of $400,000,000, closing with this clause:

And all bonds, Treasury notes, and other obligations of the United States shall be exempt from taxation by or under state or municipal authority.

There was a sharp political controversy on this question, but the House finally agreed to it by 77 to 71. Party lines were not then distinctly drawn on financial issues.

INTERNAL TAXES.

The system of internal revenue taxes imposed during the war did not evenly divide parties until near its close, when Democrats were generally arrayed against these taxes. They cannot, from the record, be correctly classed as political issues, yet their adoption and the feelings since engendered by them, makes a brief summary of the record essential.

First Session, Thirty-Seventh Congress.

The bill to provide increased revenue from imports, &c., passed the House August 2, 1861—yeas 89, nays 39.

Same day, it passed the Senate—yeas 34, nays 8, (Messrs. *Breckinridge, Bright, Johnson*, of Missouri, *Kennedy, Latham, Polk, Powell, Saulsbury*.)*

Second Session, Thirty-Seventh Congress.

The Internal Revenue Act of 1862.

1862, April 8—The House passed the bill to provide internal revenue, support the Government, and pay interest on the public debt—yeas 126, nays 15. The NAYS were:

Messrs. *William Allen, George H. Browne*, Buffinton, *Cox, Kerrigan, Knapp, Law, Norton, Pendleton, Richardson, Shiel, Vallandigham, Voorhees, Chilton A. White, Wickliffe*—15.

June 6—The bill passed in the Senate—yeas 37, nay 1, (Mr. *Powell*.)

First Session Thirty-Eighth Congress.

Internal Revenue Act of 1864.

April 28—The House passed the act of 1864—yeas 110, nays 39. The NAYS were:

Messrs. *James C. Allen, William J. Allen, Ancona, Brooks, Chanler, Cox, Dawson, Denison, Eden, Eldridge, Finck, Harrington, Benjamin G. Harris, Herrick, Philip Johnson, William Johnson, Knapp, Law, Le Blond, Long, Marcy, McDowell, McKinney, James R. Morris, Morrison, Noble, John O'Neil, Pendleton, Perry, Robinson, Ross, Stiles, Strouse, Stuart, Voorhees, Ward, Chilton A. White, Joseph W. White, Fernando Wood*—39.

* Democrats in italics.

June 6—The Senate amended and passed the bill—yeas 22, nays 3, (Messrs. *Davis, Hendricks, Powell*.)

The bill, as finally agreed upon by a Committee of Conference, passed without a division.

Second Session, Thirty-Seventh Congress.

Tariff Act of 1862.

In House—1862, July 1—The House passed, without a division, a bill increasing temporarily the duties on imports, and for other purposes.

July 8—The Senate passed it without a division.

THE TARIFF ACT OF 1864.

June 4—The House passed the bill—yeas 81, nays 28. The NAYS were:

Messrs. *James C. Allen, Bliss, James S. Brown, Cox, Edgerton, Eldridge, Finck, Grider, Harding, Harrington, Chas. M. Harris, Herrick, Holman, Hutchins, Le Blond, Long, Mallory, Marcy, McDowell, Morrison, Noble, Pendleton, Perry, Pruyn, Ross, Wadsworth, Chilton A. White, Joseph W. White*—28.

June 17—The Senate passed the bill—yeas 22, nays 5, (Messrs. *Buckalew, Hendricks, McDougall, Powell, Richardson*.)

Second Session, Thirty-Seventh Congress.

Taxes in Insurrectionary Districts, 1862.

1862, May 12—The bill for the collection of taxes in the insurrectionary districts passed the Senate—yeas 32, nays 3, as follows:

YEAS—Messrs. Anthony, Browning, Chandler, Clark, *Davis*, Dixon, Doolittle, Fessenden, Foot, Foster, Harlan, Harris, Henderson, Howe, King, Lane of Indiana, Lane of Kansas, *Latham, McDougall*, Morrill, *Nesmith*, Pomeroy, *Rice*, Sherman, Sumner, Ten Eyck, Trumbull, Wade, Wilkinson, Willey, Wilson, of Massachusetts, *Wright*—32.

NAYS—Messrs. Howard, *Powell, Saulsbury*—3.

May 28—The bill passed House—yeas 98, nays 17. The NAYS were:

Messrs. *Biddle, Calvert, Cravens, Johnson, Kerrigan, Law, Mallory, Menzies, Noble, Norton, Pendleton, Perry*, Francis Thomas *Vallandigham, Ward, Wickliffe, Wood*—17.

The Democrats who voted Aye were:

Messrs. *Ancona, Baily, Cobb, English, Haight, Holman, Lehman, Odell, Phelps*,

* Democrats in italics.

Richardson, James S. Rollins, Sheffield, Smith, John B. Steele, Wm. G. Steele.

TAXES IN INSURRECTIONARY DISTRICTS, 1864.

In Senate, June 27—The bill passed the Senate without a division.

July 2—It passed the House without a division.

Many financial measures and propositions were rejected, and we shall not attempt to give the record on these. All that were passed and went into operation can be more readily understood by a glance at our Tabulated History, in Book VII., which gives a full view of the financial history and sets out all the loans and revenues., We ought not to close this review, however, without giving here a tabulated statement, from "McPherson's History of the Great Rebellion," of

The Confederate Debt.

December 31, 1862, the receipts of the Treasury from the commencement of the "Permanent Government," (February 18, 1862,) were as follows:

RECEIPTS.

Patent fund	$13,920 00
Customs	668,566 00
Miscellaneous	2,291,812 00
Repayments of disbursing officers	3,839,263 00
Interest on loans	26,583 00
Call loan certificates	59,742,796 00
One hundred million loan	41,398,286 00
Treasury notes	215,554,885 00
Interest bearing notes	113,740.000 00
War tax	16,664,513 00
Loan 28th of February, 1861	1,375,476 00
Coin received from Bank of Louisiana	2,539,799 00
Total	$457,855,704 00
Total debt up to December 31, 1862	556,105,100 00
Estimated amount at that date necessary to support the Government to July, 1863, was	357,929,229 00

Up to December 31, 1862, the issues of the Treasury were:

Notes	$440,678,510 00
Redeemed	30,193,479 50
Outstanding	$410,485,030 50

From January 1, 1863, to September 30, 1863, the receipts of the Treasury were:

For 8 per cent. stock	$107,292,900 70
For 7 per cent. stock	38,757,650 70
For 6 per cent. stock	6,810,050 00
For 5 per cent. stock	22,992,900 00
For 4 per cent. stock	482,200 00
Cotton certificates	2,000,000 00
Interest on loans	140,210 00
War tax	4,128,988 97
Treasury notes	391,623,530 00
Sequestration	1,862,550 27
Customs	934,798 68
Export duty on cotton	8,101 78
Patent fund	10,794 04
Miscellaneous, including repayments by disbursing officers	24,498,217 93
Total	$601,522,893 12

EXPENDITURES DURING THAT TIME.

War Department	$377,988,244 00
Navy Department	38,437,661 00
Civil, miscellaneous, etc	11,629,278 00
Customs	56,636 00
Public debt	32,212,290 00
Notes cancelled and redeemed	59,044,449 00
Total expenditures	$519,368,559 00
Total receipts	601,522,893 00
Balance in treasury	$82,154,334 00

But from this amount is to be deducted the amount of all Treasury notes that have been funded, but which have not yet received a true estimation, $65,000,000; total remaining, $17,-154,334.

CONDITION OF THE TREASURY, JANUARY 1, 1864.

Jan. 25—The Secretary of the Treasury (C. G. Memminger) laid before the Senate a statement in reply to a resolution of the 20th, asking information relative to the funded debt, to call certificates, to non-interest and interest-bearing Treasury notes, and other financial matters. From this it appears that, January, 1864, the funded debt was as follows:

Act Feb 28, 1861, 8 ⅌ cent.,	15,000,000 00	
Act May 16, 1861, 8 ⅌ cent.,	8,774.900 00	
Act Aug 19, 1861, 8 ⅌ cent.,	100,000,000 00	
Act Apr. 12, 1862, 8 ⅌ cent.,	3,612,300 00	
Act Feb. 20, 1863, 8 ⅌ cent.,	95,785,000 00	
Act Feb. 20, 1863, 7 ⅌ cent.,	63.615,750 00	
Act Mar 23, 1863, 6 ⅌ cent.,	2,831,700 00	
Act April 30, 1863 (cotton interest coupons)	8,252,000 00	
		$297,871,650 00
Call certificates		69,206,770 00
Non-interest bearing Treasury notes outstanding:		
Act May 16, 1861—Payable two years after date	8,320,875 00	
Act Aug. 19, 1861—General currency	189,719,251 00	
Act Oct. 13, 1861—All denominations	131,028,366 50	
Act March 23—All denominations	391,829,702 50	
		720,898,095 00
Interest-bearing Treasury notes outstanding		102,465,450 00
Amount of Treasury notes under $5, outstanding Jan. 1, 1864, viz:		
Act April 17, 1862, denominations of $1 and $2	4,860,277 50	
Act Oct. 13, 1862, $1 and $2	2,344,800 00	
Act March 23, 1863, 50 cents	3,419,000 00	
Total under $5		10,424,077 50
Total debt, Jan. 1, 1864		$1,220,866,042 50

ITS CONDITION, MARCH 31, 1864.

The Register of the Treasury, Robert Tyler, gave a statement, which appeared in the Richmond *Sentinel* after the passage of the funding law, which gives the amount of outstanding non-interest-bearing Treasury notes, March 31, 1864, as $796,264,403, as follows:

Act May 16, 1861—Ten-year notes	$7,201,375 00
Act Aug. 19, 1861—General currency	154,365,631 00
Act Apr. 19, 1862—ones and twos	4,516,509 00
Act Oct. 18, 1862—General currency	118,997,321 50
Act Mar. 23, 1863—General currency	511,182,566 50
Total	$796,264,403 00

He also publishes this statement of the issue of non-interest-bearing Treasury notes since the organization of the "Confederate" government:

Fifty cents	$911,258 50
Ones	4,882,000 00
Twos	6,086,320 00
Fives	79,090,315 00
Tens	157,982,750 00
Twenties	217,425,120 00
Fifties	188,088,200 00
Total	$973,277,363 50

Confederate Taxes.

We also append as full and fair a statement of Confederate taxes as can be procured, beginning with a summary of the act authorizing the issue of Treasury notes and bonds, and providing a war tax for their redemption:

THE TAX ACT OF JULY, 1861.

The Richmond *Enquirer* gives the following summary of the act authorizing the issue of Treasury notes and bonds, and providing a war tax for their redemption:

Section one authorizes the issue of Treasury notes, payable to bearer at the expiration of six months after the ratification of a treaty of peace between the Confederate States and the United States. The notes are not to be of a less denomination than five dollars, to be re-issued at pleasure, to be received in payment of all public dues, except the export duty on cotton, and the whole issue outstanding at one time, including the amount issued under former acts, are not to exceed one hundred millions of dollars.

Section two provides that, for the purpose of funding the said notes, or for the purpose of purchasing specie or military stores, &c., bonds may be issued, payable not more than twenty years after date, to the amount of one hundred millions of dollars, and bearing an interest of eight per cent. per annum. This amount includes the thirty millions already authorized to be issued. The bonds are not to be issued in less amounts than $100, except when the subscription is for a less amount, when they may be issued as low as $50.

Section three provides that holders of Treasury notes may at any time exchange them for bonds.

Section four provides that, for the special purpose of paying the principal and interest of the public debt, and of supporting the Government, a war tax shall be assessed and levied of fifty cents upon each one hundred dollars in value of the following property in the Confederate States, namely: Real estate of all kinds; slaves; merchandise; bank stocks; railroad and other corporation stocks; money at interest or invested by individuals in the purchase of bills, notes, and other securities for money, except the bonds of the Confederate States of America, and cash on hand or on deposit in bank or elsewhere; cattle, horses, and mules; gold watches, gold and silver plate; pianos and pleasure carriages: *Provided, however*, That when the taxable property, herein above enumerated, of any head of a family is of value less than five hundred dollars, such taxable property shall be exempt from taxation under this act. It provides further that the property of colleges, schools, and religious associations shall be exempt.

The remaining sections provide for the collection of the tax.

THE TAX ACT OF DECEMBER 19, 1861.

An act supplementary to an act to authorize the issue of Treasury notes, and to provide a war tax for their redemption.

SEC. 1. *The Congress of the Confederate States of America do enact*, That the Secretary of the Treasury is hereby authorized to pay over to the several banks, which have made advances to the Government, in anticipation of the issue of Treasury notes, a sufficient amount, not exceeding $10,000,000, for the principal and interest due upon the said advance, according to the engagements made with them.

SEC. 2. The time affixed by the said act for making assignments is hereby extended to the 1st day of January next, and the time for the completion and delivery of the lists is extended to the 1st day of March next, and the time for the report of the said lists to the chief collector is extended to the 1st day of May next; and in cases where the time thus fixed shall be found insufficient, the Secretary of the Treasury shall have power to make further extension, as circumstances may require.

SEC. 3. The cash on hand, or on deposit in the bank, or elsewhere, mentioned in the fourth section of said act, is hereby declared to be subject to assessment and taxation, and the money at interest, or invested by individuals in the purchase of bills, notes, and other securities for money, shall be deemed to include securities for money belonging to non-residents, and such securities shall be returned, and the tax thereon paid by any agent or trustee having the same in possession or under his control. The term merchandise shall be construed to include merchandise belonging to any non-resident, and the property shall be returned, and the tax paid by any person having the same in possession as agent, attorney, or consignee: *Provided*, That the words "money at interest," as used in the act to which this act is an amendment, shall be so construed as to include all notes, or other evidences of debt, bearing interest, without reference to the consideration of the same. The exception allowed by the twentieth section for agricultural products shall be construed to embrace such products only when in the hands of the producer, or held for his account. But no tax shall be assessed or levied on any money at interest when the notes, bond, bill, or other security taken for its payment, shall be worthless from the insolvency and total inability to pay of the payer or obligor, or person liable to make such payment; and all securities for money payable under this act shall be assessed according to their value, and the assessor shall have the same power to ascertain the value of such securities as the law confers upon him with respect to other property.

SEC. 4. That an amount of money, not exceeding $25,000, shall be and the same is hereby appropriated, out of any money in the treasury not otherwise appropriated, to be disbursed under the authority of the Secretary of the Treasury, to the chief State tax collectors, for such expenses as shall be actually incurred for salaries of clerks, office hire, stationery, and incidental charges; but the books and printing required shall be at the expense of the department, and subject to its approval.

SEC. 5. The lien for the tax shall attach from the date of the assessment, and shall follow the same into every State in the Confederacy; and in case any person shall attempt to remove any property which may be liable to tax, beyond the jurisdiction of the State in which the tax is payable, without payment of the tax, the collector of the district may distrain upon and sell the same, in the same manner as is provided in cases where default is made in the payment of the tax.

SEC. 6. On the report of any chief collector, that any county, town or district, or any part thereof, is occupied by the public enemy, or has been so occupied as to occasion destruction of crops or property, the Secretary of the Treasury may suspend the collection of tax in such region until the same can be reported to Congress, and its action had thereon.

SEC. 7. In case any of the Confederate States shall undertake to pay the tax to be collected within its limits before the time at which the district collectors shall enter upon the discharge of their duties, the Secretary of the Treasury may suspend the appointment of such collectors, and may direct the chief collector to appoint assessors, and to take proper measures for the making and perfecting the returns, assessments and lists required by law; and the returns, assessments and lists so made, shall have the same legal validity, to all intents and purposes, as if made according to the provisions of the act to which this act is supplementary.

SEC. 8. That tax lists already given, varying from the provisions of this act, shall be corrected so as to conform thereto.

THE TAX ACT OF APRIL 24, 1863.

[From the Richmond Whig, April 21.]

We present below a synopsis of the bill to lay taxes for the common defence and to carry on the government of the Confederate States, which has passed both branches of Congress. It is substantially the bill proposed by the committee on conference:

1. The first section imposes a tax of eight per cent. upon the value of all naval stores, salt, wines and spirituous liquors, tobacco, manufactured or unmanufactured, cotton, wool, flour, sugar, molasses, syrup, rice, and other agricultural products, held or owned on the 1st day of July next, and not necessary for family consumption for the unexpired portion of the year 1863, and of the growth or production of any year preceding the year 1863; and a tax of one per cent. upon all moneys, bank notes or other currency on hand or on deposit on the 1st day of July next, and on the value of all credits on which the interest has not been paid, and not employed in a business, the income derived from which is taxed under the provisions of this act: *Provided*, That all moneys owned, held or deposited beyond the limits of the Confederate States shall be valued at the current rate of exchange in Confederate treasury notes. The tax to be assessed on the first day of July and collected on the first day of October next, or as soon thereafter as may be practicable.

2. Every person engaged, or intending to engage, in any business named in the fifth section, shall, within sixty days after the passage of the act, or at the time of beginning business, and on the first of January in each year thereafter, register with the district collector a true account of the

name and residence of each person, firm, or corporation engaged or interested in the business, with a statement of the time for which, and the place and manner in which the same is to be conducted, &c. At the time of the registry there shall be paid the specific tax for the year ending on the next 31st of December, and such other tax as may be due upon sales or receipts in such business.

3. Any person failing to make such registry and pay such tax, shall, in addition to all other taxes upon his business imposed by the act, pay double the amount of the specific tax on such business, and a like sum for every thirty days of such failure.

4. Requires a separate registry and tax for each business mentioned in the fifth section, and for each place of conducting the same; but no tax for mere storage of goods at a place other than the registered place of business. A new registry required upon every change in the place of conducting a registered business, upon the death of any person conducting the same, or upon the transfer of the business to another, but no additional tax.

5. Imposing the following taxes for the year ending 31st of December, 1863, and for each year thereafter:

Bankers shall pay $500.

Auctioneers, retail dealers, tobacconists, pedlers, cattle brokers, apothecaries, photographers, and confectioners, $50, and two and a half per centum on the gross amount of sales made.

Wholesale dealers in liquors, $200, and five per centum on gross amount of sales. Retail dealers in liquors, $100, and ten per centum on gross amount of sales.

Wholesale dealers in groceries, goods, wares, merchandise, &c., $200, and two and a half per centum.

Pawnbrokers, money and exchange brokers, $200.

Distillers, $200, and twenty per centum. Brewers, $100, and two and a half per centum.

Hotels, inns, taverns, and eating-houses, first class, $500; second class, $300; third class, $200; fourth class, 100; fifth class, $30. Every house where food or refreshments are sold, and every boarding house where there shall be six boarders or more, shall be deemed an eating house under this act.

Commercial brokers or commission merchants, $200, and two and a half per centum.

Theatres, $500, and five per centum on all receipts. Each circus, $100, and $10 for each exhibition. Jugglers and other persons exhibiting shows, $50.

Bowling alleys and billiard rooms, $40 for each alley or table registered.

Livery stable keepers, lawyers, physicians, surgeons, and dentists, $50.

Butchers and bakers, $50, and one per centum.

6. Every person registered and taxed is required to make returns of the gross amount of sales from the passage of the act to the 30th of June, and every three months thereafter.

7. A tax upon all salaries, except of persons in the military or naval service, of one per cent. when not exceeding $1,500, and two per cent. upon an excess over that amount: *Provided*, That no taxes shall be imposed by virtue of this act on the salary of any person receiving a salary not exceeding $1,000 per annum, or at a like rate for another period of time, longer or shorter.

8. Provides that the tax on annual incomes, between $500 and $1,500, shall be five per cent.; between $1,500 and $3,000, five per cent. on the first $1,500 and ten per cent. on the excess; between $3,000 and $5,000, ten per cent.; between $5,000 and $10,000, twelve and a half per cent.; over $10,000, fifteen per cent., subject to the following deductions: On incomes derived from rents of real estate, manufacturing, and mining establishments, &c., a sum sufficient for necessary annual repairs; on incomes from any mining or manufacturing business, the rent, (if rented,) cost of labor actually hired, and raw material; on incomes from navigating enterprises, the hire of the vessel, or allowance for wear and tear of the same, not exceeding ten per cent.; on incomes derived from the sale of merchandise or any other property, the prime cost of transportation, salaries of clerks, and rent of buildings; on incomes from any other occupation, the salaries of clerks, rent, cost of labor, material, &c.; and in case of mutual insurance companies, the amount of losses paid by them during the year. Incomes derived from other sources are subject to no deductions whatever.

All joint stock companies and corporations shall pay one tenth of the dividend and reserved fund annually. If the annual earnings shall give a profit of more than ten and less than twenty per cent. on capital stock, one eighth to be paid; if more than twenty per cent., one sixth. The tax to be collected on the 1st of January next, and of each year thereafter.

9. Relates to estimates and deductions, investigations, referees, &c.

10. A tax of ten per cent. on all profits in 1862 by the purchase and sale of flour, corn, bacon, pork, oats, hay, rice, salt, iron or the manufactures of iron, sugar, molasses made of cane, butter, woolen cloths, shoes, boots, blankets, and cotton cloths. Does not apply to regular retail business.

11. Each farmer, after reserving for his

own use fifty bushels sweet and fifty bushels Irish potatoes, one hundred bushels corn or fifty bushels wheat produced this year, shall pay and deliver to the Confederate Government one tenth of the grain, potatoes, forage, sugar, molasses, cotton, wool, and tobacco produced. After reserving twenty bushels peas or beans he shall deliver one tenth thereof.

12. Every farmer, planter, or grazier, one tenth of the hogs slaughtered by him, in cured bacon, at the rate of sixty pounds of bacon to one hundred pounds of pork; one per cent. upon the value of all neat cattle, horses, mules, not used in cultivation, and asses, to be paid by the owners of the same; beeves sold to be taxed as income.

13. Gives in detail the duties of post quartermasters under the act.

14. Relates to the duties of assessors and collectors.

15. Makes trustees, guardians, &c., responsible for taxes due from estates, &c., under their control.

16. Exempts the income and moneys of hospitals, asylums churches, schools, and colleges from taxation under the act.

17. Authorizes the Secretary of the Treasury to make all rules and regulations necessary to the operation of the act.

18. Provides that the act shall be in force for two years from the expiration of the present year, unless sooner repealed; that the tax on naval stores, flour, wool, cotton, tobacco, and other agricultural products of the growth of any year preceding 1863, imposed in the first section, shall be levied and collected only for the present year.

The tax act of February 17, 1864, levies, in addition to the above rates, the following, as stated in the Richmond *Sentinel* of February, 1864:

Sec. 1. Upon the value of real, personal, and mixed property, of every kind and description, except the exemptions hereafter to be named, five per cent.; the tax levied on property employed in agriculture to be credited by the value of property in kind.

On gold and silver ware, plate, jewels, and watches, ten per cent.

The tax to be levied on the value of property in 1860, except in the case of land, slaves, cotton, and tobacco, purchased since January 1st, 1862, upon which the tax shall be levied on the price paid.

Sec. 2. A tax of five per cent. on the value of all shares in joint stock companies of any kind, whether incorporated or not. The shares to be valued at their market value at the time of assessment.

Sec. 3. Upon the market value of gold and silver coin or bullion, five per cent.; also the same upon moneys held abroad, or all bills of exchange drawn therefor.

A tax of five per cent. on all solvent credits, and on all bank bills and papers used as currency, except non-interest-bearing Confederate Treasury notes, and not employed in a registered business taxed twenty-five per cent.

Sec. 4. Profits in trade and business taxed as follows:

On the purchase and sale of agricultural products and mercantile wares generally, from January 1, 1863, to January 1, 1865, ten per cent. in addition to the tax under the act of April 24, 1863.

The same on the purchase and sale of coin, exchange, stocks, notes, and credits of any kind, and any property not included in the foregoing.

On the amount of profits exceeding twenty-five per cent. of any bank, banking company, or joint stock company of any description, incorporated or not, twenty-five per cent. on such excess.

Sec 5. The following are exempted from taxation.

Five hundred dollars' worth of property for each head of a family, and a hundred dollars additional for each minor child; and for each son in the army or navy, or who has fallen in the service, and a member of the family when he enlisted, the further sum of $500.

One thousand dollars of the property of the widow or minor children of any officer, soldier, sailor, or marine, who has died in the service.

A like amount of property of any officer, soldier, sailor, or marine, engaged in the service, or who has been disabled therein, provided said property, exclusive of furniture, does not exceed in value $1,000.

When property has been injured or destroyed by the enemy, or the owner unable temporarily to use or occupy it by reason of the presence or proximity of the enemy, the assessment may be reduced in proportion to the damage sustained by the owner, and the tax in the same ratio by the district collector.

Sec. 6. The taxes on property for 1864 to be assessed as on the day of the passage of this act, and collected the 1st of June next, with ninety days extension west of the Mississippi. The additional tax on incomes or profits for 1863, to be paid forthwith; the tax on incomes, &c., for 1864, to be collected according to the acts of 1863.

Sec. 7. Exempts from tax on income for 1864, all property herein taxed *ad valorem*. The tax on Confederate bonds in no case to exceed the interest payable on the same; and said bonds exempt from tax when held by minors or lunatics, if the interest do not exceed one thousand dollars.

THE TAX LAW.

We learn that, according to the construction of the recent tax law in the Treasury Department, tax payers will be required to state the articles and objects subjected to a specific or *ad valorem* tax, held, owned, or possessed by them on the 17th day of February, 1864, the date of the act.

The daily wages of detailed soldiers and other employés of the Government are not liable to taxation as income, although they may amount, in the aggregate, to the sum of $1,000 per annum.

A tax additional to both the above was imposed as follows, June 1, 1864:

A bill to provide supplies for the army, and to prescribe the mode of making impressments.

SEC. 1. *The Congress of the Confederate States of America do enact*, Every person required to pay a tax in kind, under the provisions of the "Act to lay taxes for the common defense and carry on the Government of the Confederate States," approved April 24, 1863, and the act amendatory thereof, approved February 17, 1864, shall, in addition to the one tenth required by said acts to be paid as a tax in kind, deliver to the Confederate Government, of the products of the present year and of the year 1865, one other tenth of the several products taxed in kind by the acts aforesaid, which additional one tenth shall be ascertained, assessed and collected, in all respects, as is provided by law for the said tax in kind, and shall be paid for, on delivery, by the Post-Quartermasters in the several districts at the assessed value thereof, except that payment for cotton and tobacco shall be made by the agents of the Treasury Department appointed to receive the same.

SEC. 2. The supplies necessary to the support of the producer and his family, and to carry on his ordinary business, shall be exempted from the contribution required by the preceding section, and from the additional impressments authorized by the act: *Provided, however*, That nothing herein contained shall be construed to repeal or affect the provisions of an act entitled "An act to authorize the impressment of meat for the use of the army, under certain circumstances," approved Feb. 17, 1864, and if the amount of any article or product so necessary cannot be agreed upon between the assessor and the producer, it shall be ascertained and determined by disinterested freeholders of the vicinage, as is provided in cases of disagreement as to the estimates and assessments of tax in kind. If required by the assessor, such freeholder shall ascertain whether a producer, who is found unable to furnish the additional one tenth of any one product, cannot supply the deficiency by the delivery of an equivalent in other products, and upon what terms such commutation shall be made. Any commutation thus awarded shall be enforced and collected, in all respects, as is provided for any other contribution required by this act.

SEC. 3. The Secretary of War may, at his discretion, decline to assess, or, after assessment, may decline to collect the whole or any part of the additional one tenth herein provided for, in any district or locality; and it shall be his duty promptly to give notice of any such determination, specifying, with reasonable certainty, the district or locality and the product, or the proportion thereof, as to which he so declines.

SEC. 4. The products received for the contribution herein required, shall be disposed of and accounted for in the same manner as those received for the tax in kind; and the Secretary of War may, whenever the exigencies of the public service will allow, authorize the sale of products received from either source, to public officers or agents charged in any State with the duty of providing for the families of soldiers. Such sale shall be at the prices paid or assessed for the products sold, including the actual cost of collections.

SEC. 5. If, in addition to the tax in kind and the contribution herein required, the necessities of the army or the good of the service shall require other supplies of food or forage, or any other private property, and the same cannot be procured by contract, then impressments may be made of such supplies or other property, either for absolute ownership or for temporary use, as the public necessities may require. Such impressments shall be made in accordance with the provisions, and subject to the restrictions of the existing impressment laws, except so far as is herein otherwise provided.

SEC. 6. The right and the duty of making impressments is hereby confided exclusively to the officers and agents charged in the several districts with the assessment and collection of the tax in kind and of the contribution herein required; and all officers and soldiers in any department of the army are hereby expressly prohibited from undertaking in any manner to interfere with these officers and agents in any part of their duties in respect to the tax in kind, the contribution, or the impressment herein provided for: *Provided*, That this prohibition shall not be applicable to any district, county, or parish in which there shall be no officer or agent charged with the appointment and collection of the tax in kind.

SEC. 7. Supplies or other property taken by impressment shall be paid for by the post quartermasters in the several districts, and shall be disposed of and accounted for by them as is required in respect to the tax in kind and the contribution herein required; and it shall be the duty of the post quartermasters to equalize and apportion the impressments within their districts, as far as practicable, so as to avoid oppressing any portion of the community.

SEC. 8. If any one not authorized by law to collect the tax in kind or the contribution herein required, or to make impressments, shall undertake, on any pretence of such authority, to seize or impress, or to collect or receive any such property, or shall, on any such pretence, actually obtain such property, he shall, upon conviction thereof, be punished by fine not exceeding five times the value of such property, and be imprisoned not exceeding five years, at the discretion of the court having jurisdiction. And it shall be the duty of all officers and agents charged with the assessment and collection of the tax in kind and of the contribution herein required, promptly to report, through the post quartermasters in the several districts, any violation or disregard of the provisions of this act by any officer or soldier in the service of the Confederate States.

SEC. 9. That it shall not be lawful to impress any sheep, milch cows, brood mares, stud horses, jacks, bulls, or other stock kept or necessary for raising horses, mules, or cattle.

The following is the vote by which the bill passed the Senate:

YEAS — Messrs. Caperton, Graham, Haynes, Jemison, Johnson (Ark.), Johnson (Mo.), Mitchell, Orr, Walker, Watson —10.

NAYS—Messrs. Baker, Burnett, Henry, Hunter, Maxwell, Semmes, Sparrow—7.

Admitting West Virginia.

An important political movement in the early years of the war was the separation of West Virginia from the mother State, which had seceded, and her admission into the Union.

SECOND SESSION, THIRTY-SEVENTH CONGRESS.

In Senate, 1862, July 14.—The bill providing for the admission of the State of West Virginia into the Union, passed---yeas 23, nays 17, as follows:

YEAS—Messrs. Anthony, Clark, Collamer, Fessenden, Foot, Foster, Grimes, Hale, Harlan, Harris, Howe, Lane of Indiana, Lane of Kansas, Morrill, Pomeroy, *Rice*, Sherman, Simmons, Ten Eyck, Wade, Wilkinson, Willey, Wilson of Massachusetts—23.

NAYS—Messrs. *Bayard*, Browning, *Carlile*, Chandler, Cowan, *Davis*, Howard, *Kennedy*, King, *McDougal*, *Powell*, *Saulsbury*, *Stark*, Sumner, Trumbull, *Wilson* of Missouri, *Wright*—17.

During the pendency of this bill, July 14, 1862, Mr. Sumner moved to strike from the first section of the second article the words: "the children of all slaves born within the limits of said State shall be free," and insert:

Within the limits of the said State there shall be neither slavery nor involuntary servitude, otherwise than in punishment of crimes whereof the party shall be duly convicted.

Which was rejected---yeas 11, nays 24, as follows:

YEAS—Messrs. Chandler, Clark, Grimes, King, Lane of Kansas, Pomeroy, Sumner, Trumbull, Wilkinson, Wilmot, Wilson, of Massachusetts--11.

NAYS--Messrs. Anthony, *Bayard*, Browning, *Carlile*, Collamer, Doolittle, Foot Foster, Harris, Henderson, Howe, *Kennedy*, Lane of Indiana, *Powell*, *Rice*, *Saulsbury*, Sherman, Simmons, *Stark*, Ten Eyck, Wade, Wiley, *Wilson* of Missouri, *Wright* - -24.

Mr. Willey proposed to strike out all after the word "That" in the first section, and insert:

That the State of West Virginia be, and is hereby, declared to be one of the United States of America, and admitted into the Union on an equal footing with the original States in all respects whatever, and until the next general census shall be entitled to three members in the House of Representatives of the United States: *Provided always*, That this act shall not take effect until after the proclamation of the President of the United States hereinafter provided for.

SEC. 2. It being represented to Congress that since the convention of the 26th of November, 1861, that framed and proposed the constitution for the said State of West Virginia, the people thereof have expressed a wish to change the seventh section of the eleventh article of said constitution by striking out the same, and inserting the following in its place, namely, "The children of slaves born within the limits of this State after the 4th day of July, 1863, shall be free, and no slave shall be permitted to come into the State for permanent residence therein:" therefore,

Be it further enacted, That whenever the people of West Virginia shall, through their said convention, and by a vote to be taken at an election to be held within the limits of the State at such time as the convention may provide, make and ratify the change aforesaid and properly certify the same under the hand of the president of the convention, it shall be lawful for the President of the United States to issue his proclamation stating the fact, and thereupon this act shall take effect and be in force from and after sixty days from the date of said proclamation.

Mr Lane of Kansas moved to amend the amendment by inserting after the word "Herein," and before the word, "Therefore" the words:

And that all slaves within the said State who shall at the time aforesaid be under the age of ten years shall be free when they arrive at the age of twenty-one years; and all slaves over ten and under twenty-one years shall be free when they arrive at the age of twenty-five years.

Which was agreed to—yeas 25, nays 12, as follows:

YEAS—Messrs. Anthony, Clark, Collamer, Doolittle, Foot, Foster, Grimes, Harlan, Harris, Howard, Howe, King, Lane of Indiana, Lane of Kansas, Morrill, Pomeroy, Sherman, Simmons, Sumner, Ten Eyck, Trumbull, Wade, Wilkinson, Wilmot, Wilson, of Massachusetts—25.

NAYS—Messrs. Browning, *Carlile*, *Davis*, Henderson, *Kennedy*, *McDougall*, *Powell*, *Saulsbury*, *Stark* Willey, *Wilson* of Missouri, *Wright*—12.

The amendment as amended was then agreed to.

A motion to postpone the bill to the first Monday of the next December was lost—yeas 17, nays 23.

In House, July 16—The bill was postponed until the second Tuesday of the next December—yeas 63, nays 33.

THIRD SESSION, THIRTY-SEVENTH CONGRESS.

1863, Dec. 10, the House passed the bill—yeas 96, nays 57.

1863, April 20, the President issued a proclamation announcing the compliance, by West Virginia, of the conditions of admission.

COLOR IN WAR POLITICS.

Emancipation and its attendant agitations brought to the front a new class of political questions, which can best be grouped under the above caption. The following is a summary of the legislation:

Second Session, Thirty-Seventh Congress.

To Remove Disqualification of Color in Carrying the Mails.

In Senate, 1862, April 11—The Senate considered a bill "to remove all disqualification of color in carrying the mails of the United States." It directed that after the passage of the act no person, by reason of color, shall be disqualified from employment in carrying the mails, and all acts and parts of acts establishing such disqualification, including especially the seventh section of the act of March 3, 1825, are hereby repealed.

The vote in the Senate was, yeas 24, nays 11, as follows:

YEAS—Messrs. Anthony, Browning, Chandler, Clark, Collamer, Dixon, Doolittle, Fessenden, Foot, Foster, Grimes, Hale, Howard, Howe, King, Lane of Kansas, Morrill, Pomeroy, Sherman, Simmons, Sumner, Wade, Wilkinson, and Wilson of Massachusetts—24.

NAYS—Messrs. *Davis*, Henderson, *Kennedy*, Lane of Indiana, *Latham*, *Nesmith*, *Powell*, *Stark*, Willey, *Wilson* of Missouri, Wright—11.*

In House, May 21—It was considered in the House and laid on the table—yeas 83, nays 43.

First Session, Thirty-Eighth Congress.

1864, February 26—The Senate considered the bill—the question being on agreeing to a new section proposed by the Committee on Post Offices and Post Roads—as follows:

SEC. 2. That in the courts of the United States there shall be no exclusion of any witness on account of color.

Mr. Powell moved to amend by inserting after the word "States" the words: "in all cases for robbing or violating the mails of the United States."

No further progress was made on the bill.

NEGRO SUFFRAGE IN MONTANA TERRITORY.

1864, March 18—The House passed, without a division, a bill in the usual form, to provide a temporary government for the Territory of Montana.

March 31—The Senate considered it, when Mr. Wilkinson moved to strike from the second line of the fifth section, (defining the qualifications of voters,) the words "white male inhabitant" and insert the words: "male citizen of the United States, and those who have declared their intention to become such;" which was agreed to—yeas 22, nays 17, as follows:

YEAS—Messrs. Brown, Chandler, Clark, Collamer, Conness, Dixon, Fessenden. Foot, Foster, Grimes, Hale, Harlan, Harris, Howard, Howe, Morgan, Morrill, Pomeroy, Sumner, Wade, Wilkinson, Wilson—22.

NAYS—Messrs. *Buckalew*, *Carlile*, Cowan, *Davis*, Harding, Henderson, Johnson, Lane of Indiana, *Nesmith*, *Powell*, *Riddle*, *Saulsbury*, Sherman, Ten Eyck, Trumbull, Van Winkle, Willey—17.

The bill was then passed—yeas 29, nays 8, (Messrs. *Buckalew*, *Davis*, *Johnson*, *Powell*, *Riddle*, *Saulsbury*, Van Winkle, Willey.)

April 15—The Senate adopted the report of the Committee of Conference on the Montana bill, which recommended the Senate to recede from their second amendment, and the House to agree to the first and third amendments of the Senate, (including the above.)

April 15—Mr. Beaman presented the report of the Committee of Conference on the Montana bill, a feature of which was that the House should recede from its dis-

* Republicans in roman; Democrats in italics.

agreement to the Senate amendment striking out the word "white" in the description of those authorized to vote.

Mr. Holman moved that the report be tabled: which was lost by the casting vote of the Speaker—yeas 66, nays 66.

Upon agreeing to the report the yeas were 54, nays 85.

On motion to adhere to its amendments, and ask another Committee of Conference, Mr. Webster moved instructions:

And that said committee be instructed to agree to no report that authorizes any other than free white male citizens, and those who have declared their intention to become such, to vote.

Which was agreed to—yeas 75, nays 67.

April 15—The Senate declined the conference upon the terms proposed by the House resolution of that day.

April 18—The House proposed a further free conference, to which, April 25, the Senate acceded.

May 17—In Senate, Mr. Morrill submitted a report from the Conference Committee who recommend that qualified voters shall be:

All citizens of the United States, and those who have declared their intention to become such, and who are otherwise described and qualified under the fifth section of the act of Congress providing for a temporary government for the Territory of Idaho approved March 3, 1863.

The report was concurred in—yeas 26, nays 13.

May 20—The above report was made by Mr. Webster in the House, and agreed to—yeas 102, nays 26.

IN WASHINGTON CITY.*

1864, May 6—The Senate considered the bill for the registration of voters in the city of Washington, when

Mr. Cowan moved to insert the word "white" in the first section, so as to confine the right of voting to white male citizens.

May 12—Mr. Morrill moved to amend the amendment by striking out the words—

And shall have paid all school taxes and all taxes on personal property properly assessed against him, shall be entitled to vote for mayor, collector, register, members of the board of aldermen and board of common council, and assessor, and for every officer authorized to be elected at any election under any act or acts to which this is amendatory or supplementary.

and inserting the words—

And shall within the year next preceding the election have paid a tax, or been assessed with a part of the revenue of the District, county, or cities, therein, or been exempt from taxation having taxable estate, and who can read and write with facility, shall enjoy the privileges of an elector.

May 26—Mr. Sumner moved to amend the bill by adding this proviso:

Provided, That there shall be no exclusion of any person from the registry on account of color.

May 27—Mr. Harlan moved to amend the amendment by making the word "person" read "persons," and adding the words—

Who have borne arms in the military service of the United States, and have been honorably discharged therefrom.

Which was agreed to yeas 26, nays 12, as follows:

YEAS—Messrs. Anthony, Chandler, Clark, Collamer, Conness, Dixon, Fessenden, Foot, Foster, Grimes, Hale, Harlan, Harris, Johnson, Lane of Indiana, Lane of Kansas, Morgan, Morrill, Pomeroy, Ramsey, Sherman, Ten Eyck, Trumbull, Wade, Willey, Wilson—26.

NAYS—Messrs. *Buckalew*, *Carlile*, Cowan, *Davis*, *Hendricks*, *McDougall*, *Powell Richardson*, *Saulsbury*, Sumner, Van Winkle, Wilkinson—12.

May 28—Mr. Sumner moved to add these words to the last proviso:

And provided further, That all persons, without distinction of color, who shall, within the year next preceding the election, have paid a tax on any estate, or been assessed with a part of the revenue of said District, or been exempt from taxation having taxable estate, and who can read and write with facility, shall enjoy the privilege of an elector. But no person now entitled to vote in the said District, continuing to reside therein, shall be disfranchised hereby.

Which was rejected—yeas 8, nays 27, as follows:

YEAS—Messrs. Anthony, Clark, Lane of Kansas, Morgan, Pomeroy, Ramsey, Sumner, Wilkinson—8.

NAYS—Messrs. *Buckalew*, *Carlile*, Collamer, Cowan, *Davis*, Dixon, Fessenden, Foot, Foster, Grimes, Hale, Harlan, Harris, *Hendricks*, Hicks, Johnson, Lane of Indiana, *McDougall*, Morrill, *Powell*, *Sauls-*

* In 1860 a vote was had in the State of New York on a proposition to permit negro suffrage without a property qualification. The result of the city was—yeas 1,640, nays 37,471. In the State—yeas 197,505, nays 337,984. In 1864 a like proposition was defeated—yeas 85,406, nays 224,336.

In 1862, in August, a vote was, had in the State of Illinois, on several propositions relating to negroes and mulattoes, with this result:

For excluding them from the State	171,893	
Against	71,306	
		100,587
Against granting them suffrage or right to office	211,920	
For	35,649	
		176,271
For the enactment of laws to prohibit them from going to, or voting in, the State	198,938	
Against	44,414	
		154,524

—*From McPherson's History of the Great Rebellion.*

bury, Sherman, Ten Eyck, Trumbull, Van Winkle, Willey, Wilson—27.

The other proposition of Mr. Sumner, amended on motion of Mr. Harlan, was then rejected—yeas 18, nays 20, as follows:

YEAS — Messrs. Anthony, Chandler, Clark, Dixon, Foot, Foster, Hale, Harlan, Howard, Howe, Lane of Kansas, Morgan, Pomeroy, Ramsey, Sherman, Sumner, Wilkinson, Wilson—18.

NAYS—Messrs. *Buckalew*, *Carlile*, Cowan, *Davis*, Grimes, Harris, *Hendricks*, Hicks, Johnson, Lane of Indiana, *McDougall*, Morrill, *Nesmith*, *Powell*, *Richardson*, *Saulsbury*, Ten Eyck, Trumbull, Van Winkle, Willey—20.

The bill then passed the Senate, and afterward the House, without amendment.

Third Session, Thirty-Seventh Congress.

Excluding Colored Persons from Cars.

In Senate—1863, February 27—Pending a supplement to the charter of the Washington and Alexandria Railroad Company, Mr. Sumner offered this proviso to the first section:

That no person shall be excluded from the cars on account of color.

Which was agreed to—yeas 19, nays 18, as follows:

YEAS—Messrs. Arnold, Chandler, Clark, Fessenden, Foot, Grimes, Harris, Howard, King, Lane of Kansas, Morrill, Pomeroy, Sumner, Ten Eyck, Trumbull, Wade, Wilkinson, Wilmot, Wilson, of Massachusetts —19.

NAYS—Messrs. Anthony, *Bayard*, *Carlile*, Cowan, *Davis*, Henderson, Hicks, Howe, *Kennedy*, Lane of Indiana, *Latham*, *McDougall*, *Powell*, *Richardson*, *Saulsbury*, *Turpie*, Willey, *Wilson* of Missouri—18.

March 2.—The House concurred in the amendment without debate, under the previous question.

First Session, Thirty-Eighth Congress.

In Senate — 1864, February 10 — Mr. Sumner offered the following:

Resolved, That the Committee on the District of Columbia be directed to consider the expediency of further providing by law against the exclusion of colored persons from the equal enjoyment of all railroad privileges in the District of Columbia.

Which was agreed to—yeas 30, nays 10.

February 24—Mr. Willey, from the Committee on the District of Columbia, made this report, and the committee were discharged:

The Committee on the District of Columbia, who were required by resolution of the Senate, passed February 8, 1864, "to consider the expediency of further providing by law against the exclusion of colored persons from the equal enjoyment of all railroad privileges in the District of Columbia," have had the matter thus referred to them under consideration, and beg leave to report:

The act entitled "An act to incorporate the Washington and Georgetown Railroad Company," approved May 17, 1862, makes no distinction as to passengers over said road on account of the color of the passengers, and that in the opinion of the committee colored persons are entitled to all the privileges of said road which other persons have, and to all remedies for any denial or breach of such privileges which belongs to any person.

The committee therefore ask to be discharged from the further consideration of the premises.

March 17—The Senate considered the bill to incorporate the Metropolitan Railroad Company, in the District of Columbia, the pending question being an amendment, offered by Mr. Sumner, to add to the fourteenth section the words:

Provided, That there shall be no regulation excluding any person from any car on account of color.

Which was agreed to—yeas 19, nays 17, as follows:

YEAS—Messrs. Anthony, Brown, Clark, Conness, Fessenden, Foot, Foster, Grimes, Harlan, Howe, Lane of Kansas, Morgan, Morrill, Pomeroy, Ramsey, Sumner, Wade, Wilkinson, Wilson—19.

NAYS—Messrs. *Buckalew*, *Carlile*, *Davis*, Doolittle, Harding, Harris, *Hendricks*, Johnson, Lane of Indiana, *Powell*, *Riddle*, *Saulsbury*, Sherman, Ten Eyck, Trumbull, Van Winkle, Willey—17.

The bill then passed the Senate.

June 19—The House refused to strike out the proviso last adopted in the Senate —yeas 60, nays 76.

And the bill passed the House and was approved by the President.

Second Session, Thirty-Seventh Congress.

Colored Persons as Witnesses.

In Senate—Pending the confiscation bill, June 28, 1862.

Mr. Sumner moved these words as an addition to the 14th section:

And in all the proceedings under this act there shall be no exclusion of any witness on account of color.

Which was rejected—yeas 14, nays 25, as follows:

YEAS—Messrs. Chandler, Grimes, Harlan, Howard, King, Lane of Kansas, Morrill, Pomeroy, Sumner, Trumbull, Wade, Wilkinson, Wilmot—14.

NAYS—Messrs. Anthony, Browning, *Carlile*, Clark, Collamer, Cowan, *Davis*, Dixon, Doolittle, Fessenden, Foot, Foster, Harris, Henderson, Lane of Indiana, *Nesmith*, *Pearce*, *Powell*, Sherman, Simmons, *Stark*, Ten Eyck, Willey, *Wilson* of Missouri, *Wright*—25.

Pending the consideration of the supplement to the emancipation bill for the District of Columbia,

1862, July 7—Mr. Sumner moved a new section:

That in all the judicial proceedings in the District of Columbia there shall be no exclusion of any witness on account of color.

Which was adopted—yeas 25, nays 11.

The bill then passed—yeas 29, nays 6; (Messrs. *Carlile, Davis, Kennedy, Powell, Wilson*, of Missouri, *Wright.*)

July 9—The bill passed the House—yeas 69, nays 36. There was no separate vote on the above proposition.

Pending the consideration in the Senate of the House bill in relation to the competency of witnesses in trials of equity and admiralty,

1862, July 15—Mr. Sumner offered this proviso to the first section:

Provided, That there shall be no exclusion of any witness on account of color.

Which was rejected—yeas 14, nays 23.

First Session, Thirty-Eighth Congress.

1864, June 25—Pending the civil appropriation bill, in Committee of the Whole, Mr. Sumner offered this proviso:

Provided, That in the courts of the United States there shall be no exclusion of any witness on account of color.

Mr. Buckalew moved to add:

Nor in civil actions because he is a party to or interested in the issue tried.

Which was agreed to; and the amendment as amended was agreed to—yeas 22, nays 16.

The Senate subsequently concurred in this amendment—yeas 29, nays 10.

IN HOUSE.

June 29—The question being on agreeing to the amendment.

Mr. Mallory moved to add this proviso to the section amended in the Senate:

Provided, That negro testimony shall only be taken in the United States courts in those States the laws of which authorize such testimony.

Which was rejected—yeas 47, nays 66.

The amendment of the Senate was then agreed to—yeas 67, nays 48.

COLORED SCHOOLS.

June 8.—The House passed a bill to provide for the public instruction of youth in Washington city, with an amendment providing for separate schools for the colored children, by setting apart such a proportion of the entire school fund as the number of colored children between the ages of six and seventeen bear to the whole number of children in the District. The bill, with amendments, passed both Houses without a division.

On all of these questions of color, the Democrats invariably, on test votes, were found against any concession of rights to the negro. These were frequently aided by some Republicans, more conservative than their colleagues, or representing closer districts where political prejudices would affect their return to their seats. It will be observed that on nearly all these questions Senator Charles Sumner took the lead. He was at that time pre-eminently the Moses of the colored man, and led him from one right to another through Senatorial difficulties, which by the way, were never as strong as that in the House, where Thaddeus Stevens was the boldest champion of "the rights of the black man." In the field, rather in the direction of what should be done with the "contrabands" and escaped slaves, the Secretary of War, General Cameron, was their most radical friend, and his instructions were so outspoken that Lincoln had to modify them. As early as December 1, 1861, General Cameron wrote:

"While it is plain that the slave property of the South is justly subjected to all the consequences of this rebellious war, and that the Government would be untrue to its trust in not employing all the rights and powers of war to bring it to a speedy close, the details of the plan for doing so, like all other military measures, must, in a great degree, be left to be determined by particular exigencies. The disposition of other property belonging to the rebels that becomes subject to our arms is governed by the circumstances of the case. The Government has no power to hold slaves, none to restrain a slave of his liberty, or to exact his service. It has a right, however, to use the voluntary service of slaves liberated by war from their rebel masters, like any other property of the rebels, in whatever mode may be most efficient for the defence of the Government, the prosecution of the war, and the suppression of rebellion. It is clearly a right of the government to arm slaves when it may become necessary as it is to take gunpowder from the enemy. Whether it is expedient to do so is purely a military question. The right is unquestionable by the laws of war. The expediency must be determined by circumstances, keeping in view the great object of overcoming the rebels, re-establishing the laws, and restoring peace to the nation.

"It is vain and idle for the Government to carry on this war, or hope to maintain its existence against rebellious force, without enjoying all the rights and powers of war. As has been said, the right to deprive the rebels of their property in slaves and slave labor is as clear and absolute as the right to take forage from the field, or cotton from the warehouse, or powder and arms from the magazine. To leave the enemy in the possession of such property as forage and cotton and military stores, and the means of constantly reproducing them, would be madness. It is, therefore, equal madness to leave them in peaceful and secure possession of slave property, more valuable and efficient to them for war than forage, cotton and military stores. Such policy would be national suicide. What to do with that species of property is a question that time and circumstances will solve, and need not be anticipated further than to repeat that they cannot be held by the Government as slaves. It would be useless to keep them as prisoners of war; and self-preservation, the highest duty of a Government, or of individuals, demands that they should be disposed of or employed in the most effective manner that will tend most speedily to suppress the insurrection and restore the authority of the Government. If it shall be found that the men who have been held by the rebels as slaves are capable of bearing arms and performing efficient military service, it is the right, and may become the duty, of this Government to arm and equip them, and employ their services against the rebels, under proper military regulations, discipline and command.

"But in whatever manner they may be used by the Government, it is plain that, once liberated by the rebellious act of their masters, they should never again be restored to bondage. By the master's treason and rebellion he forfeits all right to the labor and service of his slave; and the slave of the rebellious master, by his service to the Government, becomes justly entitled to freedom and protection.

"The disposition to be made of the slaves of rebels, after the close of the war, can be safely left to the wisdom and patriotism of Congress. The representatives of the people will unquestionably secure to the loyal slaveholders every right to which they are entitled under the Constitution of the country."

[Subsequent events proved the wisdom of this policy, and it was eventually adopted by an Administration which proclaimed its policy "to move not ahead but with the people."]

President Lincoln and his Cabinet modified the above language so as to make it read:

"It is already a grave question what shall be done with those slaves who were abandoned by their owners on the advance of our troops into southern territory, as at Beaufort district, in South Carolina. The number left within our control at that point is very considerable, and similar cases will probably occur. What shall be done with them? Can we afford to send them forward to their masters, to be by them armed against us, or used in producing supplies to sustain the rebellion? Their labor may be useful to us; withheld from the enemy it lessens his military resources, and withholding them has no tendency to induce the horrors of insurrection, even in the rebel communities. They constitute a military resource, and, being such, that they should not be turned over to the enemy is too plain to discuss. Why deprive him of supplies by a blockade, and voluntarily give him men to produce them?

"The disposition to be made of the slaves of rebels, after the close of the war, can be safely left to the wisdom and patriotism of Congress. The Representatives of the people will unquestionably secure to the loyal slaveholders every right to which they are entitled under the Constitution of the country."

Secretary Cameron was at all times in favor of "carrying the war into Africa," and it was this stern view of the situation which eventually led him to sanction measures which brought him into plainer differences with the Administration. Lincoln took offense at the printing of his report before submitting it to him. As a result he resigned and went to Russia as Minister, on his return being again elected to the United States Senate—a place which he filled until the winter of 1877, when he resigned, and his son, J. Donald Cameron, was elected to the vacancy, and re-elected for the term ending in 1885. General B. F. Butler was the author of the "contraband" idea. A year later the views of the Administration became more radical on questions of color, and July 22, 1862, Secretary Stanton ordered all Generals in command "to seize and use any property, real or personal, which may be necessary or convenient for their several commands, for supplies, or for other military purposes; and that while property may be destroyed for proper military objects, none shall be destroyed in wantonness or malice.

"*Second.* That military and naval commanders shall employ as laborers, within and from said States, so many persons of African descent as can be advantageously used for military or naval purposes, giving them reasonable wages for their labor.

"*Third.* That, as to both property, and persons of African descent, accounts shall be kept sufficiently accurate and in detail to show quantities and amounts, and from whom both property and such persons shall have come, as a basis upon which compensation can be made in proper cases; and the several departments of this Government shall attend to and perform their appropriate parts towards the execution of these orders."

The manner and language employed by General McClellan in promulgating this order to the Army of the Potomac, led to his political differerces with the Administration, and in the end caused him to be the Democratic candidate for President in 1864, against Lincoln. His language is peculiar and some of it worthy of presentation as of political importance. He said:

"Inhabitants, especially women and children, remaining peaceably at their homes, must not be molested; and wherever commanding officers find families peculiarly exposed in their persons or property to marauding from this army, they will, as heretofore, so far as they can do with safety and without detriment to the service, post guards for their protection.

"In protecting private property, no reference is intended to persons held to service or labor by reason of African descent. Such persons will be regarded by this army, as they heretofore have been, as occupying simply a peculiar legal status under State laws, which condition the military authorities of the United States are not required to regard at all in districts where military operations are made necessary by the rebellious action of the State governments.

"Persons subject to suspicion of hostile purposes, residing or being near our forces, will be, as heretofore, subject to arrest and detention, until the cause or necessity is removed. All such arrested parties will be sent, as usual, to the Provost Marshal General, with a statement of the facts in each case.

"The general commanding takes this occasion to remind the officers and soldiers of this army that we are engaged in supporting the Constitution and the laws of the United States and suppressing rebellion against their authority; that we are not engaged in a war of rapine, revenge, or subjugation; that this is not a contest against populations, but against armed forces and political organizations; that it is a struggle carried on with the United States, and should be conducted by us upon the highest principles known to Christian civilization."

At this time such were the prejudices of Union soldiers against negroes, because of growing political agitation in the North, that many would loudly jeer them when seen within the lines. The feeling was even greater in the ranks of civilians, and yet Congress moved along, step by step. The 37th abolished slavery in the District of Columbia; prohibited it in all the territories; confirmed the freedom of the slaves owned by those in arms against the government; authorized the employment of colored men in fortifications, their enlistment, etc.; and enacted an additional article of war, which prohibited any officer from returning or aiding the return of any fugitive slave. These were rapid strides, but not as rapid as were demanded by the more radical wing of the Republican party. We have shown that most of them were opposed by the Democrats, not solidly sure where they were plainly political, but this party became less solid as the war advanced.

Senator Wilson was the author of the bill to abolish slavery in the District of Columbia. It excited much debate, and the range of the speeches covered the entire question of slavery. Those from the Border States opposed it (a few Republicans and all Democrats) but some of the Democrats of the North supported it. The vote in the Senate was 29 for to 6 against. In the House Frank P. Blair, Jr., advocated colonization in connection with the bill, but his idea met with little favor. Crittenden, Wickliffe and Vallandigham were prominent in opposition. Its most prominent advocates were Stevens of Pennsylvania, and Bingham of Ohio. The vote was 92 for to 38 against.

The bill of Arnold, of Illinois, "to render freedom national and slavery sectional," the leading idea in the platform of the convention which nominated Lincoln, prohibited slavery in "all the Territories of the United States then existing, or thereafter to be formed or acquired in any way." It was vehemently opposed, but passed with some modifications by 58 ayes to 50 noes, and it also passed the Senate.

In the Spring of 1862 General David Hunter brought the question of the enlistment of colored troops to a direct issue by raising a regiment of them. On the 9th of June following, Mr. Wickliffe of Kentucky, succeeded in getting the House to adopt a resolution of inquiry. Correspondence followed with General Hunter. He confessed the fact, stated that "he found his authority in the instructions of Secretary Cameron, and said that he hoped by fall to enroll about fifty thousand of these hardy and devoted soldiers." When this reply was read in the House it was greeted with shouts of laughter from the Republicans, and signs of anger from the others. A great debate followed on the amendment to the bill providing for the calling out of the militia, clothing the President with full power to enlist colored troops, and to proclaim "he, his mother, and wife and children forever free," after such enlistment. Preston King, of New York, was the author of this amendment. Davis, of Kentucky, and Carlisle of West Virginia, were prominent Senators in opposition; while Ten Eyck, of New Jersey, Sherman of Ohio, and Browning of Illinois sought to modify it. Garrett Davis said in opposition:

"Do you expect us to give our sanction and approval to these things? No, no! We would regard their authors as our worst enemies; and there is no foreign despotism that could come to our rescue, that we would not fondly embrace, before we would submit to any such condition of things."

Senator Fessenden of Maine, in advocacy of the amendment, said:

"I tell the President from my place here as a Senator, and I tell the generals of our army, they must reverse their practices and course of proceeding on this subject. * * * Treat your enemies as enemies, as the worst of enemies, and avail yourselves like men of every power which God has placed in your hands, to accomplish your purpose, within the rules of civilized warfare."

The bill passed, so modified, as to give freedom to all who should perform military service, but restricting liberty to the families of such only as belonged to rebel masters. It passed the House July 16th, 1862, and received the sanction of the President, who said:—"And the promise made must be kept!" General Hunter for his part in beginning colored enlistments, was outlawed by the Confederate Congress. Hunter followed with an order freeing the slaves in South Carolina.

In January, 1863, pursuant to a suggestion in the annual report of Secretary Stanton, who was by this time as radical as his predecessor in office, the House passed a bill authorizing the President to enroll into the land and naval service such number of volunteers of African descent as he might deem useful to suppress the rebellion, and for such term as he might prescribe, not exceeding five years. The slaves of loyal citizens in the Border States were excluded from the provisions of this bill. In the Senate an adverse report was made on the ground that the President already possessed these powers.

In January, 1863, Senator Wilson, who was by this time chairman of the Military Committee of the Senate, secured the passage of a bill which authorized a draft for the National forces from the ranks of all male citizens, and those of foreign birth who had declared their intentions, etc. The bill contained the usual exemptions.

CONFEDERATE USE OF COLORED MEN.

In June, 1861, the rebel Legislature of Tennessee passed this enlistment bill, which became a law:

SEC. 1. *Be it enacted by the General Assembly of the State of Tennessee,* That from and after the passage of this act the Governor shall be, and he is hereby, authorized, at his discretion, to receive into the military service of the State all male free persons of color between the ages of fifteen and fifty, or such numbers as may be necessary, who may be sound in mind and body, and capable of actual service.

2. That such free persons of color shall receive, each, eight dollars per month, as pay, and such persons shall be entitled to draw, each, one ration per day, and shall be entitled to a yearly allowance each for clothing.

3. That, in order to carry out the provisions of this act, it shall be the duty of the sheriffs of the several counties in this State to collect accurate information as to the number and condition, with the names of free persons of color, subject to the provisions of this act, and shall, as it is practicable, report the same in writing to the Governor.

4. That a failure or refusal of the sheriffs, or any one or more of them, to perform the duties required, shall be deemed an offence, and on conviction thereof shall be punished as a misdemeanor.

5. That in the event a sufficient number of free persons of color to meet the wants of the State shall not tender their services, the Governor is empowered, through the sheriffs of the different counties, to press such persons until the requisite number is obtained.

6. That when any mess of volunteers shall keep a servant to wait on the members of the mess, each servant shall be allowed one ration.

This act to take effect from and after its passage.

W. C. WHITTHORNE,
Speaker of the House of Representatives.

B. L. STOVALL,
Speaker of the Senate.

Passed June 28, 1861.

1862, November 2—Governor Joseph E. Brown, of Georgia, issued a call announcing that if a sufficient supply of negroes be not tendered within ten days, General Mercer will, in pursuance of authority given him, proceed to impress, and asking of every planter of Georgia a tender of one fifth of his negroes to complete the fortifications around Savannah. This one fifth is estimated at 15,000.

1863. The Governor of South Carolina in July, issued a proclamation for 3,000 negroes to work on the fortifications, "the need for them being pressing."

THE CHANGING SENTIMENT OF CONGRESS.

In the Rebel House of Representatives, December 29th, Mr. DARGAN, of Alabama, introduced a bill to receive into the military service all that portion of population in Alabama, Mississippi, Louisiana, and Florida, known as "Creoles."

Mr. Dargan supported the bill in some remarks. He said the Creoles were a mixed-blooded race. Under the treaty of Paris in 1803, and the treaty of Spain in 1810, they were recognized as freemen.

Many of them owned large estates, and were intelligent men. They were as much devoted to our cause as any class of men in the South, and were even anxious to go into service. They had applied to him to be received into service, and he had applied to Mr. Randolph, then Secretary of War. Mr. Randolph decided against the application, on the ground that it might furnish to the enemy a pretext of arming our slaves against us. Some time after this he was again applied to by them, and he went to the present Secretary of War, Mr. Seddon, and laid the matter before him. Mr. Seddon refused to entertain the proposition, on the ground that it did not come up before him through the military authorities. To obviate this objection, Gen. Maury, at Mobile, soon afterwards represented their wishes to the War Department. Mr. Seddon refused the offer of their services, on the ground that it would be incompatible with the position we occupied before the world; that it could not be done.

Mr. Dargan said he differed with the Secretary of War. He cared not for "the world." He cared no more for their opinions than they did for ours. He was anxious to bring into service every free man, be he who he may, willing to strike for our cause. He saw no objection to employing Creoles; they would form a potent element in our army. In his district alone a brigade of them could be raised. The crisis had been brought upon us by the enemy, and he believed the time would yet come when the question would not be the Union or no Union, but whether Southern men should be permitted to live at all. In resisting subjugation by such a barbarous foe he was for employing all our available force. *He would go further and say that he was for arming and putting the slaves into military service. He was in favor even of emlpoying them as a military arm in the defence of the country.*

1864. The Mayor of Charleston, Charles Macbeth, summons all slaveholders within the city to furnish to the military authorities forthwith, one-fourth of all their male slaves between the ages of fifteen and fifty, to labor upon the fortifications. The penalty announced, in case of failure to comply with this requisition is a fine of $200 for every slave not forthcoming. Compensation is allowed at the rate of $400 a year.

All free male persons of color between the ages of fifteen and fifty are required to give themselves up for the same purpose. Those not complying will be imprisoned, and set to work upon the fortifications along the coast. To free negroes no other compensation than rations is allowed.

NEGROES IN THE ARMY.

The Richmond press publish the official copy of "An act to increase the efficiency of the army by the employment of free negroes and slaves in certain capacities," lately passed by the Rebel Congress. The negroes are to perform "such duties as the Secretary of War or Commanding General may prescribe." The first section is as follows:

The Congress of the Confederate States of America do enact, That all male free negroes, and other free persons of color, not including those who are free under the treaty of Paris, of 1803, or under the treaty of Spain, of 1819, resident in the Confederate States, between the ages of eighteen and fifty years, shall be held liable to perform such duties with the army, or in connection with the military defences of the country, in the way of work upon the fortifications, or in government works for the production or preparation of materials of war, or in military hospitals, as the Secretary of War or the Commanding General of the Trans-Mississippi Department may, from time to time, prescribe; and while engaged in the performances of such duties shall receive rations and clothing and compensation at the rate of eleven dollars a month, under such rules and regulations as the said Secretary may establish: *Provided*, That the Secretary of War or the Commanding General of the Trans-Mississippi Department, with the approval of the President, may exempt from the operations of this act such free negroes as the interests of the country may require should be exempted, or such as he may think proper to exempt on the ground of justice, equity or necessity.

The third section provides that when the Secretary of War shall be unable to procure the services of slaves in any military department, then he is authorized to impress the services of as many male slaves, not to exceed twenty thousand, as may be required, from time to time, to discharge the duties indicated in the first section of the act.

The owner of the slave is to be paid for his services; or, if he be killed or "escape to the enemy," the owner shall receive his full value.

Governor Smith, of Virginia, has made a call for five thousand male slaves to work on the batteries, to be drawn from fifty counties. The call for this force has been made by the President under a resolution of Congress.

"CONFEDERATE" LEGISLATION UPON NEGRO PRISONERS AND THEIR WHITE OFFICERS WHEN CAPTURED.*

1863, May 1—An act was approved declaring that the commissioned officers of

*December 23, 1862—Jefferson Davis issued a proclamation of outlawry against Major General B. F. Butler, the last two clauses of which are:

the enemy ought not to be delivered to the authorities of the respective States, (as suggested in Davis's message;) but all captives taken by the Confederate forces ought to be dealt with and disposed of by the Confederate Government.

President Lincoln's emancipation proclamations of September 22, 1862, and January 1, 1863, were resolved to be inconsistent with the usages of war among civilized nations, and should be repressed by retaliation; and the President is authorized to cause full and complete retaliation for every such violation, in such manner and to such extent as he may think proper.

Every white commissioned officer commanding negroes or mulattoes in arms against the Confederate States shall be deemed as inciting servile insurrection, and shall, if captured, be put to death, or be otherwise punished, at the discretion of the court.

Every person charged with an offence made punishable under the act shall be tried by the military court of the army or corps of troops capturing him; and, *after conviction, the President may commute the punishment in such manner and on such terms as he may deem proper.*

All negroes and mulattoes who shall be engaged in war or taken in arms against the Confederate States, or shall give aid or comfort to the enemies of the Confederate States, shall, when captured in the Confederate States, be delivered to the authorities of the State or States in which they shall be captured, to be dealt with according to the present or future laws of such State or States.

Passage of the Thirteenth Amendment.

The first amendment to the Constitution growing out of the war, and one of its direct results, was that of abolishing slavery. It was first introduced to the House December 14th, 1863, by James M. Ashley of Ohio. Similar measures were introduced by James M. Wilson, Senators Henderson, Sumner and others. On the 10th of February, Senator Trumbull reported Henderson's joint resolution amended as follows:

"That the following article be proposed to the Legislatures of the several States, as an amendment to the Constitution of the United States, which, when ratified by three-fourths of said Legislatures, shall be valid to all intents and purposes as a part of the said Constitution, namely:

"ART. 13, Sec. 1. Neither slavery nor involuntary servitude except as a punishment for crime, whereof the party shall have been duly convicted, shall exist within the United States, or any place subject to their jurisdiction.

Sec. 2. Congress shall have power to enforce this article by appropriate legislation."

The Senate began the consideration of the question March 28th, Senator Trumbull opening the debate in favor of the amendment. He predicted that within a year the necessary number of States would ratify it. Wilson of Massachusetts made a long and able speech in favor. Davis of Kentucky and Saulsbury of Delaware led the opposition, but Reverdy Johnson, an independent Democratic Senator from Maryland, surprised all by his bold support of the measure. Among other things he said:

"I think history will bear me out in the statement, that if the men by whom that Constitution was framed, and the people by whom it was adopted, had anticipated the times in which we live, they would have provided by constitutional enactment, that that evil and that sin should in some comparatively unremote day be removed. Without recurring to authority, the writings public or private of the men of that day, it is sufficient for my purpose to state what the facts will justify me in saying, that every man of them who largely participated in the deliberations of the Convention by which the Constitution was adopted, earnestly desired, not only upon grounds of political economy, not only upon reasons material in their character, but upon grounds of morality and religion, that sooner or later the institution should terminate."

Senator McDougall of California, opposed the amendment. Harlan of Iowa, Hale of New Hampshire, and Sumner, made characteristic speeches in favor. Saulsbury advocated the divine right of slavery. It passed April 8th, by 38 ayes to 6 noes, the latter comprising Davis and Powell of Kentucky; McDougall of California; Hendricks of Indiana; Saulsbury and Riddle of Delaware.

Arnold of Illinois, was the first to secure the adoption in the House (Feb. 15, 1864,) of a resolution to abolish slavery; but the Constitutional amendment required a two-thirds vote, and this it was difficult to obtain, though all the power of the Administration was bent to that purpose. The discussion began May 31st; the vote was reached June 15th, but it then failed of the required two-thirds—93 for to 65 against, 23 not voting. Its more pronounced advocates were Arnold, Ashley,

Third. That all negro slaves captured in arms be at once delivered over to the executive authorities of the respective States to which they belong, to be dealt with according to the laws of said States.

Fourth. That the like orders be executed in all cases with respect to all commissioned officers of the United States when found serving in company with said slaves in insurrection against the authorities of the different States of this Confederacy.

Broomall, Stevens, and Kelly of Pennsylvania; Farnsworth and Ingersoll of Illinois, and many others. Its ablest opponents were Holman, Wood, Mallory, Cox and Pendleton—the latter rallying nearly all of the Democrats against it. Its Democratic friends were McAllister and Bailey of Pennsylvania; Cobb of Wisconsin; Griswold and Odell of New York. Before the vote was announced Ashley changed his vote so as to move a reconsideration and keep control of the question. At the next session it was passed, receiving every Republican and 16 Democratic votes, 8 Democrats purposely refraining, so that it would surely pass.

Admission of Representatives from Louisiana.

The capture of New Orleans by Admiral Farragut, led to the enrollment of 60,000 citizens of Louisiana as citizens of the United States. The President thereupon appointed a Military Governor for the entire State, and this Governor ordered an election for members of Congress under the old State constitution. This was held Dec. 3, 1862, when Messrs. Flanders and Hahn were returned, neither receiving 3,000 votes. They received certificates, presented them, and thus opened up a new and grave political question. The Democrats opposed their admission on grounds so well stated by Voorhees of Indiana, that we quote them :

"Understand this principle. If the Southern Confederacy is a foreign power, an independent nationality to-day, and you have conquered back the territory of Louisiana, you may then substitute a new system of laws in the place of the laws of that State. You may then supplant her civil institutions by institutions made anew for her by the proper authority of this *Government*—not by the executive—but by the *legislative* branch of the Government, assisted by the Executive simply to the extent of signing his name to the bills of legislation. If the Chairman of the Committee of Ways and Means, (Mr. Stevens) is correct; if the gentleman from Kansas (Mr. Conway) is correct, and this assumed power in the South is a power of the earth, and stands to-day upon equal terms of nationality with ourselves, and reconquer back State by State its territory by the power of arms, then we may govern them independently of their local laws. But if the theory we have been proceeding upon here, that this Union is unbroken; that no States have sundered the bonds that bind us together; that no successful disunion has yet taken place,—if that theory is still to prevail in these halls, then this cannot be done. You are as much bound to uphold the laws of Louisiana in all their extent and in all their parts, as you are to uphold the laws of Pennsylvania or New York, or any other State whose civil policy has not been disturbed."

Michael Hahn, one of the Representatives elect, closed a very effective speech, which secured the personal good will of the House in favor of his admission, in these words:

"And even, sir, within the limits of the dreary and desolated region of the rebellion itself, despair, which has already taken hold of the people, will gain additional power and strength, at the reception of the news that Louisiana sends a message of peace, good-will, and hearty fellowship to the Union. This intelligence will sound more joyful to patriot ears than all the oft repeated tidings of 'Union victories.' And of all victories, this will be the most glorious, useful and solid, for it speaks of *re-organization*, soon to become the great and difficult problem with which our statesmen will have to familiarize themselves, and when this shall have commenced, we will be able to realize that God, in his infinite mercy has looked down upon our misfortunes, and in a spirit of paternal love and pity, has addressed us in the language ascribed to him by our own gifted Longfellow:

> "I am weary of your quarrels,
> Weary of your wars and bloodshed,
> Weary of your prayers for vengeance,
> Of your wranglings and dissensions;
> All your strength is in your *Union*,
> All your danger is in *discord*,
> Therefore, be at peace, henceforward,
> And as *brothers* live together."

Mr. Speaker, Louisiana—ever loyal, honorable Louisiana—seeks no greater blessing in the future, than to remain a part of this great and glorious Union. She has stood by you in the darkest hours of the rebellion; and she intends to stand by you. Sir, raise your eyes to the gorgeous ceilings which ornament this Hall, and look upon her fair and lovely escutcheon. Carefully read the patriotic words which surround her affectionate pelican family, and you will find there inscribed, '*Justice, Union, Confidence.*' Those words have with us no idle meaning; and would to God that other members of this Union, could properly appreciate our motto, our motives and our position!"

The debate attracted much attention, because of the novelty of a question upon which, it has since been contended, would have turned a different plan of reconstructing the rebellious States if the President's plans had not been destroyed by his assassination. Dawes, of Massachusetts, was the Chairman of the Committee on Elections, and he closed the debate in favor of admission. The vote stood 92 for to 44 against, almost a strict party test, the Democrats voting no.

RECONSTRUCTION.

In the House as early as Dec. 15, 1863, Henry Winter Davis moved that so much of the President's message as relates to the duty of the United States to guaranty a Republican form of government to the States in which the governments recognized by the United States have been abrogated or overthrown, be referred to a select committee of nine to report the bills necessary and proper for carrying into execution the foregoing guarantee, was passed, and on May 4th, 1864, the House adopted the first reconstruction bill by 74 yeas to 66 nays—a strict party vote.* The Senate passed it by yeas 18, nays 14—Doolittle, Henderson, Lane of Indiana, Ten Eyck, Trumbull, and Van Winkle voting with the Democrats against it.

The bill authorizes the President to appoint in each of the States declared in rebellion, a Provisional Governor, with the pay and emoluments of a brigadier; to be charged with the civil administration until a State government therein shall be recognized. As soon as the military resistance to the United States shall have been suppressed, and the people sufficiently returned to their obedience to the Constitution and laws, the Governor shall direct the marshal of the United States to enroll all the white male citizens of the United States, resident in the State in their respective counties, and whenever a majority of them take the oath of allegiance, the loyal people of the State shall be entitled to elect delegates to a convention to act upon the re-establishment of a State government—the proclamation to contain details prescribed. Qualified voters in the army may vote in their camps. No person who has held or exercised any civil, military, State, or Confederate office, under the rebel occupation, and who has voluntarily borne arms against the United States, shall vote or be eligible as a delegate. The convention is required to insert in the constitution provisions—

1st. No person who has held or exercised any civil or military office, (except offices merely ministerial and military offices below a colonel,) State or Confederate, under the usurping power, shall vote for, or be a member of the legislature or governor.

2d. Involuntary servitude is forever prohibited, and the freedom of all persons is guarantied in said State.

3d. No debt, State or Confederate, created by or under the sanction of the usurping power, shall be recognized or paid by the State.

Upon the adoption of the constitution by the convention, and its ratification by the electors of the State, the Provisional Governor shall so certify to the President, who, after obtaining the assent of Congress, shall, by proclamation, recognize the government as established, and none other, as the constitutional government of the State; and from the date of such recognition, and not before, Senators and Representatives and electors for President and Vice-President may be elected in such State. Until re-organization the Provisional Governor shall enforce the laws of the Union and of the State before the rebellion.

The remaining sections are as follows:

SEC. 12. That all persons held to involuntary servitude or labor in the States aforesaid are hereby emancipated and discharged therefrom, and they and their posterity shall be forever free. And if any such persons or their posterity shall be restrained of liberty, under pretence of any claim to such service or labor, the courts of the United States shall, on *habeas corpus*, discharge them.

SEC. 13. That if any person declared free by this act, or any law of the United States, or any proclamation of the President, be restrained of liberty, with intent to be held in or reduced to involuntary servitude or labor, the person convicted before a court of competent jurisdiction of such act shall be punished by fine of not less than $1,500, and be imprisoned not less than five, nor more than twenty years.

SEC. 14. That every person who shall hereafter hold or exercise any office, civil or military, except offices merely ministerial and military offices below the grade of colonel, in the rebel service, State or Confederate, is hereby declared not to be a citizen of the United States.

Lincoln's Proclamation on Reconstruction

President Lincoln failed to sign the above bill because it reached him less than one hour before final adjournment, and thereupon issued a proclamation which closed as follows:

"Now, therefore, I, Abraham Lincoln, President of the United States, do proclaim, declare, and make known, that, while I am (as I was in December last, when by proclamation I propounded a plan for restoration) unprepared, by a formal approval of this bill, to be inflexibly committed to any single plan of restoration; and, while I am also unprepared to declare that the free State constitutions and governments already adopted and installed in Arkansas and Louisiana shall be set aside and held for nought, thereby repelling and discouraging the loyal citizens who have set up the same as to further effort, or to declare a constitutional competency in Congress to abolish slavery in States, but am at the same time sincerely hoping and

* McPherson's History, page 317.

expecting that a constitutional amendment abolishing slavery throughout the nation may be adopted, nevertheless I am fully satisfied with the system for restoration contained in the bill as one very proper plan for the loyal people of any State choosing to adopt it, and that I am, and at all times shall be, prepared to give the Executive aid and assistance to any such people, so soon as the military resistance to the United States shall have been suppressed in any such State, and the people thereof shall have sufficiently returned to their obedience to the Constitution and laws of the United States, in which cases Military Governors will be appointed, with directions to proceed according to the bill."

Admission of Arkansas.

On the 10th of June, 1864, introduced a joint resolution for the recognition of the free State government of Arkansas. A new State government had then been organized, with Isaac Murphy, Governor, who was reported to have received nearly 16,000 votes at a called election. The other State officers are:

Lieutenant Governor, C. C. Bliss; Secretary of State, R. J. T. White; Auditor, J. B. Berry; Treasurer, E. D. Ayers; Attorney General, C. T. Jordan; Judges of the Supreme Court, T. D. W. Yowley, C. A. Harper, E. Baker.

The Legislature also elected Senators, but neither Senators nor Representatives obtained their seats. Trumbull, from the Senate Judiciary Committee, made a long report touching the admission of the Senators, which closed as follows:

"When the rebellion in Arkansas shall have been so far suppressed that the loyal inhabitants thereof shall be free to re-establish their State government upon a republican foundation, or to recognize the one already set up, and by the aid and not in subordination to the military to maintain the same, they will then, and not before, in the opinion of your committee, be entitled to a representation in Congress, and to participate in the administration of the Federal Government. Believing that such a state of things did not at the time the claimants were elected, and does not now, exist in the State of Arkansas, the committee recommend for adoption the following resolution:

"*Resolved*, That William M. Fishback and Elisha Baxter are not entitled to seats as Senators from the State of Arkansas."

1864, June 29—The resolution of the Committee on the Judiciary was adopted—yeas 27, nays 6.

President Lincoln was known to favor the immediate admission of Arkansas and Louisiana, but the refusal of the Senate to admit the Arkansas Senators raised an issue which partially divided the Republicans in both Houses, some of whom favored forcible reconstruction through the aid of Military Governors and the machinery of new State governments, while others opposed. The views of those opposed to the President's policy are well stated in a paper signed by Benjamin F. Wade and Henry Winter Davis, published in the New York *Tribune*, August 5th, 1864. From this we take the more pithy extracts:

The President, by preventing this bill from becoming a law, holds the electoral votes of the rebel States at the dictation of his personal ambition.

If those votes turn the balance in his favor, is it to be supposed that his competitor, defeated by such means, will acquiesce?

If the rebel majority assert their supremacy in those States, and send votes which elect an enemy of the Government, will we not repel his claims?

And is not civil war for the Presidency inaugurated by the votes of rebel States?

Seriously impressed with these dangers, Congress, "*the proper constitutional authority*," formally declared that there are no State governments in the rebel States, and provided for their erection at a proper time; and both the Senate and the House of Representatives rejected the Senators and Representatives chosen under the authority of what the President calls the free constitution and government of Arkansas.

The President's proclamation "*holds for naught*" this judgment, and discards the authority of the Supreme Court, and strides headlong toward the anarchy his proclamation of the 8th of December inaugurated.

If electors for President be allowed to be chosen in either of those States, a sinister light will be cast on the motives which induced the President to "hold for naught" the will of Congress rather than his government in Louisiana and Arkansas.

That judgment of Congress which the President defies was the exercise of an authority exclusively vested in Congress by the Constitution to determine what is the established government in a State, and in its own nature and by the highest judicial authority binding on all other departments of the Government. * * * *

A more studied outrage on the legislative authority of the people has never been perpetrated.

Congress passed a bill; the President refused to approve it, and then by proclamation puts as much of it in force as he sees fit, and proposes to execute those parts by officers unknown to the laws of the United States and not subject to the confirmation of the Senate!

The bill directed the appointment of Provisional Governors by and with the advice and consent of the Senate.

The President, after defeating the law, proposes to appoint without law, and without the advice and consent of the Senate, *Military* Governors for the rebel States!

He has already exercised this dictatorial usurpation in Louisiana, and he defeated the bill to prevent its limitation. * * *

The President has greatly presumed on the forbearance which the supporters of his Administration have so long practiced, in view of the arduous conflict in which we are engaged, and the reckless ferocity of our political opponents.

But he must understand that our support is of a cause and not of a man; that the authority of Congress is paramount and must be respected; that the whole body of the Union men of Congress will not submit to be impeached by him of rash and unconstitutional legislation; and if he wishes our support, he must confine himself to his executive duties—to obey and execute, not make the laws—to suppress by arms armed rebellion, and leave political reorganization to Congress.

If the supporters of the Government fail to insist on this, they become responsible for the usurpations which they fail to rebuke, and are justly liable to the indignation of the people whose rights and security, committed to their keeping, they sacrifice.

Let them consider the remedy for these usurpations, and, having found it, fearlessly execute it.

The question, as presented in 1864, now passed temporarily from public consideration because of greater interest in the closing events of the war and the Presidential succession. The passage of the 14th or anti-slavery amendment by the States also intervened. This was officially announced on the 18th of December 1865, by Mr. Seward, 27 of the then 36 States having ratified, as follows: Illinois, Rhode Island, Michigan, Maryland, New York, West Virginia, Maine, Kansas, Massachusetts, Pennsylvania, Virginia, Ohio, Missouri, Nevada, Indiana, Louisiana, Minnesota, Wisconsin, Vermont, Tennessee, Arkansas, Connecticut, New Hampshire, South Carolina, Alabama, North Carolina, and Georgia.

TEXT OF THE RECONSTRUCTION MEASURES.

14th Constitutional Amendment.

Joint Resolution proposing an Amendment to the Constitution of the United States.

Be it resolved by the Senate and House of Representatives of the United States of America, in Congress assembled, (two-thirds of both houses concurring,) That the following article be proposed to the Legislatures of the several States as an amendment to the Constitution of the United States, which, when ratified by three-fourths of said Legislatures, shall be valid as part of the Constitution, namely:

[Here follows the 14th amendment. See Book IV.]

Reconstruction Act of Thirty-Ninth Congress.

An Act to provide for the more efficient government of the rebel States.

Whereas no legal State governments or adequate protection for life or property now exists in the rebel States of Virginia, North Carolina, South Carolina, Georgia, Mississippi, Alabama, Louisiana, Florida, Texas, and Arkansas; and whereas it is necessary that peace and good order should be enforced in said States until loyal and republican State governments can be legally established: Therefore

Be it enacted, &c., That said rebel States shall be divided into military districts and made subject to the military authority of the United States, as hereinafter prescribed, and for that purpose Virginia shall constitute the first district; North Carolina and South Carolina the second district; Georgia, Alabama, and Florida the third district; Mississippi and Arkansas the fourth district; and Louisiana and Texas the fifth district.

SEC. 2. That it shall be the duty of the President to assign to the command of each of said districts an officer of the army, not below the rank of brigadier general, and to detail a sufficient military force to enable such officer to perform his duties and enforce his authority within the district to which he is assigned.

SEC. 3. That it shall be the duty of each officer assigned as aforesaid to protect all persons in their rights of person and property, to suppress insurrection. disorder, and violence, and to punish, or cause to be punished, all disturbers of the public peace and criminals, and to this end he may allow local civil tribunals to take jurisdiction of and to try offenders, or, when in his judgment it may be necessary for the trial of offenders, he shall have power to organize military commissions or tribunals for that purpose; and all interference under color of State authority with the exercise of military authority under this act shall be null and void.

SEC. 4. That all persons put under military arrest by virtue of this act shall be tried without unnecessary delay, and no cruel or unusual punishment shall be inflicted; and no sentence of any military commission or tribunal hereby authorized, affecting the life or liberty of any person, shall be executed until it is approved by the officer in command of the district, and the laws and regulations for the government of the army shall not be affected by this act, except in so far as they conflict with its provisions: *Provided*, That no sentence of death under the provisions of this act shall be carried into effect without the approval of the President.

SEC. 5. That when the people of any one of said rebel States shall have formed a constitution of government in conformity with the Constitution of the United States in all respects, framed by a convention of delegates elected by the male citizens of said State twenty-one years old and upward, of whatever race, color, or previous condition, who have been resident in said State for one year previous to the day of such election, except such as may be disfranchised for participation in the rebellion, or for felony at common law, and when such constitution shall provide that the elective franchise shall be enjoyed by all such persons as have the qualifications herein stated for electors of delegates, and when such constitution shall be ratified by a majority of the persons voting on the question of ratification who are qualified as electors for delegates, and when such constitution shall have been submitted to Congress for examination and approval, and Congress shall have approved the same, and when said State, by a vote of its legislature elected under said constitution, shall have adopted the amendment to the Constitution of the United States, proposed by the Thirty-ninth Congress, and known as article fourteen, and when said article shall have become a part of the Constitution of the United States, said State shall be declared entitled to representation in Congress, and Senators and Representatives shall be admitted therefrom on their taking the oaths prescribed by law, and then and thereafter the preceding sections of this act shall be inoperative in said State: *Provided*, That no person excluded from the privilege of holding office by said proposed amendment to the Constitution of the United States shall be eligible to election as a member of the convention to frame a constitution for any of said rebel States, nor shall any such person vote for members of such convention.

SEC. 6. That until the people of said rebel States shall be by law admitted to representation in the Congress of the United States, any civil governments which may exist therein shall be deemed provisional only, and in all respects subject to the paramount authority of the United States at any time to abolish, modify, control, or supersede the same; and in all elections to any office under such provisional governments all persons shall be entitled to vote, and none others, who are entitled to vote under the provisions of the fifth section of this act; and no person shall be eligible to any office under any such provisional governments who would be disqualified from holding office under the provisions of the third article of said constitutional amendment.

Passed March 2, 1867.

Supplemental Reconstruction Act of Fortieth Congress.

AN ACT supplementary to an act entitled "An act to provide for the more efficient government of the rebel States," passed March second, eighteen hundred and sixty-seven, and to facilitate restoration.

Be it enacted, &c., That before the first day of September, eighteen hundred and sixty-seven, the commanding general in each district defined by an act entitled "An act to provide for the more efficient government of the rebel States," passed March second, eighteen hundred and sixty-seven, shall cause a registration to be made of the male citizens of the United States, twenty-one years of age and upwards, resident in each county or parish in the State or States included in his district, which registration shall include only those persons who are qualified to vote for delegates by the act aforesaid, and who shall have taken and subscribed the following oath or affirmation: "I, ——, do solemnly swear, (or affirm,) in the presence of Almighty God, that I am a citizen of the State of ——; that I have resided in said State for —— months next preceding this day, and now reside in the county of ——, or the parish of ——, in said State, (as the case may be;) that I am twenty-one years old; that I have not been disfranchised for participation in any rebellion or civil war against the United States, nor for felony commited against the laws of any State or of the United States; that I have never been a member of any State legislature, nor held any executive or judicial office in any State and afterwards engaged in insurrection or rebellion against the United States, or given aid or comfort to the enemies thereof; that I have never taken an oath as a member of Congress of the United States, or as an officer of the United States, or as a member of any State legislature, or as an executive or judicial officer of any State, to support the Constitution of the United States, and afterwards engaged in insurrection or rebellion against the United States or given aid or comfort to the enemies thereof; that I will faithfully support the Constitution and obey the laws of the United States, and will, to the best of my ability, encourage others so to do, so help me God;" which oath or affirmation may be administered by any registering officer.

SEC. 2. That after the completion of the registration hereby provided for in any State, at such time and places therein as the commanding general shall appoint and direct, of which at least thirty days' public notice shall be given, an election shall be held of delegates to a convention for the purpose of establishing a constitution and civil government for such State loyal to the Union, said convention in each State, except Virginia, to consist of the same number of members as the most numerous branch of the State legislature of such State in the year eighteen hundred and sixty, to be apportioned among the several districts, counties, or parishes of such State by the commanding general, giving to each representation in the ratio of voters or registered as aforesaid, as nearly as may be. The convention in Virginia shall consist of the same number of members as represented the territory now constituting Virginia in the most numerous branch of the legislature of said State in the year eighteen hundred and sixty, to be appointed as aforesaid.

SEC. 3. That at said election the registered voters of each State shall vote for or against a convention to form a constitution therefor under this act. Those voting in favor of such a convention shall have written or printed on the ballots by which they vote for delegates, as aforesaid, the words "For a convention," and those voting against such a convention shall have written or printed on such ballots the words "Against a convention." The person appointed to superintend said election, and to make return of the votes given thereat, as herein provided, shall count and make return of the votes given for and against a convention; and the commanding general to whom the same shall have been returned shall ascertain and declare the total vote in each State for and against a convention. If a majority of the votes given on that question shall be for a convention, then such convention shall be held as hereinafter provided; but if a majority of said votes shall be against a convention, then no such convention shall be held under this act: *Provided*, That such convention shall not be held unless a majority of all such registered voters shall have voted on the question of holding such convention.

SEC. 4. That the commanding general of each district shall appoint as many boards of registration as may be necessary, consisting of three loyal officers or persons, to make and complete the registration, superintend the election, and make return to him of the votes, lists of voters, and of the persons elected as delegates by a plurality of the votes cast at said election; and upon receiving said returns he shall open the same, ascertain the persons elected as delegates according to the returns of the officers who conducted said election, and make proclamation thereof; and if a majority of the votes given on that question shall be for a convention, the commanding general, within sixty days from the date of election, shall notify the delegates to assemble in convention, at a time and place to be mentioned in the notification, and said convention, when organized, shall proceed to frame a constitution and civil government according to the provisions of this act and the act to which it is supplementary; and when the same shall have been so framed, said constitution shall be submitted by the convention for ratification to the persons registered under the provisions of this act at an election to be conducted by the officers or persons appointed or to be appointed by the commanding general, as hereinbefore provided, and to be held after the expiration of thirty days from the date of notice thereof, to be given by said convention; and the returns thereof shall be made to the commanding general of the district.

SEC. 5. That if, according to said returns, the constitution shall be ratified by a majority of the votes of the registered electors qualified as herein specified, cast at said election, (at least one-half of all the registered voters voting upon the question of such ratification,) the president of the convention shall transmit a copy of the same, duly certified, to the President of the United States, who shall forthwith transmit the same to Congress, if then in session, and if not in session, then immediately upon its next assembling; and if it shall, moreover, appear to Congress that the election was one at which all the registered and qualified electors in the State had an opportunity to vote freely and without restraint, fear, or the influence of fraud; and if the Congress shall be satisfied that such constitution meets the approval of a majority of all the qualified electors in the State, and if the said constitution shall be declared by Congress to be in conformity with the provisions of the act to which this is supplementary, and the other provisions of said act shall have been complied with, and the said constitution shall be approved by Congress, the State shall be declared entitled to representation, and Senators and Representatives shall be admitted therefrom as therein provided.

SEC. 6. That all elections in the States mentioned in the said "Act to provide for the more efficient government of the rebel States," shall, during the operation of said act, be by ballot; and all officers making the said registration of voters and conducting said elections shall, before entering upon the discharge of their duties, take and subscribe the oath prescribed by the act approved July second, eighteen hundred and sixty-two, entitled "An act to prescribe an oath of office:* *Provided*, That if any person shall knowingly and falsely take and subscribe any oath in this act prescribed, such person so offending and being thereof duly convicted, shall be subject to the pains, penalties, and disabilities which by law are provided for the punishment of the crime of wilful and corrupt perjury.

SEC. 7. That all expenses incurred by the several commanding generals, or by virtue of any orders issued, or appointments made, by them, under or by virtue of this act, shall be paid out of any moneys in the treasury not otherwise appropriated.

SEC. 8. That the convention for each State shall prescribe the fees, salary, and compensation to be paid to all delegates and other officers and agents herein authorized or necessary to carry into effect the purposes of this act not herein otherwise provided for, and shall provide for the levy and collection of such taxes on the property in such State as may be necessary to pay the same.

SEC. 9. That the word article, in the sixth section of the act to which this is supplementary, shall be construed to mean section.

Passed March 23, 1867.

Votes of State Legislatures on the Fourteenth Constitutional Amendment.†

LOYAL STATES.

Ratified—Twenty-one States.

Maine—SENATE, January 16, 1867, yeas 31, nays 0; HOUSE, January 11, 1867, yeas 126, nays 12.

New Hampshire—SENATE, July 6, 1866, yeas 9, nays 3; HOUSE, June 28, 1866, yeas 207, nays 112.

Vermont—SENATE, October 23, 1866, yeas 28, nays 0; HOUSE, October 30, 1866, yeas 199, nays 11.

Massachusetts—SENATE, March 20, 1867, yeas 27, nays 6; HOUSE, March 14, 1867, yeas 120, nays 20.

Rhode Island—SENATE, February 5, 1867, yeas 26, nays 2; HOUSE, February 7, 1867, yeas 60, nays 9

Connecticut—SENATE, June 25, 1866, yeas 11, nays 6; HOUSE, June 29, 1866, yeas 131, nays 92.

New York—SENATE, January 3, 1867, yeas 23, nays 3; HOUSE, January 10, 1867, yeas 76, nays 40.

New Jersey—SENATE, September 11, 1866, yeas 11, nays 10; HOUSE, September 11, 1866, yeas 34, nays 24.

Pennsylvania—SENATE, January 17, 1867, yeas 20, nays 9; HOUSE, February 6, 1867, yeas 58, nays 29.

West Virginia—SENATE, January 15, 1867, yeas 15, nays 3; HOUSE, January 16, 1867, yeas 43, nays 11.

Ohio—SENATE, January 3, 1867, yeas 21, nays 12; HOUSE, January 4, 1867, yeas 54, nays 25.

Tennessee—SENATE, July 11, 1866, yeas 15, nays 6; HOUSE, July 12, 1866, yeas 43, nays 11.

Indiana—SENATE, January 16, 1867, yeas 29, nays 18; HOUSE, January 23, 1867, yeas —, nays —.

Illinois—SENATE, January 10, 1867, yeas 17, nays 7; HOUSE, January 15, 1867, yeas 59, nays 25.

Michigan—SENATE, —— 1867, yeas 25, nays 1; HOUSE, —— 1867, yeas 77, nays 15.

Missouri—SENATE, January 5, 1867, yeas 26, nays 6; HOUSE, January 8, 1867, yeas 85, nays 34.

Minnesota—SENATE, January 16, 1867, yeas 16, nays 5; HOUSE, January 15, 1867, yeas 40, nays 6.

Kansas—SENATE, January 11, 1867, unanimously; HOUSE, January 10, 1867, yeas, 75, nays 7.

Wisconsin—SENATE, January 23, 1867, yeas 22, nays 10; HOUSE, February 7, 1867, yeas 72, nays 12.

Oregon—* Senate, ——, 1866, yeas 13, nays 7; House, September 19, 1866, yeas 25, nays 22.

Nevada—* SENATE, January 22, 1867, yeas 14, nays 2; HOUSE, January 11, 1867, yeas 34, nays 4.

Rejected—Three States.

Delaware—SENATE, —— ——; HOUSE, February 7, 1867, yeas 6, nays 15.

* This act is in these words:

Be it enacted, &c., That hereafter every person elected or appointed to any office of honor or profit under the government of the United States, either in the civil, military, or naval departments of the public service, excepting the President of the United States, shall, before entering upon the duties of such office, and before being entitled to any of the salary or other emoluments thereof, take and subscribe the following oath or affirmation: "I, A B, do solemnly swear (or affirm) that I have never voluntarily borne arms against the United States since I have been a citizen thereof; that I have voluntarily given no aid, countenance, counsel, or encouragement to persons engaged in armed hostility thereto; that I have never sought nor accepted nor attempted to exercise the functions of any office whatever, under any authority or pretended authority, in hostility to the United States; that I have not yielded a voluntary support to any pretended government, authority, power, or constitution within the United States, hostile or inimical thereto; and I do further swear (or affirm) that, to the best of my knowledge and ability, I will support and defend the Constitution of the United States, against all enemies, foreign and domestic; that I will bear true faith and allegiance to the same; that I take this obligation freely, without any mental reservation or purpose of evasion, and that I will well and faithfully discharge the duties of the office on which I am about to enter; so help me God;" which said oath, so taken and signed, shall be preserved among the files of the Court, House of Congress, or Department to which the said office may appertain. And any person who shall falsely take the said oath shall be guilty of perjury, and on conviction, in addition to the penalties now prescribed for that offense, shall be deprived of his office, and rendered incapable forever after, of holding any office or place under the United States.

† Compiled by Hon. Edward McPherson in his Hand Book of Politics for 1868.

*Unofficial.

Maryland—SENATE, March 23, 1867, yeas 4, nays 13; HOUSE, March 23, 1867, yeas 12, nays 45.

Kentucky—SENATE, January 8, 1867, yeas 7, nays 24; HOUSE, January 8, 1867, yeas 26, nays 62.

Not acted—Three States.

Iowa, California, Nebraska.

INSURRECTIONARY STATES.

Rejected—Ten States.

Virginia—SENATE, January 9, 1867, unanimously; HOUSE, January 9, 1867, 1 for amendment.

North Carolina—SENATE, December 13, 1866, yeas 1, nays 44; HOUSE, December 13, 1866, yeas 10, nays 93.

South Carolina—SENATE——— ———; HOUSE, December 20, 1866, yeas 1, nays 95.

Georgia—SENATE, November 9, 1866, yeas 0, nays 36; HOUSE, November 9, 1866, yeas 2, nays 131.

Florida—SENATE, December 3, 1866, yeas 0, nays 20; HOUSE, December 1, 1866, yeas 0, nays 49.

Alabama—SENATE, December 7, 1866, yeas 2, nays 27; HOUSE, December 7, 1866, yeas 8, nays 69.

Mississippi—SENATE, January 30, 1867, yeas 0, nays 27; HOUSE, January 25, 1867, yeas 0, nays 88.

Louisiana—SENATE, February 5, 1867, unanimously; HOUSE, February 6, 1867, unanimously.

Texas—SENATE, ——— ———; HOUSE, October 13, 1866, yeas 5, nays 67.

Arkansas—SENATE, December 15, 1866, yeas 1, nays 24; HOUSE, December 17, 1866, yeas 2, nays 68.

The passage of the 14th Amendment and of the Reconstruction Acts, was followed by Presidential proclamations dated August 20, 1866, declaring the insurrection at an end in Texas, and civil authority existing throughout the whole of the United States.

PRESIDENTIAL ELECTION OF 1864.

The Republican National Convention met at Baltimore, June 7th, 1864, and renominated President Lincoln unanimously, save the vote of Missouri, which was cast for Gen. Grant. Hannibal Hamlin, the old Vice-President, was not re-nominated, because of a desire to give part of the ticket to the Union men of the South, who pressed Senator Andrew Johnson of Tennessee. "Parson" Brownlow made a strong appeal in his behalf, and by his eloquence captured a majority of the Convention.

The Democratic National Convention met at Chicago, August 29th, 1864, and nominated General George B. McClellan, of New Jersey, for President, and George H. Pendleton, of Ohio, for Vice-President. General McClellan was made available for the Democratic nomination through certain political letters which he had written on points of difference between himself and the Lincoln administration. Two of these letters are sufficient to show his own and the views of the party which nominated him, in the canvass which followed:

Gen. McClellan's Letters.

On Political Administration, July 7, 1862.

HEADQUARTERS ARMY OF THE POTOMAC, CAMP NEAR HARRISON'S LANDING, VA., *July* 7, 1862.

MR. PRESIDENT:—You have been fully informed that the rebel army is in the front, with the purpose of overwhelming us by attacking our positions or reducing us by blocking our river communications. I cannot but regard our condition as critical, and I earnestly desire, in view of possible contingencies, to lay before your excellency, for your private consideration, my general views concerning the existing state of the rebellion, although they do not strictly relate to the situation of this army, or strictly come within the scope of my official duties. These views amount to convictions, and are deeply impressed upon my mind and heart. Our cause must never be abandoned; it is the cause of free institutions and self-government. The Constitution and the Union must be preserved, whatever may be the cost in time, treasure, and blood. If secession is successful, other dissolutions are clearly to be seen in the future. Let neither military disaster, political faction, nor foreign war shake your settled purpose to enforce the equal operation of the laws of the United States upon the people of every State.

The time has come when the government must determine upon a civil and military policy, covering the whole ground of our national trouble.

The responsibility of determining, declaring, and supporting such civil and military policy, and of directing the whole course of national affairs in regard to the rebellion, must now be assumed and exercised by you, or our cause will be lost. The Constitution gives you power, even for the present terrible exigency.

This rebellion has assumed the character of a war; as such it should be regarded, and it should be conducted upon the highest principles known to Christian civilization. It should not be a war looking to the subjugation of the people of any State, in any event. It should not be at all a war upon population, but against armed forces and political organizations. Neither confiscation of property, political executions of persons, territorial organization of States, or forcible abolition of slavery, should be contemplated for a moment.

In prosecuting the war, all private property and unarmed persons should be strictly protected, subject only to the necessity of military operations; all private property taken for military use should be paid or receipted for; pillage and waste should be treated as high crimes; all unnecessary trespass sternly prohibited, and offensive demeanor by the military towards citizens promptly rebuked. Military arrests should not be tolerated, except in places where active hostilities exist; and oaths, not required by enactments, constitutionally made, should be neither demanded nor received.

Military government should be confined to the preservation of public order and the protection of political right. Military power should not be allowed to interfere with the relations of servitude, either by supporting or impairing the authority of the master, except for repressing disorder, as in other cases. Slaves, contraband under the act of Congress, seeking military protection, should receive it. The right of the government to appropriate permanently to its own service claims to slave labor should be asserted, and the the right of the owner to compensation therefor should be recognized. This principle might be extended, upon grounds of military necessity and security, to all the slaves of a particular State, thus working manumission in such State; and in Missouri, perhaps in Western Virginia also, and possibly even in Maryland, the expediency of such a measure is only a question of time. A system of policy thus constitutional, and pervaded by the influences of Christianity and freedom, would receive the support of almost all truly loyal men, would deeply impress the rebel masses and all foreign nations, and it might be humbly hoped that it would commend itself to the favor of the Almighty.

Unless the principles governing the future conduct of our struggle shall be made known and approved, the effort to obtain requisite forces will be almost hopeless. A declaration of radical views, especially upon slavery, will rapidly disintegrate our present armies. The policy of the government must be supported by concentrations of military power. The national forces should not be dispersed in expeditions, posts of occupation, and numerous armies, but should be mainly collected into masses, and brought to bear upon the armies of the Confederate States. Those armies thoroughly defeated, the political structure which they support would soon cease to exist.

In carrying out any system of policy which you may form, you will require a commander-in-chief of the army, one who possesses your confidence, understands your views, and who is competent to execute your orders, by directing the military forces of the nation to the accomplishment of the objects by you proposed. I do not ask that place for myself. I am willing to serve you in such position as you may assign me, and I will do so as faithfully as ever subordinate served superior.

I may be on the brink of eternity; and as I hope forgiveness from my Maker, I have written this letter with sincerity towards you and from love for my country.

Very respectfully, your obedient servant,
GEORGE B. McCLELLAN,
Major-General Commanding.

His Excellency A. LINCOLN, *President.*

IN FAVOR OF THE ELECTION OF GEORGE W. WOODWARD AS GOVERNOR OF PENNSYLVANIA.

ORANGE, NEW JERSEY, *October* 12, 1863.

DEAR SIR:—My attention has been called to an article in the Philadelphia *Press*, asserting that I had written to the managers of a Democratic meeting at Allentown, disapproving the objects of the meeting, and that if I voted or spoke it would be in favor of Governor Curtin, and I am informed that similar assertions have been made throughout the State.

It has been my earnest endeavor heretofore to avoid participation in party politics. I had determined to adhere to this course, but it is obvious that I cannot longer maintain silence under such misrepresentations. I therefore request you to deny that I have written any such letter, or entertained any such views as those attributed to me in the Philadelphia *Press*, and I desire to state clearly and distinctly, that having some days ago had a full conversation with Judge Woodward, I find that our views agree, and I regard his election as Governor of Pennsylvania called for by the interests of the nation.

I understand Judge Woodward to be in favor of the prosecution of the war with all the means at the command of the loyal States, until the military power of the rebellion is destroyed. I understand him to be of the opinion that while the war is urged with all possible decision and energy, the policy directing it should be in consonance with the principles of humanity and civilization, working no injury to private rights and property not demanded by military necessity and recognized by military law among civilized nations.

And, finally, I understand him to agree with me in the opinion that the sole great objects of this war are the restoration of the unity of the nation, the preservation of the Constitution, and the supremacy of the laws of the country. Believing our opinions entirely agree upon these points, I would, were it in my power, give to Judge Woodward my voice and vote.

I am, very respectfully, yours,
GEORGE B. McCLELLAN.

Hon. CHARLES J. BIDDLE.

The views of Mr. Lincoln were well known; they were felt in the general conduct of the war. The Republicans adopted as one of their maxims the words of their candidate, "that it was dangerous to swap horses while crossing a stream." The campaign was exciting, and was watched by both armies with interest and anxiety. In this election, by virtue of an act of Congress, the soldiers in the field were permitted to vote, and a large majority of every branch of the service sustained the Administration, though two years before General McClellan had been the idol of the Army of the Potomac. Lincoln and Johnson received 212 electoral votes, against 21 for McClellan and Pendleton.

Lincoln's Second Administration.

In President Lincoln's second inaugural address, delivered on the 4th of March, 1865, he spoke the following words, since oft quoted as typical of the kindly disposition of the man believed by his party to be the greatest President since Washington: "With malice toward none, with charity for all, with firmness in the right, as God gives us to see the right, let us strive on to finish the work we are in, to bind up the Nation's wounds, to care for him who shall have borne the battle, and for his widow and orphans—to do all which may achieve a just and lasting peace among ourselves and with all nations."

Lincoln could well afford to show that generosity which never comes more properly than from the hands of the victor. His policy was about to end in a great triumph. In less than five weeks later on General Lee had surrendered the main army of the South to General Grant at Appomattox, on terms at once magnanimous and so briefly stated that they won the admiration of both armies, for the rebels had been permitted to retain their horses and side arms, and to go at once to their homes, not to be disturbed by United States authority so long as they observed their paroles and the laws in force where they resided. Lee's surrender was rapidly followed by that of all Southern troops.

Next came a grave political work—the actual reconstruction of the States lately in rebellion. This work gave renewed freshness to the leading political issues incident to the war, and likewise gave rise to new issues. It was claimed at once that Lincoln had a reconstruction policy of his own, because of his anxiety for the prompt admission of Louisiana and Arkansas, but it had certainly never taken definite shape, nor was there time to get such a policy in shape, between the surrender of Lee and his own assassination. On the night of the 15th of April, six days after the surrender, J. Wilkes Booth shot him while sitting in a box in Ford's theatre. The nation stood appalled at the deed. No man was ever more sincerely mourned in all sections and by all classes. The Southern leaders thought that this rash act had lost to them a life which had never been harsh, and while firm, was ever generous. The North had looked upon him as "Father Abraham," and all who viewed the result of the shooting from sectional or partisan standpoints, thought his policy of "keeping with the people," would have shielded every proper interest. No public man ever felt less "pride of opinion" than Lincoln, and we do believe, had he lived, that he would have shaped events, as he did during the war, to the best interests of the victors, but without unnecessary agitation or harshness. All attempts of writers to evolve from his proclamation a reconstruction policy, applicable to peace, have been vain and impotent. He had none which would not have changed with changing circumstances. A "policy" in an executive office is too often but another name for executive egotism, and Lincoln was almost absolutely free from that weakness.

On the morning of Mr. Lincoln's death, indeed within the same hour (and very properly so under the circumstances), the Vice President Andrew Johnson was inaugurated as President. The excitement was painfully high, and the new President, in speeches, interviews and proclamations if possible added to it. From evidence in the Bureau of Military Justice he thought the assassination of Lincoln, and the attempted assassination of Secretary Seward had been procured by Jefferson Davis, Clement C. Clay, Jacob Thompson, Geo. N. Saunders, Beverly Tucker, Wm. C. Cleary, and "other rebels and traitors harbored in Canada." The evidence, however, fully drawn out in the trial of the co-conspirators of J. Wilkes Booth, showed that the scheme was hair-brained, and from no responsible political source. The proclamation, however, gave keenness to the search for the fugitive Davis, and he was soon captured while making his way through Georgia to the Florida coast with the intention of escaping from the country. He was imprisoned in Fortress Monroe, and an indictment for treason was found against him, but he remained a close prisoner for nearly two years, until times when political policies had been changed or modified. Horace Greeley was one of his bondsmen. By this time there was grave doubt whether he could be legally convicted, * "now that the charge of inciting Wilkes Booth's crime had been tacitly abandoned. Mr. Webster (in his Bunker Hill oration) had only given clearer expression to the American doctrine, that,

* From Greeley's Recollections of a Busy Life, page 413.

after a revolt has levied a regular army, and fought therewith a pitched battle, its champions, even though utterly defeated, cannot be tried and convicted as traitors. This may be an extreme statement; but surely a rebellion which has for years maintained great armies, levied taxes and conscriptions, negotiated loans, fought scores of sanguinary battles with alternate successes and reverses, and exchanged tens of thousands of prisoners of war, can hardly fail to have achieved thereby the position and the rights of a lawful belligerent." This view, as then presented by Greeley, was accepted by President Johnson, who from intemperate denunciation had become the friend of his old friends in the South. Greeley's view was not generally accepted by the North, though most of the leading men of both parties hoped the responsibility of a trial would be avoided by the escape and flight of the prisoner. But he was confident by this time, and sought a trial. He was never tried, and the best reason for the fact is given in Judge Underwood's testimony before a Congressional Committee (and the Judge was a Republican) "that no conviction was possible, except by packing a jury."

Andrew Johnson.

On the 29th of April, 1865, President Johnson issued a proclamation removing all restrictions upon internal, domestic and coastwise and commercial intercourse in all Southern States east of the Mississippi; the blockade was removed May 22, and on May 29 a proclamation of amnesty was issued, with fourteen classes excepted therefrom, and the requirement of an "iron-clad oath" from those accepting its provisions. Proclamations rapidly followed in shaping the lately rebellious States to the conditions of peace and restoration to the Union. These States were required to hold conventions, repeal secession ordinances, accept the abolition of slavery, repudiate Southern war debts, provide for Congressional representation, and elect new State Officers and Legislatures. The several constitutional amendments were of course to be ratified by the vote of the people. These conditions were eventually all complied with, some of the States being more tardy than others. The irreconcilables charged upon the Military officers, the Freedmen's Bureau, and the stern application of the reconstruction acts, these results, and many of them showed a political hostility which, after the election of the new Legislatures, took shape in what were in the North at the time denounced as

"THE BLACK CODES."

These were passed by all of the eleven States in the rebellion. The codes varied in severity, according to the views of the Legislatures, and for a time they seriously interfered with the recognition of the States, the Republicans charging that the design was to restore slavery under new forms. In South Carolina Gen'l Sickles issued military orders, as late as January 17, 1866, against the enforcement of such laws.

To assure the rights, of the freedmen the 14th amendment of the Constitution was passed by Congress, June 18th, 1866. President Johnson opposed it, refused to sign, but said he would submit it to the several States. This was done, and it was accepted by the required three-fourths, January 28th, 1868. This had the effect to do away with many of the "black codes," and the States which desired readmission to the Union had to finally give them up. Since reconstruction, and the political ousting of what were called the "carpet bag governments," some of the States, notably Georgia, has passed class laws, which treat colored criminals differently from white, under what are now known as the "conduct laws." Terms of sentence are served out, in any part of the State, under the control of public and private contractors, and "vagrants" are subjected to sentences which it is believed would be less extended under a system of confinement.

Johnson's Policy.

While President Johnson's policy did not materially check reconstruction, it encouraged Southern politicians to political effort, and with their well known tact they were not long in gaining the ascendancy in nearly every State. This ascendancy excited the fears and jealousies of the North, and the Republicans announced as their object and platform "that all the results of the war" should be secured before Southern reconstruction and representation in Congress should be completed. On this they were almost solidly united in Congress, but Horace Greeley trained an independent sentiment which favored complete amnesty to the South. President Johnson sought to utilize this sentiment, and to divide the Republican party through his policy, which now looked to the same ends. He had said to a delegation introduced by Gov. Oliver P. Morton, April 21, 1865:

"Your slavery is dead, but I did not murder it. As Macbeth said to Banquo's bloody ghost:

> 'Never shake thy gory locks at me;
> Thou canst not say I did it.'

"Slavery is dead, and you must pardon me if I do not mourn over its dead body; you can bury it out of sight. In restoring the State, leave out that disturbing and dangerous element, and use only those parts of the machinery which will move in harmony.

"But in calling a convention to restore the State, who shall restore and re-establish it? Shall the man who gave his influence and his means to destroy the Government? Is he to participate in the great work of reorganization? Shall he who brought this misery upon the State be permitted to control its destinies? If this be so, then all this precious blood of our brave soldiers and officers so freely poured out will have been wantonly spilled. All the glorious victories won by our noble armies will go for nought, and all the battle-fields which have been sown with dead heroes during the rebellion will have been made memorable in vain."

In a speech at Washington, Feb. 22nd, 1866, Johnson said:

"The Government has stretched forth its strong arm, and with its physical power it has put down treason in the field. That is, the section of country that arrayed itself against the Government has been conquered by the force of the Government itself. Now, what had we said to those people? We said, 'No compromise; we can settle this question with the South in eight and forty hours.'

"I have said it again and again, and I repeat it now, 'disband your armies, acknowledge the supremacy of the Constitution of the United States, give obedience to the law, and the whole question is settled.'

"What has been done since? Their armies have been disbanded. They come now to meet us in a spirit of magnanimity and say, 'We were mistaken; we made the effort to carry out the doctrine of secession and dissolve this Union, and having traced this thing to its logical and physical results, we now acknowledge the flag of our country, and promise obedience to the Constitution and the supremacy of the law.'

"I say, then, when you comply with the Constitution, when you yield to the law, when you acknowledge allegiance to the Government—I say let the door of the Union be opened, and the relation be restored to those that had erred and had strayed from the fold of our fathers."

It is not partisanship to say that Johnson's views had undergone a change. He did not admit this in his speeches, but the fact was accepted in all sections, and the leaders of parties took position accordingly —nearly all of the Republicans against him, nearly all of the Democrats for him. So radical had this difference become that he vetoed nearly all of the political bills passed by the Republicans from 1866 until the end of his administration, but such was the Republican preponderance in both Houses of Congress that they passed them over his head by the necessary two-thirds vote. He vetoed the several Freedmen's Bureau Bills, the Civil Rights Bill, that for the admission of Nebraska and Colorado, the Bill to permit Colored Suffrage in the District of Columbia, one of the Reconstruction Bills, and finally made a direct issue with the powers of Congress by his veto of the Civil Tenure Bill, March 2, 1867, the substance of which is shown in the third section, as follows:

SEC. 3. That the President shall have power to fill all vacancies which may happen during the recess of the Senate, by reason of death or resignation, by granting commissions which shall expire at the end of their next session thereafter. And if no appointment, by and with the advice and consent of the Senate, shall be made to such office so vacant or temporarily filled as aforesaid during such next session of the Senate, such office shall remain in abeyance without any salary, fees, or emoluments attached thereto, until the same shall be filled by appointment thereto, by and with the advice and consent of the Senate; and during such time all the powers and duties belonging to such office shall be exercised by such other officer as may by law exercise such powers and duties in case of a vacancy in such office.

The bill originally passed the Senate by 22 to 10—all of the nays Democrats save Van Winkle and Willey. It passed the House by 112 to 41—all of the yeas Republicans; all of the nays Democrats save Hawkins, Latham and Whaley. The Senate passed it over the veto by 35 to 11 —a strict party vote; the House by 138 to 40—a strict party vote, except Latham (Rep.) who voted nay.

The refusal of the President to enforce this act, and his attempted removal of Secretary Stanton from the Cabinet when against the wish of the Senate, led to the effort to impeach him. Stanton resisted the President, and General Grant took an active part in sustaining the War Secretary. He in fact publicly advised him to "stick," and his attitude showed that in the great political battle which must follow, they would surely have the support of the army and its great commander.

Impeachment Trial of Andrew Johnson.

* The events which led to the impeachment of President Johnson, may be briefly stated as follows: On the 21st of February, 1868, the President issued an order to Mr. Stanton, removing him from office as Secretary of War, and another to General Lorenzo Thomas, Adjutant-General of the

* From the Century of Independence by John Sully, Boston.

Army, appointing him Secretary of War *ad interim*, directing the one to surrender and the other to receive, all the books, papers, and public property belonging to the War Department. As these orders fill an important place in the history of the impeachment, we give them here. The order to Mr. Stanton reads:

"By virtue of the power and authority vested in me as President by the Constitution and laws of the United States, you are hereby removed from office as Secretary for the Department of War, and your functions as such will terminate upon the receipt of this communication. You will transfer to Brevet Major-General Lorenzo Thomas, Adjutant-General of the Army, who has this day been authorized and empowered to act as Secretary of War *ad interim*, all records, books, papers, and other public property now in your custody and charge."

The order to General Thomas reads:

"The Hon. Edwin M. Stanton having been this day removed from office as Secretary for the Department of War, you are hereby authorized and empowered to act as Secretary of War *ad interim*, and will immediately enter upon the discharge of the duties pertaining to that office. Mr. Stanton has been instructed to transfer to you all the records, books, and other public property now in his custody and charge."

These orders having been officially communicated to the Senate, that body, after an earnest debate, passed the following resolution:

"*Resolved, by the Senate of the United States*, That under the Constitution and laws of the United States the President has no power to remove the Secretary of War and designate any other officer to perform the duties of that office."

The President, upon the 24th, sent a message to the Senate, arguing at length that not only under the Constitution, but also under the laws as now existing, he had the right of removing Mr. Stanton and appointing another to fill his place. The point of his argument is: That by a special proviso in the Tenure-of-Office Bill the various Secretaries of Departments "shall hold their offices respectively for and during the term of the President by whom they may have been appointed, and for one month thereafter, subject to removal by and with the advice of the Senate." The President affirms that Mr. Stanton was appointed not by him, but by his predecessor, Mr. Lincoln, and held office only by the sufferance, not the appointment, of the present Executive; and that therefore his tenure is, by the express reading of the law excepted from the general provision, that every person duly appointed to office, "by and with the advice and consent of the Senate," etc., shall be "entitled to hold office until a successor shall have been in like manner appointed and duly qualified, except as herein otherwise provided." The essential point of the President's argument, therefore, is that, as Mr. Stanton was not appointed by him, he had, under the Tenure-of-Office Bill, the right at any time to remove him; the same right which his own successor would have, no matter whether the incumbent had, by sufferance, not by appointment of the existing Executive, held the office for weeks or even years. "If," says the President, "my successor would have the power to remove Mr. Stanton, after permitting him to remain a period of two weeks, because he was not appointed by him, I who have tolerated Mr. Stanton for more than two years, certainly have the same right to remove him, upon the same ground, namely that he was not appointed by me but by my predecessor."

In the meantime General Thomas presented himself at the War Department and demanded to be placed in the position to which he had been assigned by the President. Mr. Stanton refused to surrender his post, and ordered General Thomas to proceed to the apartment which belonged to him as Adjutant-General. This order was not obeyed, and so the two claimants to the Secretaryship of War held their ground. A sort of legal by-play then ensued. Mr. Stanton entered a formal complaint before Judge Carter, Chief Justice of the Supreme Court of the District of Columbia, charging that General Thomas had illegally exercised and attempted to exercise the duties of Secretary of War; and had threatened to "forcibly remove the complainant from the buildings and apartments of the Secretary of War in the War Department, and forcibly take possession and control thereof under his pretended appointment by the President of the United States as Secretary of War *ad interim*;" and praying that he might be arrested and held to answer this charge. General Thomas was accordingly arrested, and held to bail in the sum of $15,000 to appear before the court on the 24th. Appearing on that day he was discharged from custody and bail; whereupon he entered an action against Mr. Stanton for false imprisonment, laying his damages at $150,000.

On the 22d of February the House Committee on Reconstruction, through its Chairman, Mr. Stevens, presented a brief report, merely stating the fact of the attempted removal by the President of Mr. Stanton, and closing as follows:

"Upon the evidence collected by the Committee, which is hereafter presented, and in virtue of the powers with which they have been invested by the House, they are of the opinion that Andrew Johnson, President of the United States, should be impeached of high crimes and misdemeanors. They, therefore, recommend to the House the adoption of the following resolution:

"*Resolved*, That Andrew Johnson, President of the United States be impeached of high crimes and misdemeanors."

After earnest debate, the question on the resolution was adopted, on the 24th, by a vote of 126 to 47. A committee of two members—Stevens and Bingham—were to notify the Senate of the action of the House; and another committee of seven—Boutwell, Stevens, Bingham, Wilson, Logan, Julian, and Ward—to prepare the articles of impeachment. On the 25th (February) Mr. Stevens thus announced to the Senate the action which had been taken by the House:

"In obedience to the order of the House of Representatives we have appeared before you, and in the name of the House of Representatives and of all the people of the United States, we do impeach Andrew Johnson, President of the United States, of high crimes and misdemeanors in office. And we further inform the Senate that the House of Representatives will in due time exhibit particular articles of impeachment against him, to make good the same; and in their name we demand that the Senate take due order for the appearance of the said Andrew Johnson to answer to the said impeachment."

The Senate thereupon, by a unanimous vote, resolved that this message from the House should be referred to a select Committee of Seven, to be appointed by the chair, to consider the same and report thereon. The Committee subsequently made a report laying down the rules of procedure to be observed on the trial.

On the 29th of February the Committee of the House appointed for that purpose presented the articles of impeachment which they had drawn up. These, with slight modification, were accepted on the 2d of March. They comprise nine articles, eight of which are based upon the action of the President in ordering the removal of Mr. Stanton, and the appointment of General Thomas as Secretary of War. The general title to the impeachment is:

"Articles exhibited by the House of Representatives of the United States, in the name of themselves and all the people of the United States, against Andrew Johnson, President of the United States, as maintenance and support of their impeachment against him for high crimes and misdemeanors in office."

Each of the articles commences with a preamble to the effect that the President, "unmindful of the high duties of his office, of his oath of office, and of the requirements of the Constitution that he should take care that the laws be faithfully executed, did unlawfully and in violation of the laws and Constitution of the United States, perform the several acts specified in the articles respectively;" closing with the declaration: "Whereby the said Andrew Johnson, President of the United States, did then and there commit and was guilty of a high misdemeanor in office." The phraseology is somewhat varied. In some cases the offense is designated as a "misdemeanor," in others as a "crime." The whole closes thus:

"And the House of Representatives, by protestation, saving to themselves the liberty of exhibiting at any time hereafter any further articles or other accusation or impeachment against the said Andrew Johnson, President of the United States, and also of replying to his answers which he shall make to the articles herein preferred against him, and of offering proof to the same and every part thereof, and to all and every other article, accusation, or impeachment which shall be exhibited by them as the case shall require, do demand that the said Andrew Johnson may be put to answer the high crimes and misdemeanors in office herein charged against him, and that such proceedings, examinations, trials, and judgments may be thereupon had and given as may be agreeable to law and justice."

The following is a summary in brief of the points in the articles of impeachment, legal and technical phraseology being omitted:

Article 1. Unlawfully ordering the removal of Mr. Stanton as Secretary of War, in violation of the provisions of the Tenure-of-Office Act.—*Article* 2. Unlawfully appointing General Lorenzo Thomas as Secretary of War *ad interim*.—*Article* 3 is substantially the same as Article 2, with the addition that there was at the time of the appointment of General Thomas no vacancy in the office of Secretary of War.—*Article* 4 charges the President with "conspiring with one Lorenzo Thomas and other persons, to the House of Representatives unknown," to prevent, by intimidation and threats, Mr. Stanton, the legally-appointed Secretary of War, from holding that office.—*Article* 5 charges the President with conspiring with General Thomas and others to hinder the execution of the Tenure-of-Office Act; and, in pursuance of this conspiracy, attempting to prevent Mr. Stanton from acting as Secretary of War.—*Article* 6 charges that the President conspired with General Thomas and others to take forcible possession of the War Department.—*Article* 7 repeats the charge, in other terms, that the President conspired with General Thomas and others to hinder the execution of the Tenure-of-Office Act, and to prevent Mr. Stanton from executing the office of Secretary of War.—*Article* 8 again charges the President with conspiring with General Thomas and others to take possession of the property in the War Department.—*Article* 9 charges that the President called before him General Emory, who was in command of the forces in the Department of Washington, and declared to him that a law, passed on the 30th of June, 1867, directing that "all orders and instructions relating to military operations, issued by the President or Secretary of War, shall be issued through the General of the Army, and, in case of his inability, through the next in rank," was unconstitutional, and not binding upon General Emory; the intent being to induce General Emory to violate the law, and to obey orders issued directly from the President.

The foregoing articles of impeachment were adopted on the 2d of March, the votes upon each slightly varying, the average being 125 ayes to 40 nays. The question then came up of appointment of managers on the part of the House to conduct the impeachment before the Senate. Upon this question the Democratic members did not vote; 118 votes were cast, 60 being necessary to a choice. The following was the result, the number of votes cast for each elected manager being given: Stevens of Penn., 105; Butler, of Mass., 108; Bingham, of Ohio, 114; Boutwell, of Mass., 113; Wilson, of Iowa, 112; Williams, of Penn., 107; Logan, of Ill., 106. The foregoing seven Representatives were, therefore, duly chosen as Managers of the Bill of Impeachment. The great body of the Democratic members of the House entered a formal protest against the whole course of proceedings involved in the impeachment of the President. They claimed to represent "directly or in principle more than one-half of the people of the United States." This protest was signed by forty-five Representatives.

On the 3d the Board of Managers presented two additional articles of impeachment, which were adopted by the House. The first charges, in substance, that

"The President, unmindful of the high duties of his office and of the harmony and courtesies which ought to be maintained between the executive and legislative branches of the Government of the United States, designing to set aside the rightful authority and powers of Congress, did attempt to bring into disgrace the Congress of the United States and the several branches thereof, to impair and destroy the regard and respect of all the good people of the United States for the Congress and legislative power thereof, and to excite the odium and resentment of all the good people of the United States against Congress and the laws by it enacted; and in pursuance of his said design openly and publicly, and before divers assemblages convened in divers parts thereof to meet and receive said Andrew Johnson as the Chief Magistrate of the United States, did on the 18th day of August, in the year of our Lord 1866, and on divers other days and times, as well before as afterward, make and deliver with a loud voice certain intemperate, inflammatory, and scandalous harangues, and did therein utter loud threats and bitter menaces as well against Congress as the laws of the United States duly enacted thereby."

To this article are appended copious extracts from speeches of Mr. Johnson. The second article is substantially as follows:

"The President did, on the 18th day of August, 1866, at the City of Washington, by public speech, declare and affirm in substance that the Thirty-ninth Congress of the United States was not a Congress of the United States, authorized by the Constitution to exercise legislative power under the same, but, on the contrary, was a Congress of only a part of the States, thereby denying and intending to deny that the legislation of said Congress was valid or obligatory upon him, except in so far as he saw fit to approve the same, and did devise and contrive means by which he might prevent Edwin M. Stanton from forthwith resuming the functions of the office of Secretary for the Department of War; and, also, by further unlawfully devising and contriving means to prevent the execution of an act entitled 'An act making appropriations for the support of the army for the fiscal year ending June 30, 1868, and for other purposes,' approved March 2, 1867; and also to prevent the execution of an act entitled 'An act to provide for the more efficient government of the rebel States,' passed March 2, 1867, did commit and was guilty of a high misdemeanor in office."

On the 4th of March the Senate notified the House that they were ready to receive the Managers of the Impeachment. They appeared, and the articles were formally read. The Senate had meanwhile adopted the rules of procedure. Chief Justice Chase sent a communication to the Senate to the effect that this body, when acting upon an impeachment, was a Court presided over by the Chief Justice, and that all orders and rules should be framed by the Court. On the 5th the Court was formally organized. An exception was taken to the eligibility of Mr. Wade as a member of the Court, on the ground that he was a party interested, since, in the event of the impeachment being sustained, he, as President of the Senate, would become Acting President of the United States. This objection was withdrawn, and Mr. Wade was sworn as a member of the Court. On the 7th the summons for the President to appear was formally served upon him. On the 13th the Court was again formally reopened. The President appeared by his counsel, Hon. Henry Stanbery, of Ohio; Hon. Wm. M. Evarts, of New York; Hon. Wm. S. Groesbeck, of Ohio; Hon. Benjamin R. Curtis, of Massachusetts; Hon. Thomas A. R. Nelson, of Tennessee, who asked for forty days to prepare an answer to the indictment. This was refused, and ten days granted; it being ordered that the proceedings should reopen on the 23d. Upon that day the President appeared by his counsel, and presented his answer to the articles of impeachment. This reply was in substance as follows:

The first eight articles in the Bill of Impeachment, as briefly summed up in our last record, are based upon the action of the President in ordering the removal of Mr. Stanton, and the temporary appointment of General Thomas as Secretary of War. The gist of them is contained in the first article, charging the unlawful removal of Mr. Stanton; for, this failing, the others would fail also. To this article a considerable part of the President's answer is devoted. It is mainly an amplification of the points put forth in the Message of February 24th, in which he gave his reasons for his orders. The President cites the laws by which this department of the administration was created, and the rules laid down for the duties pertaining to it; prominent among which are: that the Secretary shall "conduct the business of the department in such manner as the President of the United States shall from time to time order and instruct;" and that he should "hold the office during the pleasure of the President;" and that Congress had no legal right to deprive the President of the power to remove the Secretary. He was, however, aware that the design of the Tenure-of-Office Bill was to vest this power of removal, in certain cases, jointly in the Executive and the Senate; and that, while believing this act to be unconstitutional, yet it having been passed over his veto by the requisite majority of two-thirds, he considered it to be his duty to ascertain in how far the case of Mr. Stanton came within the provisions of this law; after consideration, he came to the conclusion that the case did not come within the prohibitions of the law, and that, by that law he still had the right of removing Mr. Stanton; but that, wishing to have the case decided by the Supreme Court, he, on the 12th of August, issued the order merely suspending, not removing, Mr. Stanton, a power expresly granted by the Tenure-of-Office Act, and appointed General Grant Secretary of War *ad interim*. The President then recites the subsequent action in the case of Mr. Stanton; and, as he avers, still believing that he had the constitutional power to remove him from office, issued the order of February 21st, for such removal, designing to thus bring the matter before the Supreme Court. He then proceeds formally to deny that at this time Mr. Stanton was in lawful possession of the office of Secretary of War; and that, consequently, the order for his removal was in violation of the Tenure-of-Office Act; and that it was in violation of the Constitution or of any law; or that it constituted any official crime or misdemeanor.

In regard to the seven succeeding articles of impeachment the President, while admitting the facts of the order appointing General Thomas as Secretary of War *ad interim*, denies all and every of the criminal charges therein set forth. So of the ninth article, charging an effort to induce General Emory to violate the law, the President denies all such intent, and calls attention to the fact that while, for urgent reasons, he signed the bill prescribing that orders to the army should be issued only through the General, he at the same time declared it to be, in his judgment, unconstitutional; and affirms that in his interview with General Emory he said no more than he had before officially said to Congress—that is, that the law was unconstitutional.

As to the tenth article, the first of the supplementary ones, the President, while admitting that he made certain public speeches at the times and places specified, does not admit that the passages cited are fair reports of his remarks; denies that he has ever been unmindful of the courtesies which ought to be maintained between the executive and legislative departments; but he claims the perfect right at all times to express his views as to all public matters.

The reply to the eleventh article, the second supplementary one, is to the same general purport, denying that he ever affirmed that the Thirty-ninth Congress was not a valid Congress of the United States, and its acts obligatory only as they were approved by him; and denying that he had, as charged in the article, contrived unlawful means for preventing Mr. Stanton from resuming the functions of Secretary of War, or for preventing the execution of the act making appropriations for the support of the army, or that to provide for the more efficient government of the rebel States. In his answer to this article the President refers to his reply to the first article, in which he sets forth at length all the steps, and the reasons therefor, relating to the removal of Mr. Stanton. In brief, the answer of the President to the articles of impeachment is a general denial of each and every criminal act charged in the articles of impeachment.

The counsel for the President then asked for a delay of thirty days after the replication of the managers of the impeachment should have been rendered, before the trial should formally entered. This was refused, and the managers of the impeachment stated that their replication would be presented the next day; it was thus:

"The Senate will commence the trial of the President upon the articles of impeachment exhibited against him on Monday, the 30th day of March, and proceed therein with all dispatch under the rules of the Senate sitting upon the trial of an impeachment."

The replication of the House of Representatives was a simple denial of each and every averment in the answer of the President, closing thus:

"The House of Representatives . . . do say that the said Andrew Johnson, President of the United States, is guilty of the high crimes and misdemeanors mentioned in the said articles, and that the said House of Representatives are ready to prove the same."

The trial began, as appointed, on March 30. There being twenty-seven States represented, there were fifty-four Senators, who constituted the Court, presided over by Chief Justice Salmon P. Chase, of Ohio. SENATORS: *California*, Cole, Conness; *Connecticut*, Dixon, Ferry; *Delaware*, Bayard, Saulsbury; *Indiana*, Hendricks, Morton; *Illinois*, Trumbull, Yates; *Iowa*, Grimes, Harlan; *Kansas*, Pomeroy, Ross; *Kentucky*, Davis, McCreery; *Maine*, Fessenden, Morrill (Lot M.); *Maryland*, Johnson, Vickers; *Massachusetts*, Sumner, Wilson; *Michigan*, Chandler, Howard; *Minnesota*, Norton, Ramsey; *Missouri*, Drake, Henderson; *Nebraska*, Thayer, Tipton; *Nevada*, Nye, Stewart; *New Hampshire*, Cragin, Patterson (J. W.); *New Jersey*, Cattell, Frelinghuysen; *New York*, Conkling, Morgan; *Ohio*, Sherman, Wade; *Oregon*, Corbett, Williams; *Pennsylvania*, Buckalew, Cameron; *Rhode Island*, Anthony, Sprague; *Tennessee*, Fowler, Patterson (D. T.); *Vermont*, Edmunds, Morrill (J. S.); *West Virginia*, Van Winkle, Willey; *Wisconsin*, Doolittle, Howe.

Managers for the Prosecution: Messrs. Bingham, Boutwell, Butler, Logan, Stevens, Williams, Wilson.

Counsel for the President: Messrs. Curtis, Evarts, Groesbeck, Nelson, Stanbery.

The following was the order of procedure: The Senate convened at 11 or 12 o'clock, and was called to order by the president of that body, who, after prayer, would leave the chair, which was immediately assumed by the Chief Justice, who wore his official robes. The prosecution was mainly conducted by Mr. Butler, who examined the witnesses, and, in conjunction with the others, argued the points of law which came up. The defence, during the early part of the trial, was mainly conducted by Mr. Stanbery, who had resigned the office of Attorney-General for this purpose, but, being taken suddenly ill, Mr. Evarts took his place. According to the rule at first adopted, the trial was to be opened by one counsel on each side, and summed up by two on each side; but this rule was subsequently modified so as to allow as many of the managers and counsel as chose to sum up, either orally or by filing written arguments.

THE PROSECUTION.

The whole of the first day (March 30) was occupied by the opening speech of Mr. Butler. After touching upon the importance of the case, and the wisdom of the framers of the Constitution in providing for its possible occurrence, he laid down the following proposition, supporting it by a copious array of authorities and precedents:

"We define, therefore, an impeachable high crime or misdemeanor to be one, in its nature or consequences, subversive of some fundamental or essential principle of government, or highly prejudicial to the public interest, and this may consist of a violation of the Constitution, of law, of an official oath, or of duty, by an act committed or omitted, or, without violating a positive law, by the abuse of discretionary powers from improper motives, or for any improper purpose."

He then proceeded to discuss the nature and functions of the tribunal before which the trial is held. He asked: "Is this proceeding a trial, as that term is understood, so far as relates to the rights and duties of a court and jury upon an indictment for crime? Is it not rather more in the nature of an inquest?" The Constitution, he urged, "seems to have determined it to be the latter, because, under its provisions, the right to retain and hold office is the only subject to be finally adjudicated; all preliminary inquiry being carried on solely to determine that question, and that alone." He then proceeded to argue that this body now sitting to determine the accusation, is the Senate of the United States, and not a court. This question is of consequence, he argued, because, in the latter case, it would be bound by the rules and precedents of common law-statutes; the members of the court would be liable to challenge on many grounds; and the accused might claim that he could only be convicted when the evidence makes the fact clear beyond reasonable doubt, instead of by a preponderance of the evidence. The fact that in this case the Chief Justice presides, it was argued, does not constitute the Senate thus acting a court, for in all cases of impeachment, save that of the President, its regular presiding officer presides. However, the procedures have no analogy to those of an ordinary court of justice. The accused merely receives a notice of the case pending against him. He is notified

quired to appear personally, and the case will go on without his presence. Mr. Butler thus summed up his position in this regard:

"A constitutional tribunal solely, you are bound by no law, either statute or common, which may limit your constitutional prerogative. You consult no precedents save those of the law and custom of parliamentary bodies. You are a law unto yourselves, bound only by the natural principles of equity and justice, and that *salus populi suprema est lex.*"

Mr. Butler then proceeded to consider the articles of impeachment. The first eight, he says, "set out, in several distinct forms, the acts of the President in removing Mr. Stanton and appointing General Thomas, differing, in legal effect, in the purposes for which, and the intent with which, either or both of the acts were done, and the legal duties and rights infringed, and the Acts of Congress violated in so doing." In respect to all of these articles, Mr. Butler says, referring to his former definition of what constituted an impeachable high crime:

"All the articles allege these acts to be in contravention of his oath of office, and in disregard of the duties thereof. If they are so, however, the President might have the power to do them under the law. Still, being so done, they are acts of official misconduct, and, as we have seen, impeachable. The President has the legal power to do many acts which, if done in disregard of his duty, or for improper purposes, then the exercise of that power is an official misdemeanor. For example, he has the power of pardon; if exercised, in a given case, for a corrupt motive, as for the payment of money, or wantonly pardoning all criminals, it would be a misdemeanor."

Mr. Butler affirmed that every fact charged in the first article, and substantially in the seven following, is admitted in the reply of the President; and also that the general intent to set aside the Tenure-of-Office Act is therein admitted and justified. He then proceeded to discuss the whole question of the power of the President for removals from office, and especially his claim that this power was imposed upon the President by the Constitution, and that it could not be taken from him, or be vested jointly in him and the Senate, partly or in whole. This, Mr. Butler affirmed, was the real question at issue before the Senate and the American people. He said:

"Has the President, under the Constitution, the more than royal prerogative at will to remove from office, or to suspend from office, all executive officers of the United States, either civil, military or naval, and to fill the vacancies, without any restraint whatever, or possibility of restraint, by the Senate or by Congress, through laws duly enacted? The House of Representatives, in behalf of the people, join issue by affirming that the exercise of such powers is a high misdemeanor in office. If the affirmative is maintained by the respondent, then, so far as the first eight articles are concerned—unless such corrupt purposes are shown as will of themselves make the exercise of a legal power a crime—the respondent must go, and ought to go, quit and free.

This point as to the legal right of the President to make removals from office, which constitutes the real burden of the articles of impeachment, was argued at length. Mr. Butler assumed that the Senate, by whom, in conjunction with the House, the Tenure-of-Office Act had been passed over the veto of the President, would maintain the law to be constitutional. The turning point was whether the special case of the removal of Mr. Stanton came within the provisions of this law. This rested upon the proviso of that law, that—

"The Secretaries shall hold their office during the term of the President by whom they may have been appointed, and for one month thereafter, subject to removal by and with the advice and consent of the Senate."

The extended argument upon this point, made by Mr. Butler, was to the effect that Mr. Stanton having been appointed by Mr. Lincoln, whose term of office reached to the 4th of March, 1869, that of Mr. Stanton existed until a month later, unless he was previously removed by the concurrent action of the President and Senate. The point of the argument is, that Mr. Johnson is merely serving out the balance of the term of Mr. Lincoln, cut short by his assassination, so that the Cabinet officers appointed by Mr. Lincoln held their places, by this very proviso, during that term and for a month thereafter; for, he argued, if Mr. Johnson was not merely serving out the balance of Mr. Lincoln's term, then he is entitled to the office of President for four full years, that being the period for which a President is elected. If, continues the argument, Mr. Stanton's commission was vacated by the Tenure-of-Office Act, it ceased on the 4th of April, 1865; or, if the act had no retroactive effect, still, if Mr. Stanton held his office merely under his commission from Mr. Lincoln, then his functions would have ceased upon the passage of the bill, March 2, 1867; and, consequently, Mr. Johnson, in "employing" him after that date as Secretary of War, was guilty of a high misdemeanor, which would give ground for a new article of impeachment.

After justifying the course of Mr. Stanton in holding on to the secretaryship in opposition to the wish of the President, on the ground that "to desert it now would be to imitate the treachery of his accidental chief." Mr. Butler proceeded to discuss the reasons assigned by the President in his answer to the articles of impeachment for the attempt to remove Mr. Stanton. These, in substance, were, that the President believed the Tenure-of-Office Act was unconstitutional, and, therefore, void and of no effect, and that he had the right to remove him and appoint another person in his place. Mr. Butler urged that, in all of these proceedings, the President professed to act upon the assumption that the act was valid, and that his action was in accordance with its provisions. He then went on to charge that the appointment of General Thomas as Secretary of War *ad interim*, was a separate violation of law. By the act of February 20, 1863, which repealed all previous laws inconsistent with it, the President was authorized, in case of the "death, resignation, absence from the seat of Government, or sickness of the head of an executive department," or in any other case where these officers could not perform their respective duties, to appoint the head of any other executive department to fulfil the duties of the office "until a successor be appointed, or until such absence or disability shall cease." Now, urged Mr. Butler, at the time of the appointment of General Thomas as Secetary of War *ad interim*, Mr. Stanton "had neither died nor resigned, was not sick nor absent," and, consequently, General Thomas, not being the head of a department, but only of a bureau of one of them, was not eligible to this appointment, and that, therefore, his appointment was illegal and void.

The ninth article of impeachment, wherein the President is charged with endeavoring to induce General Emory to take orders directly from himself, is dealt with in a rather slight manner. Mr. Butler says, "If the transaction set forth in this article stood alone, we might well admit that doubts might arise as to the sufficiency of the proof;" but, he adds, "the surroundings are so pointed and significant as to leave no doubt in the mind of an impartial man as to the intents and purposes of the President"—these intents being, according to Mr. Butler, "to induce General Emory to take orders directly from himself, and thus to hinder the execution of the Civil Tenure Act, and to prevent Mr. Stanton from holding his office of Secretary of War."

As to the tenth article of impeachment, based upon various speeches of the President, Mr. Butler undertook to show that the reports of these speeches, as given in the article, were substantially correct; and accepted the issue made thereupon as to whether they are "decent and becoming the President of the United States, and do not tend to bring the office into ridicule and disgrace."

After having commented upon the eleventh and closing article, which charges the President with having denied the authority of the Thirty-ninth Congress, except so far as its acts were approved by him, Mr. Butler summed up the purport of the articles of impeachment in these words:

"The acts set out in the first eight articles are but the culmination of a series of wrongs, malfeasances, and usurpations committed by the respondent, and, therefore, need to be examined in the light of his precedent and concomitant acts to grasp their scope and design. The last three articles presented show the perversity and malignity with which he acted, so that the man as he is known may be clearly spread upon record, to be seen and known of all men hereafter. . . . . . We have presented the facts in the constitutional manner; we have brought the criminal to your bar, and demand judgment for his so great crimes."

The remainder of Monday, and a portion of the following day, were devoted to the presentation of documentary evidence as to the proceedings involved in the order for the removal of Mr. Stanton and the appointment of General Thomas. The prosecution then introduced witnesses to testify to the interviews between Mr. Stanton and General Thomas. They then brought forward a witness to show that General Thomas had avowed his determination to take forcible possession of the War Office. To this Mr. Stanbery, for the defense, objected. The Chief Justice decided the testimony to be admissible. Thereupon Senator Drake took exception to the ruling, on the ground that this question should be decided by the Senate—not by the presiding officer. The Chief Justice averred that, in his judgment, it was his duty to decide, in the first instance, upon any question of evidence, and then, if any Senator desired, to submit the decision to the Senate. Upon this objection and appeal arose the first conflict in the Senate as to the powers of its presiding officer. Mr. Butler argued at length in favor of the exception. Although, in this case, the decision was in favor of the prosecution, he objected to the power of the presiding officer to make it. This point was argued at length by the managers for the impeachment, who denied the right of the Chief Justice to make such decision. It was then moved that the Senate retire for private consultation on this point. There was a tie vote—25 ayes and 25 nays.—The Chief Justice gave his casting vote in favor of the motion for consultation. The Senate, by a vote of 31 to 19, sustained the Chief Justice, deciding that "the presiding officer may rule on all questions of evidence and on incidental questions, which decision will stand as the judgment of the Senate for decision, or he may, at his option in the first instance, submit any such question to a vote of the members of the Senate." In the further progress of the trial the Chief Justice, in most important cases, submitted the question directly to the Senate, without himself giving any decision. Next morning (April 1) Mr. Sumner offered a resolution to the effect that the Chief Justice, in giving a casting vote, "acted without authority of the Constition of the United States." This was negatived by a vote of 27 to 21, thus deciding that the presiding officer had the right to give a casting vote. The witness (Mr. Burleigh, delegate from Dakotah,) who had been called to prove declarations of General Thomas, was then asked whether, at an interview between them, General Thomas had said anything as "to the means by which he intended to obtain, or was directed by the President to obtain, posession of the War Department." To this question Mr. Stanbery objected, on the ground that any statements made by General Thomas could not be used as evidence against the President. Messrs. Butler and Bingham argued that the testimony was admissible, on the ground that there was, as charged, a conspiracy between the President and General Thomas, and that the acts of one conspirator were binding upon the other; and, also, that in these acts General Thomas was the agent of the President. The Senate, by 39 to 11, decided that the question was admissible. Mr. Burleigh thereupon testified substantially that General Thomas informed him that he had been directed by the President to take possession of the War Department; that he was bound to obey his superior officer; that, if Mr. Stanton objected, he should use force, and if he bolted the doors they would be broken down. The witness was then asked whether he had heard General Thomas make any statement to the clerks of the War Office, to the effect that, when he came into control, he would relax or rescind the rules of Mr. Stanton. To this question objection was made by the counsel of the President on the ground of irrelevancy. The Chief Justice was of opinion that the question was not admissible, but, if any Senator demanded, he would submit to the Senate whether it should be asked. The demand having been made, the Senate, by a vote of 28 to 22, allowed the question to be put, whereupon Mr. Burleigh testified that General Thomas, in his presence, called before him the heads of the divisions, and told them that the rules laid down by Mr. Stanton were arbitrary, and that he should relax them—that he should not hold them strictly to their letters of instruction, but should consider them as gentlemen who would do their duty—that they could come in or go out when they chose. Mr. Burleigh further testified that, subsequently, General Thomas had said to him that the only thing which prevented him from taking possession of the War Department was his arrest by the United States marshal. Other witnesses were called to prove the declarations of General Thomas. Mr. Wilkeson testified that General Thomas said to him that he should demand possession of the War Department, and, in case Mr. Stanton should refuse to give it up, he should call upon General Grant for a sufficient force to enable him to do so, and he did not see how this could be refused. Mr. Karsener, of Delaware, testified that he saw General Thomas at the President's house, told him that Delaware, of which State General Thomas is a citizen, expected him to stand firm; to which General Thomas replied that he was standing firm, that he would not disappoint his friends, but, that, in a few days, he would "kick that fellow out," meaning, as the witness supposed, Mr. Stanton.

Thursday, April 2d.—Various witnesses were introduced to testify to the occurrences when General Thomas demanded possession of the War Department. After this General Emory was called to testify to the transactions which form the ground of the ninth article of impeachment. His testimony was to the effect that the President, on the 22d of February, requested him to call; that, upon so doing, the President asked respecting any changes that had been made in the disposition of the troops around Washington; that he informed the President that no important changes had been made, and that none could be made without an order from General Grant, as provided for in an order founded upon a law sanctioned by the President. The President said that this law was unconstitutional. Emory replied that the President had approved of it, and that it was not the prerogative of the officers of the army to decide upon the constitutionality of a law, and in that opinion he was justified by the opinion of eminent counsel, and thereupon the conversation ended.

The prosecution then endeavored to introduce testimony as to the appointment of Mr. Edmund Cooper, the Private Secretary of the President, as Assistant Secretary of the Treasury, in support of the eighth and eleventh articles of impeachment, which charge the President with an unlawful attempt to control the disposition of certain public funds. This testimony, by a vote of 27 to 22, was ruled out.

The prosecution now, in support of the

tenth and eleventh articles of impeachment, charging the President with endeavoring to "set aside the rightful authority of Congress," offered a telegraphic dispatch from the President to Mr. Parsons, at that time (January 17, 1867) Provisional Governor of Alabama, of which the following is the essential part:

"I do not believe the people of the whole country will sustain any set of individuals in the attempt to change the whole character of our Government by enabling acts in this way. I believe, on the contrary, that they will eventually uphold all who have patriotism and courage to stand by the Constitution, and who place their confidence in the people. There should be no faltering on the part of those who are honest in their determination to sustain the several coördinate departments of the Government in accordance with its original design." The introduction of this was objected to by the counsel for the President, but admitted by the Senate, the vote being 27 to 17.

The whole Friday, and a great part of Saturday, (April 3d and 4th,) were occupied in the examination of the persons who reported the various speeches of the President which form the basis of the tenth article, the result being that the reports were shown to be either substantially or verbally accurate. Then, after some testimony relating to the forms in which commissions to office were made out, the managers announced that the case for the prosecution was substantially closed. The counsel for the President thereupon asked that three working days should be granted them to prepare for the defense. This, after some discussion, was granted by the Senate by a vote of 36 to 9, and the trial was adjourned to Thursday, April 9th.

THE DEFENSE.

The opening speech for the defense, occupying the whole of Thursday, and a part of Friday, was made by Mr. Curtis. Reserving, for a time, a rejoinder to Mr. Butler's argument as to the functions of the Senate when sitting as a Court of Impeachment, Mr. Curtis proceeded to a consideration of the articles of impeachment, in their order, his purpose being "to ascertain, in the first place, what the substantial allegations in each of them are, what is the legal proof and effect of these allegations, and what proof is necessary to be adduced in order to sustain them." The speech is substantially an elaboration of and argument for the points embraced in the answer of the President. The main stress of the argument related to the first article, which, as stated by Mr. Curtis, when stripped of all technical language, amounts exactly to these things:

"*First.* That the order set out in the article for the removal of Mr. Stanton, if executed, would have been a violation of the Tenure-of-Office Act.

"*Second.* That it was a violation of the Tenure-of-Office Act.

"*Third.* That it was an intentional violation of the Tenure-of-Office Act.

"*Fourth.* That it was in violation of the Constitution of the United States.

"*Fifth.* That it was intended by the President to be so.

"Or, to draw all these into one sentence, which I hope may be intelligible and clear enough, I suppose the substance of this first article is that the order for the removal of Mr. Stanton was, and was intended to be, a violation of the Constitution of the United States. These are the allegations which it is necessary for the honorable managers to make out in order to support that article."

Mr. Curtis proceeded to argue that the case of Mr. Stanton did not come within the provisions of the Tenure-of-Office Act, being expressly excepted by the proviso that Cabinet officers should hold their places during the term of the President by whom they were appointed, and for one month thereafter, unless removed by the consent of the Senate. Mr. Stanton was appointed by Mr. Lincoln, whose term of office came to an end by his death. He argued at length against the proposition that Mr. Johnson was merely serving out the remainder of Mr. Lincoln's term. The object of this exception, he said, was evident. The Cabinet officers were to be "the immediate confidential assistants of the President, for whose acts he was to be responsible, and in whom he was expected to repose the gravest honor, trust, and confidence; therefore it was that this act has connected the tenure of office of these officers with that of the President by whom they were appointed." Mr. Curtis gave a new interpretation to that clause in the Constitution which prescribes that the President "may require the opinion, in writing, of the principal officer in each of the executive departments upon any subject relating to the duties of their several offices." He understood that the word "their" included the President, so that he might call upon Cabinet officers for advice "relating to the duties of the office of these principal officers, or relating to the duties of the President himself." This, at least, he affirmed, had been the practical interpretation put upon this clause from the beginning. To confirm his position as to the intent of the Tenure-of-Office Act in this respect, Mr. Curtis quoted from speeches made in both houses at the time when the act was passed. Thus, Senator Sherman said that the act, as passed—

"Would not prevent the present President from removing the Secretary of War, the Secretary of the Navy, or the Secretary of State; and, if I supposed that either of these gentlemen was so wanting in manhood, in honor, as to hold his place after the politest intimation from the President of the United States that his services were no longer needed, I certainly, as a Senator, would consent to his removal at any time, and so would we all."

Mr. Curtis proceeded to argue that there was really no removal of Mr. Stanton; he still held his place, and so there was "no case of removal within the statute, and, therefore, no case of violation by removal." But, if the Senate should hold that the order for removal was, in effect, a removal, then, unless the Tenure-of-Office Act gave Mr. Stanton a tenure of office, this removal would not have been contrary to the provisions of this act. He proceeded to argue that there was room for grave doubt whether Mr. Stanton's case came within the provisions of the Tenure-of-Office Act, and that the President, upon due consideration, and having taken the best advice within his power, considering that it did not, and acting accordingly, did not, even if he was mistaken, commit an act "so wilful and wrong that it can be justly and properly, and for the purposes of this prosecution, termed a high misdemeanor." He argued at length that the view of the President was the correct one, and that "the Senate had nothing whatever to do with the removal of Mr. Stanton, whether the Senate was in session or not."

Mr. Curtis then went on to urge that the President, being sworn to take care that the laws be faithfully executed, must carry out any law, even though passed over his veto, except in cases where a law which he believed to be unconstitutional has cut off a power confided to him, and in regard to which he alone could make an issue which would bring the matter before a court, so as to cause "a judicial decision to come between the two branches of the Government, to see which of them is right." This, said he, is what the President has done. This argument, in effect, was an answer to the first eight articles of impeachment.

The ninth article, charging the President with endeavoring to induce General Emory to violate the law by receiving orders directly from him, was very briefly touched upon, it being maintained that, as shown by the evidence, "the reason why the President sent for General Emory was not that he might endeavor to seduce that distinguished officer from his allegiance to the laws and Constitution of his country, but because he wished to obtain information about military movements which might require his personal attention."

As to the tenth article, based upon the President's speeches, it was averred that they were in no way in violation of the Constitution, or of any law existing at the time when they were made, and were not therefore, impeachable offenses.

The reply to the eleventh article was very brief. The managers had "compounded it of the materials which they had previously worked up into others," and it "contained nothing new that needed notice." Mr. Curtis concluded his speech by saying that—"This trial is and will be the most conspicuous instance that has ever been, or even can be expected to be found, of American justice or of American injustice; of that justice which is the great policy of all civilized States; of that injustice which is certain to be condemned, which makes even the wisest man mad, and which, in the fixed and unalterable order of God's providence, is sure to return and plague the inventor."

At the close of this opening speech for the defense, General Lorenzo Thomas was brought forward as a witness. His testimony, elicited upon examination and cross-examination, was to the effect that, having received the order appointing him Secretary of War *ad interim*, he presented it to Mr. Stanton, who asked, "Do you wish me to vacate the office at once, or will you give me time to get my private property together?" to which Thomas replied, "Act your pleasure." Afterward Stanton said, "I don't know whether I will obey your instructions." Subsequently Thomas said that he should issue orders as Secretary of War. Stanton said he should not do so, and afterward gave him a written direction, not to issue any order except as Adjutant-General. During the examination of General Thomas a question came up which, in many ways, recurred upon the trial. He was asked to tell what occurred at an interview between himself and the President. Objection was made by Mr. Butler, and the point was argued. The question was submitted to the Senate, which decided, by a vote of 42 to 10, that it was admissible. The testimony of General Thomas, from this point, took a wide range, and, being mainly given in response to questions of counsel, was, apparently, somewhat contradictory. The substance was that he was recognized by the President as Secretary of War; that, since the impeachment, he had acted as such only in attending Cabinet meetings, but had given no orders; that, when he reported to the President that Mr. Stanton would not vacate the War Department, the President directed him to "take possession of the office;" that, without orders from the President, he had intended to do this by force, if necessary; that, finding that this course might involve bloodshed, he had abandoned this purpose, but that, after this, he had, in several cases, affirmed his purpose to do so, but that these declarations were "merely boast and brag." On the following day General Thomas was recalled as a witness, to enable him to correct certain points in his testimony. The first was the date of an unimportant transaction: he had given it as taking place on the 21st of February, whereas it should have been the 22d. The second was that the words of the President were that he should "take charge," not "take possession" of the War Department. In explanation of the fact that he had repeatedly sworn to the words "take possession," he said that these were "put into his mouth." Finally, General Thomas, in reply to a direct question from Mr. Butler, said that his testimony on these points was "all wrong."

Lieutenant-General Sherman was then called as a witness. After some unimportant questions, he was asked in reference to an interview between himself and the President which took place on the 14th of January: "At that interview what conversation took place between the President and you in reference to Mr. Stanton?" To this question objection was made by Mr. Butler, and the point was elaborately argued. The Chief Justice decided that the question was admissible within the vote of the Senate of the previous day; the question then was as to the admissibility of evidence as to a conversation between the President and General Thomas; the present question was as to a conversation between the President and General Sherman. "Both questions," said the Chief Justice, "are asked for the purpose of procuring the intent of the President to remove Mr. Stanton." The question being submitted to the Senate, it was decided, by a vote of 28 to 23, that it should not be admitted. The examination of General Sherman was continued, the question of the conversation aforesaid being frequently brought forward, and as often ruled out by the Senate. The only important fact elicited was that the President had twice, on the 25th and 30th of January, tendered to General Sherman the office of Secretary of War *ad interim.*

On Monday, April 13th, after transactions of minor importance, the general matter of the conversations between the President and General Sherman again came up, upon a question propounded by Senator Johnson—"When the President tendered to you the office of Secretary of War *ad interim*, did he, at the very time of making such tender, state to you what his purpose in so doing was?" This was admitted by the Senate, by a vote of 26 to 22. Senator Johnson then added to his question, "If he did, what did he state his purpose was?" This was admitted by a vote of 25 to 26. The testimony of General Sherman, relating to several interviews, was to the effect that the President said that the relations between himself and Mr. Stanton were such that he could not execute the office of President without making provision to appoint a Secretary of War *ad interim*, and he offered that office to him (General Sherman), but did not state that his purpose was to bring the matter directly into the courts. Sherman said that, if Mr. Stanton would retire, he might, although against his own wishes, undertake to administer the office *ad interim*, but asked what would be done in case Mr. Stanton would not yield. To this the President replied, "He will make no opposition; you present the order, and he will retire. I know him better than you do; he is cowardly." General Sherman asked time for reflection, and then gave a written answer, declining to accept the appointment, but stated that his reasons were mostly of a personal nature.

On the 14th the Senate adjourned, on account of the sudden illness of Mr. Stanbery. It re-assembled on the 15th, but the proceedings touched wholly upon formal points of procedure and the introduction of unimportant documentary evidence. On the 16th Mr. Sumner moved that all evidence not trivial or obviously irrelevant shall be admitted, the Senate to judge of its value. This was negatived by a vote of 23 to 11.

The 17th was mainly taken up by testimony as to the reliability of the reports of the President's speeches. Mr. Welles, Secretary of the Navy, was then called to testify to certain proceedings in Cabinet Council at the time of the appointment of General Thomas. This was objected to. The Chief Justice decided that it was admissible, and his decision was sustained by a vote of 26 to 23. The defense then endeavored to introduce several members of the Cabinet, to show that, at meetings previous to the removal of Mr. Stanton, it was considered whether it was not desirable to obtain a judicial determination of the unconstitutionality of the Tenure-of-Office Act. This question was raised in several shapes, and its admission, after thorough argument on both sides, as often refused, in the last instance by a decisive vote of 30 to 19. The defense considered this testimony of the utmost importance, as going to show that the President had acted upon the counsel of his constitutional advisers, while the prosecution claimed that he could not plead in justification of a violation of the law that he had been advised by his Cabinet, or any one else, that the law was unconstitutional. His duty was to execute the laws, and, if he failed to do this, or violated them, he did so at his own risk of the consequences. With the refusal of this testimony, the case, except the final summings up and the verdict of the Senate, was virtually closed.

The case had been so fully set forth in the opening speeches of Messrs. Butler and Curtis, and in the arguments which came up upon points of testimony, that there remained little for the other counsel except to restate what had before been said.

After the evidence had been closed the case was summed up, on the part of the managers by Messrs. Boutwell, Williams, Stevens, and Bingham in oral arguments, and Mr. Logan, who filed a written argument, and on the part of the President by Messrs. Nelson, Groesbeck, Stanbery, and Evarts. Many of these speeches were distinguished by great brilliancy and power, but, as no new points were presented, we omit any summary.

The Court decided to take a vote upon the articles on Tuesday, the 12th of May, at 12 o'clock, M. A secret session was held on Monday, during which several Senators made short speeches, giving the grounds upon which they expected to cast their votes. On Tuesday the Court agreed to postpone the vote until Saturday, the 16th. Upon that day, at 12 o'clock, a vote was taken upon the eleventh article, it having been determined to vote on that article first. The vote resulted in 35 votes for conviction, and 19 for acquittal.

The question being put to each Senator, "How say you, is the respondent, Andrew Johnson, President of the United States, guilty or not guilty of a high misdemeanor as charged in the article?"—those who responded guilty were Senators Anthony, Cameron, Cattell, Chandler, Cole, Conkling, Conness, Corbett, Cragin, Drake, Edmunds, Ferry, Frelinghuysen, Harlan, Howard, Howe, Morgan, Morrill, of Vermont, Morrill, of Maine, O. P. Morton, Nye, Patterson, N. H. Pomeroy, Sherman, Sprague, Stewart, Sumner, Thayer, Tipton, Wade, Willey, Williams, Wilson and Yates.

Those who responded not guilty were Senators Bayard, Buckalew, Davis, Dixon, Doolittle, Fessenden, Fowler, Grimes, Henderson, Hendricks, Johnson, M'Creery, Norton, Patterson of Tennessee, Ross, Saulsbury, Trumbull, Van Winkle and Vickers.

The Constitution requiring a vote of two-thirds to convict, the President was acquitted on this article. After taking this vote the Court adjourned until Tuesday, May 26th, when votes were taken upon the second and third articles, with precisely the same result as on the eleventh, the vote in each case standing 35 for conviction and 19 for acquittal. A verdict of acquittal on the second, third, and eleventh articles was then ordered to be entered on the record, and, without voting on the other articles, the Court adjourned *sine die*. So the trial was ended, and the President acquitted.

The political differences between President Johnson and the Republicans were not softened by the attempted impeachment, and singularly enough the failure of their effort did not weaken the Republicans as a party. They were so well united that those who disagreed with them passed at least temporarily from public life, some of the ablest, like Senators Trumbull and Fessenden retiring permanently. President Johnson pursued his policy, save where he was hedged by Congress, until the end, and retired to his native State, apparently having regained the love of his early political associates there.

Grant.

The Republican National Convention met at Chicago, Ill., May 20th, 1868, and nominated with unanimity, Ulysses S. Grant, of Illinois, for President, and Schuyler Colfax, of Indiana, for Vice President. The Democratic Convention met in New York City, July 4th, and after repeated ballots finally compromised on its presiding officers,* notwithstanding repeated and ap-

* The following is a correct table of the ballots in the New York Democratic Convention:

Candidates.	1.	2.	3.	4.	5.	6.	7.	8.	9.	10.	11.
Horatio Seymour	...	...	...	9	...	...	...	...	...	...	...
George H. Pendleton	105	104	119½	118½	122	122½	137½	156½	144	147½	144½
Andrew Johnson	65	52	34½	32	24	21	12½	6	5½	6	5½
Winfield S. Hancock	33½	40½	45½	43½	46	47	42½	28	34½	34	33½
Sanford E Church	33	33	33	33	33	33	33	...	...	...	...
Asa Packer	26	26	26	26	27	27	26	26	26½	27½	26
Joel Parker	13	15½	13	13	13	13	7	7	7	7	7
James E. English	16	12½	7½	7½	7	6	6	6	6	...	...
James R. Doolittle	13	12½	12	12	15	12	12	12	12	12	12½
Reverdy Johnson	8½	8	11	8	9½	...	...	...	...	...	...
Thomas A. Hendricks	2½	2	9½	11½	19½	30	39½	75	80½	82½	88
F. P. Blair, Jr	½	10½	4½	2	...	5	½	½	½	½	½
Thomas Ewing	...	½	1	1	...	...	...	...	...	...	...
J. Q. Adams	...	...	...	...	1	...	...	...	...	...	...
George B. McClellan	...	...	...	...	...	...	...	...	...	...	...
Salmon P. Chase	...	...	...	...	...	...	...	...	...	...	...
Franklin Pierce	...	...	...	...	...	...	...	...	...	...	...
John T. Hoffman	...	...	...	...	...	...	...	...	...	...	...
Stephen J. Field	...	...	...	...	...	...	...	...	...	...	...
Thomas H. Seymour	...	...	...	...	...	...	...	...	...	...	...

parently decided declarations on his part, Horatio Seymour, of New York, was therefore nominated for President, and Francis P. Blair, Jr., of Missouri, for Vice President.*

An active canvass followed, in which the brief expression—"let us have peace"—in Grant's letter of acceptance, was liberally employed by Republican journals and orators to tone down what were regarded as rapidly growing race and sectional differences, and with such effect that Grant carried all of the States save eight, receiving an electoral vote of 214 against 80.

Grant inaugurated, and the Congressional plan of reconstruction was rapidly pushed, with at first very little opposition save that manifested by the Democrats in Congress. The conditions of readmission were the ratification of the thirteenth and fourteenth constitutional amendments.

On the 25th of February, 1869, the fifteenth amendment was added to the list by its adoption in Congress and submission to the States. It conferred the right of suffrage on all citizens, without distinction of "race, color or previous condition of servitude." By the 30th of March, 1870, it was ratified by twenty-nine States, the required three-fourths of all in the Union. There was much local agitation in some of the Northern States on this new advance, and many who had never manifested their hostility to the negroes before did it now, and a portion of these passed over to the Democratic party. The issue, however, was shrewdly handled, and in most instances met Legislatures ready to receive it. Many of the Southern States were specially interested in its passage, since a denial of suffrage would abridge their representation in Congress. This was of course true of all the States, but its force was indisputable in sections containing large colored populations.

The 41st Congress met in extra session March 4th, 1869, with a large Republican majority in both branches. In the Senate there were 58 Republicans, 10 Democrats and 8 vacancies; in the House 149 Republicans, 64 Democrats and 25 vacancies, Mississippi, Texas, Virginia and Georgia not being represented. James G. Blaine, for several years previous its leading parliamentarian and orator, was Speaker of the House. All of Grant's nominations for Cabinet places were confirmed, except A. T. Stewart, of New York, nominated for Secretary of the Treasury, and being engaged in foreign commerce he was ineligible under the law, and his name was withdrawn. The names of the Cabinet will be found in the list of all Cabinet officers elsewhere given. Their announcement at first created the impression that the Grant administration was not intended to be partisan, rather personal, but if there ever was such a purpose, a little political experience on the part of the President quickly changed it. A political struggle soon followed in Congress as to the admission of Virginia, Mississippi and Texas, which had not ratified the Fourteenth Amendment or been reconstructed. A bill was passed April 10th, authorizing their people to vote on the constitutions already prepared by the State conventions, to elect members of Congress and State officers, and requiring before readmission to the Union, their Legislatures to ratify both the Fourteenth and Fifteenth Amendments. This work done, and the extra session adjourned.

In all of the Southern States, those who then prided themselves in being "unreconstructed" and "irreconcilable," bitterly opposed both the Fourteenth and Fifteenth Amendments, and on these issues excited new feelings of hostility to the "carpet baggers" and negroes of the South. With the close of the war thousands of North-

Candidates.	12.	13.	14.	15.	16.	17.	18.	19.	20.	21.	22.
Horatio Seymour	...	...	...	...	...	...	...	...	...	...	317
George H. Pendleton	145½	134½	130	129½	107½	70½	56½	...	...	...	...
Andrew Johnson	4½	4½	...	5½	5½	6	10	...	...	5	...
Winfield S. Hancock	30	48½	56	79½	113½	137½	144½	135½	142½	135½	...
Sanford E. Church	...	...	...	...	...	...	...	...	...	...	...
Asa Packer	26	26	26	...	...	...	...	22	...	...	...
Joel Parker	7	7	7	7	7	7	3½	...	...	..	...
James E. English	...	...	...	...	...	...	...	6	16	19	...
James R. Doolittle	12½	13	13	12	12	12	12	12	12	12	...
Reverdy Johnson	...	...	...	...	...	...	...	...	...	...	...
Thomas A. Hendricks	89	81	84½	82½	70½	80	87	107½	121	132	...
F. P. Blair, Jr.	½	½	...	...	...	....	...	13½	13	...	...
Thomas Ewing	...	...	...	...	...	...	...	...	...	...	...
J. Q. Adams	...	...	...	...	...	...	...	...	...	...	...
George B. McClellan	1	...	...	...	...	...	...	...	...	½	...
Salmon P. Chase	½	½	...	...	...	½	½	½	...	4	...
Franklin Pierce	...	1	...	...	...	...	...	...	...	...	...
John T. Hoffman	...	...	...	...	...	3	3	...	...	...	...
Stephen J. Field	...	...	...	...	...	...	...	15	9	8	...
Thomas H. Seymour	...	...	...	...	...	...	...	4	2	...	...

Necessary to choice........212

* General Blair was nominated unanimously on the first ballot.

ern men had settled in the South. All of them were now denounced as political adventurers by the rebels who opposed the amendments, reconstruction and freedman's bureau acts. Many of these organized themselves first into Ku Klux Klans, secret societies, organized with a view to affright negroes from participancy in the elections, and to warn white men of opposing political views to leave the country. The object of the organization broadened with the troubles which it produced. Efforts to affright were followed by midnight assaults, by horrible whippings, outrages and murders, hardly a fraction of which could be traced to the perpetrators. Doubtless many of the stories current at the time were exaggerated by partisan newspapers, but all of the official reports made then and since go to show the dangerous excesses which political and race hostilities may reach. In Georgia the whites, by these agencies, soon gained absolute political control, and this they used with more wisdom than in most Southern States, for under the advice of men like Stevens and Hill, they passed laws providing for free public schools, etc., but carefully guarded their newly acquired power by also passing tax laws which virtually disfranchised more than half the blacks. Later on, several Southern States imitated this form of political sagacity, and soon those in favor of "a white man's government," (the popular battle cry of the period) had undisputed control in Virginia, Alabama, Mississippi, Arkansas and Texas—States which the Republicans at one time had reason to believe they could control.

The Enforcement Acts.

To repress the Ku Klux outrages, Congress in May 31, 1870, passed an act giving to the President all needed powers to protect the freedmen in their newly acquired rights, and to punish the perpetrators of all outrages, whether upon whites or blacks. This was called in Congress the Enforcement Act, and an Amendatory Enforcement Act was inserted in the Sundry Civil Bill, June 10, 1872. The Ku Klux Act was passed April 20, 1871. All of these measures were strongly advocated by Senator Oliver P. Morton, who through this advocacy won new political distinction as the special champion of the rights of the blacks. Later on James G. Blaine, then the admitted leader of the House, opposed some of the supplements for its better enforcement, and to this fact is traceable the refusal on the part of the negroes of the South to give him that warm support as a Presidential candidate which his high abilities commanded in other sections.

The several Enforcement Acts and their supplements are too voluminous for insertion here, and they are of little use save as relics of the bitter days of reconstruction. They have little force now, although some of them still stand. They became a dead letter after the defeat of the "carpet-bag governments," but the President enforced them as a rule with moderation and wisdom.

The enforcement of the Ku Klux Act led to the disbanding of that organization after the trial, arrest and conviction of many of the leaders. These trials brought out the facts, and awakened many Southern minds, theretofore incredulous, to the enormity of the secret political crimes which had been committed in all the Southern States, and for a time popular sentiment even in the South, and amongst former rebel soldiers, ran strongly against the Klan. With fresh political excitements, however, fresh means of intimidation were employed at elections. Rifle clubs were formed, notably in South Carolina and Mississippi, while in Louisiana the "White League" sprang into existence, and was organized in all of the neighboring States. These were more difficult to deal with. They were open organizations, created under the semblance of State militia acts. They became very popular, especially among the younger men, and from this time until the close of the Presidential election in 1876, were potent factors in several Southern States, and we shall have occasion further on to describe their more important movements.

Readmission of Rebellious States.

Before the close of 1869 the Supreme Court, in the case of *Texas vs. White*, sustained the constitutionality of the Reconstruction acts of Congress. It held that the ordinances of secession had been "absolutely null;" that the seceding States had no right to secede and had never been out of the Union, but that, during and after their rebellion, they had no governments "competent to represent these States in their relations with the National government," and therefore Congress had the power to re-establish the relations of any rebellious State to the Union. This decision fortified the position of the Republicans, and did much to aid President Grant in the difficult work of reconstruction. It modified the assaults of the Democrats, and in some measure changed their purpose to make Reconstruction the pivot around which smaller political issues should revolve.

The regular session of the 41st Congress met Dec. 4th, 1869, and before its close Virginia, Georgia, Texas, and Mississippi had all complied with the conditions of reconstruction, and were re-admitted to the Union. This practically completed the work of reconstruction. To summarize:—

Tennessee was re-admitted July 24th, 1866; Arkansas, June 22d, 1868; North Carolina, South Carolina, Louisiana, Georgia and Florida under the act of June 25th, 1868, which provided that as soon as they fulfilled the conditions imposed by the acts of March, 1867, they should be re-admitted. All did this promptly except Georgia. Virginia was re-admitted January 25th, 1870; Mississippi, Feb. 23d, 1870; Texas, March 30th, 1870. Georgia, the most powerful and stubborn of all, had passed State laws declaring negroes incapable of holding office, in addition to what was known as the "black code," and Congress refused full admission until she had revoked the laws and ratified the 15th Amendment. The State finally came back into the Union July 15th, 1870.

The above named States completed the ratification of the 15th amendment, and the powers of reconstruction were plainly used to that end. Some of the Northern States had held back, and for a time its ratification by the necessary three-fourths was a matter of grave doubt. Congress next passed a bill to enforce it, May 30th, 1870. This made penal any interference, by force or fraud, with the right of free and full manhood suffrage, and authorized the President to use the army to prevent violations. The measure was generally supported by the Republicans, and opposed by all of the Democrats.

The Republicans through other guards about the ballot by passing an act to amend the naturalization laws, which made it penal to use false naturalization papers, authorized the appointment of Federal supervisors of elections in cities of over 20,000 inhabitants; gave to these power of arrest for any offense committed in their view, and gave alien Africans the right to naturalize. The Democrats in their opposition laid particular stress upon the extraordinary powers given to Federal supervisors, while the Republicans charged that Seymour had carried New York by gigantic naturalization frauds in New York city, and sought to sustain these charges by the unprecedented vote polled. A popular quotation of the time was from Horace Greeley, in the New York *Tribune*, who showed that under the manipulations of the Tweed ring, more votes had been cast for Seymour in one of the warehouse wards of the city, "than there were men, women, children, and cats and dogs in it."

The Legal Tender Decision.

The Act of Congress of 1862 had made "greenback" notes a legal tender, and they passed as such until 1869 against the protests of the Democrats in Congress, who had questioned the right of Congress to issue paper money. It was on this issue that Thaddeus Stevens admitted the Republicans were travelling "outside of the constitution" with a view to preserve the government, and this soon became one of his favorite ways of meeting partisan objections to war measures. At the December term of the Supreme Court, in 1869, a decision was rendered that the action of Congress was unconstitutional, the Court then being accidentally Democratic in its composition. The Republicans, believing they could not afford to have their favorite, and it must be admitted most useful financial measure questioned, secured an increase of two in the number of Supreme Justices—one under a law creating an additional Justiceship, the other in place of a Justice who had resigned—and in March, 1870, after the complexion of the Court had been changed through Republican appointments made by President Grant, the constitutionality of the legal tender act was again raised, and, with Chief Justice Chase (who had been Secretary of the Treasury in 1862 presiding) the previous decision was reversed. This was clearly a partisan struggle before the Court, and on the part of the Republicans an abandonment of old landmarks impressed on the country by the Jackson Democrats, but it is plain that without the greenbacks the war could not have been pressed with half the vigor, if at all. Neither party was consistent in this struggle, for Southern Democrats who sided with their Northern colleagues in the plea of unconstitutionality, had when "out of the Union," witnessed and advocated the issue of the same class of money by the Confederate Congress. The difference was only in the ability to redeem, and this ability depended upon success in arms—the very thing the issue was designed to promote. The last decision, despite its partisan surroundings and opposition, soon won popularity, and this popularity was subsequently taken as the groundwork for the establishment of

The Greenback Party.

This party, with a view to ease the rigors of the monetary panic of 1873, advocated an unlimited issue of greenbacks, or an "issue based upon the resources of the country." So vigorously did discontented leaders of both parties press this idea, that they soon succeeded in demoralizing the Democratic minority—which was by this time such a plain minority, and so greatly in need of new issues to make the people forget the war, that it is not surprising they yielded, at least partially, to new theories and alliances. The present one took them away from the principles of Jackson, from the hard-money theories of the early days, and would land them they knew not where, nor did many of them care, if they could once more get upon their feet. Some resisted, and comparatively few of the Democrats in the Middle States yielded, but in part of New England, the great West, and nearly all of the South, it was for several years quite difficult to draw a line between Greenbackers and Democrats. Some Republicans, too, who had tired of the "old war issues," or discontented with the management and leadership of their party, aided in the construction of the Greenback bridge, and kept upon it as long as it was safe to do so. In State elections up to as late as 1880 this Greenback element was a most important factor. Ohio was carried by an alliance of Greenbackers and Democrats, Allen being elected Governor, only to be supplanted by Hayes (afterwards President) after a most remarkable contest, the alliance favoring the Greenback, the Republicans not quite the hard-money, but a redeemable-in-gold theory. Indiana, always doubtful, passed over to the Democratic column, while in the Southern States the Democratic leaders made open alliances until the Greenbackers became over-confident and sought to win Congressional and State elections on their own merits. They fancied that the desire to repudiate ante-war debts would greatly aid them, and they openly advocated the idea of repudiation there, but they had experienced and wise leaders to cope with. They were not allowed to monopolize this issue by the Democrats, and their arrogance, if such it may be called, was punished by a more complete assertion of Democratic power in the South than was ever known before. The theory in the South was welcomed where it would suit the Democracy, crushed where it would not, as shown in the Presidential election of 1880, when Garfield, Hancock and Weaver (Greenbacker) were the candidates. The latter, in his stumping tour of the South, proclaimed that he and his friends were as much maltreated in Alabama and other States, as the Republicans, and for some cause thereafter (the Democrats alleged "a bargain and sale") he practically threw his aid to the Republicans—this when it became apparent that the Greenbackers, in the event of the election going to the House, could have no chance even there.

Gen'l Weaver went from the South to Maine, the scene of what was regarded at that moment as a pivotal struggle for the Presidency. Blaine had twice been the most prominent candidate for the Presidency—1876 and 1880—and had both times been defeated by compromise candidates. He was still, as he had been for many years, Chairman of the Republican State Committee of Maine, and now as ever before swallowed the mortification of defeat with true political grace. The Greenbackers had the year before formed a close alliance with the Democrats, and in the State election made the result so close that for many weeks it remained a matter of doubt who was elected Governor, the Democratic Greenbacker or the Republican. A struggle followed in the Legislature and before the Returning Board composed of State officers, who were Democrats, (headed by Gov. Garcelon) and sought to throw out returns on slight technicalities. Finally the Republicans won, but not without a struggle which excited attention all over the Union and commanded the presence of the State militia. Following Garfield's nomination another struggle, as we have stated, was inaugurated, with Davis as the Republican nominee for Governor, Plaisted the Democratic-Greenback, (the latter a former Republican). All eyes now turned to Maine, which voted in September. Gen'l Weaver was on the stump then, as the Greenback candidate for President, and all of his efforts were bent to breaking the alliance between the Greenbackers and Democrats.

He advocated a straight-out policy for his Greenback friends, described his treatment in the South, and denounced the Democracy with such plainness that it displayed his purpose and defeated his object. Plaisted was elected by a close vote, and the Republicans yielded after some threats to invoke the "Garcelon precedents." This was the second Democratic-Greenback victory in Maine, the first occurring two years before, when through an alliance in the Legislature (no candidate having received a majority of all the popular vote) Garland was returned.

The victory of Plaisted alarmed the Republicans and enthused the Democrats, who now denounced Weaver, but still sought alliance with his followers. General B. F. Butler, long a brilliant Republican member of Congress from Massachusetts, for several years advocated Greenback ideas without breaking from his Republican Congressional colleagues. Because of this fact he lost whatever of chance he had for a Republican nomination for Governor, "his only remaining political ambition," and thereupon headed the Greenbackers in Massachusetts, and in spite of the protests of the hard-money Democrats in that State, captured the Democratic organization, and after these tactics twice ran for Governor, and was defeated both times by the Republicans, though he succeeded, upon State and "anti-blue blood" theories, in greatly reducing their majority. In the winter of 1882 he still held control of the Democratic State Committee, after the Greenback organization had passed from view, and "what will he do next?" is one of the political questions of the hour.

The Greenback labor party ceased all Congressional alliance with the Democrats after their quarrel with General Weaver, and as late as the 47th session—1881-82—refused all alliance, and abstained from exercising what some still believe a "balance of power" in the House, though nearly half of their number were elected more as Republicans than Greenbackers.

As a party, the Greenbackers, standing alone, never carried either a State or a Congressional district. Their local successes were due to alliances with one or other of the great parties, and with the passage of the panic they dissolved in many sections, and where they still obtain it is in alliance with labor unions, or in strong mining or workingmen's districts. In the Middle States they won few local successes, but were strong in the coal regions of Pennsylvania. Advocates of similar theories have not been wanting in all the countries of Western Europe following great wars or panics, but it was reserved to the genius of Americans to establish an aggressive political party on the basis of theories which all great political economists have from the beginning antagonized as unsafe and unsound.

The Prohibitory Party.

The attempt to establish a third party in the Greenback, begot that to establish a National Prohibitory Party, which in 1880 ran James Black of Pennsylvania, as a candidate for the Presidency, and four years previous ran Neal Dow of Maine. He, however, commanded little attention, and received but sparsely scattered votes in all the States. The sentiment at the base of this party never thrived save as in States, particularly in New England, where it sought to impress itself on the prevailing political party, and through it to influence legislation. Neal Dow of Maine, first advocated a prohibitory law, and by his eloquent advocacy, secured that of Maine, which has stood for nearly thirty years. That of Massachusetts has recently been repealed. The prohibitory amendment to the Constitution of Kansas was adopted in 1881, etc. The Prohibitory Party, however, never accomplished anything by separate political action, and though fond of nominating candidates for State and local officers, has not as yet succeeded in holding even a balance of power between the political parties, though it has often confused political calculations as to results in New York, Ohio, Pennsylvania, Connecticut, Massachusetts, etc. It seems never to have taken hold in any of the Southern States, and comparatively little in the Western, until the whole country was surprised in 1880 by the passage of the Kansas amendment by over 20,000 majority in a vote of the people invoked by the Legislature. An effort followed to submit a similar amendment through the Pennsylvania Legislature in 1881. It passed the House by a large majority, but after discussion in the Senate, and amendments to indemnify manufacturers and dealers in liquor (an amendment which would cripple if it would not bankrupt the State) was adopted. Governor St. John of Kansas, a gentleman fond of stumping for this amendment, insists that the results are good in his State, while its enemies claim that it has made many criminals, that liquor is everywhere smuggled and sold, and that the law has turned the tide of immigration away from that great State. The example of Kansas, however, will probably be followed in other States, and the Prohibitory Party will hardly pass from view until this latest experiment has been fairly tested. It was also the author of "Local Option," which for a time swept Pennsylvania, but was repealed by a large majority after two years' trial.

Annexation of San Domingo.

The second session of the 41st Congress began December 5th, 1870. With all of the States represented, reconstruction being complete, the body was now divided politically as follows: Senate, 61 Republicans, 13 Democrats; House 172 Republicans, 71 Democrats. President Grant's annual message discussed a new question, and advocated the annexation of San Domingo to the United States. A treaty had been negotiated between President Grant and the President of the Republic of San Domingo as early as September 4th, 1869, looking to annexation, but it had been rejected by the Senate, Charles Sumner being prominent in his opposition to the measure. He and Grant experienced a growing personal unpleasantness, because of the President's attempt to negotiate a treaty without consulting Mr. Sumner, who was Chairman of the Committee on Foreign Affairs, and it was charged that through the influence of the President he was removed by the Republican caucus from this Chairmanship, and Senator Simon Cameron put in his place. Whether this was true or not, the differences between Grant and Sumner were universally remarked, and Sumner's imperious pride led him into a very vindictive assault upon the proposition. Grant gave few other reasons for annexation than military ones, suggested that as a naval station it would facilitate all home operations in the Gulf, while in the hands of a foreign power, in the event of war, it would prove the depot for many and dangerous warlike preparations. The question had little political significance, if it was ever designed to have any, and this second attempt to bring the scheme to the attention of Congress, was that a joint resolution (as in the annexation of Texas) might be passed. This would require but a majority, but the objection was met that no Territory could be annexed without a treaty, and this must be ratified by two-thirds of the Senate. A middle course was taken, and the President was authorized to appoint three Commissioners to visit San Domingo and ascertain the desires of its people. These reported favorably, but the subject was finally dropped, probably because the proposition could not command a two-thirds vote, and has not since attracted attention.

Amendatory Enforcement Acts.

The operation of the 15th Amendment, being still resisted or evaded in portions of the South, an Act was passed to enforce it. This extended the powers of the Federal supervisors and marshals, authorized in the first, and gave the Federal Circuit Courts exclusive jurisdiction of all cases tried under the provisions of the Act and its supplements. It also empowered these Courts to punish any State officer who should attempt to interfere with or try such cases as in contempt of the Court's jurisdiction. The Republicans sustained, the Democrats opposed the measure, but it was passed and approved February 28, 1871, and another supplement was inserted in the Sundry Civil Bill, and approved June 10th, 1872, with continued resistance on the part of the Democrats. After the appointment of a committee to investigate the condition of affairs in the Southern States, Congress adjourned March 4th, 1871.

The Alabama Claims.

During this year the long disputed Alabama Claims of the United States against Great Britain, arising from the depredations of the Anglo-rebel privateers, built and fitted out in British waters, were referred by the Treaty of Washington, dated May 8th, 1871, to arbitrators, and this was the first and most signal triumph of the plan of arbitration, so far as the Government of the United States was concerned. The arbitrators were appointed, at the invitation of the governments of Great Britain and the United States, from these powers, and from Brazil, Italy, and Switzerland. On September 14th, 1872, they gave to the United States gross damages to the amount of $15,500,000, an amount which has subsequently proved to be really in excess of the demands of merchants and others claiming the loss of property through the depredations of the rebel ram *Alabama* and other rebel privateers. We append a list of the representatives of the several governments:

Arbitrator on the part of the United States—CHARLES FRANCIS ADAMS.

Arbitrator on the part of Great Britain—The Right Honorable Sir ALEXANDER COCKBURN, Baronet, Lord Chief Justice of England.

Arbitrator on the part of Italy—His Excellency Senator Count SCLOPIS.

Arbitrator on the part of Switzerland—Mr. JACOB STAMPFLI.

Arbitrator on the part of Brazil—Baron D'ITAJUBA.

Agent on the part of the United States—J. C. BANCROFT DAVIS.

Agent on the part of Great Britain—Right Honorable LORD TENTERDEN.

Counsel for the United States—CALEB CUSHING, WILLIAM M. EVARTS, MORRISON R. WAITE.

Counsel for Great Britain—Sir ROUNDELL PALMER.

Solicitor for the United States—CHARLES C. BEAMAN, Jr.

The Force Bill.

The 42d Congress met March 4, 1871, the Republicans having suffered somewhat in their representation. In the Senate there were 57 Republicans, 17 Democrats; in the House 138 Republicans, 103 Democrats. James G. Blaine was again chosen Speaker. The most exciting political question of the session was the passage of the "Force Bill," as the Democrats called it. The object was more rigidly to enforce observance of the provisions of the 14th Amendment, as the Republicans claim; to revive a waning political power in the South, and save the "carpet-bag" governments there, as the Democrats claimed. The Act allowed suit in the Federal courts against any person who should deprive another of the rights of a citizen, and it made it a penal offense to conspire to take away any one's rights as a citizen. It also provided that inability, neglect, or refusal by any State governments to suppress such conspiracies, or their refusal to call upon the President for aid, should be deemed a denial by such State of the equal protection of the laws under the 14th Amendment. It further declared such conspiracies "a rebellion against the government of the United States," and authorized the President, when in his judgment the public safety required it, to suspend the privilege of *habeas corpus* in any district, and suppress any such insurrection by the army and navy.

President Hayes's Civil Service Order.

EXECUTIVE MANSION, Washington, *June* 22, 1877.

SIR:—I desire to call your attention to the following paragraph in a letter addressed by me to the Secretary of the Treasury, on the conduct to be observed by the officers of the General Government in relation to the elections:

"No officer should be required or permitted to take part in the management of political organizations, caucuses, conventions or election campaigns Their right to vote and to express their views on public questions, either orally or through the press, is not denied, provided it does not interfere with the discharge of their official duties. No assessment for political purposes on officers or subordinates should be allowed."

This rule is applicable to every department of the Civil Service. It should be understood by every officer of the General Government that he is expected to conform his conduct to its requirements.

Very respectfully, R. B. HAYES.

Some of the protests were strong, and it is difficult to say whether Curtis, Julian, or Eaton—its three leading advocates—or the politicians, had the best of the argument. It was not denied, however, that a strong and very respectable sentiment had been created in favor of the reform, and to this sentiment all parties, and the President as well, made a show of bowing. It was fashionable to insert civil service planks in National and State platforms, but it was was not such an issue as could livein the presence of more exciting ones; and while to this day it has earnest and able advocates, it has from year to year fallen into greater disuse. Actual trial showed the impracticability of some of the rules, and President Grant lost interest in the subject, as did Congress, for in several instances it *neglected* to appropriate the funds necessary to carry out the provisions of the law. President Arthur, in his message, to Congress in December, 1881, argued against its full application, and showed that it blocked the way to preferment, certainly of the middle-aged and older persons, who could not recall their early lessons acquired by rote; that its effect was to elevate the inexperienced to positions which required executive ability, sound judgment business aptitude, and experience. The feature of the message met the endorsment of nearly the entire Republican press, and at this writing the sentiment, at least of the Republican party, appears to favor a partial modification of the rules.

The system was begun January 1st, 1872, but in December, 1874, Congress refused to make any appropriations, and it was for a time abandoned, with slight and spasmodic revivals under the administration of President Hayes, who issued the foregoing order.

By letter from the Attorney-General, Charles Devens, August 1, 1877, this order was held to apply to the Pennsylvania Republican Association at Washington. Still later there was a further exposition, in which Attorney-General Devens, writing from Washington in October 1, 1877, excuses himself from active participation in the Massachusetts State campaign, and says: "I learn with surprise and regret that any of the Republican officials hesitate either to speak or vote, alleging as a reason the President's recent Civil Service order. In distinct terms that order states that the right of officials to vote and express their views on public questions, either orally or through the press, is not denied, provided it does not interfere with the discharge of their official duties. If such gentlemen choose not to vote, or not to express or enforce their views in support of the principles of the Republican party, either orally or otherwise, they, at least, should give a reason for such a course which is not justified by the order referred to, and which is simply a perversion of it."

Yet later, when the interest in the Pennsylvania election became general, because of the sharp struggle between Governor Hoyt and Senator Dill for Governor, a committee of gentlemen (Republicans) visited President Hayes and induced him to "suspend the operation of the order" as to Pennsylvania, where political contributions were collected.

And opposition was manifested after even the earlier trials. Benjamin F. Butler denounced the plan as English and anti-Republican, and before long some of the more radical Republican papers, which had indeed given little attention to the subject, began to denounce it as a plan to exclude faithful Republicans from and permit Democrats to enter the offices. These now argued that none of the vagaries of political dreamers could ever convince them that a free Government can be run without political parties; that while rotation in office may not be a fundamental element of republican government, yet the right of the people to recommend is its corner-stone; that civil service would lead to the creation of rings, and eventually to the purchase of places; that it would establish an aristocracy of office-holders, who could not be removed at times when it might be important, as in the rebellion fot the Administration to have only friends in public office; that it would establish grades and life-tenures in civic positions, etc.

For later particulars touching civil service, see the Act of Congress of 1883, and the regulations made pursuant to the same in Book V.

Amnesty.

The first regular session of the 42d Congress met Dec. 4th, 1871. The Democrats consumed much of the time in efforts to pass bills to remove the political disabilities of former Southern rebels, and they were materially aided by the editorials of Horace Greeley, in the New York *Tribune*, which had long contended for universal amnesty. At this session all such efforts were defeated by the Republicans, who invariably amended such propositions by adding Sumner's Supplementary Civil Rights Bill, which was intended to prevent any discrimination against colored persons by common carriers, hotels, or other chartered or licensed servants. The Amnesty Bill, however was passed May 22d, 1872, after an an agreement to exclude from its provisions all who held the higher military and civic positions under the Confederacy—in all about 350 persons. The following is a copy:

Be it enacted, etc., (two-thirds of each House concurring therein,) That all legal and political disabilities imposed by the third section of the fourteenth article of the amendments of the Constitution of the United States are hereby removed from all persons whomsoever, except Senators and Representatives of the Thirty-sixth and Thirty-seventh Congress, officers in the judicial, military, and naval service of the United States, heads of Departments, and foreign ministers of the United States.

Subsequently many acts removing the disabilities of all excepted (save Jefferson Davis] from the provisions of the above, were passed.

The Liberal Republicans.

An issue raised in Missouri gave immediate rise to the Liberal Republican party, though the course of Horace Greeley had long pointed toward the organization of something of the kind, and with equal plainness it pointed to his desire to be its champion and candidate for the Presidency. In 1870 the Republican party, then in control of the Legislature of Missouri, split into two parts on the question of the removal of the disqualifications imposed upon rebels by the State Constitution during the war. Those favoring the removal of disabilities were headed by B. Gratz Brown and Carl Schurz, and they called themselves Liberal Republicans; those opposed were called and accepted the name of Radical Republicans. The former quickly allied themselves with the Democrats, and thus carried the State, though Grant's administration "stood in" with the Radicals. As a result the disabilities were quickly removed, and those who believed with Greeley now sought to promote a reaction in Republican sentiment all over the country. Greeley was the recognized head of this movement, and he was ably aided by ex-Governor Curtin and Col. A. K. McClure in Pennsylvania; Charles Francis Adams, Massachusetts; Judge Trumbull, in Illinois; Reuben E. Fenton, in New York; Brown and Schurz in Missouri, and in fact by leading Republicans in nearly all of the States, who at once began to lay plans to carry the next Presidential election.

They charged that the Enforcement Acts of Congress were designed more for the political advancement of Grant's adherents than for the benefit of the country; that instead of suppressing they were calculated to promote a war of races in the South; that Grant was seeking the establishment of a military despotism, etc. These leaders were, as a rule, brilliant men. They had tired of unappreciated and unrewarded service in the Republican party, or had a natural fondness for "pastures new," and, in the language of the day, they quickly succeeded in making political movements "lively."

In the spring of 1871 the Liberal Republicans and Democrats of Ohio—and Ohio seems to be the most fertile soil for new ideas—prepared for a fusion, and after frequent consultations of the various leaders with Mr. Greeley in New York, a call was issued from Missouri on the 24th of January, 1872, for a National Convention of the Liberal Republican party to be held at Cincinnati, May 1st. The well-matured plans of the leaders were carried out in the nomination of Hon. Horace Greeley for President and B. Gratz Brown for Vice-President, though not without a serious struggle over the chief nomination, which was warmly contested by the friends of Charles Francis Adams. Indeed he led in most of the six ballots, but finally all the friends of other candidates voted for Greeley, and he received 482 to 187 for Adams. Dissatisfaction followed, and a later effort was made to substitute Adams for Greeley, but it failed. The original leaders now prepared to capture the Democratic Convention, which met at Baltimore, June 9th. By nearly an unanimous vote it was induced to endorse the Cincinnati platform, and it likewise finally endorsed Greeley and Brown—though not without many bitter protests. A few straight-out Democrats met later at Louisville, Ky., Sept. 3d, and nominated Charles O'Conor, of New York, for President, and John Quincy Adams, of Massachusetts, for Vice-President, and these were kept in the race to the end, receiving a popular vote of about 30,000.

The regular Republican National Convention was held at Philadelphia, June 5th. It renominated President Grant unanimously, and Henry Wilson, of Massachusetts, for Vice-President by 364½ votes to 321½ for Schuyler Colfax, who thus shared the fate of Hannibal Hamlin in his second candidacy for Vice-President on the ticket with Abraham Lincoln. This change to Wilson was to favor the solid Republican States of New England, and to prevent both candidates coming from the West.

Civil Service Reform.

After considerable and very able agitation by Geo. W. Curtis, the editor of *Harper's Weekly*, an Act was passed March 3d, 1871, authorizing the President to begin a reform in the civil service. He appointed a Commission headed by Mr. Curtis, and after more than a year's preparation this body defeated a measure which secured Congressional approval and that of President Grant.

The civil service law (and it is still a law though more honored now in the breach than the observance) embraced in a single section of the act making appropriations for sundry civil expenses for the year ending June 30, 1872, and authorize the President to prescribe such rules and regulations for admission into the civil service as will best promote the efficiency thereof, and ascertain the fitness of each candidate for the branch of service into which he seeks to enter. Under this law a commission was appointed to draft rules and regulations which were approved and are now being enforced by the President. All applicants for position in any of the government departments come under these rules:—all classes of clerks, copyists, counters; in the customs service all from deputy collector down to inspectors and clerks with the salaries of $1200 or more; in appraisers' offices all assistants and clerks; in the naval service all clerks; all light-house keepers; in the revenue, supervisors, collectors, assessors, assistants; in the postal really all postmasters whose pay is over $200, and all mail messengers. The rules apply to all new appointments in the departments or grades named, except that "nothing shall prevent the reappointment at discretion of the incumbents of any office the term of which is fixed by law." So that a postmaster or other officer escapes their application. Those specially exempt are the Heads of Departments; their immediate assistants and deputies, the diplomatic service, the judiciary, and the district attorneys. Each branch of the service is to be grouped, and admission shall always be to the lowest grade of any group. Such appointments are made for a probationary term of six months, when if the Board of Examiners approve the incumbent is continued. This Board of Examiners, three in number in each case, shall be chosen by the President from the several Departments, and they shall examine at Washington for any position there, or, when directed by an Advisory Board, shall assign places for examination in the several States. Examinations are in all cases first made of applicants within the office or department, and from the list three reported in the order of excellence; if those within fail, then outside applicants may be examined. In the Federal Blue Book, which is a part of this volume, we give the Civil Service Rules.

When first proposed, partisan politics had no part or place in civil service reform, and the author of the plan was himself a distinguished Republican. In fact both parties thought something good had been reached, and there was practically no resistance at first to a trial.

The Democrats resisted the passage of this bill with even more earnestness than any which preceded it, but the Republican discipline was almost perfect, and when passed it received the prompt approval of President Grant, who by this time was classed as "the most radical of the radicals." Opponents denounced it as little if any less obnoxious than the old Sedition law of 1798, while the Republicans claimed that it was to meet a state of growing war in the South—a war of races—and that the form of domestic violence manifested was in the highest degree dangerous to the peace of the Union and the safety of the newly enfranchised citizens.

The Credit Mobilier.

At the second session of the 42d Congress, beginning Dec. 2, 1872, the speaker (Blaine) on the first day called attention to the charges made by Democratic orators and newspapers during the Presidential campaign just closed, that the Vice President (Colfax), the Vice President elect (Wilson), the Secretary of the Treasury, several Senators, the Speaker of the House, and a large number of Representatives had been bribed, during the years 1867 and 1868, by Oakes Ames, a member of the House from Massachusetts; that he and his agents had given them presents of stock in a corporation known as the Credit Mobilier, to influence their legislative action for the benefit of the Union Pacific Railroad Company.

Upon Speaker Blaine's motion, a committee of investigation was appointed by Hon. S. S. Cox, of New York, a noted Democrat temporarily called to the Chair.

After the close of the campaign, (as was remarked by the *Republic Magazine* at the time) the dominant party might well have claimed, and would have insisted had they been opposed to a a thorough investigation and a full exposure of corruption, that the verdict of the people in the late canvss was sufficient answer to these charges; but the Republican party not merely granted all the investigations sought, but summoned on the leading committee a majority of its political foes to conduct the inquest.

The committee consisted of Messrs. Poland, of Vermont; McCreary, of Iowa; Banks, of Massachusetts; Niblack, of Indiana, and Merrick, of Maryland.

Messrs. Poland and McCreary—the two Republicans—were gentlemen of ability and standing, well known for their integrity, moderation, and impartiality. General Banks was an earnest supporter of Horace Greeley, upon the alleged ground that the Republican organization had become effete and corrupt: while Messrs. Niblack and Merrick are among the ablest representatives of the Democratic party; in fact, Mr. Merrick belonged to the extreme Southern school of political thought.

Having patiently and carefully examined and sifted the entire testimony—often "painfully conflicting," as the committee remarked—their report ought to be considered a judicial document commanding universal approval, yet scraps of the testimony and not the report itself were used with painful frequency against James A. Garfield in his Presidential canvass of 1880. There has not been a state paper submitted for many years upon a similar subject that carried with it greater weight, or which bore upon its face a fuller realization of the grave responsibilities assumed, and it is the first time in the political history of the United States that an all-important investigation has been entrusted by the dominant party to a majority of its political foes.

The report of the committee gives the best and by far the most reliable history of the whole affair, and its presentation here may aid in preventing partisan misrepresentations in the future—misrepresentations made in the heat of contest, and doubtless regretted afterwards by all who had the facilities for getting at the facts. We therefore give the

OFFICIAL REPORT OF THE CREDIT MOBILIER INVESTIGATING COMMITTEE.

Mr. Poland, from the select committee to investigate the alleged Credit Mobilier bribery, made the following report February 18, 1873:

The special committee appointed under the following resolutions of the House to wit:

WHEREAS, Accusations have been made in the public press, founded on alleged letters of Oakes Ames, a Representative of Massachusetts, and upon the alleged affidavits of Henry S. McComb, a citizen of Wilmington, in the State of Delaware, to the effect that members of this House were bribed by Oakes Ames to perform certain legislative acts for the benefit of the Union Pacific Railroad Company, by presents of stock in the Credit Mobilier of America, or by presents of a valuable character derived therefrom: therefore,

Resolved, That a special committee of five members be appointed by the Speaker pro tempore, whose duty it shall be to investigate whether any member of this House was bribed by Oakes Ames, or any other person or corporation, in any matter touching his legislative duty.

Resolved, further, That the committee have the right to employ a stenographer, and that they be empowered to send for persons and papers;

beg leave to make the following report:

In order to a clear understanding of the facts hereinafter stated as to contracts and dealings in reference to stock of the Credit Mobilier of America, between Mr. Oakes Ames and others, and members of Congress, it is necessary to make a preliminary statement of the connection of that company with the Union Pacific Railroad Company, and their relations to each other.

The company called the "Credit Mobilier of America" was incorporated by the Legislature of Pennsylvania, and in 1864 control of its charter and franchises had been obtained by certain persons interested in the Union Pacific Railroad Company, for the purpose of using it as a construction company to build the Union Pacific road. In September, 1864, a contract was entered into between the Union Pacific Company and H. M. Hoxie, for the building by said Hoxie of one hundred miles of said road from Omaha west.

This contract was at once assigned by Hoxie to the Credit Mobilier Company, as it was expected to be when made. Under this contract and extensions of it some two or three hundred miles of road were built by the Credit Mobilier Company, but no considerable profits appear to have been realized therefrom. The enterprise of building a railroad to the Pacific was of such vast magnitude, and was beset by so many hazards and risks that the capitalists of the country were generally averse to investing in it, and, notwithstanding the liberal aid granted by the Government it seemed likely to fail of completion.

In 1865 or 1866, Mr. Oakes Ames, then and now a member of the House from the State of Massachusetts, and his brother Oliver Ames became interested in the Union Pacific Company and also in the Credit Mobilier Company as the agents for the construction of the road. The Messrs. Ames were men of very large capital, and of known character and integrity in business. By their example and credit, and the personal efforts of Mr. Oakes Ames, many men of capital were induced to embark in the enterprise, and to take stock in the Union Pacific Company and also in the Credit Mobilier Company. Among them were the firm of S. Hooper & Co., of Boston, the leading member of which, Mr. Samuel Hooper, was then and is now a member of the House; Mr. John B. Alley, then a member of the House from Massachusetts, and Mr. Grimes, then a Senator from the State of Iowa. Notwithstanding the vigorous efforts of Mr. Ames and others interested with him, great difficulty was experienced in securing the required capital.

In the spring of 1867 the Credit Mobilier Company voted to add 50 per cent. to their capital stock, which was then two and a half millions of dollars; and to cause it to be readily taken each subscriber to it was entitled to receive as a bonus an equal amount of first mortgage bonds of the Union Pacific Company. The old stockholders were entitled to take this increase, but even the favorable terms offered did not induce all the old stockholders to take it, and the stock of the Credit Mobilier Company was never considered worth its par value until after the execution of the Oakes Ames contract hereinafter mentioned.

On the 16th day of August, 1867, a contract was executed between the Union Pacific Railroad Company and Oakes Ames, by which Mr. Ames contracted to build six hundred and sixty-seven miles of the Union Pacific road at prices ranging from $42,000 to $96,000 per mile. amounting in the aggregate to $47,000,000. Before the contract was entered into it was understood that Mr. Ames was to transfer it to seven trustees, who were to execute it, and the profits of the contract were to be divided among the stockholders in the Credit Mobilier Company, who should comply with certain conditions set out in the instrument transferring the contract to the trustees. The Ames contract and the transfer to trustees are incorporated in the evidence submitted, and therefore further recital of their terms is not deemed necessary.

Substantially, all the stockholders of the Credit Mobilier complied with the conditions named in the transfer, and thus became entitled to share in any profits said trustees might make in executing the contract.

All the large stockholders in the Union Pacific were also stockholders in the Credit Mobilier, and the Ames contract and its transfer to trustees were ratified by the Union Pacific, and received the assent of the great body of stockholders, but not of all.

After the Ames contract had been executed, it was expected by those interested that by reason of the enormous prices agreed to be paid for the work very large profits would be derived from building the road, and very soon the stock of the Credit Mobilier was understood by those holding it to be worth much more than its par value. The stock was not in the market and had no fixed market value, but the holders of it, in December, 1867, considered it worth at least double the par value, and in January and February, 1868, three or four times the par value, but it does not appear that these facts were generally or publicly known, or that the holders of the stock desired they should be.

The foregoing statement the committee think gives enough of the historic details, and condition and value of the stock, to make the following detailed facts intelligible.

Mr. Oakes Ames was then a member of the House of Representatives, and came to Washington at the commencement of the session, about the beginning of December, 1867. During that month Mr. Ames entered into contracts with a considerable number of members of Congress, both Senators and Representatives, to let them have shares of stock in the Credit Mobilier Company at par, with interest thereon from the first day of the previous July. It does not appear that in any instance he asked any of these persons to pay a higher price than the par value and interest, nor that Mr. Ames used any special effort or urgency to get these persons to take it. In all these negotiations Mr. Ames did not enter into any details as to the value of the stock or the amount of dividend that might be expected upon it, but stated generally that it would be good stock, and in several instances said he would guarantee that they should get at least 10 per cent. on their money.

Some of these gentlemen, in their conversations with Mr. Ames, raised the question whether becoming holders of this stock would bring them into any embarrassment as members of Congress in their legislative action. Mr. Ames quieted such suggestions by saying it could not, for the Union Pacific had received from Congress all the grants and legislation it wanted, and they should ask for nothing more. In some instances those members who contracted for stock paid to Mr. Ames the money for the price of the stock, par and interest; in others, where they had not the money, Mr. Ames agreed to carry the stock for them until they could get the money or it should be met by the dividends.

Mr. Ames was at this time a large stockholder in the Credit Mobiler, but he did not intend any of these transactions to be sales of his own stock, but intended to fulfill all these contracts from stock belonging to the company.

At this time there were about six hundred and fifty shares of the stock of the company, which had for some reason been placed in the name of Mr. T. C. Durant, one of the leading and active men of the concern.

Mr. Ames claimed that a portion of this stock should be assigned to him to enable him to fulfill engagements he had made for stock. Mr. Durant claimed that he had made similar engagements that he should be allowed stock to fulfill. Mr. McComb, who was present at the time, claimed that he had also made engagements for stock which he should have stock given him to carry out. This claim of McComb was refused, but after the stock was assigned to Mr. Ames, McComb insisted that Ames should distribute some of the stock to his (McComb's) friends, and named Senators Bayard and Fowler, and Representatives Allison and Wilson, of Iowa.

It was finally arranged that three hundred and forty-three shares of the stock of the company should be transferred to Mr. Ames to enable him to perform his engagements, and that number of shares were set over on the books of the company to Oakes Ames, trustee, to distinguish it from the stock held by him before. Mr. Ames at the time paid to the company the par of the stock and interest from the July previous, and this stock still stands on the books in the name of Oakes Ames, trustee, except thirteen shares which have been transferred to parties in no way connected with Congress. The committee do not find that Mr. Ames had any negotiation whatever with any of these members of Congress on the subject of this stock prior to the commencement of the session of December, 1867, except Mr. Scofield, of Pennsylvania, and it was not claimed that any obligation existed from Mr. Ames to him as the result of it.

In relation to the purpose and motives of Mr. Ames in contracting to let members of Congress have Credit Mobilier stock at par, which he and all other owners of it considered worth at least double that sum, the committee, upon the evidence taken by them and submitted to the House, cannot entertain doubt. When he said he did not suppose the Union Pacific Company would ask or need further legislation, he stated what he believed to be true. But he feared the interests of the road might suffer by adverse legislation, and what he desired to accomplish was to enlist strength and friends in Congress who would resist any encroachment upon or interference with the rights and privileges already secured, and to that end wished to create in them an interest identical with his own. This purpose is clearly avowed in his letters to McComb, copied in the evidence. He says he intends to place the stock "where it will do most good to us." And again, "we want more friends in this Congress." In his letter to McComb, and also in his statement prepared by counsel, he gives the philosophy of his action, to wit, "That he has found there is no difficulty in getting men to look after their own property." The committee are also satisfied that Mr. Ames entertained a fear that, when the true relations between the Credit Mobilier Company and the Union Pacific became generally known, and the means by which the great profits expected to be made were fully understood, there was danger that congressional investigation and action would be invoked.

The members of Congress with whom he dealt were generally those who had been friendly and favorable to a Pacific Railroad, and Mr. Ames did not fear or expect to find them favorable to movements hostile to it; but he desired to stimulate their activity and watchfulness in opposition to any unfavorable action by giving them a personal interest in the success of the enterprise, especially so far as it affected the interest of the Credit Mobilier Company. On the 9th day of December, 1867, Mr. C. C. Washburn, of Wisconsin, introduced in the House a bill to regulate by law the rates of transportation over the Pacific Railroad.

Mr. Ames, as well as others interested in the Union Pacific road, was opposed to this, and desired to defeat it. Other measures apparently hostile to that company were subsequently introduced into the House by Mr. Washburn of Wisconsin, and Mr. Washburne of Illinois. The committee believe that Mr. Ames, in his distributions of stock, had specially in mind the hostile efforts of the Messrs. Washburn, and desired to gain strength to secure their defeat. The reference in one of his letters to "Washburn's move" makes this quite apparent.

The foregoing is deemed by the committee a sufficient statement of facts as to Mr. Ames, taken in connection with what will be subsequently stated of his transactions with particular persons. Mr. Ames made some contracts for stock in the Credit Mobilier with members of the Senate. In public discussions of this subject the names of members of both Houses have been so connected, and all these transactions were so nearly simultaneous, that the committee deemed it their duty to obtain all evidence in their power, as to all persons then members of either House, and to report the same to the House. Having done this, and the House having directed that evidence transmitted to the Senate, the committee consider their own power and duty, as well as that of the House, fully performed, so far as members of the Senate are concerned. Some of Mr. Ames's contracts to sell stock were with gentlemen who were then members of the House, but are not members of the present Congress.

The committee have sought for and taken all the evidence within their reach as to those gentlemen, and reported the same to the House. As the House has ceased to have jurisdiction over them as members, the committee have not deemed it their duty to make any special finding of facts as to each, leaving the House and the country to their own conclusions upon the testimony.

In regard to each of the members of the present House, the committee deem it their duty to state specially the facts they find proved by the evidence, which, in some instances, is painfully conflicting.

MR. JAMES G. BLAINE, OF MAINE.

Among those who have in the public press been charged with improper participation in Credit Mobilier stock is the present Speaker, Mr. Blaine, who moved the resolution for this investigation. The committee have, therefore, taken evidence in regard to him. They find from it that Mr. Ames had conversation with Mr. Blaine in regard to taking ten shares of the stock, and recommended it as a good investment. Upon consideration Mr. Blaine concluded not to take the stock, and never did take it, and never paid or received anything on account of it; and Mr. Blaine never had any interest, direct or indirect, in Credit Mobilier stock or stock of the Union Pacific Railroad Company.

MR. HENRY L. DAWES, OF MASSACHUSETTS.

Mr. Dawes had, prior to December, 1867, made some small investments in railroad bonds through Mr. Ames. In December, 1867, Mr. Dawes applied to Mr. Ames to purchase a thousand-dollar bond of the Cedar Rapids road, in Iowa. Mr. Ames informed him that he had sold them all, but that he would let him have for his thousand dollars ten shares of Credit Mobilier stock, which he thought was better than the railroad bond. In answer to inquiries by Mr. Dawes Mr. Ames said the Credit Mobilier Company had the contract to build the Union Pacific road, and thought they would make money out of it, and that it would be a good thing; that he would guarantee that he should get 10 per cent. on his money, and that if at any time Mr. Dawes did not want the stock he would pay back his money with 10 per cent. interest. Mr. Dawes made some further inquiry in relation to the stock of Mr. John B. Alley, who said he thought it was good stock, but not as good as Mr. Ames thought, but that Mr. Ames's guarantee would make it a perfectly safe investment. Mr. Dawes thereupon concluded to purchase the ten shares, and on the 11th of January he paid Mr. Ames $800, and in a few days thereafter the balance of the price of this stock, at par and interest from July previous. In June, 1868, Mr. Ames received a dividend of 60 per cent. in money on this stock, and of it paid to Mr. Dawes $400, and applied the balance of $200 upon accounts between them. This $400 was all that was paid over to Mr. Dawes as a dividend upon this stock. At some time prior to December, 1868, Mr. Dawes was informed that a suit had been commenced in the courts of Pennsylvania by former owners of the charter of the Credit Mobilier, claiming that those then claiming and using it had no right to do so. Mr. Dawes thereupon informed Mr. Ames that as there was a litigation about the matter he did not desire to keep the stock. On the 9th of December, 1868, Mr. Ames and Mr. Dawes had a settlement of their matters in which Mr. Dawes was allowed for the money he paid for the stock with 10 per cent. interest upon it, and accounted to Mr. Ames for the $400 he had received as a dividend. Mr. Dawes received no other benefit under the contract than to get 10 per cent. upon his money, and after the settlement had no further interest in the stock.

MR. GLENNI W. SCOFIELD, OF PENNSYLVANIA.

In 1866 Mr. Scofield purchased some Cedar Rapids bonds of Mr. Ames, and in that year they had conversations about Mr. Scofield taking stock in the Credit Mobilier Company, but no contract was consummated. In December, 1867, Mr. Scofield applied to Mr. Ames to purchase more Cedar Rapids bonds, when Mr. Ames suggested he should purchase some Credit Mobilier stock, and explained generally that it was a contracting company to build the Union Pacific road; that it was a Pennsylvania corporation, and he would like to have some Pennsylvanians in it; that he would sell it to him at par and interest, and that he would guarantee he should get 8 per cent. if Mr. Scofield would give him half the dividends above that. Mr. Scofield said he thought he would take $1,000 of the stock; but before anything further was done Mr. Scofield was called home by sickness in his family. On his return, the latter part of January, 1868, he spoke to Mr. Ames about the stock, when Mr. Ames said he thought it was all sold, but he would take his money and give him a receipt, and get the stock for him if he could. Mr. Scofield thereupon paid Mr. Ames $1,041, and took his receipt therefor.

Not long after Mr. Ames informed Mr. Scofield he could have the stock, but could not give him a certificate for it until he could get a larger certificate dividend. Mr. Scofield received the bond dividend of 80 per cent., which was payable January 3, 1868, taking a bond for $1,000 and paying Mr. Ames the difference. Mr. Ames received the 60 per cent. cash dividend on the stock in June, 1868, and paid over to Mr. Scofield $600, the amount of it.

Before the close of that session of Congress, which was toward the end of July, Mr. Scofield became, for some reason, disinclined to take the stock, and a settlement was made between them, by which Mr. Ames was to retain the Credit Mobilier stock and Mr. Scofield took a thousand dollars Union Pacific bond and ten shares of Union Pacific stock.

The precise basis of the settlement does not appear, neither Mr. Ames nor Mr. Scofield having any full date in reference to it; Mr. Scofield thinks that he only received back his money and interest upon it, while Mr. Ames states that he thinks Mr. Scofield had ten shares of Union Pacific stock in addition. The committee do not deem it specially important to settle this difference of recollection. Since that settlement Mr. Scofield has had no interest in the Credit Mobilier stock and derived no benefit therefrom.

MR. JOHN A. BINGHAM, OF OHIO.

In December, 1867, Mr. Ames advised Mr. Bingham to invest in the stock of the Credit Mobilier, assuring him that it would return him his money with profitable dividends. Mr. Bingham agreed to take twenty shares, and about the 1st of February, 1868, paid to Mr. Ames the par value of the stock, for which Mr. Ames executed to him some receipt or agreement. Mr. Ames received all the dividends on the stock, whether in Union Pacific bonds, or stock, or money; some were delivered to Mr. Bingham and some retained by Mr. Ames. The matter was not finally adjusted between them until February, 1872, when it was settled, Mr. Ames retaining the twenty shares of Credit Mobilier stock, and accounting to Mr. Bingham for such dividends upon it as Mr. Bingham had not already received. Mr. Bingham was treated as the real owner of the stock from the time of the agreement to take it, in December, 1867, to the settlement in February, 1872, and had the benefit of all the dividends upon it. Neither Mr. Ames nor Mr. Bingham had such records of their dealing as to be able to give the precise amount of those dividends.

MR. WILLIAM D. KELLEY, OF PENNSYLVANIA.

The committee find from the evidence that in the early part of the second session of the Fortieth Congress, and probably in December, 1867, Mr. Ames agreed with Mr. Kelley to sell him ten shares of Credit Mobilier stock at par and interest from July 1, 1867. Mr. Kelley was not then prepared to pay for the stock, and Mr. Ames agreed to carry the stock for him until he could pay for it. On the third day of January, 1868, there was a dividend of 80 per cent. on Credit Mobilier stock in Union Pacific bonds. Mr. Ames received the bonds, as the stock stood in his name, and sold them for 97 per cent. of their face. In June, 1868, there was a cash dividend of 60 per cent., which Mr. Ames also received. The proceeds of the bonds sold, and the cash dividends received by Mr. Ames, amounted to $1,376. The par value of the stock and interest thereon from the previous July amounted to $1,047; so that, after paying for the stock, there was a balance of dividends due Mr. Kelley of $329. On the 23d day of June, 1868, Mr. Ames gave Mr. Kelley a check for that sum on the Sergeant-at-Arms of the House of Representatives, and Mr. Kelley received the money thereon.

The committee find that Mr. Kelley then understood that the money he thus received was a balance of dividends due him after paying for the stock.

All the subsequent dividends upon the stock were either in Union Pacific stock or bonds, and they were all received by Mr. Ames. In September, 1868, Mr. Kelley received from Mr. Ames $750 in money, which was understood between them to be an advance to be paid out of dividends. There has never been any adjustment of the matter between them, and there is now an entire variance in the testimony of the two men as to what the transaction between them was, but the committee are unanimous in finding the facts above stated. The evidence reported to the House gives some subsequent conversations and negotiations between Mr. Kelley and Mr. Ames on this subject. The committee do not deem it material to refer to it in their report.

MR. JAMES A. GARFIELD, OF OHIO.

The facts in regard to Mr. Garfield, as found by the committee, are identical with the case of Mr. Kelley to the point of reception of the check for $329. He agreed with Mr. Ames to take ten shares of Credit Mobilier stock, but did not pay for the same. Mr. Ames received the 80 per cent. dividend in bonds and sold them for 97 per cent., and also received the 60 per cent. cash dividend, which together paid the price of the stock and interest, and left a balance of $329. This sum was paid over to Mr. Garfield by a check on the Sergeant-at-Arms, and Mr. Garfield then understood this sum was the balance of dividends after paying for the stock. Mr. Ames received all the subsequent dividends, and the committee do not find that, since the payment of the $329, there has been any communication between Mr. Ames and Mr. Garfield on the subject until this investigation began. Some correspondence between Mr. Garfield and Mr. Ames, and some conversations between them during this investigation, will be found in the reported testimony.

The committee do not find that Mr. Ames, in his negotiations with the persons above named, entered into any detail of the relations between the Credit Mobilier Company and the Union Pacific Company, or gave them any specific information as to the amount of dividends they would be likely to receive further than has been already stated. They all knew from him, or otherwise, that the Credit Mobilier was a contracting company to build the Union Pacific road, but it does not appear that any of them knew that the profits and dividends were to be in stock and bonds of that company.

The Credit Mobilier Company was a State corporation, not subject to congressional legislation, and the fact that its profits were expected to be derived from building the Union Pacific road did not, apparently, create such an interest in that company as to disqualify the holder of Credit Mobilier stock from participating in any legislation affecting the railroad company. In his negotiations with these members of Congress, Mr. Ames made no suggestion that he desired to secure their favorable influence in Congress in favor of the railroad company, and whenever the question was raised as to whether the ownership of this stock would in any way interfere with or embarrass them in their action as members of Congress, he assured them it would not.

The committee, therefore, do not find, as to the members of the present House above named, that they were aware of the object of Mr. Ames, or that they had any other purpose in taking this stock than to make a profitable investment. It is apparent that those who advanced their money to pay for their stock present more the appearance of ordinary investors than those who did not, but the committee do not feel at liberty to find any corrupt purpose or knowledge founded upon the fact of non-payment alone.

It ought also to be observed that those gentlemen who surrendered their stock to Mr. Ames before there was any public excitement upon the subject, do not profess to have done so upon any idea of impropriety in holding it, but for reasons affecting the value and security of the investment. But the committee believe that they must have felt that there was something so out of the ordinary course of business in the extraordinary dividends they were receiving as to render the investment itself suspicious, and that this was one of the motives of their action.

The committee have not been able to find that any of these members of Congress have been affected in their official action in consequence of their interest in Credit Mobilier stock.

It has been suggested that the fact that none of this stock was transferred to those with whom Mr. Ames contracted was a circumstance from which a sense of impropriety, if not corruption, was to be inferred. The committee believe this is capable of explanation without such inference. The profits of building the road, under the Ames contract, were only to be divided among such holders of Credit Mobilier stock as should come in and become parties to certain conditions set out in the contract of transfer to the trustees, so that a transfer from Mr. Ames to new holders would cut off the right to dividends from the trustees, unless they also became parties to the agreement; and this the committee believe to be the true reason why no transfers were made.

The committee are also of opinion that there was a satisfactory reason for delay on Mr. Ames's part to close settlements with some of these gentlemen for stock and bonds he had received as dividends upon the stock contracted to them. In the fall of 1868 Mr. McComb commenced a suit against the Credit Mobilier Company, and Mr. Ames and others, claiming to be entitled to two hundred and fifty shares of the Credit Mobilier stock upon a subscription for stock to that amount. That suit is still pending. If McComb prevailed in that suit, Mr. Ames might be compelled to surrender so much of the stock assigned to him as trustee, and he was not therefore anxious to have the stock go out of his hands until that suit was terminated. It ought also to be stated that no one of the present members of the House above named appears to have had any knowledge of the dealings of Mr. Ames with other members.

The committee do not find that either of the above-named gentlemen, in contracting with Mr. Ames, had any corrupt motive or purpose himself, or was aware that Mr. Ames had any, nor did either of them suppose he was guilty of any impropriety or even indelicacy in becoming a purchaser of this stock. Had it appeared that these gentlemen were aware of the enormous dividends upon this stock, and how they were to be earned, we could not thus acquit them. And here as well as anywhere, the committee may allude to that subject. Congress had chartered the Union Pacific road, given to it a liberal grant of lands, and promised a liberal loan of Government bonds, to be delivered as fast as sections of the road were completed. As these alone might not be sufficient to complete the road, Congress authorized the company to issue their own bonds for the deficit, and secured them by a mortgage upon the road, which should be a lien prior to that of the Government. Congress never intended that the owners of the road should execute a mortgage on the road prior to that of the Government, to raise money to put into their own pockets, but only to build the road.

The men who controlled the Union Pacific seem to have adopted as the basis of their action the right to incumber the road by a mortgage prior to that of the Government to the full extent, whether the money was needed for the construction of the road or not.

It was clear enough they could not do this directly and in terms, and therefore they resorted to the device of contracting with themselves to build the road, and fix a price high enough to require the issue of bonds to the full extent, and then divide the bonds or the proceeds of them under the name of profits on the contract. All those acting in the matter seem to have been fully aware of this, and that this was to be the effect of the transaction. The sudden rise of value of Credit Mobilier stock was the result of the adoption of this scheme. Any undue and unreasonable profits thus made by themselves were as much a fraud upon the Government as if they had sold their bonds and divided the money without going through the form of denominating them profits on building the road.

Now had these facts been known to these gentlemen, and had they understood they were to share in the proceeds of the scheme, they would have deserved the severest censure.

Had they known only that the profits were to be paid in stock and bonds of the Union Pacific Company, and so make them interested in it, we cannot agree to the doctrine, which has been urged before us and elsewhere, that it was perfectly legitimate for members of Congress to invest in a corporation deriving all its rights from and subject at all times to the action of Congress.

In such case the rules of the House, as well as the rules of decency, would require such member to abstain from voting on any question affecting his interest. But, after accepting the position of a member of Congress, we do not think he has the right to disqualify himself from acting upon subjects likely to come before Congress without some higher and more urgent motive than merely to make a profitable investment. But it is not so much to be feared that in such case an interested member would vote as that he would exercise his influence by personal appeal to his fellow-members, and by other modes, which often is far more potent than a single silent vote.

We do not think any member ought to feel so confident of his own strength as to allow himself to be brought into this temptation. We think Mr. Ames judged shrewdly in saying that a man is much more likely to be watchful of his own interests than those of other people. But there is a broader view still which we think ought to be taken. This country is fast becoming filled with gigantic corporations, wielding and controlling immense aggregations of money, and thereby commanding great influence and power. It is notorious in many State legislatures that these influences are often controlling, so that in effect they become the ruling power of the State. Within a few years Congress has, to some extent, been brought within similar influences, and the knowledge of the public on that subject has brought great discredit upon the body, far more, we believe, than there were facts to justify.

But such is the tendency of the time, and the belief is far too general that all men can be ruled with money, and that the use of such means to carry public measures is legitimate and proper. No member of Congress ought to place himself in circumstances of suspicion, so that any discredit of the body shall arise on his account. It is of the highest importance that the national legislature should be free of all taint of corruption, and it is of almost equal necessity that the people should feel confident that it is so.

In a free government like ours, we cannot expect the people will long respect the laws, if they lose respect for the lawmakers.

For these reasons we think it behooves every man in Congress or in any public position to hold himself aloof, as far as possible, from all such influences, that he may not only be enabled to look at every public question with an eye only to the public good, but that his conduct and motives be not suspected or questioned. The only criticism the committee feel compelled to make on the action of these members in taking this stock is that they were not sufficiently careful in ascertaining what they were getting, and that in their judgment the assurance of a good investment was all the assurance they needed. We commend to them, and to all men, the letter of the venerable Senator Bayard, in response to an offer of some of this stock, found on page 74 of the testimony.

The committee find nothing in the conduct or motives of either of these members in taking this stock, that calls for any recommendation by the committee of the House.

MR. JAMES BROOKS, OF NEW YORK.

The case of Mr. Brooks stands upon a different state of facts from any of those already given. The committee find from the evidence as follows: Mr. Brooks had been a warm advocate of a Pacific Railroad, both in Congress and in the public press. After persons interested in the Union Pacific road had obtained control of the Credit Mobilier charter and organized under it for the purpose of making it a construction company to build the road, Dr. Durant, who was then the leading man in the enterprise, made great efforts to get the stock of the Credit Mobilier taken. Mr. Brooks was a friend of Dr. Durant, and he made some efforts to aid Dr. Durant in getting subscriptions for the stock, introduced the matter to some capitalists of New York, but his efforts were not crowned with success.

During this period Mr. Brooks had talked with Dr. Durant about taking some of the stock for himself, and had spoken of taking fifteen or twenty thousand dollars of it, but no definite contract was made between them, and Mr. Brooks was under no legal obligation to take the stock, or Durant to give it to him. In October, 1867, Mr. Brooks was appointed by the President one of the Government directors of the Union Pacific road. In December, 1867, after the stock of the Credit Mobilier was understood, by those familiar with the affairs between the Union Pacific and the Credit Mibilier, to be worth very much more than par, Mr. Brooks applied to Dr. Durant, and claimed that he should have two hundred shares of Credit Mobilier stock. It does not appear that Mr. Brooks claimed he had any legal contract for stock that he could enforce, or that Durant considered himself in any way legally bound to let him have any, but still, on account of what had been said, and the efforts of Mr. Brooks to aid him, he considered himself under obligations to satisfy Mr. Brooks in the matter.

The stock had been so far taken up, and was then in such demand, that Durant could not well comply with Brooks's demand for two hundred shares. After considerable negotiation, it was finally adjusted between them by Durant's agreeing to let Brooks have one hundred shares of Credit Mobilier stock, and giving him with it $5,000 of Union Pacific bonds, and $20,000 of Union Pacific stock. Dr. Durant testifies that he then considered Credit Mobilier stock worth double the par value, and that the bonds and stock he was to give Mr. Brooks worth about $9,000, so that he saved about $1,000 by not giving Brooks the additional hundred shares he claimed. After the negotiation had been concluded between Mr. Brooks and Dr. Durant, Mr. Brooks said that as he was a Government director of the Union Pacific road, and as the law provided such directors should not be stockholders in that company, he would not hold this stock, and directed Dr. Durant to transfer it to Charles H. Neilson, his son-in-law. The whole negotiation with Durant was conducted by Mr. Brooks himself, and Neilson had nothing to do with the transaction, except to receive the transfer. The $10,000 to pay for the one hundred shares was paid by Mr. Brooks, and he received the $5,000 of Pacific bonds which came with the stock.

The certificate of transfer of the hundred shares from Durant to Neilson is dated December 26, 1867. On the 3d of January, 1868, there was a dividend of 80 per cent. in Union Pacific bonds paid on the Credit Mobilier stock. The bonds were received by Neilson, but passed over at once to Mr. Brooks. It is claimed, both by Mr. Brooks and Neilson, that the $10,000 paid by Mr. Brooks for the stock was a loan of that sum by him to Neilson, and, that the bonds he received from Durant, and those received for the dividend, were delivered and held by him as collateral security for the loan.

No note or obligation was given for the money by Neilson, nor, so far as we can learn from either Brooks or Neilson, was any account or memorandum of the transaction kept by either of them. At the time of the arrangement or settlement above spoken of between Brooks and Durant, there was nothing said about Mr. Brooks being entitled to have 50 per cent. more stock by virtue of his ownership of the hundred shares. Neither Brooks nor Durant thought of any such thing.

Some time after the transfer of the shares to Neilson, Mr. Brooks called on Sidney Dillon, then the president of the Credit Mobilier, and claimed he or Neilson was entitled to fifty additional shares of the stock, by virtue of the purchase of the one hundred shares of Durant.

This was claimed by Mr. Brooks as his right by virtue of the 50 per cent. increase of the stock hereinbefore described. Mr. Dillon said he did not know how that was, but he would consult the leading stockholders, and be governed by them. Mr. Dillon, in order to justify himself in the transaction, got up a paper authorizing the issue of fifty shares of the stock to Mr. Brooks, and procured it to be signed by most of the principal shareholders. After this had been done, an entry of fifty shares was made on the stock-ledger to some person other than Neilson. The name in two places on the book has been erased, and the name of Neilson inserted. The committee are satisfied that the stock was first entered on the books in Mr. Brooks's name.

Mr. Neilson soon after called for the certificate for the fifty shares, and on the 29th of February, 1868, the certificate was issued to him, and the entry on the stock-book was changed to Neilson.

Neilson procured Mr. Dillon to advance the money to pay for the stock, and at the same time delivered to Dillon $4,000 Union Pacific bonds, and fifty shares of Union Pacific stock as collateral security. These bonds and stock were a portion of dividends received at the time, as he was allowed to receive the same per centage of dividends on these fifty shares that had previously been paid on the hundred. This matter has never been adjusted between Neilson and Dillon. Brooks and Neilson both testify they never paid Dillon. Dillon thinks he has received his pay, as he has not now the collaterals in his possession. If he has been paid it is probable that it was from the collaterals in some form. The subject has never been named between Dillon and Neilson since Dillon advanced the money, and no one connected with the transaction seems able to give any further light upon it. The whole business by which these fifty shares were procured was done by Mr. Brooks. Neilson knew nothing of any right to have them, and only went for the certificate when told to do so by Mr. Brooks.

The committee find that no such right to fifty shares additional stock passed by the transfer of the hundred. And from Mr. Brooks's familiarity with the affairs of the company, the committee believe he must have known his claim to them was unfounded. The question naturally arises, How was he able to procure them? The stock at this time by the stockholders was considered worth three or four times its par value. Neilson sustained no relations to any of these people that commanded any favor, and if he could have used any influence he did not attempt it; if he had this right he was unaware of it till told by Mr. Brooks, and left the whole matter in his hands. It is clear that the shares were procured by the sole efforts of Mr. Brooks, and, as the stockholders who consented to it supposed, for the benefit of Mr. Brooks. What power had Mr. Brooks to enforce an unfounded claim, to have for $5,000, stock worth $15,000 or $20,000? Mr. McComb swears that he heard conversation between Mr. Brooks and Mr. John B. Alley, a large stockholder, and one of the executive committee, in which Mr. Brooks urged that he should have the additional fifty shares, because he was or would procure himself to be made a Government director, and also that, being a member of Congress, he "would take care of the democratic side of the House."

Mr. Brooks and Mr. Alley both deny having had any such conversation, or that Mr. Brooks ever made such a statement to Mr. Alley. If, therefore, this matter rested wholly upon the testimony of Mr. McComb, the committee would not feel justified in finding that Mr. Brooks procured the stock by such use of his official position; but all the circumstances seem to point exactly in that direction, and we can find no other satisfactory solution of the question above propounded. Whatever claim Mr. Brooks had to stock, either legal or moral, had been adjusted and satisfied by Dr. Durant. Whether he was getting this stock for himself or to give to his son-in-law, we believe, from the circumstances attending the whole transaction, that he obtained it knowing that it was yielded to its official position and influence, and with the intent to secure his favor and influence in such positions. Mr. Brooks claims that he has had no interest in this stock whatever; that the benefit and advantage of his right to have it he gave to Mr. Neilson, his son-in-law, and that he has had all the dividends upon it. The committee are unable to find this to be the case, for in their judgment all the facts and circumstances show Mr. Brooks to be the real and substantial owner, and that Neilson's ownership is merely nominal and colorable.

In June, 1868, there was a cash dividend of $9,000 upon this one hundred and fifty shares of stock. Neilson received it, of course, as the stock was in his name; but on the same day it was paid over to Mr. Brooks, as Neilson says, to pay so much of the $10,000 advanced by Mr. Brooks to pay for the stock. This, then, repaid all but $1,000 of the loan; but Mr. Brooks continued to hold $16,000 of Union Pacific bonds, which Neilson says he gave him as collateral security, and to draw the interest upon all but $5,000. The interest upon the others, Neilson says, he was permitted to draw and retain, but at one time in his testimony he spoke of the amount he was allowed as being Christmas and New Year's presents. Neilson says that during the last summer he borrowed $14,000 of Mr. Brooks, and he now owes Mr. Brooks nearly as much as the collaterals; but, according to his testimony, Mr. Brooks for four years held $16,000 in bonds as security for $1,000, and received the interest on $11,000 of the collaterals. No accounts appear to have been kept between Mr. Brooks and Neilson, and doubtless what sums he has received from Mr. Brooks, out of the dividends, were intended as presents rather than as deliveries of money belonging to him.

Mr. Brooks's efforts procured the stock; his money paid for it; all the cash dividends he has received; and he holds all the bonds, except those Dillon received, which seem to have been applied toward paying for the fifty shares. Without further comment on the evidence, the committee find that the one hundred and fifty shares of stock appearing on the books of the Credit Mobilier in the name of Neilson were really the stock of Mr. Brooks, and subject to his control, and that it was so understood by both the parties. Mr. Brooks had taken such an interest in the Credit Mobilier Company, and was so connected with Dr. Durant, that he must be regarded as having full knowledge of the relations between that company and the railroad company, and of the contracts between them. He must have known the cause of the sudden increase in value of the Credit Mobilier stock, and how the large expected profits were to be made. We have already expressed our views of the propriety of a member of Congress becoming the owner of stock, possessing this knowledge.

But Mr. Brooks was not only a member of Congress, but he was a Government director of the Union Pacific Company. As such it was his duty to guard and watch over the interests of the Government in the road and to see that they were protected and preserved. To insure such faithfulness on the part of Government directors, Congress wisely provided that they should not be stockholders in the road. Mr. Brooks readily saw that, though becoming a stockholder in the Credit Mobilier was not forbidden by the letter of the law, yet it was a violation of its spirit and essence, and therefore had the stock placed in the name of his son-in-law. The transfer of the Oakes Ames contract to the trustees and the building of the road under that contract, from which the enormous dividends were derived, were all during Mr. Brooks's official life as a Government director, must have been within his knowledge, and yet passed without the slightest opposition from him. The committee believed this could not have been done without an entire disregard of his official obligation and duty, and that while appointed to guard the public interests in the road he joined himself with the promoters of a scheme whereby the Government was to be defrauded, and shared in the spoil.

In the conclusions of fact upon the evidence, the committee are entirely agreed.

In considering what action we ought to recommend to the House upon these facts, the committee encounter a question which has been much debated: Has this House power and jurisdiction to inquire concerning offenses committed by its members prior to their election, and to punish them by censure or expulsion? The committee are unanimous upon the right of jurisdiction of this House over the cases of Mr. Ames and Mr. Brooks, upon the facts found in regard to them. Upon the question of jurisdiction the committee present the following views:

The Constitution, in the fifth section of the first article, defines the power of either House as follows:

" Each House may determine the rules of its proceedings, punish its members for disorderly behavior, and with the concurrence of two-thirds expel a member.'

It will be observed that there is no qualification of the power, but there is an important qualification of the manner of its exercise—it must be done "with the concurrence of two-thirds."

The close analogy between this power and the power of impeachment is deserving of consideration.

The great purpose of the power of impeachment is to remove an unfit and unworthy incumbent from office, and though a judgment of impeachment may to some extent operate as punishment, that is not its principal object. Members of Congress are not subject to be impeached, but may be expelled, and the principal purpose of expulsion is not as punishment, but to remove a member whose character and conduct show that he is an unfit man to participate in the deliberations and decisions of the body, and whose presence in it tends to bring the body into contempt and disgrace.

In both cases it is a power of purgation and purification to be exercised for the public safety, and, in the case of expulsion, for the protection and character of the House. The Constitution defines the causes of impeachment, to wit, "treason, bribery, or other high crimes and misdemeanors." The office of the power of expulsion is so much the same as that of the power to impeach that we think it may be safely assumed that whatever would be a good cause of impeachment would also be a good cause of expulsion.

It has never been contended that the power to impeach for any of the causes enumerated was intended to be restricted to those which might occur after appointment to a civil office, so that a civil officer who had secretly committed such offense before his appointment should not be subject upon detection and exposure to be convicted and removed from office. Every consideration of justice and sound policy would seem to require that the public interests be secured, and those chosen to be their guardians be free from the pollution of high crimes, no matter at what time that pollution had attached.

If this be so in regard to other civil officers, under institutions which rest upon the intelligence and virtue of the people, can it well be claimed that the law-making Representative may be vile and criminal with impunity, provided the evidences of his corruption are found to antedate his election?

In the report made to the Senate by John Quincy Adams in December, 1807, upon the case of John Smith, of Ohio, the following language is used: "The power of expelling a member for misconduct results, on the principles of common sense, from the interests of the nation that the high trust of legislation shall be invested in pure hands. When the trust is elective, it is not to be presumed that the constituent body will commit the deposit to the keeping of worthless characters. But when a man whom his fellow-citizens have honored with their confidence on a pledge of a spotless repution, has degraded himself by the commission of infamous crimes, which become suddenly and unexpectedly revealed to the world, defective indeed would be that institution which should be impotent to discard from its bosom the contagion of such a member; which should have no remedy of amputation to apply until the poison had reached the heart."

The case of Smith was that of a Senator, who, after his election, but not during a session of the Senate, had been involved in the treasonable conspiracy of Aaron Burr. Yet the reasoning is general, and was to antagonize some positions which had been taken in the case of Marshall, a Senator from Kentucky; the Senate in that case having, among other reasons, declined to take jurisdiction of the charge for the reason that the alleged offence had been committed prior to the Senator's election, and was matter cognizable by the criminal courts of Kentucky. None of the commentators upon the Constitution or upon parliamentary law assign any such limitation as to the time of the commission of the offense, or the nature of it, which shall control and limit the power of expulsion. On the contrary they all assert that the power in its very nature is a discretionary one, to be exercised of course with grave circumspection at all times, and only for good cause. Story, Kent, and Sergeant, all seem to accept and rely upon the exposition of Mr. Adams in the Smith case as sound. May, in his Parliamentary Practice, page 59, enumerates the causes for expulsion from Parliament, but he nowhere intimates that the offense must have been committed subsequent to the election.

When it is remembered that the framers of our Constitution were familiar with the parliamentary law of England, and must have had in mind the then recent contest over Wilkes's case, it is impossible to conclude that they meant to limit the discretion of the Houses as to the causes of expulsion. It is a received principle of construction that the Constitution is to be interpreted according to the known rules of law at the time of its adoption, and therefore, when we find them dealing with a recognized subject of legislative authority, and while studiously qualifying and restricting the manner of its exercise, assigning no limitations to the subject-matter itself, they must be assumed to have intended to leave that to be determined according to established principles, as a high prerogative power to be exercised according to the sound discretion of the body. It was not to be apprehended that two-thirds of the Representatives of the people would ever exercise this power in any capricious or arbitrary manner, or trifle with or trample upon constitutional rights. At the same time it could not be foreseen what necessities for self-preservation or self-purification might arise in the legislative body. Therefore it was that they did not, and would not, undertake to limit or define the boundaries of those necessities.

The doctrine that the jurisdiction of the House over its members is exclusively confined to matters arising subsequent to their election, and that the body is bound to retain the vilest criminal as a member if his criminal secret was kept until his election was secured, has been supposed by many to have been established and declared in the famous case of John Wilkes before alluded to. A short statement of that case will show how fallacious is that supposition. Wilkes had been elected a member of Parliament for Middlesex, and in 1764 was expelled for having published a libel on the ministry. He was again elected and again expelled for a similar offense on the 3d of February, 1769. Being again elected on the 17th of February, 1769, the commons passed the following resolution: "That John Wilkes, Esq., having been in this session of Parliament expelled this house was and is incapable of being elected a member to serve in this present Parliament." Wilkes was again elected, but the House of Commons declared the seat vacant and ordered a new election. At this election Wilkes was again elected by 1,143 votes, against 296 for his competitor, Luttrell.

On the 15th of April, 1769, the house decided that by the previous action Wilkes had become ineligible, and that the votes given for him were void and could not be counted, and gave the seat to Luttrell. Subsequently, in 1783, the House of Commons declared the resolution of February 17, 1769, which had asserted the incapacity of an expelled member to be re-elected to the same Parliament, to be subversive of the rights of the electors, and expunged it from the journal. It will be seen from this concise statement of Wilkes's case that the question was not raised as to the power of the house to expel a member for offenses committed prior to his election; the point decided, and afterward most properly expunged, was that expulsion *per se* rendered the expelled member legally ineligible, and that votes cast for him could not be counted. Wilkes's offense was of purely a political character, not involving moral turpitude; he had attacked the ministry in the press, and the proceedings against him in Parliament were then claimed to be a partisan political persecution, subversive of the rights of the people and of the liberty of the press. These proceedings in Wilkes's case took place during the appearance of the famous Junius letters, and several of them are devoted to the discussion of them. The doctrine that expulsion creates ineligibility was attacked and exposed by him with great force. But he concedes that if the cause of expulsion be one that renders a man unfit and unworthy to be a member, he may be expelled for that cause as often as he shall be elected.

The case of Matteson, in the House of Representatives, has also often been quoted as a precedent for this limitation of jurisdiction. In the proceedings and debates of the House upon that case it will be seen that this was one among many grounds taken in the debate; but as the whole subject was ended by being laid on the table, it is quite impossible to say what was decided by the House. It appeared, however, in that case that the charge against Matteson had become public, and his letter upon which the whole charge rested had been published and circulated through his district during the canvass preceding his election. This fact, we judge, had a most important influence in determining the action of the House in his case.

The committee have no occasion in this report to discuss the question as to the power or duty of the House in a case where a constituency, with a full knowledge of the objectionable character of a man, have selected him to be their Representative. It is hardly a case to be supposed that any constituency, with a full knowledge that a man had been guilty of an offense involving moral turpitude, would elect him. The majority of the committee are not prepared to concede such a man could be forced upon the House, and would not consider the expulsion of such a man any violation of the rights of the electors, for while the electors have rights that should be respected, the House as a body has rights also that should be protected and preserved. But that in such case the judgment of the constituency would be entitled to the greatest consideration, and that this should form an important element in its determination, is readily admitted.

It is universally conceded, as we believe, that the House has ample jurisdiction to punish or expel a member for an offense committed during his term as a member, though committed during a vacation of Congress and in no way connected with his duties as a member. Upon what principle is it that such a jurisdiction can be maintained? It must be upon one or both of the following: that the offense shows him to be an unworthy and improper man to be a member, or that his conduct brings odium and reproach upon the body. But suppose the offense has been committed prior to his election, but comes to light afterward, is the effect upon his own character, or the reproach and disgrace upon the body, if they allow him to remain a member, any the less? We can see no difference in principle in the two cases, and to attempt any would be to create a purely technical and arbitrary distinction, having no just foundation. In our judgment, the time is not at all material, except it be coupled with the further fact that he was re-elected with a knowledge on the part of his constituents of what he had been guilty, and in such event we have given our views of the effect.

It seems to us absurd to say that an election has given a man political absolution for an offense which was unknown to his constituents. If it be urged again, as it has sometimes been, that this view of the power of the House, and the true ground of its proper exercise, may be laid hold of and used improperly, it may be answered that no rule, however narrow and limited, that may be adopted can prevent it. If two-thirds of the House shall see fit to expel a man because they do not like his political or religious principles, or without any reason at all, they have the power, and there is no remedy except by appeal to the people. Such exercise of the power would be wrongful, and violative of the principles of the Constitution, but we see no encouragement of such wrong in the views we hold.

It is the duty of each House to exercise its rightful functions upon appropriate occasions, and to trust that those who come after them will be no less faithful to duty, and no less jealous for the rights of free popular representation than themselves. It will be quite time enough to square other cases with right reason and principle when they arise. Perhaps the best way to prevent them will be to maintain strictly public integrity and public honor in all cases as they present themselves. Nor do we imagine that the people of the United States will charge their servants with invading their privileges when they confine themselves to the preservation of a standard of official integrity which the common instincts of humanity recognize as essential to all social order and good government.

The foregoing are the views which we deem proper to submit upon the general question of the jurisdiction of the House over its members. But apart from these general views, the committee are of opinion that the facts found in the present case amply justify the taking jurisdiction over them, for the following reasons:

The subject-matter upon which the action of members was intended to be influenced was of a continuous character, and was as likely to be a subject of congressional action in future Congresses as in the Fortieth. The influences brought to bear on members were as likely to be operative upon them in the future as in the present, and were so intended. Mr. Ames and Mr. Brooks have both continued members of the House to the present time, and so have most of the members upon whom these influences were sought to be exerted. The committee are, therefore, of opinion that the acts of these men may properly be treated as offenses against the present House, and so within its jurisdiction upon the most limited rule.

Two members of the committee, Messrs. Niblack and McCrary, prefer to express no opinion on the general jurisdictional questions discussed in the report, and rest their judgment wholly on the ground last stated.

In relation to Mr. Ames, he sold to several members of Congress stock of the Credit Mobilier Company, at par, when it was worth double that amount or more, with the purpose and intent thereby to influence their votes and decisions upon matters to come before Congress.

The facts found in the report as to Mr. Brooks, show that he used the influence of his official positions as member of Congress and Government director in the Union Pacific Railroad Company, to get fifty shares of the stock of the Credit Mobilier Company, at par, when it was worth three or four times that sum, knowing that it was given to him with intent to influence his votes and decisions in Congress, and his action as a Government director.

The sixth section of the act of February 26, 1853, 10 Stat. United States, 171, is in the following words:

"If any person or persons shall, directly or indirectly, promise, offer, or give, or cause or procure to be promised, offered, or given, any money, goods, right in action, bribe, present, or reward, or any promise, contract, undertaking, obligation, or security for the payment or delivery of any money, goods, right in action, bribe, present, or reward, or any other valuable thing whatever, to any member of the Senate or House of Representatives of the United States, after his election as such member, and either before or after he shall have qualified and taken his seat, or to any officer of the United States, or person holding any place of trust or profit, or discharging any official function under or in connection with any Department of the Government of the United States, or under the Senate or House of Representatives of the United States, after the passage of this act, with intent to influence his vote or decision on any question, matter, cause, or proceeding which may then be pending, or may by law, or under the Constitution of the United States, be brought before him in his official capacity, or in his place of trust or profit, and shall thereof be convicted, such person or persons so offering, promising, or giving, or causing or procuring to be promised, offered, or given, any such money, goods, right in action, bribe, present, or reward, or any promise, contract, undertaking, obligation, or security for the payment or delivery of any money, goods, right in action, bribe, present, or reward, or other valuable thing whatever, and the member, officer, or person who shall in anywise accept or receive the same, or any part thereof, shall be liable to indictment as for a high crime and misdemeanor in any of the courts of the United States having jurisdiction for the trial of crimes and misdemeanors; and shall, upon conviction thereof, be fined not exceeding three times the amount so offered, promised, or given, and imprisoned in the penitentiary not exceeding three years; and the person so convicted of so accepting or receiving the same, or any part thereof, if an officer or person holding any such place of trust or profit as aforesaid, shall forfeit his office or place; and any person so convicted under this section shall forever be disqualified to hold any office of honor, trust, or profit under the United States."

In the judgment of the committee, the facts reported in regard to Mr. Ames and Mr. Brooks would have justified their conviction under the above-recited statute and subjected them to the penalties therein provided.

The committee need not enlarge npon the dangerous character of these offenses. The sense of Congress is shown by the severe penalty denounced by the statute itself. The offenses were not violations of private rights, but were against the very life of a constitutional Government by poisoning the fountain of legislation.

The duty devolved upon the committee has been of a most painful and delicate character. They have performed it to the best of their ability. They have proceeded with the greatest care and deliberation, for while they desired to do their full duty to the House and the country, they were most anxious not to do injustice to any man. In forming their conclusions they have intended to be entirely cool and dispassionate, not to allow themselves to be swerved by any popular fervor on the one hand, or any feeling of personal favor and sympathy on the other.

The committee submit to the House and recommend the adoption of the following resolutions.

"1. Whereas Mr. Oakes Ames, a Representative in this House from the State of Massachusetts, has been guilty of selling to members of Congress shares of stock in the Credit Mobilier of America, for prices much below the true value of such stock, with intent thereby to influence the votes and decisions of such members in matters to be brought before Congress for action: Therefore,

Resolved, That Mr. Oakes Ames be, and he is hereby, expelled from his seat as a member of this House.

2. Whereas Mr. James Brooks, a Representative in this House from the State of New York, did procure the Credit Mobilier Company to issue and deliver to Charles H. Neilson, for the use and benefit of said Brooks, fifty shares of the stock of said company, at a price much below its real value, well knowing that the same was so issued and delivered with intent to influence the votes and decisions of said Brooks, as a member of the House, in matters to be brought before Congress for action, and also to influence the action of said Brooks as a Government director in the Union Pacific Railroad Company: Therefore,

Resolved, That Mr. James Brooks be, and he is hereby, expelled from his seat as a member of this House."

The House, after much discussion, modified the propositions of the committee of investigation, and subjected Oakes Ames and James Brooks to the "absolute condemnation of the House." Both members died within three months thereafter.

The session was full of investigations, but all the others failed to develop any tangible scandals. The Democrats demanded and secured the investigation of the New York custom-house; the United States Treasury; the use of Seneca sandstone; the Chorpenning claim, and the Navy Department, etc. They were, as stated, fruitless.

The "Salary Grab."

At the same session—1871-'73, acts were passed to abolish the franking privilege, to increase the President's salary from $25-000 to $50,000, and that of Senators and Representatives from $5,000 to $7,500. The last proved quite unpopular, and was generally denounced as "The Salary Grab," because of the feature which made it apply to the Congressmen who passed the bill, and of course to go backward to the beginning of the term. This was not new, as earlier precedents were found to excuse it, but the people were nevertheless dissatisfied, and it was made an issue by both parties in the nomination and election of Representatives. Many were defeated, but probably more survived the issue, and are still enjoying public life. Yet the agitation was kept up until the obnoxious feature of the bill and the Congressional increase of salary were repealed, leaving it as now at the rate of $5,000 a year and mileage.

A House committee, headed by B. F. Butler, on Feb. 7th, 1873, made a report which gave a fair idea of the expenses under given circumstances—the increase to be preserved, but the franking privilege and mileage to be repealed. We quote the figures:

Increase of President's salary	$25,000 00
Increase of Cabinet ministers' salary	14,000 00
Increase of salary of judges United States Supreme Court	18,500 00
Increase of salary of Senators, Members, and Delegates	972,000 00
Total increase	$1,029,500 00
Saving to the Government, according to the official statement of the Postmaster-General, per annum, by the abolition of the franking privilege	$2,543,327 72
Saving to the Government by abolition of mileage, stationery, postage, and newspaper accounts (estimated)	200 000 00
	$2,753,327 72
	1,029,500 00
Total net saving	$1,713,827 72

The House passed a bill for the abolition of mileage, but in the Senate it was referred to the Committee on Civil Service and Retrenchment, and not again heard from. So that the increased pay no longer obtains, the franking privilege only to the extent of mailing actual Congressional documents, and mileage remains.

The following curious facts relating to these questions we take from Hon. Edward McPherson's admirable compilation in his "Hand-Book of Politics" for 1874.

Statement of Compensation and Mileage.

Drawn by U. S. Senators under the various Compensation Acts.

Mr. Gorham, Secretary of the Senate, prepared, under date of January 3, 1874, a statement, in answer to a resolution of the Senate, covering these points:

I.—*The several rates of compensation fixed by various laws, and the cases in which the same were retroactive, and for what length of time.*

1. By the act of September 22, 1789, the compensation of Senators and Representatives in Congress was fixed at six dollars a day, and thirty cents a mile for traveling to and from the seat of Government. This rate was to continue until March 4, 1795. The same act fixed the compensation from March 4, 1795, to March 4, 1796, (at which last-named date, by its terms, it expired,) at seven dollars a day, and thirty-five cents a mile for travel. This act was retroactive, extending back six months and eighteen days, namely, to March 4, 1789.

2. The act of March 10, 1796, fixed the compensation at six dollars a day, and thirty cents a mile for travel. (This act extended back over six days only.)

3. The act of March 19, 1816, fixed the compensation at $1,500 a year, "instead of the daily compensation," and left the mileage unchanged. This act was retroactive, extending back one year and fifteen days, namely to March 4, 1815. (This act was repealed by the act of February 6, 1817, but it was expressly declared that no former act was thereby revived.)

4. The act of January 22, 1818, fixed the compensation at eight dollars a day, and forty cents a mile for travel. This act was retroactive, extending back fifty-three days, namely, to the assembling of Congress, December 1, 1817.

5. The act of August 16, 1856, fixed the compensation at $3,000 a year, and left the mileage unchanged. This act was retroactive, extending back one year, five months, and twelve days, namely, to March 4, 1855.

6. The act of July 28, 1866, fixed the compensation at $5,000 a year, and twenty cents a mile for travel, (not to affect mileage accounts already accrued.) This act was retroactive, extending back one year, four months, and twenty-four days, namely, to March 4, 1865.

7. The act of March 3, 1873, fixed the compensation at $7,500 a year, and actual traveling expenses; the mileage already paid for the Forty-Second Congress to be deducted from the pay of those who had received it. This act was retroactive, extending back two years, namely, to March 4, 1871.

NOTE.—Stationery was allowed to Senators and Representatives without any special limit until March 3, 1868, when the amount for stationery and newspapers for each Senator and Member was limited to $125 a session. This was changed by a subsequent act, taking effect July 1, 1869, to $125 a year. The act of 1873 abolished all allowance for stationery and newspapers.

II.—*Names of Senators who drew pay under the retroactive provisions of the several laws, amounts drawn, and dates of same.*

ACT OF 1789.—The records of my office do not furnish the exact information desired under this head concerning the First Congress, the compensation of which was fixed by act of September 22, 1789. It appears, however, that the account of each Senator was made up, and that each received the amount allowed by law. The following is a copy from the record:

January 19, 1790.—That there is due to the Senators of the United States for attendance in Congress the present session, to the 31st of March inclusive, and expenses of travel to Congress, as allowed by law, as follows, to wit:

Messrs. Richard Basset, $496.50; Pierce Butler, $796; Charles Carroll, $186; Tristram Dalton, $612; Oliver Ellsworth, $546.50; Jonathan Elmer, $414; William Few, $833.50; John Henry, $596.50; Benjamin Hawkins, $615; William S. Johnson, $544; Samuel Johnson, $534; Rufus King, $522; John Langdon, $618; William Maclay, $585; Robert Morris, $430.50; William Paterson, $514.50; George Read, $195; Caleb Strong, $575.50; Philip Schuyler, $571.50; Paine Wingate, $616.50.

ACT OF 1816.—The record contains no showing as to the amount paid to Senators under the retroactive provision of the act of March 19, 1816. The following, taken from the books, shows the amount of compensation paid to each Senator for the entire Congress, exclusive of mileage:

Messrs. Eli P. Ashmun, $920; James Barbour, $2,859; William T. Barry, $2,080; William W. Bibb, $2,070; James Brown, $2,980; George W. Campbell, $2,950; Dudley Chace, $3,000; John Condit, $2,980; David Daggett, $3,000; Samuel W. Dana, $2,640; Elegius Fromentin, $3,000; John Gaillard, President, $6,000; Robert H. Goldsborough, $2,840; Christopher Gore, $1,940; Alexander Contee Hanson, $530; Martin D. Hardin, $900; Robert G. Harper, $1,450; Outerbridge Horsey, $3,000; Jeremiah B. Howell, $3,000; William Hunter, $2,930; Rufus King, $2,660; Abner Lacock, $3,000; Nathaniel Macon, $2,946; Jeremiah Mason of New Hampshire, $2,680; Armistead T. Mason of Virginia, $2,360; Jeremiah Morrow, $3,000; James Noble, $920; Jonathan Roberts, $3,000; Benjamin Ruggles, $3,000; Nathan Sanford, $2,720; William Smith, $540; Montfort Stokes, $810; Charles Tait, $3,000; Isham Talbot, $2,730; John Taylor of South Carolina, $1,990; Waller Taylor of Indiana, $920; Thomas W. Thompson, $2,850; Isaac Tichenor, $3,000; George M. Troup, $830; James Turner, $2,060; Joseph B. Varnum, $3,000; William H.

Wells, $2,610; John Williams, $3,000; James J. Wilson, $3,000.

Act of 1818.—Under the retroactive provision of the act of January 22, 1818, the following named Senators drew the amounts for compensation and mileage opposite their respective names:

Messrs. Eli P. Ashmun, $668; James Barbour, $520; James Burril, $762; George W. Campbell, $1,008; John J. Crittenden, $1,007.20; David Daggett, $690.40; Samuel W. Dana, $283.20; Mahlon Dickerson, $628.80; John W. Eppes, $584; James Fisk, $848; Elegius Fromentin, $1,393.60; John Gaillard, $880; Robert H. Goldsborough, $483.20; Outerbridge Horsey, $485.60; William Hunter, $543.20; Henry Johnson, $1,273.60; Rufus King, $627.20; Abner Lacock, $649.60; Walter Leake, $1,384; Nathaniel Macon, $600; David L. Morril, $876; Jeremiah Morrow, $776; James Noble, $918.40; Harrison Gray Otis, $7[illegible]2.80; Jonathan Roberts, $564.80; Benjamin Ruggles, $688; Nathan Sanford, $616; William Smith, $774.40; Montfort Stokes, $745.60; Clement Storer, $875.20; Charles Tait, $952; Isham Talbot, $872; Waller Taylor, $1,080; Isaac Tichenor, $784; George M. Troup, $952;——Van Dyke, $380.80; Thomas H. Williams of Mississippi, $1,433.60; John Williams of Tennessee, $861.60; James J. Wilson, $568.

Act of 1856.—Under the retroactive provision of the act of August 16, 1856, the following named Senators drew the amounts opposite their respective names:

Messrs. Stephen Adams, $2,243.77; Philip Allen, $2,202.79; James A. Bayard, $2,088.03; James Bell, $1,083.93; John Bell, $2,268.36; J. P. Benjamin, $2,210.99; Asa Biggs, $2,161.81; William Bigler, $1,594.24; Jesse D. Bright, president *pro tempore*, $6,772.40; R. Brodhead, $2,251.97; A. G. Brown, $2,251.97; A. P. Butler, $2,202.70; Lewis Cass, $2,251.97; C. C. Clay, jr., $2,251.97; J. M. Clayton, $2,292.95; J. Collamer, $2,219.18; J. J. Crittenden, $2,243.79; H. Dodge, $2,292.95; S. A. Douglas, $2,268.36; C. Durkee, $2,235.56; J. J. Evans, $2,121.70; W. S. Fessenden, $2,276.56; H. Fish, $2,237.28; B. Fitzpatrick, $2,194.59; S. Foot, $2,292.94; L. F. S. Foster, $2,112.62; H. S. Geyer, $2,276.56; J. P. Hale, $887.10; H. Hamlin, $1,989.68; J. Harlan, $2,268.36; S. Houston, $2,292.95; R. M. T. Hunter, 2,210.99; A. Iverson, $2,210.99; C. T. James, $2,210.99; R. W. Johnson, $632.21; G. W. Jones, $2,235.58; J. C. Jones, $2,047.05; S. R. Mallory, $2,276.56; J. M. Mason, $2,170; J. A. Pearce, $2,1[illegible].59; T. G. Pratt, $2,129.02; G. E. Pugh, $2,096.21; D. S. Reid, $2,235.58; T. J. Rusk, $2,292.95; W. K. Sebastian, $2,137.22; W. H. Seward, $2,292.95; John Slidell, $2,276.56; C. E. Stuart, $2,292.95; C. Sumner, $2,292.95; J. B. Thompson, $2,235.57; John R. Thomson, $2,022.46; Robert Toombs, $2,006.07; Isaac Toucey, $2,292.65; L. Trumbull, $2,251.97; B. F. Wade, $2,202.79; J. B. Weller, $2,251 97; H. Wilson, $2,178.20; W. Wright, $2,120.82; D. L. Yulee, $2,194.59.

Act of 1866.—Under the retroactive provision of the act of July 28, 1866, the following named Senators received the amounts opposite their respective names:

Messrs. H. B. Anthony, $2.805 56; B. Gratz Brown, $2,805 56; C. R. Buckalew, $2,805 56; Z. Chandler, $2,805 56; D. Clark, $2,805 56; J. Collamer, $1,366 15; J. Conness, $2,805 56; E. Cowan, $2,805 56; A. H. Cragin, $2,805 56; J. A. J. Creswell, $2,805, 56; G. Davis, $2,805 56; J. Dixon, $2,805 56; J. R. Doolittle, $2,805 56; W. P. Fessenden, $2,805 56; S. Foot, $2,136 76; L. F. S. Foster, President *pro tempore*, $261 93; J. W. Grimes, $2,805 56; J. Guthrie, $2,805 56; I. Harris, $2,805 56; J. B. Henderson, $2,805 56; T. A. Hendricks, $2,805.56; J. M. Howard, $2,805 56; T. O. Howe, $2,805 56; R. Johnson, $2,805 56; H. S. Lane, $2,805 56; J. H. Lane, $2,710 49; James A. McDougall, $2,805 56; E. D. Morgan, $2,805 56; L. M. Morrill, $2,805 56; J. W. Nesmith, $2,805 56; D. S. Norton, $2,805 56; J. W. Nye, $2,805 56; S. C. Pomeroy, $2, 805 56; A. Ramsey, $2,805 56; G. R. Riddle, $2,805 56; W. Saulsbury, $2,805 56; J. Sherman, $2,805 56; W. M. Stewart, $2,805 56; C. Sumner, $2,805 56; L. Trumbull, $2,805 56; P. G. VanWinkle, $2,805 56; B. Wade, $2,805 56; W. T. Willey, $2,805 56; G. H. Williams, $2,805 56; H. Wilson, $2,805 56; W. Wright, $2,805 56; R. Yates, $2,805 56; J. Harlan, $350; L. P. Poland, $1,361; John P. Stockton, $2,131 20; S. J. Kirkwood, $2,361 10; G. F. Edmunds, $666 66; E. G. Ross, $180 40.

Act of 1873.—Under the retroactive provision of the act of March 3, 1873, the following named Senators received the sums set opposite their respective names:

Messrs. A. Ames, $2,840; J. L. Alcorn, $2,312 39; J. T. Bayard, $4,865 60; F. P. Blair, $3,761 60; A. I. Boreman, $4,514; W. G. Brownlow, $4,588; A. Caldwell, $2,647 60; S. Cameron, $4,856; M. H. Carpenter, $3,887 60; E. Casserly, $970 40; Z. Chandler, $3,906 80; P. Clayton, $2,600; C. Cole, $970 40; H. Cooper, $3,760; H. G. Davis, $4,635 20; O. S. Ferry, $4,652; T. W. Ferry, $3,920; J. W. Flanagan, $2,000; A. Gilbert, $3,680; George Goldthwaite, $3,924 80; M. C. Hamilton, $2,480; Joshua Hill, $4,083 20; P. W. Hitchcock, $2,852 80; T. O. Howe, $3,689 60, J. W. Johnston, $4,705 60; John T. Lewis, $4,804 40; John A. Logan, $3,800; W. B. Machen, $552 98; L. M. Morrill, $4,190; J. S. Morrill, (draft in favor of the treasurer of the State of Vermont,) $4,386 80; T. M. Norwood, $4,169 60; J. W. Nye, $2,076 80; T. W. Osborn, $3,440; J. W. Patterson, $4,280; S. C. Pomeroy, $3,320; John Pool, $4,620 80; M. W. Ransom, $4,817 60; B. F. Rice, $3,200; T. J. Robertson, $4,374 80; F. A. Sawyer, $4,294 40; George E. Spencer, $4,106; W. Sprague, $4,508; W. M. Stewart, $1,486 40; J. P. Stockton, $4,790; T. W. Tipton, $3,358; Lyman Trumbull, $3,980; G. Vickers, $4,880; J. R. West, $2,468 80.

III.—*Names of Senators who covered into the Treasury amounts due them under retroactive provisions of law, with date of such action.*

There is no record in my office showing that any Senator covered into the Treasury any money to which he was entitled by the retroactive provisions of either of the acts of September 22, 1789, March 19, 1816, January 22, 1818, August 16, 1856, or July 28, 1866.

The following Senators covered into the Treasury the amounts due them under the retroactive provision of the act of March 3, 1873, namely:

1873.—May 26, H. B. Anthony, $4,497 20; June 23, W. A. Buckingham, $4,553 60; May 21, R. E. Fenton, $4,184; June 2, F. T. Frelinghuysen, $4,644 80; May 19, H. Hamlin, $4,136; August 14, O. P. Morton, $3,922 40; April 9, D. D. Pratt, $4,121 60; August 25, A. Ramsey, $3,041 40; March 28, C. Schurz, $3,761 60; May 9, John Scott, $4,733 06; July 11, John Sherman, $4,336 40; May 2, C. Sumner, $4,445 60; May 22, A. G. Thurman, $4,359 20; March 28, Henry Wilson, $4,448; September 6, George G. Wright, $3,140 80.

NOTE.—Several of these Senators, as well as others who have not either drawn or covered into the Treasury the amounts due them under the retroactive provision of the act of 1873, expressed to me their intention to allow the money to lapse into the Treasury by the ordinary operation of law, which they supposed would occur July 3, 1873. After learning that it could not be covered in, except by their order, before July 3, 1875, some gave me written instructions to anticipate the latter date. I am unable to furnish from any information in my office the names of Senators who themselves paid into the Treasury salary drawn under the act of 1873 or previous acts. I have not furnished the names of Senators who have left increased salary undrawn, as this information was not called for in the resolution.

IV.—*A Comparative Statement.*

Total compensation and allowance of Senators, under act of July 28, 1866, from March 4, 1871, to March 3, 1872: Compensation, $370,000; mileage, $37,041 20; stationery and newspapers, $9,250; total, $416,291 20; average per Senator, $5,625 55$\frac{45}{74}$.

Under same act, from March 4, 1872, to March 3, 1873, during which year members of the Senate received mileage for attending the special session of the Senate, held in May, 1872, the following amounts were paid: Compensation, $370,000; mileage, $59,002 80; newspapers and stationery, $9,250; total, $438,252 80; average per Senator, $5,922 23$\frac{1}{3}\frac{8}{7}$.

Total compensation and allowance of Senators under act of March 3, 1873: Compensation, $555,000; traveling expenses, based upon the certificates of forty-six Senators, (twenty-eight having presented none,) amounting to $4,607 95, giving an average of $100 17x74=$7,412 58; total, $562,412 58; average per Senator, $7,600 17.

In connection with this were statements, prepared by the Secretary of the Senate, and laid before that body by Senator CAMERON, January 9, 1874, of the amounts of mileage paid in dollars (cents omitted) at particular dates under the acts of 1856 and 1866, are given. The act of 1856 fixed mileage at forty cents per mile each way, and the act of 1866 fixed it at twenty cents per mile each way.

Returning Boards.

At the second session of the 42d Congress that body, and the President as well, were compelled to consider a new question in connection with politics—an actual conflict of State Governments. There had always been, in well regulated State governments, returning boards, but with a view the better to guard the newly enfranchised citizens of the South from intimidation, the Louisiana Republicans, under very bold and radical leaders, had greatly strengthened the powers of her returning boards. It could canvass the votes, reject the returns in part or as a whole of parishes where force or fraud had been used, and could declare results after such revision. The Governor of Louisiana had made several removals and appointments of State officers for the purpose mainly of making a friendly majority in the returning board, and this led to the appointment of two bodies, both claiming to be the legitimate returning board. There soon followed two State governments and legislatures, the Democratic headed by Governor John McEnery, the Republican by Governor Wm. Pitt Kellogg, later in the U. S. Senate. Kellogg brought suit against the Democratic officers before Judge Durell, of the Federal District Court, and obtained an order that the U. S. Marshal (S. B. Packard, afterwards Governor), should seize the State House and prevent the meetings of the McEnery legislature. Then both governments were hastily inaugurated, and claimed the recognition of Congress. The Senate Committee reported that Judge Durell's decision was not warranted, but the report refused a decisive recognition of either government. A bill was introduced declaring the election of Nov. 4, 1872, on which this condition of affairs was based, null and void, and providing for a new election, but this bill was defeated by a close vote. Later on, Louisiana claimed a large share in National politics. Somewhat similar troubles occurred in Alabama, Arkansas, and Texas, but they were settled with far greater ease than those of Louisiana. The correspondence in all of these cases was too voluminous to reproduce here, and we shall dismiss the subject until the period of actual hostilities were reached in Louisiana.

The Grangers.

So early as 1867 a secret society had been formed first in Washington, known as the Patrons of Husbandry, and it soon succeeded in forming subordinate lodges or granges in Illinois, Wisconsin, and other States. It was declared not to be political; that its object was co-operation among farmers in purchasing supplies from first hands, so as to do away with middle-men, but, like many other secret organizations, it was soon perverted to political purposes, and for a time greatly disturbed the political parties of the Western States. This was especially true of the years 1873–74, when the Grangers announced a contemplated war on railroad corporations, and succeeded in carrying the legislatures of Illinois and Wisconsin, and inducing them subsequently to pass acts, the validity of which the Supreme Courts of the State, under a temporary popular pressure which was apparently irresistible, could not sustain. The effect of these laws was to almost bankrupt the Illinois Central, theretofore wealthy, to cripple all railroads, to interfere largely with foreign exports, and to react against the interests of the people of the States passing them, that the demand for repeal was soon very much greater than the original demand for passage. As these laws, though repealed, are still often referred to in the discussion of political and corporate questions, we give the text of one of them:

Illinois Railroad Act of 1873.

An Act to prevent extortion and unjust discrimination in the rates charged for the transportation of passengers and freights on railroads in this State, and to punish the same, and prescribe a mode of procedure and rules of evidence in relation thereto, and to repeal an act entitled "An act to prevent unjust discrimination and extortions in the rates to be charged by the different railroads in this State for the transportation of freights on said roads," approved April 7, A. D. 1871.

SECTION 1. *Be it enacted by the People of the State of Illinois, represented in the General Assembly,* If any railroad corporation, organized or doing business in this State under any act of incorporation, or general law of this State now in force, or which may hereafter be enacted, or any railroad corporation organized or which may hereafter be organized under the laws of any other State, and doing business in this State, shall charge, collect, demand, or receive more than a fair and reasonable rate of toll or compensation for the transportation of passengers or freight of any description, or for the use and transportation of any railroad car upon its track, or any of the branches thereof, or upon any railroad within this State which it has the right, license, or permission to use, operate, or control, the same shall be deemed guilty of extortion, and upon conviction thereof shall be dealt with as hereinafter provided.

SEC. 2. If any such railroad corporation aforesaid shall make any unjust discrimination in its rates or charges of toll, or compensation, for the transportation of passengers or freight of any description, or for the use and transportation of any railroad car upon its said road, or upon any of the branches thereof, or upon railroads connected therewith, which it has the right, license, or permission to operate, control, or use, within this State, the same shall be deemed guilty of having violated the provisions of this act, and upon conviction thereof shall be dealt with as hereinafter provided.

SEC. 3. If any such railroad corporation shall charge, collect, or receive for the transportation of any passenger, or freight of any description, upon its railroad, for any distance within this State, the same or a greater amount of toll or compensation than is at the same time charged, collected, or received for the transportation, in the same direction, of any passenger, or like quantity of freight of the same class, over a greater distance of the same railroad; or if it shall charge, collect, or receive at any point upon this railroad a higher rate of toll or compensation for receiving, handling, or delivering freight of the same class and quantity than it shall at the same time charge, collect, or receive at any other point upon the same railroad; or if it shall charge, collect or receive for the transportation of any passenger, or freight of any description, over its railroad a greater amount as toll or compensation than shall at the same time be charged, collected, or received by it for the transportation of any passenger or like quantity of freight of the same class, being transported in the same direction over any portion of the same railroad of equal distance; or if it shall charge, collect, or receive from any person or persons a higher or greater amount of toll or compensation than it shall at the same time charge, collect, or receive from any other person or persons for receiving, handling, or delivering freight of the same class and like quantity at the same point upon its railroad; or if it shall charge, collect, or receive from any person or persons for the transportation of any freight upon its railroad a higher or greater rate of toll or compensation than it shall at the same time charge, collect, or receive from any other person or persons for the transportation of the like quantity of freight of the same class being transported from the same direction over equal distances of the same railroad; or if it shall charge, collect, or receive from any person or persons for the use and transportation of any railroad car or cars upon its railroad for any distance the same or a greater amount of toll or compensation than is at the same time charged, collected, or received from any person or persons for the use and transportation of any railroad car of the same class or number, for a like purpose, being transported in the same direction over a greater distance of the same railroad; or if it shall charge, collect, or receive from any person or persons for the use and transportation of any railroad car or cars upon its railroad a higher or greater rate of toll or compensation than it shall at the same time charge, collect, or receive from any other person or persons for the use and transportation of any railroad car or cars of the same class or number, for a like purpose, being transported from the same point in the same direction over an equal distance of the same railroad; all such discriminating rates, charges, collections, or receipts, whether made directly or by means of any rebate, drawback, or other shift or evasion, shall be deemed and taken against such railroad corporation as *prima facie* evidence of the unjust discriminations prohibited by the provisions of this act, and it shall not be deemed a sufficient excuse or justification of such discriminations on the part of such railroad corporation, that the railway station or point at which it shall charge, collect, or receive the same or less rates of toll or compensation for the transportation of such passenger or freight, or for the use and transportation of such railroad car the greater distance than for the shorter distance, is a railway station or point at which there exists competition with any other railroad or means of transportation. This section shall not be construed so as to exclude other evidence tending to show any unjust discrimination in freight and passenger rates. The provisions of this section shall extend and apply to any railroad, the branches thereof, and any road or roads which any railroad corporation has the right, license, or permission to use, operate, or control, wholly or in part, within the State: *Provided, however*, That nothing herein contained shall be so construed as to prevent railroad corporations from issuing commutation, excursion, or thousand mile tickets, as the same are now issued by such corporations.

SEC. 4. Any such railroad corporation guilty of extortion, or of making any unjust discrimination as to passenger or freight rates, or the rates for the use and transportation of railroad cars, or in receiving, handling, or delivering freights shall, upon conviction thereof, be fined in any sum not less than one thousand dollars ($1,000) nor more than five thousand dollars ($5,000) for the first offense; and for the second offense not less than five thousand dollars ($5,000) nor more than ten thousand dollars ($10,000;) and for the third offense not less than ten thousand dollars ($10,000) nor more than twenty thousand dollars ($20,000;) and for every subsequent offense and conviction thereof shall be liable to a fine of twenty-five thousand dollars ($25,000:) *Provided*, That in all cases under this act either party shall have the right of trial by jury.

SEC. 5. The fines hereinbefore provided for may be recovered in an action of debt in the name of the people of the State of Illinois, and there may be several counts joined in the same declaration as to extortion and unjust discrimination, and as to passenger and freight rates, and rates for the use and transportation of railroad cars, and for receiving, handling, or delivering freights. If, upon the trial of any case instituted under this act, the jury shall find for the people, they shall assess and return with their verdict the amount of the fine to be imposed upon the defendant, at any sum not less than one thousand dollars ($1,000) nor more than five thousand dollars ($5,000,) and the court shall render judgment accordingly; and if the jury shall find for the people, and that the defendant has been once before convicted of a violation of the provisions of this act, they shall return such finding with their verdict, and shall assess and return with their verdict the amount of the fine to be imposed upon the defendant, at any sum not less than five thousand dollars ($5,000) nor more than ten thousand dollars ($10,000,) and the court shall render judgment accordingly; and if the jury shall find for the people, and that the defendant has been twice before convicted of a violation of the provisions of this act, with respect to extortion or unjust discrimination, they shall return such finding with their verdict, and shall assess and return with their verdict the amount of the fine to be imposed upon the defendant, at any sum not less than ten thousand dollars ($10,000) nor more than twenty thousand dollars ($20,000;) and in like manner for every subsequent offense and conviction such defendant shall be liable to a fine of twenty-five thousand dollars ($25,000.) *Provided*, That in all cases under the provisions of this act a preponderance of evidence in favor of the people shall be sufficient to authorize a verdict and judgment for the people.

SEC. 6. If any such railroad corporation shall, in violation of any of the provisions of this act, ask, demand, charge, or receive of any person or corporation, any extortionate charge or charges for the transportation of any passengers, goods, merchandise, or property, or for receiving, handling, or delivering freights, or shall make any unjust discrimination against any person or corporation in its charges therefor, the person or corporation so offended against may for each offense recover of such railroad corporation, in any form of action, three times the amount of the damages sustained by the party aggrieved, together with cost of suit and a reasonable attorney's fee, to be fixed by the court where the same is heard, on appeal or otherwise, and taxed as a part of the costs of the case.

SEC. 7. It shall be the duty of the railroad and warehouse commissioners to personally investigate and ascertain whether the provisions of this act are violated by any railroad corporation in this State, and to visit the various stations upon the line of each railroad for that purpose, as often as practicable; and whenever the facts in any manner ascertained by said commissioners shall in their judgment warrant such prosecution, it shall be the duty of said commissioners to immediately cause suits to be commenced and prosecuted against any railroad corporation which may violate the provisions of this act. Such suits and prosecutions may be instituted in any county in the State, through or into which the line of the railroad corporation sued for violating this act may extend. And such railroad and warehouse commissioners are hereby authorized, when the facts of the case presented to them shall, in their judgment, warrant the commencement of such action, to employ counsel to assist the Attorney General in conducting such suit on behalf of the State. No such suits commenced by said commissioners shall be dismissed, except said railroad and warehouse commissioners and the Attorney General shall consent thereto.

SEC. 8. The railroad and warehouse commissioners are hereby directed to make for each of the railroad corporations doing business in this State, as soon as practicable, a schedule of reasonable maximum rates of charges for the transportation of passengers and freight and cars on each of said railroads; and said schedule shall, in all suits brought against any such railroad corporations, wherein is in any way involved the charges of any such railroad corporation for the transportation of any passenger or freight or cars, or unjust discrimination in relation thereto, be deemed and taken, in all courts of this State, as *prima facie* evidence that the rates therein fixed are reasonable maximum rates of charges for the transportation of passengers and freights and cars upon the railroads for which said schedules may have been respectively prepared. Said commissioners shall, from time to time, and as often as circumstances may require, change and revise said schedules. When such schedules shall have been made or revised as aforesaid, it shall be the duty of said commissioners to cause publication thereof to be made for three successive weeks, in some public newspaper published in the city of Springfield in this state: "*Provided*, That the schedules thus prepared shall not be taken as *prima facie* evidence as herein provided until schedules shall have been prepared and published as aforesaid for all the railroad companies now organized under the laws of this State, and until the fifteenth day of January, A. D. 1874, or until ten days after the meeting of the next session of this General Assembly, provided a session of the General Assembly shall be held previous to the fifteenth day of January aforesaid." All such schedules, purporting to be printed and published as aforesaid, shall be received and held, in all such suits, as *prima facie* the schedules of said commissioners, without further proof than the production of the paper in which they were published, together with the certificate of the publisher of said paper that the schedule therein contained is a true copy of the schedule furnished for publication by said commissioners, and that it has been published the above specified time; and any such paper purporting to have been published at said city, and to be a public newspaper, shall be presumed to have been so published at the date thereof, and to be a public newspaper.

SEC. 10. In all cases under the provisions of this act, the rules of evidence shall be the same as in other civil actions, except as hereinbefore otherwise provided. All fines recovered under the provisions of this act shall be paid into the county treasury of the county in which the suit is tried, by the person collecting the same, in the manner now provided by law, to be used for county purposes. The remedies hereby given shall be regarded as cumulative to the remedies now given by law against railroad corporations, and this act shall not be construed as repealing any statute giving such remedies. Suits commenced under the provisions of this act shall have precedence over all other business, except criminal business.

SEC. 11. The term "railroad corporation," contained in this act, shall be deemed and taken to mean all corporations, companies, or individuals now owning or operating, or which may hereafter own or operate any railroad, in whole or in part, in this State; and the provisions of this act shall apply to all persons, firms, and companies, and to all associations of persons, whether incorporated or otherwise, that shall do business as common carriers upon any of the lines of railways in this State (street railways excepted) the same as to railroad corporations thereinbefore mentioned.

SEC. 12. An act entitled "An act to prevent unjust discriminations and extortions in the rates to be charged by the different railroads in this State for the transportation of freight on said roads," approved April 7, A. D. 1871, is hereby repealed, but such repeal shall not affect nor repeal any penalty incurred or right accrued under said act prior to the time this act takes effect, nor any proceedings or prosecutions to enforce such rights or penalties.

Approved May 2, 1873.

S. M. CULLOM,
Speaker House of Representatives.

JOHN EARLY,
President of the Senate.

JOHN L. BEVERIDGE,
Governor.

The same spirit, if not the same organization, led to many petitions to Congress for the regulation of inter-state commerce and freight rates, and to some able reports on the subject. Those which have commanded most attention were by Senator Windom of Minnesota and Representative Reagan of Texas, the latter being the author of a bill which commanded much consideration from Congress in the sessions of 1878–'80, but which has not yet secured favorable action. In lieu of such bill Senator Cameron, of Pennsylvania, introduced a joint resolution for the appointment of a Commission to investigate and report upon the entire question. Final action has not yet been taken, and at this writing interest in the subject seems to have flagged.

The disastrous political action attempted by the Grangers in Illinois and Wisconsin, led to such general condemnation that subsequent attempts were abandoned save in isolated cases, and as a rule the society has passed away. The principle upon which it was based was wholly unsound, and if strictly carried out, would destroy all home improvements and enterprise. Parties and societies based upon a class, and directed or perverted toward political objects, are very happily short-lived in this Republic of ours. If they could thrive, the Republic could not long endure.

Supplementary Civil Rights Bill.

Senator Sumner's Supplementary Civil Rights Bill was passed by the second session of the 43d Congress, though its great author had died the year before—March 11th, 1874. The text of the Act is given in Book V. of this volume, on Existing Political Laws. Its validity was sustained by the U. S. District Courts in their instructions to grand juries. The first conviction under the Act was in Philadelphia, in February, 1876. Rev. Fields Cook, pastor of the Third Baptist colored church of Alexandria, Virginia, was refused sleeping and eating accommodations at the Bingham House, by Upton S. Newcomer, one of its clerks; and upon the trial of the case, in the U. S. District Court, JOHN CADWALADER, Judge, instructed the jury as follows:

The fourteenth amendment of the Constitution of the United States makes all persons born or naturalized in the United States, and subject to the jurisdiction thereof, citizens of the United States, and provides that no State shall make or enforce any law which shall abridge the privileges or immunities of citizens of the United States; nor shall any State * * * deny to any person within its jurisdiction the equal protection of the laws. This amendment expressly gives to Congress the power to enforce it by appropriate legislation. An act of Congress of March 1, 1875, enacts that all persons within the jurisdiction of the United States shall be entitled to the full and equal enjoyment of the accommodations, advantages, facilities and privileges of inns, public conveyances on land or water, theatres and other places of public amusement, subject only to the conditions and limitations established by law, and applicable alike to citizens of every race and color, and makes it a criminal offense to violate these enactments by denying to any citizen, except for reasons by law applicable to citizens of every race and color, * * * the full enjoyment of any of the accommodations, advantages, facilities or privileges enumerated. As the law of Pennsylvania had stood until the 22d of March, 1867, it was not wrongful for innkeepers or carriers by land or water to discriminate against travelers of the colored race to such an extent as to exclude them from any part of the inns or public conveyances which was set apart for the exclusive accommodation of white travelers. The Legislature of Pennsylvania, by an act of 22d of March, 1867, altered the law in this respect as to passengers on railroads. But the law of the State was not changed as to inns by any act of the State Legislature. Therefore, independently of the amendment of the Constitution of the United States and of the act of Congress now in question, the conduct of the defendant on the occasion in question might, perhaps, have been lawful. It is not necessary to express an opinion upon this point, because the decision of the case depends upon the effect of this act of Congress. I am under opinion that under the Fourteenth Amendment of the Constitution the enactment of this law was within the legislative power of Congress, and that we are bound to give effect to the act of Congress according to its fair meaning. According to this meaning of the act I am of opinion that if this defendant, being in charge of the business of receiving travelers in this inn, and of providing necessary and proper accommodations for them in it, refused such accommodations to the witness Cook, then a traveler, by reason of his color, the defendant is guilty in manner and form as he stands indicted. If the case depended upon the unsupported testimony of this witness alone, there might be some reason to doubt whether this defendant was the person in charge of this part of the business. But under this head the additional testimony of Mr. Annan seems to be sufficient to remove all reasonable doubt. If the jury are convinced of the defendant's identity, they will consider whether any reasonable doubt of his conduct or motives in refusing the accommodations to Fields Cook can exist. The case appears to the court to be proved; but this question is for the jury, not for the court. If the jury have any reasonable doubt, they should find the defendant not guilty; otherwise they will find him guilty.

The jury brought in a verdict of guilty, March 1, 1876, and the Court imposed a fine of $500.

The Morton Amendment.

In the session of '73, Senator Morton, of Indiana, introduced an amendment to the Constitution providing for the general choice of Presidential Electors by Congressional districts, and delivered several speeches on the subject which attracted much attention at the time. Since then many amendments have been introduced on the subject, and it is a matter for annual discussion. We quote the Morton Amendment as the one most likely to command favorable action:

"*Resolved by the Senate and House of Representatives of the United States of America in Congress assembled*, (two-thirds of each House concurring therein:) That the following article is hereby proposed as an amendment to the Constitution of the United States, and, when ratified by the Legislatures of three-fourths of the several States, shall be valid, to all intents and purposes, as a part of the Constitution, to wit:

"ARTICLE —.

"I. The President and Vice-President shall be elected by the direct vote of the people in the manner following: Each State shall be divided into districts, equal in number to the number of Representatives to which the State may be entitled in the Congress, to be composed of contiguous territory, and to be as nearly equal in population as may be; and the person having the highest number of votes in each district for President shall receive the vote of that district, which shall count one presidential vote.

"II. The person having the highest number of votes for President in a State shall receive two presidential votes from the State at large.

"III. The person having the highest number of presidential votes in the United States shall be President.

"IV. If two persons have the same number of votes in any State, it being the highest number, they shall receive each one presidential vote from the State at large; and if more than two persons shall have each the same number of votes in any State, it being the highest number, no presidential vote shall be counted from the State at large. If more persons than one shall have the same number of votes, it being the highest number in any district, no presidential vote shall be counted from that district.

"V. The foregoing provisions shall apply to the election of Vice-President.

"VI. The Congress shall have power to provide for holding and conducting the elections of President and Vice-President, and to establish tribunals for the decision of such elections as may be contested."

VII. The States shall be divided into districts by the legislatures thereof, but the Congress may at any time by law make or alter the same.

The present mode of election is given in Book V. of this volume.

The Whisky Ring.

During 1875 an extensive Whisky Ring, organized to control revenue legislation and avoidance of revenue taxes, was discovered in the West. It was an association of distillers in collusion with Federal officers, and for a time it succeeded in defrauding the government of the tax on distilled spirits. This form of corruption, after the declaration by President Grant—"let no guilty man escape"—was traced by detectives to the portals of the White House, but even partisan rancor could not connect the President therewith. O. E. Babcock, however, was his private Secretary, and upon him was charged complicity with the fraud. He was tried and acquitted, but had to resign. Several Federal officers were convicted at St. Louis.

Impeachment of Belknap.

Another form of corruption was discovered in 1876, when the House impeached Wm. W. Belknap, the Secretary of War, on the charge of selling an Indian trading establishment. The first and main specification was, that—

On or about the second day of November, eighteen hundred and seventy, said William W. Belknap, while Secretary of War as aforesaid, did receive from Caleb P. Marsh fifteen hundred dollars, in consideration of his having appointed said John S. Evans to maintain a trading-establishment at Fort Sill aforesaid, and for continuing him therein.

The following summary of the record shows the result, and that Belknap escaped punishment by a refusal of two-thirds to vote "guilty:"

The examination of witnesses was begun, and continued on various days, till July 26, when the case was closed.

August 1.—The SENATE voted. On the first article, thirty-five voted guilty, and twenty-five not guilty. On the second, third and fourth, Mr. MAXEY made the thirty-sixth who voted guilty. On the fifth, Mr. MORTON made the thirty-seventh who voted guilty. The vote on first was:

VOTING GUILTY — Messrs. *Bayard*, BOOTH, Cameron of Pennsylvania, *Cockrell*, *Cooper*, *Davis*, Dawes, *Dennis*, Edmunds, *Gordon*, Hamilton, Harvey, Hitchcock, *Kelly*, *Kernan*, *Key*, *McCreery*, *McDonald*, *Merrimon*, Mitchell, Morrill of Vermont, *Norwood*, Oglesby, *Randolph*, *Ransom*, Robertson, Sargent, *Saulsbury*, Sherman, *Stevenson*, *Thurman*, Wadleigh, *Wallace*, *Whyte*, *Withers*—35.

VOTING NOT GUILTY—Messrs. Allison, Anthony, Boutwell, Bruce, Cameron of Wisconsin, Christiancy, Conkling, Conover, Cragin, Dorsey, *Eaton*, Ferry of Michigan, Frelinghuysen, Hamlin, Howe, Ingalls, Jones of Nevada, Logan, McMillan, Paddock, Patterson, Spencer, West, Windom, Wright—25.

Mr. JONES of Florida declined to vote. Those "voting not guilty" generally denied jurisdiction, and so voted accordingly. Belknap had resigned and the claim was set up that he was a private citizen.

The White League.

By 1874 the Democrats of the South, who then generally classed themselves as Conservatives, had gained control of all the State governments except those of Louisiana, Florida and South Carolina. In nearly all, the Republican governments had called upon President Grant for military aid in maintaining their positions, but this was declined except in the presence of such outbreak as the proper State authorities could not suppress. In Arkansas, Alabama, Mississippi, and Texas, Grant declined to interfere save to cause the Attorney General to give legal advice. The condition of all these governments demanded constant attention from the Executive, and his task was most difficult and dangerous. The cry came from the Democratic partisans in the South for home-rule; another came from the negroes that they were constantly disfranchised, intimidated and assaulted by the White League, a body of men organized in the Gulf States for the purpose of breaking up the "carpet-bag governments." So conflicting were the stories, and so great the fear of a final and destructive war of races, that the Congressional elections in the North were for the first time since the war greatly influenced. The Forty-fourth Congress, which met in December, 1875, had been changed by what was called "the tidal wave," from Republican to Democratic, and M. C. Kerr, of Indiana, was elected Speaker. The Senate remained Republican with a reduced margin.

The troubles in the South, and especially in Louisiana, had been in the year previous and were still of the gravest character. Gen'l Sheridan had been sent to New Orleans and on the 10th of January, 1875, made a report which startled the country as to the doings of the White League. As it still remains a subject for frequent quotation we give its text:

SHERIDAN'S REPORT.

NEW ORLEANS, January 10, 1875.

HON. W. W. BELKNAP, *Secretary of War:*

Since the year 1866, nearly thirty-five hundred persons, a great majority of whom were colored men, have been killed and wounded in this State. In 1868 the official record shows that eighteen hundred and eighty-four were killed and wounded. From 1868 to the present time, no official investigation has been made, and the civil authorities in all but a few cases have been unable to arrest, convict and punish perpetrators. Consequently, there are no correct records to be consulted for information. There is ample evidence, however, to show that more than twelve hundred persons have been killed and wounded during this time, on account of their political sentiments. Frightful massacres have occurred in the parishes of Bossier, Caddo, Catahoula, Saint Bernard, Saint Landry, Grant and Orleans. The general character of the massacres in the above named parishes is so well known that it is unnecessary to describe them. The isolated cases can best be illustrated by the following instances which I have taken from a mass of evidence now lying before me of men killed on account of their political principles. In Natchitoches Parish, the number of isolated cases reported is thirty-three. In the parish of Bienville, the number of men killed is thirty. In Red River Parish the number of isolated cases of men killed is thirty-four. In Winn Parish the number of isolated cases where men were killed is fifteen. In Jackson Parish the number killed is twenty; and in Catahoula Parish the number of isolated cases reported where men were killed is fifty; and most of the country parishes throughout the State will show a corresponding state of affairs. The following statement will illustrate the character and kind of these outrages. On the 29th of August, 1874, in Red River Parish, six State and parish officers, named Twitchell, Divers, Holland, Howell, Edgerton and Willis, were taken, together with four negroes, under guard, to be carried out of the State, and were deliberately murdered on the 30th of August, 1874. The White League tried, sentenced, and hung two negroes on the 28th of August, 1874. Three negroes were shot and killed at Brownsville, just before the arrival of the United States troops in the parish. Two White Leaguers rode up to a negro cabin and called for a drink of water. When the old colored man turned to draw it, they shot him in the back and killed him. The courts were all broken up in this district, and the district judge driven out. In the parish of Caddo, prior to the arrival of the United States troops, all of the officers at Shreveport were compelled to abdicate by the White League, which took possession of the place. Among those obliged to abdicate were Walsh, the mayor, Rapers, the sheriff, Wheaton, clerk of the court, Durant, the recorder, and Ferguson and Renfro, administrators. Two colored men, who had given evidence in regard to frauds committed in the parish, were compelled to flee for their lives and reached this city last night, having been smuggled through in a cargo of cotton. In the parish of Bossier the White League have attempted to force the abdication of Judge Baker, the United States Commissioner and parish judge, together with O'Neal, the sheriff, and Walker, the clerk of the court; and they have compelled the parish and district courts to suspend operations. Judge Baker states that the White Leaguers notified him several times that if he became a candidate on the republican ticket, or if he attempted to organize the republican party, he should not live until election.

They also tried to intimidate him through his family by making the same threats to his wife, and when told by him that he was a United States commissioner, they notified him not to attempt to exercise the functions of his office. In but few of the country parishes can it be truly said that the law is properly enforced, and in some of the parishes the judges have not been able to hold court for the past two years. Human life in this State is held so cheaply, that when men are killed on account of political opinions, the murderers are regarded rather as heroes than as criminals, in the localities where they reside, and by the White League and their supporters. An illustration of the ostracism that prevails in the State may be found in a resolution of a White League club in the parish of De Soto, which states, "That they pledge themselves under (no?) circumstances after the coming election to employ, rent land to, or in any other manner give aid, comfort, or credit, to any man, white or black, who votes against the nominees of the white man's party." Safety for individuals who express their opinion in the isolated portion of this State has existed only when that opinion was in favor of the principles and party supported by the Ku-Klux and White League organizations. Only yesterday Judge Myers, the parish judge of the parish of Natchitoches, called on me upon his arrival in this city, and stated that in order to reach here alive, he was obliged to leave his home by stealth, and after nightfall, and make his way to Little Rock, Arkansas, and come to this city by way of Memphis. He further states that while his father was lying at the point of death in the same village, he was unable to visit him for fear of assassination; and yet he is a native of the parish, and proscribed for his political sentiments only. It is more than probable that if bad government has existed in this State it is the result of the armed organizations, which have now crystallized into what is called the White League; instead of bad government developing them, they have by their terrorism prevented to a considerable extent the collection of taxes, the holding of courts, the punishment of criminals, and vitiated public sentiment by familiarizing it with the scenes above described. I am now engaged in compiling evidence for a detailed report upon the above subject, but it will be some time before I can obtain all the requisite data to cover the cases that have occurred throughout the State. I will also report in due time upon the same subject in the States of Arkansas and Mississippi.

P. H. SHERIDAN,
Lieutenant-General.

President Grant said in a special message to Congress, January 13, 1875:—

"It has been bitterly and persistently alleged that Kellogg was not elected. Whether he was or not is not altogether certain, nor is it any more certain that his competitor, McEnery, was chosen. The election was a gigantic fraud, and there are no reliable returns of its result. Kellogg obtained possession of the office, and in my opinion has more right to it than his competitor.

"On the 20th of February, 1873, the Committee on Privileges and Elections of the Senate made a report, in which they say they were satisfied by testimony that the manipulation of the election machinery by Warmoth and others was equivalent to twenty thousand votes; and they add, to recognize the McEnery government 'would be recognizing a government based upon fraud, in defiance of the wishes and intention of the voters of the State.' Assuming the correctness of the statements in this report, (and they seem to have been generally accepted by the country,) the great crime in Louisiana, about which so much has been said, is, that one is holding the office of governor who was cheated out of twenty thousand votes, against another whose title to the office is undoubtedly based on fraud, and in defiance of the wishes and intentions of the voters of the State.

"Misinformed and misjudging as to the nature and extent of this report, the supporters of McEnery proceeded to displace by force in some counties of the State the appointees of Governor Kellogg; and on the 13th of April, in an effort of that kind, a butchery of citizens was committed at Colfax, which in blood-thirstiness and barbarity is hardly surpassed by any acts of savage warfare.

"To put this matter beyond controversy, I quote from the charge of Judge Woods, of the United States circuit court, to the jury in the case of the United States *vs.* Cruikshank and others, in New Orleans, in March, 1874. He said:

"'In the case on trial there are many facts not in controversy. I proceed to state some of them in the presence and hearing of counsel on both sides; and if I state as a conceded fact any matter that is disputed, they can correct me.'

"After stating the origin of the difficulty, which grew out of an attempt of white persons to drive the parish judge and sheriff, appointees of Kellogg, from office, and their attempted protection by colored persons, which led to some fighting in which quite a number of negroes were killed, the judge states:

"'Most of those who were not killed were taken prisoners. Fifteen or sixteen of the blacks had lifted the boards and taken refuge under the floor of the court-house. They were all captured. About thirty-seven men were taken prisoners; the number is not definitely fixed. They were kept under guard until dark. They were led out, two by two, and shot. Most of the men were shot to death. A few were wounded, not mortally, and by pretending to be dead were afterward, during the night, able to make their escape. Among them was the Levi Nelson named in the indictment.

"'The dead bodies of the negroes killed in this affair were left unburied until Tuesday, April 15, when they were buried by a deputy marshal and an officer of the militia from New Orleans. These persons found fifty-nine dead bodies. They showed pistol-shot wounds, the great majority in the head, and most of them in the back of the head. In addition to the fifty-nine dead bodies found, some charred remains of dead bodies were discovered near the court-house. Six dead bodies were found under a warehouse, all shot in the head but one or two, which were shot in the breast.

"'The only white men injured from the beginning of these troubles to their close were Hadnot and Harris. The court-house and its contents were entirely consumed.

"'There is no evidence that any one in the crowd of whites bore any lawful warrant for the arrest of any of the blacks. There is no evidence that either Nash or Cazabat, after the affair, ever demanded their offices, to which they had set up claim, but Register continued to act as parish judge, and Shaw as Sheriff.

"'These are facts in this case, as I understand them to be admitted.'

"To hold the people of Louisiana generally responsible for these atrocities would not be just; but it is a lamentable fact that insuperable obstructions were thrown in the way of punishing these murderers, and the so-called conservative papers of the State not only justified the massacre, but denounced as Federal tyranny and despotism the attempt of the United States officers to bring them to justice. Fierce denunciations ring through the country about office-holding and election matters in Louisiana, while every one of the Colfax miscreants goes unwhipped of justice, and no way can be found in this boasted land of civilization and Christianity to punish the perpetrators of this bloody and monstrous crime.

"Not unlike this was the massacre in August last. Several northern young men of capital and enterprise had started the little and flourishing town of Coushatta. Some of them were republicans and office-holders under Kellogg. They were therefore doomed to death. Six of them were seized and carried away from their homes and murdered in cold blood. No one has been punished; and the conservative press of the State denounced all efforts to that end, and boldly justified the crime."

The House on the 1st of March, 1875, by a strict party vote, 155 Republicans to 86 Democrats, recognized the Kellogg government. The Senate did the same on March 5th, by 33 to 23, also a party vote.

Under the influence of the resolution unanimously adopted by the House of Representatives of the United States, recommending that the House of Representatives of that State seat the persons rightfully entitled thereto from certain districts, the whole subject was, by consent of parties, referred to the Special Committee of the House who examined into Louisiana affairs, viz.: Messrs. George F. Hoar, William A. Wheeler, William P. Frye, Charles Foster, William Walter Phelps, Clarkson N. Potter and Samuel S. Marshall, who, after careful examination, made an award, which was adopted by the Legislature in April, 1875. It is popularly known as the "Wheeler Compromise."

Text of the Wheeler Compromise.

New Orleans, March, 1875.

Whereas, It is desirable to adjust the difficulties growing out of the general election in this State, in 1872, the action of the Returning Board in declaring and promulgating the results of the general election, in the month of November last, and the organization of the House of Representatives, on the 4th day of January last, such adjustment being deemed necessary to the re-establishment of peace and order in this State.

Now, therefore, the undersigned members of the Conservative party, claiming to have been elected members of the House of Representatives, and that their certificates of election have been illegally withheld by the Returning Board, hereby severally agree to submit their claims to seats in the House of Representatives to the award and arbitrament of George F. Hoar, William A. Wheeler, William P. Frye, Charles Foster, William Walter Phelps, Clarkson N. Potter, and Samuel S. Marshall, who are hereby authorized to examine and determine the same upon the equities of the several cases; and when such awards shall be made, we hereby severally agree to abide by the same:

And such of us as may become members of the House of Representatives, under this arrangement, hereby severally agree to sustain by our influence and votes the joint resolution herein set forth.

[Here follow the signatures of the Democrats who claimed that their certificates of election as members of the House of Representatives had been illegally withheld by the Returning Board.]

And the undersigned claiming to have been elected Senators from the Eighth and Twenty-Second Senatorial Districts, hereby agree to submit their claims to the foregoing award and arbitrament, and in all respects to abide the results of the same.

[Here follow the signatures of the Democrats, who made a like claim as to seats in the Senate.]

And the undersigned, holding certificates of election from the Returning Board, hereby severally agree that upon the coming in of the award of the foregoing arbitrators they will, when the same shall have been ratified by the report of the Committee on Elections and Qualifications of the body in session at the State House claiming to be the House of Representatives, attend the sitting of the said House for the purpose of adopting said report, and if said report shall be adopted, and the members embraced in the foregoing report shall be seated, then the undersigned severally agree that immediately upon the adoption of said report they will vote for the following joint resolution:

[Here follow the signatures of the Democratic members of the House of Representatives in relation to whose seats there was no controversy.]

JOINT RESOLUTION.

Resolved, by the General Assembly of the State of Louisiana, That said Assembly, without approving the same, will not disturb the present State Government claiming to have been elected in 1872, known as the Kellogg Government, or seek to impeach the Governor for any past official acts, and that henceforth it will accord to said Governor all necessary and legitimate support in maintaining the laws and advancing the peace and prosperity of the people of this State: and that the House of Representatives, as to its members, as constituted under the award of George F. Hoar, W. A. Wheeler, W. P. Frye, Charles Foster, Samuel S. Marshall, Clarkson N. Potter, and William Walter Phelps, shall remain without change except by resignation or death of members until a new general election, and that the Senate, as now organized, shall also remain unchanged except so far as that body shall make changes on contests.

TEXT OF THE AWARD.

NEW YORK, March 13, 1875.

The undersigned having been requested to examine the claims of the persons hereinafter named to seats in the Senate and House of Representatives of the State of Louisiana, and having examined the returns and the evidence relating to such claims, are of opinion, and do hereby find, award and determine, that F. S. Goode is entitled to a seat in the Senate from the Twenty-second Senatorial District; and that J. B. Elam is not entitled to a seat in the Senate from the Eighth Senatorial District; and that the following named persons are entitled to seats in the House of Representatives from the following named parishes respectively: From the Parish of Assumption, R. R. Beaseley, E. F. X. Dugas; from the Parish of Bienville, James Brice; from the Parish of De Soto, J. S. Scales, Charles Schuler; from the Parish of Jackson, E. Kidd; from the Parish of Rapides, James Jeffries, R. C. Luckett, G. W. Stafford; from the Parish of Terrebone, Edward McCollum, W. H. Keyes; from the Parish of Winn, George A. Kelley. And that the following named persons are not entitled to seats which they claim from the following named parishes respectively, but that the persons now holding seats from said parishes are entitled to retain the seats now held by them; from the Parish of Avoyelles, J. O. Quinn; from the Parish of Iberie, W. F. Schwing; from the Parish of Caddo, A. D. Land, T. R. Vaughan, J. J. Horan. We are of opinion that no person is entitled to a seat from the Parish of Grant.

In regard to most of the cases, the undersigned are unanimous; as to the others the decision is that of a majority.

GEORGE F. HOAR,
W. A. WHEELER,
W. P. FRYE,
CHARLES FOSTER,
CLARKSON N. POTTER,
WILLIAM WALTER PHELPS,
SAMUEL S. MARSHALL.

This adjustment and award were accepted and observed, until the election in November, 1876, when a controversy arose as to the result, the Republicans claiming the election of Stephen B. Packard as Governor by about 3,500 majority, and a Republican Legislature; and the Democrats claiming the election of Francis T. Nicholls as Governor, by about 8,000 majority, and a Democratic Legislature. Committees of gentlemen visited New Orleans, by request of President Grant and of various political organizations, to witness the count of the votes by the Returning Board. And in December, 1876, on the meeting of Congress, committees of investigation were appointed by the Senate and by the House of Representatives. Exciting events were now daily transpiring. On the 1st of January, 1877, the Legislature organized in the State House without exhibitions of violence. The Democrats did not unite in the proceedings, but met in a separate building, and organized a separate Legislature. Telegraphic communication was had between the State House and the Custom House, where was the office of Marshal Pitkin, who with the aid of the United States troops, was ready for any emergency. About noon the Democratic members, accompanied by about 500 persons, called at the State House and demanded admission. The officer on duty replied that the members could enter, but the crowd could not. A formal demand was then made upon General Badger and other officials, by the spokesman, for the removal of the obstructions, barricades, police, etc., which prevented the ingress of members, which being denied, Col. Bush, in behalf of the crowd, read a formal protest, and the Democrats retired. Gov. Kellogg was presented by a committee with a copy of the protest, and he replied, that as chief magistrate and conservator of the peace of the State, believing that there was danger of the organization of the General Assembly being violently interfered with, he had caused a police force to be stationed in the lower portion of the building; that he had no motive but to preserve the peace; that no member or attache of either house will be interfered with in any way, and that no United States troops are stationed in the capitol building. Clerk Trezevant declined to call the House to order unless the policemen were removed. Upon the refusal to do so, he withdrew, when Louis Sauer, a member, called the roll, and 68 members—a full House being 120—answered to their names. Ex-Gov. Hahn was elected Speaker, receiving 53 votes as against 15 for Ex-Gov. Warmoth.

The Senate was organized by Lieutenant-Governor Antoine with 19 present—a full Senate being 30—eight of whom held over, and 11 were returned by the Board. Gov. Kellogg's message was presented to each House.

The Democrats organized their Legislature in St. Patrick's hall. The Senators were called to order by Senator Ogden. Nineteen Senators, including nine holding over, and four, who were counted out by the board, were present.

The Democratic members of the House were called to order by Clerk Trezevant, and 61 answered to their names. Louis Bush was elected Speaker.

January 3d—Republican Legislature passed a resolution asking for military protection against apprehended Democratic violence, and it was telegraphed to the President.

On Sunday, January 8th, Gov. Kellogg telegraphed to President Grant to the same effect.

January 8th—Stephen B. Packard took the oath of office as Governor, and C. C. Antoine as Lieutenant-Governor, at the State House at 1:30, in the presence of the Legislature.

January 8—Francis T. Nicholls and L. A. Wiltz to-day took the oath of office of Governor and Lieutenant-Governor, respectively, on the balcony of St. Patrick's hall.

By the 11th of January both parties were waiting for the action of the authorities at Washington. Gov. Packard to-day commissioned A. S. Badger Major-General of the State National Guard, and directed him to organize the first division at once. Two members of the Packard Legislature, Mr. Barrett, of Rapides, and Mr. Kennedy, of St. Charles, had withdrawn from that body and gone over to the Nicholls Legislature.

Messrs. Breux, Barrett, Kennedy, Estopival, Wheeler, and Hamlet, elected as Republicans, under the advice of Pinchback—a defeated Republican candidate for U. S. Senator, left the Packard or Republican, and joined the Nicholls Legislature.

On the 15th, Governor Packard, after receiving a copy of the telegram of the President to General Augur, issued a proclamation aimed at the "organized and armed combination and conspiracy of men now offering unlawful and violent resistance to the lawful authority of the State government."

The Nicholls court issued an order to Sheriff Handy to provide the means for protecting the court from any violence or intrusion on the part of the adherents of "S. B. Packard, a wicked and shameless impostor."

Governor Packard on the 16th, in a letter to Gen. Augur, acknowledges the receipt of a communication from his aide-de-camp asking for assurances from him that the President's wishes concerning the preservation of the present *status* be respected, and says that the request would have been more appropriate if made immediately after his installation as Governor and before many of the main branches of the Government had been forcibly taken possession of by the opposition. He says: "I had scarcely taken the oath of office when the White League were called to arms; the Court room and the records of the Supreme Court of the State were forcibly taken possession of, and various precinct police-stations were captured in like manner by overwhelming forces. Orders had been issued by the Secretary of War early on that day that all unauthorized armed bodies should desist. A dispatch from yourself of the same date to the Secretary of War, conveyed the assurances that Nicholls had promised the disbandment of his armed forces. * * * * It was my understanding, that neither side should be permitted to interfere with the *status* of the other side. Yet the day after this order was received and the pledge given by Nicholls, a force of several hundred armed White Leaguers repaired to the State Arsenal and took therefrom into their own keeping five pieces of artillery, and a garrison of armed men was placed in and around the Supreme Court building. That on the following day, January 11, an armed company of the White League broke into and took possession of the office of the Recorder of Mortgages. * * * * In view of all these facts it seemed to me that to give the pledge verbally asked of me this morning would be to sanction revolution, and by acquiescence give it the force of accomplished fact, and I therefore declined."

Many telegrams followed between the Secretary of War, J. Don. Cameron, Gen'l Augur and Mr. Packard, the latter daily complaining of new "outrages by the White League," while the Nicholls government professed to accord rights to all classes, and to obey the instructions from Washington, to faithfully maintain the *status* of affairs until decisive action should be taken by the National government. None was taken, President Grant being unwilling to outline a Southern policy for his successor in office.

Election of Hayes and Wheeler.

The troubles in the South, and the almost general overthrow of the "carpet bag government," impressed all with the fact that the Presidential election of 1876 would be exceedingly close and exciting, and the result confirmed this belief. The Greenbackers were the first to meet in National Convention, at Indianapolis, May 17th. Peter Cooper of New York was nominated for President, and Samuel F. Cary of Ohio, for Vice President.

The Republican National Convention met at Cincinnati, June 14th, with James G. Blaine recognized as the leading candidate. Grant had been named for a third term, and there was a belief that his name would be presented. Such was the feeling on this question that the House of Congress and a Republican State Convention in Pennsylvania, had passed resolutions declaring that a third term for President would be a violation of the "unwritten law" handed down through the examples of Washington, and Jackson. His name, however, was not then presented. The "unit rule" at this Convention was for the first time resisted, and by the friends of Blaine, with a view to release from instructions of State Conventions some of his friends. New York had instructed for Conkling, and Pennsylvania for Hartranft. In both of these states some delegates had been chosen by their respective Congressional districts, in advance of any State action, and these elections were as a rule confirmed by the State bodies. Where they were not, there were contests, and the right of district representation was jeopardized if not destroyed by the reinforcement of the unit rule. It was therefore thought to be a question of much importance by the warring interests. Hon. Edw. McPherson was the temporary Chairman of the Convention, and he took the earliest opportunity presented to decide against the binding force of the unit rule, and to assert the liberty of each delegate to vote as he pleased. The Convention sustained the decision on an appeal.

Ballots of the Cincinnati Republican Convention, 1876:

Ballots,	1	2	3	4	5	6	7
Blaine,	285	296	292	293	287	308	351
Conkling,	113	114	121	126	114	111	21
Bristow,	99	93	90	84	82	81	
Morton,	124	120	113	108	95	85	
Hayes,	61	64	67	68	102	113	384
Hartranft,	58	63	68	71	69	50	
Jewell,	11						
Washb'ne,		1	1	3	3	4	
Wheeler,	3	3	2	2	2	2	

Gen. Rutherford B. Hayes, of Ohio, was nominated for President, and Hon. Wm. A. Wheeler, of New York, for Vice President.

The Democratic National Convention met at St. Louis, June 28th. Great interest was excited by the attitude of John Kelly, the Tammany leader of New York, who was present and opposed with great bitterness the nomination of Tilden. He afterwards bowed to the will of the majority and supported him. Both the unit and the two-thirds rule were observed in this body, as they have long been by the Democratic party. On the second ballot, Hon. Samuel J. Tilden, of New York, had 535 votes to 203 for all others. His leading competitor was Hon. Thomas A. Hendricks, of Indiana, who was nominated for Vice President.

The Electoral Count.

The election followed Nov. 7th, 1876, Hayes and Wheeler carrying all of the Northern States except Connecticut, New York, New Jersey and Indiana; Tilden and Hendricks carried all of the Southern States except South Carolina, Florida and Louisiana. The three last named States were claimed by the Democrats, but their members of the Congressional Investigating Committee quieted rival claims as to South Carolina by agreeing that it had fairly chosen the Republican electors. So close was the result that success or failure hinged upon the returns of Florida and Louisiana, and for days and weeks conflicting stories and claims came from these States. The Democrats claimed that they had won on the face of the returns from Louisiana, and that there was no authority to go behind these. The Republicans publicly alleged frauds in nearly all of the Southern States; that the colored vote had been violently suppressed in the Gulf States, but they did not formally dispute the face of the returns in any State save where the returning boards gave them the victory. This doubtful state of affairs induced a number of prominent politicians of both the great parties to visit the State capitals of South Carolina, Florida and Louisiana to witness the count. Some of these were appointed by President Grant; others by the Democratic National Committee, and both sets were at the time called the "visiting statesmen," a phrase on which the political changes were rung for months and years thereafter.

The electoral votes of Florida were decided by the returning board to be Republican by a majority of 926,—this after throwing out the votes of several districts where fraudulent returns were alleged to be apparent or shown by testimony. The Board was cited before the State Supreme Court, which ordered a count of the face of the returns; a second meeting only led to a second Republican return, and the Republican electors were then declared to have been chosen by a majority of 206, though before this was done, the Electoral College of the State had met and cast their four votes for Hayes and Wheeler. Both parties agreed very closely in their counts, except as to Baker county, from which the Republicans claimed 41 majority, the Democrats 95 majority—the returning board accepting the Republican claim.

In Louisiana the Packard returning board was headed by J. Madison Wells, and this body refused to permit the Democrats to be represented therein. It was in session three weeks, the excitement all the time being at fever heat, and finally made the following average returns: Republican electors, 74,436; Democratic, 70,505; Republican majority, 3,931. McEnery, who claimed to be Governor, gave the Democratic electors a certificate based on an average vote of 83,635 against 75,759, a Democratic majority of 7,876.

In Oregon, the three Republican electors had an admitted majority of the popular vote, but on a claim that one of the number was a Federal office-holder and therefore ineligible, the Democratic Governor gave a certificate to two of the Republican electors, and a Mr. Cronin, Democrat. The three Republican electors were certified by the Secretary of State, who was the canvassing officer by law. This Oregon business led to grave suspicions against Mr. Tilden, who was thereafter freely charged by the Republicans with the use of his immense private fortune to control the result, and thereafter, the New York *Tribune*, with unexampled enterprise, exposed and reprinted the "cipher dispatches" from Gramercy, which Mr. Pelton, the nephew and private secretary of Mr. Tilden, had sent to Democratic "visiting statesmen" in the four disputed sections. In 1878, the Potter Investigating Committee subsequently confirmed the "cipher dispatches" but Mr. Tilden denied any knowledge of them.

The second session of the 44th Congress met on Dec. 5th, 1876, and while by that time all knew the dangers of the approaching electoral count, yet neither House would consent to the revision of the joint rule regulating the count. The Republicans claimed that the President of the Senate had the sole authority to open and announce the returns in the presence of the two Houses; the Democrats plainly disputed this right, and claimed that the joint body could control the count under the law. Some Democrats went so far as to say that the House (which was Democratic, with Samuel J. Randall in the Speaker's chair) could for itself decide when the emergency had arrived in which it was to elect a President.

There was grave danger, and it was asserted that the Democrats, fearing the President of the Senate would exercise the power of declaring the result, were preparing first to forcibly and at least with secrecy swear in and inaugurate Tilden. Mr. Watterson, member of the House from Kentucky, boasted that he had completed arrangements to have 100,000 men at Washington on inauguration day, to see that Tilden was installed. President Grant and Secretary of War Cameron, thought the condition of affairs critical, and both made active though secret preparations to secure the safe if not the peaceful inauguration of Hayes. Grant, in one of his sententious utterances, said he "would have peace if he had to fight for it." To this end he sent for Gov. Hartranft of Pennsylvania, to know if he could stop any attempted movement of New York troops to Washington, as he had information that the purpose was to forcibly install Tilden. Gov. Hartranft replied that he could do it with the National Guard and the Grand Army of the Republic. He was told to return to Harrisburg and prepare for such an emergency. This he did, and as the Legislature was then in session, a Republican caucus was called, and it resolved, without knowing exactly why, to sustain any action of the Governor with the resources of the State. Secretary Cameron also sent for Gen'l Sherman, and for a time went on with comprehensive preparations, which if there had been need for completion, would certainly have put a speedy check upon the madness of any mob. There is a most interesting unwritten history of events then transpiring which no one now living can fully relate without unjustifiable violations of political and personal confidences. But the danger was avoided by the patriotism of prominent members of Congress representing both of the great political parties. These gentlemen held several important and private conferences, and substantially agreed upon a result several days before the exciting struggle which followed the introduction of the Electoral Commission Act. The leaders on the part of the Republicans in these conferences were Conkling, Edmunds, Frelinghuysen; on the part of the Democrats Bayard, Gordon, Randall and Hewitt, the latter a member of the House and Chairman of the National Democratic Committee.

The Electoral Commission Act, the basis of agreement, was supported by Conkling in a speech of great power, and of all men engaged in this great work he was at the time most suspected by the Republicans, who feared that his admitted dislike to Hayes would cause him to favor a bill which would secure the return of Tilden, and as both of the gentlemen were New Yorkers, there was for several days grave fears of a combination between the two. The result showed the injustice done, and convinced theretofore doubting Republicans that Conkling, even as a partisan, was faithful and far-seeing. The Electoral Commission measure was a Democratic one, if we are to judge from the character of the votes cast for and against it. In the Senate the vote stood 47 for to 17 against. There were 21 Republicans for it and 16 against, while there were also 26 Democrats for it to only 1 (Eaton) against. In the House much the same proportion was maintained, the bill passing that body by 191 to 86. The following is the text of the

ELECTORAL COMMISSION ACT.

An act to provide for and regulate the counting of votes for President and Vice-President, and the decision of questions arising thereon, for the term commencing March fourth, Anno Domini eighteen hundred and seventy-seven.

Be it enacted by the Senate and House of Representatives of the United States of America in Congress assembled, That the Senate and House of Representatives shall meet in the hall of the House of Representatives, at the hour of one o'clock post meridian, on the first Thursday in February, Anno Domini eighteen hundred and seventy-seven; the President of the Senate shall be their presiding officer. Two tellers shall be previously appointed on the part of the Senate, and two on the part of the House of Representatives, to whom shall be handed, as they are opened by the President of the Senate, all the certificates, and papers purporting to be certificates, of the electoral votes, which certificates and papers shall be opened, presented and acted upon in the alphabetical order of the States, beginning with the letter A; and said tellers having then read the same in presence and hearing of the two Houses, shall make a list of the votes as they shall appear from the said certificates; and the votes having been ascertained and counted as in this act provided, the result of the same shall be delivered to the President of the Senate, who shall thereupon announce the state of the vote, and the names of the persons, if any elected, which announcement shall be deemed a sufficient declaration of the persons elected President and Vice-President of the United States, and, together with a list of the votes, be entered on the journals of the Houses. Upon such reading of any such certificate or paper when there shall only be one return from a State, the President of the Senate shall call for objections, if any. Every objection shall be made in writing, and shall state clearly and concisely, and without argument, the ground thereof, and shall be signed by at least one Senator and one Member of the House of Representatives before the same shall be received. When all objections so made to any vote or paper from a State shall have been received and read, the Senate shall thereupon withdraw, and such objections shall be submitted to the Senate for its decision; and the Speaker of the House of Representatives shall, in like manner, submit such objections to the House of Representatives for its decision; and no electoral vote or votes from any State from which but one return has been received shall be rejected, except by the affirmative vote of the two Houses. When the two Houses have votes, they shall immediately again meet, and the presiding officer shall then announce the decision of the question submitted.

SEC. 2. That if more than one return, or paper purporting to be a return from a State, shall have been received by the President of the Senate, purporting to be the certificate of electoral votes given at the last preceding election for President and Vice-President in such State (unless they shall be duplicates of the same return), all such returns and papers shall be opened by him in the presence of the two Houses when met as aforesaid, and read by the tellers, and all such returns and papers shall thereupon be submitted to the judgment and decision as to which is the true and lawful electoral vote of such State, of a commission constituted as follows, namely: During the session of each House, on the Tuesday next preceding the first Thursday in February, eighteen hundred and seventy-seven, each House shall, by viva voce vote, appoint five of its members, with the five associate justices of the Supreme Court of the United States to be ascertained as hereinafter provided, shall constitute a commission for the decision of all questions upon or in respect of such double returns named in this section. On the Tuesday next preceding the first Thursday in February, Anno Domini, eighteen hundred and seventy-seven, or as soon thereafter as may be, the associate justices of the Supreme Court of the United States now assigned to the first, third, eighth, and ninth circuits shall select, in such manner as a majority of them shall deem fit, another of the associate justices of said court, which five persons shall be members of said commission; and the person longest in commission of said five justices shall be the president of said commission. The members of said commission shall respectively take and subscribe the following oath: "I——— do solemnly swear (or affirm, as the case may be,) that I will impartially examine and consider all questions submitted to the commission of which I am a member, and a true judgment give thereon, agreeably to the Constitution and the laws: so help me God;" which oath shall be filed with the Secretary of the Senate. When the commission shall have been thus organized, it shall not be in the power of either House to dissolve the same, or to withdraw any of its members; but if any such Senator or member shall die or become physically unable to perform the duties required by this act, the fact of such death or physical inability shall be by said commission, before it shall proceed further, communicated to the Senate or House of Representatives, as the case may be, which body shall immediately and without debate proceed by viva voce vote to fill the place so vacated, and the person so appointed shall take and subscribe the oath hereinbefore prescribed, and become a member of said commission; and in like manner, if any of said justices of the Supreme Court shall die or become physically incapable of performing the duties required by this act, the other of said justices, members of the said commission, shall immediately appoint another justice of said court a member of said commission, and in like manner, if any of said justices of the Supreme Court shall die or become physically incapable of performing the duties required by this act, the other of said justices, members of the said commission, shall immediately appoint another justice of said court a member of said commission, and, in such appointment, regard shall be had to the impartiality and freedom from bias sought by the original appointments to said commission, who shall thereupon immediately take and subscribe the oath hereinbefore prescribed, and become a member of said commission to fill the vacancy so occasioned. All the certificates and papers purporting to be certificates of the electoral votes of each State shall be opened, in the alphabetical order of the States, as provided in section one of this act; and when there shall be more than one such certificate or paper, as the certificates and papers from such State shall so be opened (excepting duplicates of the same return), they shall be read by the tellers, and thereupon the President of the Senate shall call for objections, if any. Every objection shall be made in writing, and shall state clearly and concisely, and without argument, the ground thereof, and shall be signed by at least one Senator and one member of the House of Representatives before the same shall be received. When all such objections so made to any certificate, vote, or paper from a State shall have been received and read, all such certificates, votes and papers so objected to, and all papers accompanying the same, together with such objections, shall be forthwith submitted to said commission, which shall proceed to consider the same, with the same powers, if any, now possessed for that purpose by the two Houses acting separately or together, and, by a majority of votes, decide whether any and what votes from such State are the votes provided for by the Constitution of the United States, and how many and what persons were duly appointed electors in such State, and may therein take into view such petitions, depositions, and other papers, if any, as shall, by the Constitution and now existing law, be competent and pertinent in such consideration; which decision shall be made in writing, stating briefly the ground thereof, and signed by the members of said commission agreeing therein; whereupon the two Houses shall again meet, and such decision shall be read and entered in the journal of each house, and the counting of the vote shall proceed in conformity therewith, unless, upon objection made thereto in writing by at least five Senators and five members of the House of Representatives, the two Houses shall separately concur in ordering otherwise, in which case such concurrent order shall govern. No votes or papers from any other State shall be acted upon until the objections previously made to the votes or papers from any State shall have been finally disposed of.

SEC. 3. That, while the two Houses shall be in meeting, as provided in this act, no debate shall be allowed and no question shall be put by the presiding officer, except to either House on a motion to withdraw; and he shall have power to preserve order.

SEC. 4. That when the two Houses separate to decide upon an objection that may have been made to the counting of any electoral vote or votes from any State, or upon objection to a report of said commission, or other question arising under this act, each Senator and Representative may speak to such objection or question ten minutes, and not oftener than once; but after such debate shall have lasted two hours, it shall be the duty of each House to put the main question without further debate.

SEC. 5. That at such joint meeting of the two Houses, seats shall be provided as follows: For the President of the Senate, the Speaker's chair; for the Speaker, immediately upon his left; the Senators in the body of the hall upon the right of the presiding officer; for the Representatives, in the body of the hall not provided for the Senators; for the tellers, Secretary of the Senate, and Clerk of the House of Representatives, at the Clerk's desk; for the other officers of the two Houses, in front of the Clerk's desk and upon each side of the Speaker's platform. Such joint meeting shall not be dissolved until the count of electoral votes shall be completed and the result declared; and no recess shall be taken unless a question shall have arisen in regard to counting any such votes, or otherwise under this act, in which case it shall be competent for either House, acting separately, in the manner hereinbefore provided, to direct a recess of such House not beyond the next day, Sunday excepted, at the hour of ten o'clock in the forenoon. And while any question is being considered by said commission, either House may proceed with its legislative or other business.

SEC. 6. That nothing in this act shall be held to impair or affect any right now existing under the Constitution and laws to question, by proceeding in the judicial courts of the United States, the right or title of the person who shall be declared elected, or who shall claim to be President or Vice-President of the United States, if any such right exists.

SEC. 7. That said commission shall make its own rules, keep a record of its proceedings, and shall have power to employ such persons as may be necessary for the transaction of its business and the execution of its powers.

Approved, January 29, 1877.

Members of the Commission.

HON. NATHAN CLIFFORD, *Associate Justice Supreme Court, First Circuit.*

Hon. WILLIAM STRONG, *Associate Justice Supreme Court, Third Circuit.*

Hon. SAMUEL F. MILLER, *Associate Justice Supreme Court, Eighth Circuit.*

Hon. STEPHEN J. FIELD, *Associate Justice Supreme Court, Ninth Circuit.*

Hon. JOSEPH P. BRADLEY, *Associate Justice Supreme Court, Fifth Circuit.*

Hon. GEORGE F. EDMUNDS, *United States Senator.*

Hon. OLIVER P. MORTON, *United States Senator.*

Hon. FREDERICK T. FRELINGHUYSEN, *United States Senator.*

Hon. ALLEN G. THURMAN, *United States Senator.*

Hon. THOMAS F. BAYARD, *United States Senator.*

Hon. HENRY B. PAYNE, *United States Representative.*

Hon. EPPA HUNTON, *United States Representative.*

Hon. JOSIAH G. ABBOTT, *United States Representative.*

Hon. JAMES A. GARFIELD, *United States Representative.*

Hon. GEORGE F. HOAR, *United States Representative.*

The Electoral Commission met February 1st, and by uniform votes of 8 to 7, decided all objections to the Electoral votes of Florida, Louisiana, South Carolina, and Oregon, in favor of the Republicans, and while the two Houses disagreed on nearly all of these points by strict party votes, the electoral votes were, under the provisions of the law, given to Hayes and Wheeler, and the final result declared to be 185 electors for Hayes and Wheeler, to 184 for Tilden and Hendricks. Questions of eligibility had been raised against individual electors from Michigan, Nevada, Pennsylvania, Rhode Island, Vermont and Wisconsin, but the Commission did not sustain any of them, and as a rule they were unsupported by evidence. Thus closed the gravest crisis which ever attended an electoral count in this country, so far as the Nation was concerned; and while for some weeks the better desire to peacefully settle all differences prevailed, in a few weeks partisan bitterness was manifested on the part of a great majority of Northern Democrats, who believed their party had been deprived by a partisan spirit of its rightful President.

The Title of President Hayes.

The uniform vote of 8 to 7 on all important propositions considered by the Electoral Commission, to their minds showed a partisan spirit, the existence of which it was difficult to deny. The action of the Republican "visiting statesmen" in Louisiana, in practically overthrowing the Packard or Republican government there, caused distrust and dissatisfaction in the minds of the more radical Republicans, who contended with every show of reason that if Hayes carried Louisiana, Packard must also have done so. The only sensible excuse for seating Hayes on the one side and throwing out Governor Packard on the other, was a patriotic desire for peace in the settlement of both Presidential and Southern State issues. This desire was plainly manifested by President Hayes on the day of his inauguration and for two years thereafter. He took early occasion to visit Atlanta, Ga., and while at that point and *en route* there made the most conciliatory speeches, in which he called those who had engaged in the Rebellion, "brothers," "gallant soldiers," etc. These speeches excited much attention. They had little if any effect upon the South, while the more radical Republicans accused the President of "slopping over." They did not allay the hostility of the Democratic party, and did not restore the feeling in the South to a condition better than that which it had shown during the exciting days of the Electoral count. The South then, under the lead of men like Stephens, Hill and Gordon, in the main showed every desire for a peaceful settlement. As a rule only the Border States and Northern Democrats manifested extreme distrust and bitterness, and these were plainly told by some of the leaders from the Gulf States, that so far as they were concerned, they had had enough of civil war.

As late as April 22, 1877, the Maryland Legislature passed the following:

Resolved by the General Assembly of Maryland, That the Attorney General of the State be, and he is hereby, instructed, in case Congress shall provide for expediting the action, to exhibit a bill in the Supreme Court of the United States, on behalf of the State of Maryland, with proper parties thereto, setting forth the fact that due effect has not been given to the electoral vote cast by this State on the 6th day of December, 1876, by reason of fraudulent returns made from other States and allowed to be counted provisionally by the Electoral Commission, and subject to judicial revision, and praying said court to make the revision contemplated by the act establishing said commission; and upon such revision to declare the returns from the States of Louisiana and Florida, which were counted for Rutherford B. Hayes and William A. Wheeler, fraudulent and void, and that the legal electoral votes of said States were cast for Samuel J. Tilden as President, and Thomas A. Hendricks as Vice President, and that by virtue thereof and of 184 votes cast by other States, of which 8 were cast by the State of Maryland, the said Tilden and Hendricks were duly elected, and praying said Court to decree accordingly.

It was this resolution which induced the Clarkson N. Potter resolution of investigation, a resolution the passage of which was resisted by the Republicans through filibustering for many days, but was finally passed by 146 Democratic votes to 2 Democratic votes (Mills and Morse) against, the Republicans not voting.

The Cipher Despatches.

An amendment offered to the Potter resolution but not accepted, and defeated by the Democratic majority, cited some fair specimens of the cipher dispatches exposed by the New York *Tribune.* These are matters of historical interest, and convey information as to the methods which politicians will resort to in desperate emergencies. We therefore quote the more pertinent portions.

Resolved, That the select committee to whom this House has committed the investigation of certain matters affecting, as is alleged, the legal title of the President of the United States to the high office which he now holds, be and is hereby instructed in the course of its investigations to fully inquire into all the facts connected with the election in the State of Florida in November, 1876, and especially into the circumstances attending the transmission and receiving of certain telegraphic dispatches sent in said year between Tallahassee in said State and New York City, viz.:

"TALLAHASSEE, *November* 9, 1876.

"A. S. HEWITT, *New York:*

"Comply if possible with my telegram.
"GEO. P. RAREY."

Also the following:

"TALLAHASSEE, *December* 1, 1876.

"W. T. PELTON, *New York:*

"Answer Mac's dispatch immediately, or we will be embarrasssed at a critical time. WILKINSON CALL."

Also the following:

"TALLAHASSEE, *December* 4, 1876.

"W. T. PELTON:

"Things culminating here. Answer Mac's despatch to-day. W. CALL."

And also the facts connected with all telegraphic dispatches between one John F. Coyle and said Pelton, under the latter's real or fictitious name, and with any and all demands for money on or about December 1, 1876, from said Tallahassee, on said Pelton, or said Hewitt, or with any attempt to corrupt or bribe any official of the said State of Florida by any person acting for said Pelton, or in the interest of Samuel J. Tilden as a presidential candidate.

Also to investigate the charges of intimidation at Lake City, in Columbia county, where Joel Niblack and other white men put ropes around the necks of colored men and proposed to hang them, but released them on their promise to join a Democratic club and vote for Samuel J. Tilden.

Also the facts of the election in Jackson county, where the ballot-boxes were kept out of the sight of voters, who voted through openings or holes six feet above the ground, and where many more Republican votes were thus given into the hands of the Democratic inspectors than were counted or returned by them.

Also the facts of the election in Waldo precinct, in Alachua county, where the passengers on an emigrant-train, passing through on the day of election, were allowed to vote.

Also the facts of the election in Manatee county, returning 235 majority for the Tilden electors, where there were no county officers, no registration, no notice of the election, and where the Republican party, therefore, did not vote.

Also the facts of the election in the third precinct of Key West, giving 342 Democratic majority, where the Democratic inspector carried the ballot-box home, and pretended to count the ballots on the next day, outside of the precinct and contrary to law.

Also the facts of the election in Hamilton, where the election-officers exercised no control over the ballot-box, but left it in unauthorized hands, that it might be tampered with.

Also the reasons why the Attorney-General of the State, Wm. Archer Cocke, as a member of the Canvassing Board, officially advised the board, and himself voted, to exclude the Hamilton county and Key West precinct returns, thereby giving, in any event, over 500 majority to the Republican electoral ticket, and afterwards protested against the result which he had voted for, and whether or not said Cocke was afterward rewarded for such protest by being made a State Judge.

OREGON.

And that said committee is further instructed and directed to investigate into all the facts connected with an alleged attempt to secure one electoral vote in the State of Oregon for Samuel J. Tilden for President of the United States, and Thomas A. Hendricks for Vice-President, by unlawfully setting up the election of E. A. Cronin as one of such presidential electors elected from the State of Oregon on the 7th of November, the candidates for the presidential electors on the two tickets being as follows:

On the Republican ticket: W. C. Odell, J. C. Cartwright, and John W. Watts.

On the Democratic ticket: E. A. Cronin, W. A. Laswell, and Henry Klippel.

The votes received by each candidate, as shown by the official vote as canvassed, declared, and certified to by the Secretary of State under the seal of the State,—the Secretary being under the laws of Oregon sole canvassing-officer, as will be shown hereafter,—being as follows:

W. K. Odell received............15,206 votes
John C. Cartwright received....15,214 "
John W. Watts received.........15,206 "
E. A. Cronin received...........14,157 "
W. A. Laswell received..........14,149 "
Henry Klippel received.........14,136 "

And by the unlawful attempt to bribe one of said legally elected electors to recognize said Cronin as an elector for President and Vice-President, in order that one of the electoral votes of said State might be cast for said Samuel J. Tilden as President and for Thomas A. Hendricks as Vice-President; and especially to examine and inquire into all the facts relating to the sending of money from New York to some place in said Oregon for the purposes of such bribery, the parties sending and receiving the same, and their relations to and agency for said Tilden, and more particularly to investigate into all the circumstances attending the transmission of the following telegraphic despatches:

"PORTLAND, Oregon, *Nov.* 14, 1876.

"Gov. L. F. GROVER:

"Come down to-morrow if possible.
"W. H. EFFINGER,
"A. NOLTNER,
"C. P. BELLINGER."

"PORTLAND, *November* 16, 1876.

"To Gov. GROVER, *Salem:*

"We want to see you particularly on account of despatches from the East.

"WILLIAM STRONG, S. H. REED,
"C. P. BELLINGER, W. W. THAYER,
"C. E. BRONAUGH."

Also the following cipher despatch sent from Portland, Oregon, on the 28th day of November, 1876, to New York City:

"PORTLAND, *November* 28, 1876.

"To W. T. Pelton, *No.* 15 *Gramercy Park, New York:*

"By vizier association innocuous negligence cunning minutely previously readmit doltish to purchase afar act with cunning afar sacristy unweighed afar pointer tigress cattle superannuated syllabus dilatoriness misapprehension contraband Kountz bisulcuous top usher spiniferous answer. J. H. N. PATRICK.

"I fully endorse this.
"JAMES K. KELLY."

Of which, when the key was discovered, the following was found to be the true intent and meaning:

"PORTLAND, *November* 28, 1876.

"To W. T. PELTON, *No.* 15 *Gramercy Park, New York:*

"Certificate will be issued to one Democrat. Must purchase a Republican elector to recognize and act with Democrats and secure the vote and prevent trouble. Deposit $10,000 to my credit with Kountz Brothers, Wall Street. Answer.
J. H. N. PATRICK.

"I fully endorse this.
"JAMES K. KELLY."

Also the following:

"NEW YORK, *November* 25, 1876.

"A. BUSH, *Salem:*

"Use all means to prevent certificate. Very important. C. E. TILTON."

Also the following:

"*December* 1, 1876.

"To Hon. SAM. J. TILDEN, *No.* 15 *Gramercy Park, New York:*

"I shall decide every point in the case of post-office elector in favor of the highest Democratic elector, and grant certificate accordingly on morning of 6th instant. Confidential. GOVERNOR."

Also the following:

"SAN FRANCISCO, *December* 5.

"LADD & BUSH, *Salem:*

"Funds from New York will be deposited to your credit here to-morrow when bank opens. I know it. Act accordingly. Answer. W. C. GRISWOLD."

Also the following, six days before the foregoing:

"NEW YORK, *November* 29, 1876.

"To J. H. N. PATRICK, *Portland, Oregon:*

"Moral hasty sideral vizier gabble cramp by hemistic welcome licentiate muskeete compassion neglectful recoverable hathouse live innovator brackish association dime afar idolator session hemistic mitre."
[No signature.]

Of which the interpretation is as follows:

"NEW YORK, *November* 29, 1876.

"To J. H. N. PATRICK, *Portland, Oregon:*

"No. How soon will Governor decide certificate? If you make obligation contingent on the result in March, it can be done, and slightly if necessary."
[No signature.]

Also the following, one day later:

"PORTLAND, *November* 30, 1876.

"TO W. T. PELTON, *No.* 15 *Gramercy Park, New York:*

"Governor all right without reward. Will issue certificate Tuesday. This is a secret. Republicans threaten if certificate issued to ignore Democratic claims and fill vacancy, and thus defeat action of Governor. One elector must be paid to recognize Democrat to secure majority. Have employed three lawyers, editor of only Republican paper as one lawyer, fee $3,000. Will take $5,000 for Republican elector; must raise money; can't make fee contingent. Sail Saturday. Kelly and Bellinger will act. Communicate with them. Must act promptly." [No signature].

Also the following:

"SAN FRANCISCO, *December* 5, 1876.

"TO KOUNTZE BROS., *No.* 12 *Wall St., New York:*

"Has my account credit by any funds lately? How much?

"J. H. N. PATRICK."

Also the following:

"NEW YORK, *December* 6.

"J. H. N. PATRICK, *San Francisco:*

"Davis deposited eight thousand dollars December first. KOUNTZE BROS."

Also the following:

"SAN FRANCISCO, *December* 6.

"TO JAMES K. KELLY:

"The eight deposited as directed this morning. Let no technicality prevent winning. Use your discretion."

[No signature.]

And the following:

"NEW YORK, *December* 6.

"HON. JAS. K. KELLY:

"Is your matter certain? There must be no mistake. All depends on you. Place no reliance on any favorable report from three southward. Sonetter. Answer quick."

[No signature.]

Also the following:

"DECEMBER 6, 1876.

"TO Col. W. T. PELTON, 15 *Gramercy Park, N. Y.:*

"Glory to God! Hold on to the one vote in Oregon! I have one hundred thousand men to back it up!

"CORSE."

And said committee is further directed to inquire into and bring to light, so far as it may be possible, the entire correspondence and conspiracy referred to in the above telegraphic despatches, and to ascertain what were the relations existing between any of the parties sending or receiving said despatches and W. T. Pelton, of New York, and also what relations existed between said W. T. Pelton and Samuel J. Tilden, of New York.

April 15, 1878, Mr. Kimmel introduced a bill, which was never finally acted upon, to provide a mode for trying and determining by the Supreme Court of the United States the title of the President and Vice-President of the United States to take their respective offices when their election to such offices is denied by one or more of the States of the Union.

The question of the title of President was finally settled June 14, 1878, by the following report of the House Judiciary Commitee:

Report of the Judiciary Committee.

June 14—Mr. HARTRIDGE, from the Committee on the Judiciary, made the following report:

The Committee on the Judiciary, to whom were referred the bill (H. R. No. 4315) and the resolutions of the Legislature of the State of Maryland directing judicial proceedings to give effect to the electoral vote of that State in the last election of President and Vice-President of the United States, report back said bill and resolutions with a recommendation that the bill do not pass.

Your committee are of the opinion that Congress has no power, under the Constitution, to confer upon the Supreme Court of the United States the original jurisdiction sought for it by this bill. The only clause of the Constitution which could be plausibly invoked to enable Congress to provide the legal machinery for the litigation proposed, is that which gives the Supreme Court original jurisdiction in "cases" or "controversies" between a State and the citizens of another State. The committee are of the opinion that this expression "cases" and "controversies" was not intended by the framers of the Constitution to embrace an original proceeding by a State in the Supreme Court of the United States to oust any incumbent from a political office filled by the declaration and decision of the two Houses of Congress clothed with the constitutional power to count the electoral votes and decide as a final tribunal upon the election for President and Vice-President. The Forty-fourth Congress selected a commission to count the votes for President and Vice-President, reserving to itself the right to ratify or reject such count, in the way prescribed in the act creating such commission. By the joint action of the two Houses it ratified the count made by the commission, and thus made it the expression of its own judgment.

All the Departments of the Federal

Government, all the State governments in their relations to Federal authority, foreign nations, the people of the United States, all the material interests and industries of the country, have acquiesced in, and acted in accordance with, the pronounced finding of that Congress. In the opinion of this committee, the present Congress has no power to undo the work of its predecessor in counting the electoral vote, or to confer upon any judicial tribunal the right to pass upon and perhaps set aside the action of that predecessor in reference to a purely political question, the decision of which is confided by the Constitution in Congress.

But apart from these fundamental objections to the bill under consideration, there are features and provisions in it which are entirely impracticable. Your committee can find no warrant of authority to summon the chief-justices of the supreme courts of the several States to sit at Washington as a jury to try any case, however grave and weighty may be its nature. The right to summon must carry with it the power to enforce obedience to the mandate, and the Committee can see no means by which the judicial officers of a State can be compelled to assume the functions of jurors in the Supreme Court of the United States.

There are other objections to the practical working of the bill under consideration, to which we do not think it necessary to refer.

It may be true that the State of Maryland has been, in the late election for President and Vice-President, deprived of her just and full weight in deciding who were legally chosen, by reason of frauds perpetrated by returning boards in some of the States. It may also be true that these fraudulent acts were countenanced or encouraged or participated in by some who now enjoy high offices as the fruit of such frauds. It is due to the present generation of the people of this country and their posterity, and to the principles on which our Government is founded, that all evidence tending to establish the fact of such fraudulent practices should be calmly, carefully, and rigorously examined.

But your committee are of the opinion that the consequence of such examination, if it discloses guilt upon the part of any in high official position, should not be an effort to set aside the judgment of a former Congress as to the election of a President and Vice-President, but should be confined to the punishment, by legal and constitutional means, of the offenders, and to the preservation and perpetuation of the evidences of their guilt, so that the American people may be protected from a recurrence of the crime.

Your committee, therefore, recommend the adoption of the accompanying resolution:

Resolved, That the two Houses of the Forty-fourth Congress having counted the votes cast for President and Vice-President of the United States, and having declared Rutherford B. Hayes to be elected President, and William A. Wheeler to be elected Vice-President, there is no power in any subsequent Congress to reverse that declaration, nor can any such power be exercised by the courts of the United States, or any other tribunal that Congress can create under the Constitution.

We agree to the foregoing report so far as it states the reasons for the resolution adopted by the committee, but dissent from the concluding portion, as not having reference to such reasons, as not pertinent to the inquiry before us, and as giving an implied sanction to the propriety of the pending investigation ordered by a majority vote of the House of Representatives, to which we were and are opposed.

Wm. P. Frye.
O. D. Conger.
E. G. Lapham.

Leave was given to Mr. Knott to present his individual views, also to Mr. Butler (the full committee consisting of Messrs. *Knott, Lynde, Harris*, of Virginia, *Hartridge, Stenger, McMahon, Culberson*, Frye, Butler, Conger, Lapham.)

The question being on the resolution reported by the committee, it was agreed to —yeas 235, nays 14, not voting 42.

The Hayes Administration.

It can be truthfully said that from the very beginning the administration of President Hayes had not the cordial support of the Republican party, nor was it solidly opposed by the Democrats, as was the last administration of General Grant. His early withdrawal of the troops from the Southern States,—and it was this withdrawal and the suggestion of it from the "visiting statesmen" which overthrew the Packard government in Louisiana,—embittered the hostility of many radical Republicans. Senator Conkling was conspicuous in his opposition, as was Logan of Illinois; and when he reached Washington, the younger Senator Cameron, of Pennsylvania. It was during this administration, and because of its conservative tendencies, that these three leaders formed the purpose to bring Grant again to the Presidency. Yet the Hayes' administration was not always conservative, and many Republicans believed that its moderation had afforded a much needed breathing spell to the country. Toward its close all became better satisfied, the radical portion by the President's later efforts to prevent the intimidation of negro voters in the South, a form of intimidation which was now accomplished by means of rifle clubs, still another advance from the White League and the Ku Klux. He made this a leading feature in his annual message to the Congress which began December 2d, 1878, and by a virtual abandonment of his earlier policy he succeeded in reuniting what were then fast separating wings of his own party. The conference report on the Legislative Appropriation Bill was adopted by both Houses June 18th, and approved the 21st. The Judicial Expenses Bill was vetoed by the President June 23d, on the ground that it would deprive him of the means of executing the election laws. An attempt on the part of the Democrats to pass the Bill over the veto failed for want of a two-thirds vote, the Republicans voting solidly against it. June 26th the veltoed bill was divided, the second division still forbidding the pay of deputy marshals at elections. This was again vetoed, and the President sent a special message urging the necessity of an appropriation to pay United States marshals. Bills were accordingly introduced, but were defeated. This failure to appropriate moneys called for continued until the end of the session. The President was compelled, therefore, to call an extra session, which he did March 19th, 1879, in words which briefly explain the cause:—

THE EXTRA SESSION OF 1879.

"The failure of the last Congress to make the requisite appropriation for legislative and judicial purposes, for the expenses of the several executive departments of the Government, and for the support of the Army, has made it necessary to call a special session of the Forty-sixth Congress.

"The estimates of the appropriations needed, which were sent to Congress by the Secretary of the Treasury at the opening of the last session, are renewed, and are herewith transmitted to both the Senate and the House of Representatives.

"Regretting the existence of the emergency which requires a special session of Congress at a time when it is the general judgment of the country that the public welfare will be best promoted by permanency in our legislation, and by peace and rest, I commend these few necessary measures to your considerate attention."

By this time both Houses were Democratic. In the Senate there were 42 Democrats, 33 Republicans and 1 Independent (David Davis). In the House 149 Democrats, 130 Republicans, and 14 Nationals—a name then assumed by the Greenbackers and Labor-Reformers. The House passed the Warner Silver Bill, providing for the unlimited coinage of silver, the Senate Finance Committee refused to report it, the Chairman, Senator Bayard, having refused to report it, and even after a request to do so from the Democratic caucus,—a course of action which heralded him every where as a "hard-money" Democrat.

The main business of the extra session was devoted to the consideration of the Appropriation Bills which the regular session had failed to pass. On all of these the Democrats added "riders" for the purpose of destroying Federal supervision of the elections, and all of these political riders were vetoed by President Hayes. The discussions of the several measures and the vetoes were highly exciting, and this excitement cemented afresh the Republicans, and caused all of them to act in accord with the administration. The Democrats were equally solid, while the Nationals divided—Forsythe, Gillette, Kelley, Weaver, and Yocum generally voting with the Republicans; De La Matyr, Stevenson, Ladd and Wright with the Democrats.

President Hayes, in his veto of the Army Appropriation Bill, said:

"I have maturely considered the important questions presented by the bill entitled 'An Act making appropriations for the support of the Army for the fiscal year ending June 30, 1880, and for other purposes,' and I now return it to the House of Representatives, in which it originated, with my objections to its approval.

"The bill provides, in the usual form, for the appropriations required for the support of the Army during the next fiscal year. If it contained no other provisions, it would receive my prompt approval. It includes, however, further legislation, which, attached as it is to appropriations which are requisite for the efficient performance of some of the most necessary duties of the Government, involves questions of the gravest character. The sixth section of the bill is amendatory of the statute now in force in regard to the authority of persons in the civil, military and naval service of the United States 'at the place where any general or special election is held in any State.' This statute was adopted February 25, 1865, after a protracted debate in the Senate, and almost without opposition in the House of Representatives, by the concurrent votes of both of the leading political parties of the country, and became a law by the approval of President Lincoln. It was re-enacted in 1874 in the Revised Statutes of the United States, sections 2002 and 5528.

* * * * * * * *

"Upon the assembling of this Congress, in pursuance of a call for an extra session, which was made necessary by the failure of the Forty-fifth Congress to make the needful appropriations for the support of the Government, the question was presented whether the attempt made in the last Congress to engraft, by construction, a new principle upon the Constitution should be persisted in or not. This Congress has ample opportunity and time to pass the appropriation bills, and also to enact any political measures which may be determined upon in separate bills by the usual and orderly methods of proceeding. But the majority of both Houses have deemed it wise to adhere to the principles asserted and maintained in the last Congress by the majority of the House of Representatives. That principle is that the House of Representatives has the sole right to originate bills for raising revenue, and therefore has the right to withhold appropriations upon which the existence of the Government may depend, unless the Senate and the President shall give their assent to any legislation which the House may see fit to attach to appropriation bills. To establish this principle is to make a radical, dangerous, and unconstitutional change in the character of our institutions. The various Departments of the Government, and the Army and Navy, are established by the Constitution, or by laws passed in pursuance thereof. Their duties are clearly defined, and their support is carefully provided for by law. The money required for this purpose has been collected from the people, and is now in the Treasury, ready to be paid out as soon as the appropriation bills are passed. Whether appropriations are made or not, the collection of the taxes will go on. The public money will accumulate in the Treasury. It was not the intention of the framers of the Constitution that any single branch of the Government should have the power to dictate conditions upon which this treasure should be applied to the purpose for which it was collected. Any such intention, if it had been entertained, would have been plainly expressed in the Constitution."

The vote in the House on this Bill, notwithstanding the veto, was 148 for to 122 against—a party vote, save the division of the Nationals, previously given. Not receiving a two-thirds vote, the Bill failed.

The other appropriation bills with political riders shared the same fate, as did the bill to prohibit military interference at elections, the modification of the law touching supervisors and marshals at congressional elections, etc. The debates on these measures were bitterly partisan in their character, as a few quotations from the Congressional *Record* will show:

The Republican view was succinctly and very eloquently stated by General Garfield, when, in his speech of the 29th of March, 1879, he said to the revolutionary Democratic House:

"The last act of Democratic domination in this Capitol, eighteen years ago, was striking and dramatic, perhaps heroic. Then the Democratic party said to the Republicans, 'If you elect the man of your choice as President of the United States we will shoot your Government to death;' and the people of this country, refusing to be coerced by threats or violence, voted as they pleased, and lawfully elected Abraham Lincoln President of the United States.

"Then your leaders, though holding a majority in the other branch of Congress, were heroic enough to withdraw from their seats and fling down the gage of mortal battle. We called it rebellion; but we recognized it as courageous and manly to avow your purpose, take all the risks, and fight it out on the open field. Notwithstanding your utmost efforts to destroy it, the Government was saved. Year by year since the war ended, those who resisted you have come to believe that you have finally renounced your purpose to destroy, and are willing to maintain the Government. In that belief you have been permitted to return to power in the two Houses.

"To-day, after eighteen years of defeat, the book of your domination is again opened, and your first act awakens every unhappy memory and threatens to destroy the confidence which your professions of patriotism inspired. You turned down a leaf of the history that recorded your last act of power in 1861, and you have now signalized your return to power by beginning a second chapter at the same page; not this time by a heroic act that declares war on the battle-field, but you say if all the legislative powers of the Government do not consent to let you tear certain laws out of the statute-book, you will not shoot our Government to death as you tried to do in the first chapter; but you declare that if we do not consent against our will, if you cannot coerce an independent branch of this Government against its will, to allow you to tear from the statute-books some laws put there by the will of the people, you will starve the Government to death. [Great applause on the Republican side.]

"Between death on the field and death by starvation, I do not know that the American people will see any great difference. The end, if successfully reached, would be death in either case. Gentlemen, you have it in your power to kill this Government; you have it in your power, by withholding these two bills, to smite the nerve-centres of our Constitution with the paralysis of death; and you have declared your purpose to do this, if you cannot break down that fundamental element of free consent which up to this hour has always ruled in the legislation of this Government."

The Democratic view was ably given by Representative Tucker of Virginia, April 3, 1879: "I tell you, gentlemen of the House of Representatives, *the Army dies on the 30th day of June, unless we resuscitate it by legislation.* And what is the question here on this bill? Will you resuscitate the Army after the 30th of June, with the power to use it as keepers of the polls? That is the question. It is not a question of repeal. It is a question of re-enactment. If you do not appropriate this money, there will be no Army after the 30th of June to be used at the polls. The only way to secure an Army at the polls is to appropriate the money. *Will you appropriate the money for the Army in order that they may be used at the polls? We say no, a thousand times no.* * * * The gentlemen on the other side say there must be no coercion. Of whom? Of the President? But what right has the President to coerce us? There may be coercion one way or the other. He demands an unconditional supply. *We say we will give him no supply but upon conditions.* * * * When, therefore, vicious laws have fastened themselves upon the statute-book which imperil the liberty of the people, this House is bound to say it will appropriate no money to give effect to such laws until and except upon condition that they are repealed. [Applause on the Democratic side.] * * We will give him the Army on a single condition that it shall never be used or be present at the polls when an election is held for members of this House, or in any presidential election, or in any State or municipal election. * * * Clothed thus with unquestioned power, bound by clear duty, to expunge these vicious laws from the statute-book, following a constitutional method sanctioned by venerable precedents in English history, we feel that we have the undoubted right, and are beyond cavil in the right, in declaring that with our grant of supply there must be a cessation of these grievances, and we make these appropriations conditioned on securing a free ballot and fair juries for our citizens."

The Senate, July 1, passed the House bill placing quinine on the free list.

The extra session finally passed the Appropriation bills without riders, and adjourned July 1st, 1879, with the Republican party far more firmly united than at the beginning of the Hayes administration. The attempt on the part of the Democrats to pass these political riders, and their threat, in the words of Garfield, who had then succeeded Stevens and Blaine as the Republican Commoner of the House, reawakened all the partisan animosities which the administration of President Hayes had up to that time allayed. Even the President caught its spirit, and plainly manifested it in his veto messages. It was a losing battle to the Democrats, for they had, with the view not to "starve the government," to abandon their position, and the temporary demoralization which followed bridged over the questions pertaining to the title of President Hayes, overshadowed the claims of Tilden, and caused the North to again look with grave concern on the establishment of Democratic power. If it had not been for this extra session, it is asserted and believed by many, the Republicans could not have so soon gained control of the lower House, which they did in the year following; and that the plan to nominate General Hancock for the Presidency, which originated with Senator Wallace of Pennsylvania, could not have otherwise succeeded if Tilden's cause had not been kept before his party, unclouded by an extra session which was freighted with disaster to the Democratic party.

The Negro Exodus.

During this summer political comment, long after adjournment, was kept active by a great negro exodus from the South to the Northwest, most of the emigrants going to Kansas. The Republicans ascribed this to ill treatment, the Democrats to the operations of railroad agents. The people of Kansas welcomed them, but other States, save Indiana, were slow in their manifestations of hospitality, and the exodus soon ceased for a time. It was renewed in South Carolina in the winter of 1881–82, the design being to remove to Arkansas, but at this writing it attracts comparatively little notice. The Southern journals generally advise more liberal treatment of the blacks in matters of education, labor contracts, etc., while none of the Northern or Western States any longer make efforts to get the benefit of their labor, if indeed they ever did.

Closing Hours of the Hayes Administration.

At the regular session of Congress, which met December 1st, 1879, President Hayes advised Congress against any further legislation in reference to coinage, and favored the retirement of the legal tenders.

The most important political action taken at this session was the passage, for Congress was still Democratic, of a law to prevent the use of the army to keep the peace at the polls. To this was added the Garfield proviso, that it should not be construed to prevent the Constitutional use of the army to suppress domestic violence in a State—a proviso which in the view of the Republicans rid the bill of material partisan objections, and it was therefore passed and approved. The "political riders" were again added to the Appropriation and Deficiency bills, but were again vetoed and failed in this form to become laws. Upon these questions President Hayes showed much firmness. During the session the Democratic opposition to the General Election Law was greatly tempered, the Supreme Court having made an important decision, which upheld its constitutionality. Like all sessions under the administration of President Hayes and since, nothing was done to provide permanent and safe methods for completing the electoral count. On this question each party seemed to be afraid of the other. The session adjourned June 16th, 1880.

The second session of the 46th Congress began December 1st, 1880. The last annual message of President Hayes recommended the earliest practicable retirement of the legal-tender notes, and the maintenance of the present laws for the accumulation of a sinking fund sufficient to extinguish the public debt within a limited period. The laws against polygamy, he said, should be firmly and effectively executed. In the course of a lengthy discussion of the civil service the President declared that in his opinion "every citizen has an equal right to the honor and profit of entering the public service of his country. The only just ground of discrimination is the measure of character and capacity he has to make that service most useful to the people. Except in cases where, upon just and recognized principles, as upon the theory of pensions, offices and promotions are bestowed as rewards for past services, their bestowal upon any theory which disregards personal merit is an act of injustice to the citizen, as well as a breach of that trust subject to which the appointing power is held. Considerable space was given in the Message to the condition of the Indians, the President recommending the passage of a law enabling the government to give Indians a title-fee, inalienable for twenty-five years, to the farm lands assigned to them by allotment. He also repeats the recommendation made in a former message that a law be passed admitting the Indians who can give satisfactory proof of having by their own labor supported their families for a number of years, and who are willing to detach themselves from their tribal relations, to the benefit of the Homestead Act, and authorizing the government to grant them patents containing the same provision of inalienability for a certain period.

The Senate, on the 19th, appointed a committee of five to investigate the causes of the recent negro exodus from the South. On the same day a committee was appointed by the House to examine into the subject of an inter-oceanic ship-canal.

The payment of the award of the Halifax Fisheries Commission—$5,500,000—to the British government was made by the American minister in London, November 23, 1879, accompanied by a communication protesting against the payment being understood as an acquiescence in the result of the Commission "as furnishing any just measure of the value of a participation by our citizens in the inshore fisheries of the British Provinces."

On the 17th of December 1879, gold was sold in New York at par. It was first sold at a premium January 13, 1862. It reached its highest rate, $2.85, July 11, 1864.

The electoral vote was counted without any partisan excitement or disagreement. Georgia's electoral college had met on the second instead of the first Wednesday of December, as required by the Federal law. She actually voted under her old Confederate law, but as it could not change the result, both parties agreed to the count of the vote of Georgia "in the alternative," *i. e.*—"if the votes of Georgia were counted the number of votes for A and B. for President and Vice-President would be so many, and if the votes of Georgia were not counted, the number of votes for A and B. for President and Vice-President would be so many, and that in either case A and B are elected."

Among the bills not disposed of by this session were the electoral count joint rule; the funding bill; the Irish relief bill; the Chinese indemnity bill; to restrict Chinese immigration; to amend the Constitution as to the election of President; to regulate the pay and number of supervisors of election and special deputy-marshals; to abrogate the Clayton-Bulwer Treaty; to prohibit military interference at elections; to define the terms of office of the Chief Supervisors of elections; for the appointment of a tariff commission; the political assessment bill; the Kellogg-Spofford case; and the Fitz-John Porter bill.

The regular appropriation bills were all completed. The total amount appropriated was about $186,000,000. Among the special sums voted were $30,000 for the centennial celebration of the Yorktown victory, and $100,000 for a monument to commemorate the same.

Congress adjourned March 3d, 1881, and President Hayes on the following day retired from office. The effect of his administration was, in a political sense, to strengthen a growing independent sentiment in the ranks of the Republicans—an element more conservative generally in its views than those represented by Conkling and Blaine. This sentiment began with Bristow, who while in the cabinet made a show of seeking out and punishing all corruptions in government office or service. On this platform and record he had contested with Hayes the honors of the Presidential nominations, and while the latter was at the time believed to well represent the same views, they were not urgently pressed during his administration. Indeed, without the knowledge of Hayes, what is believed to be a most gigantic "steal," and which is now being prosecuted under the name of the Star Route cases, had its birth, and thrived so well that no important discovery was made until the incoming of the Garfield administration. The Hayes administration, it is now fashionable to say, made little impress for good or evil upon the country, but impartial historians will give it the credit of softening party asperities and aiding very materially in the restoration of better feeling between the North and South. Its conservatism, always manifested save on extraordinary occasions, did that much good at least.

The Campaign of 1880.

The Republican National Convention met June 5th, 1880, at Chicago, in the Exposition building, capable of seating 20,000 people. The excitement in the ranks of the Republicans was very high, because of the candidacy of General Grant for what was popularly called a "third term," though not a third consecutive term. His three powerful Senatorial friends, in the face of bitter protests, had secured the instructions of their respective State Conventions for Grant. Conkling had done this in New York, Cameron in Pennsylvania, Logan in Illinois, but in each of the three States the opposition was so impressive that no serious attempts were made to substitute other delegates for those which had previously been selected by their Congressional districts. As a result there was a large minority in the delegations of these States opposed to the nomination of General Grant, and the votes of them could only be controlled by the enforcement of the unit rule. Senator Hoar of Massachusetts, the President of the Convention, decided against its enforcement, and as a result all of the delegates were free to vote upon either State or District instructions, or as they chose. The Convention was in session three days. We present herewith the

BALLOTS.

Ballots.	1	2	3	4	5	6
Grant,	304	305	305	305	305	305
Blaine,	284	282	282	281	281	281
Sherman,	93	94	93	95	95	95
Edmunds,	34	32	32	32	32	31
Washburne,	30	32	31	31	31	31
Windom,	10	10	10	10	10	10
Garfield,		1	1	1	2	2
Harrison,		1				

Ballots.	7	8	9	10	11	12
Grant,	305	306	308	305	305	304
Blaine,	281	284	282	282	281	283
Sherman,	94	91	90	91	62	93
Edmunds,	32	31	31	30	31	31
Washburne,	31	32	32	22	32	33
Windom,	10	10	10	10	10	10
Garfield,	1	1	1	2	2	1
Hayes,					1	2

Ballots,	13	14	15	16	17	18
Grant,	305	305	309	306	303	305
Blaine,	285	285	281	283	284	283
Sherman,	89	89	88	88	90	92
Edmunds,	31	31	31	31	31	31
Washburne,	33	35	36	36	34	35
Windom,	10	10	10	10	10	10
Garfield,	1					
Hayes,	1	1				
Davis,					1	
McCrary,	1					

Ballots,	19	20	21	22	23	24
Grant,	305	308	305	305	304	305
Blaine,	279	276	276	275	274	279
Sherman,	95	93	96	95	98	93
Edmunds,	31	31	31	31	31	31
Washburne,	31	35	35	35	36	35
Windom,	10	10	10	10	10	10
Garfield,	1	1	1	1	2	2
Hartranft,	1	1	1	1		

Ballots,	25	26	27
Grant,	302	303	306
Blaine,	281	280	277
Sherman,	94	93	93
Edmunds,	31	31	31
Washburne,	36	35	36
Windom,	10	10	10
Garfield,	2	2	2

There was little change from the 27th ballot until the 36th and final one, which resulted as follows:

Whole number of votes	755
Necessary to a choice	378
Grant	306
Blaine	42
Sherman	3
Washburne	5
Garfield	399

As shown, General James A. Garfield, of Ohio, was nominated on the 36th ballot, the forces of General Grant alone remaining solid. The result was due to a sudden union of the forces of Blaine and Sherman, it is believed with the full consent of both, for both employed the same wire leading from the same room in Washington in telegraphing to their friends at Chicago. The object was to defeat Grant. After Garfield's nomination there was a temporary adjournment, during which the friends of the nominee consulted Conkling and his leading friends, and the result was the selection of General Chester A. Arthur of New York, for Vice-President. The object of this selection was to carry New York, the great State which was then almost universally believed to hold the key to the Presidential position.

The Democratic National Convention met at Cincinnati, June 22d. Tilden had up to the holding of the Pennsylvania State Convention been one of the most prominent candidates. In this Convention there was a bitter struggle between the Wallace and Randall factions, the former favoring Hancock, the latter Tilden. Wallace, after a contest far sharper than he expected, won, and bound the delegation by the unit rule. When the National Convention met, John Kelly, the Tammany leader of New York, was again there, as at St. Louis four years before, to oppose Tilden, but the latter sent a letter disclaiming that he was a candidate, and yet really inviting a nomination on the issue of "the fraudulent counting in of Hayes." There were but two ballots, as follows:

FIRST BALLOT.

Hancock	171	Randall	6
Bayard	153½	Loveland	5
Payne	81	McDonald	3
Thurman	63½	McClellan	3
Field	66	English	1
Morrison	62	Jewett	1
Hendricks	49½	Black	1
Tilden	38	Lothrop	1
Ewing	10	Parker	1
Seymour	8		

SECOND BALLOT.

Hancock	705
Tilden	1
Bayard	2
Hendricks	30

Thus General Winfield S. Hancock, of New York, was nominated on the second ballot. Wm. H. English, of Indiana, was nominated for Vice-President.

The National Greenback-Labor Convention, held at Chicago, June 11, nominated General J. B. Weaver, of Iowa, for President, and General E. J. Chambers, of Texas, for Vice-President.

In the canvass which followed, the Republicans were aided by such orators as Conkling, Blaine, Grant, Logan, Curtis, Boutwell, while the Camerons, father and son, visited the October States of Ohio and Indiana, as it was believed that these would determine the result, Maine having in September very unexpectedly defeated the Republican State ticket by a small majority. The Democrats were aided by Bayard, Voorhees, Randall, Wallace, Hill, Hampton, Lamar, and hosts of their best orators. Every issue was recalled, but for the first time in the history of the Republicans of the West, they accepted the tariff issue, and made open war on Watterson's plank in the Democratic platform—"a tariff for revenue only." Iowa, Ohio, and Indiana, all elected the Republican State tickets with good margins; West Virginia went Democratic, but the result was, notwithstanding this, reasonably assured to the Republicans. The Democrats, however, feeling the strong personal popularity of their leading candidate, persisted with high courage to the end. In November all of the Southern States, with New Jersey, California,* and Nevada in the North, went Democratic; all of the others Republican. The Greenbackers held only a balance of power, which they could not exercise, in California, Indiana, and New Jersey. The electoral vote of Garfield and Arthur was 214, that of Hancock and English 155. The popular vote was Republican, 4,442,950; Democratic, 4,442,035; Greenback or National, 306,867; scattering, 12,576. The Congressional elections in the same canvass gave the Republicans 147 members; the Democrats, 136; Greenbackers, 9; Independents, 1.

Fifteen States elected Governors, nine of them Republicans and six Democrats.

General Garfield, November 10, sent to Governor Foster, of Ohio, his resignation as a Senator, and John Sherman, the Secretary of the Treasury, was in the winter following elected as his successor.

The third session of the Forty-sixth Congress was begun December 6. The President's Message was read in both Houses. Among its recommendations to Congress were the following: To create the office of Captain-General of the Army for General Grant; to defend the inviolability of the constitutional amendments; to promote free popular education by grants of public lands and appropriations from the United States Treasury; to appropriate $25,000 annually for the expenses of a Commission to be appointed by the President to devise a just, uniform, and efficient system of competitive examinations, and to supervise the application of the same throughout the entire civil service of the government; to pass a law defining the relations of Congressmen to appointments to office, so as to end Congressional encroachment upon the appointing power; to repeal the Tenure-of-office Act, and pass a law protecting office-holders in resistance to political assessments; to abolish the present system of executive and judicial government in Utah, and substitute for it a government by a commission to be appointed by the President and confirmed by the Senate, or, in case the present government is continued, to withhold from all who practice

* One Democratic elector was defeated, being cut by over 500 voters on a local issue.

polygamy the right to vote, hold office, and sit on juries; to repeal the act authorizing the coinage of the silver dollar of 412½ grains, and to authorize the coinage of a new silver dollar equal in value as bullion with the gold dollar; to take favorable action on the bill providing for the allotment of lands on the different reservations.

Two treaties between this country and China were signed at Pekin, November 17, 1881, one of commerce, and the other securing to the United States the control and regulation of the Chinese immigration.

President Hayes, February 1, 1881, sent a message to Congress sustaining in the main the findings of the Ponca Indian Commission, and approving its recommendation that they remain on their reservation in Indian Territory. The President suggested that the general Indian policy for the future should embrace the following ideas: First, the Indians should be prepared for citizenship by giving to their young of both sexes that industrial and general education which is requisite to enable them to be self-supporting and capable of self-protection in civilized communities; second, lands should be allotted to the Indians in severalty, inalienable for a certain period; third, the Indians should have a fair compensation for their lands not required for individual allotments, the amount to be invested, with suitable safeguards, for their benefit; fourth, with these prerequisites secured, the Indians should be made citizens, and invested with the rights and charged with the responsibilities of citizenship.

The Senate, February 4, passed Mr. Morgan's concurrent resolution declaring that the President of the Senate is not invested by the Constitution of the United States with the right to count the votes of electors for President and Vice-President of the United States, so as to determine what votes shall be received and counted, or what votes shall be rejected. An amendment was added declaring in effect that it is the duty of Congress to pass a law at once providing for the orderly counting of the electoral vote. The House concurred February 5, but no action by bill or otherwise has since been taken.

Senator Pendleton, of Ohio, December 15, 1881, introduced a bill to regulate the civil service and to promote the efficiency thereof, and also a bill to prohibit Federal officers, claimants, and contractors from making or receiving assessments or contributions for political purposes.

The Burnside Educational Bill passed the Senate December 17, 1881. It provides that the proceeds of the sale of public land and the earnings of the Patent Office shall be funded at four per cent., and the interest divided among the States in proportion to their illiteracy. An amendment by Senator Morgan provides for the instruction of women in the State agricultural colleges in such branches of technical and industrial education as are suited to their sex. No action has yet been taken by the House.

On the 9th of February the electoral votes were counted by the Vice-President in the presence of both Houses, and Garfield and Arthur were declared elected President and Vice-President of the United States. There was no trouble as to the count, and the result previously stated was formally announced.

The Three Per Cent. Funding Bill.

The 3 per cent. Funding Bill passed the House March 2, and was on the following day vetoed by President Hayes on the ground that it dealt unjustly with the National Banks in compelling them to accept and employ this security for their circulation in lieu of the old bonds. This feature of the bill caused several of the Banks to surrender their circulation, conduct which for a time excited strong political prejudices. The Republicans in Congress as a rule contended that the debt could not be surely funded at 3 per cent.; that 3½ was a safer figure, and to go below this might render the bill of no effect. The same views were entertained by President Hayes and Secretary Sherman. The Democrats insisted on 3 per cent., until the veto, when the general desire to fund at more favorable rates broke party lines, and a 3½ per cent. funding bill was passed, with the feature objectionable to the National Banks omitted.

The Republicans were mistaken in their view, as the result proved. The loan was floated so easily, that in the session of 1882 Secretary Sherman, now a Senator, himself introduced a 3 per cent. bill, which passed the Senate Feb. 2d, 1882, in this shape:—

Be it enacted, &c. That the Secretary of the Treasury is hereby authorized to receive at the Treasury and at the office of any Assistant Treasurer of the United States and at any postal money order office, lawful money of the United States to the amount of fifty dollars or any multiple of that sum or any bonds of the United States, bearing three and a-half per cent. interest, which are hereby declared valid, and to issue in exchange therefore an equal amount of registered or coupon bonds of the United States, of the denomination of fifty, one hundred, five hundred, one thousand and ten thousand dollars, of such form as he may prescribe, bearing interest at the rate three per centum per annum, payable either quarterly or semi-annually, at the Treasury of the United

States. Such bonds shall be exempt from all taxation by or under state authority, and be payable at the pleasure of the United States. "Provided, That the bonds herein authorized shall not be called in and paid so long as any bonds of the United States heretofore issued bearing a higher rate of interest than three per centum, and which shall be redeemable at the pleasure of the United States, shall be outstanding and uncalled. The last of the said bonds originally issued and their substitutes under this act shall be first called in and this order of payment shall be followed until all shall have been paid."

The money deposited under this act shall be promptly applied solely to the redemption of the bonds of the United States bearing three and a-half per centum interest, and the aggregate amount of deposits made and bonds issued under this act shall not exceed the sum of two hundred million dollars. The amount of lawful money so received on deposit, as aforesaid, shall not exceed, at any time, the sum of twenty-five million dollars. Before any deposits are received at any postal money office under this act, the postmaster at such office shall file with the Secretary of the Treasury his bond, with satisfactory security, conditioned that he will promptly transmit to the Treasury of the United States the money received by him in conformity with regulations to be prescribed by such secretary; and the deposit with any postmaster shall not at any time, exceed the amount of his bond.

SECTION 2. Any national banking association now organized or hereafter organized desiring to withdraw its circulating notes upon a deposit of lawful money with the Treasury of the United States as provided in section 4 of the Act of June 20, 1874, entitled "An act fixing the amount of United States notes providing for a redistribution of National bank currency and for other purposes," shall be required to give thirty days' notice to the Controller of the Currency of its intention to deposit lawful money and withdraw its circulating notes; provided that not more than five million of dollars of lawful money shall be deposited during any calender month for this purpose; and provided further, that the provisions of this section shall not apply to bonds called for redemption by the Secretary of the Treasury.

SECTION 3. That nothing in this act shall be so construed as to authorize an increase of the public debt.

In the past few years opinions on the rates of interest have undergone wonderful changes. Many supposed—indeed it was a "standard" argument—that rates must ever be higher in new than old countries, that these higher rates comported with and aided the higher rates paid for commodities and labor. The funding operations since the war have dissipated this belief, and so shaken political theories that no party can now claim a monopoly of sound financial doctrine. So high is the credit of the government, and so abundant are the resources of our people after a comparatively short period of general prosperity, that they seem to have plenty of surplus funds with which to aid any funding operation, however low the rate of interest, if the government—State or National—shows a willingness to pay. As late as February, 1882, Pennsylvania funded seven millions of her indebtedness at 3, 3½ and 4 per cent., the two larger sums commanding premiums sufficient to cause the entire debt to be floated at a little more than 3 per cent., and thus floating commands an additional premium in the money exchanges.

History of the National Loans.

In Book VII of this volume devoted to Tabulated History, we try to give the reader at a glance some idea of the history of our National finances. An attempt to go into details would of itself fill volumes, for no class of legislation has taken so much time or caused such a diversity of opinion Yet it is shown, by an admirable review of the loans of the United States, by Rafael A. Bayley, of the Treasury Department published in the February (1882) number of the *International Review*, that the "financial system of the government of the United States has continued the same from its organization to the present time." Mr. Bayley has completed a history of our National Loans, which will be published in the Census volume on "Public Debts." From his article in the *Review* we condense the leading facts bearing on the history of our national loans.

The financial system of the United States, in all its main features, is simple and well defined, and its very simplicity may probably be assigned as the reason why it appears so difficult of comprehension by many people of intelligence and education. It is based upon the principles laid down by Alexander Hamilton, and the practical adoption of the fundamental maxim which he regarded as the true secret for rendering public credit immortal, viz., "that the creation of the debt should always be accompanied with the means of extinguishment." A faithful adherence to this system by his successors has stood the test of nearly a century, with the nation at peace or at war, in prosperity or adversity; so that, with all the change that progress has entailed upon the people of the age, no valid grounds exist for any change here.

"During the colonial period, and under

the confederation, the financial operations of the Government were based on the law of necessity, and depended for success upon the patriotism of the people, the co-operation of the several States, and the assistance of foreign powers friendly to our cause.

"It was the willingness of the people to receive the various kinds of paper money issued under authority of the Continental Congress, and used in payment for services and supplies, together with the issue of similar obligations by the different States, for the redemption of which they assumed the responsibility; aided by the munificent gift of money from Louis XVI. of France, followed by loans for a large amount from both France and Holland, that made victory possible, and laid the foundations for the republic of to-day, with its credit unimpaired, and with securities commanding a ready sale at a high premium in all the principal markets of the world.

"Authorities vary as to the amount of paper money issued and the cost of the war for independence. On the 1st of September, 1779, Congress resolved that it would 'on no account whatever emit more bills of credit than to make the whole amount of such bills two hundred millions of dollars.' Mr. Jefferson estimates the value of this sum *at the time of its emission* at $36,367,719.83 in specie, and says; 'If we estimate at the same value the like sum of $200,000,000 supposed to have been emitted by the States, and reckon the Federal debt, foreign and domestic, at about $43,000,000, and the State debt at $25,000,000, it will form an amount of $140,000,000, the total sum which the war cost the United States. It continued eight years, from the battle of Lexington to the cessation of hostilities in America. The annual expense was, therefore, equal to about $17,500,000 in specie.'

"The first substantial aid rendered the colonies by any foreign power was a free gift of money and military supplies from Louis XVI. of France, amounting in the aggregate to 10,000,000 livres, equivalent to $1,815,000.

"These supplies were not furnished openly, for the reason that France was not in a position to commence a war with Great Britain. The celebrated Caron de Beaumarchais was employed as a secret agent, between whom and Silas Deane, as the political and commercial agent of the United States, a contract was entered into whereby the former agreed to furnish a large amount of military supplies from the arsenals of France, and to receive American produce in payment therefor.

"Under this arrangement supplies were furnished by the French Government to the amount of 2,000,000 livres. An additional 1,000,000 was contributed by the Government of Spain for the same purpose, and through the same agency. The balance of the French subsidy was paid through Benjamin Franklin. In 1777 a loan of 1,000,000 livres was obtained from the 'Farmers General of France' under a contract for its repayment in American tobacco at a stipulated price. From 1778 to 1783, additional loans were obtained from the French King, amounting to 34,000,000 livres. From 1782 to 1789, loans to the amount of 9,000,000 guilders were negotiated in Holland, through the agency of John Adams, then the American Minister to the Hague.

"The indebtedness of the United States at the organization of the present form of government (including interest to December 31, 1790) may be briefly stated, as follows:

Foreign debt....................	$11,883,315.96
Domestic debt..................	40,256,802.45
Debt due foreign officers...	198,208.10
Arrears outstanding (since discharged).................	450,395.52
Total..........................	$52,788,722.03

To this should be added the individual debts of the several States, the precise amount and character of which was then unknown, but estimated by Hamilton at that time to aggregate about $25,000,000.

"The payment of this vast indebtedness was virtually guarantied by the provisions of Article VI. of the Constitution, which says: 'All debts contracted, and engagements entered into, before the adoption of this Constitution shall be as valid against the United States under this Constitution as under the confederation.' On the 21st of September, 1789, the House of Representatives adopted the following resolutions:

Resolved, That this House consider an adequate provision for the support of the public credit as a matter of high importance to the national honor and prosperity.

Resolved, That the Secretary of the Treasury be directed to prepare a plan for that purpose, and to report the same to this House at its next meeting.

"In reply thereto Hamilton submitted his report on the 9th of January, 1790, in which he gave many reasons for assuming the debts of the old Government, and of the several States, and furnished a plan for supporting the public credit. His recommendations were adopted, and embodied in the act making provision for the payment of the debt of the United States, approved August 4, 1790.

"This act authorized a loan of $12,000,000, to be applied to the payment of the foreign debt, principal and interest; a loan equal to the full amount of the domestic debt, payable in certificates issued for its amount according to their specie value, and computing the interest to December 31, 1791, upon such as bore interest; and a further loan of $21,500,000, payable in the principal and interest of the certificates or notes which, prior to January 1, 1790, were issued by the respective States as evidences of indebtedness incurred by them for the expenses of the late war. 'In the case of the debt of the United States, interest upon two-thirds of the principal only, at 6 per cent., was immediately paid; interest upon the remaining third was deferred for ten years, and only three per cent. was allowed upon the arrears of interest, making one-third of the whole debt. In the case of the separate debts of the States, interest upon four-ninths only of the entire sum was immediately paid; interest upon two-ninths was deferred for ten years, and only 3 per cent. allowed on three-ninths.' Under this authority 6 per cent. stock was issued to the amount of $30,060,-511, and deferred 6 per cent. stock, bearing interest from January 1, 1800, amounting to $14,635,386. This stock was made subject to redemption by payments not exceeding, in one year, on account both of principal and interest, the proportion of eight dollars upon a hundred of the sum mentioned in the certificates; $19,719,237 was issued in 3 per cent. stock, subject to redemption whenever provision should be made by law for that purpose.

"The money needed for the payment of the principal and interest of the foreign debt was procured by new loans negotiated in Holland and Antwerp to the amount of $9,400,000, and the issue of new stock for the balance of $2,024,900 due on the French debt, this stock bearing a rate of interest one-half of one per cent. in advance of the rate previously paid, and redeemable at the pleasure of the Government. Subsequent legislation provided for the establishment of a sinking fund, under the management of a board of commissioners, consisting of the President of the Senate, Chief Justice of the Supreme Court, Secretary of State, Secretary of the Treasury, and Attorney General, for the time being, who, or any three of whom, were authorized, under the direction of the President of the United States, to make purchases of stock, and otherwise provide for the gradual liquidation of the entire debt, from funds set apart for this purpose. On assuming the position of Secretary of the Treasury, Hamilton found himself entirely without funds to meet the ordinary expenses of the Government, except by borrowing, until such time as the revenues from duties on imports and tonnage began to come into the Treasury. Under these circumstances, he was forced to make arrangements with the Bank of New York and the Bank of North America for temporary loans, and it was from the moneys received from these banks that he paid the first installment of salary due President Washington, Senators, Representatives and officers of Congress, during the first session under the Constitution, which began at the city of New York, March 4, 1789.

"The first 'Bank of the United States' appears to have been proposed by Alexander Hamilton in December, 1790, and it was incorporated by an act of Congress, approved February 25, 1791, with a capital stock of $10,000,000 divided into 25,-000 shares at $400 each. The government subscription of $2,000,000, under authority of the act, was paid by giving to the bank bills of exchange on Holland equivalent to gold, and borrowing from the bank a like sum for ten years at 6 per cent. interest. The bank went into operation very soon after its charter was obtained, and declared its first dividend in July, 1792. It was evidently well managed, and was of great benefit to the Government and the people at large, assisting the Government by loans in cases of emergency, and forcing the 'wildcat' banks of the country to keep their issues 'somewhere within reasonable bounds.' More than $100,000,-000 of Government money was received and disbursed by it without the loss of a single dollar. It made semi-annual dividends, averaging about 8½ per cent., and its stock rose to a high price. The stock belonging to the United States was sold out at different times at a profit, 2,220 shares sold in 1802 bringing an advance of 45 per cent. The government subscription, with ten years' interest amounted to $3,200-000, while there was received in dividends and for stock sold $3,773,580, a profit of nearly 28.7 per cent. In 1796 the credit of the Government was very low, as shown by its utter failure to negotiate a loan for the purpose of paying a debt to the Bank of the United States for moneys borrowed and used, partly to pay the expenses of suppressing the whisky insurrection in Pennsylvania and to buy a treaty with the pirates of Algiers. On a loan authorized for $5,000,000, only $80,000 could be obtained, and this at a discount of 12½ per cent.; and, there being no other immediate resource, United States Bank stock to the amount of $1,304,260 was sold at a premium of 25 per cent.

"Under an act approved June 30, 1798, the President was authorized to accept such vessels as were suitable to be armed for the public service, not exceeding twelve in number, and to issue certificates, or other evidences of the public debt of the United States, in payment. The ships George Washington, Merrimack, Maryland and Patapsco, brig Richmond, and frigates Boston, Philadelphia, John Adams, Essex and New York, were purchased, and 6 per cent. stock, redeemable at the pleasure of Congress, was issued in payment to the amount of $711,700.

"The idea of creating a navy by the purchase of vessels built by private parties and issuing stock in payment therefor, seems to have originated with Hamilton.

"In the years 1797 and 1798 the United States, though nominally at peace with all the world, was actually at war with France—a war not formally declared, but carried on upon the ocean with very great virulence. John Marshall, Elbridge Gerry and Charles C. Pinckney were appointed envoys extraordinary to the French Republic, with power for terminating all differences and restoring harmony, good understanding and commercial and friendly intercourse between the two nations; but their efforts were in vain, and extensive preparations were made to resist a French invasion. It was evident that the ordinary revenues of the country would be inadequate for the increased expenditure, and a loan of $5,000,000 was authorized by an act approved July 16, 1798, redeemable at pleasure after fifteen years. The rate of interest was not specified in the act, and the market rate at the time being 8 per cent. this rate was paid, and it was thought by a committee of Congress that the loan was negotiated 'upon the best terms that could be procured, and with a laudable eye to the public interest.' A loan of $3,500,000 was authorized by an act approved May 7, 1800, for the purpose of meeting a large deficit in the revenues of the preceding year, caused by increased expenditures rendered necessary on account of the difficulties with France, and stock bearing 8 per cent. interest, reimbursable after fifteen years, was issued to the amount of $1,481,700, on which a premium was realized of nearly 5¾ per cent. These are the only two instances in which the Government has paid 8 per cent. interest on its bonds.

"The province of Louisiana was ceded to the United States by a treaty with France, April 30, 1803, in payment for which 6 per cent. bonds, payable in fifteen years, were issued to the amount of $11,-250,000, and the balance which the Government agreed to pay for the province, amounting to $3,750,000, was devoted to reimbursing American citizens for French depredations on their commerce. These claims were paid in money, and the stock redeemed by purchases made under the direction of the Commissioners of the Sinking Fund within twelve years. Under an act approved February 11, 1807, a portion of the 'old 6 per cent.' and 'deferred stocks" was refunded into new stock, bearing the same rate of interest, but redeemable at the pleasure of the United States. This was done for the purpose of placing it within the power of the Government to reimburse the amount refunded within a short time, as under the old laws these stocks could only be redeemed at the rate of 2 per cent. annually. Stock was issued amounting to $6,294,051, nearly all of which was redeemed within four years. Under the same act old '3 per cent. stock' to the amount of $2,861,309 was converted into 6 per cents., at sixty-five cents on the dollar, but this was not reimbursable without the assent of the holder until after the whole of certain other stocks named in the act was redeemed. The stock issued under this authority amounted to $1,859,871. It would appear that the great majority of the holders of the "old stock" preferred it to the new. A loan equal to the amount of the principal of the public debt reimbursable during the current year was authorized by an act approved May 1, 1810, and $2,-750,000 was borrowed at 6 per cent. interest from the Bank of the United States, for the purpose of meeting any deficiency arising from increased expenditures on account of the military and naval establishments. This was merely a temporary loan, which was repaid the following year.

"The ordinary expenses for the year 1812 were estimated by the Committee of Ways and Means of the House of Representatives at $1,200,000 more than the estimated receipts for the same period, and the impending war with Great Britain made it absolutely necessary that some measures should be adopted to maintain the public credit, and provide the requisite funds for carrying on the Government. Additional taxes were imposed upon the people, but as these could not be made immediately available there was no other resource but new loans and the issue of Treasury notes. This was the first time since the formation of the new Government that the issue of such notes had been proposed, and they were objected to as engrafting on our system of finance a new and untried measure.

"Under various acts of Congress approved between March 4, 1812, and February 24, 1815, 6 per cent. bonds were issued to the amount of $50,792,674. These bonds were negotiated at rates varying from 20 per cent. discount to par, the net cash realized amounting to $44,530,123. A further sum of $4,025,000 was obtained by temporary loans at par, of which sum $225,000 was for the purpose of repairing the public buildings in Washington, damaged by the enemy on the night of August 24, 1814. These 'war loans' were all made redeemable at the pleasure of the Government after a specified date, and the faith of the United States was solemnly pledged to provide sufficient revenues for this purpose. The 'Treasury note system' was a new feature, and its success was regarded as somewhat doubtful.

"Its subsequent popularity, however, was owing to a variety of causes. The notes were made receivable everywhere for dues and customs, and in payment for public lands. They were to bear interest from the day of issue, at the rate of 5 2-5 per cent. per annum, and their payment was guaranteed by the United States, principal and interest, at maturity. They thus furnished a circulating medium to the country, superior to the paper of the suspended and doubtful State banks. These issues were therefore considered more desirable than the issue of additional stock, which could be realized in cash only by the payment of a ruinous discount. The whole amount of Treasury notes issued during the war period was $36,680,794. The Commissioners of the Sinking Fund were authorized to provide for their redemption by purchase, in the same manner as for other evidences of the public debt, and by authority of law $10,575,738 was redeemed by the issue of certificates of funded stock, bearing interest at from 6 to 7 per cent. per annum, redeemable at any time after 1824.

"During the years 1812-13 the sum of $2,934,747 of the old 6 per cent. and deferred stocks were refunded into new 6 per cent. stock redeemable in twelve years; and by an act approved March 31, 1814, Congress having authorized a settlement of the 'Yazoo claims' by an issue of non-interest-bearing stock, payable out of the first receipts from the sale of public lands in the Missisipi territory, $4,282,037 was issued for this purpose. On the 24th of February, 1815, Secretary Dallas reported to Congress that the public debt had been increased, in consequence of the war with Great Britain, $68,783,122, a large portion of which was due and unpaid, while another considerable proportion was fast becoming due. These unpaid or accruing demands were in part for temporary loans, and the balance for Treasury notes either due or maturing daily. To provide for their payment a new loan for the full amount needed was authorized by act of March 3, 1815, and six per. cent stock redeemable in fifteen years, was issued in the sum of $12,288,148. This stock was sold at from 95 per cent. to par, and was nearly all redeemed in 1820 by purchases made by the Commissioners of the Sinking Fund.

"The Government became a stockholder in the second Bank of the United States, to the amount of 70,000 shares, under the act of incorporation, approved April 10, 1816. The capital stock was limited to $35,000,000, divided into 350,000 shares of $100 each. The Government subscription was paid by the issue of 5 per cent. stock to the amount of $7,000,000, redeemable at the pleasure of the Government. This was a profitable investment for the United States, as in addition to $1,500,000 which the bank paid as a bonus for its charter, the net receipts over and above disbursements amounted to $4,993,167. The available funds in the Treasury on the 1st of January, 1820, were less than $250,000, and the estimated deficiency for the year amounted to nearly $4,000,000. This state of affairs was owing partly to the disastrous effects of the commercial crisis of 1819, heavy payments for the redemption of the public debt, continued through a series of years, and large outstanding claims, amounting to over $30,000,000, resulting from the late war with Great Britain. To meet the emergency, a loan was authorized by act of May 15, 1820, and $999,999.13 was borrowed at 5 per cent., redeemable in twelve years, and $2,000,000 at 6 per cent., reimbursable at pleasure, this latter stock realizing a premium of 2 per cent. By act of March 3, 1821, 5 per cent. stock amounting to $4,735,276 was issued at a premium of over 5½ per cent., and the proceeds used in payment of the principal and interest of the public debt falling due within the year.

"An effort was made in 1822 to refund a portion of the 6 per cent. war loans of 1812-14 into 5 per cents., but only $56,705 could be obtained. Two years later the Government was more successful, and, under the act of May 26, 1824, 6 per cent. stock of 1813 to the amount of $4,454,728 was exchanged for new stock bearing 4½ per cent. interest, redeemable in 1833-34. During the same year $5,000,000 was borrowed at 4½ per cent. to provide for the payment of the awards made by the Commissioners under the treaty with Spain of February 22, 1819, and a like amount, at the same rate of interest, to be applied in paying off that part of the 6 per cent. stock of 1812 redeemable the following year. The act of March 3, 1825, authorized a loan of $12,000,000, at 4½ per cent. interest, the money borrowed to be applied in paying off prior loans, but only $1,539,336 was exchanged for an equal amount of 6 per cent. stock of 1813.

"In the year 1836 the United States was, for the first time in the history of the country, practically out of debt. Secretary Woodbury, in his report of December 8, 1836, estimated the amount of public debt still outstanding at about $328,582, and this remained unpaid solely because payment had not been demanded, ample funds to meet it having been deposited in the United States Bank and loan offices. The debt outstanding consisted mainly of unclaimed interest and dividends, of claims for services and supplies during the Revolution, and of old Treasury notes, and it is supposed that payment of these had not been asked for solely because the evidences of the debt had been lost or destroyed. The estimates showed the probability of a surplus of at least $14,000,000 in the Treasury at the close of the year 1836, and this estimate proved to be far below the truth. In this favorable condition of the public finances, Congress adopted the extraordinary resolution of depositing the surplus over $5,000,000 with the several States, and under the act of June 23, 1836, surplus revenue amounting to $28,101,644.91 was so deposited.

"In 1837, however, the state of the country had changed. The 'flush' times of 1835 and 1836 had been succeeded by extraordinary depression, which ultimately produced a panic. In May most of the banks suspended specie payments. The sales of public lands, and the duties on the importations of foreign goods, which had helped to swell the balance in the Treasury to over $42,000,000, had fallen off enormously. Even on the goods that were imported it was difficult to collect the duties, for the law compelled them to be paid in specie, and specie was hard to obtain. It had become impossible not only to pay the fourth installment of the surplus at the end of 1836 to the several States, but even to meet the current expenses of the Government from its ordinary revenues. In this emergency the Secretary of the Treasury suggested that contingent authority be given the President to cause the issue of Treasury notes. This measure was generally supported on the ground of absolute necessity, as there was a large deficit already existing, and this was likely to increase from the condition of the country at that time. The measure was opposed, however, by some who thought that greater economy in expenditures would relieve the Treasury, while others denounced it as an attempt "to start a Treasury bank."

"However, an act was approved October 12, 1837, authorizing an issue of $10,000,000 in Treasury notes in denominations not less than fifty dollars, redeemable in one year from date, with interest at rates fixed by the Secretary, not exceeding 6 per cent. These notes, as usual, were receivable in payment of all duties and taxes levied by the United States, and in payment for public lands. Prior to 1846, the issue of notes of this character amounted to $47,002,900, bearing interest at rates varying from one-tenth of one per cent. to 6 per cent. To provide in part for their redemption, authority was granted for the negotiation of several loans, and $21,021,094 was borrowed for this purpose, bonds being issued for a like sum, bearing interest at from 5 to 6 per cent., redeemable at specified dates. These bonds were sold at from 2½ per cent. discount to 3¾ per cent. premium, and redeemed at from par to 19¾ per cent. advance.

"War with Mexico was declared May 13, 1846, and in order to provide against a deficiency a further issue of $10,000,000 in Treasury notes was authorized by act of July 22, 1846, under the same limitations and restrictions as were contained in the act of October, 1837, except that the authority given was to expire at the end of one year from the passage of the act. The sum of $7,687,800 was issued in Treasury notes, and six per cent. bonds having ten years to run were issued under the same act to the amount of $4,999,149. These were sold at a small advance, and redeemed at various rates from par to eighteen and two-thirds per cent. premium.

"The expenses incurred on account of the war with Mexico were much greater than the original estimates, and the failure to provide additional revenues sufficient to meet the increased demands made a new loan necessary, as well as an additional issue of notes, which had now become a popular method of obtaining funds. Under the authority granted by act of January 28, 1847, Treasury notes to the amount of $26,122,100 were issued at par, redeemable one and two years from date, with interest at from 5 2–5 to 6 per cent. More money still being needed, a 6 per cent. loan, having twenty years to run, was placed upon the market, under the authority of the same act, and bonds to the amount of $28,230,350 were sold at various rates, ranging from par to 2 per cent. premium. Of this stock the sum of $18,815,100 was redeemed at an advance of from 1¼ to 21¼ per cent., the premium paid (exclusive of commissions) amounting to $3,466,107. Under the act of March 31, 1848, 6 per cent. bonds, running twenty years, were issued to the amount of $16,000,000, and sold at a premium ranging from 3 to 4.05 per cent. This loan was made for the same purpose as the preceding one, and $7,091,658 was redeemed by purchase at an advance ranging from 8 to 22.46 per cent., the premium paid amounting to $1,251,258.

"The widespread depression of trade and commerce which occurred in 1857 was severely felt by the Government, as well as by the people, and so great was the decrease in the revenues from customs that it became absolutely necessary to provide the Treasury with additional means for meeting the demands upon it. Treasury notes were considered as preferable to a new loan, and by the act of December 23, 1857, a new issue was authorized for such an amount as the exigencies of the public service might require, but not to exceed at any one time $20,000,000. These notes were receivable in payment for all debts due the United States, including customs, and were issued at various rates of interest, ranging from 3 to 6 per cent., to the amount of $52,778,900, redeemable one year from date, the interest to cease at the expiration of sixty days' notice after maturity. In May, 1858, the Secretary of the Treasury informed Congress that, owing to the appropriations having been increased by legislation nearly $10,000,000 over the estimates, while the customs revenue had fallen off to a like amount, it would be necessary to provide some means to meet the deficit. In these circumstances, a new loan was authorized by act of June 14, 1858, and 5 per cent. bonds amounting to $20,000,000, redeemable in fifteen years, were sold at an average premium of over 3½ per cent. Under the act of December 17, 1873, $13,957,000 in bonds of the loan of 1881, and $260,000 in bonds of a loan of 1907, were issued in exchange for a like amount of bonds of this loan.

"The act of June 22, 1860, authorized the President to borrow $21,000,000 on the credit of the United States, the money to be used only in the redemption of Treasury notes, and to replace any amount of such notes in the Treasury which should have been paid in for public dues. Only $7,022,000 was borrowed at 5 per cent. interest, the certificates selling at from par to 1.45 per cent. premium. The failure to realize the whole loan was caused by the political troubles which culminated in the civil war. In September, bids were invited for $10,000,000, and the whole amount offered was speedily taken. It soon became evident, however, that war was inevitable, and a commercial crisis ensued, during which a portion of the bidders forfeited their deposits, and the balance of the loan was withdrawn from the market. Authority was granted by the act of December 17, 1860, for a new issue of Treasury notes, redeemable in one year from date, but not to exceed $10,000,000 at any one time, with interest at such rates as might be offered by the lowest responsible bidders after advertisement. An unsuccessful attempt was made to pledge the receipts from the sale of public lands specifically for their redemption. The whole amount of notes issued under this act was $10,010,900, of which $4,840,000 bore interest at 12 per cent. Additional offers followed, ranging from 15 to 36 per cent., but the Treasury declined to accept them.

"Up to this period of our national existence the obtaining of the money necessary for carrying on the Government and the preservation inviolate of the public credit had been comparatively an easy task. The people of the several States had contributed in proportion to their financial resources; and a strict adherence to the fundamental maxim laid down by Hamilton had been maintained by a judicious system of taxation to an extent amply sufficient to provide for the redemption of all our national securities as they became due. But the time had come when we were no longer a united people, and the means required for defraying the ordinary expenses of the Government were almost immediately curtailed and jeopardized by the attitude of the States which attempted to secede. The confusion which followed the inauguration of the administration of President Lincoln demonstrated the necessity of providing unusual resources without delay. A system of internal revenue taxation was introduced, and the tariff adjusted with a view to increased revenues from customs. As the Government had not only to exist and pay its way, but also to provide for an army and navy constantly increasing in numbers and equipment, new and extraordinary methods were resorted to for the purpose of securing the money which must be had in order to preserve the integrity of the nation. Among these were the issue of its own circulating medium in the form of United States notes* and circulating notes,† for the redemption of which the faith of the nation was solemnly pledged. New loans were authorized to an amount never before known in our history, and the success of our armies was assured by the determination manifested by the people themselves to sustain the Government at all hazards. A brief review of the loan transactions during the period covered by the war is all that can be attempted within the limited space afforded this article. The first war loan may be considered as having been negotiated under the authority of an act approved February 8, 1861. The credit of the Government at this time was very low, and a loan of $18,415,000, having twenty years to run, with 6 per cent. interest, could only be negotiated at a discount of $2,019,776.10, or at an average rate of $89.03 per one hundred dollars. From this time to June 30, 1865, Government securities of various descriptions were issued under authority of law to the amount of $3,888,686,575, including the several issues of bonds, Treasury notes, seven-thirties, legal tenders and fractional currency. The whole amount issued under the same authority to June 30, 1880, was $7,137,646,836, divided as follows:

Six per cent. bonds	$1,130,279,000
Five per cent. bonds	196,118,300
Temporary loan certificates	969,992,250
Seven-thirty notes	716,099,247
Treasury notes and certificates of indebtedness	1,074,713,132
Old demand notes, legal tenders, coin certificates and fractional currency	3,050,444,907
Total	$7,137,646,836

"This increase may be readily accounted for by the continued issue of legal tenders,

* Commonly called "Greenbacks," or "Legal Tender notes."

† Commonly called "National Bank notes."

compound interest notes, fractional currency and coin certificates, together with a large amount of bonds issued in order to raise the money necessary to pay for military supplies, and other forms of indebtedness growing out of the war. The rebellion was practically at an end in May, 1865, yet the large amount of money required for immediate use in the payment and disbandment of our enormous armies necessitated the still further negotiation of loans under the several acts of Congress then in force, and it was not until after the 31st of August, 1865, that our national debt began to decrease. At that time the total indebtedness, exclusive of the "old funded and unfunded debt" of the Revolution, and of cash in the Treasury, amounted to $2,844,646,626.56. The course of our financial legislation since that date has been constantly toward a reduction of the interest, as well as the principal of the public debt.

"By an act approved March 3, 1865, a loan of $600,000,000 was authorized upon similar terms as had been granted for previous loans, with the exception that nothing authorized by this act should be made a legal tender, or be issued in smaller denominations than fifty dollars. The rate of interest was limited to 6 per cent. in coin, or 7.3 per cent. in currency, the bonds issued to be redeemable in not less than five, nor more than forty, years. Authority was also given for the conversion of Treasury notes or other interest-bearing obligations into bonds of this loan. An amendment to this act was passed April 12, 1866, authorizing the Secretary of the Treasury, at his discretion, to receive any Treasury notes or other obligations issued under any act of Congress, whether bearing interest or not, in exchange for any description of bonds authorized by the original act; and also to dispose of any such bonds, either in the United States or elsewhere, to such an amount, in such manner, and at such rates as he might deem advisable, for lawful money, Treasury notes, certificates of indebtedness, certificates of deposit, or other representatives of value, which had been or might be issued under any act of Congress; the proceeds to be used only for retiring Treasury notes or other national obligations, provided the public debt was not increased thereby. As this was the first important measure presented to Congress since the close of the war tending to place our securities upon a firm basis, the action of Congress in relation to it was looked forward to with a great deal of interest. The discussion took a wide range, in which the whole financial administration of the Government during the war was reviewed at length. After a long and exciting debate the bill finally passed, and was approved by the President. Under the authority of these two acts, 6 per cent. bonds to the amount of $958,483,550 have been issued to date. These bonds were disposed of at an aggregate premium of $21,522,074, and under the acts of July 14, 1870, and January 20, 1871, the same bonds to the amount of $725,582,400 have been refunded into other bonds bearing a lower rate of interest. The success of these several loans was remarkable, every exertion being used to provide for their general distribution among the people.

"In 1867 the first issue of 6 per cent. bonds, known as five-twenties, authorized by the act of Feb. 25, 1862, became redeemable, and the question of refunding them and other issues at a lower rate of interest had been discussed by the Secretary of the Treasury in his annual reports, but the agitation of the question as to the kinds of money in which the various obligations of the Government should be paid, had so excited the apprehension of investors as to prevent the execution of any refunding scheme.

"The act to strengthen the public credit was passed March 18, 1869, and its effect was such as secured to the public the strongest assurances that the interest and principal of the public debt outstanding at that time would be paid in coin, according to the terms of the bonds issued, without any abatement.

"On the 12th of January, 1870, a bill authorizing the refunding and consolidation of the national debt was introduced in the Senate, and extensively debated in both Houses for several months, during which the financial system pursued by the Government during the war was freely reviewed. The adoption of the proposed measure resulted in an entire revolution of the refunding system, under which the public debt of the United States at that time was provided for, by the transmission of a large amount of debt to a succeeding generation. The effect of this attempt at refunding the major portion of the public debt was far more successful than any similar effort on the part of any Government, so far as known.

The act authorizing refunding certificates convertible into 4 per cent. bonds, approved February 26, 1879, was merely intended for the benefit of parties of limited means, and was simply a continuation of the refunding scheme authorized by previous legislation.

"The period covered precludes any attempt toward reviewing the operation by which the immediate predecessor of the present Secretary reduced the interest on some six hundred millions of 5 and 6 per cent. bonds to 3½ per cent. It is safe to say, however, that under the administration of the present Secretary there will be no deviation from the original law laid down by Hamilton.

James A. Garfield.

James A. Garfield and Chester A. Arthur were publicly inaugurated President and Vice President of the United States March 4, 1881.

President Garfield in his inaugural address promised full and equal protection of the Constitution and the laws for the negro, advocated universal education as a safeguard of suffrage, and recommended such an adjustment of our monetary system "that the purchasing power of every coined dollar will be exactly equal to its debt-paying power in all the markets of the world." The national debt should be refunded at a lower rate of interest, without compelling the withdrawal of the National Bank notes, polygamy should be prohibited, and civil service regulated by law.

An extra session of the Senate was opened March 4. On the 5th, the following cabinet nominations were made and confirmed: Secretary of State, James G. Blaine, of Maine; Secretary of the Treasury, William Windom, of Minnesota; Secretary of the Navy, William H. Hunt, of Louisiana; Secretary of War, Robert T. Lincoln, of Illinois; Attorney General, Wayne MacVeagh, of Pennsylvania; Postmaster General, Thomas L. James, of New York; Secretary of the Interior, Samuel J. Kirkwood, of Iowa.

In this extra session of the Senate Vice President Arthur had to employ the casting vote on all questions where the parties divided, and he invariably cast it on the side of the Republicans. The evenness of the parties caused a dead-lock on the question of organization, for when David Davis, of Illinois, voted with the Democrats, the Republicans had not enough even with the Vice President, and he was not, therefore, called upon to decide a question of that kind. The Republicans desired new and Republican officers; the Democrats desired to retain the old and Democratic ones.

Republican Factions.

President Garfield, March 23d, sent in a large number of nominations, among which was that of William H. Robertson, the leader of the Blaine wing of the Republican party in New York, to be Collector of Customs. He had previously sent in five names for prominent places in New York, at the suggestion of Senator Conkling, who had been invited by President Garfield to name his friends. At this interview it was stated that Garfield casually intimated that he would make no immediate change in the New York Collectorship, and both factions seemed satisfied to allow Gen'l Edwin A. Merritt to retain that place for a time at least. There were loud protests, however, at the first and early selection of the friends of Senator Conkling to five important places, and these protests were heeded by the President. With a view to meet them, and, doubtless, to quiet the spirit of faction rapidly developing between the Grant and anti-Grant elements of the party in New York, the name of Judge Robertson was sent in for the Collectorship. He had battled against the unit rule at Chicago, disavowed the instructions of his State Convention to vote for Grant, and led the Blaine delegates from that State while Blaine was in the field, and when withdrawn went to Garfield. Senator Conkling now sought to confirm his friends, and hold back his enemy from confirmation; but these tactics induced Garfield to withdraw the nomination of Conkling's friends, and in this way Judge Robertson's name was alone presented for a time. Against this course Vice-President Arthur and Senators Conkling and Platt remonstrated in a letter to the President, but he remained firm. Senator Conkling, under the plea of "the privilege of the Senate,"—a courtesy and custom which leaves to the Senators of a State the right to say who shall be confirmed or rejected from their respective States if of the same party—now sought to defeat Robertson. In this battle he had arrayed against him the influence of his great rival, Mr. Blaine, and it is presumed the whole power of the administration. He lost, and the morning following the secret vote, May 17th, 1881, his own and the resignation of Senator Platt were read. These resignations caused great excitement throughout the entire country. They were prepared without consultation with any one—even Vice-President Arthur, the intimate friend of both, not knowing anything of the movement until the letters were opened at the chair where he presided. Logan and Cameron—Conkling's colleagues in the great Chicago battle—were equally unadvised. The resignations were forwarded to Gov. Cornell, of New York, who, by all permissible delays, sought to have them reconsidered and withdrawn, but both Senators were firm. The Senate confirmed Judge Robertson for Collector, and General Merritt as Consul-General at London, May 18th, President Garfield having wisely renewed the Conkling list of appointees, most of whom declined under the changed condition of affairs.

These events more widely separated the factions in New York—one wing calling itself "Stalwart," the other "Half-Breed," a term of contempt flung at the Independents by Conkling. Elections must follow to fill the vacancies, the New York Legislature being in session. These vacancies gave the Democrats for the time control of the United States Senate, but they thought it unwise to pursue an advantage which would compel them to show their hands for or against one or other of the opposing Republican factions. The extra session of the Senate adjourned May 20th.

The New York Legislature began balloting for successors to Senators Conkling and Platt on the 31st of May. The majority of the Republicans (Independents or "Half-breeds") supported Chauncey M. Depew as the successor of Platt for the long term, and William A. Wheeler as the successor of Conkling for the short term, a few supporting Cornell. The minority (Stalwarts) renominated Messrs. Conkling and Platt. The Democrats nominated Francis Kernan for the long term, and John C. Jacobs for the short term; and, on his withdrawal, Clarkson N. Potter. The contest lasted until July 22, and resulted in a compromise on Warner A. Miller as Platt's successor, and Elbridge G. Lapham as Conkling's successor. In Book VII., our Tabulated History of Politics, we give a correct table of the ballots. These show at a single glance the earnestness and length of the contest.

The factious feelings engendered thereby were carried into the Fall nominations for the Legislature, and as a result the Democrats obtained control, which in part they subsequently lost by the refusal of the Tammany Democrats to support their nominees for presiding officers. This Democratic division caused a long and tiresome deadlock in the Legislature of New York. It was broken in the House by a promise on the part of the Democratic candidate for Speaker to favor the Tammany men with a just distribution of the committees — a promise which was not satisfactorily carried out, and as a result the Tammany forces of the Senate joined hands with the Republicans. The Republican State ticket would also have been lost in the Fall of 1881, but for the interposition of President Arthur, who quickly succeeded in uniting the warring factions. This work was so well done, that all save one name on the ticket (Gen'l Husted) succeeded.

The same factious spirit was manifested in Pennsylvania in the election of U. S. Senator in the winter of 1881, the two wings taking the names of "Regulars" and "Independents." The division occurred before the New York battle, and it is traceable not alone to the bitter nominating contest at Chicago, but to the administration of President Hayes and the experiment of civil service reform. Administrations which are not decided and firm upon political issues, invariably divide their parties, and while these divisions are not always to be deplored, and sometimes lead to good results, the fact that undecided administrations divide the parties which they represent, ever remains. The examples are plain: Van Buren's, Tyler's, Fillmore's, Buchanan's, and Hayes'. The latter's indecision was more excusable than that of any of his predecessors. The inexorable firmness of Grant caused the most bitter partisan assaults, and despite all his efforts to sustain the "carpet-bag governments" of the South, they became unpopular and were rapidly supplanted. As they disappeared, Democratic representation from the South increased, and this increase continued during the administration of Hayes—the greatest gains being at times when he showed the greatest desire to conciliate the South. Yet his administration did the party good, in this, that while at first dividing, it finally cemented through the conviction that experiments of that kind with a proud Southern people were as a rule unavailing. The re-opening of the avenues of trade and other natural causes, apparently uncultivated, have accomplished in this direction much more than any political effort.

In Pennsylvania a successor to U. S. Senator Wm. A. Wallace was to be chosen. Henry W. Oliver, Jr., received the nomination of the Republican caucus, the friends of Galusha A. Grow refusing to enter after a count had been made, and declaring in a written paper that they would not participate in any caucus, and would independently manifest their choice in the Legislature. The following is the first vote in joint Convention:

OLIVER.		WALLACE.	
Senate	20	Senate	16
House	75	House	77
Total	95	Total	93
GROW.		**AGNEW.**	
Senate	12	Senate	1
House	44	House	...
Total	56	Total	1
BREWSTER.		**BAIRD.**	
Senate	...	Senate	...
House	1	House	1
Total	1	Total	1
M'VEAGH.			
Senate	...		
House	1		
Total	1		

Whole number of votes cast, 248; necessary to a choice, 125.

On the 17th of January the two factions issued opposing addresses. From these we quote the leading ideas, which divided the factions. The "Regulars" said:

"Henry W. Oliver, jr., of Allegheny county, was nominated on the third ballot, receiving 79 of the 95 votes present. Under the rules of all parties known to the present or past history of our country, a majority of those participating should have been sufficient; but such was the desire for party harmony and for absolute fairness, that a majority of all the Republican members of the Senate and House was required to nominate. The effect of this was to give those remaining out a negative voice in the proceedings, the extent of any privilege given them in regular legislative sessions by the Constitution. In no other caucus or convention has the minority ever found such high consideration, and we believe there remains no just cause of complaint against the result. Even captious faultfinding can find no place upon which to hang a sensible objection. Mr. Oliver was, therefore, fairly nominated by the only body to which is delegated the power of nomination and by methods which were more than just, which, from every standpoint, must be regarded as generous; and in view of these things, how can we, your Senators and Representatives, in fairness withhold our support from him in open sessions; rather how can we ever abandon a claim established by the rules regulating the government of all parties, accepted by all as just, and which are in exact harmony with that fundamental principle of our Government which proclaims the right of the majority to rule? To do otherwise is to confess the injustice and the failure of that principle—something we are not prepared to do. It would blot the titles to our own positions. There is not a Senator or member who does not owe his nomination and election to the same great principle. To profit by its acceptance in our own cases and to deny it to Mr. Oliver would be an exhibition of selfishness too flagrant for our taste. To acknowledge the right to revolt when no unfairness can be truthfully alleged and when more than a majority have in the interest of harmony been required to govern, would be a travesty upon every American notion and upon that sense of manliness which yields when fairly beaten."

The "Independent" address said:

"*First.* We recognize a public sentiment which demands that in the selection of a United States Senator we have regard to that dignity of the office to be filled, its important duties and functions, and the qualifications of the individual with reference thereto. This sentiment is, we understand, that there are other and higher qualifications for this distinguished position than business experience and success, and reckons among these the accomplishments of the scholar, the acquirements of the student, the mature wisdom of experience and a reasonable familiarity with public affairs. It desires that Pennsylvania shall be distinguished among her sister Commonwealths, not only by her populous cities, her prosperous communities, her vast material wealth and diversified industries and resources, but that in the wisdom, sagacity and statesmanship of her representative she shall occupy a corresponding rank and influence. To meet this public expectation and demand we are and have at all times been willing to subordinate our personal preferences, all local considerations and factional differences, and unite with our colleagues in the selection of a candidate in whom are combined at least some of these important and essential qualifications. It was only when it became apparent that the party caucus was to be used to defeat this popular desire and to coerce a nomination which is conspicuously lacking in the very essentials which were demanded, that we determined to absent ourselves from it. * * * *

"*Second,* Having declined to enter the caucus, we adhere to our determination to defeat, if possible, its nominee, but only by the election of a citizen of unquestioned fidelity to the principles of the Republican party. In declaring our independency from the caucus domination we do not forget our allegiance to the party whose chosen representatives we are. The only result of our policy is the transfer of the contest from the caucus to the joint convention of the two houses. There will be afforded an opportunity for the expression of individual preferences and honorable rivalry for an honorable distinction. If the choice shall fall upon one not of approved loyalty and merit, the fault will not be ours."

After a long contest both of the leading candidates withdrew, and quickly the Regulars substituted General James A. Beaver, the Independent Congressman, Thomas M. Bayne. On these names the dead-lock remained unbroken. Without material change the balloting continued till February 17th, when both Republican factions agreed to appoint conference committees of twelve each, with a view to selecting by a three-fourths vote a compromise candidate. The following were the respective committees: For the Independents: Senators Davis, Bradford; Lee, Venango; Stewart, Franklin; Lawrence, Washington; Representatives Wolfe, Union; Silverthorne, Erie; Mapes, Venango; McKee, Philadelphia; Slack, Allegheny; Stubs, Chester; Niles, Tioga; and Derickson, Crawford. For the Regulars: Senators Greer, Butler; Herr, Dauphin; Smith, Philadelphia; Keefer, Schuylkill; Cooper, Delaware; Representatives Pollock, Philadelphia; Moore, Allegheny; Marshall, Huntingdon; Hill, Indiana; Eshleman, Lancaster; Thomson, Armstrong; and Billingsley, Washington.

The joint convention held daily sessions and balloted without result until February

22d, when John I. Mitchell, of Tioga, Congressman from the 16th district, was unanimously agreed upon as a compromise candidate. He was nominated by a full Republican caucus on the morning of February 23d, and elected on the first ballot in joint convention on that day, the vote standing: Mitchell, 150; Wallace, 92; MacVeagh, 1; Brewster, 1.

The spirit of this contest continued until fall. Senator Davies, a friend of Mr. Grow, was a prominent candidate for the Republican nomination for State Treasurer. He was beaten by General Silas M. Baily, and Davies and his friends cordially made Baily's nomination unanimous. Charles S. Wolfe, himself the winter before a candidate for United States Senator, was dissatisfied. He suddenly raised the Independent flag, in a telegram to the Philadelphia *Press*, and as he announced was "the nominee of a convention of one" for State Treasurer. After a canvass of remarkable energy on the part of Mr. Wolfe, General Baily was elected, without suffering materially from the division. Mr. Wolfe obtained nearly 50,000 votes, but as almost half of them were Democratic, the result was, as stated, not seriously affected.

The Independents in Pennsylvania, however, were subdivided into two wings, known as the Continental and the Wolfe men—the former having met since the election last fall, (State Senator John Stewart, chairman) and proclaimed themselves willing and determined to abide all Republican nominations fairly made, and to advocate "reform within the party lines." These gentlemen supported Gen. Baily and largely contributed to his success, and as a rule they regard with disfavor equal to that of the Regulars, what is known as the Wolfe movement. These divisions have not extended to other States, nor have they yet assumed the shape of third parties unless Mr. Wolfe's individual canvass can be thus classed. Up to this writing (March 10, 1882,) neither wing has taken issue with President Arthur or his appointments, though there were some temporary indications of this when Attorney General MacVeagh, of Pennsylvania, persisted in having his resignation accepted. President Arthur refused to accept, on the ground that he desired MacVeagh's services in the prosecution of the Star Route cases, and Mr. MacVeagh withdrew for personal and other reasons not yet fully explained. In this game of political fence the position of the President was greatly strengthened.

Singularly enough, in the only two States where factious divisions have been recently manifested in the Republican ranks, they effected almost if not quite as seriously the Democratic party. There can be but one deduction drawn from this, to wit:—That a number in both of the great parties, were for the time at least, weary of their allegiance. It is possible that nothing short of some great issue will restore the old partisan unity, and partisan unity in a Republic, where there are but two great parties, is not to be deplored if relieved of other than mere political differences. The existence of but two great parties, comparatively free from factions, denotes government health; where divisions are numerous and manifest increasing growth and stubbornness, there is grave danger to Republican institutions. We need not, however, philosophize when Mexico and the South American Republics are so near.

The Caucus.

Both the "Independents" of Pennsylvania and the "Half-Breeds" of New York at first proclaimed their opposition to the caucus system of nominating candidates for U. S. Senators, and the newspapers in their interest wrote as warmly for a time against "King Caucus" as did the dissatisfied Democratic journals in the days of De Witt Clinton. The situation, however, was totally different, and mere declamation could not long withstand the inevitable. In Pennsylvania almost nightly "conferences" were held by the Independents, as indeed they were in New York, though in both States a show of hostility was kept up to nominating in party caucus men who were to be elected by representative, more plainly legislative votes. It was at first claimed that in the Legislature each man ought to act for himself or his constituents, but very shortly it was found that the caucuses of the separate wings were as binding upon the respective wings as they could have been upon the whole. Dead-locks were interminable as long as this condition of affairs obtained, and hostility to the caucus system was before very long quietly discouraged and finally flatly abandoned, for each struggle was ended by the ratification of a general caucus, and none of them could have been ended without it. The several attempts to find other means to reach a result, only led the participants farther away from the true principle, under republican forms at least, of the right of the majority to rule. In Pennsylvania, when Mr. Oliver withdrew, fifty of his friends assembled and informally named General Beaver, and by this action sought to bind the original 95 friends of Oliver. Their conduct was excused by the plea that they represented a majority of their faction. It failed to bind all of the original number, though some of the Independents were won. The Independents, rather the original 44, bound themselves in writing not to change their course of action unless there was secured the previous concurrence of two-thirds, and this principle was extended to the 56 who supported Mr. Bayne. Then when the joint committee of 24 was agreed upon, it was bound by a rule requiring three-fourths to recommend a candidate. All of these were plain departures from a great principle, and the deeper the contest became, the greater the departure. True, these were but voluntary forms, but they were indefensible, and are only referred to now to show the danger of mad assaults upon great principles when personal and factious aims are at stake. Opposition to the early Congressional caucus was plainly right, since one department of the Government was by voluntary agencies actually controlling another, while the law gave legal forms which could be more properly initiated through voluntary action. The writer believes, and past contests all confirm the view that the voluntary action can only be safely employed by the power by the law with the right of selection. Thus the people elect township, county and State officers, and it is their right and duty by the best attainable voluntary action to indicate their choice. This is done through the caucus or convention, the latter not differing from the former save in extent and possibly breadth of representation. The same rule applies to all offices elective by the people. It cannot properly apply to appointive offices, and while the attempt to apply it to the election of U. S. Senators shows a strong desire on the part, frequently of the more public-spirited citizens, to exercise a greater share in the selection of these officers than the law directly gives them, yet their representatives can very properly be called upon to act as they would act if they had direct power in the premises, and such action leads them into a party caucus, where the will of the majority of their respective parties can be fairly ascertained, and when ascertained respected. The State Legislatures *appoint* U. S. Senators, and the Representatives and Senators of the States are bound to consider in their selection the good of the entire State. If this comports with the wish of their respective districts, very well; if it does not, their duty is not less plain. Probably the time will never come when the people will elect United States Senators; to do that is to radically change the Federal system, and to practically destroy one of the most important branches of the Government; yet he is not a careful observer who does not note a growing disposition on the part of the people, and largely the people of certain localities, and imaginary political sub-divisions, to control these selections. The same is true of Presidential nominations, where masses of people deny the right of State Conventions to instruct their delegates-at-large. In many States the people composing either of the great parties now select their own representative delegates to National Conventions, and where their selections are not respected, grave party danger is sure to follow. There is nothing wrong in this, since it points to, and is but paving the way for a more popular selection of Presidents and Vice Presidents—to an eventual selection of Presidential electors probably by Congressional districts. Yet those to be selected at large must through practical voluntary forms be nominated in that way, and the partisan State Convention is the best method yet devised for this work, and its instructions should be as binding as those of the people upon their representatives. In this government of ours there is voluntary and legal work delegated to the people directly; there is legal work delegated to appointing powers, and an intelligent discrimination should ever be exercised between the two. "Render unto Cæsar those things which are Cæsar's," unless there be a plain desire, backed by a good reason, to promote popular reforms as enduring as the practices and principles which they are intended to support.

Fredrick W. Whitridge, in an able review of the caucus system published * in Lalor's *Encyclopædia of Political Science*, says:

"A caucus, in the political vocabulary of the United States, is primarily a private meeting of voters holding similar views, held prior to an election for the purpose of furthering such views at the election. With the development of parties, and the rule of majorities, the caucus or some equivalent has become an indispensable adjunct to party government, and it may now be defined as a meeting of the majority of the electors belonging to the same party in any political or legislative body held preliminary to a meeting thereof, for the purpose of selecting candidates to be voted for, or for the purpose of determining the course of the party at the meeting of the whole body. The candidates of each party are universally selected by caucus, either directly or indirectly through delegates to conventions chosen in caucuses. In legislative bodies the course of each party is often predetermined with certainty in caucus, and often discussion between parties has been, in consequence, in some degree superseded. The caucus system is, in short, the basis of a complete electoral system which has grown up within each party, side by side with that which is alone contemplated by the laws. This condition has in recent years attracted much attention, and has been bitterly announced as an evil. It was, however, early foreseen. John Adams, in 1814, wrote in the "Tenth

* By Rand & McNally, Chicago, Ill., 1882.

Letter on Government:" "They have invented a balance to all balance in their caucuses. We have congressional caucuses, state caucuses, county caucuses, city caucuses, district caucuses, town caucuses, parish caucuses, and Sunday caucuses at church doors, and in these aristocratical caucuses *elections have been decided*." The caucus is a necessary consequence of majority rule. If the majority is to define the policy of a party, there must be some method within each party of ascertaining the mind of the majority, and settling the party programme, before it meets the opposing party at the polls. The Carlton and Reform clubs discharge for the Tories and Liberals many of the functions of a congressional caucus. Meetings of the members of the parties in the *reichstag*, the *corps legislatif* and the chamber of deputies are not unusual, although they have generally merely been for consultation, and neither in England, France, Germany or Italy, has any such authority been conceded to the wish of the majority of a party as we have rested in the decision of a caucus. What has been called a caucus has been established by the Liberals of Birmingham, England, as to which, see a paper by W. Fraser Rae, in the "International Review" for August, 1880. The origin of the term caucus is obscure. It has been derived from the Algonquin word *Kaw-kaw-wus*—to consult, to speak—but the more probable derivation makes it a corruption of caulkers. In the early politics of Boston, and particularly during the early difficulties between the townsmen and the British troops, the seafaring men and those employed about the ship yards were prominent among the town-people, and there were numerous gatherings which may have very easily come to be called by way of reproach a meeting of caulkers, after the least influential class who attended them, or from the caulking house or caulk house in which they were held. What was at first a derisive description, came to be an appellation, and the gatherings of so-called caulkers became a caucus. John Pickering, in a vocabulary of words and phrases peculiar to the United States (Boston, 1816), gives this derivation of the word, and says several gentlemen mentioned to him that they had heard this derivation. Gordon, writing in 1774, says: "More than fifty years ago Mr. Samuel Adams' father and twenty others, one or two from the north end of the town where all the ship business is carried on, used to meet, make a caucus and lay their plan for introducing certain persons into places of trust and power. When they had settled it they separated, and each used their particular influence within his own circle. He and his friends would furnish themselves with ballots, including the names of the parties fixed upon, which they distributed on the days of election. By acting in concert, together with a careful and extensive distribution of ballots, they generally carried their elections to their own mind. In like manner it was that Mr. Samuel Adams first became a representative for Boston." (*History of the American Revolution*, vol. i., p. 365.) February, 1763, Adams writes in his diary: "This day I learned that the caucus club meets at certain times in the garret of Tom Dawes, the adjutant of the Boston regiment. He has a large house and he has a movable partition in his garret which he takes down and the whole club meets in his room. There they smoke tobacco until they cannot see one end of the room from another. There they drink flip, I suppose, and there they choose a moderator who puts questions to the vote regularly; and selectmen, assessors, collectors, wardens, fire wards and representatives are regularly chosen in the town. Uncle Fairfield, Story, Ruddock, Adams, Cooper, and a *rudis indigestaques moles* of others, are members. They send committees to wait on the merchants' club, and to propose in the choice of men and measures. Captain Cunningham says, they have often solicited him to go to the caucuses; they have assured him their benefit in his business, etc." (*Adams' Works*, vol. ii., p. 144.) Under the title caucus should be considered the congressional nominating caucus; the caucuses of legislative assemblies; primary elections, still known outside the larger cities as caucuses; the evils which have been attributed to the latter, and the remedies which have been proposed. These will accordingly be mentioned in the order given.

"The democratic system is the result of the reorganization of the various anti-Tammany democratic factions, brought about, in 1881, by a practically self-appointed committee of 100. Under this system primary elections are to be held annually in each of 678 election districts, at which all democratic electors resident in the respective districts may participate, provided they were registered at the last general election. The persons voting at any primary shall be members of the election district association for the ensuing year, which is to be organized in January of each year. The associations may admit democratic residents in their respective districts, who are not members, to membership, and they have general supervision of the interests of the party within their districts. Primaries are held on not less than four days' public notice, through the newspapers, of the time and place, and at the appointed time the meeting is called to order by the chairman of the election district association, provided twenty persons be present; if that number shall not be present, the meeting may be called to order with a less number, at the end of fifteen minutes. The first business of the meeting is to select a chairman, and all elections of delegates or committeemen shall take place in open meeting. Each person, as he offers to vote, states his name and residence, which may be compared with the registration list at the last election, and each person shall state for whom he votes, or he may hand to the judges an open ballot, having designated thereon the persons for whom he votes, and for what positions. Nominations are all made by conventions of delegates from the districts within which the candidate to be chosen is to be voted for. There is an assembly district committee in each assembly district, composed of one delegate for each 100 votes or fraction thereof, from each election district within the assembly district. There is also a county committee composed of delegates from each of the assembly district committees. The function of these committees is generally to look after the interests of the parties within their respective spheres. This system is too new for its workings to be as yet fairly criticised. It may prove a really popular system, or it may prove only an inchoate form of the other systems. At present it can only be said that the first primaries under it were participated in by 27,000 electors.

"The evils of the caucus and primary election systems lie in the stringent obligation which is attached to the will of a formal majority; in the fact that the process of ascertaining what the will of the majority is, has been surrounded with so many restrictions that the actual majority of votes are disfranchised, and take no part in that process, so that the formal majority is in consequence no longer the majority in fact, although it continues to demand recognition of its decisions as such.

"The separation between the organization and the party, between those who nominate and those who elect, is the sum of the evils of the too highly organized caucus system. It has its roots in the notion that the majority is right, because it is the majority, which is the popular view thus expressed by Hammond: 'I think that when political friends consent to go into caucus for the nomination of officers, every member of such caucus is bound in honor to support and carry into effect its determination. If you suspect that determination will be so preposterous that you cannot in conscience support it, then you ought on no account to become one of its members. To try your chance in a caucus, and then, because your wishes are not gratified, to attempt to defeat the result of the deliberation of your friends, strikes me as a palpable violation of honor and good faith. You caucus for no other possible purpose than under the implied argument that the opinion and wishes of the minority shall be yielded to the opinions of the majority, and the sole object of caucusing is to ascertain what is the will of the majority. I repeat that unless you intend to carry into effect the wishes of the majority, however contrary to your own, you have no business at a caucus.' (*Political History of New York*, vol. i., p. 192).—In accordance with this theory, the will of the majority becomes obligatory as soon as it is made known, and one cannot assist at a caucus in order to ascertain the will of the majority, without thereby being bound to follow it; and the theory is so deeply rooted that, under the caucus and primary election system, it has been extended to cases in which the majorities are such only in form.

"The remedies as well as the evils of the caucus and nominating system have been made the subject of general discussion in connection with civil service reform. It is claimed that that reform, by giving to public officers the same tenure of their positions which is enjoyed by the employes of a corporation or a private business house, or during the continuance of efficiency or good behaviour, would abolish or greatly diminish the evils of the caucus system by depriving public officers of the illegitimate incentive to maintain it under which they now act. Other more speculative remedies have been suggested. It is proposed, on the one hand, to very greatly diminish the number of elective officers, and, in order to do away with the pre-determination of elections, to restrict the political action of the people in their own persons to districts so small that they can meet together and act as one body, and that in all other affairs than those of these small districts the people should act by delegates. The theory here seems to be to get rid of the necessity for election and nominating machinery. (See '*A True Republic*,' by Albert Strickney, New York, 1879; and a series of articles in *Scribner's Monthly* for 1881, by the same writer). On the other hand, it is proposed to greatly increase the number of elections, by taking the whole primary system under the protection of the law.* This plan proposes: 1. The direct nomination of candidates by the members of the respective political parties in place of nominations by delegates in conventions. 2. To apply the election laws to primary elections. 3. To provide that both political parties shall participate in the same primary election instead of having a different caucus for each party. 4. To provide for a final election to be held between two candidates, each representative of a party

* This was partially done by the Legislature of Pennsylvania in 1881.

who have been selected by means of the primary election. This plan would undoubtedly do away with the evils of the present caucus system, but it contains no guarantee that a new caucus system would not be erected for the purpose of influencing 'the primary election' in the same manner in which the present primary system now influences the final election. (See however '*The Elective Franchise in the United States*,' New York, 1880, by D. C. McClellan.)—The effective remedy for the evils of the caucus system will probably be found in the sanction of primary elections by law. * * * Bills for this purpose were introduced by the Hon. Erastus Brooks in the New York Legislature in 1881, which provided substantially for the system proposed by Mr. McClellan, but they were left unacted upon, and no legislative attempt to regulate primaries, except by providing for their being called, and for their procedeure, has been made elsewhere. In Ohio what is known as the Baber law provides that where any voluntary political association orders a primary, it must be by a majority vote of the central or controlling committee of such party or association; that the call must be published for at least five days in the newspapers, and state the time and place of the meeting, the authority by which it was called, and the name of the person who is to represent that authority at each poll. The law also provides for challenging voters, for punishment of illegal voting, and for the bribery or intervention of electors or judges. (*Rev. Stat. Ohio*, secs. 2916–2921.) A similar law in Missouri is made applicable to counties only of over 100,000 inhabitants, but by this law it is made optional with the voluntary political association whether it will or not hold its primaries under the law, and if it does, it is provided that the county shall incur no expense in the conduct of such elections. (*Laws of Missouri*, 1815, p. 54.) A similar law also exists in California. (*Laws of California*, 1865–1866, p. 438.) These laws comprise all the existing legislation on the subject, except what is known as the Landis Bill of 1881, which requires primary officers to take an oath, and which punishes fraud."

Assassination of President Garfield.

At 9 o'clock on the morning of Saturday, July 2d, 1881, President Garfield, accompanied by Secretary Blaine, left the Executive Mansion to take a special train from the Baltimore and Potomac depot for New England, where he intended to visit the college from which he had graduated. Arriving at the depot, he was walking arm-in-arm through the main waiting-room, when Charles J. Guiteau, a persistent applicant for an office, who had some time previously entered through the main door, advanced to the centre of the room, and having reached within a few feet of his victim, fired two shots, one of which took fatal effect. The bullet was of forty-four calibre, and striking the President about four inches to the right of the spinal column, struck the tenth and badly shattered the eleventh rib. The President sank to the floor, and was conveyed to a room where temporary conveniences were attainable, and a couch was improvised. Dr. Bliss made an unsuccessful effort to find the ball. The shock to the President's system was very severe, and at first apprehensions were felt that death would ensue speedily. Two hours after the shooting, the physicians decided to remove him to the Executive Mansion. An army ambulance was procured, and the removal effected. Soon after, vomiting set in, and the patient exhibited a dangerous degree of prostration, which threatened to end speedily in dissolution. This hopeless condition of affairs continued until past midnight, when more favorable symptoms were exhibited. Dr. Bliss was on this Sunday morning designated to take charge of the case, and he called Surgeon-General Barnes, Assistant Surgeon-General Woodward, and Dr. Reyburn as consulting physician. To satisfy the demand of the country, Drs. Agnew, of Philadelphia, and Hamilton, of New York, were also summoned by telegraph, and arrived on a special train over the Pennsylvania Railroad, Sunday afternoon. For several days immediately succeeding the shooting, the patient suffered great inconvenience and pain in the lower limbs. This created an apprehension that the spinal nerves had been injured, and death was momentarily expected. On the night of July 4th a favorable turn was observed, and the morning of the 5th brought with it a vague but undefined hope that a favorable issue might ensue. Under this comforting conviction, Drs. Agnew and Hamilton, after consultation with the resident medical attendants, returned to their homes; first having published to the country an indorsement of the treatment inaugurated. During July 5th and 6th the patient continued to improve, the pulse and respiration showing a marked approach to the condition of healthfulness, the former being reported on the morning of the 6th at 98, and in the evening it only increased to 104. On the 7th Dr. Bliss became very confident of ultimate triumph over the malady. In previous bulletins meagre hope was given, and the chances for recovery estimated at one in a hundred.

From July 7th to the 16th there was a slight but uninterrupted improvement, and the country began to entertain a confident hope that the patient would recover.

Hope and fear alternated from day to day, amid the most painful excitement. On the 8th of August Drs. Agnew and Hamilton had to perform their second operation to allow a free flow of pus from the wound. This resulted in an important discovery. It was ascertained that the track of the bullet had turned from its downward deflection to a forward course. The operation lasted an hour, and ether was administered, the effect of which was very unfortunate. Nausea succeeded, and vomiting followed every effort to administer nourishment for some time. However, he soon rallied, and the operation was pronounced successful, and, on the following day, the President, for the first time, wrote his name. On the 10th he signed an important extradition paper, and on the 11th wrote a letter of hopefulness to his aged mother. On the 12th Dr. Hamilton expressed the opinion that the further attendance of himself and Dr. Agnew was unnecessary. The stomach continued weak, however, and on the 15th nausea returned, and the most menacing physical prostration followed the frequent vomiting, and the evening bulletin announced that "the President's condition, on the whole, is less satisfactory."

Next a new complication forced itself upon the attention of the physicians. This was described as "inflammation of the right parotid gland." On August 24th it was decided to make an incision below and forward of the right ear, in order to prevent suppuration. Though this operation was pronounced satisfactory, the patient gradually sank, until August 25th, when all hope seemed to have left those in attendance.

Two days of a dreary watch ensued; on the 27th an improvement inspired new hope. This continued throughout the week, but failed to build up the system. Then it was determined to remove the patient to a more favorable atmosphere. On the 6th of September this design was executed, he having been conveyed in a car arranged for the purpose to Long Branch, where, in a cottage at Elberon, it was hoped vigor would return. At first, indications justified the most sanguine expectations. On the 9th, however, fever returned, and a cough came to harass the wasted sufferer. It was attended with purulent expectoration, and became so troublesome as to entitle it to be regarded as the leading feature of the case. The surgeons attributed it to the septic condition of the blood. The trouble increased until Saturday, September 10th, when it was thought the end was reached. He rallied, however, and improved rapidly, during the succeeding few days, and on Tuesday, the 13th, was lifted from the bed and placed in a chair at the window. The improvement was not enduring, however, and on Saturday, September 17th, the rigor returned. During the nights and days succeeding, until the final moment, hope rose and fell alternately, and though the patient's spirits fluctuated to justify this change of feeling, the improvement failed to bring with it the strength necessary to meet the strain.

President Garfield died at 10.35 on the night of Sept. 19th, 1881, and our nation mourned, as it had only done once before, when Abraham Lincoln also fell by the hand of an assassin. The assassin Guiteau was tried and convicted, the jury rejecting his plea of insanity.

President Arthur.

Vice-President Arthur, during the long illness of the President, and at the time of his death, deported himself so well that he won the good opinion of nearly all classes of the people, and happily for weeks and months all factious or partisan spirit was hushed by the nation's great calamity. At midnight on the 19th of September the Cabinet telegraphed him from Long Branch to take the oath of office, and this he very properly did before a local judge. The Government cannot wisely be left without a head for a single day. He was soon afterwards again sworn in at Washington, with the usual ceremonies, and took occasion to make a speech which improved the growing better feeling. The new President requested the Cabinet to hold on until Congress met, and it would have remained intact had Secretary Windom not found it necessary to resume his place in the Senate. The vacancy was offered to ex-Governor Morgan, of New York, who was actually nominated and confirmed before he made up his mind to decline it. Judge Folger now fills the place. The several changes since made will be found in the Tabulated History, Book VII.

It has thus far been the effort of President Arthur to allay whatever of factious bitterness remains in the Republican party. In his own State of New York the terms "Half-Breed" and "Stalwart" are passing into comparative disuse, as are the terms "Regulars" and "Independents" in Pennsylvania.

"Boss Rule."

The complaint of "Boss Rule" in these States—by which is meant the control of certain leaders—still obtains to some extent. Wayne MacVeagh was the author of this very telling political epithet, and he used it with rare force in his street speeches at Chicago when opposing the nomination of Grant. It was still further cultivated by Rufus E. Shapley, Esq,, of Philadelphia, the author of "Solid for Mulhooly," a most admirable political satire, which had an immense sale. Its many hits were freely quoted by the Reformers of Philadelphia, who organized under the Committee of One Hundred, a body of merchants who first banded themselves together to promote reforms in the municipal government. This organization, aided by the Democrats, defeated Mayor Wm. S. Stokley for his third term, electing Mr. King, theretofore a very popular Democratic councilman. In return for this support, the Democrats accepted John Hunter, Committee's nominee for Tax Receiver, and the combination succeeded. In the fall of 1881 it failed on the city ticket, but in the spring of 1882 secured material successes in the election of Councilmen, who were nominees of both parties, but aided by the endorsement of the Committee of One Hundred. A similar combination failed as between Brown (Rep.) and Eisenbrown (Dem.) for Magistrate. On this part of the ticket the entire city voted, and the regular Republicans won by about 500 majority.

The following is the declaration of principles of the Citizens' Republican Association of Philadelphia, which, under the banner of Mr. Wolfe, extended its organization to several counties:

I. We adhere to the platform of the National Convention of the Republican party, adopted at Chicago, June 2d, 1880, and we proclaim our unswerving allegiance to the great principles upon which that party was founded, to wit: national supremacy, universal liberty, and governmental probity.

II. The Republican party, during its glorious career, having virtually established its principles of national supremacy and universal liberty as the law of the land, we shall, while keeping a vigilant watch over the maintenance of those principles, regard the third one, viz.: governmental probity, as the living issue to be struggled for in the future; and as the pure administration of government is essential to the permanence of Republican institutions, we consider this issue as in no way inferior in importance to any other.

III. The only practical method of restoring purity to administration is through the adoption of a system of civil service, under which public officials shall not be the tools of any man or of any clique, subject to dismissal at their behest, or to assessment in their service; nor appointment to office be "patronage" at the disposal of any man to consolidate his power within the party.

IV. It is the abuse of this appointing power which has led to the formation of the "machine," and the subjection of the party to "bosses." Our chosen leader, the late President Garfield, fell a martyr in his contest with the "bosses." We take up the struggle where he left it, and we hereby declare that we will own no allegiance to any "boss," nor be subservient to any "machine;" but that we will do our utmost to liberate the party from the "boss" domination under which it has fallen.

V. Recognizing that political parties are simply instrumentalities for the enforcement of certain recognized principles, we shall endeavor to promote the principles of the Republican party by means of that party, disenthralled and released from the domination of its "bosses." But should we fail in this, we shall have no hesitation in seeking to advance the principles of the party through movements and organizations outside of the party lines.

The idea of the Committee of One Hundred is to war against "boss rule" in municipal affairs. James McManes has long enjoyed the leadership of the Republican party in Philadelphia, and the reform element has directed its force against his power as a leader, though he joined at Chicago in the MacVeagh war against the form of "boss rule," which was then directed against Grant, Conkling, Logan and Cameron. This episode has really little, if anything, to do with Federal politics, but the facts are briefly recited with a view to explain to the reader the leading force which supported Mr. Wolfe in his independent race in Pennsylvania. Summed up, it is simply one of those local wars against leadership which precede and follow factions.

The factious battles in the Republican party, as we have stated, seem to have spent their force. The assassination of President Garfield gave them a most serious check, for men were then compelled to look back and acknowledge that his plain purpose was to check divisions and heal wounds. Only haste and anger assailed, and doubtless as quickly regretted the assault. President Arthur, with commendable reticence and discretion, is believed to be seeking the same end. He has made few changes, and these reluctantly. His nomination of ex-Senator Conkling to a seat in the Supreme Bench, which, though declined, is generally accepted as an assurance to New Yorkers that the leader hated by one side and loved by the other, should be removed from partisan politics peculiar to his own State, but removed with the dignity and honor becoming his high abilities. It has ever been the policy of wise administrations, as with wise generals, to care for the wounded, and Conkling was surely and sorely wounded in his battle against the confirmation of Robertson and his attempted re-election to the Senate. He accepted the situation with quiet composure, and saw his friend Arthur unite the ranks which his resignation had sundered. After this there remained little if any cause for further quarrel, and while in writing history it is dangerous to attempt a prophecy, the writer believes that President Arthur will succeed in keeping his party, if not fully united, at least as compact as the opposing Democratic forces.

The Readjusters.

This party was founded in 1878 by Gen'l William Mahone, a noted Brigadier in the rebel army. He is of Scotch-Irish descent, a man of very small stature but most remarkable energy, and acquired wealth in the construction and development of Southern railroads. He sounded the first note of revolt against what he styled the Bourbon rule of Virginia, and being classed as a Democrat, rapidly divided that party on the question of the Virginia debt. His enemies charge that he sought the repudiation of this debt, but in return he not only denied the charge, but said the Bourbons were actually repudiating it by making no provision for its payment, either in appropriations or the levying of taxes needed for the purpose. Doubtless his views on this question have undergone some modification, and that earlier in the struggle the uglier criticisms were partially correct. Certain it is that he and his friends now advocate full payment less the proportion equitably assigned to West Virginia, which separated from the parent State during the war, and in her constitution evaded her responsibility by declaring that the State should never contract a debt except one created to resist invasion or in a war for the government. This fact shows how keenly alive the West Virginians were to a claim which could very justly be pressed in the event of Virginia being restored to the Union, and this claim Gen'l Mahone has persistently pressed, and latterly urged a funding of the debt of his State at a 3 per cent. rate, on the ground that the State is unable to pay more and that this is in accord with proper rates of interest on the bonds of State governments—a view not altogether fair or sound, since it leaves the creditors powerless to do otherwise than accept. The regular or Bourbon Democrats proclaimed in favor of full payment, and in this respect differed from their party associates as to ante-war debts in most other Southern States.

Gen. Mahone rapidly organized his revolt, and as the Republican party was then in a hopeless minority in Virginia, publicly invited an alliance by the passage of a platform which advocated free schools for the blacks and a full enforcement of the National laws touching their civil rights. The Legislature was won, and on the 16th of December, 1880, Gen'l Mahone was elected to the U. S. Senate to succeed Senator Withers, whose term expired March 4, 1881.

In the Presidential campaign of 1880, the Readjusters supported Gen'l Hancock, but on a separate electoral ticket, while the Republicans supported Garfield on an electoral ticket of their own selection. This division was pursuant to an understanding, and at the time thought advisable by Mahone, who, if his electors won, could go for Hancock or not, as circumstances might suggest; while if he failed the Republicans might profit by the separation. There was, however, a third horn to this dilemma, for the regular Democratic electors were chosen, but the political complexion of the Legislature was not changed. Prior to the Presidential nominations Mahone's Readjuster Convention had signified their willingness to support Gen'l Grant if he should be nominated at Chicago, and this fact was widely quoted by his friends in their advocacy of Grant's nomination, and in descanting upon his ability to carry Southern States.

The Readjuster movement at first had no other than local designs, but about the time of its organization there was a great desire on the part of the leading Republicans to break the "Solid South," and every possible expedient to that end was suggested. It was solid for the Democratic party, and standing thus could with the aid of New York, Indiana and New Jersey (them all Democratic States) assure the election of a Democratic President.

One of the favorite objects of President Hayes was to break the "Solid South." He first obtained it by conciliatory speeches, which were so conciliatory in fact that they angered radical Republicans, and there were thus threatened division in unexpected quarters. He next tried it through Gen'l Key, whom he made Postmaster General in the hope that he could resurrect and reorganize the old Whig elements of the South. Key was to attend to Southern postal patronage with this end in view, while Mr. Tener, his able First Assistant, was to distribute Northern or Republican patronage. So far as dividing the South was concerned, the scheme was a flat failure.

The next and most quiet and effectual effort was made by Gen'l Simon Cameron, Ex-Senator from Pennsylvania. He started on a brief Southern tour, ostensibly for health and enjoyment, but really to meet Gen'l Mahone, his leading Readjuster friends, and the leading Republicans. Conferences were held, and the union of the two forces was made to embrace National objects. This was in the Fall of 1879.

Not long thereafter Gen'l Mahone consulted with Senator J. Don. Cameron, who was of course familiar with his father's movements, and he actively devised and carried out schemes to aid the new combination by which the "Solid South" was to be broken. In the great State campaign of 1881, when the Bourbon and anti-Bourbon candidates for Governor, were stumping the State, Gen'l Mahone found that a large portion of his colored friends were handicapped by their inability to pay the taxes imposed upon them by the laws of Virginia, and this threatened defeat. He sought aid from the National administration. President Garfield favored the combination, as did Secretary Windom, but Secretary Blaine withheld his support for several months, finally, however, acceding to the wishes of the President and most of the Cabinet. Administration influences caused the abandonment of a straight-out Republican movement organized by Congressman Jorgensen and others, and a movement which at one time threatened a disastrous division was overcome. The tax question remained, and this was first met by Senator J. Don. Cameron, who while summering at Manhattan Island, was really daily engaged in New York City raising funds for Mahone, with which to pay their taxes. Still, this aid was insufficient, and in the heat of the battle the revenue officers throughout the United States, were asked to contribute. Many of them did so, and on the eve of election all taxes were paid and the result was the election of William E. Cameron (Readjuster) as Governor by about 20,000 majority, with other State officers divided between the old Readjusters and Republicans. The combination also carried the Legislature.

In that great struggle the Readjusters became known as the anti-Bourbon movement, and efforts are now being made to extend it to other Southern States. It has taken root in South Carolina, Georgia, Tennessee, Arkansas, Mississippi, and more recently in Kentucky, where the Union War Democrats in State Convention as late as March 1, 1882, separated from the Bourbon wing of the party. For a better idea of these two elements in the South, the reader is referred to the recent speeches of Hill and Mahone in the memorable Senate scene directly after the latter took the oath of office, and cast his vote with the Republicans. These speeches will be found in Book III of this volume.

Suppressing Mormonism.

Polygamy, justly denounced as "the true relic of barbarism" while slavery existed, has ever since the settlement of the Mormons in Utah, been one of the vexed questions in American politics. Laws passed for its suppression have proved, thus far, unavailing; troops could not crush it out, or did not at a time when battles were fought and won; United States Courts were powerless where juries could not be found to convict. Latterly a new and promising effort has been made for its suppression. This was begun in the Senate in the session of 1882. On the 16th of February a vote was taken by sections on Senator Edmunds' bill, which like the law of 1862 is penal in its provisions; but directly aimed against the crime of polygamy.

President Arthur signed the Edmunds anti-polygamy bill on the 23d of March, 1882.

Delegate Cannon of Utah, was on the floor of the Senate electioneering against the bill, and he plead with some success, for several Democratic Senators made speeches against it. The Republicans were unanimously for the bill, and the Democrats were not solidly against it, though the general tenor of the debate on this side was against it.

Senator Vest (Democrat) of Missouri, said that never in the darkest days of the rule of the Tudors and Stuarts had any measure been advocated which came so near a bill of attainder as this one. It was monstrous to contend that the people of the United States were at the mercy of Congress without any appeal. If this bill passed it would establish a precedent that would come home to plague us for all time to come. The pressure against polygamy to-day might exist to-morrow against any church, institution or class in this broad land, and when the crested waves of prejudice and passion mounted high they would be told that the Congress of the United States had trampled upon the Constitution. In conclusion, he said: "I am prepared for the abuse and calumny that will follow any man who dares to criticise any bill against polygamy, and yet, if my official life had to terminate to-morrow, I would not give my vote for the unconstitutional principles contained in this bill." Other speeches were made by Messrs. Morgan, Brown, Jones, of Florida, Saulsbury, Call, Pendleton, Sherman, and Lamar, and the debate was closed by Mr. Edmunds in an eloquent fifteen-minutes' speech, in which he carefully reviewed and controverted the objections urged against the bill of the committee.

He showed great anxiety to have the measure disposed of at once and met a request from the Democratic side for a postponement till other features should be embodied in the bills with the remark that this was the policy that had hitherto proven a hindrance to legislation on this subject and that he was tired of it. In the bill as amended the following section provoked more opposition than any other, although the Senators refrained from making any particular mention of it: "That if any male person in a Territory or other place over which the United States have exclusive jurisdiction hereafter cohabits with more than one woman he shall be deemed guilty of a misdemeanor, and on conviction thereof he shall be punished by a fine of not more than $300 or by imprisonment for not more than six months, or by both said punishments in the discretion of the court." The bill passed viva voce vote after a re-arrangement of its sections, one of the changes being that not more than three of the commissioners shall be members of the same party. The fact that the yeas and nays were not called, shows that there is no general desire on either side to make the bill a partisan measure.

The Edmunds Bill passed the House March 14, 1882, without material amendment, the Republican majority, refusing to allow the time asked by the Democrats for discussion. The vote was 193 for to only 45 against, all of the negative votes being Democratic save one, that of Jones, Greenbacker from Texas.

The only question was whether the bill, as passed by the Senate, would accomplish that object, and whether certain provisions of this bill did not provide a remedy which was worse than the disease. Many Democrats thought that the precedent of interfering with the right of suffrage at the polls, when the voter had not been tried and convicted of any crime, was so dangerous that they could not bring themselves to vote for the measure. Among these democrats were Belmont and Hewitt, of New York, and a number of others equally prominent. But they all professed their readiness to vote for any measure which would affect the abolition of polygamy without impairing the fundamental rights of citizens in other parts of the country.

THE TEXT OF THE BILL.

Be it enacted, &c., That section 5,352 of the Revised Statutes of the United States be, and the same is hereby amended so as to read as follows, namely:

"Every person who has a husband or wife living who, in a Territory or other place over which the United States have exclusive jurisdiction, hereafter marries another, whether married or single, and any man who hereafter simultaneously, or on the same day, marries more than one woman, in a Territory or other place over which the United States has exclusive jurisdiction, is guilty of polygamy, and shall be punished by a fine of not more than $500 and by imprisonment for a term of not more than five years; but this section shall not extend to any person by reason of any former marriage whose husband or wife by such marriage shall have been absent for five successive years, and is not known to such person to be living, and is believed by such person to be dead, nor to any person by reason of any former marriage which shall have been dissolved by a valid decree of a competent court, nor to any person by reason of any former marriage which shall have been pronounced void by a valid decree of a competent court, on the ground of nullity of the marriage contract."

SEC. 2. That the foregoing provisions shall not affect the prosecution or punishment of any offence already committed against the section amended by the first section of this act.

SEC. 3. That if any male person, in a Territory or other place over which the United States have exclusive jurisdiction, hereafter cohabits with more than one woman, he shall be deemed guilty of a misdemeanor, and on conviction thereof shall be punished by a fine of not more than $300, or by imprisonment for not more than six months, or by both said punishments in the discretion of the court.

SEC. 4. That counts for any or all of the offences named in sections 1 and 3 of this act may be joined in the same information or indictment.

SEC. 5. That in any prosecution for bigamy, polygamy or unlawful cohabitation under any statute of the United States, it shall be sufficient cause of challenge to any person drawn or summoned as a juryman or talesman, first, that he is or has been living in the practice of bigamy, polygamy, or unlawful cohabitation with more than one woman, or that he is or has been guilty of an offence punishable by either of the foregoing sections or by section 5352 of the Revised Statutes of the United States or the act of July 1, 1862, entitled "An act to punish and prevent the practice of polygamy in the Territories of the United States and other places, and disapproving and annulling certain acts of the Legislative Assembly of the Territory of Utah;" or, second, that he believes it right for a man to have more than one living and undivorced wife at the same time, or to live in the practice of cohabiting with more than one woman, and any person appearing or offered as a juror or talesman and challenged on either of the foregoing grounds may be questioned on his oath as to the existence of any such cause of challenge, and other evidence may be introduced bearing upon the question raised by such challenge, and this question shall be tried by the court. But as to the first ground of challenge before mentioned the person challenged shall be bound to answer if he shall say upon his oath that he declines on the ground that his answer may tend to criminate himself, and if he shall answer to said first ground his answer shall not be given in evidence in any criminal prosecution against him for any offense named in sections 1 or 3 of this act, but if he declines to answer on any ground he shall be rejected as incompetent.

SEC. 6. That the President is hereby authorized to grant amnesty to such classes of offenders guilty before the passage of this act of bigamy, polygamy, or unlawful cohabitation before the passage of this act, on such conditions and under such limitations as he shall think proper; but no such amnesty shall have effect unless the conditions thereof shall be complied with.

SEC. 7. That the issue of bigamous or polygamous marriages known as Mormon marriages, in cases in which such marriages have been solemnized according to the ceremonies of the Mormon sect, in any Territory of the United States, and such issue shall have been born before the 1st day of January, A. D. 1883, are hereby legitimated.

SEC. 8. That no polygamist, bigamist, or any person cohabiting with more than one woman, and no woman cohabiting with any of the persons described as aforesaid in this section, in any Territory or other place over which the United States have exclusive jurisdiction, shall be entitled to vote at any election held in any such Territory or other place, or be eligible for election or appointment to or be entitled to hold any office or place of public trust, honor or emolument in, under, or for such Territory or place, or under the United States.

SEC. 9. That all the registration and election offices of every description in the Territory of Utah are hereby declared vacant, and each and every duty relating to the registration of voters, the conduct of elections, the receiving or rejection of votes, and the canvassing and returning of the same, and the issuing of certificates or other evidence of election in said Territory, shall, until other provision be made by the Legislative Assembly of said Territory as is hereinafter by this section provided, be performed under the existing laws of the United States and of said Territory by proper persons, who shall be appointed to execute such offices and perform such duties by a board of five persons, to be appointed by the President, by and with the advice and consent of the Senate, and not more than three of whom shall be members of one political party, and a majority of whom shall constitute a quorum. The members of said board so appointed by the President shall each receive a salary at the rate of $3,000 per annum, and shall continue in office until the Legislative Assembly of said Territory shall make provision for filling said offices as herein authorized. The secretary of the Territory shall be the secretary of said board, and keep a journal of its proceedings, and attest the action of said board under this section. The canvass and return of all the votes at elections in said Territory for members of the Legislative Assembly thereof shall also be returned to said board, which shall canvass all such returns and issue certificates of election to those persons who, being eligible for such election, shall appear to have been lawfully elected, which certificate shall be the only evidence of the right of such persons to sit in such Assembly: *Provided*, That said board of five persons shall not exclude any person otherwise eligible to vote from the polls on account of any opinion such person may entertain on the subject of bigamy or polygamy, nor shall they refuse to count any such vote on account of the opinion of the person casting it on the subject of bigamy or polygamy; but each house of such Assembly, after its organization, shall have power to decide upon the elections and qualifications of its members. And at or after the first meeting of said Legislative Assembly whose members shall have been elected and returned according to the provisions of this act, said Legislative Assembly may make such laws, conformable to the organic act of said Territory and not inconsistent with other laws of the United States, as it shall deem proper concerning the filling of the offices in said Territory declared vacant by this act.

John R. McBride writing in the February number (1882) of *The International Review*, gives an interesting and correct view of the obstacles which the Mormons have erected against the enforcement of United States laws in the Territory. It requires acquaintance with these facts to fully comprehend the difficulties in the way of what seems to most minds a very plain and easy task. Mr. McBride says: Their first care on arriving in Utah was to erect a "free and Independent State," called the "State of Deseret." It included in its nominal limits, not only all of Utah as it now is, but one-half of California, all of Nevada, part of Colorado, and a large portion of four other Territories now organized. Brigham Young was elected Governor, and its departments, legislative and judicial, were fully organized and put into operation. Its legislative acts were styled "ordinances," and when Congress, disregarding the State organization, instituted a Territorial Government for Utah, the legislative body chosen by the Mormons adopted the ordinances of the "State of Deseret." Many of these are yet on the statute book of Utah. They show conclusively the domination of the ecclesiastical idea, and how utterly insignificant in comparison was the power of the civil authority. They incorporated the Mormon Church into a body politic and corporate, and by the third section of the act gave it supreme authority over its members in everything temporal and spiritual, and assigned as a reason for so doing that it was because the powers confirmed were in "support of morality and virtue, and were founded on the revelations of the Lord." Under this power to make laws and punish and forgive offenses, to hear and determine between brethren, the civil law was superseded. The decrees of the courts of this church, certified under seal, have been examined by the writer, and he found them exercising a jurisdiction without limit except that of appeal to the President of the church. That the assassinations of apostates, the massacres of the Morrisites at Morris Fort and of the Arkansas emigrants at Mountain Meadows, were all in pursuance of church decrees, more or less formal, no one acquainted with the system doubts. This act of incorporation was passed February 8, 1851, and is found in the latest compilation of Utah statutes. It is proper also to observe that, for many years after the erection of the Territorial Government by Congress, the "State of Deseret" organization was maintained by the Mormons, and collision was only prevented because Brigham was Governor of both, and found it unnecessary for his purpose to antagonize either. His church organization made both a shadow, while *that* was the substance of all authority. One of the earliest of their legislative acts was to organize a Surveyor General's Department,[1] and title to land was declared to be in the persons who held a certificate from that office.[2] Having instituted their own system of government and taken possession of the land, and assumed to distribute that in a system of their own, the next step was to vest certain leading men with the control of the timbers and waters of the country. By a series of acts granting lands, waters and timber to individuals, the twelve apostles became the practical proprietors of the better and more desirable portions of the country. By an ordinance dated October 4, 1851, there was granted to Brigham Young the "sole control of City Creek and Cañon for the sum of five hundred dollars." By an ordinance dated January 9, 1850, the "waters of North Mill Creek and the waters of the Cañon next north" were granted to Heber C. Kimball. On the same day was granted to George A. Smith the "sole control of the cañons and timber of the east side of the 'West Mountains." On the 18th of January, 1851, the North Cottonwood Cañon was granted exclusively to Williard Richards. On the 15th of January, 1851, the waters of the "main channel" of Mill Creek were donated to Brigham Young. On the 9th of December, 1850, there was granted to Ezra T. Benson the exclusive control of the waters of Twin Springs and Rock Springs, in Tooelle Valley; and on the 14th of January, 1851, to the same person was granted the control of all the cañons of the "West Mountain" and the timber therein. By the ordinance of September 14, 1850, a "general conference of the Church of Latter Day Saints" was authorized to elect thirteen men to become a corporation, to be called the Emigration Company; and to this company, elected exclusively by the church, was secured and appropriated the two islands in Salt Lake known as Antelope and Stansberry Islands, to be under the exclusive control of President Brigham Young. These examples are given to show that the right of the United States to the lands of Utah met no recognition by these people. They appropriated them, not only in a way to make the people slaves, but indicated their claim of sovereignty as superior to any. Young, Smith, Benson and Kimball were apostles. Richards was Brigham Young's counselor. By an act of December 28, 1855, there was granted to the "University of the State of Deseret" a tract of land amounting to about five hundred acres, inside the city limits of Salt Lake City, without any reservation to the occupants whatever; and everywhere was the authority of the United States over the country and its soil and people utterly ignored.

Not satisfied with making the grants referred to, the Legislative Assembly entered upon a system of municipal incorporations, by which the fertile lands of the Territory were withdrawn from the operation of the preëmptive laws of Congress; and thus while *they* occupied these without title, non-Mormons were unable to make settlement on them, and they were thus engrossed to Mormon use. From a report made by the Commissioner of the General Land Office to the United States Senate,[1] it appears that the municipal corporations covered over 400,000 acres of the public lands, and over 600 square miles of territory. These lands[2] are not subject to either the Homestead or Preëmption laws, and thus the non-Mormon settler was prevented from attempting, except in rare instances, to secure any lands in Utah. The spirit which prompted this course is well illustrated by an instance which was the subject of an investigation in the Land Department, and the proofs are found in the document just referred to. George Q. Cannon, the late Mormon delegate in Congress, was called to exercise his

[1] Act of March 2, 1850. [2] Act of January 19, 1866.

[1] Senate doc. 181, 46th Congress.
[2] Sec. 2, 258, Rev. Stat. U.S.

duties as an apostle to the Tooelle "Stake" at the city of Grantville. In a discourse on Sunday, the 20th day of July, 1875, Mr. Cannon said:[1] "God has given us (meaning the Mormon people) this land, and, if any outsider shall come in to take land which we claim, a piece *six feet* by *two* is all they are entitled to, and that will last them to all eternity."

By measures and threats like these have the Mormons unlawfully controlled the agricultural lands of the Territory and excluded therefrom the dissenting settler. The attempt of the United States to establish a Surveyor-General's office in Utah in 1855, and to survey the lands in view of disposing of them according to law, was met by such opposition that Mr. Burr, the Surveyor-General, was compelled to fly for life. The monuments of surveys made by his order were destroyed, and the records were supposed to have met a like fate, but were afterwards restored by Brigham Young to the Government. The report of his experience by Mr. Burr was instrumental in causing troops to be sent in 1857 to assert the authority of the Government. When this army, consisting of regular troops, was on the way to Utah, Brigham Young, as Governor, issued a proclamation, dated September 15, 1857, declaring martial law and ordering the people of the Territory to hold themselves in readiness to march to repel the invaders, and on the 29th of September following addressed the commander of United States forces an order forbidding him to enter the Territory, and directing him to retire from it by the same route he had come. Further evidence of the Mormon claim that they were independent is perhaps unnecessary. The treasonable character of the local organization is manifest. It is this organization that controls, not only the people who belong to it, but the 30,000 non-Mormons who now reside in Utah.

Every member of the territorial Legislature is a Mormon. Every county officer is a Mormon. Every territorial officer is a Mormon, except such as are appointive. The schools provided by law and supported by taxation are Mormon. The teachers are Mormon, and the sectarian catechism affirming the revelations of Joseph Smith is regularly taught therein. The municipal corporations are under the control of Mormons. In the hands of this bigoted class all the material interests of the Territory are left, subject only to such checks as a Federal Governor and a Federal judiciary can impose. From beyond the sea they import some thousands of ignorant converts annually, and, while the non-Mormons are increasing, they are overwhelmed by the muddy tide of fanaticism shipped in upon them. The suffrage has been bestowed upon all classes by a statute so general that the ballot box is filled with a mass of votes which repels the free citizen from the exercise of that right. If a Gentile is chosen to the Legislature (two or three such instances have occurred), he is not admitted to the seat, although the act of Congress (June 23, 1874) requires the Territory to pay all the expenses of the enforcement of the laws of the Territory, and of the care of persons convicted of offenses against the laws of the Territory. Provision is made for jurors' fees in criminal cases only, and none is made for the care of criminals.[1] While Congress pays the legislative expenses, amounting to $20,000 per session, the Legislature defiantly refuses to comply with the laws which its members are sworn to support. And the same body, though failing to protect the marriage bond by any law whatever requiring any solemnities for entering it, provided a divorce act which practically allowed marriages to be annulled at will.[2] Neither seduction, adultery nor incest find penalty or recognition in its legal code. The purity of home is destroyed by the beastly practice of plural marriage, and the brows of innocent children are branded with the stain of bastardy to gratify the lust which cares naught for its victims. Twenty-eight of the thirty-six members of the present Legislature of Utah are reported as having from two to seven wives each. While the Government of the United States is paying these men their mileage and *per diem* as law-makers in Utah, those guilty of the same offense outside of Utah are leading the lives of felons in convict cells. For eight years a Mormon delegate has sat in the capitol at Washington having four living wives in his harem in Utah, and at the same time, under the shadow of that capitol, lingers in a felon's prison a man who had been guilty of marrying a woman while another wife was still living.

For thirty years have the Mormons been trusted to correct these evils and put themselves in harmony with the balance of civilized mankind. This they have refused to do. Planting themselves in the heart of the continent, they have persistently defied the laws of the land, the laws of modern society, and the teachings of a common humanity. They degrade woman to the office of a breeding animal, and, after depriving her of all property rights in her husband's estate,[3] all control of her children,[4] they, with ostentation, bestow upon her the ballot in a way that makes it a nullity if contested, and compels her to use it to perpetuate her own degradation if she avails herself of it.

[1] According to the affidavits of Samuel Howard and others, page 14.

[1] See Report of Attorney-General United States, 1880-81.
[2] Act of March 6, 1852. [3] Act of February 16, 1872.
[4] Secs. 1 and 2, act of February 3, 1852.

No power has been given to the Mormon Hierarchy that has not been abused. The right of representation in the legislative councils has been violated in the apportionment of members so as to disfranchise the non-Mormon class.[1] The system of revenue and taxation was for twenty-five years a system of confiscation and extortion.[2] The courts were so organized and controlled that they were but the organs of the church oppressions and ministers of its vengeance.[3] The legal profession was abolished by a statute that prohibited a lawyer from recovering on any contract for service, and allowed every person to appear as an attorney in any court.[4] The attorney was compelled to present "all the facts in the case," whether for or against his client, and a refusal to disclose the confidential communications of the latter subjected the attorney to fine and imprisonment.[5] No law book except the statutes of Utah and of the United States, "when applicable," was permitted to be read in any court by an attorney, and the citation of a decision of the Supreme Court of the United States, or even a quotation from the Bible, in the trial of any cause, subjected a lawyer to fine and imprisonment.[6] The practitioners of medicine were equally assailed by legislation. The use of the most important remedies known to modern medical science, including all anæsthetics, was prohibited except under conditions which made their use impossible, "and if death followed" the administration of these remedies, the person administering them was declared guilty of manslaughter or murder.[7] The Legislative Assembly is but an organized conspiracy against the national law, and an obstacle in the way of the advancement of its own people. For sixteen years it refused to lay its enactments before Congress, and they were only obtained by a joint resolution demanding them. Once in armed rebellion against the authority of the nation, the Mormons have always secretly struggled for, as they have openly prophesied, its entire overthrow. Standing thus in the pathway of the material growth and development of the Territory, a disgrace to the balance of the country, with no redeeming virtue to plead for further indulgence, this travesty of a local government demands radical and speedy reform.

The South American Question.

If it was not shrewdly surmised before it is now known that had President Garfield lived he intended to make his administration brilliant at home and abroad—a view confirmed by the policy conceived by Secretary Blaine and sanctioned, it must be presumed, by President Garfield. This policy looked to closer commercial and political relations with all of the Republics on this Hemisphere, as developed in the following quotations from a correspondence, the publication of which lacks completeness because of delays in transmitting all of it to Congress.

Ex-Secretary Blaine on the 3d of January sent the following letter to President Arthur:

"The suggestion of a congress of all the American nations to assemble in the city of Washington for the purpose of agreeing on such a basis of arbitration for international troubles as would remove all possibility of war in the Western hemisphere was warmly approved by your predecessor. The assassination of July 2 prevented his issuing the invitations to the American States. After your accession to the Presidency I acquainted you with the project and submitted to you a draft for such an invitation. You received the suggestion with the most appreciative consideration, and after carefully examining the form of the invitation directed that it be sent. It was accordingly dispatched in November to the independent governments of America North and South, including all, from the Empire of Brazil to the smallest republic. In a communication addressed by the present Secretary of State on January 9, to Mr. Trescot and recently sent to the Senate I was greatly surprised to find a proposition looking to the annulment of these invitations, and I was still more surprised when I read the reasons assigned. If I correctly apprehend the meaning of his words it is that we might offend some European powers if we should hold in the United States a congress of the "selected nationalities" of America.

"This is certainly a new position for the United States to assume, and one which I earnestly beg you will not permit this government to occupy. The European powers assemble in congress whenever an object seems to them of sufficient importance to justify it. I have never heard of their consulting the government of the United States in regard to the propriety of their so assembling, nor have I ever known of their inviting an American representative to be present. Nor would there, in my judgment, be any good reason for their so doing. Two Presidents of the United States in the year 1881 adjudged it to be expedient that the American powers should meet in congress for the sole purpose of agreeing upon some basis for arbitration of differences that may arise between them and for the prevention, as far as possible,

1 See act of January 17. 1862.
2 Act of January 7, 1854, sec. 14.
3 Acts of Jan 21, 1853, and of January, 1855, sec. 29.
4 Act of Februury 18, 1852.
5 Act of February 18, 1852.
6 Act of January 14, 1854.
7 Sec. 106, Act March 6, 1852.

of war in the future. If that movement is now to be arrested for fear that it may give offense in Europe, the voluntary humiliation of this government could not be more complete, unless we should press the European governments for the privilege of holding the congress. I cannot conceive how the United States could be placed in a less enviable position than would be secured by sending in November a cordial invitation to all the American governments to meet in Washington for the sole purpose of concerting measures of peace and in January recalling the invitation for fear that it might create "jealousy and ill will" on the part of monarchical governments in Europe. It would be difficult to devise a more effective mode for making enemies of the American Government and it would certainly not add to our prestige in the European world. Nor can I see, Mr. President, how European governments should feel "jealousy and ill will" towards the United States because of an effort on our own part to assure lasting peace between the nations of America, unless, indeed, it be to the interest of European power that American nations should at intervals fall into war and bring reproach on republican government. But from that very circumstance I see an additional and powerful motive for the American Governments to be at peace among themselves.

"The United States is indeed at peace with all the world, as Mr. Frelinghuysen well says, but there are and have been serious troubles between other American nations. Peru, Chili and Bolivia have been for more than two years engaged in a desperate conflict. It was the fortunate intervention of the United States last spring that averted war between Chili and the Argentine Republic. Guatemala is at this moment asking the United States to interpose its good offices with Mexico to keep off war. These important facts were all communicated in your late message to Congress. It is the existence or the menace of these wars that influenced President Garfield, and as I supposed influenced yourself, to desire a friendly conference of all the nations of America to devise methods of permanent peace and consequent prosperity for all. Shall the United States now turn back, hold aloof and refuse to exert its great moral power for the advantage of its weaker neighbors?

If you have not formally and finally recalled the invitations to the Peace Congress, Mr. President, I beg you to consider well the effect of so doing. The invitation was not mine. It was yours. I performed only the part of the Secretary—to advise and to draft. You spoke in the name of the United States to each of the independent nations of America. To revoke that invitation for any cause would be embarrassing; to revoke it for the avowed fear of "jealousy and ill will" on the part of European powers would appeal as little to American pride as to American hospitality. Those you have invited may decline, and having now cause to doubt their welcome will, perhaps, do so. This would break up the congress, but it would not touch our dignity.

"Beyond the philanthropic and Christian ends to be obtained by an American conference devoted to peace and good-will among men, we might well hope for material advantages, as the result of a better understanding and closer friendship with the nation of America. At present the condition of trade between the United States and its American neighbors is unsatisfactory to us, and even deplorable. According to the official statistics of our own Treasury Department, the balance against us in that trade last year was $120,000,000—a sum greater than the yearly product of all the gold and silver mines in the United States. This vast balance was paid by us in foreign exchange, and a very large proportion of it went to England, where shipments of cotton, provisions and breadstuffs supplied the money. If anything should change or check the balance in our favor in European trade our commercial exchanges with Spanish America would drain us of our reserve of gold at a rate exceeding $100,000,000 per annum, and would probably precipitate a suspension of specie payment in this country. Such a result at home might be worse than a little jealousy and ill-will abroad. I do not say, Mr. President, that the holding of a peace congress will necessarily change the currents of trade, but it will bring us into kindly relations with all the American nations; it will promote the reign of peace and law and order; it will increase production and consumption and will stimulate the demand for articles which American manufacturers can furnish with profit. It will at all events be a friendly and auspicious beginning in the direction of American influence and American trade in a large field which we have hitherto greatly neglected and which has been practically monopolized by our commercial rivals in Europe.

As Mr. Frelinghuysen's dispatch, foreshadowing the abandonment of the peace congress, has been made public, I deem it a matter of propriety and justice to give this letter to the press. JAS. G. BLAINE.

The above well presents the Blaine view of the proposition to have a Congress of the Republics of America at Washington, and under the patronage of this government, with a view to settle all difficulties by arbitration, to promote trade, and it is presumed to form alliances ready to suit a new and advanced application of the Monroe doctrine.

The following is the letter proposing a conference of North and South American Republics sent to the U. S. Ministers in Central and South America:

SIR: The attitude of the United States with respect to the question of general peace on the American Continent is well known through its persistent efforts for years past to avert the evils of warfare, or, these efforts failing, to bring positive conflicts to an end through pacific counsels or the advocacy of impartial arbitration. This attitude has been consistently maintained, and always with such fairness as to leave no room for imputing to our Government any motive except the humane and disinterested one of saving the kindred States of the American Continent from the burdens of war. The position of the United States, as the leading power of the new world, might well give to its Government a claim to authoritative utterance for the purpose of quieting discord among its neighbors, with all of whom the most friendly relations exist. Nevertheless the good offices of this Government are not, and have not at any time, been tendered with a show of dictation or compulsion, but only as exhibiting the solicitous good will of a common friend.

THE CENTRAL AND SOUTH AMERICAN STATES.

For some years past a growing disposition has been manifested by certain States of Central and South America to refer disputes affecting grave questions of international relationship and boundaries to arbitration rather than to the sword. It has been on several occasions a source of profound satisfaction to the Government of the United States to see that this country is in a large measure looked to by all the American powers as their friend and mediator. The just and impartial counsel of the President in such cases, has never been withheld, and his efforts have been rewarded by the prevention of sanguinary strife or angry contentions between peoples whom we regard as brethren. The existence of this growing tendency convinces the President that the time is ripe for a proposal that shall enlist the good will and active co-operation of all the States of the Western Hemisphere both North and South, in the interest of humanity and for the common weal of nations.

He conceives that none of the Governments of America can be less alive than our own to the dangers and horrors of a state of war, and especially of war between kinsmen. He is sure that none of the chiefs of Government on the Continent can be less sensitive than he is to the sacred duty of making every endeavor to do away with the chances of fratricidal strife, and he looks with hopeful confidence to such active assistance from them as will serve to show the broadness of our common humanity, the strength of the ties which bind us all together as a great and harmonious system of American Commonwealths.

A GENERAL CONGRESS PROPOSED.

Impressed by these views, the President extends to all the independent countries of North and South America an earnest invitation to participate in a general Congress, to be held in the city of Washington, on the 22d of November, 1882, for the purpose of considering and discussing the methods of preventing war between the nations of America. He desires that the attention of the Congress shall be strictly confined to this one great object; and its sole aim shall be to seek a way of permanently averting the horrors of a cruel and bloody contest between countries oftenest of one blood and speech, or the even worse calamity of internal commotion and civil strife; that it shall regard the burdensome and far-reaching consequences of such a struggle, the legacies of exhausted finances, of oppressive debt, of onerous taxation, of ruined cities, of paralyzed industries, of devastated fields, of ruthless conscriptions, of the slaughter of men, of the grief of the widow and orphan, of embittered resentments that long survive those who provoked them and heavily afflict the innocent generations that come after.

THE MISSION OF THE CONGRESS.

The President is especially desirous to have it understood that in putting forth this invitation the United States does not assume the position of counseling or attempting, through the voice of the Congress, to counsel any determinate solution of existing questions which may now divide any of the countries. Such questions cannot properly come before the Congress. Its mission is higher. It is to provide for the interests of all in the future, not to settle the individual differences of the present. For this reason especially the President has indicated a day for the assembling of the Congress so far in the future as to leave good ground for the hope that by the time named the present situation on the South Pacific coast will be happily terminated, and that those engaged in the contest may take peaceable part in the discussion and solution of the general question affecting in an equal degree the well-being of all.

It seems also desirable to disclaim in advance any purpose on the part of the United States to prejudge the issues to be presented to the Congress. It is far from the intent of this Government to appear before the Congress as in any sense the protector of its neighbors or the predestined and necessary arbitrator of their disputes. The United States will enter into the deliberations of the Congress on the same footing as other powers represented, and with the loyal determination to approach any proposed solution, not merely in its own interest, or with a view to asserting its own power, but as a single member among many co-ordinate and co-equal States. So far as the influence of this Government may be potential, it will be exerted in the direction of conciliating whatever conflicting interests of blood, or government, or historical tradition that may necessarily come together in response to a call embracing such vast and diverse elements.

INSTRUCTIONS TO THE MINISTERS.

You will present these views to the Minister of Foreign Affairs of Costa Rica, enlarging, if need be, in such terms as will readily occur to you upon the great mission which it is within the power of the proposed Congress to accomplish in the interest of humanity, and the firm purpose of the United States of America to maintain a position of the most absolute and impartial friendship toward all. You will, therefore, in the name of the President of the United States, tender to his Excellency, the President of ———, a formal invitation to send two commissioners to the Congress, provided with such powers and instructions on behalf of their Government as will enable them to consider the questions brought before that body within the limit of submission contemplated by this invitation.

The United States, as well as the other powers, will in like manner be represented by two commissioners, so that equality and impartiality will be amply secured in the proceedings of the Congress.

In delivering this invitation through the Minister of Foreign Affairs, you will read this despatch to him and leave with him a copy, intimating that an answer is desired by this Government as promptly as the just consideration of so important a proposition will permit.

I am, sir, your obedient servant,

JAMES G. BLAINE.

Minister Logan's Reply.

The following is an abstract of the reply of Minister Logan to the above.

"From a full review of the situation, as heretofore detailed to you, I am not clear as to being able to obtain the genuine co-operation of all the States of Central America in the proposed congress.—Each, I have no doubt, will ultimately agree to send the specified number of commissioners and assume, outwardly, an appearance of sincere co-operation, but, as you will perceive from your knowledge of the posture of affairs, all hope of effecting a union of these States except upon a basis the leaders will never permit—that of a free choice of the whole people—will be at an end. The obligation to keep the peace, imposed by the congress, will bind the United States as well as all others, and thus prevent any efforts to bring about the desired union other than those based upon a simple tender of good offices—this means until the years shall bring about a radical change—must be as inefficient in the future as in the past. The situation, as it appears to me, is a difficult one. As a means of restraining the aggressive tendency of Mexico in the direction of Central America, the congress would be attended by the happiest results, should a full agreement be reached. But as the Central American States are now in a chaotic condition, politically considered, with their future status wholly undefined, and as a final settlement can only be reached, as it now appears, through the operation of military forces, the hope of a Federal union in Central America would be crushed, at least in the immediate present. Wiser heads than my own may devise a method to harmonize these difficulties when the congress is actually in session, but it must be constantly remembered that so far as the Central American commissioners are concerned they will represent the interests and positive mandates of their respective government chiefs in the strictest and most absolute sense. While all will probably send commissioners, through motives of expediency, they may possibly be instructed to secretly defeat the ends of the convention. I make these suggestions that you may have the whole field under view.

"I may mention in this connection that I have received information that up to the tenth of the present month only two members of the proposed convention at Panama had arrived and that it was considered as having failed."

Contemporaneous with these movements or suggestions was another on the part of Mr. Blaine to secure from England a modification or abrogation of the Clayton-Bulwer treaty, with the object of giving to the United States, rather to the Republics of North and South America, full supervision of the Isthmus and Panama Canal when constructed. This branch of the correspondence was sent to the Senate on the 17th of February. Lord Granville, in his despatch of January 7th to Minister West in reference to the Clayton-Bulwer

Treaty controversy, denies any analogy between the cases of the Panama and Suez Canals. He cordially concurs in Mr. Blaine's statement in regard to the unexampled development of the Pacific Coast, but denies that it was unexpected.

He says the declaration of President Monroe anterior to the treaty show that he and his Cabinet had a clear prevision of the great future of that region. The development of the interests of the British possessions also continued, though possibly less rapidly. The Government are of the opinion that the canal, as a water way between the two great oceans and Europe and Eastern Asia, is a work which concerns not only the American Continent, but the whole civilized world. With all deference to the considerations which prompted Mr. Blaine he cannot believe that his proposals will be even beneficial in themselves. He can conceive a no more melancholy spectacle than competition between nations in the construction of fortifications to command the canal. He cannot believe that any South American States would like to admit a foreign power to erect fortifications on its territory, when the claim to do so is accompanied by the declaration that the canal is to be regarded as a part of the American coast line. It is difficult to believe, he says, that the territory between it and the United States could retain its present independence. Lord Granville believes that an invitation to all the maritime states to participate in an agreement based on the stipulations of the Convention of 1850, would make the Convention adequate for the purposes for which it was designed. Her Majesty's Government would gladly see the United States take the initiative towards such a convention, and will be prepared to endorse and support such action in any way. provided it does not conflict with the Clayton-Bulwer treaty.

Lord Granville, in a subsequent despatch, draws attention to the fact that Mr. Blaine, in using the argument that the treaty has been a source of continual difficulties, omits to state that the questions in dispute which related to points occupied by the British in Central America were removed in 1860 by the voluntary action of Great Britain in certain treaties concluded with Honduras and Nicaragua, the settlement being recognized as perfectly satisfactory by President Buchanan. Lord Granville says, further, that during this controversy America disclaimed any desire to have the exclusive control of the canal.

The Earl contends that in cases where the details of an international agreement have given rise to difficulties and discussions to such an extent as to cause the contracting parties at one time to contemplate its abrogation or modification as one of several possible alternatives, and where it has yet been found preferable to arrive at a solution as to those details rather than to sacrifice the general bases of the engagement, it must surely be allowed that such a fact, far from being an argument against that engagement, is an argument distinctly in its favor. It is equally plain that either of the contracting parties which had abandoned its own contention for the purpose of preserving the agreement in its entirety would have reason to complain if the differences which had been settled by its concessions were afterwards urged as a reason for essentially modifying those other provisions which it had made this sacrifice to maintain. In order to strengthen these arguments, the Earl reviews the correspondence, quotes the historical points made by Mr. Blaine and in many instances introduces additional data as contradicting the inferences drawn by Mr. Blaine and supporting his own position.

The point on which Mr. Blaine laid particular stress in his despatch to Earl Granville, is the objection made by the government of the United States to any concerted action of the European powers for the purpose of guarantying the neutrality of the Isthmus canal or determining the conditions of its use.

CHILI AND PERU.

The entire question is complicated by the war between Chili and Peru, the latter owning immense guano deposits in which American citizens have become financially interested. These sought the friendly intervention of our government to prevent Chili, the conquering Republic, from appropriating these deposits as part of her war indemnity. The Landreau, an original French claim, is said to represent $125,-000,000, and the holders were prior to and during the war pressing it upon Calderon, the Peruvian President, for settlement; the Cochet claim, another of the same class, represented $1,000,000,000. Doubtless these claims are speculative and largely fraudulent, and shrewd agents are interested in their collection and preservation. A still more preposterous and speculative movement was fathered by one Shipherd, who opened a correspondence with Minister Hurlburt, and with other parties for the establishment of the Credit Industriel, which was to pay the $20,000,000 money indemnity demanded of Peru by Chili, and to be reimbursed by the Peruvian nitrates and guano deposits.

THE SCANDAL.

All of these things surround the question with scandals which probably fail to truthfully reach any prominent officer of our government, but which have nevertheless attracted the attention of Congress to such an extent that the following action has been already taken:

On February 24th Mr. Bayard offered in the Senate a resolution reciting that whereas publication has been widely made by the public press of certain alleged public commercial contracts between certain companies and copartnerships of individuals relative to the exports of guano and nitrates from Peru, in which the mediation by the Government of the United States between the Governments of Peru, Bolivia and Chili is declared to be a condition for the effectuation and continuance of the said contracts: therefore be it resolved, that the Committee on Foreign Relations be instructed to inquire whether any promise or stipulation by which the intervention by the United States in the controversies existing between Chili and Peru or Chili and Bolivia has been expressly or impliedly given by any person or persons officially connected with the Government of the United States, or whether the influence of the Government of the United States has been in any way exerted, promised or intimated in connection with, or in relation to the said contracts by any one officially connected with the Government of the United States, and whether any one officially connected with the Government of the United States is interested, directly or indirectly, with any such alleged contracts in which the mediation as aforesaid of the United States is recited to be a condition, and that the said committee have power to send for persons and paper and make report of their proceedings in the premises to the Senate at the earliest possible day.

Mr. Edmunds said he had drafted a resolution covering all the branches of "that most unfortunate affair" to which reference was now made, and in view of the ill policy of any action which would commit the Senate to inquiries about declaring foreign matters in advance of a careful investigation by a committee, he now made the suggestion that he would have made as to his own resolution, if he had offered it, namely, that the subject be referred to the Committee on Foreign Relations. He intimated that the proposition prepared by himself would be considered by the committee as a suggestion bearing upon the pending resolution.

Mr. Bayard acquiesced in the reference with the remark that anything that tended to bring the matter more fully before the country was satisfactory to him.

The resolution accordingly went to the Committee on Foreign Relations.

In the House Mr. Kasson, of Iowa, offered a resolution reciting that whereas, it is alleged, in connection with the Chili Peruvian correspondence recently and officially published on the call of the two Houses of Congress, that one or more Ministers Plenipotentiary of the United States were either personally interested or improperly connected with a business transaction in which the intervention of this Government was requested or expected and whereas, it is alleged that certain papers in relation to the same subject have been improperly lost or removed from the files of the State Department, that therefore the Committee on Foreign Affairs be instructed to inquire into said allegations and ascertain the facts relating thereto, and report the same with such recommendations as they may deem proper, and they shall have power to send for persons and papers. The resolution was adopted.

THE CLAIMS.

The inner history of what is known as the Peruvian Company reads more like a tale from the Arabian Nights than a plain statement of facts. The following is gleaned from the prospectus of the company, of which only a limited number of copies was printed. According to a note on the cover of these "they are for the strictly private use of the gentlemen into whose hands they are immediately placed."

The prospects of the corporation are based entirely upon the claims of Cochet and Landreau, two French chemists, residents of Peru. In the year 1833, the Peruvian government, by published decree, promised to every discoverer of valuable deposits upon the public domain a premium of one-third of the discovery as an incentive to the development of great natural resources vaguely known to exist. In the beginning of 1830, Alexandre Cochet, who was a man of superior information, occupied himself in the laborious work of manufacturing nitrate of soda in a small *oficina* in Peru, and being possessed with quick intelligence and a careful observer he soon came to understand that the valuable properties contained in the guano—an article only known to native cultivators of the soil—would be eminently useful as a restorative to the exhausted lands of the old continent. With this idea he made himself completely master of the mode of application adopted by the Indians and small farmers in the province where he resided, and after a careful investigation of the chemical effects produced on the land by the proper application of the regenerating agent, he proceeded in the year 1840 to the capital (Lima) in order to interest some of his friends in this new enterprise. Not without great persuasion and much hesitation, he induced his countryman, Mr. Achilles Allier, to take up the hazardous speculation and join with him in his discovery. He succeeded, however, and toward the end of the same year the firm of Quiros & Allier obtained a concession for six years from the government of Peru for the exportation of all the guano existing in the afterwards famous islands of Chinchi for the sum of sixty thousand dollars. In consequence of the refusal of that firm to admit Cochet, the discoverer, to a participation in the profits growing out of this contract a series of lawsuits resulted and a paper war ensued in which Cochet was baffled. In vain he called the attention of the government to the nature and value of this discovery; he was told that he was a "visionary." In vain he demonstrated that the nation possessed hundreds of millions of dollars in the grand deposits: this only confirmed the opinion of the Council of State that he was a madman. In vain he attempted to prove that one cargo of guano was equal to fourteen cargoes of grain; the Council of State cooly told him that guano was an article known to the Spaniards, and of no value: that Commissioner Humbolt had referred to it, and that they could not accept his theory respecting its superior properties, its value and its probable use in foreign agriculture at a period when no new discovery could be made relative to an article so long and of so evident small value.

At length a new light began to dawn on the lethargic understanding of the officials in power, and as rumors continued to arrive from Europe confirming the asseverations of Cochet, and announcing the sale of guano at from $90 to $120 per ton, a degree of haste was suddenly evinced to secure once more to the public treasury this new and unexpected source of wealth; and at one blow the contract with Quiroz & Allier, which had previously been extended, was reduced to one year. Their claims were cancelled by the payment of ten thousand tons of guano which Congress decreed them. There still remained to be settled the just and acknowledged indebtedness for benefits conferred on the country by Cochet, benefits which could not be denied as wealth and prosperity rolled in on the government and on the people. But few, if any, troubled themselves about the question to whom they were indebted for so much good fortune, nor had time to pay particular attention to Cochet's claims. Finally, however, Congress was led to declare Cochet the true discoverer of the value, uses and application of guano for European agriculture, and a grant of 5,000 tons was made in his favor September 30th, 1849, but was never paid him. After passing a period of years in hopeless expectancy—from 1840 to 1851—his impoverished circumstances made it necessary for him to endeavor to procure, through the influence of his own government, that measure of support in favor of his claims which would insure him a competency in his old age.

He resolved upon returning to France, after having spent the best part of his life in the service of a country whose cities had risen from desolation to splendor under the sole magic of his touch—a touch that had in it for Peru all the fabled power of the long-sought "philosopher's stone." In 1853 Cochet returned to France, but he was then already exhausted by enthusiastic explorations in a deadly climate and never rallied. He lingered in poverty for eleven painful years and died in Paris in an almshouse in 1864, entitled to an estate worth $500,000,000—the richest man in the history of the world—and was buried by the city in the Potters' Field; his wonderful history well illustrating that truth is stranger than fiction.

THE LANDREAU CLAIM.

About the year 1844 Jean Theophile Landreau, also a French citizen, in partnership with his brother, John C. Landreau, a naturalized American citizen, upon the faith of the promised premium of 33⅓ per cent. entered upon a series of extended systematic and scientific explorations with a view to ascertaining whether the deposits of guano particularly pointed out by Cochet constituted the entire guano deposit of Peru, and with money furnished by his partner, John, Theophile prosecuted his searches with remarkable energy and with great success for twelve years, identifying beds not before known to the value of not less than $400,000,000. Well aware, however, of the manner in which his fellow-countryman had been neglected by an unprincipled people, he had the discretion to keep his own counsel and to extort from the Peruvian authorities an absolute agreement in advance before he revealed his treasure. This agreement was, indeed, for a royalty of less than one-sixth the amount promised, but the most solemn assurances were given that the lessened amount would be promptly and cheerfully paid, its total would give the brothers each a large fortune, and payments were to begin at once. The solemn agreement having been concluded and duly certified, the precious deposits having been pointed out and taken possession of by the profligate government, the brothers were at first put off with plausible pretexts of delay, and when these grew monotonous the government calmly issued a decree recognizing the discoveries, accepting the treasure, and annulling the contract, with a suggestion that a more suitable agreement might be arranged in the future.

It will be seen that these two men, Cochet and Landreau, have been acknowledged by the Peruvian government as claimants. No attempt has ever been made to deny the indebtedness. The very decree of repudiation reaffirmed the obligation, and all the courts refused to pronounce against the plaintiffs. Both of these claims came into the possession of Mr. Peter W. Hevenor, of Philadelphia. Cochet left one son whom Mr. Hevenor found in poverty in Lima and advanced money to push his father's claim of $500,000,000 against the government. After $50,000 were spent young Cochet's backer was surprised to learn of the Laudreaus and their claim. Not wishing to antagonize them, he advanced them money, and in a short time owned nearly all the fifteen interests in the Landreau claim of $125,000,000.

To the Peruvian Company Mr. Hevenor has transferred his titles, and on the basis of these that corporation maintains that eventually it will realize not less than $1,-200,000,000, computed as follows:

The amount of guano already taken out of the Cochet Islands—including the Chinchas—will be shown by the Peruvian Custom House records, and will aggregate, it is said, not far from $1,200,000,000 worth. The discoverer's one-third of this would be $400,000,000, and interest upon this amount at six per cent. - say for an equalized average of twenty years—would be $480,000,000 more. The amount remaining in these islands is not positively known, and is probably not more than $200,000,000 worth; and in the Landreau deposits say $300,000,-000 more. The Chilian plenipotentiary recently announced that his government are about opening very rich deposits on the Lobos Islands—which are included in this group. It is probably within safe limits, says the Peruvian Company's prospectus, to say that, including interest to accrue before the claim can be fully liquidated, its owners will realize no less than $1,200,000,000.

THE COUNTRIES INVOLVED.

In South America there are ten independent governments; and the three Guianas which are dependencies on European powers. Of the independent governments Brazil is an empire, having an area of 3,609,160 square miles and 11,058,000 inhabitants. The other nine are republics. In giving area and population we use the most complete statistics at our command, but they are not strictly reliable, nor as late as we could have wished. The area and the population of the republics are: Venzuela, 426,712 square miles and 2,200,-000 inhabitants; United States of Colombia, 475,000 square miles and 2,900,000 inhabitants; Peru, 580,000 square miles and 2,500,000 inhabitants; Ecuador, 208,000 square miles and 1,300,000 inhabitants; Bolivia, 842,730 square miles and 1,987,352 inhabitants; Chili, 200,000 square miles and 2,084,960 inhabitants; Argentine Republic, 1,323,560 square miles and 1,887,-000 inhabitants; Paraguay, 73,000 square miles and 1,337,439 inhabitants; Uruguay, 66,716 square miles and 240,000 inhabitants, or a total in the nine republics of 3,789,220 square miles and 16,436,751 inhabitants. The aggregate area of the nine republics exceeds that of Brazil 180,060 square miles, and the total population exceeds that of Brazil 5,069,552. Brazil, being an empire, is not comprehended in the Blaine proposal—she rather stands as a strong barrier against it. Mexico and Guatamala are included, but are on this continent, and their character and resources better understood by our people. In the South American countries generally the Spanish language is spoken. The educated classes are of nearly pure Spanish extraction. The laboring classes are of mixed Spanish and aboriginal blood, or of pure aboriginal ancestry. The characteristics of the Continent are emphatically Spanish. The area and population we have already given. The territory is nearly equally divided between the republics and the empire, the former having a greater area of only 180,060 square miles; but the nine republics have an aggregate population of 5,059,522 more than Brazil. The United States has an area of 3,634,797 square miles, including Alaska; but excluding Alaska, it has 3,056,797 square miles. The area of Brazil is greater than that of the United States, excluding Alaska, by 552,-363 square miles, and the aggregate area of the nine republics is greater by 732,423 square miles. This comparison of the area of the nine republics and of Brazil with that of this nation gives a definite idea of their magnitude. Geographically, these republics occupy the northern, western and southern portions of South America, and are contiguous. The aggregate exports and imports of South America, according to the last available data, were $529,300,000; those of Brazil, $168,930,000; of the nine republics, $360,360,000.

These resolutions will bring out voluminous correspondence, but we have given the reader sufficient to reach a fair understanding of the subject. Whatever of scandal may be connected with it, like the Star Route cases, it should await official investigation and condemnation. Last of all should history condemn any one in advance of official inquiry. None of the governments invited to the Congress had accepted formally, and in view of obstacles thrown in the way by the present administration, it is not probable they will.

Accepting the proposition of Mr. Blaine as stated in his letter to President Arthur, as conveying his true desire and meaning, it is due to the truth to say that it comprehends more than the Monroe doctrine, the text of which is given in President Monroe's own words in this volume. While he contended against foreign intervention with the Republics on this Hemisphere, he never asserted the right of our government to participate in or seek the control either of the internal, commercial or foreign policy of any of the Republics of America, by arbitration or otherwise. So that Mr. Blaine is the author of an advance upon the Monroe doctrine, and what seems at this time a radical advance. What it may be when the United States seeks to "spread itself" by an aggressive foreign policy, and by aggrandizement of new avenues of trade, possibly new acquisitions of territory, is another question. It is a policy brilliant beyond any examples in our history, and a new departure from the teachings of Washington, who advised absolute non-intervention in foreign affairs. The new doctrine might thrive and acquire great popularity under an administration friendly to it; but President Arthur has already intimated his hostility, and it is now beyond enforcement during his administration. The views of Congress also seem to be adverse as far as the debates have gone into the question, though it has some warm friends who may revive it under more favorable auspices.

The Star Route Scandal.

Directly after Mr. James assumed the position of Postmaster-General in the Cabinet of President Garfield, he discovered a great amount of extravagance and probably fraud in the conduct of the mail service known as the Star Routes, authorized by act of Congress to further extend the mail facilities and promote the more rapid carriage of the mails. These routes proved to be very popular in the West and South-west, and the growing demand for mail facilities in these sections would even in a legitimate way, if not closely watched, lead to unusual cost and extravagance; but it is alleged that a ring was formed headed by General Brady, one of the Assistant Postmaster-Generals under General Key, by which routes were established with the sole view of defrauding the Government—that false bonds were given and enormous and fraudulent sums paid for little or no service. This scandal was at its height at the time of the assassination of President Garfield, at which time Postmaster-General James, Attorney-General MacVeagh and other officials were rapidly preparing for the prosecution of all charged with the fraud. Upon the succession of President Arthur he openly insisted upon the fullest prosecution, and declined to receive the resignation of Mr. MacVeagh from the Cabinet because of a stated fear that the prosecution would suffer by his withdrawal. Mr. MacVeagh, however, withdrew from the Cabinet, believing that the new President should not by any circumstance be prevented from the official association of friends of his own selection; and at this writing Attorney-General Brewster is pushing the prosecutions.

On the 24th of March, 1882, the Grand Jury sitting at Washington presented indictments for conspiracy in connection with the Star Route mail service against the following named persons: Thomas J. Brady, J. W. Dorsey, Henry M. Vail, John W. Dorsey, John R. Miner, John M. Peck, M. C. Rerdell, J. L. Sanderson, Wm. H. Turner. Also against Alvin O. Buck, Wm. S. Barringer and Albert E. Boone, and against Kate M. Armstrong for perjury. The indictment against Brady, Dorsey and others, which is very voluminous, recites the existence, on March 10, 1879, of the Post Office Department, Postmaster-General and three assistants, and a Sixth Auditor's office and Contract office and division.

"To the latter was subject," the indictment continues, "the arrangement of the mail service of the United States and the letting out of the same on contract." It then describes the duties of the inspecting division. On March 10, 1879, the grand jurors represent, Thomas J. Brady was the lawful Second Assistant Postmaster-General engaged in the performance of the duties of that office. William H. Turner was a clerk in the Second Assistant Postmaster-General's office, and attended to the business of the contract division relating to the mail service over several post routes in California, Colorado, Oregon, Nebraska, and the Territories. On the 16th of March, 1879, the indictment represents Thomas J. Brady as having made eight contracts with John W. Dorsey to carry the mails from July 1, 1878, to June 30, 1882, from Vermillion, in Dakota Territory, to Sioux Falls and back, on a fourteen hour time schedule, for $398 each year; on route from White River to Rawlins, Colorado, once a week of 108 hours' time, for $1,700 a year; on route from Garland, Colorado, to Parrott City, once a week, on a schedule of 168 hours' time, for $2,745; on route from Ouray, Colorado, to Los Pinos, once a week, in 12 hours' time, for $348; on route from Silverton, Colorado, to Parrott City, twice a week, on 36 hours' time, for $1,488; on route from Mineral Park, in Arizona Territory, to Pioche and back, once a week, in 84 hours' time, $2,982; on route from Tres Almos to Clifton and back, once a week, of 84 hours' time, for $1,568.

It further sets forth that the Second Assistant Postmaster-General entered into five contracts with John R. Miner on June 13, 1878, on routes in Dakota Territory and Colorado, and on March 15, 1879, with John M. Peck, over eight post routes. In the space of sixty days after the making of these contracts they were in full force. On March 10, 1879, John W. Dorsey, John R. Miner, and John M. Peck, with Stephen W. Dorsey and Henry M. Vaile, M. C. Rerdell and J. L. Sanderson, mutually interested in these contracts and money, to be paid by the United States to the three parties above named, did unlawfully and maliciously combine and conspire to fraudulently write, sign, and cause to be written and signed, a large number of fraudulent letters and communications and false and fraudulent petitions and applications to the Postmaster-General for additional service and increase of expenditure on the routes, which were purported to be signed by the people and inhabitants in the neighborhood of the routes, which were filed with the papers in the office of the Second Assistant Postmaster-General. Further that these parties swore falsely in describing the number of men and animals required to perform the mail service over the routes and States as greater than was necessary.

These false oaths were placed on file in the Second Assistant Postmaster-General's office; and by means of Wm. H. Turner falsely making and writing and endorsing these papers, with brief and untrue statements as to their contents, and by Turner preparing fraudulent written orders for allowances to be made to these contractors and signed by Thomas J. Brady fraudulently, and for the benefit and gain of all the parties named in this bill, the service was increased over these routes; and that Brady knew it was not lawfully needed and required. That he caused the order for increasing to be certified to and filed in the Sixth Auditor's office for fraudulent additional compensation. That Mr. Brady gave orders to extend the service so as to include other and different stations than those mentioned in the contract, that he and others might have the benefits and profits of it: that he refused to impose fines on these contracts for failures and delinquencies, but allowed them additional pay for the service over these routes. During the continuance of these contracts the parties acquired unto themselves several large and excessive sums of money, the property of the United States, fraudulently and unlawfully ordered to be paid them by Mr. Brady.

These are certainly formidable indictments. Others are pending against persons in Philadelphia and other cities, who are charged with complicity in these Star Route frauds, in giving straw bonds, &c. The Star Route service still continues, the Post Office Department under the law having sent out several thousand notifications this year to contractors, informing them of the official acceptance of their proposals, and some of these contractors are the same named above as under indictment. This well exemplifies the maxim of the law relative to innocence until guilt be shown.

The Coming States.

Bills are pending before Congress for the admission of Dakota, Wyoming, New Mexico and Washington Territories. The Bill for the admission of Dakota divides the old Territory, and provides that the new State shall consist of the territory included within the following boundaries: Commencing at a point on the west line of the State of Minnesota where the forty-sixth degree of north latitude intersects the same; thence south along the west boundary lines of the States of Minnesota and Iowa to the point of intersection with the northern boundary line of the State of Nebraska; thence westwardly along the northern boundary line of the State of Nebraska to the twenty-seventh meridian of longitude west from Washington; thence north along the said twenty-seventh degree of longitude to the forty-sixth degree of north latitude; to the place of beginning. The bill provides for a convention of one hundred and twenty delegates, to be chosen by the legal voters, who shall adopt the United States Constitution and then proceed to form a State Constitution and government. Until the next census the State shall be entitled to one representative, who, with the Governor and other officials, shall be elected upon a day named by the Constitutional Convention. The report sets apart lands for school purposes, and gives the State five per centum of the proceeds of all sales of public lands within its limits subsequent to its admission as a State, excluding all mineral lands from being thus set apart for school purposes. It provides that portion of the the Territory not included in the proposed new State shall continue as a Territory under the name of the Territory of North Dakota.

The proposition to divide comes from Senator McMillan, and if Congress sustains the division, the portion admitted would contain 100,000 inhabitants, the entire estimated population being 175,000—a number in excess of twenty of the present States when admitted, exclusive of the original thirteen; while the division, which shows 100,000 inhabitants, is still in excess of sixteen States when admitted.

Nevada, with less than 65,000 population, was admitted before the close Presidential election of 1876, and it may be said that her majority of 1,075, in a total poll of 19,691 votes, decided the Presidential result in favor of Hayes, and these votes counteracted the plurality of nearly 300,000 received by Mr. Tilden elsewhere. This fact well illustrates the power of States, as States, and however small, in controlling the affairs of the country. It also accounts for the jealousy with which closely balanced political parties watch the incoming States.

Population is but one of the considerations entering into the question of admitting territories, State sovereignty does not rest upon population, as in the make-up of the U. S. Senate neither population, size, nor resources are taken into account. Rhode Island, the smallest of all the States, and New York, the great Empire State, with over 5,000,000 of inhabitants, stand upon an equality in the conservative branch of the Government. It is in the House of Representatives that the population is considered. Such is the jealousy of the larger States of their representation in the U. S. Senate, that few new ones would be admitted without long and continuous knocking if it were not for partisan interests, and yet where a fair number of people demand State Government there is no just cause for denial. Yet all questions of population, natural division, area and resources should be given their proper weight.

The area of the combined territories—Utah, Washington, New Mexico, Dakota, Arizona, Montana, Idaho, Wyoming and Indian is about 900,000 square miles. We exclude Alaska, which has not been surveyed.

Indian Territory and Utah are for some years to come excluded from admission—the one being reserved to the occupancy of the Indians, while the other is by her peculiar institution of polygamy, generally thrown out of all calculation. And yet it may be found that polygamy can best be made amenable to the laws by the compulsory admission of Utah as a State—an idea entertained by not a few who have given consideration to the question. Alaska may also be counted out for many years to come. There are but 30,000 inhabitants, few of these permanent, and Congress is now considering a petition for the establishment of a territorial government there.

Next to Dakota, New Mexico justly claims admission. The lands comprised within its original area were acquired from Mexico, at the conclusion of the war with that country, by the treaty of Guadalupe Hidalgo in 1848, and by act of September 9, 1850, a Territorial government was organized. By treaty of December 30, 1853, the region south of the Gila river—the Gadsden purchase, so called—was ceded by Mexico, and by act of August 4, 1854, added to the Territory, which at that time included within its limits the present Territory of Arizona. Its prayer for admission was brought to the serious attention of Congress in 1874. The bill was presented in an able speech by Mr. Elkins, then delegate from the Territory, and had the warm support of many members. A bill to admit was also introduced in the Senate, and passed that body February 25, 1875, by a vote of thirty-two to eleven, two of the present members of that body, Messrs. Ingalls and Windom, being among its supporters. The matter of admission came up for final action in the House at the same session, just prior to adjournment, and a motion to suspend the rules, in order to put it upon its final passage, was lost by a vote of one hundred and fifty-four to eighty-seven, and the earnest efforts to secure the admission of New Mexico were thus defeated. A bill for its admission is now again before Congress, and it is a matter of interest to note the representations as to the condition of the Territory then made, and the facts as they now exist. It has, according to the census of 1880, a population of 119,565. It had in 1870 a population of 91,874. It was claimed by the more moderate advocates of the bill that its population then numbered 135,000 (15,435 more than at present), while others placed it as high as 145,000. Of this population, 45,000 were said to be of American and European descent. It was stated by Senator Hoar, one of the opponents of the bill, that, out of an illiterate population of 52,220, by far the larger part were native inhabitants of Mexican or Spanish origin, who could not speak the English language. This statement seems to be in large degree confirmed by the census of 1880, which shows a total native white population of 108,721, of whom, as nearly as can be ascertained, upward of 80 per cent. are not only illiterates of Mexican and Spanish extraction, but as in 1870, speaking a foreign language. The vote for Mr. Elkins, Territorial Delegate in 1875, was reported as being about 17,000. The total vote in 1878 was 18,806, and in 1880, 20,397, showing a comparatively insignificant increase from 1875 to 1880.

The Territory of Washington was constituted out of Oregon, and organized as a Territory by act of March 2, 1853. Its population by the census of 1880 was 75,116, an increase from 23,955 in 1870. Of this total, 59,313 are of native and 15,803 of foreign nativity. Its total white population in the census year was 67,119; Chinese, 3,186; Indian, 4,105; colored, 326, and its total present population is probably not far from 95,000. Its yield of precious metals in 1880, and for the entire period since its development, while showing resources full of promise, has been much less than that of any other of the organized Territories. Its total vote for Territorial Delegate in 1880, while exceeding that of the Territories of Arizona, Idaho, and Wyoming, was but 15,823.

The Territory of Arizona, organized out of a portion of New Mexico, and provided with a territorial government in 1863, contains about 5,000,000 acres less than the Territory of New Mexico, or an acreage exceeded by that of only five States and Territories. Its total population in 1870 was 9,658, and in 1880, 40,440, 351,60 of whom were whites. Of its total population in the census year, 24,391 were of native and 16,049 of foreign birth, the number of

Indians, Chinese, and colored being 5,000.

Idaho was originally a part of Oregon, from which it was separated and provided with a territorial government by the act of March 3, 1863. It embraces in its area a little more than 55,000,000 acres, and had in 1880 a total population of 32,610, being an increase from 14,999 in 1870. Of this population, 22,636 are of native and 9,974 of foreign birth; 29,013 of the total inhabitants are white, 3,379 Chinese and 218 Indians and colored.

The Territory of Montana, organized by act of May 26, 1864, contains an acreage larger than that of any other Territory save Dakota. While it seems to be inferior in cereal producing capacity, in its area of valuable grazing lands it equals, if it does not excel, Idaho. The chief prosperity of the Territory, and that which promises for it a future of growing importance, lies in its extraordinary mineral wealth, the productions of its mines in the year 1880 having been nearly twice that of any other Territory, with a corresponding excess in its total production, which had reached, on June 30, 1880, the enormous total of over $53,000,000. Its mining industries represent in the aggregate very large invested capital, and the increasing products, with the development of new mines, are attracting constant additions to its population, which in 1880 showed an increase, as compared with 1870, of over 90 per cent. For particulars see census tables in tabulated history.

Wyoming was constituted out of the Territory of Dakota, and provided with territorial government July 25, 1868. Lying between Colorado and Montana, and adjoining Dakota and Nebraska on the east, it partakes of the natural characteristics of these States and Territories, having a fair portion of land suitable for cultivation, a large area suitable for grazing purposes, and a wealth in mineral resources whose development, although of recent beginning, has already resulted in an encouraging yield in precious metals. It is the fifth in area.

Henry Randall Waite, in an able article in the March number of the International Review (1882,) closes with these interesting paragraphs:

"It will be thus seen that eleven States organized from Territories, when authorized to form State governments, and the same number when admitted to the Union, had free populations of less than 60,000, and that of the slave States included in this number, seven in all, not one had the required number of free inhabitants, either when authorized to take the first steps toward admission or when finally admitted; and that both of these steps were taken by two of the latter States with a total population, free and slave, below the required number. Why so many States have been authorized to form State governments, and have been subsequently admitted to the Union with populations so far below the requirements of the ordinance of 1787, and the accepted rules for subsequent action may be briefly explained as follows: 1st, by the ground for the use of a wide discretion afforded in the provisions of the ordinance of 1787, for the admission of States, when deemed expedient, before their population should equal the required number; and 2d, by the equally wide discretion given by the Constitution in the words, 'New States may be admitted by Congress into this Union,' the only provision of the Constitution bearing specifically upon this subject. Efforts have been made at various times to secure the strict enforcement of the original rules, with the modification resulting from the increase in the population of the Union, which provided that the number of free inhabitants in a Territory seeking admission should equal the number established as the basis of representation in the apportionment of Representatives in Congress, as determined by the preceding census. How little success the efforts made in this direction have met, may be seen by a comparison of the number of inhabitants forming the basis of representation, as established by the different censuses, and the free population of the Territories admitted at corresponding periods.

"At this late date, it is hardly to be expected that rules so long disregarded will be made applicable to the admission of the States to be organized from the existing Territories. There is, nevertheless, a growing disposition on the part of Congress to look with disfavor upon the formation of States whose population, and the development of whose resources, render the expediency of their admission questionable; and an increasing doubt as to the propriety of so dividing the existing Territories as to multiply to an unnecessary extent the number of States, with the attendant increase in the number of Representatives in the National Legislature.

"To recapitulate the facts as to the present condition of the Territories with reference to their admission as States, it may be said that only Dakota, Utah, New Mexico and Washington are in possession of the necessary population according to the rule requiring 60,000; that only the three first named conform to the rule demanding a population equal to the present basis of representation; that only Dakota, Utah and Washington give evidence of that intelligence on the part of their inhabitants which is essential to the proper exercise, under favorable conditions, of the extended rights of citizenship, and of that progress in the development of their resources which makes self-government essential, safe, or in any way desirable; and that only Dakota can be said, unquestionably, to possess all of the requirements which, by the dictates of a sound policy, should be demanded of a Territory at this time seeking admission to the Union.

"Whatever the response to the Territorial messengers now waiting at the doors of Congress, a few years, at most, will bring an answer to their prayers. The stars of a dozen proud and prosperous States will soon be added to those already blazoned upon the blue field of the Union, and the term Territory, save as applied to the frozen regions of Alaska, will disappear from the map of the United States."

The Chinese Question.

Since 1877 the agitation of the prohibition of Chinese immigration in California and other States and Territories on the Pacific slope has been very great. This led to many scenes of violence and in some instances bloodshed, when one Dennis Kearney led the Workingmen's party in San Francisco. On this issue an agitator and preacher named Kalloch was elected Mayor. The issue was carried to the Legislature, and in the vote on a constitutional amendment it was found that not only the labor but nearly all classes in California were opposed to the Chinese. The constitutional amendment did not meet the sanction of the higher courts. A bill was introduced into Congress restricting Chinese immigrants to fifteen on each vessel. This passed both branches, but was vetoed by President Hayes on the ground that it was in violation of the spirit of treaty stipulations. At the sessions of 1881-82 a new and more radical measure was introduced. This prohibits immigration to Chinese or Coolie laborers for twenty years. The discussion in the U. S. Senate began on the 28th of February, 1882, in a speech of unusual strength by Senator John F. Miller, the author of the Bill. From this we freely quote, not alone to show the later views entertained by the people of the Pacific slope, but to give from the lips of one who knows the leading facts in the history of the agitation.

Abstracts from the Text of Senator Miller's Speech.

On his Bill to Prohibit Chinese Immigration.

In the Senate, Feb. 28th, 1882, Mr. Miller said:

"This measure is not a surprise to the Senate, nor a new revelation to the country. It has been before Congress more than once, if not in the precise form in which it is now presented, in substance the same, and it has passed the ordeal of analytical debate and received the affirmative vote of both Houses. Except for the Executive veto it would have been long ago the law of the land. It is again presented, not only under circumstances as imperative in their demands for its enactment, but with every objection of the veto removed and every argument made against its approval swept away. It is an interesting fact in the history of this measure, that the action which has cleared its way of the impediments which were made the reasons for the veto, was inaugurated and consummated with splendid persistance and energy by the same administration whose executive interposed the veto against it. Without stopping to inquire into the motive of the Hayes administration in this proceeding, whether its action was in obedience to a conviction that the measure was in itself right and expedient, or to a public sentiment, so strong and universal as to demand the utmost vigor in the diplomacy necessary for the removal of all impediments to its progress, it must be apparent that the result of this diplomatic action has been to add a new phase to the question in respect of the adoption of the measure itself.

"In order to fully appreciate this fact it may be proper to indulge in historical reminiscence for a moment. For many years complaints had been made against the introduction into the United States of the peculiar people who come from China, and the Congress, after careful consideration of the subject, so far appreciated the evil complained of as to pass a bill to interdict it.

"The Executive Department had, prior to that action, with diplomatic finesse, approached the imperial throne of China, with intent, as was said, to ascertain whether such an interdiction of coolie importation, or immigration so called, into the United States would be regarded as a breach of friendly relations with China, and had been informed by the diplomat, to whom the delicate task had been committed, that such interdiction would not be favorably regarded by the Chinese Government. Hence, when Congress, with surprising audacity, passed the bill of interdiction the Executive, believing in the truth of the information given him, thought it prudent and expedient to veto the bill, but immediately, in pursuance of authority granted by Congress, he appointed three commissioners to negotiate a treaty by which the consent of China should be given to the interdiction proposed by Congress. These commissioners appeared before the Government of China upon this special mission, and presented the request of the Government of the United States affirmatively, positively, and authoritatively made, and after the usual diplomatic ceremonies, representations, misrepresentations, avowals, and concealments, the treaty was made, the concession granted, and the interdiction agreed upon. This treaty was presented here and ratified by the Senate, with what unanimity Senators know, and which the rules of the Senate forbid me to describe.

"The new phase of this question, which we may as well consider in the outset, suggests the spectacle which this nation should present if Congress were to vote this or a similar measure down. A great nation cannot afford inconsistency in action, nor betray a vacillating, staggering, inconstant policy in its intercourse with other nations. No really great people will present themselves before the world through their government as a nation irresolute, fickle, feeble, or petulant; one day eagerly demanding of its neighbor an agreement or concession, which on the next it nervously repudiates or casts aside. Can we make a solemn request of China, through the pomp of an extraordinary embassy and the ceremony of diplomatic negotiation, and with prudent dispatch exchange ratifications of the treaty granting our request, and within less than half a year after such exchange is made cast aside the concession and, with childish irresolution, ignore the whole proceeding? Can we afford to make such a confession of American imbecility to any oriental power? The adoption of this or some such measure becomes necessary, it seems to me, to the intelligent and consistent execution of a policy adopted by this Government under the sanction of a treaty with another great nation.

"If the Executive department, the Senate, and the House of Representatives have all understood and appreciated their own action in respect of this measure; if in the negotiation and ratification of the new treaty with China, the Executive and the Senate did not act without thought, in blind, inconsiderate recklessness—and we know they did not—if the Congress of the United States in the passage of the fifteen passenger bill had the faintest conception of what it was doing—and we know it had —then the policy of this Government in respect of so-called Chinese immigration has been authoritatively settled.

"This proposition is submitted with the greater confidence because the action I have described was in obedience to, and in harmony with, a public sentiment which seems to have permeated the whole country. For the evidence of the existence of such a sentiment, it is only necessary to produce the declarations upon this subject of the two great historical parties of the country, deliberately made by their national conventions of 1880. One of these (the Democratic convention) declared that there shall be—

"'No more Chinese immigration except for travel, education, and foreign commerce, and therein carefully guarded.'

"The other (the Republican) convention declared that—

"'Since the authority to regulate immigration and intercourse between the United States and foreign nations rests with Congress, or with the United States and its treaty-making power, the Republican party, regarding the unrestricted immigration of the Chinese as an evil of great magnitude, invokes the exercise of these powers to restrain and limit the immigration by the enactment of such just, humane, and reasonable provisions as will produce that result.'

"These are the declarations of the two great political parties, in whose ranks are enrolled nearly all the voters of the United States; and whoever voted at the last Presidential election voted for the adoption of the principles and policy expressed by those declarations, whether he voted with the one or the other of the two great parties. Both candidates for the Presidency were pledged to the adoption and execution of the policy of restriction thus declared by their respective parties, and the candidate who was successful at the polls, in his letter of acceptance, not only gave expression to the sentiment of his party and the country, but with a clearness and conciseness which distinguished all his utterances upon great public questions, gave the reasons for that public sentiment." He said:

"'The recent movement of the Chinese to our Pacific Coast partakes but little of the qualities of an immigration, either in its purposes or results. It is too much like an importation to be welcomed without restriction; too much like an invasion to be looked upon without solicitude. We cannot consent to allow any form of servile labor to be introduced among us under the guise of immigration.'

* * * * * * * *

"In this connection it is proper also to consider the probable effect of a failure or refusal of Congress to pass this bill, upon the introduction of Chinese coolies into the United States in the future. An adverse vote upon such a measure, is an invitation to the Chinese to come, It would be interpreted to mean that the Government of the United States had reversed its policy, and is now in favor of the unrestricted importation of Chinese; that it looks with favor upon the Chinese invasion now in progress. It is a fact well known that the hostility to the influx of Chinese upon the Pacific coast displayed by the people of California has operated as a restriction, and has discouraged the importation of

Chinese to such a degree that it is probable that there are not a tenth part the number of Chinese in the country there would have been had this determined hostility never been shown. Despite the inhospitality, not to say resistance, of the California people to the Chinese, sometimes while waiting for the action of the General Government difficult to restrain within the bounds of peaceable assertion, they have poured through the Golden Gate in constantly increased numbers during the past year, the total number of arrivals at San Francisco alone during 1881 being 18,561. Nearly two months have elapsed since the 1st of January, and there have arrived, as the newspapers show, about four thousand more.

"The defeat of this measure now is a shout of welcome across the Pacific Ocean to a myriad host of these strange people to come and occupy the land, and it is a rebuke to the American citizens, who have so long stood guard upon the western shore of this continent, and who, seeing the danger, have with a fortitude and forbearance most admirable, raised and maintained the only barrier against a stealthy, strategic, but peaceful invasion as destructive in its results and more potent for evil, than an invasion by an army with banners. An adverse vote now, is to commission under the broad seal of the United States, all the speculators in human labor, all the importers of human muscle, all the traffickers in human flesh, to ply their infamous trade without impediment under the protection of the American flag, and empty the teeming, seething slave pens of China upon the soil of California! I forbear further speculation upon the results likely to flow from such a vote, for it presents pictures to the mind which one would not willingly contemplate.

"These considerations which I have presented ought to be, it seems to me, decisive of the action of the Senate upon this measure; and I should regard the argument as closed did I not know, that there still remain those who do not consider the question as settled, and who insist upon further inquiry into the reasons for a policy of restriction, as applied to the Chinese. I am not one of those who would place the consideration of consistency or mere appearances above consideration of right or justice; but since no change has taken place in our relations with China, nor in our domestic concerns which renders a reversal of the action of the government proper or necessary, I insist that if the measure of restriction was right and good policy when Congress passed the fifteenth passenger bill, and when the late treaty with China was negotiated and ratified, it is right and expedient now.

"This measure had its origin in California. It has been pressed with great vigor by the Representatives of the Pacific coast in Congress, for many years. It has not been urged with wild vehement declamation by thoughtless men, at the behest of an ignorant unthinking, prejudiced constituency. It has been supported by incontrovertible fact and passionless reasoning and enforced by the logic of events. Behind these Representatives was an intelligent, conscientious public sentiment—universal in a constituency as honest, generous, intelligent, courageous, and humane as any in the Republic.

"It had been said that the advocates of Chinese restriction were to be found only among the vicious, unlettered foreign element of California society. To show the fact in respect of this contention, the Legislature of California in 1878 provided for a vote of the people upon the question of Chinese immigration (so called) to be had at the general election of 1879. The vote was legally taken, without excitement, and the response was general. When the ballots were counted, there were found to be 883 votes for Chinese immigration and 154,638 against it. A similar vote was taken in Nevada and resulted as follows: 183 votes for Chinese immigration and 17,259 votes against. It has been said that a count of noses is an ineffectual and illusory method of settling great questions, but this vote of these two States settled the contention intended to be settled; and demonstrated that the people of all others in the United States who know most of the Chinese evil, and who are most competent to judge of the necessity for restriction are practically unanimous in the support of this measure.

"It is to be supposed that this vote of California was the effect of an hysterical spasm, which had suddenly seized the minds of 154,000 voters, representing the sentiment of 800,000 people. For nearly thirty years this people had witnessed the effect of coolie importation. For more than a quarter of a century these voters had met face to face, considered, weighed, and discussed the great question upon which they were at last called upon, in the most solemn and deliberate manner, to express an opinion. I do not cite this extraordinary vote as a conclusive argument in favor of Chinese restriction; but I present it as an important fact suggestive of argument. It may be that the people who have been brought face to face with the Chinese invasion are all wrong, and that those who have seen nothing of it, who have but heard something of it, are more competent (being disinterested) to judge of its possible, probable, and actual effects, than those who have had twenty or thirty years of actual continuous experience and contact with the Chinese colony in America;

and it may be that the Chinese question is to be settled upon considerations other than those practical common sense reasons and principles which form the basis of political science.

"It has sometimes happened in dealing with great questions of governmental policy that sentiment, or a sort of emotional inspiration, has seized the minds of those engaged in the solution of great problems, by which they have been lifted up into the ethereal heights of moral abstraction. I trust that while we attempt the path of inquiry in this instance we shall keep our feet firmly upon the earth. This question relates to this planet and the temporal government of some of its inhabitants; it is of the earth earthly; it involves principles of economic, social, and political science, rather than a question of morals; it is a question of national policy, and should be subjected to philosophical analysis. Moreover, the question is of to-day. The conditions of the world of mankind at the present moment are those with which we have to deal. If mankind existed now in one grand co-operative society, in one universal union, under one system of laws, in a vast homogeneous brotherhood, serenely beatified, innocent of all selfish aims and unholy desires, with one visible temporal ruler, whose judgments should be justice and whose sway should be eternal, then there would be no propriety in this measure.

"But the millennium has not yet begun, and man exists now, as he has existed always—in the economy of Providence—in societies called nations, separated by the peculiarities if not the antipathies of race. In truth the history of mankind is for the most part descriptive of racial conflicts and the struggles between nations for existence. By a perfectly natural process these nations have evolved distinct civilizations, as diverse in their characteristics as the races of men from which they have sprung. These may be properly grouped into two grand divisions, the civilization of the East and the civilization of the West. These two great and diverse civilizations have finally met on the American shore of the Pacific Ocean.

"During the late depression in business affairs, which existed for three or four years in California, while thousands of white men and women were walking the streets, begging and pleading for an opportunity to give their honest labor for any wages, the great steamers made their regular arrivals from China, and discharged at the wharves of San Francisco their accustomed cargoes of Chinese who were conveyed through the city to the distributing dens of the Six Companies, and within three or four days after arrival every Chinaman was in his place at work, and the white people unemployed still went about the streets. This continued until the white laboring men rose in their desperation and threatened the existence of the Chinese colony when the influx was temporarily checked; but now since business has revived, and the pressure is removed, the Chinese come in vastly increased numbers, the excess of arrivals over departures averaging about one thousand per month at San Francisco alone. The importers of Chinese had no difficulty in securing openings for their cargoes now, and when transportation from California to the Eastern States is cheapened, as it soon will be, they will extend their operations into the Middle and Eastern States, unless prevented by law, for wherever there is a white man or woman at work for wages, whether at the shoe bench, in the factory, or on the farm, there is an opening for a Chinaman. No matter how low the wages may be, the Chinaman can afford to work for still lower wages, and if the competition is free, he will take the white man's place.

"At this point we are met by the query from a certain class of political economists, 'What of it? Suppose the Chinese work for lower wages than white men, is it not advantageous to the country to employ them?' The first answer to such question is, that by this process white men are supplanted by Chinese. It is a substitution of Chinese and their civilization for white men and Anglo-Saxon civilization. This involves considerations higher than mere economic theories. If the Chinese are as desirable as citizens, if they are in all the essential elements of manhood the peers or the superiors of the Caucasian; if they will protect American interests, foster American institutions, and become the patriotic defenders of republican government; if their civilization does not antagonize ours nor contaminate it; if they are free, independent men, fit for liberty and self-government as European immigrants generally are, then we may begin argument upon the question whether it is better or worse, wise or unwise, to permit white men, American citizens, or men of kindred races to be supplanted and the Chinese to be substituted in their places. Until all this and more can be shown the advocates of Chinese importation or immigration have no base upon which to even begin to build argument.

"The statistics of the manufacture of cigars in San Francisco are still more suggestive. This business was formerly carried on exclusively by white people, many hundreds finding steady and lucrative employment in that trade. I have here the certified statement from the office of the collector of internal revenue at San Francisco, showing the number of white people and Chinese, relatively, employed on the 1st of November last in the manufacture of cigars. The statement is as follows:

Number of white men employed.....	493
Number of white women employed.	170
Total whites......................	663
Number of Chinese employed........	5 182

"The facts of this statement were carefully ascertained by three deputy collectors. The San Francisco Assembly of Trades certify that there are 8,265 Chinese employed in laundries. It is a well-known fact that white women who formerly did this work have been quite driven out of that employment. The same authority certifies that the number of Chinese now employed in the manufacture of clothing in San Francisco, is 7,510, and the number of whites so employed is 1,000. In many industries the Chinese have entirely supplanted the white laborers, and thousands of our white people have quit California and sought immunity from this grinding competition in other and better-favored regions."

* * * * * * * *

"If you would 'secure the blessings of liberty to ourselves and our posterity,' there must be some place reserved in which, and upon which, posterity can exist. What will the blessings of liberty be worth to posterity if you give up the country to the Chinese? If China is to be the breeding-ground for peopling this country, what chance of American posterity? We of this age hold this land in trust for our race and kindred. We hold republican government and free institutions in trust for American posterity. That trust ought not to be betrayed. If the Chinese should invade the Pacific coast with arms in their hands, what a magnificent spectacle of martial resistance would be presented to a startled world! The mere intimation of an attempt to make conquest of our western shore by force would rouse the nation to a frenzy of enthusiasm in its defense. For years a peaceful, sly, strategic conquest has been in progress, and American statesmanship has been almost silent, until the people have demanded action.

"The land which is being overrun by the oriental invader is the fairest portion of our heritage. It is the land of the vine and the fig tree; the home of the orange, the olive, and the pomegranate. Its winter is a perpetual spring, and its summer is a golden harvest. There the northern pine peacefully sways against the southern palm; the tender azalea and the hardy rose mingle their sweet perfume, and the tropic vine encircles the sturdy oak. Its valleys are rich and glorious with luscious fruits and waving grain, and its lofty

> Mountains like giants stand,
> To sentinel the enchanted land.

"I would see its fertile plains, its sequestered vales, its vine-clad hills, its deep blue canons, its furrowed mountain-sides, dotted all over with American homes—the homes of a free, happy people, resonant with the sweet voices of flaxen-haired children, and ringing with the joyous laughter of maiden fair—

> Soft as her clime, and sunny as her skies—

like the homes of New England; yet brighter and better far shall be the homes which are to be builded in that wonderland by the sunset sea, the homes of a race from which shall spring

> The flower of men,
> To serve as model for the mighty world,
> And be the fair beginning of a time."

Reply of Senator Geo. F. Hoar.

Senator Hoar, of Massachusetts, replied to Senator Miller, and presented the supposed view of the Eastern States in a masterly manner. The speech covered twenty-eight pamphlet pages, and was referred to by the newspaper as an effort equal to some of the best by Charles Sumner. We make liberal extracts from the text, as follows:

"Mr. President: A hundred years ago the American people founded a nation upon the moral law. They overthrew by force the authority of their sovereign, and separated themselves from the country which had planted them, alleging as their justification to mankind certain propositions which they held to be self-evident.

"They declared—and that declaration is the one foremost action of human history—that all men equally derive from their Creator the right to the pursuit of happiness; that equality in the right to that pursuit is the fundamental rule of the divine justice in its application to mankind; that its security is the end for which governments are formed, and its destruction good cause why governments should be overthrown. For a hundred years this principle has been held in honor. Under its beneficent operation we have grown almost twenty-fold. Thirteen States have become thirty-eight; three million have become fifty million; wealth and comfort and education and art have flourished in still larger proportion. Every twenty years there is added to the valuation of this country a wealth enough to buy the whole German Empire, with its buildings and its ships and its invested property. This has been the magnet that has drawn immigration hither. The human stream, hemmed in by banks invisible but impassable, does not turn toward Mexico, which can feed and clothe a world, or South America, which can feed and clothe a hundred worlds, but seeks only that belt of States where it finds this law in operation. The marvels of comfort and happiness it has wrought for us scarcely surpass what it has done for other countries. The immigrant sends back the message to those he has left behind. There is scarcely a nation in Europe west of Russia which has not felt the force of our example and whose institutions are not more or less slowly approximating to our own.

"Every new State as it takes its place in the great family binds this declaration as a frontlet upon its forehead. Twenty-four of the States, including California herself, declare it in the very opening sentence of their constitutions. The insertion of the phrase 'the pursuit of happiness,' in the enumeration of the natural rights for securing which government is ordained, and the denial of which constitutes just cause for its overthrow, was intended as an explicit affirmation that the right of every human being who obeys the equal laws to go everywhere on the surface of the earth that his welfare may require is beyond the rightful control of government. It is a birthright derived immediately from him who 'made of one blood all nations of men for to dwell on all the face of the earth, and hath determined the times before appointed and the bounds of their habitation.' He made, so our fathers held, of one blood all the nations of men. He gave them the whole face of the earth whereon to dwell. He reserved for himself by his agents heat and cold, and climate, and soil, and water, and land to determine the bounds of their habitation. It has long been the fashion in some quarters, when honor, justice, good faith, human rights are appealed to, and especially when the truths declared in the opening sentences of the Declaration of Independence are invoked as guides in legislation to stigmatize those who make the appeal as sentimentalists, incapable of dealing with practical affairs. It would be easy to demonstrate the falsehood of this notion. The men who erected the structure of this Government were good, practical builders and knew well the quality of the corner-stone when they laid it. When they put forth for the consideration of their contemporaries and of posterity the declaration which they thought a decent respect for the opinions of mankind required of them, they weighed carefully the fundamental proposition on which their immortal argument rested. Lord Chatham's famous sentence will bear repeating again:

When your lordships look at the papers transmitted to us from America, when you consider their decency, firmness, and wisdom, you cannot but respect their cause and wish to make it your own. For myself I must declare and avow that in all my reading and observation—and it has been my favorite study, I have read Thucydides, and have studied and admired the master states of the world—that for solidity of reasoning, force of sagacity, and wisdom of conclusion, under such a complication of difficult circumstances, no nation or body of men can stand in preference to the general Congress assembled at Philadelphia.

The doctrine that the pursuit of happiness is an inalienable right with which men are endowed by their Creator, asserted by as religious a people as ever lived at the most religious period of their history, propounded by as wise, practical, and far-sighted statesmen as ever lived as the vindication for the most momentous public act of their generation, was intended to commit the American people in the most solemn manner to the assertion that the right to change their homes at their pleasure is a natural right of all men. The doctrine that free institutions are a monopoly of the favored races, the doctrine that oppressed people may sever their old allegiance at will, but have no right to find a new one, that the bird may fly but may never light, is of quite recent origin.

California herself owing her place in our Union to the first victory of freedom in the great contest with African slavery, is pledged to repudiate this modern heresy, not only by her baptismal vows, but by her share in the enactment of the statute of 1868. Her constitution read thus until she took Dennis Kearney for her law-giver:

We, the people of California, grateful to Almighty God for our freedom, in order to secure its blessings, do establish this constitution.

DECLARATION OF RIGHTS.

SECTION 1. All men are by nature free and independent, and have certain inalienable rights, among which are those of enjoying and defending life and liberty, acquiring, possessing, and defending property, and pursuing and obtaining safety and happiness.

* * * * * * *

SEC. 17. Foreigners who are or who may hereafter become bona fide residents of this State, shall enjoy the same rights in respect to the possession, enjoyment, and inheritance of property, as native born citizens.

In the Revised Statutes, section 1999, Congress in the most solemn manner declare that the right of expatriation is beyond the lawful control of government:

SEC. 1999. Whereas the right of expatriation is a natural and inherent right of all people, indispensable to the enjoyment of the rights of life, liberty, and the pursuit of happiness; and

Whereas in the recognition of this principle this Government has freely received emigrants from all nations, and invested them with the rights of citizenship.

This is a re-enactment, in part, of the statute of 1868, of which Mr. Conness, then a California Senator, of Irish birth, was, if not the author, the chief advocate.

The California Senator called up the bill day after day. The bill originally provided that the President might order the arrest and detention in custody of "any subject or citizen of such foreign government" as should arrest and detain any naturalized citizen of the United States under the claim that he still remained subject to his allegiance to his native sovereign. This gave rise to debate.

But there was no controversy about the part of the bill which I have read. The preamble is as follows:

Whereas the right of expatriation is a natural and inherent right of all people, indispensable to the enjoyment of the rights of life, liberty, and the pursuit of happiness, for the protection of which the Government of the United States was established; and whereas in the recognition of this principle this Government has freely received emigrants from all nations and vested them with the rights of citizenship, &c.

Mr. Howard declares that—

The absolute right of expatriation is the great leading American principle.

Mr. Morton says:

That a man's right to withdraw from his native country and make his home in another, and thus cut himself off from all connection with his native country, is a part of his natural liberty, and without that his liberty is defective. We claim that the right to liberty is a natural, inherent, God-given right, and his liberty is imperfect unless it carries with it the right of expatriation.

The bill containing the preamble above recited passed the Senate by a vote of 39 to 5.

The United States of America and the Emperor of China cordially recognize the inherent and inalienable right of man to change his home and allegiance, and also the mutual advantage of the free migration and emigration of their citizens and subjects respectively from the one country to the other for purposes of curiosity, of trade, or as permanent residents.

"The bill which passed Congress two years ago and was vetoed by President Hayes, the treaty of 1881, and the bill now before the Senate, have the same origin and are parts of the same measure. Two years ago it was proposed to exclude Chinese laborers from our borders, in express disregard of our solemn treaty obligations. This measure was arrested by President Hayes. The treaty of 1881 extorted from unwilling China her consent that we might regulate, limit, or suspend the coming of Chinese laborers into this country—a consent of which it is proposed by this bill to take advantage. This is entitled "A bill to enforce treaty stipulations with China."

"It seems necessary in discussing the statute briefly to review the history of the treaty. First let me say that the title of this bill is deceptive. There is no stipulation of the treaty which the bill enforces. The bill where it is not inconsistent with the compact only avails itself of a privilege which that concedes. China only relaxed the Burlingame treaty so far as to permit us to 'regulate, limit, or suspend the coming or residence' of Chinese laborers, 'but not absolutely to prohibit it.' The treaty expressly declares 'such limitation or suspension shall be reasonable.' But here is proposed a statute which for twenty years, under the severest penalties, absolutely inhibits the coming of Chinese laborers to this country. The treaty pledges us not absolutely to prohibit it. The bill is intended absolutely to prohibit it.

"The second article of the treaty is this:

"Chinese subjects, whether proceeding to the United States as traders, students, or merchants, or from curiosity, together with their body and household servants, and Chinese laborers, who are now in the United States, shall be allowed to go and come of their own free will and accord, and shall be accorded all the rights, privileges, immunities, and exemptions which are accorded to the citizens and subjects of the most favored nations.

"Yet it is difficult to believe that the complex and cumbrous passport system provided in the last twelve sections of the bill was not intended as an evasion of this agreement. Upon what other nation, favored or not, is such a burden imposed? This is the execution of a promise that they may come and go 'of their own free will.'

"What has happened within thirteen years that the great Republic should strike its flag? What change has come over us that we should eat the bravest and the truest words we ever spoke? From 1858 to 1880 there was added to the population of the country 42,000 Chinese.

"I give a table from the census of 1880 showing the Chinese population of each State:

Statement showing the Chinese population in each State and Territory, according to the United States censuses of 1870 *and of* 1880.

Alabama	——	4
Alaska	——	——
Arizona	20	1,630

Arkansas	98	134
California	49,310	75,025
Colorado	7	610
Connecticut	2	124
Dakota	——	238
Delaware	——	1
District of Columbia	3	13
Florida	——	18
Georgia	1	17
Idaho	4,274	3,378
Illinois	1	210
Indiana	——	33
Iowa	3	47
Kansas	——	19
Kentucky	1	10
Louisiana	71	481
Maine	1	9
Maryland	2	5
Massachusetts	97	237
Michigan	2	27
Minnesota	——	53
Mississippi	16	52
Missouri	3	94
Montana	1,949	1,764
Nebraska	——	18
Nevada	3,152	5,420
New Hampshire	——	14
New Jersey	15	176
New Mexico	——	55
New York	29	924
North Carolina	——	——
Ohio	1	114
Oregon	3,330	9,513
Pennsylvania	14	160
Rhode Island	——	27
South Carolina	1	9
Tennessee	——	26
Texas	25	141
Utah	445	501
Vermont	——	——
Virginia	4	6
Washington	234	3,182
West Virginia	——	14
Wisconsin	——	16
Wyoming	143	914
Total	63,254	105,463

"By the census of 1880 the number of Chinese in this country was 105,000—one five-hundredth part of the whole population. The Chinese are the most easily governed race in the world. Yet every Chinaman in America has four hundred and ninety-nine Americans to control him.

The immigration was also constantly decreasing for the last half of the decade. The Bureau of Statistics gives the numbers as follows, (for the first eight years the figures are those of the entire Asiatic immigration:)

The number of immigrants from Asia, as reported by the United States Bureau of Statistics is as follows, namely:

1871	7.236
1872	7,825
1873	20,326
1874	13,857
1875	16,498
1876	22,943
1877	10,640
1878	9,014
Total	108,339

And from China for the year ended June 30—

1879	9,604
1880	5,802
Total	15,406
Grand Total	123,745

"See also, Mr. President, how this class of immigrants, diminishing in itself, diminishes still more in its proportion to the rapidly increasing numbers who come from other lands. Against 22,943 Asiatic immigrants in 1876, there are but 5,802 in 1880. In 1878 there were 9,014 from Asia, in a total of 153,207, or one in seventeen of the entire immigration; and this includes all persons who entered the port of San Francisco to go to any South American country. In 1879 there were 9,604 from China in a total of 250,565, or one in twenty-six. In 1880 there were 5,802 from China in a total immigration of 593,359, or one in one hundred and two. The whole Chinese population, then, when the census of 1880 was taken, was but one in five hundred of our people. The whole Chinese immigration was but one in one hundred and two of the total immigration; while the total annual immigration quadrupled from 1878 to 1880, the Chinese was in 1880 little more than one-half what it was in 1878, and one-fourth what it was in 1876.

"The number of immigrants of all nations was 720,045 in 1881. Of these 20,711 were Chinese. There is no record in the Bureau of Statistics of the number who departed within the year. But a very high anti-Chinese authority places it above 10,000. Perhaps the expection that the hostile legislation under the treaty would not affect persons who entered before it took effect stimulated somewhat their coming. But the addition to the Chinese population was less than one seventy-second of the whole immigration. All the Chinese in the country do not exceed the population of its sixteenth city. All the Chinese in California hardly surpass the number which is easily governed in Shanghai by a police of one hundred men. There are as many pure blooded Gypsies wandering about the country as there are Chinese in California. What an insult to American intelligence to ask leave of China to keep out her people, because this little handful of almond-eyed Asiatics threaten to destroy our boasted civilization. We go boasting of our democracy, and our superiority, and our strength. The flag bears the stars of hope to all nations. A hundred thousand Chinese land in California and everything is changed. God has not made of one blood all the nations any longer. The self-evident truth becomes a self-evident lie. The golden rule does not apply to the natives of the continent where it was first uttered. The United States surrender to China, the Republic to the despot, America to Asia, Jesus to Joss.

"There is another most remarkable example of this prejudice of race which has happily almost died out here, which has come down from the dark ages and which survives with unabated ferocity in Eastern Europe. I mean the hatred of the Jew. The persecution of the Hebrew has never, so far as I know, taken the form of an affront to labor. In every other particular the reproaches which for ten centuries have been leveled at him are reproduced to do service against the Chinese. The Hebrew, so it was said, was not a Christian. He did not affiliate or assimilate into the nations where he dwelt. He was an unclean thing, a dog, to whom the crime of the crucifixion of his Saviour was never to be forgiven. The Chinese quarter of San Francisco had its type in every city of Europe. If the Jew ventured from his hiding-place he was stoned. His wealth made him the prey of the rapacity of the noble, and his poverty and weakness the victim of the rabble. Yet how has this Oriental conquered Christendom by the sublimity of his patience? The great poet of New England, who sits by every American fireside a beloved and perpetual guest, in that masterpiece of his art, the Jewish Cemetery at Newport, has described the degradation and the triumph of these persecuted children of God.

How came they here? What burst of Christian hate,
What persecution, merciless and blind,
Drove o'er the sea—that desert desolate—
These Ishmaels and Hagars of mankind?
They lived in narrow streets and lanes obscure,
Ghetto and Judenstrass, in mirk and mire;
Taught in the school of patience to endure
The life of anguish and the death of fire.

* * * * * * * *

Anathema maranatha! was the cry
That rang from town to town, from street to street;
At every gate the accursed Mordecai
Was mocked and jeered, and spurned by Christian feet.

Pride and humiliation hand in hand
Walked with them through the world where'er they went;
Trampled and beaten were they as the sand,
And yet unshaken as the continent.

Forty years ago—
Says Lord Beaconsfield, that great Jew who held England in the hollow of his hand, and who played on her aristocracy as on an organ, who made himself the master of an alien nation, its ruler, its oracle, and through it, and in despite of it, for a time the master of Europe—

Forty years ago—not a longer period than the children of Israel were wandering in the desert—the two most dishonored races in Europe were the Attic and the Hebrew. The world has probably by this discovered that it is impossible to destroy the Jews. The attempt to extirpate them has been made under the most favorable auspices and on the largest scale; the most considerable means that man could command have been pertinaciously applied to this object for the longest period of recorded time. Egyptian Pharaohs, Assyrian kings, Roman emperors, Scandinavian crusaders, Gothic princes, and holy inquisitors, have alike devoted their energies to the fulfillment of this common purpose. Expatriation, exile, captivity, confiscation, torture on the most ingenious and massacre on the most extensive scale, a curious system of degrading customs and debasing laws which would have broken the heart of any other people, have been tried, and in vain.

"Lord Beaconsfield admits that the Jews contribute more than their proportion to the aggregate of the vile; that the lowest class of Jews are obdurate, malignant, odious, and revolting. And yet this race of dogs, as it has been often termed in scorn, furnishes Europe to-day its masters in finance and oratory and statesmanship and art and music. Rachel, Mozart, Mendelssohn, Disraeli, Rothschild, Benjamin, Heine, are but samples of the intellectual power of a race which to-day controls the finance and the press of Europe.

"I do not controvert the evidence which is relied upon to show that there are great abuses, great dangers, great offenses, which have grown out of the coming of this people. Much of the evil I believe might be cured by State and municipal authority. Congress may rightfully be called upon to go to the limit of the just exercise of the powers of government in rendering its aid.

"We should have capable and vigilant consular officers in the Asiatic ports from which these immigrants come, without whose certificate they should not be received on board ship, and who should see to it that no person except those of good character and no person whose labor is not his own property be allowed to come over. Especially should the trade in human labor under all disguises be suppressed. Filthy habits of living must surely be within the control of municipal regulation. Every State may by legislation or by municipal ordinance in its towns and cities prescribe the dimension of dwellings and limit the number who may occupy the same tenement.

"But it is urged—and this in my judgment is the greatest argument for the bill—

that the introduction of the labor of the Chinese reduces the wages of the American laborer. 'We are ruined by Chinese cheap labor" is a cry not limited to the class to whose representative the brilliant humorist of California first ascribed it. I am not in favor of lowering any where the wages of any American labor, skilled or unskilled. On the contrary, I believe the maintenance and the increase of the purchasing power of the wages of the American working man should be the one principal object of our legislation. The share in the product of agriculture or manufacture which goes to labor should, and I believe will, steadily increase. For that, and for that only, exists our protective system. The acquisition of wealth, national or individual, is to be desired only for that. The statement of the accomplished Senator from California on this point meets my heartiest concurrence. I have no sympathy with any men, if such there be, who favor high protection and cheap labor.

"But I believe that the Chinese, to whom the terms of the California Senator attribute skill enough to displace the American in every field requiring intellectual vigor, will learn very soon to insist on his full share of the product of his work. But whether that be true or not, the wealth he creates will make better and not worse the condition of every higher class of labor. There may be trouble or failure in adjusting new relations. But sooner or later every new class of industrious and productive laborers elevates the class it displaces. The dread of an injury to our labor from the Chinese rests on the same fallacy that opposed the introduction of labor-saving machinery, and which opposed the coming of the Irishman and the German and the Swede. Within my memory in New England all the lower places in factories, all places of domestic service, were filled by the sons and daughters of American farmers. The Irishmen came over to take their places; but the American farmer's son and daughter did not suffer; they were only elevated to a higher plane. In the increased wealth of the community their share is much greater. The Irishman rose from the bog or the hovel of his native land to the comfort of a New England home, and placed his children in a New England school. The Yankee rises from the loom and the spinning-jenny to be the teacher, the skilled laborer in the machine shop, the inventor, the merchant, or the opulent landholder and farmer of the West.

* * * * * * * *

A letter from F. A. Bee, Chinese Consul, approving the management of the estate, accompanied the report of the referee:

"Mr. President, I will not detain the Senate by reading the abundant testimony, of which this is but the sample, of the possession by the people of this race of the possibility of a development of every quality of intellect, art, character, which fits them for citizenship, for republicanism, for Christianity.

"Humanity, capable of infinite depths of degradation, is capable also of infinite heights of excellence. The Chinese, like all other races, has given us its examples of both. To rescue humanity from this degradation is, we are taught to believe, the great object of God's moral government on earth. It is not by injustice, exclusion, caste, but by reverence for the individual soul that we can aid in this consummation. It is not by Chinese policies that China is to be civilized. I believe that the immortal truths of the Declaration of Independence came from the same source with the Golden Rule and the Sermon on the Mount. We can trust Him who promulgated these laws to keep the country safe that obeys them. The laws of the universe have their own sanction. They will not fail. The power that causes the compass to point to the north, that dismisses the star on its pathway through the skies, promising that in a thousand years it shall return again true to its hour and keep His word, will vindicate His own moral law. As surely as the path on which our fathers entered a hundred years ago led to safety, to strength, to glory, so surely will the path on which we now propose to enter bring us to shame, to weakness, and to peril."

On the 3d of March the debate was renewed. Senator Farley protested that unless Chinese immigration is prohibited it will be impossible to protect the Chinese on the Pacific coast. The feeling against them now is such that restraint is difficult, as the people, forced out of employment by them, and irritated by their constantly increasing numbers, are not in a condition to submit to the deprivations they suffer by the presence of a Chinese population imported as slaves and absorbing to their own benefit the labor of the country. A remark of Mr. Farley about the Chinese led Mr. Hoar to ask if they were not the inventors of the printing press and of gunpowder. To this question Mr. Jones, of Nevada, made a brief speech, which was considered remarkable, principally because it was one of the very few speeches of any length that he has made since he became a Senator. Instead of agreeing with Mr. Hoar that the Chinese had invented the printing press and gunpowder, he said that information he had received led him to believe that the Chinese were not entitled to the credit of either of these inventions. On the contrary, they had stolen them from Aryans or Caucasians who wandered into the kingdom. Mr. Hoar smiled incredulously and made a remark to the effect that he had never heard of those Aryans or Caucasians before.

Continuing his remarks, Mr. Farley expressed his belief that should the Mongolian population increase and the Chinese come in contact with the Africans, the contact would result in demoralization and bloodshed which the laws could not prevent. Pig-tailed Chinamen would take the place everywhere of the working girl unless Congress extended its protection to California and her white people, who had by their votes demanded a prohibition of Chinese immigration. Mr. Maxey, interpreting the Constitution in such a way as to bring out of it an argument against Chinese immigration, said he found nothing in it to justify the conclusion that the framers of it intended to bring into this country all nations and races. The only people the fathers had in view as citizens were those of the Caucasian race, and they contemplated naturalization only for such, for they had distinctly set forth that the heritage of freedom was to be for their posterity. Nobody would pretend to express the opinion that it was expected that the American people should become mixed up with all sorts of races and call the result "our posterity." While the American people had, in consequence of their Anglo-Saxon origin, been able to withstand the contact with the African, the Africans would never stand before the Chinese. Mr. Maxey opposed the Chinese because they do not come here to be citizens, because the lower classes of Chinese alone are immigrants, and because by contact they poison the minds of the less intelligent.

Mr. Saulsbury had something to say in favor of the bill, and Mr. Garland, who voted against the last bill because the treaty had not been modified, expressed his belief that the Government could exercise properly all the powers proposed to be bestowed by this bill. Some time was consumed by Mr. Ingalls in advocacy of an amendment offered by him, proposing to limit the suspension of immigration to 10 instead of 20 years. Mr. Miller and Mr. Bayard opposed the amendment, Mr. Bayard taking the ground that Congress ought not to disregard the substantially unanimous wish of the people of California, as expressed at the polls, for absolute prohibition. The debate was interrupted by a motion for an executive session, and the bill went over until Monday, to be taken up then as the unfinished business.

On March 6th a vote was ordered on Senator Ingalls' amendment. It was defeated on a tie vote—yeas 23, nays 23.

The vote in detail is as follows:

Yeas—Messrs. Aldrich, Allison, Blair, Brown, Cockrell, Conger, Davis of Illinois, Dawes, Edmunds, Frye, Harris, Hoar, Ingalls, Jackson, Lapham, McDill, McMillan, Mitchell, Morrell, Saunders, Sewell, Sherman and Teller—23.

Nays—Messrs. Bayard, Beck, Call, Cameron of Wisconsin, Coke, Fair, Farley, Garland, George, Hale, Hampton, Hill of Colorado, Jonas, Jones of Nevada, McPherson, Marcy, Miller of California, Miller of New York, Morgan, Ransom, Slater, Vest and Walker—23.

Pairs were announced between Davis, of West Virginia, Saulsbury, Butler, Johnson, Kellogg, Jones, of Florida, and Grover, against the amendment, and Messrs. Windom, Ferry, Hawley, Platt, Pugh, Rollins and Van Wyck in the affirmative. Mr. Camden was also paired.

Mr. Edmunds, partially in reply to Mr. Hoar argued that the right to decide what constitutes the moral law was one inherent in the Government, and by analogy the right to regulate the character of the people who shall come into it belonged to a Government. This depended upon national polity and the fact as to most of the ancient republics that they did not possess homogeneity was the cause of their fall. As to the Swiss Republic, it was untrue that it was not homogeneous. The difference there was not one of race but of different varieties of the same race, all of which are analogous and consistent with each other. It would not be contended that it is an advantage to a republic that its citizens should be made of diverse races, with diverse views and diverse obligations as to what the common prosperity of all required. Therefore there was no foundation for the charge of a violation of moral and public law in our making a distinction as to the foreigners we admit. He challenged Mr. Hoar to produce an authority on national law which denied the right of one nation to declare what people of other nations should come among them. John Hancock and Samuel Adams, not unworthy citizens of Massachusetts, joined in asserting in the Declaration of Independence the right of the colonies to establish for themselves, not for other peoples, a Government of their own, not the Government of somebody else. The declaration asserted the family or consolidated right of a people within any Territory to determine the conditions upon which they would go on, and this included the matter of receiving the people from other shores into their family. This idea was followed in the Constitution by requiring naturalization. The Chinaman may be with us, but he is not of us. One of the conditions of his naturalization is that he must be friendly to the institutions and intrinsic polity of our Government. Upon the theory of the Massachusetts Senators, that there is a universal oneness of one human being with every other human being on the globe, this traditional and fundamental principle was entirely ignored. Such a theory as applied to Government was contrary to all human experience, to all discussion, and to every step of the founders of our Government. He said that Mr. Sumner, the predecessor of Mr. Hoar, was the author of the law on the coolie traffic, which imposes fines and penalties more severe than those in this bill upon any master of an American vessel carrying a Chinaman who is a servant. The present bill followed that legislation. Mr. Edmunds added that he would vote against the bill if the twenty-year clause was retained, but would maintain the soundness of principle he had enunciated.

Mr. Hoar argued in reply that the right of expatriation carried with it the right to a home for the citizen in the country to which he comes, and that the bill violated not only this but the principles of the Fourteenth and Fifteenth Amendments which made citizenship the birthright of every one born on our soil, and prohibited an abridgement of the suffrage because of race, color, etc.

Mr. Ingalls moved an amendment postponing the time at which the act shall take effect until sixty days after information of its passage has been communicated to China.

After remarks by Messrs. Dawes, Teller and Bayard, at the suggestion of Mr. Brown Mr. Ingalls modified his amendment by providing that the act shall not go into effect until ninety days after its passage, and the amendment was adopted.

On motion of Mr. Bayard, amendments were adopted making the second section read as follows: "That any master of any vessel of whatever nationality, who shall knowingly on such vessel bring within the jurisdiction of the United States and permit to be landed any Chinese laborer," &c.

Mr. Hoar moved to amend by adding the following: "Provided, that this bill shall not apply to any skilled laborer who shall establish that he comes to this country without any contract beyond which his labor is the property of any person besides himself."

Mr. Farley suggested that all the Chinese would claim to be skilled laborors.

Mr. Hoar replied that it would test whether the bill struck at coolies or at skilled labor.

The amendment was rejected—Yeas, 17; nays, 27.

Mr. Call moved to strike out the section which forfeits the vessel for the offense of the master. Lost.

Mr. Hoar moved to amend by inserting: "Provided that any laborer who shall receive a certificate from the U. S. Consul at the port where he shall embark that he is an artisan coming to this country at his own expense and of his own will, shall not be affected by this bill." Lost—yeas 19, nays 24.

On motion of Mr. Miller, of California, the provision directing the removal of any Chinese unlawfully found in a Customs Collection district by the Collector, was amended to direct that he shall be removed to the place from whence he came.

On motion of Mr. Brown an amendment was adopted providing that the mark of a Chinese immigrant, duly attested by a witness, may be taken as his signature upon the certificate of resignation or registration issued to him.

The question then recurred on the amendment offered by Mr. Farley that hereafter no State Court or United States Court shall admit Chinese to citizenship.

Mr. Hawley, of Conn., on the following day spoke against what he denounced as "a bill of iniquities."

On the 9th of March what proved a long and interesting debate was closed, the leading speech being made by Senator Jones (Rep.) of Nevada, in favor of the bill. After showing the disastrous effects of the influx of the Chinese upon the Pacific coast and answering some of the arguments of the opponents of restriction, Mr. Jones said that he had noticed that most of those favoring Chinese immigration were advocates of a high tariff to protect American labor. But, judging from indications, it is not the American laborer, but the lordly manufacturing capitalist who is to be protected as against the European capitalist, and who is to sell everything he has to sell in an American market, one in which other capitalists cannot compete with him, while he buys that which he has to buy—the labor of men—in the most open market. He demands for the latter free trade in its broadest sense, and would have not only free trade in bringing in laborers of our own race, but the Chinese, the most skilful and cunning laborers of the world. The laborer, however, is to buy from his capitalist master in a protective market, but that which he himself has to sell, his labor, and which he must sell every day (for he cannot wait, like the capitalist, for better times or travel here and there to dispose of it), he must sell in the openest market of the world. When the artisans of this country shall be made to understand that the market in which they sell the only thing they have to sell is an open one they will demand, as one of the conditions of their existence, that they shall have an open market in which to buy what they want. As the Senator from Massachusetts (Mr. Dawes) said he wanted the people to know that the bill was a blow struck at labor, Mr. Jones said he reiterated the assertion with the qualification that it was not a blow at our own, but at underpaid pauper labor. That cheap labor produces national wealth is a fallacy, as shown by the home condition of the 350,000,000 of Chinamen.

"Was the bringing of the little brown man a sort of counter balance to the trades unions of this country? If he may be brought here, why may not the products of his toil come in? Now, when the laborer is allowed to get that share from his labor that civilization has decided he shall have, the little brown man is introduced. He (Mr. Jones) believed in protection, and had no prejudice against the capitalist, but he would have capital and labor equally protected. Enlarging upon the consideration that the intelligence or creative genius of a country in overcoming obstacles, not its material resources, constitutes its wealth, and that the low wages of the Chinese, while benefiting individual employers, would ultimately impoverish the country by removing the stimulant to create labor-saving machinery and like inventions. Mr. Jones spoke of what he called the dearth of intellectual activity in the South in every department but one, that of politics.

"This was because of the presence of a servile race there. The absence of Southern names in the Patent Office is an illustration. We would not welcome the Africans here. Their presence was not a blessing to us, but an impediment in our way. The relations of the white and colored races of the South were now no nearer adjustment than they were years ago. He would prophesy that the African race would never be permitted to dominate any State of the South. The experiment to that end had been a dismal failure, and a failure not because we have not tried to make it succeed, but because laws away above human laws have placed the one race superior to and far above the other. The votes of the ignorant class might preponderate, but intellect, not numbers, is the superior force in this world. We clothed the African in the Union blue and the belief that he was one day to be free was the candle-light in his soul, but it is one thing to aspire to be free and another thing to have the intelligence and sterling qualities of character that can maintain free government. Mr. Jones here expressed his belief that, if left alone to maintain a government, the negro would gradually retrograde and go back to the methods of his ancestors. This, he added, may be heresy, but I believe it to be the truth. If, when the first shipload of African slaves came to this country the belief had spread that they would be the cause of political agitation, a civil war, and the future had been foreseen, would they have been allowed to land?

How much of this country would now be worth preserving if the North had been covered by Africans as is South Carolina to-day, in view of their non-assimilative character? The wisest policy would have been to exclude them at the outset. So we say of the Chinese to-day, he exclaimed, and for greater reason, because their skill makes them more formidable competitors than the negro. Subtle and adept in manipulation, the Chinaman can be put into almost any kind of a factory. His race is as obnoxious to us and as impossible for us to assimilate with as was the negro race. His race has outlived every other because it is homogeneous, and for that reason alone. It has imposed its religion and peculiarities upon its conquerors and still lived. If the immigration is not checked now, when it is within manageable limits, it will be too late to check it. What do we find in the condition of the Indian or the African to induce us to admit another race into our midst? It is because the Pacific coast favor our own civilization, not that of another race, that they discourage the coming of these people. They believe in the homogeneity of our race, and that upon this depends the progress of our institutions and everything on which we build our hopes.

Mr. MORRILL, (Rep.) of Vt., said he appreciated the necessity of restricting Chinese immigration, but desired that the bill should strictly conform to treaty requirements and be so perfected that questions arising under it might enable it to pass the ordeal of judicial scrutiny.

Mr. SHERMAN, (Rep.) of Ohio, referring to the passport system, said the bill adopted some of the most offensive features of European despotism. He was averse to hot haste in applying a policy foreign to the habits of our people, and regarded the measure as too sweeping in many of its provisions and as reversing our immigration policy.

After remarks by Messrs. Ingalls, Farley, Maxey, Brown and Teller, the amendment of Mr. Farley, which provides that hereafter no court shall admit Chinese to citizenship, was adopted—yeas 25, nays 22.

The following is the vote:

YEAS—Messrs. Bayard, Beck, Call, Cameron of Wisconsin, Cockrell, Coke, Fair, Farley, Garland, George, Gorman, Harris, Jackson, Jonas, Jones of Nevada, Maxey, Morgan, Pugh, Ransom, Slater, Teller, Vance, Vest, Voorhees and Walker—25.

NAYS—Messrs. Aldrich, Allison, Blair, Brown, Conger, Davis of Illinois, Dawes, Edmunds, Frye, Hale, Hill of Colorado, Hoar, Ingalls, Lapham, McDill, McMillan, Miller of New York, Mitchell, Morrill, Plumb, Saunders and Sawyer—22.

Mr. Grover's amendment construing the words "Chinese laborers," wherever used in the act, to mean both skilled and unskilled laborers and Chinese employed in mining prevailed by the same vote—yeas 25, nays 22.

Mr. BROWN, (Dem.) of Ga., moved to strike out the requirement for the production of passports by the permitted classes whenever demanded by the United States authorities. Carried on a *viva voce* vote, the Chair (Mr. Davis, of Illinois) creating no little merriment by announcing, "The nays are loud but there are not many of them."

MR. INGALLS' AMENDMENT.

Upon the bill being reported to the Senate from the Committee of the Whole Mr. INGALLS again moved to limit the suspension of the coming of Chinese laborers to ten years.

Mr. JONES, of Nevada, said this limit would hardly have the effect of allaying agitation on the subject as the discussion would be resumed in two or three years, and ten years, he feared, would not even be a long enough period to enable Congress intelligently to base upon it any future policy.

Mr. MILLER, of California, also urged that the shorter period would not measurably relieve the business interest of the Pacific slope, inasmuch as the white immigrants, who were so much desired, would not come there if they believed the Chinese were to be again admitted in ten years. Being interrupted by Mr. Hoar, he asserted that that Senator and other republican leaders, as also the last republican nominee for President, had heretofore given the people of the Pacific slope good reason to believe that they would secure to them the relief they sought by the bill.

Mr. HOAR, (Rep.) of Mass., briefly replied.

The amendment was lost—yeas 20, nays 21.

The vote is as follows:

YEAS—Messrs. Aldrich, Allison, Blair, Brown, Conger, Davis of Illinois, Dawes, Edmunds, Frye, Hale, Hoar, Ingalls, Lapham, McDill, McMillan, Mahone, Morrill, Plumb, Sawyer and Teller—20.

NAYS—Messrs. Bayard, Beck, Call, Cameron of Wisconsin, Coke, Fair, Farley, Garland, George, Gorman, Jackson, Jonas, Jones of Nevada, Miller of California, Miller of New York, Morgan, Ransom, Slater, Vance, Voorhees and Walker—21.

Messrs. Butler, Camden, McPherson, Johnston, Davis of West Virginia, Pendleton and Ransom were paired with Messrs. Hawley, Anthony, Sewell, Platt, Van Wyck, Windom and Sherman.

Messrs. Hampton, Pugh, Vest, Rollins and Jones of Florida were paired with absentees.

PASSAGE OF THE BILL.

The question recurred on the final passage of the bill, and Mr. EDMUNDS closed the debate. He would vote against the bill as it now stood, because he believed it to be an infraction of good faith as pledged by the last treaty; because he believed it injurious to the welfare of the people of the United States, and particularly the people on the Pacific coast, by preventing the development of our great trade with China.

The vote was then taken and the bill was passed—yeas 29, nays 15.

The following is the vote in detail:—

YEAS—Messrs. Bayard, Beck, Call, Cameron of Wisconsin, Cockrell, Coke, Fair, Farley, Garland, George, Gorman, Hale, Harris, Hill of Colorado, Jackson, Jonas, Jones of Nevada, Miller of California, Miller of New York, Morgan, Pugh, Ransom, Sawyer, Teller, Vance, Vest, Voorhees and Walker—29.

NAYS—Messrs. Aldrich, Allison, Blair, Brown, Conger, Davis of Illinois, Dawes, Edmunds, Frye, Hoar, Ingalls, Lapham, McDill, McMillan and Morrill—15.

Pairs were announced of Messrs. Camden, Davis of West Virginia, Grover, Hampton, Butler, McPherson, Johnston, Jones of Florida and Pendleton in favor of the bill, with Messrs. Anthony, Windom, Van Wyck, Mitchell, Hawley, Sewell, Platt, Rollins and Sherman against it.

Mr. FRYE, (Rep.) of Me., in casting his vote, stated that he was paired with Mr. Hill, of Georgia, on all political questions, but that he did not consider this a political question, and besides, had express permission from Senator Hill to vote upon it.

Mr. MITCHELL, (Rep.) of Pa., in announcing his pair with Mr. Hampton stated that had it not been for that fact he would vote against the bill, regarding it as un-American and inconsistent with the principles which had obtained in the government.

The title of the bill was amended so as to read, "An act to execute certain treaty stipulations relating to Chinese," though Mr. Hoar suggested that "execute" ought to be stricken out and "violate" inserted.

The Senate then, at twenty minutes to six, adjourned until to-morrow.

PROVISIONS OF THE BILL.

The Chinese Immigration bill as passed provides that from and after the expiration of ninety days after the passage of this act and until the expiration of twenty years after its passage the coming of Chinese laborers to the United States shall be suspended, and prescribes a penalty of imprisonment not exceeding one year and a fine of not more than $500 against the master of any vessel who brings any Chinese laborer to this country during that period. It further provides that the classes of Chinese excepted by the treaty from such prohibition—such as merchants, teachers, students, travelers, diplomatic agents and Chinese laborers who were in the United States on the 17th of November, 1880 —shall be required, as a condition for their admission, to procure passports from the government of China personally identifying them and showing that they individually belong to one of the permitted classes, which passports must have been indorsed by the diplomatic representative of the United States in China or by the United States Consul at the port of departure. It also provides elaborate machinery for carrying out the purposes of the act, and additional sections prohibit the admission of Chinese to citizenship by any United States or State court and construes the words "Chinese laborers" to mean both skilled and unskilled laborers and Chinese employed in mining.

The sentiment in favor of the passage of this bill has certainly greatly increased since the control of the issue has passed to abler hands than those of Kearney and Kalloch, whose conduct intensified the opposition of the East to the measure, which in 1879 was denounced as "violating the conscience of the nation." Mr. Blaine's advocacy of the first bill limiting emigrants to fifteen on each vessel, at the time excited much criticism in the Eastern states, and was there a potent weapon against him in the nominating struggle for the Presidency in 1880; but on the other hand it is believed that it gave him strength in the Pacific States.

Chinese immigration and the attempt to restrict it presents a question of the gravest importance, and was treated as such in the Senate debate. The friends of the bill, under the leadership of Senators Miller and Jones, certainly stood in a better and stronger attitude than ever before.

The anti-Chinese bill passed the House just as it came from the Senate, after a somewhat exended debate, on the 23d of March, 1882. Yeas 167, nays 65, (party lines not being drawn) as follows:

Yeas—Messrs. Aikin, Aldrich, Armfield, Atkins, Bayne, Belford, Belmont, Berry, Bingham, Blackburn, Blanchard, Bliss, Blount, Brewer, Brumm, Buckner, Burrows, of Missouri; Butterworth, Cabell, Caldwell, Calkins, Campbell, Cannon, Casserley, Caswell, Chalmers, Chapman, Clark, Clements, Cobb, Converse, Cook, Cornell, Cox, of New York; Cox, of North Carolina; Covington, Cravens, Culbertson, Curtin, Darrell, Davidson; Davis, of Illinois; Davis, of Missouri; Demotte, Deuster, Dezendorf, Dibble, Dibrell, Dowd, Dugro, Ermentrout, Errett, Farwell, of Illinois; Finley, Flowers, Ford, Forney, Fulkerson, Garrison, Geddes, George, Gibson, Guenther, Gunter, Hammond, of Georgia; Hardy, Harmer, Harris, of New Jersey; Haseltine, Hatch, Hazelton, Heilman, Herndon, Hewitt, of New York; Hill, Hiscock, Hoblitzell, Hoge, Hollman, Horr, Houk, House, Hubbell, Hubbs, Hutchins, Jones, of Texas; Jones, of Arkansas; Jorgenson, Kenna, King, Klotz, Knott, Ladd, Leedom, Lewis, Marsh, Martin, Matson, McClure, McCook, McKenzie, McKinley, McLane, McMillan, Miller, Mills, of Texas; Money, Morey, Moulton, Murch, Mutchler, O'Neill, Pacheco, Page, Paul, Payson, Pealse, Phelps, Phister, Pound, Randall, Reagan, Rice of Missouri, Richardson, Robertson, Robinson, Rosecrans, Scranton, Shallenberger, Sherwin, Simonton, Singleton, of Mississippi, Smith of Pennsylvania, Smith of Illinois, Smith of New York, Sparks, Spaulding, Spear, Springer, Stockslager, Strait, Talbott, Thomas, Thompson of Kentucky, Tillman, Townsend of Ohio, Townsend of Illinois, Tucker, Turner of Georgia, Turner of Kentucky, Updegraff, of Ohio, Upson, Valentine, Vance, Van Horn, Warner, Washburne, Webber, Welborn, Whitthorne, Williams of Alabama, Willis, Willetts, Wilson, Wise of Pennsylvania, Wise of Virginia, and W. A. Wood of New York—167.

The nays were Messrs. Anderson, Barr, Bragg, Briggs, Brown, Buck, Camp, Candler, Carpenter, Chase, Crapo, Cullen, Dawes, Deering, Dingley, Dunnell, Dwight, Farwell of Iowa, Grant, Hall, Hammond, of New York, Hardenburgh, Harris, of Massachusetts, Haskell, Hawk, Henderson, Hepburn, Hooker, Humphrey, Jacobs, Jones of New Jersey, Joyce, Kasson, Ketchum, Lord, McCoid, Morse, Norcross, Orth, Parker, Ramsey, Rice of Ohio, Rice of Massachusetts, Rich, Richardson of New York, Ritchie, Robinson of Massachusetts, Russel, Ryan, Shultz, Skinner, Scooner, Stone, Taylor, Thompson of Iowa, Tyler, Updegraff of Iowa, Urner, Wadsworth, Wait, Walker, Ward, Watson, White and Williams of Wisconsin—65.

In the House the debate was participated in by Messrs. Richardson, of South Carolina; Wise and Brumm, of Pennsylvania; Joyce, of Vermont; Dunnell, of Minnesota; Orth, of Indiana; Sherwin, of Illinois; Hazelton, of Wisconsin; Pacheco, of California, and Townsend, of Illinois, and others. An amendment offered by Mr. Butterworth, of Ohio, reducing the period of suspension to fifteen years, was rejected. Messrs. Robinson, of Massachusetts; Curtin, of Pennsylvania, and Cannon, of Illinois, spoke upon the bill, the two latter supporting it. The speech of Ex-Governor Curtin was strong and attracted much attention. Mr. Page closed the debate in favor of the measure. An amendment offered by Mr. Kasson, of Iowa, reducing the time of suspension to ten years, was rejected—yeas 100, nays 131—and the bill was passed exactly as it came from the Senate by a vote of 167 to 65. The House then adjourned.

Our Merchant Marine.

An important current issue is the increase of the Navy and the improvement of the Merchant Marine, and to these questions the National Administration has latterly given attention. The New York *Herald* has given much editorial ability and research to the advocacy of an immediate change for the better in these respects, and in its issue of March 10th, 1882, gave the proceedings of an important meeting of the members of the United States Naval Institute held at Annapolis the day before, on which occasion a prize essay on the subject—"Our Merchant Marine; the Cause of its Decline and the Means to be Taken for its Revival," was read. The subject was chosen nearly a year ago, because it was the belief of the members of the institute that a navy cannot exist without a merchant marine. The naval institute was organized in 1873 for the advancement of professional and scientific knowledge in the navy. It has on its roll 500 members, principally naval officers, and its proceedings are published quarterly. Rear Admiral C. R. P. Rodgers is president; Captain J. M. Ramsay, vice president; Lieutenant Commander C. M. Thomas, secretary; Lieutenant Murdock, corresponding secretary, and Paymaster R. W. Allen, treasurer. There were eleven competitors for the prize, which is of $100, and a gold medal valued at $50. The judges were Messrs. Hamilton Fish, A. A. Low and J. D. Jones. They awarded the prize to Lieutenant J. D. J. Kelley, U. S. N., whose motto was "Nil Clarius Æquore," and designated Master C. T. Calkins, U. S. N., whose motto was "Mais il faut cultiver notre jardin" as next in the order of merit, and further mentioned the essays of Lieutenant R. Wainwright, United States Navy, whose motto was "Causa latet, vis est notissima," and Lieutenant Commander J. E. Chadwick, United States Navy, whose motto was "Spes Meliora," as worthy of honorable mention, without being entirely agreed as to their comparative merits.

STRIKING PASSAGES FROM THE PRIZE ESSAY.

From Lieut. Kelley's prize essay many valuable facts can be gathered, and such of these as contain information of permanent value we quote:

"So far as commerce influences this country has a vital interest in the carrying trade, let theorists befog the cool air as they may. Every dollar paid for freight imported or exported in American vessels accrues to American labor and capital, and the enterprise is as much a productive industry as the raising of wheat, the spinning of fibre or the smelting of ore. Had the acquired, the 'full' trade of 1860 been maintained without increase $80,000,000 would have been added last year to the national wealth, and the loss from diverted shipbuilding would have swelled the sum to a total of $100,000,000.

"Our surplus products must find foreign markets, and to retain them ships controlled by and employed in exclusively American interests are essential instrumentalities. Whatever tends to stimulate competition and to prevent combination benefits the producer, and as the prices abroad establish values here, the barter we obtain for the despised one-tenth of exports—$665,000,000 in 1880—determines the profit or loss of the remainder in the home market. During the last fiscal year 11,500,000 gross tons of grain, oil, cotton, tobacco, precious metals, &c., were exported from the United States, and this exportation increases at the rate of 1,500,000 tons annually; 3,800,000 tons of goods are imported, or in all about 15,000,000 tons constitute the existing commerce of this country.

"If only one-half of the business of carrying our enormous wealth of surplus products could be secured for American ships, our tonnage would be instantly doubled, and we would have a greater fleet engaged in a foreign trade, legitimately our own, than Great Britain has to-day. The United States makes to the ocean carrying-trade its most valuable contribution, no other nation giving to commerce so many bulky tons of commodities to be transported those long voyages which in every age have been so eagerly coveted by marine peoples. Of the 17,000 ships which enter and clear at American ports every year, 4,600 seek a cargo empty and but 2,000 sail without obtaining it.

"Ships are profitable abroad and can be made profitable here, and in truth during the last thirty years no other branch of industry has made such progress as the carrying trade. To establish this there are four points of comparison—commerce, railways, shipping tonnage and carrying power of the world, limited to the years between 1850 and 1880:—

	1850.	1880.	*Increase Per Cent.*
Commmerce of all nations	$4,280,000,000	$14,405,000,000	240
Railways (miles open)	44,400	222,[illegible]00	398
Shipping tonnage	6,905,000	18,720,000	171
Carrying tonnage	8,464,000	34,280,060	304

"In 1850, therefore, for every $5,000,000 of international commerce there were fifty-four miles of railway and a maritime carrying power of 9,900 tons; and in 1880 the respective ratios had risen to seventy-seven miles and 12,000 tons; this has saved one-fourth freight and brought producer and consumers into such contact that we no longer hear "of the earth's products being wasted, of wheat rotting in La Mancha, wool being used to mend wads and sheep being burned for fuel in the Argentine Republic." England has mainly profited by this enormous development, the shipping of the United Kingdom earning $300,000,000 yearly, and employing 200,000 seamen, whose industry is therefore equivalent to £300 per man, as compared with £190 for each of the factory operatives. The freight earned by all flags for sea-borne merchandise is $500,000,00, or about 8 per cent. of the value transported. Hence the toll which all nations pay to England for the carrying trade is equal to 4 per cent (nearly) of the exported values of the earth's products and manufactures; and pessimists who declare that ship owners are losing money or making small profits must be wrong, for the merchant marine is expanding every year.

"The maximum tonnage of this country at any time registered in the foreign trade was in 1861, and then amounted to 5,539,813 tons; Great Britain in the same year owning 5,895,369 tons, and all the other nations 5,800,767 tons. Between 1855 and 1860 over 1,300,000 American tons in excess of the country's needs were employed by foreigners in trades with which we had no legitimate connection save as carriers. In 1851 our registered steamships had grown from the 16,000 tons of 1848 to 63,920 tons—almost equal to the 65,920 tons of England, and in 1855 this had increased to 115,000 tons and reached a maximum, for in 1862 we had 1,000 tons less. In 1855 we built 388 vessels, in 1856 306 vessels and in 1880 26 vessels—all for the foreign trade. The total tonnage which entered our ports in 1856 from abroad amounted to 4,464,038, of which American built ships constituted 3,194,375 tons, and all others but 1,259,762 tons. In 1880 there entered from abroad 15,240,534 tons, of which 3,128,374 tons were American and 12,112,000 were foreign—that is, in a ratio of seventy-five to twenty-five, or actually 65,901 tons less than when we were twenty-four years younger as a nation. The grain fleet sailing last year from the port of New York numbered 2,897 vessels, of which 1,822 were sailing vessels carrying 59,822,033 bushels, and 1,075 were steamers laden with 42,426,533 bushels, and among all these there were but seventy-four American sailing vessels and not one American steamer.

"While this poison of decay has been eating into our vitals the possibilities of the country in nearly every other industry have reached a plane of development beyond the dreams of the most enthusiastic theorizers. We have spread out in every direction and the promise of the future beggars imaginations attuned even to the key of our present and past development. We have a timber area of 560,000,000 acres, and across our Canadian border there are 900,000,000 more acres; in coal and iron production we are approaching the Old World.

	1842.	1879.
Coal—	*Tons.*	*Tons.*
Great Britain...	35,000,000	135,000,000
United States...	2,000,000	60,000,000
Iron—		
Great Britain...	2,250,000	6,300,000
United States...	564,000	2,742,000

During these thirty-seven years the relative increase has been in coal 300 to 2,900 per cent., in iron 200 to 400 per cent., and all in our favor. But this is not enough, for England, with a coal area less than either Pennsylvania or Kentucky, has coaling stations in every part of the world and our steamers cannot reach our California ports without the consent of the English producers. Even if electricity takes the place of steam it must be many years before the coal demand will cease, and to-day, of the 36,000,000 tons of coal required by the steamers of the world, three-fourths of it is obtained from Great Britain.

"It is unnecessary to wire-draw statistics, but it may, as a last word, be interesting to show, with all our development, the nationality and increase of tonnage entering our ports since 1856:—

Country.	*Increase.*	*Decrease.*
England	6,977,163	—
Germany	922,903	—
Norway and Sweden	1,214,008	—
Italy	596,907	—
France	208,412	—
Spain	164,683	—
Austria	226,277	—
Belgium	204,872	—
Russia	104,009	—
United States	—	65,901

"This," writes Lindsay, "is surely not decadence, but defeat in a far nobler conflict than the wars for maritime supremacy between Rome and Carthage, consisting as it did in the struggle between the skill and industry of the people of two great nations."

We have thus quoted the facts gathered from a source which has been endorsed by the higher naval authorities. Some reader will probably ask, "What relation have these facts to American politics?" We answer that the remedies proposed constitute political questions on which the great parties are very apt to divide. They have thus divided in the past, and parties have turned "about face" on similar questions.

Just now the Democratic party inclines to "free ships" and hostility to subsidies—while the Republican party as a rule favors subsidies. Lieutenant Kelley summarized his proposed remedies in the two words: "free ships."

Mr. Blaine would solve the problem by bounties, for this purpose enacting a general law that should ignore individuals and enforce a policy. His scheme provides that any man or company of men who will build in an American yard, with American material, by American mechanics, a steamship of 3,000 tons and sail her from any port of the United States to any foreign port, he or they shall receive for a monthly line a mail allowance of $25 per mile per annum for the sailing distance between the two ports; for a semi-monthly line $45 per mile, and for a weekly line $75 per mile. Should the steamer exceed three thousand tons, a small advance on these rates might be allowed; if less, a corresponding reduction, keeping three thousand as the average and standard. Other reformers propose a bounty to be given by the Government to the shipbuilder, so as to make the price of an American vessel the same as that of a foreign bought, equal, but presumably cheaper, ship.

Mr. Blaine represents the growing Republican view, but the actual party views can only be ascertained when bills covering the subject come up for consideration.

Current Politics.

We shall close this written history of the political parties of the United States by a brief statement of the present condition of affairs, as generally remarked by our own people, and by quoting the views of an interesting cotemporaneous English writer.

President Arthur's administration has had many difficulties to contend with. The President himself is the legal successor of a beloved man, cruelly assassinated, whose well-rounded character and high abilities had won the respect even of those who defamed him in the heat of controversy, while they excited the highest admiration of those who shared his political views and thoughts. Stricken down before he had time to formulate a policy, if it was ever his intention to do so, he yet showed a proper appreciation of his high responsibilities, and had from the start won the kindly attention of the country. Gifted with the power of saying just the right thing at the right moment, and saying it with all the grace and beauty of oratory, no President was better calculated to make friends as he moved along, than Garfield. The manifestations of factional feeling which immediately preceded his assassination, but which cannot for a moment be intelligently traced to that cause, made the path of his successor far more difficult than if he had been called to the succession by the operation of natural causes. That he has met these difficulties with rare discretion, all admit, and at this writing partisan interest and dislike are content to "abide a' wee" before beginning an assault. He has sought no changes in the Cabinet, and thus through personal and political considerations seems for the time to have surrendered a Presidential prerogative freely admitted by all who understand the wisdom of permitting an executive officer to seek the advice of friends of his own selection. Mr. Blaine and Mr. MacVeagh, among the ablest of the late President's Cabinet, were among the most emphatic in insisting upon the earliest possible exercise of this prerogative—the latter upon its immediate exercise. Yet it has been withheld in several particulars, and the Arthur administration has sought to unite, wherever divided (and now divisions are rare), the party which called it into existence, while at the same time it has by careful management sought to check party strife at least for a time, and devoted its attention to the advancement of the material interests of the country. Appointments are fairly distributed among party friends, not divided as between factions; for such a division systematically made would disrupt any party. It would prove but an incentive to faction for the sake of a division of the spoils. No force of politics is or ought to be better understood in America than manufactured disagreements with the view to profitable compromises. Fitness, recognized ability, and adequate political service seem to constitute the reasons for Executive appointments at this time.

The Democratic party, better equipped in the National Legisture than it has been for years—with men like Hill, Bayard, Pendleton, Brown, Voorhees, Lamar and Garland in the Senate—Stephens, Randall, Hewitt, Cox, Johnson in the House—with Tilden, Thurman, Wallace and Hancock in the background—is led with rare ability, and has the advantage of escaping responsibilities incident to a majority party. It has been observed that this party is pursuing the traditional strategy of minorities in our Republic. It has partially refused a further test on the tariff issue, and is seeking a place in advance of the Republicans on refunding questions—both popular measures, as shown in all recent elections. It claims the virtue of sympathy with the Mormons by questioning the propriety of legal assaults upon the liberty of conscience, while not openly recording itself as a defender of the crime of polygamy. As a solid minority it has at least in the Senate yielded to the appeal of the States on the Pacific slope, and favored the abridgment of Chinese immigration. On this question, however, the Western Republican Senators as a rule were equally active in support of the Miller Bill, so that whatever the result, the issue can no longer be a political one in the Pacific States. The respectable support which the measure has latterly received has cast out of the struggle the Kearneys and Kallochs, and if there be demagoguery on either side, it comes in better dress than ever before.

Doubtless the parties will contest their claims to public support on their respective histories yet a while longer. Party history has served partisan purposes an average of twenty years, when with that history recollections of wars are interwoven, and the last war having been the greatest in our history, the presumption is allowable that it will be freely quoted so long as sectional or other forms of distrust are observable any where. When these recollections fail, new issues will have to be sought or accepted. In the mere search for issues the minority ought always to be the most active; but their wise appropriation, after all, depends upon the wisdom and ability of leadership. It has ever been thus, and ever will be. This is about the only political prophecy the writer is willing to risk —and in risking this he but presents a view common to all Americans who claim to be "posted" in the politics of their country.

What politicians abroad think of our "situation" is well told, though not always accurately, by a distinguished writer in the January (1882) number of "*The London Quarterly Review.*" From this we quote some very attractive paragraphs, and at the same time escape the necessity of descriptions and predictions generally believed to be essential in rounding off a political volume, but which are always dangerous in treating of current affairs. Speaking of the conduct of both parties on the question of Civil Service Reform, the writer says:

"What have they done to overthrow the celebrated Jacksonian precept, 'to the victors belongs the spoils?' What, in fact, is it possible for them to do under the present system? The political laborer holds that he is worthy of his hire, and if nothing is given to him, nothing will he give in return. There are tens of thousands of offices at the bestowal of every administration, and the persons who have helped to bring that administration into power expect to receive them. 'In Great Britain," once remarked the American paper which enjoys the largest circulation in the country, 'the ruling classes have it all to themselves, and the poor man rarely or never gets a nibble at the public crib. Here we take our turn. We know that, if our political rivals have the opportunity to-day, we shall have it to-morrow. This is the philosophy of the whole thing compressed into a nutshell.' If President Arthur were to begin to-day to distribute offices to men who were most worthy to receive them, without reference to political services, his own party would rebel, and assuredly his path would not be strewn with roses. He was himself a victim of a gross injustice perpetrated under the name of reform. He filled the important post of Collector of the Port of New York, and filled it to the entire satisfaction of the mercantile community. President Hayes did not consider General Arthur sufficiently devoted to his interests, and he removed him in favor of a confirmed wire-puller and caucus-monger, and the administration papers had the address to represent this as the outcome of an honest effort to reform the Civil Service. No one really supposed that the New York Custom House was less a political engine than it had been before. The rule of General Arthur had been, in point of fact, singularly free from jobbery and corruption, and not a breath of suspicion was ever attached to his personal character. If he had been less faithful in the discharge of his difficult duties, he would have made fewer enemies. He discovered several gross cases of fraud upon the revenue, and brought the perpetrators to justice; but the culprits were not without influence in the press, and they contrived to make the worse appear the better cause. Their view was taken at second-hand by many of the English journals, and even recently the public here were gravely assured that General Arthur represented all that was base in American politics, and moreover that he was an enemy of England, for he had been elected by the Irish vote. The authors of these foolish calumnies did not perceive that, if their statements had been correct, General Garfield, whom they so much honored, must also have been elected by the Irish vote; for he came to power on the very same 'ticket.' In reality, the Irish vote may be able to accomplish many things in America, but we may safely predict that it will never elect a President. General Arthur had not been many weeks in power, before he was enabled to give a remarkable proof of the injustice that had been done to him in this particular respect. The salute of the English flag at Yorktown is one of the most graceful incidents recorded in American history, and the order originated solely with the President. A man with higher character or, it may be added, of greater accomplishments and fitness for his office, never sat in the Presidential chair. His first appointments are now admitted to be better than those which were made by his predecessor for the same posts. Senator Frelinghuysen, the new Secretary of State, or Foreign Secretary, is a man of great ability, of most excellent judgment, and of the highest personal character. He stands far beyond the reach of all unworthy influences. Mr. Folger, the Secretary of the Treasury, possesses the confidence of the entire country, and the nomination of the new Attorney-General was received with universal satisfaction. All this little accords with the dark and forbidding descriptions of President Arthur which were placed before the public here on his accession to office. It is surely time that English writers became alive to the danger of accepting without question the distorted views which they find ready to their hands in the most bigoted or most malicious of American journals.

"Democrats and Republicans, then, alike profess to be in favor of a thorough reform in the Civil Service, and at the present moment there is no other very prominent question which could be used as a test for the admission of members into either party. The old issue, which no one could possibly mistake, is gone. How much the public really care for the new one, it would be a difficult point to decide. A Civil Service system, such as that which we have in England, would scarcely be suited to the "poor man," who, as the New York paper says, thinks he has a right occasionally to 'get a nibble at the public crib.' If a man has worked hard to bring his party into power, he is apt, in the United States, to think that he is entitled to some 'recognition,' and neither he nor his friends would be well pleased if they were told that, before anything could be done for him, it would be necessary to examine him in modern languages and mathematics. Moreover, a service such as that which exists in England requires to be worked with a system of pensions; and pensions, it is held in America, are opposed to the Republican idea.* If it were not for this objection, it may be presumed that some provision would have been made for more than one of the ex-Presidents, whose circumstances placed them or their families much in need of it. President Monroe spent his last years in wretched circumstances, and died bankrupt. Mrs. Madison 'knew what it was to want bread.' A negro servant, who had once been a slave in the family, used furtively to give her 'small sums'—they must have been very small—out of his own pocket. Mr. Pierce was, we believe, not far removed from indigence; and it has been stated that after Andrew Johnson left the White House, he was reduced to the necessity of following his old trade. General Grant was much more fortunate; and we have recently seen that the American people have subscribed for Mrs. Garfield a sum nearly equal to £70,000. But a pension system for Civil Servants is not likely to be adopted. Permanence in office is another principle which has found no favor with the rank and file of either party in America, although it has sometimes been introduced into party platforms for the sake of producing a good effect. The plan of 'quick rotation' is far more attractive to the popular sense. Divide the spoils, and divide them often. It is true that the public indignation is sometimes aroused, when too eager and rapacious a spirit is exhibited. Such a feeling was displayed in 1873, in consequence of an Act passed by Congress increasing the pay of its own members and certain officers of the Government. Each member of Congress was to receive $7,500 a year, or £1,500. The sum paid before that date, down to 1865, was $5000 a year, or £1000, and 'mileage' free added — that is to say, members were entitled to be paid twenty cents a mile for traveling expenses to and from Washington. This Bill soon became known as the 'Salary Grab' Act, and popular feeling against it was so great that it was repealed in the following Session, and the former pay was restored. As a general rule, however, the 'spoils' system has not been heartily condemned by the nation; if it had been so condemned, it must have fallen long ago.

"President Arthur has been admonished by his English counsellors to take heed that he follows closely in the steps of his predecessor. General Garfield was not long enough in office to give any decided indications of the policy which he intended to pursue; but, so far as he had gone, impartial observers could detect very little difference between his course of conduct in regard to patronage and that of former Presidents. He simply preferred the friends of Mr. Blaine to the friends of Mr. Conkling; but Mr. Blaine is a politician of precisely the same class as Mr. Conkling—both are men intimately versed in all the intricacies of 'primaries,' the 'caucus,' and the general working of the 'machine.' They are precisely the kind of men which American politics, as at present practised and understood, are adapted to produce. Mr. Conkling, however, is of more imperious a disposition than Mr. Blaine; the first disappointment or contradiction turns him from a friend into an enemy. President Garfield removed the Collector of New York—the most lucrative and most coveted post in the entire Union—and in-

* Enormous sums are, however, given to soldiers who were wounded during the war, or who pretend that they were—for jobbery on an unheard of scale is practised in connection with these pensions. It is estimated that $120,000,000 (24,000,000*l.*) will have to be paid during the present fiscal year, for arrears of pension, and the number of claimants is constantly increasing. [The writer evidently got these "facts" from sensational sources.] —*Am. Pol.*

stead of nominating a friend of Mr. Conkling's for the vacancy, he nominated a friend of Mr. Blaine's. Now Mr. Conkling had done much to secure New York State for the Republicans, and thus gave them the victory; and he thought himself entitled to better treatment than he received. But was it in the spirit of true reform to remove the Collector, against whom no complaint had been made, merely for the purpose of creating a vacancy, and then of putting a friend of Mr. Blaine's into it—a friend, moreover, who had been largely instrumental in securing General Garfield's own nomination at Chicago? * Is this all that is meant, when the Reform party talk of the great changes which they desire to see carried out? Again, the new President has been fairly warned by his advisers in this country, that he must abolish every abuse, new or old, connected with the distribution of patronage. If he is to execute this commission, not one term of office, nor three terms, will be sufficient for him. Over every appointment there will inevitably arise a dispute; if a totally untried man is chosen, he will be suspected as a wolf coming in sheep's clothing; if a well known partizan is nominated, he will be denounced as a mere tool of the leaders, and there will be another outcry against 'machine politics.' 'One party or other,' said an American journal not long ago, 'must begin the work of administering the Government on business principles,' and the writer admitted that the work would 'cost salt tears to many a politician.' The honor of making this beginning has not yet been sought for with remarkable eagerness by either party; but seems to be deemed necessary to promise that something shall be done, and the Democrats, being out of power, are naturally in the position to bid the highest. The reform will come, as we have intimated, when the people demand it; it cannot come before, for few, indeed, are the politicians in the United States who venture to trust themselves far in advance of public opinion. And even of that few, there are some who have found out, by hard experience, that there is little honor or profit to be gained by undertaking to act as pioneers.

"It is doubtless a step in advance, that both parties now admit the absolute necessity of devising measures to elevate the character of the public service, to check the progress of corruption, and to introduce a better class of men into the offices which are held under the Government. The necessity of great reforms in these respects has been avowed over and over again by most of the leading journals and influential men in the country. The most radical of the Republicans, and the most conservative of the Democrats, are of one mind on this point. Mr. Wendell Phillips, an old abolitionist and Radical, once publicly declared that Republican government in cities had been a complete failure.* An equally good Radical, the late Mr. Horace Greeley, made the following still more candid statement:—'There are probably at no time less than twenty thousand men in this city [New York] who would readily commit a safe murder for a hundred dollars, break open a house for twenty, and take a false oath for five. Most of these are of European birth, though we have also native miscreants who are ready for any crime that will pay.' † Strong testimony against the working of the suffrage—and it must have been most unwilling testimony—was given in 1875 by a politician whose long familiarity with caucuses and 'wire-pulling' in every form renders him an undeniable authority. Let it be widely proclaimed,' he wrote, 'that the experience and teachings of a republican form of government prove nothing so alarmingly suggestive of and pregnant with danger as that cheap suffrage involves and entails cheap representation.' ‡ Another Republican, of high character, has stated that 'the methods of politics have now become so repulsive, the corruption so open, the intrigues and personal hostilities are so shameless, that it is very difficult to engage in them without a sense of humiliation.'" §

Passing to another question, and one worthy of the most intelligent discussion, but which has never yet taken the shape of a political demand or issue in this country, this English writer says:

"Although corruption has been suspected at one time or other in almost every Department of the Government, the Presidential office has hitherto been kept free from its stain. And yet, by an anomaly of the Constitution, the President has sometimes been exposed to suspicion, and still more frequently to injustice and misrepresentation, in consequence of the practical irresponsibility of his Cabinet officers. They are his chief advisers in regard to the distribution of places, as well as in the higher affairs of State, and the discredit of any mismanagement on their part falls upon him. It is true that he chooses them, and may dismiss them, with the concurrence of the Senate; but, when once appointed, they are beyond reach of all effective criticism—for newspaper attacks are easily explained by the suggestion of party malice. They cannot be questioned in

* The undeniable facts of the case were as we have briefly indicated above. See, for example, a letter to the 'New York Nation,' Nov. 3, 1881.

* Speech in New York, March 7, 1881.
† 'New York Tribune,' Feb. 25, 1870.
‡ Letter in New York papers, Feb. 20, 1875.
§ Mr. George William Curtis, in 'Harper's Magazine,' 1870.

Congress, for they are absolutely prohibited from sitting in either House.

For months together it is quite possible for the Cabinet to pursue a course which is in direct opposition to the wishes of the people. This was seen, among other occasions, in 1873–4, when Mr. Richardson was Secretary of the Treasury, and at a time when his management of the finances caused great dissatisfaction. At last a particularly gross case of negligence, to use no harsher word, known as the 'Sanborn contracts,' caused his retirement; that is to say, the demand for his withdrawal became so persistent and so general, that the President could no longer refuse to listen to it. His objectionable policy might have been pursued till the end of the Presidential term, but for the accidental discovery of a scandal, which exhausted the patience of his friends as well as his enemies. Now had Mr. Richardson been a member of either House, and liable to be subjected to a rigorous cross-questioning as to his proceedings, the mismanagement of which he was accused, and which was carried on in the dark, never could have occurred. Why the founders of the Constitution should have thrown this protection round the persons who happen to fill the chief offices of State, is difficult to conjecture, but the clause is clear:—'No person holding any office under the United States shall be a member of either House during his continuance in office.'* Mr. Justice Story declares that this provision 'has been vindicated upon the highest grounds of public authority,' but he also admits that, as applied to the heads of departments, it leads to many evils. He adds a warning which many events of our own time have shown to be not unnecessary:—'if corruption ever eats its way silently into the vitals of this Republic, it will be because the people are unable to bring responsibility home to the Executive through his chosen Ministers. They will be betrayed when their suspicions are most lulled by the Executive, under the guise of an obedience to the will of Congress.'† The inconveniences occasioned to the public service under the present system are very great. There is no official personage in either House to explain the provisions of any Bill, or to give information on pressing matters of public business. Cabinet officers are only brought into communication with the nation when they send in their annual reports, or when a special report is called for by some unusual emergency. Sometimes the President himself goes down to the Capitol to talk over the merits of a Bill with members. The Department which happens to be interested in any particular measure puts it under the charge of some friend of the Administration, and if a member particularly desires any further information respecting it he may, if he thinks proper, go to the Department and ask for it. But Congress and Ministers are never brought face to face. It is possible that American 'Secretaries' may escape some of the inconvenience which English Ministers are at times called upon to undergo; but the most capable and honest of them forfeit many advantages, not the least of which is the opportunity of making the exact nature of their work known to their countrymen, and of meeting party misrepresentations and calumnies in the most effectual way. In like manner, the incapable members of the Cabinet would not be able, under a different system, to shift the burden of responsibility for their blunders upon the President. No President suffered more in reputation for the faults of others than General Grant. It is true that he did not always choose his Secretaries with sufficient care or discrimination, but he was made to bear more than a just proportion of the censure which was provoked by their mistakes. And it was not in General Grant's disposition to defend himself. In ordinary intercourse he was sparing of his words, and could never be induced to talk about himself, or to make a single speech in defense of any portion of his conduct. The consequence was, that his second term of office was far from being worthy of the man who enjoyed a popularity, just after the war, which Washington himself might have envied, and who is still, and very justly, regarded with respect and gratitude for his memorable services in the field.

"The same sentiment, to which we have referred as specially characteristic of the American people—hostility to all changes in their method of government which are not absolutely essential—will keep the Cabinet surrounded by irresponsible, and sometimes incapable, advisers. Contrary to general supposition, there is no nation in the world so little disposed to look favorably on Radicalism and a restless desire for change, as the Americans. The Constitution itself can only be altered by a long and tedious process, and after every State in the Union has been asked its opinion on the question. There is no hesitation in enforcing the law in case of disorder, as the railroad rioters in Pennsylvania found out a few years ago. The state of affairs, which the English Government has permitted to exist in Ireland for upwards of a year, would not have been tolerated twenty-four hours in the United States. The maintenance of the law first, the discussion of grievances afterwards; such is, and always has been, the policy of every American Government, until the evil day of

* Article I. sect. vi. 2.

† 'Commentaries,' I., book iii. sect. 869.

James Buchanan. The governor of every State is a real ruler, and not a mere ornament, and the President wields a hundred-fold more power than has been left to the Sovereign of Great Britain. Both parties as a rule, combine to uphold his authority, and, in the event of any dispute with a foreign Power, all party distinctions disappear as if by magic. There are no longer Democrats and Republicans, but only Americans. The species of politician, who endeavors to gain a reputation for himself by destroying the reputation of his country was not taken over to America in the 'Mayflower,' and it would be more difficult than ever to establish it on American ground to-day. A man may hold any opinions that may strike his fancy on other subjects, but in reference to the Government, he is expected, while he lives under it, to give it his hearty support, especially as against foreign nations. There was once a faction called the 'Know Nothings,' the guiding principle of which was inveterate hostility to foreigners; but a party based upon the opposite principle, of hostility to one's own country, has not yet ventured to lift up its head across the Atlantic. That is an invention in politics which England has introduced, and of which she is allowed to enjoy the undisputed monopoly. * * *

"Display and ceremonial were by no means absent from the Government in the beginning of its history. President Washington never went to Congress on public business except in a State coach, drawn by six cream-colored horses. The coach was an object which would excite the admiration of the throng even now in the streets of London. It was built in the shape of a hemisphere, and its panels were adorned with cupids, surrounded with flowers worthy of Florida, and of fruit not to be equalled out of California. The coachman and postillions were arrayed in gorgeous liveries of white and scarlet. The Philadelphia 'Gazette,' a Government organ, regularly gave a supply of Court news for the edification of the citizens. From that the people were allowed to learn as much as it was deemed proper for them to know about the President's movements, and a fair amount of space was also devoted to Mrs. Washington—who was not referred to as Mrs. Washington, but as 'the amiable consort of our beloved President.' When the President made his appearance at a ball or public reception, a dais was erected for him upon which he might stand apart from the vulgar throng, and the guests or visitors bowed to him in solemn silence. 'Republican simplicity' has only come in later times. In our day, the hack-driver who takes a visitor to a public reception at the White House, is quite free to get off his box, walk inside by side with his fare, and shake hands with the President with as much familiarity as anybody else. Very few persons presumed to offer to shake hands with General Washington. One of his friends, Gouverneur Morris, rashly undertook, for a foolish wager, to go up to him and slap him on the shoulder, saying, 'My dear General, I am happy to see you look so well.' The moment fixed upon arrived, and Mr. Morris, already half-repenting of his wager, went up to the President, placed his hand upon his shoulder, and uttered the prescribed words. 'Washington,' as an eye-witness described the scene, 'withdrew his hand, stepped suddenly back, fixed his eye on Morris for several minutes with an angry frown, until the latter retreated abashed, and sought refuge in the crowd.' No one else ever tried a similar experiment. It is recorded of Washington, that he wished the official title of the President to be 'High Mightiness,' * and at one time it was proposed to engrave his portrait upon the national coinage. No royal levées were more punctiliously arranged and ordered than those of the First President. It was Jefferson, the founder of the Democratic party, who introduced Democratic manners into the Republic. He refused to hold weekly receptions, and when he went to Congress to read his Address, he rode up unattended, tied his horse to a post, and came away with the same disregard for outward show. After his inauguration, he did not even take the trouble to go to Congress with his Message, but sent it by the hands of his Secretary—a custom which has been found so convenient that it has been followed ever since. A clerk now mumbles through the President's Message, while members sit at their desks writing letters, or reading the Message itself, if they do not happen to have made themselves masters of its contents beforehand."

The writer, after discussing monopolies and tariffs, closes with hopes and predictions so moderately and sensibly stated that any one will be safe in adopting them as his own.

"The controversies which have yet to be fought out on these issues [the tariff and corporate power] may sometimes become formidable, but we may hope that the really dangerous questions that once confronted the American people are set at rest for ever. The States once more stand in their proper relation to the Union, and any interference with their self-government is never again likely to be attempted, for the feeling of the whole people would condemn it. It was a highly Conservative system which the framers of the Constitution adopted, when they decided that each State should be entitled to make its own laws,

* [These are mere traditions tinged with the spirit of some of the assaults made in the "good old days" even against so illustrious a man as Washington.—*Am. Pol.*]

to regulate its own franchise, to raise its own taxes, and settle everything in connection with its own affairs in its own way. The general government has no right whatever to send a single soldier into any State, even to preserve order, until it has been called upon to act by the Governor of that State. The Federal Government, as it has been said by the Supreme Court, is one of enumerated powers;' and if it has ever acted in excess of those powers, it was only when officers in States broke the compact which existed, and took up arms for its destruction. They abandoned their place in the Union, and were held to have thereby forfeited their rights as States. In ordinary times there is ample security against the abuse of power in any direction. If a State government exceeds its authority, the people can at the next election expel the parties who have been guilty of the offense; if Congress trespasses upon the functions of the States, there is the remedy of an appeal to the Supreme Court, the 'final interpreter of the Constitution;' if usurpation should be attempted in spite of these safeguards, there is the final remedy of an appeal to the whole nation under the form of a Constitutional Amendment, which may at any time be adopted with the consent of three-fourths of the States. Only, therefore, as Mr. Justice Story has pointed out, when three-fourths of the States have combined to practice usurpation, is the case 'irremediable under any known forms of the Constitution.' It would be difficult to conceive of any circumstances under which such a combination as this could arise. No form of government ever yet devised has proved to be faultless in its operation; but that of the United States is well adapted to the genius and character of the people, and the very dangers which it has passed through render it more precious in their eyes than it was before it had been tried in the fire. It assures freedom to all who live under it; and it provides for the rigid observance of law, and the due protection of every man in his rights. There is much in the events which are now taking place around us to suggest serious doubts, whether these great and indispensable advantages are afforded by some of the older European systems of government which we have been accustomed to look upon as better and wiser than the American Constitution."

A final word as to a remaining great issue—that of the tariff. It must ever be a political issue, one which parties cannot wholly avoid. The Democratic party as a mass, yet leans to Free Trade; the Republican party, as a mass, favors Tariffs and high ones, at least plainly protective. Within a year, two great National Conventions were held, one at Chicago and one at New York, both in former times, Free Trade centres, and in these Congress was petitioned either to maintain or improve the existing tariff. As a result we see presented and advocated at the current session the Tariff Commission Bill, decisive action upon which has not been taken at the time we close these pages. The effect of the conventions was to cause the Democratic Congressional caucus to reject the effort of Proctor Knott, to place it in its old attitude of hostility to protection. Many of the members sought and for the time secured an avoidance of the issue. Their ability to maintain this attitude in the face of Mr. Watterson's* declaration that the Democratic party must stand or fall on that issue, remains to be seen.

* Mr. Watterson, formerly a distinguished member of Congress, is the author of the "tariff for revenue only" plank in the Democratic National Platform of 1880, and is now, as he has been for years, the chief editor of the *Louisville Courier Journal.*

POLITICAL CHANGES IN 1882.

With a view to carry this work through the year 1882 and into part of 1883, very plain reference should be made to the campaign of 1882, which in several important States was fully as disastrous to the Republican party as any State elections since the advent of that party to national supremacy and power. In 1863 and 1874 the Republican reverses were almost if not quite as general, but in the more important States the adverse majorities were not near so sweeping. Political "tidal waves" had been freely talked of as descriptive of the situation in the earlier years named, but the result of 1882 has been pertinently described by Horatio Seymour as the "groundswell," and such it seemed, both to the active participants in, and lookers-on, at the struggle.

Political discontent seems to be periodical under all governments, and the periods are probably quite as frequent though less violent under republican as other forms. Certain it is that no political party in our history has long enjoyed uninterrupted success. The National success of the Republicans cannot truthfully be said to have been uninterrupted since the first election of Lincoln, as at times one or the other of the two Houses of Congress have been in the hands of the Democratic party, while since the second Grant administration there has not been a safe working majority of Republicans in either House. Combinations with Greenbackers, Readjusters, and occasionally with dissenting Democrats have had to be employed to preserve majorities in behalf of important measures, and these have not always succeeded, though the general tendency of side-parties has been to support the majority, for the very plain reason that majorities can reward with power upon committees and with patronage.

Efforts were made by the Democrats in the first session of the 47th Congress to reduce existing tariffs, and to repeal the internal revenue taxes. The Republicans met the first movement by establishing a Tariff Commission, which was appointed by President Arthur, and composed mainly of gentlemen favorable to protective duties. In the year previous (1881) the income from internal taxes was $135,264,385.51, and the cost of collecting $4,327,793.24, or 3.20 per cent. The customs revenues amounted to $198,159,676.02, the cost of collecting the same $6,383,288.10, or 3.22 per cent. There was no general complaint as to the cost of collecting these immense revenues, for this cost was greatly less than in former years, but the surplus on internal taxes (about $146,000,000) was so large that it could not be profitably employed even in the payment of the public debt, and as a natural result all interests called upon to pay the tax (save where there was a monopoly in the product or the manufacture) complained of the burden as wholly unnecessary, and large interests and very many people demanded immediate and absolute repeal. The Republicans sought to meet this demand half way by a bill repealing all the taxes, save those on spirits and tobacco, but the Democrats obstructed and defeated every attempt at partial repeal. The Republicans thought that the moral sentiment of the country would favor the retention of the internal taxes upon spirits and tobacco (the latter having been previously reduced) but if there was any such sentiment it did not manifest itself in the fall elections. On the contrary, every form of discontent, encouraged by these great causes, took shape. While the Tariff Commission, by active and very intelligent work, held out continued hope to the more confident industries, those which had been threatened or injured by the failure of the crops in 1881, and by the assassination of President Garfield, saw only prolonged injury in the probable work of the Commission, for to meet the close Democratic sentiment and to unite that which it was hoped would be generally friendly, moderate tariff rates had to be fixed; notably upon iron, steel, and many classes of manufactured goods. Manufacturers of the cheaper grades of cotton goods were feeling the pressure of competition from the South—where goods could be made from a natural product close at hand—while those of the North found about the same time that the tastes of their customers had improved, and hence their cheaper grades were no longer in such general demand. There was overproduction, as a consequence grave depression, and not all in the business could at once realize the cause of the trouble. Doubt and distrust prevailed, and early in the summer of 1882, and indeed until late in the fall, the country seemed upon the verge of a business panic. At the same time the leading journals of the country seemed to have joined in a crusade against all existing political methods, and against all statutory and political abuses. The cry of "Down with Boss Rule!" was heard in many States, and this rallied to the swelling ranks of discontent all who are naturally fond of pulling down leaders—and the United States Senatorial elections of 1883 quickly showed that the blow was aimed at all leaders, whether they were alleged Bosses or not. Then, too, the forms of discontent which could not take practical shape in the great Presidential contest between Garfield and Hancock, came to the front with cumulative force after the assassination. There is little use in philosophizing and searching for sufficient reasons leading to a fact, when the fact itself must be confessed and when its force has been felt. It is a plain fact that many votes in the fall of 1882 were determined by the nominating struggle for the Presidency in 1880, by the quarrels which followed Garfield's inauguration, and by the assassination. Indeed, the nation had not recovered from the shock, and many very good people looked with very grave suspicion upon every act of President Arthur after he had succeeded to the chair. The best informed, broadest and most liberal political minds saw in his course an honest effort to heal existing differences in the Republican party, but many acts of recommendation and appointment directed to this end were discounted by the few which could not thus be traced, and suspicion and discontent swelled the chorus of other injuries. The result was the great political changes of 1882. It began in Ohio, the only important and debatable October State remaining at this time. The causes enumerated above (save the assassination and the conflict between the friends of Grant and Blaine) operated with less force in Ohio than any other section—for here leaders had not been held up as "Bosses;" civil service reform had many advocates among them; the people were not by interest specially wedded to high tariff duties, nor were they large payers of internal revenue taxes. But the liquor issue had sprung up in the Legislature the previous winter, the Republicans attempting to levy and collect a tax from all who sold, and to prevent the sale on Sundays. These brief facts make strange reading to the people of other States, where the sale of liquor has generally been licensed, and forbidden on Sundays. Ohio had previously passed a prohibitory constitutional amendment, in itself defective, and as no legislation had been enacted to enforce it, those who wished began to sell as though the right were natural, and in this way became strong enough to resist taxation or license. The Legislature of 1882, the majority controlled by the Republicans, attempted to pass the Pond liquor tax act, and its issue was joined. The liquor interests organized, secured control of the Democratic State Convention, nominated a ticket pledged to their interests, made a platform which pointed to unrestricted sale, and by active work and the free use of funds, carried the election and reversed the usual majority. Governor Foster, the boldest of the Republican leaders, accepted the issue as presented, and stumped in favor of license and the sanctity of the Sabbath; but the counsels of the Republican leaders were divided, Ex-Secretary Sherman and others enacting the role of "confession and avoidance." The result carried with it a train of Republican disasters. Congressional candidates whom the issue could not legimately touch, fell before it, probably on the principle that "that which strikes the head injures the entire body." The Democratic State and Legislative tickets succeeded, and the German element, which of all others is most favorable to freedom in the observance of the Sabbath, transferred its vote almost as an entirety from the Republican to the Democratic party.

Ohio emboldened the liquor interests, and in their Conventions and Societies in other States they agreed as a rule to check and, if possible, defeat the advance of the prohibitory amendment idea. This started in Kansas in 1880, under the lead of Gov. St. John, an eloquent temperance advocate. It was passed by an immense majority, and it was hardly in force before conflicting accounts were scattered throughout the country as to its effect. Some of the friends of temperance contended that it improved the public condition; its enemies all asserted that in the larger towns and cities it produced free and irresponsible instead of licensed sale. The latter seem to have had the best of the argument, if the election result is a truthful witness. Gov. St. John was again the nominee of the Republicans, but while all of the remainder of the State-ticket was elected, he fell under a majority which must have been produced by a change of forty thousand votes. Iowa next took up the prohibitory amendment idea, secured its adoption, but the result was injurious to the Republicans in the Fall elections, where the discontent struck at Congressmen, as well as State and Legislative officers.

The same amendment had been proposed in Pennsylvania, a Republican House in 1881 having passed it by almost a solid vote (Democrats freely joining in its support), but a Republican Senate defeated, after it had been loaded down with amendments. New York was coquetting with the same measure, and as a result the liquor interests—well-organized and with an abundance of money, as a rule struck at the Republican party in both New York and Pennsylvania, and thus largely aided the groundswell. The same interests aided the election of Genl. B. F. Butler of Massachusetts, but from a different reason. He had, in one of his earlier canvasses, freely advocated the right of the poor to sell equally with those who could pay heavy license fees, and had thus won the major sympathy of the interest. Singularly enough, Massachusetts alone of all the Republican States meeting with defeat in 1882, fails to show in her result reasons which harmonize with those enumerated as making up the elements of discontent. Her people most do favor high tariffs, taxes on liquors and luxuries, civil service reforms, and were supposed to be more free from legal and political abuses than any other. Massachusetts had, theretofore, been considered to be the most advanced of all the States—in notions, in habit, and in law—yet Butler's victory was relatively more pronounced than that of any Democratic candidate, not excepting that of Cleveland over Folger in New York, the Democratic majority here approaching two hundred thousand. How are we to explain the Massachusetts' result? Gov. Bishop was a high-toned and able gentleman, the type of every reform contended for. There is but one explanation. Massachusetts had had too much of reform; it had come in larger and faster doses than even her progressive people could stand—and an inconsistent discontent took new shape there—that of very plain reaction. This view is confirmed by the subsequent attempt of Gov. Butler to defeat the re-election of Geo. F. Hoar to the U. S. Senate, by a combination of Democrats with dissatisfied Republicans. The movement failed, but it came very near to success, and for days the result was in doubt. Hoar had been a Senator of advanced views, of broad and comprehensive statesmanship, but that communistic sentiment which occasionally crops out in our politics and strikes at all leaders, merely from the pleasure of asserting the right to tear down, assailed him with a vigor almost equal to that which struck Windom of Minnesota, a statesman of twenty-four years' honorable, able and sometimes brilliant service. To prejudice the people of his State against him, a photograph of his Washington residence had been scattered broadcast. The print in the photograph intended to prejudice being a coach with a liveried lackey It might have been the coach and lackey of a visitor, but the effect was the same where discontent had run into a fever.

Political discontent gave unmistakable manifestations of its existence in Ohio, Massachusetts, New York (where Ex-Governor Cornell's nomination had been defeated by a forged telegram), Michigan, Nebraska, Kansas, Iowa, Connecticut, California, Colorado, Pennsylvania, and Indiana. The Republican position was well maintained in New Hampshire, Vermont, Rhode Island, Minnesota, Illinois, and Wisconsin. It was greatly improved in Virginia, where Mahone's Republican Readjuster ticket carried the State by nearly ten thousand, and where a United States' Senator and Congressman-at-large were gained, as well as some of the District Congressmen. The Republicans also improved the situation in North Carolina and Tennessee, though they failed to carry either. They also gained Congressmen in Mississippi and Louisiana, but the Congressional result throughout the country was a sweeping Democratic victory, the 48th Congress, beginning March 4, 1883, showing a Democratic majority of 71 in a total membership of 325.

In Pennsylvania alone of all the Northern States, were the Republican elements of discontent organized, and here they were as well organized as possible under the circumstances. Charles S. Wolfe had the year previous proclaimed what he called his "independence of the Bosses," by declaring himself a candidate for State Treasurer, "nominated in a convention of one." He secured 49,984 votes, and this force was used as the nucleus for the better organized Independent Republican movement of 1882. Through this a State Convention was called which placed a full ticket in the field, and which in many districts nominated separate legislative candidates.

The complaints of the Independent Republicans of Pennsylvania were very much like those of dissatisfied Republicans in other Northern States, where no adverse organizations were set up, and these can best be understood by giving the official papers and correspondence connected with the revolt, and the attempts to conciliate and suppress it by the regular organization. The writer feels a delicacy in appending this data, inasmuch as he was one of the principals in the negotiations, but formulated complaints, methods and principles peculiar to the time can be better understood as presented by organized and official bodies, than where mere opinions of cotemporaneous writers and speakers must otherwise be given. A very careful summary has been made by Col. A. K. McClure, in the Philadelphia *Times Almanac*, and from this we quote the data connected with the—

The Independent Republican Revolt in Pennsylvania.

The following call was issued by Chairman McKee, of the committee which conducted the Wolfe campaign in 1881:

HEADQUARTERS STATE COMMITTEE,
CITIZENS' REPUBLICAN ASSOCIATION,
GIRARD HOUSE,
PHILADELPHIA, December 16, 1881.

To the Independent Republicans of Pennsylvania:

You are earnestly requested to send representatives from each county to a State conference, to be held at Philadelphia, Thursday, January 12th, 1882, at 10 o'clock A. M., to take into consideration the wisdom of placing in nomination proper persons for the offices of Governor, Lieutenant Governor, Secretary of Internal Affairs and Supreme Court Judge, and such other matters as may come before the conference, looking to the overthrow of "boss rule," and the elimination of the pernicious "spoils system," and its kindred evils, from the administration of public affairs. It is of the utmost importance that those fifty thousand unshackled voters who supported the independent candidacy of Hon. Charles S. Wolfe for the office of State Treasurer as a solemn protest against ring domination, together with the scores of thousands of liberty-loving citizens who are ready to join in the next revolt against "bossism," shall be worthily represented at this conference.

I. D. MCKEE, Chairman.
FRANK WILLING LEACH, Secretary.

Pursuant to the above call, two hundred and thirteen delegates, representing thirty-three of the sixty-six counties, met at the Assembly Building, January 12th, 1882, and organized by the election of John J. Pinkerton as chairman, together with a suitable list of vice-presidents and secretaries. After a general interchange of views, a resolution was adopted directing the holding of a State Convention for the nomination of a State ticket, May 24th. An executive committee, with power to arrange for the election of delegates from each Senatorial district, was also appointed, consisting of Messrs. I. D. McKee, of Philadelphia; Wharton Barker, of Montgomery; John J. Pinkerton, of Chester; F. M. Nichols, of Luzerne; H. S. McNair, of York, and C. W. Miller, of Crawford. Mr. Nichols aftewards declining to act, George E. Mapes, of Venango, was substituted in his place. Before the time arrived for the meeting of the convention of May 24th, several futile efforts were made to heal the breach between the two wings of the Republican party. At a conference of leading Independents held in Philadelphia, April 23d, at which Senator Mitchell was present, a committee was appointed for the purpose of conferring with a similar committee from the regular organization, upon the subject of the party differences. The members of the Peace Conference, on the part of the Independents, were Charles S. Wolfe, I. D. McKee, Francis B. Reeves, J. W. Lee, and Wharton Barker. The committee on the part of the Stalwarts were M. S. Quay, John F. Hartranft, C. L. Magee, Howard J. Reeder, and Thomas Cochran. A preliminary meeting was held at the Continental Hotel, on the evening of April 29th, which adjourned to meet at the same place on the evening of May 1st; at which meeting the following peace propositions were agreed upon:

Resolved, That we recommend the adoption of the following principles and methods by the Republican State Convention of May 10th.

First. That we unequivocally condemn the use of patronage to promote personal political ends, and require that all offices bestowed within the party shall be upon the sole basis of fitness.

Second. That competent and faithful officers should not be removed except for cause.

Third. That the non-elective minor offices should be filled in accordance with rules established by law.

Fourth. That the ascertained popular will shall be faithfully carried out in State and National Conventions, and by those holding office by the favor of the party.

Fifth. That we condemn compulsory assessments for political purposes, and proscription for failure to respond either to such assessments or to requests for voluntary contributions, and that any policy of political proscription is unjust, and calculated to disturb party harmony.

Sixth. That public office constitutes a high trust to be administered solely for the people, whose interests must be paramount to those of persons or parties, and that it should be invariably conducted with the same efficiency, economy, and integrity as are expected in the execution of private trusts.

Seventh. That the State ticket should be such as by the impartiality of its constitution and the high character and acknowledged fitness of the nominees will justly commend itself to the support of the united Republican party.

Resolved, That we also recommend the adoption of the following permanent rules for the holding of State Conventions, and the conduct of the party:

First. That delegates to State Conventions shall be chosen in the manner in which candidates for the General Assembly are nominated, except in Senatorial districts composed of more than one county, in which conferees for the selection of Senatorial delegates shall be chosen in the manner aforesaid, and the representation of each county shall be based upon its Republican vote cast at the Presidential election next preceding the convention.

Second. Hereafter the State Convention of the Republican party shall be held on the second Wednesday of July, except in the year of the Presidential election, when it shall be held not more than thirty days previous to the day fixed for the National Convention, and at least sixty days' notice shall be given of the date of the State Convention.

Third. That every person who voted the Republican electoral ticket at the last Presidential election next preceding any State Convention shall be permitted to participate in the election of delegates to State and National Conventions, and we recommend to the county organizations that in their rules they allow the largest freedom in the general participation in the primaries consistent with the preservation of the party organization.

M. S. QUAY,
J. F. HARTRANFT,
THOMAS COCHRAN,
HOWARD J. REEDER,
C. L. MAGEE,

On the part of the Republican State Committee, appointed by Chairman Cooper.

CHARLES S. WOLFE,
I. D. MCKEE,
FRANCIS B. REEVES,
WHARTON BARKER,
J. W. LEE,

On the part of Senator Mitchell's Independent Republican Committee.

The following resolution was adopted by the joint conference:

Resolved, That we disclaim any authority to speak or act for other persons than ourselves, and simply make these suggestions as in our opinion are essential to the promotion of harmony and unity.

In order, however, that there might be no laying down of arms on the part of the Independents, in the false belief that the peace propositions had ended the contest, without regard to whether they were accepted in good faith, and put in practice by the regular convention, the following call was issued by the Independent Executive Committee:

EXECUTIVE COMMITTEE,
CITIZENS' REPUBLICAN ASSOCIATION OF PENNSYLVANIA, GIRARD HOUSE.

PHILADELPHIA, May 3d, 1882.

To the Independent Republicans of Pennsylvania:

At a conference of Independent Republicans held in Philadelphia, on January 12th, 1882, the following resolution was adopted, to wit:

Resolved, That a convention be held on the 24th day of May, 1882, for the purpose of placing in nomination a full Independent Republican ticket for the offices to be filled at the general election next November.

In pursuance and by the authority of the above resolution the undersigned, the State Executive Committee appointed at the said conference, request the Independent Republicans of each county of the Commonwealth of Pennsylvania to send delegates to the Independent Convention of May 24th, the basis of representation to be the same as that fixed for Senators and Representatives of the General Assembly of Pennsylvania.

Should the convention of May 10th fail to nominate as its candidates men who in their character, antecedents and affiliations are embodiments of the principles of true Republicanism free from the iniquities of bossism, and of an honest administration of public affairs free from the evils of the spoils system, such nominations, or any such nomination, should be emphatically repudiated by the Independent Convention of May 24th, and by the Independent Republicans of Pennsylvania in November next.

The simple adoption by the Harrisburg Convention of May 10th of resolutions of plausible platitudes, while confessing the existence of the evils which we have strenuously opposed, and admitting the justice of our position in opposing them, will not satisfy the Independent Republicans of this Commonwealth. We are not battling for the construction of platforms, but for the overthrow of bossism, and the evils of the spoils system, which animated a despicable assassin to deprive our loved President Garfield of his life, and our country of its friend and peacemaker.

The nomination of slated candidates by machine methods, thereby tending to the perpetuation of boss dominion in our Commonwealth, should never be ratified by the Independent Republicans in convention assembled or at the polls. Upon this very vital point there should be no mistake in the mind of any citizen of this State. The path of duty in this emergency leads forward, and not backward, and forward we should go until bossism and machineism and stalwartism—aye, and Cameronism—are made to give way to pure Republicanism. The people will not submit to temporizing or compromising.

We appeal to the Independent Republicans of Pennsylvania to take immediate steps toward perfecting their organization in each county, and completing the selection of delegates to the Independent State Convention. Use every exertion to secure the choice as delegates of representative, courageous men, who will not falter when the time arrives to act—who will not desert into the ranks of the enemy when the final time of testing comes. Especially see to it that there shall not be chosen as delegates any Pharisaical Independents, who preach reform, yet blindly follow boss leadership at the crack of the master's whip. Act quickly and act discreetly.

A State Campaign Committee of fifty, comprising one member from each Senatorial district, has been formed, and any one desiring to co-operate with us in this movement against the enemies of the integrity of our State, who shall communicate with us, will be immediately referred to the committeeman representing the district in which he lives. We urgently invite a correspondence from the friends of political independence from all sections of the State.

Again we say to the Independent Republicans of Pennsylvania in the interest of justice and the Commonwealth's honor, leave no stone unturned to vindicate the rights of the people.

I. D. MCKEE, Chairman.
WHARTON BARKER.
JOHN J. PINKERTON.
GEO. E. MAPES.
H. S. MCNAIR.
CHARLES W. MILLER.
FRANK WILLING LEACH, Secretary.

In pursuance of the above call, the Independent Convention met, May 24th, in Philadelphia, and deciding that the action of the regular Republican Convention, held at Harrisburg on May 10th, did not give the guarantee of reform demanded by the Independents, proceeded to nominate a ticket and adopt a platform setting forth their views.

Although the break between the two wings of the party was thus made final to all appearances, yet all efforts for a reconciliation were not entirely abandoned. Thos. M. Marshall having declined the nomination for Congressman at Large on the Republican ticket, the convention was reconvened June 21st, for the purpose of filling the vacancy, and while in session, instructed the State Central Committee to use all honorable means to secure harmony between the two sections of the party. Accordingly, the Republican State Committee was called to meet in Philadelphia, July 13th. At this meeting the following propositions were submitted to the Independents:

Pursuant to the resolution passed by the Harrisburg Convention of June 21st, and authorizing the Republican State Committee to use all honorable means to promote harmony in the party, the said committee, acting in conjunction with the Republican candidates on the State ticket, respectfully submit to the State Committee and candidates of the Independents the following propositions:

First. The tickets headed by James A. Beaver and John Stewart, respectively, be submitted to a vote of the Republican electors of the State, at primaries, as hereinafter provided for.

Second. The selection of candidates to be voted for by the Republican party in November to be submitted as aforesaid, every Republican elector, constitutionally and legally qualified, to be eligible to nomination.

Third. A State Convention to be held, to be constituted as recommended by the Continental Hotel Conference, whereof Wharton Barker was chairman and Francis B. Reeves secretary, to select candidates to be voted for by the Republican party in November, its choice to be limited to the candidates now in nomination, or unlimited, as the Independent State Committee may prefer.

The primaries or convention referred to in the foregoing propositions to be held on or before the fourth Wednesday of August next, under regulations or apportionment to be made by Daniel Agnew, Hampton L. Carson, and Francis B. Reeves, not in conflict, however, with the acts of Assembly regulating primary elections, and the candidates receiving the highest popular vote, or the votes of a majority of the members of the convention, to receive the united support of the party.

Resolved, That in the opinion of the Republican State Committee the above propositions fully carry out, in letter and spirit, the resolution passed by the Harrisburg Convention, June 21st, and that we hereby pledge the State Committee to carry out in good faith any one of the foregoing propositions which may be accepted.

Resolved, That the chairman of the Republican State Committee be directed to forward an official copy of the proceedings of this meeting, together with the foregoing propositions, to the Independent State Committee and candidates.

Whereupon, General Reeder, of Northampton, moved to amend by adding a further proposition, as follows.

Fourth. A State Convention, to be constituted as provided for by the new rules adopted by the late Republican State Convention, to select candidates to be voted for by the Republican party in November, provided, if such convention be agreed to, said convention shall be held not later than the fourth Wednesday in August. Which amendment was agreed to, and the preamble and resolutions as amended were agreed to.

This communication was addressed to the chairman of the Independent State Committee, I. D. McKee, who called the Independent Committee to meet July 27th, to consider the propositions. In the meantime the Independent candidates held a conference on the night of July 13th, and four of them addressed the following propositions to the candidates of the Stalwart wing of the party:

PHILADELPHIA, July 13th, 1882.

To General James A. Beaver, Hon. William T. Davies, Hon. John M. Greer, William Henry Ra[illegible]e, Esq., and Marriott Brosius, Esq.

Gentlemen: By a communication received from the Hon. Thomas V. Cooper, addressed to us as candidates of the Independent Republicans, we are advised of the proceedings of the State Committee, which assembled in this city yesterday.

Without awaiting the action of the Independent State Committee, to which we have referred the communication, and attempting no discussion of the existing differences, or the several methods proposed by which to secure party unity, we beg to say that we do not believe that any of the propositions, if accepted, would produce harmony in the party, but on the contrary, would lead to wider divisions. We therefore suggest that the desired result can be secured by the hearty co-operation of the respective candidates. We have no authority to speak for the great body of voters now giving their support to the Independent Republican ticket, nor can we include them by any action we may take. We are perfectly free, however, to act in our individual capacity, and desire to assure you that we are not only willing, but anxious to co-operate with you in the endeavor to restore peace and harmony to our party. That this can be accomplished beyond all doubt we feel entirely assured, if you, gentlemen, are prepared to yield, with us, all personal considerations, and agree to the following propositions:

First. The withdrawal of both tickets.

Second. The several candidates of these tickets to pledge themselves not to accept any subsequent nomination by the proposed convention.

Under these conditions we will unite with you in urging upon our respective constituencies the adoption of the third proposition submitted by your committee, and conclude the whole controversy by our final withdrawal as candidates. Such withdrawal of both tickets would remove from the canvass all personal as well as political antagonisms, and leave the party united and unembarrassed.

We trust, gentlemen, that your judgment will approve the method we have suggested, and that, appreciating the importance of concluding the matter with as little delay as possible, you will give us your reply within a week from this date.

Very respectfully, your obedient servants,
JOHN STEWART,
LEVI BIRD DUFF.
GEORGE W. MERRICK.
GEORGE JUNKIN.

William McMichael, Independent candidate for Congressman at Large, dissented from the proposition of his colleagues, and addressed the following communication to Chairman Cooper:

PHILADELPHIA, July 13th, 1882.

Hon. Thomas V. Cooper, Chairman, etc.

Dear Sir: Your letter of July 12th is received, addressed to the chairman of the State Committee of the Independent Republicans and their candidates, containing certain propositions of your committee. I decline those propositions, because they involve an abandonment of the cause of the Independent Republicans.

If a new convention, representing all Republicans, had nominated an entirely new ticket, worthy of popular support, and not containing the name of any candidate on either of the present tickets, and sincerely supporting the principles of the Independent Republicans, the necessity for a separate Independent Republican movement would not exist. Your proposition, however, practically proposes to re-nominate General Beaver, and reaffirm the abuse which we oppose.

The convention of Independent Republicans which met in Philadelphia on May 24th, announced principles in which I believe. It nominated me for Congressman at Large, and I accepted that nomination. It declared boldly against bossism, the spoils system, and all the evils which impair Republican usefulness, and in favor of popular rule, equal rights of all, national unity, maintenance of public credit, protection to labor, and all the great principles of true Republicanism. No other ticket now in the field presents those issues. The people of Pennsylvania can say at the polls, in November, whether they approve of those principles, and will support the cause which represents them. I will not withdraw or retire unless events hereafter shall give assurance that necessary reform in the civil service shall be adopted; assessments made upon office-holders returned, and not hereafter exacted; boss, machine, and spoils methods forever abandoned; and all our public offices, from United States Senator to the most unimportant officials, shall be filled only by honest and capable men, who will represent the people, and not attempt to dictate to or control them.

I shall go on with the fight, asking the support of all my fellow-citizens who believe in the principles of the Independent Republican Convention of May 24th.

Yours truly,
WILLIAM MCMICHAEL.

To these propositions General Beaver and his colleagues replied in the following communication:

PHILADELPHIA, July 15th, 1882.

Hon. Thomas V. Cooper, Chairman Republican State Committee, Philadelphia, Pa.

Sir: We have the honor to acknowledge the receipt through you of a communication addressed to us by the Hon. John Stewart, Colonel Levi Bird Duff, Major G. W. Merrick, and George Junkin, Esq., in response to certain propositions submitted by the Republican State Committee, representing the Republican party of Pennsylvania, looking to an amicable and honorable adjustment of whatever differences there may be among the various elements of the party. Without accepting any of the propositions submitted by your committee, this communication asks us, as a condition precedent to any recommendation on the part of the writers thereof, to declare that in the event of the calling of a new convention, we will severally forbid the Republicans of Pennsylvania to call upon us for our services as candidates for the various positions to be filled by the people at the coming election. To say that in the effort to determine whether or not our nomination was the free and unbiased choice of the Republican party we must not be candidates, is simply to try the question at issue. We have no desire to discuss the question in any of its numerous bearings. We have placed ourselves unreservedly in the hands of the Republicans of Pennsylvania. We have pledged ourselves to act concurrently with your committee, and are bound by its action. We therefore respectfully suggest that we have no power or authority to act independently of the committee, or make any declaration at variance with the propositions submitted in accordance with its action. There ought to be and can be no such thing as personal antagonism in this contest. We socially and emphatically disclaim even the remotest approach to a feeling of this kind toward any person. We fraternize with and are ready to support any citizen who loves the cause of pure Republicanism, and with this declaration we submit the whole subject to your deliberate judgment and wise consideration.

James A. Beaver.
William Henry Rawle,
Marriott Brosius.
W. T. Davies.
John M. Greer.

At the meeting of the Independent State Committee, July 27th, the propositions of the Regular Committee were unanimously rejected, and a committee appointed to draft a reply, which was done in the following terms:

Thomas V. Cooper, Esq., Chairman Republican State Committee.

Dear Sir: I am instructed to advise you that the Independent Republican State Committee have considered the four suggestions contained in the minutes of the proceedings of your committee, forwarded to me by you on the 12th instant.

I am directed to say that this committee find that none of the four are methods fitted to obtain a harmonious and honorable unity of the Republican voters of Pennsylvania. All of them are inadequate to that end, for the reason that they afford no guarantee that, being accepted, the principles upon which the Independent Republicans have taken their stand would be treated with respect or put into action. All of them contain the probability that an attempt to unite the Republicans of the State by their means would either result in reviving and strengthening the political dictatorship which we condemn or would permanently distract the Republican body, and insure the future and continued triumph of our common opponent, the Democratic party.

Of the four suggestions, the first, second and fourth are so inadequate as to need no separate discussion: the third, which alone may demand attention, has the fatal defect of not including the withdrawal of that "slated" ticket which was made up many months ago, and long in advance of the Harrisburg Convention, to represent and to maintain the very evils of control and abuses of method to which we stand opposed. This proposition, like the others, supposing it to have been sincerely put forward, clearly shows that you misconceive the cause of the Independent Republican movement, as well as its aims and purposes. You assume that we desire to measure the respective numbers of those who support the Harrisburg ticket and those who find their principles expressed by the Philadelphia Convention. This is a complete and fatal misapprehension. We are organized to promote certain reforms, and not to abandon them in pursuit of votes. Our object is the overthrow of the "boss system" and of the "spoils system."

In behalf of this we are willing and anxious to join hands with you whenever it is assured that the union will be honestly and earnestly for that purpose. But we cannot make alliances or agree to compromises that in their face threaten the very object of the movement in which we have engaged. Whether your ticket has the support of many or few, of a majority or a minority of the Republican voters, does not affect in the smallest degree the duty of every citizen to record himself against the abuses which it represents. Had the gentlemen who compose it been willing to withdraw themselves from the field, as they were invited to join in doing, for the common good, by the Independent Republican candidates, this act would have encouraged the hope that a new convention, freely chosen by the people, and unembarrassed by claims of existing candidates, might have brought forth the needed guarantee of party emancipation and public reform.

This service, however, they have declined to render their party; they not only claim and receive your repeated assurances of support, but they permit themselves to be put forward to secure the use of the Independent Republican votes at the same time that they represent the "bossism," the "spoils" methods, and the "machine" management which we are determined no longer to tolerate. The manner in which their candidacy was decreed, the means employed to give it convention formality, the obligations which they incur by it, the political methods with which it identifies them, and the political and personal plans for which their official influence would be required, all join to make it the most imperative public duty not to give them support at this election under any circumstances.

In closing this note, this committee must express its regret, that, having considered it desirable to make overtures to the Independent Republicans, you should have so far misapprehended the facts of the situation. It is our desire to unite the Republican party on the sure ground of principle, in the confidence that we are thus serving it with the highest fidelity, and preserving for the future service of the Commonwealth that vitality of Republicanism which has made the party useful in the past, and which alone confers upon it now the right of continued existence. The only method which promises this result in the approaching election is that proposed by the Independent Republican candidates in their letter of July 13th, 1882, which was positively rejected by your committee.

On behalf of the Independent Republican State Committee of Pennsylvania,

I. D. McKee, Chairman.

With this communication ended all efforts at conciliation.

* * * * * * * *

The election followed, and the Democratic ticket, headed by Robert E. Pattison of Philadelphia, received an average plurality of 40,000, and the Independent Republican ticket received an average vote of about 43,000—showing that while Independence organized did not do as well in a gubernatorial as it had in a previous off-year, it yet had force enough to defeat the Republican State ticket headed by Gen. James A. Beaver. All of the three several State tickets were composed of able men, and the force of both of the Republican tickets on the hustings excited great interest and excitement; yet the Republican vote, owing to the division, was not out by nearly one hundred thousand, and fifty thousand more Republicans than Democrats remained at home, many of them purposely. In New York, where dissatisfaction had no rallying point, about two hundred thousand Republicans remained at home, some because of anger at the defeat of Gov. Cornell in the State nominating convention—some in protest against the National Administrations, which was accused of the desire for direct endorsement where it presented the name of Hon Chas. J. Folger, its Secretary of the Treasury, as the home gubernatorial candidate,—others because of some of the many reasons set forth in the bill of complaints which enumerates the causes of the dissatisfaction within the party.

At this writing the work of Republican repair is going on. Both the Senate and House at Washington are giving active work to the passage of a tariff bill, the repeal of the revenue taxes, and the passage of a two-cent letter postage bill—measures anxiously hastened by the Republicans in order to anticipate friendly and defeat unfriendly attempts on the part of the Democratic House, which comes in with the first session of the 48th Congress.

In Pennsylvania, as we close this review of the struggle of 1882, the Regular and Independent Republican State Committees—at least the heads thereof—are devising a plan to jointly call a Republican State Convention to nominate the State ticket to be voted for in November, 1883. The groundswell was so great that it had no sooner passed, than Republicans of all shades of opinion, felt the need of harmonious action, and the leaders everywhere set themselves to the work of repair.

The Republicans in the South differed from those of the North in the fact that their complaints were all directed against a natural political enemy—the Bourbons—and wherever there was opportunity they favored and entered into movements with Independent and Readjuster Democrats, with the sole object of revolutionizing political affairs in the South. Their success in these combinations was only great in Virginia, but it proved to be promising in North Carolina, Mississippi, and Louisiana, and may take more definite and general shape in the great campaign of 1884.

The Democratic party was evidently surprised at its great victory in 1882, and has not yet formally resolved what it will do with it. The Congress beginning with December, 1883, will doubtless give some indication of the drift of Democratic events.

The most notable law passed in the closing session of the 47th Congress, was the Civil Service Reform Bill, introduced by Senator Geo. H. Pendleton of Ohio, but prepared under the direction of the Senate Judiciary Committee. The Republicans, feeling that there was some public demand for the passage of a measure of the kind, eagerly rushed to its support, at a time when it was apparent that the spoils of office might slip from their hands. From opposite motives the Democrats, who had previously encouraged, now ran away from it, but it passed both Houses with almost a solid Republican vote, a few Democrats in each House voting with them. President Arthur signed the bill, but at this writing the Commission which it creates has not been appointed, and of course none of the rules and constructions under the act have been formulated. Its basic principles are fixed tenure in minor places, competitive examinations, and non-partisan selections.

PART III.

POLITICAL PLATFORMS.

COMPARISONS AND DESCRIPTION OF ALL LEADING ISSUES.
WITH TABLES FOR READY REFERENCE.

POLITICAL PLATFORMS.

THE FIRST POLITICAL PLATFORM ENUNCIATED IN THE UNITED STATES TO COMMAND GENERAL ATTENTION WAS DRAWN BY MR. MADISON IN 1798, WHOSE OBJECT WAS TO PRONOUNCE THE ALIEN AND SEDITION LAWS UNCONSTITUTIONAL, AND TO DEFINE THE RIGHTS OF THE STATES.

Virginia Resolutions of 1798.

Pronouncing the Alien and Sedition Laws to be unconstitutional, and Defining the rights of the States.—Drawn by Mr. Madison.

In the Virginia House of Delegates,
Friday, Dec. 21, 1798.

Resolved, That the General Assembly of Virginia doth unequivocally express a firm resolution to maintain and defend the Constitution of the United States, and the constitution of this state, against every aggression either foreign or domestic; and that they will support the government of the United States in all measures warranted by the former.

That this Assembly most solemnly declares a warm attachment to the Union of the states, to maintain which it pledges its powers; and, that for this end, it is their duty to watch over and oppose every infraction of those principles which constitute the only basis of that Union, because a faithful observance of them can alone secure its existence and the public happiness.

That this Assembly doth explicitly and peremptorily declare, that it views the powers of the federal government, as resulting from the compact to which the states are parties, as limited by the plain sense and intention of the instrument constituting that compact, as no farther valid than they are authorized by the grants enumerated in that compact; and that in case of a deliberate, palpable, and dangerous exercise of other powers, not granted by the said compact, the states, who are parties thereto, have the right, and are in duty bound, to interpose, for arresting the progress of the evil, and for maintaining within their respective limits the authorities, rights, and liberties appertaining to them.

That the General Assembly doth also express its deep regret, that a spirit has, in sundry instances, been manifested by the federal government, to enlarge its powers by forced constructions of the constitutional charter which defines them; and, that indications have appeared of a design to expound certain general phrases (which, having been copied from the very limited grant of powers in the former Articles of Confederation, were the less liable to be misconstrued) so as to destroy the meaning and effect of the particular enumeration which necessarily explains, and limits the general phrases, and so as to consolidate the states by degrees into one sovereignty, the obvious tendency and inevitable result of which would be, to transform the present republican system of the United States into an absolute, or at best, a mixed monarchy.

That the General Assembly doth particularly protest against the palpable and alarming infractions of the Constitution, in the two late cases of the "Alien and Sedition Acts," passed at the last session of Congress; the first of which exercises a power nowhere delegated to the federal government, and which, by uniting legislative and judicial powers to those of executive, subverts the general principles of free government, as well as the particular organization and positive provisions of the Federal Constitution; and the other of which acts exercises, in like manner, a power not delegated by the Constitution, but on the contrary, expressly and positively forbidden by one of the amendments thereto; a power which, more than any other, ought to produce universal alarm, because it is levelled against the right of freely examining public characters and measures, and of free communication among the people thereon, which has ever been justly deemed the only effectual guardian of every other right.

That this state having by its Convention, which ratified the Federal Constitution, expressly declared, that among other essential rights, "the liberty of conscience and the press cannot be cancelled, abridged, restrained, or modified by any authority of the United States," and from its extreme anxiety to guard these rights from every possible attack of sophistry and ambition, having with other states recommended an amendment for that purpose, which amendment was, in due time, annexed to the Constitution, it would mark a reproachful inconsistency, and criminal degeneracy, if an indifference were now shown to the most palpable violation of one of the rights, thus declared and secured; and to the establishment of a precedent which may be fatal to the other.

That the good people of this commonwealth, having ever felt, and continuing to feel the most sincere affection for their brethren of the other states; the truest anxiety for establishing and perpetuating the Union of all: and the most scrupulous fidelity to that Constitution, which is the pledge of mutual friendship, and the instrument of mutual happiness; the General Assembly doth solemnly appeal to the like dispositions in the other States, in confidence that they will concur with this commonwealth, in declaring, as it does hereby declare, that the acts aforesaid are unconstitutional; and, that the necessary and proper measures will be taken by each for co-operating with this state, in maintaining unimpaired the authorities, rights, and liberties, reserved to the states, respectively, or to the people.

That the governor be desired to transmit a copy of the foregoing resolutions to the executive authority of each of the other states, with a request that the same may be communicated to the legislature thereof; and that a copy be furnished to each of the Senators and Representatives representing this state in the Congress of the United States.

Attest, JOHN STEWART.

1798. December 24th. Agreed to by the Senate. H. BROOKE.

A true copy from the original deposited in the office of the General Assembly.

JOHN STEWART, Keeper of Rolls.

Extracts from the Address to the People, which accompanied the foregoing resolutions:—

Fellow-Citizens: Unwilling to shrink from our representative responsibility, conscious of the purity of our motives, but acknowledging your right to supervise our conduct, we invite your serious attention to the emergency which dictated the subjoined resolutions. Whilst we disdain to alarm you by ill-founded jealousies, we recommend an investigation, guided by the coolness of wisdom, and a decision bottomed, on firmness but tempered with moderation.

It would be perfidious in those intrusted with the guardianship of the state sovereignty, and acting under the solemn obligation of the following oath: "I do swear, that I will support the Constitution of the United States," not to warn you of encroachments, which, though clothed with the pretext of necessity, or disguised by arguments of expediency, may yet establish precedents, which may ultimately devote a generous and unsuspicious people to all the consequences of usurped power.

Encroachments, springing from a government whose organization cannot be maintained without the co-operation of the states, furnish the strongest incitements upon the state legislatures to watchfulness, and impose upon them the strongest obligation to preserve unimpaired the line of partition.

The acquiescence of the states under infractions of the federal compact, would either beget a speedy consolidation, by precipitating the state governments into impotency and contempt; or prepare the way for a revolution, by a repetition of these infractions, until the people are aroused to appear in the majesty of their strength. It is to avoid these calamities, that we exhibit to the people the momentous question, whether the Constitution of the United States shall yield to a construction which defies every restraint and overwhelms the best hopes of republicanism.

Exhortations to disregard domestic usurpations until foreign danger shall have passed, is an artifice which may be for ever used; because the possessors of power, who are the advocates for its extension, can ever create national embarrassments, to be successively employed to soothe the people into sleep, whilst that power is swelling silently, secretly, and fatally. Of the same character are insinuations of a foreign influence, which seize upon a laudable enthusiasm against danger from a broad, and distort it by an unnatural application, so as to blind your eyes against danger at home.

The sedition act presents a scene which was never expected by the early friends of the Constitution. It was then admitted that the state sovereignties were only diminished by powers specifically enumerated, or necessary to carry the specified powers into effect. Now federal authority is deduced from implication, and from the existence of state law it is inferred that Congress possesses a similar power of legislation; whence Congress will be endowed with a power of legislation in all cases whatsoever, and the states will be stript of every right reserved by the concurrent claims of a paramount legislature.

The sedition act is the offspring of these tremendous pretensions, which inflict a death wound on the sovereignty of these states.

For the honor of American understanding, we will not believe that the people have been allured into the adoption of the Constitution by an affectation of defining powers, whilst the preamble would admit a construction which would erect the will of Congress into a power paramount in all cases, and therefore limited in none. On the contrary, it is evident that the objects for which the Constitution was formed were deemed attainable only by a particular enumeration and specification of each power granted to the federal government; reserving all others to the people, or to the states. And yet it is in vain we search for any specified power, embracing the right of legislation against the freedom of the press.

Had the states been despoiled of their sovereignty by the generality of the preamble, and had the federal government been endowed with whatever they should judge to be instrumental towards union, justice, tranquillity, common defence, general welfare, and the preservation of liberty nothing could have been more frivolous than an enumeration of powers.

All the preceding arguments rising from a deficiency of constitutional power in Congress, apply to the alien act, and this act is liable to other objections peculiar to itself. If a suspicion that aliens are dangerous constitute the justification of that power exercised over them by Congress, then a similar suspicion will justify the exercise of a similar power over natives. Because there is nothing in the Constitution distinguishing between the power of a state to permit the residence of natives and aliens. It is therefore a right originally possessed, and never surrendered by the respective states, and which is rendered dear and valuable to Virginia, because it is assailed through the bosom of the Constitution, and because her peculiar situation renders the easy admission of artisans and laborers an interest of vast importance.

But this bill contains other features, still more alarming and dangerous. It dispenses with the trial by jury: it violates the judicial system; it confounds legislative, executive, and judicial powers; it punishes without trial; and it bestows upon the President despotic power over a numerous class of men. Are such measures consistent with our constitutional principles? And will an accumulation of power so extensive in the hands of the executive, over aliens, secure to natives the blessings of republican liberty?

If measures can mould governments, and if an uncontrolled power of construction is surrendered to those who administer them, their progress may be easily foreseen and their end easily foretold. A lover of monarchy, who opens the treasures of corruption, by distributing emolument among devoted partisans, may at the same time be approaching his object, and deluding the people with professions of republicanism. He may confound monarchy and republicanism, by the art of definition. He may varnish over the dexterity which ambition never fails to display, with the pliancy of language, the seduction of expediency, or the prejudices of the times. And he may come at length to avow that so extensive a territory as that of the United States can only be governed by the energies of monarchy; that it cannot be defended, except by standing armies; and that it cannot be united, except by consolidation.

Measures have already been adopted which may lead to these consequences. They consist:

In fiscal systems and arrangements, which keep a host of commercial and wealthy individuals, embodied and obedient to the mandates of the treasury.

In armies and navies, which will, on the one hand, enlist the tendency of man to pay homage to his fellow creature who can feed or honor him; and on the other, employ the principle of fear, by punishing imaginary insurrections, under the pretext of preventive justice.

In swarms of officers, civil and military, who can inculcate political tenets tending to consolidation and monarchy, both by indulgences and severities; and can act as spies over the free exercise of human reason.

In restraining the freedom of the press, and investing the executive with legislative, executive, and judicial powers, over a numerous body of men.

And, that we may shorten the catalogue, in establishing by successive precedents such a mode of construing the Constitution as will rapidly remove every restraint upon federal power.

Let history be consulted; let the man of experience reflect; nay, let the artificers of monarchy be asked what farther materials they can need for building up their favorite system?

These are solemn, but painful truths; and yet we recommend it to you not to forget the possibility of danger from without, although danger threatens us from within. Usurpation is indeed dreadful, but against foreign invasion, if that should happen, let us rise with hearts and hands united, and repel the attack with the zeal of freemen, who will strengthen their title to examine and correct domestic measures by having defended their country against foreign aggression.

Pledged as we are, fellow-citizens, to these sacred engagements, we yet humbly and fervently implore the Almighty Disposer of events to avert from our land war and usurpation, the scourges of mankind; to permit our fields to be cultivated in peace; to instill into nations the love of friendly intercourse; to suffer our youth to be educated in virtue; and to preserve our morality from the pollution invariably incident to habits of war; to prevent the laborer and husbandman from being harassed by taxes and imposts; to remove from ambition the means of disturbing the commonwealth; to annihilate all pretexts for power afforded by war; to maintain the Constitution; and to bless our nation with tranquillity, under whose benign influence we may reach the summit of happiness and glory, to which we are destined by Nature and Nature's God.

Attest. JOHN STEWART, C. H. D.

1799, Jan. 23. Agreed to by the Senate.

H. BROOKE, C. S.

A true copy from the original deposited in the office of the General Assembly.

JOHN STEWART, Keeper of Rolls.

Answers of the several State Legislatures.

STATE OF DELAWARE.—In the House of Representatives, Feb. 1, 1799. Resolved, By the Senate and House of Representatives of the state of Delaware, in General Assembly met, that they consider the resolutions from the state of Virginia as a very unjustifiable interference with the general government and constituted authorities of the United States, and of dangerous tendency, and therefore not fit subject for the further consideration of the General Assembly.

ISAAC DAVIS, Speaker of the Senate.

STEPHEN LEWIS, Speaker of the H. of R's. Test—

JOHN FISHER, C. S.
JOHN CALDWELL, C. H. R.

STATE OF RHODE ISLAND AND PROVIDENCE PLANTATIONS.—In General Assembly, February, A. D. 1799. Certain resolutions of the Legislature of Virginia, passed on 21st of December last, being communicated to this Assembly,

1. *Resolved*, That in the opinion of this legislature, the second section of third article of the Constitution of the United States in these words, to wit: The judicial power shall extend to all cases arising under the laws of the United States, vests in the federal courts, exclusively, and in the Supreme Court of the United States ultimately, the authority of deciding on the constitutionality of any act or law of the Congress of the United States.

2. *Resolved*, That for any state legislature to assume that authority, would be,

1st. Blending together legislative and judicial powers.

2d. Hazarding an interruption of the peace of the states by civil discord, in case of a diversity of opinions among the state legislatures; each state having, in that case, no resort for vindicating its own opinions, but to the strength of its own arm.

3d. Submitting most important questions of law to less competent tribunals; and

4th. An infraction of the Constitution of the United States, expressed in plain terms.

3. *Resolved*, That although for the above reasons this legislature, in their public capacity, do not feel themselves authorized to consider and decide on the constitutionality of the sedition and alien laws (so called); yet they are called upon by the exigency of this occasion, to declare, that in their private opinions these laws are within the powers delegated to Congress, and promotive of the welfare of the United States.

4. *Resolved*, That the governor communicate these resolutions to the supreme executive of the state of Virginia, and at the same time express to him that this legislature cannot contemplate, without extreme concern and regret, the many evil and fatal consequences which may flow from the very unwarrantable resolutions aforesaid, of the legislature of Virginia, passed on the twenty-first day of December last.

A true copy. SAMUEL EDDY, Sec.

COMMONWEALTH OF MASSACHUSETTS.—In Senate, Feb. 9, 1799. The legislature of Massachusetts having taken into serious consideration the resolutions of the State of Virginia, passed the 21st day of December last, and communicated by his excellency the governor, relative to certain supposed infractions of the Constitution of the United States, by the government thereof, and being convinced that the Federal Constitution is calculated to promote the happiness, prosperity, and safety of the people of these United States, and to maintain that union of the several states, so essential to the welfare of the whole; and being bound by solemn oath to support and defend that Constitution, feel it unnecessary to make any professions of their attachment to it, or of their firm determination to support it against every aggression, foreign or domestic.

But they deem it their duty solemnly to declare, that while they hold sacred the principle, that consent of the people is the only pure source of just and legitimate power, they cannot admit the right of the state legislatures to denounce the administration of that government to which the people themselves, by a solemn compact, have exclusively committed their national concerns: That, although a liberal and enlightened vigilance among the people is always to be cherished, yet an unreasonable jealousy of the men of their choice, and a recurrence to measures of extremity, upon groundless or trivial pretexts, have a strong tendency to destroy all rational liberty at home, and to deprive the United States of the most essential advantages in their relations abroad: That this legislature are persuaded that the decision of all cases in law and equity, arising under the Constitution of the United States, and the construction of all laws made in pursuance thereof, are exclusively vested by the people in the judicial courts of the United States.

That the people in that solemn compact, which is declared to be the supreme law of the land, have not constituted the state legislatures the judges of the acts or measures of the federal government, but have confided to them the power of proposing such amendments of the Constitution, as shall appear to them necessary to the interests, or conformable to the wishes of the people whom they represent.

That by this construction of the Constitution, an amicable and dispassionate remedy is pointed out for any evil which experience may prove to exist, and the peace and prosperity of the United States may be preserved without interruption.

But, should the respectable state of Virginia persist in the assumption of the right to declare the acts of the national government unconstitutional, and should she oppose successfully her force and will to those of the nation, the Constitution would be reduced to a mere cipher, to the form and pageantry of authority, without the energy of power. Every act of the federal government which thwarted the views or checked the ambitious projects of a particular state, or of its leading and influential members, would be the object of opposition and of remonstrance; while the people, convulsed and confused by the conflict between two hostile jurisdictions, enjoying the protection of neither, would be wearied into a submission to some bold leader, who would establish himself on the ruins of both.

The legislature of Massachusetts, although they do not themselves claim the right, nor admit the authority of any of the state governments, to decide upon the constitutionality of the acts of the federal government, still, lest their silence should be construed into disapprobation, or at best into a doubt of the constitutionality of the acts referred to by the State of Virginia; and, as the General Assembly of Virginia has called for an expression of their sentiments, do explicitly declare, that they consider the acts of Congress, commonly called "the alien and sedition acts," not only constitutional, but expedient and necessary: That the former act respects a description of persons whose rights were not particularly contemplated in the Constitution of the United States, who are entitled only to a temporary protection, while they yield a temporary allegiance; a protection which ought to be withdrawn whenever they become "dangerous to the public safety," or are found guilty of "treasonable machination" against the government: That Congress having been especially intrusted by the people with the general defence of the nation, had not only the right, but were bound to protect it against internal as well as external foes. That the United States, at the time of passing the *act concerning aliens*, were threatened with actual invasion, had been driven by the unjust and ambitious conduct of the French government into warlike preparations, expensive and burthensome, and had then, within the bosom of the country, thousands of aliens, who, we doubt not, were ready to co-operate in any external attack.

It cannot be seriously believed, that the United States should have waited till the poignard had in fact been plunged. The removal of aliens is the usual preliminary of hostility, and is justified by the invariable usages of nations. Actual hostility had unhappily long been experienced, and a formal declaration of it the government had reason daily to expect. The law, therefore, was just and salutary, and no officer could, with so much propriety, be intrusted with the execution of it, as the one in whom the Constitution has reposed the executive power of the United States.

The *sedition act*, so called, is, in the opinion of this legislature, equally defensible. The General Assembly of Virginia, in their resolve under consideration, observe, that when that state by its convention ratified the Federal Constitution, it expressly declared, "That, among other essential rights, the liberty of conscience and of the press cannot be cancelled, abridged, restrained, or modified by any authority of the United States," and from its extreme anxiety to guard these rights from every possible attack of sophistry or ambition, with other states, recommend an amendment for that purpose: which amendment was, in due time, annexed to the Constitution; but they did not surely expect that the proceedings of their state convention were to explain the amendment adopted by the Union. The words of that amendment, on this subject, are, "Congress shall make no law abridging the freedom of speech or of the press."

The act complained of is no abridgment of the freedom of either. The genuine liberty of speech and the press, is the liberty to utter and publish the truth; but the constitutional right of the citizen to utter and publish the truth, is not to be confounded with the licentiousness in speaking and writing, that is only employed in propagating falsehood and slander. This freedom of the press has been explicitly secured by most, if not all, the state constitutions; and of this provision there has been generally but one construction among enlightened men; that it is a security for the rational use and not the abuse of the press; of which the courts of law, the juries, and people will judge; this right is not infringed, but confirmed and established by the late act of Congress.

By the Constitution, the legislative, executive, and judicial departments of government are ordained and established; and general enumerated powers vested in them respectively, including those which are prohibited to the several states. Certain powers are granted in general terms by the people to their general government, for the purposes of their safety and protection. The government is not only empowered, but it is made their duty to repel invasions and suppress insurrections; to guaranty to the several states a republican form of government; to protect each state against invasion, and, when applied to, against domestic violence; to hear and decide all cases in law and equity, arising under the Constitution, and under any treaty or law made in pursuance thereof; and all cases of admiralty and maritime jurisdiction, and relating to the law of nations. Whenever, therefore, it becomes necessary to effect any of the objects designated, it is perfectly consonant to all just rules of construction, to infer, that the usual means and powers necessary to the attainment of that object, are also granted: But the Constitution has left no occasion to resort to implication for these powers; it has made an express grant of them, in the 8th section of the first article, which ordains, "That Congress shall have power to make all laws which shall be necessary and proper for carrying into execution the foregoing powers, and all other powers vested by the Constitution in the government of the United States or in any department or officer thereof."

This Constitution has established a Supreme Court of the United States, but has made no provisions for its protection, even against such improper conduct in its presence, as might disturb its proceedings, unless expressed in the section before recited. But as no statute has been passed on this subject, this protection is, and has been for nine years past, uniformly found in the application of the principles and usages of the common law. The same protection may unquestionably be afforded by a statute passed in virtue of the before-mentioned section, as necessary and proper, for carrying into execution the powers vested in that department. A construction of the different parts of the Constitution, perfectly just and fair, will, on analogous principles, extend protection and security against the offences in question, to the other departments of government, in discharge of their respective trusts.

The President of the United States is bound by his oath "to preserve, protect, and defend the Constitution," and it is expressly made his duty, "to take care that the laws be faithfully executed;" but this would be impracticable by any created being, if there could be no legal restraint of those scandalous misrepresentations of his measures and motives, which directly tend to rob him of the public confidence. And equally impotent would be every other public officer, if thus left to the mercy of the seditious.

It is holden to be a truth most clear, that the important trusts before enumerated cannot be discharged by the government to which they are committed, without the power to restrain seditious practices and unlawful combinations against itself, and to protect the officers thereof from abusive misrepresentations. Had the Constitution withheld this power, it would have made the government responsible for the effects without any control over the causes which naturally produce them, and would have essentially failed of answering the great ends for which the people of the United States declare, in the first clause of that instrument, that they establish the same, viz: "To form a more perfect union, establish justice, insure domestic tranquillity, provide for the common defence, promote the general warfare, and secure the blessings of liberty to ourselves and posterity."

Seditious practices and unlawful combinations against the federal government, or any officer thereof, in the performance of his duty, as well as licentiousness of speech and of the press, were punishable on the principles of common law in the courts of the United States, before the act in question was passed. This act then is an amelioration of that law in favor of the party accused, as it mitigates the punishment which that authorizes, and admits of any investigation of public men and measures which is regulated by truth. It is not intended to protect men in office, only as they are agents of the people. Its object is to afford legal security to public offices and trusts created for the safety and happiness of the people, and therefore the security derived from it is for the benefit of the people, and is their right.

The construction of the Constitution and of the existing law of the land, as well as the act complained of, the legislature of Massachusetts most deliberately and firmly believe results from a just and full view of the several parts of the Constitution: and they consider that act to be wise and necessary, as an audacious and unprincipled spirit of falsehood and abuse had been too long unremittingly exerted for the purpose of perverting public opinion, and threatened to undermine and destroy the whole fabric of government.

The legislature further declare, that in the foregoing sentiments they have expressed the general opinion of their constituents, who have not only acquiesced without complaint in those particular measures of the federal government, but have given their explicit approbation by re-electing those men who voted for the adoption of them. Nor is it apprehended, that the citizens of this state will be accused of supineness or of an indifference to their constitutional rights; for while, on the one hand, they regard with due vigilance the conduct of the government, on the other, their freedom, safety and happiness require, that they should defend that government and its constitutional measures against the open or insidious attacks of any foe, whether foreign or domestic.

And, lastly, that the legislature of Massachusetts feel a strong conviction, that the several United States are connected by a common interest which ought to render their union indissoluble, and that this state will always co-operate with its confederate states in rendering that union productive of mutual security, freedom, and happiness.

Sent down for concurrence.

SAMUEL PHILIPS, President.

In the House of Representatives, Feb. 13, 1799.

Read and concurred.

EDWARD H. ROBBINS, Speaker.

A true copy. Attest,

JOHN AVERY, Secretary.

STATE OF NEW YORK.—In Senate, March 5, 1799.—Whereas, the people of the United States have established for themselves a free and independent national government: And whereas it is essential to the existence of every government, that it have authority to defend and preserve its constitutional powers inviolate, inasmuch as every infringement thereof tends to its subversion: And whereas the judicial power extends expressly to all cases of law and equity arising under the Constitution and the laws of the United States whereby the interference of the legislatures of the particular states in those cases is manifestly excluded: And whereas our peace, prosperity, and happiness, eminently depend on the preservation of the Union, in order to which, a reasonable confidence in the constituted authorities and chosen representatives of the people is indispensable: And whereas every measure calculated to weaken that confidence has a tendency to destroy the usefulness of our public functionaries, and to excite jealousies equally hostile to rational liberty, and the principles of a good republican government: And whereas the Senate, not perceiving that the rights of the particular states have been violated, nor any unconstitutional powers assumed by the general government, cannot forbear to express the anxiety and regret with which they observe the inflammatory and pernicious sentiments and doctrines which are contained in the resolutions of the legislatures of Virginia and Kentucky—sentiments and doctrines, no less repugnant to the Constitution of the United States, and the principles of their union, than destructive to the Federal government and unjust to those whom the people have elected to administer it: wherefore, *Resolved*, That while the Senate feel themselves constrained to bear unequivocal testimony against such sentiments and doctrines, they deem it a duty no less indispensable, explicitly to declare their incompetency, as a branch of the legislature of this state, to supervise the acts of the general government.

Resolved, That his Excellency, the Governor, be, and he is hereby requested to transmit a copy of the foregoing resolution to the executives of the states of Virginia and Kentucky, to the end that the same may be communicated to the legislatures thereof.

A true copy.

ABM. B. BAUCKER, Clerk.

STATE OF CONNECTICUT.—At a General Assembly of the state of Connecticut, holden at Hartford, in the said state, on the second Thursday of May, Anno Domini 1799, his excellency the governor having communicated to this assembly sundry resolutions of the legislature of Virginia, adopted in December, 1798, which relate to the measures of the general government; and the said resolutions having been considered, it is

Resolved, That this Assembly views with deep regret, and explicitly disavows, the principles contained in the aforesaid resolutions; and particularly the opposition to the "Alien and Sedition Acts"—acts which the Constitution authorized; which the exigency of the country rendered necessary; which the constituted authorities have enacted, and which merit the entire approbation of this Assembly. They, therefore, decidedly refuse to concur with the legislature of Virginia, in promoting any of the objects attempted in the aforesaid resolutions.

And it is further resolved, That his excellency the governor be requested to transmit a copy of the foregoing resolution to the governor of Virginia, that it may be communicated to the legislature of that state.

Passed in the House of Representatives unanimously.

Attest, JOHN C. SMITH, Clerk.

Concurred, unanimously, in the upper House.

Teste, SAM. WYLLYS, Sec'y.

STATE OF NEW HAMPSHIRE.—In the House of Representatives, June 14, 1799.—The committee to take into consideration the resolutions of the General Assembly of Virginia, dated December 21, 1798; also certain resolutions of the legislature of Kentucky, of the 10th of November, 1798; report as follows:—

The legislature of New Hampshire, having taken into consideration certain resolutions of the General Assembly of Virginia, dated December 21, 1798; also certain resolutions of the legislature of Kentucky, of the 10th of November, 1798,—

Resolved, That the legislature of New Hampshire unequivocally express a firm resolution to maintain and defend the Constitution of the United States, and the constitution of this state, against every aggression, either foreign or domestic, and that they will support the government of the United States in all measures warranted by the former.

That the state legislatures are not the proper tribunals to determine the constitutionality of the laws of the general government; that the duty of such decision is properly and exclusively confided to the judicial department.

That if the legislature of New Hampshire, for mere speculative purposes, were to express an opinion on the acts of the general government, commonly called "the Alien and Sedition Bills," that opinion would unreservedly be, that those acts are constitutional and, in the present critical situation of our country, highly expedient.

That the constitutionality and expediency of the acts aforesaid have been very ably advocated and clearly demonstrated by many citizens of the United States, more especially by the minority of the General Assembly of Virginia. The legislature of New Hampshire, therefore, deem it unnecessary, by any train of arguments, to attempt further illustration of the propositions, the truth of which, it is confidently believed, at this day, is very generally seen and acknowledged.

Which report, being read and considered, was unanimously received and accepted, one hundred and thirty-seven members being present.

Sent up for concurrence.

JOHN PRENTICE, Speaker.

In Senate, same day, read and concurred in unanimously.

AMOS SHEPARD, President.

Approved June 15, 1799.

J. T. GILMAN, Governor.

A true copy.

Attest, JOSEPH PEARSON, Sec'y.

STATE OF VERMONT.—In the House of Representatives, October 30, A. D. 1799.—The House proceeded to take under their consideration the resolutions of the General Assembly of Virginia, relative to certain measures of the general government, transmitted to the legislature of this state for their consideration; whereupon,

Resolved, that the General Assembly of the state of Vermont do highly disapprove of the resolutions of the General Assembly of the state of Virginia, as being unconstitutional in their nature and dangerous in their tendency. It belongs not to state legislatures to decide on the constitutionality of the laws made by the general government; this power being exclusively vested in judiciary courts of the Union.

That his excellency the governor be requested to transmit a copy of this resolution to the executive of Virginia, to be communicated to the General Assembly of that state; and that the same be sent to the Governor and Council for their concurrence.

SAMUEL C. CRAFTS, Clerk.

In Council, October 30, 1799.—Read and concurred in unanimously.

RICHARD WHITNEY, Sec'y.

Resolutions of 1798 and 1799.

(The original draught prepared by Thomas Jefferson.)

The following resolutions passed the House of Representatives of Kentucky, Nov. 10, 1798. On the passage of the first resolution, one dissentient; 2d, 3d, 4th, 5th, 6th, 7th, 8th, two dissentients; 9th, three dissentients.

1. *Resolved*, That the several states composing the United States of America, are not united on the principle of unlimited submission to their general government;

but that by compact under the style and title of a Constitution for the United States, and of amendments thereto, they constituted a general government for special purposes, delegated to that government certain definite powers, reserving, each state to itself, the residuary mass of right to their own self-government: and, that whensoever the general government assumes undelegated powers, its acts are unauthoritative, void, and of no force; that to this compact each state acceded as a state, and is an integral party; that this government, created by this compact, was not made the exclusive or final judge of the extent of the powers delegated to itself; since that would have made its discretion, and not the Constitution, the measure of its powers; but, that as in all other cases of compact among parties having no common judge, each party has an equal right to judge for itself, as well of infractions as of the mode and measure of redress.

2. *Resolved,* That the Constitution of the United States having delegated to Congress a power to punish treason, counterfeiting the securities and current coin of the United States, piracies and felonies committed on the high seas, and offences against the laws of nations, and no other crimes whatever; and it being true, as a general principle, and one of the amendments to the Constitution having also declared, "that the powers not delegated to the United States by the Constitution, nor prohibited by it to the states, are reserved to the states respectively, or to the people," therefore also the same act of Congress, passed on the 14th day of July, 1798, and entitled "An act in addition to the act entitled An act for the punishment of certain crimes against the United States;" as also the act passed by them on the 27th day of June, 1798, entitled "An act to punish frauds committed on the Bank of the United States," (and all other their acts which assume to create, define, or punish crimes other than those enumerated in the Constitution), are altogether void and of no force, and that the power to create, define, and punish such other crimes is reserved, and of right appertains solely and exclusively to the respective states, each within its own territory.

3. *Resolved,* That it is true, as a general principle, and is also expressly declared by one of the amendments to the Constitution, that "the powers not delegated to the United States by the Constitution, nor prohibited by it to the states, are reserved to the states respectively, or to the people;" and that no power over the freedom of religion, freedom of speech, or freedom of the press being delegated to the United States by the Constitution, nor prohibited by it to the states, all lawful powers respecting the same did of right remain, and were reserved to the states or to the people; that thus was manifested their determination to retain to themselves the right of judging how far the licentiousness of speech and of the press may be abridged without lessening their useful freedom, and how far those abuses which cannot be separated from their use should be tolerated rather than the use be destroyed; and thus also they guarded against all abridgment by the United States, of the freedom of religious principles and exercises, and retained to themselves the right of protecting the same, as this, stated by a law passed on the general demand of its citizens, had already protected them from all human restraint or interference: and that, in addition to this general principle and express declaration, another and more special provision has been made by one of the amendments to the Constitution, which expressly declares, that "Congress shall make no laws respecting an establishment of religion, or prohibiting the free exercise thereof, or abridging the freedom of speech, or of the press," thereby guarding in the same sentence, and under the same words, the freedom of religion, of speech, and of the press, insomuch that whatever violates either, throws down the sanctuary which covers the others; and that libels, falsehood, and defamation, equally with heresy and false religion, are withheld from the cognisance of federal tribunals. That therefore the act of the Congress of the United States, passed on the 14th of July, 1798, entitled "An act in addition to the act entitled An act for the punishment of certain crimes against the United States," which does abridge the freedom of the press, is not law, but is altogether void and of no force.

4. *Resolved,* That alien friends are under the jurisdiction and protection of the laws of the state wherein they are: that no power over them has been delegated to the United States, nor prohibited to the individual states distinct from their power over citizens; and it being true, as a general principle, and one of the amendments to the Constitution having also declared, that "the powers not delegated to the United States by the Constitution, nor prohibited to the states, are reserved to the states respectively, or to the people," the act of the Congress of the United States, passed the 22d day of June, 1798, entitled "An act concerning aliens," which assumes power over alien friends not delegated by the Constitution, is not law, but is altogether void and of no force.

5. *Resolved,* That in addition to the general principle as well as the express declaration, that powers not delegated are reserved, another and more special provision inferred in the Constitution, from abundant caution has declared, "that the migra-

tion or importation of such persons as any of the states now existing shall think proper to admit, shall not be prohibited by the Congress prior to the year 1808." That this commonwealth does admit the migration of alien friends described as the subject of the said act concerning aliens; that a provision against prohibiting their migration, is a provision against all acts equivalent thereto, or it would be nugatory; that to remove them when migrated is equivalent to a prohibition of their migration, and is, therefore, contrary to the said provision of the Constitution, and void.

6. *Resolved*, That the imprisonment of a person under the protection of the laws of this commonwealth on his failure to obey the simple order of the President to depart out of the United States, as is undertaken by the said act, entitled, "An act concerning aliens," is contrary to the Constitution, one amendment in which has provided, that "no person shall be deprived of liberty without due process of law," and, that another having provided, "that in all criminal prosecutions, the accused shall enjoy the right to a public trial by an impartial jury, to be informed as to the nature and cause of the accusation, to be confronted with the witnesses against him, to have compulsory process for obtaining witnesses in his favor, and to have assistance of counsel for his defence," the same act undertaking to authorize the President to remove a person out of the United States who is under the protection of the law, on his own suspicion, without jury, without public trial, without confrontation of the witnesses against him, without having witnesses in his favor, without defence, without counsel, is contrary to these provisions also of the Constitution, is therefore not law, but utterly void and of no force.

That transferring the power of judging any person who is under the protection of the laws, from the courts to the President of the United States, as is undertaken by the same act concerning aliens, is against the article of the Constitution which provides, that "the judicial power of the United States shall be vested in the courts, the judges of which shall hold their office during good behavior," and that the said act is void for that reason also; and it is further to be noted that this transfer of judiciary power is to that magistrate of the general government who already possesses all the executive, and a qualified negative in all the legislative powers.

7. *Resolved*, That the construction applied by the general government (as is evident by sundry of their proceedings) to those parts of the Constitution of the United States which delegate to Congress power to lay and collect taxes, duties, imposts, excises; to pay the debts, and provide for the common defence and general welfare of the United States, and to make all laws which shall be necessary and proper for carrying into execution the powers vested by the Constitution in the government of the United States, or any department thereof, goes to the destruction of all the limits prescribed to their power by the Constitution: That words meant by that instrument to be subsidiary only to the execution of the limited powers, ought not to be so construed as themselves to give unlimited powers, nor a part so to be taken as to destroy the whole residue of the instrument: That the proceedings of the general government under color of those articles, will be a fit and necessary subject for revisal and correction at a time of greater tranquillity, while those specified in the preceding resolutions call for immediate redress.

8. *Resolved*, That the preceding resolutions be transmitted to the Senators and Representatives in Congress from this commonwealth, who are enjoined to present the same to their respective Houses, and to use their best endeavors to procure at the next session of Congress a repeal of the aforesaid unconstitutional and obnoxious acts.

9. *Resolved lastly*, That the governor of this commonwealth be, and is hereby authorized and requested to communicate the preceding resolutions to the legislatures of the several states, to assure them that this commonwealth considers union for special national purposes, and particularly for those specified in their late federal compact, to be friendly to the peace, happiness, and prosperity of all the states—that, faithful to that compact, according to the plain intent and meaning in which it was understood and acceded to by the several parties, it is sincerely anxious for its preservation; that it does also believe, that to take from the states all the powers of self-government, and transfer them to a general and consolidated government, without regard to the special delegations and reservations solemnly agreed to in that compact, is not for the peace, happiness, or prosperity of these states; and that, therefore, this commonwealth is determined, as it doubts not its co-states are, to submit to undelegated and consequently unlimited powers in no man, or body of men on earth: that if the acts before specified should stand, these conclusions would flow from them; that the general government may place any act they think proper on the list of crimes and punish it themselves, whether enumerated or not enumerated by the Constitution as cognisable by them; that they may transfer its cognisance to the President or any other person, who may himself be the accuser, counsel, judge, and jury, whose suspicions may be the evidence, his order the sentence, his officer the executioner, and

his breast the sole record of the transaction; that a very numerous and valuable description of the inhabitants of these states, being by this precedent reduced as outlaws to the absolute dominion of one man and the barriers of the Constitution thus swept from us all, no rampart now remains against the passions and the power of a majority of Congress, to protect from a like exportation or other grievous punishment the minority of the same body, the legislatures, judges, governors, and counsellors of the states, nor their other peaceable inhabitants who may venture to reclaim the constitutional rights and liberties of the states and people, or who, for other causes, good or bad, may be obnoxious to the view or marked by the suspicions of the President, or to be thought dangerous to his or their elections or other interests, public or personal; that the friendless alien has been selected as the safest subject of a first experiment; but the citizen will soon follow, or rather has already followed; for, already has a sedition act marked him as a prey: that these and successive acts of the same character, unless arrested on the threshold, may tend to drive these states into revolution and blood, and will furnish new calumnies against republican governments, and new pretexts for those who wish it to be believed, that man cannot be governed but by a rod of iron; that it would be a dangerous delusion were a confidence in the men of our choice to silence our fears for the safety of our rights; that confidence is everywhere the parent of despotism; free government is found in jealousy and not in confidence; it is jealousy and not confidence which prescribes limited constitutions to bind down those whom we are obliged to trust with power; that our Constitution has accordingly fixed the limits to which, and no farther, our confidence may go; and let the honest advocate of confidence read the alien and sedition acts, and say if the Constitution has not been wise in fixing limits to the government it created, and whether we should be wise in destroying those limits? Let him say what the government is, if it be not a tyranny, which the men of our choice have conferred on the President, and the President of our choice has assented to and accepted over the friendly strangers, to whom the mild spirit of our country and its laws had pledged hospitality and protection; that the men of our choice have more respected the bare suspicions of the President than the solid rights of innocence, the claims of justification, the sacred force of truth, and the forms and substance of law and justice. In questions of power, then, let no more be said of confidence in man, but bind him down from mischief by the chains of the Constitution. That this Commonwealth does therefore call on its co-states for an expression of their sentiments on the acts concerning aliens, and for the punishment of certain crimes hereinbefore specified, plainly declaring whether these acts are or are not authorized by the federal compact. And it doubts not that their sense will be so announced as to prove their attachment to limited government, whether general or particular, and that the rights and liberties of their co-states will be exposed to no dangers by remaining embarked on a common bottom with their own: but they will concur with this commonwealth in considering the said acts as so palpably against the Constitution as to amount to an undisguised declaration, that the compact is not meant to be the measure of the powers of the general government, but that it will proceed in the exercise over these states of all powers whatsoever. That they will view this as seizing the rights of the states and consolidating them in the hands of the general government, with a power assumed to bind the states (not merely in cases made federal) but in all cases whatsoever, by laws made, not with their consent, but by others against their consent; that this would be to surrender the form of government we have chosen, and live under one deriving its powers from its own will, and not from our authority; and that the co-states recurring to their natural rights in cases not made federal, will concur in declaring these void and of no force, and will each unite with this Commonwealth in requesting their repeal at the next session of Congress.

EDMUND BULLOCK, S. H. R.
JOHN CAMPBELL, S. P. T.

Passed the House of Representatives, Nov. 10, 1798.

Attest, THOS. TODD, C. H. R.

In Senate, Nov. 13, 1798.—Unanimously concurred in.

Attest, B. THURSTON, C. S.

Approved, Nov. 19, 1798.
JAS. GARRARD, Gov. of Ky.

By the Governor,
HARRY TOULMIN, Sec. of State.

House of Representatives, Thursday, Nov. 14, 1799.

The House, according to the standing order of the day, resolved itself into a committee of the whole House, on the state of the commonwealth, Mr. Desha in the chair; and after some time spent therein, the speaker resumed the chair, and Mr. Desha reported that the committee had taken under consideration sundry resolutions passed by several state legislatures, on the subject of the alien and sedition laws, and had come to a resolution thereupon, which he delivered in at the clerk's table, where it was read and *unanimously* agreed to by the House, as follows:—

The representatives of the good people of this commonwealth, in General Assembly convened, having maturely considered the answers of sundry states in the Union, to their resolutions passed the last session, respecting certain unconstitutional laws of Congress, commonly called the alien and sedition laws, would be faithless, indeed, to themselves and to those they represent, were they silently to acquiesce in the principles and doctrines attempted to be maintained in all those answers, that of Virginia only excepted. To again enter the field of argument, and attempt more fully or forcibly to expose the unconstitutionality of those obnoxious laws, would, it is apprehended, be as unnecessary as unavailing. We cannot, however, but lament that, in the discussion of those interesting subjects by sundry of the legislatures of our sister states, unfounded suggestions and uncandid insinuations, derogatory to the true character and principles of this commonwealth, have been substituted in place of fair reasoning and sound argument. Our opinions of these alarming measures of the general government, together with our reasons for those opinions, were detailed with decency and with temper, and submitted to the discussion and judgment of our fellow-citizens throughout the Union. Whether the like decency and temper have been observed in the answers of most of those states who have denied or attempted to obviate the great truths contained in those resolutions, we have now only to submit to a candid world. Faithful to the true principles of the Federal Union, unconscious of any designs to disturb the harmony of that Union, and anxious only to escape the fangs of despotism, the good people of this commonwealth are regardless of censure or calumniation. Lest, however, the silence of this commonwealth should be construed into an acquiescence in the doctrines and principles advanced and attempted to be maintained by the said answers, or lest those of our fellow-citizens throughout the Union who so widely differ from us on those important subjects, should be deluded by the expectation, that we shall be deterred from what we conceive our duty, or shrink from the principles contained in those resolutions—therefore,

Resolved, That this commonwealth considers the Federal Union, upon the terms and for the purposes specified in the late compact, as conducive to the liberty and happiness of the several states: That it does now unequivocally declare its attachment to the Union, and to that compact, agreeably to its obvious and real intention, and will be among the last to seek its dissolution: That if those who administer the general government be permitted to transgress the limits fixed by that compact, by a total disregard to the special delegations of power therein contained, an annihilation of the state governments, and the creation upon their ruins of a general consolidated government, will be the inevitable consequence: That the principle and construction contended for by sundry of the state legislatures, that the general government is the exclusive judge of the extent of the powers delegated to it, stop nothing short of despotism—since the discretion of those who administer the government, and not the Constitution, would be the measure of their powers: That the several states who formed that instrument being sovereign and independent, have the unquestionable right to judge of the infraction; and that a nullification by those sovereignties of all unauthorized acts done under color of that instrument is the rightful remedy: That this commonwealth does, under the most deliberate reconsideration, declare that the said alien and sedition laws are, in their opinion, palpable violations of the said Constitution; and, however cheerfully it may be disposed to surrender its opinion to a majority of its sister states, in matters of ordinary or doubtful policy, yet in momentous regulations like the present, which so vitally wound the best rights of the citizen, it would consider a silent acquiescence as highly criminal: That although this commonwealth, as a party to the federal compact, will bow to the laws of the Union, yet it does, at the same time, declare that it will not now, or ever hereafter, cease to oppose in a constitutional manner every attempt, at what quarter soever offered, to violate that compact. And, finally, in order that no pretext or arguments may be drawn from a supposed acquiescence on the part of this commonwealth in the constitutionality of those laws, and be thereby used as precedents for similar future violations of the federal compact—this commonwealth does now enter against them its solemn protest.

Extract, &c. Attest. T. TODD, C. H. R.

In Senate, Nov. 22, 1799—Read and concurred in.

Attest, B. THURSTON, C. S.

Washington's Farewell Address to the People of the United States, Sept. 17, 1796.

Accepted as a Platform for the People of the Nation, regardless of party.

FRIENDS AND FELLOW-CITIZENS:—

The period for a new election of a citizen to administer the executive government of the United States being not far distant, and the time actually arrived when your thoughts must be employed in designating the person who is to be clothed with that important trust, it appears to me proper, especially as it may conduce to a more distinct expression of the public voice, that I should now apprise you of the resolution I have formed to decline being considered among the number of those out of whom a choice is to be made. I beg you, at the same time, to do me the justice to be assured that this resolution has not been taken without a strict regard to all the considerations appertaining to the relation which binds a dutiful citizen to his country; and that in withdrawing the tender of service, which silence, in my situation, might imply, I am influenced by no diminution of zeal for your future interests; no deficiency of grateful respect of your past kindness; but am supported by a full conviction that the step is compatible with both.

The acceptance of, and continuance hitherto in, the office to which your suffrages have twice called me, have been a uniform sacrifice of inclination to the opinion of duty, and to a deference for what appeared to be your desire. I constantly hoped that it would have been much earlier in my power, consistently with motives which I was not at liberty to disregard, to return to that retirement from which I had been reluctantly drawn. The strength of my inclination to do this, previous to the last election, had even led to the preparation of an address to declare it to you; but mature reflection on the then perplexed and critical posture of our affairs with foreign nations, and the unanimous advice of persons entitled to my confidence, impelled me to abandon the idea.

I rejoice that the state of your concerns, external as well as internal, no longer renders the pursuit of inclination incompatible with the sentiment of duty or propriety; and am persuaded, whatever partiality may be retained for my services, that, in the present circumstances of our country, you will not disapprove my determination to retire.

The impressions with which I first undertook the arduous trust were explained on the proper occasion. In the discharge of this trust, I will only say, that I have with good intentions contributed towards the organization and administration of the government the best exertions of which a very fallible judgment was capable. Not unconscious in the outset of the inferiority of my qualifications, experience, in my own eyes—perhaps still more in the eyes of others—has strengthened the motives to diffidence of myself; and every day the increasing weight of years admonishes me, more and more, that the abode of retirement is as necessary to me as it will be welcome. Satisfied that if any circumstances have given peculiar value to my services, they were temporary, I have the consolation to believe that, while choice and prudence invite me to quit the political scene, patriotism does not forbid it.

In looking forward to the moment which is intended to terminate the career of my public life, my feelings do not permit me to suspend the deep acknowledgment of that debt of gratitude which I owe to my beloved country for the many honors it has conferred upon me; still more for the steadfast confidence with which it has supported me; and for the opportunities I have thence enjoyed of manifesting my inviolable attachment, by services faithful and persevering, though in usefulness unequal to my zeal. If benefits have resulted to our country from these services, let it always be remembered to your praise, and as an instructive example in our annals, that under circumstances in which the passions, agitated in every direction, were liable to mislead; amidst appearances sometimes dubious, vicissitudes of fortune often discouraging; in situations in which, not unfrequently, want of success has countenanced the spirit of criticism,—the constancy of your support was the essential prop of the efforts, and a guarantee of the plans, by which they were effected. Profoundly penetrated by this new idea, I shall carry it with me to my grave, as a strong incitement to unceasing vows, that Heaven may continue to you the choicest tokens of its beneficence; that union and brotherly affection may be perpetual; that the free Constitution, which is the work of your hands, may be sacredly maintained; that its administration, in every department, may be stamped with wisdom and virtue; that in fine, the happiness of the people of these states, under the auspices of liberty, may be made complete, by so careful a preservation and so prudent a use of this blessing as will acquire to them the glory of recommending it to the applause, the affection, and the adoption of every nation which is yet a stranger to it.

Here, perhaps, I ought to stop; but a solicitude for your welfare, which cannot end but with my life, and the apprehension of danger natural to that solicitude, urge me, on an occasion like the present, to offer to your solemn contemplation, and to recommend to your frequent review, some sentiments, which are the result of much reflection, of no inconsiderable observation, and which appear to me all-important to the permanency of your felicity as a people. These will be afforded to you with the more freedom, as you can only see in them the disinterested warning of a parting friend, who can possibly have no personal motive to bias his counsel; nor can I forget, as an encouragement to it, your indulgent reception of my sentiments on a former and not dissimilar occasion.

Interwoven as is the love of liberty with

every ligament of your hearts, no recommendation of mine is necessary to fortify or confirm the attachment.

The unity of government which constitutes you one people, is also now dear to you. It is justly so; for it is a main pillar in the edifice of your real independence—the support of your tranquillity at home, your peace abroad, of your safety, of your prosperity, of that very liberty which you so highly prize. But as it is easy to foresee that, from different causes and from different quarters, much pains will be taken, many artifices employed, to weaken in your minds the conviction of this truth: as this is the point in your political fortress against which the batteries of internal and external enemies will be most constantly and actively, (though often covertly and insidiously) directed,—it is of infinite moment that you should properly estimate the immense value of your national union to your collective and individual happiness; that you should cherish a cordial, habitual, and immovable attachment to it; accustoming yourself to think and speak of it as of the palladium of your political safety and prosperity, watching for its preservation with jealous anxiety; discountenancing whatever may suggest even a suspicion that it can, in any event, be abandoned; and indignantly frowning upon the first dawning of every attempt to alienate any portion of our country from the rest, or to enfeeble the sacred ties which now link together the various parts.

For this you have every inducement of sympathy and interest. Citizens, by birth or choice, of a common country, that country has a right to concentrate your affections. The name of *American*, which belongs to you in your national capacity, must always exalt the just pride of patriotism, more than appellations derived from local discriminations. With slight shades of difference, you have the same religion, manners, habits, and political principles. You have, in a common cause, fought and triumphed together; the independence and liberty you possess are the work of joint counsels and joint efforts, of common dangers, sufferings, and successes. But these considerations, however powerfully they address themselves to your sensibility, are generally outweighed by those which apply more immediately to your interest; here every portion of our country finds the most commanding motives for carefully guarding and preserving the union of the whole.

The North, in an unrestrained intercourse with the South, protected by the equal laws of a common government, finds, in the productions of the latter, great additional resources of maritime and commercial enterprise, and precious materials of manufacturing industry. The South, in the same intercourse benefiting by the agency of the North, sees its agriculture grow, and its commerce expanded. Turning partly into its own channels the seamen of the North, it finds its particular navigation invigorated; and while it contributes, in different ways, to nourish and increase the general mass of the national navigation, it looks forward to the protection of a maritime strength to which itself is unequally adapted. The East, in like intercourse with the West, already finds, and in the progressive improvement of interior communication, by land and by water, will more and more find, a valuable vent for the commodities which each brings from abroad or manufactures at home. The West derives from the East supplies requisite to its growth or comfort, and what is perhaps of still greater consequence, it must, of necessity, owe the secure enjoyment of indispensable outlets for its own productions, to the weight, influence, and the maritime strength of the Atlantic side of the Union, directed by an indissoluble community of interests as one nation. Any other tenure by which the West can hold this essential advantage, whether derived from its own separate strength, or from an apostate and unnatural connexion with any foreign power, must be intrinsically precarious.

While, then, every part of our country thus feels an immediate and particular interest in union, all the parts combined cannot fail to find, in the united mass of means and efforts, greater strength, greater resource, proportionably greater security from external danger, a less frequent interruption of their peace by foreign nations; and what is of inestimable value, they must derive from union an exemption from those broils and wars between themselves, which so frequently afflict neighboring countries, not tied together by the same government; which their own rivalship alone would be sufficient to produce, but which opposite foreign alliances, attachments and intrigues, would stimulate and embitter. Hence, likewise, they will avoid the necessity of those overgrown military establishments, which, under any form of government, are inauspicious to liberty, and which are to be regarded as particularly hostile to republican liberty; in this sense it is that your union ought to be considered as a main prop of your liberty, and that the love of one ought to endear to you the preservation of the other.

These considerations speak a persuasive language to every reflecting and virtuous mind, and exhibit the continuance of the Union as a primary object of patriotic desire. Is there a doubt, whether a common government can embrace so large a sphere? Let experience solve it. To listen to mere speculation, in such a case, were criminal.

We are authorized to hope, that a proper organization of the whole, with the auxiliary agency of governments for the respective subdivisions, will afford a happy issue to the experiment. It is well worth a fair and full experiment. With such powerful and obvious motives to Union, affecting all parts of our country, while experience shall not have demonstrated its impracticability, there will always be reason to distrust the patriotism of those who, in any quarter, may endeavor to weaken its bands.

In contemplating the causes which may disturb our Union, it occurs as a matter of serious concern, that any ground should have been furnished for characterizing parties by geographical discriminations—Northern and Southern—Atlantic and Western: whence designing men may endeavor to excite a belief that there is a real difference of local interests and views. One of the expedients of party to acquire influence within particular districts, is to misrepresent the opinions and aims of other districts. You cannot shield yourselves too much against the jealousies and heart-burnings which spring from these misrepresentations; they tend to render alien to each other those who ought to be bound together by paternal affection. The inhabitants of our Western country have lately had a useful lesson on this head; they have seen in the negotiation by the executive, and in the unanimous ratification by the Senate, of the treaty with Spain, and in the universal satisfaction at that event throughout the United States, decisive proof how unfounded were the suspicions propagated among them, of a policy in the general government, and in the Atlantic States, unfriendly to their interest in regard to the Mississippi—that with Great Britain, and that with Spain, which secure to them everything they could desire in respect to our foreign relations, towards confirming their prosperity. Will it not be their wisdom to rely for the preservation of these advantages on the Union by which they were procured? Will they not henceforth be deaf to those advisers, if such there are, who would sever them from their brethren, and connect them with aliens?

To the efficacy and permanency of your Union a government of the whole is indispensable. No alliance, however strict between the parties, can be an adequate substitute; they must inevitably experience the infractions and interruptions which all alliances, in all time, have experienced. Sensible of this momentous truth, you have improved upon your first essay, by the adoption of a Constitution of government, better calculated than your former for an intimate union, and for the efficacious management of your common concerns. This government, the offspring of our own choice, uninfluenced and unawed—adopted upon full investigation and mature deliberation, completely free in its principles, in the distribution of its powers—uniting security with energy, and containing within itself a provision for its own amendment, has a just claim to your confidence and your support. Respect for its authority, compliance with its laws, acquiescence in its measures, are duties enjoined by the fundamental maxims of true liberty. The basis of our political system is the right of the people to make and to alter their Constitutions of government; but the Constitution which at any time exists, till changed by an explicit and authentic act of the whole people, is sacredly obligatory upon all. The very idea of the power and right of the people to establish government, presupposes the duty of every individual to obey the established government.

All obstruction to the execution of laws, all combinations and associations under whatever plausible character, with the real design to direct, control, counteract, or awe the regular deliberation and action of the constituted authorities, are destructive to this fundamental principle, and of fatal tendency. They serve to organize faction, to give it an artificial and extraordinary force, to put in the place of the delegated will of the nation, the will of a party, often a small but artful and enterprising minority of the community; and, according to the alternate triumphs of different parties, to make the public administration the mirror of the ill-concerted and incongruous projects of fashion, rather than the organ of consistent and wholesome plans, digested by common counsels and modified by mutual interests.

However combinations or associations of the above description may now and then answer popular ends, they are likely, in the course of time and things, to become potent engines, by which cunning, ambitious, and unprincipled men will be enabled to subvert the power of the people, and to usurp for themselves the reins of government; destroying, afterwards, the very engines which had lifted them to unjust dominion.

Towards the preservation of your government, and the permanency of your present happy state, it is requisite, not only that you steadily discountenance irregular oppositions to its acknowledged authority, but also that you resist with care the spirit of innovation upon its principles, however specious the pretexts. One method of assault may be to effect, in the forms of the Constitution, alterations which will impair the energy of the system, and thus to undermine what cannot be directly overthrown. In all the changes to which you may be invited, remember that time and habit are at least as necessary to fix the true character of governments as of other human institutions; that experience is the surest standard by which to test the real tendency of the existing constitution of a country; that facility in changes, upon the credit of mere hypothesis and opinion, exposes to perpetual change, from the endless variety of hypothesis and opinion; and remember, especially, that for the efficient management of your common interests, in a country so extensive as ours, a government of as much vigor as is consistent with the perfect security of liberty is indispensable. Liberty itself will find in such a government, with powers properly distributed and adjusted, its surest guardian. It is, indeed, little else than a name, where the government is too feeble to withstand the enterprise of faction, to confine each member of the society within the limits described by the laws, and to maintain all in the secure and tranquil enjoyment of the rights of person and property.

I have already intimated to you the danger of parties in the state, with particular reference to the founding of them on geographical discriminations. Let me now take a more comprehensive view, and warn you, in the most solemn manner, against the baneful effects of the spirit of party generally.

This spirit, unfortunately, is inseparable from our nature, having its root in the strongest passions of the human mind. It exists under different shapes in all governments, more or less stifled, controlled, or repressed; but in those of the popular form it is seen in its greatest rankness, and is truly their worst enemy.

The alternate domination of one faction over another, sharpened by the spirit of revenge, natural to party dissensions, which, in different ages and countries, has perpetrated the most horrid enormities, is itself a frightful despotism. But this leads, at length, to a more formal and permanent despotism. The disorders and miseries which result, gradually incline the minds of men to seek security and repose in the absolute power of an individual: and sooner or later, the chief of some prevailing faction, more able or more fortunate than his competitors, turns this disposition to the purposes of his own elevation on the ruins of public liberty.

Without looking forward to an extremity of this kind (which, nevertheless, ought not to be entirely out of sight), the common and continual mischiefs of the spirit of party are sufficient to make it the interest and duty of a wise people to discourage and restrain it.

It serves always to distract the public councils, and enfeeble the public administration. It agitates the community with ill-founded jealousies and false alarms; kindles the animosity of one part against another; foments, occasionally, riot and insurrection. It opens the door to foreign influence and corruption, which find a facilitated access to the government itself, through the channels of party passions. Thus the policy and the will of one country are subjected to the policy and will of another.

There is an opinion that parties in free countries, are useful checks upon the administration of the government, and serve to keep alive the spirit of liberty. This, within certain limits, is probably true; and in governments of a monarchical cast, patriotism may look with indulgence, if not with favor, upon the spirit of party. But in those of the popular character, in governments purely elective, it is a spirit not to be encouraged. From their natural tendency, it is certain there will always be enough of that spirit for every salutary purpose. And there being constant danger of excess, the effort ought to be, by force of public opinion, to mitigate and assuage it. A fire not to be quenched, it demands a uniform vigilance to prevent its bursting into a flame, lest, instead of warming, it should consume.

It is important, likewise, that the habits of thinking, in a free country, should inspire caution in those intrusted with its administration, to confine themselves within their respective constitutional spheres, avoiding, in the exercise of the powers of one department, to encroach upon another. The spirit of encroachment tends to consolidate the powers of all the departments in one, and thus to create, whatever the form of government, a real despotism. A just estimate of that love of power, and proneness to abuse it, which predominates in the human heart, is sufficient to satisfy us of the truth of this position.

The necessity of reciprocal checks in the exercise of political power, by dividing and distributing it into different depositories, and constituting each the guardian of the public weal, against invasions by the others, has been evinced by experiments, ancient and modern; some of them in our own country, and under our own eyes. To preserve them must be as necessary as to institute them. If, in the opinion of the people, the distribution or modification of the constitutional powers be, in any particular, wrong, let it be corrected by an amendment in the way which the Constitution designates. But let there be no change by usurpation; for though this, in one instance, may be the instrument of good, it is the customary weapon by which free governments are destroyed. The precedent must always greatly overbalance, in permanent evil, any partial or transient benefit which the use can at any time yield.

Of all the dispositions and habits which lead to political prosperity, religion and morality are indispensable supports. In vain would that man claim the tribute of patriotism, who should labor to subvert these great pillars of human happiness, these firmest props of the duties of men and citizens. The mere politician, equally with the pious man, ought to respect and cherish them. A volume could not trace all their connexions with private and public felicity. Let it simply be asked, where is the security for property, for reputation, for life, if the sense of religious obligation desert the oaths which are the instruments of investigation in courts of justice? And let us with caution indulge the supposition, that morality can be maintained without religion. Whatever may be conceded to the influence of refined education on minds of peculiar structure, reason and experience both forbid us to expect that national morality can prevail in exclusion of religious principles. It is substantially true, that virtue or morality is a necessary spring of popular government. The rule, indeed, extends with more or less force to every species of free government. Who, that is a sincere friend to it, can look with indifference upon attempts to shake the foundation of the fabric?

Promote then, as an object of primary importance, institutions for the general diffusion of knowledge. In proportion as the structure of a government gives force to public opinion, it is essential that public opinion should be enlightened.

As a very important source of strength and security, cherish public credit. One method of preserving it is to use it as sparingly as possible, avoiding occasions of expense by cultivating peace, but remembering also that timely disbursements to prepare for danger frequently prevent much greater disbursements to repel it; avoiding, likewise, the accumulation of debt, not only by shunning occasions of expense, but by vigorous exertions in time of peace to discharge the debts which unavoidable wars may have occasioned; not ungenerously throwing upon posterity the burden which we ourselves ought to bear. The execution of these maxims belongs to your representatives, but it is necessary that public opinion should co-operate. To facilitate to them the performance of their duty, it is essential that you should practically bear in mind, that toward the payments of debts there must be revenues; that to have revenue there must be taxes; that no taxes can be devised, which are not more or less inconvenient and unpleasant; that the intrinsic embarrassment inseparable from the selection of the proper objects (which is always a choice of difficulties) ought to be a decisive moment for a candid construction of the conduct of the government in making it, and for a spirit of acquiescence in the measure for obtaining revenue, which the public exigencies may at any time dictate.

Observe good faith and justice towards all nations; cultivate peace and harmony with all; religion and morality enjoin this conduct; and can it be that good policy does not equally enjoin it? It will be worthy of a free, enlightened, and at no distant period a great nation, to give to mankind the magnanimous and too novel example of a people always guided by an exalted justice and benevolence. Who can doubt that, in the course of time and things, the fruits of such a plan would richly repay any temporary advantages which might be lost by a steady adherence to it? Can it be that Providence has not connected the permanent felicity of a nation with its virtue? The experiment, at least, is recommended by every sentiment which ennobles human nature. Alas! is it rendered impossible by its vices?

In the execution of such a plan, nothing is more essential than that permanent, inveterate antipathies against particular nations, and passionate attachment for others, should be excluded: and that in place of them, just and amicable feelings towards all should be cultivated. The nation which indulges towards another an habitual hatred, or an habitual fondness, is, in some degree, a slave. It is a slave to its animosity or to its affection; either of which is sufficient to lead it astray from its duty and its interest. Antipathy in one nation against another, disposes each more readily to offer insult and injury, to lay hold of slight causes of umbrage, and to be haughty and untractable, when accidental or trifling occasions of dispute occur. Hence frequent collisions, obstinate, envenomed, and bloody contests. The nation, prompted by ill-will and resentment, sometimes impels to war the government, contrary to the best calculations of policy. The government sometimes participates in the national propensity, and adopts, through passion, what reason would reject; at other times it makes the animosity of the nation subservient to projects of hostility, instigated by pride, ambition, and other sinister and pernicious motives. The peace often, sometimes perhaps the liberty, of nations has been the victim.

So likewise a passionate attachment of one nation to another produces a variety of evils. Sympathy for the favorite nation, facilitating the illusion of an imaginary common interest, in cases where no real common interest exists, and infusing into one the enmities of the other, betrays the former into a participation in the quarrels and wars of the latter, without adequate inducement or justification. It leads also to concessions to the favorite nation of privileges denied to others, which is apt doubly to injure the nation making the concessions; by unnecessarily parting with what ought to have been retained, and by exciting jealousy, ill-will, and a disposition to retaliate, in the parties from whom equal privileges are withheld; and it gives to ambitious, corrupted, or deluded citizens (who devote themselves to the favorite nation) facility to betray, or sacrifice the interest of their own country, without odium; sometimes even with popularity; gilding with the appearance of a virtuous sense of obligation, a commendable deference for public opinion, or a laudable zeal for public good, the base or foolish compliances of ambition, corruption, or infatuation.

As avenues to foreign influence in innumerable ways, such attachments are particularly alarming to the truly enlightened and independent patriot. How many opportunities do they afford to tamper with domestic factions, to practice the art of seduction, to mislead public opinion, to influence or awe the public councils? Such an attachment of a small or weak, towards a great and powerful nation, dooms the former to be the satellite of the latter.

Against the insidious wiles of foreign influence (I conjure you to believe me, fellow-citizens), the jealousy of a free people ought to be constantly awake; since history and experience prove that foreign influence is one of the most baneful foes of republican government. But that jealousy, to be useful, must be impartial; else it becomes the instrument of the very influence to be avoided, instead of a defence against it. Excessive partiality for one foreign nation, and excessive dislike for another, cause those whom they actuate to see danger only on one side, and serve to veil, and even second, the arts of influence on the other. Real patriots, who may resist the intrigues of the favorite, are liable to become suspected and odious; while its tools and dupes usurp the applause and confidence of the people, to surrender their interests.

The great rule of conduct for us, in regard to foreign nations, is, in extending our commercial relations, to have with them as little political connexion as possible. So far as we have already formed engagements, let them be fulfilled with perfect good faith. There let us stop.

Europe has a set of primary interests, which to us have none, or a very remote relation. Hence she must be engaged in frequent controversies, the causes of which are essentially foreign to our concerns. Hence, therefore, it must be unwise in us to implicate ourselves, by artificial ties, in the ordinary vicissitudes of her politics, or the ordinary combinations and collisions of her friendships or enmities.

Our detached and distant situation invites and enables us to pursue a different course. If we remain one people under an efficient government, the period is not far off when we may defy material injury from external annoyance; when we may take such an attitude as will cause the neutrality we may at any time resolve upon, to be scrupulously respected; when belligerent nations, under the impossibility of making acquisitions upon us, will not lightly hazard the giving us provocation; when we may choose peace or war, as our interests, guided by justice, shall counsel.

Why forego the advantages of so peculiar a situation? Why quit our own to stand upon foreign ground? Why, by interweaving our destiny with that of any part of Europe, entangle our peace and prosperity in the toils of European ambition, rivalship, interest, humor, or caprice?

It is our true policy to steer clear of permanent alliances with any portion of the foreign world; so far, I mean, as we are now at liberty to do it; for let me not be understood as capable of patronizing infidelity to existing engagements. I hold the maxim no less applicable to public than to private affairs, that honesty is always the best policy. I repeat it, therefore, let those engagements be observed in their genuine sense. But, in my opinion, it is unnecessary, and would be unwise to extend them.

Taking care always to keep ourselves, by suitable establishments, on a respectable defensive posture, we may safely trust to temporary alliances for extraordinary emergencies.

Harmony, and a liberal intercourse with all nations, are recommended by policy, humanity, and interest. But even our commercial policy should hold an equal and impartial hand; neither seeking nor granting exclusive favors or preferences; consulting the natural cause of things; diffusing and diversifying, by gentle means, the streams of commerce, by forcing nothing; establishing, with powers so disposed, in order to give trade a stable course, to define the rights of our merchants, and to enable the government to support them, conventional rules of intercourse, the best that present circumstances and mutual opinions will permit, but temporary, and liable to be, from time to time, abandoned or varied, as experience and circumstances shall dictate; constantly keeping in view, that it is folly in one nation to look for disinterested favors from another; that it must pay, with a portion of its independence, for whatever it may accept under that character; that by such acceptance it may place itself in the condition of having given equivalents for nominal favors, and yet of being reproached with ingratitude for not giving more. There can be no greater error than to expect, or calculate upon, real favors from nation to nation. It is an illusion which experience must cure, which a just pride ought to discard.

In offering to you, my countrymen, these counsels of an old and affectionate friend, I dare not hope they will make the strong and lasting impression I could wish; that they will control the usual current of the passions, or prevent our nation from running the course which has hitherto marked the destiny of nations; but if I may even flatter myself that they may be productive of some partial benefit, some occasional good; that they may now and then recur to moderate the fury of party spirit, to warn against the mischiefs of foreign intrigues, to guard against the impostures of pretended patriotism; this hope will be a full recompense for the solicitude for your welfare by which they have been dictated.

How far, in the discharge of my official duties, I have been guided by the principles which have been delineated, the public records, and other evidences of my conduct, must witness to you and the world. To myself, the assurance of my own conscience is, that I have at least believed myself to be guided by them.

In relation to the still subsisting war in Europe, my proclamation of the 23d of April, 1793, is the index to my plan. Sanctioned by your approving voice, and by that of your representatives in both Houses of Congress, the spirit of that measure has continually governed me, uninfluenced by any attempts to deter or divert me from it.

After deliberate examination, with the aid of the best lights I could obtain, I was well satisfied that our country, under all the circumstances of the case, had a right to take, and was bound in duty and interest to take a neutral position. Having taken it, I determined, as far as should depend upon me, to maintain it with moderation, perseverance, and firmness.

The considerations which respect the right to hold this conduct, it is not necessary on this occasion to detail. I will only observe, that, according to my understanding of the matter, that right, so far from being denied by any of the belligerent powers, has been virtually admitted by all.

The duty of holding neutral conduct may be inferred, without anything more, from the obligation which justice and humanity impose on every nation, in cases in which it is free to act, to maintain inviolate the relations of peace and unity towards other nations.

The inducements of interests, for observing that conduct, will best be referred to your own reflections and experience. With me, a predominant motive has been to endeavor to gain time to our country to settle and mature its yet recent institutions, and to progress, without interruption, to that degree of strength and consistency which is necessary to give it, humanly speaking, the command of its own fortunes.

Though, in reviewing the incidents of my administration, I am unconscious of intentional error; I am, nevertheless, too sensible of my defects not to think it probable that I may have committed many errors. Whatever they may be, I fervently beseech the Almighty to avert or mitigate the evils to which they may tend. I shall also carry with me the hope, that my country will never come to view them with indulgence; and that, after forty-five years of my life dedicated to its service with an upright zeal, the faults of incompetent abilities will be consigned to oblivion, as myself must soon be to the mansions of rest.

Relying on its kindness in this, as in other things, and actuated by that fervent love towards it which is so natural to a man who views in it the native soil of himself and his progenitors for several generations, I anticipate, with pleasing expectation, that retreat in which I promise myself to realize, without alloy, the sweet enjoyment of partaking, in the midst of my fellow-citizens, the benign influence of good laws under a free government—the ever favorite object of my heart—and happy reward, as I trust, of our mutual cares, labors, and dangers.

George Washington.

United States, 17th of Sept., 1796.

1800.—No Federal Platform.

Republican Platform, Philadelphia.

Adopted in Congressional Caucus.

1. An inviolable preservation of the Federal constitution, according to the true sense in which it was adopted by the states, that in which it was advocated by its friends, and not that which its enemies apprehended, who, therefore, became its enemies.

2. Opposition to monarchizing its features by the forms of its administration, with a view to conciliate a transition, first, to a president and senate for life; and, secondly, to an hereditary tenure of those offices, and thus to worm out the elective principle.

3. Preservation to the states of the powers not yielded by them to the Union, and to the legislature of the Union its constitutional share in division of powers; and resistance, therefore, to existing movements for transferring all the powers of the states

to the general government, and all of those of that government to the executive branch.

4. A rigorously frugal administration of the government, and the application of all the possible savings of the public revenue to the liquidation of the public debt; and resistance, therefore, to all measures looking to a multiplication of officers and salaries, merely to create partisans and to augment the public debt, on the principle of its being a public blessing.

5. Reliance for internal defense solely upon the militia, till actual invasion, and for such a naval force only as may be sufficient to protect our coasts and harbors from depredations; and opposition, therefore, to the policy of a standing army in time of peace which may overawe the public sentiment, and to a navy, which, by its own expenses, and the wars in which it will implicate us, will grind us with public burdens and sink us under them.

6. Free commerce with all nations, political connection with none, and little or no diplomatic establishment.

7. Opposition to linking ourselves, by new treaties, with the quarrels of Europe, entering their fields of slaughter to preserve their balance, or joining in the confederacy of kings to war against the principles of liberty.

8. Freedom of religion, and opposition to all maneuvers to bring about a legal ascendency of one sect over another.

9. Freedom of speech and of the press; and opposition, therefore, to all violations of the constitution, to silence, by force, and not by reason, the complaints or criticisms, just or unjust, of our citizens against the conduct of their public agents.

10. Liberal naturalization laws, under which the well disposed of all nations who may desire to embark their fortunes with us and share with us the public burdens, may have that oppportunity, under moderate restrictions, for the development of honest intention, and severe ones to guard against the usurpation of our flag.

11 Encouragement of science and the arts in all their branches, to the end that the American people may perfect their independence of all foreign monopolies, institutions and influences.

1801–1811.—No Platforms.

(No Convention or Caucus held.)

1812.—No Republican Platform.

No Federal Platform.

Clintonian Platform.

New York, August 17.

1. Opposition to nominations of chief magistrates by congressional caucuses, as well because such practices are the exercise of undelegated authority, as of their repugnance to the freedom of elections.

2. Opposition to all customs and usages in both the executive and legislative departments which have for their object the maintenance of an official regency to prescribe tenets of political faith, the line of conduct to be deemed fidelity or recreancy to republican principles, and to perpetuate in themselves or families the offices of the Federal government.

3. Opposition to all efforts on the part of particular states to monopolize the principal offices of the government, as well because of their certainty to destroy the harmony which ought to prevail amongst all the constituent parts of the Union, as of their leanings toward a form of oligarchy entirely at variance with the theory of republican government; and, consequently, particular opposition to continuing a citizen of Virginia in the executive office another term, unless she can show that she enjoys a corresponding monopoly of talents and patriotism, after she has been honored with the presidency for twenty out of twenty-four years of our constitutional existence, and when it is obvious that the practice has arrayed the agricultural against the commercial interests of the country.

4. Opposition to continuing public men for long periods in offices of delicate trust and weighty responsibility as the reward of public services, to the detriment of all or any particular interest in, or section of, the country; and, consequently, to the continuance of Mr. Madison in an office which, in view of our pending difficulties with Great Britain, requires an incumbent of greater decision, energy and efficiency.

5. Opposition to the lingering inadequacy of preparation for the war with Great Britain, now about to ensue, and to the measure which allows uninterrupted trade with Spain and Portugal, which, as it can not be carried on under our flag, gives to Great Britain the means of supplying her armies with provisions, of which they would otherwise be destitute, and thus affording aid and comfort to our enemy.

6. Averment of the existing necessity for placing the country in a condition for aggressive action for the conquest of the British American Provinces and for the defence of our coasts and exposed frontiers: and of the propriety of such a levy of taxes as will raise the necessary funds for the emergency.

7. Advocacy of the election of De Witt Clinton as the surest method of relieving the country from all the evils existing and

prospective, for the reason that his great talents and inflexible patriotism guaranty a firm and unyielding maintenance of our national sovereignty, and the protection of those commercial interests which were flagging under the weakness and imbecility of the administration.

1815.—Resolutions passed by the Hartford Convention, January 4.

Resolved, That it be and is hereby recommended to the legislatures of the several states represented in this convention, to adopt all such measures as may be necessary effectually to protect the citizens of said states from the operation and effects of all acts which have been or may be passed by the Congress of the United States, which shall contain provisions subjecting the militia or other citizens to forcible drafts, conscriptions, or impressments not authorized by the constitution of the United States.

Resolved, That it be and is hereby recommended to the said legislatures, to authorize an immediate and an earnest application to be made to the government of the United States, requesting their consent to some arrangement whereby the said states may, separately or in concert, be empowered to assume upon themselves the defense of their territory against the enemy, and a reasonable portion of the taxes collected within said states may be paid into the respective treasuries thereof, and appropriated to the balance due said states and to the future defense of the same. The amount so paid into said treasuries to be credited, and the disbursements made as aforesaid to be charged to the United States.

Resolved, That it be and hereby is recommended to the legislatures of the aforesaid states, to pass laws where it has not already been done, authorizing the governors or commanders-in-chief of their militia to make detachments from the same, or to form voluntary corps, as shall be most convenient and conformable to their constitutions, and to cause the same to be well armed, equipped, and held in readiness for service, and upon request of the governor of either of the other states, to employ the whole of such detachment or corps, as well as the regular forces of the state, or such part thereof as may be required, and can be spared consistently with the safety of the state, in assisting the state making such request to repel any invasion thereof which shall be made or attempted by the public enemy.

Resolved, That the following amendments of the constitution of the United States be recommended to the states represented as aforesaid, to be proposed by them for adoption by the state legislatures, and in such cases as may be deemed expedient by a convention chosen by the people of each state. And it is further recommended that the said states shall persevere in their efforts to obtain such amendments, until the same shall be effected.

First. Representatives and direct taxes shall be apportioned among the several states which may be included within this Union, according to their respective numbers of free persons, including those bound to serve for a term of years, and excluding Indians not taxed, and all other persons;

Second. No new state shall be admitted into the Union by Congress, in virtue of the power granted in the constitution, without the concurrence of two-thirds of both houses;

Third. Congress shall not have power to lay an embargo on the ships or vessels of the citizens of the United States, in the ports or harbors thereof, for more than sixty days;

Fourth. Congress shall not have power, without the concurrence of two-thirds of both houses, to interdict the commercial intercourse between the United States and any foreign nation or the dependencies thereof;

Fifth. Congress shall not make nor declare war, nor authorize acts of hostility against any foreign nation, without the concurrence of two-thirds of both houses, except such acts of hostility be in defense of the territories of the United States when actually invaded;

Sixth. No person who shall hereafter be naturalized shall be eligible as a member of the Senate or House of Representatives of the United States, or capable of holding any civil office under the authority of the United States;

Seventh. The same person shall not be elected President of the United States a second time, nor shall the President be elected from the same state two terms in succession.

Resolved, That if the application of these states to the government of the United States, recommended in a foregoing resolution, should be unsuccessful, and peace should not be concluded, and the defense of these states should be neglected, as it has been since the commencement of the war, it will, in the opinion of this convention, be expedient for the legislatures of the several states to appoint delegates to another convention, to meet at Boston, in the state of Massachusetts, on the third Monday of June next, with such powers and instructions as the exigency of a crisis so momentous may require.

Resolved, That the Honorable George Cabot, the Honorable Chauncey Goodrich, the Honorable Daniel Lyman, or any two of them, be authorized to call another meeting of this convention, to be holden in Boston at any time before new delegates shall be chosen as recommended in the above resolution, if in their judgment the situation of the country shall urgently require it.

From 1813-1829.—No Platforms by either political party, except that at Hartford by Federalists, given above.

1830.—Anti-masonic resolution,

Philadelphia, September.

Resolved, That it is recommended to the people of the United States, opposed to secret societies, to meet in convention on Monday, the 26th day of September, 1831, at the city of Baltimore, by delegates equal in number to their representatives in both Houses of Congress, to make nominations of suitable candidates for the offices of President and Vice-President, to be supported at the next election, and for the transaction of such other business as the cause of Anti-Masonry may require.

1832.—National Democratic Platform, adopted at a ratification Meeting

at Washington City, May 11.

Resolved, That an adequate protection to American industry is indispensable to the prosperity of the country; and that an abandonment of the policy at this period would be attended with consequences ruinous to the best interests of the nation.

Resolved, That a uniform system of internal improvements, sustained and supported by the general government, is calculated to secure, in the highest degree, the harmony, the strength and permanency of the republic.

Resolved, That the indiscriminate removal of public officers for a mere difference of political opinion, is a gross abuse of power; and that the doctrine lately boldly preached in the United States Senate, that "to the victors belong the spoils of the vanquished," is detrimental to the interests, corrupting to the morals, and dangerous to the liberties of the country.

1836.—"Locofoco" Platform,

New York, January.

We hold these truths to be self-evident, that all men are created free and equal; that they are endowed by their Creator with certain inalienable rights, among which are life, liberty, and the pursuit of happiness; that the true foundation of republican government is the equal rights of every citizen in his person and property, and in their management; that the idea is quite unfounded that on entering into society we give up any natural right; that the rightful power of all legislation is to declare and enforce only our natural rights and duties, and to take none of them from us; that no man has the natural right to commit aggressions on the equal rights of another, and this is all from which the law ought to restrain him; that every man is under the natural duty of contributing to the necessities of society, and this all the law should enforce on him; that when the laws have declared and enforced all this, they have fulfilled their functions.

We declare unqualified hostility to bank notes and paper money as a circulating medium, because gold and silver is the only safe and constitutional currency; hostility to any and all monopolies by legislation, because they are violations of equal rights of the people; hostility to the dangerous and unconstitutional creation of vested rights or prerogatives by legislation, because they are usurpations of the people's sovereign rights; no legislative or other authority in the body politic can rightfully, by charter or otherwise, exempt any man or body of men, in any case whatever, from trial by jury and the jurisdiction or operation of the laws which govern the community.

We hold that each and every law or act of incorporation, passed by preceding legislatures, can be rightfully altered and repealed by their successors; and that they should be altered or repealed, when necessary for the public good, or when required by a majority of the people.

1836.—Whig Resolutions,

Albany, N. Y., February 3.

Resolved, That in support of our cause, we invite all citizens opposed to Martin Van Buren and the Baltimore nominees.

Resolved, That Martin Van Buren, by intriguing with the executive to obtain his influence to elect him to the presidency, has set an example dangerous to our freedom and corrupting to our free institutions.

Resolved, That the support we render to William H. Harrison is by no means given to him solely on account of his brilliant and successful services as leader of our armies during the last war, but that in him we view also the man of high intellect, the stern patriot, uncontaminated by the machinery of hackneyed politicians—a man of the school of Washington.

Resolved, That in Francis Granger we recognize one of our most distinguished fellow-citizens, whose talents we admire, whose patriotism we trust, and whose principles we sanction.

1839.—Abolition Resolution,

Warsaw, N. Y., November 13.

Resolved, That, in our judgment, every consideration of duty and expediency which ought to control the action of Christian freemen, requires of the Abolitionists of the United States to organize a distinct and independent political party, embracing all the necessary means for nominating candidates for office and sustaining them by public suffrage.

Abolition Platforms.

The first national platform of the Abolition party upon which it went into the contest in 1840, favored the abolition of slavery in the District of Columbia and Territories; the inter-state slave-trade, and a general opposition to slavery to the full extent of constitutional power.

In 1848, that portion of the party which did not support the Buffalo nominees took the ground of affirming the constitutional authority and duty of the General Government to abolish slavery in the States.

Under the head of "Buffalo," the platform of the Free Soil party, which nominated Mr. Van Buren, will be found.

1840.—Democratic Platform,

Baltimore, May 5.

Resolved, That the Federal government is one of limited powers, derived solely from the constitution, and the grants of power shown therein ought to be strictly construed by all the departments and agents of the government, and that it is inexpedient and dangerous to exercise doubtful constitutional powers.

2. *Resolved*, That the constitution does not confer upon the general government the power to commence and carry on a general system of internal improvements.

3. *Resolved*, That the constitution does not confer authority upon the Federal government, directly or indirectly, to assume the debts of the several states, contracted for local internal improvements or other state purposes; nor would such assumption be just or expedient.

4. *Resolved*, That justice and sound policy forbid the Federal government to foster one branch of industry to the detriment of another, or to cherish the interests of one portion to the injury of another portion of our common country—that every citizen and every section of the country has a right to demand and insist upon an equality of rights and privileges, and to complete and ample protection of persons and property from domestic violence or foreign aggression.

5. *Resolved*, That it is the duty of every branch of the government to enforce and practice the most rigid economy in conducting our public affairs, and that no more revenue ought to be raised than is required to defray the necessary expenses of the government.

6. *Resolved*, That Congress has no power to charter a United States bank; that we believe such an institution one of deadly hostility to the best interests of the country, dangerous to our republican institutions and the liberties of the people, and calculated to place the business of the country within the control of a concentrated money power, and above the laws and the will of the people.

7. *Resolved*, That Congress has no power under the constitution, to interfere with or control the domestic institutions of the several states; and that such states are the sole and proper judges of everything pertaining to their own affairs, not prohibited by the constitution; that all efforts, by Abolitionists or others, made to induce Congress to interfere with questions of slavery, or to take incipient steps in relation thereto, are calculated to lead to the most alarming and dangerous consequences, and that all such efforts have an inevitable tendency to diminish the happiness of the people, and endanger the stability and permanence of the Union, and ought not to be countenanced by any friend to our political institutions.

8. *Resolved*, That the separation of the moneys of the government from banking institutions is indispensable for the safety of the funds of the government and the rights of the people.

9. *Resolved*, That the liberal principles embodied by Jefferson in the Declaration of Independence, and sanctioned in the constitution, which makes ours the land of liberty and the asylum of the oppressed of every nation, have ever been cardinal principles in the democratic faith; and every attempt to abridge the present privilege of becoming citizens, and the owners of soil among us, ought to be resisted with the same spirit which swept the alien and sedition laws from our statute book.

Whereas, Several of the states which have nominated Martin Van Buren as a candidate for the presidency, have put in nomination different individuals as candidates for Vice-President, thus indicating a diversity of opinion as to the person best entitled to the nomination; and whereas, some of the said states are not represented in this convention; therefore,

Resolved, That the convention deem it

expedient at the present time not to choose between the individuals in nomination, but to leave the decision to their republican fellow-citizens in the several states, trusting that before the election shall take place, their opinions will become so concentrated as to secure the choice of a Vice-President by the electoral college.

1843.—Liberty Platform.

Buffalo, August 30.

1. *Resolved*, That human brotherhood is a cardinal principle of true democracy, as well as of pure Christianity, which spurns all inconsistent limitations; and neither the political party which repudiates it, nor the political system which is not based upon it, can be truly democratic or permanent.

2. *Resolved*, That the Liberty party, placing itself upon this broad principle, will demand the absolute and unqualified divorce of the general government from slavery, and also the restoration of equality of rights among men, in every state where the party exists, or may exist.

3. *Resolved*, That the Liberty party has not been organized for any temporary purpose by interested politicians, but has arisen from among the people in consequence of a conviction, hourly gaining ground, that no other party in the country represents the true principles of American liberty, or the true spirit of the constitution of the United States.

4. *Resolved*, That the Liberty party has not been organized merely for the overthrow of slavery; its first decided effort must, indeed, be directed against slaveholding as the grossest and most revolting manifestation of despotism, but it will also carry out the principle of equal rights into all its practical consequences and applications, and support every just measure conducive to individual and social freedom.

5. *Resolved*, That the Liberty party is not a sectional party but a national party; was not originated in a desire to accomplish a single object, but in a comprehensive regard to the great interests of the whole country; is not a new party, nor a third party, but is the party of 1776, reviving the principles of that memorable era, and striving to carry them into practical application.

6. *Resolved*, That it was understood in the times of the declaration and the constitution, that the existence of slavery in some of the states was in derogation of the principles of American liberty, and a deep stain upon the character of the country, and the implied faith of the states and the nation was pledged that slavery should never be extended beyond its then existing limits, but should be gradually, and yet, at no distant day, wholly abolished by state authority.

7. *Resolved*, That the faith of the states and the nation thus pledged, was most nobly redeemed by the voluntary abolition of slavery in several of the states, and by the adoption of the ordinance of 1787, for the government of the territory northwest of the river Ohio, then the only territory in the United States, and consequently the only territory subject in this respect to the control of Congress, by which ordinance slavery was forever excluded from the vast regions which now compose the states of Ohio, Indiana, Illinois, Michigan, and the territory of Wisconsin, and an incapacity to bear up any other than freemen was impressed on the soil itself.

8. *Resolved*, That the faith of the states and the nation thus pledged, has been shamefully violated by the omission, on the part of many of the states, to take any measures whatever for the abolition of slavery within their respective limits; by the continuance of slavery in the District of Columbia, and in the territories of Louisiana and Florida; by the legislation of Congress; by the protection afforded by national legislation and negotiation to slaveholding in American vessels, on the high seas, employed in the coastwise Slave Traffic; and by the extension of slavery far beyond its original limits, by acts of Congress admitting new slave states into the Union.

9. *Resolved*, That the fundamental truths of the Declaration of Independence, that all men are endowed by their Creator with certain inalienable rights, among which are life, liberty, and the pursuit of happiness, was made the fundamental law of our national government, by that amendment of the constitution which declares that no person shall be deprived of life, liberty, or property, without due process of law.

10. *Resolved*, That we recognize as sound the doctrine maintained by slaveholding jurists, that slavery is against natural rights, and strictly local, and that its existence and continuance rests on no other support than state legislation, and not on any authority of Congress.

11. *Resolved*, That the general government has, under the constitution, no power to establish or continue slavery anywhere, and therefore that all treaties and acts of Congress establishing, continuing or favoring slavery in the District of Columbia, in the territory of Florida, or on the high seas, are unconstitutional, and all attempts to hold men as property within the limits of exclusive national jurisdiction ought to be prohibited by law.

12. *Resolved*, That the provisions of the

constitution of the United States which confers extraordinary political powers on the owners of slaves, and thereby constituting the two hundred and fifty thousand slaveholders in the slave states a privileged aristocracy; and the provisions for the reclamation of fugitive slaves from service, are anti-republican in their character, dangerous to the liberties of the people, and ought to be abrogated.

13. *Resolved*, That the practical operation of the second of these provisions, is seen in the enactment of the act of Congress respecting persons escaping from their masters, which act, if the construction given to it by the Supreme Court of the United States in the case of Prigg *vs.* Pennsylvania be correct, nullifies the habeas corpus acts of all the states, takes away the whole legal security of personal freedom, and ought, therefore, to be immediately repealed.

14. *Resolved*, That the peculiar patronage and support hitherto extended to slavery and slaveholding, by the general government, ought to be immediately withdrawn, and the example and influence of national authority ought to be arrayed on the side of liberty and free labor.

15. *Resolved*, That the practice of the general government, which prevails in the slave states, of employing slaves upon the public works, instead of free laborers, and paying aristocratic masters, with a view to secure or reward political services, is utterly indefensible and ought to be abandoned.

16. *Resolved*, That freedom of speech and of the press, and the right of petition, and the right of trial by jury, are sacred and inviolable; and that all rules, regulations and laws, in derogation of either, are oppressive, unconstitutional, and not to be endured by a free people.

17. *Resolved*, That we regard voting, in an eminent degree, as a moral and religious duty, which, when exercised, should be by voting for those who will do all in their power for immediate emancipation.

18. *Resolved*, That this convention recommend to the friends of liberty in all those free states where any inequality of rights and privileges exists on account of color, to employ their utmost energies to remove all such remnants and effects of the slave system.

Whereas, The constitution of these United States is a series of agreements, covenants or contracts between the people of the United States, each with all, and all with each; and,

Whereas, It is a principle of universal morality, that the moral laws of the Creator are paramount to all human laws; or, in the language of an Apostle, that "we ought to obey God rather than men;" and,

Whereas, The principle of common law —that any contract, covenant, or agreement, to do an act derogatory to natural right, is vitiated and annulled by its inherent immorality—has been recognized by one of the justices of the Supreme Court of the United States, who in a recent case expressly holds that "*any* contract that rests upon such a basis is *void*;" and,

Whereas, The third clause of the second section of the fourth article of the constitution of the United States, when construed as providing for the surrender of a fugitive slave, *does* "rest upon such a basis," in that it is a contract to rob a man of a natural right—namely, his natural right to his own liberty—and is therefore absolutely *void*. Therefore,

19. *Resolved*, That we hereby give it to be distinctly understood by this nation and the world, that, as abolitionists, considering that the strength of our cause lies in its righteousness, and our hope for it in our conformity to the laws of God, and our respect for the rights of man, we owe it to the Sovereign Ruler of the Universe, as a proof of our allegiance to Him, in all our civil relations and offices, whether as private citizens, or public functionaries sworn to support the constitution of the United States, to regard and to treat the third clause of the fourth article of that instrument, whenever applied to the case of a fugitive slave, as utterly null and void, and consequently as forming no part of the constitution of the United States, whenever we are called upon or sworn to support it.

20. *Resolved*, That the power given to Congress by the constitution, to provide for calling out the militia to suppress insurrection, does not make it the duty of the government to maintain slavery by military force, much less does it make it the duty of the citizens to form a part of such military force; when freemen unsheathe the sword it should be to strike for liberty, not for despotism.

21. *Resolved*, That to preserve the peace of the citizens, and secure the blessings of freedom, the legislature of each of the free states ought to keep in force suitable statutes rendering it penal for any of its inhabitants to transport, or aid in transporting from such state, any person sought to be thus transported, merely because subject to the slave laws of any other state; this remnant of independence being accorded to the free states by the decision of the Supreme Court, in the case of Prigg *vs.* the state of Pennsylvania.

1844.—Whig Platform.

Baltimore, May 1.

1. *Resolved*, That these principles may

be summed as comprising a well-regulated national currency: a tariff for revenue to defray the necessary expenses of the government, and discriminating with special reference to the protection of the domestic labor of the country; the distribution of the proceeds from the sales of the public lands; a single term for the presidency; a reform of executive usurpations; and generally such an administration of the affairs of the country as shall impart to every branch of the public service the greatest practical efficiency, controlled by a well-regulated and wise economy.

1844.—Democratic Platform.

Baltimore, May 27.

Resolutions 1, 2, 3, 4, 5, 6, 7, 8 and 9, of the platform of 1840, were reaffirmed, to which were added the following:

10. *Resolved*, That the proceeds of the public lands ought to be sacredly applied to the national objects specified in the constitution, and that we are opposed to the laws lately adopted, and to any law for the distribution of such proceeds among the states, as alike inexpedient in policy and repugnant to the constitution.

11. *Resolved*, That we are decidedly opposed to taking from the President the qualified veto power by which he is enabled, under restrictions and responsibilities amply sufficient to guard the public interest, to suspend the passage of a bill whose merits can not secure the approval of two-thirds of the Senate and House of Representatives, until the judgment of the people can be obtained thereon, and which has thrice saved the American people from the corrupt and tyrannical domination of the bank of the United States.

12. *Resolved*, That our title to the whole of the territory of Oregon is clear and unquestionable; that no portion of the same ought to be ceded to England or any other power, and that the reoccupation of Oregon and the reannexation of Texas at the earliest practicable period, are great American measures, which this convention recommends to the cordial support of the democracy of the Union.

1848.—Democratic Platform.

Baltimore, May 22.

1. *Resolved*, That the American democracy place their trust in the intelligence, the patriotism, and the discriminating justice of the American people.

2. *Resolved*, That we regard this as a distinctive feature of our political creed, which we are proud to maintain before the world, as the great moral element in a form of government springing from and upheld by the popular will; and contrast it with the creed and practice of federalism, under whatever name or form, which seeks to palsy the will of the constituent, and which conceives no imposture too monstrous for the popular credulity.

3. *Resolved*, Therefore, that entertaining these views, the Democratic party of this Union, through the delegates assembled in general convention of the states, coming together in a spirit of concord, of devotion to the doctrines and faith of a free representative government, and appealing to their fellow-citizens for the rectitude of their intentions, renew and reassert before the American people, the declaration of principles avowed by them on a former occasion, when, in general convention, they presented their candidates for the popular suffrage.

Resolutions 1, 2, 3 and 4, of the platform of 1840, were reaffirmed.

8. *Resolved*, That it is the duty of every branch of the government to enforce and practice the most rigid economy in conducting our public affairs, and that no more revenue ought to be raised than is required to defray the necessary expenses of the government, and for the gradual but certain extinction of the debt created by the prosecution of a just and necessary war.

Resolution 5, of the platform of 1840, was enlarged by the following:

And that the results of democratic legislation, in this and all other financial measures, upon which issues have been made between the two political parties of the country, have demonstrated to careful and practical men of all parties, their soundness, safety and utility in all business pursuits.

Resolutions 7, 8 and 9, of the platform of 1840, were here inserted.

13. *Resolved*, That the proceeds of the public lands ought to be sacredly applied to the national objects specified in the constitution; and that we are opposed to any law for the distribution of such proceeds among the states as alike inexpedient in policy and repugnant to the constitution.

14. *Resolved*, That we are decidedly opposed to taking from the President the qualified veto power, by which he is enabled, under restrictions and responsibilities amply sufficient to guard the public interests, to supend the passage of a bill whose merits can not secure the approval of two-thirds of the Senate and House of Representatives, until the judgment of the people can be obtained thereon, and which has saved the American people from the corrupt and tyrannical domination of the Bank of the United States, and from a corrupting system of general internal improvements.

15. *Resolved,* That the war with Mexico, provoked on her part by years of insult and injury, was commenced by her army crossing the Rio Grande, attacking the American troops, and invading our sister state of Texas, and upon all the principles of patriotism and the laws of nations, it is a just and necessary war on our part, in which every American citizen should have shown himself on the side of his country, and neither morally nor physically, by word or by deed, have given "aid and comfort to the enemy."

16. *Resolved,* That we would be rejoiced at the assurance of peace with Mexico, founded on the just principles of indemnity for the past and security for the future; but that while the ratification of the liberal treaty offered to Mexico remains in doubt, it is the duty of the country to sustain the administration and to sustain the country in every measure necessary to provide for the vigorous prosecution of the war, should that treaty be rejected.

17. *Resolved,* That the officers and soldiers who have carried the arms of their country into Mexico, have crowned it with imperishable glory. Their unconquerable courage, their daring enterprise, their unfaltering perseverance and fortitude when assailed on all sides by innumerable foes and that more formidable enemy—the diseases of the climate—exalt their devoted patriotism into the highest heroism, and give them a right to the profound gratitude of their country, and the admiration of the world.

18. *Resolved,* That the Democratic National Convention of thirty states composing the American Republic, tender their fraternal congratulations to the National Convention of the Republic of France, now assembled as the free suffrage representative of the sovereignty of thirty-five millions of Republicans, to establish government on those eternal principles of equal rights, for which their La Fayette and our Washington fought side by side in the struggle for our national independence; and we would especially convey to them, and to the whole people of France, our earnest wishes for the consolidation of their liberties, through the wisdom that shall guide their councils, on the basis of a democratic constitution, not derived from the grants or concessions of kings or dynasties, but originating from the only true source of political power recognized in the states of this Union—the inherent and inalienable right of the people, in their sovereign capacity, to make and to amend their forms of government in such manner as the welfare of the community may require.

19. *Resolved,* That in view of the recent development of this grand political truth, of the sovereignty of the people and their capacity and power for self-government, which is prostrating thrones and erecting republics on the ruins of despotism in the old world, we feel that a high and sacred duty is devolved, with increased responsibility, upon the Democratic party of this country, as the party of the people, to sustain and advance among us constitutional liberty, equality, and fraternity, by continuing to resist all monopolies and exclusive legislation for the benefit of the few at the expense of the many, and by a vigilant and constant adherence to those principles and compromises of the constitution, which are broad enough and strong enough to embrace and uphold the Union as it was, the Union as it is, and the Union as it shall be in the full expansion of the energies and capacity of this great and progressive people.

20. *Resolved,* That a copy of these resolutions be forwarded, through the American minister at Paris, to the National Convention of the Republic of France.

21. *Resolved,* That the fruits of the great political triumph of 1844, which elected James K. Polk and George M. Dallas, President and Vice-President of the United States, have fulfilled the hopes of the democracy of the Union in defeating the declared purposes of their opponents in creating a National Bank; in preventing the corrupt and unconstitutional distribution of the land proceeds from the common treasury of the Union for local purposes; in protecting the currency and labor of the country from ruinous fluctuations, and guarding the money of the country for the use of the people by the establishment of the constitutional treasury; in the noble impulse given to the cause of free trade by the repeal of the tariff of '42, and the creation of the more equal, honest, and productive tariff of 1846; and that, in our opinion, it would be a fatal error to weaken the bands of a political organization by which these great reforms have been achieved, and risk them in the hands of their known adversaries, with whatever delusive appeals they may solicit our surrender of that vigilance which is the only safeguard of liberty.

22. *Resolved,* That the confidence of the democracy of the Union in the principles, capacity, firmness, and integrity of James K. Polk, manifested by his nomination and election in 1844, has been signally justified by the strictness of his adherence to sound democratic doctrines, by the purity of purpose, the energy and ability, which have characterized his administration in all our affairs at home and abroad; that we tender to him our cordial congratulations upon the brilliant success which has hitherto crowned his patriotic efforts, and assure him in advance, that at the expiration of his presidential term he will carry with him

to his retirement, the esteem, respect and admiration of a grateful country.

23. *Resolved*, That this convention hereby present to the people of the United States Lewis Cass, of Michigan, as the candidate of the Democratic party for the office of President, and William O. Butler, of Kentucky, for Vice-President of the United States.

1848.—Whig Principles Adopted at a Ratification Meeting,

Philadelphia, June 9.

1. *Resolved*, That the Whigs of the United States, here assembled by their representatives, heartily ratify the nominations of General Zachary Taylor as President, and Millard Fillmore as Vice-President, of the United States, and pledge themselves to their support.

2. *Resolved*, That in the choice of General Taylor as the Whig candidate for President, we are glad to discover sympathy with a great popular sentiment throughout the nation—a sentiment which having its origin in admiration of great military success, has been strengthened by the development, in every action and every word, of sound conservative opinions, and of true fidelity to the great example of former days, and to the principles of the constitution as administered by its founders.

3. *Resolved*, That General Taylor, in saying that, had he voted in 1844, he would have voted the Whig ticket, gives us the assurance—and no better is needed from a consistent and truth-speaking man—that his heart was with us at the crisis of our political destiny, when Henry Clay was our candidate, and when not only Whig principles were well defined and clearly asserted, but Whig measures depended on success. The heart that was with us then is with us now, and, we have a soldier's word of honor, and a life of public and private virtue, as the security.

4. *Resolved*, That we look on General Taylor's administration of the government as one conducive of peace, prosperity and union; of peace, because no one better knows, or has greater reason to deplore, what he has seen sadly on the field of victory, the horrors of war, and especially of a foreign and aggressive war; of prosperity, now more than ever needed to relieve the nation from a burden of debt, and restore industry—agricultural, manufacturing, and commercial—to its accustomed and peaceful functions and influences; of union, because we have a candidate whose very position as a southwestern man, reared on the banks of the great stream whose tributaries, natural and artificial, embrace the whole Union, renders the protection of the interests of the whole country his first trust, and whose various duties in past life have been rendered, not on the soil, or under the flag of any state or section, but over the wide frontier, and under the broad banner of the nation.

5. *Resolved*, That standing, as the Whig party does, on the broad and firm platform of the constitution, braced up by all its inviolable and sacred guarantees and compromises, and cherished in the affections, because protective of the interests of the people, we are proud to have as the exponent of our opinions, one who is pledged to construe it by the wise and generous rules which Washington applied to it, and who has said—and no Whig desires any other assurance—that he will make Washington's administration his model.

6. *Resolved*, That as Whigs and Americans, we are proud to acknowledge our gratitude for the great military services which, beginning at Palo Alto, and ending at Buena Vista, first awakened the American people to a just estimate of him who is now our Whig candidate. In the discharge of a painful duty—for his march into the enemy's country was a reluctant one; in the command of regulars at one time, and volunteers at another, and of both combined; in the decisive though punctual discipline of his camp, where all respected and loved him; in the negotiation of terms for a dejected and desperate enemy; in the exigency of actual conflict when the balance was perilously doubtful—we have found him the same—brave, distinguished, and considerate, no heartless spectator of bloodshed, no trifler with human life or human happiness; and we do not know which to admire most, his heroism in withstanding the assaults of the enemy in the most hopeless fields of Buena Vista—mourning in generous sorrow over the graves of Ringgold, of Clay, of Hardin—or in giving, in the heat of battle, terms of merciful capitulation to a vanquished foe at Monterey, and not being ashamed to avow that he did it to spare women and children, helpless infancy and more helpless age, against whom no American soldier ever wars. Such a military man, whose triumphs are neither remote nor doubtful, whose virtues these trials have tested, we are proud to make our candidate.

7. *Resolved*, That in support of this nomination, we ask our Whig friends throughout the nation to unite, to co-operate zealously, resolutely, with earnestness, in behalf of our candidate, whom calumny can not reach, and with respectful demeanor to our adversaries, whose candidates have yet to prove their claims on the gratitude of the nation.

1848.—Buffalo Platform.

Utica, June 22.

Whereas, We have assembled in convention as a union of freemen, for the sake of freedom, forgetting all past political difference, in a common resolve to maintain the rights of free labor against the aggression of the slave power, and to secure free soil to a free people; and,

Whereas, The political conventions recently assembled at Baltimore and Philadelphia—the one stifling the voice of a great constituency, entitled to be heard in its deliberations, and the other abandoning its distinctive principles for mere availability—have dissolved the national party organization heretofore existing, by nominating for the chief magistracy of the United States, under the slaveholding dictation, candidates, neither of whom can be supported by the opponents of slavery extension, without a sacrifice of consistency, duty, and self-respect; and,

Whereas, These nominations so made, furnish the occasion, and demonstrate the necessity of the union of the people under the banner of free democracy, in a solemn and formal declaration of their independence of the slave power, and of their fixed determination to rescue the Federal government from its control,

1. *Resolved, therefore*, That we, the people here assembled, remembering the example of our fathers in the days of the first Declaration of Independence, putting our trust in God for the triumph of our cause, and invoking His guidance in our endeavors to advance it, do now plant ourselves upon the national platform of freedom, in opposition to the sectional platform of slavery.

2. *Resolved*, That slavery in the several states of this Union which recognize its existence, depends upon the state laws alone, which can not be repealed or modified by the Federal government, and for which laws that government is not responsible. We therefore propose no interference by Congress with slavery within the limits of any state.

3. *Resolved*, That the proviso of Jefferson, to prohibit the existence of slavery, after 1800, in all the territories of the United States, southern and northern; the votes of six states and sixteen delegates in Congress of 1784, for the proviso, to three states and seven delegates against it; the actual exclusion of slavery from the Northwestern Territory, by the Ordinance of 1787, unanimously adopted by the states in Congress; and the entire history of that period, clearly show that it was the settled policy of the nation not to extend, nationalize or encourage, but to limit, localize and discourage, slavery; and to this policy, which should never have been departed from, the government ought to return.

4. *Resolved*, That our fathers ordained the constitution of the United States, in order, among other great national objects, to establish justice, promote the general welfare, and secure the blessings of liberty; but expressly denied to the Federal government, which they created, all constitutional power to deprive any person of life, liberty, or property, without due legal process.

5. *Resolved*, That in the judgment of this convention, Congress has no more power to make a slave than to make a king; no more power to institute or establish slavery than to institute or establish a monarchy; no such power can be found among those specifically conferred by the constitution, or derived by just implication from them.

6. *Resolved*, That it is the duty of the Federal government to relieve itself from all responsibility for the existence or continuance of slavery wherever the government possesses constitutional power to legislate on that subject, and it is thus responsible for its existence.

7. *Resolved*, That the true, and, in the judgment of this convention, the only safe means of preventing the extension of slavery into territory now free, is to prohibit its extension in all such territory by an act of Congress.

8. *Resolved*, That we accept the issue which the slave power has forced upon us; and to their demand for more slave states, and more slave territory, our calm but final answer is, no more slave states and no more slave territory. Let the soil of our extensive domains be kept free for the hardy pioneers of our own land, and the oppressed and banished of other lands, seeking homes of comfort and fields of enterprise in the new world.

9. *Resolved*, That the bill lately reported by the committee of eight in the Senate of the United States, was no compromise, but an absolute surrender of the rights of the non-slaveholders of all the states; and while we rejoice to know that a measure which, while opening the door for the introduction of slavery into the territories now free, would also have opened the door to litigation and strife among the future inhabitants thereof, to the ruin of their peace and prosperity, was defeated in the House of Representatives, its passage, in hot haste, by a majority, embracing several senators who voted in open violation of the known will of their constituents, should warn the people to see to it that their representatives be not suffered to betray them. There must be no more compromises with slavery; if made, they must be repealed.

10. *Resolved*, That we demand freedom and established institutions for our brethren in Oregon, now exposed to hardships, peril, and massacre, by the reckless hostility of the slave power to the establishment of free government and free territo-

ries; and not only for them, but for our brethren in California and New Mexico.

11. *Resolved*, It is due not only to this occasion, but to the whole people of the United States, that we should also declare ourselves on certain other questions of national policy; therefore,

12. *Resolved*, That we demand cheap postage for the people; a retrenchment of the expenses and patronage of the Federal government; the abolition of all unnecessary offices and salaries; and the election by the people of all civil officers in the service of the government, so far as the same may be practicable.

13. *Resolved*, that river and harbor improvements, when demanded by the safety and convenience of commerce with foreign nations, or among the several states, are objects of national concern, and that it is the duty of Congress, in the exercise of its constitutional power, to provide therefor.

14. *Resolved*, That the free grant to actual settlers, in consideration of the expenses they incur in making settlements in the wilderness, which are usually fully equal to their actual cost, and of the public benefits resulting therefrom, of reasonable portions of the public lands, under suitable limitations, is a wise and just measure of public policy, which will promote in various ways the interests of all the states of this Union; and we, therefore, recommend it to the favorable consideration of the American People.

15. *Resolved*, That the obligations of honor and patriotism require the earliest practical payment of the national debt, and we are, therefore, in favor of such a tariff of duties as will raise revenue adequate to defray the expenses of the Federal government, and to pay annual installments of our debt and the interest thereon.

16. *Resolved*, That we inscribe on our banner, "Free Soil, Free Speech, Free Labor, and Free Men," and under it we will fight on, and fight ever, until a triumphant victory shall reward our exertions.

1852.—Democratic Platform.

Baltimore, June 1.

Resolutions 1, 2, 3, 4, 5, 6 and 7, of the platform of 1848, were reaffirmed, to which were added the following:

8. *Resolved*, That it is the duty of every branch of the government to enforce and practice the most rigid economy in conducting our public affairs, and that no more revenue ought to be raised than is required to defray the necessary expenses of the government, and for the gradual but certain extinction of the public debt.

9. *Resolved*, That Congress has no power to charter a National Bank; that we believe such an institution one of deadly hostility to the best interests of the country, dangerous to our republican institutions and the liberties of the people, and calculated to place the business of the country within the control of a concentrated money power, and that above the laws and will of the people; and that the results of Democratic legislation, in this and all other financial measures, upon which issues have been made between the two political parties of the country, have demonstrated to candid and practical men of all parties, their soundness, safety, and utility, in all business pursuits.

10. *Resolved*, That the separation of the moneys of the government from banking institutions is indispensable for the safety of the funds of the government and the rights of the people.

11. *Resolved*, That the liberal principles embodied by Jefferson in the Declaration of Independence, and sanctioned in the constitution, which makes ours the land of liberty and the asylum of the oppressed of every nation, have ever been cardinal principles in the Democratic faith; and every attempt to abridge the privilege of becoming citizens and the owners of the soil among us, ought to be resisted with the same spirit that swept the alien and sedition laws from our statute books.

12. *Resolved*, That Congress has no power under the constitution to interfere with, or control, the domestic institutions of the several states, and that such states are the sole and proper judges of everything appertaining to their own affairs, not prohibited by the constitution; that all efforts of the Abolitionists or others, made to induce Congress to interfere with questions of slavery, or to take incipient steps in relation thereto, are calculated to lead to the most alarming and dangerous consequences; and that all such efforts have an inevitable tendency to diminish the happiness of the people, and endanger the stability and permanency of the Union, and ought not to be countenanced by any friend of our political institutions.

13. *Resolved*, That the foregoing proposition covers, and is intended to embrace, the whole subject of slavery agitation in Congress; and therefore the Democratic party of the Union, standing on this national platform, will abide by, and adhere to, a faithful execution of the acts known as the Compromise measures settled by last Congress, "the act for reclaiming fugitives from service labor" included; which act, being designed to carry out an express provision of the constitution, can not, with fidelity thereto, be repealed, nor so changed as to destroy or impair its efficiency.

14. *Resolved*, That the Democratic party

will resist all attempts at renewing in Congress, or out of it, the agitation of the slavery question, under whatever shape or color the attempt may be made.

[Here resolutions 13 and 14, of the platform of 1848, were inserted.]

17. *Resolved*, That the Democratic party will faithfully abide by and uphold the principles laid down in the Kentucky and Virginia resolutions of 1792 and 1798, and in the report of Mr. Madison to the Virginia Legislature in 1799; that it adopts those principles as constituting one of the main foundations of its political creed, and is resolved to carry them out in their obvious meaning and import.

18. *Resolved*, That the war with Mexico, upon all the principles of patriotism and the law of nations, was a just and necessary war on our part, in which no American citizen should have shown himself opposed to his country, and neither morally nor physically, by word or deed, given aid and comfort to the enemy.

19. *Resolved*, That we rejoice at the restoration of friendly relations with our sister Republic of Mexico, and earnestly desire for her all the blessings and prosperity which we enjoy under republican institutions, and we congratulate the American people on the results of that war which have so manifestly justified the policy and conduct of the Democratic party, and insured to the United States indemnity for the past and security for the future.

20. *Resolved*, That, in view of the condition of popular institutions in the old world, a high and sacred duty is devolved with increased responsibility upon the Democracy of this country, as the party of the people, to uphold and maintain the rights of every state, and thereby the union of states, and to sustain and advance among them constitutional liberty, by continuing to resist all monopolies and exclusive legislation for the benefit of the few at the expense of the many, and by a vigilant and constant adherence to those principles and compromises of the constitution which are broad enough and strong enough to embrace and uphold the Union as it is, and the Union as it should be, in the full expansion of the energies and capacity of this great and progressive people.

1852.—Whig Platform.

Baltimore, June 16.

The Whigs of the United States, in convention assembled adhering to the great conservative principles by which they are controlled and governed, and now as ever relying upon the intelligence of the American people, with an abiding confidence in their capacity for self-government and their devotion to the constitution and the Union, do proclaim the following as the political sentiments and determination for the establishment and maintenance of which their national organization as a party was effected:

First. The government of the United States is of a limited character, and is confined to the exercise of powers expressly granted by the constitution, and such as may be necessary and proper for carrying the granted powers into full execution, and that powers not granted or necessarily implied are reserved to the states respectively and to the people.

Second. The state governments should be held secure to their reserved rights, and the General Government sustained in its constitutional powers, and that the Union should be revered and watched over as the palladium of our liberties.

Third. That while struggling freedom everywhere enlists the warmest sympathy of the Whig party, we still adhere to the doctrines of the Father of his Country, as announced in his Farewell Address, of keeping ourselves free from all entangling alliances with foreign countries, and of never quitting our own to stand upon foreign ground; that our mission as a republic is not to propagate our opinions, or impose on other countries our forms of government, by artifice or force, but to teach by example, and show by our success, moderation and justice, the blessings of self-government, and the advantages of free institutions.

Fourth. That, as the people make and control the government, they should obey its constitution, laws and treaties as they would retain their self-respect and the respect which they claim and will enforce from foreign powers.

Fifth. Governments should be conducted on the principles of the strictest economy; and revenue sufficient for the expenses thereof, in time of peace, ought to be derived mainly from a duty on imports, and not from direct taxes; and on laying such duties sound policy requires a just discrimination, and, when practicable, by specific duties, whereby suitable encouragement may be afforded to American industry, equally to all classes and to all portions of the country.

Sixth. The constitution vests in Congress the power to open and repair harbors, and remove obstructions from navigable rivers, whenever such improvements are necessary for the common defense, and for the protection and facility of commerce with foreign nations or among the states, said improvements being in every instance national and general in their character.

Seventh. The Federal and state governments are parts of one system, alike necessary for the common prosperity, peace and security and ought to be regarded alike with a cordial, habitual and immovable attachment. Respect for the authority of each, and acquiescence in the just constitutional measures of each, are duties required by the plainest considerations of national, state and individual welfare.

Eighth. That the series of acts of the 32d Congress, the act known as the Fugitive Slave Law included, are received and acquiesced in by the Whig party of the United States as a settlement in principle and substance of the dangerous and exciting questions which they embrace; and, so far as they are concerned, we will maintain them, and insist upon their strict enforcement, until time and experience shall demonstrate the necessity of further legislation to guard against the evasion of the laws on the one hand and the abuse of their powers on the other—not impairing their present efficiency; and we deprecate all further agitation of the question thus settled, as dangerous to our peace, and will discountenance all efforts to continue or renew such agitation whenever, wherever or however the attempt may be made; and we will maintain the system as essential to the nationality of the Whig party, and the integrity of the Union.

1852.—Free-soil Platform.

Pittsburg, August 11.

Having assembled in national convention as the free democracy of the United States, united by a common resolve to maintain right against wrong, and freedom against slavery; confiding in the intelligence, patriotism, and discriminating justice of the American people; putting our trust in God for the triumph of our cause, and invoking His guidance in our endeavors to advance it, we now submit to the candid judgment of all men, the following declaration of principles and measures:

1. That governments, deriving their just powers from the consent of the governed, are instituted among men to secure to all those inalienable rights of life, liberty, and the pursuit of happiness, with which they are endowed by their Creator, and of which none can be deprived by valid legislation, except for crime.

2. That the true mission of American democracy is to maintain the liberties of the people, the sovereignty of the states, and the perpetuity of the Union, by the impartial application of public affairs, without sectional discriminations, of the fundamental principles of human rights, strict justice, and an economical administration.

3. That the Federal government is one of limited powers derived solely from the constitution, and the grants of power therein ought to be strictly construed by all the departments and agents of the government, and it is inexpedient and dangerous to exercise doubtful constitutional powers.

4. That the constitution of the United States, ordained to form a more perfect Union, to establish justice, and secure the blessings of liberty, expressly denies to the general government all power to deprive any person of life, liberty, or property, without due process of law; and, therefore, the government, having no more power to make a slave than to make a king, and no more power to establish slavery than to establish a monarchy, should at once proceed to relieve itself from all responsibility for the existence of slavery, wherever it possesses constitutional power to legislate for its extinction.

5. That, to the persevering and importunate demands of the slave power for more slave states, new slave territories, and the nationalization of slavery, our distinct and final answer is—no more slave states, no slave territory, no nationalized slavery, and no national legislation for the extradition of slaves.

6. That slavery is a sin against God, and a crime against man, which no human enactment nor usage can make right: and that Christianity, humanity, and patriotism, alike demand its abolition.

7. That the Fugitive Slave Act of 1850 is repugnant to the constitution, to the principles of the common law, to the spirit of Christianity, and to the sentiments of the civilized world; we, therefore, deny its binding force on the American people, and demand its immediate and total repeal.

8. That the doctrine that any human law is a finality, and not subject to modification or repeal, is not in accordance with the creed of the founders of our government, and is dangerous to the liberties of the people.

9. That the acts of Congress, known as the Compromise measures of 1850, by making the admission of a sovereign state contingent upon the adoption of other measures demanded by the special interests of slavery; by their omission to guarantee freedom in the free territories; by their attempt to impose unconstitutional limitations on the powers of Congress and the people to admit new states; by their provisions for the assumption of five millions of the state debt of Texas, and for the payment of five millions more, and the cession of large territory to the same state under menace, as an inducement to the relinquishment of a groundless claim; and by their invasion of the sovereignty of the states and the liberties of the people, through the enactment of an unjust, oppressive, and unconstitutional fugitive

slave law, are proved to be inconsistent with all the principles and maxims of democracy, and wholly inadequate to the settlement of the questions of which they are claimed to be an adjustment.

10. That no permanent settlement of the slavery question can be looked for except in the practical recognition of the truth that slavery is sectional and freedom national; by the total separation of the general government from slavery, and the exercise of its legitimate and constitutional influence on the side of freedom; and by leaving to the states the whole subject of slavery and the extradition of fugitives from service.

11. That all men have a natural right to a portion of the soil; and that as the use of the soil is indispensable to life, the right of all men to the soil is as sacred as their right to life itself.

12. That the public lands of the United States belong to the people and should not be sold to individuals nor granted to corporations, but should be held as a sacred trust for the benefit of the people, and should be granted in limited quantities, free of cost, to landless settlers.

13. That due regard for the Federal constitution, a sound administrative policy, demand that the funds of the general government be kept separate from banking institutions; that inland and ocean postage should be reduced to the lowest possible point; that no more revenue should be raised than is required to defray the strictly necessary expenses of the public service and to pay off the public debt; and that the power and patronage of the government should be diminished by the abolition of all unnecessary offices, salaries and privileges, and by the election of the people of all civil officers in the service of the United States, so far as may be consistent with the prompt and efficient transaction of the public business.

14. That river and harbor improvements, when necessary to the safety and convenience of commerce with foreign nations, or among the several states, are objects of national concern; and it is the duty of Congress, in the exercise of its constitutional powers, to provide for the same.

15. That emigrants and exiles from the old world should find a cordial welcome to homes of comfort and fields of enterprise in the new; and every attempt to abridge their privilege of becoming citizens and owners of soil among us ought to be resisted with inflexible determination.

16. That every nation has a clear right to alter or change its own government, and to administer its own concerns in such manner as may best secure the rights and promote the happiness of the people; and foreign interference with that right is a dangerous violation of the law of nations, against which all independent governments should protest, and endeavor by all proper means to prevent; and especially is it the duty of the American government, representing the chief republic of the world, to protest against, and by all proper means to prevent, the intervention of kings and emperors against nations seeking to establish for themselves republican or constitutional governments.

17. That the independence of Hayti ought to be recognized by our government, and our commercial relations with it placed on the footing of the most favored nations.

18. That as by the constitution, "the citizens of each state shall be entitled to all the privileges and immunities of citizens in the several states," the practice of imprisoning colored seamen of other states, while the vessels to which they belong lie in port, and refusing the exercise of the right to bring such cases before the Supreme Court of the United States, to test the legality of such proceedings, is a flagrant violation of the constitution, and an invasion of the rights of the citizens of other states, utterly inconsistent with the professions made by the slaveholders, that they wish the provisions of the constitution faithfully observed by every state in the Union.

19. That we recommend the introduction into all treaties hereafter to be negotiated between the United States and foreign nations, of some provision for the amicable settlement of difficulties by a resort to decisive arbitrations.

20. That the free democratic party is not organized to aid either the Whig or Democratic wing of the great slave compromise party of the nation, but to defeat them both; and that repudiating and renouncing both as hopelessly corrupt and utterly unworthy of confidence, the purpose of the Free Democracy is to take possession of the Federal government and administer it for the better protection of the rights and interests of the whole people.

21. That we inscribe on our banner Free Soil, Free Speech, Free Labor, and Free Men, and under it will fight on and fight ever, until a triumphant victory shall reward our exertions.

22. That upon this platform, the convention presents to the American people, as a candidate for the office of President of the United States, John P. Hale, of New Hampshire, and as a candidate for the office of Vice-President of the United States, George W. Julian, of Indiana, and earnestly commend them to the support of all freemen and all parties.

1856.—The American Platform.

Adopted at Philadelphia February 21.

1. An humble acknowledgment to the

Supreme Being for His protecting care vouchsafed to our fathers in their successful revolutionary struggle, and hitherto manifested to us, their descendants, in the preservation of the liberties, the independence, and the union of these states.

2. The perpetuation of the Federal Union and constitution, as the palladium of our civil and religious liberties, and the only sure bulwarks of American independence.

3. *Americans must rule America;* and to this end *native*-born citizens should be selected for all state, federal, and municipal offices of government employment, in preference to all others. *Nevertheless,*

4. Persons born of American parents residing temporarily abroad, should be entitled to all the rights of native-born citizens.

5. No person should be selected for political station (whether of native or foreign birth), who recognizes any allegiance or obligation of any description to any foreign prince, potentate, or power, or who refuses to recognize the federal and state constitutions (each within its sphere) as paramount to all other laws, as rules of political action.

6. The unequaled recognition and maintenance of the reserved rights of the several states, and the cultivation of harmony and fraternal good-will between the citizens of the several states, and, to this end, non-interference by Congress with questions appertaining solely to the individual states, and non-intervention by each state with the affairs of any other state.

7. The recognition of the right of native-born and naturalized citizens of the United States, permanently residing in any territory thereof, to frame their constitution and laws, and to regulate their domestic and social affairs in their own mode, subject only to the provisions of the federal constitution, with the privilege of admission into the Union whenever they have the requisite population for one Representative in Congress: *Provided, always,* that none but those who are citizens of the United States under the constitution and laws thereof, and who have a fixed residence in any such territory, ought to participate in the formation of the constitution or in the enactment of laws for said territory or state.

8. An enforcement of the principles that no state or territory ought to admit others than citizens to the right of suffrage or of holding political offices of the United States.

9. A change in the laws of naturalization, making a continued residence of twenty-one years, of all not heretofore provided for, an indispensable requisite for citizenship hereafter, and excluding all paupers and persons convicted of crime from landing upon our shores; but no interference with the vested rights of foreigners.

10. Opposition to any union between church and state; no interference with religious faith or worship; and no test-oaths for office.

11. Free and thorough investigation into any and all alleged abuses of public functionaries, and a strict economy in public expenditures.

12. The maintenance and enforcement of all laws constitutionally enacted, until said laws shall be repealed, or shall be declared null and void by competent judicial authority.

13. Opposition to the reckless and unwise policy of the present administration in the general management of our national affairs, and more especially as shown in removing "Americans" (by designation) and conservatives in principle, from office, and placing foreigners and ultraists in their places; as shown in a truckling subserviency to the stronger, and an insolent and cowardly bravado towards the weaker powers; as shown in reopening sectional agitation, by the repeal of the Missouri Compromise; as shown in granting to unnaturalized foreigners the right of suffrage in Kansas and Nebraska; as shown in its vacillating course on the Kansas and Nebraska question; as shown in the corruptions which pervade some of the departments of the government; as shown in disgracing meritorious naval officers through prejudice or caprice; and as shown in the blundering mismanagement of our foreign relations.

14. Therefore, to remedy existing evils and prevent the disastrous consequences otherwise resulting therefrom, we would build up the "American Party" upon the principles hereinbefore stated.

15. That each state council shall have authority to amend their several constitutions, so as to abolish the several degrees, and substitute a pledge of honor, instead of other obligations, for fellowship and admission into the party.

16. A free and open discussion of all political principles embraced in our platform.

1856.—Democratic Platform,

Adopted at Cincinnati, June 6.

Resolved, That the American democracy place their trust in the intelligence, the patriotism, and discriminating justice of the American people.

Resolved, That we regard this as a distinctive feature of our political creed, which we are proud to maintain before the world as a great moral element in a form of government springing from and upheld by the popular will; and we contrast it with the creed and practice of federalism, under whatever name or form, which seeks to palsy the will of the constituent, and which conceives no imposture too monstrous for the popular credulity.

Resolved, therefore, That entertaining these views, the Democratic party of this Union, through their delegates, assembled in general convention, coming together in a spirit of concord, of devotion to the doctrines and faith of a free representative government, and appealing to their fellow citizens for the rectitude of their intentions, renew and reassert, before the American people, the declaration of principles avowed by them, when, on former occasions, in general convention, they have presented their candidates for the popular suffrage.

1. That the Federal government is one of limited power, derived solely from the constitution, and the grants of power made therein ought to be strictly construed by all the departments and agents of the government, and that it is inexpedient and dangerous to exercise doubtful constitutional powers.

2. That the constitution does not confer upon the general government the power to commence and carry on a general system of internal improvements.

3. That the constitution does not confer authority upon the Federal government, directly or indirectly, to assume the debts of the several states, contracted for local and internal improvements or other state purposes; nor would such assumption be just or expedient.

4. That justice and sound policy forbid the Federal government to foster one branch of industry to the detriment of another, or to cherish the interests of one portion of our common country; that every citizen and every section of the country has a right to demand and insist upon an equality of rights and privileges, and a complete and ample protection of persons and property from domestic violence and foreign aggression.

5. That it is the duty of every branch of the government to enforce and practice the most rigid economy in conducting our public affairs, and that no more revenue ought to be raised than is required to defray the necessary expenses of the government and gradual but certain extinction of the public debt.

6. That the proceeds of the public lands ought to be sacredly applied to the national objects specified in the constitution, and that we are opposed to any law for the distribution of such proceeds among the states, as alike inexpedient in policy and repugnant to the constitution.

7. That Congress has no power to charter a national bank; that we believe such an institution one of deadly hostility to the best interests of this country, dangerous to our republican institutions and the liberties of the people, and calculated to place the business of the country within the control of a concentrated money power and above the laws and will of the people; and the results of the democratic legislation in this and all other financial measures upon which issues have been made between the two political parties of the country, have demonstrated to candid and practical men of all parties their soundness, safety, and utility in all business pursuits.

8. That the separation of the moneys of the government from banking institutions is indispensable to the safety of the funds of the government and the rights of the people.

9. That we are decidedly opposed to taking from the President the qualified veto power, by which he is enabled, under restrictions and responsibilities amply sufficient to guard the public interests, to suspend the passage of a bill whose merits can not secure the approval of two-thirds of the Senate and House of Representatives, until the judgment of the people can be obtained thereon, and which has saved the American people from the corrupt and tyrannical dominion of the Bank of the United States and from a corrupting system of general internal improvements.

10. That the liberal principles embodied by Jefferson in the Declaration of Independence, and sanctioned in the Constitution, which makes ours the land of liberty and the asylum of the oppressed of every nation, have ever been cardinal principles in the democratic faith; and every attempt to abridge the privilege of becoming citizens and owners of soil among us, ought to be resisted with the same spirit which swept the alien and sedition laws from our statute books.

And whereas, Since the foregoing declaration was uniformly adopted by our predecessors in national conventions, an adverse political and religious test has been secretly organized by a party claiming to be exclusively Americans, and it is proper that the American democracy should clearly define its relations thereto; and declare its determined opposition to all secret political societies, by whatever name they may be called—

Resolved, That the foundation of this union of states having been laid in, and its prosperity, expansion, and pre-eminent example in free government built upon, entire freedom of matters of religious concernment, and no respect of persons in regard to rank or place of birth, no party can justly be deemed national, constitutional, or in accordance with American principles, which bases its exclusive organization upon religious opinions and accidental birth-place. And hence a political crusade in the nineteenth century, and in the United States of America, against Catholics and foreign-born, is neither justified by the past history or future prospects of the country, nor in unison with the spirit of toleration and enlightened freedom which peculiarly distinguishes the American system of popular government.

Resolved, That we reiterate with renewed energy of purpose the well-considered declarations of former conventions upon the sectional issue of domestic slavery, and concerning the reserved rights of the states—

1. That Congress has no power under the constitution to interfere with or control the domestic institutions of the several states, and that all such states are the sole and proper judges of everything appertaining to their own affairs not prohibited by the constitution; that all efforts of the Abolitionists or others, made to induce Congress to interfere with questions of slavery, or to take incipient steps in relation thereto, are calculated to lead to the most alarming and dangerous consequences, and that all such efforts have an inevitable tendency to diminish the happiness of the people and endanger the stability and permanency of the Union, and ought not to be countenanced by any friend of our political institutions.

2. That the foregoing proposition covers and was intended to embrace the whole subject of slavery agitation in Congress, and therefore the Democratic party of the Union, standing on this national platform, will abide by and adhere to a faithful execution of the acts known as the compromise measures, settled by the Congress of 1850—"the act for reclaiming fugitives from service or labor" included; which act, being designed to carry out an express provision of the constitution, can not, with fidelity thereto, be repealed, or so changed as to destroy or impair its efficiency.

3. That the Democratic party will resist all attempts at renewing in Congress, or out of it, the agitation of the slavery question, under whatever shape or color the attempt may be made.

4. That the Democratic party will faithfully abide by and uphold the principles laid down in the Kentucky and Virginia resolutions of 1792 and 1798, and in the report of Mr. Madison to the Virginia legislature in 1799; that it adopts these principles as constituting one of the main foundations of its political creed, and is resolved to carry them out in their obvious meaning and import.

And that we may more distinctly meet the issue on which a sectional party, subsisting exclusively on slavery agitation, now relies to test the fidelity of the people, north and south, to the constitution and the Union—

1. *Resolved*, That claiming fellowship with and desiring the co-operation of all who regard the preservation of the Union under the constitution as the paramount issue, and repudiating all sectional parties and platforms concerning domestic slavery which seek to embroil the states and incite to treason and armed resistance to law in the territories, and whose avowed purpose, if consummated, must end in civil war and disunion, the American democracy recognize and adopt the principles contained in the organic laws establishing the territories of Nebraska and Kansas, as embodying the only sound and safe solution of the slavery question, upon which the great national idea of the people of this whole country can repose in its determined conservation of the Union, and non-interference of Congress with slavery in the territories or in the District of Columbia.

2. That this was the basis of the compromise of 1850, confirmed by both the Democratic and Whig parties in national conventions, ratified by the people in the election of 1852, and rightly applied to the organization of the territories in 1854.

3. That by the uniform application of the Democratic principle to the organization of territories and the admission of new states, with or without domestic slavery, as they may elect, the equal rights of all the states will be preserved intact, the original compacts of the constitution maintained inviolate, and the perpetuity and expansion of the Union insured to its utmost capacity of embracing, in peace and harmony, every future American state that may be constituted or annexed with a republican form of government.

Resolved, That we recognize the right of the people of all the territories, including Kansas and Nebraska, acting through the legally and fairly expressed will of the majority of the actual residents, and whenever the number of their inhabitants justifies it, to form a constitution, with or without domestic slavery, and be admitted into the Union upon terms of perfect equality with the other states.

Resolved, finally, That in view of the condition of the popular institutions in the old world (and the dangerous tendencies of sectional agitation, combined with the attempt to enforce civil and religious disabilities against the rights of acquiring and enjoying citizenship in our own land), a high and sacred duty is devolved, with increased responsibility, upon the Democratic party of this country, as the party of the Union, to uphold and maintain the rights of every state, and thereby the union of the states, and to sustain and advance among us constitutional liberty, by continuing to resist all monopolies and exclusive legislation for the benefit of the few at the expense of the many, and by a vigilant and constant adherence to those principles and compromises of the constitution which are broad enough and strong enough to embrace and uphold the Union as it was, the Union as it is, and the Union as it shall be, in the full expression of the energies and capacity of this great and progressive people.

1. *Resolved*, That there are questions connected with the foreign policy of this country which are inferior to no domestic questions whatever. The time has come for the people of the United States to declare themselves in favor of free seas and progressive free trade throughout the world, and, by solemn manifestations, to place their moral influence at the side of their successful example.

2. *Resolved*, That our geographical and political position with reference to the other states of this continent, no less than the interest of our commerce and the development of our growing power, requires that we should hold sacred the principles involved in the Monroe doctrine. Their bearing and import admit of no misconstruction, and should be applied with unbending rigidity.

3. *Resolved*, That the great highway which nature, as well as the assent of states most immediately interested in its maintenance, has marked out for free communication between the Atlantic and Pacific oceans, constitutes one of the most important achievements realized by the spirit of modern times, in the unconquerable energy of our people; and that result would be secured by a timely and efficient exertion of the control which we have the right to claim over it; and no power on earth should be suffered to impede or clog its progress by any interference with relations that may suit our policy to establish between our government and the governments of the states within whose dominions it lies; we can under no circumstances surrender our preponderance in the adjustment of all questions arising out of it.

4. *Resolved*, That in view of so commanding an interest, the people of the United States cannot but sympathize with the efforts which are being made by the people of Central America to regenerate that portion of the continent which covers the passage across the inter-oceanic isthmus.

5. *Resolved*, That the Democratic party will expect of the next administration that every proper effort be made to insure our ascendency in the Gulf of Mexico, and to maintain permanent protection to the great outlets through which are emptied into its waters the products raised out of the soil and the commodities created by the industry of the people of our western valleys and of the Union at large.

6. *Resolved*, That the administration of Franklin Pierce has been true to Democratic principles, and, therefore, true to the great interests of the country; in the face of violent opposition, he has maintained the laws at home and vindicated the rights of American citizens abroad, and, therefore, we proclaim our unqualified admiration of his measures and policy.

1856.—Republican Platform,

Adopted at Philadelphia, June 17.

This convention of delegates, assembled in pursuance of a call addressed to the people of the United States, without regard to past political differences or divisions, who are opposed to the repeal of the Missouri Compromise, to the policy of the present administration, to the extension of slavery into free territory; in favor of admitting Kansas as a free state, of restoring the action of the Federal government to the principles of Washington and Jefferson; and who purpose to unite in presenting candidates for the offices of President and Vice-President, do resolve as follows:

Resolved, That the maintenance of the principles promulgated in the Declaration of Independence, and embodied in the federal constitution, is essential to the preservation of our Republican institutions, and that the federal constitution, the rights of the states, and the union of the states, shall be preserved.

Resolved, That with our republican fathers we hold it to be a self-evident truth that all men are endowed with the inalienable rights to life, liberty, and the pursuit of happiness, and that the primary object and ulterior design of our Federal government were, to secure these rights to all persons within its exclusive jurisdiction; that as our republican fathers, when they had abolished slavery in all our national territory, ordained that no person should be deprived of life, liberty, or property, without due process of law, it becomes our duty to maintain this provision of the constitution against all attempts to violate it for the purpose of establishing slavery in any territory of the United States, by positive legislation, prohibiting its existence or extension therein. That we deny the authority of Congress, of a territorial legislature, of any individual or association of individuals, to give legal existence to slavery in any territory of the United States, while the present constitution shall be maintained.

Resolved, That the constitution confers upon Congress sovereign power over the territories of the United States for their government, and that in the exercise of this power it is both the right and the imperative duty of Congress to prohibit in the territories those twin relics of barbarism—polygamy and slavery.

Resolved, That while the constitution of the United States was ordained and established, in order to form a more perfect union, establish justice, insure domestic tranquillity, provide for the common defense, promote the general welfare, and secure the blessings of liberty, and contains ample provisions for the protection of the life, liberty, and property of every citizen, the dearest constitutional rights of the people of Kansas have been fraudulently and violently taken from them; their territory has been invaded by an armed force; spurious and pretended legislative, judicial, and executive officers have been set over them, by whose usurped authority, sustained by the military power of the government, tyrannical and unconstitutional laws have been enacted and enforced; the rights of the people to keep and bear arms have been infringed; test oaths of an extraordinary and entangling nature have been imposed, as a condition of exercising the right of suffrage and holding office; the right of an accused person to a speedy and public trial by an impartial jury has been denied; the right of the people to be secure in their persons, houses, papers, and effects against unreasonable searches and seizures, has been violated; they have been deprived of life, liberty, and property without due process of law; that the freedom of speech and of the press has been abridged; the right to choose their representatives has been made of no effect; murders, robberies, and arsons have been instigated or encouraged, and the offenders have been allowed to go unpunished; that all these things have been done with the knowledge, sanction, and procurement of the present national administration; and that for this high crime against the constitution, the Union, and humanity, we arraign the administration, the President, his advisers, agents, supporters, apologists, and accessories, either before or after the facts, before the country and before the world; and that it is our fixed purpose to bring the actual perpetrators of these atrocious outrages, and their accomplices, to a sure and condign punishment hereafter.

Resolved, That Kansas should be immediately admitted as a state of the Union with her present free constitution, as at once the most effectual way of securing to her citizens the enjoyment of the rights and privileges to which they are entitled, and of ending the civil strife now raging in her territory.

Resolved, That the highwayman's plea that "might makes right," embodied in the Ostend circular, was in every respect unworthy of American diplomacy, and would bring shame and dishonor upon any government or people that gave it their sanction.

Resolved, That a railroad to the Pacific ocean, by the most central and practicable route, is imperatively demanded by the interests of the whole country, and that the Federal government ought to render immediate and efficient aid in its construction, and, as an auxiliary thereto, the immediate construction of an emigrant route on the line of the railroad.

Resolved, That appropriations of Congress for the improvement of rivers and harbors of a national character, required for the accommodation and security of our existing commerce, are authorized by the constitution, and justified by the obligation of government to protect the lives and property of its citizens.

Resolved, That we invite the affiliation and co-operation of the men of all parties, however differing from us in other respects, in support of the principles herein declared; and believing that the spirit of our institutions, as well as the constitution of our country, guarantees liberty of conscience and equality of rights among citizens, we oppose all proscriptive legislation affecting their security.

1856.—Whig Platform.

Baltimore, September 13.

Resolved, That the Whigs of the United States, now here assembled, hereby declare their reverence for the constitution of the United States, their unalterable attachment to the National Union, and a fixed determination to do all in their power to preserve them for themselves and their posterity. They have no new principles to announce; no new platform to establish; but are content to broadly rest—where their fathers rested—upon the constitution of the United States, wishing no safer guide, no higher law.

Resolved, That we regard with the deepest interest and anxiety the present disordered condition of our national affairs—a portion of the country ravaged by civil war, large sections of our population embittered by mutual recriminations; and we distinctly trace these calamities to the culpable neglect of duty by the present national administration.

Resolved, That the government of the United States was formed by the conjunction in political unity of wide-spread geographical sections, materially differing, not only in climate and products, but in social and domestic institutions; and that any cause that shall permanently array the different sections of the Union in political hostility and organize parties founded only on geographical distinctions, must inevitably prove fatal to a continuance of the National Union.

Resolved, That the Whigs of the United States declare, as a fundamental article of political faith, an absolute necessity for avoiding geographical parties. The danger, so clearly discerned by the Father of his Country, has now become fearfully apparent in the agitation now convulsing the nation, and must be arrested at once if we would preserve our constitution and our Union from dismemberment, and the name of America from being blotted out from the family of civilized nations.

Resolved, That all who revere the constitution and the Union, must look with alarm at the parties in the field in the present presidential campaign—one claiming only to represent sixteen northern states, and the other appealing mainly to the passions and prejudices of the southern states; that the success of either faction must add fuel to the flame which now threatens to wrap our dearest interests in a common ruin.

Resolved, That the only remedy for an evil so appalling is to support a candidate pledged to neither of the geographical sections nor arrayed in political antagonism, but holding both in a just and equal regard. We congratulate the friends of the Union that such a candidate exists in Millard Fillmore.

Resolved, That, without adopting or referring to the peculiar doctrines of the party which has already selected Mr. Fillmore as a candidate, we look to him as a well tried and faithful friend of the constitution and the Union, eminent alike for his wisdom and firmness—for his justice and moderation in our foreign relations—calm and pacific temperament, so well becoming the head of a great nation—for his devotion to the constitution in its true spirit—his inflexibility in executing the laws but, beyond all these attributes, in possessing the one transcendent merit of being a representative of neither of the two sectional parties now struggling for political supremacy.

Resolved, That, in the present exigency of political affairs, we are not called upon to discuss the subordinate questions of administration in the exercising of the constitutional powers of the government. It is enough to know that civil war is raging, and that the Union is in peril; and we proclaim the conviction that the restoration of Mr. Fillmore to the presidency will furnish the best if not the only means of restoring peace.

1860.—Constitutional Union Platform.

Baltimore, May 9.

Whereas, Experience has demonstrated that platforms adopted by the partisan conventions of the country have had the effect to mislead and deceive the people, and at the same time to widen the political divisions of the country, by the creation and encouragement of geographical and sectional parties; therefore,

Resolved, That it is both the part of patriotism and of duty to *recognize* no political principles other than THE CONSTITUTION OF THE COUNTRY, THE UNION OF THE STATES, AND THE ENFORCEMENT OF THE LAWS; and that as representatives of the Constitutional Union men of the country, in national convention assembled, we hereby pledge ourselves to maintain, protect, and defend, separately and unitedly, these great principles of public liberty and national safety against all enemies at home and abroad, believing that thereby peace may once more be restored to the country, the rights of the people and of the states re-established, and the government again placed in that condition of justice, fraternity, and equality, which, under the example and constitution of our fathers, has solemnly bound every citizen of the United States to maintain a more perfect union, establish justice, insure domestic tranquillity, provide for the common defense, promote the general welfare, and secure the blessings of liberty to ourselves and our posterity.

1860.—Republican Platform,

Chicago, May 17.

Resolved, That we, the delegated representatives of the Republican electors of the United States, in convention assembled, in discharge of the duty we owe to our constituents and our country, unite in the following declarations:

1. That the history of the nation, during the last four years, has fully established the propriety and necessity of the organization and perpetuation of the Republican party, and that the causes which called it into existence are permanent in their nature, and now, more than ever before, demand its peaceful and constitutional triumph.

2. That the maintenance of the principles promulgated in the Declaration of Independence and embodied in the federal constitution, "That all men are created equal; that they are endowed by their Creator with certain inalienable rights; that among these are life, liberty, and the pursuit of happiness; that to secure these rights, governments are instituted among men, deriving their just powers from the consent of the governed," is essential to the preservation of our republican institutions; and that the federal constitution, the rights of the states, and the union of the states, must and shall be preserved.

3. That to the union of the states this nation owes its unprecedented increase in population, its surprising development of

material resources, its rapid augmentation of wealth, its happiness at home and its honor abroad; and we hold in abhorrence all schemes for disunion, come from whatever source they may; and we congratulate the country that no Republican member of Congress has uttered or countenanced the threats of disunion so often made by Democratic members, without rebuke and with applause from their political associates; and we denounce those threats of disunion, in case of a popular overthrow of their ascendency, as denying the vital principles of a free government, and as an avowal of contemplated treason, which it is the imperative duty of an indignant people sternly to rebuke and forever silence.

4. That the maintenance inviolate of the rights of the states, and especially the right of each state to order and control its own domestic institutions according to its own judgment exclusively, is essential to that balance of powers on which the perfection and endurance of our political fabric depends; and we denounce the lawless invasion, by armed force, of the soil of any state or territory, no matter under what pretext, as among the gravest of crimes.

5. That the present Democratic administration has far exceeded our worst apprehensions, in its measureless subserviency to the exactions of a sectional interest, as especially evinced in its desperate exertions to force the infamous Lecompton constitution upon the protesting people of Kansas; in construing the personal relations between master and servant to involve an unqualified property in persons; in its attempted enforcement, everywhere, on land and sea, through the intervention of Congress and of the federal courts, of the extreme pretensions of a purely local interest; and in its general and unvarying abuse of the power entrusted to it by a confiding people.

6. That the people justly view with alarm the reckless extravagance which pervades every department of the Federal government; that a return to rigid economy and accountability is indispensable to arrest the systematic plunder of the public treasury by favored partisans; while the recent startling developments of frauds and corruptions at the federal metropolis, show that an entire change of administration is imperatively demanded.

7. That the new dogma, that the constitution, of its own force, carries slavery into any or all of the territories of the United States, is a dangerous political heresy, at variance with the explicit provisions of that instrument itself, with contemporaneous exposition, and with legislative and judicial precedent—is revolutionary in its tendency, and subversive of the peace and harmony of the country.

8. That the normal condition of all the territory of the United States is that of freedom; that as our republican fathers, when they had abolished slavery in all our national territory, ordained that "no person shall be deprived of life, liberty, or property, without due process of law," it becomes our duty, by legislation, whenever such legislation is necessary, to maintain this provision of the constitution against all attempts to violate it; and we deny the authority of Congress, of a territorial legislature, or of any individuals, to give legal existence to slavery in any territory of the United States.

9. That we brand the recent reopening of the African slave trade, under the cover of our national flag, aided by perversions of judicial power, as a crime against humanity and a burning shame to our country and age; and we call upon Congress to take prompt and efficient measures for the total and final suppression of that execrable traffic.

10. That in the recent vetoes, by their federal governors, of the acts of the legislatures of Kansas and Nebraska, prohibiting slavery in those territories, we find a practical illustration of the boasted Democratic principle of non-intervention and popular sovereignty, embodied in the Kansas-Nebraska bill, and a demonstration of the deception and fraud involved therein.

11. That Kansas should, of right, be immediately admitted as a state under the constitution recently formed and adopted by her people, and accepted by the House of Representatives.

12. That, while providing revenue for the support of the general government by duties upon imports, sound policy requires such an adjustment of these imports as to encourage the development of the industrial interest of the whole country; and we commend that policy of national exchanges which secures to the working men liberal wages, to agriculture remunerative prices, to mechanics and manufacturers an adequate reward for their skill, labor, and enterprise, and to the nation commercial prosperity and independence.

13. That we protest against any sale or alienation to others of the public lands held by actual settlers, and against any view of the homestead policy which regards the settlers as paupers or suppliants for public bounty; and we demand the passage by Congress of the complete and satisfactory homestead measure which has already passed the House.

14. That the republican party is opposed to any change in our naturalization laws, or any state legislation by which the rights of citizenship hitherto accorded to immigrants from foreign lands shall be abridged or impaired; and in favor of giving a full and efficient protection to the rights of all

classes of citizens, whether native or naturalized, both at home and abroad.

15. That appropriations by Congress for river and harbor improvements of a national character, required for the accommodation and security of an existing commerce, are authorized by the constitution and justified by the obligations of government to protect the lives and property of its citizens.

16. That a railroad to the Pacific ocean is imperatively demanded by the interest of the whole country; that the Federal government ought to render immediate and efficient aid in its construction; and that as preliminary thereto, a daily overland mail should be promptly established.

17. Finally, having thus set forth our distinctive principles and views, we invite the co-operation of all citizens, however differing on other questions, who substantially agree with us in their affirmance and support.

1860.—Democratic (Douglas) Platform,

Charleston, April 23, and Baltimore, June 18.

1. *Resolved,* That we, the Democracy of the Union, in convention assembled, hereby declare our affirmance of the resolutions unanimously adopted and declared as a Platform of principles by the Democratic convention at Cincinnati, in the year 1856, believing that democratic principles are unchangeable in their nature when applied to the same subject-matters; and we recommend, as the only further resolutions, the following:

Inasmuch as differences of opinion exist in the Democratic party as to the nature and extent of the powers of a territorial legislature, and as to the powers and duties of Congress, under the constitution of the United States, over the institution of slavery within the territories:

2. *Resolved,* That the Democratic party will abide by the decisions of the Supreme Court of the United States on the questions of constitutional law.

3. *Resolved,* That it is the duty of the United States to afford ample and complete protection to all its citizens, whether at home or abroad, and whether native or foreign.

4. *Resolved,* That one of the necessities of the age, in a military, commercial, and postal point of view, is speedy communication between the Atlantic and Pacific states; and the Democratic party pledge such constitutional government aid as will insure the construction of a railroad to the Pacific coast at the earliest practicable period.

5. *Resolved,* That the Democratic party are in favor of the acquisition of the island of Cuba, on such terms as shall be honorable to ourselves and just to Spain.

6. *Resolved,* That the enactments of state legislatures to defeat the faithful execution of the Fugitive Slave Law are hostile in character, subversive of the constitution, and revolutionary in their effect.

7. *Resolved,* That it is in accordance with the true interpretation of the Cincinnati platform, that, during the existence of the territorial governments, the measure of restriction, whatever it may be, imposed by the federal constitution on the power of the territorial legislature over the subject of domestic relations, as the same has been, or shall hereafter be, finally determined by the Supreme Court of the United States, shall be respected by all good citizens, and enforced with promptness and fidelity by every branch of the general government.

1860.—Democratic (Breckinridge) Platform.

Charleston and Baltimore.

Resolved, That the platform adopted by the Democratic party at Cincinnati be affirmed, with following explanatory resolutions:

1. That the government of a territory, organized by an act of Congress, is provisional and temporary; and, during its existence, all citizens of the United States have an equal right to settle, with their property, in tho territory, without their rights, either of person or property, being destroyed or impaired by congressional or territorial legislation.

2. That it is the duty of the Federal government, in all its departments, to protect, when necessary, the rights of persons and property in the territories, and wherever else its constitutional authority extends.

3. That when the settlers in a territory having an adequate population form a state constitution in pursuance of law, the right of sovereignty commences, and, being consummated by admission into the Union, they stand on an equal footing with the people of other states, and the state thus organized ought to be admitted into the Federal Union, whether its constitution prohibits or recognizes the institution of slavery.

4. That the Democratic party are in favor of the acquisition of the island of Cuba, on such terms as shall be honorable to ourselves and just to Spain, at the earliest practicable moment.

5. That the enactments of state legislatures to defeat the faithful execution of the Fugitive Slave Law are hostile in character, subversive of the constitution, and revolutionary in their effect.

6. That the Democracy of the United States recognize it as the imperative duty of this government to protect the natural-

ized citizen in all his rights, whether at home or in foreign lands, to the same extent as its native-born citizens.

Whereas, One of the greatest necessities of the age, in a political, commercial, postal, and military point of view, is a speedy communication between the Pacific and Atlantic coasts; therefore, be it

Resolved, That the Democratic party do hereby pledge themselves to use every means in their power to secure the passage of some bill, to the extent of the constitutional authority of Congress, for the construction of a Pacific railroad from the Mississippi river to the Pacific ocean, at the earliest practicable moment.

1864.—Radical Platform.

Cleveland, May 31.

1. That the Federal Union shall be preserved.

2. That the constitution and laws of the United States must be observed and obeyed.

3. That the Rebellion must be suppressed by force of arms, and without compromise.

4. That the rights of free speech, free press and the *habeas corpus* be held inviolate, save in districts where martial law has been proclaimed.

5. That the Rebellion has destroyed slavery; and the federal constitution should be so amended as to prohibit its re-establishment, and to secure to all men absolute equality before the law.

6. That integrity and economy are demanded, at all times in the administration of the government, and that in time of war the want of them is criminal.

7. That the right of asylum, except for crime and subject to law, is a recognized principle of American liberty; and that any violation of it can not be overlooked, and must not go unrebuked.

8. That the national policy known as the "Monroe Doctrine" has become a recognized principle; and that the establishment of an anti-republican government on this continent by any foreign power can not be tolerated.

9. That the gratitude and support of the nation are due to the faithful soldiers and the earnest leaders of the Union army and navy, for their heroic achievements and deathless valor in defense of our imperiled country and of civil liberty.

10. That the one-term policy for the presidency, adopted by the people, is strengthened by the force of the existing crisis, and should be maintained by constitutional amendment.

11. That the constitution should be so amended that the President and Vice-President shall be elected by a direct vote of the people.

12. That the question of the reconstruction of the rebellious states belongs to the people, through their representatives in Congress, and not to the Executive.

13. That the confiscation of the lands of the rebels, and their distribution among the soldiers and actual settlers, is a measure of justice.

1864.—Republican Platform.

Baltimore, June 7.

Resolved, That it is the highest duty of every American citizen to maintain, against all their enemies, the integrity of the union and the paramount authority of the constitution and laws of the United States; and that, laying aside all differences of political opinions, we pledge ourselves, as Union men, animated by a common sentiment and aiming at a common object, to do everything in our power to aid the government in quelling, by force of arms, the Rebellion now raging against its authority, and in bringing to the punishment due to their crimes the rebels and traitors arrayed against it.

Resolved, That we approve the determination of the government of the United States not to compromise with rebels, nor to offer them any terms of peace, except such as may be based upon an "unconditional surrender" of their hostility and a return to their allegiance to the constitution and laws of the United States; and that we call upon the government to maintain this position, and to prosecute the war with the utmost possible vigor to the complete suppression of the Rebellion, in full reliance upon the self-sacrificing patriotism, the heroic valor, and the undying devotion of the American people to the country and its free institutions.

Resolved, That as slavery was the cause, and now constitutes the strength, of this Rebellion, and as it must be always and everywhere hostile to the principles of republican government, justice and the national safety demand its utter and complete extirpation from the soil of the Republic; and that we uphold and maintain the acts and proclamations by which the government, in its own defense, has aimed a death-blow at the gigantic evil. We are in favor, furthermore, of such an amendment to the constitution, to be made by the people in conformity with its provisions, as shall terminate and forever prohibit the existence of slavery within the limits or the jurisdiction of the United States.

Resolved, That the thanks of the American people are due to the soldiers and sailors of the army and navy, who have periled their lives in defense of their country and in vindication of the honor of its flag; that the nation owes to them some permanent recognition of their patriotism and their valor, and ample and permanent provision for those of their survivors who have received disabling and honorable wounds in the service of the country; and that the memories of those who have fallen in its defense shall be held in grateful and everlasting remembrance.

Resolved, That we approve and applaud the practical wisdom, the unselfish patriotism, and the unswerving fidelity to the constitution and the principles of American liberty with which Abraham Lincoln has discharged, under circumstances of unparalleled difficulty, the great duties and responsibilities of the presidential office; that we approve and indorse, as demanded by the emergency and essential to the preservation of the nation, and as within the provisions of the constitution, the measures and acts which he has adopted to defend the nation against its open and secret foes; that we approve, especially, the Proclamation of Emancipation, and the employment, as Union soldiers, of men heretofore held in slavery; and that we have full confidence in his determination to carry these, and all other constitutional measures essential to the salvation of the country, into full and complete effect.

Resolved, That we deem it essential to the general welfare that harmony should prevail in the national councils, and we regard as worthy of public confidence and official trust those only who cordially indorse the principles proclaimed in these resolutions, and which should characterize the administration of the government.

Resolved, That the government owes to all men employed in its armies, without regard to distinction of color, the full protection of the laws of war; and that any violation of these laws, or of the usages of civilized nations in the time of war, by the rebels now in arms, should be made the subject of prompt and full redress.

Resolved, That foreign immigration, which in the past has added so much to the wealth, development of resources, and increase of power to this nation—the asylum of the oppressed of all nations—should be fostered and encouraged by a liberal and just policy.

Resolved, That we are in favor of the speedy construction of the railroad to the Pacific coast.

Resolved, That the national faith, pledged for the redemption of the public debt, must be kept inviolate; and that, for this purpose, we recommend economy and rigid responsibility in the public expenditures and a vigorous and just system of taxation; and that it is the duty of every loyal state to sustain the credit and promote the use of the national currency.

Resolved, That we approve the position taken by the government, that the people of the United States can never regard with indifference the attempt of any European power to overthrow by force, or to supplant by fraud, the institutions of any republican government on the western continent, and that they will view with extreme jealousy, as menacing to the peace and independence of this, our country, the efforts of any such power to obtain new footholds for monarchical governments, sustained by a foreign military force, in near proximity to the United States.

1864.—Democratic Platform.

Chicago, August 29.

Resolved, That in the future, as in the past, we will adhere with unswerving fidelity to the Union under the constitution, as the only solid foundation of our strength, security, and happiness as a people, and as a frame-work of government equally conducive to the welfare and prosperity of all the states, both northern and southern.

Resolved, That this convention does explicitly declare, as the sense of the American people, that after four years of failure to restore the Union by the experiment of war, during which, under the pretense of a military necessity of a war power higher than the constitution, the constitution itself has been disregarded in every part, and public liberty and private right alike trodden down, and the material prosperity of the country essentially impaired, justice, humanity, liberty, and the public welfare demand that immediate efforts be made for a cessation of hostilities, with a view to an ultimate convention of all the states, or other peaceable means, to the end that, at the earliest practicable moment, peace may be restored on the basis of the federal union of all the states.

Resolved, That the direct interference of the military authority of the United States in the recent elections held in Kentucky, Maryland, Missouri, and Delaware, was a shameful violation of the constitution; and the repetition of such acts in the approaching election will be held as revolutionary, and resisted with all the means and power under our contrel.

Resolved, That the aim and object of the Democratic party is to preserve the Federal Union and the rights of the states unimpaired; and they hereby declare that they consider the administrative usurpation of extraordinary and dangerous powers not granted by the constitution, the subversion of the civil by the military law in states not in insurrection, the arbitrary military arrest, imprisonment, trial, and sentence of American citizens in states where civil law exists in full force, the suppression of freedom of speech and of the press, the denial of the right of asylum, the open and avowed disregard of state rights, the employment of unusual test-oaths, and the interference with and denial of the right of the people to bear arms in their defense, as calculated to prevent a restoration of the Union and the perpetuation of a government deriving its just powers from the consent of the governed.

Resolved, That the shameful disregard of the administration to its duty in respect to our fellow-citizens who now are, and long have been, prisoners of war, in a suffering condition, deserves the severest reprobation, on the score alike of public policy and common humanity.

Resolved, That the sympathy of the Democratic party is heartily and earnestly extended to the soldiery of our army and the sailors of our navy, who are and have been in the field and on the sea under the flag of their country; and, in the event of our attaining power, they will receive all the care and protection, regard and kindness, that the brave soldiers of the Republic have so nobly earned.

1868. Republican Platform.

Chicago, May 20.

1. We congratulate the country on the assured success of the reconstruction policy of Congress, as evinced by the adoption, in the majority of the states lately in rebellion, of constitutions securing equal civil and political rights to all; and it is the duty of the government to sustain those institutions and to prevent the people of such states from being remitted to a state of anarchy.

2. The guarantee by Congress of equal suffrage to all loyal men at the south was demanded by every consideration of public safety, of gratitude, and of justice, and must be maintained; while the question of suffrage in all the loyal states properly belongs to the people of those states.

3. We denounce all forms of repudiation as a national crime; and the national honor requires the payment of the public indebtedness in the uttermost good faith to all creditors at home and abroad, not only according to the letter but the spirit of the laws under which it was contracted.

4. It is due to the labor of the nation that taxation should be equalized and reduced as rapidly as the national faith will permit.

5. The national debt, contracted as it has been for the preservation of the Union for all time to come, should be extended over a fair period for redemption; and it is the duty of Congress to reduce the rate of interest thereon whenever it can be honestly done.

6. That the best policy to diminish our burden of debts is to so improve our credit that capitalists will seek to loan us money at lower rates of interest than we now pay, and must continue to pay, so long as repudiation, partial or total, open or covert, is threatened or suspected.

7. The government of the United States should be administered with the strictest economy; and the corruptions which have been so shamefully nursed and fostered by Andrew Johnson call loudly for radical reform.

8. We profoundly deplore the tragic death of Abraham Lincoln, and regret the accession to the presidency of Andrew Johnson, who has acted treacherously to the people who elected him and the cause he was pledged to support; who has usurped high legislative and judicial functions; who has refused to execute the laws; who has used his high office to induce other officers to ignore and violate the laws; who has employed his executive powers to render insecure the property, the peace, liberty, and life of the citizen; who has abused the pardoning power; who has denounced the national legislature as unconstitutional; who has persistently and corruptly resisted, by every means in his power, every proper attempt at the reconstruction of the states lately in rebellion; who has perverted the public patronage into an engine of wholesale corruption; and who has been justly impeached for high crimes and misdemeanors, and properly pronounced guilty thereof by the vote of thirty-five Senators.

9. The doctrine of Great Britain and other European powers, that because a man is once a subject he is always so, must be resisted at every hazard by the United States, as a relic of feudal times, not authorized by the laws of nations, and at war with our national honor and independence. Naturalized citizens are entitled to protection in all their rights of citizenship as though they were native-born; and no citizen of the United States, native or naturalized, must be liable to arrest and imprisonment by any foreign power for acts done or words spoken in this country; and, if so arrested and imprisoned, it is the duty of the government to interfere in his behalf.

10. Of all who were faithful in the trials of the late war, there were none entitled to more special honor than the brave soldiers and seamen who endured the hardships of campaign and cruise, and imperiled their lives in the service of the country. The

bounties and pensions provided by the laws for these brave defenders of the nation are obligations never to be forgotten; the widows and orphans of the gallant dead are the wards of the people—a sacred legacy bequeathed to the nation's protecting care.

11. Foreign immigration, which in the past has added so much to the wealth, development, and resources, and increase of power to this Republic, the asylum of the oppressed of all nations, should be fostered and encouraged by a liberal and just policy.

12. This convention declares itself in sympathy with all oppressed people who are struggling for their rights.

13. That we highly commend the spirit of magnanimity and forbearance with which men who have served in the Rebellion, but who now frankly and honestly co-operate with us in restoring the peace of the country and reconstructing the southern state governments upon the basis of impartial justice and equal rights, are received back into the communion of the loyal people; and we favor the removal of the disqualifications and restrictions imposed upon the late rebels, in the same measure as the spirit of disloyalty shall die out, and as may be consistent with the safety of the loyal people.

14. That we recognize the great principles laid down in the immortal Declaration of Independence, as the true foundation of democratic government; and we hail with gladness every effort toward making these principles a living reality on every inch of American soil.

1868.—Democratic Platform.

New York, July 4.

The Democratic party, in national convention assembled, reposing its trust in the intelligence, patriotism, and discriminating justice of the people, standing upon the constitution as the foundation and limitation of the powers of the government and the guarantee of the liberties of the citizen, and recognizing the questions of slavery and secession as having been settled, for all time to come, by the war or voluntary action of the southern states in constitutional conventions assembled, and never to be revived or reagitated, do, with the return of peace, demand—

1. Immediate restoration of all the states to their rights in the Union under the constitution, and of civil government to the American people.

2. Amnesty for all past political offenses, and the regulation of the elective franchise in the states by their citizens.

3. Payment of all the public debt of the United States as rapidly as practicable—all money drawn from the people by taxation, except so much as is requisite for the necessities of the government, economically administered, being honestly applied to such payment; and where the obligations of the government do not expressly state upon their face, or the law under which they were issued does not provide that they shall be paid in coin, they ought, in right and in justice, to be paid in the lawful money of the United States.

4. Equal taxation of every species of property according to its real value, including government bonds and other public securities.

5. One currency for the government and the people, the laborer and the officeholder, the pensioner and the soldier, the producer and the bondholder.

6. Economy in the administration of the government; the reduction of the standing army and navy; the abolition of the Freedmen's Bureau and all political instrumentalities designed to secure negro supremacy; simplification of the system and discontinuance of inquisitorial modes of assessing and collecting internal revenue; that the burden of taxation may be equalized and lessened, and the credit of the government and the currency made good; the repeal of all enactments for enrolling the state militia into national forces in time of peace; and a tariff for revenue upon foreign imports, and such equal taxation under the internal revenue laws as will afford incidental protection to domestic manufactures, and as will, without impairing the revenue, impose the least burden upon, and best promote and encourage, the great industrial interests of the country.

7. Reform of abuses in the administration; the expulsion of corrupt men from office; the abrogation of useless offices; the restoration of rightful authority to, and the independence of, the executive and judicial departments of the government; the subordination of the military to the civil power, to the end that the usurpations of Congress and the despotism of the sword may cease.

8. Equal rights and protection for naturalized and native-born citizens, at home and abroad; the assertion of American nationality which shall command the respect of foreign powers, and furnish an example and encouragement to people struggling for national integrity, constitutional liberty and individual rights; and the maintenance of the rights of naturalized citizens against the absolute doctrine of immutable allegiance and the claims of foreign powers to punish them for alleged crimes committed beyond their jurisdiction.

In demanding these measures and reforms, we arraign the Radical party for its disregard of right and the unparalleled oppression and tyranny which have marked its career. After the most solemn and unanimous pledge of both Houses of Congress to prosecute the war exclusively for the maintenance of the government and the preservation of the Union under the constitution, it has repeatedly violated the most sacred pledge under which alone was rallied that noble volunteer army which carried our flag to victory. Instead of restoring the Union, it has so far as in its power, dissolved it and subjected ten states in time of profound peace, to military despotism and negro supremacy. It has nullified there the right of trial by jury; it has abolished the *habeas corpus*, that most sacred writ of liberty; it has overthrown the freedom of speech and press; it has substituted arbitrary seizures and arrests, and military trials and secret star-chamber inquisitions, for the constitutional tribunals; it has disregarded in time of peace, the right of the people to be free from searches and seizures; it has entered the post and telegraph offices, and even the private rooms of individuals, and seized their private papers and letters without any specific charge or notice of affidavit, as required by the organic law. It has converted the American capitol into a bastile; it has established a system of spies and official espionage to which no constitutional monarchy of Europe would now dare to resort. It has abolished the right of appeal on important constitutional questions to the supreme judicial tribunals, and threatens to curtail or destroy its original jurisdiction, which is irrevocably vested by the constitution; while the learned Chief Justice has been subjected to the most atrocious calumnies, merely because he would not prostitute his high office to the support of the false and partisan charges preferred against the President. Its corruption and extravagance have exceeded anything known in history; and, by its frauds and monopolies, it has nearly doubled the burden of the debt created by the war. It has stripped the President of his constitutional power of appointment, even of his own cabinet. Under its repeated assaults, the pillars of the government are rocking on their base; and should it succeed in November next, and inaugurate its President, we will meet, as a subjected and conquered people, amid the ruins of liberty and the scattered fragments of the constitution.

And we do declare and resolve that ever since the people of the United States threw off all subjection to the British crown, the privilege and trust of suffrage have belonged to the several states, and have been granted, regulated, and controlled exclusively by the political power of each state respectively; and that any attempt by Congress, on any pretext whatever, to deprive any state of this right, or interfere with its exercise, is a flagrant usurpation of power which can find no warrant in the constitution, and, if sanctioned by the people will subvert our form of government, and can only end in a single centralized and consolidated government in which the separate existence of the states will be entirely absorbed, and an unqualified despotism be established in place of a federal union of co-equal states. And that we regard the reconstruction acts (so called) of Congress as usurpations and unconstitutional, revolutionary and void.

That our soldiers and sailors, who carried the flag of our country to victory against the most gallant and determined foe, must ever be gratefully remembered, and all the guarantees given in their favor must be faithfully carried into execution.

That the public lands should be distributed as widely as possible among the people, and should be disposed of either under the pre-emption of homestead lands or sold in reasonable quantities and to none but actual occupants at the minimum price established by the government. When grants of public lands may be allowed, necessary for the encouragement of important public improvements, the proceeds of the sale of such lands, and not the lands themselves should be so applied.

That the President of the United States, Andrew Johnson, in exercising the power of his high office in resisting the aggressions of Congress upon the constitutional rights of the states and the people, is entitled to the gratitude of the whole American people, and on behalf of the Democratic party, we tender him our thanks for his patriotic efforts in that regard.

Upon this platform, the Democratic party appeal to every patriot, including all the conservative element and all who desire to support the constitution and restore the Union, forgetting all past differences of opinion, to unite with us in the present great struggle for the liberties of the people; and that to all such, to whatever party they may have heretofore belonged, we extend the right hand of fellowship, and hail all such co-operating with us, as friends and brethren.

Resolved, That this convention sympathizes cordially with the workingmen of the United States in their efforts to protect the rights and interests of the laboring classes of the country.

Resolved, That the thanks of the convention are tendered to Chief Justice Salmon P. Chase, for the justice, dignity, and impartiality with which he presided over the court of impeachment on the trial of President Andrew Johnson.

1872.—Labor Reform Platform.

Columbus, February 21.

We hold that all political power is inherent in the people, and free government founded on their authority and established for their benefit; that all citizens are equal in political rights, entitled to the largest religious and political liberty compatible with the good order of society, as also the use and enjoyment of the fruits of their labor and talents; and no man or set of men is entitled to exclusive separable endowments and privileges or immunities from the government, but in consideration of public services; and any laws destructive of these fundamental principles are without moral binding force, and should be repealed. And believing that all the evils resulting from unjust legislation now affecting the industrial classes can be removed by the adoption of the principles contained in the following declaration: therefore,

Resolved, That it is the duty of the government to establish a just standard of distribution of capital and labor, by providing a purely national circulating medium, based on the faith and resources of the nation, issued directly to the people without the intervention of any system of banking corporations, which money shall be legal tender in the payment of all debts, public and private, and interchangeable, at the option of the holder, for government bonds bearing a rate of interest not to exceed 3.65 per cent., subject to future legislation by Congress.

2. That the national debt should be paid in good faith, according to the original contract, at the earliest option of the government, without mortgaging the property of the people or the future exigencies of labor to enrich a few capitalists at home and abroad.

3. That justice demands that the burdens of government should be so adjusted as to bear equally on all classes, and that the exemption from taxation of government bonds bearing extravagant rates of interest, is a violation of all just principles of revenue laws.

4. That the public lands of the United States belong to the people, and should not be sold to individuals nor granted to corporations, but should be held as a sacred trust for the benefit of the people, and should be granted to landless settlers only, in amounts not exceeding one hundred and sixty acres of land.

5. That Congress should modify the tariff so as to admit free such articles of common use as we can neither produce nor grow, and lay duties for revenue mainly upon articles of luxury and upon such articles of manufacture as will, we having the raw materials, assist in further developing the resources of the country.

6. That the presence in our country of Chinese laborers, imported by capitalists in large numbers for servile use is an evil entailing want and its attendant train of misery and crime on all classes of the American people, and should be prohibited by legislation.

7. That we ask for the enactment of a law by which all mechanics and day-laborers employed by or on behalf of the government, whether directly or indirectly, through persons, firms, or corporations, contracting with the state, shall conform to the reduced standard of eight hours a day, recently adopted by Congress for national employes; and also for an amendment to the acts of incorporation for cities and towns, by which all laborers and mechanics employed at their expense shall conform to the same number of hours.

8. That the enlightened spirit of the age demands the abolition of the system of contract labor in our prisons and other reformatory institutions.

9. That the protection of life, liberty, and property are the three cardinal principles of government, and the first two are more sacred than the latter; therefore, money needed for prosecuting wars should, as it is required, be assessed and collected from the wealthy of the country, and not entailed as a burden on posterity.

10. That it is the duty of the government to exercise its power over railroads and telegraph corporations, that they shall not in any case be privileged to exact such rates of freight, transportation, or charges, by whatever name, as may bear unduly or unequally upon the producer or consumer.

11. That there should be such a reform in the civil service of the national government as will remove it beyond all partisan influence, and place it in the charge and under the direction of intelligent and competent business men.

12. That as both history and experience teach us that power ever seeks to perpetuate itself by every and all means, and that its prolonged possession in the hands of one person is always dangerous to the interests of a free people, and believing that the spirit of our organic laws and the stability and safety of our free institutions are best obeyed on the one hand, and secured on the other, by a regular constitutional change in the chief of the country at each election; therefore, we are in favor of limiting the occupancy of the presidential chair to one term.

13. That we are in favor of granting general amnesty and restoring the Union at once on the basis of equality of rights and privileges to all, the impartial administration of justice being the only true bond of union to bind the states together and restore the government of the people.

14. That we demand the subjection of

the military to the civil authorities, and the confinement of its operations to national purposes alone.

15. That we deem it expedient for Congress to supervise the patent laws so as to give labor more fully the benefit of its own ideas and inventions.

16. That fitness, and not political or personal considerations, should be the only recommendation to public office, either appointive or elective; and any and all laws looking to the establishment of this principle are heartily approved.

1872.—Prohibition Platform.

Columbus, Ohio, February 22.

The preamble recites that protection and allegiance are reciprocal duties; and every citizen who yields obedience to the full commands of government should be protected in the enjoyment of personal security, personal liberty, and private property. That the traffic in intoxicating drinks greatly impairs the personal security and personal liberty of a great mass of citizens, and renders private property insecure. That all political parties are hopelessly unwilling to adopt an adequate policy on this question: Therefore, as a national convention, we adopt the following declaration of principles:

That while we acknowledge the pure patriotism and profound statesmanship of those patriots who laid the foundation of this government, securing at once the rights of the states severally and their inseparable union by the federal constitution, we would not merely garnish the sepulchres of our republican fathers, but we do hereby renew our pledges of solemn fealty to the imperishable principles of civil and religious liberty embodied in the Declaration of Independence and our federal constitution.

That the traffic in intoxicating beverages is a dishonor to Christian civilization, a political wrong of unequalled enormity, subversive of ordinary objects of government, not capable of being regulated or restrained by any system of license whatever, and imperatively demands, for its suppression, effective legal prohibition, both by state and national legislation.

That there can be no greater peril to a nation than existing party competition for the liquor vote. That any party not opposed to the traffic, experience shows will engage in this competition—will court the favor of criminal classes—will barter away the public morals, the purity of the ballot, and every object of good government, for party success.

That, as prohibitionists, we will individually use all efforts to persuade men from the use of intoxicating liquors; and we invite all persons to assist in this movement.

That competence, honesty, and sobriety are indispensable qualifications for holding office.

That removals from public office for mere political differences of opinion are wrong.

That fixed and moderate salaries of public officers should take the place of fees and perquisites; and that all means should be taken to prevent corruption and encourage economy.

That the President and Vice-President should be elected directly by the people.

That we are in favor of a sound national currency, adequate to the demands of business, and convertible into gold and silver at the will of the holder, and the adoption of every measure compatible with justice and public safety to appreciate our present currency to the gold standard.

That the rates of ocean and inland postage, and railroad telegraph lines and water transportation, should be made as low as possible by law.

That we are opposed to all discrimination in favor of capital against labor, as well as all monopoly and class legislation.

That the removal of the burdens imposed by the traffic in intoxicating drinks will emancipate labor, and will practically promote labor reform.

That suffrage should be granted to all persons, without regard to sex.

That the fostering and extension of common schools is a primary duty of the government.

That a liberal policy should be pursued to promote foreign immigration.

1872.—Liberal Republican Platform.

Cincinnati, May 1.

We, the Liberal Republicans of the United States, in national convention assembled at Cincinnati, proclaim the following principles as essential to just government.

1. We recognize the equality of all men before the law, and hold that it is the duty of government, in its dealings with the people, to mete out equal and exact justice to all, of whatever nativity, race, color, or persuasion, religious or political.

2. We pledge ourselves to maintain the union of these states, emancipation, and enfranchisement, and to oppose any reopening of the questions settled by the thirteenth, fourteenth, and fifteenth amendments of the constitution.

3. We demand the immediate and absolute removal of all disabilities imposed on account of the Rebellion, which was finally subdued seven years ago, believing that

universal amnesty will result in complete pacification in all sections of the country.

4. Local self-government, with impartial suffrage, will guard the rights of all citizens more securely than any centralized power. The public welfare requires the supremacy of the civil over the military authority, and the freedom of person under the protection of the *habeas corpus.* We demand for the individual the largest liberty consistent with public order, for the state self-government, and for the nation a return to the methods of peace and the constitutional limitations of power.

5. The civil service of the government has become a mere instrument of partisan tyranny and personal ambition, and an object of selfish greed. It is a scandal and reproach upon free institutions, and breeds a demoralization dangerous to the perpetuity of republican government. We, therefore, regard a thorough reform of the civil service as one of the most pressing necessities of the hour; that honesty, capacity, and fidelity constitute the only valid claims to public employment; that the offices of the government cease to be a matter of arbitrary favoritism and patronage, and that public station shall become again a post of honor. To this end, it is imperatively required that no President shall be a candidate for re-election.

6. We demand a system of federal taxation which shall not unnecessarily interfere with the industry of the people, and which shall provide the means necessary to pay the expenses of the government, economically administered, the pensions, the interest on the public debt, and a moderate reduction annually of the principal thereof; and recognizing that there are in our midst honest but irreconcilable differences of opinion with regard to the respective systems of protection and free trade, we remit the discussion of the subject to the people in their congressional districts and the decision of Congress thereon, wholly free from Executive interference or dictation.

7. The public credit must be sacredly maintained, and we denounce repudiation in every form and guise.

8. A speedy return to specie payment is demanded alike by the highest considerations of commercial morality and honest government.

9. We remember with gratitude the heroism and sacrifices of the soldiers and sailors of the Republic; and no act of ours shall ever detract from their justly earned fame or the full rewards of their patriotism.

10. We are opposed to all further grants of lands to railroads or other corporations. The public domain should be held sacred to actual settlers.

11. We hold that it is the duty of the government, in its intercourse with foreign nations, to cultivate the friendships of peace, by treating with all on fair and equal terms, regarding it alike dishonorable either to demand what is not right or submit to what is wrong.

12. For the promotion and success of these vital principles and the support of the candidates nominated by this convention, we invite and cordially welcome the co-operation of all patriotic citizens, without regard to previous political affiliations.

1872.—Democratic Platform,

Baltimore, July 9.

We, the Democratic electors of the United States, in convention assembled, do present the following principles, already adopted at Cincinnati, as essential to just government:

[Here followed the "Liberal Republican Platform;" which see above.]

1872.—Republican Platform,

Philadelphia, June 5.

The Republican party of the United States, assembled in national convention in the city of Philadelphia, on the 5th and 6th days of June, 1872, again declares its faith, appeals to its history, and announces its position upon the questions before the country;

1. During eleven years of supremacy it has accepted, with grand courage, the solemn duties of the time. It suppressed a gigantic rebellion, emancipated four millions of slaves, decreed the equal citizenship of all, and established universal suffrage. Exhibiting unparalleled magnanimity, it criminally punished no man for political offenses, and warmly welcomed all who proved their loyalty by obeying the laws and dealing justly with their neighbors. It has steadily decreased, with firm hand, the resultant disorders of a great war, and initiated a wise and humane policy toward the Indians. The Pacific railroad and similar vast enterprises have been generously aided and successfully conducted, the public lands freely given to actual settlers, immigration protected and encouraged, and a full acknowledgment of the naturalized citizen's rights secured from European powers. A uniform national currency has been provided, repudiation frowned down, the national credit sustained under the most extraordinary burdens, and new bonds negotiated at lower rates. The revenues have been carefully collected and honestly applied. Despite annual large reductions of the rates of taxation, the public debt has been reduced during General Grant's presidency at the rate of a hundred millions a year, great financial

crises have been avoided, and peace and plenty prevail throughout the land. Menacing foreign difficulties have been peacefully and honorably compromised, and the honor and power of the nation kept in high respect throughout the world. This glorious record of the past is the party's best pledge for the future. We believe the people will not intrust the government to any party or combination of men composed chiefly of those who have resisted every step of this beneficent progress.

2. The recent amendments to the national constitution should be cordially sustained because they are right, not merely tolerated because they are law, and should be carried out according to their spirit by appropriate legislation, the enforcement of which can safely be intrusted only to the party that secured those amendments.

3. Complete liberty and exact equality in the enjoyment of all civil, political, and public rights should be established and effectually maintained throughout the Union by efficient and appropriate state and federal legislation. Neither the law nor its administration should admit any discrimination in respect to citizens by reason of race, creed, color, or previous condition of servitude.

4. The national government should seek to maintain honorable peace with all nations, protecting its citizens everywhere, and sympathizing with all peoples who strive for greater liberty.

5. Any system of civil service under which the subordinate positions of the government are considered rewards for mere party zeal is fatally demoralizing; and we, therefore, favor a reform of the system, by laws which shall abolish the evils of patronage, and make honesty, efficiency, and fidelity the essential qualifications for public positions, without practically creating a life tenure of office.

6. We are opposed to further grants of the public lands to corporations and monopolies, and demand that the national domain be set apart for free homes for the people.

7. The annual revenue, after paying current expenditures, pensions, and the interest on the public debt, should furnish a moderate balance for the reduction of the principal; and that revenue, except so much as may be derived from a tax upon tobacco and liquors, should be raised by duties upon importations, the details of which should be so adjusted as to aid in securing remunerative wages to labor, and promote the industries, prosperity, and growth of the whole country.

8. We hold in undying honor the soldiers and sailors whose valor saved the Union. Their pensions are a sacred debt of the nation, and the widows and orphans of those who died for their country are entitled to the care of a generous and grateful people. We favor such additional legislation as will extend the bounty of the government to all our soldiers and sailors who were honorably discharged, and who in the line of duty became disabled, without regard to the length of service or the cause of such discharge.

9. The doctrine of Great Britain and other European powers concerning allegiance—"once a subject always a subject"—having at last, through the efforts of the Republican party, been abandoned, and the American idea of the individual's right to transfer allegiance having been accepted by European nations, it is the duty of our government to guard with jealous care the rights of adopted citizens against the assumption of unauthorized claims by their former governments, and we urge continued careful encouragement and protection of voluntary immigration.

10. The franking privilege ought to be abolished, and a way prepared for a speedy reduction in the rates of postage.

11. Among the questions which press for attention is that which concerns the relations of capital and labor; and the Republican party recognizes the duty of so shaping legislation as to secure full protection and the amplest field for capital, and for labor, the creator of capital, the largest opportunities and a just share of the mutual profits of these two great servants of civilization.

12. We hold that Congress and the President have only fulfilled an imperative duty in their measures for the suppression of violence and treasonable organizations in certain lately rebellious regions, and for the protection of the ballot-box; and, therefore, they are entitled to the thanks of the nation.

13. We denounce repudiation of the public debt, in any form or disguise, as a national crime. We witness with pride the reduction of the principal of the debt, and of the rates of interest upon the balance, and confidently expect that our excellent national currency will be perfected by a speedy resumption of specie payment.

14. The Republican party is mindful of its obligations to the loyal women of America for their noble devotion to the cause of freedom. Their admission to wider fields of usefulness is viewed with satisfaction; and the honest demand of any class of citizens for additional rights should be treated with respectful consideration.

15. We heartily approve the action of Congress in extending amnesty to those lately in rebellion, and rejoice in the growth of peace and fraternal feeling throughout the land.

16. The Republican party proposes to respect the rights reserved by the people to

themselves as carefully as the powers delegated by them to the states and to the federal government. It disapproves of the resort to unconstitutional laws for the purpose of removing evils, by interference with rights not surrendered by the people to either the state or national government.

17. It is the duty of the general government to adopt such measures as may tend to encourage and restore American commerce and ship-building.

18. We believe that the modest patriotism, the earnest purpose, the sound judgment, the practical wisdom, the incorruptible integrity, and the illustrious services of Ulysses S. Grant have commended him to the heart of the American people; and with him at our head, we start to-day upon a new march to victory.

19. Henry Wilson, nominated for the Vice-Presidency, known to the whole land from the early days of the great struggle for liberty as an indefatigable laborer in all campaigns, an incorruptible legislator and representative man of American institutions, is worthy to associate with our great leader and share the honors which we pledge our best efforts to bestow upon them.

1872.—Democratic (Straight-out) Platform,

Louisville, Ky., September 3.

Whereas, A frequent recurrence to first principles and eternal vigilance against abuses are the wisest provisions for liberty, which is the source of progress, and fidelity to our constitutional system is the only protection for either: therefore,

Resolved, That the original basis of our whole political structure is consent in every part thereof. The people of each state voluntarily created their state, and the states voluntarily formed the Union; and each state provided by its written constitution for everything a state could do for the protection of life, liberty, and property within it; and each state, jointly with the others, provided a federal union for foreign and inter-state relations.

Resolved, That all governmental powers, whether state or federal, are trust powers coming from the people of each state, and that they are limited to the written letter of the constitution and the laws passed in pursuance of it; which powers must be exercised in the utmost good faith, the constitution itself stating in what manner they may be altered and amended.

Resolved, That the interests of labor and capital should not be permitted to conflict, but should be harmonized by judicious legislation. While such a conflict continues, labor, which is the parent of wealth, is entitled to paramount consideration.

Resolved, That we proclaim to the world that principle is to be preferred to power; that the Democratic party is held together by the cohesion of time-honored principles, which they will never surrender in exchange for all the offices which Presidents can confer. The pangs of the minorities are doubtless excruciating; but we welcome an eternal minority, under the banner inscribed with our principles, rather than an almighty and everlasting majority, purchased by their abandonment.

Resolved, That, having been betrayed at Baltimore into a false creed and a false leadership by the convention, we repudiate both, and appeal to the people to approve our platform, and to rally to the polls and support the true platform and the candidates who embody it.

1875.—The American National Platform,

Adopted in Mass Meeting, Pittsburg, June 9.

We hold:

1. That ours is a Christian and not a heathen nation, and that the God of the Christian Scriptures is the author of civil government.

2. That God requires and man needs a Sabbath.

3. That the prohibition of the importation, manufacture, and sale of intoxicating drinks as a beverage, is the true policy on the temperance question.

4. The charters of all secret lodges granted by our federal and state legislatures should be withdrawn, and their oaths prohibited by law.

5. That the civil equality secured to all American citizens by articles 13th, 14th, and 15th of our amended constitution should be preserved inviolate.

6. That arbitration of differences with nations is the most direct and sure method of securing and perpetuating a permanent peace.

7. That to cultivate the intellect without improving the morals of men is to make mere adepts and experts: therefore, the Bible should be associated with books of science and literature in all our educational institutions.

8. That land and other monopolies should be discountenanced.

9. That the government should furnish the people with an ample and sound currency and a return to specie payment, as soon as practicable.

10. That maintenance of the public credit, protection to all loyal citizens, and justice to Indians are essential to the honor and safety of our nation.

11. And, finally, we demand for the American people the abolition of electoral colleges, and a direct vote for President and Vice-President of the United States.

[Their candidates were James B. Walker, Wheaton, Illinois, for President; and Donald Kirkpatrick, Syracuse, New York, for Vice-President.]

1876.—Prohibition Reform Platform,

Cleveland, Ohio, May 17.

The Prohibition Reform party of the United States, organized in the name of the people, to revive, enforce, and perpetuate in the government the doctrines of the Declaration of Independence, submit, in this centennial year of the republic, for the suffrages of all good citizens, the following platform of national reforms and measures:

First. The legal prohibition in the District of Columbia, the territories, and in every other place subject to the laws of Congress, of the importation, exportation, manufacture, and traffic of all alcoholic beverages, as high crimes against society; an amendment of the national constitution, to render these prohibitory measures universal and permanent; and the adoption of treaty stipulations with foreign powers, to prevent the importation and exportation of all alcoholic beverages.

Second. The abolition of class legislation, and of special privileges in the government, and the adoption of equal suffrage and eligibility to office, without distinction of race, religious creed, property, or sex.

Third. The appropriation of the public lands, in limited quantities, to actual settlers only; the reduction of the rates of inland and ocean postage; of telegraphic communication; of railroad and water transportation and travel, to the lowest practical point, by force of laws, wisely and justly framed, with reference, not only to the interest of capital employed, but to the higher claims of the general good.

Fourth. The suppression, by laws, of lotteries and gambling in gold, stocks, produce, and every form of money and property, and the penal inhibition of the use of the public mails for advertising schemes of gambling and lotteries.

Fifth. The abolition of those foul enormities, polygamy and the social evil; and the protection of purity, peace, and happiness of homes, by ample and efficient legislation.

Sixth. The national observance of the Christian Sabbath, established by laws prohibiting ordinary labor and business in all departments of public service and private employment (works of necessity, charity, and religion excepted) on that day.

Seventh. The establishment, by mandatory provisions in national and state constitutions, and by all necessary legislation, of a system of free public schools for the universal and forced education of all the youth of the land.

Eighth. The free use of the Bible, not as a ground of religious creeds, but as a text-book of the purest morality, the best liberty, and the noblest literature in our public schools, that our children may grow up in its light, and that its spirit and principles may pervade our nation.

Ninth. The separation of the government in all its departments and institutions, including the public schools and all funds for their maintenance, from the control of every religious sect or other association, and the protection alike of all sects by equal laws, with entire freedom of religious faith and worship.

Tenth. The introduction into all treaties hereafter negotiated with foreign governments of a provision for the amicable settlement of international difficulties by arbitration.

Eleventh. The abolition of all barbarous modes and instruments of punishment; the recognition of the laws of God and the claims of humanity in the discipline of jails and prisons, and of that higher and wiser civilization worthy of our age and nation, which regards the reform of criminals as a means for the prevention of crime.

Twelfth. The abolition of executive and legislative patronage, and the election of President, Vice-President, United States Senators, and of all civil officers, so far as practicable, by the direct vote of the people.

Thirteenth. The practice of a friendly and liberal policy to immigrants from all nations, the guaranty to them of ample protection, and of equal rights and privileges.

Fourteenth. The separation of the money of government from all banking institutions. The national government, only, should exercise the high prerogative of issuing paper money, and that should be subject to prompt redemption on demand, in gold and silver, the only equal standards of value recognized by the civilized world.

Fifteenth. The reduction of the salaries of public officers in a just ratio with the decline of wages and market prices; the abolition of sinecures, unnecessary offices, and official fees and perquisites; the practice of strict economy in government expenses; and a free and thorough investigation into any and all alleged abuses of public trusts.

1876.—Independent (Greenback) Platform,

Indianapolis, Ind., May 17.

The Independent party is called into existence by the necessities of the people, whose industries are prostrated, whose labor is deprived of its just reward by a ruinous policy which the Republican and Democratic parties refuse to change; and, in view of the failure of these parties to furnish relief to the depressed industries of the country, thereby disappointing the just hopes and expectations of the suffering people, we delare our principles, and invite all independent and patriotic men to join our ranks in this movement for financial reform and industrial emancipation.

First. We demand the immediate and unconditional repeal of the specie resumption act of January 14, 1875, and the rescue of our industries from ruin and disaster resulting from its enforcement; and we call upon all patriotic men to organize in every congressional district of the country, with a view of electing representatives to Congress who will carry out the wishes of the people in this regard and stop the present suicidal and destructive policy of contraction.

Second. We believe that a United States note, issued directly by the government, and convertible, on demand, into United States obligations, bearing a rate of interest not exceeding one cent a day on each one hundred dollars, and exchangeable for United States notes at par, will afford the best circulating medium ever devised. Such United States notes should be full legal tenders for all purposes, except for the payment of such obligations as are, by existing contracts, especially made payable in coin; and we hold that it is the duty of the government to provide such a circulating medium, and insist, in the language of Thomas Jefferson, that "bank paper must be suppressed, and the circulation restored to the nation, to whom it belongs."

Third. It is the paramount duty of the government, in all its legislation, to keep in view the full development of all legitimate business, agricultural, mining, manufacturing, and commercial.

Fourth. We most earnestly protest against any further issue of gold bonds for sale in foreign markets, by which we would be made, for a long period, "hewers of wood and drawers of water" to foreigners, especially as the American people would gladly and promptly take at par all bonds the government may need to sell, provided they are made payable at the option of the holder, and bearing interest at 3.65 per cent. per annum or even a lower rate.

Fifth. We further protest against the sale of government bonds for the purpose of purchasing silver to be used as a substitute for our more convenient and less fluctuating fractional currency, which, although well calculated to enrich owners of silver mines, yet in operation it will still further oppress, in taxation, an already overburdened people.

1876.—Republican Platform,

Cincinnati, Ohio, June 14.

When, in the economy of Providence, this land was to be purged of human slavery, and when the strength of the government of the people, by the people, and for the people, was to be demonstrated, the Republican party came into power. Its deeds have passed into history, and we look back to them with pride. Incited by their memories to high aims for the good of our country and mankind, and looking to the future with unfaltering courage, hope, and purpose, we, the representatives of the party, in national convention assembled, make the following declaration of principles:

1. The United States of America is a nation, not a league. By the combined workings of the national and state governments, under their respective constitutions, the rights of every citizen are secured, at home and abroad, and the common welfare promoted.

2. The Republican party has preserved these governments to the hundredth anniversary of the nation's birth, and they are now embodiments of the great truths spoken at its cradle—"That all men are created equal; that they are endowed by their Creator with certain inalienable rights, among which are life, liberty, and the pursuit of happiness; that for the attainment of these ends governments have been instituted among men, deriving their just powers from the consent of the governed." Until these truths are cheerfully obeyed, or, if need be, vigorously enforced, the work of the Republican party is unfinished.

3. The permanent pacification of the southern section of the Union, and the complete protection of all its citizens in the free enjoyment of all their rights, is a duty to which the Republican party stands sacredly pledged. The power to provide for the enforcement of the principles embodied in the recent constitutional amendments is vested, by those amendments, in the Congress of the United States; and we declare it to be the solemn obligation of the legislative and executive departments of the government to put into immediate and vigorous exercise all their constitutional powers for removing any just causes of discontent on the part of any class, and for securing to every American citizen complete liberty and exact equality in the exercise of all civil, political, and public rights. To this end we imperatively demand a Congress and a Chief Executive whose courage and fidelity to these duties shall not falter until these results are placed beyond dispute or recall.

4. In the first act of Congress signed by President Grant, the national government assumed to remove any doubt of its pur-

pose to discharge all just obligations to the public creditors, and "solemnly pledged its faith to make provision at the earliest practicable period for the redemption of the United States notes in coin." Commercial prosperity, public morals, and national credit demand that this promise be fulfilled by a continuous and steady progress to specie payment.

5. Under the constitution, the President and heads of departments are to make nominations for office, the Senate is to advise and consent to appointments, and the House of Representatives is to accuse and prosecute faithless officers. The best interest of the public service demand that these distinctions be respected; that Senators and Representatives who may be judges and accusers should not dictate appointments to office. The invariable rule in appointments should have reference to the honesty, fidelity, and capacity of the appointees, giving to the party in power those places where harmony and vigor of administration require its policy to be represented, but permitting all others to be filled by persons selected with sole reference to the efficiency of the public service, and the right of all citizens to share in the honor of rendering faithful service to the country.

6. We rejoice in the quickened conscience of the people concerning political affairs, and will hold all public officers to a rigid responsibility, and engage that the prosecution and punishment of all who betray official trusts shall be swift, thorough, and unsparing.

7. The public school system of the several states is the bulwark of the American Republic; and, with a view to its security and permanence, we recommend an amendment to the constitution of the United States, forbidding the application of any public funds or property for the benefit of any schools or institutions under sectarian control.

8. The revenue necessary for current expenditures, and the obligations of the public debt, must be largely derived from duties upon importations, which, so far as possible, should be adjusted to promote the interests of American labor and advance the prosperity of the whole country.

9. We reaffirm our opposition to further grants of the public lands to corporations and monopolies, and demand that the national domain be devoted to free homes for the people.

10. It is the imperative duty of the government so to modify existing treaties with European governments, that the same protection shall be afforded to the adopted American citizen that is given to the native-born; and that all necessary laws should be passed to protect emigrants in the absence of power in the states for that purpose.

11. It is the immediate duty of Congress to fully investigate the effect of the immigration and importation of Mongolians upon the moral and material interests of the country.

12. The Republican party recognizes, with approval, the substantial advances recently made towards the establishment of equal rights for women by the many important amendments effected by Republican legislatures in the laws which concern the personal and property relations of wives, mothers, and widows, and by the appointment and election of women to the superintendence of education, charities, and other public trusts. The honest demands of this class of citizens for additional rights, privileges, and immunities, should be treated with respectful consideration.

13. The constitution confers upon Congress sovereign power over the territories of the United States for their government; and in the exercise of this power it is the right and duty of Congress to prohibit and extirpate, in the territories, that relic of barbarism—polygamy; and we demand such legislation as shall secure this end and the supremacy of American institutions in all the territories.

14. The pledges which the nation has given to her soldiers and sailors must be fulfilled, and a grateful people will always hold those who imperiled their lives for the country's preservation in the kindest remembrance.

15. We sincerely deprecate all sectional feeling and tendencies. We, therefore, note with deep solicitude that the Democratic party counts, as its chief hope of success, upon the electoral vote of a united south, secured through the efforts of those who were recently arrayed against the nation; and we invoke the earnest attention of the country to the grave truth that a success thus achieved would reopen sectional strife, and imperil national honor and human rights.

16. We charge the Democratic party with being the same in character and spirit as when it sympathized with treason; with making its control of the House of Representatives the triumph and opportunity of the nation's recent foes; with reasserting and applauding, in the national capital, the sentiments of unrepentant rebellion; with sending Union soldiers to the rear, and promoting Confederate soldiers to the front; with deliberately proposing to repudiate the plighted faith of the government; with being equally false and imbecile upon the overshadowing financial questions; with thwarting the ends of justice by its partisan mismanagement and obstruction of investigation; with proving itself

through the period of its ascendency in the lower house of Congress, utterly incompetent to administer the government; and we warn the country against trusting a party thus alike unworthy, recreant, and incapable.

17. The national administration merits commendation for its honorable work in the management of domestic and foreign affairs, and President Grant deserves the continued hearty gratitude of the American people for his patriotism and his eminent services in war and in peace.

18. We present, as our candidates for President and Vice-President of the United States, two distinguished statesmen, of eminent ability and character, and conspicuously fitted for those high offices, and we confidently appeal to the American people to intrust the administration of their public affairs to Rutherford B. Hayes and William A. Wheeler.

1876.—Democratic Platform.

St. Louis, Mo., June 27.

We, the delegates of the Democratic party of the United States, in national convention assembled, do hereby declare the administration of the Federal government to be in urgent need of immediate reform; do hereby enjoin upon the nominees of this convention, and of the Democratic party in each state, a zealous effort and co-operation to this end; and do hereby appeal to our fellow-citizens of every former political connection to undertake, with us, this first and most pressing patriotic duty.

For the Democracy of the whole country, we do here reaffirm our faith in the permanence of the Federal Union, our devotion to the constitution of the United States, with its amendments universally accepted as a final settlement of the controversies that engendered civil war, and do here record our steadfast confidence in the perpetuity of republican self-government.

In absolute acquiescence in the will of the majority—the vital principle of republics; in the supremacy of the civil over the military authority; in the total separation of church and state, for the sake alike of civil and religious freedom; in the equality of all citizens before just laws of their own enactment; in the liberty of individual conduct, unvexed by sumptuary laws; in the faithful education of the rising generation, that they may preserve, enjoy, and transmit these best conditions of human happiness and hope—we behold the noblest products of a hundred years of changeful history; but while upholding the bond of our Union and great charter of these our rights, it behooves a free people to practice also that eternal vigilance which is the price of liberty.

Reform is necessary to rebuild and establish in the hearts of the whole people the Union, eleven years ago happily rescued from the danger of a secession of states, but now to be saved from a corrupt centralism which, after inflicting upon ten states the rapacity of carpet-bag tyranny, has honey-combed the offices of the Federal government itself, with incapacity, waste, and fraud; infected states and municipalities with the contagion of misrule; and locked fast the prosperity of an industrious people in the paralysis of "hard times."

Reform is necessary to establish a sound currency, restore the public credit, and maintain the national honor.

We denounce the failure, for all these eleven years of peace, to make good the promise of the legal tender notes, which are a changing standard of value in the hands of the people, and the non-payment of which is a disregard of the plighted faith of the nation.

We denounce the improvidence which, in eleven years of peace, has taken from the people, in federal taxes, thirteen times the whole amount of the legal-tender notes, and squandered four times their sum in useless expense without accumulating any reserve for their redemption.

We denounce the financial imbecility and immorality of that party which, during eleven years of peace, has made no advance toward resumption, no preparation for resumption, but, instead, has obstructed resumption, by wasting our resources and exhausting all our surplus income; and, while annually professing to intend a speedy return to specie payments, has annually enacted fresh hinderances thereto. As such hinderance we denounce the resumption clause of 1875, and we here demand its repeal.

We demand a judicious system of preparation, by public economies, by official retrenchments, and by wise finance, which shall enable the nation soon to assure the whole world of its perfect ability and of its perfect readiness to meet any of its promises at the call of the creditor entitled to payment. We believe such a system, well devised, and, above all, intrusted to competent hands for execution, creating, at no time, an artificial scarcity of currency, and at no time alarming the public mind into a withdrawal of that vaster machinery of credit by which ninety-five per cent. of all business transactions are performed. A system open, public, and inspiring general confidence, would, from the day of its adoption, bring healing on its wings to all our harassed industries—set in motion the wheels of commerce, manufactures, and the mechanic arts—restore employment to labor—and, renew, in all its natural sources, the prosperity of the people.

Reform is necessary in the sum and

modes of federal taxation, to the end that capital may be set free from distrust and labor lightly burdened.

We denounce the present tariff, levied upon nearly four thousand articles, as a masterpiece of injustice, inequality, and false pretence. It yields a dwindling, not a yearly rising, revenue. It has impoverished many industries to subsidize a few. It prohibits imports that might purchase the products of American labor. It has degraded American commerce from the first to an inferior rank on the high seas. It has cut down the sales of American manufactures at home and abroad, and depleted the returns of American agriculture—an industry followed by half our people. It costs the people five times more than it produces to the treasury, obstructs the processes of production, and wastes the fruits of labor. It promotes fraud, fosters smuggling, enriches dishonest officials, and bankrupts honest merchants. We demand that all custom-house taxation shall be only for revenue.

Reform is necessary in the scale of public expense—federal, state, and municipal. Our federal taxation has swollen from sixty millions gold, in 1860, to four hundred and fifty millions currency, in 1870; our aggregate taxation from one hundred and fifty-four millions gold, in 1860, to seven hundred and thirty millions currency, in 1870—or, in one decade, from less than five dollars per head to more than eighteen dollars per head. Since the peace, the people have paid to their tax-gatherers more than thrice the sum of the national debt, and more than twice that sum for the Federal government alone. We demand a rigorous frugality in every department and from every officer of the government.

Reform is necessary to put a stop to the profligate waste of public lands, and their diversion from actual settlers, by the party in power, which has squandered 200,000,000 of acres upon railroads alone, and, out of more than thrice that aggregate, has disposed of less than a sixth directly to tillers of the soil.

Reform is necessary to correct the omission of a Republican Congress, and the errors of our treaties and our diplomacy which have stripped our fellow-citizens of foreign birth and kindred race, recrossing the Atlantic, of the shield of American citizenship, and have exposed our brethren of the Pacific coast to the incursions of a race not sprung from the same great parent stock, and in fact now, by law, denied citizenship through naturalization, as being neither accustomed to the traditions of a progressive civilization nor exercised in liberty under equal laws. We denounce the policy which thus discards the liberty-loving German and tolerates a revival of the coolie trade in Mongolian women, imported for immoral purposes, and Mongolian men, held to perform servile labor contracts and demand such modification of the treaty with the Chinese Empire, or such legislation within constitutional limitations, as shall prevent further importation or immigration of the Mongolian race.

Reform is necessary, and can never be effected but by making it the controlling issue of the elections, and lifting it above the two false issues with which the office-holding class and the party in power seek to smother it:

1. The false issue with which they would enkindle sectarian strife in respect to the public schools, of which the establishment and support belongs exclusively to the several states, and which the Democratic party has cherished from their foundation, and is resolved to maintain, without prejudice or preference for any class, sect, or creed, and without largesses from the treasury to any.

2. The false issue by which they seek to light anew the dying embers of sectional hate between kindred peoples once estranged, but now reunited in one indivisible republic and a common destiny.

Reform is necessary in the civil service. Experience proves that efficient, economical conduct of the governmental business is not possible if its civil service be subject to change at every election, be a prize fought for at the ballot-box, be a brief reward of party zeal, instead of posts of honor assigned for proved competency, and held for fidelity in the public employ; that the dispensing of patronage should neither be a tax upon the time of all our public men nor the instrument of their ambition. Here, again, promises, falsified in the performance, attest that the party in power can work out no practical or salutary reform.

Reform is necessary, even more, in the higher grades of the public service. President, Vice-President, Judges, Senators, Representatives, Cabinet officers—these, and all others in authority—are the people's servants. Their offices are not a private perquisite; they are a public trust. When the annals of this Republic show the disgrace and censure of a Vice-President; a late Speaker of the House of Representatives marketing his rulings as a presiding officer; three Senators profiting secretly by their votes as law-makers; five chairmen of the leading committees of the late House of Representatives exposed in jobbery; a late Secretary of the Treasury forcing balances in the public accounts; a late Attorney-General misappropriating public funds; a Secretary of the Navy enriched, or enriching friends, by percentages levied off the profits of contractors with his department; an Ambassador to England concerned in a dishonorable speculation; the

President's private secretary barely escaping conviction upon trial for guilty complicity in frauds upon the revenue; a Secretary of War impeached for high crimes and misdemeanors—the demonstration is complete, that the first step in reform must be the people's choice of honest men from another party, lest the disease of one political organization infect the body politic, and lest by making no change of men or parties we get no change of measures and no real reform.

All these abuses, wrongs, and crimes—the product of sixteen years' ascendency of the Republican party—create a necessity for reform, confessed by the Republicans themselves; but their reformers are voted down in convention and displaced from the cabinet. The party's mass of honest voters is powerless to resist the 80,000 office-holders, its leaders and guides.

Reform can only be had by a peaceful civic revolution. We demand a change of system, a change of administration, a change of parties, that we may have a change of measures and of men.

Resolved, That this convention, representing the Democratic party of the United States, do cordially indorse the action of the present House of Representatives, in reducing and curtailing the expenses of the Federal government, in cutting down salaries and extravagant appropriations, and in abolishing useless offices and places not required by the public necessities; and we shall trust to the firmness of the Democratic members of the House that no committee of conference and no misinterpretation of the rules will be allowed to defeat these wholesome measures of economy demanded by the country.

Resolved, That the soldiers and sailors of the Republic, and the widows and orphans of those who have fallen in battle, have a just claim upon the care, protection, and gratitude of their fellow-citizens.

1878.—National Platform.

Toledo, Ohio, February 22.

Whereas, Throughout our entire country the value of real estate is depreciated, industry paralyzed, trade depressed, business incomes and wages reduced, unparalleled distress inflicted upon the poorer and middle ranks of our people, the land filled with fraud, embezzlement, bankruptcy, crime, suffering, pauperism, and starvation; and

Whereas, This state of things has been brought about by legislation in the interest of, and dictated by, money-lenders, bankers and bondholders; and

Whereas, While we recognize the fact that the men in Congress connected with the old political parties have stood up manfully for the rights of the people, and met the threats of the money power, and the ridicule of an ignorant and subsidized press, yet neither the Republican nor the Democratic parties, in their policies, propose remedies for the existing evils; and

Whereas, The Independent Greenback party, and other associations more or less effective, have been unable, hitherto, to make a formidable opposition to old party organizations; and

Whereas, The limiting of the legal-tender quality of the greenbacks, the changing of currency bonds into coin bonds, the demonetization of the silver dollar, the exempting of bonds from taxation, the contraction of the circulating medium, the proposed forced resumption of specie payments, and the prodigal waste of the public lands, were crimes against the people; and, as far as possible, the results of these criminal acts must be counteracted by judicious legislation:

Therefore, We assemble in national convention and make a declaration of our principles, and invite all patriotic citizens to unite in an effort to secure financial reform and industrial emancipation. The organization shall be known as the "National Party," and under this name we will perfect, without delay, national, state, and local associations, to secure the election to office of such men only as will pledge themselves to do all in their power to establish these principles:

First. It is the exclusive function of the general government to coin and create money and regulate its value. All bank issues designed to circulate as money should be suppressed. The circulating medium, whether of metal or paper, shall be issued by the government, and made a full legal-tender for all debts, duties, and taxes in the United States, at its stamped value.

Second. There shall be no privileged class of creditors. Official salaries, pensions, bonds, and all other debts and obligations, public and private, shall be discharged in the legal-tender money of the United States strictly according to the stipulations of the laws under which they were contracted.

Third. The coinage of silver shall be placed on the same footing as that of gold.

Fourth. Congress shall provide said money adequate to the full employment of labor, the equitable distribution of its products, and the requirement of business, fixing a minimum amount *per capita* of the population as near as may be, and otherwise regulating its value by wise and equitable provisions of law, so that the rate of interest will secure to labor its just reward.

Fifth. It is inconsistent with the genius of popular government that any species of private property should be exempt from bearing its proper share of the public burdens. Government bonds and money should be taxed precisely as other property, and a graduated income tax should be levied for the support of the government and the payment of its debts.

Sixth. Public lands are the common property of the whole people, and should not be sold to speculators nor granted to railroads or other corporations, but should be donated to actual settlers, in limited quantities.

Seventh. The government should, by general enactments, encourage the development of our agricultural, mineral, mechanical, manufacturing, and commercial resources, to the end that labor may be fully and profitably employed; but no monopolies should be legalized.

Eighth. All useless offices should be abolished, the most rigid economy favored in every branch of the public service, and severe punishment inflicted upon public officers who betray the trusts reposed in them.

Ninth. As educated labor has devised means for multiplying productions by inventions and discoveries, and as their use requires the exercise of mind as well as body, such legislation should be had that the number of hours of daily toil will be reduced, giving to the working classes more leisure for mental improvement and their several enjoyments, and saving them from premature decay and death.

Tenth. The adoption of an American monetary system, as proposed herein, will harmonize all differences in regard to tariff and federal taxation, reduce and equlize the cost of transportation by land and water, distribute equitably the joint earnings of capital and labor, secure to the producers of wealth the results of their labor and skill, and muster out of service the vast army of idlers, who, under the existing system, grow rich upon the earnings of others, that every man and woman may, by their own efforts, secure a competency, so that overgrown fortunes and extreme poverty will be seldom found within the limits of our republic.

Eleventh. Both national and state governments should establish bureaus of labor and industrial statistics, clothed with the power of gathering and publishing the same.

Twelfth. That the contract system of employing labor in our prisons and reformatory institutions works great injustice to our mechanics and artisans, and should be prohibited.

Thirteenth. The importation of servile labor into the United States from China is a problem of the most serious importance, and we recommend legislation looking to its suppression.

Fourteenth. We believe in the supremacy of law over and above all perishable material, and in the necessity of a party of united people that will rise above old party lines and prejudices. We will not affiliate in any degree with any of the old parties, but, in all cases and localities, will organize anew, as united National men—nominate for office and official positions only such persons as are clearly believers in and identified with this our sacred cause; and, irrespective of creed, color, place of birth, or past condition of political or other servitude, vote only for men who entirely abandon old party lines and organizations.

1879.—National Liberal Platform.

Cincinnati, Ohio, September 14.

1. Total separation of Church and State, to be guaranteed by amendment of the United States constitution; including the equitable taxation of church property, secularization of the public schools, abrogation of Sabbatarian laws, abolition of chaplaincies, prohibition of public appropriations for religious purposes, and all measures necessary to the same general end.

2. National protection for national citizens in their equal civil, political, and religious rights, to be guaranteed by amendment of the United States constitution and afforded through the United States courts.

3. Universal education, the basis of universal suffrage in this secular Republic, to be guaranteed by amendment of the United States constitution, requiring every state to maintain a thoroughly secularized public school system, and to permit no child within its limits to grow up without a good elementary education.

1880.—Independent Republican Principles.

I. Independent Republicans adhere to the republican principles of national supremacy, sound finances, and civil service reform, expressed in the Republican platform of 1876, in the letter of acceptance of President Hayes, and in his message of 1879; and they seek the realization of those principles in practical laws and their efficient administration. This requires,

1. The continuance on the statute-book of laws protecting the rights of voters at national elections. But national supremacy affords no pretext for interference with the local rights of communities; and the development of the south from its present defective civilization can be secured only under constitutional methods, such as those of President Hayes.

2. The passage of laws which shall deprive greenbacks of their legal-tender quality, as a first step toward their ulti-

mate withdrawal and cancellation, and shall maintain all coins made legal tender at such weight and fineness as will enable them to be used without discount in the commercial transactions of the world.

3. The repeal of the acts which limit the terms of office of certain government officials to four years; the repeal of the tenure-of-office acts, which limit the power of the executive to remove for cause; the establishment of a permanent civil service commission, or equivalent measures to ascertain, by open competition, and certify to the President or other appointing power the fitness of applicants for nomination or appointment to all non-political offices.

II. Independent Republicans believe that local issues should be independent of party. The words Republican and Democrat should have no weight in determining whether a school or city shall be administered on business principles by capable men. With a view to this, legislation is asked which shall prescribe for the voting for local and for state officers upon separate ballots.

III. Independent Republicans assert that a political party is a co-operation of voters to secure the practical enactment into legislation of political convictions set forth as its platform. Every voter accepting that platform is a member of that party; any representative of that party opposing the principles or evading the promises of its platform forfeits the support of its voters. No voter should be held by the action or nomination of any caucus or convention of his party against his private judgment. It is his duty to vote against bad measures and unfit men, as the only means of obtaining good ones; and if his party no longer represents its professed principles in its practical workings, it is his duty to vote against it.

IV. Independent Republicans seek good nominations through participation in the primaries and through the defeat of bad nominees; they will labor for the defeat of any local Republican candidate, and, in co-operation with those holding like views elsewhere, for the defeat of any general Republican candidate whom they do not deem fit.

1880. Republican Platform.

Chicago, Illinois, June 2.

The Republican party, in national convention assembled, at the end of twenty years since the Federal government was first committed to its charge, submits to the people of the United States its brief report of its administration:

It suppressed a rebellion which had armed nearly a million of men to subvert the national authority. It reconstructed the union of the states with freedom, instead of slavery, as its corner-stone. It transformed four million of human beings from the likeness of things to the rank of citizens. It relieved Congress from the infamous work of hunting fugitive slaves, and charged it to see that slavery does not exist.

It has raised the value of our paper currency from thirty-eight per cent. to the par of gold. It has restored, upon a solid basis, payment in coin for all the national obligations, and has given us a currency absolutely good and equal in every part of our extended country. It has lifted the credit of the nation from the point where six per cent. bonds sold at eighty-six to that where four per cent. bonds are eagerly sought at a premium.

Under its administration railways have increased from 31,000 miles in 1860, to more than 82,000 miles in 1879.

Our foreign trade has increased from $700,000,000 to $1,150,000,000 in the same time; and our exports, which were $20,000,000 less than our imports in 1860, were $264,000,000 more than our imports in 1879.

Without resorting to loans, it has, since the war closed, defrayed the ordinary expenses of government, besides the accruing interest on the public debt, and disbursed, annually, over $30,000,000 for soldiers' pensions. It has paid $888,000,000 of the public debt, and, by refunding the balance at lower rates, has reduced the annual interest charge from nearly $151,000,000 to less than $89,000,000.

All the industries of the country have revived, labor is in demand, wages have increased, and throughout the entire country there is evidence of a coming prosperity greater than we have ever enjoyed.

Upon this record, the Republican party asks for the continued confidence and support of the people; and this convention submits for their approval the following statement of the principles and purposes which will continue to guide and inspire its efforts:

1. We affirm that the work of the last twenty years has been such as to commend itself to the favor of the nation, and that the fruits of the costly victories which we have achieved, through immense difficulties, should be preserved; that the peace regained should be cherished; that the dissevered Union, now happily restored, should be perpetuated, and that the liberties secured to this generation should be transmitted, undiminished, to future generations; that the order established and the credit acquired should never be impaired; that the pensions promised should be paid; that the debt so much reduced should be extinguished by the full payment of every dollar thereof; that the reviving industries should be further promoted; and that the

commerce, already so great, should be steadily encouraged.

2. The constitution of the United States is a supreme law, and not a mere contract; out of confederate states it made a sovereign nation. Some powers are denied to the nation, while others are denied to states; but the boundary between the powers delegated and those reserved is to be determined by the national and not by the state tribunals.

3. The work of popular education is one left to the care of the several states, but it is the duty of the national government to aid that work to the extent of its constitutional ability. The intelligence of the nation is but the aggregate of the intelligence in the several states; and the destiny of the nation must be guided, not by the genius of any one state, but by the average genius of all.

4. The constitution wisely forbids Congress to make any law respecting an establishment of religion; but it is idle to hope that the nation can be protected against the influences of sectarianism while each state is exposed to its domination. We, therefore, recommend that the constitution be so amended as to lay the same prohibition upon the legislature of each state, to forbid the appropriation of public funds to the support of sectarian schools.

5. We reaffirm the belief, avowed in 1876, that the duties levied for the purpose of revenue should so discriminate as to favor American labor; that no further grant of the public domain should be made to any railway or other corporation; that slavery having perished in the states, its twin barbarity—polygamy—must die in the territories; that everywhere the protection accorded to citizens of American birth must be secured to citizens by American adoption. That we esteem it the duty of Congress to develop and improve our water-courses and harbors, but insist that further subsidies to private persons or corporations must cease. That the obligations of the republic to the men who preserved its integrity in the day of battle are undiminished by the lapse of fifteen years since their final victory—to do them perpetual honor is, and shall forever be, the grateful privilege and sacred duty of the American people.

6. Since the authority to regulate immigration and intercourse between the United States and foreign nations rests with the Congress of the United States and its treaty-making powers, the Republican party, regarding the unrestricted immigration of the Chinese as an evil of great magnitude, invoke the exercise of that power to restrain and limit that immigration by the enactment of such just, humane, and reasonable provisions as will produce that result.

That the purity and patriotism which characterized the early career of Rutherford B. Hayes in peace and war, and which guided the thoughts of our immediate predecessors to select him for a presidential candidate, have continued to inspire him in his career as chief executive, and that history will accord to his administration the honors which are due to an efficient, just, and courteous discharge of the public business, and will honor his interposition between the people and proposed partisan laws.

8. We charge upon the Democratic party the habitual sacrifice of patriotism and justice to a supreme and insatiable lust for office and patronage. That to obtain possession of the national and state governments, and the control of place and position, they have obstructed all efforts to promote the purity and to conserve the freedom of suffrage; have devised fraudulent certifications and returns; have labored to unseat lawfully-elected members of Congress, to secure, at all hazards, the vote of a majority of the states in the House of Representatives; have endeavored to occupy, by force and fraud the places of trust given to others by the people of Maine, and rescued by the courageous action of Maine's patriotic sons; have, by methods vicious in principle and tyrannical in practice, attached partisan legislation to appropriation bills, upon whose passage the very movements of government depend; have crushed the rights of the individual; have advocated the principle and sought the favor of rebellion against the nation, and have endeavored to obliterate the sacred memories of the war, and to overcome its inestimably valuable results of nationality, personal freedom, and individual equality. Equal, steady, and complete enforcement of the laws, and protection of all our citizens in the enjoyment of all privileges and immunities guaranteed by the constitution, are the first duties of the nation. The danger of a solid south can only be averted by the faithful performance of every promise which the nation made to the citizen. The execution of the laws, and the punishment of all those who violate them, are the only safe methods by which an enduring peace can be secured, and genuine prosperity established throughout the south. Whatever promises the nation makes, the nation must perform; and the nation can not with safety relegate this duty to the states. The solid south must be divided by the peaceful agencies of the ballot, and all opinions must there find free expression; and to this end honest voters must be protected against terrorism, violence, or fraud. And we affirm it to be the duty and the purpose of the Republican party to use all legitimate means to restore all the states of this Union to the most perfect harmony

which may be practicable; and we submit to the practical, sensible people of the United States to say whether it would not be dangerous to the dearest interests of our country, at this time to surrender the administration of the national government to a party which seeks to overthrow the existing policy, under which we are so prosperous, and thus bring distrust and confusion where there is now order, confidence, and hope.

9. The Republican party, adhering to a principle affirmed by its last national convention, of respect for the constitutional rule covering appointments to office, adopts the declaration of President Hayes, that the reform of the civil service should be thorough, radical, and complete. To this end it demands the co-operation of the legislative with the executive department of the government, and that Congress shall so legislate that fitness, ascertained by proper practical tests, shall admit to the public service; and that the power of removal for cause, with due responsibility for the good conduct of subordinates, shall accompany the power of appointment.

1880.—National (Greenback) Platform,

Chicago, Illinois, June 9.

The civil government should guarantee the divine right of every laborer to the results of his toil, thus enabling the producers of wealth to provide themselves with the means for physical comfort, and facilities for mental, social, and moral culture; and we condemn, as unworthy of our civilization, the barbarism which imposes upon wealth-producers a state of drudgery as the price of a bare animal existence. Notwithstanding the enormous increase of productive power by the universal introduction of labor-saving machinery and the discovery of new agents for the increase of wealth, the task of the laborer is scarcely lightened, the hours of toil are but little shortened, and few producers are lifted from poverty into comfort and pecuniary independence. The associated monopolies, the international syndicates, and other income classes demand dear money, cheap labor, and a strong government, and, hence, a weak people. Corporate control of the volume of money has been the means of dividing society into hostile classes, of an unjust distribution of the products of labor, and of building up monopolies of associated capital, endowed with power to confiscate private property. It has kept money scarce; and the scarcity of money enforces debt-trade, and public and corporate loans; debt engenders usury, and usury ends in the bankruptcy of the borrower. Other results are—deranged markets, uncertainty in manufacturing enterprises and agriculture, precarious and intermittent employment for the laborer, industrial war, increasing pauperism and crime, and the consequent intimidation and disfranchisement of the producer, and a rapid declension into corporate feudalism. Therefore, we declare—

First. That the right to make and issue money is a sovereign power, to be maintained by the people for their common benefit. The delegation of this right to corporations is a surrender of the central attribute of sovereignty, void of constitutional sanction, and conferring upon a subordinate and irresponsible power an absolute dominion over industry and commerce. All money, whether metallic or paper, should be issued, and its volume controlled, by the government, and not by or through banking corporations; and, when so issued, should be a full legal tender for all debts, public and private.

Second. That the bonds of the United States should not be refunded, but paid as rapidly as practicable, according to contract. To enable the government to meet these obligations, legal-tender currency should be substituted for the notes of the national banks, the national banking system abolished, and the unlimited coinage of silver, as well as gold, established by law.

Third. That labor should be so protected by national and state authority as to equalize its burdens and insure a just distribution of its results. The eight hour law of Congress should be enforced, the sanitary condition of industrial establishments placed under the rigid control, the competition of contract convict labor abolished, a bureau of labor statistics established, factories, mines, and workshops inspected, the employment of children under fourteen years of age forbidden, and wages paid in cash.

Fourth. Slavery being simply cheap labor, and cheap labor being simply slavery, the importation and presence of Chinese serfs necessarily tends to brutalize and degrade American labor; therefore, immediate steps should be taken to abrogate the Burlingame treaty.

Fifth. Railroad land grants forfeited by reason of non-fulfillment of contract should be immediately reclaimed by the government, and, henceforth, the public domain reserved exclusively as homes for actual settlers.

Sixth. It is the duty of Congress to regulate inter-state commerce. All lines of communication and transportation should be brought under such legislative control as shall secure moderate, fair, and uniform rates for passenger and freight traffic.

Seventh. We denounce as destructive to property and dangerous to liberty the action of the old parties in fostering and sustaining gigantic land, railroad, and money corporations, and monopolies invested with and exercising powers belonging to the government, and yet not responsible to it for the manner of their exercise.

Eighth. That the constitution, in giving Congress the power to borrow money, to declare war, to raise and support armies, to provide and maintain a navy, never intended that the men who loaned their money for an interest-consideration should be preferred to the soldiers and sailors who periled their lives and shed their blood on land and sea in defense of their country; and we condemn the cruel class legislation of the Republican party, which, while professing great gratitude to the soldier, has most unjustly discriminated against him and in favor of the bondholder.

Ninth. All property should bear its just proportion of taxation, and we demand a graduated income tax.

Tenth. We denounce as dangerous the efforts everywhere manifest to restrict the right of suffrage.

Eleventh. We are opposed to an increase of the standing army in time of peace, and the insidious scheme to establish an enormous military power under the guise of militia laws.

Twelfth. We demand absolute democratic rules for the government of Congress, placing all representatives of the people upon an equal footing, and taking away from committees a veto power greater than that of the President.

Thirteenth. We demand a government of the people, by the people, and for the people, instead of a government of the bondholder, by the bondholder, and for the bondholder; and we denounce every attempt to stir up sectional strife as an effort to conceal monstrous crimes against the people.

Fourteenth. In the furtherance of these ends we ask the co-operation of all fair-minded people. We have no quarrel with individuals, wage no war on classes, but only against vicious institutions. We are not content to endure further discipline from our present actual rulers, who, having dominion over money, over transportation, over land and labor, over the press and the machinery of government, wield unwarrantable power over our institutions and over life and property.

1880.—Prohibition Reform Platform,

Cleveland, Ohio, June 17.

The prohibition Reform party of the United States, organized, in the name of the people, to revive, enforce, and perpetuate in the government the doctrines of the Declaration of Independence, submit, for the suffrage of all good citizens, the following platform of national reforms and measures:

In the examination and discussion of the temperance question, it has been proven, and is an accepted truth, that alcoholic drinks, whether fermented, brewed, or distilled, are poisonous to the healthy human body, the drinking of which is not only needless but hurtful, necessarily tending to form intemperate habits, increasing greatly the number, severity, and fatal termination of diseases, weakening and deranging the intellect, polluting the affections, hardening the heart and corrupting the morals, depriving many of reason and still more of its healthful exercise, and annually bringing down large numbers to untimely graves, producing, in the children of many who drink, a predisposition to intemperance, insanity, and various bodily and mental diseases, causing diminution of strength, feebleness of vision, fickleness of purpose, and premature old age, and inducing, in all future generations, deterioration of moral and physical character. Alcoholic drinks are thus the implacable foe of man as an individual.

First. The legalized importation, manufacture, and sale of intoxicating drinks ministers to their use, and teaches the erroneous and destructive sentiment that such use is right, thus tending to produce and perpetuate the above mentioned evils.

Second. To the home it is an enemy—proving itself to be a disturber and destroyer of its peace, prosperity, and happiness; taking from it the earnings of the husband; depriving the dependent wife and children of essential food, clothing, and education; bringing into it profanity, abuse, and violence; setting at naught the vows of the marriage altar; breaking up the family and sundering the children from the parents, and thus destroying one of the most beneficent institutions of our Creator, and removing the sure foundation of good government, national prosperity, and welfare.

Third. To the community it is equally an enemy—producing vice, demoralization, and wickedness; its places of sale being resorts of gaming, lewdness, and debauchery, and the hiding-place of those who prey upon society; counteracting the efficacy of religious effort, and of all means of intellectual elevation, moral purity, social happiness, and the eternal good of mankind, without rendering any counteracting or compensating benefits; being in its influence and effect evil and only evil, and that continually.

Fourth. To the state it is equally an enemy—legislative inquiries, judicial investigations, and official reports of all penal, reformatory, and dependent institutions showing that the manufacture and sale of such beverages is the promoting cause of intemperance, crime, and pauperism, and of demands upon public and private charity, imposing the larger part of taxation, paralyzing thrift, industry, manufactures, and commercial life, which, but for it, would be unnecessary; disturbing the peace of streets and highways; filling prisons and poor-houses; corrupting politics, legislation, and the execution of the laws; shortening lives; diminishing health, industry, and productive power in manufactures and art; and is manifestly unjust as well as injurious to the community upon which it is imposed, and is contrary to all just views of civil liberty, as well as a violation of the fundamental maxim of our common law, to use your own property or liberty so as not to injure others.

Fifth. It is neither right nor politic for the state to afford legal protection to any traffic or any system which tends to waste the resources, to corrupt the social habits, and to destroy the health and lives of the people; that the importation, manufacture, and sale of intoxicating beverages is proven to be inimical to the true interests of the individual home, community, and state, and destructive to the order and welfare of society, and ought, therefore, to be classed among crimes to be prohibited.

Sixth. In this time of profound peace at home and abroad, the entire separation of the general government from the drink-traffic, and its prohibition in the District of Columbia, territories, and in all places and ways over which, under the constitution, Congress has control and power, is a political issue of the first importance to the peace and prosperity of the nation. There can be no stable peace and protection to personal liberty, life, or property, until secured by national or state constitutional provisions, enforced by adequate laws.

Seventh. All legitimate industries require deliverance from the taxation and loss which the liquor traffic imposes upon them; and financial or other legislation could not accomplish so much to increase production and cause a demand for labor, and, as a result, for the comforts of living, as the suppression of this traffic would bring to thousands of homes as one of its blessings.

Eighth. The administration of the government and the execution of the laws are through political parties; and we arraign the Republican party, which has been in continuous power in the nation for twenty years, as being false to duty, as false to loudly-proclaimed principles of equal justice to all and special favors to none, and of protection to the weak and dependent, insensible to the mischief which the trade in liquor has constantly inflicted upon industry, trade, commerce, and the social happiness of the people; that 5,652 distilleries, 3,830 breweries, and 175,266 places for the sale of these poisonous liquors, involving an annual waste to the nation of one million five hundred thousand dollars, and the sacrifice of one hundred thousand lives, have, under its legislation, grown up and been fostered as a legitimate source of revenue; that during its history, six territories have been organized and five states been admitted into the Union, with constitutions provided and approved by Congress, but the prohibition of this debasing and destructive traffic has not been provided, nor even the people given, at the time of admission, power to forbid it in any one of them. Its history further shows, that not in a single instance has an original prohibitory law been passed by any state that was controlled by it, while in four states, so governed, the laws found on its advent to power have been repealed. At its national convention in 1872, it declared, as part of its party faith, that "it disapproves of the resort to unconstitutional laws for the purpose of removing evils, by interference with rights not surrendered by the people to either the state or national government," which, the author of this plank says, was adopted by the platform committee with the full and implicit understanding that its purpose was the discountenancing of all so-called temperance, prohibitory, and Sunday laws.

Ninth. We arraign, also, the Democratic party as unfaithful and unworthy of reliance on this question; for, although not clothed with power, but occupying the relation of an opposition party during twenty years past, strong in numbers and organization, it has allied itself with liquor-traffickers, and become, in all the states of the Union, their special political defenders, and in its national convention in 1876, as an article of its political faith, declared against prohibition and just laws in restraint of the trade in drink, by saying it was opposed to what it was pleased to call "all sumptuary laws." The National party has been dumb on this question.

Tenth. Drink-traffickers, having the history and experience of all ages, climes, and conditions of men, declaring their business destructive of all good—finding no support in the Bible, morals, or reason—appeal to misapplied law for their justification, and intrench themselves behind the evil elements of political party for defense, party tactics and party inertia become battling forces, protecting this evil.

Eleventh. In view of the foregoing facts and history, we cordially invite all voters, without regard to former party affiliations, to unite with us in the use of the ballot for the abolition of the drinking system, under the authority of our national and state governments. We also demand, as a right, that women, having the privileges of citizens in other respects, be clothed with the ballot for their protection, and as a rightful means for the proper settlement of the liquor question.

Twelfth. To remove the apprehension of some who allege that a loss of public revenue would follow the suppression of the direct trade, we confidently point to the experience of governments abroad and at home, which shows that thrift and revenue from the consumption of legitimate manufactures and commerce have so largely followed the abolition of drink as to fully supply all loss of liquor taxes.

Thirteenth. We recognize the good providence of Almighty God, who has preserved and prospered us as a nation; and, asking for His Spirit to guide us to ultimate success, we all look for it, relying upon His omnipotent arm.

1880.—Democratic Platform,

Cincinnati, Ohio, June 22.

The Democrats of the United States, in convention assembled, declare:

First. We pledge ourselves anew to the constitutional doctrines and traditions of the Democratic party, as illustrated by the teachings and examples of a long line of Democratic statesmen and patriots, and embodied in the platform of the last national convention of the party.

Second. Opposition to centralization, and to that dangerous spirit of encroachment which tends to consolidate the powers of all the departments in one, and thus to create, whatever the form of government, a real despotism; no sumptuary laws; separation of the church and state for the good of each; common schools fostered and protected.

Third. Home rule; honest money, consisting of gold and silver, and paper, convertible into coin on demand; the strict maintenance of the public faith, state and national; and a tariff for revenue only; the subordination of the military to the civil power; and a general and thorough reform of the civil service.

Fourth. The right to a free ballot is a right preservative of all rights; and must and shall be maintained in every part of the United States.

Fifth. The existing administration is the representative of conspiracy only; and its claim of right to surround the ballot-boxes with troops and deputy marshals, to intimidate and obstruct the elections, and the unprecedented use of the veto to maintain its corrupt and despotic power, insults the people and imperils their institutions. We execrate the course of this administration in making places in the civil service a reward for political crime; and demand a reform, by statute, which shall make it forever impossible for a defeated candidate to bribe his way to the seat of a usurper by billeting villains upon the people.

Sixth. The great fraud of 1876-7, by which, upon a false count of the electoral votes of two states, the candidate defeated at the polls was declared to be President, and, for the first time in American history, the will of the people was set aside under a threat of military violence, struck a deadly blow at our system of representative government. The Democratic party, to preserve the country from the horrors of a civil war, submitted for the time, in the firm and patriotic belief that the people would punish the crime in 1880. This issue precedes and dwarfs every other. It imposes a more sacred duty upon the people of the Union than ever addressed the consciences of a nation of freemen.

Seventh. The resolution of Samuel J. Tilden, not again to be a candidate for the exalted place to which he was elected by a majority of his countrymen, and from which he was excluded by the leaders of the Republican party, is received by the Democrats of the United States with deep sensibility; and they declare their confidence in his wisdom, patriotism, and integrity unshaken by the assaults of the common enemy; and they further assure him that he is followed into the retirement he has chosen for himself by the sympathy and respect of his fellow-citizens, who regard him as one who, by elevating the standard of the public morality, and adorning and purifying the public service, merits the lasting gratitude of his country and his party.

Eighth. Free ships, and a living chance for American commerce upon the seas; and on the land, no discrimination in favor of transportation lines, corporations, or monopolies.

Ninth. Amendments of the Burlingame treaty; no more Chinese immigration, except for travel, education, and foreign commerce, and, therein, carefully guarded.

Tenth. Public money and public credit for public purposes solely, and public land for actual settlers.

Eleventh. The Democratic party is the friend of labor and the laboring man, and pledges itself to protect him alike against the cormorants and the commune.

Twelfth. We congratulate the country upon the honesty and thrift of a Democratic Congress, which has reduced the public expenditure $10,000,000 a year; upon the continuation of prosperity at home and the national honor abroad; and, above all, upon the promise of such a change in the administration of the government as shall insure a genuine and lasting reform in every department of the public service.

Virginia Republican.

[*Adopted August* 11.]

Whereas, It is proper that when the people assemble in convention they should avow distinctly the principles of government on which they stand; now, therefore, be it,

Resolved, That we, the Republicans of Virginia, hereby make a declaration of our allegiance and adhesion to the principles of the Republican party of the country, and our determination to stand squarely by the organization of the Republican party of Virginia, always defending it against the assaults of all persons or parties whatsoever.

Second. That amongst the principles of the Republican party none is of more vital importance to the welfare and interest of the country in all its parts than that which pertains to the sanctity of Government contracts. It therefore becomes the special duty and province of the Republican party of Virginia to guard and protect the credit of our time-honored State, which has been besmirched with repudiation, or received with distrust, by the gross mismanagement of various factions of the Democratic party, which have controlled the legislation of the State.

Third. That the Republican party of Virginia hereby pledges itself to redeem the State from the discredit that now hangs over her in regard to her just obligations for moneys loaned her for constructing her internal improvements and charitable institutions, which, permeating every quarter of the State, bring benefits of far greater value than their cost to our whole people, and we in the most solemn form pledge the Republican party of the State to the full payment of the whole debt of the State, less the one-third set aside as justly falling on West Virginia; that the industries of the country should be fostered through protective laws, so as to develop our own resources, employ our own labor, create a home market, enhance values, and promote the happiness and prosperity of the people.

Fourth. That the public school system of Virginia is the creature of the Republican party, and we demand that every dollar the Constitution dedicates to it shall be sacredly applied thereto as a means of educating the children of the State, without regard to condition or race.

Fifth. That the elective franchise as an equal right should be based on manhood qualification, and that we favor the repeal of the requirements of the prepayment of the capitation tax as a prerequisite to the franchise as opposed to the Constitution of the United States, and in violation of the condition whereby the State was readmitted as a member of our Constitutional Union, as well as against the spirit of the Constitution; but demand the imposition of the capitation tax as a source of revenue for the support of the public schools without its disfranchising effects.

Sixth. That we favor the repeal of the disqualification for the elective franchise by a conviction of petty larceny, and of the infamous laws which place it in the power of a single justice of the peace (ofttimes being more corrupt than the criminal before him) to disfranchise his fellow-man.

Seventh. Finally, that we urge the repeal of the barbarous law permitting the imposition of stripes as degrading and inhuman, contrary to the genius of a true and enlightened people, and a relic of barbarism.

[The Convention considered it inexpedient to nominate candidates for State officers.]

Virginia Readjuster.

[*Adopted June* 2.]

First. We recognize our obligation to support the institution for the deaf, dumb and blind, the lunatic asylum, the public free schools and the Government out of the revenues of the State; and we deprecate and denounce that policy of ring rule and subordinated sovereignty which for years borrowed money out of banks at high rates of interest for the discharge of these paramount trusts, while our revenues were left the prey of commercial exchanges, available to the State only at the option of speculators and syndicates.

Second. We reassert our purpose to settle and adjust our State obligations on the principles of the "Bill to re-establish public credit," known as the "Riddleberger bill," passed by the last General Assembly and vetoed by the Governor. We maintain that this measure recognizes the just debt of Virginia, in this, that it assumes two-thirds of all the money Virginia borrowed, and sets aside the other third to West Virginia to be dealt with by her in her own way and at her own pleasure; that it places those of her creditors who have received but 6 per cent. instalments of interest in nine years upon an exact equality with those who by corrupt agencies were enabled to absorb and monopolize our means of payment; that it agrees to pay such rate of interest on our securities as can with certainty be met out of the revenues of the State, and that it contains all the essential features of finality.

Third. We reassert our adherence to the Constitutional requirements for the "equal and uniform" taxation of property, exempting none except that specified by the Constitution and used exclusively for "religious, charitable and educational purposes."

Fourth. We reassert that the paramount obligation of the various works of internal improvement is to the people of the State, by whose authority they were created, by whose money they were constructed and by whose grace they live; and it is enjoined upon our representative and executive officers to enforce the discharge of that duty; to insure to our people such rates, facilities and connections as will protect every industry and interest against discrimination, tend to the development of our agricultural and mineral resources, encourage the investment of active capital in manufactures and the profitable employment of labor in industrial enterprises, grasp for our city and our whole State those advantages to which by their geographical position they are entitled, and fulfil all the great public ends for which they were designed.

Fifth. The Readjusters hold the right to a free ballot to be the right preservative of all rights, and that it should be maintained in every State in the Union. We believe the capitation tax restriction upon the suffrage in Virginia to be in conflict with the XIVth Amendment to the Constitution of the United States. We believe that it is a violation of that condition of reconstruction wherein the pledge was given not so to amend our State Constitution as to deprive any citizen or class of citizens of a right to vote, except as punishment for such crimes as are felony at common law. We believe such a prerequisite to voting to be contrary to the genius of our institutions, the very foundation of which is representation as antecedent to taxation. We know that it has been a failure as a measure for the collection of revenue, the pretended reason for its invention in 1876, and we know the base, demoralizing and dangerous uses to which it has been prostituted. We know it contributes to the increase of monopoly power, and to corrupting the voter. For these and other reasons we adhere to the purpose hitherto expressed to provide more effectual legislation for the collection of this tax, dedicated by the Constitution to the public free schools, and to abolish it as a qualification for and restriction upon suffrage.

Sixth. The Readjusters congratulate the whole people of Virginia on the progress of the last few years in developing mineral resources and promoting manufacturing enterprises in the State, and they declare their purpose to aid these great and growing industries by all proper and essential legislation, State and Federal. To this end they will continue their efforts in behalf of more cordial and fraternal relations between the sections and States, and especially for that concord and harmony which will make the country to know how earnestly and sincerely Virginia invites all men into her borders as visitors or to become citizens without fear of social or political ostracism; that every man, from whatever section of country, shall enjoy the fullest freedom of thought, speech, politics and religion, and that the State which first formulated these principles as fundamental in free government is yet the citadel for their exercise and protection.

Virginia Democratic.

[*Adopted August 4.*]

The Conservative Democratic party of Virginia—Democratic in its Federal relations and Conservative in its State policy—assembled in convention, in view of the present condition of the Union and of this Commonwealth, for the clear and distinct assertion of its political principles, doth declare that we adopt the following articles of political faith:

First. Equality of right and exact justice to all men, special privileges to none; freedom of religion, freedom of the press, and freedom of the person under the protection of the habeas corpus; of trial by juries impartially selected, and of a pure, upright and non-partisan judiciary; elections by the people, free from force or fraud of citizens or of the military and civil officers of Government; and the selection for public offices of those who are honest and best fitted to fill them; the support of the State governments in all their rights as the most competent administrations of our domestic concerns and the surest bulwarks against anti-republican tendencies; and the preservation of the General Government in its whole constitutional vigor as the best sheet-anchor of our peace at home and our safety abroad.

Second. That the maintenance of the public credit of Virginia is an essential means to the promotion of her prosperity. We condemn repudiation in every shape and form as a blot upon her honor, a blow at her permanent welfare, and an obstacle to her progress in wealth, influence and power; and that we will make every effort to secure a settlement of the public debt, with the consent of her creditors, which is consistent with her honor and dictated by justice and sound public policy; that it is eminently desirable and proper that the several classes of the debt now existing should be unified, so that equality, which is equity, may control in the annual payment of interest and the ultimate redemption of principal; that, with a view of securing such equality, we pledge our party to use all lawful authority to secure a settlement of the State debt so that there shall be but one class of the public debt; that we will use all lawful and constitutional means in our power to secure a settlement of the State debt upon the basis of a 3 per cent. bond, and that the Conservative-Democratic party pledges itself, as a part of its policy, not to increase the present rate of taxation.

Third. That we will uphold, in its full constitutional integrity and efficiency, our public-school system for the education of both white and colored children—a system inaugurated by the Constitution of the State and established by the action of the Conservative party years before it was required by the Constitution; and will take the most effectual means for the faithful execution of the same by applying to its support all the revenues set apart for that object by the Constitution or otherwise.

Fourth. Upon this declaration of principles we cordially invite the co-operation of all Conservative Democrats, whatever may have been or now are their views upon the public debt, in the election of the nominees of this Convention and in the maintenance of the supremacy of the Democratic party in this State.

Resolved, further, That any intimation, coming from any quarter, that the Conservative-Democratic party of Virginia has been, is now, or proposes to be, opposed to an honest ballot and a fair count, is a calumny upon the State of Virginia as unfounded in fact as it is dishonorable to its authors.

That special efforts be made to foster and encourage the agricultural, mechanical, mining, manufacturing and other industrial interests of the State.

That, in common with all good citizens of the Union, we reflect with deep abhorrence upon the crime of the man who aimed a blow at the life of the eminent citizen who was called by the constitutional voice of fifty millions of people to be the President of the United States; and we tender to him and to his friends the sympathy and respect of this Convention and of those we represent, in this great calamity, and our hearty desire for his complete restoration to health and return to the discharge of his important duties, for the welfare and honor of our common country.

COMPARISON OF PLATFORM PLANKS ON GREAT POLITICAL QUESTIONS.

General Party Doctrines.

DEMOCRATIC.	REPUBLICAN.
1856—That the liberal principles embodied by Jefferson in the Declaration of Independence, and sanctioned in the Constitution, which makes ours the land of liberty and the *asylum of the oppressed* of every nation, have ever been cardinal principles in the Democratic faith; and every attempt to abridge the present privilege of becoming citizens and the owners of soil among us ought to be resisted with the same spirit which swept the alien and sedition laws from our statute books. [Plank 8.	1856—That the maintenance of the principles promulgated in the Declaration of Independence and embodied in the Federal Constitution, is essential to the preservation of our Republican institutions, and that the Federal Constitution, the rights of the States, and the union of the States shall be preserved; that with our Republican fathers, we hold it to be a self-evident truth that all men are endowed with the inalienable rights to life, liberty, and the pursuit of happiness, and that the primary object and ulterior design of our Federal Government were to secure these rights to all persons within its exclusive jurisdiction. [Plank 1.
1860—Reaffirmed.	1860—That the maintenance of the principles promulgated in the Declaration of Independence and embodied in the Federal Constitution. "That all men are created equal; that they are endowed by their Creator with certain inalienable rights; that among these are life, liberty, and the pursuit of happiness; that to secure these rights governments are instituted among men, deriving their just powers from the consent of the governed," is essential to the preservation of our Republican institutions; and that the Federal Constitution, the rights of the States, and the Union of the States must and shall be preserved. [Plank 2.
1864—	1864—
1868—	1868—
1872—We recognize the equality of all men before the law, and hold that	1872—Complete liberty and exact equality in the enjoyment of all civil,

DEMOCRATIC.

it is the duty of Government in its dealings with the people to mete out equal and exact justice to all, of whatever nativity, race, color, or persuasion, religious or political. [Plank 1.

1876—

1880—Opposition to centralizationism, and to that dangerous spirit of encroachment which tends to consolidate the powers of all the departments in one, and thus to create, whatever be the form of Government, a real despotism. [Plank 2.

REPUBLICAN.

political and public rights should be established and effectually maintained throughout the Union by efficient and appropriate State and Federal Legislation. Neither the law nor its administration should admit any discrimination in respect of citizens by reasons of race, creed, color or previous condition of servitude. [Plank 3.

1876—*The United States of America is a Nation not a league.* By the combined workings of the National and State Governments, under their respective constitutions, the rights of every citizen are secured at home or abroad, and the common welfare promoted.

1880—*The constitution of the United States is a supreme law and not a mere contract.* Out of confederate States it made a sovereign nation. Some powers are denied to the nation, while others are denied to the States, but the boundary between the powers delegated and those reserved is to be determined by the National, and not by the State tribunal. [Cheers.] [Plank 2.

The Rebellion.

DEMOCRATIC.

1864—That this convention does *explicitly declare*, as the sense of the American people, that *after four years of failure to restore the Union by the experiment of war*, during which, under the pretense of a military necessity or war-power higher than the Constitution, the Constitution itself has been disregarded in every part, and public liberty and private right alike trodden down, and the material prosperity of the country essentially impaired, justice, humanity, liberty, and the public welfare demand that *immediate efforts be made for a cessation of hostilities*, with a view to the ultimate convention of the States, or other peaceable means, to the end that, at the earliest practicable moment peace may be restored on the basis of the Federal Union of the States. [1st resolution.

REPUBLICAN.

1864—That it is the highest duty of every American citizen to maintain against all their enemies the integrity of the Union and the paramount authority of the Constitution and laws of the United States; and that laying aside all differences of political opinions, we pledge ourselves as Union men, animated by a common sentiment, and aiming at a common object, to do everything in our power to aid the Government, in quelling by force of arms the rebellion now raging against its authority, and in bringing to the punishment due to their crimes the rebels and traitors arrayed against it.

That we approve the determination of the Government of the United States not to compromise with rebels, or to offer them any terms of peace, except such as may be based upon an unconditional surrender of their hostility and a return to their just allegiance to the Constitution and laws of the United States; and that we call upon the Government to maintain this position and to prosecute the war with the utmost possible vigor to the complete suppression of the rebellion, in full reliance upon the self-sacrificing patriotism, the heroic valor, and the undying devotion of the American people to the country and its free institutions.

[1st and 2d resolutions.]

Home Rule.

DEMOCRATIC.

1856—That we recognize the right

REPUBLICAN.

1856— * * * The dearest consti-

DEMOCRATIC.

of the people in all the Territories, including Kansas and Nebraska, acting through the legally and fairly expressed will of a majority of actual residents, and wherever the number of their inhabitants justifies it, to form a constitution * * * and be admitted into the Union upon terms of perfect equality with the other States.

REPUBLICAN.

tutional rights of the people of Kansas have been fraudulently and violently taken from them; their territory has been invaded by an armed force; spurious and pretended legislative, judicial, and executive officers have been set over them, by whose usurped authority, sustained by the military power of the Government, tyrannical and unconstitutional laws have been enacted and enforced; the right of the people to keep and bear arms has been infringed; test-oaths of an extraordinary and entangling nature have been imposed as a condition of exercising the right of suffrage and holding office; the right of an accused person to a speedy and public trial by an impartial jury has been denied; the right of the people to be secure in their persons, houses, papers, and effects against unreasonable searches and seizures, has been violated; they have been deprived of life, liberty, and property without due process of law; that the freedom of speech and of the press has been abridged; the right to choose their representatives has been made of no effect; murders, robberies, and arsons have been instigated and encouraged, and the offenders have been allowed to go unpunished; that all these things have been done

DEMOCRATIC.

1860—That when the settlers in a Territory, having an adequate population, form a State Constitution, the right of sovereignty commences, and, being consummated by admission into the Union, they stand on an equal footing with the people of other States; and the State thus organized ought to be admitted into the Federal Union, whether its constitution prohibits or recognizees the institution of slavery. [Plank 3, Breckinridge, Dem.

1864—

1868—After the most solemn and unanimous pledge of both Houses of Congress to prosecute the war exclusively for the maintenance of the Government and the preservation of the Union under the Constitution, it [the Republican party] has repeatedly vio-

REPUBLICAN.

with the knowledge, sanction, and procurement of the present Administration, and that for this high crime against the Constitution, the Union, and humanity, we arraign the Administration, the President, his advisers, agents, supporters, apologists, and accessories, either *before* or *after* the fact, before the country and before the world; and that it is our fixed purpose to bring the actual perpetrators of these atrocious outrages and their accomplices to a sure and condign punishment. [Plank 3.

1860—That the maintenance inviolate of the rights of the States, and especially the right of each State to order and control its own domestic institutions according to its own judgment exclusively, is essential to that balance of power on which the perfection and endurance of our political fabric depends; and we denounce the lawless invasion by armed force of the soil of any State or Territory, no matter under what pretext, as among the gravest of crimes. [Plank 4.

1864—

1868—We congratulate the country on the assured success of the reconstruction policy of Congress, as evinced by the adoption, in the majority of the States lately in rebellion, of constitutions securing equal civil and political rights to all; and it

DEMOCRATIC.

lated that most sacred pledge under which alone was rallied that noble volunteer army which carried our flag to victory. Instead of restoring the Union, it has, so far as in its power, dissolved it, and subjected ten States, in time of profound peace, to military despotism and negro supremacy. It has nullified there the right of trial by jury; it has abolished the *habeas corpus*, that most sacred writ of liberty; it has overthrown the freedom of speech and the press; it has substituted arbitrary seizures and arrests, and military trials and secret star-chamber inquisitions for the constitutional tribunals; it has disregarded in time of peace the right of the people to be free from searches and seizures; it has entered the post and telegraph offices, and even the private rooms of individuals, and seized their private papers and letters without any specific charge or notice of affidavit, as required by the organic law; it has converted the American Capitol into a bastile; it has established a system of spies and official espionage to which no constitutional monarchy of Europe would now dare to resort; it has abolished the right of appeal on important constitutional questions to the supreme judicial tribunals, and threatens to curtail or destroy its original jurisdiction, which is irrevocably vested by the Constitution, while the learned Chief Justice has been subjected to the most atrocious calumnies, merely because he would not prostitute his high office to the support of the false and partisan charges preferred against the President. * * * Under its repeated assaults the pillars of the Government are rocking on their base, and should it succeed in November next and inaugurate its President, we will meet as a subjected and conquered people, amid the ruins of liberty and the scattered fragments of the Constitution.

REPUBLICAN.

is the duty of the Government to sustain those institutions and prevent the people of such States from being remitted to a state of anarchy.

DEMOCRATIC.

1872—Local self-government, with impartial suffrage, will guard the rights of all citizens more securely than any centralized power. The public welfare requires the supremacy of the civil over the military authority, and freedom of persons under the protection of the *habeas corpus*. We demand for the individual the largest liberty consistent with public order; for the State self-government, and for the nation a return to the methods of peace and the constitutional limitations of power. [Plank 4.

1880—* * "Home Rule." [Plank 3.

REPUBLICAN.

1872—We hold that Congress and the President have only fulfilled an imperative duty in their measures for the suppression of violent and treasonable organizations in certain lately rebellious regions, and for the protection of the ballot-box; and, therefore, they are entitled to the thanks of the nation. [Plank 12.

1880—

Internal Improvements.

DEMOCRATIC.

1856—That the Constitution does not confer upon the general Government the power to com-

REPUBLICAN.

1856—That appropriations by congress for the improvement of rivers and harbors of a na-

DEMOCRATIC.

mence and carry on a general system of internal improvements. [Plank 2.

1860—Reaffirmed.

1864—
1868—
1872—
1876—
1880—Plank 2 of 1856 reaffirmed.

REPUBLICAN.

tional character, required for the accommodation and security of our existing commerce, are authorized by the Constitution and justified by the obligation of Government to protect the lives and property of its citizens. [Plank 7.

1860—That appropriations by Congress for river and harbor improvements of a national character, required for the accommodation and security of an existing commerce, are authorized by the Constitution and justified by the obligation of Government to protect the lives and property of its citizens. [Plank 15.

1864—
1868—
1872—
1876—
1880— * * * That we deem it the duty of Congress to develop and improve our seacoast and harbors, but insist that further subsidies to private persons or corporations must cease.

The National Debt and Interest, the Public Credit, Repudiation, etc.

DEMOCRATIC.

1864—

1868—Payment of the public debt of the United States as rapidly as practicable; all moneys drawn from the people by taxation, except so much as is requisite for the necessities of the Government, economically administered, being honestly applied to such payment, and where the obligations of the Government do not expressly state upon their face, or the law under which they were issued does not provide that they shall be paid in coin, they ought, in right and in justice, to be paid in the *lawful money* of the United States. [Plank 3.

Equal taxation of every species of property according to its real value, including Government bonds and other public securities. [Plank 4.

1872 — We demand a system of Federal taxation which shall not unnecessarily interfere with the industries of the people, and

REPUBLICAN.

1864—That the National faith, pledged for the redemption of the public debt, must be kept inviolate, and that for this purpose we recommend economy and rigid responsibility in the public expenditures, and a vigorous and just system of taxation; and that it is the duty of every loyal State to sustain the credit and promote the use of the National currency. [Plank 10.

1868 — We denounce all forms of repudiation as a National crime; and the National honor requires the payment of the public indebtedness in the uttermost good faith to all creditors at home and abroad, not only according to the letter, but the spirit of the laws under which it was contracted. [Plank 3.

It is due to the labor of the nation that taxation should be equalized and reduced as rapidly as the national faith will permit. [Plank 4.

The national debt, contracted as it has been for the preservation of the Union for all time to come, should be extended over a fair period for redemption; and it is the duty of Congress to reduce the rate of interest thereon whenever it can be honestly done. [Plank 5.

That the best policy to diminish our burden of debt is to so improve our credit that capitalists will seek to loan us money at lower rates of interest than we now pay and must continue to pay so long as repudiation, partial or total, open or covert, is threatened or suspected. [Plank 6.

1872— * * * A uniform national currency has been provided, repudiation frowned down, the national credit sustained under the

DEMOCRATIC.

which shall provide the means necessary to pay the expenses of the Government, economically administered, the pensions, the interest on the public debt, and a moderate reduction annually of the principal thereof. * * *

The public credit must be sacredly maintained, and we denounce repudiation in every form and guise. [Plank 7.

1876—Reform is necessary to establish a sound currency, restore the public credit, and maintain the national honor.

1880—* * * Honest money—the strict maintenance of the public faith—consisting of gold and silver, and paper convertible into coin on demand; the strict maintenance of the public faith, State and national. [Plank 3.

REPUBLICAN.

most extraordinary burdens, and new bonds negotiated at lower rates. * * [Plank 1.

We denounce repudiation of the public debt, in any form of disguise, as a national crime. We witness with pride the reduction of the principal of the debt, and of the rates of interest upon the balance. [Plank 13.

1876—In the first act of Congress signed by President Grant, the National Government assumed to remove any doubts of its purpose to discharge all just obligations to the public creditors, and "solemnly pledged its faith to make provision at the earliest practicable period for the redemption of the United States notes in coin." Commercial prosperity, public morals, and national credit demand that this promise be fulfilled by a continuance and steady progress to specie payment. [Plank 4.

1880—It [the Republican party] has raised the value of our paper currency from 38 per cent. to the par of gold [applause]; it has restored, upon a solid basis, payment in coin of all national obligations, and has given us a currency absolutely good and equal in every part of our extended country [applause]; it has lifted the credit of the nation from the point of where 6 per cent. bonds sold at 86, to that where 4 per cent. bonds are eagerly sought at a premium. [Preamble.

Resumption.

DEMOCRATIC.

1872 — A speedy return to specie payment is demanded alike by the highest considerations of commercial morality and honest government. [Plank 8.

1876 — We denounce the financial imbecility and immorality of that party, which, during eleven years of peace, has made no advance toward resumption, no preparation for resumption, but instead has obstructed resumption, by wasting our resources and exhausting all our surplus income; and, while annually professing to intend a speedy return to specie payments, has annually enacted fresh hindrances thereto. As such hindrance *we denounce the resumption clause of the act of* 1875, *and we here demand its repeal.*

1880—* * * Honest money, * * * consisting of gold, and silver, and paper convertible into coin on demand.

REPUBLICAN.

1872—* * * Our excellent national currency will be perfected by a speedy resumption of specie payment. [Plank 13.

1876—In the first act of Congress signed by President Grant, the National Government assumed to remove any doubts of its purpose to discharge all just obligations to the public creditors, and solemnly pledged its faith to make provision at the "earliest practicable period for the redemption of the United States notes in coin." Commercial prosperity, public morals and national credit demand that this promise be fulfilled *by a continuous and steady progress to specie payment.*

1880— * * * It [the Republican party] has restored, upon a solid basis, payment in coin of all National obligations, and has given us a currency absolutely good and equal in every part of our extended country.

Capital and Labor.

DEMOCRATIC.

1868 — *Resolved*, That this convention sympathize cordially with the working men of the United States in

REPUBLICAN.

1868—

DEMOCRATIC.	REPUBLICAN.
their efforts to protect the rights and interests of the laboring classes of the country.	
1872—	1872—Among the questions which press for attention is that which concerns the relations of capital and labor, and the Republican party recognizes the duty of so shaping legislation as to secure full protection and the amplest field for capital, and for labor, the creator of capital the largest opportunities and a just share of the mutual profits of these two great servants of civilization. [Plank 11.
1880—The Democratic party is the friend of labor and the laboring man, and pledges itself to protect him alike against the cormorant and the commune. [Plank 13.	1880—

Tariff.

DEMOCRATIC.	REPUBLICAN.
1856 — The time has come for the people of the United States to declare themselves in favor of * * * progressive free trade throughout the world, by solemn manifestations, to place their moral influence at the side of their successful example. [Resolve I. That justice and sound policy forbid the Federal Government to foster one branch of industry to the detriment of any other, or to cherish the interests of one portion to the injury of another portion of our common country. [Plank 4.	1856—
1860—Reafirmed.	1860—That, while providing revenue for the support of the general Government by duties upon imports, sound policy requires such an adjustment of these imposts as to encourage the development of the industrial interests of the whole country; and we commend that policy of national exchanges which secures to the workingmen liberal wages, to agriculture remunerative prices, to mechanics and manufacturers an adequate reward for their skill, labor, and enterprise, and to the nation commercial prosperity and independence. [Plank 12.
1864—	1864—
1868— * * * A tariff for revenue upon foreign imports, and such equal taxation under the Internal Revenue laws as will afford incidental protection to domestic manufactures, and as will, without impairing the revenue, impose the least burden upon and best promote and encourage the great industrial interests of the country. [Plank 6.	1868—
1872— * * * * Recognizing that there are in our midst honest but irreconcilable differences of opinion with regard to the respective systems of protection and free trade, we remit the discussion of the subject to the people in their Congressional districts, and to the decision of the Congress thereon, wholly free from executive in-	1872— * * * * Revenue except so much as may be derived from a tax upon tobacco and liquors, should be raised by duties upon importations, the details of which should be so adjusted as to aid in securing remunerative wages to labor, and promote the industries, prosperity, and growth of the whole country. [Plank 7.

DEMOCRATIC.

terference or dictation. [Plank 6.

1876—* * * * *We demand that all custom-house taxation shall be only for revenue.* [Plank 11.

1880— * * * * A tariff for revenue only. [Plank 3.

REPUBLICAN.

1876—The revenue necessary for current expenditures and the obligations of the public debt must be largely derived from duties upon importations, which so far as possible, should be adjusted to promote the interests of American labor and advance the prosperity of the whole country. [Plank 8.

1880—Reaffirmed.

Education.

DEMOCRATIC.

1876—The false issue with which they [the Republicans] would enkindle sectarian strife in respect to the public schools, of which the establishment and support belong exclusively to the several States, and which *the Democratic party has cherished from their foundation*, and is resolved to maintain without prejudice or preference for any class, sect, or creed, and without largesses from the Treasury to any.

1880—* * * Common Schools fostered and protected. [Plank 2.

REPUBLICAN.

1876—The public school system of the several States is the bulwark of the American Republic, and with a view to its security and permanence we recommend an Amendment to the Constitution of the United States, forbidding the application of any public funds or property for the benefit of any schools or institutions under sectarian control. [Plank 4.

1880—The work of popular education is one left to the care of the several States, but it is the duty of the National Government to aid that work to the extent of its constitutional ability. The intelligence of the nation is but the aggregate of the intelligence in the several States, and the destiny of the Nation must be guided, not by the genius of any one State, but by the average genius of all. [Plank 3.

Duty to Union Soldiers and Sailors.

DEMOCRATIC.

1864 — That the sympathy of the Democratic party is heartily and earnestly extended to the soldiery of our army and sailors of our navy, who are and have been in the field and on the sea under the flag of our country, and, in the event of its attaining power, they will receive all the care, protection, and regard that the brave soldiers and sailors of the Republic so nobly earned. [Plank 6.

1868— * * * * * * * That our soldiers and sailors, who carried the flag of our country to victory, against a most gallant and determined foe, must ever be gratefully remembered, and all the guarantees given in their favor must be faithfully carried into execution.

REPUBLICAN.

1864—That the thanks of the American people are due to the soldiers and sailors of the army and navy, who have periled their lives in defense of the country and in vindication of the honor of its flag; that the nation owes to them some permanent recognition of their patriotism and their valor, and ample and permanent provision for those of their survivors who have received disabling and honorable wounds in the service of the country; and that the memories of those who have fallen in its defence shall be held in grateful and everlasting remembrance. [Plank 4.

1868—Of all who were faithful in the trials of the late war, there were none entitled to more especial honor than the brave soldiers and seamen who endured the hardships of campaign and cruise and imperiled their lives in the service of their country; the bounties and pensions provided by the laws for these brave defenders of the nation are obligations never to be forgotten; the widows and orphans of the gallant dead are the wards of the people—a sacred legacy bequeathed to the nation's care. [Plank 10.

DEMOCRATIC.

1872— * We remember with gratitude the heroism and sacrifices of the soldiers and sailors of the Republic, and no act of ours shall ever detract from their justly earned fame for the full reward of their patriotism [Plank 9.

1876— * * * The soldiers and sailors of the Republic, and the widows and orphans of those who have fallen in battle, have a just claim upon the care, protection, and gratitude of their fellow-citizens.
[Last resolution.

1880—

REPUBLICAN.

1872—We hold in undying honor the soldiers and sailors whose valor saved the Union. Their pensions are a sacred debt of the nation, and the widows and orphans of those who died for their country are entitled to the care of a generous and grateful people. We favor such additional legislation as will extend the bounty of the Government to all our soldiers and sailors who were honorably discharged, and who in the line of duty became disabled, without regard to the length of service or the cause of such discharge.
[Plank 8.

1876—The pledges which the nation has given to her soldiers and sailors must be fulfilled, and a grateful people will always hold those who imperiled their lives for the country's preservation, in the kindest remembrance.
[Plank 14.

1880—That the obligations of the Republic to the men who preserved its integrity in the day of battle are undiminished by the lapse of fifteen years since their final victory. To do them honor is and shall forever be the grateful privilege and sacred duty of the American people.

Naturalization and Allegiance.

DEMOCRATIC.

1860—That the Democracy of the United States recognize it as the imperative duty of this Government to protect the naturalized citizen in all his rights, whether at home or in foreign lands, to the same extent as its native-born citizens. [Plank 6.

1864—

1868 — Equal rights and protection for naturalized and native-born citizens at home and abroad, the assertion of American nationality which shall command the respect of foreign powers, and furnish an example and encouragement to people struggling for national integrity, constitutional liberty, and individual rights and the maintenance of the rights of naturalized citizens against the absolute doctrine of immutable allegiance, and the claims of foreign powers to punish them for alleged crime committed beyond their jurisdiction.
[Plank 8.

1872—

REPUBLICAN.

1860 — The Republican party is opposed to any change in our naturalization laws, or any State legislation by which the rights of citizenship hitherto accorded to immigrants from foreign lands shall be abridged or impaired; and in favor of giving a full and efficient protection to the right of all classes of citizens, whether native or naturalized, both home and abroad.
[Plank 14.

1864—

1868—The doctrine of Great Britain and other European Powers, that because a man is once a subject he is always so, must be resisted at every hazard by the United States, as a relic of feudal times, not authorized by the laws of nations, and at war with our national honor and independence. Naturalized citizens are entitled to protection in all their rights of citizenship as though they were native-born; and no citizen of the United States, native or naturalized, must be liable to arrest and imprisonment by any foreign power for acts done or words spoken in this country; and, if so arrested and imprisoned, it is the duty of the Government to interfere in his behalf.
[Plank 9.

1872 — The doctrine of Great Britain and other European Powers concerning allegiance —"once a subject always a subject"— *having at last, through the efforts of the Republican party, been aban-*

DEMOCRATIC. | REPUBLICAN.

REPUBLICAN. — *doned*, and the American idea of the individual's right to transfer allegiance having been accepted by European nations, it is the duty of our Government to guard with jealous care the rights of adopted citizens against the assumption of unauthorised claims by their former Governments, and we urge continued careful encouragement and protection of voluntary immigration. [Plank 9.

1876—

REPUBLICAN. — 1876—It is the imperative duty of the Government so to modify existing treaties with European governments, that the same protection shall be afforded to the adopted American citizen that is given to the native-born, and that all necessary laws should be passed to protect emigrants in the absence of power in the State for that purpose. [Plank 10.

1880—

REPUBLICAN. — 1880— * * * * Everywhere the protection accorded to a citizen of American birth must be secured to citizens by American adoption. [Plank 5.

The Chinese.

DEMOCRATIC.

1876—Reform is necessary to correct the omissions of a Republican Congress, and the errors of our treaties and our diplomacy, which have stripped our fellow-citizens of foreign birth and kindred race recrossing the Atlantic, of the shield of American citizenship, and have exposed our brethren of the Pacific coast to the incursions of a race not sprung from the same great parent stock, and in fact now by law denied citizenship through naturalization as being neither accustomed to the traditions of a progressive civilization nor exercised in liberty under equal laws. We denounce the policy which thus discards the liberty-loving German and tolerates a revival of the coolie trade in Mongolian women imported for immoral purposes, and Mongolian men held to perform servile labor contracts, and demand such modification of the treaty with the Chinese Empire, or such legislation within constitutional limitations, as shall prevent further importation or immigration of the Mongolian race.

1880 — Amendment of the Burlingame Treaty. No more Chinese immigration, except for travel, education, and foreign commerce, and therein carefully guarded. [Plank 11.

REPUBLICAN.

1876—It is the immediate duty of Congress to fully investigate the effect of the immigration and importation of Mongolians upon the moral and material interests of the country. [Plank 11.

1880—Since the authority to regulate immigration and intercourse between the United States and foreign nations rests with the Congress of the United States and the treaty-making power, the Republican party, regarding the unrestricted immigration of Chinese as a matter of grave concernment under the exercise of both these powers, would limit and restrict that immigration by the enactment of such just, humane, and reasonable laws and treaties as will produce that result. [Plank 6.

Civil Service.

DEMOCRATIC.

1872 — The civil service of the government has become a mere instrument of partisan tyranny and personal ambition and an object of selfish greed. It is a scandal and reproach upon free institutions and breeds a demoralization dangerous to the perpetuity of Republican Government. We therefore regard a thorough reform of the civil service as one of the most pressing necessities of the hour; that honesty, capacity and fidelity constitute the only valid claim to public employment; and the offices of the Government cease to be a matter of arbitrary favoritism and patronage, and public station become again a post of honor. To this end it is imperatively required that no President shall be a candidate for reelection.

REPUBLICAN.

1872—Any system of the civil service, under which the subordinate positions of the Government are considered rewards for mere party zeal is fatally demoralizing, and we therefore favor a reform of the system by laws which shall abolish the evils of patronage and make honesty, efficiency and fidelity the essential qualifications for public positions, without practically creating a life tenure of office.

[Plank 5.

DEMOCRATIC.

1876—Reform is necessary in the civil service. Experience that proves efficient, economical conduct of Governmental business is not possible if the civil service be subject to change at every election, be a prize fought for at the ballot-box, be a brief reward of party zeal, instead of posts of honor assigned for proved competency, and held for fidelity in the public employ; that the dispensing of patronage should neither be a tax upon the time of all our public men, nor the instrument of their ambition.

REPUBLICAN.

1876—Under the Constitution the President and heads of Departments are to make nominations for office; the Senate is to advise and consent to appointments, and the House of Representatives to accuse and prosecute faithless officers. The best interest of the public service demands that these distinctions be respected; that Senators and Representatives who may be judges and accusers should not dictate appointments to office. The invariable rule in appointments should have reference to the honesty, fidelity and capacity of the appointees, giving to the party in power those places where harmony and vigor of administration require its policy to be represented, but permitting all others to be filled by persons selected with sole reference to the efficiency of the public service, and the right of all citizens to share in the honor of rendering faithful service to the country.

[Plank 5.

DEMOCRATIC.

1880— * * Thorough reform in the civil service.

REPUBLICAN.

1880 — The Republican party, adhering to the principles affirmed by its last National Convention of respect for the Constitutional rules governing appointments to office, adopts the declaration of President Hayes, that the reform of the civil service should be thorough, radical and complete. To this end it demands the co-operation of the legislative with the executive departments of the Government, and that Congress shall so legislate that fitness, ascertained by proper practical tests, shall admit to the public service.

ELECTORAL VOTES FOR PRESIDENTS AND VICE-PRESIDENTS.

	CANDIDATES.	Maine.	N. Hamp.	Vermont	Mass.	R. Island	Conn.	N. York	N. Jersey	Penna.	Delaware	Maryl'nd	Virginia	N. C.	S. C.	Georgia	Alabama	Miss.	Louisiana	Tenn.	Kent'cky	Ohio	Indiana	Illinois	Missouri	Arkansas	Michigan	W. Va.	Florida	Texas	Iowa	Wis.	Minn.	Nebraska	Kansas	Colorado	Nevada	Oregon	Cal.	Total.
1788	Washington, Va. (Fed.)		5		10		7		6	10	3	6	10		7	5																								69
	John Adams, Mass. (Fed.)		5		10		5		1	8			5																											34
	Scattering						2		5	2	3	6	5		7	5																								35
1792	Washington, Va. (Fed.)		6	4	16	4	9	12	7	15	3	8	21	12	7	4					4																			182
	John Adams, Mass. (Fed.)		6	4	16	4	9		7	14	3	8			6																									77
	George Clinton, N. Y. (Rep.)							12		1			21	12	sc	4					sc																			50
1796	Adams, Mass. (Fed.)		6	4	16	4	9	12	7	1	3	7	1	1																										71
	Jefferson, Va. (Rep.)									14		4	20	11	8	4				3	4																			68
	Pinckney, S. C. (Fed.)			4	13		4	12	7	2	3	4	1	1	8																									59
	Burr, N. Y. (Rep.)									13		3	1	6						3	4																			30
	Scattering		6		3	4	5					2	19	5		4																								48
1800	Jefferson, Va. (Rep.)							12		6		5	21	8	8	4				5	4																			78
	Adams, Mass. (Fed.)		6	4	16	4	9		7	7	3	5		4																										65
	Burr, N. Y. (Rep.)					sc		12		8		5	21	8	8	4				3	4																			73
	Pinckney, S. C. (Rep.)		6	4	16	3	9		7	7	3	5		4																										64
1804 Pres.	Jefferson, Va. (Rep.)		7	6	19	4		19	8	20		9	24	14	10	6				5	8	3																		162
	Pinckney, S. C. (Fed.)						9				3	2																												14
Vice-Pres.	Clinton, N. Y. (Rep.)		7	6	19	4		19	8	20		9	24	14	10	6				5	8	3																		162
	King, N. Y. (Fed.)						9				3	2																												14
1808 Pres.	Madison, Va. (Rep.)			6				13	8	20		9	24	11	10	6				5	7	3																		122
	Pinckney, S. C. (Fed.)		7		19	4	9	sc			3	2		3																										47
Vice-Pres.	Clinton, N. Y. (Rep.)							13	8	20		9	24	11	10	6				5	7	sc																		113
	King, N. Y. (Fed.)		7	sc	19	4	9	sc			3	2		3																										47
1812 Pres.	Madison, Va. (Rep.)			8						25		6	25	15	11	8			3	8	12	7																		128
	De Witt Clinton, N. Y. (Cl. Dem.)		8		22	4	9	29	8		4	5																												89
Vice-Pres.	Gerry, Mass. (Rep.)		1	8	2					25		6	25	15	11	8			3	8	12	7																		131
	Ingersoll, Pa. (Cl. Dem)		7		20	4	9	29	8		4	5																												86
1816 Pres.	Monroe, Va. (Dem.)		8	8		4		29	8	25		8	25	15	11	8			3	8	12	8	3																	183
	King, N. Y. (Fed.)				22		9				3																													34
Vice-Pres.	Daniel D. Tompkins, N. Y. (Dem.)		8	8	sc	4	sc	29	8	25	sc	8	25	15	11	8			3	8	12	8	3																	183

ELECTORAL VOTES FOR PRESIDENTS AND VICE-PRESIDENTS.—(Continued).

	CANDIDATES.	Maine	N. Hamp.	Vermont	Mass.	R. Island	Conn.	N. York	N. Jersey	Penna.	Delaware	Maryl'nd	Virginia	N. C.	S. C.	Georgia	Alabama	Miss.	Louisiana	Tenn.	Kent'cky	Ohio	Indiana	Illinois	Missouri	Arkansas	Michigan	Florida	Texas	Iowa	Wis.	W. Va.	Minn.	Nebraska	Kansas	Colorado	Nevada	Oregon	Cal.	Total.
1820 Pres.	James Monroe, Va. (Dem.)	9	7 sc	8	15	4	9	29	8	25	4	11	25	15	11	8	3	3	3	8	12	8	3	3																231
Vice-Pres.	Daniel D. Tompkins, N. Y. (Dem.)	9	7 sc	8	7 sc	4	9	29	8	25	sc	10 s	25	15	11	8	3	3	3	8	12	8	3	3																218
1824 Pres.	Jackson, Tenn. (Dem.)							1	8	28		7		15	11		5	3	3	11			5	2																99
	John Q. Adams, Mass. (Fed.)	9	8	7	15	4	8	26			1	3							2					1																84
	Crawford, Ga. (Dem.)							5			2	1	24			9																								41
	Clay, Ky. (Whig)	8						4													14	16			3															37
Vice-Pres.	Calhoun, S. C. (Dem.)	9	7	7	15	3		29	8	28	1	10		15	11		5	3	5	11	7		5	3																183
	Sanford, N. Y.		sc				sc	7			sc	sc	sc			sc					7	16			sc															30
Vote House Rep. States	Adams (Fed.)	7	6	5	12	2	6	18	1	1		5	1	1			3		2		8	10			1															13
	Jackson (Dem.)							2	5	25		3	1	2	9			1	1	9	4	2	3	1																7
	Crawford (Dem.)				1			14			1	1	12	10		7						2																		4
1828 Pres.	Jackson, Tenn. (Dem.)	1						20		28		5	24	15	11	9	5	3	5	11	14	16	5	3	3															178
	Adams, Mass. (Fed.)	8	8	7	15	4	8	16	8		3	6																												83
Vice-Pres.	J. C. Calhoun, S. C. (Dem.)	1						20		28		5	24	15	11	2	5	3	5	11	14	16	5	3	3															171
	Rush, Pa. (Fed.)	8	8	7	15	4	8	16	8		3	6																												83
	Smith, S. C.																																							7
1832 Pres.	Jackson, Tenn. (Dem.)	10	7					42	8	30		3	23	15	sc	11	7	4	5	15		21	9	5	4															219
	Clay, Ky. (Whig.)			sc	14	4	8				3	5									15																			49
Vice-Pres.	Van Buren, N. Y. (Dem.)	10	7					42	8			3	23	15		11	7	4	5	15		21	9	5	4															189
	Sergeant, Pa. (Whig.)			sc	14	4	8			sc	3	5			sc						15																			49
1836 Pres.	Van Buren, N. Y. (Dem.)	10	7			4	8	42		30			23	15	sc	7	4	5	sc				5	4	3	3														170
	Harrison, Ohio (Whig.)			7	sc				8		3	10								15	21	9																		73
Vice-Pres.	Johnson, Ky. (Dem.)	10	7			4	8	42		30				15		7	4	5					5	4	3	3														147
	Francis Granger, N. Y. (Whig)			7	14				8		3	sc	sc		sc				sc	15	21	9																		77
1840 Pres.	Harrison, Ohio (Whig)	10		7	14	4	8	42	8	30	3	10		15		11		4	5	15	15	21	9				3													234
	Van Buren, N. Y. (Dem.)		7										23		11		7							5	4	3														60
Vice-Pres.	Tyler, Va. (Whig)	10		7	14	4	8	42	8	30	3	10		15		11		4	5	17	15	21	9				3													234
	Johnson, Ky. (Dem.)		7										23		sc		7							5	4	3														48

1844 Pres.	Polk, Tenn. (Dem.)	9	6	...	...	...	...	36	...	26	...	...	17	...	9	10	9	6	6	...	...	...	12	9	7	3	5	...	...	...	...	...	...	...	...	...	...	...	...	170
	Clay, Ky. (Whig)	...	...	6	12	4	6	...	7	...	3	8	...	11	...	...	...	...	...	13	12	23	...	...	...	...	...	...	...	...	...	...	...	...	...	...	...	...	...	105
Vice-Pres.	Dallas, Pa. (Dem.)	9	6	...	...	...	...	36	...	26	...	...	17	...	9	10	9	6	6	...	...	...	12	9	7	3	5	...	...	...	...	...	...	...	...	...	...	...	...	170
	Frelinghuysen, N. Y. (Whig)	...	...	6	12	4	6	...	7	...	3	8	...	11	...	...	...	...	...	13	12	23	...	...	...	...	...	...	...	...	...	...	...	...	...	...	...	...	...	105
1848 Pres.	Taylor, La. (Whig)	...	...	6	12	4	6	...	7	26	...	8	...	11	...	10	...	...	6	13	12	...	...	...	...	...	...	...	3	...	...	...	...	...	...	...	...	...	...	163
	Cass, Mich. (Dem.)	9	6	...	...	...	...	...	...	...	...	...	17	...	9	...	9	6	...	...	...	23	12	9	7	3	5	...	...	4	4	4	...	...	...	...	...	...	...	127
Vice-Pres.	Fillmore, N. Y. (Whig)	...	...	6	12	4	6	36	7	26	3	8	...	11	...	10	...	...	6	13	12	...	...	...	...	...	...	...	3	...	...	...	...	...	...	...	...	...	...	163
	Butler, Ky. (Dem.)	9	6	...	...	...	...	...	...	...	...	...	17	...	9	...	9	6	...	...	...	23	12	9	7	3	5	...	...	4	4	4	...	...	...	...	...	...	...	127
1852 Pres.	Pierce, N. H. (Dem.)	8	5	...	...	4	6	35	7	27	3	8	15	10	8	10	9	7	6	...	...	23	13	11	9	4	6	...	3	4	4	5	...	...	...	...	...	...	...	254
	Scott, Va. (Whig)	...	...	5	13	...	...	...	...	...	...	...	...	...	...	...	...	...	...	12	12	...	...	...	...	...	...	...	...	...	...	...	...	...	...	...	...	...	...	42
Vice-Pres.	King, Ala. (Dem.)	8	5	...	...	4	6	35	7	27	3	8	15	10	8	10	9	7	6	...	...	23	13	11	9	4	6	...	3	4	4	5	...	...	...	...	...	...	...	254
	Graham, N. C. (Whig)	...	...	5	13	...	...	...	...	...	...	...	...	...	...	...	...	...	...	12	12	...	...	...	...	...	...	...	...	...	...	...	...	...	...	...	...	...	...	42
1856 Pres.	Buchanan, Pa. (Dem.)	...	...	...	...	...	...	...	7	27	3	...	15	10	8	10	9	7	6	12	12	...	13	11	9	4	...	...	3	4	...	...	...	...	...	...	...	...	4	174
	J. C. Fremont, N. Y. (Rep.)	8	5	5	13	4	6	35	...	...	...	...	...	...	...	...	...	...	...	...	...	23	...	...	...	...	6	...	...	...	4	5	...	...	...	...	...	...	...	114
	Fillmore, N. Y. (Am.)	...	...	...	...	...	...	...	...	...	...	8	...	...	...	...	...	...	...	...	...	...	...	...	...	...	...	...	...	...	...	...	...	...	...	...	...	...	...	8
Vice-Pres.	Breckinridge, Ky. (Dem.)	...	...	...	...	...	...	...	7	27	3	...	15	10	8	10	9	7	6	12	12	...	13	11	9	4	...	...	3	4	...	...	...	...	...	...	...	...	4	174
	Dayton, Ohio (Rep.)	8	5	5	13	4	6	35	...	...	...	...	...	...	...	...	...	...	...	...	...	23	...	...	...	...	6	...	...	...	4	5	...	...	...	...	...	...	...	114
	Donnelson, Tenn. (Am.)	...	...	...	...	...	...	...	...	...	...	8	...	...	...	...	...	...	...	...	...	...	...	...	...	...	...	...	...	...	...	...	...	...	...	...	...	...	...	8
1860 Pres.	Lincoln, Ill. (Rep.)	8	5	5	13	4	6	35	4	27	...	...	...	...	...	...	...	...	...	...	...	23	13	11	...	...	6	...	...	...	4	5	4	...	...	...	...	3	4	180
	Breckinridge, Ky. (Dem.)	...	...	...	...	...	...	...	...	...	3	8	...	10	8	10	9	7	6	...	...	...	...	...	...	4	...	...	3	4	...	...	...	...	...	...	...	...	...	72
	Bell, Tenn. (Am.)	...	...	...	...	...	...	...	...	...	...	...	15	...	...	...	...	...	...	12	12	...	...	...	...	...	...	...	...	...	...	...	...	...	...	...	...	...	...	39
	Douglas, Ill. (Dem.)	...	...	...	...	...	...	...	3	...	...	...	...	...	...	...	...	...	...	...	...	...	...	...	...	...	...	...	...	...	...	...	9	...	...	...	...	...	...	12
Vice-Pres.	Hamlin, Me. (Rep.)	8	5	5	13	4	6	35	4	27	...	...	...	...	...	...	...	...	...	...	...	23	13	11	...	...	6	...	...	...	4	5	4	...	...	...	...	3	4	180
	Lane, Oregon (Dem.)	...	...	...	...	...	...	...	...	...	3	8	...	10	8	10	9	7	6	...	...	...	...	...	4	...	...	...	3	4	...	...	...	...	...	...	...	...	...	72
	Everett, Mass. (Am.)	...	...	...	...	...	...	...	...	...	...	...	15	...	...	...	...	...	...	12	12	...	...	...	...	...	...	...	...	...	...	...	...	...	...	...	...	...	...	39
	Johnson, Geo. (Dem.)	...	...	...	...	...	...	...	3	...	...	...	...	...	...	...	...	...	...	...	...	...	...	...	...	...	...	...	...	...	...	...	9	...	...	...	...	...	...	12
1864 Pres.	Lincoln, Ill. (Rep.)	7	5	5	12	4	6	33	...	26	...	7	...	...	...	...	...	...	...	...	...	21	13	16	11	...	8	5	...	...	8	8	4	...	3	...	2	3	5	212
	McClellan, N. J. (Dem.)	...	...	...	...	...	...	...	7	...	3	...	...	...	...	...	...	...	...	...	11	...	...	...	...	...	...	...	...	...	...	...	...	...	...	...	...	...	...	21
	Vacancies. Seceded States	...	...	...	...	...	...	...	...	...	...	...	10	9	6	9	8	7	7	10	...	...	...	...	...	5	...	...	3	6	8	...	...	...	...	...	1	...	...	81
Vice-Pres.	Johnson, Tenn. (Rep.)	7	5	5	12	4	6	33	...	26	...	7	...	...	...	...	...	...	...	...	...	21	13	16	11	...	8	5	...	...	...	8	4	...	8	...	2	3	5	212
	Pendleton, Ohio (Dem.)	...	...	...	...	...	...	...	7	...	3	...	...	...	...	...	...	...	...	...	11	...	...	...	...	...	...	...	...	...	...	...	...	...	...	...	...	...	...	21
	Vacancies	...	...	...	...	...	...	...	...	...	...	...	10	9	6	9	8	7	7	10	...	...	...	...	...	5	...	...	3	6	...	...	...	1	...	...	...	...	...	81
1868 Pres.	Grant, Ill. (Rep.)	7	5	5	12	4	6	...	...	26	...	...	...	9	6	...	8	...	...	10	...	21	18	16	11	5	8	5	3	...	8	8	4	3	3	...	3	...	5	214
	Seymour, N. Y. (Dem.)	...	...	...	...	...	...	33	7	...	3	7	...	...	...	9	...	...	7	...	11	...	...	...	...	...	...	...	...	...	...	...	...	...	...	...	...	3	...	80
	Vacancies	...	...	...	...	...	...	...	...	...	...	...	10	...	...	...	...	7	...	...	...	...	...	...	...	...	...	...	...	6	...	...	...	...	...	...	...	...	...	23

ELECTORAL VOTES FOR PRESIDENTS AND VICE-PRESIDENTS.—[Continued.]

	CANDIDATES.	Maine.	N.Hamp.	Vermont	Mass.	R. Island	Conn.	N. York	N. Jersey	Penna.	Delaware	Maryl'nd	Virginia	N. C.	S. C.	Georgia	Alabama	Miss.	Louisi'na	Tenn.	Kent'cky	Ohio	Indiana	Illinois	Missouri	Arkansas	Michigan	W. Va.	Florida	Texas	Iowa	Wis.	Minn.	Nebraska	Kansas	Colorado	Nevada	Oregon	Cal.	Total.
Vice-Pres.	Colfax, Ind. (Rep.)	7	5	5	12	4	6			26				9	6		8			10		21	13	16	11	5	8	5	3		8	8	4	3	3		3		5	214
	Blair, Me. (Dem.)							33	7		3	7				9			7		11																	3		80
	Vacancies												10					7												6										23
1872 Pres.	Grant, Ill. (Rep.)	7	5	5	13	4	6	35	9	29	3		11	10	7		10	8				22	15	21		6	11	5	4		11	10	5	3	5		3	3		286
	Hendricks, Ind. (Dem.)											8								12	8				6					8										42
	Brown, Mo. (Lib. Rep.)															6					4				8															18
	Perkins, Ga. (Dem.)															2																								2
	Davis, Ill. (Lib. Rep.)																								1															1
	Not counted															3			8							6														17
	Horace Greeley, N. Y. (Lib. Rep.) died before meeting of electoral college																																							......
Vice-Pres.	Wilson, Mass. (Rep.)	7	5	5	13	4	6	35	9	29	3		11	10	7		10	8				22	15	21		6	11	5	4		11	10	5	3	5		3	3		286
	Brown, Mo. (Lib. Rep.)											8				5				12	8				6					8										47
	Julian, Ind. (Dem.)																																	5						5
	Colquitt, Ga. (Dem.)															5																								5
	Palmer, Ill. (Dem.)																								3															3
	Bramlette, Ky. (Dem.)																				3																			3
	Groesbeck, Ohio (Dem.)																								1															1
	Macken, Ky. (Dem.)																		1																					1
	Banks, Mass. (Lib. Rep.)															1																								1
	Not counted																6		8																					14
1876 Pres.	Hayes, Ohio (Rep.)	7	5	5	13	4				29					7				8			22		21			11		4		11	10	5	3	5	3	3	3	6	185
	Tilden, N. Y. (Dem.)						6	35	9		3	8	11	10		11	10	8		12	12		15		15	6		5		8										184
Vice-Pres.	Wheeler, N. Y. (Rep.)	7	5	5	13	4				29					7							22		21			11		4		11	10	5	3	5	3	3	3	6	185
	Hendricks, Ind. (Dem.)						6	35	9		3	8	11	10		11	10	8	8	12	12		15		15	6		5		8										184
1880 Pres.	Garfield, Ohio (Rep.)	7	5	5	13	4	6	35		29												22	15	21			11		4		11	3	5	3	5	3		8	1	214
	Hancock, N. Y. (Dem.)								9		3	8	11	10	7	11	10	8	8	12	12				15	5		8		10							3		5	155
	Weaver, Iowa (Gr.)																																							......
Vice-Pres.	Arthur, N. Y. (Rep.)	7	5	5	13	4	6	35		29												22	15	21			11		4		11	3	5	3	5	3		3	1	214
	English, Ind. (Dem.)								9		3	8	11	10	7	11	10	8	8	12	12				15	5		8		10							3			155
	Chambers, Tex. (Gr.)																																							......

APPORTIONMENT UNDER TENTH CENSUS.

Present apportionment, (293), and proposed apportionment under Census of 1880 from 293 to 325 Representatives, based on a population of 49,371,340 in the States.

STATES.	Pres No.	293	294	295	296	297	298	299	300	301	302	303	304	305	306	307	308	309	310	311	312	313	314	315	316	317	318	319	320	321	322	323	324	325
Alabama	8	7	7	7	7	7	7	8	7	8	8	8	8	8	8	8	8	8	8	8	8	8	8	8	8	8	8	8	8	8	8	8	8	8
Arkansas	4	5	5	5	5	5	5	5	5	5	5	5	5	5	5	5	5	5	5	5	5	5	5	5	5	5	5	5	5	5	5	5	5	5
California	4	5	5	5	5	5	5	5	5	5	5	5	5	5	5	5	5	5	5	5	6	6	6	6	6	6	6	6	6	6	6	6	6	6
Colorado	1	1	1	1	1	1	1	1	1	1	1	1	1	1	1	1	1	1	1	1	1	1	1	1	1	1	1	1	1	1	1	1	1	1
Connecticut	4	4	4	4	4	4	4	4	4	4	4	4	4	4	4	4	4	4	4	4	4	4	4	4	4	4	4	4	4	4	4	4	4	4
Delaware	1	1	1	1	1	1	1	1	1	1	1	1	1	1	1	1	1	1	1	1	1	1	1	1	1	1	1	1	1	1	1	1	1	1
Florida	2	1	1	1	1	1	1	1	1	1	2	2	2	2	2	2	2	2	2	2	2	2	2	2	2	2	2	2	2	2	2	2	2	2
Georgia	9	9	9	9	9	9	9	9	9	9	9	9	9	9	9	9	10	10	10	10	10	10	10	10	10	10	10	10	10	10	10	10	10	10
Illinois	19	18	18	18	18	18	18	18	19	19	19	19	19	19	19	19	19	19	19	19	19	20	20	20	20	20	20	20	20	20	20	20	20	20
Indiana	13	12	12	12	12	12	12	12	12	12	12	12	12	12	12	12	12	12	12	13	13	13	13	13	13	13	13	13	13	13	13	13	13	13
Iowa	9	10	10	10	10	10	10	10	10	10	10	10	10	10	10	10	10	10	10	10	10	10	10	10	10	10	10	10	11	11	11	11	11	11
Kansas	3	6	6	6	6	6	6	6	6	6	6	6	6	6	6	6	6	6	6	6	6	6	6	6	6	6	6	6	6	6	7	7	7	7
Kentucky	10	10	10	10	10	10	10	10	10	10	10	10	10	10	10	10	10	10	10	10	10	10	11	11	11	11	11	11	11	11	11	11	11	11
Louisiana	6	5	5	6	6	6	6	6	6	6	6	6	6	6	6	6	6	6	6	6	6	6	6	6	6	6	6	6	6	6	6	6	6	6
Maine	5	4	4	4	4	4	4	4	4	4	4	4	4	4	4	4	4	4	4	4	4	4	4	4	4	4	4	4	4	4	4	4	4	4
Maryland	6	5	5	5	5	6	6	6	6	6	6	6	6	6	6	6	6	6	6	6	6	6	6	6	6	6	6	6	6	6	6	6	6	6
Massachusetts	11	10	11	11	11	11	11	11	11	11	11	11	11	11	11	11	11	11	11	11	11	11	11	11	11	11	11	12	12	12	12	12	12	12
Michigan	9	10	10	10	10	10	10	10	10	10	10	10	10	10	10	10	10	10	10	10	10	10	10	11	11	11	11	11	11	11	11	11	11	11
Minnesota	3	5	5	5	5	5	5	5	5	5	5	5	5	5	5	5	5	5	5	5	5	5	5	5	5	5	5	5	5	5	5	5	5	5
Mississippi	6	7	7	7	7	7	7	7	7	7	7	7	7	7	7	7	7	7	7	7	7	7	7	7	7	7	7	7	7	7	7	7	7	7
Missouri	13	13	13	13	13	13	13	13	13	13	13	13	13	13	13	13	13	14	14	14	14	14	14	14	14	14	14	14	14	14	14	14	14	14
Nebraska	1	3	3	3	3	3	3	3	3	3	3	3	3	3	3	3	3	3	3	3	3	3	3	3	3	3	3	3	3	3	3	3	3	3
Nevada	1	1	1	1	1	1	1	1	1	1	1	1	1	1	1	1	1	1	1	1	1	1	1	1	1	1	1	1	1	1	1	1	1	1
New Hampshire	3	2	2	2	2	2	2	2	2	2	2	2	2	2	2	2	2	2	2	2	2	2	2	2	2	2	2	2	2	2	2	2	2	2
New Jersey	7	7	7	7	7	7	7	7	7	7	7	7	7	7	7	7	7	7	7	7	7	7	7	7	7	7	7	7	7	7	7	7	7	7
New York	33	30	30	30	30	30	31	31	31	31	31	31	31	31	31	32	32	32	32	32	32	32	32	32	33	33	33	33	33	33	33	33	33	34
North Carolina	8	8	8	8	8	8	8	8	8	8	8	8	9	9	9	9	9	9	9	9	9	9	9	9	9	9	9	9	9	9	9	9	9	9
Ohio	20	19	19	19	19	19	19	19	19	19	19	20	20	20	20	20	20	20	20	20	20	20	20	20	20	21	21	21	21	21	21	21	21	21
Oregon	1	1	1	1	1	1	1	1	1	1	1	1	1	1	1	1	1	1	1	1	1	1	1	1	1	1	1	1	1	1	1	1	1	1
Pennsylvania	27	25	25	25	26	26	26	26	26	26	26	26	26	26	26	27	27	27	27	27	27	27	27	27	27	27	28	28	28	28	28	28	28	28
Rhode Island	2	2	2	2	2	2	2	2	2	2	2	2	2	2	2	2	2	2	2	2	2	2	2	2	2	2	2	2	2	2	2	2	2	2
South Carolina	5	6	6	6	6	6	6	6	6	6	6	6	6	6	6	6	6	6	6	6	6	6	6	6	6	6	6	6	6	6	6	7	7	7
Tennessee	10	9	9	9	9	9	9	9	9	9	9	9	9	10	10	10	10	10	10	10	10	10	10	10	10	10	10	10	10	10	10	10	10	10
Texas	6	9	9	9	9	9	9	9	10	10	10	10	10	10	10	10	10	10	10	10	10	10	10	10	10	10	10	10	10	10	10	10	11	11
Vermont	3	2	2	2	2	2	2	2	2	2	2	2	2	2	2	2	2	2	2	2	2	2	2	2	2	2	2	2	2	2	2	2	2	2
Virginia	9	9	9	9	9	9	9	9	9	9	9	9	9	9	9	9	9	9	10	10	10	10	10	10	10	10	10	10	10	10	10	10	10	10
West Virginia	3	4	4	4	4	4	4	4	4	4	4	4	4	4	4	4	4	4	4	4	4	4	4	4	4	4	4	4	4	4	4	4	4	4
Wisconsin	8	8	8	8	8	8	8	8	8	8	8	8	8	8	8	8	8	8	8	8	8	8	8	8	8	8	8	8	8	9	9	9	9	9

TABLE SHOWING THE DUTIES LEVIED ON THE FOLLOWING LEADING ARTICLES FROM 1789 TO 1867.

Date of Tariffs.	Sugar.	Coffee.	Tea—Souchong.	Salt (in bulk.)	Pig Iron.	Bar Iron.	Glass Manufactures.	Cotton M'nufc's.	Woolen Manufactures.	Silk Goods.
July 4, 1789	1 cent p. lb	2½ cts. p. lb	13 cts. p. lb	6 cts. p. bush.	5 per cent.	5 per cent.	10 per cent.	5 p. ct.	5 per cent.	5 per ct.
August 10, 1790	1½ "	4 "	18 "	12 "	5 "	7½ "	12½ "	7½ "	7½ "	7½ "
May 2, 1792	1½ "	4 "	18 "	12 "	10 "	10 "	15 "	10 "	10 "	10 "
June 7, 1794	1½ "	5 "	18 "	12 "	15 "	15 "	20 "	12½ "	12½ to 15 per cent.	10 "
March 3, 1797	2 "	5 "	18 "	20 "	15 "	15 "	20 "	15 "	12½ to 15 "	10 "
May 13, 1800	2½ "	5 "	18 "	20 "	15 "	15 "	20 "	15 "	12½ to 15 "	12½ "
March 26, 1804	2½ "	5 "	18 "	Free.	17½ "	17½ "	22½ "	17½ "	15 to 17 "	15 "
July 1, 1812	5 "	10 "	36 "	*20 cents p. lb.	30 "	30 "	40 "	30 "	30 per cent.	25 "
April 27, 1816	3 "	5 "	25 "	20 "	20 "	$30 p. ton.	20 "	25 "	25 "	25 "
May 22, 1824	3 "	5 "	25 "	20 "	20 "	30 "	30 p. ct. & 3 cts. p. lb	25 "	30 "	25 "
May 19, 1828	3 "	5 "	25 "	20 "	$12½ p. ton.	37 "	30 p. ct. & 3 "	25 "	45 "	30 "
May, 1830	3 "	2 "	10 "	15 "	12½ "	37 "	30 p. ct. & 3 "	25 "	45 "	30 "
July 14, 1832	2½ "	Free.	Free.	10 "	10 "	30 "	30 p. ct. & 3 "	25 "	50 "	10 "
September 11, 1841	20 per cent.	"	"	10 "	20 per cent.	20 per cent.	20 per cent.	20 "	20 "	20 "
August 30, 1842	2½ cts. p. lb	"	"	8 cents p. bush.	$9 p. ton.	$25 p. ton.	30 "	30 "	40 "	$2.50 p. lb.
August 6, 1846	30 per cent.	"	"	20 per cent.	30 per cent.	30 per cent.	40 "	25 "	30 "	25 per ct.
March 3, 1857	24 "	"	"	15 "	24 "	24 "	30 "	19 "	24 "	19 "
March 2, 1861	¾ ct. per lb.	"	"	4 cents p. bush.	$6 per ton.	$15 p. ton.	30 "	25 "	25 p. c. & 12 cts. p. lb	20 "
August 5, 1861	2 cts. p. lb.	4 cts. p. lb	15 cts. p. lb	12 cts. p. 100 lbs	6 "	15 "	30 "	25 "	25 " "	30 "
December 24, 1861	2½ "	4 "	15 "	12 "	6 "	15 "	30 "	25 "	25 " "	30 "
July 14, 1862	3 "	5 "	20 "	18 "	6 "	17 "	35 "	30 "	30 p. c. & 18 cts. p. lb	30 "
June 30, 1864	3 "	5 "	25 "	18 "	9 "	1a1½ c. p. lb	40 "	35 "	40 p. c. & 24 "	60 "
March 2, 1867	....	....	....	....	....	....	....	....	35 p. c. & 50 "	60 "

* Imposed July 27, 1813.

NOTE.—In 1833 the Sliding Scale was introduced, by which, in cases where the duty exceeds 20 per cent., the excess should be reduced biennially.

For later duties see Table of Tariffs in succeeding pages.

STATUTES OF LIMITATIONS.

State Laws with reference to limitations of actions, showing the limit of time on which action may be brought.

States and Territories.	Assault, slander, replevin, etc.	Open accounts.	Notes.	Judgments.	Sealed and witnessed instruments.
	Yrs	Yrs.	Yrs.	Yrs.	Yrs.
Alabama	1	3	6	20	10
Arkansas	1	3	5	10	10
California	3	2	4	5	5
Colorado	1	2	2	3	3
Connecticut	1	6	6	6	17
Dakota	2	6	6	20	20
Delaware	1	3	6	20	20
Dist. of Columbia	1	3	3	12	12
Florida	2	5	3	20	20
Georgia	1	4	6	7	20
Idaho	3	2	4	5	5
Illinois	1	5	10	20	10
Indiana	2	6	20	20	20
Iowa	2	5	10	20	10
Kansas	1	3	5	5	15
Kentucky	1	5	5	15	15
Louisiana	1	3	5	10	20
Maine	2	6	20	20	20
Maryland	3	3	3	12	12
Massachusetts	2	6	20	20	20
Michigan	2	6	6	10	10
Minnesota	2	6	6	10	20
Mississippi	1	3	6	7	7
Missouri	1	4	5	5	10
Montana	2	2	4	5	4
Nebraska	2	6	20	20	10
Nevada	2, 6	6	20	20	20
New Hampshire	1	—	—	10	10
New Jersey	2	6	6	20	20
New Mexico	1	3	10	10	10
New York	1	6	15	15	15
North Carolina	1	3	10	10	10
Ohio	1	6	15	15	15
Ontario (U. Canada	1	5	5	20	30
Oregon	2	1	6	10	20
Pennsylvania	1	6	6	20	20
Quebec (L. Canada)	1, 2	5	5	30	30
Rhode Island	1	6	6	20	20
South Carolina	2	6	6	20	20
Tennessee	1	6	6	20	—
Texas	1	2	4	10	10
Utah	1	2	4	5	7
Vermont	2	6	14	8	8
Virginia	5	5	5	10	20
Washington Terr'y	2	3	6	9	20
West Virginia	5	5	6	10	10
Wisconsin	2	6	6	20	20
Wyoming	1	6	15	10	21

The Recent American Tariffs, under Revised Statutes, Sec. 2491, et seq.

COMMODITIES.	RATE OF DUTY.
Ale, porter, and beer—in bottles	35 c. per gall.
" " " in casks	25 c. per gall.
Aniline dyes or colors	50 c. per lb. and 35 p. c.
Animals, living — cattle, hogs, horses, sheep, etc	20 per cent.
Barley	15 c. per bush.
Books and other printed matter	25 per cent.
Braids of straw	30 per cent.
Brushes	40 per cent.
Buttons	30 per cent.
Cheese	4 c. per lb.
China, porcelain and parian ware, plain, white, and not decorated in any manner	45 per cent.
Do. gilded, ornamented or decorated in any manner	50 per cent.
Do. other earthen, stone, or crockery ware, white, glazed, edged, printed, or dipped, or cream colored	40 per cent.
Coal, bitumen, and shale	75 c. per ton.
Corsets and corset-cloth, valued at $6 per dozen, or less	$2 per doz.
Do. valued over $6 per dozen	35 per cent.
Cotton, manufactures of — plain bleached, value 20 cents or less per square yard	5½ c. per sq. yd.
Do. printed or colored, value 25 cents or less per square yard	5½ c. per sq. yd. & 20 p. c.
Do. Hosiery	35 per cent.
Do. Laces, cords, braids, gimps, galloons and cotton laces, colored and insertings	35 per cent.
Do. Thread-yarn, warps, or warp-yarn not wound on spools, valued at over 60 and not exceeding 80 cents per pound	30 c. per lb. and 20 p. c.
Cotton, valued at over 80 cents per pound	40 c. per lb. and 20 p. c.
Do. Velvet, velveteens, velvet bindings, ribbons, and vestings	35 per cent.
Currants, Zante, or other	1 c. per lb.
Diamonds (cut), cameos, mosaics, gems, pearls, rubies, and other precious stones, not set	10 per cent.
Dolls	35 per cent.
Embroideries, of cotton or wool	35 per cent.
Fans	35 per cent.
Feathers, ostrich, cock, and other ornamental	25 per cent.
Feathers and flowers, artificial and ornamental, not otherwise provided for	50 per cent.
Figs	2½ c. per lb.
Fire-crackers, in boxes of 40 packs, not exceeding 80 to the pack	$1 per box.
Flax linens, valued at 30 cents or less per square yard	35 per cent.
Do. valued at above 30 cents per square yard	40 per cent.
Do. Burlaps, and like manufactures of flax, jute, or hemp, of which either shall be the component of chief value (except bagging for cotton	30 per cent
Do. Duck, canvas, paddings, cotton bottoms, diapers, crash, huckabacks, handkerchiefs (not hemmed), lawns, or other manufactures of flax, jute, or hemp, valued at 30 cents or less per square yard	35 per cent.
Do. valued at above 30 cents per square yard	40 per cent.
Do. Thread, twine and pack-thread	40 per cent.
Do. all other manufactures of flax not otherwise provided for	40 per cent.
Fruits and nuts:—	
Almonds, not shelled	6 c. per lb.
" shelled	10 c. per lb.
Filberts and walnuts	3 c. per lb.
Prunes	1 c. per lb.
Raisins	2½ c. per lb.
Furs, and manufactures of	20 per cent.
Glass-ware:—	
Porcelain, Bohemian, cut, engraved, painted, colored, printed, stained, silvered, or gilded, not including plate-glass silvered, or looking-glass plates	40 per cent.
Plate-glass, cast, polished, not silvered, above 24 by 30, and not above 24 by 60	25 c. per sq. ft.
Above 24 by 60	50 c per sq. ft.
Window-glass, cylinder, crown, or common, unpolished, above 10 by 15 and not above 16 by 24	2 c. per lb.
Above 16 by 24 and not above 24 by 30	2½ c. per lb.
Above 24 by 30	3 c. per lb.
Manufactures of, not otherwise specified	40 per cent.
Hats, bonnets, and hoods, straw	40 per cent.
Hemp, jute, and other fibre:—	
Bags, cotton-bags, and bagging (except bagging for cotton)	40 per cent.
Jute and sunn-hemp	$15 per ton.
Jute butts	$6 per ton.
Manila, India, and other like substitutes for hemp	$25 per ton.
India Rubber, manufactures of:—	
Braces, webbing, etc	35 per cent.
Iron and steel, manufactures of:—	
In slabs, blooms, loops, etc	35 per cent.
Pig-iron	$7 per ton.
Scrap-iron, old, wrought	$8 per ton.
Manufactures of iron, not otherwise provided for	35 per cent.

COMMODITIES.	RATE OF DUTY.
Iron and steel, manufactures of:—	
Steel, and manufactures of penknives, jack-knives and pocket-knives	50 per cent.
All other cutlery, including sword blades	35 per cent.
In ingots, bars, coils, sheets, and steel-wire, not less than ¼ inch diameter, valued at 7 cents per pound or less	2¼ c. per lb.
Valued at above 7 cents and not over 11 cents per pound	3 c. per lb.
Muskets, rifles, and other fire-arms	35 per cent.
Railway bar, or rails, wholly of steel	1¼ c. per lb.
Manufactures of steel, not otherwise provided for	45 per cent.
Jewelry of gold, silver, or other metal, or imitations of	25 per cent.
Lead, and manufactures of:—	
Pigs and bars, and molten	2 c. per lb.
Leather, and manufactures of:—	
Calf-skins, tanned, or tanned and dressed	25 per cent.
Gloves, of kid or leather, of all descriptions	50 per cent.
Upper leather of all kinds, and skins, dressed and finished, of all kinds, not otherwise provided for	20 per cent.
Manufactures of, and articles of leather, or of which leather shall be a component part, not otherwise provided for	35 per cent.
Lemons and oranges	20 per cent.
Marble, and manufactures of:	
Veined and all other, in block, roughed or squared, not otherwise specified	50 c. per cu. ft. & 20 p. c. per cu. ft.
Mats of cocoa-nut, china, and all other floor-matting, of flags, jute, or grass	30 per cent.
Metal, manufactures of, not otherwise provided for	35 per cent.
Musical instruments	30 per cent.
Oils, olive, salad, in bottles or flasks	$1 per gall.
Opium	$1 per lb.
Opium prepared for smoking	$6 per lb.
Paintings and statuary, not by American artists	10 per cent.
Papier-mache, manufactures, articles, and wares of	35 per cent.
Pickles, sauces, and capers	35 per cent.
Rice, cleaned	2½ c. per lb.
Salt, in bags, sacks, barrels, or other packages	12 c. per 100 lbs.
Salt, in bulk	8 c. per 100 lbs.
Sardines and anchovies, packed in oil or otherwise	4 c. per box.
Seeds, flaxs. or lins. (56 lbs. to bush.)	20 c. per bush.
Silk:—	
Braids, laces, fringes, galloons, buttons, and ornaments, dress and piece goods	60 per cent.
Velvets	60 per cent.
Ribbons	60 per cent.
Ribbons (edge of cotton)	50 per cent.
Silk manufactures not otherwise provided for, made of silk, or of which silk is the component or chief value	60 per cent.
Manufactures of, which have as a component thereof 25 per cent., or over, in value of cotton, flax, wool, or worsted	50 per cent.
Soda caustic	1½ c. per lb.
Soda ash	¼ c. per lb.
Spices:	
Cassia, and Cassia Vera	10 c. per lb.
Nutmegs	20 c. per lb.
Pepper, black and white grain	5 c. per lb.
Spirits and wines:—	
Brandy, proof	$2 per gall.
Cordials, liqueurs, arrack, absinthe, kirschwasser, ratafia	$2 per gall.
Spirits, other, manufactured or distilled from grain	$2 per gall.
Spirits, other (except brandy), manufactured or distilled from other materials	$2 per gall.
Cologne-water and other perfumery, of which alcohol forms the principal ingredient	$3 per gall. and 50 per c. per gall.

COMMODITIES.	RATE OF DUTY.
Sugar and molasses:—	
Molasses	5 c. plus 25 per cent. per lb.
Molasses concentrated, tank-bottoms, sirup of sugar-cane, and melado	1½ c. plus 25 c. per lb.
Sugar:	
All not above No. 7 Dutch standard	1¾ c. plus 25 p. c. p. lb.
Above No. 7 and not above No. 10	2 c. plus 25 p. c. per lb.
Above No. 7 and not above No. 10	2 c per lb.
Above No. 13 and not above No. 16	2¾ c. plus 25 p. c. per lb.
Tartar, cream of	10 c. per lb.
Tartar, argols, other than crude	6 c. per lb.
Tin, plates or sheets	1 1-10 c. per lb.
Tobacco, and manufactures of:—	
Leaf, unmanufactured and not stemmed	35 c. per lb.
Cigars, cigarettes, and cheroots	$2.50 per lb. and 25 p. c. per lb.
Toys, wooden and other	50 per cent.
Watches, of gold or silver	25 per cent.
Wines, Champagne, and all other sparkling, in bottles, containing not more than 1 pint each and more than ½ pint	$3 per dozen.
Wines, Champagne, and all other sparkling, in bottles, containing not more than 1 quart and more than 1 pint ... dozens	$6 per doz.
" Still wines, in casks ... galls.	40 c. per gall.
" in bottles, containing each not more than 1 quart and not more than 1 pint ... doz. bots.	$1.60 per doz.
Wood: Boards, planks, deals, and other lumber ... M. ft.	$2 per M. ft.
" Manufactures of, not otherwise provided for	35 per cent.
Wools, hair of the alpaca, goat, etc.: Raw and manufactured, Class No. 1, clothing wool, value 32 cents or less per lb ... lbs.	10 c. per lb. & 11 p. c.
" Value 32 cents or less per pound ... lbs.	10 c. p. lb. & 11 p. c., less 10 per c.
" Value over 32 cents per pound ... lbs.	12 c. per lb. & 10 p. c.
" Class No. 2, value over 32 cents per pound ... lbs.	12 c. per lb. & 10 p. c.
" Class No. 3, carpet and other similar wools, valued at 12 cents or less per lb ... lbs.	3 c. per lb.
" Value over 12 cents per pound ... lbs.	6 c. per lb.
" Carpets and carpetings of all kinds, Aubusson and Axminster, and carpets woven whole for rooms ... sq. yds.	50 per cent.
" Brussels carpet wrought by Jacquard machine ... sq. yd.	44 c. per sq. yd. & 35 p. c.
" Brussels tapestry, printed on the warp or otherwise ... sq. yds.	28 c. per sq. yd. & 35 p. c.
" Patent velvet and tapestry velvet, printed on the warp or otherwise ... sq. yds.	40 c. per sq. yd. & 35 p. c.
" Dress goods, women and children's, and real or imitation Italian cloths, valued at not exceeding 20 cents per sq. yd ... sq. yds.	6 c. per sq. yd. & 35 p. c.
" Valued at above 20 cents per square yd ... sq. yds.	8 c. per sq. yd. & 40 p. c.
" Dress goods, women and children's, and real or imitation Italian cloths, weighing 4 ounces and over per square yard ... lbs.	50 c. per lb. & 35 p. c.
" Hosiery, valued at above 80 cents per pound ... lbs.	50 c. per lb. & 35 p. c.
" Manufactures not otherwise specified, valued at above 80 cents per pound ... lbs.	50 c. per lb. & 35 p. c.
Wool cloths ... lbs.	50 c. per lb. & 35 p. c.
" Cloths ... lbs.	50 c. per lb. & 35 p. c., less 10 p. c.
" Clothing—articles of wear ... lbs.	50 c. per lb. & 40 p. c.
" Clothing—ready-made ... lbs.	50 c. per lb. & 40 p. c.

Commodities.	Rate of Duty.	Commodities.	Rate of Duty.
Wool, manufactures wholly or in part of, not otherwise provided for ....lbs.	50 c. per lb. & 35 p. c.	" Webbings, beltings, bindings, braids, galloons, fringes, cords, buttons, etc.... lbs.	50 c. per lb. & 50 p. c
" Shawls, woolen....lbs.	50 c. per lb. & 35 p. c.	" Yarns, valued at above 80 cents per pound ....lbs.	50 c. per lb. & 50 p. c.
" Worsted, etc., not otherwise provided for....lbs.	50 c. per lb. & 40 p. c.	Zinc, in sheets....	2¼ c. per lb.

THE CUSTOMS TARIFF OF GREAT BRITAIN.

No protective duties are now levied on goods imported, Customs duties being charged solely for the sake of revenue. Formerly the articles subject to duty numbered nearly a thousand; now they are only twenty-two, the chief being tobacco, spirits, tea, and wine. The following is a complete list:

Articles.	£	s.	d.
Ale or beer, spec. gravity not exceeding 1065°, per bbl....	0	8	0
Ale or beer, spec. gravity not exceeding 1090°, per bbl....	0	11	0
Ale or beer, spec. gravity exceeding 1090°, per bbl....	0	16	0
Beer, Mum, per bbl....	1	1	0
Beer, spruce, spec. gravity not exceeding 1190°, per bbl....	1	1	0
Beer, spruce, exceeding 1190°, per barrel..	1	4	0
Cards, playing, per doz. packs....	0	3	9
Chickory (raw or kiln-dried), cwt....	0	13	3
Chicory (roasted or ground), lb....	0	0	2
Chloral hydrate, pound....	0	1	3
Chloroform, pound....	0	3	0
Cocoa, pound....	0	0	1
Cocoa, cwt., husks and shells....	0	2	0
Cocoa paste and chocolate, pound....	0	0	2
Coffee, raw, cwt....	0	14	0
Coffee, kiln-dried, roasted or ground, per pound....	0	0	2
Collodion, gallon....	0	1	4
Essence of spruce, 10 per cent. ad valorem			
Ethyl, iodide of, gallon....	0	13	0
Ether, gallon....	0	1	5
Fruit, dried, cwt....	0	7	0

Articles.	£	s.	s.
Malt, per quarter....	1	4	9
Naphtha, purified, gallon....	0	10	5
Pickles, in vinegar, gallon....	0	0	1
Plate, gold, ounce....	0	17	0
Plate, silver, ounce....	0	1	6
Spirits, brandy, Geneva, rum, etc., gallon.	0	10	5
Spirits, rum, from British Colonies, gallon	0	10	2
Spirits, cologne water, gallon....	0	16	6
Tea, pound....	0	0	6
Tobacco, unmanufactured, lb....	0	3	1¾
Tobacco, containing less than ten per ct. of moisture, lb....	0	3	6
Cavendish or Negro head....	0	4	6
Other manufactured tobacco....	0	4	0
Snuff, containing more than 13 per cent. of moisture, lb....	0	3	9
Snuff, less than 13 per cent. of moisture, lb.	0	4	6
Tobacco, cigars, pound....	0	5	0
Varnish, containing alcohol, gallon....	0	12	0
Vinegar, gallon....	0	0	3
Wine, containing less than 26° proof spirit, gallon....	0	1	0
Wine, containing more than 26° and less than 42 spirit, gallon....	0	2	6
Wine, for each additional degree of strength beyond 42°, gallon....	0	0	3

PRESIDENTS AND VICE-PRESIDENTS.

Term	Presidents. Name.	Qualified.	Vice-Presideets. Name.	Qualified.
*1	George Washington....	April 30, 1789	John Adams....	June 3, 1789
2	" "	March 4, 1793	" "	Dec. 2, 1793
3	John Adams....	March 4, 1797	Thomas Jefferson....	March 4, 1797
4	Thomas Jefferson....	March 4, 1801	Aaron Burr....	March 4, 1801
5	" "	March 4, 1805	George Clinton....	March 4, 1805
6	James Madison....	March 4, 1809	" "	March 4, 1809
7	" "	March 4, 1813	Elbridge Gerry....	March 4, 1813
			John Gaillard....	Nov. 25, 1814
8	James Monroe....	March 4, 1817	Daniel D. Tompkins....	March 4, 1817
9	" "	March 5, 1821	" "	March 5, 1821
10	John Q. Adams....	March 4, 1825	John C. Calhoun....	March 4, 1825
11	Andrew Jackson....	March 4, 1829	" "	March 4, 1829
12	" "	March 4, 1833	Martin Van Buren....	March 4, 1833
13	Martin Van Buren....	March 4, 1837	Richard M. Johnson....	March 4, 1837
14	Wm. H. Harrison....	March 4, 1841	John Tyler....	March 4, 1841
14a	John Tyler....	April 6, 1841	†Samuel L. Southard....	April 6, 1841
			†Willie P. Mangum....	May 31, 1842
15	James K. Polk....	March 4, 1845	George M. Dallas....	March 4, 1845
16	Zachary Taylor....	March 5, 1849	Millard Fillmore....	March 5, 1849
16a	Millard Fillmore....	July 10, 1850	†William R. King....	July 11, 1850
17	Franklin Pierce....	March 4, 1853	William R. King....	March 4, 1853
			†David R. Atchison....	April 18, 1853
			†Jesse D Bright....	Dec. 5, 1854
18	James Buchanan....	March 4, 1857	John C. Breckinridge....	March 4, 1857
19	Abraham Lincoln....	March 4, 1861	Hannibal Hamlin....	March 4, 1861
20	" "	March 4, 1865	Andrew Johnson....	March 4, 1865
20a	Andrew Johnson....	April 15, 1865	†Lafayette S. Foster....	April 15, 1865
			†Benjamin F. Wade....	March 2, 1867
21	Ulysses S. Grant....	March 4, 1869	Schuyler Colfax....	March 4, 1869
22	" "	March 4, 1873	Henry Wilson....	March 4, 1873
			†Thomas W. Ferry....	Nov. 22, 1875
23	Rutherford B. Hayes....	March 5, 1877	William A. Wheeler....	March 5, 1877
24	James A. Garfield....	March 4, 1881	Chester A. Arthur....	March 4' 1881
24a	Chester A. Arthur....	Oct. 20, 1881	†Thomas F. Bayard....	Oct. 12, 1881
			†David Davis....	Oct. 13, 1881

* The figures in this column mark the terms held by the Presidents.

† Acting Vice-President and President *pro tem.* of the Senate.

SUMMARY OF POPULAR AND ELECTORAL VOTES IN PRESIDENTIAL ELECTIONS, 1789-1880.

Year.	Number of States.	Total Elect. Vote.	Party.	Candidates.	States.	Popular Vote.	Elect. Vote.
1789	10	73		George Washington			69
				John Adams			34
				John Jay			9
				R. R. Harrison			6
				John Rutledge			6
				John Hancock			4
				George Clinton			3
				Samuel Huntington			2
				John Milton			2
				Benjamin Lincoln			1
				James Armstrong			1
				Edward Telfair			1
				Vacancies			4
1792	15	135	Federalist	George Washington			132
			Federalist	John Adams			77
			Republican	George Clinton			50
			Republican	Thomas Jefferson			4
			Republican	Aaron Burr			1
				Vacancies			3
1796	16	138	Federalist	John Adams			71
			Republican	Thomas Jefferson			68
			Federalist	Thomas Pinckney			59
			Republican	Aaron Burr			30
				Samuel Adams			15
				Oliver Ellsworth			11
				George Clinton			7
				John Jay			5
				James Iredell			3
				George Washington			2
				John Henry			2
				S. Johnson			2
				Charles C. Pinckney			1
1800	16	138	Republican	Thomas Jefferson			73
			Republican	Aaron Burr			73
			Federalist	John Adams			65
			Federalist	Charles C. Pinckney			64
			Federalist	John Jay			1

Year.	Number of States.	Total Elect. Vote.	Party.	For President.	States.	Popular Vote.	Elect. Vote.	For Vice-President.	Elect. Vote.
1804	21	176	Republican	Thomas Jefferson	15		162	George Clinton	162
			Federalist	Chas. C. Pinckney	2		14	Rufus King	14
1808	17	176	Republican	James Madison	12		122	George Clinton	113
			Republican	George Clinton			6	James Madison	3
			Federalist	Chas. C Pinckney	5		47	Rufus King	47
								John Langdon	9
								James Monroe	3
				Vacancy			1		1
1812	18	218	Republican	James Madison	11		128	Elbridge Gerry	131
			Federalist	De Witt Clinton	7		89	Jared Ingersoll	86
				Vacancy			1		1
1816	19	221	Republican	James Monroe	16		183	D. D. Tompkins	183
			Federalist	Rufus King	3		34	John E. Howard	22
								James Ross	5
								John Marshall	4
								Robt. G. Harper	3
				Vacancies			4		4
1820	24	235	Republican	James Monroe	24		231	D. D. Tompkins	218
				John Q. Adams			1	Rich. Stockton	8
								Daniel Rodney	4
								Robt. G. Harper	1
								Richard Rush	1
				Vacancies			3		3
1824	24	261	Republican	Andrew Jackson	10	155,872	99	John C. Calhoun	182
			Republican	John Q. Adams	8	105,321	84	Nathan Sanford	30
			Republican	Wm. H Crawford	3	44,282	41	Nathaniel Macon	24
			Republican	Henry Clay	3	46,587	37	Andrew Jackson	13
								M. Van Buren	9
								Henry Clay	2
				Vacancy					1

SUMMARY OF POPULAR AND ELECTORAL VOTES.—[Continued.]

Year.	Number of States.	Total Elect. Vote.	Party.	For President.	States.	Popular Vote.	Elect Vote.	For Vice-President.	Elect. Vote.
1828	24	261	Democratic	Andrew Jackson	15	647,231	178	John C. Calhoun	171
			Nat. Republican	John Q. Adams	9	509,097	83	Richard Rush	83
								William Smith	7
1832	24	288	Democratic	Andrew Jackon	15	687,502	219	M. Van Buren	189
			Nat. Republican	Henry Clay	7	530,189	49	John Sergeant	49
			Anti-Mason	William Wirt	1	33,108	7	Amos Ellmaker	7
			e	John Floyd	1		11	Henry Lee	11
								William Wilkins	30
				Vacancies.			2		2
1836	26	294	Democratic	Martin Van Buren	15	761,549	170	R. M. Johnson	147
			Whig	Wm. H. Harrison	7		73	Francis Granger	77
				Hugh L. White	2	736,656	26	John Tyler	47
				Daniel Webster	1		14	William Smith	23
				W. P. Mangum	1		11		
1840	26	294	Whig	Wm. H. Harrison	19	1,275,017	234	John Tyler	234
			Democratic	Martin Van Buren	7	1,128,702	60	R. M. Johnson	48
			Liberty	James G. Birney		7,059			
								L. W. Tazewell	11
								James K. Polk	1
1844	26	275	Democratic	James K. Polk	15	1,337,243	170	Geo. M. Dallas	170
			Whig	Henry Clay	11	1,299,068	105	T. Frelinghuysen	105
			Liberty	James G. Birney		62,300			
1848	30	290	Whig	Zachary Taylor	15	1.360,101	163	Millard Fillmore	163
			Democratic	Lewis Cass	15	1,220,544	127	Wm. O. Butler	127
			Free Soil	Martin Van Buren		291,263		Chas. F. Adams	
1852	31	296	Democratic	Franklin Pierce	27	1.601,474	254	Wm. R. King	254
			Whig	Winfield Scott	4	1,386,578	42	Wm. A. Graham	42
			Free Democracy	John P. Hale		156,149		Geo. W. Julian	
1856	31	296	Democratic	James Buchanan	19	1,838,169	174	J. C. Breckinridge	174
			Republican	John C. Fremont	11	1,341.264	114	Wm. L. Dayton	114
			American	Millard Fillmore	1	874,534	8	A. J. Donelson	8
1860	33	303	Republican	Abraham Lincoln	17	1,866,352	180	Hannibal Hamlin	180
			Democratic	J. C. Breckinridge	11	845,763	72	Joseph Lane	72
			Democratic	S. A. Douglas	2	1,375,157	12	H. V. Johnson	12
			"Const. Union"	John Bell	3	589,581	39	Edward Everett	39
1864	36	314	Republican	Abraham Lincoln	22	2,216,067	212	Andrew Johnson	212
			Democratic	Geo. B. McClellan	3	1,808,725	21	Geo. H. Pendleton	21
				Vacancies*	11		81		81
1868	37	317	Republican	Ulysses S. Grant	26	3,015,071	214	Schuyler Colfax	214
			Democratic	Horatio Seymour	8	2,709,613	80	F. P. Blair, Jr.	80
				Vacancies†	3		23		23
1872	37	366	Republican	Ulysses S. Grant	31	3,597,070	286	Henry Wilson	286
			Dem. and Lib. Rep.	Horace Greeley	6	2.834,079		B. Gratz Brown	47
			Democratic	Chas. O'Conor		29,408		John Q. Adams	
			Temperance	James Black		5,608		A. H. Colquite	5
				T. A. Hendricks			42	Iohn M. Palmer	3
				B. Gratz Brown			18	Geo. W. Julian	5
				Chas. J. Jenkins			2	T. E. Bramlette	3
				David Davis			1	W. S. Groesbeck	1
								Willis B. Machen	1
								N. P. Banks	1
				Not counted‡			17		14
1876	38	369	Republican	R. B. Hayes	21	4.033,950	185	Wm. A. Wheeler	185
			Democratic	S. J. Tilden	17	4,284.885	184	T. A. Hendricks	184
			"Greenback"	Peter Cooper		81,740		S. F. Cary	
			"Prohibition"	Green C. Smith		9,522		R. T. Stewart	
1880	38	369	Republican	James A. Garfield	19	4,442,950	214	Chester A. Arthur	214
			Democratic	W. S. Hancock,	19	4,442,035	155	Wm. H. English	155
			"Greenback"	James B. Weaver		306,867		B. J. Chambers	
				Scattering		12,576			

* Not voting—Alabama, Arkansas, Florida, Georgia. Louisiana, Mississippi, North Carolina, South Carolina, Tennessee, Texas, and Virginia.

† Not voting—Mississippi, Texas, and Virginia.

‡ Seventeen votes rejected, viz.: 3 from Georgia for Horace Greeley (dead), and 8 from Louisiana, and 6 from Arkansas for U. S. Grant.

CABINET OFFICERS OF THE ADMINISTRATIONS.

GEORGE WASHINGTON, President.

I. and II.; 1789-1797.

Secretary of State, Thomas Jefferson, Virginia, September 26th, 1789; Edmund Randolph, Virginia, January 2d, 1794; Timothy Pickering, Pennsylvania, December 10th, 1795. *Secretary of Treasury*, Alexander Hamilton, New York, September 11th, 1789; Oliver Wolcott, Connecticut, February 2d, 1795. *Secretary of War*, Henry Knox, Massachusetts, September 12th, 1789; Timothy Pickering, Pennsylvania, January 2d, 1795; James McHenry, Maryland, January 27th, 1796. *Attorney General*, Edmund Randolph, Virginia, September 26th, 1789; William Bradford, Pennsylvania, January 27th, 1794; Charles Lee, Virginia, December 10th, 1795. *Postmaster-General*,* Samuel Osgood, Massachusetts, September 26th, 1789; Timothy Pickering, Pennsylvania, August 12th, 1791; Joseph Habersham, Georgia, February 25th, 1795.

JOHN ADAMS, President.

III.; 1797-1801.

Secretary of State, Timothy Pickering, continued; John Marshall, Virginia, May 13th, 1800. *Secretary of Treasury*, Oliver Wolcott, continued; Samuel Dexter, Massachusetts, January 1st, 1801. *Secretary of War*, James McHenry, continued; Samuel Dexter, Massachusetts, May 13th, 1800; Roger Griswold, Connecticut, February 3d, 1801. *Secretary of Navy*,† George Cabot, Massachusetts, May 3d, 1798; Benjamin Stoddert, Maryland, May 21st, 1798. *Attorney-General*, Charles Lee, continued; Theophilus Parsons, Massachusetts, February 20th, 1801. *Postmaster-General*, Joseph Habersham, continued.

THOMAS JEFFERSON, President.

IV. and V.; 1801-1809.

Secretary of State, James Madison, Virginia, March 5th, 1801. *Secretary of Treasury*, Samuel Dexter, continued; Albert Gallatin, Pennsylvania, May 14th, 1801. *Secretary of War*, Henry Dearborn, Massachusetts, March 5th, 1801. *Secretary of Navy*, Benjamin Stoddart, continued; Robert Smith, Maryland, July 15th, 1801; Jacob Crowninshield, Massachusetts, May, 3d, 1805. *Attorney-General*, Levi Lincoln, Massachusetts, March 5th, 1801; Robert Smith, Maryland, March 3d, 1805; John Breckinridge, Kentucky, August 7th, 1805; Cæsar A. Rodney, Pennsylvania, January 20th, 1807. *Postmaster-General*, Joseph Habersham, continued; Gideon Granger, Connecticut, November 28th, 1801.

JAMES MADISON, President.

VI. and VII.; 1809-1817.

Secretary of State, Robert Smith, Maryland, March 6th, 1809; James Monroe, Virginia, April 2d, 1811. *Secretary of Treasury*, Albert Gallatin, continued; George W. Campbell, Tennessee, February 9th, 1814; A. J. Dallas, Pennsylvania, October 6th, 1814; William H. Crawford, Georgia, October 22d, 1816. *Secretary of War*, William Eustis, Massachusetts, March 7th, 1809; John Armstrong, New York, January 13th, 1813; James Monroe, Virginia, September 27th, 1814; William H. Crawford, Georgia, August 1st, 1815. *Secretary of Navy*, Paul Hamilton, South Carolina, March 7th, 1809; William Jones, Pennsylvania, January 12th, 1813; B. W. Crowninshield, Massachusetts, December 19th, 1814. *Attorney-General*, C. A. Rodney, continued; William Pinckney, Maryland, December 11th, 1811; Richard Rush, Pennsylvania, February 10th, 1814. *Postmaster-General*, Gideon Granger, continued; Return J. Meigs, Ohio, March 17th, 1814.

---

*Not a Cabinet officer, but a subordinate of the Treasury Department until 1829.

† Naval affairs were under the control of the Secretary of War until a separate Navy Department was organized by Act of April 30th, 1798. The Acts organizing the other Departments were of the following dates: *State*, September 15th, 1789: *Treasury*, September 2d, 1789; *War*, August 7th, 1789. The Attorney-General's duties were regulated by the Judiciary Act of September 24th, 1789.

JAMES MONROE, President.

VIII. and IX.; 1817-1825.

Secretary of State, John Quincy Adams, Massachusetts, March 5th, 1817. *Secretary of Treasury*, William H. Crawford, continued. *Secretary of War*, George Graham, Virginia, April 7th, 1817; John C. Calhoun, South Carolina, October 8th, 1817. *Secretary of Navy*, B. W. Crowninshield, continued; Smith Thompson, New York, November 9th, 1818; John Rogers, Massachusetts, September 1st, 1823; Samuel L. Southard, New Jersey, September 16th, 1823. *Attorney-General*, Richard Rush, continued; William Wirt, Virginia, November 13th, 1817. *Postmaster-General*, R. J. Meigs, continued; John McLean, Ohio, June 26th, 1823.

JOHN QUINCY ADAMS, President.

X.; 1825-1829.

Secretary of State, Henry Clay, Kentucky, March 7th, 1825. *Secretary of Treasury*, Richard Rush, Pennsylvania, March 7th, 1825. *Secretary of War*, James Barbour, Virginia, March 7th, 1825; Peter B. Porter, New York, May 26th 1828. *Secretary of Navy*, S. L. Southard, continued. *Attorney-General*, William Wirt, continued. *Postmaster-General*, John McLean, continued.

ANDREW JACKSON, President.

XI. and XII.; 1829-1837.

Secretary of State, Martin Van Buren, New York, March 6th, 1829; Edward Livingston, Louisiana, May 24th, 1831; Louis McLane, Delaware, May 29th, 1833; John Forsyth, Georgia, June 27th, 1834. *Secretary of Treasury*, Samuel D. Ingham, Pennsylvania, March 6th, 1829; Louis McLane, Delaware, August 8th, 1831; William J. Duane, Pennsylvania, May 29th, 1833; Roger B. Taney, Maryland, September 23d, 1833; Levi Woodbury, New Hampshire, June 27th, 1834. *Secretary of War*, John H. Eaton, Tennessee, March 9th, 1829; Lewis Cass, Michigan, August 1st, 1831; Benjamin F Butler, New York, March 3d, 1837. *Secretary of Navy*, John Branch, North Carolina, March 9th, 1829; Levi Woodbury, New Hampshire, May 23d, 1831; Mahlon Dickerson, New Jersey, June 30th, 1834. *Attorney-General*, John M. Berrien, Georgia. March 9th, 1829; Roger B. Taney, Maryland, July 20th, 1831; Benjamin F. Butler, New York, November 15th, 1833. *Postmaster-General*, William T. Barry, Kentucky, March 9th, 1829; Amos Kendall, Kentucky, May 1st, 1835.

MARTIN VAN BUREN, President.

XIII.; 1837-1841.

Secretary of State, John Forsyth, continued. *Secretary of Treasury*, Levi Woodbury continued. *Secretary of War*, Joel R. Poinsett, South Carolina, March 7th, 1837. *Secretary of Navy*, Mahlon Dickerson, continued; James K. Paulding, New York, June 25th, 1838. *Attorney-General*, Benjamin F Butler; Felix Grundy, Tennessee, July 5th, 1838; Henry D. Gilpin, Pennsylvania. January 11th, 1840. *Postmaster-General*, Amos Kendall, continued; John M. Niles, Connecticut, May 19th, 1840.

WM. H. HARRISON AND JOHN TYLER, Presidents.

XIV.; 1841-1845.

Secretary of State, Daniel Webster, Massachusetts, March 5th, 1841; Hugh S. Legare, South Carolina, May 9th, 1843; A. P Upshur, Virginia, July 24th, 1843; John C. Calhoun, South Carolina, March 6th, 1844. *Secretary of Treasury*, Thomas Ewing, Ohio, March 5th, 1841; Walter Forward, Pennsylvania, September 13th, 1841; John C. Spencer, New York, March 3d, 1843; George M. Bibb, Kentucky, June 15th, 1844. *Secretary of War*, John Bell, Tennessee, March 5th, 1841; John McLean, Ohio, September 13th, 1841; John C. Spencer, New York, October 12th, 1841; James M. Porter, Pennsylvania, March 8th, 1843; William Wilkins, Pennsylvania, February 15th, 1844. *Secretary of Navy*, G. E. Badger, North Carolina, March 5th, 1841; A. P Upshur, Virginia, September 13th, 1841; David Henshaw, Massachusetts, July 24th, 1843; T. W. Gilmer, Virginia, February 15th, 1844; John Y. Mason, Virginia, March 14th, 1844. *Attorney-General*, John J. Crittenden, Kentucky, March 5th, 1841; Hugh S. Legare, South Carolina, September 13th, 1841; John Nelson, Maryland, July 1st, 1843. *Postmaster-General*, Francis Granger, New York, March 6th, 1841; Charles A. Wickliffe, Kentucky, September 13th, 1841.

JAMES K. POLK, PRESIDENT.

XV.; 1845-1849.

Secretary of State, James Buchanan, Pennsylvania, March 6th, 1845. *Secretary of Treasury*, Robert J. Walker, Mississippi, March 6th, 1845. *Secretary of War*, William L. Marcy, New York, March 6th, 1845. *Secretary of Navy*, George Bancroft, Massachusetts, March 10th, 1845; John Y. Mason, September 9th, 1846. *Attorney-General*, John Y Mason, Virginia, March 5th, 1845; Nathan Clifford, Maine, October 17th, 1846. *Postmaster-General*, Cave Johnson, Tennessee, March 6th, 1845.

ZACHARY TAYLOR AND MILLARD FILLMORE, Presidents

XVI.; 1849-1853.

Secretary of State, John M. Clayton, Delaware, March 7th, 1849; Daniel Webster, Massachusetts, July 22d, 1850; Edward Everett, Massachusetts, December 6th, 1852. *Secretary of Treasury*, W. M. Meredith, Pennsylvania, March 8th, 1849; Thomas Corwin, Ohio, July 23d, 1850. *Secretary of War*, George W. Crawford, Georgia, March 8th, 1849; Winfield Scott (*ad interim*), July 23d, 1850; Charles M Conrad, Louisiana, August 15th, 1850. *Secretary of Navy*, William B. Preston, Virginia, March 8th, 1849; William A. Graham, North Carolina, July 22d, 1850; J. P. Kennedy, Maryland, July 22d, 1852. *Secretary of Interior*, Thomas H. Ewing, Ohio, March 8th, 1849; A. H H. Stuart, Virginia, September 12th, 1850 *Attorney-General*, Reverdy Johnson, Maryland, March 8th, 1849; John J Crittenden, Kentucky, July 22d, 1850. *Postmaster-General*, Jacob Collamer, Vermont, March 8th, 1849; Nathan K. Hall, New York, July 23d, 1850; S. D Hubbard, Connecticut, August 31st, 1852.

FRANKLIN PIERCE, President.

XVII.; 1853-1857.

Secretary of State, William L. Marcy, New York, March 7th, 1853. *Secretary of Treasury*, James Guthrie, Kentucky, March 7th, 1853. *Secretary of War*, Jefferson Davis, Mississippi, March 7th, 1853 *Secretary of Navy*, James C. Dobbin, North Carolina, March 7th, 1853. *Secretary of Interior*, Robert McClelland, Michigan, March 7th, 1853; Jacob Thompson, Mississippi, March 6th, 1856. *Attorney-General*, Caleb Cushing, Massachusetts, March 7th, 1853. *Postmaster General*, James Campbell, Pennsylvania, March 7th, 1853.

JAMES BUCHANAN, President.

XVIII.; 1857-1861.

Secretary of State, Lewis Cass, Michigan, March 6th, 1857; J. S. Black, Pennsylvania, December 17th, 1860. *Secretary of Treasury*, Howell Cobb, Georgia, March 6th, 1857; Philip F. Thomas, Maryland, December 12th, 1860; John A. Dix, New York, January 11th, 1861. *Secretary of War*, John B. Floyd, Virginia, March 6th, 1857; Joseph Holt, Kentucky, January 18th, 1861. *Secretary of Navy*, Isaac Toucey, Connecticut, March 6th, 1857. *Secretary of Interior* Jacob Thompson, continued. *Attorney-General*, J. S. Black, Pennsylvania, March 6th, 1857; E. M. Stanton, Pennsylvania, December 20th, 1860. *Postmaster-General*, Aaron V. Brown, Tennessee, March 6th, 1857; Joseph Holt, Kentucky, March 14th, 1859; Horatio King, Maine, February 12th, 1861.

ABRAHAM LINCOLN AND ANDREW JOHNSON, Presidents.

XIX. and XX.; 1861-1869.

Secretary of State, William H. Seward, New York, March 5th, 1861. *Secretary of Treasury*, S. P. Chase, Ohio, March 5th, 1861; W. P. Fessenden, Maine, July 1st, 1864; Hugh McCulloch, Indiana, March 7th, 1865. *Secretary of War*, Simon Cameron, Pennsylvania, March 5th, 1861; Edwin M. Stanton, Pennsylvania, January 15th, 1862; U. S Grant (*ad interim*), August 12th, 1867; Edwin M. Stanton (reinstated), January 14th, 1868; J. M. Schofield, Illinois, May 28th, 1868. *Secretary of Navy*, Gideon Welles, Connecticut, March 5th, 1861. *Secretary of Interior*, Caleb P. Smith, March 5th, 1861; John P. Usher, Indiana, January 8th, 1863; James Harlan, Iowa, May 15th, 1865; O. H. Browning, Illinois, July 27th, 1866. *Attorney-General*, Edward Bates, Missouri, March 5th, 1861; Titian J. Coffee, June 22d, 1863; James Speed, Kentucky, December 2d, 1864; Henry Stanbery, Ohio, July 23d, 1866; William M. Evarts, New York, July 15th, 1868. *Postmaster-General*, Montgomery Blair, Maryland, March 5th, 1861; William Dennison, Ohio, September 24th, 1864; Alexander W. Randall, Wisconsin, July 25th, 1866.

ULYSSES S. GRANT, President.

XXI. and XXII.; 1869-1877.

Secretary of State, E. B. Washburne, Illinois, March 5th, 1869; Hamilton Fish, New York, March 11th, 1869. *Secretary of Treasury*, George S. Boutwell, Massachusetts, March 11th, 1869; William A. Richardson, Massachusetts, March 17th, 1873; Benjamin H Bristow, Kentucky, June 2d, 1874; Lot M. Morrill, Maine, June 21st, 1876 *Secretary of War*, John A. Rawlins, Illinois, March 11th, 1869; William T. Sherman, Ohio, September 9th, 1869; William W. Belknap, Iowa, October 25th, 1869; Alphonso Taft, Ohio, March 8th, 1876; J. D. Cameron, Pennsylvania, May 22d, 1876. *Secretary of Navy*, Adolph E. Borie, Pennsylvania, March 5th, 1869; George M. Robeson, New Jersey, June 25th, 1869. *Secretary of Interior*, Jacob D. Cox, Ohio, March 5th, 1869; Columbus Delano, Ohio, November 1st, 1870; Zachariah Chandler, Michigan, October 19th, 1875. *Attorney-General*, E. R. Hoar, Massachusetts, March 5th, 1869; Amos T. Akerman, Georgia, June 23d, 1870; George H. Williams, Oregon, December, 14th, 1871; Edwards Pierrepont, New York, April 26th, 1875; Alphonso Taft, Ohio, May 22d, 1876. *Postmaster-General*, J. A. J. Creswell, Maryland, March 5th, 1869; Marshall Jewell, Connecticut, August 24th, 1874; James M. Tyner, Indiana, July 12th, 1876.

RUTHERFORD B. HAYES, President.

XXIII.; 1877-1881.

Secretary of State, William M. Evarts, New York, March 12th, 1877. *Secretary of Treasury*, John Sherman, Ohio, March 8th, 1877. *Secretary of War*, George W. McCrary, Iowa, March 12th, 1877; Alexander Ramsey, Minnesota, December 12th, 1879. *Secretary of Navy*, Richard W. Thompson, Indiana, March 12th, 1877; Nathan Goff, Jr., West Virginia, January 6th, 1881. *Secretary of Interior*, Carl Schurz, Missouri, March 12th, 1877. *Attorney-General*, Charles Devens, Massachusetts, March 12th, 1877. *Postmaster-General*, David M. Key, Tennessee, March 12th, 1877; Horace Maynard, Tennessee, August 25th, 1880.

JAMES A. GARFIELD AND CHESTER A. ARTHUR.

Presidents.

XXIV.; 1881-1885.

Secretary of State, James G. Blaine, Maine, March 5th, 1881; Frederick T. Frelinghuysen, New Jersey, December 12th, 1881. *Secretary of Treasury*, William H Windom, Minnesota, March 5th, 1881; Charles J. Folger, New York, October 27th, 1881. *Secretary of War*, Robert T. Lincoln, Illinois, March 5th, 1881. *Secretary of Navy*, W. H. Hunt, Louisiana, March 5th, 1881. *Secretary of Interior*, S. J. Kirkwood, Iowa, March 5th, 1881. *Attorney-General*, Wayne MacVeagh, Pennsylvania, March 5th, 1881; Benjamin H. Brewster, Pennsylvania, December 16th, 1881. *Postmaster-General*, Thomas L. James, New York, March 5th, 1881; Timothy O. Howe, Wisconsin, December 20th, 1881.

FOREIGN IMMIGRATION SINCE 1870, BY FISCAL YEARS.—Official.

Years.	Number.	Years.	Number.	Years.	Number.
1870	387,203	1874	313,339	1878	138,469
1871	321,350	1875	227,498	1879	177,826
1872	404,806	1876	169,986	1880	457,257
1873	459,803	1877	141,857	1881	669,431

Of the arrivals in 1881, 410,729 were males and 258,702 females. There were 153,718 from Great Britain and Ireland; 210,485 from Germany; 21,109 from Austria; 11,890 from China; 102,922 from Quebec and Ontario; 14,437 from Nova Scotia; 49,760 from Sweden; 22,705 from Norway; 15,387 from Italy; 5,227 from France; 9,117 from Denmark, and 11,293 from Switzerland.

SIGNERS OF THE DECLARATION OF INDEPENDENCE. IN CONGRESS ASSEMBLED JULY 4th, 1776.

The following list of members of the Continental Congress, who signed the Declaration of Independence (although the names are included in the general list of that Congress, from 1774 to 1778), is given separately for the purpose of showing the places and dates of their birth, and the times of their respective deaths, for convenient reference:

Names of the Signers.	Born at	Delegated From	Died.
Adams, John	Braintree, Mass., 19 Oct. 1735	Massachusetts	4 July, 1826.
Adams, Samuel	Boston, Mass., 27 Sept. 1722	Massachusetts	2 Oct. 1803.
Bartlett, Josiah	Amesbury, Mass. in Nov. 1729	New Hampshire	19 May 1795.
Braxton, Carter	Newington, Va., 10 Sept. 1736	Virginia	10 Oct. 1797.
Carroll, Chas of Carrollton	Annapolis, Md., 20 Sept. 1737	Maryland	14 November, 1832.
Chase, Samuel	Somerset Co., Md., 17 Apr. 1741	Maryland	19 June, 1811.
Clark, Abraham	Elizabethtown, N. J., 15 Feb. 1726	New Jersey	— September, 1794.
Clymer, George	Philadelphia, Pa., in 1739	Pennsylvania	23 Jan. 1813.
Ellery, William	Newport, R. I., 22 Dec. 1727	R. I. & Prov. Pl	15 Feb. 1820.
Floyd, William	Suffolk Co., N. Y., 17 Dec. 1734	New York	4 Aug 1821.
Franklin, Benjamin	Boston, Mass., 17 Jan. 1706	Pennsylvania.	17 April, 1790.
Gerry, Elbridge	Marblehead, Mass., 1 July 1744	Massachusetts	23 November, 1814.
Gwinnet, Button	England, in 1732	Georgia	27 May, 1777.
Hall, Lyman	Connecticut, in 1731	Georgia	— Feb. 1790.
Hancock, John	Braintree, Mass., in 1737	Massachusetts	8 Oct 1793.
Harrison, Benjamin.	Berkley, Va., ——— ———	Virginia	— April, 1791.
Hart, John	Hopewell, N. J., in 1715	New Jersey	1880.
Heyward, Thomas, Jr	St. Luke's, S. C., in 1746	South Carolina	— March, 1809.
Hewes, Joseph	Kingston, N. J., in 1730	North Carolina	10 Oct. 1779.
Hooper, William	Boston, Mass., 17 June, 1742	North Carolina	— Oct. 1790.
Hopkins, Stephen	Scituate, Mass., 7 Mar., 1707	R. I. & Prov. Pl	13 July, 1785.
Huntington, Samuel	Windham, Conn., 3 July 1732	Connecticut	5 Jan. 1796.
Hopkinson, Francis	Philadelphia, Pa., in 1737	New Jersey	9 May, 1790.
Jefferson, Thomas	Shadwell, Va., 13 Apr. 1734	Virginia	4 July, 1826.
Lee, Richard Henry	Stratford, Va., 20 Jan. 1732	Virginia	19 June, 1794.
Lee, Francis Lightfoot	Stratford, Va., 14 Oct. 1734	Virginia	— April, 1797.
Lewis, Francis F	Landaff, Wales, in Mar. 1713	New York	30 Dec. 1803.
Livingston, Philip	Albany, N. Y., 15 Jan. 1716	New York	12 June, 1778.
Lynch, Thomas, Jr	St. George's, S. C., 5 Aug. 1749	South Carolina	Lost at sea, 1779
McKean, Thomas	Chester Co., Pa., 19 Mar 1734	Delaware	24 June, 1817.
Middleton, Arthur	Middleton Place, S. C., in 1743	South Carolina	1 Jan. 1787.
Morris, Lewis	Morrissianna, N. Y., in 1726	New York	22 Jan. 1798.
Morris, Robert	Lancashire, Eng., Jan. 1733-4	Pennsylvania	8 May, 1806
Morton, John	Ridley, Pa., in 1724	Pennsylvania	— April, 1777.
Nelson, Thomas, Jr	York, Va., 26 Dec. 1738	Virginia	4 Jan. 1789.
Paca, Wm.	Wye-Hill, Md., 31 Oct. 1740	Maryland	— ———, 1799.
Paine, Robert Treat	Boston, Mass., in 1731	Massachusetts	11 May, 1804.
Penn, John	Caroline Co., Va., 17 May 1741	North Carolina	26 Oct. 1809.
Read, George	Cecil Co., Md., in 1734	Delaware	— ———, 1798.
Rodney, Cæsar	Dover, Del., in 1730	Delaware	— ———, 1783.
Ross, George	New Castle, Del. in 1730	Pennsylvania	— July, 1779.
Rush, Benjamin, M. D.	Byberry, Pa., 24 Dec. 1745	Pennsylvania	19 April, 1813.
Rutledge, Edward	Charleston, S. C., in Nov. 1749	South Carolina	23 Jan. 1800.
Sherman, Roger	Newton, Mass., 19 Apr. 1721	Connecticut	23 July, 1793.
Smith, James	———, Ireland, ——— ———	Pennsylvania	11 July, 1806.
Stockton, Richard	Princeton, N. J., 1 Oct. 1730	New Jersey	28 Feb. 1781.
Stone, Thomas	Charles Co., Md., in 1742	Maryland	5 Oct. 1787.
Taylor, George	———, Ireland, in 1716	Pennsylvania	23 Feb. 1781.
Thornton, Matthew	———, Ireland, in 1714	New Hampshire	24 June, 1803.
Walton, George	Frederick Co., Va., in 1740	Georgia	2 Feb. 1804
Whipple, Wm	Kittery, Maine, in 1730	New Hampshire	28 Nov. 1785.
Williams, Wm	Lebanon, Conn., 8 Apr. 1731	Connecticut	2 Aug. 1811.
Wilson, James	Scotland, about 1742	Pennsylvania	28 Aug. 1798.
Witherspoon, John	Yester, Scotland, 5 Feb. 1722	New Jersey	15 Nov. 1794.
Wolcott, Oliver	Windsor, Conn., 26 Nov. 1726.	Connecticut	1 Dec. 1797.
Wythe, George	Elizabeth City Co., Va., in 1726	Virginia	8 June, 1806.

ANTE-WAR DEBTS OF THE SEVERAL STATES.

TABLE showing the Debts of the several States before the war (1860-61).

STATES.	In 1860-61.	STATES.	In 1860-61.
Maine	$699,500	Iowa	200,000
New Hampshire	31,669	Missouri	24,734,000
Vermont	none.	Kansas	150,000
Massachusetts	7,132,627	Kentucky	4,729,234
Rhode Island	none,	California	....
Connecticut	none.	Oregon	55,372
New York	34,182,976	Virginia	33,248.141
New Jersey	104,000	North Carolina	9,129,505
Pennsylvania	37,964,602	South Carolina	3,691,574
Delaware	none.	Georgia	2,670,750
Maryland	....	Florida	363 000
Ohio	14.250,173	Alabama	5,048,000
Indiana	7,770,233	Mississippi	none.
Michigan	2,388,843	Louisiana	10,023,903
Illinois	10,277,161	Texas	....
Wisconsin	100,000	Arkansas	3,092,622
Minnesota	250,000	Tennessee	16,643,668

CANDIDATES FOR PRESIDENT AND VICE PRESIDENT,

Since the adoption of the *Federal Constitution*, March 1st, 1789.

The following is a *list* of the *Presidents* and *Vice-Presidents* of the *United States*, as well as those who were candidates for each office, since the organization of the Government: (*vide* pp. 21-25, 62.)

1789—George Washington* and John Adams, two terms, no opposition.

1797—John Adams, opposed by Thomas Jefferson,* who, having the next highest electoral vote, became Vice President.

1801—Thomas Jefferson* and Aaron Burr; beating John Adams and Charles C. Pinckney.*

1805—Thomas Jefferson* and George Clinton; beating Charles C. Pinckney* and Rufus King.

1809—James Madison* and George Clinton; beating Charles C. Pinckney.*

1813—James Madison* and Eldridge Gerry; beating DeWitt Clinton.

1817—James Monroe* and Daniel D. Tompkins; beating Rufus King.

1821—James Monroe* and Daniel D. Tompkins; beating John Quincy Adams.

1825—John Quincy Adams and John C. Calhoun;* beating Andrew Jackson,* Henry Clay,* and William H. Crawford;* there being four candidates for President, and Albert Gallatin for Vice President.

1829—Andrew Jackson* and John C. Calhoun*; beating John Quincy Adams and Richard Rush.

1833—Andrew Jackson* and Martin Van Buren; beating Henry Clay,* John Floyd,* and William Wirt for President; and William Wilkins, John Sergeant, and Henry Lee* for Vice President.

1837—Martin Van Buren and Richard M. Johnson*; beating William H. Harrison, Hugh L. White, and Daniel Webster for President, and John Tyler* for Vice President.

1841—William H. Harrison and John Tyler*; beating Martin Van Buren and Littleton W. Tazewell.* Harrison died one month after his inauguration and John Tyler* became President for the rest of the term.

1845—James K. Polk* and George M. Dallas; beating Henry Clay* and Theodore Frelinghuysen.

1849—Zachary Taylor* and Millard Fillmore; beating Lewis Cass and Martin Van Buren for President, and William O. Butler* and C. F. Adams, for Vice President.

1853—Franklin Pierce and William R. King*; beating Winfield Scott and William A. Graham.*

1857—James Buchanan and John C. Breckinridge*; beating John C. Fremont and Millard Fillmore for President, and William L. Dayton and A. J. Donaldson* for Vice President.

1861—Abraham Lincoln and Hannibal Hamlin; beating John Bell, Stephen A. Douglas, and J. C. Breckinridge* for President.

1865—Abraham Lincoln and Andrew Johnson,* Union candidates; beating G. B. McClellan and G. H. Pendleton.

1869—Ulysses S Grant and Schuyler Colfax; beating Horatio Seymour and Frank P. Blair, jr.

1873—Ulysses S. Grant and Henry Wilson; beating Horace Greeley and B. Gratz Brown, for President and Vice President.

1877—Rutherford B. Hayes and Wm. A. Wheeler; beating Samuel Tilden and Thomas A. Hendricks.

1881—James A. Garfield and Chester A. Arthur; beating General W. S. Hancock and W. H. English. Arthur succeeded Garfield, after his death from assassination, Sept. 19, 1881, and David Davis is now Acting Vice President.

* Candidates from Southern States.

NUMBER OF ELECTORAL VOTES TO WHICH EACH STATE HAS BEEN ENTITLED, AT EACH ELECTION, 1789-1876.

States.	1789	1792	1796	1800	1804	1808	1812	1816	1820	1824	1828	1832	1836	1840	1844	1848	1852	1856	1860	1864	1868	1872	1876	1880
Alabama	....	....	....	....	....	....	....	....	3	5	5	7	7	7	9	9	9	9	9	8	8	10	10	12
Arkansas	....	....	....	....	....	....	....	....	....	....	....	....	3	3	3	3	4	4	4	5	5	6	6	7
California	....	....	....	....	....	....	....	....	....	....	....	....	....	....	....	....	...4	4	4	5	5	6	6	8
Colorado	....	....	....	....	....	....	....	....	....	....	....	....	....	....	....	....	....	....	....	....	....	....	3	3
Connecticut	7	9	9	9	9	9	9	9	9	8	8	8	8	8	6	6	6	6	6	6	6	6	6	6
Delaware	3	3	3	3	3	3	4	4	4	3	3	3	3	3	3	3	3	3	3	3	3	3	3	3
Florida	....	....	....	....	....	....	....	....	....	....	....	....	....	....	....	3	3	3	3	3	3	4	4	4
Georgia	5	4	4	4	6	6	8	8	8	9	9	11	11	11	10	10	10	10	10	9	9	11	11	12
Illinois	....	....	....	....	....	....	....	....	3	3	3	5	5	5	9	9	11	11	11	16	16	21	21	22
Indiana	....	....	....	....	....	....	....	3	3	5	5	9	9	9	12	12	13	13	13	13	13	15	15	15
Iowa	....	....	....	....	....	....	....	....	....	....	....	....	....	....	....	4	4	4	4	8	8	11	11	13
Kansas	....	....	....	....	....	....	....	....	....	....	....	....	....	....	....	....	....	....	....	3	3	5	5	9
Kentucky	....	4	4	4	8	8	12	12	12	14	14	15	15	15	12	12	12	12	12	11	11	12	12	13
Louisiana	....	....	....	....	....	....	3	3	3	5	5	5	5	5	6	6	6	6	6	7	7	8	8	8
Maine	....	....	....	....	....	....	....	....	9	9	9	10	10	10	9	9	8	8	8	7	7	7	7	6
Maryland	8	10	10	10	11	11	11	11	11	11	11	10	10	10	8	8	8	8	8	7	7	8	8	8
Massachusetts	10	16	16	16	19	19	22	22	15	15	15	14	14	14	12	12	13	13	13	12	12	13	13	14
Michigan	....	....	....	....	....	....	....	....	....	....	....	....	3	3	5	5	6	6	6	8	8	11	11	13
Minnesota	....	....	....	....	....	....	....	....	....	....	....	....	....	....	....	....	....	....	4	4	4	5	5	7
Mississippi	....	....	....	....	....	....	....	....	3	3	3	4	4	4	6	6	7	7	7	7	7	8	8	9
Missouri	....	....	....	....	....	....	....	....	3	3	3	4	4	4	7	7	9	9	9	11	11	15	15	16
Nebraska	....	....	....	....	....	....	....	....	....	....	....	....	....	....	....	....	....	....	....	....	3	3	3	5
Nevada	....	....	....	....	....	....	....	....	....	....	....	....	....	....	....	....	....	....	....	3	3	3	3	3
New Hampshire	5	6	6	6	7	7	8	8	8	8	8	7	7	7	6	6	5	5	5	5	5	5	5	4
New Jersey	6	7	7	7	8	8	8	8	8	8	8	8	8	8	7	7	7	7	7	7	7	9	9	9
New York	8	12	12	12	19	19	29	29	29	36	36	42	42	42	36	36	35	35	35	33	33	35	35	36
North Carolina	7	12	12	12	14	14	15	15	15	15	15	15	15	15	11	11	10	10	10	9	9	10	10	11
Ohio	....	....	....	....	3	3	8	8	8	16	16	21	21	21	23	23	23	23	23	21	21	22	22	23
Oregon	....	....	....	....	....	....	....	....	....	....	....	....	....	....	....	....	....	....	3	3	3	3	3	3
Pennsylvania	10	15	15	15	20	20	25	25	25	28	28	30	30	30	26	26	27	27	27	26	26	29	29	30
Rhode Island	3	4	4	4	4	4	4	4	4	4	4	4	4	4	4	4	4	4	4	4	4	4	4	4
South Carolina	7	8	8	8	10	10	11	11	11	11	11	11	11	11	.9	9	8	8	8	6	6	7	7	9
Tennessee	....	....	3	3	5	5	8	8	8	11	11	15	15	15	13	13	12	12	12	10	10	12	12	12
Texas	....	....	....	....	....	....	....	....	....	....	....	....	....	....	....	4	4	4	4	6	6	8	8	13
Vermont	....	4	4	4	6	6	8	8	8	7	7	7	7	7	6	6	5	5	5	5	5	5	5	4
Virginia	12	21	21	21	24	24	25	25	25	24	24	23	23	23	17	17	15	15	15	10	10	11	11	12
West Virginia	....	....	....	....	....	....	....	....	....	....	....	....	....	....	....	....	....	....	....	5	5	5	5	6
Wisconsin	....	....	....	....	....	....	....	....	....	....	....	....	....	....	....	4	5	5	5	8	8	10	10	11
Total	91	135	138	138	176	176	218	221	235	261	261	288	294	294	275	290	296	296	303	314	317	366	369	401
Number of States	13	15	16	16	17	17	18	19	24	24	24	24	26	26	26	30	31	31	33	36	37	37	38	38

www.ingramcontent.com/pod-product-compliance
Lightning Source LLC
LaVergne TN
LVHW010524100826
845148LV00001B/89

9781425573676